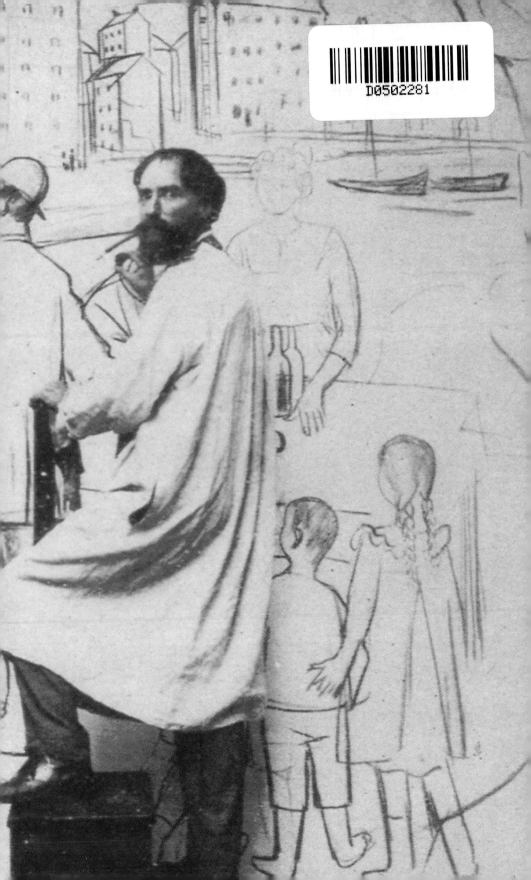

AUGUSTUS JOHN

AUGUSTUS JOHN

MICHAEL HOLROYD

Farrar, Straus and Giroux
NEW YORK

This edition first published 1996

Augustus John: A Biography by Michael Holroyd was originally
published in two volumes, *Volume 1 The Years of Innocence* and
Volume 2 The Years of Experience, by William Heinemann Ltd
in 1974 and 1975. The two volumes were published together as
one volume in the USA by Holt, Rinehart & Winston Inc. in 1975
as *Augustus John: A Biography*. A revised one-volume edition
was published in paperback by Penguin Books Ltd in 1976.
Copyright © Michael Holroyd 1974, 1975, 1976.
This present edition combines the contents of all previous
editions, revised, rearranged and cut, and with substantial
new material added by the author.

This edition copyright © 1996 by Michael Holroyd

First published in the United Kingdom in 1996 by
Chatto & Windus Limited
Random House, 20 Vauxhall Bridge Road
London SW1V 2SA

First published in the United States in 1996 by
Farrar, Straus and Giroux, New York

Library of Congress Cataloging-in-Publication Data
Holroyd, Michael.
Augustus John : the new biography / Michael Holroyd.—1st ed.
p. cm.
Includes bibliographical references and index.
 1. John, Augustus, 1878–1961. 2. Painters—Great Britain—
Biography. I. Title.
ND497.J8H64 1996 759.2—dc20 [B] 96–17251 CIP

Index by Vicki Robinson

Phototypeset by Intype London Ltd
Printed in Great Britain by
Mackays of Chatham PLC, Chatham, Kent

CONTENTS

CONTENTS

LIST OF ILLUSTRATIONS

Colour plates, between pages 318 and 319, of paintings by Augustus John

Black and white plates, between pages 94 and 95

'I inherited a vile melancholy from my father, which has made me mad all my life, at least not sober.'

Samuel Johnson, Boswell's *Tour of the Hebrides* (16 September 1773)

'Poor soul, the centre of my sinful earth,
Fool'd by these rebel powers that thee array,
Why dost thou pine within and suffer dearth,
Painting thy outward walls so costly gay?'

Shakespeare, Sonnet CXLVI

'So must pure lovers soules descend
T'affections, and to faculties,
Which sense may reach and apprehend,
Else a great Prince in prison lies.'

John Donne, 'The Extasie'

PREFACE

'If an idea's worth having once, it's worth having twice.'

Tom Stoppard

While I was working on my biography of Lytton Strachey during the 1960s, Dorelia John let me see some correspondence from Strachey and Carrington. After I finished the book I sent her a copy. It was so weighty a work, she wrote, that she could read it only in bed. That was where I had written much of it, I replied: in bed. We had never met, but almost at once what felt like an intimacy sprang up between us. There were some impressive protests when *Lytton Strachey* was published. 'Can't think what the fuss is about,' Dorelia commented. She wanted to know who my next subject would be. 'What about Augustus John?' I asked. Dorelia told me she would think about it and that I must come and see her when the winter was over.

By a coincidence, the first person invited to write a book about Augustus John – it was probably no more than an introduction and commentary to a volume of drawings – was Lytton Strachey. That had been in 1913, and Strachey (though he wished John to draw his portrait) refused on the grounds that it was too early for such a publication – a verdict with which John agreed.

Nearly forty years later Alan Moorehead started a biography, but came to a halt under the abrupt pressure of John's co-operation. Then, following John's death in 1961, Dylan Thomas's biographer Constantine FitzGibbon began flirting with the idea, but the affair turned sour. There was also the fashion expert and museum keeper James Laver, who had written books on Tissot and Whistler and who began looking into John's life too, but his researches turned up very little.

Augustus John had been dead for not much more than half a dozen years – the very period when I had been writing *Lytton Strachey* – and it seemed to me that my Strachey researches might be a good preparation for a book on John. I liked the idea of a significant minor character from one book evolving into the subject of the next. The process gave me a feeling that they were choosing me rather than the other way around. Besides, some of the Bloomsbury background extended into Bohemian

Chelsea where John held court, and I had met a number of people who knew them both. On one occasion in the late 1950s I had even collided with John himself. There had been no formal introductions. The impact took place on the edge of a pavement in Chelsea. John, in his young eighties, had 'lunched well'. He hesitated tremendously on the kerb. Like a great oak tree, blasted, doomed, he seemed precariously rooted there until, unintentionally assisted by his future biographer, and to a cacophony of shouting brakes and indignant hooting, a whiff of burnt rubber, he propelled himself triumphantly across the road, and was gone. I stood there wondering how he had survived so long. Even in those few blurred moments, his extraordinary physical presence had struck me forcibly. I mentioned the incident to my father, and he remarked that I was bumping into the right people.

How similar, I wondered, were Strachey and John? When Strachey turned up at Roger Fry's Second Post-Impressionist Exhibition in 1912, he was immediately recognized by the porter on duty – as Augustus John. It was an understandable mistake since they were both sporting earrings at the time. 'In our house at Frognal,' wrote Stephen Spender in his autobiography *World Within World*, 'the names of Augustus John, Bernard Shaw, Lytton Strachey, Van Gogh, stood for a diabolic, cunning depravity, a plot of bearded demons against all which should be held sacred.'[1] But individually Strachey and John were so dissimilar, I thought, that even their silences were different: Strachey's an intellectual scorched earth of dismay; John's an animal brooding which he communicated to the whole pack. As for Bernard Shaw, so I later discovered, he was never silent. But all of them campaigned in their work and lives, or some combination of both, for greater tolerance in a repressive age – then tested our powers of tolerance in more relaxed times, so offering a biographer, in the interests of historical perspective, opportunities for narrative irony.

I filled the interval before meeting Dorelia by studying in the Reading Room of the British Museum, and by learning to drive. The Stracheys had lived not far from London and reaching them, though always problematical, had involved a fleet of trains and buses which the Stracheys enjoyed haphazardly plotting for me. Dorelia lived almost a hundred miles west of London, somewhat inaccessibly placed beyond Fordingbridge on the border of Hampshire and Dorset. I had the loan of a car, but no knowledge of it. So I sent myself to driving school. It was an episode that soon took on allegorical significance. Never having been to a university, I have used my biographical subjects as if they were my professors. But the road adventures to which I treated my instructor, and the ordeal through which I put my examiner, became a parody of the teacher–pupil relationship, indicating my natural ineptitude, vulnerability to boredom, and a pedantic ability to take obedience to subversive lengths. Between each agonizing lesson I continued my reading. By the time I drove off to meet Dorelia in the early summer of 1968 I had become quite scholarly.

I went first to gaze at the memorial statue of Augustus John by Ivor Roberts-Jones, standing like some chocolate pugilist near the river. This statue had been the seat of some recent embarrassments. Originally the memorial was to have been of Augustus and Dorelia, but Augustus was such a big fellow that, to Dorelia's relief, there wasn't enough money or materials for anyone else. The single figure was discreetly placed behind a large tree by the parish council. But one night shortly after the unveiling ceremony there had been a violent thunderstorm, and in the morning the tree lay on the ground while Augustus stood dramatically revealed. It was, everyone said, typical of him. But the question that occurred to me was: could I do something equivalent in a biography?

Next I went to his grave, a simple white stone in a triangular field. Finally I came to Fryern Court, Dorelia's home and her creation. The lane coiled between azaleas and magnolias, then opened out into a crunchy gravel sweep with a fringe of grass. I parked flamboyantly, but there was no one to see me. Except for a small herd of kittens, the place seemed deserted. On the walls hung pink roses and an ancient clematis in whose matted stems the cats had made their nests. They lay, sleepy in the sun, watching me as I hammered at the open door. Through the windows, which were also open, I could see dark empty rooms. I called, but no one answered. I retreated a little into the foliage, and when I turned back there was Dorelia watching me from the doorway.

The purpose of our interview, she explained, was to find out if my 'intentions were honourable'. She led me into the dining-room and sat down at the end of a long refectory table. I was seating myself on her left when she shook her head and pointed to a chair on her right. 'Sit there,' she said, 'where the light is on your face.' As we were rearranging ourselves, her son Romilly edged in, apologized for being late, and took off his hat. Since Romilly, then in his early sixties, was the writer in the family – at that time, he told me, he was contemplating a humorous work on engineering – his involvement in our discussion seemed sensible. But not to Dorelia. Gently, firmly, she suggested he should run out into the garden and amuse himself there – perhaps even do something useful – while we debated literary and artistic matters indoors. We would come and see how he was getting on when we had finished. He went out as obediently as a child.

Our talk was not a very precise affair. Dorelia asked me several questions and I explained that I wanted to present an accurate account of Augustus John's life, correcting the wayward chronology of his own writings. Since he was largely an autobiographical artist, obsessively drawing and painting his family and friends, I hoped that the story of his life might prepare readers for looking again at his work. Was not the work of a portrait painter analogous to that of a biographer? George Steiner had recently argued that 'it is the minor master . . . whose career may be important in that it has crystallized the manners of a period, the tone of a particular milieu', who makes the most valid subject for biography. My belief was that Augustus John's career would provide a natural frame for a number of pen-portraits and conversation pieces, and enable me to exhibit a post-Victorian, pre-modern phase of our cultural history, a transition period, the tone and manners of which he had greatly influenced. The challenge was to find an imaginative means of recreating the milieu of someone whose concepts appeared primarily in pictures rather than as words.

Dorelia listened politely, but she was more interested, I sensed, in finding out what sort of person I was than what sort of book I wanted to write. Perhaps, to an extent, the two are the same. We spoke a little of Lytton Strachey and Carrington, of my contact with Augustus John in Chelsea, and the peculiar habits of motor cars. The whole John family, I gathered, were fearless and imaginative drivers, and it struck me that by immersing myself in their world I might gain some of their wit and inventiveness behind the wheel. Yet it was difficult for me to understand how any of this conversation could help Dorelia – unless it was to discover how I might apply my biographical methods to myself. Dorelia, however, had her own method for determining things. This made use of a ring and a piece of cotton – equipment that never failed her. She would tie the cotton to the ring, suspend it between two fingers, and examine the direction in which the ring floated. Since she said little to me that day, I had no doubt that my fate depended upon the behaviour of this pendulum. I felt we had got on well, and my hope was that, below the ritual of these magic operations, lay a subconscious willpower that would direct the movements of the ring.

At any rate I could do no more. We went out into the garden to find out how Romilly was getting on. Dorelia was at home in that garden. Though smaller than I had imagined, and white-haired, she looked more like the mythical Dorelia of Augustus John's pictures than I had thought possible – perhaps she had grown to look like this. We followed a path that ended in nettles and a rubbish dump where we found Romilly. He sprang up as we approached and walked back eagerly with us for tea. Dorelia, like a good general, never wasted words. A few syllables, and I was put to work cutting the bread. But when I showed her the slices, immaculate to my eye, she raised her hands to her face and hooted with laughter. We ate what she called my 'doorsteps', while the cats weaved in and out among the plates and cups, and outside the light began to fade.

Before I left, Romilly took me to one side. Should I in the heat and struggle of my researches, he asked, stumble across the date of his birth, would I let him have it? They both came out to hear me race the engine and waved as I started back to London. It had been a strange day, a journey into a world very different from my own, which is one of the fascinations of writing biography.

After this there was a Dorelian silence. Then in June a letter arrived. 'I am very sorry to be so long answering . . . But I am advised *not* to give you permission to write a book about A.J.' the first paragraph began. In despair I read on: '. . . until I have an agreement that it will not be published unless approved of by me or my executors Sir Caspar and Romilly.' My spirits rose. At the end of this formal note, Dorelia had added a conspiratorial postscript. 'I hope you don't mind. I will help you in any way I can.'

So I began my research. There were periods in Somerset House, the Public Record Office, in the storage rooms of museums and galleries, the cellars of solicitors' offices, the reference sections of libraries, or simply at home writing questionnaire letters, when this research seemed particularly dusty and unrewarding. But then came moments of discovery, like delayed dividends from an arduous investment of time.

From my accumulating knowledge I mapped out a number of research trips into Wales, to the United States and through Europe. *Augustus John* was to be my road book, my sea-and-air book. It began with a wonderful summer in Tenby and Haverfordwest, and became, despite the inevitable anxieties, the most purely enjoyable of my books to write.

In the United States, lecturing as I went to help pay for my travels, I took my first tentative steps into some of the famous manuscript libraries: the Harry Ransom Humanities Research Center at the University of Texas at Austin, the Widener and Houghton Libraries at Harvard, Cornell University Library, Yale University and the Paul Mellon Center for British Art at Yale, and the 'Morgue' at *Life* magazine in New York. I had been used to working in the casual surroundings of people's houses, and I found it somewhat intimidating to be searched for concealed guns or photographed for police records before I entered these halls of scholarship. Such precautions, I reflected, support the illusion that the written word is greatly in demand. Once inside, I might have any sharp object confiscated together with part of my clothing, and be required to sign forms that were linguistically more interesting than the documents I wanted to consult. I found it sometimes difficult to account for myself in a convincing style on these forms or as I sat in windowless cells scribbling against time with borrowed pencils on pencil-coloured paper. But I was a hardened scholar by the end.

After reading through the Augustus John–John Quinn correspondence at the Berg Collection in the New York Public Library, looked down on by John's intimidating portrait of Quinn, I took a train to Schenectady and spent a few hours with the poet Jeanne Foster, who had been Quinn's mistress. In the 1920s she had met Gwen John in Paris and also Augustus John in New York, and though she was now in her early eighties and I in my early thirties, we seemed to hit it off very well. Afterwards we wrote one or two letters to each other, but I did not see her again. A few years later I received a letter from an American lawyer, and an explanatory note from Quinn's biographer B. L. Reid, to say that Jeanne Foster was dead and that she had added a codicil to her will leaving me her Gwen John papers and pictures. The pictures arrived in their original 1920s frames as I was finishing my biography. I was infinitely touched by this gift from beyond the grave in memory of our day together, which now appeared like an augury for the book itself.

I had always been taught with some pride that the English are the most insular race in the world. But in matters of art and literature, I discovered, the French are much superior. The indifference with which the English treat all artists, the French reserve for foreign artists alone. There is a special blank look, a specially emphatic shake of the head they use when you mention an artist who is not French. They love to smile incredulously when they hear of such phenomena, and lingeringly mispronounce the names. It was not even possible for them to confuse Augustus John with Jasper Johns: they knew of neither. They knew nothing too of Gwen John, who had spent most of her painting life in Paris – nothing beyond the fact that she was one of Rodin's models catalogued under the more easily pronounceable name Mary Jones.

Before I set off for France I had armed myself with bilingual letters of introduction and permission statements from various keepers, curators and copyright holders. These gained me a number of appointments, in particular with one *conservatrice* who, it was said, saw no one. As I entered her office, she rose from her chair to tell me she was off that very hour for Venezuela. I sat down as if for life; she reluctantly subsided and continued talking French. But I was equal to this. My French, in which I never make a mistake, is completely silent (the result of having been taught it as a dead language for ten years at privileged preparatory and public schools). She, equally well-educated, spoke no English. We had therefore equipped ourselves with seconds: she with a teddy bear of an old gentleman twice the age of anyone and deaf; I with a girl, indispensable I hoped to the pursuit of John scholarship, who was afflicted in several languages with an ingenious grasp of malapropism ('masturbate' for 'masticate' was one I remember with affection). The contest between the four of us was fantastic, but finally the girl's misnomers won over the teddy bear's mishearings, and I triumphantly entered the archive.

Further south I was met by the drastic improvements inflicted by the French on the fishing villages Augustus John had sought out as refuges from twentieth-century commercialism. Aerodromes, huge glue factories, bauxite hills, red, barren and misshapen, had obliterated much that he had loved and painted in Provence. But it had not been possible to erase everything, and I saw a little of what he had tried to celebrate: the curious blue light over the inland sea at Martigues; and the Alpilles, spotted with green aromatic scrub and the spiky plumes of the cypress trees above St-Rémy.

Over several years I was to be paid advances on royalties of £4,000 from Heinemann in Britain and $40,000 from Holt, Rinehart in the United States. A good part of this money was not due until completion and delivery of the book, but I was also given several hundred pounds as the recipient of a Winston Churchill Fellowship. With some of this money I extended my travels into Italy, where I saw the pictures that had inspired some of Augustus John's most ambitious work, and to Spain where I made a short attempt to live a simple mountain life as the guest of some quite genuine demi-Johns. I was not very good at this. To earn goodwill I took on the duties of gardener, a job that needed the skills of an alpinist. I could spy the sea, glimmering with the prospect of escape. But among outdoor people there appears to be a rule of timelessness any interruption of which is judged to be bad manners. As I scaled the rocks with my watering-can, I plotted an acceptable escape. A telegram to my mother requesting her to send an urgent SOS mentioning illness seemed, at that height, the most sensible arrangement. I sent it from a village near by, but it arrived in England reading as if I were gravely ill and requesting her presence at my deathbed. She set out and, miraculously, she found me. She had expected a vigil beside some hospital bed. I was delighted to see, in the face of such a dismal prospect, she had not omitted to pack bathing suits and evening dresses.

One of the privileges of writing biographies is that you meet, often on friendly terms, some extraordinary people. In Liverpool I came across the legendary 'Romani Rawnie' Dora Yates, incredibly old but still very game, who introduced me to that sane centre of nomad studies, the Gypsy Lore Society. Later on there was the fine sight of Anthony Powell dancing over a Somerset lawn wearing a striped apron, a Burmese cat on his shoulders, in his hand a wooden spoon, asking me whether I liked curry. Rather different was an afternoon on the floor of David Jones's room trying to coax tea out of some primitive machinery. Then there were some rain-swept Welsh days with the novelist Richard Hughes and his wife Frances, a painter of bonfires and waterfalls. We passed much of the time reconstructing a farcical drama, complete with doors, windows and haunted shrubbery, that Augustus John and Dylan Thomas had waged at their home nearly forty years earlier. The bearded Hughes was excellent in the role of Caitlin Thomas.

Finally there was the voluminous John family. Dorelia sent word to them all and they collaborated with varying degrees of enthusiasm. 'What shall I tell him?' cried her daughter Poppet. 'Tell him,' Dorelia replied, 'that Augustus was a *monster!*' The implication was that they could tell me whatever they wanted, and though Poppet and her sister Vivien awaited me with alarm, they both talked and wrote freely once we had got to know one another. There were also their half-sisters, children 'not of the whole blood', for whom I posed more of a problem.

And there were the sons. The eldest, David John, I used to visit near the river in Chelsea. He had begun his career as an architect, dreaming of the grand lunatic asylum he would one day build for his family. But instead he had taken to music, then become a postman, and after narrowly missing an opening as lavatory attendant, so he told me, gone into retirement, though occasionally moving furniture and giving parties. I caught up with Robin John on his silent wanderings at a pub in Piccadilly. From Paris came his brother Edwin John, once a prizefighter, later a watercolourist, who was Gwen John's executor. After an initial meeting in a pub, Edwin's daughter, the dashing Sara John, gave a supper party for her father and myself, together with Mary Taubman, the leading authority on Gwen John. We all brought bottles of wine and I have little memory of how the evening went, except that it signalled the beginning of a very happy working relationship.

Mary Taubman was herself a painter and had written a thesis on Gwen John at Edinburgh University. In 1953, her final year as a student, she had gone out to see Edwin John in France. 'He was installed in the little pavilion which Gwen John had built among the tall trees of her garden-plot at Meudon and where she had spent the last years of a reclusive life,' she remembered. 'As the heir to Gwen John's estate, Edwin, more than any other person, could help or hinder my researches. That our meeting should happen in this place was an unlooked-for bonus and, I felt, an auspicious one.

'He was waiting on the platform of Meudon's small station when I arrived. It was characteristic of him to have come in person to escort me to his door and a sort of old-world courtesy was a facet of the kindness he showed throughout our meeting . . . I was relieved to notice that not only my training in drawing and painting but also my rural upbringing seemed to be counting in my favour and I sensed that, among the jokey references to bagpipes, Calvinism and haggis, my Scottishness was being marked up as a plus, even if only because it reinforced the likelihood of independence from what he called "the London world".

It strikes me now that each aspect of his personality remembered from that first meeting was, in its own way, to impinge on the course of all my future Gwen John studies. Alongside the generosity and the teasing sense of humour (I hadn't yet heard of his fame as a practical joker) there was his self-deprecating manner and his scorn for pretentiousness. This in turn was linked to an impassioned integrity in his approach to his role as custodian of Gwen John's oeuvre and reputation. It was his most impressive, if at times disquieting, characteristic and the one which, in the end, and in spite of difficulties it raised, I valued most.

As we looked out over Gwen John's garden, drinking tea from her teacups, we discussed the enigma of her last decade. Edwin . . . was unwilling to make a pronouncement, far less a guess, as to why she had virtually given up painting towards the end of her life. I asked about the surviving pictures and learned that they were now dispersed, some in London, some in Cornwall, some still in Meudon, though these were not at present accessible. However there were more gouaches and drawings we could look at. I was impressed by his discerning appreciation of these pictures as we went through them one by one . . .

One of my objectives in coming to Meudon was to see a collection of Gwen John's letters and notes already glimpsed in some tantalising extracts published by Augustus John and, more recently, elaborated upon by Sir John Rothenstein . . . Edwin supplied the additional fact that the suitcase containing these papers was at present in the care of Sir Caspar John and was no doubt lodged somewhere in the corridors of the Admiralty in London . . . Before I left, he asked me to choose a little picture from a group of her gouaches and presented it to me in a cardboard portfolio she herself had made and decorated. My request to be allowed to study the papers in Sir Caspar's charge was something he felt unable to agree to.

Back in Edinburgh I was met by a letter from Edwin enclosing Sir Caspar's address and giving me permission to make use of the Gwen John documents. That letter and the papers it gave access to were to be the key to all my future research.'[2]

I was meeting Edwin John and Mary Taubman fifteen years later. There had been several interruptions to Mary's work on Gwen John. She had intended to go back to her own painting, she told me, and had also taught at the Cardiff College of Art. But while she was living in France she had come across a privately owned cache of Gwen John's pictures, and felt there was no escape. In one sense, it seemed to me, Edwin was her jailer, and the key he provided all those years ago sometimes liberated her, sometimes locked her away. Not all Gwen John papers were 'in the corridors of the Admiralty'. From time to time Edwin alluded to other material. Like a character in a fairy story, Edwin would release these papers and pictures to Mary by instalments, as if frightened that she might vanish once she had seen everything and published her book. I remember her telling me that after more than a dozen years, he had casually mentioned a most important batch of letters while they were riding on the top of a bus. Partly because of this complex style of collaboration, and partly because of her own perfectionism, Mary's progress on her Gwen John book was slow. The six or seven years I spent on Augustus John did not particularly impress her.

Each of us worked as the other's part-time research assistant. I came back from France and the United States with Gwen John material; she managed to get Edwin John's general agreement to help me, and would let me have copies of items she thought might be useful. It was a rare sympathetic arrangement, with much unspoken, and no sense of rivalry, that did nothing to prepare me for the rigours of academic competitiveness that surrounded Bernard Shaw. I found it encouraging to have someone like this working in tandem and I remember our time together as being full of discovery, excitement and laughter. Were we being affected in any way, we wondered, by our subjects? People said that Mary had begun to look like a Gwen John model, perhaps look like Gwen John – she said it wryly herself, challenging some response. I could point to my clean-shaven chin as a sign of my immaculate independence, a sign that was to become even more remarkable after a third bearded subject. But I could remember that, when I was deep in Lytton Strachey's early 'black period', with all its detail of late-Victorian neurasthenia, I had begun to feel infected with several long out-of-date diseases. The fact is that no writer knows how he or she is being invaded by the subject of a book – at least not at the time of writing it.

Another invaluable colleague was Malcolm Easton, author of an extraordinary book on Aubrey Beardsley. He was twenty-five years older than I was, had scraped a living as an artist in Soho in the 1930s, gone under the sea to serve in submarines during the war, and then emerged as an art historian at the University of Hull. His exhibition there in 1970 entitled 'Augustus John: Portraits of the Artist's Family' was an eye-opener for me, showing a selection of John's best pictures that no one of my generation had had an opportunity of seeing. A lonely, difficult, admirable man, with a tendency to misunderstand or mishear things to his own disadvantage, and no element of self-seeking in his nature, Malcolm preferred to write to people rather than see them – he had beautiful handwriting and designed his own writing-paper. When we met, it was at the Charing Cross Hotel, and from those meetings and our letters came a book on John's work, and a couple of exhibitions: 'Augustus John: Early Drawings and Etchings' at Colnaghi's in 1974; and a large two-part show the following year at the National Portrait Gallery.

From my adventures I would return from time to time to Fryern Court. 'Still more letters have turned up,' Dorelia would write, and I would go down and load them into the car. On these occasions, followed by the curious gaze of the family, Dorelia would take me into a small room behind the kitchen where she was popularly supposed to be spilling the beans. In fact she was neither eloquent nor exact. Some of her answers were masterpieces of brevity. Her best comments would come in response to stories I told her of people I had met whom she had not seen for many years. She liked travelling back into the past, having grown frailer and feeling sometimes irritated by the limitations of old age. I remember driving away one evening in July 1969. She was sitting in a chair in front of the house in the sunlight, smiling her self-contained smile. A fortnight later she was dead. She died as she had lived, without fuss. On the evening of 23 July, Romilly had found her on the dining-room floor, and he put her to bed. That night she died in her sleep. When Romilly told me, I felt the shock as if I had known her a long time.

She had not expected to live to read my biography, she once told me, and the arrangement we had made concerning her executors now came into force. From Fryern, Romilly reported that he had 'a pillowcase full of letters' for me. Over the next year, a number of these pillowcases would bloom from time to time. The other executor, Admiral of the Fleet Sir Caspar John, lived in London. Our first encounter had been an abrupt affair, but I knew enough of Augustus by then to realize that I must not submit, and at the end of our meeting the Admiral generously conceded: 'I always say if you can't beat 'em, join 'em: so I join you.' At various stages of the book's progress he would get through to me on 'the blower' and I would sail over. There might be red wine or beer, an exchange of questions and answers, occasionally a broadside. After an hour or two of these engagements, I would stagger out and navigate my way back as best I might.

As I worked away I accumulated many scholarly encumbrances. Huge filing cabinets appeared; concertina files and coloured pens lay on every surface. It was impossible to open any drawer or cupboard without an avalanche of old photographs and microfilms spilling out. The whole place was cluttered with good intentions unfulfilled – they spread over the desk and chairs and floor, and began growing up the walls.

There is a paradox about research: the more you do, the more you appear to give yourself to do. I have met scholars who pass their lives in research without ever reaching the writing stage. What carries me from one stage to the next is anxiety. There are many strains to the anxiety virus. I remember how, one blustery day in France, my pleasure at watching some beautifully coloured butterflies moving between the trees turned to horror on realizing that they were specimens of French currency that had blown out of my pocket. Other forms of anxiety strike even deeper than the financial one. All length is torture, and the biographer tunnels on so long that, like Macbeth, returning is as tedious as to go on. There is no sighting the end, no remembering the beginning, and he is alone. Not quite alone, of course: he has the dead for company, and his work is to resurrect the dead.

After my travels, I reverted to old habits and wrote in bed. It was the only place where I could resolve my natural laziness with an obstinate streak of conscientiousness. But it was surprising how this sensible arrangement provoked people. It infuriated my father who was determined, as it were, to catch me napping, though no one was 'at his desk' earlier than I was.

A morning bedful of two or three hundred words was by the end no longer a disgraceful total, followed by afternoons among the files. There is nothing like the preparation of a chronology or the copying down of passages from letters for teaching me about my subject. Life itself slipped past as I bent over these mechanical exercises that alone enabled me to spot unexpected connections and give the work tension and design.

The transference of a book from private to public property can be alarming, but I was fortunate in that, despite many difficulties, the John family had really 'joined me' and weathered the ordeal so well.

*

Augustus John was published in Britain and the United States in 1974–5. Shortly afterwards Caspar John commissioned a friend, Ronald Hamand, to make a catalogue of the John family papers. This job took some three years, and when it was completed, Caspar delivered the catalogue,[3] together with all the papers themselves, to his co-executor and half-brother Romilly John, leaving him to sort out what should be done with them. What Romilly did was to appeal somewhat desperately ('I have a problem . . . they're often so illegible') to the National Museum of Wales at Cardiff.

The National Museum of Wales was then in the process of rediscovering and establishing both Augustus John's and Gwen John's identities as native-born Welsh artists. Early in 1976, the centenary of Gwen's birth, the museum had acquired from Edwin John more than a thousand of her drawings, together with sketchbooks and several oil paintings – this being material found in her Paris studio after her death in 1939. Before this acquisition, Cardiff held only a small representation of her pictures. But 'the huge collection the Museum now houses is by far the greatest number of her works anywhere,' wrote the Assistant Keeper of Art, A. D. Fraser Jenkins, in a booklet accompanying the Gwen John centenary exhibition.

Two years later, during the centenary year of Augustus's birth, the National Museum of Wales put on 'Augustus John: Studies for Composition', an exhibition that was also shown in England and at the Yale Center for British Art in the United States. To pay off death duties, there had been two Augustus John studio sales at Christie's in 1962 and 1963. One hundred and thirteen paintings and two hundred and eighteen drawings were auctioned for a total, in those pre-VAT days, of almost £135,000 (equivalent to £1½ million in 1996). One of the best paintings, 'Dorelia in the Garden at Alderney Manor', was bought by the National Museum of Wales which, in 1972, also acquired from the executors of Dorelia's estate the remainder of what was left in Augustus's studio at Fryern Court – over a thousand drawings, one hundred and ten paintings, and three bronzes. The oil paintings in this collection 'were nearly all unfinished or rejected portraits, mostly later than 1920', wrote A. D. Fraser Jenkins in his introduction to the catalogue. Among the drawings he found 'a quantity of slight sketches or first ideas for paintings, many of them stained, dusty or torn'. While sorting through this part of the collection, Fraser Jenkins formed a plan for comparing a number of John's initial ideas with the completed paintings (sometimes shown as photographs) and charting the progress of these compositions in a way that had not previously been examined.

The block purchase of Augustus John's studio contents had established the National Museum of Wales as what Mark L. Evans, one of the future Assistant Keepers in the Department of Art, described as 'the principal repository of [Augustus] John's work and the main centre for research on his art'.[4] It had already become such a repository and centre for the art of Gwen John.

But the group of papers in Romilly John's keeping was not chiefly associated with the art of Augustus John. It did contain a few sketchbooks and some correspondence from painters (including Carrington, Epstein, J. D. Innes, Wyndham Lewis, William Rothenstein and Matthew Smith), but most of the fifteen hundred letters written by John or addressed to him involved writers (James Joyce, T. E. Lawrence, Sean O'Casey, John

Cowper Powys, Bernard Shaw, the Sitwells, Lytton Strachey, Dylan Thomas), members of the Gypsy Lore Society (Scott Macfie, John Sampson, Dora Yates) and his family (Ida John, Gwen John and Dorelia McNeill). As he went through this archive, Romilly John began to think that 'perhaps the National Library of Wales would be the right depository'.[5]

It was expected that the National Library of Wales at Aberystwyth would purchase these papers when they came up for auction at Sotheby's on 17 December 1979. But the library was outbid, and the archive went for £52,000 ($127,600) to an anonymous bidder from the United States who employed the booksellers Bernard Quaritch Ltd to act as his agent. The papers then mysteriously went missing. Several national newspapers attempted to follow the trail, but got no further than discovering that the material had been taken to Ireland from where it was illegally exported to the United States. The matter was reported to the Reviewing Committee on the Export of Works of Art, but since no special licence for export had been applied for, and since Quaritch could not professionally reveal the identity of the collector for whom they had acted (the ethics of manuscript dealers being similar to those of journalists and unlike those of biographers and historians, who must constantly refer to their sources), there seemed nothing that could be done.

But something, drop by drop like a Chinese torture, was to be done over the next few years. The newspaper speculation persisted. There were plans for a film by Robert Bolt, a play by Peter Terson, and continual inquiries from scholars and writers who wanted to edit a selection of Augustus John's correspondence, or publish a biography of Ida John, or write books about John's contemporaries. Such people were told that the owner of the archive 'wishes to retain his anonymity' and 'is unwilling to share any of that material'. Fortunately there was one important exception to this dull rule of non-cooperation. This was Cecily Langdale, whose scholarly and substantial *Gwen John*, which included a valuable *catalogue raisonné* of the paintings and a selection of the drawings, was published in 1987. 'The A[ugustus] J[ohn] papers are in storage,' she wrote to me from New York that year, 'and the owner, I fear, really doesn't want to be bothered with requests for information.' But, she added, 'he has been extremely nice to me and has helped me in every possible way.'

A fortnight after getting this letter, I received a telephone call from the recently retired Chairman of the Board of Customs and Excise, Sir Angus Fraser, soon to be appointed Adviser to the Prime Minister on Efficiency and Effectiveness in Government. Was I, he wanted to know, Augustus John's biographer? He had used that invaluable reference work, the telephone directory, and having assured himself that I was the right chap, he wrote me a letter asking whether I knew of any British institution that might be interested in purchasing the Augustus John archive. 'I happen to know that the American purchaser of 1979 is divesting himself of a number of his collections and would be willing to part with this one too,' he explained. He had sent this purchaser an article I had written in the *Sunday Times*[6] mentioning the disappearance of the John papers.

'The trouble is likely to be the dollar price expected, given the way the dollar/sterling exchange rate has moved since 1979. As I understand it, the present owner wants to recover his original payment plus an allowance for notional interest over the intervening years. When he bought the John material, the dollar stood at well over $2 to £1. Allowing for eight years' interest, the selling price he is looking for is in the range of $200,000–250,000, i.e. about £123,000–154,000 at today's exchange rates. It is going to be very difficult to identify a British institution which can afford that kind of money . . . I have absolutely no financial interest in this matter; it is simply that, having becoming aware of the opening for a sale, I would be glad to see the papers come back to the U.K.'

Apart from the Tate Gallery, I thought there were two places where these papers would find a good home: the British Library, and the National Library of Wales, which had been the underbidder at Sotheby's. Unknown to me at that time, the National Library of Wales had started building a Gwen John archive. It rivalled in interest the New York Public Library's holding of her correspondence with the American patron John Quinn, and her letters to Rodin at the Musée Rodin in Meudon. Edwin John had died in 1978, and half a dozen years later his son and daughter completed the sale of the correspondence, notes and other personal papers that Mary Taubman had been working on, and that had been in Gwen John's studio along with the pictures bought in 1976 by the National Museum of Wales.

Having made my suggestions I heard nothing more for the rest of the year, and began ruminating on the curiosities of the international manuscript market and the peculiar motives of private collectors.

I remembered that one cold January day in the early 1970s as I was working on *Augustus John*, I had received a letter from an Australian university saying that I might like to know that while I was enduring the snows and winds of an English winter, the manuscript, galleys and page proofs of my *Lytton Strachey* 'sit comfortably at a constant temperature in our Rare Book Room'. It had the advantage of me. I would never have thought such a thing possible when I started writing. I believed then that I could steer clear of most libraries except my own, assembled over the years from secondhand bookshops. Almost all Strachey's letters had been in private hands and, once I had prised them out of attics, cellars and studios, I was often permitted to cart them back to my room. But those amateur days, with their privileged access, were coming to an end. Augustus John's papers were divided between private houses and public institutions, and continually on the move from the former to the latter where they would be more professionally managed.

Manuscript libraries are somewhat like laboratories where, with thousands of fragments, you experiment in the hope of a resurrection miracle. But such sombre places of scholarship often rely on contemporary business of one sort or another for their derivative funds. Business and scholarship are not always easy companions. I first became aware of the difficulties that may arise from these partnerships while tracking down some of Augustus John's correspondence to a library that informed me I could not examine it because everything was embargoed. I happened to know the original seller of this material. When I asked her about the embargo she was unable to explain it. After further investigations I found out that the dealers themselves had imposed the embargo either because they were shocked by the illustrated contents or more probably because by 'hotting up' the material they also hotted up the price. In this case I was able to break the embargo but, having had no description of the material, was disappointed after all my stubborn detective work to discover that the letters were of no real use – until perhaps now – though the temptation to force some of them into my book after such a struggle was strong.

Once a manuscript is sold at auction to a dealer there is no certain way of tracing its destination. The mail is crammed with blind letters of inquiry, and there are many culs-de-sac. I remember sending one of these letters myself and, receiving no answer, following it up after an interval with a second inquiry. This time the answer was swift and helpful. The librarian stated that he had one unspecified item that might be useful. I offered to pay the fee and was eventually rewarded with a luxurious folder complete with a covering letter explaining that, since there was only a single uncatalogued item involved, the library had waived its fee. Full of gratitude I opened the folder and found inside, beautifully copied and presented, my own original unanswered letter stamped with a warning that I did not have copyright permission to quote it.

About the motives of private collectors I find it difficult to speculate. No person who buys the correspondence of the dead can be prevented from doing what he likes with it, except of course publish it: that is the prerogative of the copyright holder. But since holographs lose some of their financial value when published, a period of hibernation may very well suit someone who buys for capital appreciation. Though he may not legally quote anything much without copyright permission, an owner may, without breaking any law I know, burn or otherwise destroy his papers, thereby robbing himself. Or he may lock everything away in a bank vault. That is the law of property some call theft.

Original manuscripts never lose their power of attracting textual critics, biographers and historians because handling such material is usually the nearest that they come to their subjects. They are almost literally in touch with them. Manuscript research, as Philip Larkin pointed out, can reveal the genesis and evolution of a work of literature and provide us with an archive of the writer's life as the background of his works. 'All literary manuscripts', Larkin argued, 'have two kinds of value.'[7] He called them the magical and meaningful values. The first, which is older and universal, kindles research with a peculiar excitement and intimacy; the second, which is more technical and modern, contributes to our understanding of a writer's intentions. Together they may enlarge our knowledge of the creative process, while contributing to the recreative process of non-fiction literature.

All this was being frustrated while the Augustus John papers remained in limbo. What I did not know was that the National Library of Wales had been contacted by a third party acting on behalf of the purchaser. Negotiations for a private-treaty sale had started, proceeded, then stopped: and silence fell. Then at the beginning of 1988 I was contacted by a manuscript librarian at the British Library asking me to write in support of his objection, addressed to the Reviewing Committee of Works of Art, to the export of the Augustus John papers. The position seemed somewhat topsy-turvy since we were lodging an objection to something that was apparently being proposed eight years after it had actually happened. Reading between the lines, I guessed that the papers had somehow been smuggled back into the country and now posed something of a problem. In the event, the hearing in front of the Reviewing Committee never took place since the exporters agreed to sell the papers to the National Library of Wales after representatives from its Department of Manuscripts and Records had inspected the collection at Sotheby's London office. This sale was completed in June 1988 by Sotheby's, which had now sold the same papers twice.

The price was not quite what the owner had wanted, but then the collection itself was no longer so comprehensive. Only photocopies, for example, of letters from members of the Gypsy Lore Society were included, the originals having been retained by the anonymous American collector. Like Sir Angus Fraser (who edited George Borrow's letters and published a book on gypsies), he obviously kept up a special interest in travelling people and 'the affairs of Egypt'.

My biography had gone into paperback in the 1970s and was last reprinted in 1987. The publication of Ceridwen Lloyd-Morgan's *Gwen John Papers at the National Museum of Wales* the following year, and the schedule of *Gwen John Papers* and catalogue of *Augustus John Papers* which she compiled in 1988 and 1991, alerted me to the large archive of both artists that had been formed at Aberystwyth since my biography was written. After being given advance notice of a further reprint in 1992, I decided to go and have a look at these collections. What I saw during this reconnaissance persuaded me to buy back the rights in my book and prepare this new edition.

The Augustus John collection has changed considerably since I was handed it in instalments by Dorelia and Romilly John at Fryern, and drove it in great disorder to my room in London. Then the papers had been all muddled together and posted into shopping bags and pillowcases; now they were sorted and filed, bound and guarded by what at first gasp appeared a formidable set of regulations. Traces of their old happy-go-lucky days could be detected in Caspar John's flowing pencil dates and occasionally, I was surprised to see, my own more tortuous ones. But now there was a systematic dating guide provided by the catalogue calendar, this being all the more necessary because many of the envelopes that had existed twenty-five years before had gone missing. There were a few other items missing from the papers after their long journeys by car, ship or plane, but documents had been added in the mid-1970s when Ronald Hamand was going round the family preparing his catalogue. This material was new to me, as were some of the Nettleship and John papers donated to or bought by the National Library of Wales between the mid-1970s and the early 1990s.[8] This group includes approximately three hundred and twenty-five Augustus John letters.

Even more interesting to me was the Gwen John archive. I had used some of the contents and could recognize Mary Taubman's handwritten dates. But there was a good deal of material I had not seen, including papers that no one else had used while they were in private hands (such as Augustus John's letters to his son Edwin). There are more than seventy-five letters from Augustus John in the Gwen John archive, as well as correspondence from her father, her brother Thornton and sister Winifred, her nephew (Augustus's son) Henry John, and from Ida and Dorelia.

For the first time I was able to examine holographs the contents of which had previously been given to me as copies. For example, there was the single long letter to Gwen John from the painter with whom Dorelia had eloped to Bruges in 1904.[9] His first name was Leonard and his family name (indicated by another piece of correspondence) began with the letter B. Looking at the written copy I was given in the early 1970s, it had seemed to me that his address had been shortened to 'kplaas 5'. So I had gone to Bruges, found the only 'plaats' or square beginning with the letter K and deduced that Leonard and Dorelia were living in a house belonging to Lodewyck Van den Broucke and his wife Leonie (née Huys). The records that might have revealed their son's name had been destroyed, but I surmised that he might have been named after his mother and was therefore Leonard Broucke. Thus he stands as a hypothesis in my footnote and more definitively in the index.

But when Ceridwen Lloyd-Morgan came to examine the holograph, she saw that a corner of the letter had been torn and that 'kplaas 5' or 'kplaats 5' was not the whole address. It was now a matter of searching for a plaats the previous syllable of which ended with a k. There were three such addresses in Bruges: Jan van Eyckplaats 5, for which the records were destroyed by fire in the 1940s; Memlinckplaats 5 (now Woensdagmarkt) which was a convent occupied by five nuns; and Park-plaats 5 which had no identifiable occupants. So in this edition of my biography Leonard fades away more deeply unremembered, which is aesthetically fitting if bibliographically unsatisfactory. 'It would be ironical if a pile of Leonard's paintings were one day discovered in a barn and found to be great masterpieces!' Romilly John had written to me. Unfortunately I have been unable to find any artist of the right period and nationality with such a name and initial. So Romilly's discovery remains to be made.

Altogether I worked for some eighty hours in the Department of Manuscripts and Records at Aberystwyth quarrying out new material. There also turned out to be John correspondence I had not seen first time round at the Royal Academy of Arts, University of Reading Library, University of Liverpool Library, BBC Written Archives Centre, as well as in two private collections. I had kept, in desultory fashion, a file in which I placed, as if for oblivion, letters from readers with corrections and additions. This I retrieved from the dark and put to use. Finally I brought myself up to date by reading those publications on Gwen and Augustus John and their contemporaries that had appeared over the last twenty years.

There is much that is new.

In 1974 Caspar and Romilly John had consulted lawyers about some aspects of my typescript and requested me to remove passages that might have made the family liable to financial penalties. Caspar wrote to thank me for 'so readily, if so reluctantly' agreeing to this excision. 'We are both sorry to have had to ask you to do this, but in view of the enclosed lawyer's letter we had small option.' That legal threat has now lapsed with time, and I have restored my original account of, for example, how Augustus John was awarded the Order of Merit.

After drastic cutting, the biography remains approximately the same length. There are new pages on Augustus John's family, on Gwen John and their Slade School friends; new information concerning artists, such as Henry Lamb and Wyndham Lewis, who played significant roles in his life, and other supporting characters – for example Dylan and Caitlin Thomas, and the great gypsy scholar John Sampson – all of which has enabled me to improve the continuity of the narrative. That narrative is cast as comedy: romantic comedy, domestic comedy, the comedy of morals and of manners, absurdist comedy, black comedy, tragi-comedy.

Some papers I saw twenty-five years ago have disappeared but more have risen to the surface, and this shifting archaeology of sources has inevitably altered John's place in the artistic landscape. There are new passages about some of his pictures and those, from W. B. Yeats and Sean O'Casey to the Marchesa Casati, Eve Fleming, Lady Ottoline Morrell and Madame Suggia, who sat for his portraits.

John's artistic reputation, once so high, has plummeted. In place of 'the last of the great masters' who worked directly from life in the manner of Rembrandt, Tiepolo or Watteau, stands a banal and flashy manufacturer of pastiches and the simulacra of genuine masterworks. The famously gifted painter who led the revolutionary artists in Britain into the twentieth century has by the end of the century retrospectively dwindled to an inferior talent which in old age grew more obviously vulgar and sentimental.

Neither judgement is definitive. John's work, blown here and there by contemporary criticism and conventional art history, appeared to fall off the map when in 1987 it was omitted from the Royal Academy exhibition 'British Art in the Twentieth Century: the Modern Movement'. This technical knockout, unthinkable during the first half of this century, emphasized the difficulty critics and historians have when treating individual talents that do not fit into ideological or narrative patterns. But John's exclusion was felt to be unsatisfactory, and the placing of his work remains a problem unsolved. Nor are those proper judges of his work who presume to say, as Samuel Johnson wrote of his biographical subject Richard Savage: 'Had I been in Savage's condition, I should have lived or written better than Savage.'

John's artistic reputation is a background theme in my book, charted through the contemporary criticism of Roger Fry and Clive Bell, Sickert, Rothenstein and Wyndham Lewis, Anthony Blunt, Herbert Read and others. It is the story of a visual lyricist whose early accomplishment, interpreting English, French and Welsh landscape through poetic eyes, belonged 'essentially to youth (as so often in poetry)',[10] Richard Shone has argued. His inability to transform these 'magnificent beginnings' into a mature body of work in later years clouded his life and moves as a shadow through this book.

But this is a biography, not an art book, and I have used the pictures to illumine the life. For me the virtue of biography is the humanizing effect it can bring to history. To see people as being 'worth' a Life on account of their greatness and goodness is a nineteenth-century concept. The aim, I believe, of modern biographers, who live so long with their subjects, is to find some connecting current of energy, travel with it across time, as it were, and, from loneliness perhaps, make contact with other human beings. In that contact, if they are fortunate, may be found a literary pattern, a story with clues and signposts that forms a parallel world to that of the subject's work. Biography is no longer simply an instrument of information retrieval, though historical and cultural information that is retrieved from these expeditions is a bonus. The biographer's prime purpose is to recreate a world into which readers may enter, and where, interpreting messages from the past, they may experience feelings and thoughts that remain with them after the book is closed.

PART I

'The most innocent, wicked man I have ever met.'
W. B. Yeats to John Quinn (4 October 1907)

THE YEARS OF INNOCENCE

ONE

Little England Beyond Wales

I

'MAMA'S DEAD!'

'Who *am* I in the first place?'

Augustus John, *Finishing Touches*

A regiment of women, monstrously feathered and furred, waited at Tenby railway station. The train that pulled in one autumn day in the year 1877 carried among its passengers a young solicitor and his wife, Edwin and Augusta John. With his upright figure, commanding nose, his ginger whiskers, he had more the bearing of a soldier than lawyer. She was a pale woman of twenty-nine, with small features, rather fragile-looking, her hair in ringlets. She was expecting their third child.

The landladies of Tenby fell upon the new arrivals. But the Johns stood aloof. By prior arrangement the most regal of these beldames escorted them to her carriage and drove them up the Esplanade along the 'fine houses of coherent design' fronting the sea to a building on the edge of South Cliffs: No. 50 Rope Walk Field.[1] From their windows they looked over to Caldy Island and to a smaller island, St Margarets, later a bird sanctuary, that at low tide seemed to attach it to the mainland of Wales.

Augusta's other children were born in Haverfordwest in Pembrokeshire. But she and Edwin had decided that, for safety, she should give birth to their third child in Tenby, Haverfordwest having recently been hit by an epidemic of scarlet fever. Soon after the New Year her labour pains began, and at five-thirty on the morning of 4 January 1878 the new baby was born. It was a boy, and they named him after both of them: Augustus Edwin John.

*

Victoria Place, Haverfordwest, had been built in 1839 to commemorate the opening of the new toll bridge. The houses were narrow, and all had small square windows with wooden frames that sloped inwards, and window-sills a child could sit on.

The John family lived at No. 7.[2] Almost immediately behind the front

3

door ascended a steep staircase. Small alcoves had been cut into the wall. From the second floor it was possible to see into Castle Square opposite, one side of which was formed by the Castle Inn, with its ramparts and its archway through which coaches drove to the stables behind. Above the inn rose the ruined Norman castle, its stone windows gaping at the sky. All around stretched the uneven slate roofs of the houses, now high, now low, undulating away to the perimeter of the town. And beyond the town lay green hills that on summer evenings grew blue and hazy, and in winter, when there was frost, stood out hard.

In the eleven years of their marriage Edwin and Augusta John had two boys and two girls. Thornton was nearly three years older than Augustus: Gwen eighteen months older; and Winifred was born almost two years later.[3]

For all of them, Haverfordwest was an exciting town in which to grow up. On market days the streets and square heaved with a pandemonium of people and animals – women from Llangwm in short skirts, bright shawls and billycock hats carrying baskets of oysters on their backs; philosophical-looking tramps wandering through with an air of detachment and no obvious purpose; and gypsies, mysterious and aloof, shooting down sardonic glances as they rode by in ragged finery on their horse-drawn carts. From this continuous perambulation rose a cacophony of barking dogs, playing children, the perpetual lowing of cattle, screaming of pigs and the loud vociferation of the Welsh drovers.

Papa warned all his children against walking abroad on market days in case they should be kidnapped by the gypsies and spirited away in their caravans, no one knew where.[4] The lure of danger made it a warning Augustus never forgot.

At weekends, Edwin John would lead out his children on well conducted expeditions in the outskirts of the town. Augustus loved these walks. One of his favourites was along a path known as 'the frolic' which ran southeast, parallel to the River Cleddau, where barges were pulled in over the marshy ground to dilapidated wharves. Beyond the tidal flats, in the middle distance, a railway train would sometimes seem to issue from the ruins of an ancient priory and rumble on under its white banner till, with a despairing wail, it hurled itself into the hillside: and vanished.

Another popular walk was along a right-of-way called 'the scotchwells'. Under a colonnade of trees this path followed the millstream past the booming flour mill from which the terrifying figure of its miller, white from head to toe, might emerge. Sometimes, too, Papa would take them high above the Cleddau valley and perilously close to the cottage of a known witch.

On all these walks Edwin John marched in front, preserving a moderate speed – the pace of a gentleman – only halting, in primrose time, to pick a few of his favourite flowers and make a nosegay against the frightful exhalations of the tannery, or, when on the seashore, to gather shells for his collection. Behind him, heard but not seen, the children crocodiled out in an untidy line, darting here and there in a series of guerrilla raids.

On Sundays there was church. Augustus preferred being sent with the servants to their Nonconformist chapels, bethels, zions and bethesdas. He loved the sonorous unintelligible language, the fervour of the singing, the obstinacy of prayer, the surging and resurging crescendos of the orator as he worked himself towards that divine afflatus with which good Welsh sermons terminated.

The religious atmosphere of Victoria Place was for several years fortified by two aunts, Rosina and Leah Smith – Aunts 'Rose' and 'Lily'. They were younger sisters of Augusta, both in their twenties, and both ablaze for God. They had come to Haverfordwest from Brighton when Augusta's health began to fail. After the birth of Winifred, Augusta seldom seemed well. She suffered from chronic rheumatism which the damp climate of Haverfordwest was thought to aggravate, and she travelled much in search of a cure.

In her absence Rosina and Leah took charge of the children's upbringing. One of the aunts' first demands was for the dismissal of the nurse, on the grounds that she had permitted the children to grow abnormally fond of her. They had gone to her cottage on the lonely moors above the Prescelly Mountains north of Haverfordwest, where they would sit wide-eyed over their bowls of *cawl*, staring at the dark-bearded woodmen with their clogs, thin-pointed and capped with brass, and then argue on the way home whether their feet were the same shape. Few of these men knew a word of English. Old pagan festivals still flourished, and on certain dates the children were given sprigs of box plant and mugs of water, and told to run along the stone flags of the streets asperging any stranger they met. These were habits of which the aunts could not approve.

The new regime under aunts was a bewildering change. Both were Salvationists and held rank in General Booth's army. Aunt Leah, a lady of ruthless cheerfulness and an alarming eloquence, had once 'tried the spirits' but found them wanting. Also found wanting was a young man who had had the temerity to propose marriage to her. But she had been seduced by the Princess Adelaide's Circle, of which she soon became a prominent member.

Aunt Rosina – 'a little whirlwind', Winifred remembered her, 'battering everyone to death'[5] – had a curious ferret-like face which, the children speculated, might cause her to get shot one day by mistake. Her choice of religion seemed to depend on her digestion, which was erratic. 'At one time it might be "The Countess of Huntingdon's Connexion", with raw beef and hot water, at another Joanna Southcote and grapes, or again, The Society of Friends plus charcoal biscuits washed down with Rowntree's Electric Cocoa."[6]

The two aunts toured the neighbourhood of Haverfordwest in a wicker pony-trap known locally as 'the Hallelujah Chariot', bringing souls to Jesus. Strong men, it was said, pickled in sin, fell prostrate to the ground before them, weeping miserably. Their presence dominated Victoria Place. Each day began with morning prayers, and continued with the aid of improving tracts, *Jessica's First Prayer* and *The Lamplighter*.

Although the theatre was out of bounds, the children were permitted to attend an entertainment called 'Poole's Diorama'. This was a precursor of the cinema -- a vast historical picture, or series of pictures which, to music and other sound effects, was gradually unrolled on an apparently endless canvas across the stage. At one corner a man with a wand pointed to features of interest and shouted out his explanations to the audience. But when 'The Bombardment of Alexandria' was depicted the aunts judged matters had gone far enough and bustled the children outside.

Even more exciting, though viewed with some family misgivings, was the children's first visit to the circus. Though later in life Augustus used to object to 'that cruel and stupid convention of strapping the horses' noses down to their chests', this circus, he claimed, corrupted him for life. It wasn't simply a question of the animals, but the dazzling appearance of a beautiful woman in tights, and of other superb creatures, got up in full hunting kit and singing 'His Moustache was Down to Heah, Tiddy-foll-ol' and 'I've a Penny in my Pocket, La-de-dah'.

In summer the family used to go off to Broad Haven, twelve miles away, where Edwin had a one-storey house specially built for him out of the local stone.[7] And the aunts came too. But here the regime was less strict and the children happier. Their house on St Bride's Bay had a large lawn and faced the sea, in which the children spent much of their time. Yet even in the waves they were not beyond religious practices which extended offshore with dangerous ceremonies of Baptism by Total Immersion.

The Johns at this time were an isolated family. The uncompromising reputation of the aunts, the formidable respectability of Edwin, and their rather lowly origins, limited the number of their friends while failing to win them entry into the upper reaches of Haverfordwest society. The children were at ease only in the sea or roaming the wilds at Broad Haven. 'Our invincible shyness,' Augustus later recorded, 'comparable only to that of the dwarf inhabitants of Equatorial Africa, resisted every advance on the part of strangers.' Their grandfather, William John, used to exhort them: 'Talk! If you can't think of anything to say tell a lie!' And: 'If you make a mistake, make it with authority!' But the children were speechless.

The only adults with whom Augustus appears to have formed any friendly contact were the servants. At Victoria Place the one room where he felt at home was the kitchen. He passed many hours sitting on a 'skew' by the kitchen fire, listening to the quick chatter and watching the comings and goings. Sometimes an intoxicated groom would stagger in, and the women would dance and sing to him till his eyes filled with remorse. It was natural theatre, full of melodrama and comedy, and the fascination of half-understood stories.

The children needed the influence of their mother, but she was absent more and more. One day, in the second week of August 1884, the servants were lined up in the hall of Victoria Place, and Edwin John informed the household that his wife had died. The servants stood in their line, some of them crying quietly; but the children ran from room to room, chanting with senseless excitement: 'Mama's dead! Mama's dead!'

2

THE RESPONSIBLE PARTIES

'Have I any claim to the throne? My father kept everything dark,
but I had an uncle descended from Owen Glyndwr.'
Augustus John to Caspar John (16 February 1951)

'We come from a long line of professional people,' Edwin John would tell Augustus when questioned about their antecedents. Since he was seeking to enter fashionable Pembrokeshire society, he had his reasons for not being more explicit. Augustus, who had little sense of belonging to his parents' families, did not probe further. They couldn't *all* have been middle-class lawyers, he thought; then he would glance at his father again and reflect that perhaps it was better to remain in the dark. At least *he* would be different.

Both his paternal grandfathers, William John[8] and David Davies, had been Welsh labourers living in Haverfordwest; while on his mother's side he came from a long line of Sussex plumbers, all unhelpfully bearing the name Thomas Smith. William John's son, who was named after him, was born in 1818. At the age of twenty-two he married a local seamstress, Mary Davies, the same age as himself. On the marriage certificate he described himself as a 'writer', which probably meant attorney's clerk (the occupation he gave on his children's birth certificates). That he had cultural interests, however, is certain. By the end of his life he had collected a fair library including leather-bound volumes of Dickens, Scott, Smollett and an edition of Dante's *Inferno* with terrifying illustrations by Gustave Doré; and he had done something rather unusual for a man of his class in the mid-nineteenth century: he had travelled through Italy, bringing back with him a fund of Italian stories and a counterfeit Vandyke to hang in his dining-room.

William and Mary John had begun their married life in a workman's cottage in Chapel Street, then moved to Prendergast Hill and in 1850 were living at 5 Gloster Terrace. Each move, though only a few hundred yards, denoted a rise in the world, and the climax was reached when, in 1855, they transferred to Victoria Place. The basis of their fortune was an investment in a new bank which had turned out well. In 1854 William was admitted a solicitor and shortly afterwards started his own legal firm in Quay Street. He served for several years as town clerk of Haverfordwest, bought a number of properties and, on his death, left a capital sum of nearly eight thousand pounds (equivalent to £300,000 in 1996). In politics he was a Liberal, had acted as Lord Kensington's agent in all his contests up to the late 1870s and was well known for his speeches in Welsh at the Quarter Sessions. But although, in the various directories of the time, he is listed among the attorneys, he is not among the gentry.[9]

Between 1840 and 1856 William and Mary had six children who survived, three sons and three daughters. Edwin William John, the fourth child and second son, was born on 18 April 1847. No. 5 Gloster Terrace, where his earliest years were spent, was a tall thin house into which were crammed five children,[10] their parents and a maternal aunt, Martha Davies, who helped to look after her nephews and nieces. There was also another Martha Davies of about the same age, who acted as a general servant.

In later years Edwin John let it be known that he was an old Cheltonian. In fact he was at Cheltenham College for only three terms and, according to his younger sister Clara, this year produced a devastating effect upon him. His disposition, tolerable before he attended public school, was 'impossible' ever afterwards. He fell victim to the cult of appearances, forgetting all he knew of the Welsh language and becoming obsessed by his social reputation.

Edwin's main education had been conducted locally in Haverfordwest. He knew Lloyd George's father, William George, a Unitarian schoolmaster at a private school in Upper Market Street where Edwin went for several years. William George 'was a severe disciplinarian', he recalled, ' – rather passionate, sometimes having recourse to the old-fashioned punishment of caning.'

It was the eldest son Alfred, not Edwin, who had originally been intended for the law.[11] Alfred married a Swansea girl and had three children in three years, but after a period working in his father's law office his spirit suddenly revolted. While still in his twenties he ran away to London – and eventually to Paris – to play the flute, first in an orchestra, later in bed.[12] The burden of family responsibility then passed to Edwin who, leaving Cheltenham at the age of sixteen, was immediately articled to his father and, in the Easter term of 1870, became a solicitor. On his twenty-fifth birthday, William John made him a partner, and the practice became known as William John and Son. When the father retired seven years later, the son took it over entirely. He had done all that could have been expected of him.

He had even married with his father's 'lawful consent'. The legal atmosphere was so pervasive that, on the marriage certificate, his wife accidentally gave her own profession as that of solicitor.[13] Her father Thomas Smith's profession she described as 'Lead Merchant'.

*

Thomas and Zadock Smith had been born at Chiddingly in Sussex, the sons of Thomas Smith, a village plumber. The elder son, who inherited his father's business, moved to Brighton and in 1831, at the age of twenty-two, married Augusta Phillips. They lived in Union Street, and between 1832 and 1840, Augusta gave birth to three children, Sarah Ann, Emily and Thomas, who was later to inherit the Smith plumbing business. Early in 1843, she was again pregnant and her condition must have been serious. She was given an abortion, but afterwards was attacked by violent fevers. On 25 May, at the age of thirty-two, she died.

A year later Thomas Smith married again. His second wife was a twenty-six-year-old girl, Mary Thornton, the daughter of William Vincent Thornton, a cupper from Cheltenham. Before her marriage she was living in Ship Street, Brighton, and it was here that Thomas Smith and his three children now moved. In the next fourteen years they had at least ten children, but the mortality rate among the boys was high, four of them dying before their twelfth birthday.[14] Thomas Smith was 'a person of full habit of body' and outlived nine of his seventeen children.

In its way Thomas Smith's career was comparable to that of William John. From humble beginnings he became a successful and respected local figure. By the age of fifty he was a Master Plumber, glazier and painter, employing ten men and three boys in the painter's shop he had bought next door in Ship Street, and in the home a cook, housemaid and nursemaid. His will might have drawn a nod of approval from the Town Clerk of Haverfordwest. In one respect at least it is superior to William John's:

he left a sum of almost fourteen thousand pounds (equivalent in 1996 to approximately £522,000).

Mary Smith's third child, born on 22 September 1848, was named Augusta after her father's first wife. From a comparatively early age she appears to have shown a talent for art. She was sent to 'Mrs Leleux's Establishment' at Eltham House in Foxley Road, North Brixton, and here, in December 1862, she was presented with a book, *Wayside Flowers*, as a 'Reward for Improvement in Drawing'.

She continued drawing and painting up to the time of her marriage, and to some extent afterwards. The few examples of her work that survive show her subjects to have been mostly pastoral scenes. A study of Gras-mere church, seen across a tree-lined river and executed in soft cool colours, is signed 'Augusta Smith' and dated 1865;[15] a picture of cattle with friendly faces, painted three years later when she was nineteen, is signed 'Gussie'. But a charming 'Landscape with Cows' painted after marriage and simply signed 'A. John' is part of the Dalton Collection in Charlotte, North Carolina, where, attributed to her son, it hangs happily in company with Constables, Rembrandts, Sickerts and Turners.

For Augusta, painting was only a pastime. Her father's taste for biblical Christian names, and the fact that almost none of his daughters married before his death, suggests an Old Testament view of women's place in the scheme of things to which, while he lived, Augusta was obedient. But on the night of Thursday, 20 February 1873, Thomas Smith suffered a stroke. For five days he lay paralysed on his bed, gradually sinking until, at four o'clock on the following Thursday afternoon, he died.

His relatives filled three mourning coaches at the cemetery. Such was his reputation as an honest tradesman that, despite appalling weather, a great concourse of people gathered at the grave, while in Brighton itself nearly every shop in his part of the town had one or two shutters up. 'In fact,' the *Brighton Evening News* (4 March 1873) commented, 'so general a display of shutters is seldom to be seen on the occasion of a funeral of a tradesman, only but honourably distinguished by his strict and uniform integrity during a long business career.'

Four months later, on 3 July, Augusta married Edwin John at St Peter's Church in Brighton. It was said to be a love match. One of the tastes they held in common was music: she would play Chopin on the piano, while he preferred religious music and in later life wrote a number of 'chaste and tuneful compositions' for the organ, including a setting for the Te Deum and a berceuse. The three eldest children, who were unmu-sical, were all encouraged to draw and, to amuse them, Augusta 'painted all round the walls of their nursery'.[16]

But the strongest reaction Augusta produced on all her children was through her absence. She died, apparently among strangers, at Ferney Bottom, Hartington, in Derbyshire. The cause of her death was given as rheumatic gout and exhaustion. She was thirty-five years old;[17] her daughter Gwen was eight and Augustus was six-and-a-half.

3

LIFE WITH FATHER

'The bubble of a life-time of respectability burst without trace. There seemed no answer to it but ridicule. That was your answer and I approve of it – that or silence.'
Thornton John to Augustus John (25 June 1959)

The year 1884 was for Edwin John a particularly unhappy one. His marriage, ruined latterly by his wife's ill-health, was at an end; and his father, who had been suffering from what the locals called 'water on the brain', had died in the previous month.[18] He had four children, two fanatical sisters-in-law, few friends.

That autumn Edwin made a great decision. He gave up his legal practice in Victoria Place, sold his house at Broad Haven and, taking with him two Welsh servants from Haverfordwest, moved to Tenby where, for a short spell, he had enjoyed some happiness with Augusta. Leah and Rosina left too, transferring their proselytizing zeal to the wider horizons of the New World,[19] and leaving Edwin to lapse back into the bosom of the orthodox church.[20]

But there may have been another reason why Edwin wanted to get away from Haverfordwest. He had inherited almost all his father's fortune of some eight thousand pounds. His two brothers, Alfred and Frederick, were each left only a small annual income provided that, at the time of William John's death, neither was 'an uncertified bankrupt or through his own act or default or by operation or process of law or otherwise disentitled personally to receive or enjoy the same during his life or until he shall become bankrupt'.[21] It seems that in their father's opinion Alfred, who had gone to Paris, was a ne'er-do-well; Frederick, who served time in prison (and was to die in 1896 aged thirty-nine), was a criminal; and Edwin was his good son. Two of their sisters, Joanna and Emma, were already dead, but another sister, Clara, was alive. She did not go to her father's funeral, and neither did Alfred or Frederick, for there was bad feeling between them and Edwin. Clara never enlarged 'upon the rift which separated them', Thornton wrote to Augustus, ' – hatred perhaps would be a better word. I suspected money.'[22]

Clara felt she had a moral claim on her brother, but Edwin knew she had no legal claim. He was now a comparatively wealthy man, having also inherited his wife Augusta's money (partly held in trust for their children). He was thirty-seven years of age – not too late to start another life in a new place.

Victoria House, 32 Victoria Street, into which he and his young family now moved was an ordinary mid-nineteenth-century terrace house, with three main floors, a basement for servants and an attic for children.

Augustus disliked his new home almost from the beginning. Dark and cube-like, with a peeling façade, it was like a cage and he a bird caught within it. Set in a dreary little street off the Esplanade, from where you could hear but not see the waters of Carmarthen Bay, it was furnished without taste or imagination, its dull mahogany tables and chairs, its heavy shelves of law tomes and devotional works, its conglomeration of inauthentic Italian pottery, pseudo-ivory elephants and fake Old Masters – all tourist souvenirs from William John's European wanderings – reinforcing the atmosphere of mediocrity and gloom. In the twelve years he lived here, Augustus came to feel that this was not a proper home nor was Edwin John a real father. 'I felt at last that I was living in a kind of mortuary where everything was dead,' he records, 'like the stuffed doves in their glass dome in the drawing-room, and fleshless as the abominable "skeleton-clock" on the mantelpiece: this museum of rubbish, changing only in the imperceptible process of its decay, reflected the frozen immobility of its curator's mind.'[23]

Edwin John was afflicted by a form of acute anxiety from which he protected himself with a straitjacket of respectability. For what he had lost with the death of his wife, for all he had seemed prevented from attaining by his terrible reserve, he found solace in the contemplation of a stubbornly unspent bank balance.

The regime at Victoria House was an expression of this financial and emotional stringency. Sometimes, at night, the children were so cold that they would pile up furniture on their beds. Though timid in public, Edwin was something of an authoritarian at home and demanded of his children an unquestioning obedience. He was determined to do the right thing – and the right thing so often combined unpleasantness with parsimony. Gwen, who abhorred rice pudding, was required to swallow it to the last mouthful; Winifred, who was rather fragile when young, was specially fed on a diet of bread-and-butter pudding full of raisins which she was convinced were dead flies. More awful than anything else were the silences. Whether because of his shyness or of some wall of melancholia, Edwin seemed shut off from his children, unable to mix or communicate with them. Breakfast, lunch and eventually dinner were sometimes eaten without a word spoken. Once, when Winifred hazarded some whispered remark, Edwin turned on her and asked with facile sarcasm: 'Oh, so you've found it at last, have you?'

'Found what?'

'Your tongue.'

It was after this that Gwen and Winifred invented a language based on touch and facial expressions, but they were forbidden to use it in the house since it made them look so hideous. So they would go upstairs before each meal and try to decide what each would say.

'I'm going to say . . .'

'No. I want to say that.'

'I thought of it first.'

'Well, I'm the eldest.'

Augustus's silence was more complicated. He had seen a boy of about his own age fall off a roundabout at a fairground and be led away bleeding at the mouth. This scene had so impressed him that he later transferred it to himself. When called upon to answer some question he would struggle gallantly with his partly amputated tongue but utter only a few grunts. This handicap left him at last when he became a self-elected son of the Antelope Comanche Indians, and was required to cry 'Ugh! Ugh!'

Birthdays were times of unbearable excitement. Though excessively formal, Edwin John was not an unkind man. At night, the children would tell him what to play on the piano, and the sound of his scrupulous rendering would float up to their icy bedrooms. He also read to them in the evenings from *Jane Eyre*, and Mme Blavatsky's *Isis Unveiled*, from bowdlerized versions of *The Arabian Nights* and, more haltingly, from the complete works of a Flemish writer, Hendrik Conscience, translated into French – a language in which Edwin was being tutored by Monsieur de Berensburg, a Belgian exile in Tenby. Gwen and Winifred were for a time taught by a French governess who was delighted by their progress and told their father it must be due to some French ancestry. This intended compliment dismayed Edwin who discontinued the lessons and substituted instruction in German grammar.

As at Haverfordwest, it was the servants who enjoyed themselves most and they were much envied by other servants in Tenby. Shrieks of laughter were often to be heard rising from the basement and invading the stillness of Edwin John's rooms. Occasionally relatives called, and the children would be dragged out from behind furniture and under beds to deliver their cold kisses.

But it was not an unhappy life. Their emotions were chiefly directed to their animals, the sea, to wild stretches of the country and the occasional best friend. Gwen had a cat, Mudge, who was a famous fighter. Out walking, Edwin would meet him on the town wall looking so disreputable that he refused to recognize the animal, quickening his pace to shake him off. But when Winifred lost her spaniel Floss, Edwin arranged for the town crier to walk through Tenby ringing his bell and shouting out the news. Once Floss was found, he hurried round to her school, accompanied by a maid, interrupting her lessons to tell her the good news.

Thornton grew into a small quiet boy, more at home in the sea than on land. Rather slow and precise in his speech, he would provoke Augustus into all sorts of exasperating tricks to discover the limits of his endurance. Destined by his father to be an engineer, he cherished a romantic ambition to live the life of a gold prospector, and before the age of twenty left, luggageless, for Canada, sprouted a moustache and spent many years unsuccessfully digging.*

The two girls, Winnie with long fair hair down her back, and Gwen who was dark, used to walk about Tenby alone, which was regarded as very peculiar. Both were intensely shy. As they grew older they were allowed to go for bicycle rides together along the green Pembrokeshire lanes, climbing on to the stone walls whenever they met a flock of sheep. Once they encountered a company of soldiers, whose officer gave a word of command as they approached so that the columns of men separated, allowing them to ride down the centre at full speed, blushing furiously.

Winifred, who was to become an accomplished violinist in the United

---

* Either he would discover a good partner and no gold, or some gold and a partner who ran off with it. But, except for a brief period when he dreamed of starting a tobacco factory in Ireland, he seemed to have found what he really loved – mountains, prairies, horses and empty spaces. Among the trappers, cowboys and prospectors he earned the title of 'the rider from away back', and, in company with a band of them, crossed Canada on horseback, fording rivers and bathing in hot springs till his skin turned dark orange. Above all he relished solitude and for some years before 1914 went to live beside an Indian encampment, whose inhabitants would appear outside his tent, sit for hours smoking their long pipes, then vanish. He also travelled through Montana 'and always on horseback'; he wrote: 'I used to make my bed on the ground without a tent, and the dawn was the most important part of the day.' He married late in life a woman who had had two previous husbands and whom he discovered after her death to have been twenty years older than he thought. He had no children, but one foster daughter. He died in British Columbia on 19 March 1968, aged ninety-two.

States,* and who also loved dancing, shared her sister's affinity for the sea and passion for flowers. But Gwen's need for sea and flowers, nurtured in greater solitude, was obsessive. She used to dream of flowers and if she could not pick them, she would spend her pocket-money buying them.

Out of sight of her father and the well-dressed persons of Tenby, Gwen would strip off her clothes and run along the empty beaches. In this wildness, and the quick switchback of her emotions, she resembled Augustus more closely than Winifred or Thornton who were both softer personalities. But as children Gwen and Winifred paired off together while Thornton and Augustus, wearing their dark-blue schoolboy caps at the very backs of their heads, trailed groups of girls across the sandhills. At home Gwen and Gus would stage elaborate arguments as to who was really the elder, neither of them appealing for judgement to Papa because they would then have to find something else to argue over.

Much of Augustus's life at this time passed in fantasy. He would ransack his father's library for books and, poring over them, would seem to hover on the threshold of other worlds. When he read the story of Gerda and Little Kay, he was overcome by ungovernable tears, and had to shut himself away in his room. His favourite author was Gustave Aimard, whose tales of 'Red Indians' so absorbed him that he took to studying his father's features in the hope of discovering in them some trace of Antelope blood.

But it was outside Victoria House that Gus came fully alive. Striding through the streets of Tenby on the tallest stilts, diving off rocks and swimming far out into the cold bay, gathering wild strawberries that overhung the cliff tops, gazing fearfully down disused coal pits or up through the terrifying blow-holes that bellowed out volumes of yellow sea-spume over the fields, wandering across the salt-marshes to the rock-pools

---

* From Paris, Winifred crossed the Atlantic while still in her early twenties. By the summer of 1905 she had reached Montana, living some months with Thornton surrounded by Indians, 'rattlesnakes and all sorts of wild animals'. The two of them planned to travel to Mexico by boat along the Mississippi. 'The idea of orange groves and sunlight is *enchanting*,' Augustus wrote to her, '– but too remote from *my* experience to be anything but a lovely dream. But depend on it, you have only to perjure yourselves to its reality to bring this family at any rate helter skelter on your tracks ... I can *see* you and Thornton installed on the top of some crumbling teocalli with the breath of the Pacific in your nostrils.' Eventually this plan was abandoned, and Winifred journeyed instead to Vancouver where 'the weather was perfect: it rained every day', and to San Francisco, 'a beastly town'. For a number of years she gave violin lessons in California, and on 30 January 1915 married one of her pupils, Victor Lauder Shute, a failed painter who had turned engineer and worked mostly for the railroads. They had three children, Dale, Betty and Muriel, a fourth child being still-born in 1924. Although she claimed to have developed 'such strong nerves I have played to a room full of people and forgot everybody', she remained shy.

She never returned to Wales or England, but died in Martinez (California) on 12 April 1967, aged eighty-seven.

in the hills where the snow outlasted the winter – Augustus was in his element.

At home he appeared to shrink; outdoors he seemed fearless. One day, coming across an untethered horse, without a word he jumped on its back. As it started to gallop, he slowly began sliding off until he was eventually hanging under its neck. So this odd pair hurtled towards the horizon. But in the end, when the horse finally came to a halt, Augustus was still clasped there. He was always climbing. He would descend the dizzy rock-cliffs between Giltar and Lydstep to wet shingle beaches and, like Gwen, fling off his clothes and throw himself in and out of the water while the tide advanced, giving him that special thrill which comes from not being quite sure of getting back.

In particular, he loved the harbour at Tenby with its fleet of luggers and fishing-smacks, and the russet sails of the trawlers; and the long expanse of Tenby beaches, their sand spongy like cake – a golden play-ground two miles long. Here, while still very young, Gus would play all day with his brother and sisters, catching shrimps in the tidal pools where the sea-urchins delicately flowered, paddling through the waves that seethed and criss-crossed the shore, and elaborately hauling buckets of sand up the blue slate-coloured cliffs. Where the sea had worn these cliffs away, devious caves had been hollowed out, as if gnawed by giant sea-mice – dark, dangerous and exciting. Slabs of slate rock lay bundled at the entrances, covered with barnacles and emerald seaweed.

The beach was a fashionable meeting place for all Tenby. Under the cliffs a band played patriotic airs and 'nigger minstrels' sang and danced; donkeys, led by donkey-boys and ridden by well-dressed infants, trotted obediently to and fro; gentlemen in boaters or top hats, and ladies in long skirts with wasp waists, balancing parasols, promenaded the sands. Bathing – a complicated procedure in voluminous blue serge costumes or long combinations – was permitted between special hours. Horse-drawn bath-ing machines, strewn along the sands, were used – bathing from boats was not lawful within two hundred yards of the shore. These bathing machines were upright carriages on wheels, advertising the benefits of Beecham's Pills and Pears Soap. They were looked after by a large uncorseted woman and a company of boys, celebrated for their vulgarity, who shocked Augus-tus by whispering unheard-of obscenities in his ears. A frantic man, sum-moned by the shouts of these boys, would canter up and down the sands harnessing horses to the vehicles which were then pulled out into the deep water. The occupants could thus enter the water with the least possible hazard to modesty. Once they had completed their swimming, they would re-enter their horse-drawn dressing-room, regain their clothes, then raise a flag as a signal that they were ready to be towed back.

As he grew older, Augustus began to avoid this beach, roaming beyond North Cliff Point where he and his companions could bathe from the rocks and lie naked in the sun. He longed for a wider world than that enclosed by the walls of Tenby and was happiest when he and his brother and sisters were invited to stay at Begelly, in a house overlooking an infertile common populated by geese, cattle and the caravans of romantic-looking gypsies. Here, and with the Mackenzie family at Manorbier, the rules and repressions of Tenby were forgotten, Papa was left behind, and the strangely brooding children of Victoria Street were transformed into a turbulent tribe of Johns.

One of Gus's best friends at this time was a boy, eighteen months younger than he, called Arthur Morley. With their butterfly nets, the two boys spent much of their time playing along the dunes. 'We used to go for walks together, sometimes to a place known as Hoyle's Mouth, a cave in a limestone cliff about $1^1/_2$ miles from the town near a marsh where flew many orange-tip butterflies,' Morley recalled. 'On the floor of the cave we used to dig pre-historic animals . . . We found that leading out of this cave there was a second which we could reach by crawling along a very small passage with a lighted candle.'[24]

His greatest friend was Robert Prust, whose family occupied, with their parrot, a fine house on the south cliff. Robert Prust was keen on 'Red Indians', and for a long time Augustus hero-worshipped him. The two of them would lead a pack of braves along the rough grass tracks, across the sand dunes known as 'the Burrows' to advance upon the army encampment at Penally. No one took his Indian life more seriously than Augustus. 'Under the discipline of the Red Man's Code,' he wrote, 'I practised severe austerities, steeled myself against pain and danger, was careful not to betray any emotion and wasted few words.'[25] Such a regime was too much for his companions who, one by one, abandoned the warpath to chase the paleface Tenby girls. At last, only the two of them were left. The final betrayal came when, having helped Augustus set fire to a wood, Robert Prust revealed a most un-Indian lack of stoicism. Thereafter Augustus was left to roam the Burrows with only a phantom tribe of Comanches.

The cult of the 'Red Indian' gave Augustus an alternative world to Tenby. Yet everywhere there were encroachments. His hunting ground, the Burrows, was converted into a golf-links; the 'nigger minstrels' under the cliffs were replaced by a refined troupe of pierrots who could be invited with impunity to tea; flower shows took over the ice-rink and the annual fair, with its blaring roundabouts spinning away late into the night, was removed from under the old town walls.

Tenby, in the last two decades of the nineteenth century, was becoming a town patronized by relatives of the county landowners of Pembrokeshire, by retired field officers and elderly sea-dogs. It was also a holiday resort for the upper-middle classes, who arrived each summer to play their golf, badminton and high-lobbing lawn tennis, to shoot sea-birds and hunt foxes. There were regattas, picnics and water-parties, much blowing of marine music, balls with polkas and galops at the Royal Assembly Rooms and, in the evening, the twilight ritual of promenades along the cliffs.

Everywhere strict rules of etiquette were observed. One of the first things Edwin John did was to throw away his professional brass plate – though he continued to practise law from his home as if it were merely a gentleman's whim or hobby, like his shell collecting. He volunteered as assistant organist at St Mary's, and every Sunday morning lined up his children, like small soldiers, in the hall, to be inspected before taking them off for the service. He himself, in a top hat and frock coat, led the way, and drew many curious glances. He did more: he took up photography; he played the harmonium; he had cold baths in the early morning; above all he did – and was conspicuously seen to do – absolutely nothing whatsoever. His manner was unapproachable: and no one approached him. It was very odd. He redoubled his efforts. His hair grew white, his cheeks turned pink, his collection of cowries multiplied, his solitary walks towards Giltar or along the road to Gumfreston became longer, his collars, always of the stiffest, stiffened further: throughout the district his gentility and rectitude were freely acknowledged. But with the élite of Tenby – the Prusts and Swinburnes, the Morleys and Massays and Hannays and de Burghs, whose children were his children's companions – Edwin was never on visiting terms. For although his propriety was unexampled, curious rumours persisted of some scandal back at Haverfordwest – rumours fanned into life by Gus and Gwen, Thornton and Winifred.

So Edwin John, who hated eccentricity, took his place among the town's most bizarre characters: with the gentleman who tied a rope to his topmost window and, shunning stairs, swarmed up and down it; and with another who wore socks on his hands; with the lady who struggled to keep an airless house, stuffing paper into every crevice of window and door; with Cadwalladyr, the speechless shrimper, massive and hairy and never less than up to his waist in water; and with Mr Prydderch, bank manager and Captain of the Fire, who, 'swaggering fantastically, his buttocks strangely protuberant', paraded the town to the music of a brass band until confined in Carmarthen Asylum.

Edwin John made sure that his children were seen to be educated. Nothing excessive was required; in particular the girls' education was so reticent as to be almost invisible. As soon as the family had settled into their house at Tenby, Gwen and Winifred were sent to what was referred to as a 'private school' a few yards down Victoria Street. It consisted of three pupils, the mother of the third one, a German lady married to a philosopher named Mackenzie, acting as teacher. This arrangement combined for Edwin the advantages of cheapness with those of social prestige in claiming for his daughters a foreign 'governess', optimistically described as 'Swiss'. Mrs Mackenzie was a kind and homely woman who, to a limited extent and more especially with Winifred, took the place of a mother. Her daughter Irene became a particular friend of Winifred's – the two of them laughed so much together that if one caught sight of the other even on the horizon she would be convulsed with giggles. Gwen, at this time, suffered from back trouble that gave Mrs Mackenzie's lessons a drastic appearance as she lay, on doctor's advice, stretched out on the schoolroom floor where Irene and Winifred insisted on joining her.

When they were older the two sisters attended Miss Wilson's Academy,[26] a school that placed more emphasis on deportment than scholarship. Miss Wilson herself was a stern-looking woman of unguessable age, who later committed suicide in the sea.

Gus's education was also unusual. Late in 1884 he went to an infant school in Victoria Street, and at the age of ten was sent to join his brother at Greenhill, a rambling building set on a plateau on the slopes of lower Tenby.[27] This school catered for the sons both of tradesmen and of the middle classes, and its pupils, faithfully mimicking the ways of their parents, segregated themselves into two classes: 'gentlemen' and 'cads'. It was run by Mr Goward, a tiny man with a large spectacled face topped by a flame of hair, dressed in mock-clerical neckwear and curiously short turned-down trousers. An ardent Liberal and Congregationalist, he began each day with a Gladstonian homily, followed, according to his mood, by hymns or a rendering of 'Scots, Wha Hae'.

Gussie, as everyone called him, was a mutinous pupil, often in trouble for breaking school rules, caricaturing the masters and retaliating when corrected. With the other boys he seems to have been popular. It was here that he won his first serious stand-up fight, collapsing into uncontrollable tears after his victory as if in sympathy with the loser.

It was here, too, that he received from the drill master a smashing blow on his ear that, for the rest of his life, made him partially deaf.

Regularly, each term, his misdeeds were reported to his father who meticulously committed them to paper. Then, one day, something shocking happened: Augustus struck the second master – instead of the other way about – and Edwin felt he could ignore these delinquencies no longer. Having entered this last enormity in his ledger, he summoned Augustus to his study, read out the full catalogue of his crimes over the years and with a cry of 'Now, sir!' had, in his own words, 'recourse to the old-fashioned punishment of caning'.

Shortly after this incident, Mr Goward left Greenhill for British Columbia, and both Thornton and Augustus were sent to boarding school at Clifton College, near Bristol. The new school took a number of pupils from Pembrokeshire and was well thought of in Tenby, from where it was seen as a minor Eton College turning out middle-class stalwarts who played the game and administered the Empire.

Augustus never fitted into this school. The top hat, Eton jacket and collar made him feel uncomfortable and faintly ridiculous. At football, which he liked, he achieved some success. But cricket seemed elaborately unspontaneous: he could never bowl, the long drudgery of fielding bored him, and at batting, which appeared more promising, he was always being given out. It was while day-dreaming on the cricket field that a ball struck him on his ear and did for that one what the drill instructor's baton had done for the other at Greenhill.

Though strong for his age, Augustus seldom entered into the games of the other boys and he made no lasting friendships. The only boy for whom he cared at all was, like himself, an outcast in this foreign atmosphere of an English preparatory school, being a 'half-wit', but so sweet-natured that Augustus befriended him.

Everything that appealed to him at this time seemed to lead him away from Clifton: the River Avon flowing westwards under wooded cliffs towards the Golden Valley and the sea; the docks of Bristol where, for a few pence, it was possible to watch a platoon of rats being mauled to death by a dog or ferret; and, in the dark autumn evenings, while he was dreaming over his homework, the distant wail of an itinerant street vendor, which stirred in him a painful longing.

'Gloom, boredom and anguish of mind'[28] were his predominant moods at Clifton, but they did not last long. Early in 1891 he left to continue his schooling back at Tenby which, for all its disadvantages, was still the only home he knew.

St Catherine's, where he passed the next two-and-a-half years, had recently opened on the north-east corner of Victoria Street.[29] There was one classroom and seven pupils – though this number doubled later on – and the atmosphere, far happier than at Clifton, was like that of a family party.

'A lonely adolescent' was how Augustus later described himself in his early teens. Sometimes he was rebellious, sometimes quiet, at all times conspicuous. He liked to claim that he was a descendant of Owen Glendower, the fourteenth-century Welsh 'prince'. When one boy expressed scepticism, Augustus marched up to him glaring terrifically and waving his fists before his nose, and the doubter was convinced.

The school was so small it could not raise a full team for any game, and they devised all sorts of miniature variations – hockey on roller skates; four-a-side football; golf along the sand dunes with one club; and a game with wooden sticks with which you endeavoured, without being hit yourself, to hit your opponent's elbow. Augustus enjoyed these sports without going out of his way to excel in them. But there was one game at which he did excel. 'We each had to make a shield of some sort and were given six tennis balls,' Arthur Morley remembered.

'We were then divided into two sides . . . The idea was to attack the other side with the tennis balls. Anyone who was hit was out. Gussie naturally was captain of one side, but instead of trying to take his enemies by surprise he stood on the highest dune challenging them all loudly – he had, I think, been studying The Lady of the Lake. He was a striking figure.'[30]

With such small numbers and a wide span of ages, little teaching in class was practical, and the boys worked on individual lines under the headmaster's supervision. Augustus was largely innumerate, maintaining his place in arithmetic at the bottom of the school. But his reading and writing improved greatly. He devoured almost every book he could lay his hands on, especially any volume of poetry, and his stories and essays were so vividly written that the headmaster, who thought he might become a novelist, used to read them to the class.

It was not long before Augustus established himself as a star pupil. With the headmaster, Allen Evans, a clever Welshman who had passed his written examination for the Indian Civil Service but failed to pass the medical, he was an obvious favourite. On one occasion Evans delivered to the class a triumphal address in which he expatiated on the boldness and idealism of Augustus's aspirations, picturing him with one foot on Giltar Point and the other on Caldy Island, and in effect comparing him to the Colossus of Rhodes.

To these encomiums, which might have embarrassed another boy, Augustus responded like a bud in the sun. He had longed for encouragement from his father, but Edwin's lack of interest had closed him up. The hero-worship he had wanted to fix upon his father he now transferred to Allen Evans. Their special friendship lasted more than a year, but eventually ended painfully. 'One day when we were at work in the classroom the headmaster and Gussie stood together in a quiet but very bitter argument,' Arthur Morley remembered.

'I think that the former was accusing the latter of some offence which Gussie was vehemently denying. In the end the headmaster no doubt feeling that the argument had gone beyond the bounds of reason turned towards me and said: "Morley, did you hear what we were saying?" This was embarrassing, but I said: "I could not help hearing, sir." He then turned to Gussie and said: "There is a boy who talks the truth." '

For Augustus, the effect of this scene was devastating. He had been accused of dishonesty and his plea of absent-mindedness over a new school regulation was brushed aside as a lie. Charged publicly with deceit by the man whom he idolized, he was unable to find words to defend himself and broke down before the school.

This incident appears to have had a lasting effect on him. Episodes in later life would press upon this bruise and unaccountably cause him pain, giving rise to blasts of anger, grating sarcasm. Fifty years later, when writing the first draft of an autobiography, he cursed this 'amateur pedagogue', his former hero long since dead, for his 'appalling meanness of soul'.

At the age of sixteen, he left school, and a little later, while he was away from Tenby, heard that Allen Evans had committed suicide. Half-seriously, he began to wonder whether he possessed the evil eye. In his fragmentary autobiography, *Chiaroscuro*, he alludes briefly to the headmaster's 'unhappy end'.[31] But there is also a sentence, not eventually included in the book, that expresses his sense of retribution: 'Not long did my master (whom I had loved) enjoy his satisfacton and when he had punctiliously cut his throat, I grieved no more.'

4

A CRISIS OF IDENTITY

'We don't go to Heaven in families now -- but one by one.'
Gwen John to Ursula Tyrwhitt

'I am visiting my father,' Augustus John wrote to William Rothenstein during a stay in Tenby over thirty years later, 'and suffering again from the same condition of frantic boredom and revolt from which I escaped so long ago. My antecedents are really terrifying.'

Yet he loved Pembrokeshire, the exultant strangeness of the place, its exuberance of shadow and light; and since he was never cruelly treated some other factor must have accounted for this extremity of 'boredom and revolt'.

It was the *indoorness* of late Victorian life, the conformity and constraint of his oddly patriarchal background that affected him. For almost forty years, from the death of the Prince Consort in 1861, Britain had been in mourning. Despite the heavy new buildings, the heavy industry, everything seemed at a standstill – everything except for military developments across the Empire. This atmosphere of stagnation was eccentrically reproduced at Victoria House after the death of Augusta John. The widower did something of what Queen Victoria had done. There were no exaggerated manifestations of feeling. The iron will within Edwin John held firm. But though he was calm, he filled the house with darkness – out of which Augustus would burst rather like Edward VII escaping from the formalities of Windsor Castle into the new century.

'Too shy to be sociable, he made few friends; and these few he often found an embarrassment. Walking at his side through the town, I would be surprised by a sudden quickening of pace on his part, while at the same time he would be observed to consult his watch anxiously as if late for an important appointment: after a few minutes' spurt he would slow down and allow me to catch up with him. This manoeuvre pointed to the presence of a friend in the vicinity . . . he was delighted when a bemused soldier from Penally Barracks, mistaking him for a retired officer of high rank, saluted him. In reality he lacked every martial quality, except, of course, honour. Excessively squeamish, he would never have been able to accustom himself to the licence of the camp; even the grossness of popular speech shocked him . . .'[32]

To what extent is this picture of his father accurate? Winifred, who was probably Edwin's favourite but who saw less of him than the others, told her daughters she felt Augustus had been rather unfair. But Thornton approved, and Gwen's attitude to their father exceeded Gus's. 'I think the Family has had its day,' she wrote.

Edwin had two ambitions. The first was the revival of an old day-dream: to enter the church. All his life he entertained an admiration for churchmen, and had once considered preparing himself for the priesthood. In his fifties, he became organist at Gumfreston, a tiny inaccessible church two miles from Tenby. Every Sunday morning, wet or fine, he would make his way there, play the hymns and the psalms loud and slow; then walk back along the fields. He persisted with these duties until he was almost ninety.

His other ambition was to remarry. For a short time he seems to have become engaged to Alice Jones-Lloyd, and on another occasion was said to have proposed marriage to Teresa George. Both women were considerably younger than himself, handsome and of good family. These matrimonial skirmishes were always discreet, but news of them eventually leaked out bringing down on him the combined rage of Gwen and Winifred. 'I was furious at this heartless and extravagant outburst, and took his part,' Augustus records, 'but my overheated intervention only earned me the disapproval of all three.'[33]

The ordinary people of Tenby quite liked Edwin. They liked the look of him. 'I am not clever,' he boasted, 'but I am independent, and I believe in a good appearance all the time. With a good appearance I can accomplish much.' His chief accomplishment was to convert this good appearance into the appearance of goodness. His stamina for church-going, his cast-iron empty routine, above all his unrelenting loneliness and longevity excited a respect uncomplicated by envy. He was no trouble and he seemed a kindly man. He offered to pay for the education of his housekeeper's son; he taught a number of local children to play the organ; and when he wished to try out some new air he would call on a young chorister and present him afterwards with a shilling. Another of his pupils in the neighbourhood, John Leach, remembers that:

'my own father in spring and summer often took my sister and me to evensong . . . and usually we walked home with Edwin John through the woods and lanes. It came about through these walks that he asked my sister and me to go with him to the cinema, of which he appeared to be very fond. These were the days of the early Chaplins, the Keystone cops and the serial with its weekly threat to the life or virtue of the heroine. Perhaps Edwin John was fortified by the presence of children on these occasions . . . Besides being generous, one recalls [him] as a quiet, gentle, soft-voiced courteous man, who talked to children without condescension.'

But his own children he could not love. He was faced with the obstacle of their existence: an obstacle to remarriage, to the church and to almost any ambition he may have had. 'He became an object only,' commented Thornton. 'Is it any wonder we felt the effects of this?'[34]

'What damned ancestral strain is at work?'[35] Augustus later demanded. All of them were afflicted by melancholia. Winifred was probably the most successful at shedding what Augustus called this 'gloom by day and horror by night'.[36] She was to bring up a conventional American family and nourish a belief in the rigorous simplicities of psychic religion. Though she developed 'strong nerves'[37] to combat her timidity, she shared with Gwen, so she felt, a lifetime's devotion to privacy and the wish 'to be forgotten'[38] after death. But Gwen, who thought 'aloneness' rather than family life 'is nearer God',[39] believed in the value of her work after death. Gwen's self-neglect worried Gus and he worried her about it. 'Leave everybody and let them leave you,' she exhorted herself. 'Then only will you be without fear.'[40] Thornton, too, came to agree 'about solitude being a good thing. I didn't always think so.'[41] He would pass much of his own life 'alone but I am not at all lonely'[42] or fishing from his sailing boat.

Winifred, after escaping to the United States in her twenties, was obliged, like all the children, to keep up a regular correspondence with her father so as to receive the quarterly allowance from her mother's estate. 'Papa worries me to go home,' she wrote to Gwen in 1910. 'I don't want to'[43] – and she didn't. But Thornton, who left for Canada at the same time as Winifred, did return to Tenby at the end of the First World War. For Edwin still wanted his sons and daughters round him, even if he could not show them affection. He took the opportunity to remind Thornton that he was an executor of his will and, despite there being no work for his son in Tenby, advanced this as a proper reason for his staying there. 'I said I could return in the event of his death,' remembered Thornton who, on getting back to Canada, realized that he would never return. 'Do you think I should write to tell him so?'[44] he questioned Gwen.

Gwen, who went to live in France, could not avoid seeing her father occasionally. 'My father is here,' she wrote from Paris to her friend Ursula Tyrwhitt, ' – not because he has wished to see me or I to see him, but because other relations and people he knows think better of him if he has been to see me. And for that I have to be tired out and unable to paint for days. And he never helps me to live materially – or cares how I live.'[45] Gwen hardly ever referred to her childhood and her few references to Wales – 'the mild climate of Tenby means that one has little energy there'[46] – are polite metaphors. For ten years, in the optimistic belief that their father was dying, Gus would try to arrange a farewell meeting between the three of them. But he failed, and when eventually the old man died in 1938 Gwen did not go over for his funeral. He had been no more than an 'unwanted interruption to her work'.[47]

'I hold no grudge against him,' Thornton wrote of Edwin after his death. Nor did Winifred. But Gwen, who spent more precious energy in escaping from him, and Gus, who never really escaped and sometimes felt 'I ought to have stopped' in 'my native town',[48] did hold a grudge.

Augustus had needed a hero, and the hope that his father might somehow reveal himself as this hero had died a slow death. He described his father to the painter Darsie Japp as 'a revolting personage'[49] and was anxious to erase signs of involuntary attachment. 'I wanted to be my own unadulterated self, and no one else. And so, taking my father as a model, I watched him carefully, imitating his tricks as closely as I could, but in reverse. By this method I sought to protect myself from the intrusions of the uninvited dead.'[50]

His actions represented not simply a wish to be different from his father, but to be someone other than his father's son. His claim to be a descendant of Owen Glendower; his vivid fantasy life, nourished by books, which developed into the cult of the 'Red Indian': these were symptoms of his identification with non-John people. The kinship he felt for gypsies, too, and which later became so close that many people believed him to have gypsy blood, arose not just from the fact that Edwin John disapproved of them but from his having warned his son they might capture him and bring him up as one of their own. He longed to be kidnapped. At home he felt an outcast, and at school it was with the outcast he grew most sympathetic – the 'half-wit' at Clifton, even the boy he beat in a fight at Greenhill.

This drive to be someone else grew more complicated in adult life. To know Augustus John was to know not a single man, but a crowd of people, none of them quite convincing. His reaction against the paternal environment of his early years was in perpetual conflict with the melancholy characteristics he inherited from his father. Between the two opposing forces in this civil war stretched a no man's land where Augustus pitched his tent. But this battling against himself produced a state of crisis. In later years everyone else would recognize readily enough the manly and melodramatic form of Augustus John – but he himself did not know who he was. His lack of stylistic conviction as a painter, the frequent changes of handwriting and signature in his letters, his surprising passivity and lack of initiative in everyday matters, the abrupt changes of mood, the sense of strain and vacancy, the theatricality: all these suggested a lack of self-knowledge. 'When I am in Ireland I'm an Irishman,' he told Reginald Pound, and it was partly true. He was a chameleon. He had half turned his back on Wales and, while continuing to make sentimental visits, chose to live fifty years of his life amid the lushness of Hampshire and Dorset – a green-tree country he seldom painted and to whose beauty he was not particularly responsive. Like his brother and sisters, he too dreamed of exiling himself far off from the land of their father. But having 'got stuck'[51] in England, he later resented the parental contamination of his homeland. 'I wish to the Devil I were in Wales again instead of this blighted country,'[52] he wrote from Hampshire to his friend John Sampson in 1913. In such moods of disgruntled nostalgia his thoughts veered wistfully to the Prescelly Mountains and the west coast – and he would suddenly 'make a dash' there ('a pony trap and a spell of irresponsibility'[53]). But when in 1929 Sylvia Townsend Warner advised him to 'go back to Wales' permanently, he replied that this was 'impossible' because his father was there and he 'was still afraid of him'.[54] Yet, had it been possible, it would have been 'better to try and make the best of one's own country',[55] he acknowledged. Indeed, he sometimes felt it would have been really best of all if he had never left Wales.

Over the years Augustus became more imaginative at changing his past. He claimed not to know the date of his birthday, and declared that he never celebrated it. In 1946 he told a *Time* magazine interviewer, Alfred Wright, that his mother's name was Augusta Petulengro; and six years later (14 May 1952) he wrote to John Rothenstein: 'As for Gypsies, I have not encountered a sounder "Gypsy" than myself. My mother's name was Petulengro, remember, and we descend from Tubal-Cain via Paracelsus.' What he did not tell Alfred Wright or John Rothenstein (saving the inverted commas) was that Petulengro was the Romany version of Smith.[56] It was deliberate teasing, a fantasy that was irresistible to him but in which he did not actually believe. His real state of mind concerning who he was seems to have been a genuine bewilderment. 'I am in a curious state,' he confessed to Lady Cynthia Asquith in 1918, ' – wondering who I am. I watch myself closely without yet being able to classify myself. I evade definition – and that must mean I *have no character*. Do you understand yours?'

This void seems to have been created through the rejection of all Augustus knew of his background. He could not remember his mother; he knew nothing of his origins; he disliked his father. Victoria House appeared to enclose him in darkness. His shyness and anxiety cut him off from other people, cut them all off from everyone except themselves. Gwen was to make solitude part of her way of life. Edwin had done much the same but, probably in reaction to him, Augustus could not come to terms with this legacy of melancholia, endeavouring by force of energy to hurl it from him, or to outpace it, like a boy running against his shadow which at evening lengthens and overtakes him. To many who, like William Rothenstein, believed that Augustus had been born 'with a whole series of silver spoons between his gums',[57] this stampeding through life seemed a thoughtless squandering of his natural gifts. But Augustus took a more sombre view of himself: 'I am not so perverse as unfortunate,' he wrote (15 September 1899). All the children had been unfortunate in losing their mother and in having to contend with the family's isolation. But Augustus seemed particularly unfortunate in having been afflicted while at school by partial deafness that raised another invisible barrier between him and the world.

'If our mother had lived it would have been different,' Thornton wrote to Augustus over seventy years after her death (3 February 1959). She had encouraged them to draw and paint and, surrounded by her pictures, Gwen and Gus continued drawing and painting, using the attic at Victoria House as their studio. 'Wherever they went their sketch-books went with them,' their father liked to recall.

'In their walks along the beach . . . on excursions into the country, wherever they went the sketch-books went too, and were used. They sketched everything they saw – little scenes, people, animals . . . I can remember when they were a little older, and I sometimes used to take them to the theatre in London, how, even here, the inevitable sketch-books turned up as well. Then in the few minutes interval between the acts they worked feverishly to draw some person who had interested them.'[58]

Although he conceded 'it was possible that I was a less keen observer of the boy's work than his mother would have been', Edwin took pride in having failed to put a stop to all this sketching. He had left his children's talent 'to develop freely and naturally'. But one day on Tenby beach, Gwen, who 'was always picking up beautiful children to draw and adore',[59] came across Jimmy, a twelve-year-old boy with a pale haunting face and corkscrew curls down to his shoulders, dressed in a costume of old green velvet. Having made friends with him, she invited him back to her attic, and, in the hope of some payment for these sessions, his mother came too – rather to Gwen's disgust. But Edwin disapproved of strollers, and the sight of this woman wandering into his house was open to misinterpretation. He therefore decided to put his foot down and forbid Gwen inviting 'models' home. But already it was too late. He objected; Gwen insisted; and he gave way. It was the pattern of things to come.

In their adolescence the children began to pair off differently, Thornton and Winifred, both small and quiet, spending more time together, and Gwen growing more involved with Gus. They needed someone to replace their mother and displace their father, someone to love and from whom to learn. Gwen appears to have hoped that Augustus might be this person, but his needs were similar to hers and he responded fretfully to Gwen's attentions, undermining her confidence by making her feel ignorant. She was older, but he was bigger. 'I suffered a long time because of him,' she wrote in her early thirties, 'it's like certain illnesses which recur in time . . . I revolted against him at the beginning of each holiday, but he won by telling me horrible things and when I threw myself on him to fight him and pull his hair . . . he always won, for of course he was the stronger.'[60] Gwen was often in tears over this period, and Gus in angry despair.

Like Gwen, Gus saw life in terms of pictures. 'Once when we were walking together over the sand dunes and saw a piece of hard perpendicular sand,' Arthur Morley recalled, 'Gussie pulled out his penknife and very rapidly carved out an attractive hand and face. On another occasion when he was sitting on my right in class he seized my Latin Grammar book and on the first empty page drew in ink with amazing speed two comic faces very different from each other, face to face.'[61]

At Greenhill there had been art classes in which the pupils, armed with coloured chalks, copied lithographs of Swiss scenery. But Augustus also practised drawing from life, discovering from among the masters some challenging models. At Clifton he had been given no encouragement and no instruction. 'Philosophy was eschewed,' he afterwards wrote, 'Art apologized for, and Science summarized in a series of smelly parlour tricks.'[62]

Back at Tenby, while studying at St Catherine's, he endured a course of 'stumping' under the tuition of a Miss O'Sullivan. 'Stumping' was a substitute for drawing prescribed by the State Art Education Authorities. The stumps were spiral cones of paper, and the stumping powder a box of pulverized chalk. With these materials, some charcoal, an indiarubber and a sheet of cartridge paper, students would reproduce the objects placed before them by means of a prolonged smudging, rubbing and stippling that gave him a method of representing form without risking the use of line. At first he copied simple cones, pyramids and cylinders, then gradually advanced, via casts of fruit and flowers, to Greco-Roman statuary until he finally arrived at the Life Room, where he spent several months studying a fully clothed model almost as bored as himself. At this stage his work was submitted to the Central Authority, since each successful student received a certificate qualifying him to indoctrinate others in the Theory and Practice of Stumping, while the school received a grant from the Exchequer. Augustus was awarded his certificate and, at the age of sixteen, became a Master Stumper, Third Class.

He was more than ever anxious to leave Tenby. But what was he to do? He no longer thought of becoming a trapper on the Red River, or of leading a revolt of the Araucanian Indians, but dreamed of exploring the exotic possibilities of China. He would join the Civil Service perhaps, if that would carry him to such enchanted lands: he would do *anything* to get far enough away from this stagnant little backwater. He still loved parts of Tenby, the wooded valleys inland and the wild sea coast and rocky country along it, but the meanness of his life at home constricted him unbearably, and his hunger for a larger world grew every day more acute. His father, who would have preferred to launch him on a barrister's career, had to acknowledge that he was unfitted by nature to such a profession, and for a short time it was agreed between them that he should join the army. Augustus began his army training locally, and in the evenings the respective merits of the officer-training establishments at Sandhurst and Woolwich were weighed.

Then he changed his mind. He had decided, he said, not to join the army, but to study art. Edwin had never, he later admitted, 'taken their drawing seriously'. But for some months Augustus had been going to an art school in Tenby run by Edward J. Head, a Royal Academician, who reported very favourably on his progress. Edwin was impressed by these reports. He was an annual visitor to the Royal Academy and had read in *The Times* accounts of various sales and successes in the art world. Pastoral painting and conversation pieces in particular recommended themselves to him as gentlemanly pursuits. These days, it seemed, the artist's profession might be tolerably respectable, provided it was practised with financial success. Mr Head himself, if not exactly a gentleman, managed to live comfortably. When a number of his pictures had first been hung at the Academy, Edwin's civic pride vibrated. Here was an example his son might strive to emulate. Naturally he would have preferred Augustus to go for a soldier, but he was such a temperamental fellow, so moody and mutinous and with no head for serious business: art might be just the job for him. One thing still bothered Edwin: had he been sufficiently unenthusiastic? Certainly he had failed to encourage his son, but was that by itself enough? He had no wish to appear irresponsible in the way of putting up difficulties. In his own account of this time, Edwin explained his position by means of paradox:

'Obstacles put in his [Augustus's] way would only have strengthened his determination to become an artist . . . He suggested being allowed to attend the Slade School in London. The earnestness he put into this request made me first think he might after all make an artist . . . he could display plenty of determination when necessary, and his whole childhood had proved that he could give untiring application to either drawing or painting. This, combined with his obvious eagerness, made me give my consent quite willingly.'[63]

It was Mr Head who had recommended the Slade. The fees, Edwin discovered, were pretty stiff, but the legacy of forty pounds from Augusta would see to his son's upkeep – and there was always the possibility of a scholarship. Besides, it would put an end to the rows that were now breaking out between them. On the whole, things could have turned out worse.

TWO

'Slade School Ingenious'

I

NEW STUDENTS – OLD MASTERS

'What a brood I have raised!'

Henry Tonks

On his first day at the Slade, in October 1894, Augustus was led into the Antique Room, presided over by Henry Tonks – and almost at once a rumpus broke out. Some of the new students, who had already worked for several months in Paris, were objecting at not being allowed straight into the Life Class. Professor Tonks, however, was adamant: the students' taste must first be conditioned by Greco-Roman sculpture before it was fit to deal with the raw materials of life. And against this judgement there was no appeal.

Augustus was not one of those who objected. To him the absence of stumping was in itself wonderful enough. Far from having been to Paris, he had scarcely been to London and he felt his immense ignorance of everything. To the others he appeared a rather spruce and silent figure, white-collared, clean-shaven, guarding his dignity. Tonks placed him on one of the wooden 'donkeys', next to another new student, Ethel Hatch. 'I found myself sitting next to a boy about sixteen', she recalled, 'with chestnut hair and very brown [*sic*] eyes who had the name "John" written in large letters on his paper . . . He was very neatly dressed, and was very quiet and polite, and on the following mornings he never failed to say good morning when he came in.'[1]

He seemed out of the ordinary in so far as he was quieter than other students, and perhaps more timid. But one of them, Michel Salaman, noticed that, when he called for an indiarubber one day and someone threw it to him, he caught it and began rubbing out in a single movement. He was supremely well co-ordinated.

Every student had been instructed to provide himself with a box of charcoals, some sheets of *papier Ingres*, and a chunk of bread. Their first task was to make what they could of the discobolus. Augustus fixed it with a stare, then using a few sweeping strokes, polished it off, as he thought, in a couple of minutes. Tonks, however, thought differently. It was bold, certainly, but far too summary. Yet he was interested by Augustus's sketch.

Everything at the Slade dazzled Augustus. The spirit of dedication by which he felt himself to be surrounded, thrilled and abashed him. He hardly knew where to look. The girls were so eye-catching and the men apparently so self-assured that whatever imperfections he observed in their work he attributed to his own lack of understanding.

The teaching of Tonks gave Augustus the sense of direction he had so far lacked. In such a place he seemed to know who he was and the part he had to play. Whatever successes he gained later in his career, he remained to a certain extent a Slade student all his life. In its strengths and limitations, this was the single most important influence on him.

*

When Augustus John came to London, the Slade School was twenty-three years old, and about to enter one of its most brilliant phases. Its tradition was founded upon the study of the Old Masters, and laid special emphasis on draughtsmanship – on the interpretation of line as the Old Masters understood line, and of anatomical construction. 'Drawing is an explanation of the form,' Augustus was told. This was the Slade motto, and he never forgot it.

The school had opened in 1871, at a time when British art was at a low ebb. Cut off by its indifference from the exciting developments taking place on the Continent, the Royal Academy with its English literary tradition was all-powerful. The time was ripe for some form of revolution.

The new school took its name from Felix Slade, a wealthy connoisseur of the arts, who, on his death in 1868, had left £35,000 to found professorships of art at Oxford, Cambrige and the University of London. The Oxford and Cambridge chairs – the former taken by Ruskin – were to be solely for lecturing. In London the executors were asked to found a 'Felix Slade Faculty of Fine Arts', and University College voted £5,000 for building the Slade School as part of the college quadrangle off Gower Street.

The first professor, Edward Poynter, was an unlikely choice. A fellow student of George du Maurier, he was portrayed in *Trilby* as Lorimer, the 'Industrious Apprentice'. In his inaugural address he attacked the teaching in schools, where months were spent upon a single elaborate drawing, and recommended 'the "free and intelligent manner of drawing" ... of the French ateliers, of which he had experience as a pupil of Gleyre ...'[2] He recommended other innovations too: men and women must be offered the same opportunities; students were not examined on admission; and all the teachers had to be practising artists.[3]

Poynter did not remain long at the Slade. He became President of the Royal Academy, and in 1876 handed over the Slade torch to Alphonse Legros. Much in the condition of British art over the next fifty years is suggested by his career.

Legros taught his students to draw freely with the point, and to build up their drawings by observing the broad planes of the model. A friend of the great French artists of the period – Degas, Fantin-Latour, Manet, Rodin – he was himself a good draughtsman, a disciple of Raphael and Rembrandt, of Ingres and Delacroix. One of his pupils, William Rothenstein, has described his methods of teaching drawing:

'As a rule we drew larger than sight-size, but Legros would insist that we studied the relations of light and shade and half-tone, at first indicating these lightly, starting as though from a cloud, and gradually coaxing the solid forms into being by superimposed hatching. This was a severe and logical method of constructive drawing – academic in the true sense of the word . . . He urged us to train our memories, to put down in our sketch-books things seen in the streets . . . to copy, during school hours, in the National Gallery and in the Print Room of the British Museum . . .'[4]

Legros took no trouble to hide his hostility to the Royal Academy which, he believed, represented neither tradition nor scholarship, and he encouraged his students to be independent of Burlington House. He was close neither to the Salon painters nor to the Impressionists, and eventually he became an isolated figure. His instruction in painting, as opposed to drawing, was later described by Walter Sickert as 'almost a model of how not to do it'.

Legros retired from the Slade a year before Augustus arrived, but his principles were firmly established there. He and Poynter had been trained in the studio schools of Paris, and were in a line of studio teachers stretching back to the Renaissance. This was the atmosphere in which Augustus found himself at the age of sixteen – that of a medieval-Renaissance workshop school, which launched him on his Renaissance life.

By the time Legros retired, the Royal Academy had become aware of the Slade's growing strength, but despite its efforts to get one of its men appointed, the chair was offered to Frederick Brown. Brown was then forty-two, 'a gruff, hard-bitten man, of great feeling, with something of the Victorian military man about him, such as the colonel who had spent his life on the North-West Frontier, surrounded by savages, which indeed his life as a progressive artist and teacher during the 'seventies and 'eighties must have rather resembled.'[5] This somewhat grim figure, with his greying hair, chin-tuft, prognathous jaw and grave bespectacled eyes, was invariably dressed in a black frock coat. His teeth seemed permanently clenched, giving him the appearance of a man who would stand no nonsense – nor would he. He had studied in Paris under Robert-Fleury and Bouguereau, and for the past fifteen years had been head of the Westminster School of Art, which he expanded from evening classes and ran on the lines of a French school. He was popular with his students, many of whom followed him from Westminster to the Slade. His severe expression and high standards were complemented by great patience and he endeared himself to students by his wonderful memory – he would often refer to drawings they had done years before, and he became a great collector of their work.

One of these students who was to follow Brown to the Slade was a young Fellow of the Royal College of Surgeons, Henry Tonks. Tonks, who had become increasingly attracted to the artist's life, was eloquent in persuading his patients to pose as models and, when obliged to fall back on the dead, he seized every opportunity to draw the corpses that were dissected in his class. In about 1890, while Senior Resident Medical Officer at the Royal Free Hospital, he had started to attend the Westminster School of Art as a part-time student, hurrying off to its evening classes smelling strongly of carbolic.

Tonks was exactly the person Brown felt he needed to support him at the Slade. He was well educated, businesslike, and had a gift for teaching and a knowledge of anatomy that gave him special insight into the process of figure-drawing. Like Brown, he was dissatisfied with the mechanical methods of instruction employed in most art schools. If Brown resembled a Victorian colonel, Tonks, who was tall and gaunt, had the commanding presence of a nineteenth-century cardinal.

In the late autumn of 1893 Brown offered him the post of his assistant. Tonks was 'amazed, almost beside himself with pleasure'. A few months before Augustus arrived there, he took up his new career at the Slade. So began the famous partnership of Brown and Tonks, those two lean and rock-like bachelors, which was to carry on the teaching reforms of Legros, establish the Slade tradition of constructive drawing, and influence generations of British art.

*

From morning till late afternoon, Augustus toiled over the casts of Greek, Roman and Renaissance heads. Then, initially for short twenty-minute poses, he and the other new students were allowed down into the Life

Class. Augustus entered this studio for the first time with feelings of awe. Seated on the 'throne', he saw a girl, Italian and completely naked. 'Perfect beauty always intimidates,' he wrote. 'Overcome for a moment by a strange sensation of weakness at the knees, I hastily seated myself and with trembling hand began to draw, or pretend to draw this dazzling apparition.'[6] Looking round, he was astonished to observe that the other students appeared almost indifferent to the spectacle, and his respect for them mounted even higher.

The regime at the Slade was still austere. Men and women worked together only in the Antique Rooms. They were segregated elsewhere and rarely met in the evenings. 'This is not a matrimonial agency,' Brown told Alfred Hayward, a student whom he had come across saying good morning to a young girl in one of the corridors. Models and students were forbidden to speak to one another; older students in the Life Rooms had little communication with the new pupils, and the hierarchy was like that of a public school. Augustus seemed fixed in his work all day long and half the night. Wherever he went he took his sketchbook, filling it with rapid drawings of his fellow students.

In criticizing their monthly compositions one day, Tonks had said he wanted his students to go to the National Gallery more often and look less at the *Yellow Book*, with its drawings by Aubrey Beardsley. Augustus passed much of his free time at the National Gallery, the British Museum and other permanent collections in London. What he saw in these places overwhelmed him. He could not sort out his ideas, could not decide what excited him most or what suited his own talent best – the treasures of Europe were at the end of a bus ride to Trafalgar Square. He flitted from picture to picture. Should he be a Pre-Raphaelite or a latter-day disciple of Rembrandt? Or both – or something else again? Looking back at this period years later, he concluded: 'A student should devote himself to one Master only; or one at a time.'[7] His earliest master, on whom he began modelling his drawing, was Watteau.

The crowded cosmopolitan streets of London stimulated and confused him during these first months. The pervading smell of chipped potatoes, horse dung and old leather; the leaping naphtha flames along the main roads; the wood-block paving of the streets looking like squares from a Battenburg cake; the glittering multicoloured music halls; the costermongers with their barrows of fruit and flowers; the vendors of pickled eels, ices and meat pies; the jugglers and conjurors who performed for pennies: it was too foreign for him to absorb. He walked everywhere – from Bermondsey to Belgravia, from the narrow streets of cobblestones where chickens scavenged and the shabby slum children played to fashionable Hyde Park where men and women, glossily hatted, rode to and fro, their horses gleaming with health, their coachmen decked out in author-itative livery. It seemed that no encounter was impossible, and every adventure for the asking – if only he had the courage to find his voice.

But he was boorishly shy, and also poor. Most evenings he would return after dark to a dreary little villa, 8 Milton Road, Acton, where he lived with one of his 'Jesus Christ Aunts'; and every morning he left early on his long day's journey into town to reach the Slade long before ten o'clock when classes officially began. Occasionally his father would send him a small amount of money and he would hurry off to the music halls. In the melodramas and variety shows at the Alhambra, the Old Mogul, the Metropolitan, the Bedford, Collins's and Old Sadler's Wells, where a crowd of students could take a box for a shilling, he sketched the buskers and comedians, including the legendary buffoon Arthur Roberts, and the singers and dancers with their magical names, Cissy Loftus, Cadieux and Mary Belfont, who held him in thrall.[8] They were more real than reality. One student later remembered him shouting out his own line in one of the songs, and the singer improvising her refrain to cap it, and then the two of them keeping up the repartee, she in her harsh cockney, he in his vibrant Welsh, among the cheering and stampeding audience. He went to these music halls whenever he could afford it, and sometimes when he could not: and once or twice was ignominiously thrown out.

But he was much alone. On Sundays he would often wander round Speakers' Corner, listen to the orators, join the crowds and gaze at the outlandish sights – then, bursting with nervous energy, march all the way home. Often he travelled great distances, staring into people's faces, carrying under his arm one or other of his two favourite books – Walt Whitman's *Leaves of Grass* and *Hamlet*.

Increasingly during this first year, he sought the company of two other Slade students, Ambrose McEvoy and Benjamin Evans. McEvoy was a short-sighted youth, with a low dark Phil May fringe, an oddly cracked voice and spare, limp body, who improbably became something of a dandy, with his dancing pumps, monocle, high collar and black suit. In deference to Whistler, he converted himself into an almost perfect 'arrangement in black and white'. His natural amiability, talent for quick design (which led to early employment as comic-strip draughtsman for a paper called *Nuts*), and gift for comedy all endeared him to the solitary Augustus.

Benjamin Evans, who had been at the same 'frightful school' as Augustus at Clifton, was an intelligent and witty draughtsman, deeply versed in Rembrandt. The three of them went everywhere together. Some-times they would start out in the small hours of the morning and walk to Hampton Court or Dulwich; then, after breakfasting at a cabman's pull-up, spend the rest of the day at the picture gallery. At other times they would take their sketchbooks to the anarchist clubs off the Tottenham Court Road. In the mild climate of England, the foreign desperadoes who gathered here seemed to have grown curiously genial. Augustus saw many sinister celebrities including Louise Michel, 'the Red Virgin', who had once fought on the barricades during the Paris Commune of 1870 in the uniform of a man, and was now a little old lady in black; and that doyen of revolutionaries, Peter Kropotkin, dressed in a frock coat and radiating goodwill to everyone. Most innocent of all were the American anarchists – not a bomb, not an ounce of nitro-glycerine, between them. The leader of the English group was David Nichols, founder of 'Freedom', whose rashest act was to recite some passages from Swinburne in cockney. Despite a vehement Spanish contingent, the general atmosphere was one of sturdy handclasps, singing and dancing, and voluble monologues in indistinct dialects.

Augustus's tendency was to hero-worship those whom he liked, but since few people are natural heroes, this idolatry was often replaced by an aggressive disillusionment. Friendship with him was an erratic business. McEvoy, once known as the Shelley of British Art, whose ambition, it was later said, was to paint every holder of the Victoria Cross and every leading débutante, became the wrong type of success; and Evans who (Augustus believed) gave up art to became a sanitary engineer, turned out the wrong sort of failure.

Almost the only person who seemed capable of sustaining Augustus's adulation was Tonks himself. Tonks was a scathing critic, his drastic comments, like amputations, cutting off many a career. 'What is it?' he would ask after closely examining some student's drawing. '. . . *What is it?* . . . It is an *insect?*' Mere accuracy never satisfied him. 'Very good,' he remarked of one competent drawing – then added with a deep sigh: 'But can't you see the *beauty* in that boy's arm?' He would reduce many of the students to tears. But behind the Dantesque mask lay a benevolent nature. Sometimes he would have brief flirtations with the girl students, but his lasting passion was for the teaching of drawing and, as Augustus observed, 'the Slade was his mistress'.[9]

In Augustus's second term at the Slade two new teachers arrived. Both taught painting. Philip Wilson Steer was already one of the most celebrated artists in the country, and one of the worst art teachers in the world. But Augustus liked his quiet humour. He was a large, friendly, small-headed, slow-moving man, inarticulate and easygoing. When he was appointed to the Order of Merit he took the insignia along to show Tonks and asked: 'Have you received one of these?' Although he was England's most distinguished living painter, no one would ever guess he painted – or at least he hoped not. He travelled the country with his painting materials locked up in a cricket bag, explaining: 'I get better service that way.' It was true that he had studied in Paris, but he never troubled to learn French. England's most revolutionary artist was a deeply conservative man. He gained a reputation for wisdom yet scarcely ever spoke. Of his own fame he seemed unaware and would refer to his job (if there were no avoiding it) as 'muddling along with paint'. Yet he could be witty and had a sharp sense of character. 'Will Rothenstein paints pretty well like the rest of us,' he once murmured, ' – but from higher motives, of course.' Asked one evening what was wrong with an artist who had made an attempt upon the virtue of a servant girl, and who entered his drawing-room leaning upon a stick, he hazarded: 'Housemaid's knee, I suppose.' His chief enemy was draughts, and to outwit them he would dress, at the height of summer, in a heavy overcoat, yachting cap and policeman's boots.

At the Slade, Steer gave full expression to his inertia. Students awaiting his criticism as he sat behind them would turn at last to find him apparently asleep. As a result of such methods, Augustus was never taught very seriously to paint. His technique in oils remained rather clumsy at the Slade. But he was impressed by the 'flickering and voluptuous' touch with which Steer reworked his students' paintings and was part of a rococo style that had replaced his impressionistic use of colour.

The other new teacher was Walter Russell, a dry unmemorable man. Only three years after joining Brown's team, Russell, a member of the New English Art Club, was exhibiting his work at the Royal Academy. Since the New English was the chief rallying ground for opposition to the Academy, and since the Slade of Brown and Tonks was a nursery for this opposition, Russell's career seems to suggest an extraordinary contradiction. Increasingly he became a link between the Royal Academy and the forces that had set themselves up to oppose it. He remained at the Slade for thirty-two years and was knighted as a senior Academician, his career providing an index to the condition of painting in England.

The ties that Russell formed between the Slade and the Royal Academy enabled new talent to be directed towards the academic tradition of art in Britain. So when at last the 'Roger Fry rabble', as Tonks captioned them, advanced across the country after 1910 with their rallying cry of 'Cézanna!' they were opposed not just by the diehards at the Royal Academy, but by alert and combative reformers such as Tonks, who had behind him some of the most gifted young artists in the country and who, for the next twenty years, fought a vigorous defensive campaign against the invasion of Post-Impressionism, futurism and all abstract art. 'It is interesting to observe, and this is a fine lesson, how degradation sets in at once with the coming in of contempt for Nature,' Tonks wrote to the artist Albert

Rutherston (5 January 1932). 'We are no good without it, we are like children, without guardians. The last twenty years have been I believe the worst on record, speaking generally, and because of this Roger Fry has upset the applecart.'

Those who, like Augustus, owed their loyalty to Tonks, were to find that the solid ground under their feet was no longer connected to the mainland of contemporary art. 'I was never apprenticed to a master whom I might follow humbly and perhaps overtake.' Tonks, remarkable man though he was, could only act as go-between, pointing his way back to the Old Masters. But the Old Masters were many, and all of them were dead. Augustus needed a living master. With patience, he might have found a new guardian for his talent. But in the summer of 1895 he suffered an accident, the long-term effects of which were to remove the quality of patience he needed.

2

WATER-LEGEND

'The Slade continues to produce geniuses, we turn them out every year.'
Henry Tonks to Ronald Gray (November 1901)

Augustus was happy at the Slade. In his second year he won a certificate for figure drawing, a prize for advanced antique drawing and, much to his father's gratification, a Slade scholarship of thirty-five pounds a year for two years. But at home he was discontented. Never had Tenby seemed so provincial, Victoria House so mean and squalid. Whenever possible he would avoid staying there, and go off on expeditions in Wales and England, and later to Belgium and Holland, with his two friends Ambrose McEvoy and Benjamin Evans.

When it was not possible to escape, he occasionally invited a friend down to share his exile. One winter his fellow student Michel Salaman came for a week. It was an alarming holiday. Salaman was the same age as Augustus and belonged to a large and distinguished red-haired fox-hunting family that had made its fortune in ostrich feathers. The atmosphere of Victoria House was unlike anything he had experienced. Edwin, very dry and upright, made all conversation, even in whispers, sound a vulgarity. Thornton appeared to be a sort of hobbledehoy, utterly miserable when not playing cards. Winifred seemed dull and musical except in the presence of Gwen, when the two girls would giggle continuously, much

40

to Salaman's dismay. Gus, he thought, was quite out of place in these strange surroundings. Between dismal meals, the two boys would hurry off to the caves where Gus flew from rock to rock with the most agile and dangerous leaps. They also penetrated deep into the blackness of these caves, using up all their matches and unnerving Salaman with the thought that they'd be discovered, two heaps of bones, fifty years later. On another occasion, seeing a navvy who was bullying a child in the street, Augustus strode up and, while Salaman looked on in horror, put a stop to the affair by challenging the navvy to a fight. By the end of his visit Salaman was exhausted. He never went back.

At the beginning of the summer holidays of 1895 Augustus set off on a camping trip round Pembrokeshire with McEvoy, Evans and a donkey. It was in keeping with his Whitmanesque spirit of freedom. At Haverfordwest they fell in with a party of Irish tinkers 'rich in the wisdom of the road'; at Solva they were taught by a tramp how to snare rabbits. They drank beer in wayside inns, entered themselves unsuccessfully in village regattas, joined with more success in old-fashioned games 'which included a good deal of singing and kissing',[10] and painted 'the Rape of the Sabine Women'. It was an exhilarating summer. 'My friends and myself are encamped in a place called Newgate with two cottages and one partially built and a stretch of sand two miles long,' Augustus wrote to another student, Ursula Tyrwhitt.

'The Atlantic continually plays music on the beach. Outside browses the Donkey, our hope and pride. On this animal we depend to draw our cart and baggage . . . Outside the tent the odour of the fragrant onion arises on the summer air, it is McEvoy who cooks. One night we slept under the eternal stars, one of which alone was visible – Venus – and that I regret was placed exactly over my head.'

When they arrived back in Tenby, McEvoy and Evans left for London. Augustus expected to join them again shortly at the Slade. Meanwhile he had to steel himself for a week or two at Victoria House. The boredom was excruciating. He felt tempted to do all manner of wild things, but did nothing – there was nothing to do. One afternoon towards the end of his vacation he went to bathe on the South Sands with Gwen, Winifred and their friend Irene Mackenzie. The tide was far out but on the turn, and he decided to go off on his own and practise diving from Giltar Point. He climbed the rock and looked down. The surface of the water was strewn with seaweed. He stripped off his clothes and dived in. 'Instantly I was made aware of my folly,' he later wrote. 'The impact of my skull on a hidden rock was terrific. The universe seemed to explode!'[11] Possibly because of the cold water he did not lose consciousness and somehow managed to drag himself to the shore. Part of his scalp had been torn away and lay flapping over one eye. The ebb and flow of his blood was everywhere. He did what first aid he could, dressed slowly, turbaned his towel round his head and set off back to the South Sands. 'Presently he came running back,' Irene Mackenzie recalled, 'with blood pouring from his forehead.'[12] Edwin, who had joined his daughters on the beach, was greatly alarmed. They must get him back to the privacy of the house as discreetly as possible. Augustus was already feeling very weak. They hurried him back by a curious zig-zag route to his bed. Here he seems to have lost consciousness for a time. The next thing he knew was that he was being examined, rather to his gratification, not by the family's usual practitioner, but by Dr Lock, a far more eminent and romantic figure. Dr Lock stitched his wound, told him that he probably owed his life to his uncommonly thick skull, and left. Little more needed to be done. It was essential, however, that he have a period of convalescence in Victoria House. This 'durance vile'[13] was by far the worst part of his accident. 'As my brain clears I find my confinement here more galling,' he complained to Ursula Tyrwhitt.

'But I'm healing like a dog – the doctor is amazed at the way I heal. The wound is the worst of its kind he has had to deal with. If I appear at all cracked at any time in the future, I trust you will put it down to my knock on the head and not to any original madness. The worst part of it is the beef tea, I think. I am not allowed to remain long in peace without the slavey bearing in an enormous cup of that beverage . . . Man cannot live by beef tea alone.'

The students gathered at the Slade, but Augustus was not among them. Even Gwen had gone to London. He perspired with impatience. His wound was healing, it seemed, by the force of willpower. Even so it was a slow business. For a time Augustus tried working on his own. 'I have been doing sketches for a Poster for cocoa,' he told Ursula Tyrwhitt. '. . . It's great fun, but difficult – like everything else.' Then suddenly he tired of this: 'I'm sick of doing comic sketches . . . I don't feel in a comic mood at all.' His feelings were of colossal tedium and colossal revolt. Once he was free from this appalling imprisonment he would do such things . . . In the meantime: 'I am horribly dull. I was hoping for some signs that my brain was affected – a little madness is so enlivening. I do hope this dullness is not permanent.'

His handwriting in these letters to Ursula Tyrwhitt grows increasingly wild and there are drawings of himself, like a wounded soldier, with a bandage round his head and the beginnings of a beard. 'You must have lots of news to tell me, if only you would,' he pleads. 'I am insatiable.' And when Ursula does write to him he calls her 'an angel' and feels better. 'In fact I got up this morning before the doctor came and he was quite annoyed . . . they've cut away a great patch of my hair which will look funny I daresay. I'm longing to see a good picture again . . . I'm going to paint next term. Hurrah! How exciting it is . . . I feel sure *another* letter would complete the cure.'

His own letters also contain a rather tentative declaration of love. He recalls the last romantic evening of the summer term. 'How the strawberries sweetened one's sorrow! – how the roses made one's despair almost acceptable! How you extinguished everybody at the Soirée! Before you came it was night – a starry beautiful night, but you brought as it were the dawn which made the stars turn pale and flee, remaining alone with its own glorious roseate luminescence. Selah!'

At first he is merely in love with love itself, but soon he becomes more practical. He wants to extract from her 'like a tooth' the pledge that he may keep company with her once he returns. Is he to be allowed 'to take you home', he asks. 'I mean to accompany you?' In return he will lend her his Rembrandt book. They must have an understanding.

When he does go back to the Slade that autumn he is transformed. Upon his head he wears a smoking-cap of black velvet and gold embroidery to conceal his wound; and round his cheeks and chin sprout small tufts of red hair. He had become, Ethel Hatch noticed, extremely untidy – quite unlike the spruce, clean-shaven youth whom she had met the previous year.

The Augustus John legend was beginning.

This legend is a good example of how a remarkable man may be simplified into a popular myth. In the public imagination he was to represent the Great Artist, the Great Lover and the Great Bohemian. It was an ironic comment on his actual career, one which he did not accept himself but never effectively contradicted.

The story is perhaps more succinctly told on the back of a Brooke Bond tea card, as one of a series of fifty Famous People. Here Virginia Shankland wrote that Augustus John 'hit his head on a rock whilst diving, and emerged from the water a genius!'[14] To this must be added one further ingredient of the legend, perhaps not palatable to Brooke Bond tea drinkers. 'As a man he was larger than life-size,' wrote a *Daily Telegraph* leader writer. 'Even while still young his prowess with the fair sex was legendary and the stories about him legion. He attacked everything with vigour.'[15]

It seems clear that from 1897 onwards Augustus was a changed man. He was changed not only in appearance, but also in his work and behaviour. In his first year at the Slade, Tonks had described his work as 'methodical'. Now his drawings, remarkable for their firm, fluent, lyrical line, and executed with assurance and spontaneity, seemed to promise a new force in British art. What excited his contemporaries was 'his skill in making very beautiful line drawings of nudes and of portrait heads', writes the critic A. D. Fraser Jenkins. His large life studies revealed great delicacy and he continued 'compulsively to draw from the female nude. In drawing with line rather than shadow, John turned his attention to the rhythm of the outline, and his fascination with this later became dominant.'[16] Spencer Gore, who went up to the Slade in 1896, remembered him making 'hundreds of the most elaborate and careful drawings . . . sketch-books full of the drawings of people's arms and feet, of guitars and pieces of furniture, copies of old masters'. Whenever he moved his rooms, people would go and pick up the 'torn-up scraps on the floor which was always littered with them & piece them together. I know people who got many wonderful drawings that way.'[17]

As his beard formed, so his clothes became shabbier, his manner more unpredictable. For long periods he was still very quiet: but suddenly there would be a rush of high spirits, some outrageous exploit: then again silence. In his earlier years, according to Edwin, he had been 'a happy healthy child, not at all given to brooding or moodiness, who loved games and in every way was much the same as other children . . . a docile tractable child not subject to passionate outbursts'.[18] Edwin was anxious to present the picture of an ordinary respectable family. But Augustus's energies were increasingly directed against everything he held in common with his father, and in appearance he now began to resemble what Wyndham Lewis was to call 'a great man of action into whose hands the fairies had stuck a brush instead of a sword'.

Augustus disliked this description, for much the same reason that he disliked the portrait painted of him in 1900 by William Orpen,[19] which did not show the uncertain, dreamy person he knew himself to be. Already by then he was paling to invisibility in the sunlight of the John reputation. 'I am just a legend,' he once said. 'I am not a real person at all.'

The essence of Augustus's performance at the Slade, which was to nourish this larger-than-life legend, was *impatience*. His bang on the head had not infected him with a genius for draughtsmanship. Augustus himself described the theory of a rock releasing hidden springs of genius as 'nonsense', and he added: 'I was in no way changed, unless my fitful industry with its incessant setbacks, my wool-gathering and squandering of time, my emotional ups and downs and general inconsequence can be charitably imputed to this mishap.'[20]

The claustrophobia of his convalescence was what most strongly affected him. It did not confer extra qualities, but magnified certain traits, leaving him with an obsession against being confined and an additional sense of isolation. He was unable to tolerate stress, but had to outpace his anxieties. The assurance of his early drawings testifies to the speed with which he did them. His natural doubts and hesitations had no time to crowd in on him and when they began to do so, he put on an extra burst of speed. In a letter written by Charles Morgan to the art critic D. S. MacColl, he recalled some words of Wilson Steer's: 'Do you remember that drawing by John? It was done at a time when he drew with many lines and many of those lines were superfluous or even wrong, but then at the last moment, he would select among them and emphasize those which were right, and so, by an act of genius save a drawing which, in the hands of any other man, would have become a mess and a failure.' This technique of acceleration served him magnificently while he was still young. He raised the standard of work at the Slade, lifted other students to a new level. 'We can't teach students,' acknowledged Frederick Brown, 'they learn from one another.'

It was the vitality and restlessness that impressed other students. Everything seemed to contribute to his God-like aspect: his very name, Augustus, suggested the deified Roman Emperor.[21] By his eighteenth birthday he was an imposing figure: a picturesque figure nearly six feet tall, with a Christ-like beard, roving eyes and beautiful hands with long nervous fingers that gave a look of intelligence to everything he did. He was not talkative. But sometimes his eyes would light up, and he would speak eloquently in a deep flowing Welsh voice.

Physically he was the stuff from which heroes are made, and the age was right for theatrical heroes. From Oscar Wilde, who put his genius into his life and only his talent into his work, to the Sitwells with their genius for publicity, English civilization was presenting a fantastic gallery of 'characters' – dandies and eccentrics, prophets and impresarios of the arts. The age was becoming more mechanical, personal liberty restricted, behaviour uniform. The collective frustration of Edwardian England was soon to focus upon Augustus and elect him as a symbol of free man. Through him people lived out their fantasies; for what they dared not do, it seemed he did fearlessly and instinctively. There was nothing mechanical, nothing restricted or uniform about him; there was *wildness*. Wyndham Lewis, who first saw him at the Slade, was to describe Augustus as 'the most notorious nonconformist England has known for a long time.

'Following in the footsteps of Borrow, he was one of those people who always set out to do the thing that "is not done", according to the British canon. He swept aside the social conventions, which was a great success, and he became a public lion practically on the spot. There was another reason for this lionization (which is why he has remained a lion): he happened to be an unusually fine artist.

Such a combination was rare . . . Here was one who had gigantic earrings, a ferocious red beard, a large angry eye, and who barked beautifully at you from his proud six foot, and, marvellously, was a great artist too. He was reported to like women and wine and song and to be by birth a gypsy.'[22]

The triumphal progress had started.

3

A SINGULAR GROUP

'We were much together on and off.'

Augustus John, Chiaroscuro

No one could have appeared more at odds with Augustus than his sister Gwen. Physically, she looked fragile. Her figure was slender; she had tiny hands and feet; her oval face was very pale, and her soft Pembrokeshire voice almost inaudible. She dressed carefully in dark colours, and latterly in black. Her hair was brown, neatly arranged, with a bow on top. But this modest impression was corrected by a look of extreme determination. The receding John chin, which Augustus now camouflaged, seemed to symbolize Gwen's withdrawn nature. Socially ill at ease, she presented an air of aloofness.

Both their personalities were elusive: hers, in its reticence, manifestly so; his, more deceptively behind the theatricality of his 'reputation'. Despite appearances, they had much in common – an essentially simple interpretation of life, a singular sensitivity to beauty: the beauty of nature and of people, especially women, sometimes the same women. 'With our common contempt for sentimentality, Gwen and I were not opposites but much the same really, but we took a different attitude,' Augustus later wrote. 'I am rarely "exuberant". She was always so; latterly in a tragic way. She wasn't chaste or subdued, but amorous and proud. She didn't steal through life but preserved a haughty independence which people mistook for humility. Her passions for both men and women were outrageous and irrational.'[23]

Both, in their fashion, were set apart. But Augustus's separateness had been complicated by his partial deafness and made hysterical by the aftermath of his bathing accident. There was a disconnectedness to much that he did. Unlike Gwen, he could not bear to contain his emotions, but had to disburden himself immediately. So, although they were confronted by many similar problems, their methods of dealing with them differed.

Before Augustus had been at the Slade many months, he was urging Gwen to join him. Her need to escape from Victoria House was as compelling as his had been, and, as he later implied, she would have joined him anyway: 'She wasn't going to be left out of it!'[24] But there was the matter of persuading her father. Finishing schools for girls, especially in London, were a mark of social prestige. But art schools were more problematical. The Female School of Art and Design turned out to be mainly a craft academy training students as professional designers, while Queen's and Bedford Colleges offered only a few drawing classes for women. There were also some private art schools which prepared women for the Royal Academy Schools, which had reluctantly admitted them ten years earlier – yet they still excluded them from the Life Room. The Slade was an obvious choice. The insistence on high seriousness and its connection with a university were reassuring. The women came from good families and were said to be brought there each morning by carriages or escorted by servants – a duty that Gus could freely undertake for Gwen. The Life Class itself was always conducted in silence, with the professor alone permitted to speak. Altogether it sounded an excellent establishment.

So Gwen came to London, staying first at 'Miss Philpot's Educational Establishment' at 10 Princes Square, Bayswater. But during the autumn of 1895, when she started to attend the Slade, she moved to 23 Euston Square,* near University College. By this time Augustus had left Acton, his paganism having proved too much for his aunt, and was living at 20 Montague Place, a superior lodging house in a street of temperance hotels, private apartments and the occasional bootmaker or surgeon. In *Chiaroscuro* he described himself and Gwen sharing rooms together a little later and, like monkeys, living off fruit and nuts. Early in 1897 they took the first-floor flat of 21 Fitzroy Street, a house that had recently been bought by a Mrs Everett, mother of one of their friends at the Slade, who hurriedly converted it from a brothel (the proprietress of which had described herself as 'feather dresser') into a series of flats and studios. Here they seem to have lived intermittently for over a year, sharing it with Grace Westray, another Slade student, and with Winifred John who

---

* On the University College, London, form she crossed out '10 Princes Square' and substituted '23 Euston Square', apartments rented by a Charles Smith.

47

had then come up to London to study music. Apart from this, and a flat over a tobacconist's in which they lived briefly after leaving the Slade, the only rooms they shared were other people's. They were close to each other, yet it was not practicable for them to remain together long.

Although Gwen seldom appeared to take Gus's advice and sometimes ridiculed his opinions (such as that she substitute an 'athletic' for her 'unhygienic' way of life) she was agitated by his presence, being unable to retain her single-mindedness when he was near. In any case they dared not stay too close – there was the danger of emotional trespass with all its trailing difficulties of guilt and regret. In her letters to him Gwen would occasionally call Gus 'dear love' and Gus would occasionally send her 'a kiss'. They understood each other: but their 'attitudes' being so different they also upset each other. Gus's impatient and demanding personality influenced Gwen when they were together so that she would adopt his 'attitude' rather than developing her own. Like him, she loved the sea, but later trained herself to paint indoors, often solitary figures, even empty rooms, sometimes a child praying in church, a vase of flowers on a table, a wide-awake cat on a cushion – all simple love objects. But Gus could never bear to stay indoors. 'I feel acutely what I am missing all the time shut up in my studio,' he told Robert Gregory, ' – all the sights & delights of the high road or any road . . .'[25] So while she, shunning delight and living laborious days, would gather herself in solitude, he was off along all roads and any roads that might lead him to visions and symbols of what he missed: phantasmagorical gatherings of open-air men and women – gypsies, strollers, musicians and mothers with children of around the age he had been when his mother died: all dreams of wish-fulfilment. In actual life Gus agreed with Gwen that 'loneliness is a great thing . . . let your neighbour be at the other end of the earth.'[26] But he wanted to transcend actual life in his imagination and to lose himself perpetually in other people; whereas Gwen, desiring a more interior life, wanted to 'go and live somewhere', as she confided to their friend Ursula Tyrwhitt, 'where I met nobody I know till I am so strong that people and things could not affect me beyond reason'.[27]

People were frequently threatening to affect Gwen beyond reason, and she did not recover from her passions so easily as Gus appeared to do. 'I was born to love,'[28] she wrote, but how could she put all this energy of loving into her work? While at the Slade she formed an attachment to another girl.[29] When this girl began a love affair with a married man, Gwen decided that it must be stopped. Failing to persuade her, she declared an ultimatum: either the affair must cease or she herself would commit suicide. There was no doubting her sincerity. 'The atmosphere of our group now became almost unbearable,' Augustus records, 'with its frightful tension, its terrifying excursions and alarms. Had my sister gone mad? At one moment Ambrose McEvoy thought so, and, distraught himself, rushed to tell me the dire news: but Gwen was only in a state of spiritual exaltation, and laughed at my distress.'[30]

From dramatic involvements of this kind Gwen had to protect herself. Only then could she control her energy, limit misfortunes and pursue her search for 'the strange form'.[31] She had to fight the terrible tendency towards 'impatience and angoisse'[32] she shared with Gus, learn to prepare slowly and paint quickly. In this lifelong acquiring of patience lay her belief that 'my vision will have some value in the world . . . I think it will count because I am patient and recueillée in some degree.'[33]

She was not naturally sombre – Augustus testifies to her 'native gaiety and humour'. Ruthless towards those who bothered her – 'I will not be troubled by people'[34] – she remained obstinately vulnerable to those whom she loved and admired. 'I am ridiculous,' she wrote. 'I can't refuse anything that is asked of me.'[35]

About Augustus's pictures Gwen said little – neither of them talked to each other much about painting. Besides she was always being sent newspaper cuttings from her father about Gus's spectacular successes. But in a letter she sent Ursula Tyrwhitt in the winter of 1914–15 she wrote: 'I think them rather good. They want something which perhaps will come soon!' Of her work Augustus was a consistent admirer from early days. 'Gwen has done a wonderful masterpiece,' he wrote to Michel Salaman of her 'Self-Portrait in a Red Blouse'[36] in 1902. In his last years, after Gwen had died, this admiration curdled into a sentimentalized concoction – 'Fifty years after my death I shall be remembered as Gwen John's brother' – reminiscent of Bernard Shaw's theatrical exit line after his visit to Meudon ('Shaw, Bernard: subject of a bust by Rodin: otherwise unknown').[37] Yet Augustus's admiration was genuine, often expressed and acted upon during her lifetime. 'I have seen him peer fixedly, almost obsessively, at pictures by Gwen as though he could discern in them his own temperament in reverse,' John Rothenstein recalls: 'as though he could derive from the act satisfaction in his own wider range, greater natural endowment, tempestuous energy, and at the same time be reproached by her single-mindedness, her steadiness of focus, above all by the sureness with which she attained her simpler aims.'[38]

*

Round Gwen and Gus there soon gathered a group of talented young artists. A new spirit of comradeship, unknown in Legros's time, invaded the Slade. 'The girls were supreme,' Augustus recalled. Among this 'remarkably brilliant group of women students', in what Augustus called

'the Grand Epoch of the Slade', were Ida Nettleship and Gwen Salmond,[39] the latter a self-possessed and outspoken girl whose 'Descent
from the Cross' was much admired. But perhaps the most precocious of
all was Edna Waugh, very pretty and petite and with long hair down to
her waist, who had gone there in 1893 at the age of fourteen, won a
scholarship and in 1897 scored a dramatic triumph with her watercolour
'The Rape of the Sabines', showing women in traumatic positions being
carried off by strange men for 'purposes unspecified'. She was proclaimed
an infant prodigy, another Slade School 'genius'. The poetic imaginings
with which she filled her notebooks particularly impressed Tonks, with
whom she was a favourite and who predicted she would be a second
Burne-Jones, to which she replied that on the contrary she would be 'the
first Edna Waugh'. But to many people's dismay she did not long remain
Edna Waugh.

For no one, unless it was to be Augustus's own wife, better illustrated
the heavy burdens of domesticity upon artistic endeavour. In the spring
of 1896, a young barrister, William Clarke Hall, had written to Edna's
parents formally requesting permission to propose marriage to her. He
was more than a dozen years older than she was, but had admired her
since she was thirteen – 'the child for whom of all things in the world I
care most'. This was a big shock for Edna. She liked Willie when he used
to come and see her father. She was struck by his piercing blue eyes, but
could not tell whether or not she loved him. Did she like him simply
because he worshipped her so extravagantly? She was so young she did
not know what she felt. 'You occupy more than half my imaginings,' she
assured him. But he, offended by her fractional hesitation, accused her of
being 'completely self-absorbed'; and because he 'seemed so much more
mature than myself', she felt he must be able to 'understand so truly
what is wrong with me'. Her mother considered her to be engaged and
so apparently did everyone else. So presumably she was – at any rate it
seemed inevitable. 'Don't bother your head whether you care for Willie
with lasting love,' her friend Ida Nettleship counselled her, '. . . when
you love you will know.' But Edna did not know, perhaps because,
as Ida explained to William Clarke Hall, 'it's a child's love that Edna bears
you.'[40]

In her last year at the Slade, Edna asked Gwen John for advice on oil
painting. Gwen had learnt from Ambrose McEvoy the Old Master technique of putting on fluid paint in layers, modifying the underlying colour
(a green monochrome wash) with a series of semi-transparent glazes. But
Edna found that this 'was not the right medium for me', and that ink
and watercolour suited her best. Her talent had more in common with
Augustus's. 'I wanted to draw a subject quickly,' she wrote, 'seize it,

convey my impression.'[41] The aim of all these students on leaving the Slade was to have their pictures exhibited by the New English Art Club. Early in 1899 Gus and Edna, the two hares in the race, would be the first to get their work accepted. It was the beginning and almost the end of Edna's artistic life. For, a few months earlier, on 22 December 1898, she became the first of this group of students to be married. William Clarke Hall was thirty-two, Edna nineteen: a confused Victorian adolescent bride desperately missing her artistic friends and feeling 'in a shadow full of weight and strange lurking despair'.[42]

Beside these women, according to Augustus, 'the male students cut a poor figure.' Chief among them was William Orpen, the son of an Irish solicitor, who arrived at the Slade in 1897 encrusted with prizes from the Metropolitan School of Art in Dublin. With his arrival, a new force made itself felt in Gower Street. It was the force, primarily, of tireless industry and ambition. Orpen was a gnome-like, slim and active figure, very popular with the other students. His high cheekbones were given prominence by sunken pale cheeks, light grey eyes, and thick brown unkempt hair. He wore a small blue serge jacket without lapels – of a type usually worn by engineers. In 1899, he was to win the Summer Composition Prize with his outstanding 'The Play Scene in *Hamlet*', which uses the open auditorium of the Sadler's Wells Theatre to depict a rehearsal of Act III with diverse groups of figures, including Augustus embracing Ida Nettleship. But his father had by now had enough of his son's painting and gave him the alternative of taking up some serious business or being cut off with a hundred pounds. Orpen took the hundred pounds and never looked back. There seemed nothing he could not accomplish. He was a devoted disciple of William Rothenstein, and after a successful proposal of marriage was to become his brother-in-law. Later, while in Ireland working as an art teacher, he met an American patron, a specimen comparatively rare before the transatlantic jet. This was the stylishly beautiful Mrs St George, who became his mistress and the guide to his successful professional career. 'You are certainly the most wonderful thing that ever happened,' he acknowledged.[43]

At first Augustus took to Orpen. He was an easy companion, spontaneous, whimsical, high-spirited. But after Orpen became what Augustus called 'the protégé of big business', their ways diverged. Orpen himself was modest about his talent. He did not seek to rival John Singer Sargent whose position as England's pre-eminent portrait painter nevertheless would come to him as next in succession. 'I am not fit to tie Augustus John's shoe-laces,'[44] he told Robert Gregory in 1910. Yet even in these early days at the Slade, people, it was said, came to praise John's pictures but went away with Orpen's.* He cut his hair short as a soldier's, perched on his shaven dome a small bowler hat, encircled his neck with a stiff white collar and worked like a businessman. The artist, Augustus believed, was lost to sight.

Orpen had few prejudices, fewer opinions. His rapid-fire, staccato conversation had about it the suggestion of epigrams but was confined to subjects of triviality. If the talk threatened to turn serious, he would fall into extravagant feats of horseplay. It was not beyond him to get down on all fours at dinner and bark like a dog, or to produce from his pocket some new mechanical toy and set it spinning across the table. He also developed, his nephew John Rothenstein remembers, a 'habit of speaking of himself, in the third person, as "little Orps" or even as "Orpsie boy". It would be difficult to imagine a more effective protection against intimacy.'45 He caricatured the collective wish of all these Slade students to stay young forever. Even his professional career was somehow juvenile. Money, fame, success were like delicious sweets to him: he could not resist them.

Orpen and Augustus were often together during these student days, and in 1898 they were joined by a third companion, Albert Rutherston.† 'Little Albert', as he was called, was the younger brother of William Rothenstein, very pink and small and regarded as rather a rake. 'Not content with working all day,' William Rothenstein recorded, 'they used to meet in some studio and draw at night. They picked up strange and unusual models; but I was shy, after seeing John's brilliant nudes, of drawing in his company.'46

Above the studio at 21 Fitzroy Street lived their landlady, Mrs Everett, an improbable woman in her forties, fat and vigorous, her cheeks aflame, her eyes intensely blue, unevenly dressed in widow's weeds and men's boots. Her son Henry and niece Kathleen Herbert had recently gone to the Slade where she now attempted to join them, arriving with a Gladstone bag containing one large bible, a loaf of bread, Spanish dagger, spirit lamp and saucepan, and a dilapidated eighteenth-century volume on art. Here was a phenomenon unique in Tonks's experience. In desperation he banished her to the Skeleton Room in the cellar of the Slade. Interpreting this as a privilege, she garishly transformed the place by introducing there

---

* Hence E. X. Kapp's masterly clerihew:

> When Augustus John
> Really does slap it on,
> His price is within 4d.
> Of Orpen's.

† Albert Rothenstein changed his named to Rutherston during the First World War, and is generally now remembered by that name. To avoid unnecessary complication I have called him Rutherston throughout.

various brass Buddhas, stuffed peacocks and a small organ, two grand-father armchairs loosely covered with gold-encrusted priests' vestments and a slow-dying palm tree, like a monstrous spider, from which she suspended religious texts decorated and mounted on cardboard. Some nights she slept there; some days she entertained her pack of dogs there; often, night or day, her voice could be heard among the skeletons singing lustily: 'Oh, make those dry bones live again, Great Lord of Hosts!' – to which the students above would add their refrain, clapping wildly and chanting ribald choruses.

Excommunicated at last from the Slade, Mrs Everett started a 'Sunday School' in the converted brothel at Fitzroy Street. Here, and later at 101 Charlotte Street, she encouraged the art students to gather for bread and jam, hot sweet tea and intimate talk of the Almighty. These teas or 'bun-worries', as they were called, were lively affairs, especially when Augustus and Orpen turned up, and would last late into the night, culminating in the singing of 'Are You Washed?' with its confident refrain: 'Yes, I'm washed!' For Augustus the atmosphere was uncomfortably like that sur-rounding his Salvationist aunts, but Mrs Everett was such a fascinating subject to draw from so many angles that he often came. 'One lovely day early in May,' Ethel Hatch remembered,

'Mrs Everett invited us all to a picnic in the country . . . she met us with a large yellow farm cart, she herself was wearing a sun-bonnet, and the driver a smock . . . After lunch we wandered about in the lovely park and grounds, and some of them ran races round the trees; John was a very good runner, and most graceful. I can see him now, chasing a red-haired girl through the trees at the bottom of the lawn.

. . . afterwards a photograph was taken of the party in the wagon, with John sitting astride a horse. I shall never forget the journey home in the train, when John and Orpen entertained us by standing up in the carriage singing all the latest songs from Paris, with a great deal of action.'[47]

At another of her gatherings, Mrs Everett, drawing on her artistic knowledge, extolled John's great talent and informed him: 'God loves you.' But Augustus, suddenly embarrassed, mumbled: 'I don't think he has bestowed any particular favours on me.' He was overwhelmed during this period by avalanches of flattery. When Tonks declared that he would be the greatest draughtsman since Michelangelo, he replied simply: 'I can't agree with what you said.' It was this modesty that helped to endear him to his fellow students. One summer big baskets of roses were imported to decorate the gaunt walls of the Slade. 'Several of us were standing about outside the Portrait Room with baskets of festoons,' Edna Clarke

Hall remembered.[48] '. . . We were considering a pedestal, from which the statue for some unknown reason had been removed, when Profesor Tonks came suddenly out of the Portrait Class. He stopped and from his height looked down on me, and with one of his sardonic smiles and indicating the empty pedestal asked "Is that for John?" '[49]

Excelling *au premier coup*, Augustus went on collecting certificates and prizes at the Slade; and Gwen, too, was successful, most notably winning the Melville Nettleship Prize for figure composition.[50] When Sargent, the American portrait painter then at the height of his fame in London, visited the Slade, he said that Augustus's drawings were beyond anything that had been done since the Italian Renaissance. 'Not only were his drawings of heads and of the nude masterly,' wrote William Rothenstein, 'he poured out compositions with extraordinary ease; he had the copiousness which goes with genius, and he himself had the eager understanding, the imagination, the readiness for intellectual and physical adventure one associates with genius.'[51]

After leaving the Slade in the late afternoon, Gus and his friends McEvoy and Salaman, Ursula Tyrwhitt and Edna Waugh, would go back to his rooms and continue drawing and painting and acting as one another's models. 'Their faces, seen through one another's eyes,' wrote Mary Taubman, 'and especially through the eyes of Augustus John, are part of our consciousness of that famous epoch in the Slade's history.'[52] On one famous occasion when Augustus lost his key, he leapt on to the railings in front of the house and then, like a monkey, scaled up the outside of the building to the top floor. Having got through an attic window, a minute later he was opening the door to the other students standing there amazed by his acrobatics.

In 1897, when Augustus was nineteen, Tonks offered his students a prize for copies after Rubens, Watteau, Michelangelo and Raphael. Augustus won it with a charcoal study after Watteau. His dexterity was dazzling. Whatever style he adopted, he did it supremely well and his work seemed to act on the other students as a catalyst. Before joining the Slade he had studied reproductions of Pre-Raphaelite paintings in magazines and been enormously impressed by them. Now this influence was passing. Gainsborough had become his favourite British artist; but he had also developed an admiration for Reynolds, in particular his power of combining fine design with psychological insight. The more he saw, the more he admired. He would, he told William Rothenstein, have given 'five years to watch Titian paint a picture'. But at the same time he claimed that 'J. F. Millet was a master I bowed before.' But Watteau was probably still the chief influence upon him, though he was about to be introduced by William Rothenstein to the work of Goya whom he later considered superior to all these. Rothenstein's book on Goya opened up for Augustus a venturous world on which he would have liked to model his own career.

He was contemptuous of convention but admired tradition. 'We may say that the whole of art which preceded it has influenced the work of John, in the sense that he has continued a universal tradition,' wrote the critic T. W. Earp. But although he was an amalgam of so many Old Masters, he was beginning to produce unmistakable 'Johns'. After years of anecdotal Victorian pictures, his lightning facility was extraordinarily refreshing. He wanted to register the mood of a passing moment in a fit of seeing. His drawings were less analyses of character than aesthetic statements. Draughtsmanship was not primarily for him an intellectual exercise, but a matter of passionate observation involving the co-ordination of hand, eye and brain.[53] 'Does it not seem,' he once asked, 'as if the secret of the artist lies in the prolongation of the age of adolescence with whatever increase of technical skill and sophistication the lessons of the years may bring?'[54]

But while his drawings and pastels improved, his paintings remained uncertain. He found it difficult to control his palette. The Slade had taught him little of the relation of one colour to another and he had no natural sense of tone. Sometimes he would ruin a picture for the sake of a gesture which took his fancy.

In the autumn of 1898 he set off with Evans and McEvoy for Amsterdam, where a large Rembrandt exhibition was being held at the Stedelijk Museum. 'This was a great event,' he recorded. 'As I bathed myself in the light of the Dutchman's genius, the scales of aesthetic romanticism fell from my eyes, disclosing a new and far more wonderful world.'[55] They slept in a lodging house, wandered by the canals of old Amsterdam, lived off herrings and schnapps, and every day went to the galleries and museums. It was now that the last wraiths of Pre-Raphaelitism, the spell of Malory's dim and lovely world, faded in his imagination and began to be replaced by the poetry of common humanity. Not long afterwards, he travelled through Belgium with the same companions, immersing himself in the Flemish masters for whom he also felt an affinity. 'Bruges, Anvers, Gand, Bruxelles have seen me and I have beheld them,' he wrote to Will Rothenstein. 'Rubens I have expostulated with, been chidden by, and loved. Jack Jordaens has been my boon companion and I have wept beside the Pump of Quinton Matzys.'

He returned to Tenby. Edwin had recently moved from 32 Victoria Street to a house round the corner in South Cliff Street. Southbourne, as it was called, was almost identical to Victoria House: a similar narrow, dark, cube-like prison. Augustus felt all the old sensations of claustrophobia, the panic and emptiness. 'An exile in my native place I greet you from afar and tearfully,' he wrote to Will Rothenstein.

'Rain has set in and I feel cooped up and useless. What we have seen of the country has been wonderful. But it is ten minutes walk to the rocky landscape with figures.

Pembrokeshire has never appeared so fine to me before, nor the town so smugly insignificant, nor the paternal roof so tedious and compromising a shelter. Trinkets which in a lodging house would be amusing insult my eye here and the colloquy of the table compels in me a blank mask of attention only relieved now and then by hysterical and unreasonable laughter.

The great solace is to crouch in the gloom of a deserted brick kiln amongst the debris of gypsies and excrete under the inspiration of lush Nature without, to the accompaniment of a score of singing birds.

I hope to quit this place shortly and come home to London where I can paint off my humours.'

In a letter to Michel Salaman of about the same date Augustus wrote: 'I intend coming up to London in a week or so when I shall start that Holy Moses treat.' He had chosen, from among the alternatives set for the Slade Summer Competition that year, Poussin's theme 'Moses and the Brazen Serpent'. The bustling bravura composition he now produced, five feet by seven feet, was by far his most ambitious painting as a student. Heavily influenced by the Italian Renaissance, the composition is very obviously an exercise – 'an anthology of influences' Andrew Forge described it – and, though not wholly imitative, it lacks the originality of, say, Stanley Spencer's prize paintings at the Slade a few years later, 'The Apple Gatherers' and 'The Nativity'. Built up from individual life studies and showing Augustus's debt to Wilson Steer, its dramatic effect resembles a sixteenth-century mannerist painting. 'It is a *competition style* in which the figures are drawn in particularly difficult poses,' writes A. D. Fraser Jenkins, 'and in many of them are pastiches, no doubt unintentionally, of figures by Michelangelo, Tintoretto, Raphael and other old masters.'[56] This *tour de force* of eclecticism won Augustus the Summer Prize and he left the Slade in glory.

Two years before, while he was at work in the Life Class, Augustus had seen Brown usher in a jaunty little man in black, wearing a monocle: James McNeill Whistler. 'It is difficult to imagine the excitement that name aroused in those days,' he recalled.[57] They had all heard and read so much about this miniature Mephistopheles; had spent so many hours in the Print Room of the British Museum studying his etchings of the

Thames and of Venice; had seen in the galleries from time to time some
reticent new stain from his brush – the image of a tired old gentleman
sitting by a wall, or a young one obtruding no more than cuffs and a
violin; or of a *jeune fille* poised in immobility, or some dim river in the
dusk, washed with silver. 'An electric shock seemed to galvanize the class:
there was a respectful demonstration: the Master bowed genially and
retired.' A few years later Augustus himself would be an idol of the Slade.
The students loved him for his good, bad and indifferent drawings, for
his undiscriminating vitality, his willingness to destroy so much that he
did and his challenge to them to take risks. For those in need of a hero,
he was the obvious choice, and his entrance into the Slade Life Class at the
beginning of the twentieth century was as exciting to the next generation of
students as that of the *fin-de-siècle* butterfly with his famous sting. 'When
I first saw this extraordinary individual was while I was a student at the
Slade school,' Wyndham Lewis later wrote:

'... the walls bore witness to the triumphs of this "Michelangelo" ... A
large charcoal drawing in the centre of the wall of the life-class of a hairy
male nude, arms defiantly folded and a bristling moustache, commemorated his powers with almost a Gascon assertiveness: and fronting the stairs
that lead upwards where the ladies were learning to be Michelangelos,
hung a big painting of Moses and the Brazen Serpent ...

... One day the door of the life-class opened and a tall bearded figure,
with an enormous black Paris hat, large gold ear-rings decorating his
ears, with a carriage of the utmost arrogance, strode in and the whisper
"John" went round the class. He sat down on a donkey – the wooden
chargers astride which we sat to draw – tore a page of banknote paper
out of a sketch-book, pinned it upon a drawing-board, and with a ferocious
glare at the model (a female) began to draw with an indelible pencil. I
joined the group behind this redoubtable personage ... John left as
abruptly as he had arrived. We watched in silence this mythological figure
depart.'58

4

FLAMMONDISM

'And women, young and old, were fond
Of looking at the man Flammonde.'

Edward Arlington Robinson

Augustus's growing renown in the late 1890s and early 1900s was partly based upon his extreme visibility. In a uniform world of braced and tied, well-waistcoated, buttoned-down men, it was impossible to overlook him. His shoes, created specially to his own design, were unpolished; the gold earrings he was soon to pin on were second-hand; he wore no collar and was contemptuous of those who did – in its place he fastened a black silk scarf with a silver brooch; he did wear a hat but it was of gypsy design, patina'd with age; his eyes were restless, his hair alarmingly uncut. 'We are the sort of people', he told another Bohemian Welsh artist, Nina Hamnett, 'our fathers warned us against.'

He walked the streets with a terrific stride, as if raising his own morale, protecting himself against other people. One day a gang of children fell in behind him shouting: 'Get yer 'air cut, mister.' He halted, turned on them, and growled: 'Get your throats cut!'

His reputation seemed to depend on deliberate neglect. He neglected to shave; he neglected caution and convention and common sense. There was no telling what he would say or do next – though very often he said and did nothing. The barometer of his moods shot up and down with extraordinary rapidity. Periods of charm, even tenderness, would vanish suddenly before convulsions of temper; days of leaden gloom suddenly dispersed, and he would glow with geniality. There seemed nothing to account for these alterations, or to connect them.

Wherever he went he struck sparks of romance. William Rothenstein remembered him at the age of twenty-one, looking like 'a young fawn. He had beautiful eyes, almond-shaped and with lids defined like those Leonardo drew, a short nose, broad cheek-bones, while over a fine forehead fell thick brown hair, parted in the middle. He wore a light curling beard (he had never shaved) and his figure was lithe and elegant. I was at once attracted to John . . . A dangerous breaker of hearts, he would be, I thought, with his looks and his ardour . . . [He] was full of plans for future work; but he was poor and needed money for models.'[59]

Augustus was indeed ambitious. He felt eager to develop his talent as a means of fixing his identity. His world was full of echoes and reflections.

He saw himself in other people's looks, heard himself in their replies, recognized himself through their attitudes. Many of his portraits, such as 'The Smiling Woman', were in this oblique fashion autobiographical.

Under the flamboyant exterior there was much uncertainty. He invented a part, complete with theatrical costume, that acted as an eye-catching form of concealment. Unsure of so much, he was dynamic in one thing: the pursuit of beauty, in particular beautiful women. Round him there gathered, wrote Lord David Cecil, a following of 'magnificent goddesses who, with kerchiefed heads and flowing, high-waisted dresses, stand gazing into the distance in reverie or look down pensively at the children who run and leap and wrestle round their feet. Wild and regal, at once lover, mother and priestess, woman dominates Mr John's scene.'

Like his maternal grandfather Thomas Smith, Augustus was a man 'of full habit of body'. But his view of women was idealistic rather than sensual, and had been formed by the early death of his mother. Back in Tenby, he had been drawn towards full-bosomed mature women, admiring from afar and usually while in church their rich proportions that seemed to offer the warmth and consolation he desired. Typical of these women had been the headmaster's wife at his unsympathetic school near Bristol, on whose generous bosom, he remembered, 'in great distress, I once laid my head and wept'.[60]

With adolescence his world had become invaded by disturbing forces. Whether upon the beach or in the streets of Tenby, it seemed his fate to encounter at every turn the mocking glance of some girl. His awkwardness was painful and the old-fashioned clothes his father made him wear an unspeakable constraint. He would have felt less sensitive if, while wandering alone on the marshes, he had come across some faerie's child lingering disconsolately amid the sedge. For she, like him, would have been silent, would not have laughed, but taken him into her embrace. Such phantoms peopled his imagination. Prevented by his timidity from making contact with actual girls, he kept company with imaginary creatures who had travelled from the reveries of Burne-Jones and Rossetti.

The conflict between reality and his fastidiously romantic dreamland gradually intensified. On Sunday afternoons in the early 1890s Geraldine de Burgh, her elder sister and a friend of theirs used to walk from Tenby over the sand dunes and rough grass tracks of the Burrows towards Penally and Giltar. And almost every Sunday they were secretly met by 'Gussie', Thornton and their friend Robert Prust. Geraldine was partnered by Gussie – the routine was invariable – though she would have preferred Robert Prust. Gussie, she thought, was terribly backward: they did not even hold hands. But as the youngest, it was not hers to choose. Over sixty-five years later, Augustus wrote to her: 'You are one of the big landmarks of my early puberty. I was intensely shy then, besides you generally had your brother with you to add to my confusion. Perhaps your noble name intimidated me too. But I was always afraid of girls then – girls and policemen . . .'

By this time Augustus had experienced what he called 'the dawn of manhood'. The mysteries of reproduction were explained to him with much raucous humour by the other boys in Tenby. He was horrified. It was impossible to imagine his father involving himself with his mother in this way. Gloom, terror and bewilderment mounted in him. To such improbable coupling did he owe his very existence! It seemed as if he would never be free from the burden of his origins. It was with this knowledge that he tortured Gwen.

But gradually the guilt and disgust receded. 'Further investigations both in Art and Nature,' he wrote, 'completing the process of enlightenment thus begun, brought me down from cloud cuckooland to the equally treacherous bed-rock of Mother Earth.'[61]

To Augustus, all women were mothers, with himself either as child or God-the-Father. Not long content to figure in the public eye as doubtful or baffled, he presented himself as robustly pagan with a creed that personified Nature as a mother. She was an object of desire, but also a goddess of fertility, a symbolic yet physical being capable of answering all needs: a woman to be celebrated and enjoyed. This he was to express most lyrically in the small figure-in-landscape panels – usually not more than twenty inches by fifteen inches – that he painted in the years before the First World War. Here women and children, like trees or hills, appear as an integral part of the Mother Earth – a connection he specifically and sexually makes in some of his letters. 'This landscape,' he wrote to Wyndham Lewis (October 1946) from Provence, 'like some women I have heard of, takes a deal of getting into. I am making the usual awkward approaches – and soon hope to dispense with these manoeuvres and get down to bed-rock, but the preliminaries are tiresome.'

These preliminaries grew increasingly tiresome after his third year at the Slade. An occasional glass of wine or whisky or, when in France, of absinthe or calvados or even, at the Café Royal, hock-and-seltzer or crème de menthe frappé, helped him to accelerate past this awful shyness. His first serious girlfriend was the bird-like Ursula Tyrwhitt who, responding to his letters of entreaty, allowed him to walk her home after school. When they were together they drew and painted each other's portraits; and wrote love-letters to each other when they were apart. 'How is it pray, that your letters have the scent of violets? Violets that make my heart beat,' Augustus asked her. '. . . Write again sans blague Ursula Ursula Ursula.' She was six years older than he was and she dazzled him. He

wrote praising her 'glorious roseate luminescence'. But their affair ended
when, in panic, her clergyman father sent her off to Paris. In one of his
last letters to her, while they were both still students, Augustus enclosed
a charming self-portrait, pen and brush in black ink, inscribed 'Au Revoir,
Gus'.

Before leaving the Slade, Augustus had taken up with another student,
Ida Nettleship, one of Ursula's best friends. Ida, with her 'beautiful warm
face', was a sexually attractive girl, with slanted eyes, a sensuous mouth,
curly hair and a dark complexion. There seemed an incandescent quality
about her, yet for the time being the fires flickered dreamily. She was very
quiet – 'tongueless' she calls herself – and when she did speak it was with
a soft, cultured voice. She had been brought up in a Pre-Raphaelite
atmosphere and, at the age of four, was snatched from the nursery floor
to be kissed by Robert Browning – an experience she was told never to
forget. By her mother, who made clothes for ladies connected with the
theatre, including Ellen Terry and Oscar Wilde's wife Constance, Ida was
worshipped and perhaps a little spoilt. Her father, Jack Nettleship, once
the creator of imaginative Blake-like designs, had by now turned painter
of melodramatic zoo-animals, leopards and polar bears, hyenas and stal-
lions, all lavishly reproduced in *Boy's Own Paper*. 'Father is painting a girl
and a lion,' Ida wrote to Gus. He had preferred painting to a career as a
writer[62] and became one of a group known as 'the Brotherhood' which
included John Butler Yeats, Edwin Ellis and George Wilson. 'George
Wilson was our born painter,' Yeats used to say, 'but Nettleship our
genius.' But as the Pre-Raphaelite spirit ebbed out of British art, Jack
Nettleship had lost confidence and painted only what Rossetti called 'his
pot-boilers'.

He sent Ida to the Slade in 1892; in 1895 she won a three-year
scholarship and remained there altogether six years. From most of the
students she held aloof, cultivating a small circle of friends – Gwen
Salmond, Edna Waugh and the Salaman family. They were known collectively as 'the nursery' because they were, or behaved as if they were,
younger than the other students. Kipling's two *Jungle Books* had come
out in the mid-1890s and were immensely popular with these children of
the Empire. Ida, having grown up surrounded by her father's pictures
of animals, named each of her special friends after one of Kipling's jungle
creatures, she herself being Mowgli, the man cub. Her early letters seem
exaggeratedly fey. She is frequently exchanging with 'Baloo' the big brown
bear (Dorothy Salaman) tokens of 'friendship for always' which take the
form of rosaries made from eucalyptus, pin cushions, ivy leaves and
lavender and all manner of flowers and plants 'rich in purple bells, a joy
to the eyes'. She ends these letters on a high note of jungle euphoria:

'Bless you with jungle joy, Your bad little man cub, Mistress Mowgli Nettleship'. When 'Bagheera', the pantheress (Bessie Salaman) marries, Ida writes: 'I think you are a charmer – but oh you *are* married – never girl Bessie again. Do you know you are different? . . . Mowgli will be so lonely in the jungle without the queen panthress. Oh you're worth a kiss sweet, tho' you are grown into a wife.'

Ida herself carefully avoided growing into a wife. All her intimate friends were girls. They lived in a golden world with the timeless prospect of being girls eternal. Their mood was that of Polixenes in *The Winter's Tale*:

> We were as twinn'd lambs that did frisk i' the sun,
> And bleat the one at the other: what we chang'd
> Was innocence for innocence; we knew not
> The doctrines of ill-doing, no, nor dream'd
> That any did.

Men had no place in this sentimental paradise. The only creature to be apportioned some degree of masculinity was Ida herself, the man cub. At the Slade she had many admirers, but she shrugged them all off – all except one. This was Clement Salaman, elder brother of Augustus's friend Michel Salaman, who had got to know her through his sisters. It was not long before he fell in love and, for a short time, they were rather unrealistically engaged to be married. Ida seems to have consented to this partly for his sister's sake. Since she was not in love with him, she could not really believe he was in love with her. Naturally she would always want to be his friend, as she was Baloo's and Bagheera's friend. But he was not part of her jungle life. She created more trouble by discussing it all with Edna Waugh. This displeased Edna's fiancé William Clarke Hall, who accused Ida of 'falseness and fickleness' and of causing him to lose his faith in women. But Ida believed she must 'go through life aiming for the highest'. When Clement's sister Bessie became engaged, Ida had exhorted her not to 'fall from what is possible for you . . . don't slip – strive high for others'. But was Clement the highest? Was she herself not falling from what was possible?

In February 1897 she formally broke off the engagement, explaining in a letter to the pantheress Bagheera that this was 'a good and pleasant thing for both'. 'Don't you think a great friendship could come out of it?' she queried. 'The soft side surely can be conquered – indeed I think he has conquered it. It would be a life joy, a friendship between us. Think how splendid. No thought of marriage or softness to spoil.'

Shortly before the end of this engagement, Ida's sister Ethel 'happened to go into the room where they were spooning and I roared with laughter', she recalled, 'and afterwards Ida said to me: "You mustn't laugh at that, it's holy." '[63] From both parents she had imbibed religion. Jack Nettleship had once confessed: 'My mother cannot endure the God of the Old Testament, but likes Jesus Christ; whereas I like the God of the Old Testament, and cannot endure Jesus Christ; and we have got into the way of quarrelling about it at lunch.'[64] Ida herself was very High Church when young. In vermilion and black inks she prepared a manual for use at Mass and Benediction, 'The Little Garden of the Soul', seventy-five pages long and done with scrupulous care: 'Ida Nettleship her book'. In everyday matters she was not above sermonizing to her friends. Girls still at school were warned to beware of 'affections', advised to walk a lot and play plenty of lawn tennis. She herself had taken to practising the fiddle as a means of avoiding temptation. 'Keep a brave true heart and be brave and kind to all other people,' she instructed Bessie Salaman, ' – And think of making happiness and not taking it.'

In March 1897, following the break-up of her engagement, Ida left England for Florence, moving among various *pensioni* and reassuring her 'dear sweet mother' that she must not 'let the proprieties worry you – I do assure you there's nothing to fear'. Superficially there did seem cause for anxiety since here, as at the Slade, Ida quickly attracted a swarm of young admirers, poets and Americans, who brought her almond blossom, purple anemones and full-blown roses; and a red-haired student, less romantic and with a funny face, 'who began talking smart to me – and ended by being melancholy and thirsty'. Most persistent of all was a peevish musician called Knight, 'very friendly and bothersome', who, she explained to her sister Ethel, 'plays the piano, and reads Keats and cribs other people's ideas on art. He looks desperately miserable . . . His complaints and sorrows weary my ears so continually – and "oh, he is so constant and so kind". They all are.' But her virtue vanquished them all.

Ida's letters from Italy[65] show that, on the whole, the girls in the *pensione* took her fancy more than the men – one very beautiful 'like a Botticelli with great grey eyes'; and a pretty American one, 'dark eyed and languid in appearance', who sat next to her at meals and 'says sharp things in a subdued trickle of a voice'; even 'the little chambermaid here with little curls hanging about her face and great dark eyes' who 'takes a great interest in me'. Almost the only woman she did not find sympathetic was the fidgety little Signorina who gave her lessons in Italian and self-control, and who 'says eh? in a harsh tone between every sentence – I pinch myself black and blue to keep from dancing round the table in an agony of exasperation'.

When she was not learning Italian she was drawing and painting –

'dashing my head against an impenetrable picture I am attempting to reproduce in the Pitti', as she described it. '. . . I am so bold and unafraid in the way I work that all the keepers and all the visitors and all the copyists come and gape . . . they think I am either a fool or a genius.' Every day she worked six or seven hours, copying Old Masters or sketching out of doors. But, she warned her mother, '*don't* expect great things – it's fatal . . . it's no easier to do in Italy than in England'.

Yet Italy enchanted her: bells on the mules passing below her window; chatter of carts and of people that carried along the stone streets on the evening air; sight of a dazzling green hill under olive trees; the river careering down by the *pensione*, swollen and yellow with rain – all these sights and sounds stirred longings in her, she scarcely knew for what. 'I simply gasp things in now, in my effort to live as much as possible these last weeks,' she wrote towards the end of her time there. 'I can't believe I shall ever be here again in this life – anyway it's not to be counted on. And it's like madness to think how soon I shall be away, and it going on just the same . . . I suppose Italy must have some intoxication for people – some remarkable fascination. She certainly has converted me to be one of her lovers.'

After her return to England, Ida felt flat. Her drawing and painting left her dissatisfied. 'We have a model like a glorious southern sleek beauty, so hard it is to do anything but look,' she wrote to Bessie Salaman. 'To put her in harsh black and white – ugh, it's dreadful.' Tonks had become rather discouraging. She grew uncertain in a way she never had been. 'Some days I look and wonder and say "Why paint?" ' she admitted to Dorothy Salaman. 'There are such beautiful things, are they not enough? It seems like fools' madness to ever desire to put them down.'

Always before she had been swept upwards by gushes of enthusiasm. Now she felt herself being suffocated by an 'eternal ennui' which seemed to come between her and the life her vigorous nature needed. There must be more to living than copying Old Masters and exchanging flowers. Her boredom – 'a giant who is difficult to cope with' – overshadowed everything.

It was about this time that she started to become involved with Augustus. His personality was like a light that flooded into her life, banishing this gloomy giant. He was made for open spaces. He strode capaciously through the streets, taking her arm with a sudden thrust of initiative, as one who might say: 'Come on now, we'll show them what we can do!' Never had she known such an exhilarating companion. He was unlike any of the rather starched and stiff young men who had admired her – and so funny she sometimes cried with laughter. He did not treat her as a child, was never superior, but seemed to have a penetrating need of her to which she could not help opening up. 'When she is passionate,' her friend Edna Waugh told the disapproving William Clarke Hall, 'she is wonderful. She rises like a wild spirit.' Many people felt overwhelmed by her: but Augustus was not overwhelmed. The stale familiarity of London vanished when they were together and sudden energy flooded through her. He was, she thought, a wonderfully romantic creature with just that trace of feminine delicacy which made him so sympathetic. It was as if they were discovering life together as no one else had done. Without him, existence grew doubly tedious. She was also beginning to recognize certain frontiers that she must cross. 'There are myriads of things one can give oneself to,' she told Dorothy Salaman, ' – one can make oneself a friend of the universe – but talking is no good. A want *is* a want – and when one is hungry it's no good – or not much – to hear someone singing a fine song.' Only Augustus, it seemed, could assuage her hunger. Once, when she was playing with her sisters the game of 'What-do-you-like-doing-best-in-the-World', Ida gave her choice in a low whisper: 'Going to a picture gallery with Gus John.'

Augustus was the first and only man Ida loved. They did not become engaged. Their situation was awkward, for the Nettleships would have much preferred their daughter to remain engaged to Clement Salaman who came from a wealthy family and, like William Clarke Hall, had qualified as a barrister. Augustus's introduction into their Victorian household had been a disaster. It was Ada Nettleship,[66] Ida's mother, who chiefly objected to him; and her objections were not easily to be overcome. Since her husband's lions and tigers did not sell, she had become the 'business person' in the family. Her dressmaking trade took up almost the whole of their house – a barrack-like building at No. 58 Wigmore Street. Her husband and daughters were confined to the fourth floor, ill lit by gas-jets, and her domestic life was likewise thinly sandwiched in between her business pursuits.

Ada Nettleship was fat and soft and looked older than her age. For many years she had been careful to take no exercise and moved, when obliged to do so, with extreme slowness. She appeared a formidable dumpling of a woman, with short grey hair, a round face, retroussé nose and plump capable hands. She dressed in a uniform of heavy black brocade made in one piece from neck to hem, with a little jabot of lace and a collar of net drawn up and tied under her chin with a narrow black velvet ribbon. Her voice was high-pitched but rather flat; her expression serious; her temper not at all good – except towards her family for whose welfare she was responsible. She worked her staff of skirt-girls, pin-girls and the embroideresses whom she had imported from the Continent very hard and, before their hours were altered by Act of Parliament, very long. But though feared, she was respected by these girls for she was an imaginative dressmaker and competent businesswoman, her one weakness being a liking for society people with titles who often postponed paying their bills.

Ada Nettleship was horrified by Augustus. It is doubtful whether, in her opinion, anyone would have been good enough for her favourite daughter, but Augustus was too bad to be true – she had no use for him at all. The person she saw was no romantic Christ-like figure, simply a lanky unwashed youth, shifty-eyed and uncouth to the point of rudeness, with a scraggy, reddish beard, long hair, and scruffy clothes. She could not understand what Ida saw in him. She was confident, however, that her daughter's peculiar affection would not last. As for Jack Nettleship, he was more dismayed than horrified. 'I do wish he'd clean his shoes,' he kept complaining, ' – it's so bad for the leather.' But he spoke with little authority, generally going barefoot round the house himself.

'I always felt', Ida's sister Ethel Nettleship later wrote, 'that Gus being so young, & with so much fine feeling, perhaps his breaking into our Victorian family might not have caused such a wreckage!'[67] But Augustus was at his worst in Wigmore Street. His love for Ida, combined with her mother's antagonism, made him wretchedly ill at ease. Max Beerbohm, who saw him there, noted that he was 'pale – sitting in window seat – sense of something powerful – slightly sinister – Lucifer'. Old Nettleship, though everyone agreed he was the salt of the earth, only added to this embarrassment. With bald head, grey-bearded chin and nose 'like an opera-glass',[68] he presented an eccentric spectacle within this conventional setting. 'Years before he had been thrown from his horse, while hunting, and broke his arm, and because it had been badly set suffered great pain for a long time,' wrote another visitor to the house, W. B. Yeats. 'A little whisky would always stop the pain, and soon a little became a great deal and he found himself a drunkard.'[69] Having put himself into an institution for some months, he emerged completely cured, though still with the need for some liquid to sip constantly. This craving he assuaged by continual cocoa, hot or cold, which he drank from a gigantic jorum eight inches in diameter and eight inches deep. An alarmingly modest man, he would show Augustus his carnivorous paintings, begging for criticism. These pictures left Augustus cold, but if he ventured any criticism, Nettleship would rush for his palette and brushes and begin the laborious business of repainting. It was blasphemy for Augustus to hear him describe Beardsley's creatures as 'damned ugly women'. Yet he first met many celebrities here, from the old William Michael Rossetti to the young Walter Sickert, 'the latter just emerging from the anonymity of *élève de Whistler*'.[70]

In a rough synopsis[71] for his autobiography, scribbled on Eiffel Tower Restaurant paper some time during the 1920s, Augustus introduces Ida's name together with the word 'torture'. He was violently attracted to her. Her mature body, so chaste and erotic, the muted intensity of her quiet manner, those strangely slanting eyes, that ingenuous mind: all this was throbbingly exciting to him. His happiness seemed to depend upon possessing the secret of her beauty, and he pursued her with unpredictable persistence. One day, for example, he turned up at St Albans, where she had gone to a party of Edna Clarke Hall's. 'Ida and I had not seen each other for some time, so, to get away from the others, we climbed up a ladder to the top of a great haystack . . . We had hardly settled there when up the ladder came Augustus John,' Edna remembered.

'Ida told John very definitely that we wanted to be alone and he told us no less definitely that he wanted to be there, and to put an end to the matter he gave a great heave and it [the ladder] fell to the ground. And there we were! Ida was extremely vexed and told him so in no uncertain terms. John took umbrage and said that if we did not want him he would go. He flung himself on to the steep thatch and proceeded to slide down head first. We were horrified! The stack was a very high one, and the ground seemed a long way off. Securing ourselves as best we could, we both got hold of a foot – his shoes, then his socks came off, – we frantically seized his trousers. He wriggled like an eel and his trousers began to come off. Then we cried aloud for help and some of the party came running, put up the ladder and rescued the crazy fellow!
But the peace of our solitude was completely shattered.'[72]

Augustus was tortured not by unrequited love but unconsummated sex. Ida loved him, but she refused to commit herself to him. She still hoped that her mother would come to like him. Meanwhile their love affair, for all its passion, seemed to have reached a dead end. Augustus was not faithful. He behaved as nature intended. Sight was mind, and out of sight was sometimes out of mind. On his journey through the Netherlands with Evans and McEvoy he responded to the beauty of the people he saw as much as to the Flemish masters. The two were jumbled together in his letters as if there were no difference. He writes, for example, of Rembrandt's wife, Saskia van Uylenborch:

'She was sweeter than honey, more desirable than beauty, more profound than the Cathedral. And in Brussels lives an old woman with faded eyes who made me blush for thinking so much of the young wenches.

But there was one in Antwerp I think Rembrandt would have cared for, Gabrielle Madeleine by name. She had azure under her eyes and her veins were blue and such a good stout mask withal, and she spoke French only as a Flamande can. Unfortunately she wore fashionable boots of a pale buff tint. (Besides which her room lay within that of her white haired bundle of a Mama.) You will shrug your shoulders hearing of my aberrations but I feel more competent for them, and that is the main thing.'

Women continued to inspire Augustus as custodians of a happiness he could divine but never completely enjoy. They symbolized for him an ideal state of being that formed the subject of his painting. Yet his most immediate need was for a physical union that would dissolve his loneliness. But while his body was comforted by these affairs, his spirit lost something. The penalty he paid for being unable to endure isolation was a gradual theft from his artistic imagination of its stimulus. For his ideal concept of 'beauty', once divested of its symbolic majesty and enigmatic life, was in danger of becoming sentimental and empty.

5

FROM AMONG THE LIVING . . .

'Wonderful days and wonderful nights these were.'
William Rothenstein, *Men and Memories*

'I am taking a studio with McEvoy,' Augustus had written to Michel Salaman in the summer of 1898. This was 76 Charlotte Street, once used by Constable, and now, over the next two years, to be shared intermittently with Orpen, Benjamin Evans and Albert Rutherston. All of them were desperately poor, but full of plans for future work. Most helpful to Augustus was Albert's elder brother William Rothenstein. His admiration for Augustus's work was tireless. To his many artist friends, including Sargent, Charles Conder and Charles Furse, Rothenstein began showing Augustus's drawings, and a number were sold in this way – though Furse was taken aback at the price of two pounds apiece. It was mainly on this money, together with what he received each quarter through his grand-father Thomas Smith's will, that Augustus subsisted.

'John – Orpen – McEvoy and myself are going to get up a class,' Albert Rutherston wrote to his father (20 January 1899), 'and have a model in John's studio once a week at night – it will come to about 7d each.'

Because the studio was small, Augustus spent a good deal of time roaming the streets with his sketchbook. He had been reading Heine's *Florentine Nights* and was particularly drawn to a tattered band of strolling players he met in Hyde Park, and eventually succeeded in persuading the principal dancer to pose for him. 'Those flashing eyes, that swart mongolian face (the nose seemed to have been artificially flattened), framed in a halo of dark curls, made an impression not to be shaken off lightly.'[73]

'I hate Gus doing replicas', Ida was to write. Yet he had to paint portraits to make money. His first commission was to paint an old lady living in Eaton Square for a fee of forty pounds (equivalent to £2,140 in 1996), half of which was paid in advance. 'As the work went on I began to tire of the old lady's personality,' he remembered; 'she too, I could see, was bored by mine, and getting restless. She even spoke rather sharply to me now and then. This didn't encourage me at all. One day, having made a date for the next sitting, I departed never to return. I had got her head done pretty well at any rate and the old lady got her picture at half price.'[74] Looked at today, the picture seems surprisingly close in style and feeling to some of Gwen John's portraiture. The colour has been toned down – monochrome with silvery-white flesh tones and slight touches of warm ochre. In the middle of an area of black dress, the old lady holds a red book. An orange frill on the cushion behind her head gives colour to her face and follows the line of her smile. Augustus's treatment of the face, which is modelled in the yellow-brown against darker brown of Rembrandt, conveys an air of beauty in decay, and the impression is one of restrained sadness. But Augustus could not endure sadness – he had to get away. His 'tiredness', like the 'boredom' that assailed him during his convalescence in Tenby, was a phobia that would threaten all his loves and friendships, and change the impetus of his work.

About the same time, through the mediation of a fashionable lady in Hampstead, Augustus was commissioned to do some drawings in the west of England. His first destination was a large mausoleum of a house set in parkland that resembled a cemetery. On arriving there, he was struck by the good looks of his young hostess, which seemed, after a cocktail or two, very visibly to increase. After the drawing was done she took him upstairs to show him her home-made chapel fitted into the attic. Her husband was away shooting, she explained – he often was – and during the dull days she would seek consolation here. Within the wall, Augustus spied a recess – perhaps a confessional, or a boudoir . . . But soon he had to be on his way for the next assignment. Here, too, there was much architectural magnificence. His new hostess, unencumbered with religiosity, was as amiable as the first. There seemed to be an epidemic of 'shooting' in the district, for her husband also had been carried off by it.

When the drawing was done, Augustus returned to London with two cheques in his pocket, and richer in more ways than one.

Perhaps because of the emotional deprivation of his mother, Augustus seemed to be missing a source of self-esteem. He was like a leaking vessel that needed continual attention. But now, to his surprise and delight, other people were beginning to find him to be a marvellous proper man. He sensed some of the power he could exert. So much that he had missed at Tenby, even at the Slade, seemed within his possession. It was dangerous knowledge. Such was the charm of his presence that old ladies on buses, it was rumoured, would get up blushing to offer him their seats; and young girls at the Café Royal fainted when he made his legendary entrances there.

The letters that Augustus and his friends wrote at this time show them drawing and painting all day. In the evening they would hurry off to the Empire to listen to Yvette Guilbert sing, or go to the Hippodrome to see a splendid troupe of Japanese acrobats, tightrope walkers, nightingale-clowns and high-diving swimmers. Best of all, Augustus loved the Sadler's Wells music hall in Islington, London's oldest surviving theatre. He went almost every week, taking there for a shilling a box from the front of which he would fling his hat in the air whenever he approved of a turn. The crowd in the stalls, believing him to be a tremendous swell, nicknamed him 'Algy'. One night, when their teasing became too personal, Augustus rose and delivered a drunken speech. The crowd, after listening for a minute, went for him, but he emptied his beer over them and, like the Scarlet Pimpernel, escaped.

After such breathless entertainments, whenever they could afford it, Augustus and his friends would go to the Café Royal, eat sandwiches, drink lager beer and sit up late gazing at the celebrities. Orpen, Albert Rutherston and Augustus were together so much of the time that they became known as 'the three musketeers'; but on less rowdy evenings they would be joined by McEvoy and Gwen John, Ida Nettleship and some of her special friends. Sometimes, too, by Mrs Everett, her hair decorated with arum lilies, anxious to spirit them away to Salvationist meetings where men with sturdy legs and women with complexions joined in brass and tambourine choruses.

On 14 September 1898 Ida and Gwen Salmond crossed over to Paris, Gwen to stay there for six months, Ida for three. They put up temporarily at what Ida called a 'very old lady style of pension' at 226 boulevard Raspail on the outskirts of the Latin quarter; 'such a healthy part of Paris!' she reassured her mother (15 September 1898) who was worried by their proximity to the bars and restaurants of the boulevard Montparnasse. They had invited Gwen John to join them, but when she mentioned the plan to her father, Edwin automatically opposed it. She was, however, undeterred; went round the house singing 'To Paris! To Paris!'; and wrote to Ida in the third week of September announcing that she was on her way. 'Gwen John is coming – hurrah,' Ida told her mother. '. . . We *are* so glad Gwen is coming. It makes all the difference – a complete trio.'[75]

Gwen arrived carrying a large marmalade cake, and the three of them set off to look at flats – 'such lovely bare places furnished only with looking-glases'[76] – soon finding what they wanted on the top floor of 12 rue Froideveau, or 'Cold Veal Street' as Ida called it. In a letter to her mother she described the moral architecture of the place, which was

'on the 5th floor – overlooking a large open space [the Montparnasse cemetery] – right over the market roof. It has 3 good rooms, a kitchen and W.C. and water and gas – and a balcony. Good windows – very light and airy. Nothing opposite for miles – very high up. The woman (concierge) is very clean and exceedingly healthy looking. The proprietress is rather swell – an old lady – she lives this end of Paris and we went to see her. She asked questions, and especially that *we received nobody* – '*Les dames* oui. Mais les messieurs? Non! *Jamais!*' . . . She wants to keep her apartments very high in character. All this is rather amusing, but it will show you it is a respectable place. It *is* over a café – but the entrance is right round the corner – quite separate . . . We want all the paper scraped and the place whitewashed . . . It is near the Louvre and Julian's – and is very open.'[77]

Gwen Salmond had sixty pounds and wanted to study at the Académie Julian under Benjamin Constant. Ida had thirty pounds and thought of going to either Delécluze or Colarossi, both of which were less expensive. Gwen John had less money still and could not afford to attend any school. But by a fortunate chance another studio was just opening in Paris that autumn – the Académie Carmen at 6 passage Stanislas. It was to be run by a luxuriant Italian beauty, Carmen Rossi, the one-time model of Whistler who, it was announced, would himself attend twice a week to instruct the pupils. Such was Whistler's reputation that many students came from the other schools, the carriages of the more wealthy ones blocking the narrow entrance. The price was the same as Julian's – too expensive for Ida: but Gwen Salmond, changing her mind at the last moment, decided to go there. 'Whistler has been twice to the studio – and Gwen finds him very beautiful and just right,' Ida wrote to her mother. '. . . [he] is going to paint a picture of Madame la Patronne of the studio, his model, and hang it in the studio for the students to learn from. Isn't it fine? He's a regular first rate Master and, according to Gwen, knows how to teach.' So enthusiastic was Gwen Salmond that she insisted that Gwen

John accompany her, smuggling her in as an afternoon pupil and helping her financially.

The rules of the Académie Carmen were stricter than those of the Slade. Smoking was outlawed; singing and even talking prohibited; charcoal drawings on the walls forbidden; studies from the nude in mixed classes banned – and the sexes segregated into different ateliers. Whistler himself insisted on being received not as a companion in shirtsleeves, but as the Master visiting his apprentices. What Gwen John learnt from him was the 'good habit' of orderliness. He offered no magical short cuts: on the contrary he would have liked to teach his students from the very beginning, even the grinding and mixing of the colours. Tintoretto, he reminded them, had never done any work of his own until he was forty, and that was the way he wished them to work for him. His larks, which always contained some serious matter, often bewildered them. The palette, not the canvas, was the field of experiment, he told them, and he would sometimes ignore their pictures altogether, earnestly studying their palettes to detect what progress was being made. His monocled sarcasms and the need which his rootless nature felt for a band of dedicated disciples, antagonized the men. But many of the women students adored him, understanding the poignancy and hidden kindness of his character and responding to his courtesy and wit. 'Whistler is worth living for,' Gwen Salmond declared simply in a letter to Michel Salaman. At any criticism, she and the others rushed to Whistler's defence. 'I hear there is a blasphemous letter about Whistler's teaching in one of the English papers,' Ida fulminated to her mother. 'It is very stupid and unkind.'[78]

In Augustus, too, Whistler inspired the veneration due to one who has been a famous rebel victorious against the social conventions, and a dedicated Master in his own right. With the money he had won for 'Moses and the Brazen Serpent',* he followed the three girls to Paris that autumn, and in the Salon Carré of the Louvre the two painters met formally for the first time: Whistler a small, neat, erect old gentleman in black, with crisp curly hair containing one white lock, and a flashing monocle; Augustus tall, dishevelled, trampish. After some ceremony and a contest of compliments on behalf of Gwen, Augustus ventured to suggest that his sister's work showed a sense of character. 'Character? What's character?' Whistler demanded. 'It's *tone* that matters. Your sister shows a sense of tone.'

Augustus seems to have spent his short time in Paris looking at

---

* 'We have now the news of John's prize,' Ida wrote from 12 rue Froideveau to Michel Salaman. 'He sent a delicious pen and ink sketch of himself with 1st prize £30 stuck in his hat as sole intimation of what had befallen him. We were so awfully glad.'

Rembrandt, Leonardo, Raphael and Velázquez. His sister also took him to meet Carmen, and together they visited Whistler in his studio, then at work on an immense self-portrait – a ghostly face set upon a body hardly discernible in the gloom. To explain her attendance at the Académie Carmen, Gwen had written home to say that she had won a scholarship there. By this imaginary triumph she may have hoped to reconcile Edwin to the notion of giving her a small allowance. But Edwin decided to do better than this – that was, to come and see for himself how she was getting along. His arrival probably accounted for Augustus's quick departure from Paris. To welcome him, Gwen arranged a small supper party, putting on a new dress designed by herself from one in a picture by Manet – possibly his 'Bar at the Folies Bergère'. 'You look like a prostitute in that dress,' Edwin greeted her: after which she decided she could never accept money from such a man. Despite this setback, she continued going to Whistler's school and, in order to earn enough money, began posing as a model.

Whistler's teaching was a perfect corrective to that of Brown and Tonks at the Slade. Painting, not drawing, came first. 'I do not teach art,' Whistler declared, ' – I teach the scientific application of paint and brushes.' In this laboratory atmosphere, to which Augustus never subjected himself, where students could paint in the dark if need be, Gwen developed her methodical technique 'to a point of elaboration undreamt of by her Master'.[79] It was a short period of vital importance in her career, though much of her work was done independently. 'Gwen John is well and has not been lonely,' Ida reported to her mother. 'She has many more friends – one Alsatian girl [Mlle Marthe] whom we are painting in the mornings. Such a beauty she is.'[80]

Breakfast-time in Cold Veal Street was given over to reading Shakespeare: *King Lear* and *King John*; while in the evening the three of them sometimes ate at an anarchists' restaurant where grubbily dressed girls fetched their own food to avoid being waited upon. Between these times they painted. 'Gwen S. and J. are painting me,' Ida told her mother, 'and we are all 3 painting Gwen John.' Their life together, with all its excitements and difficulties, dedication and triviality is charmingly described in a letter of Ida's to Michel Salaman:

'We are having a very interesting time and working hard. I almost think I am beginning to paint – but I have not begun to really draw yet. We have a very excellent flat, and a charming studio room – so untidy – so unfurnished – and nice spots of drawings and photographs on the walls – half the wall is covered with brown paper, and when we have spare time and energy we are going to cover the other half . . . Gwen John is sitting before a mirror carefully posing herself. She has been at it for half an hour. It is for an "interior". We all go suddenly daft with lovely pictures we can see or imagine, and want to do ... We want to call Gwen John "Anne" – but have not the presence of mind or memory. And I should like to call Gwen Salmond Cynthia. These are merely ideals. As a matter of fact we are very unideal, and have most comically feminine rubs, at times; which make one feel like a washerwoman or something common. But as a whole it is a most promising time ...'

It came to an end early in 1899. Ida returned to Wigmore Street and Gwen John established herself in a cellar below the dressmakers and decorators of Howland Street. Augustus, who disapproved of most places in which his sister decided to live, tried to include her in some of the invitations he was now receiving and the following spring the two of them went down to stay at Pevril Tower, a boarding house which Mrs Everett had opened at Swanage. Suffering from conjunctivitis, Augustus could do little work; and Gwen too was listless, wandering along the cliffs by moonlight, catching fireflies and putting them in her hair and in Mrs Everett's. 'I have not done anything,' she confessed to Michel Salaman. Most days she would go off into the country, through an old wood full of anemones and primroses to the sea three miles away – and plunge in. 'The rocks are treacherous there, & the sea unfathomable,' she wrote to Michel Salaman, '... but there is no delicious danger about it, so yesterday I sat on the edge of the rock to see what would happen – & a great wave came & rolled me over & over which was humiliating & *very* painful & then it washed me out to sea – & that was terrifying – but I was washed up again. Today the sky is low, everything is grey & covered in mist – it is a good day to paint – but I think of people.'[81]

Augustus, too, seemed involved with people. Together with Orpen, Albert Rutherston and others, he had helped to organize a revolutionary campaign against the mosaic decorations of St Paul's Cathedral by Sir William Richmond. During April and May he was busy dragooning students from all the art schools round London into meetings, trying to raise funds for the printing of notices and arranging for a public petition to be presented to the Dean and Chapter of the cathedral. 'Sir William Richmond R.A. has for five years been decorating St Paul's Cathedral and last year the mosaics were discovered to the Public,' Albert Rutherston explained to his father. 'The place has been utterly spoilt and looks now like a 2nd rate Café – it is a mass of glittering gold etc. – he has also had the cheek to cut away pieces of Wren's sculpture and replace it by his own mosaics ... Even Sir Edward Poynter P.R.A. has asked Richmond to stop his decorations.'*

The other excitement of these months was Augustus's first one-man show at the Carfax Gallery in Ryder Street, off St James's. This gallery had recently been opened by John Fothergill, a young painter, archaeologist and author, famous for his dandified clothes and later as a connoisseur of innkeeping.[82] Robert Sickert, younger brother of Walter, acted as manager: and the choice of artists was left to William Rothenstein. Rodin, Conder, Orpen, Max Beerbohm all held exhibitions there as well as Rothenstein himself. By the spring of 1899 it was Augustus's turn. 'There is to be a show of my drawings at Carfax and Co.,' he had written from Swanage to Michel Salaman. 'I hope to Gaud I shan't have all back on my hands. There is however not much fear of that as Carfax himself would probably annex them in consideration of the considerable sum advanced to me in the young and generous days of his debut.' Singled out for praise by the didactic New English Art critic D. S. MacColl, the show was a success, earning Augustus another thirty pounds (equivalent to £1,600 in 1996).

With this sum in his pocket he set off to join a large painting party at Vattetot-sur-Mer, a village near Étretat on the Normandy coast. William Rothenstein and his new wife, the former actress Alice 'Kingsley'; his brother Albert Rutherston, now prophetically nicknamed 'All but Rothenstein'; Orpen and his future wife (Alice Kingsley's sister), Grace Knewstub, unfortunately known as 'Newslut'; Arthur Clifton, the business manager of the Carfax Gallery, and his red-haired wife: all these Augustus knew already. But in Charles Conder he met a wistful, tentative, ailing man, his hair luxuriant but lifeless, a brown lock perpetually over one malicious blue eye, who admitted in an exhausted voice to being a little 'gone at the knees'.

Every morning the company rose at half-past seven, drank a cup of chocolate, and painted until eleven. Conder worked at his exquisite silk fans; Orpen was still labouring over his 'Hamlet' and making preliminary studies for his oil portrait of Augustus; Rothenstein painted 'The Doll's House' in which Alice Rothenstein and Augustus posed on the little staircase leading up from the sitting-room;[83] Augustus himself did no painting, but drew, mostly landscapes. 'As for us,' he wrote to Michel Salaman, 'we grow more delighted with this place daily. The country is wonderfully fine in quality. In addition we have a charming model in the person of Mrs R's sister [Grace] who serves to represent Man in relation to Nature. Orpen and I have been drawing with a certain industry, I think. Albert reads Balzac without cessation. Occasionally his brother drives him

* See Appendix One, 'Desecration of Saint Paul's'.

out into the fields with a stick but he returns in good time for the next meal with half a tree trunk gradated with straight lines to show.'

Vattetot was a village of austere buildings with small windows and steeply pitched roofs set on the cliffs above Vaucottes and shielded by double and triple lines of trees from the persistent winds. Farms and apple-orchards surrounded them, gentle hills and, along the coastline a quarter of a mile away, small shingle bays. Among the local farmers and fishermen the visitors attracted a good deal of notice. At eleven o'clock on most mornings, the colony would lay down brushes, make for the rocky cliffs, and dive into the breakers. Augustus was a fearless swimmer, crawling far out until he became a speck in the distance. 'Albert and I were seduced by that old succubus the Sea – the other day,' he wrote to Michel Salaman. 'The waves were tremendous and the shore being very sloping there was a very great backwash – it required all our virtue to prevail in the struggle.'

Conder preferred Orpen's work, but everything Augustus did appealed to Rothenstein. His drawings proclaimed an amazing genius, his actions an incredible recklessness. One day he jumped into a bucket at the top of a deep well and went crashing down to the bottom. It was all that the others could do – Rothenstein perspiring with admiration among them – to haul him back to the surface. And when he sprinted, stark naked, along the beach, it seemed to Rothenstein, paddling and prawn-catching near by, that he had never seen so faun-like a figure. The coastguards, too, ogled these antics through their glasses, and all the more attentively when the girls undressed in a cave under the cliffs and raced through the waves. There was a threat of court action – but the pagan goings-on went on.

'Under this discipline we all ripened steadily,' Augustus recorded.[84] In the evenings they sat, Orpen, little Albert and himself, in the café singing, smoking, drinking their calvados, and listening to Conder, a bottle of Pernod at his elbow, telling his muffled stories of nights with Toulouse-Lautrec and sinister experiences in Paris. He used these stories to hold his young friends late into the night, dreading to be alone. But Orpen would steal away early to get on with his work, while Augustus was always last to leave. Conder's reliance on Pernod, which he used both as a drink and as a medium for his brush, sent tremors of apprehension through Augustus, and he told the Rothensteins that, in the event of his ever feeling tempted to drink, Conder's example would be a powerful disincentive. As for calvados, that was rather different: he felt bound to use its quickening properties to draw nearer the soil and, by a kind of chemical magic, grow fruitful. Seeing the way things were going, Alice Rothenstein began to import quantities of restorative tea from England.

Sometimes they would set off for long walks: to Fécamp, for the sake of the incomparable *pâtisserie*; to the little casino at Vaucottes, Conder always leading; to Étretat, a charming place with high cliffs at both ends of the promenade, full of smart people and mixed bathing ('the women all wear black silk stockings with their bathing costumes', Albert Rutherston reported); and to Yport, four miles away, where lived a tailor who decked Augustus out in a dazzling pale-blue corduroy suit with tight jacket and wide pegtop trousers. 'He looks splendid,' Orpen had reported to John Everett, 'and is acting up to his clothes' – much to the terror of Alice Rothenstein. Fearful that he or Conder would seduce her sister Grace, she decided to send her back to London in what she supposed to be the more harmless company of Orpen. Late at night, and chaperoned by the Rothensteins, they would all wander back from Yport along the beach, sometimes bathing again by moonlight: 'wonderful days and wonderful nights these were,' remembered Will Rothenstein,[85] who had begun his honeymoon with hay fever and ended it with jaundice.

In August, Orpen returned to complete his 'Hamlet' and Augustus travelled with him and Grace Knewstub as far as Paris. They stayed close to Montparnasse station, and the two painters spent their nights on the town, their days half-asleep in the Louvre. 'It was so pleasant there,' Augustus wrote to Ursula Tyrwhitt. 'I wish you had been with us to wander in the Louvre, after the hot sun and dazzling light outside to be in the cool sculpture galleries . . . I envy the sleeping Hermaphrodite its frozen passion, its marble self-sufficiency, its eternal languor.'

Augustus's own passions were sleepless. He returned to Vattetot and was soon addressing rhapsodies to Grace Knewstub's chiffon scarf. 'Seeing it round your neck and tinted with your blood, it was unto me even Beauty's embellishment.' But his drawing of Grace, done in his new etching style, was to be given with 'unhesitating devotion' to Orpen's new young model Emile Scobel. 'Mr Augustus is very well,' Orpen reported to Michel Salaman on his return from France. 'I left him with a lady! He was to come to the station to see me off (myself and Miss Knewstub) but did not turn up.' Everything seemed to be going wrong for Orpen. He was using Augustus's studio in Charlotte Street which had no gas stove. 'When I return I'll get a more presentable machine,' Augustus assured him, 'which will make the house sweet and render the studio an absolute trap for pretty girls.' But Orpen was then more interested in his summer composition for the Slade. 'My Hamlet would kill high morality,' he wrote in another letter to Salaman that September, ' – Hamlet ought to be treated like a "Day of Judgement". Miss John is settled in 122 Gower Street. She is a most beautiful lady! Miss Nettleship I have seen but she has not posed yet, to tell the truth I am afraid to ask her to take the pose as she has seen my Hamlet – I will wait till Gus comes back I think – Miss John says she would not take it.'

Ida, however, agreed to take the pose which would involve her and Gus leaning together, with their arms round each other. Then Orpen fell ill. 'The wretched Orpen has got jaundice or verdigris or something horrible,' Augustus later told Ursula Tyrwhitt. According to Orpen his complaint was more complicated, and not unconnected with Augustus. 'My illness [jaundice] has been very severe. I was not able to eat for nearly ten days, but everything has started going down now! – I am still yellow – I have also got some nasty animals on a certain portion of my body – Gus's doing – Dog that he is – this is my judgement for Paris! Tell him not!'

Augustus himself appeared wonderfully unaffected by these adventures, as if protected by unthinking innocence. 'How he escaped getting the Ladies Fever we couldn't make out,' John Everett noted with irritation in his journal (1899). 'Tonks used to say it must be his natural dirt.'

At the end of September, Augustus, Conder, Alice and the convalescent Will left for Paris where, over the next ten days, they fell in with that 'distinguished reprobate' Oscar Wilde. Wilde had recently been released from prison and was living in a small hotel on the Left Bank. Though appreciative of him as 'a great man of inaction' and a 'big and good-natured fellow with an enormous sense of fun, impeccable bad taste, and a deeply religious apprehension of the Devil',[86] Augustus felt embarrassed by his elaborate performances of wit, not knowing how to respond. 'I could think of nothing whatever to say. Even my laughter sounded hollow.' Despite this, Wilde seems to have been much taken with 'the charming Celtish poet in colour',[87] as he described Augustus. Alice Rothenstein, noticing this friendliness, grew unexpectedly fearful for his reputation and hurried Augustus along to the hairdresser. Next day Oscar looked grave. 'You should have consulted me', he said, laying a hand reproachfully on Augustus's shoulder, 'before taking this important step.'

Stifled by these long unspontaneous lunches at the Café de la Régence and the Café Procope, Augustus was on the lookout to escape with Conder and find 'easier if less distinguished company'. The two of them would go off 'whoring', as Conder called it, visiting a succession of *boîtes de nuit* in Montmartre until the first pale gleams of the Parisian dawn showed in the sky, and each with a companion went his way. Once again much of the waking and sleeping day was spent in the Louvre, of which Augustus never seemed to tire. 'Imagine,' he wrote to Ursula Tyrwhitt, 'we were on the top of the Louvre yesterday! On the roof, and grapes and flowers are there. The prospect was wonderful – Paris at one's feet!'

Two painters made a special impression on him. The first was Honoré Daumier who 'reinforced with immense authority the lesson he had begun to learn from Rembrandt, of seeing broadly and simply, and who taught him to interpret human personality boldly, without fearing to pass, if need be, the arbitrary line commonly held to divide objective representation from caricature'.[88] The second was Puvis de Chavannes whose pictures of an idealized humanity and the relationship between figures and landscape were to be a lifelong inspiration to him.

After he had spent his money from the Carfax exhibition, Augustus borrowed twenty pounds from Michel Salaman with the intention of travelling back via Brussels and Antwerp. But the life in Montmartre held him until his last pound note was gone. 'I've had a fantastic time here,' he told Ursula Tyrwhitt (October 1899) ' – we spent all our money and can't go to Belgium so we're off home tonight.'

6

. . . INTO 'MORAL LIVING'

'I have no ability for affairs.'
Augustus John to Michel Salaman (1902)

The legend that was sown when Augustus dived on to a rock at the age of seventeen had by now bloomed. Only after he left the Slade, and the exterior discipline of Tonks and Brown had been removed, did he, in Michel Salaman's words, 'kick over the traces'. This transformation particularly astonished John Everett,[89] who had met Augustus in October 1896, shared 21 Fitzroy Street with him during part of 1897, and who had left England for a year at sea in 1898. On his return to London in 1899 the first person he met was Orpen, who eagerly apprised him of all the scandalous things Augustus was up to: how he went pub-crawling and got gloriously drunk; how he knew a prostitute who would always go back to him if she could not pick up anyone in the streets; how he had careered all over the flowerbeds in Hyde Park with the police in hot pursuit – and other marvels. Remembering his companion of two or three years ago – 'a poor physical specimen [who] never played any games . . . a very quiet boy, a great reader, a studious youth' who avoided all the organized rags and tugs-of-war and was thought by some to be 'a nonentity' – Everett was nonplussed. 'If you had told me that of any man at the Slade I'd have believed you,' he replied to Orpen. 'But not John.'

Over the next year Everett saw a lot of Augustus. 'All the things Orpen had told me about John were true,' he wrote in his journal. 'His character had completely changed. It was not the John I'd known in the early days at the Slade.' He was getting commissions for portraits and drawings and the quality of his work had never been higher. He seemed, however, quite irresponsible. In some ways he was like the sailors Everett rubbed shoulders with during his voyages. He would make an appointment with some sitter for the following morning, go off drinking half the night with his friends, then wake up grumpily next afternoon. Yet he was not really a heavy drinker. Very little alcohol got the better of him and he could quickly become morose; unlike Conder, who drank far more, remained cheerful, but had a tendency to see yellow-striped cats. Sometimes Augustus stayed out all night, and more than once he was arrested by the police and not released with a caution until the next day. Despite his broken appointments, he was making a reasonable income, though often obliged to borrow from his friends. Money had only one significance for him: it meant freedom of action. To his friends he was open-handed, and when in funds it was generally he who, at restaurants, demanded the bill, or was left with it. Other bills, such as the rent, he sometimes omitted to pay. 'Gus says you need never pay Mrs Everett!' Orpen assured Michel Salaman. Some landladies were more exigent. 'I want to talk to you about this studio [76 Charlotte Street],' Orpen wrote in another letter to Salaman on his return from Vattetot. 'There is great trouble going on about Gus. I'm afraid he will not get back here.' Mrs Laurence, who kept the house, had grown alarmed by what she called 'Mr John's saturnalias'. One night, simply it appears in order to terrify her, he had danced on the roof of the Church of St John the Evangelist next door. Other times he was apparently more conscientious, working late into the night with a nude model over his composition of 'Adam and Eve', and, in the heat of inspiration, stripping off his own clothes. Woken from her sleep by sounds of revelry from this Garden of Eden, Mrs Laurence, chaperoned by her friend old Mrs Young, went to investigate and, without benefit of art training, was shocked by what she found. When Augustus had left suddenly for France with the Carfax money in his pocket, he had paid her nothing; and so, when he returned in October, she refused him entry. He retreated, therefore, to old territory: 21 Fitzroy Street – 'comfortless quarters', as Will Rothenstein described them, but economical.

Here was Will Rothenstein's cue once more to hurry to the rescue by generously offering his own house, No. 1 Pembroke Cottages, off Edwardes Square in Kensington, to Gus and Gwen. Augustus used the house only spasmodically, preferring to sleep in Orpen's Fitzroy Street cellar rather than trudge back to Kensington late at night. The springs of this bed had collapsed at the centre, so only the artist who reached it first and sank into the precipitous valley of the mattress was comfortable. Neither liked early nights, but Orpen was eventually driven by lack of sleep to extraordinary ingenuities, falling into bed in the afternoon twilight, bolting doors, undressing in the dark, anything at all, to win a restful night. Augustus would then mount the stairs to John Everett's room, drink rum in front of his fire till past midnight, and suddenly jump up exclaiming: 'My God! I've missed the last train!' For weeks on end he slept on two of Everett's armchairs.

When Will Rothenstein returned to London, 'I found the house empty and no fire burning. In front of a cold grate choked with cinders lay a collection of muddy boots . . . late in the evening John appeared, having climbed through a window; he rarely, he explained, remembered to take the house-key with him.'[90] This was a sincere test of Rothenstein's hero-worship. 'There were none I loved more than Augustus and Gwen John,' he admitted, 'but they could scarcely be called "comfortable" friends.'[91] As for his wife Alice, she insisted that the walls must be whitewashed and the floors scrubbed before their little home would again be habitable.

Will Rothenstein had recently finished, for the New English Art Club, a portrait of Augustus[92] that won the difficult approbation of Tonks and, more difficult still, avoided the disapprobation of Augustus himself. It shows a soft and dreamy young man whose efforts to roughen and toughen himself are visibly unconvincing. Yet the life he was now leading was certainly rough. After a last effort to recapture 76 Charlotte Street – from which he was repelled 'with a charming County Court summons beautifully printed'[93] – he took up fresh quarters at 61 Albany Street, by the side of Regent's Park. 'I've abandoned my kopje in Charlotte Street,' he told Will Rothenstein in the new Boer War language, 'trekked and laagered up at the above, strongly fortified but scantily supplied. Generals Laurence and Young hover at my rear . . . the garrison [is] in excellent spirits.'

He had briefly taken up with a Miss Simpson who, dismissing him as hopelessly impoverished, decided to marry a bank clerk – and invited Augustus to her wedding. Except for his pale-blue corduroys he had nothing to wear. What happened was described by Orpen in a letter to John Everett:

'I met John last night – he had been to Miss Simpson's wedding, drunk as a lord. Dressed out in Conder's clothes, check waistcoat, high collar, tail coat, striped trousers. He seemed to say he was playing a much more important part than the bridegroom at the wedding and spoke with commiseration at the thought of how bored they must be getting at each other's society . . . He almost wept over this, gave long lectures on moral living, and left us.'

Augustus's theories of 'moral living' had strained his relationship with Ida almost to breaking point. He was painting a portrait of her which 'has clothed itself in scarlet', she told Michel Salaman (1 February 1900), adding: 'Gwen John has gone back to 122 Gower Street.[94] John sleeps, apparently, anywhere.'

The break between them came after an eventful trip Augustus took with Conder that spring to Mrs Everett's boarding house at Swanage. His hair was now cut short, his beard trimmed and he went everywhere in part of Conder's wedding equipment – tail coat, high collar and cap. After the dissipations of London, both painters tried hard to discipline themselves. 'I am quite well now and had almost a providential attack of measles which left me for some days to do my work,' Conder wrote from Swanage to Will Rothenstein. Not since his early days had he worked so consistently out of doors, painting at least nine views of Swanage.[95] He seemed to have found a technique for combining life and work. He would sit painting at the very centre of a rowdy group of friends. 'There would be a whole lot of us smoking, talking, telling good stories,' Everett optimistically recorded. 'Conder would join in the conversation, talk the whole time, yet his hand would go on doing the fan. At times it really seemed as if somebody else was doing the watercolour.'

'We drink milk and soda and tea in large quantities,' Augustus solemnly confided to Orpen. 'I must confess to a pint of beer occasionally on going into the town.' As at Vattetot, both painters worked hard. Conder reported that Augustus was painting 'a decoration 8 ft by 6 . . . with a score of figures half life size'. Though this was 'no easy matter', he nevertheless appeared to 'work away with great ease' and, Conder concluded, large composition 'seems to be his forte'.

Augustus too was impressed by Conder's painting 'which becomes everyday more beautiful', he told Will Rothenstein. 'The country here is lovely beyond words. Corfe Castle and the neighbourhood would make you mad with painter's cupidity! . . . I have started a colossal canvas whereon I depict Dr Faust on the Brocken. I sweat at it from morn till eve.' Not even an attack of German measles could interrupt such work. 'Conder had them some weeks ago,' he reported to Will Rothenstein.

'I had quite forgotten about it when I woke up one morning horrified to find myself struck of a murrain – I have been kept in ever since, shut off from the world. In the daylight it isn't so bad, but I dread the night season which means little sleep and tragic horrors of dreams at that. I mean in the day I work desperately hard at my colossal task. I can say at any rate Faust has benefited by my malady. In fact it is getting near the finish. There are about 17 figures in it not to speak of a carrion-laden gibbet.'⁹⁶

Illness benefited their painting, but the renewal of good health, seasoned by the salt air, brought its problems. Mrs Everett, protected from a knowledge of their world by her harmonium, had invited down two fine-looking Slade girls, Elie Monsell and Daisy Legge, to keep them all company. John Everett, who visited Pevril Tower during weekends, watched the danger approaching gloomily. It seemed inevitable that some romantic entanglements would develop, and before long Conder, to his dismay, found himself engaged to the Irish art student Elie Monsell. Hauled up to London for a difficult interview with the girl's mother (who seems to have been younger than himself), he shortly afterwards fled across the Channel to join Orpen in France. The engagement appeared to lapse, and the following year Conder found himself married to Stella Bedford.

Augustus was also experiencing what he called 'the compulsion of sea-air'⁹⁷ directed towards 'a superb woman of Vienna',⁹⁸ Maria Katerina, an aristocrat employed by Mrs Everett in the guise of parlourmaid. 'A beautiful Viennese lady here has had the misfortune to wrench away a considerable portion of my already much mutilated heart,' was how he broke the news to Orpen. 'Misfortune because such things cannot be brooked too complacently ... Conder is engaged on an even more beautiful fête galante.'

In a letter written nearly twenty years later (2 February 1918) to his friend Alick Schepeler, Augustus was to make a unique admission. 'The sort of paranoia or mental hail storm from which I suffer continually', he told her, '... means that each impression I receive is immediately obliterated by the next girl's, irrespective of its importance. Other people have remarked upon my consistent omission to keep appointments but only to you have I ever confessed the real and dreadful reason.'

This new mental hailstorm temporarily obliterated his feelings for Ida. It was as if he had never met her, as if he had been blinded and could no longer see her. Possibly his confinement with measles – 'German measles please!' he reminded Will Rothenstein, 'I did not catch them in Vienna' – had helped to bring about the dreadful impatience of his emotions; and this impatience was exacerbated by the girl's elusiveness. The letters he wrote to his friends reverberate with the echoes of this passion. 'It was without surprise I learnt she was descended from the old nobility of Austria. Her uncle, the familiar of Goethe, was Count von Astz,' he admitted to Michel Salaman. 'This damnably aristocratic pedigree, you will understand, only goes to make her more fatally attractive to my perverse self . . . She wears patent leather shoes with open work stockings and – '

On Conder's advice, he bought a ring and presented it to her one dark night at the top of a drainpipe that led to her bedroom window. This gesture had a telling effect upon Maria Katerina's defences, which 'proved in the end to be not insurmountable'.[99] She 'has sucked the soul out of my lips', Augustus boasted to Will Rothenstein. 'I polish up my German lore. I spend spare moments trying to recall phrases from Ollendorf and am so grateful for your lines of Schiller which are all that remain to me of the *Lied von der Glocke*.' But with the very instant of success, perhaps even fractionally preceding it, came the first encroachment of boredom.

'Sometimes when I surprise myself not quite happy tho' alone I begin to fear I have lost that crown of youth, the art of loving fanatically. I begin to suspect I have passed the virtues of juvenescence and that its follies are all that remain to me. Write to me dear Will and tell me . . . those little intimacies which are the salt of friendship and the pepper of love.'

On his last night in Swanage, Augustus and Maria met secretly on the cliffs. She was wearing her ring and promised to meet him in France where he was shortly to go with Michel Salaman. Back in London he felt desolate, and more than usually unself-sufficient. On 18 May, Mafeking Night, he strolled down to Trafalgar Square to see the fun, as people celebrated the lifting of the seven-month siege of Mafeking by the Boers. London had gone mad with excitement. Bells rang, guns were being fired, streamers waving; people danced in groups, clapping, shouting, kissing. The streets filled with omnibuses, people of all sorts, policemen without helmets. As if by magic, whistles appeared in everyone's mouths, Union Jacks in their hands, and in the tumult of tears and laughter and singing complete strangers threw their arms about one another's necks; it was, as Winston Churchill said, a most 'unseemly' spectacle. Some were shocked by such a 'frantic and hysterical outburst of patriotic enthusiasm', as Arnold Bennett called it. '[Trafalgar] Square, the Strand and all the adjacent avenues were packed with a seething mass of patriots celebrating the great day in a style that would have made a "savage" blush,' Augustus wrote.

'Mad with drink and tribal hysteria, the citizens formed themselves into solid phalanxes, and plunging at random this way and that, swept all before them. The women, foremost in this mêlée, danced like Maenads, their shrill cat-calls swelling the general din. Feeling out of place and rather scared, I extricated myself from this pandemonium with some difficulty, and crept home in a state of dejection.'[100]

*

'You have evidently forgotten my address,' Augustus remarked with surprise to Michel Salaman. This was not difficult. By June 1900, shortly before he was due to join Salaman in France, he had reached the same point of crisis at Albany Street as had been achieved the previous year in Charlotte Street, and by much the same methods. 'We all went back to John's place in Albany Street,' John Everett wrote in his journal. 'On the way they picked up an old whore, made some hot whisky. The result was John fell on the floor paralytic, the old whore on top of him in the same condition . . . Orpen and [Sidney] Starr tried to pull the old whore's drawers off, but she was too heavy to move.'

'I cannot come just yet,' Augustus wrote to Michel Salaman in France, ' – I have some old commissions to finish amongst other deterrents to immediate migration. Yet in a little while I have hopes of being able to join you. I have had notice to quit this place. I think I will take a room somewhere in Soho if I can find one – a real "mansarde" I hope – I want to hide myself away for some time . . . I shall have to see my Pa before I would come as it is now a long while since I have seen him . . . it would be nice if Gwen could come too and good for her too me thinks.' Salaman had taken rooms at a house called Cité Titand in Le Puy-en-Velay, a medieval village in the Auvergne built about a central rock and dominated by a colossal Virgin in cast iron with doors opening into her body. Augustus arrived early in August. 'It is a wonderful country I assure you – unimaginably wonderful!' he wrote to Ursula Tyrwhitt on 19 September 1900.

'. . . There are most exquisite hills, little and big, Rembrandtesque, Titianesque, Giorgionesque, Turneresque, growing out from volcanic rocks, dominating the fat valleys watered by pleasant streams, tilled by robust peasants bowed by labour and age or upright with the pride of youth and carrying things on their heads. I have bathed in the waters of the Borne and have felt quite Hellenic! At first the country gave me indigestion; used to plainer fare it proved too rich, too high for my northern stomach; now I begin to recover and will find a lifetime too short to assimilate its menu of many courses . . .'[101]

To the golden-haired Alice Rothenstein, who had recommended Le

Puy, he wrote with equal enthusiasm. 'Really, you have troubled my peace with your golden hills and fat valleys of Burgundy! . . .

'I work indoors mostly now. I am painting Michel's portrait. I hope to make a success of it. If when finished it will be as good as it is now I may count on that. I am also painting Polignac castle which ought to make a fine picture . . .'[102]

The very excellent military band plays in the park certain nights, and we have enjoyed sitting listening to it. It is very beautiful to watch the people under the trees. At intervals the attention of the populace is diverted from following the vigorous explanatory movements of the conductor by an appeal to patriotism, effected by illuminating the flag by Bengal lights at the window of the museum! It is dazzling and undeniable! The band plays very well. Rendered clairvoyant by the music one feels very intimate with humanity, only Michel's voice when he breaks in with a laborious attempt at describing how beautifully the band played 3 years ago at the Queen's Hall that time he took Edna Waugh – is rather disturbing – or is it that I am becoming ill-tempered?'

Where Augustus went, could Will be far behind? He turned up with Alice early in September and stayed two weeks at the Grand Hôtel des Ambassadeurs. 'Every day we met at lunch in a vast kitchen, full of great copper vessels, a true rôtisserie de la Reine Pédauque,' Will Rothenstein remembered, 'presided over by a hostess who might have been mother to Pantagruel himself, so heroic in size she was, and of so genial and warm a nature.'[103]

On their bicycles, the four of them pedalled as far south as Notre-Dame-des-Neiges, where Stevenson had once stayed on his travels with a donkey. Augustus on wheels was a fabulous sight, and Will noticed that the girls minding their cattle in the fields crossed themselves as he whizzed past, and that the men in horror would exclaim: 'Quel type de rapin!' At Arlempdes, a village of such devilish repute it went unmarked on any map, they were entertained by the *curé*, who commented ecstatically upon Augustus's fitness for the principal role in their Passion play. 'Who does he remind you of?' he asked his sister. 'Notre Seigneur, le bon Dieu,' she answered without hesitation. 'I take it as a compliment,' Augustus remarked, but refused the part – understandably, since the previous year, in the heat of the occasion, Christ had been stabbed in the side. On reaching Notre-Dame-des-Neiges, Alice took sanctuary at an inn while the three men spent the night in a Trappist monastery where Will believed he might see Huysmans. Though rising early, he saw no one. Augustus lay abed in his cell where he was served by the silent monks with a breakfast of wine and cheese.

After returning to Le Puy, Will and Alice wheeled their machines over the horizon and were gone. 'Is it that I am becoming ill-tempered?' Augustus had queried. His temper was affected by the failure of Maria Katerina to appear. He had written long letters urging her to meet him in Paris, but these were intercepted by Mrs Everett who, after Augustus left Swanage, had discovered hairpins in his bed. Brandishing these instruments she had extracted from her servant a full confession. Her duty now was clear. From reading Augustus's letters it was a small step to writing Maria's, the tone of which, Augustus noticed, suddenly changed. 'When you will no longer have me – what will I do then?' she asked. 'What will become of me then? Repudiated by my husband who loves me? Can you answer that?' Augustus did answer it according to his lights, but at such a distance, and screened by Mrs Everett, they were not strong enough. 'Women always suspect me of fickleness,' he explained to Alice Rothenstein, 'but will they never give me a chance of vindicating myself? They are too modest, too cautious, for to do that they would have to give their lives. I am not an exponent of the faithful dog business.'

Michel Salaman, who was financing their holiday, suffered grievously from his disappointment. Almost every day Augustus complained of ailments and accidents. His womanizing brought out in him a satyr-like quality. Some women were alarmed, others hypnotized. Michel Salaman was shocked.

Augustus did his best to pull himself together. 'I am painting beyond Esplay,' he wrote to Will Rothenstein.[104] '. . . I want to travel again next year hitherwards and be a painter. I am, dear Will, full of ideas for work.' He read – in particular Balzac's *Vie conjugale* which 'pains and makes me laugh at the same time'. He travelled – to Paris for a few days to see some Daumiers and Courbets and 'was profoundly moved'.

He was soon joined by 'the waif of Pimlico' as he called his sister Gwen, and by 'the gentle Ambrose McEvoy'. Salaman was rather on his guard with Gwen. She had once had a crush on him and he found her exacting. When she and McEvoy arrived at Le Puy, he returned to England. 'I am conducted about by McEvoy and Gwen,' Augustus wrote to Salaman, 'who explain the beauties and show me new and ever more surprising spots.' After a long evening walk they would hurry back 'to cook a dinner which is often successful in some items'. Sometimes the two men – 'the absinthe friends' – would sit in a café where, Augustus told Ursula Tyrwhitt, 'a young lady exquisitely beautiful, attired as a soldier, sings songs of dubious meaning'.

By October, Augustus had become, according to McEvoy, a 'demon' for work, refusing to budge from his easel. He was as quick to infatuation as to anger: and quick to forget both. But for McEvoy and for Gwen it was a less happy time. McEvoy seemed in a dream. 'After a strange period of mental and physical bewilderment I am beginning to regain some of my normal senses,' he wrote to Salaman. '. . . At first I felt like some animal and incapable of expressing anything. Drawing was quite impossible. I should like to live here for years and then I might hope to paint pictures that would have something of the grand air of the Auvergne – but now! Gus seems to retain his self-control. Perhaps he has been through my stage. He constantly does the most wonderful drawings. Oh, it is most perplexing.'

During this month at Le Puy, McEvoy's relationship with Gwen appears to have reached some sort of crisis. For much of the time he was silent, 'a mere wreck', drinking himself gently into oblivion; while Gwen, who spent many days in tears, seemed inconsolable. Having known Whistler, McEvoy had been able to give Gwen help with her oil painting technique at the Slade; but she had nothing more to learn from him after returning from Whistler's own tuition at the Académie Carmen. She seemed too demanding, he too immature – besides, he was under Gus's spell.

'It will be a frightful job seeking for rooms in London,' Augustus wrote to Salaman shortly before his return. But by November he had found what he wanted at 39 Southampton Street above the Economic Cigar Company. This was no 'mansarde', but would serve for a time. Many of the drawings he had done at Le Puy were now put on exhibition at the Carfax Gallery. 'Tonks has bought 2 drawings. Brown thinks of doing so too,' he wrote to Will Rothenstein. 'I have a great number if you like to come and amuse yourself.' It was again partly owing to Rothenstein's advocacy that the drawings sold so well. 'John is the great one at present,' Orpen assured Everett, 'making a lot of money and doing splendid drawing.' Augustus himself was delighted by this success – in a restrained way. 'The run on my drawings tho' confined to a narrow circle has been very pleasant,' he wrote in another letter to Will Rothenstein that autumn. 'People however seem better at bargaining than I am.'

People also seemed better, it struck him, at arranging their lives. He was growing increasingly dissatisfied by the series of pursuing landladies and girlfriends in retreat. Perhaps, after all, there was something to be said for 'moral living'. At any rate the novelty was appealing.

He began to see Ida again. Although she had few illusions about the sort of life he had been leading, she still loved him. But he was dangerous. He knew he was dangerous and did not attempt to conceal it. In one of the limericks he was fond of composing, he scribbled:

There was a young woman named Ida
Who had a porcelain heart inside her
But she met a young card
Who hugged her so hard
He smashed up her crockery, Poor Ida!

Soon the two of them were together again on the old basis. 'John is once more in the embrace of Miss Nettleship – the reunion is "Complet",' Orpen informed Everett. 'Marie (la Belle) has faded into the dark of winter, and disappeared . . .'

But the old basis was no longer good enough. Since the Nettleships would never agree to their 'living in sin', and since Ida would never consent to distressing them in this way, 'moral living', as Augustus had called it, seemed the one solution. Having decided this, he acted at once. He conceded the formality of a civil ceremony but insisted on an elopement, and set off with Ida early one Saturday morning for the Borough of St Pancras where they celebrated the event in secret. 'I have news to tell you,' he wrote the following week to his sister Winifred. 'Ida Nettleship and I got spliced at the St Pancras Registry Office last Saturday! McEvoy and Evans and Gwen aided and abetted us. Everyone agreed it was a beautiful wedding – there was a wonderful fog which lent an air of mystery unexpectedly romantic.' This letter he illustrated with a drawing of himself standing on his head.

Jack Nettleship, when he discovered what had happened, took the news philosophically: his wife less so. 'It might have been worse,' Augustus commented.[105] That evening Ida went up to the bedroom of one of her mother's employees, Elspeth Phelps. 'I want to tell you something, Elspeth,' she said, taking her hands. 'I want to tell you – ' and then burying her face in her hands she broke into great heaving sobs. After a few moments she continued: 'I want to tell you I've married Gussie – and I think I'm a little frightened.'[106]

She gave no sign of this fear in public. After the wedding they went round to tell Will and Alice Rothenstein the news. 'How pleased we were, and what mysterious things Ida and my wife had to talk over!' Will wrote.[107] That evening the Rothensteins gave them a party. Ida looked 'exquisitely virginal in her simple white dress'. 'Mr & Mrs Nettleship, Mrs Beerbohm and Neville [Lytton], Miss Salmond, Misses John, Salaman, Messrs Steer, Tonks, McEvoy, Salaman and myself were there,' Albert Rutherston wrote to his parents. But Augustus himself was not there. The last anyone had seen of him was on his way that afternoon to a bath. Late that night, he turned up wearing a bright check suit and earrings. 'We were very gay,' remembered Albert Rutherston. 'We had scherades [*sic*] towards the end of the evening which was great fun. Mr and Mrs John were radiant.' One of these charades represented Steer teaching at the Slade – a long silence, then: 'How's your sister?' This, Augustus swore, was a perfect example of Steer's methods.

'I pray the marriage may be a splendid thing for both parties,' Orpen wrote to Will Rothenstein. Augustus himself had no doubts. At last someone had given him the chance of vindicating himself. Though Ida and he had undergone a more or less conventional wedding, neither of them were conventional people: they simply loved each other.

For their honeymoon, he took his wife to Swanage, and they stayed at Pevril Tower.

THREE

Love for Art's Sake

I

EVIL AT WORK

'For an idea of the Academy they deplored, we can turn to the Catalogue of Harry Furniss's spoof Academy exhibition of 1887 – Alma-Tadema's Roman Ladies, Stacy Mark's gnarled birds, a laborious allegory by Watts, cattle shows, whiskery portraits, a besotted cavalier, and the minutely painted floorboards of Orchardson.'

Bevis Hillier, *The Early Years of the New English Art Club*

The New English Art Club, by the time Augustus John officially became a member in 1903, was seventeen years old. It had been founded, after some half-dozen years of discussions, by a number of artists who had worked in the Parisian schools and who wanted an exhibiting society run on the French democratic lines of elective juries as against the appointed privileged committee of Burlington House. During the mid-nineteenth century the Royal Academy had been perfecting its policy of caution. It had been slow to welcome the Pre-Raphaelites until Pre-Raphaelitism became diluted – by which time it welcomed little else. To many of the Academy's forty immortals, Paris was still a name of dread, to be associated with lubricity, bloodshed and bad colour.

But to the mob of disgruntled outsiders Paris was an Elysium. They found their inspiration not so much in Impressionism as in the ennobling realism of Millet and Corot, in the 'pleinairism' of Jules Bastien-Lepage and the Barbizon School. Their movement was formalized in 1886 when the New English Art Club came into being.

For a quarter of a century the club was to act as a *salon des refusés*. The exhibitions were shown at the Dudley Gallery in the Egyptian Hall, the 'Hall of Mystery'. Its original members numbered many hardened sentimentalists. Chief among them at the start was the 'Newlyn Group', whose watchword was 'values'. They were not, in any exaggerated way, revolutionaries. The pictures of Frank Bramley, in the matter of domestic sentiment, could rival those of most academicians; while George Clausen,

Stanhope Forbes and H. H. La Thanghe's large-scale, open-air paintings of country and fisher folk, which excited much popular acclaim, contained little to vex the Academy of Sir John Millais. It was not long before all these artists drifted off to Burlington House.

This dangerous contact with the open air, this accent on 'realism' and concentration upon rustic themes, seem at first sight to have something in common with Augustus's spontaneous landscapes. These pleinair Victorian painters were *theatrical* realists, and their pictures were carefully staged. Sickert explained the artificial nature of the Newlyn Group when he wrote:

'Your subject is a real peasant in his own natural surroundings, and not a model from Hatton Garden. But what is he doing? He is posing for a picture as best he can, and he looks it. That woman stooping to put potatoes into a sack will never rise again. The potatoes, portraits every one, will never drop into the sack, and never a breath of air circulates around that painful rendering in the flat of the authentic patches on the very gown of a real peasant. What are the truths you have gained, a handful of tiresome little facts, compared to the truths you have lost? To life and spirit, light and air?'[1]

Augustus abandoned storytelling altogether. Simply the thing itself was what he saw. His figures seldom touch or focus on each other. They appear as single shapes caught in preparatory gestures, or are arranged as in a ballet performed within the landscape of his imagination.

By the early 1890s control of the NEAC had passed to another group, sometimes called 'the London Impressionists', the leading figures of which were Steer and Sickert. They, too, looked to France for their inspiration – not to Millet and Corot, but to Monet, Manet and Degas. London Impressionism had little in common with Monet's 1874 landscape entitled 'Une Impression', from which the name literally derived. It was impressionism relying on line and tonality, and dominated by the influence of Whistler. Whistler himself had ceased to exhibit at the club in 1889, 'disapproving, perhaps, a society so less than republican in constitution as to have no president'.[2] But Sickert was still a faithful disciple and, moreover, a severe critic of Bastien-Lepage. The sentiment and invention of narrative painting were on the way out before impartiality and an insistence upon 'the thing there'. When D. S. MacColl praised Whistler on the aptness of a bit of wall-skirting in a portrait, he retorted severely: 'But it's *there.*' And Sickert, too, shared this principle. 'Supposing', he explained, 'that you paint a woman carrying a pail of water through the door, and drops are spilt upon the planks. There is a natural necessary rhythm about the pattern they make much better than anything you could invent.'

Hampered by difficulties over galleries, and weakened by their aesthetic differences, the New English failed to make an early impact. But then, in 1890, the Scottish painter D. S. MacColl became Art Critic of the *Spectator*, and shortly afterwards the Irish novelist George Moore was appointed to a similar post on the *Speaker*. Both writers gave a leading place to the NEAC shows.

Moore, who had studied as a painter in Paris, re-emphasized the French influence of the NEAC over the lingering Nazarene culture in Burlington House. He had been educated, he liked to point out, not round the lawns and cloisters of Oxford or Cambridge but at the marble tables of the Nouvelles Athènes, a café on the Place Pigalle, sitting through the morning idleness and long summer evenings until completely 'aestheticized' by two o'clock the following morning. D. S. MacColl revived the antagonism between the club and the Academy, provoking anger among academic reactionaries. Sir Frederic Leighton predicted that the club would soon be disbanded. Sir William Richmond was heard to say of John Singer Sargent: 'I should like to set him copying Holbeins for a year.' The climax came in 1893 over Degas's inaccurately named picture 'L'Absinthe'. During one of the fiercest aesthetic battles in the history of modern art, MacColl, Degas and the whole of the NEAC were abused 'from Budapest to Aberdeen'. This controversy had the result of placing the New English Art Club at the forefront of non-academic painting – even Aubrey Beardsley joined it. 'Degradation to suit a decadent civilization,' thundered the *Westminster Gazette*. 'No longer does nobility of idea dictate subjects to authors; sex is over-emphasized; the peak of abomination has been reached by the *Yellow Book* . . . All this relates to the evil at work as expressed by the New English Art Club.'

By the turn of the century, when Augustus began to exhibit, the club was about to enter a new phase in its history. Alphonse Legros had disliked the aims of the NEAC, but Brown was an original member, a close associate of Sickert's, and the man who had drafted the club's rules. Tonks, too, became a member in 1895 and was elected to the jury, on which he represented the revolutionary element in many an argument with Roger Fry – roles that were later dramatically to be reversed. It was therefore not surprising that the Slade should emerge as the chief nursery of young talent, and that people should look to Augustus, as the spoilt child of this crèche, to lead the way.

He and Gwen and other ex-students were soon exhibiting there. 'Gwen has had a portrait hung in the NEAC,' Augustus wrote to Michel Salaman from Swanage. 'I don't know yet whether they have hung mine . . . Orpen has sent also and Everett so that there should be a healthy inoculation of new and Celtic blood into the Aged New English at last. The jurors have rejected both Mr Nettleship and Ida's works. I can't see why the former should wish to seek laurels in this direction . . . I have returned now . . . The New English has opened its doors on the flabber-gasted.'[3]

From this time onward a change began to pass over the appearance of the NEAC exhibitions: more drawings and watercolours were seen and the club became, in the words of D. S. MacColl, 'a school of drawing'.[4] Then Roger Fry's appointment as Art Critic of the *Athenaeum* gained for the New English another platform. The Winter Exhibition of 1904, Fry wrote, was its most important one yet. 'Mr Sargent, Mr Steer, Mr Rothenstein, Mr John, Mr Orpen, to mention only the best known artists, are all seen here at their best.' But the older members belonged to a group, he continued, 'whose traditions and methods are already being succeeded by a new set of ideas. They are no longer *le dernier cri* – that is given by a group of whom Mr John is the most remarkable member.'

There was nothing inimical in Augustus's work to Sickert's London Impressionists whose pursuit was 'life' and whose object was to draw it feverishly, Quentin Bell has explained, 'capturing at high speed the essentials of the situation'.[5] Between Sickert and himself there developed a respect tinged with irony. Sickert was amused by Augustus's moody character. 'I am proud to say', he boasted, 'that I once succeeded in bringing a smile to the somewhat difficult lips of Mr Augustus John.'[6] Yet he saw the value of his work, describing him as 'the first draughtsman that we have . . . the most sure and able of our portrait painters'.[7] And in the *New Age* he paid generous tribute to Augustus's 'intensity and virtuosity [which] have endued his peculiar world of women, half gypsy, half model, with a life of their own. But his whole make-up is personal to himself, and the last thing a wary young man had better do is to imitate John . . . [he is] incessantly provisioning himself from the inexhaustible and comfortable cupboard of nature.'[8]

Perversely, Augustus dismissed Sickert's writings as 'elegant drivel'.[9] Though he liked Sickert's work, he felt impatience with his aesthetic intrigues. Augustus seldom interested himself in art politics. While other painters held stormy meetings about New Rules and Old Prejudices, the only record of Augustus intercepting their discussions is in the spring of 1903 when, so Orpen told Conder (2 May 1903), he 'demanded to know why after accepting Miss Gwendolen John's pictures – they [the NEAC Committee] had not hung them. But alas this question was out of order . . .'[10]

But Gwen was thankful to be free of the New English. 'I think I can paint better than I used – I know I can,' she told Ursula Tyrwhitt (8 July

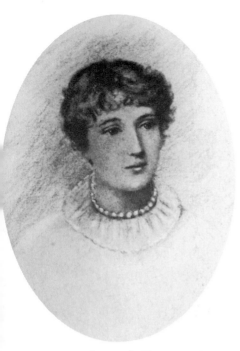

Augusta Smith.

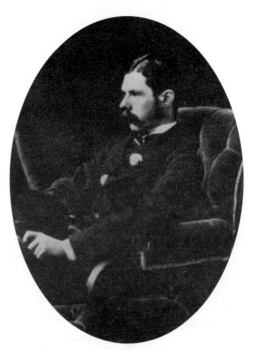

Edwin John.

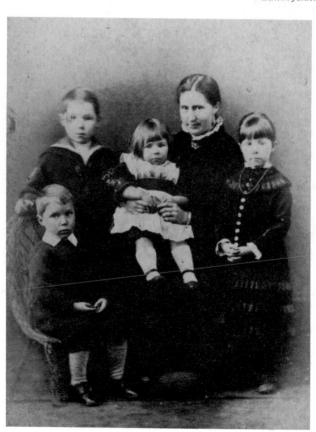

The four John children (left to right, Augustus, Thornton, Winifred and Gwen,) with their nurse (c. 1880).

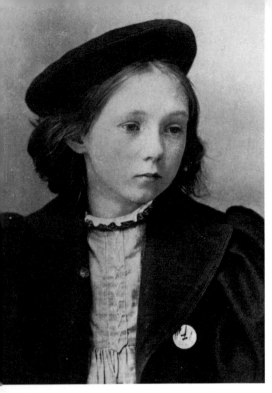

Gwen.

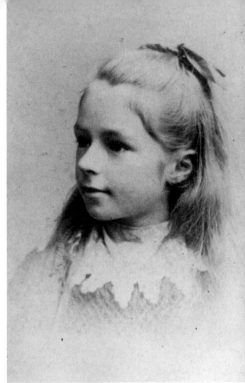

Winifred.

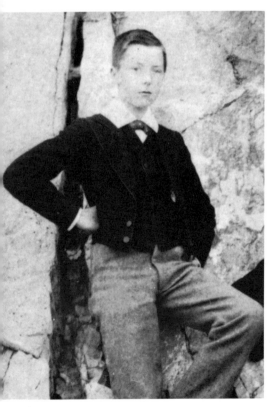

Augustus.

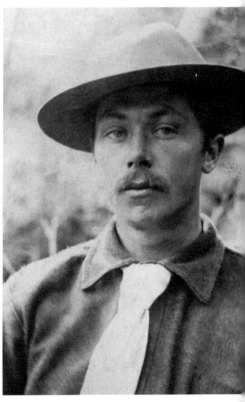

Thornton.

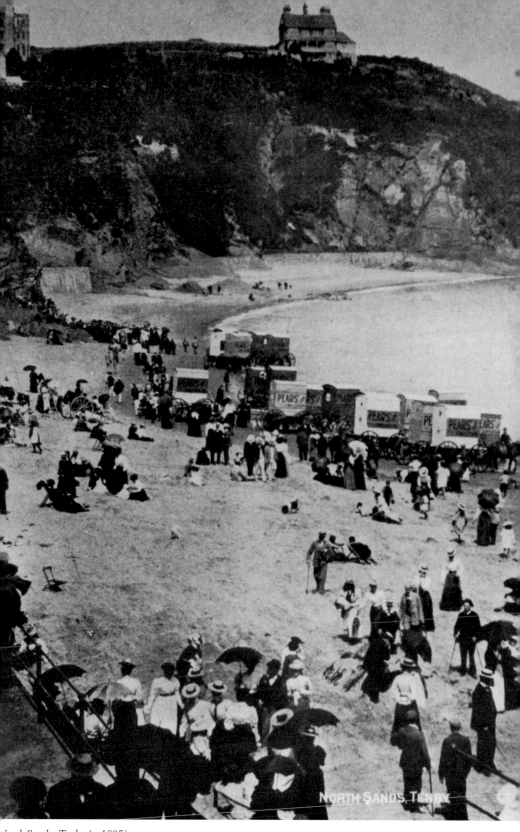

North Sands, Tenby (c. 1895).

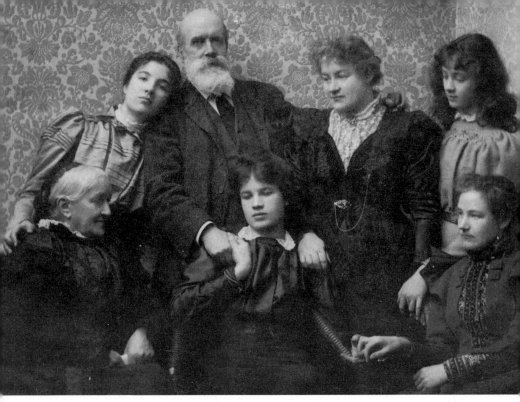

The Nettleship family, left to right, Granny Hinton, Ethel, Jack, Ida, Ada, Ursula, Margaret Hinton (c.1890).

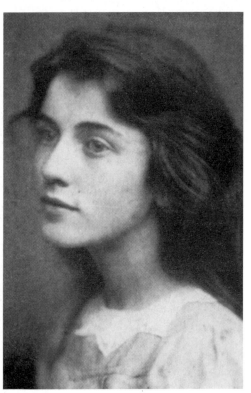

Edna Waugh (later Clarke Hall).

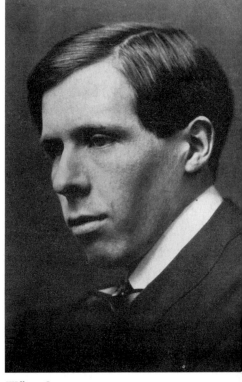

William Orpen.

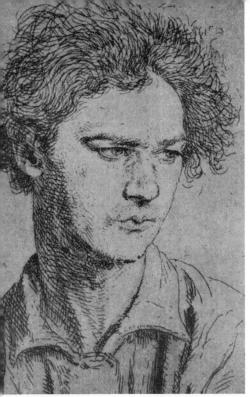

Jacob Epstein.

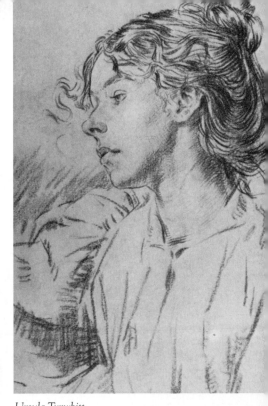

Ursula Tyrwhitt.

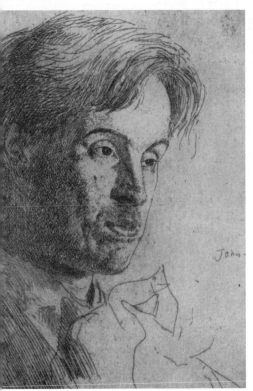

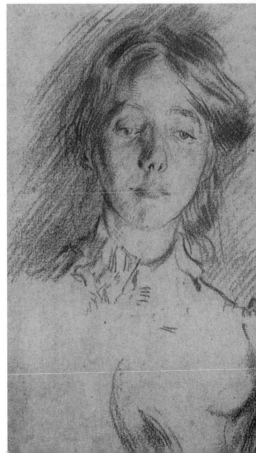

ABOVE W.B. Yeats. RIGHT Gwen John.

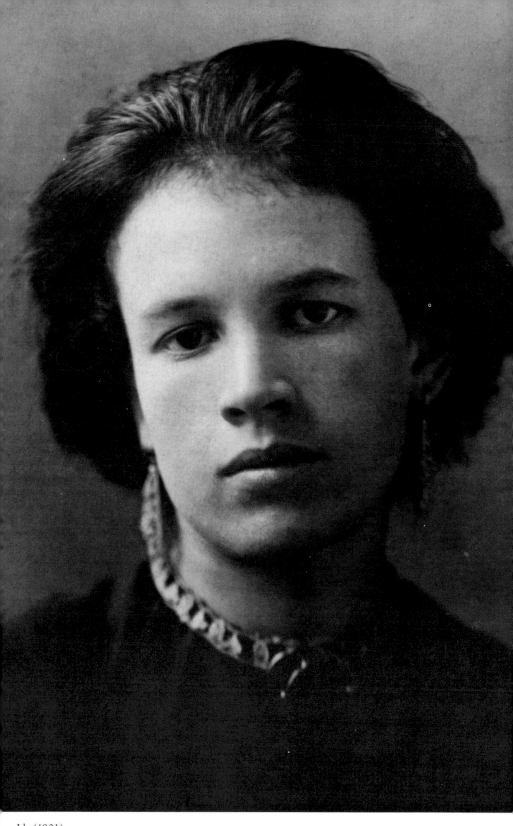

Ida (1901).

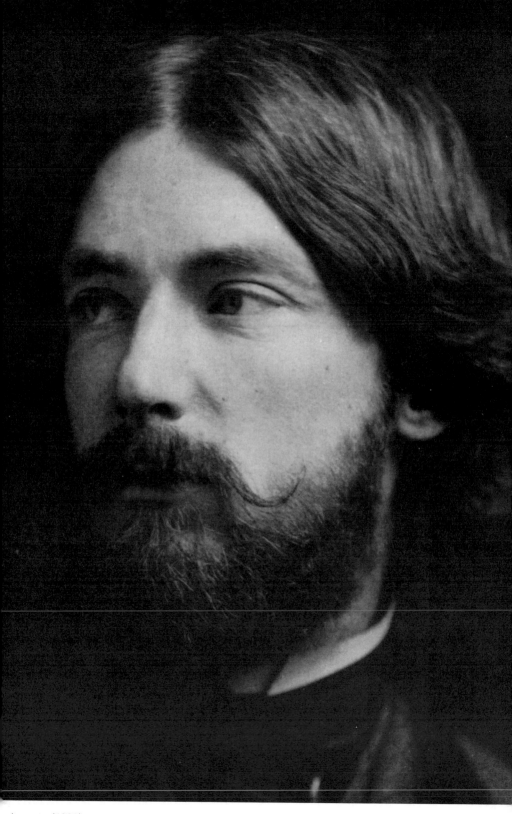

Augustus (1901).

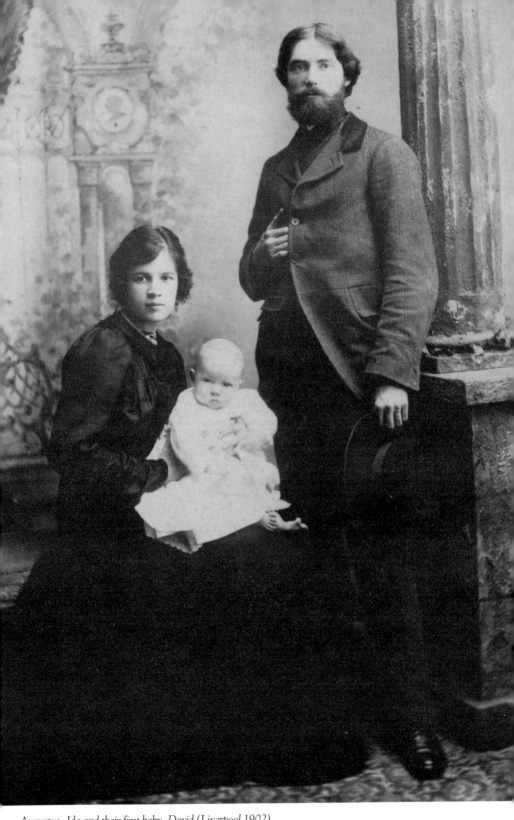

Augustus, Ida and their first baby, David (Liverpool 1902).

1904); 'it has been such a help not to think of the N.E.A.C. – and not to hurry over something to get it in – I shall never do anything for an exhibition again – but when the exhibitions come round send anything I happen to have.'

Gwen finally ceased showing her pictures at the club in the winter of 1911. 'I paint a good deal,' she wrote to Margaret Sampson after the last show (5 December 1911), 'but I don't often get a picture done – that requires, for me, a very long time of a quiet mind, and never to think of exhibitions.'

Augustus continued regularly showing his work at the NEAC until the large Retrospective Exhibition of 1925, and intermittently afterwards.* His attitude to the New English was the same as his attitude would be to the Royal Academy. 'Over here paltry little clubs & exhibitions agitate the artistic climate,' he wrote to Gwen in 1904. As for the Royal Academy, it was unthinkable that he would ever belong to an institution whose shows were simply 'a vast collection of wrong-minded stuff'. Sargent, who had joined the Royal Academy in 1897, was he told Gwen, 'the cleverest of the spoilers, moilers & toilers [who] with infallible judgement leaves out everything that makes a face interesting. His art is merely "the glass of fashion" but hardly "the mould of form".'

Augustus envied Gwen's quiet as opposed to his own agitated atmosphere. He wanted her to be recognized and he worried about her neglect, over which he sometimes felt odd sensations of responsibility. But she was almost impossible to help either with gifts of money, which put her awkwardly in his debt, or with offers to manage exhibitions on her behalf, which troubled her as much as the exhibitions themselves. His moods of responsibility came and went, and she was affected both by their coming and their going.

And he was affected by Gwen's tenuous self-sufficiency. Her attitude, if he could have attained it, would surely have furthered his own talent. But with such a lifestyle, such an entourage, he could never afford it. For she, in her prison-like rooms, was comparatively free; while he, restlessly patrolling here and darting somewhere else, would be encumbered by the claims of voluminous and irregular families.

* See Appendix Two, 'John's Pictures at the New English Art Club'.

2

LIVERPOOL SHEDS AND ROMANY FLOTSAM

'I become more rebellious in Liverpool.'
Augustus John to Alice Rothenstein (December 1905)

'We have taken the most convenient flat imaginable in Fitzroy Street,' Augustus wrote to his sister Winifred a few days after his marriage. 'It has an excellent studio. The whole most cheap.'

By the time they returned from their honeymoon at Swanage, this flat – three rooms and a huge studio in the top part of 18 Fitzroy Street – had been redecorated and stood ready for them. But no sooner had they got there than Ida fell ill with the Swanage complaint – measles – and returned to Wigmore Street, leaving Augustus alone. It was not a good omen.

Money was now their chief worry. Well though Augustus's work had sold at his exhibitions, it was not admired by everyone and could scarcely earn him enough to keep a wife, let alone children. He applied for a British Institute scholarship but did not get one. Then, that February 1901, shortly after Ida returned, a new opportunity for making a living suddenly presented itself. Albert Rutherston, having staggered round to deliver his wedding present of a kitchen table, reported that 'there is just a chance of John going to Liverpool for a year to act as Professor in the school of art there during the absence of the present one – it would be very nice for him as he will get a studio free and at least £300 or £400 [equivalent to £15,500–£20,500 in 1996] for the year.'

What had happened was that Herbert Jackson, the art instructor at the art school affiliated to University College, Liverpool, had gone off to the Boer War. When asked to recommend someone temporarily to fill his place, D. S. MacColl had put Augustus's name forward;[11] and, since there was no time to be lost, his proposal was at once accepted.

Augustus arrived in Liverpool late that winter, 'a heartening sight', one student recalled, '. . . striding across the drab quad to the studios in his grey fisherman's jersey and with golden rings* in his ears'.[12] The university staff were rather flustered by this spectacle, enhanced by the beard, long hair and large magnetic eyes, and by the sonorous voice with which he sang his repertoire of ballads romantic and bawdy – rollicking songs from the old troubadours and suggestive ones imported from Parisian

---

* Later on at Liverpool Augustus wore only one earring, having, so the story goes, gallantly presented the other one to a lady who admired their design.

cabarets, little verses from Villon and whining cockney limericks with their cringing refrain:

'I'm a man as done wrong to my paryents'.

'Liverpool is a most gorgeous place,' Augustus immediately wrote to Michel Salaman. He had been warned that it was an ugly city but he did not find it ugly. It enthralled him. Over the last quarter of the nineteenth century, it had been rising from a 'black hole' as Nathaniel Hawthorne, the US Consul there in the 1850s, called it, into a prosperous and dignified Victorian trading city. Its prosperity depended upon its port, one of the largest in the world, which made it a cosmopolitan meeting place 'full of European enclaves and strange languages, while the steamships and sailing barques brought sailors' stories, rhymes and riddles from all over the world'.[13]

Lytton Strachey, who left the university a few months before Augustus John arrived there, had recoiled from the groups of starving children, drunken sailors, beggars with their dingy barrel organs, that infested the stinking slum streets and tenements that lay behind and around Liverpool's grand façade. The crowds at the docks were 'appalling', he noted, and 'all hideous. It gave me the shivers and in ten minutes I fled.'[14] But Augustus revelled in this spectacle of human diversity: the knife grinders, umbrella makers, ship owners, Celtic scholars, soap kings. The only place that gave him the shivers was the Walker Art Gallery – 'a stinking hole'[15] he called it in a letter to Michel Salaman.

'The docks are wondrous,' Augustus was soon writing to Will Rothenstein. 'The college is quite young, so are its professors and they are very anxious to make it an independent seat of learning . . . The town is full of Germans, Jews, Welsh and Irish and Dutch.' Everything seemed to delight him. Whatever was new appeared exciting – and there was much that was new to him, much that smelt of adventure here. He explored the sombre district of the Merseyside with its migrant population of Scandinavians on their way to the New World, and reported to Alice Rothenstein, 'the Mersey is grand – vast – in a golden haze – a mist of love in the great blue eye of heaven.' He nosed around the Goree Piazza, still faintly reeking of the slave trade; he reconnoitred the Chinese Quarter off Pitt Street and Upper Frederick Street, with its whiff of opium, and looked in on the lodging houses of the tinkers round Scotland Road. Even the art school – a collection of wooden sheds on Brownlow Hill – appealed to him. 'It is amusing teaching,' he told Will Rothenstein.

Over the first few weeks he and Ida put up at 9 St James's Street, and it was here that Augustus's one complaint lay. 'It has been impossible to do much work yet – living as a guest in somebody's house – a great bore.' He was hungry for work, especially since there was soon to be another show of his pictures at the Carfax Gallery. But already by April they had found 'very good rooms', he reported, 'in the house of an absent-minded and charming Professor, one Mackay'.

'Some of the College professors are charming men,' Augustus wrote to Michel Salaman. John MacDonald Mackay, Rathbone Professor of Ancient History, was 'the leading spirit of the College', he assured Will Rothenstein shortly after moving to his house at 4 St James's Road. 'He avoids coming to the practical point most tenaciously – when arranging about taking these rooms he refused to consider terms but referred us to the Swedish Consul – who was extremely surprised when Ida spoke to him on the subject.'

Mackay combined two qualities that appealed to Augustus's divided nature: comedy and idealism. With his right hand raised, half to his audience, half to the sky visible through the window, a faraway look in his eyes, he would discourse in a weird moustachioed chant, interrupting himself with bursts of sing-song laughter or rhetorical indignation, often abandoning the line of his argument, yet always struggling back to First Principles. Within the chemistry of his strange, broken-back eloquence, Liverpool was transformed into a new Athens destined to save the country from materialism by the luminescence of its thought, the excellence of its work, the beauty of its art and architecture. Whatever nominal positions others may have held, Mackay was the patron of the university while Augustus lived there.

Mackay was important to Augustus in two respects. First, he became the subject of one of his strongest portraits. He had a magnificent head, with fair unkempt hair, a powerful jaw and square chin, and the broad shoulders and torso of someone altogether larger. Augustus's 'official' portrait – a three-quarter view of him decked out in his red academic robes – catches the spiritual energy of the man.[16]

Secondly, he introduced Augustus and Ida to people whom, in their peculiar shyness, they might otherwise never have known. A number of these Augustus drew and painted, and a few became close friends. 'We are to dine with the Dowdalls on Friday which I dread,' Ida wrote to her mother. 'They are very nice, but I would rather hide.' A little later she is writing: 'We had a nice little dinner with the Dowdalls on Saturday. He is a lawyer, I think, with a taste for painting – and he has a little auburn-haired wife who spends most of her time being painted by different people. Gus is to draw Dowdall's mother.'

Harold Chaloner Dowdall, later to become a County Court judge and, as Lord Mayor of Liverpool, the subject of one of Augustus's most controversial portraits, was a pompous good-natured barrister, very loyal to the Johns but with a tendency to dilate, perhaps for an entire day, on the extreme freshness of that morning's eggs at breakfast. His wife Mary, nicknamed 'the Rani', was 'the most charming and entertaining character in Liverpool', Augustus asserted. She soon became Ida's most devoted confidante. 'The Rani has beautiful browny-red hair and is quite exceptional, and reminds me of the grass and the smell of the earth,' Ida wrote. As always with those she admired, she likened the Rani to an animal in its natural surroundings. 'Certainly you belong to the woods and where creatures start and hide away at any alien sound.'

As the daughter of Lord Borthwick, the Hon. Mrs Dowdall was Liverpool's aristocrat. But she shocked Liverpool society dreadfully. Respectable people were put out by her habit of walking barefoot through the mud – 'the gentle stimulant of cold mud welling between one's toes is a clarifier of thought', she informed them, 'after a day's perfect irresponsibility'. They were dismayed when, at the fashionable hour, she was to be seen swinging her stockingless legs from the back of a gypsy caravan trundling down Bold Street. They disliked her involvement with the repertory theatre which gave theatrical performances on Good Friday, her frequent modelling for dubious artists such as Charles Shannon, her awful wit, her sheer attractiveness, her unaccountable failure to take Liverpool society seriously. Above all, Liverpool was appalled by the books she wrote – novels they were, with such titles as *Three Loving Ladies* and, most notoriously, *The Book of Martha*, which, embellished with a frontispiece by Augustus, dealt with tradesmen and servants. She was also the author of *Joking Apart*, and her jokes, delivered in the mock-magisterial tones of her husband, were introduced by: 'All virgins will kindly leave the Court.' No wonder she emptied the drawing-rooms of Edwardian Liverpool.

Augustus's contacts with the university staff were not pushed to extremes, but among the exceptions were the Professor of Modern Literature, Walter Raleigh, who abashed him with his early morning brilliance – 'he shone even at breakfast!'[17] – Charles Bonnier, the French professor, a victim to the theory and practice of *pointillisme*, who 'has been producing a most astoundingly horrible marmalade of spots yellow, purple, blue and green in my studio';[18] and Herbert MacNair, Instructor in Design and Stained Glass, a lusty bicyclist who, in later life, became a postman. He and his wife Frances, working in perfect unison, involved themselves with a peculiar form of art nouveau, producing, to Augustus's dismay, friezes of quaint mermaids designed after the MacNair crest, staircases encrusted in sheet lead, lamps of fancifully twisted wrought iron, symbolic watercolours on vellum, embroideries depicting bulbous gnomes and fairies prettily arranged, and as their *pièce de résistance* a burly door-knocker 18 inches long, the delight of small boys who used it 'to keep themselves in constant touch with the most advanced Art movement', Augustus told Will Rothenstein. '. . . Between them [they] have produced one baby [Sylvan] and a multitude of spooks – their drawing-room is very creepy and the dinner-table was illuminated with two rows of nightlights in a lantern of the "MacNair" pattern . . .'

By far the most valuable new friend Augustus made was the university Librarian, John Sampson. A portly man, almost twice Augustus's age, Sampson was ponderous in his manner but at heart a poet, a romantic and a rebel. His influence on Augustus over the next two years was to change his life. The two men met in the late spring of 1901 and struck up an immediate friendship.

Sampson was almost pedantically self-taught. He had left school at fourteen, been apprenticed to a lithographer and engraver in Liverpool, read literature at night and, having learnt the aesthetic disciplines of typography and design, set up a small business as printer in the Liverpool Corn Exchange. He had ambitions to become an artist – ambitions which Augustus quickly quelled. But his abiding passion was the pursuit of lost languages, the unknown vocabularies and grammars of ancient mother tongues still miraculously to be heard across woods and fields and mountainsides in the heart of Wales. These fugitive words – 'ablatives or adverbs or queer things of that sort' – spread through him an extraordinary pleasure, especially when their curators turned out to be those 'exasperating lovely creatures', the gypsy girls; for 'man does not live by philology alone.' Sampson seemed to regard the rhyming slang and 'flying cant', the beautiful grand syllables of forgotten tongues, as orchestrated clues to some treasure. It was, he later said, 'like finding a tribe of organ-grinders who among themselves spoke Ciceronian Latin'. He particularly relished the challenge of locating Shelta, the obscure uncorrupted jargon in which the tinkers communicated their secret messages, tracking it down 'from one squalid lodging house and thieves' kitchen to another'.[19] His search had led him to a great Celtic scholar from Leipzig, Kuno Meyer, then teaching German at University College, Liverpool. It was through Meyer's influence that Sampson was appointed the first Librarian at the university.

There was much in the huge and gentle figure of Sampson for Augustus to admire: the sardonic humour, the irresistible lure of the fields and hills, the vast accumulation of odd knowledge. 'You are a learned man,' Walter Raleigh wrote to Sampson (16 July 1908), 'and a rogue, one of the sort of fellows who think they can conduct the business of life on inspirationist principles, and who run an office pretty well much the same way as they make love to a woman.'[20] He was said to write seventy-seven love letters a year, and looked a commanding figure as he strode through the streets of Liverpool in his old velvet jacket, disgracefully baggy trousers, with his muff and gin bottle and a battered slouch hat set at an angle, his chest thrust out, legs moving powerfully. He knew how to drink, was a great smoker, liked reading Romany poems amid clouds of strong tobacco smoke. 'A heavy figure with a florid countenance', Geoffrey Keynes remembered him, 'hunched in an armchair at a great desk covered with papers, a gold-rimmed pince-nez dripping off his nose over a wide waistcoat scattered with portions of food . . .'[21] Despite his intimidating scholarship, a rather overbearing manner and fierce temper, there was something lovable about him: a gentleness in his voice and much boyish ardour. He was followed everywhere by devoted women with exotic names – Damaris, Doonie, Kish – who dedicated themselves to him and his work.

'The majestic Sampson' reminded Augustus of 'a magnificent ship on a swelling sea'. His chief influence in the first year or two of their friendship lay in the refreshing new model of married life he presented. Augustus was fearful of domesticity; the long dark imprisonment of wedlock filled him with unease. Sampson, though never indiscreet, showed him a freer, more open-air version of marriage. Seven years ago he had married a pretty Scottish girl, Meg Sprunt, much younger than himself and famed for her flying hair. Now they had two sons and a daughter. 'I really must abandon these casual wandering ways now that I am a husband and parent,' Sampson admitted. But he could not help slipping off for a day or a week to the favoured camping places of the travellers, gazing at their long black hair glittering with gold coins, their fields ablaze with quilts and tents. He would sit eating the delicious *otchi-witches* (hedgehogs) and listen in ecstasy to their riddles, folk-tales and songs played on harps and on fiddles improvised from an ashplant and a few hairs from the tail of a horse. To hear the lovely words, the marvellous rising sounds of their language, became a linguistic passion for Sampson, guiding him to happiness or to madness – perhaps both. His face lit up, he was overcome by an immense emotion. 'Did you hear him use the ablative – how perfectly beautiful!' He was a very perfect *Rai* (gentleman scholar): 'the large and rolling Rai', Augustus called him, or 'Rai of Rai's' as he was known in wild places beyond the university.

Augustus had a quick ear for languages and under Sampson's tutelage he soon picked up the English dialect of Romany and later something of the deep inflected Welsh dialect. When he arrived in Liverpool he had been reading the novels of Turgenev in the recent translations by Constance Garnett, and Kropotkin's *Memoirs of a Revolutionist*. Now he turned to *Kriegspiel*, the unique gypsy novel by Francis Hindes Groome, and to the picaresque romances of George Borrow, 'the prince among vagabonds', who could make his readers hear 'the music of the wind on the heath'. Like Augustus, Borrow had suffered from 'the Horrors'; and like Sampson he found relief in 'a dream partly of study, partly of adventure'. For both Augustus and Sampson, united by a longing for poetic escapades, Borrow became an inspiration, replacing bourgeois with bohemian life, promising nothing, beckoning his followers away from the ethics of nineteenth-century empire-building and the commercial practices of twentieth-century industrialism.

As a learned guide to the ways of the road, 'Beloved Sampson' became a new kind of hero for Augustus. Their friendship was to be interrupted by glaring quarrels and rivalries, but it lasted a lifetime. They exchanged passwords and countersigns and indelicate verses in Romany. 'You must hate my jargon compounded of all the dialects in Europe,'[22] Augustus acknowledged. It was not really a letter-writing relationship. 'Many a time have I started writing to you and in many places,' Augustus assured him the following year, ' – but my pockets are always full of unfinished letters.'[23] Sampson seldom got so far as beginning letters. 'You will never write to me I suppose,' Augustus lamented; 'all I can do is to write to *you* and assure you of the sweet pleasure it would always be for me to hear from you, a pleasure which might well come at a time when blank glooms shut out the beauty of the world – one cannot *always* keep the horizon clear. It is as well to have a pal a long way off when those at hand and in sight are . . . rather spectral and unconvincing shapes!'[24]

And yet, because there would be long wandering intervals between their meetings, and distance was always precious to them and separation a necessity, the letters they did eventually send each other over thirty years possessed a special value. 'What's the point of seeing Gypsies if I can't talk to you about them?'[25] Augustus demanded. So, with long meditative silences, they did talk a little, partly in Romany, partly in English, through their correspondence. Sampson's letters, with their reminiscences of sunlight and tobacco smoke, green leaves and wayside pubs, were a magical pick-me-up for Augustus, like an old perfume invading his mind. 'I shall count the hours till I hear from you,' he implored, '. . . don't keep me in suspense.' It was important to him that Sampson 'remember your brother of the Predilection' and send him news of 'little Egypt'. From time to time he would fire back 'a pack of Romani stuff' from his travels through Europe, and Sampson would examine it through his pince-nez and surround it all with his illuminating annotations.

Augustus venerated Sampson's eclectic scholarship, ranging from the *Lyrical Poems of William Blake* which he was preparing when they met, to his subversive *Poachers' Calendar* and collection of 'songs for singing at encampments'. Augustus put him on to W. H. Hudson's *The Purple*

Land ('a beautiful book') and Sampson introduced him to Hardy's poems ('wonderful things', Augustus discovered). On good days they felt each was the other's kindred spirit in art and letters, two names that should be coupled down the long ages. 'Now partner, you must play straight, no publishing songs without my collaboration – that is the bond,'[26] Augustus exhorted Sampson. He provided lyrical or bawdy frontispieces for several of Sampson's books: his Romany version of *Omar Khayyám*, his volume of poems *Romane Gilia*, and gypsy anthology *The Wind on the Heath* which, Sampson assured Augustus, was a 'strictly amoral' book, and therefore 'an excellent one to give to chyes [children]'.[27]

But what Augustus chiefly prized was Sampson's massive masterpiece-to-be, *The Dialect of the Gypsies of Wales*, tracing the connections between Romany, Sanskrit, Persian and the languages of Europe. 'It will be a masterpiece old pal,' Augustus confidently assured his friend, 'and will probably make Romani in future an indispensable adjunct of a gentleman's education – like Greek used to be.'[28] Augustus was all impatience to see the book – 'how is the great book going on? Surely you are near Z by now' – but impatience was inappropriate. In Sampson's opinion 'no time or trouble should be grudged to make the book a perfect specimen of its kind.'[29] It was a good corrective to Augustus's hasty spirit. Early in 1924 Sampson wrote: 'My vocab. has now reached p. 368, beginning of letter T. I send you a proof of an earlier sheet – R being rather an interesting letter – to show you what it's like. References to "o Janos" [John] wind through the pages "like a golden thread".'[30]

'How delighted I was to receive the specimen sheets!' Augustus replied. '. . . It's always a joy to me to read a word of the old tongue and now soon we shall have the big book at last . . . It's a fine thing to have accomplished so complete a thing in one's life.' The implication was that Augustus's life had become scattered with too many unaccomplished, or at least unfinished, things.

Augustus was Sampson's most eclectic disciple. When, falling one day in later life into despair after a gypsy informed him that he was getting bald at the top of his head, Sampson turned and asked Augustus: 'What should I do?' he was sternly instructed, 'Return to your innocence' – by which Augustus meant 'sin openly and scandalize the world.'[31] But Sampson could not do this: his flirtations were furtive and he led a secret life. Augustus seemed to him exorbitantly favoured by the gods. It was almost impossible not to sentimentalize over him. Sampson described him as 'strong, handsome, a genius, beloved by many men and women with a calling which is also his chief pleasure and allows him the most entire freedom, successful beyond his dreams or needs and assured of immortality as long as art lasts'. This was the legendary being Sampson was to celebrate in his poem 'The Apotheosis of Augustus John'. 'It is almost more than one mortal deserves,' Sampson wrote to his son Michael, 'but somehow it seems all right in his case.'[32]

Augustus needed to put himself in the service of some master. And if the service was intermittent and Sampson a master in the wrong artistic medium, nevertheless the older man's influence was strong in those early Liverpool days. By the gypsies themselves, Sampson was already admitted as one of their own. Augustus had been attracted to gypsies since childhood, but always from a distance. Now, as the Rai's friend, he was welcomed by these 'outlandish and despised people' as a fellow vagrant. He could not keep away. Sampson would take him to Cabbage Hall, a strip of wasteland beyond Liverpool where there was no hall and no cabbages, only the tents and caravans of the gypsy tribes which congregated there throughout the winter; and their visits were rich in speculation and adventure.

There was something strangely satisfying in this life of singing and dancing and odd journeys. The tents, the wagons, the gaily painted carts and great shining flanks of the horses, the sight of the women with their children, stirred Augustus in a way he could not explain. They were so fine-looking, these weathered people, as they crowded round, their language flying everywhere, their beauty intensified by a proud and enigmatic bearing. 'From fairest creatures we desire increase' – the possibilities seemed endless. Noah, Kenza, Eros and Bohemia; Sinfai, Athaliah, Counseletta and Tihanna – their extraordinary names, and the mystery and antiquity of their origins conjured up a world, remote yet sympathetic, to which he should have belonged.

When he left them to return to the university and to Ida, he would try to reason out why he felt these tremors of fascination and what the true significance of it might be. They seemed to have much in common with him; they were natural exhibitionists, yet deeply secretive; they were quick-witted, courteous, yet temperamental and with a dark suspicion of strangers; they were essentially honest, almost naïve, yet prevaricating; they loved children, yet without sentimentality. All this he knew, and yet it still left unexplained that painful hammering of his heart whenever he approached their camps. His excitement came from desires damped down in childhood now magically rekindled. In the sun and wind, like the trees and fields around them, these travellers seemed truly alive. There was nothing confined, nothing claustrophobic here: they did what they wanted, went where they wished – over the next hill, far away – and they were answerable to nobody.

He was exhilarated.

*

At 4 St James's Road life had begun to follow a steady pattern. 'We have callers pretty often,' Ida informed Alice Rothenstein, 'University men and their wives. Our room is always in disorder when they come as Gus is generally painting – but they survive it.' Generally he was painting Ida, but she also found time to continue with her painting and 'have an old man model, who goes to lectures on Dante, and takes part in play-readings. He sits like a rock, occasionally wiping his old eyes when they get moist.'

Augustus's father came to see them, and so did Ida's mother. The Nettleships had not come round to Ida's marriage. Very little was said, but Mrs Nettleship's work-girls felt her disapproval and whispered among themselves that it was 'a shame', that Augustus was 'not half good enough' for Ida and had taken her to live in a slum. Ida's sister Ursula was still disappointed that there had been no smart wedding; but her other sister Ethel[33] bravely came to stay for a week and observed Augustus working hard. It was an uneventful time, but not unhappy. 'I am afraid I haven't started a baby yet,' Ida apologized to Alice. 'I want one.'

The first variations in this routine came that summer. Ida 'looks suspiciously pregnant', Augustus suddenly remarked to Will Rothenstein. The doctor soon confirmed her pregnancy, but in these early months there was a rumour of complications and, so this doctor warned her, the risk of a miscarriage. For this reason she passed the summer months quietly, first at Wigmore Street, then with Edwin and Winifred John in Tenby.

Liberated from domesticity on doctor's orders, Augustus felt he had been let out from a narrow place. He could go where he wanted, be what he liked. One morning he set out intending to go for a short walk 'but instead went to Bruges and stood amazed before the works of Van Eyck and Memling', he explained to Will Rothenstein. 'The Belgians are as shoddy as they were formerly magnificent. Maeterlinck needs all his second sight.'

His truancy over, he joined Ida in Tenby 'feeling rather metagrabolized', and carried her off for a month's rest-and-painting to New Quay. 'Now the child has quickened, I suppose there is very small fear of a miscarriage,' Ida reassured her mother that September. '. . . I have been very well here – no indigestion and very regular bowels. The baby moves from time to time – and I am growing very big and hard.' Every morning Augustus would go bathing and, during the afternoons 'have models in a disused school room'. Ida sat at home, letting out her skirts and creating new clothes for the baby, and these she would take up to the schoolroom at tea time, when the painting had to stop.

In the last week of September they returned to Liverpool – but not to St James's Road, since Ida could no longer manage the stairs there. For two weeks they put up with John and Margaret Sampson – 'delightful people', Ida promised her mother – at 146 Chatham Street, a semi-slum. Then they moved off to rather grander accommodation, 66 Canning Street, a three-storeyed, red-brick house, complete with art nouveau metalwork on the doors and railings, and a black projecting portico with Doric cornices.

So much, this autumn, augured well for Augustus. Ida's pregnancy inflamed him with excitement – a sense of power, tenderness, and some curious feeling of fulfilment, almost as if it were he who was being born again. They had been fortunate in finding Canning Street, and Augustus himself had at last discovered a good studio[34] and was making it habitable.

The university, too, had 'raised my dole by a smug £200 and a day less in the week than last term'.[35] This increase reflected the excellent work he was doing at the Art Sheds. His predecessor, Herbert Jackson, had been an uninspiring teacher. He would slump down by a student's drawing board, sketch an ear or a foot, examine it, then remark: 'It's not much good, I suppose, but it'll do.' Augustus's methods marked a great improvement. 'Alas, how many brilliant drawings have I done on the boards of my pupils!' he commented. It was as though he was learning from his own instruction. Above all he stressed the importance of observation. 'When you draw,' he told his class, 'don't look at the model for one second and five minutes at your drawing, but five minutes at the model and one second at your drawing.' He was immensely pleased when his pupils did well, and he was responsible for several gifted young artists later leaving the School of Art and throwing in their lot with the Sandon Studios Society.[36]

Despite the incursion which teaching made into his time, his own work was also going well. Liverpool stimulated him, made him more keenly responsive to the visible world. 'For my part a fine morning fills me with unspeakable joy,' he wrote to Will Rothenstein, ' – a tender sky tethers me to childhood, a joyous countenance is an obstacle on the road to old age.'

His letters during this first year at Liverpool are congested with happiness. 'It has seemed to me of late I've been passing through a transition stage,' he confided to Rothenstein (4 May 1901),

'taking my leave lingeringly and spasmodically, and with many runs backward, of old traditions . . . Something stirs within me which makes me think so long and passionate company with so many loves as I have kept has not left me barren. Hitherto I have been Art's most devoted concubine, but now at length the seed takes root. I *am*, O Will, about to become a *mother* – the question of paternity must be left to the future. I suspect at least 4 old masters.'

Between the winter exhibitions of 1900 and 1902, greatly to Brown's disappointment, Augustus sent in nothing to the New English. Instead he relied on the Carfax Gallery and in particular on Rothenstein. To him Augustus would dispatch what he called his 'parcels of fancies' and 'pastels of sluts' – beggar girls, ballet girls and all manner of remarkable-looking models he had collided with in the streets of Liverpool. His purpose was to record as directly as possible the natural beauty he saw around him, without any message or moral, any attitude or intervening glaze of intellectuality. Yet it is 'a strange, troubled feeling for beauty' these pictures reveal, with 'undefined hungers and raptures hinted at', Laurence Binyon was to write.[37]

With these pastels Rothenstein was most successful, especially in selling them to other artists – Charles Ricketts and Charles Shannon, Brown and Tonks. 'Such power, combined with a marvellous subtlety, such drawing, astonished me more than ever,' Rothenstein recorded; 'no one living had his range of sensuous, lofty and grotesque imagination.' But the contrast he regularly showed between crabbed age and youth struck the Royal Academician landscape artist Sir George Clausen as 'deplorable'. His pastels were not pornographic – they were not even pretty (in the manner of Russell Flint's watercolours). 'His work antagonised people; it was deemed *deliberately* ugly,' Rothenstein recorded. 'Were people altogether blind to beauty?'[38] he wondered, looking at these lyrical nudes. Augustus's gratitude, both to Rothenstein and to his models, swelled to its most rhapsodic vein:

'Beloved Will,
    You know nothing delights my soul more than your laudation! you have made me tickle and thrill, and gulp tears to eye and water to lip. And have my poor girls served me so well! Blessing on you Maggie and Ellen Jones![39] Daughters of Cardigan I thank ye! And you Queen of the Brook whose lewd leer captured me in my dreams, may your lusty honest blood be never denied the embrace it tingles for!
    . . . I pant to do a superb decoration.'

The most important development in Augustus's art during this Liverpool period was his work as an etcher. He had taken up etching at the suggestion of his friend Benjamin Evans, one of his first plates being a portrait of Evans.[40] He grew immensely enthusiastic over this new medium. 'I have been etching a good deal,' he told Will Rothenstein. It was Rembrandt's example[41] that Evans had extolled and that now fired off this activity. Like Rembrandt, Augustus's first experiments included a number of portrait studies of himself in various poses and costumes – fur caps and wide-brimmed hats, bare-headed and in a black gown. But there were also several portraits of Ida, very plump and maternal, in a fur-tipped cape or with a special necklace, or simply as 'a brown study': and the macabre or eccentric figures of drapers, chandlers, old haberdashers, young serving-maids, ragamuffin children and all the cosmopolitan population of Liverpool whom he saw on the wasteground of Cabbage Hall, or wandering through the university, or at the working-men's dining-rooms and doss houses along Scotland Road – gypsies and mulattos, the frock-coated bourgeois, the black women, muffin men, charwomen and old people with fierce hopeless expressions.

Augustus had made so close a study of Rembrandt's method, and assimilated it to such an extent, that many of his etchings look like imitations. Yet however derivative his technique, these etchings do reveal a great deal about his work. In a perceptive introduction to the Catalogue of Augustus's etchings, Campbell Dodgson wrote:

'There are certain features in his work which make it unlike that of his contemporaries. His choice of figure subjects in preference to the land-scape or architectural motives which are so much in vogue to-day is one of them. His consistency in restricting the size of his plates to small, or even tiny, dimensions is another. Both are significant traits which link his work to the great tradition of the painter-etchers of four centuries . . . But a fault common to many of them is a fault that runs through Mr John's paintings and drawings as well, lack of concentration and acquiescence in an apparent finish, a facile substitute for true perfection. Or if we consider the subjects themselves, rather than the manner in which he treats them, is there not something unsatisfying, superficial, betraying lack of "funda-mental brainwork" in most of the compositions containing two or more figures? There is no apparent motive for bringing them together, and Mr John, with all his intense interest in single types, and his power, unequalled among etchers of to-day, of expressing individual character, lacks the imaginative, constructive, or dramatic gift of showing several characters in action.'

The fruit-sellers, street-philosophers, tramps and coster-girls who figure in so many of Augustus's visual lyrics were in fact poor subjects – elusive, self-conscious, shy of being stared at. He had taught his students the value of observation but this lesson was difficult to put into practice.

He could catch them all right, these reluctant sitters, but well before the five minutes were up they were off. He was therefore thrown back on memory and imagination, and to some extent these failed him. Everything made its impact at once, and seemed to last only so long as it remained in front of him. Some of these studies of gypsies or fisher folk lack atmosphere. The oxygen has gone out of their world, and they wilt. This seepage of vitality is particularly noticeable in his etchings because the medium was so slow. To fill the emptiness, he overworked them with a turmoil of feathery cross-hatching.[42] He could not decide on the right moment to stop. 'It is only that I feel ever inclined to add a few scratches on the plate that I husband them in this way,' he told Will Rothenstein.

Campbell Dodgson's other criticism Augustus would have refuted. It was not his desire artifically to inject action or drama into these studies; it was not his wish to apply sophisticated 'brainwork' to simple people. What action or drama or brainwork is there in a tree, the corner of a field, a standing woman? What intellectual 'purpose' may be divined in such everyday shapes and ordinary sights? Augustus did not plot his pictures. His groups are deliberately motiveless. He etches them because they're there – and because he loves them being there. In a sense, the superficiality of which Campbell Dodgson accuses him is exactly what he sets out to achieve. His theme is the profundity of the superficial. He makes the aesthetic statement that passing sights of no special significance have the power to move us beyond explanation or understanding. So far as the artist is concerned, Augustus believed, the 'meaning' of his studies should be left to the unconscious. His intention was to fix the passing moment and make it timeless, and in that timeless moment discover 'a romantic world composed in the image of his desire'.[43] But when the magic of timelessness fails and the passing moment will not pose for him, time hangs heavy, and we feel betrayed by the pointlessness of this empty life.

*

So much this autumn promised well; so much seemed to trail its shadow of disappointment: and as the autumn changed to winter, these shadows began to stretch out.

The turning point came in October. It was in the second week of this month that Augustus sustained a bang on the head, reminiscent of his bathing accident at Tenby. Ida, in a letter to her mother (16 October 1901), explained what happened:

'Gus has broken his nose and put his finger out of joint by falling from a ladder in the studio. The doctor came – a splendid big red-brown man

– and sewed up the cut on his nose in two exquisite stitches. Poor Gus was very white, and bloody in parts. He is now a lovely sight, very much swollen and one red eye. His profile is like a lion. They say the scar will not show, and he will be well in a fortnight. The bone was a little damaged but it won't make any difference – we think his nose may be straighter after!'

After the first shock had passed, Augustus resolved not to be pinned down by his injury. 'My dear!' he wrote to Will Rothenstein, 'a bang on the head has never and will never down me. Au contraire I feel double the *übermensch* with a great patch on my nose! I have paraded it before my students with great effect. At the Sketch Club the other night it must have been grand to see me point a dislocated finger of scorn and turn up a broken nose at these purblind gropings in pictorial darkness.'

Such was the devastating effect of this patch and bandage, he claimed, that students hurried over to see it from other art schools, and his class overflowed. But what is evident from his letters is that this fall had brought back memories of his accident at Tenby, and that he was theatrically over-reacting to it. He wore his misfortune, humorously enough, like some sartorial accomplishment. But an extra wildness entered into his behaviour, as if he were pushing frantically against a door he feared might close on him.

Up till now he had seemed to share the biological adventure of Ida's pregnancy, but suddenly it threatened him with confinement. The whole process was too long – a nine-*days*' wonder was what he would have liked. He felt hemmed in. 'I really must come to town and see what my contemporaries are about,' he wrote that October to Will Rothenstein. But the following month he was writing: 'I fear I cannot come to London before our baby has squeezed its way through the narrow portals of life.'

London, now that he could not reach it, was marvellously desirable to him; while over Liverpool, so fresh and enthralling only that spring, a cloud had begun to settle. London bought his pictures – sometimes the very pictures which Liverpool rejected. The Liverpool Academy refused him membership. He felt himself among Philistines. 'I come now shattered from a visit to the Walker Art Gallery,' he wrote to Will Rothenstein. 'It contains the Ox Bovril of the R.A. shambles.'[44]

Because of Liverpool's hostility to his work and because of his own spendthrift ways, he was often pressed for money and, on one occasion, obliged to settle a huge milk bill by handing over to the disgruntled milkman a number of masterpieces. 'I would paint any man a nice big picture for £50, if he paid down 25 first,' he complained to Rothenstein this winter. 'That's to say a good big nude.' But no one wanted his nudes. They were big, certainly; but they were not good, Liverpool decided.

He began to feel that his teaching was holding up the work he really wanted to do. 'What output can be expected of one who works at a school for 3 days!' he expostulated.[45] Mackay's lofty ideas now seemed peculiarly misleading. 'Mackay talks grandiosely of a great art school with 300 a year for me and studio and my own to follow – But I trust him not,' he confided to Will Rothenstein (16 April 1902). Against Mackay's vision of a university palace with towers raised above the clouds and a studio at the top of them for every face of the day stood Augustus's actual curriculum – a treadmill that grew more irksome to him each week. 'The three days I prostitute to foul faced commodity weigh on my soul terribly,' he confessed. 'My conscience is awakening and I see the evil of my ways.'[46] By the early spring of 1902 his university career had reached a point of crisis. 'I am now expected to examine *all* the work done by every student (50–60) during the past Session and choose an example of *each* to send to the National Competition S. Kensington,' he complained to Rothenstein (9 March 1902). 'You can imagine the brilliant result of such a rummage. I draw the line at that.' But if he drew the line too firmly he would be out of a job. He was trapped.

The most respectable, and therefore most despicable, elements of university life had begun to infiltrate their home. The wives of professors made it their duty to call regularly on Ida carrying with them useful pieces of black net, warm flannel nightgowns and wool socks; also disused blankets, nondescript fragments of lace, second-hand pin-cushions, half the veil of a deceased nun (rumoured to have special properties), and a miniature stove for preparing baby's food. Whenever Augustus returned from his studio, there they were, these clusters of affable vague women, tousled, dusty and bespectacled, parading their offerings and chattering about Ida's baby – when would it arrive? Would it be a boy? Would it be born before, after, or at the same time as the other University College baby that winter, Mrs Boyce's? Under this pressure Ida began to have fantastic nightmares about her baby. 'I dreamt last night that the baby came – an immense girl, the size of a 1 year old child – with thick lips, the under one hanging – little black eyes near together and a big fine nose,' she wrote to her mother. 'Altogether very like a savage – and most astonishing to us.'[47]

Avoiding these Liverpool ladies, Augustus spent more time with his gypsies. That autumn there was a fair on Cabbage Hall. The place was filled up with carts and wagons, booths and cheap-jacks; and everywhere the animal – both horse and human – was magnificently exhibited. How tawdry the tea-party wives who filled his home seemed when contrasted with those pictures of sin and supernatural knowledge, the gypsy fortune-tellers, with their stately bearing and unreadable eyes like black coals burning with concentrated hate – terrible to behold! Augustus would linger there till the fields and hills grew dark, a heavy mist enshrouded the tents, and the fiddlers one by one stopped their playing.

Like a gypsy himself, Augustus was growing ever more elusive. Ida seldom knew where he was. It was not only Cabbage Hall that he preferred to his own home, but other people's homes – the Rani's at 28 Alexandra Drive which, according to Albert Rutherston, 'is good for the moral tone of us all'; and the defunct Gothic school near Rodney Street where lived the 'Doonie', the artist Albert Lipczinski's generous blue-eyed wife to whom, in order to avoid trouble, Augustus wrote his letters in Romany. 'The hospitality of Liverpool is truly wonderful,' Albert Rutherston told Max Beerbohm, 'the women more so.'

Ida took it all calmly, though her dreams grew still more fantastic. She dreamt of a tiny man, 'the size of the 1st joint of a finger', immensely charming, who drank milk out of a miniature saucer, like a cat, and who had a little boat in which he sailed off alone. He was very plucky, but eventually got lost and exhausted, frightened by the prickly larch trees, until he came across a tent in which lived Jack Nettleship, who took him up and carried him home, quite naked. 'Do you think the baby will be a lunatic, having such a mother?' she asked her father.[48] The baby was born, weighing 6 pounds exactly, on 6 January 1902. 'My wife gave birth to a little boy yesterday,' Augustus wrote to Albert Rutherston (7 January 1902), 'and seems none the worse.' But his casual tone concealed real excitement.

The birth of Ida's son affected the Nettleships' attitude to Ida's marriage. Even Mrs Nettleship was prepared to bury her doubts and put the best face on it as she arrived in Liverpool with a special nurse. While Ida rested in bed, Augustus sat downstairs listening to his mother-in-law strumming cheerful tunes on the piano. They reminded him of his father. After a fortnight Ida was allowed up. 'It was lovely,' she wrote to her sister Ursula. 'But I felt as if I were too light to keep down on the floor.' Her letters over the next few weeks were full of baby-news in which Augustus took as keen an interest as she did, approving each grunt, each ounce. 'I cannot realise I have a little boy yet,' she told Ursula (21 January 1902). 'I *cannot* believe I am his mother. I love him very much. He has an intelligent little face – but looks, nearly always, perplexed, or contemplative. I do not think he has smiled yet. He is a wonderful mixture of Nettleship-John.'

What exercised Augustus's mind more than anything else was the choice of a name. It was another sign of his own lack of identity that, with all his children, this choice should be such a perplexing matter. By the time the child's birth came to be registered, one name alone had been settled upon – and that was compulsory: Nettleship. As a preliminary name, Augustus had given a good deal of consideration to Lewis. But no sooner had he decided upon this than the baby would physiognomically alter so as to resemble an Anthony or a Peter. Then a new conviction would seize him; he would fix upon his son a good Welsh name – Llewelyn or maybe Owen or even Evan . . . But which? Perhaps, since the child would after all be only one-quarter Welsh, this too was wrong. Whichever way he looked at it, the problem appeared insoluble – yet it had to be solved. He read books, he strode off for long contemplative walks and on his return he tried out names in the proximity of the baby as it slept. By March, Honoré was in the lead and seemed almost certain to win. But by May, Ida was writing to Alice Rothenstein: 'Really I cannot tell you the baby's name, as we can't decide. Gus has said Pharaoh for the last few days. But it changes every week. I don't mind what it is.' To meet the pressure of such inquiries, Augustus was eventually hurried into accepting David by the end of the year. But for much of his childhood David was called Tony, then reverted to David – with the occasional variant of Dafydd, being one-quarter Welsh.

At the beginning of March 1902, Augustus, Ida and 'Llewelyn de Wet Ravachol John' (temporarily named after an uncaptured Boer leader and an anarchist bomber) left Canning Street and moved to 138 Chatham Street very near the Sampsons. Here, for five months, they went through the rigours of family life. 'I wish you would tell me something about your baby,' Ida asked Alice Rothenstein. 'Does he often cry? Ours *howls*. He is howling now. I have done all I can for him, and I know he is not hungry. I suppose the poor soul is simply unhappy.' Augustus too was not happy. The birth of his son, with all its novelty and curiosity, had turned his attention back into their home, but now the noise began to drive him out again. Ida sometimes felt that she had more to do than she could manage. There was no opportunity for painting. 'Baby takes so much time – and the rooms we are in are not kept very clean, so I am always dusting and brushing. Also we have a puppy, who adds to the difficulties,' she told Alice. But, she went on: 'I think I enjoy working hard really.'

Augustus's pictures of Ida often show her with children. But she was far from being a conventional mother-figure. In a sense she was more of a mother to Augustus than to his sons. She did not feel about her first-born, she told the Rothensteins, as they did about theirs. 'I have not had any ecstasies over him,' she confessed. 'He is a comic little fellow, but he grumbles such a fearful lot. I think he would very much rather not have been created.' She never experienced the physical, possessive love of her children that the Rothensteins appeared to enjoy. 'How wonderful it seems to me how you and others love their children,' she wrote again to Alice about three years later. 'Somehow I don't, like you do. I love only my husband and the children as being a curious – most curious – result of part of that love.'

Augustus was one of those fathers who, while his children were very small with little developed character of their own, felt towards them a primitive and protective love. Whereas Ida could not believe she was their mother, Augustus in certain moods almost seemed to believe it was he who had given birth to them and at the start he was more physically close than she was. 'Honoré is becoming a surprising bantling with muscles like an amorillo,' he wrote proudly to Will Rothenstein that spring. His new role as parent fortified his self-confidence. 'The arrival of Honoré gives me to see I cannot dally and temporize with Fate.'

One consideration prevented him from severing his connection with the University Art School. 'I am wondering,' he confided to Rothenstein, 'which is the best way to get out of this school, whether to be chucked out or resign . . . the former I think would look best in the end.' He had made a number of friends in Liverpool, but they were all rebels in the university or individualists outside it. The very qualities that provoked hero-worship also created aversion in people such as Charles Allen, who taught sculpture at the university, and F. M. Simpson who held the Chair of Architecture. 'I become more rebellious in Liverpool,' he was to tell Alice Rothenstein – and it was true. He did dreadful things there, such as failing to rise to his feet when the King's health was drunk – 'it took some doing'. His name was a trigger for all sorts of scandalous gossip. 'Mr [Wyndham] Lewis has been spreading very bad reports about everybody in London,' Orpen wrote a little later this year to Albert Rutherston, '. . . his last was that John had been kicked out of Liverpool and that he was going to leave his wife.'

But Augustus was unrepentant. 'The school may go to hell,' he announced – and suddenly he felt much better. Even his work improved. 'I have started some startling pictures,' he claimed. 'Ah! if they would emerge triumphantly from the ordeal of completion.'

To make up for the loss of his salary, he was arranging to paint a series of portraits. 'I have some jobs on hand now, enfin, mon cher!' he told Rothenstein in May, 'les pommes de terre enterrées si longtemps commencent à pousser.' He had also made some rapid decisions on the art of portrait painting to fit in with these new commissions. 'Nowadays, I fancy, portraits should be painted in an hour or two,' he decided (16 April 1902). 'The brush cannot linger over shabby and ephemeral garments.' Of the intermittent series of Liverpool portraits he now began, three were to be outstanding – those of Mackay, completed in June this year, and of Kuno Meyer and Chaloner Dowdall done several years later. Some of the other portraits[49] give a feeling that he had made a brief effort to become interested in his subject, and failed. Soon, however, they were 'bubbling with sovereigns and cheques', Ida wrote to Michel Salaman, 'caused by the disturbance Gus's work has created in the rich Liverpool waters'.[50]

But he was no longer painting Ida. 'I have not sat to Gus for ages,' she wrote to Alice. Although matters were far from being so bad as Wyndham Lewis reported, Ida felt acutely the need of sympathetic companionship. 'I long for Gwen [John],' she had written the previous summer. Winifred had stayed that autumn, making two flannel nightgowns and some woollen socks for the baby; and 'Gwen will be up here soon,' Gus assured Michel Salaman. Now, at long last she arrived by steamer from New Quay. Her life, too, had not been easy. During the summer of 1901 she had still shared an address – 39 Southampton Street – with Ambrose McEvoy; but two months after their tearful holiday at Le Puy, at the end of 1900, McEvoy became engaged to Mary Edwards, a damp-looking woman, nine years older than himself, who lived near the Thames. 'We were quite surprised,' Everett noted with relish in his journal, 'as he'd been running round before with Gwen John.' It had been Augustus who introduced them to each other. Mary Edwards had declared her love for McEvoy at 21 Fitzroy Street, where Gus and Gwen were sharing rooms. But they did not marry immediately, and an awkward period ensued with Gwen living at 41 Colville Terrace, the McEvoy family home in Bayswater, where, as if in mourning, the shutters were always closed to avoid paying the rates. It was from here that she had come to Chatham Street; and it was from Chatham Street that she wrote to Michel Salaman a letter that indicates the direction in which her life was to move.

'As to being happy, you know, don't you, that when a picture is done – whatever it is, it might as well not be as far as the artist is concerned – and in all the time he has taken to do it, it has only given him a few seconds' pleasure. To me the writing of a letter is a very important event! I try to say what I mean exactly, it is the only chance I have – for in talking, shyness and timidity distort the very meaning of my words in people's ears – that I think is one reason I am such a waif ... I don't pretend to know anybody well. People are like shadows to me and I am like a shadow.'

But with a few people, mostly women, Gwen was at ease – and one of them was Ida. She could trust Ida, she told Salaman, 'with all my thoughts and feelings and secrets'; and Ida felt she could trust Gwen. Gwen had been hurt by McEvoy – 'sister Gwen upset', Augustus noted.[51] An etching he did of her probably during this visit[52] shows her as a contained and upright figure, on her guard, the daughter of Edwin John. Her expression is impassive, giving nothing away. On her head sits a pancake hat; her hair is pinned into a tight bun; her dress firmly tied at the neck; her lips buttoned. There is an impression of solitude. No gentleness.

'I have been very busy with the baby,' Gwen wrote to Salaman. She would take him out for 'air', and scandalize the neighbourhood by sitting unconcernedly on a doorstep whenever she felt like a rest. But for the sake of their families there was also a formal occasion when they stood shoulder to shoulder, Gus, Gwen and Ida (holding the baby), all looking to their front, present and correct, in the photographer's studio.

After Gwen left, Ida felt her own isolation with fresh sharpness. In the middle of April she went with 'her dearest and wickedest' baby for a few days to London to see her father, who had not been well. 'I am left deserted,' Augustus exclaimed to Will Rothenstein (16 April 1902). 'As a consequence I lay abed last night with a moonlit sky in front of me and chased infinite thoughts. Decidedly it is inspiring to lie alone at times. I fear continued cosiness is risky . . . I wish I had somebody to think with.'

He had never pretended to be an 'exponent of the faithful dog business'. Ida knew this when she married him. He trusted her to recognize that the overpowering attraction of other women did not diminish his loyalty to her. He loved Ida and would always love her – it was important she understood this. But he needed to play truant. Then he would return to her, choosing the moment that best suited him. But if his freedom were curtailed, if he were prevented from acting as his nature demanded, then a hot-and-cold madness would break out in him and instinctively he would say and do things for which he felt hardly responsible. It was as if another being had taken control and he was no longer 'himself'. The last thing he wanted to do was to hurt Ida, but too much 'moral living' might imperil them both.

At the end of July they left Liverpool[53] and returned to live in Fitzroy Street. 'We are in a great turmoil packing,' Augustus wrote to Michel Salaman. Liverpool was 'fresh and airy with a clean blue and white sky',[54] but it was no longer the 'gorgeous place' it had been eighteen months earlier. Both of them, for rather different reasons, were happy to be back in London. The 'cosiness' of their married life was almost at an end.

3

WHAT COMES NATURALLY

'An artist is at the mercy of his temperament and his preferences
are apt to be purely personal, quite disproportionate and utterly
unhistorical.'

Augustus John (William Rothenstein Memorial
Exhibition Catalogue, Tate Gallery 1950)

In the eighteen months since her marriage Ida had changed considerably.
'Ida with her shock of black hair, as wild as a Maenad in a wood pursued
by Pan,' Arthur Symons had romantically pictured her.[55] 'Intractable, a
creature of uncertain moods and passion. One never knew what she was
going to say or do . . . She had – to me – the almost terrible fascination
of the Wild Beast. There was something almost Witch-like in her.' This
had been her fascination for Augustus. But with the metamorphosis from
Ida Nettleship to Mrs John she had developed into a more substantial
figure – both physically, following the birth of David, but also in character.
Gone was the feyness, the whimsicality of her early Mowgli letters; and
gone too was much of her moralizing. Her moods and passion had been
the longing of a vigorous nature for everything from which young Victorian ladies were hermetically protected. Now there was reality enough –
she was glutted with it. Her character gained unexpected depths in
grappling with new problems; she grew more resilient, more direct, at
times more ironical. But, in Augustus's eyes, she lost something of her
wild mystery. She was obliged to give up painting in order to become a
mother, and her letters from Liverpool had been full of baby news. 'Mr
Dafydd John is very well & fat & cheeky, & oh how he laughs,' she wrote
to Gus's sister Winifred. 'He plays bo-peep. He sits up, but does not
crawl at all yet.' By the time they returned to London, the novelty was
gone. Motherhood was a full-time job to which she did not easily resign
herself – 'I certainly was not made for a mother,' she admitted to Alice
Rothenstein (1903). She was made, she felt, for Augustus, and wanted to
be his mistress. But the roles of mistress and of mother were often in
conflict, and in the nature of things – though not in her nature – the
mother began to overshadow the mistress.

'Look what a grand life she had,' her sister Ethel later wrote, 'going full
tilt.'[56] But really it was life that had gone full tilt into her. The first blow
came shortly after her return from Liverpool when her father became ill.
Though having great difficulty in breathing, he would gasp out page after
page of Browning each day, until gradually he grew too weak. Ida and

Augustus were with him during this final illness, though for much of the time he was barely conscious and could recognize no one. Once he called out: 'Are you there, Ethel?' and, after a silence, called back: 'Yes, I thought you might come and see us through this risk.' His daughters Ethel and Ursula were abroad ('If there had been time,' their mother wrote, 'I would have sent for you'), but Ida was at Wigmore Street all week. 'Old Nettleship is at his last,' Augustus told Will Rothenstein. 'He will die before the morning it is thought. Ida and I go round at midnight to see him. He has been in a high temperature . . . and his mind has not been clear.'

He survived that night, and in a moment of consciousness assured Augustus that God was 'nearer to me than the door'. Next morning his arm went up like a semaphore and could not be kept down until suddenly he died. 'It was a very wonderful experience,' Augustus wrote to Michel Salaman. 'Mrs N. is immensely philosophical.' For Ida it was a deep loss. 'The dear old chap was quite unconscious,' she wrote afterwards to Will Rothenstein (1 September 1902), 'and did not suffer, except in the struggle for breath, and at the end he was quite peaceful. He was so grand and simple.' The day before the funeral, at her request, Gus drew the dead man's head. Then they carried him off to Kensal Green.

Besides Gus, her father had been the only man who meant anything to Ida. Now she would have to rely on Augustus alone. As if sensing this extra responsibility, he grew wilder. He was meant to be hanging his pictures in the Carfax Gallery, but this depressed him and to rid himself of this depression he was drinking more. 'I thank you sincerely for bearing me home in safety,' he afterwards wrote to Will. 'I was utterly incapable. I had been imbibing a quantity of bad rum. I knew it to be poison yet drank it with relish . . . After having slept 3 hours I awoke perfectly well again.' His powers of recovery were remarkable, and he tested them to the full. 'John had the drinks,' L. A. G. Strong wryly noted in his diary, 'and his friends had the headache.'[57]

The pattern that had established itself in Liverpool was now broadly repeated in London. By the autumn Ida was pregnant again. She was visited at Fitzroy Street by all her old jungle friends, Gwen Salmond, Edna Clarke Hall, Bessie Salaman, Ursula Tyrwhitt, and by her family, in particular her mother who brought along, brightly intact, all her old grievances. She didn't like the poor district they lived in and she didn't like Augustus. It was as if the two of them were in a tug-of-war over the possession of Ida – but however attached Ida was to her mother, she had given herself to Gus. He tried to get on with Mrs Nettleship, but she was so reproving that he would storm out of the house.

'Our life flows so evenly and regularly, I love it,' Ida wrote to the Rani, Mary Dowdall, soon after returning to London. 'But', she added, 'I'm afraid Gus finds it rather a bore.' They still lived in 'that varied harmony', as Augustus described it to Michel Salaman, 'which is the essence of great music'. But he was growing 'very staid and old fashioned in my ways', he liked to claim. 'A french maid cooks my meals. Beer, tobacco & slippers figure largely in my existence. A parrot tempers my solitude and occasionally screeches. Sometimes [Wyndham] Lewis & Albert [Rutherston] or Will or McEvoy call, and arrest my incipient vegetation.'[58]

He had begun to find something of a home from home in the Café Royal which, by the beginning of the century, had become the rendezvous of many artists and writers living in London. With its exuberant neo-classical ornament, its abundance of gilt, its ubiquitous flashing mirrors and surfaces of crimson velvet, it formed a cosily grandiose setting for their gatherings. It was unique in Britain, a café–restaurant on the French pattern where people could wander from table to table. 'If you want to see English people at their most English, go to the Café Royal,' Beerbohm Tree advised Hesketh Pearson, 'where they are trying their hardest to be French.' The atmosphere owed something to the nineties – crème de menthe frappé drunk through straws; the clatter of dominoes; and drawings on menus. Through its 'smoky acres of painted goddesses and cupids and tarnished gilding, its golden caryatids and garlands, and its filtered submarine illumination, composed of tobacco smoke, of the flames from chafing dishes and the fumes from food, of the London fog outside and the dim electric light within', Augustus appeared a monumental figure 'like some kind of Rasputin-Jehovah', Osbert Sitwell remembered.[59]

He liked the place for its casualness, for the easy coming-and-going, the undemanding companionship. He liked it because, by simple force of personality, he dominated the place. His observant eyes, his voice so confiding and laconic, ruminating, rumbling; his manners, formal yet large; the beautiful hands which threw a spell about his conversation; and that alarming residue of rage and outrage which could be so innocently stirred up: all these ingredients contributed to a physical presence that could pull you into its orbit. 'Of all the men I have met,' wrote Frank Harris, who claimed to have met everyone, 'Augustus John has the most striking personality.'

Though he tended to be silent at home, at the Café Royal he was a different person and, after a few drinks, wonderfully exuberant. Here, by popular acclaim, he was acknowledged a Bohemian king, with the waiters his courtiers, all his companions guests. In such a genial climate, his uncertainties dissolved, his morale rose and he inflated himself terrifically. He could be arrogant, sometimes childishly offensive to people, and he would grow sullen if others became too talkative. He liked to be at the centre of things, and because this suited him so well and he had charm and was such fun, people were generally happy for him to be a star. And there was another reason. Almost always he was left with the bill, and would pay it uncomplainingly with a huge fistful of notes that was sometimes all the money he possessed. In a sense he paid friends to entertain him, and he valued them as entertainers more than friends. His generosity was agreeably complicated by a vein of sardonic humour. One evening in the Domino Room, George Moore was denigrating him to Steer and Rothenstein – 'Why, the man can no more draw than I can!' – when Augustus himself walked in and sat down at their table. He took no notice of Moore, who tried to engage his attention, but in silence, Will Rothenstein recorded, 'he took out a sketch book, and made as if to draw, doing nothing, however, but scribble. Moore, flattered, imagining John to be sketching him, sat bolt upright not moving a muscle. When John, tired of scribbling, shut up his book, Moore asked to see it, and turning over the pages, said unctuously, "One can see the man can *draww*." '[60]

In the three most famous paintings of the Café Royal, those by Adrian Allinson, Charles Ginner and William Orpen, Augustus is prominently depicted. He liked best the company of other artists and of models – though he did not talk much about painting. Writers, preferably of the romantic school; decaying aristocrats, circus people, magicians and vagabonds, Celtic gentlemen with a knowledge of archaeology, some philosophical or mathematical ambitions or perhaps a smattering of Sanskrit or Hindi; Social Creditors, practical jokers, picturesque anarchists of the Kropotkin school, flamenco dancers, Buddhists: these were his crew. He welcomed anyone stranded in a tributary off the mainstream of twentieth-century commercial advancement.

With such companions he felt a natural affinity – for was he not also an exile from the modern world, however loudly, in fits and starts, it might applaud him? Was he not a revolutionary in almost everything except perhaps his painting? 'Be regular and ordinary in your life, like a bourgeois,' Flaubert had advised artists, 'so that you can be violent and original in your works.' But Augustus often squandered his vitality in acts of nonconformity. 'Perfect conformity', he remarked, 'is perhaps only possible in prison.'[61] His whole life was directed to avoiding, or escaping from, any form of imprisonment; and his revolutionary energies were to be directed as much against the bureaucratic future as the restrictive past. 'The flower of art blooms only where the soil is deep,' Henry James wrote. In England (especially after the First World War) Augustus would find little depth of soil. 'The march of progress will leave the struggling artist behind,' he warned.

'He is always an outsider, shunning the crowd, wandering off the beaten track and dodging the official guide and the policeman. Perhaps in a dream he has caught a glimpse of the Golden Age and is in search of it; everywhere he hits on mysterious clues to a lost world; sometimes he hears low music which seems to issue from the hills; the trees confabulate, the waters murmur of a secret which the sky has not forgotten.'[62]

The Rothensteins had begun the habit of entertaining a small group of artists and writers at their house in Church Row, Hampstead, and it was here that Augustus met W. B. Yeats. 'With his lank hair falling over his brow, his myopic eyes, his hieratic gestures,' Augustus later wrote, 'he looked every inch a poet of the twilight.'[63] Policemen and official guides were no obstacles to him, and his poetic vision held steady while for Augustus, looking every inch a romantic painter, it became 'a passing light . . . a dream that lingers a moment, retreating in the dawn, incomplete, aimless.'[64]

Among the other visitors to the Rothensteins' house were Max Beerbohm, with his immaculately tailored human nature, so amusing at a distance, so invisible near to; the naturalist W. H. Hudson, hopelessly and eternally in love with Alice Rothenstein; Robert Cunninghame Graham, the traveller, adventurer and friend of 'Buffalo Bill', delivering a string of improper stories clothed in impenetrable layers of Scottish dialect; Walter Sickert, decked out in a roaring check shirt and leggings, looking like some farmer from a comic opera; Jacob Epstein, as innocent and truculent as Augustus himself, smelling like a polecat; and William Nicholson and James Pryde, the dandified Castor and Pollux of poster art.

With Wyndham Lewis, to whom the Rothensteins had also introduced him, Augustus now struck up a long precarious friendship.[65] Lewis had come from Rugby to the Slade, a good-looking, gloweringly ambitious young man, who drew with thick black contours resembling the lead in a stained glass window. In Tonks's opinion, he had the finest sense of line of all his students. Rothenstein took him to Augustus's top-floor flat (which he himself would later occupy), probably in the summer of 1902. 'There was a noise of children', Lewis afterwards recalled, 'for this patriarch had already started upon his Biblical courses'.

For a time Lewis, made heady by the John atmosphere, became a formidable disciple. 'I was with John a great deal in those early days in London,' he wrote in *Rude Assignment*. '. . . Unlike most painters, John was very intelligent. He read much and was of remarkable maturity.' They stimulated and exasperated each other in equal measures. Lewis was much impressed by all that Augustus had so rapidly achieved. His success in art and with women appeared phenomenal, and by associating with him, Lewis seems to have felt, some of this success might fall his way. Augustus, on his side, was flattered by Lewis's veneration. Here was someone mysterious and remarkable, a poet hesitating between literature and painting, whose good opinion served to increase Augustus's self-esteem. He seemed a valuable ally. For whatever else he felt, Augustus was never bored by Lewis, whose dynamic progress through life was conducted as if to outwit some invisible foe. This involved a series of aggressive retreats – to neutral Scandinavia for example, where he would find a letter from Augustus demanding: 'Is Sweden safe?' Such places were not only safe, Lewis would hint in his replies, but the arenas of unimaginable conquests.

'Have patience with this literature of our misunderstanding,' Lewis appealed.[66] Aware of his friend's superior education, Augustus strove to match Lewis's 'calligraphic obscurity' by what he called 'linguistic licence' – that is, a fantastic prolixity which he considered the intellectual tenor of their relationship required. The result was an exchange of letters, part undiscoverable, part indecipherable, covering over fifty years, that is almost complete in its comic density. Both were flamboyantly secretive men with bombardier tempers, and their friendship, which somehow endured all its volcanic quarrels, kept being arrested by declarations that it was at an end – an event upon which they would with great warmth congratulate themselves. Yet such was the good feeling generated by these separations and congratulations that they quickly came together again, when all the damning-and-blasting of their complicated liaison would start up once more.[67]

Their correspondence is extremely generous with offensive advice which they attempt to make more palatable by adding the odd 'mon vieux' or 'old fellow'. Augustus frequently intends to return Lewis's letters by post in order to get him to 'admit [that] no more offensive statement could be penned'; but almost always he mislays the letter or, in his first fit of uncontrollable fury, flings it irrecoverably into some fire or sea. Besides, Lewis is always offering to provide batches of duplicates by special courier. Augustus is constantly being dumbfounded by Lewis's requests for money coupled with his forgetfulness in repaying it; and by his insistence that Augustus was influencing mutual friends to his discredit. Augustus's style grows more and more convoluted in grappling with these charges. Then, suddenly, the clouds clear and in a succinct moment of retaliation he announces that Lewis's drawings 'lack *charm*, my dear fellow'.[68]

The whole relationship is bedevilled by ingenious dissension. Each credits the other with Machiavellian cunning. Lewis is amazed that Augustus never invites him for a drink; Augustus is perplexed that Lewis is never able to visit him – when he does so, Augustus is always out; while Lewis, on principle, never answers his doorbell. They make elaborate plans to meet on neutral territory, but then something goes wrong – the wrong time, the wrong place, the wrong mood. Lewis becomes increasingly irritated that Augustus so seldom writes. Augustus becomes irritated because when he does write his letters go astray, Lewis in the meantime having moved in darkest secrecy to some unknown address such as the Pall Mall Deposit. The letters which do arrive express very adequately this irritation fanned, in Lewis's case, by eloquent invective, and in Augustus's by a circumlocution that ingeniously avoids answering any of Lewis's inquiries. It is a most stimulating exchange.

Life itself – beyond Fitzroy Street – was variously stimulating: but at home it was the old fruitful routine. On 11 March 1903 Ida's second child was born. Gus had confidently predicted a girl, but 'instead of Esther, a roaring boy has forced admittance to our household,' he told Will Rothenstein. '. . . Ida welcomes him heartily. But what will David say?' It was '*much* nicer', Ida had told the Rani, 'to have Gussie than the doctor, and a gamp twice a day than a hovering nurse in a starched cap. Lorenzo Paganini is quite lovely and so quiet.' The boy, also referred to as 'nice fat slug' or 'pig face' ('his face is like a pink pig's,' Ida boasted to Margaret Sampson), was eventually saddled with the name Caspar – nicknamed Capper (and occasionally 'Caper Sauce') – and a gate was fitted at the top of the stairs outside their flat to prevent the children from falling. Suddenly their home seemed very crowded. 'I emerged into a melodramatic scene of human frailty,' Caspar later wrote.[69]

In a highly oblique passage of *Finishing Touches*,[70] his posthumous and unfinished volume of memoirs, Augustus refers to himself under the pseudonym of 'George'. George, a new recruit of Will Rothenstein's and said to be on the threshold of a brilliant career, is 'only just recovering from the nervous breakdown following his recent marriage'. At the informal parties in Will Rothenstein's house, finding 'an atmosphere no doubt very different from the climatic conditions of the home-life to which he was as yet uninured . . . he began to expand and blossom forth himself, in a style combining scholarship with an attractive diffidence and humour. He felt perhaps that here was a means of escape from the insidious encroachments of domesticity, and accordingly attached himself to Will Rothenstein with the desperate haste of a man caught in the quicksands.'

If he expanded here and at the Café Royal, he often contracted again when he got home. This concertina motion, to which Ida responded with a mixture of excitement and dread, had by 1903 produced a strange fragmentation of himself. He became subject to sudden withdrawals from human contact. It seemed baffling that someone of such intelligence and strong physique could at times be so will-less. The only Will he had, apparently, was Rothenstein, whose remedy was to send him off on marathon walks round Hampstead Heath.

Yet Augustus was not indolent. He could work well if tactfully organized. But to organize him was an operation needing remorseless diplomacy. Will Rothenstein, for all his energy and enthusiasm, could not begin to do this, and even Ida, continually pregnant and fretted by domestic duties, was unable to manage such an extra task. It needed a team to organize Augustus, and a team was precisely what he was about to assemble round him: a team of exasperated patrons and art dealers and dedicated women. He did not know why he needed this entourage, only that he must have it. His first steps to get what he wanted imperilled his marriage and brought him to a state which, in his autobiographical synopsis, he described as 'madness'.

4

TEAM SPIRIT

'What inconsiderate buggers we males are.'
Augustus John to Mary Dowdall

'Gus is painting several Masterpieces,' Ida notified Gwen John. '. . . We are as happy as larks.' To the winter exhibition of the New English Art Club, late in 1902, he sent two major pictures. The first of these, 'Merikli',[71] was a portrait of Ida holding a basket of flowers and fruit painted as if by an Old Master: Rembrandt, with a helping hand from Velasquez. Ida's figure, touched by warm light, emerges enthusiastically from the dark shadows of the background. The colouring is sombre, the tone low; the handling is accomplished but conventional and the pose rather artificial. Yet there are a number of peculiar elements in the painting that give it a veil of mystery. In John Sampson's *The Dialect of the Gypsies of Wales, merikli* is defined as: 'Connected with the Sanscrit "pearl", "gem" or "jewel" ie., ornament worn round the neck'. In the picture Ida is wearing a necklace of coral (not precious stone but a once-live substance). Then, from the plaited-straw basket, full of roses and cherries, she proffers a 'daisy' – probably a pun on the slang use of 'daisy' meaning a first-rate specimen of anything. Ida also wears a wedding ring on the right hand. Such unorthodoxes and *double entendres* suggest a less conventional set of values than the pastiche seventeenth-century manner first conveys, and also reveals the literary methods by which he was attempting to combine new ideas with old forms.

It was voted Picture of the Year at the exhibition.

His other portrait at the NEAC was of an Italian girl, Signorina Estella Cerutti. In the opinion of John Rothenstein, this picture 'proclaimed him a master in the art of painting',[72] being 'clearly stamped with that indefinable largeness of form characteristic of major paintings'. The major painter it brings to mind is Ingres, and its striking dissimilarity to 'Merikli' (which also recalls Hals) shows a painter still in search of his own idiom. Estella Cerutti is a splendidly buxom woman, whose creamy-golden silhouette is rendered more piquant by the ballooning curves of her ribbed muslin dress. Whereas Ida's features were painted broadly and spontaneously and looked somewhat masculine in their strength, all is subordinate in the portrait of Estella Cerutti to sinuous contour and the mapping of the shadows. She is not held in the frame but seems to be moving past a window, a self-assured figure holding a handkerchief in her hands (perhaps a reference to *Othello*) and casting a languorous backward glance.

It was a glance that Augustus followed. 'Esther' Cerutti, as he called her – the very name he was to have given his second child had it been a daughter – lived below them at Fitzroy Street. In the spring and summer of 1903 he made numerous drawings of her and at least one etching.[73] Two or three times a week she would come up to their flat, and he would sometimes descend to hers. 'The Cerutti's vices necessitate frequent purchases of Turkish cigarettes,' Augustus explained to Michel Salaman, 'which act as a sedative.' They were a sedative for him rather than her. Ida admired, envied, and was irritated by Esther in the most confusing way. What style she had! She was an accomplished pianist, dressed superbly well and suffered from such appealing illnesses. It was almost impossible not to be provoked.

Augustus seemed held in tension between the two of them, motionlessly suspended within their opposing fields of attraction. 'For days I have been inert and dejected,' he confessed to the Rani in Liverpool.

'I cannot account for the dejection except as the necessary complement of inanition, for my reasons to hope remain palpable and the same. Dearest Lady! How we married people need to cling and pull together and so make this holy state by union a force – for I begin now and then to suspect its weakening – or perhaps it is that I am a weak member, but then at least I am a link in the nuptial chain. But I think we ought to plan it so that we have the laugh on the others . . . As to Miss Esther I don't know whether to be mühen [to exert himself] again or not to be mühen, both courses being fraught with problems distant and immediate. At present I slumber in the studio surrounded by my works.'

To escape these problems he went that summer on a 'short but brilliant campaign in Wales with the admirable Sampson'. But when he returned, the problems were still waiting for him, so he immediately set off again, this time for Liverpool with his sister Winifred, who was sailing to join Thornton in North America. Once he had put her on board, he combed the town for old friends. 'The Town proved most inhospitable,' he complained to the Rani. '. . . I had hoped to see Sampson – but alas! his house proved nothing but a silent tomb of memories with those wonderful blinds drawn gloomily down.' The Rani herself was away in the country, though her elusiveness, he admitted, was stimulating in a disappointing sort of way. 'Curiously enough 'tis to a dream I owe my most vivid, most tender recollection of you. (And they call dreams vague . . . hazy . . .) It happened in Liverpool the last night I spent there. (Heaven knows how I spent the next!)' Afterwards he 'fled down Brownlow Hill to the station and so home again'.

A letter Ida sent Alice Rothenstein about this time gives some of the changes in the John household. From her mother Ida had got a few pieces of furniture, including their bed; on the walls of each room she had put plain white paper, and suspended baskets of roses from the ceiling. To do the cooking she had employed a rabbity young girl named Maggie – tempted by 'friendly lettuce' – and a maid called Alice whom David insisted on calling 'Aunt Alice'.

Ida's day began at 5.30 a.m. and ended at 7.30 p.m. Between day and night came three delightful hours of idleness: then at 10.30 p.m. the night work began – 'it is the hardest part,' she told the Rani. 'I am breaking the baby of having a bottle at 3 a.m., and it entails a constant hushing off to sleep again – as he keeps waking expecting it. Also he has not yet begun to turn himself over in bed, and requires making comfortable 2 or 3 times before 3 a.m. This is not grumbling but bragging.' Nevertheless, it was a tremendous relief to her to get rid of the two children for short spells. That summer they went down with Maggie to stay at Tenby with Edwin John, and Ida felt almost guilty at her sense of liberation. 'It is most delightful without them,' she admitted to Alice Rothenstein.

As soon as their flat was emptied of children, it filled up again with 'aunts' – that is, models for Augustus. Esther, magnificently attired in expensive dresses almost bursting at their fastenings, presented herself and posed, while Ida, who was not Mrs Nettleship's daughter for nothing, set to work creating clothes for herself so as 'to have at least one pretty feather to Esther's hundred lovely costumes. I shall have to come down naked in my fichu [scarf or small shawl], for how can one wear grey linen by her silks and laces?'

But while Ida was anxious at being outshone by Esther, Esther was about to be eclipsed by another girl. In the same letter to Alice Rothenstein, Ida mentions that 'Gus and the beautiful Dorelia McNeill are here . . . Gus is painting Dorelia'. He was, she adds, feeding up Dorelia for her portrait. This is the first mention of the legendary Dorelia, who was to find a place at the centre of the lives of Ida and Augustus and play a short intense part in the life of Gwen John.

Who was Dorelia? Over a period of sixty years, Augustus drew and painted her obsessively. Yet what these pictures convey is not her identity but her enchantment and mysteriousness. The most celebrated portrait of them all, 'The Smiling Woman',[74] shows what Roger Fry called a 'gypsy Giaconda'[75] whose smile was often likened to that of the 'Mona Lisa'. Another picture, 'Dorelia Standing Before a Fence', is more mellow and depicts her as a dream creature who, on our waking, continues to baffle and beguile us.

In this sense, Dorelia was a creation of Augustus's. He made her enigmatic; he made her his ideal woman. What he desired from women was at once simple and impossible to achieve; it was the unknown, timelessly preserved intact; a fantasy blended with reality; a symbol of creativity and nature; mistress and mother. Though he felt a romantic reverence for high birth – 'you darling little aristocratic love', he used to call the Rani – he disliked sophisticated women on the whole, and avoided women famous for their intellect. Cleverness he could find elsewhere, if he needed it: he could even occasionally find it in men. But before the inscrutable beauty of a few women he could lose and renew himself, feel his imagination come alive in inexplicable ways.

All that Augustus aspired to is suggested by the fantasies he wove around Dorelia. In his pictures we see Dorelia as tall, with a swan's neck and well-proportioned head, often the mother-figure seen against a vibrant landscape. In truth she lived in town, was rather short, and no more the conventional mother than Ida. In his paintings he dressed her in broad-rimmed straw hats, their sweeping lines like those of the French peasants; and in long skirts that reached the ground, with high waistlines and tight bodices, like the costumes of the peasant women of Connemara: but she was not a peasant, French or Celt. He laid a false trail across the life of a gypsy girl called Dorelia Boswell, so that many concluded that his Dorelia was probably a Boswell and certainly a gypsy: she was neither. He called her 'Ardor'; he called her 'Relia' and he called her Dorelia, and finally he called her 'Dodo': but none of these were her actual names.

Dorothy McNeill had been born on 19 December 1881 at 97 Bellenden Road, Camberwell. Her father, William George McNeill, was a mercantile clerk, a position he held until promoted, through age, to the rank of retired mercantile clerk. Son of the stationmaster at Peckham, he had married a local girl, Kate Florence Neal, the daughter of a dairy farmer.[76] They were an unremarkable couple given the collective nickname 'Mr and Mrs Brown'. But all their seven children (of whom Dorothy was the fourth) were extraordinarily handsome – mostly small with dark complexions, prominent mouths curving downwards, voices gentle and low, black hair and large brooding eyes.

Each of the four daughters had been taught some profession. Dorothy learnt to type. Her first job, at the age of sixteen, was for the editor of a magazine called *The Idler*. Then, for a short time, she worked for a writer. By 1902 she had become a junior secretary copying legal documents in the office of a solicitor, G. Watson Brown, in Basinghall Street. She did not appear discontented, but since her personality was very passive and she was not communicative, it was difficult to know what she felt. Another young typist in the office, Muriel Alexander, remembers that Dora, as everyone there called her, always dressed 'artistically' in a style entirely her own, wearing long full-skirted dresses and having her hair parted in the middle and drawn in a knot at the back of her head. Everyone liked her; no one knew much about her. On the surface, it seemed, she had accepted a secretarial career, to be followed in the ordinary way by one as housewife. She was not ambitious in the usual sense; but she felt certain another kind of life awaited her, and that she belonged to the world of art. How this was she could not say; nor did she speak about it. But instinctively she felt it to be her destiny. This was her secret, the source of her patience, her means of emancipation. It was Dorothy who typed each day; but it was Dorelia who dreamed.

And it was Dorelia who, in the evenings after the office closed, went off to the late classes at the Westminster School of Art. Here she got to know a number of artists and began to be invited to their parties, at one of which she met Gwen John. Gwen was then using a 'most exquisite looking pupil of about 15 years old' as a model in exchange for drawing lessons. 'Gwen makes her draw the most hideous and wicked of the Roman emperors in the British Museum,'[77] Ida reported. Dorelia had already seen Gwen's brother at an exhibition of Spanish paintings at the Guildhall near her office, but they had not spoken and he did not see her. Yet she remembered this first glimpse of him as if, without words or contact of any kind, she had chosen him as the vehicle of her destiny.

There are many stories of how they met. A popular one was that Augustus overtook her wearing a black hat in Holborn one day, looked back, and was unable to look away. They must have met early in 1903 while she was living in a basement in Fitzroy Street. By the summer he was already writing her passionate letters:

'The smell of you is in my nostrils and it will never go and I am sick for love of you. What are the great beneficent influences I owe a million thanks to who have brought you in my way, Ardor my little girl, my love, my spouse whose smile opens infinite vistas to me, enlarges, intensifies existence like a strain of music. I want to look long and solemnly at you. I want to hear you laugh and sigh. My breath is upon your cheek – do you feel it? I kiss you on the lips – do you kiss me back? Yes I possess you as you possess me and I will hear you laugh again and worship your eyes again and touch you again and again and again and again . . . your love Gustavus . . .'

She was hypnotically beautiful – almost embarrassingly so: 'one could not take one's eyes off her,' Will Rothenstein remembered.[78] In his portraits of her, Augustus gave her a sultry look, with high rounded cheekbones, slanting eyes and an air of devastating refinement.[79] A painting entitled 'Ardor'[80] shows a full dimpled face, eyes that solicit, pink cheeks and mouth. It is the portrait of a seductress, a comparable subject technically to 'Merikli'. In his portraiture, Augustus was like a stage director, assigning his subjects a variety of short dramatic roles. Dorelia, it seemed, acquiesced in them all. She sprang from the natural and the mythic world. She became all things to him; she was Everywoman.

It was not by her looks alone that she dazzled him. Beauty is not so scarce. What was uncommon about Dorelia was the serenity that gave her beauty its depth – a quality he so conspicuously lacked. She was not witty or articulate; and certainly not sentimental. It was her *presence* that was so powerful, her vitality and above all her magical peace-giving qualities. People who were miserable could come to her, relax, absorb something of her extraordinary calm. All manner of disasters, tragedies, crises appeared to shrivel up within the range of her personality. She guarded her secrets well, like a cat.

Augustus did not conceal from Ida his sudden flaring infatuation for Dorelia: concealment did not come easily to him – it was something he would learn, rather inadequately, later on. Besides, he might as well have tried to hide a forest fire. He presented Ida with the facts; he introduced her to Dorelia; and he left her to decide what should be done. Of the three of them, Ida was the most likely to take a positive decision about the future. Augustus and Dorelia acted on impulse in a way that might appear decisive, but which was often a simple reflex.

The upheaval of Ida's feelings was painful. Upon the decision she had to make depended the future of their marriage. She knew Augustus better than anyone – 'our child-genius' as she was soon to call him – and she had to accept that she could not hope to confine his incendiary passions within the grate of married life. He maddened her, but she loved him. And she *liked* Dorelia. When the two women were together – it was strange – Ida's difficulties seemed less acute and she was almost happy. Reason therefore told her that, if Augustus's feelings persisted, some form of *ménage-à-trois* was the only practical solution. Reason told her this; but sometimes a violent jealousy would surge through her, drowning reason. She felt ugly. She felt useless. Marriage, which had imprisoned her, left Augustus free, since her love for him excluded other romantic and sexual feelings, while his for her did not. The quasi-religious advice she had poured forth in earlier days on her aunts and sisters she now turned upon herself. Her moral duty was to accept these awkward complications as a part of her love. Whatever happened she must fight against jealousy, since that was the voice of the devil. So, for the time being, she appeared philosophical: 'Men must play,' she wrote, improving the quotation from Charles Kingsley, 'and women must weep.'

With Ida apparently raising no objections, Dorelia began moving into their married life. At first the part she played, though a vital one, was intermittent. She never lived in their flat, though she visited Augustus most weeks to be drawn and painted by him. He loved to dress her up, buying her bright petticoats down to her knees, gay ribbons to tie in her hair, and he relied on Ida to help him choose the costumes. 'Don't forget to come on Sunday,' he reminded Dorelia. 'I want to get a new dress made for you, white stockings and little black boots and lots of silly little things for your hair . . . Sleep well Relia and don't forget me when you go to sleep.' But sometimes, without warning, she did forget him. 'In the devil's name! Why did you not come? Are you ill? . . . or did you dance too much the night before, so you were [too] tired to come up here . . . A true young wife and a lady you are . . . Are your new clothes made [yet]? I should like to see you on the high road all dressed in fire-red. Are you coming next Sunday?' But already by Monday he found he could not wait till next Sunday.

'I went last night down to Westminster to find you but you were not there. When are you going there again? as I would like to see your pretty eyes again. If you'll believe me my girl, I liked more than I can say sitting with you on the grass on the ferns. As you say, you are a young wild tree, my Relia. I love to kiss you just as I love to feel the warmth of the sun, just as I like to smell the good earth. One gets used to the afterwards, my girl, and then they need not be so very damned. My wife and I have been ransacking shops to find a certain stuff for your picture . . . I am getting excited over the picture. I will do it better now after I have kissed you several times.'

He longed to paint her in the nude, but she was unwilling. 'Why not sit for me in your soft skin, and no other clothes – are you ashamed? Nonsense! It is not as if you were very fat.' But still she would not.

At each point his excitement was matched by her imperturbability; his passion by her elusiveness; his doubts and speculations by her compliance. She had cast a spell on him, and he began to weave one for her. 'How would you like yourself as a Romany lady?' he asked. To Dorelia, who was rather dismissive of her anonymous parents, here was an intriguing question. Under Augustus's tuition she began learning the language. All these early letters he sent her were written in Romany,* mixed with odd English words, and with word-lists attached. Whatever Augustus learnt from Sampson he passed on to Dorelia – and Ida picked up some of the words too, though she never dared write to Sampson in Romany as Dorelia was soon doing. Romany became their secret code, as the *Jungle Book* language had once been for Ida's friends. But Ida was not at the centre of this Romany conspiracy as she had been in the recreated world of Kipling. That centre was for Augustus and Dorelia alone. He was delighted how swiftly she learnt, how eager she was to enter this make-believe. 'Sit and write down another letter for me,' he urged her. 'Put in it all the Romany words you know, then a little tale about yourself, and send it to me.' She wrote and told him about an old woman who drank whisky and had fallen in love with her – and he was enchanted.

So his love grew. He could think of almost nothing else, could scarcely endure being parted from her. 'Dear sweetheart Dorelia,' he wrote to her early that summer on a short visit to Littlehampton.

'Now I am going to bed, now I am under the blankets, and I wish that you were here too, you sweet girl-wife. I want to kiss you again on the lips, and eyes, and neck and nose and all over your bare fiery body. When our faces touch, my blood burns with a wild fire of love, so much I love you my wild girl. I don't speak falsely. If you laugh you cannot love. Now I see your white teeth. Why are you not here with me? I hear the sea that sings and cries in the old way, my own great sad mother. Send me word very soon – Tell me that you love me a bit. Yours Gustavus Janik.'

It was not long before rumours of Augustus's romance began to be whispered among his friends, and among Ida's. 'I have come to the conclusion that it is very difficult to deceive anyone,' Ida wrote to Alice

---

* They are written partly in the inflected Romany, like the so-called 'Welsh Romany' which is really an older form of English Romany, partly in the broken English Romany, and partly in English. The versions quoted here were done into English by the gypsy scholar Ferdinand G. Hugh who wrote that 'I have made the translation as near as possible to the actual Romany words'.

Rothenstein, 'and that people know one's own business almost as well as one knows it oneself. I suppose you know that, as you know most things (I am not sarcastic). In a certain way you are a very wise person.' This was Ida's difficulty: she had no one in whom she could confide. Alice was a loyal friend, but perhaps not a very understanding one. Her own life was so different and so safe. There was about her a suspicion of vicarious living, of looking with disapproving relish at other people's goings-on. Nobody could doubt that Alice had Ida's interests sincerely at heart, but Ida tried to avoid revealing her problems. Besides, Alice seethed with high-principled gossip. She invariably counselled prudence, now that she had married Will. 'I ask you why should a healthy young woman be particularly "prudent",' complained the Rani to Ida, ' – or was Alice herself ever – such rot!' On the whole Ida preferred Will's counsel and companionship. He too could lecture her, but when he addressed himself to young women his romanticism quite dissolved his moralizing. They were a strange couple, Alice and Will – she still so beautiful, a faintly overblown conventional pink rose 'large and fair and cushiony and sleepy', as Ida had written; he 'a hideous little Jew with a wonderful mind – as quick as a sewing-machine, and with the quality of Bovril'.

Partly because of Alice, Ida was shy of disclosing her secrets to Will. And to Augustus himself it was always difficult to speak of anything intimate for long. It was like sending one's words down a dark well. When he did talk, it was usually to deliver some laconic sentence that put an end to discussion. She was aware of becoming less attractive in his eyes when she tried to speak to him seriously. He seemed to believe that any talk about their problems could only exacerbate them. This was one of the reasons he drank – to be blind to his problems: to be rid of himself.

Although she would have preferred a man to talk to, Ida confided most to the Rani. To her she felt she might occasionally 'grumple' without disloyalty. The Rani could be trusted, and her humour made everything easier – 'my heart's blood to you', she ended one of her letters, 'and my liver to Augustus'. The world seemed a brighter place after one of her letters. 'Yours is the proper way to have babies,' she told Ida, 'one after the other without fuss and let them roll around together and squabble and eat and be kissed and otherwise not bother.' She would write of the entertaining disasters that had befallen her, such as poisoning her family with mushrooms; she sent Ida appalling photographs of herself 'looking like the Virgin Mary with indigestion'; she told her how common her own children were becoming and how she disliked the Liverpool middle classes, 'all bandy-legged and floppy nosed and streaky haired', with their 'jocky caps and sham pearls and bangles and dogs and three-quarter coats' – they made her ache with anger, causing 'the glands behind my ears to swell'. Finally she would apologize for failing, despite everything, to be discontented. 'I am sorry I am so happy and you so much the reverse – I think I really am too stupid to be anything else. You must pay the penalty for having the intelligence, I suppose – the lady Dorelia is a strange creature.'

Dorelia's strangeness – 'her face is a mystery', Ida remarked, 'like everyone else's' – and the uneasy partnership to which she had been admitted were increasingly the subject of speculation. 'I saw John last week and he doesn't seem to have been pulling himself together as he should have done,' lamented Will Rothenstein to his brother Albert (3 June 1903), ' – he seems as restless as ever, and looks no better than he should do. Ida has gone off to Tenby for a month with her babes, so he is alive just now.'

A few weeks after Ida returned, Albert Rutherston went to dine with them at Fitzroy Street one evening. 'They are well,' he told Michel Salaman (9 August 1903), 'and John showed me some exceedingly good starts of paintings – they have bred at least a dozen canaries from the original twain which fly about the room – perch on the rafters and sit on one's head while one dines – it really was amusing . . . Miss MacNeill came after dinner – she . . . seems to be a great friend of all the Johns – I think John must have a secret agreement with that lady and Mrs J – but not a word to anyone of this – it is only my notion and a mad one at that.'

Others who saw this crowded household, with its multiplying flocks of canaries, women and children, were sadder and more critical. 'Really matrimony is not a happy subject to talk about at present,' Tonks wrote to Will Rothenstein (15 September 1903). 'The John establishment makes me feel very melancholy, and I do not see that the future shines much.'

But Augustus loved Fitzroy Street. Before Whistler died that summer, he would occasionally meet him there and they would have lunch together. He had always been amused by Whistler's panache, but no longer had quite the same reverence for him. Whistler had been a man of cities; his curiosity 'stopped short at dockland to the east and Battersea to the west'.[81] He belonged to the urban cult of Decadence, against which Augustus had now started to rebel.

The flat at Fitzroy Street was obviously too small for them all. Augustus felt unable to breathe in that bricked-up atmosphere. He dreamt of wide spaces, 'the broad, open road, with the yellowhammer in the hedge and the blackthorn showing flower'.[82] As the summer wore on, this feeling grew insupportable. 'I have fled the town and my studio; dreary shed void of sunlight and the song of birds and the aspirant life of plants,' he told

Will Rothenstein from Westcot, in Berkshire, where he had gone to see Charles McEvoy.[83]

'Nor shall I soon consent to exchange the horizons that one can never reach for four mournful walls and a suffocating roof – where one's thoughts grow pale and poisonous as fungi in dark cellars, and the Breath of the Almighty is banished, and shut off the vision of a myriad world in flight. Little Egypt for me – the land without bounds or Parliaments or Priests, the Primitive world of a people without a History, the country of the Pre-Adamites!'

The difference between town and country was like that between sleep and waking life. 'Don't get up so much,' he advised Dorelia from Fitzroy Street, 'it's better to sleep. What beautiful weather we are having – it makes me dream of woods and wind and running water. I would like to live in any wooded place where the singing birds are heard, where you could smoke and sleep and stop without being stared at.'

The best plan, he suddenly decided, was to find some house in the country not far from London that would accommodate as many as might reasonably find themselves there – women, children, animals, friends, family, servants and, more intermittently, Augustus himself. Ida, who had recently completed her decorations to Fitzroy Street, agreed. 'We have been house hunting,' she wrote to Michel Salaman.

But Dorelia had other plans.

5

CANDID WHITE AND MATCHING GREEN

'Everything is happy and inevitable here – one cannot quarrel with an invisible hand nor need one call it the Devil's . . .'
Augustus John to John Sampson (n.d. [1904])

'I hope for a different life later on – I think it can only be postponed.'
Ida John to Gwen John (21 September 1904)

'Leave everybody and let them leave you. Then only will you be without fear.'
Gwen John, Diary

The Carfax Gallery, in the spring of 1903, had held a joint show of Gwen and Gus's pictures. 'I am devilish tired of putting up my exhibits,' Augustus complained to Dorelia. 'I would like to burn the bloody lot.' Of the forty-eight pictures – paintings, pastels, drawings and etchings – forty-five were by Augustus, and Gwen withdrew one of hers. Nevertheless, he told Rothenstein, 'Gwen has the honours or should have – for alas our smug critics don't appear to have noticed the presence in the Gallery of two rare blossoms from the most delicate of trees. The little pictures to me are almost painfully charged with feeling; even as their neighbours are empty of it. And to think that Gwen so rarely brings herself to paint! We others are always in danger of becoming professional and to detect oneself red-handed in the very act of professional industry is a humiliating experience!'

Gwen had closed down her feelings for Ambrose McEvoy. But she needed to love someone. Until recently she had continued living in the McEvoy family home in Colville Terrace, while Ambrose and Mary moved down to Shrivenham in Oxfordshire, an address used by Gwen's former friend Grace Westray. It was possibly at this time that Gwen went back to the cellar in Howland Street – 'a kind of dungeon', as Augustus described it, '. . . into which no ray of sunlight could ever penetrate'. Indifferent to physical discomfort, she seemed filled with a strange elation. 'I have never seen her [Gwen] so well or so gay,' Albert Rutherston told Michel Salaman (9 August 1903). 'She was fat in the face and merry to a degree.'

The source of Gwen's happiness was Dorelia. On an impulse, she proposed that the two of them should leave London and walk to Rome – and Dorelia calmly agreed. There was nothing, there was no one, to hold Gwen in England. She was to celebrate the opening of a new chapter in her life with a pilgrimage that cut her off geographically, physically and emotionally from her past. But for Dorelia the decision is less understandable since it meant abandoning Augustus, perhaps for months, at a critical stage of their relationship. With a man so volatile, what guarantee was there he would feel the same when she arrived back? Yet Dorelia's mind did not work along these lines. If Fate intended her to live with Augustus, then that was how it would be – and nothing could alter this. Although she seldom revealed her thoughts, there can be little doubt that she was feeling the strain of being a visitor to Gus and Ida's married life. Once they had settled into a house in the country perhaps everything would be different. All Dorelia knew was that her life, whatever form it took, would be involved with art, and that there was nothing inconsistent with this in going off for an adventure with Gwen.

The two girls were as excited as if it were an elopement. But Augustus found himself occupying a parental role, advising caution, good sense, second thoughts. Their plan was impossible, he promised: it was also mad. Should they not at least pack a pistol? But Gwen would not listen to his arguments – 'she never did'.[84] Finally, he relented, giving them a little money and some cake. They set off that August, 'carrying a minimum of belongings and a great deal of painting equipment',[85] and boarded a steamer in the Thames.

'Give my love to that dear girl Dorelia,' Ida wrote to Gwen. '. . . Aurevoir mes deux amies . . . Aurevoir encore.' Ida hardly knew what to think, so confused were her feelings. She had been glad Dorelia was going abroad and yet she felt envious of her, and also curious about this escapade with Gwen. 'Is Dorelia much admired?' she questioned Gwen. 'I can't believe you tell me *everything*, it is all so golden. I suppose you will come with bags of money, & bank notes sewn about you.'[86] But actually she was rather surprised to hear they had landed intact at Bordeaux and started walking up the Garonne. 'What a success!' she congratulated them. 'I am so glad & I . . . long to be with you (now I know its nice). To sleep out in the middle of a river & have a great roaring wave at 3 in the morning – Really it must be gorgeous.' In comparison her own life seemed tame. Now that Thornton and Winifred were across the Atlantic, Gwen and Dorelia across the Channel, and even Wyndham Lewis in Spain with his fellow artist Spencer Gore, Fitzroy Street filled up rapidly with Nettleships. 'My tribe came round as usual tonight and assisted at the bathing etc.,' Ida wrote to Gwen. 'Gus lay on the bed – Ursula knelt by me – Ethel reclined by Gus – Mother loomed large on the other side of the bath.' The good news was that Ida wasn't pregnant again ('So I feel very light hearted'); the bad news that Gus hadn't found a house for them in the country. And then there was some further news. Esther Cerutti had stepped back into their lives, 'as full of that curious thing called style as ever. I believe that is why I tolerate her nonsense.'[87]

From time to time over the next weeks, Gus and Ida would get morsels of news about the 'crazy walkers' as they made their way from village to village towards Toulouse. Sometimes they received odd letters themselves; sometimes they heard from Ursula Tyrwhitt who was also in correspondence with Gwen. The two girls obviously found the going hard. Once they travelled in a motor car – 'till it broke down'; and more than once they were offered lifts in carts – 'every lift seems saving of time and therefore money too so we always take them', Gwen explained to Ursula. At each village they would try to earn some money by going to the inn and either singing or drawing portraits of those men who would pose. But their motives were sometimes misconstrued. At night they slept in the fields, under haystacks, on the icy stone flags beside the Garonne or, when they were lucky, in stables, lying on each other to feel a little warmer, covering themselves with their portfolios and waking up encircled by congregations of farmers, gendarmes and stray animals. Between the villages, bowed beneath bundles of possessions that seemed larger than themselves, they would practise their singing. They lived mostly on grapes and bread, a little beer, some lemonade. There were many adventures; losing their tempers with the women, outwitting the men, shaking with fright at phantom shapes in the night, tearful with laughter when these turned out to be harmless pieces of farm machinery.

Near Meilhan they met a sculptor who told Gwen her lines were too short ('it is good to have things pointed out'); at La Réole they met a young artist who 'came to look at us in the stable' and 'gave us his address in Paris so we can be models if we like in Paris',[88] Gwen reported to Ursula.

By the end of November they reached Toulouse where they hired a room 'from a tiny little old woman dressed in black . . . she is very very wicked'. Here they stayed and worked. 'We shall never get to Rome I'm afraid,' Gwen wrote to Ursula, 'it seems further away than it did in England . . . the country round is wonderful especially now – the trees are all colours – I paint my picture on the top of a hill – Toulouse lies below and all round we can see the country for many miles and in the distance the Pyrenees. I cannot tell you how wonderful it is when the sun goes down, the last two evenings we have had a red sun – lurid I think is the word, the scene is sublime then, it looks like Hell or Heaven.'[89]

Augustus noted their progress with a mixture of amusement and irritation. 'I congratulate you both on having thus far preserved body and soul intact,' he wrote to them when they were about halfway to Toulouse. 'But with all my growing sedulity I find it difficult to believe you are really growing fat on a diet of wine and onions and under a burden of $\frac{1}{2}$ a hundredweight odd.' He also congratulated them on having escaped the importunities of an old man in a barn 'with true womanly ingenuity', and he enclosed five pounds for Dorelia – 'a modest instalment of my debt to you'.[90] But already small misunderstandings had begun to creep into their exchanges. In any event, Dorelia decided she did not want random gifts of money accompanied by jokes she did not care for – and wrote to tell him so.

Gus was mainly concerned, at this stage, with Gwen's pictures. He himself was contributing half a dozen works to the Winter Show of the NEAC, including portraits of Mackay, Rothenstein and Sampson: he was eager for Gwen to submit at least one of her own so that she should not be forgotten. 'The day for the NEAC is Nov. 9.,' he reminded both girls. 'I hope Gwen will do a good picture of you, and that it will contain all the Genius of Guienne and Languedoc. I hope it will be as wild as your travels and as unprecedented.' But Gwen refused to be rushed. 'The New English sending day is next Monday,' Augustus wrote again more urgently, 'and Gwen's picture doesn't seem to arrive.' When it did arrive – a glowing portrait of Dorelia entitled 'L'Étudiante' – it was almost six years late, and was shown at the NEAC Winter Exhibition of 1909.

Soon after Gwen and Dorelia left, Augustus and Ida had taken a two-year lease on what seemed a perfect house, with a large orchard and stables, at Matching Green in Essex. 'It is lovely here,' Ida wrote to the Rani, '. . . to go out into the quiet evenings and see the moon floating up above and feel the cold air.' They moved in with a lawnmower, their canaries, Gwen's cats and a dog called Bobster during late November. Elm House stood next to a the Chequers Inn, had a studio but no telephone or electric light, and overlooked the village green. 'Several gypsies have been already,' Ida informed Margaret Sampson. 'Our house is one of the two ugly ones. Inside it is made bearable by our irreproachable taste.' Four-and-a-half miles from Harlow, their nearest town, and twenty from London, Matching Green stood in a tract of land, Augustus told Will Rothenstein, 'abundant in such things as trees, ponds, streams, hillocks, barns etc. . . . Pines amaze me growing stiff and lofty like Phallic symbols. I get dangerous classic tendencies out here I fear. London is perhaps on the whole a safer place for me.'

Since leaving his Liverpool job, Augustus's income had been erratic, while his responsibilities steadily mounted. It was this state of affairs – 'living as I do in such insecurity', he described it[91] – that now persuaded him to collaborate in a scheme of Orpen's. 'I have committed myself to one day a week teaching at a school Orpen initiates with Knewstub as secretary,' he wrote to Will Rothenstein. 'We hope to make pocket money out of it at least. It is a very respectable undertaking with none of the perfection you had insisted on. It is Knewstub who makes things feasible with his capacity for organising and letter writing.'

Jack Knewstub was the brother-in-law of both Orpen and Will Rothenstein. Nicknamed 'Curly' Knewstub, he had fair wavy hair, boyish good looks and a rather tough North Country manner. For a time he had acted as secretary to a Welsh Member of Parliament and it was here that he learnt his skills as letter-writer. In his organizing capacity he was certainly superior to Augustus, but he was no businessman. His father had been both pupil and assistant to Rossetti – old Knewstub, it was said, could draw but not colour, and Rossetti, a superb colourist, could not draw: it was an ideal partnership. But Curly Knewstub, brought up in this Pre-Raphaelite world, could neither draw nor colour. He was an artist *manqué*, a dreamer with ambitious cultural fantasies to which this new school now acted as a focus. In the firmament of his imagination, Augustus shone like the moon. Over the years, he schooled his own six children to draw in the John manner, until they came to loathe John's very name.

If Knewstub worshipped Augustus, Augustus tolerated Knewstub. Admittedly he was 'a tactless idiot', 'exasperating' and 'difficult to avoid'; and also so 'damned incompetent' that it was as well to have nothing to do with him in financial matters. Yet no one was perfect and Knewstub proved an agreeable drinking companion, useful in countless little ways – the paper and sealing-wax of life.

The Chelsea Art School, as it was called, opened in the autumn of 1903 at numbers 4 and 5 Rossetti Studios in Flood Street. It was, Augustus wrote to Gwen, 'a bold enterprise by which we expect to replenish our coffers'. On the prospectus* Augustus and Orpen were named as its principals. Knewstub, who began by using 18 Fitzroy Street as his office, acted as secretary and general manager. The sexes were segregated, Gwen Salmond conscripted as 'lady superintendent' and various other 'Sladers', including Michel Salaman and Will Rothenstein, drafted to give lectures.

In some ways this generation of British artists was to remain a band of eternal students. Perhaps it was because their training at the Slade, where they were so happy, had been incomplete. Gwen Salmond, for example, after leaving the Chelsea Art School, was to study with the Spanish-born, French-trained artist Leandro Ramon Garrido and then, after the war, enrol in a school run by the French cubist painter André Lhote, whose classes Gwen John also attended 'ill or well' as late as 1936.

Another Slade student, Edna Clarke Hall, who was to join the Central School of Art and Design in the 1920s, decided to enrol in the Orpen and John Chelsea Art School. 'The great are following,' Orpen shouted across to Augustus as she entered the Flood Street studios, 'we shall succeed.' Having drifted into her respectable marriage five years earlier Edna had been 'put on a pedestal and forgotten' by her husband. But she was not forgotten by Augustus. He would turn up unexpectedly at her home from time to time, sit in the garden drawing her, filling up sheet after sheet compulsively with 'little wonders'. She watched with fascination, having no idea what was coming next. 'He talked as he drew,' she remembered, 'swiftly and casually but with such a learned hand.'[92] He always came on weekday afternoons and she would make sure he had gone and all evidence of his work – and hers – been hidden away by the time her husband got back from his law office. For William Clarke Hall continued to disapprove of her art-student friends, especially Augustus John, and

* See Appendix Three.

to discourage her from painting and drawing. 'What is all this rubbish lying around?' he had demanded, looking at her pens and paints. So she put them away, but went on longing 'for the old Slade days when we were all drawing together'.

It was Gwen Salmond who arranged the life-drawing classes for Edna at the Chelsea Art School – just as she had arranged for Gwen John to attend the Académie Carmen in Paris – so enabling her to escape for a time the 'great solitude' of her marriage. Edna enjoyed returning to school. But nothing could conceal the fact that 'those happy days' at the Slade were 'gone for ever'. So much had been happening to her friends in her absence. Gwen Salmond had become an art teacher, taking classes for the London County Council and the Clapham School of Art; Gwen John had disappeared with the mysterious Dorelia, 'the queen of all waterlilies' as Ida called her; and Ida herself had started a large family because, as she explained, 'there is nothing else to do now that painting is not practicable, and I must create something.'[93] Such news of Ida's domestic routine of washing and sewing and baby-minding as Edna picked up 'strengthened a longing I have often felt to take you right away from those boys of yours'.[94] But where could she take her? Edna herself had no babies. She was merely a child-wife and Edwardian hostess.

'The school idea receives great encouragement from all sides,'[95] Augustus had reported to Michel Salaman. No one was more excited than Edna. She liked the way Augustus taught by demonstration, re-drawing the students' work with extraordinary skill. He made obvious efforts to be tolerant and enthusiastic but, like Tonks at the Slade, he could also be sarcastic. Having reduced a pupil to tears, he would then become riddled with guilt and, as an act of contrition, find himself inviting the tearful student out for 'a drink or a day trip up the river on a steamer',[96] during which he would recite Romany verses in his rumbling bass voice – an impressive sound drifting incomprehensibly along the water.

Everything began promisingly at the Chelsea Art School. 'They have 35 students – but need to double the money to make it pay,' Ida wrote to Winifred John in January 1904. 'They have fine studios in Chelsea. Gwen Salmond is the chief girl and looks after the women's affairs. Isn't it mad?'

One person who thought the arrangement dangerously mad was Alice Rothenstein. Did Ida, she wondered, know *nothing* about men? It was inviting trouble, this burying herself in the country and permitting Augustus to roam the streets of London alone. Her head swam at the pure folly of it. So strongly did she feel, that she would have intervened had she not been weightily pregnant at the time. As it was, the very least she could do from her bed of confinement was to pepper Ida with warnings. Of course, it was none of her business, but then what were friends for? Alice had been on the stage before she married Will. Ida had had a sheltered upbringing and was an innocent creature – she must be protected by post. Ida endured these reprimands stoically, then retaliated (12 December 1903):

'You are quite quite wrong, but I will not scold you now as you are just going to have a baby. In the first place I prefer being here. And healthy or no, Gus enjoys being in London alone.

Think it pride if you will, but the truth is I would not come back if I had the chance. You do not understand, and you need not add my imaginary troubles to your worries. If I had not known it was alright I should not have come here. *I always know.* So there. Cease your regrets and all the rest of it. Yrs. Ida.'

Alice was shocked. This was the last thing she had expected. The temptation to appear more offended than she actually felt was almost irresistible. Ida, however, was having no nonsense. She refused to be seen as forlorn, abandoned or irresponsible, as Alice's theatrical imagination demanded. 'Dear Alice, I was not in the least vexed,' she replied, 'and you know I was not. And please always say exactly what you feel. Only I can't help doing the same and disagreeing. And I know it is such a good thing we came here, and you say it is a bad thing.'

Thereafter, whenever Alice's volleys of questions grew too intense, Ida would put up a smokescreen. Had Alice observed how lovely the trees were looking just now? Would she like news of the two piebald pigs she owned ('they grunt very nicely') and about the terrific number of black-and-white cats Gwen John had left with them? Sometimes Ida would post her 'several pages of nothing': at other times she would reveal that, with many disheartening interruptions, she was learning the piano or making a hat. She sent flowers and embroidery and lists of 'scattered visitors – all very pale' to Elm House: her mother and sisters, Margaret Sampson, the Rani – 'we have giggled and been stupid and feminine all the time'. She invited Alice to visit her also and see the elm trees, the green, the open skies: 'The geese still cackle and waddle on the green, and the bony horses graze. All the buds are coming out, and the birds beginning to sing long songs.'

But by far the best method of deflecting Alice's formidable pity was to introduce the ever-interesting subject of children. Alice, who was extremely proud of her children, simply could not resist it. Ida is careful to establish that her two sons are in no way comparable to the magnificent Rothenstein boys. David, who 'is spoiled – or any rate he is difficile', shouts whenever the sun comes out, loves nursery rhymes with any mention of dying in them, says 'NO' a great many times each day and has taken to drawing, making their lives terrible with his ceaseless howls for pictures of hyenas, cows and 'taegers'. Caspar is enormous, struggles with a free style on his tummy across the floor exclaiming 'Mama' as if it were some kind of joke, remains perfectly toothless at ten months old, but has developed two fat and rosy cheeks from perpetually blowing a trumpet – 'his first and only accomplishment'. He is strong as a bull and has achieved a 'long dent in his forehead from a knock . . . [which] really must have dented his skull as it still shows after several weeks'.

But sometimes her stream of domestic trivia runs dry, and we catch sight of other aspects of Ida's life. 'Dear Alice, I have nothing to say – do forgive me. I am very tired.' The children dominated her night and day, sucking away all energy. Never, it seemed, could she escape from their noise, their eternal need for food and attention. 'I am getting a little restive sometimes,' she admitted (15 February 1904), 'but what I chiefly long for is 2 or 3 quiet nights. Not that they are restless in the night – but as you know they require attention several times.' She was a conscientious mother, determined to make the best of it. Motherhood was a medicine she had to swallow, and to judge from its bitter taste it must be improving her character. 'All my energies go to controlling my own children's passions,' she explained to Alice. 'I do get angry and irritable sometimes, but I am getting slowly better, and it is a discipline worth having. I have been so used to looking upon life as a means to get pleasure, but I am coming round to another view of it. And it is a limitless one.'

Intermittently this glow of moral optimism would fade and she envied Gwen John her painting, Dorelia her freedom. Both Ida and Gus would have preferred to be in France with Gwen and Dorelia, whatever the emotional complications. 'It's all very well talking about Toulouse,' Gus reprimanded Gwen that autumn. 'Naturally I prefer Toulouse to Didcot myself. But there's the question d'enfants.'[97] How he survived the Nettleship family Christmas was a wonder. 'We are very silly and Gussy has many disdainful smiles,' Ida wrote to Gwen. '. . . [He] is drawing animals & people for Davie to recognise.'[98]

There were plenty of animals and people for David and Caspar to recognize at Matching Green: their lunatic of a dog, now called Jack and 'too silly for words'; and Gwen's family of ten cats (some of the kittens Augustus drowned in a kettle); and six breeding canaries. 'Domesticities amongst the birds are going on all around me,' Ida wrote to Margaret Sampson. Then there was Maggie, the cook; and Lucy Green who came in 'shining with soap' to help with the housework; and various visitors including Esther Cerutti, who arrived from London in all her finery and played the piano.

Almost the only person whom the children did not see so much was the 'father of the family' who was 'generally in London',[99] Ida explained to Winifred. Augustus loved Matching Green – 'I see things so beautiful sometimes,' he confessed to Sampson, 'I wonder my poor eyes don't drop out.'[100] But you could have too much of a good thing. Besides, he had to work at the new art school and make some money for them all. In some ways he was like an extra child for Ida, or an adolescent, who could seldom tell her when he was coming back for supper because he did not know himself.

Ida would have liked to be as free and easy herself. 'I get very little time for contemplation now-a-days – and if I do get half-an-hour I am certain to tear my dress and have to mend it, or spill a box of pins, or something.' She had given up painting altogether. 'For the first time in my life Matching Green bores me – to extinction almost,' she told the Rani who came down from Liverpool to stay with her. 'I wish it did quite. It would be quite a pleasant way of dying – to be bored away into nothing.' She longed for a more adventurous life, and more adult companionship. 'I am "comblé de travail" ', she wrote to Dorelia. 'I am usually so tired that if I sit down I doze . . . My thoughts are often with you.'[101] When she compared their lives in her imagination, 'I long to come over,' she told Gwen and Dorelia in the spring of 1904. '. . . Your life is romantic, mine a pigstye with the stye overhead.'[102] She was getting too little of Gus's company and far too much of his children's. 'I am beginning to wonder if my head will stand much more of the babies' society.'

From the nursery she began escaping into the kitchen. Though Alice, their maid at Fitzroy Street, had left, their young cook Maggie, now very 'fat and attractive' and nicknamed 'Minger', had come with them to Elm House. As the weeks went by, Ida did more cooking and Maggie more looking after the boys. 'I have begun to learn to cook,' she announced triumphantly (15 February 1904), 'and can make several puddings and most delicious pastry.' Cooking was so much quieter than children, so much – despite what everyone said – more creative. 'I have been cooking and cooking and cooking – and have been so successful. I want to try and make Maggie nurse, and be cook and odd woman [myself] . . . And cooking is so charming . . . However, it is not settled yet.' By the spring it was settled: 'Maggie is Nurse entirely now – and I am Cook General. It is so much less wearing.'

She also took up gardening, became a 'scientific laundress', grew 'mad on polishing furniture', involved herself in the manufacture of loud check coats. Guilt often stabbed at her: she was a poor mother, a reluctant 'housewife', despite being better off than many others. Besides Maggie, she was soon regularly employing Lucy Green, 'a very large and conscientious child of 14' to act as housemaid. Yet still she seemed to suffer from overwork. 'Matching Green is quite drunk to-day,' she wrote to Alice at Easter. '. . . Soon the woman who lives on our other side will be helping herself home by our garden railings. It is remarkable the way they all make for the pub. Overwork. I know the necessity. I go to domestic novels – quite as unwholesome in another way. For my part I could not be really at leisure and able to follow my own desires with less than 4 servants. So what can these poor people do without one? And yet how gorgeous life is.'

Then again this glow would darken and apathy would sweep over her. 'I should like to have gone to Michel [Salaman]'s marriage feast but they will do well enough without me, and nothing matters.'

But one person still mattered to her: Gus. All winter he had been subject to dark moods, and when spring came these moods grew blacker and more frequent. Her inability to pull him out of these depressions was a source of self-reproach. She lost confidence – perhaps she was the wrong person; perhaps only Dorelia could help him – help both of them. Ida's exhaustion was added to Gus's listlessness, and together they seemed like two ships becalmed, waiting. 'Dorelia and Gwen, when are you coming back?' Ida asked; and Gus added his appeal to the same letter: 'I wish you two would come back & be painted – with your faces towards Spain if you like.'[103]

*

The Chelsea Art School absorbed much of Augustus's energy during its first two terms. For his own work he used a studio above the school, and would often spend a full week, or even a fortnight, in town. 'London is very beautiful,' he wrote to Dorelia, 'it becomes more like home every day.'

Orpen's chief contribution to the school was a series of lectures on anatomy. All pupils had to draw from the model, then 'skin him' and draw the muscles employed in his posture.

As at Liverpool, Augustus stressed the value of observation. He discouraged the use of red chalk because it tended to make a bad drawing look pretty. Every line should carry meaning, nothing be left vague. Students were taught to keep their drawings broad and simple, avoiding too much detail, to use a hard piece of charcoal, to draw with the point and to perfect 'the delicate line'.

Perhaps because it diverted his mind from personal worries, Augustus enjoyed his teaching. The division of his life between town and country seemed to suit him: he never quite had time to grow tired of either. In London he was meeting many people – Gordon Craig, Arthur Symons, Charles Ricketts, Lady Gregory.[104] In March he dined at the house of art collector and critic Hugh Lane, and Lady Gregory noted: 'We went upstairs after dinner to look at the Titian – Philip II, and I speaking to John for the first time said "How can the wonderful brilliancy of that colour keep its freshness so long?" And John said "Ah-h-h".'

From remarkable exchanges such as this, he would return with relief to the freshness of Essex. 'It has been wondrous fine in the country these last few days – a white frost over everything, our humble garden transformed; every leaf and twig rimed with crystal; in the moonlight things sparkled subtly and any old outhouse became the repository of unguessable secrets,' he wrote to Will Rothenstein. 'To-day all changed into the dreariness of mud – the green a morass – the sky all gone, and grey expressionless vapour instead . . . I am bent on etching now and mark me Will I will have a new set out before it is time to think of potato planting. This bald little house is becoming trim and homely and you will not find it inhospitable when you seek its shelter.'

Armchairs and green-baize tables, a light-oak bureau and a cottage piano had made their appearance there. Augustus's pipes and slippers littered the rooms; breeding cages for the canaries were raised upon the walls, each suspended by a single nail – 'they are charming and make an awful mess', the Rani wrote when she came to stay. The little brown bookshelves in the chimney corners were filled with many of the books he was reading in tandem with Wyndham Lewis: books by Baudelaire, Verlaine and Huysmans; also Stendhal, Turgenev and Borrow, Darwin, Balzac, Flaubert and Maupassant, as well as elaborate works on Italian painters, cookbooks, domestic novels and volumes about Wales. The white-papered walls of the drawing-room were covered with rows of Goya and Rembrandt etchings 'and part of a Raphael cartoon in one corner'. But his own work was subject to fitful delays. 'Rumbling home in a bus in a state of blank misery I found myself opposite a perfect queen among women, a Beatrice, a Laura, a Blessed Virgin!' he exclaimed to Will Rothenstein that winter. 'The sight of her loveliness, the depth of her astonished eyes, her movements of a captured nymph dispelled the turgid clouds from my mind, leaving an exquisite calm which became by the time I got to bed a contradiction of almost religious exaltation. Would I could repay my debt to the enchantress! Would that I too were a wizard!'

But he could summon up no wizardry to control his own emotions. Visual experiences affected him as a switch controls an electric light. Without these, he was nothing. Clouds of 'blank misery' rushed in to fill the vacuum. They came and went again, forming and dissolving according to no obvious laws, but massing more densely, taking longer to evaporate. For Dorelia, like a sun beyond the horizon, was out of sight: and he was miserable without her. 'What can have taken place in Relia's [Dorelia's] head', he asked Gwen, 'that she never writes to me?'[105]

He had hoped she would return for a belated house-warming party at Matching Green. 'Of course Dorelia you are coming here,' Ida wrote. 'Gus says you are well worth your keep only as a model – and I can give you plenty to do too. But what would your family say? Gwen would love this place.' Augustus also loved this apple-and-pear country. 'The village seems to me curiously beautiful in a humble way,' he wrote to the two girls, ' – the Green is now full of ponds. At night the little lighted tenements are reflected in the water in a very grave and secret way.'[106]

He longed to finish his portrait of Dorelia. 'Your fat excites me enormously and I am dying to inspect it,' he wrote to her.

'I am itching to resume that glorious counterfeit of you which has already cost me too many sighs. I have a feeling that the solitude of Matching Green will do much towards its perfection. The thought of this picture came upon me with an inward fluttering and I am fond to believe that the problem will now find its final solution in your newly acquired tissue. When are you two going to turn your backs on Pyrenean vistas? How is it you are not going to assist at the warming and consecration of Elm House? I imagine new papers in the ladies smoking room with ribbons and roses on it and new chintz on the chairs and sofa again with roses and ribbons. Ida has commissioned me to paint a silk panel for the piano, and the front door is already a pure and candid white behind which no hypocrisy can harbour.'

He asked to be told of their exploits, but all he received was a package of out-of-date Christmas presents – bonbons and toys for the children, and some cakes for him and Ida. 'Gwen is still in Toulouse I believe,' Ida told Alice (January 1904), 'painting hard – and anxious as soon as her 5 pictures are finished, to go to Paris.' 'They have a dog who is naughty *always*, Gwen says,' she wrote to Winifred the same month. And that, it seems, was all they knew.

Even before the end of the year Augustus had been growing impatient at their prolonged absence. 'The spring days stir my bowels subtly,' he had confided to Sampson. '. . . My palate begins to water to lusty appetites.'[107] The weeks went by; he heard almost nothing, and what news did trickle through tantalized him. 'It was a bloody long time before I heard from you,' he burst out in a letter to Dorelia from the Chelsea Art School.

'Gwendolina says that you get prettier and prettier ... When are you coming back again? You are tired of running about those foreign places I know ... I have stayed up here now for many days, laudably attempting to get things done, but these models, drat them, don't give a man a chance with all this employment. However I am gettting into a weedy condition. My studio is grimey, my bed is unmade, my hair uncombed, my nails unpared, my teeth uncleaned, my boots unblacked, my socks unfresh, my collar unchanged, my hose undarned, my tie unsafety pinned (I wish you'd send me some safety pins, it's not too much to ask) – lastly, my purse unlined.'

It was true that Gwen and Dorelia were by now growing tired of Toulouse. Their room was bare; they bathed, when it was not too frigid, in the river; and subsisted mainly on a diet of old bread, new cheese and middle-aged figs – though there were also evenings over a bottle of wine and a bowl of soup. Gwen, Dorelia observed, was becoming very strict and demanding. She disapproved of the theatre and spoke with disgust of the 'vulgar red lips' of a girl they used as a model. Yet she was not unattractive to men, and never careless of her appearance – 'in fact', Dorelia noted, 'rather vain'.[108] To maintain themselves the two girls made portrait sketches in the cafés for three francs each. The rest of the time Gwen worked at her five paintings, at least four of which were portraits of Dorelia.[109] 'I look forward to a little time in which I can try to express in some way my thoughts,' she wrote to Ursula Tyrwhitt. 'I am hurrying so because we are so tired of Toulouse - we do not want to stay a day longer than necessary – I do nothing but paint – but you know how slowly that gets on – a week is nothing.'

'Is Dorelia much admired ... She must look gorgeous,'[110] Ida had written to Gwen. Gwen's portraits of Dorelia were gorgeous and show someone admired and loved. She was working with layers of paint over a fast-drying base of burnt umber, the technique she had apparently picked up from Ambrose McEvoy. These pictures are less oblique than anything she was to paint over the next thirty-five years in France. Together with her two self-portraits (the first an extraordinarily confident bravura work akin to the portraiture of Augustus, who owned it all his life; the second, which Augustus had described as a 'masterpiece' and which resembles an English governess, owned by Frederick Brown of the Slade), they represent the crown of Gwen John's 'English' period.

By the end of February 1904, Gwen's pictures being for the time being finished, the two girls bundled their possessions on to their backs again, and made their way north in the direction of London. 'What a surprise to hear from you in Paris,' Augustus wrote at the end of March. 'I suppose you willed yourself there . . . I trust you are careful to pose only to good young artists. They must find you two quite épatant [dumbfounding].'[111]

He was overjoyed that they were on their way back. It could not be long now before they arrived in England. 'I have ordered a mighty canvas against your coming,' he wrote to Dorelia, '. . . so better go in for Ju-Jitsu at once, dear, for you will have to fill it spreadeagle wise.' But when Gwen and Dorelia reached Paris, they stopped. The Rani, who was staying at Elm House in the last week of March, describes what the atmosphere was like in a letter to her husband (24 March 1904):

'Mr Augustus's habits are really remarkable. He came on Tuesday with a bad cold and all Wednesday morning he stayed in bed and played the concertina and we had to take turns to provide him with gossip. All afternoon he read Balzac – never moved from his chair – went out for a walk just before supper in piercing cold – read all evening including meals – said "I want to make some more sketches of you" and dropped the subject. All Thursday (yesterday) he stayed in bed and asked for no one – played the most melancholy tunes on his concertina and got up at tea time – very silent, read his book but as good as gold and ready to nail up bird cages or anything – after tea went out – at tea he said "Good God is it Thursday? – I thought of doing that sketch to-day." At 6.15 he appeared with a block and some red chalk and began to draw me as I sat by the fire. I said "I hope you are not doing it unless you feel inclined" to which a growl and "I do feel inclined – that is I shan't know if I do until I've done." He drew furiously by firelight and the last glimmer from the window and fetched a lamp and drew by that until supper – 7 o'clock – three sketches – I didn't ask to see them knowing better – at supper we both took our life in our hands . . . and asked to see the sketches he had done. He produced them . . . each more charming than the other . . . He worked with the tension and rapidity of ten Shannons [Charles Shannon, lithographer and painter] rolled into one – scraped and tore away at it in the most marvellous way and did I should think fully six more of which I only saw one – too exquisitely squirrelly and funny for description but beautiful. They were mostly put in the coal scuttle as he did them but preserved all right. It must have been about 12 when he suddenly stopped, said "thank you for sitting" and went off to bed.'

The next day, 25 March, the Chelsea Art School officially ended its term, and Augustus began to spend more days at Matching Green. 'The school is going on rather dully,' he wrote to Gwen. 'I'm trying to think of some startling innovation to buck people up, like having a family of boys & girls posing in groups now. But we need another studio for portraits.'[112] Time hung heavy. For a while he stayed mild and good, only half-aware, it seemed, of the terrible clamour of children, cats, canaries, chickens and other cattle that reverberated through Elm House.

'Mrs John is beating the baby to sleep which always amuses me and appears to succeed very well – she is so earnest over it that the baby seems to gather that she means business,' the Rani wrote to her husband a few days later (27 March 1904).

'. . . The baby is simply roaring its head off and no one paying any attention – it is in another room . . . You would hate to be here. Mr Augustus looks sometimes at the baby and says "Well darling love – dirty little beast" at the same time. He is the sweetest natured person in the world. It is all indescribable and full of shades and contrasts and the whole is just like his pictures. He looks so beautiful and never takes a bath so far as I can make out. At least I know he is not three minutes dressing but always looks clean. He has cut his hair by the way a good deal – Ida likes it. I haven't made up my mind yet – I think she must have sat on the baby – it has suddenly stopped crying.'

The sweetness slipped out of his nature on learning what Gwen and Dorelia were up to in Paris. They had settled into a single room at 19 boulevard Edgar-Quinet. 'I am getting on with my painting, that makes me happy,' Gwen wrote to Alice Rothenstein. She had been followed from Toulouse by a married woman who, falling under her spell, had abandoned her husband to be with Gwen. But in Paris Gwen, happy now with her painting and with Dorelia, would have nothing to do with the woman. 'She [Gwen] was extremely queer and hard,' Dorelia remembered,[113] 'always attracted to the wrong people, for their beauty alone.' In many ways she was as overpowering as Gus.

In their spare time the two girls made clothes. 'The room is full of pieces of dresses – we are making new dresses,' Gwen told Alice. 'Dorelia's is pink with a skirt of three flounces. She will look lovely in it. Our two painters will want her as a model I am sure when we go home.' They had taken with them the address of the young artist they had met at La Réole who had offered them jobs as models in Paris. The news that agitated Augustus was that Dorelia was posing in the nude – something she had never consented to do for him. What were the two of them up to? 'You tell me not to be alarmed,' Ida had written to Dorelia. ' – I am not – only mystified.' For weeks Gwen had been tantalizing Augustus with bulletins of Dorelia's marvellous efflorescence. 'Dora mustn't grow any prettier or she will burst,' Ida replied that spring. '. . . oh my dears – come back before it's too late . . .'[114]

Suddenly Augustus could stand it no more. 'Why the devil don't I hear from you, you bad fat girl?' he reprimanded Dorelia.

'You sit in the nude for those devilish foreign people, but you do not want to sit for me when I asked you, wicked little bloody harlot ['lũbni'] that you are. You exhibit your naked fat body for money, not for love. So much for you! How much do you show them for a franc? I am sorry that I never offered to give you a shilling or two for a look at your minj [middle part]. That was all you were waiting for. The devil knows I might have bought the minj and love together. I am sorry that I was so foolish to love you. Well if you are not a whore, truly tell me why not. Gustavus.'

Dorelia's reply, when it arrived, was little more than a scribble. In the heat of the moment, Augustus had forgotten to enclose his usual word-list, so much of his Romany invective had gone astray. Certain phrases in his letter puzzled Dorelia. What, for example, did *lũbni* mean? But Augustus already felt rather ashamed of his outburst and refused to answer. All this letter-writing was getting him nowhere. He needed to *see* Dorelia. It was eight months since he had seen her. What was he to do? It was Ida who decided. 'Paris is quite near,' she reminded him. She would have liked to go herself, but it was better that he go – he could see the show of Primitives there at the same time. The idea was very appealing. 'Do you see any Géricaults?' he asked Gwen. 'He was a very wonderful man and liked to use plenty of paint. Courbet also is a man that flies to my head when I think of France. I suppose there are no wonderful young painters in Paris . . . I want to see you and the *Primitiffs* . . . you and that pretty slut Dorelia, she who is too lazy to answer my frequent gracious and affectionate letters.'[115]

As soon as Ida had spoken, Augustus reacted. He was like a dynamo – one that needed someone else to turn the switch before it burst into life. A week before he came to Paris, Gwen had written to Alice Rothenstein: 'We are getting homesick I think, we are always talking of beautiful places we know of beyond the suburbs of London and Fitzroy St and Howland St seem to me more than ever charming and interesting.' They would soon, she added, be coming home.

This was their intention shortly before Augustus turned up in Paris in the second week of May. But afterwards they did something different. That another man might take his place in Dorelia's life had not seriously occurred to Augustus. But this was what was happening in Paris while he lay lugubriously playing the concertina at Matching Green. His rival seems to have been a young artist – half artist and half farmer – possibly the man she and Gwen had met at La Réole. His name was Leonard, and from Dorelia's point of view he had some advantages over Augustus: he was not married; and life with him, while not contradicting her sense of destiny, might involve a farming background, which appealed to her.

Augustus arrived in Paris and a few days later Dorelia left boulevard Edgar-Quinet – not with Augustus back to England, but to Belgium with Leonard. She fled with him secretly, telling no one, leaving no address. She had gone, they discovered, to Bruges, was living with Leonard and for the time being could only be reached through a poste restante. She would stay with him three months – or a lifetime: it depended how things worked out. It was, she afterwards remarked, 'one of my two discreditable episodes'.[116]

Exasperated, agitated, almost beside himself, Gus hung on in Paris, seeing Gwen, doing nothing. He was reduced once more to writing letters – not in prose this time, but page after page of poems, ballads and sonnets, odd rhymes running in his head which he stored up and subsequently sent Dorelia.

> But for the woman I hold in my heart,
> Whose body is a flame, whose soul a flower,
> Whose smile beguiled me in the wood, the smart
> Of kisses of her red lips every hour
> Branding me lover anew, is she to be,
> Being my Mistress, my Fatality?

In the stream of his passion there are already odd pebbles of pedantry. At one point, he interrupts an anguished appeal to instruct Dorelia that 'the word "ardent" in the first sonnet I sent you should be changed to "nodding". Kindly make that correction.'*

So numerous were these poems that there seems to have been one left over for Ida who, he now learnt, was pregnant again. Possibly on Gwen's advice, he appears to have written little but verse to Dorelia at her poste restante. But to Ida he explained all that was happening, and so did Gwen. 'Darling Gwen', Ida answered, 'Your letter was such a comfort and made things so much simpler. I get brooding here. I am inclined to agree that D[orelia] will turn up one day & oh how happy we might be.'[117]

Augustus's letters revealed how Gwen herself was suffering over Dorelia's disappearance. 'Gussie tells me you do not eat,' Ida wrote. 'Little girl what is the matter? Poor little thing, it is really hardest on you that she went. It was a *shame*. Did you over-drive her? I know you are a beauty

---

* She did.

once you start. But you are worth devoting yourself to, & she should not have given up.'[118]

Upon Ida's reaction the whole course of their collective future hung. She found herself longing for Dorelia to come back. The last weeks at Matching Green had been miserable. She felt that she had even lost the ability of sitting to Augustus, and with it her last connection with art. Perhaps it was a temporary incapacity due to her new pregnancy but, she told Gwen, 'I would rather lose a child than the power of sitting.' For it *was* a power, this gift of inspiring painting, and Ida felt critical of Dorelia for abandoning it voluntarily, however difficult Gus and Gwen might be.

Ida herself had no intention of giving up. If Dorelia was added to their household, and Gwen herself returned, they could control these Johns, even in overdrive. Her confidence reaching a state of exaltation, she sent Gus and Gwen two letters that were dramatically to alter the course of events.

It was Gwen who put herself in charge of these events with a letter to Dorelia. 'Dorelia, something has happened which takes my breath away so beautiful it is,' she began. 'Ida wants you to go to Gussy – not only wants it but desires it passionately. She has written to him and to me. She says "She [Dorelia] is ours and she knows it. By God I will haunt her till she comes back."

'She also said to Gussy, "I have discovered I love you and what you want I want passionately. She, Dorelia, shall have pleasure with you eh?" She said much more but you understand what she means.

Gus loves you in a much more noble way than you may think – he will not ask you now because he says perhaps you are happy with your artist and because of your worldly welfare – but he only says that last – because he knows you – we know you too and we do ask.

You are necessary for his development and for Ida's, and he is necessary for yours – I have known that a long time – but I did not know how much. Dorelia you know I love you, you do not know how much. I should think it the greatest crime to take with intention anyone's happiness away even for a little time – it is to me the only thing that would matter.

. . . I know of course from one point of view you will have to be brave and unselfish – but I have faith in you. Ida's example makes me feel that some day I shall be unselfish too.

I would not write this if I knew you have no affection for Gussy. You are his aren't you?

You might say I write this because I love you all – if you were strangers to me, I would try to write in the same way so much I feel in my heart that it [is] right what I say, and good.

I am sorry for Leonard, but he has had his happiness for a time what more can he expect? We do not expect more. And all the future is yours to do what you like. Do not think these are my thoughts only – they are my instincts and inspired by whatever we have in us divine. I know what I write is for the best, more than I have ever known anything. If you are perplexed, trust me. . . . Gussy is going home to-night. Come by the first train to me. I shall be at the gare to meet you. When you are here you will know what to do . . .

Do not put it off a minute simply because I shall then think you have not understood this letter – that it has not conveyed the truth to you. I fear that, because I know how weak words are sometimes – and yet it would be strange if the truth is not apparent here in every line.

You will get this to-morrow morning perhaps – I shall be in the evening at the gare du nord. I would not say goodbye to Leonard. Your Gwen.'[119]

It was not simply that Gwen wanted Dorelia to return to Gus, but that she believed Dorelia belonged to the John tribe and that by running away she had contradicted her nature. Her letter, and the others she wrote over this period, are remarkable for their fundamentalist attitude to Dorelia's future. Hers was no ordinary religion, it was the religion of love for art's sake. Were not art and religious experience much the same thing? Was not Dorelia an idol in the Temple of Art, a rare *femme inspiratrice*?

But it is Gwen's tone of didactic certainty that is so remarkable. The other side of this moral conviction was a callousness that shows itself in her attitude to Leonard – 'what more can he expect?'

Gwen took over and organized everything. Augustus's absence from the battlefield of negotiations avoided any hint of a sexual tug-of-war, of a man-versus-man contest. Nor was Gwen acting for herself. Was she not surrendering Dorelia to Gus and Ida?

If Dorelia was subject to anyone's will, it must have been Gwen's, whose hard queer intimate company she had kept over the last eight months, and who, alone of all the John tribe, knew Leonard. The timing of her first letter, too, was good: no appeal until Ida's sanction had been obtained. Finally, Gwen called upon the one strain stronger than any other in Dorelia's character, one that Gwen understood well: her sense of destiny. There was only one weakness in Gwen's position, and that was inevitable: while she could only send 'weak words' on pieces of paper, Leonard was actually with Dorelia. It was to be her words against his presence. But what she could do to offset this disadvantage she did, recommending Dorelia to tell Leonard nothing, to leave him in the same secret way as she had left Paris. For this too was in Dorelia's character, and to have a weakness recommended as one's duty can be irresistible.

When Gwen went to the Gare du Nord the following evening to meet her, Dorelia was not there. But she had sent a letter. To go back, she wrote, would be to curtail her freedom. With Leonard she was free of the overwhelming passions of Gus and Gwen, who together so excited and exhausted her. 'God, I'm tired of being weak, of depending on people, of being dragged this way & that by my feelings, of listening to everybody but myself. I must be free – *I will be.* I wonder if you will understand . . . I am afraid you will not understand. Gussie will perhaps, he knows me, how I am.'[120]

Like the other Gwen, Gwen Salmond, who was soon to liberate Matthew Smith from nervous paralysis and fill him with confidence in his artistic talent, Dorelia believed in her possession of a vicarious ability that was the special gift of some women, perhaps even some men. She had served Gwen John, but her relationship with Augustus entangled her in Ida's peculiar destiny. Besides, she did not want to be a slave to this gift, and sensed the danger of her love for Gus and Gwen – that it would devour and damage others. 'You must know that I love you all – I cannot say how much,' she replied to Gwen. 'You say I must be unselfish and brave. I must, but not in the way you mean . . .

'Whatever I do there must be something false; let me choose the least false, the most natural, let me? If I loved Gussie & you & Ida twenty times more – though I cannot love you more than I do – I would not come back . . . I see how wonderful it would be – it cannot be.'

All this, Dorelia felt, 'must sound horrible to you but I must write it'. It was essential that she resist the potent spell of these Johns. Gwen had written her letter in 'an ecstasy': it was not reasonable; it was not practicable. Whatever happened, she concluded, Gwen must not seek her out in Bruges: 'it would be useless.'[121]

If Gwen had not won as easily as she appears to have expected, she already sensed victory. Dorelia had asked for her permission, and she refused to give it. In her answer she brushed aside all these objections. She understood Dorelia's position, Dorelia did not understand hers. She returned to the attack, reiterating and elaborating her previous arguments. 'I must speak plainly for you to know everything before you choose. Leonard cannot help you, he would have to know Gussie for that and Ida and you a long, long time, he never could understand unless he was our brother or a great genius.

'Strength and weakness, selfishness and unselfishness are only words – our work in life was to develop ourselves and so fulfil our destiny. And when we do this we are of use in the world, then *only* can we help our friends and develop them. I *know* that Gussie and Ida are more parts of you than Leonard is for ever. When you leave him you will perhaps make a great character of him – if he has faith in you that you are acting according to your truest self – and what good could you do him if he had no faith in you – by being always with him? But faith or no faith he would know some day the truth – and that is the highest good that can happen to us. To 'wholly develop' a man is nonsense – all events help to do that. I know as certainly as the day follows the night that you would develop him and all your friends as far as one human being can another by *being yourself. That is what you have to think of,* Dorelia. To do this is hard – that is what I meant by saying you must be brave and strong. I am sorry for people who suffer but that is how we learn all we know nearly – and that is the great happiness – knowledge of the truth!

You know you are Gussy's as well as I do. Did you do wisely in going away like that without telling him? Do you dare spend a week with him or a day, or a few hours? Forgive me for speaking like this darling Dorelia – I only want to help you to know yourself. I love you so much that if I never saw you again and knew you were happy I should be happy too . . . It makes it simple to know all we have to do is to be true to the feelings that have been ours longest and most consistently.'[122]

While Gwen was writing this to Dorelia, Leonard had posted an answer to her first letter which, disobeying Gwen's instructions, Dorelia had shown him. 'Leonard has written to you too,' Dorelia informed Gwen, ' – do not think he has influenced me.' Written in halting English, by now partly indecipherable, it is couched as a rebuke yet struggles to maintain a sense of fairness in grappling with Gwen's philosophy:

'Dear Miss John,

Dorelia got your letter to-day and showed it to me. Your letter forces me to explain to you several things you forgot, as well as I can do.

Of course you don't know me neither do you know my sentiments to Dor; but this is the other side of the facts, at which you did not like to look, anyway it exists and it is as true as your words, if I allow myself to talk a little bit of myself.

You say L. has had his happiness for a time, what more can he expect? Do you really think . . . that Dorelia's feelings are small enough to love a man like this? People like me don't love often and a woman like Dorelia will not pass my way again; you would better understand, if you would know my life.

Your letter is full of love, the love of a woman for another one, now imagine mine if you can. I am no ordinary man as you may think, who loves a girl because she is beautiful or whatever. I tell you and you are Dory's friend so you must understand it, I am an artist and cannot live without her and I will not live without her – I think this is clear. Very right if you say "it is the greatest crime to take with intention anyone's happiness". You might say as you did I had my hapiness. Do you think hapiness is a thing that you take like café after dinner, a thing that you enjoy a few times and something you can get sick of? Not my hapiness by God; I suffered enough before and I don't let escape something from me that I created myself with all my love and all my strength. Well, all those words are only an answer to yours, but something else that you forgot.

We cannot force the fate to go our ways, fate forces us . . .

That's all I have to tell you, compare now my fate with that of John and his family perhaps you will see where it is heavier. My words seem hard to you, but they are the expression of my feelings as well as I can say it. I think it is not necessary to talk about Dorelias feelings and thoughts. I did *not* tell her what to do, I told her she might do what she thinks right and naturel, but remember your words of the crime and think that there are greater crimes which are against the rules of nature.

If you want wright to me your thoughts about everything and dont get mad against me, you must see that there is no world that [is] absolutely right.'[123]

Wisely Gwen did not accept this invitation to write to Leonard. She was not interested in a discussion of 'thoughts about everything', but in outcomes; not in fairness, but rightness. Leonard's letter arrived in Paris before Gwen had posted her second letter to Dorelia, so she slipped into the envelope an extra pitiless page deflecting his arguments to her own ends. What he had written disappointed her, she claimed, and made her 'more certain if certainty can be more certain of everything I have told you'. Leonard's love was, after all, nothing better than possessiveness. She had supposed it to have been finer – perhaps he'd climb to better things in time, given the adversity. He loved her of course, no one denied that. But his love was selfish, like that of the Pebble of the brook in Blake's *The Clod and the Pebble*, while Augustus's, 'much more noble', resembled the little Clod of Clay's.[124] For, whatever his faults, Augustus was an artist; while Leonard was still a part of the bourgeoisie.

'I have just read Leonard's letter. In self-justification I must answer a few things to you. I don't know what he thinks I mean – he does not understand certainly . . . He says "you are not free anymore you are his,

his body and soul". He says there are greater crimes than breaking another's happiness that is to do things against the rules of nature.

He limits the laws of nature. You are bound to those whom you are in sympathy by laws much stronger than the most apparent ones. The laws of nature are infinite and some are so delicate they have no names but they are strong. We are more than intellectual and animal beings we are spiritual also. Men don't know this so well as women, and I am older than Leonard.

He said "I *could* not live without her and *will not* live without her – this is clear." Well a man who talks like that ought to be left to walk and stand and work alone – by every woman. Only when he can will he do good work.'[125]

Gwen's shock tactics exploded powerful doubts within Dorelia. And to Gwen's philosophy were now added Augustus's poetry, and letters of entreaty from Ida. Ida had already dispatched Augustus back to the front line of combat in Paris so that, when the critical moment came, he could advance upon Bruges with all haste. 'Aurevoir,' she wrote to him, 'and don't come here again alone. Mrs Dorel Harem must be with you.'

From Dorelia herself little or nothing was heard. She was floundering, quietly, hopelessly and without comment. Then, suddenly, she capitulated. 'I have given in and am going back with Gus soon,' she wrote to Gwen. How and when she was going back were still uncertain; hers was a conditional surrender of which no one quite knew the conditions. It was now that Augustus decided to move from France into Belgium, while from further back, the John artillery still kept up its hail of letters. Ida was insistent that Dorelia should return, not simply to England, but to Elm House itself. The three of them must live together in Augustus's 'wonderful concubinage'. This would be infinitely preferable to a dreary segregation, with its periodic loneliness, dullness, incompleteness – almost respectability. If Dorelia were elsewhere, Ida could never be sure what Augustus would do. This at least was part of her reason for welcoming Dorelia into the home. But the prospect of it also curiously excited her. She had begun to identify her feelings for Dorelia with Gwen's, and to suspect that in some extraordinary way she loved her too. 'Darling Dorel,' she wrote:

'Please do not forget that you are coming back – or get spirited away before – as I should certainly hang myself in an apple tree. Whenever I write to you I think you will be annoyed or bored – I seem to have written so often and said the same thing. But for the last time O my honey let me say it – I *crave* for you to come here. I don't expect you will and I

don't want you to if – well if you don't. But I do want you to understand
it is all I want. I now feel incomplete and thirsty without you. I don't
know why – and in all probability I shall have to continue so – as of
course it will probably be impractical or something and naturally there
are your people – and Gus will want you to be in town.

But I want you to know how it is Mrs Harem – only you needn't come
for 10 days as I am curing freckles on my face and shall be hideous until
I blossom out afresh.

I heard from Gwen "Dorelia writes she has given in". Were you then
holding out against Gus, you little bitch? You are a mystery, but you are
ours. I don't know if I love you for your own sake or for his. Aurevoir –
I wish I could help that Leonard. It is so sad.'

It seems probable that Leonard still did not know what was happening.
Dorelia kept everything secret – in a sense even from herself. She put
herself in the path of the greatest current of energy, and let events take
their course. Augustus by this time had reached Antwerp where he halted,
expecting some news. 'I am getting to know every stone of Antwerp,' he
complained.

'. . . The Devil keeps you away from me Ardor McNeill. Sometimes I talk
to you while walking along and laugh so heartily all the people stare. All
night I have strange dreams . . . You have only written once and how
many letters I have sent you. You make me feel like Jesus Christ sometimes.
I sit and sip and call for paper and ink . . . I think of the portrait I shall
paint of you – there is a painting here by Rembrandt of little Saskia – a
wondrous work – it is the repository of the inmost secret in the heart of
a great artist. It is like the Cathedral here only more intimate more
personal more subtle. In it is the principle of man's love of woman. You
call me pirino – beloved, but do you love me enough . . . Beloved Beloved
your hands are laid on my head and everything fades . . . Ardor thou
sylph with a secret for me let me hear you breathe. Gustavus.'[126]

He kept on writing letters – what else could he do? But 'have you taken
the trouble to go to the Post Office for them?' he asked. Once, to his
dismay, he forgot to go to the post office himself and found his letter still
in his pocket two days later – then posted it out of sequence. But his
outpourings had no sequence. They all said the same thing. 'Why did you
desert me before – why, I cannot think. Don't trouble to find an impossible
answer. If anyone can understand you I can. Love, I know you – Know
me. Know me.'[127]

Dorelia did not trouble to find an answer. In a sense Augustus's letters were complete in themselves. During the whole of this episode while Gwen, Ida and Gus were discharging their emotions on to paper, Dorelia confined herself to little more than the odd postcard – a time, a place, a piece of luggage, some weather, part of a dream, sometimes simply nothing at all but the picture on one side, her signature on the other. Augustus dashed from place to place – Antwerp, Brussels, Ghent – endeavouring to catch these elusive cards, endeavouring to discover in them some clue as to what was going on. 'I hope you haven't sent word to Antwerp now that I have left,' he wrote from Ghent. But how would he know without travelling back to Antwerp?

It appears that Dorelia had consented to see him, but only outside Bruges. 'I can come then on Tuesday morning?' he asked, perplexed, exasperated. 'Why come here, this isn't the way home, at least not the shortest. Beloved tell me where to find you – but if you can come here before *come in the name of all the Gods* – wait for me here opposite the station.'[128] They met, almost by accident it seemed, certainly by good luck, but even now nothing was fixed. Dorelia needed more time: a week. Allowing her to return was a torture to Augustus. 'What am I to do these last days?' he demanded. She did not reply. 'The time is nearly up – Ardor,' he wrote again. 'Gand [the French spelling of Ghent] is very near Bruges. I am to rejoin you on Tuesday morning. So be it.'[129]

They set off on their return journey from Bruges station on 1 August 1904. They were to travel, not via Paris, but direct to London. Before leaving, Augustus wrote to Gwen arranging for Dorelia's belongings in the boulevard Edgar-Quinet to be sent to the studio in Flood Street. On the platform, waiting for their train, Dorelia also wrote to Gwen. Her postcard reads: 'How is the cat? Dorelia.'[130]

Whether Leonard understood, until after she left, that Dorelia had 'given in' and chosen Augustus, is unclear. He returned to Paris, imagining perhaps he was following her. But he only saw Gwen, who told him nothing. His name does not appear in their correspondence again: except once at the end of the summer. 'Leonard came up to me a few days ago,' Gwen wrote to Dorelia. 'I should write him a nice letter if I were you. He will get very ill otherwise I think.'[131] After this he vanishes, his identity lost, with the unsettling echo of his words to Gwen: 'I will not live without her.'

Gwen's letter to Dorelia passes on to details of a skirt Dorelia has promised to make for her and a request for some more 'earrings like Gussie's' which she has lost. Also there is news of four 'Toulousians with umbrellas' whom they had met on their uncompleted walk to Rome. They had turned up in Paris and Gwen had been able to take them to Rodin's studio, 'a great favour, as he does not see students now.' As a result, they were growing 'so enthusiastic that they are almost unintelligible'.

*

'Why not call on Rodin?' Augustus had asked Gwen on hearing at the end of March that she and Dorelia had reached Paris. 'He loves English young ladies.'[132]

While Dorelia was at Leonard's Paris studio, Gwen had taken Gus's advice and gone to see Rodin. 'I am at Rodin's nearly every day now,'[133] she informed Ursula Tyrwhitt a little later. The extraordinary assurance of her letters to Dorelia in Bruges and her resolute attitude to Leonard may well have sprung from her elation over Rodin. Dorelia had observed that she had written in an 'ecstasy' and though she later denied this ('I haven't been in one for ages'), it was certainly true.

Auguste Rodin was sixty-three when they became lovers that summer, more than six years older than Gwen's father. For a decade he would be everything to her that her father had not been and everything that she had failed to find in Ambrose McEvoy. She became his model, his pupil, his mistress, his little girl. The loving care over her work and welfare that Edwin John had never shown, and Augustus only intermittently ('I must urge you to eat generously . . . Do do some drawings of nudes. Goodbye and a kiss from Gustavus'),[134] was now assumed by Rodin, who found himself urging her to eat, wash, work, brush her hair, tidy her room; who made timetables for her and ('wasn't it kind of him?' Gwen asked Ursula Tyrwhitt) paid for the rent of her new lodgings. She was in such an excited state, she could not keep it wholly secret. Gus watched what was happening with a mixture of admiration, envy and concern. 'How delightful to have a drawing given you by Rodin – does he give all his sitters drawings?' he asked on arriving back at Matching Green. ' . . . When you have exhausted Rodin's resources let me know.'[135]

Augustus felt grateful to Gwen for all she had done to reclaim Dorelia. He understood that Rodin might develop his sister's talent as she believed Dorelia would develop his – indeed, this was the sort of master-and-student arrangement from which he himself would have liked to benefit. 'Give my homage to dear master Rodin. I salute him and wish I could serve him as you do,' he wrote to Gwen that autumn. ' . . . You are evidently becoming indispensable to Auguste Rodin. It must indeed be a pleasure to be of service to such a man.'[136]

It was a startling coincidence, this fact that Rodin's Christian name should be the same as his own. Gwen would use episodes from their adolescence to stir Rodin's sympathy and protection. 'J'étais pensant avant de dormir de mon frère,' she wrote to him, ' . . . et comment j'étais misérable en Angleterre.'[137] Sometimes, when she waited for Rodin and he did not come, morbid dreams would rise from her childhood involving Gus's 'méchanceté' (wickedness). 'I torment myself . . . because of my brother – and if I had seen my *Maitre* these last few days I wouldn't have had these feelings, for they are feelings rather than thoughts,' she noted in a draft letter for Rodin. '. . . I suffered a long time ago because of him [Augustus], it's like certain illnesses which recur in time. When they return I believe that my brother is my evil Genius and that he will do me harm – perhaps, without wishing to – if I do not avoid him . . .'[138]

Though Augustus sincerely wished Gwen well, she did not want to accept money from him. She wanted to be free, rather than caught up, as her sister Winifred found herself in relation to Thornton. All four of them experienced great difficulties forming loving relationships outside the family. Gwen had lent Winifred some money the previous year when she joined Thornton in North America, and Winifred had recently written to her about a young man called Philip. 'Thornton must guess Philip is in love with me & I really must tell him soon. I keep putting it off. I hate to tell him. I'd rather tell Papa a thing like that.'[139] A little later, when Philip left and Paul arrived, it was the same story ('he said he wished it was Papa he had to tell instead of Thornton').[140] Eventually Paul disappeared and 'I don't want to ever "fall in love again",' Winifred informed Gwen. 'Don't be soft on the subject of R[odin] be firm – sacrifice all to work. I am going to . . .' Thornton, she added, was 'rather lonely'.[141]

Gwen's love for Rodin – like Gus's for Ida and Dorelia, and Winifred's marriage later on to one of her violin pupils – was part of the intimacy of her work. She elected him her good genius, learning from him how to concentrate her powers of observation by the repetition of images and how to simplify her work with strong contours. She had 'un corps admirable', Rodin told her, and it was appropriate that he should use her as a model for his unfinished monument to Whistler. For Gwen's painting technique in France, almost the opposite of her English work, relied on her own version of what she had learnt at the Académie Carmen about Whistler's preparation of paint mixtures.

'Je vous aime et je vous désire heureuse,'[142] Rodin assured Gwen. In London she had been 'shy as a sheep'; in Paris she grew, in Augustus's words, 'amorous and proud'. The Jane Eyre governess of her self-portrait was replaced by a rather brazen female speaking of 'things I never thought of before'.[143] Under Rodin's spell she spent hours on her appearance, buying new clothes, pinching her breasts to ensure they did not grow smaller, and commanding Rodin to save his energy for their next lovemaking.

But their lovemaking, which rejuvenated her, aged him. Her passion, like that of Augustus, was a compulsive and demanding force that grew from the aridity of their upbringing. 'Love is my illness,' Gwen told Rodin, 'and there is no cure till you come.'[144] She wore him out with her obsession, haunting the café opposite his studio, camping in the bushes outside his fence at night, and writing hundreds of adoring letters in a handwriting that became pathetically schoolgirlish. 'Vous avez de grandes facultés de sentir et de penser,' he replied. 'Courage, petite amie, moi je suis si fatigué et vieux . . . mais j'aime votre petit coeur si devoué, patience et pas de violence.'[145]

'I don't think we change but we disappear sometimes,'[146] Gwen was to tell Michel Salaman. Before meeting Rodin she had confessed to getting rather homesick for London. 'We shall be going home in the Autumn I think if not before,' she had written earlier in the year to Alice Rothenstein. Rodin changed her plans. She anchored herself in Paris which became her new home, a home in exile, and so escaped from 'not only the overpowering influence of Augustus', wrote Mary Taubman, 'but also from the curiously vapid atmosphere of the English art world . . .'[147]

*

'Maintenant il faut travailler un peu,'[148] Augustus wrote to Gwen after arriving back in England with Dorelia. He had been inspired by the precision and simplicity of L'Exposition des Primitifs Français he had seen at the Palais du Louvre and Bibliothèque Nationale – 'a magnificent exhibition', Gwen had called it. 'I've been leading a reckless life in the Louvre, & so am on the brink of ruin,'[149] she told Dorelia. Augustus felt similarly – in his fashion. 'Oh yes I am going to do the Louvre,' he had written to Gwen, 'but I must have air air air! Studios are sickening.'[150]

From some letters he wrote to Charles Rutherston, it seems that in the autumn of 1904 Augustus took a studio on the other side of the King's Road from the Chelsea Art School – No. 4 Garden Studios in Manresa Road. Dorelia spent some of her time there ('Dorelia is practising Chopin in the Studio in London') and some time at Elm House, as Ida had desired. 'They are putting up a hen run in the garden here,' Ida wrote to welcome the returning couple. '. . . The hammock is up and there are some canvas chairs and we are becoming quite like a "country house" – and now the rain has come.'

Ida was anxious for Gwen to 'come & pay us a little visit & go back again', but instead of Gwen, Edwin John arrived. He had been searching Paris for Gwen, but she had not sent him her new address. He became convinced she was back in England. 'Father called yesterday & received a great shock on not finding you here,' Augustus notified Gwen that September. 'He suspected some dark plot but I assured him there was none, impossible as it appeared. He is a strange unique little man, all silver pink & black. He is unparalleled in simplicity and only needs a good deal more of another sort to be quite perfect.'[151] Having inspected the household in Dorelia's absence, Edwin reported to Winifred that the two boys, David and Caspar, 'are completely spoilt by over indulgence', and then returned to Wales.

Ida had welcomed Gus and Dorelia at Matching Green. 'Gus came back so well from Paris,' she wrote to Gwen. '. . . It goes without saying he loves Dorelia – but then he always did.'[152] All of them appeared happy. Augustus's happiness shines through the letters he wrote that late summer. 'The country here is like a new America to discover every evening on a walk at sundown,' he wrote to Gwen on 29 August. 'Sometimes I come to the conclusion that nothing could be near so beautiful as our poultry run – it seems so marvellous, so removed from human interestedness, so remote & magical – the fowls, carrying with them ever the stigma of the Orient, move about their concerns under the slanting golden rays of the sun and are golden & soft & dappled under the gilded green of alders. I am painting of course. Dorelia's face is a mystery – just like others perhaps.'[153]

But Dorelia's mysteriousness was sometimes provoking. 'You keep your movements & impressions enveloped in mystery – why?' Gwen demanded that August. '. . . *What is London like after France?* & how do you like being in the bosom of your family?'[154] Those were complicated, almost impossible, questions. Ida had desired Dorelia to come back, but now that she was back, clouds of anxiety were already forming. After the strain of the past months, Ida felt exhausted. That autumn she seems to have come near a breakdown. 'Ida has her moments of défaillance [weakness],' Augustus admitted to Gwen, 'but the burden she carries [her pregnancy] accounts for them.'[155] Worried by the tone of Ida's letters, and perhaps curious about Dorelia too, Gwen did come over to Matching Green for three days in September.

But what Ida really wanted was to come out and join Gwen in Paris – as Gwen Salmond had done in July, and Ursula Tyrwhitt was planning to do later in the year. 'How I wish I were with you,' she wrote to Gwen. 'Aurevoir my darling.'[156] She seemed to be saying goodbye to freedom; to be cutting herself off from the life Dorelia enjoyed with Gus in London and Gwen in Paris. 'You have Rodin & work & streets & museums,' she told Gwen. '. . . The children are back tomorrow & nous voilà pour tout l'hiver. Cela me donne des frissons d'ennui.'[157]

This need to cut loose for a time ran strongly in Ida. 'Matching Green seems a grave now, but I live in hope of a resurrection.'[158] Eventually she put the question to Gus. Should she go to Paris? He didn't say yes and he didn't say no. He didn't say that he thought she had gone slightly mad. So she pressed him as to what he would truly prefer, and he said stay, '& so I could not come, could I?' Ida explained to Gwen.

There were reasons for staying. She was seven-and-a-half months pregnant; one of the children was sick; and there was a portrait of her that Augustus promised urgently to finish. He had not tried to forbid her going. It seemed to him 'the only course to take', and she reluctantly agreed. But 'I know I shall regret not coming many times unless I get very strong,'[159] Ida confided to Gwen.

What Augustus recognized was that he and Dorelia must be specially attentive to Ida during these final weeks of her pregnancy. To 'preserve her mental equilibrium', they took her for 'frequent diversions' up to London and 'it is nicer here now,' she admitted to Gwen. '. . . We stay in Gus's new studio . . . Dorelia & Gus are very kind & when I do not think it is compassion I am happy enough.' Back at Matching Green she reflected that she would probably manage to get through this period of instability 'if I always remember he *does* want me here – it is only when I think he doesn't it becomes unbearable.'[160]

And it was true he did want her there. After the baby was born, he assured her, she could buzz off to Paris, though really she doubted if 'I shall be well able to leave it'. Meanwhile he went on treating her to 'little journeys to London' where she could help Dorelia make curtains for his studio, and taking her back to their gypsy garden at Matching Green where the hens continued 'moving among medicine bottles, and broken pots and pans, crockery, meat cans, old boots and ancient dirt and indescribable debris – the uncatalogued tales of a human abode'.[161]

So this first crisis evaporated. Augustus looked, and saw that all was good. 'Never have the beauties of the outer world moved me as of late,' he wrote to Will Rothenstein. '. . . I have worked at my women painfully, laboriously, with alternations of achievement and failure, impotence and power – you know the grinding see-saw – under a studio light, cold, informal, meaningless – a studio – what is it? a habitation – no – not even a *cowshed* – 'tis a box wherein miserable painters hide themselves and shut the door on nature. I have imprisoned myself in my particular dungeon all day to-day for example – on my sitters' faces naught but the shifting light of reminiscence and that narrowed and distorted . . .'[162]

This, until too late, was to be Gwen's route rather than his own: the shutting away of her impatience, the search for strange form, the 'narrow talent, sharpened as a pencil',[163] as Sylvia Townsend Warner described it. 'What I don't like is to see people and much light,'[164] Gwen was to tell Ursula Tyrwhitt. Augustus needed people and light. 'This evening at sundown I escaped at last to the open, to the free air of space, where things have their proportion and place and are articulate,' he continued his letter to Will Rothenstein, ' – so by the roadside I came upon my women and my barking dog seated on the dark grass in the dusk, and sitting with them I was aware of spirits present – old spirits, ancient, memorable, familiar spirits, consulted in boyhood – insulted in manhood – bright, good, clear, beneficent spirits, ever-loving and loved spirits of Beauty and Truth and Mystery. And so we are going for a picnic to-morrow – and I will make sketches, God-willing. I wish we might never come back to dust-heap-making again. The call of the road is on me. Why do we load ourselves with the chains of commodities when the trees live rent free, and the river pays no toll?'

So with ominous foreboding, he signs his letter: 'Yours with the Unrest of Ahasuerus in his bones, "John".'

FOUR

Men Must Play and Women Weep

I

KEEPING UP THE GAME

'A little restraint would not be a bad thing in my friends I'm thinking.'

Augustus John to Michel Salaman (n.d. [1905])

'My baby is getting so heavy I do not know how I shall bear him (or them) by October,' Ida had written to Alice Rothenstein (August 1904). 'The two outside are splendid and well,' she added, but 'I am such a size I think I am going to have a litter instead of the usual.'

The usual ('much to our bewilderment'), another boy of heroic proportions – he weighed 9 pounds at birth – eventually called Robin (or Robyn) or even for a short time 'Paganini, the great future musician', was born at Elm House on 23 October. He was so punctual that everyone was taken by surprise. 'I had to race across the green for the wise woman,' Augustus told Margaret Sampson. 'The doctor, with truly professional promptitude, arrived in his express 16 horse motor car immediately after the event was successfully accomplished.' Despite these emergencies 'there was less fuss than usually accompanies the advent of an ordinary hen's egg,' he assured the Rani. '. . . Of course it's staggering to be confronted with a boy after all our prayers for a girl. Ida started the life of Frederick the Great last night which I think must have determined the sex of the infant. It was very rash . . . Ida has just remarked "Tell her she can have it if she likes." '

The unconventionality of her married life distanced Ida from her family and cut her off from a number of her friends. She felt held down by her 'blundering career', like 'a bird sitting on its eggs'.

'I have arrived at the point of eating toasted cheese and stout for supper,' she darkly confessed to the Rani. 'It is a horrible thing to do, but shows to what a pitch animal spirits can arrive in this country.' It was not especially for love, she explained, that 'I am hungry and thirsty, but for ethics and life and rainbows and colours – butterflies and shimmering seas and human intercourse'. She prized her friends, even when they did

166

not approve of her Matching Green *ménage*. 'As you know,' she wrote to Will Rothenstein, 'the communicable part of my life is very narrow, and I have nothing to tell you about it. As to the other, you must understand that without telling or you would never count me one of your "dearest of friends" – a privilege of which I am only worthy in my most silent moments.'

Ida did take some pleasure in her children. Robin was 'most beautiful [and] sleeps for hours', she wrote to Winifred. 'He is no trouble. If David had been like that how happy we should have been. But there, poor Davy was the first – & I did not know anything.' Now that she knew more and had 'such a good little nurse for them', she could enjoy watching David and Caspar scrambling in and out of the pram 'pretending to be bears or monkeys'. They were both 'much entertained' by the mysterious new baby. 'I am nursing him & hope to keep on,' Ida told Winifred. 'He is thriving . . .'[1]

The new baby delighted them all. 'He has Gus's eyes,' Ida reported, '. . a large long nose turned down at the end . . . my mouth & upper lip [and] he is decidedly pretty.' Whenever the nurse was away, Dorelia would come and help, shining the furniture with beeswax and turpentine, wheeling the boys out in their overcrowded pram, clearing the debris after a gas explosion. 'Dorelia is here & so angelic,' Ida wrote to Gwen in the first week of November, '. . . she does so much . . . It is a glorious day & the dogs are barking & the rooks cawing. I shall be getting up about Saturday I think. I feel very well . . . How domestic we all are, oh Lord.'[2]

All the domestic news she felt able to communicate to her family was packed into a letter Ida wrote in the spring of 1905 to her aunt, Margaret Hinton:

'Robin is quite a man! He crawls about and eats bread and butter, and this evening he sat on the grass in the front garden and interviewed several boys who stopped on their way from school to talk to him. He makes so many noises, and laughs and wags his head about. You say you wonder what we do all day. About 6.30 Robin wakes and crawls about the floor, and grunts and says ah and eh and daddle and silly things like that. About 7 D[avid] and C[aspar] wake and say more silly things, and get dressed, and have a baked apple, or a pear or something, and play about with toys and run up and down. Breakfast about 8.30. Go out in the garden, Robin washed and put to bed about 9.30. D and C go out for a walk, or to the shop, and to post. Bring in letters at 11. We have dinner about 1, and they wake up about 2., have dinner, go out, and so on and so on till 7 when they're all in bed, sometimes dancing about and shouting, sometimes going to sleep. Robin now joins in the fray and shouts too.'[3]

It was an Allen and Hanbury world. Ida's letters reveal her increasing need to break free from this round of cooking-and-children and create a life with other adults, especially women. There must be 'something that is behind the ordinary aspect of things', she wrote. 'I think it is reality.' The trivialities she could document; the reality which lay barricaded behind them was receding. What worried her was the question of whether she could come to terms with the facts of her life as they now existed. 'Some days the curtain seems to lift a little for me,' she told her aunt, 'and they are days of inspiration and clearer knowledge. Those days I seem to walk on a little way. The other days I simply fight to keep where I am . . . I can understand the saints and martyrs and great men suffering everything for their idea of truth. It is more difficult, once you have given it some life – to go back on your idea than to stick to it. It torments you and worries you and tears you to pieces if you do not live up to it . . . it must sound mad to you, especially talking of fighting. It's wonderful what a different life one leads inside, to outside – at least how unknown the inside one is.'

It was impossible, in England in 1905, for people to understand, or to admit they understood, her inside life – as yet she hardly comprehended it herself. By admitting her husband's mistress into the home had she made the supreme sacrifice for love, or acted with inexcusable weakness? On the whole, in England in 1905, people would believe the latter, and blame the women. Even in Paris, men and women were hardly so brazen! Her unknown life, therefore, had to stay unknown – especially to the Nettleships. In defiance of the social conventions, Ida believed – was determined to believe – that she lived a natural life: natural for her. But, as her reference to saints and martyrs implies, it was not easy and she embraced with some readiness the notion of self-sacrifice. Unfortunately, triviality filled up each day. She rushed from crises over the children's tadpoles to crises about the canaries' eggs. 'What with babies, toothache and a visitation of *fleas* (where from we do not know) I am fast losing my reason,' she exclaimed to Alice.

Alice had grown curious again, but was dismayed when Ida in a dignified, faintly exasperated letter, went some way to satisfying her curiosity. 'Gus and Dorelia are up in town,' she wrote this winter, 'from which you may draw your own conclusions, and not bother me any more to know "where Dorelia sleeps" – You know we are not a *conventional* family, you have heard Dorelia is beautiful and most charming, and you must learn that my only happiness is for him to be happy and complete, and that far from diminishing our love it appears to augment it. I have my bad times it is only honest to admit. She is *so* remarkably charming. But those times are the devil and not the truth of light. You are large minded enough to conceive the amazement [? arrangement] as beautiful and possible – and would not think more of it than you would of any other madness which is really sanity. You will not gossip I know as that implies something brought to light which one wants hidden. All this we do not wish to hide, though there is no need to publish it, as after all it is a private matter. This letter is intended to be most discreet. It really expresses the actual state of affairs and you need not consider there is any bitterness or heartache behind, as, though there *is* occasionally, it is a weakness *not to be tolerated* and which is gradually growing less and will cease when my understanding is quite cleared of its many weeds . . .'

The response from Alice was an unprecedented silence. 'Alice Rothenstein has at last shut up,' Ida reported triumphantly to Augustus. To Alice herself she wrote: 'You and Will both ignore my letter but I suppose you don't know what to say – and really there is nothing. I hope you showed it to Will . . . Write again and tell me about someone – anyone – and all the horrid gossip you can think of.'

But the only gossip Alice could think of was Ida's. She could think of nothing else. What Ida really needed from her friends were stories about their own lives, or other people's, so irresistible that they would draw her out of the shell of her own existence. She wanted her friends' letters to be like chapters from a serialized novel, so absorbing, so full of detail and suspense, that they supplied a complete new fabric in which to wrap herself. What she got from the red-haired Rani was only a sweet exuberant amusement, eccentrically mistyped ('diving room' for dining-room), proclaiming Ida's situation as far too interesting to leave for a second. This was some comfort – 'only one is apt to drown the interest in tears', Ida confided to her – 'how natural and how foolish this is you will know'. The Rani's letters from Liverpool read as if the two of them were spectators at a Matching Green theatre. But Ida could not see it that way. If only she *could* be a spectator instead of taking everything with such 'pudding-like gravity'. Yet the Rani was the best of her friends: 'Your letters make green places in my life,' she told her. It was only in moments of crisis that she fell beyond their reach 'like a stone falling down a well'.

From Alice she received advice: cautionary advice, reproachful advice, advice that ran contrary to everything she had already done. All Alice's advice was seasoned with a flavour of inquisitiveness. 'She [Alice] is so – oh I don't know – she wants to know *why* and *how* – as if Chinese Ladies had answers to their riddles,' Ida complained to the Rani. 'The only nuisance about a riddle is its answer. Riddles are most fascinating by themselves.' Yet although she was always unsettled by Alice – as Alice was by her – somehow they maintained a 'tremendous admiration of each other' so that, worse than all Alice's reproaches, were no letters. Alice's silence seemed to deafen Ida with her own doings. 'Your silence is chilling,' she wrote to her. 'I do not think, if it is caused by displeasure, that it is fair . . . Please to write at once, and tell me you adore me and everything I do is right . . . Oh Alice Alice Alice why don't you write and tell me all your Nurse's faults and all about Johnnie – and how you hope I am well and are longing to see me – *Darling* don't be cross – I can't help it. My heart is a well of deep happiness and this makes me malicious.' Did she mean 'unhappiness'? Here was another riddle.

What bewildered Alice was Ida's attitude. Otherwise everything was melodramatically clear. Ida was the victim, noble but misguided; Dorelia the culprit who, if she had any decency, would take herself off; and Augustus was the man, a stereotypical artist whom Ida must control as Alice controlled poor Will. She knew the cast well enough. Will, however, disagreed and blamed Augustus. 'Ida is simply an angel,' he wrote to Alice (19 October 1905), ' – I think you are most unjust to Dorelia, who is looking after the children all the time and helping everything on, – Heaven knows she gets little for doing so.'

The friendship between the Johns and the Rothensteins was by the beginning of 1905 developing symptoms of burlesque. Ida, being especially fond of Will, was besieged by Alice; Augustus, attracted to the 'mortal pretty' Alice, was fêted by Will. It was as if each Rothenstein sought to protect the other from these explosive Johns. Ida's correspondence to 'darling Will' contains what are almost love letters and these would be dutifully answered – by Alice. But when Alice sat to Augustus, Will objected to her expression – the head flung back, the eyes closed – and would turn up at Augustus's studio to escort his wife home so punctually that sometimes Alice had not yet arrived there.

'You are a dear good friend to Gus,' Ida had written to Will. But Augustus, though he could not disagree, sometimes wished it were otherwise. He could not feel what he knew he was expected to feel. He could not pretend. He knew very well that he should feel grateful – Will needed to be kept well oiled with gratitude – but so often it was irritation that swarmed through him. His fate was to be helped, with extreme magnanimity, at many twists and crises of his career, by someone whose personality he increasingly disliked. Wherever he turned he seemed unable to avoid the rigours of Rothenstein's generosity, and his reaction, as he was well aware, appeared mean. A number of times he tried to end their relationship. 'I have broken with Rothenstein by the bye which of course is base ingratitude,' he later told Lady Ottoline Morrell (8 February 1909), ' – in extenuation I must say the sensation so far has been quite tolerable'. But breaking with Rothenstein was no easy matter. He was like a boxer for ever turning the other cheek to his assailant, yet never to be knocked out: a nightmare figure.

'It is more difficult to receive than to give,' Augustus wrote.[4] This was the lesson many of Rothenstein's beneficiaries had to learn. Epstein, for example, who once assured him: 'Your help so freely given me has been of the greatest service to me,' was also to write (20 June 1911):

'Dear Rothenstein –
I want no more of your damned insincere invitations.
This pretence of friendship has gone on far enough.
Yours etc Jacob Epstein.
It is the comic element in your attitude that has prevented me writing the above before this. I did not believe till now you could have gone on with it.'

Augustus's reaction was similar to Epstein's. 'How I wish someone would record the diverting history of Rothenstein's career – it would be the most ludicrous, abject and scurrilous psychological document ever penned,' Augustus assured Ottoline Morrell (23 March 1909). 'He is I think . . . Le Sale Juif par excellence de notre siècle. There is I think one man only who could write adequately about him and that's [Wyndham] Lewis . . .'

According to his son, John Rothenstein, 'no-one among his contemporaries had shown such perceptive generosity towards his brother artists of succeeding generations from Augustus John and Epstein to Henry Moore and Ceri Richards'. This is true, yet in the opinion of Max Beerbohm he had no friends at all.* What, then, was the secret of this gift for unpopularity? He was a figure somewhat similar to that, in the literary world, of Hugh Walpole, increasingly the patron rather than the creative artist, fixing his personal ambitions on the performance of his protégés. It was as if he sought to ride to immortality on their backs. Will Rothenstein's two prize rebellious steeds were Augustus John and Stanley Spencer, whom he entered against the rival stables of Roger Fry. But of all his string, Augustus was the greatest disappointment to him, winning in brilliant fashion so many of the minor races, running under false colours, starting favourite for the classics but seldom running to form.

During 1905, disillusionment had begun to set in. 'I am sorry John has no success,' Will wrote to Alice (19 October 1905). 'I slid some advice

---

* One of the guests at a dinner in honour of Will Rothenstein remarked: 'We ought really to have been at a dinner composed of his enemies.' To which his companion replied: 'They'd be precisely the same people.'

in on the subject before the Puvis [de Chavannes] decoration at the Sorbonne, and I still think he may do great work – at any rate he feels it, and can do it.'

Will's advice, like Alice's, was a formidable commodity. A Max Beerbohm multiple caricature shows him advising poets how to write poetry, playwrights how to stage their plays, painters how to paint, and himself (looking into a mirror) on modesty. Augustus, unfortunately, was not susceptible to advice. He preferred to use Rothenstein for money. 'I had a letter from John – not one I cared for much, for there was a hint of further pecuniary needs,' Will complained to his brother Albert (10 September 1908). What Will traded in, what he purchased, was gratitude. But this was not a quality with which Augustus was richly endowed. 'I have not found him [Augustus] the most grateful of men in the days of his splendour,' Will sorrowfully confided to the Rani years later (19 August 1933). But then, who was properly grateful? Gwen John, he thought, was the exception. 'No shadow, I thank Heaven, has ever come between us,' he wrote to her in 1926. 'The years have gone by, but our hearts remain the same, and people like you, in whom no mean thought can ever find a resting place, become ever more precious.'[5] In fact it was people like the Rothensteins who made Gwen feel happy she had left England. She had 'a contempt', she told Augustus, for Will's brother Albert; and as for Alice Rothenstein, 'I hope she is not coming over here or if she does, I shall not have to see her.'[6]

Rothenstein was always being short-changed because, he felt, he lacked the mysterious spirit of charm. 'The Gods who made me energetic & gave me a little passion & a little faith did me an ill turn when they made me ugly & charmless,' he confessed (28 July 1915) to Rabindranath Tagore.[7] The gratitude he squeezed out of people was a substitute for the love he felt he could never attract. He had been brought up in the Whistlerian tradition where the slightest whisper of criticism was intolerable. To this sensitivity was added an exceptional sanctimoniousness. He seemed to view everything through a mist of high-mindedness. In the racialist climate of Edwardian England, though he was not a practising Jew, he started off with disadvantages, and built them into a positive handicap.

For Augustus there was also the embarrassing problem of Rothenstein's praise. He needed praise. But he was not so susceptible as to think more highly of those who provided it. He imbibed Rothenstein's praise for a time: then suddenly it sickened him.[8]

It was partly because Will had made such an aesthetic investment in Augustus's future that he welcomed the presence of Dorelia. The inspiration which Augustus originally found in Ida had begun to fail; but, in 'the matchless Dorelia', Rothenstein later rhapsodized, 'in her dazzling beauty, now lyrical, now dramatic, John found constant inspiration. Who, indeed, could approach John in the interpretation of a woman's sensuous charm? No wonder fair ladies besieged his studio, and his person, too; for John had other magic than that of his brush; no one so irresistible as he, or with such looks, such brains, such romantic and reckless daring and indifference to public opinion.'[9]

The Winter Show of the New English Art Club at the end of 1904 included two paintings of Dorelia. 'This year for the first time Mr John gives promise of becoming a painter,' Roger Fry wrote in the *Athenaeum*. '. . . At last he has seen where the logic of his views as a draughtsman should lead him . . . he has already arrived at a control of his medium which astonishes one by comparison with the work of a year or two back . . . One must go back to Alfred Stevens or Etty or the youthful Watts to find its like . . . People will no doubt . . . complain of his love of low life, just as they complain of Rubens's fat blondes; but in the one case as in the other they will have to bow to the mastery of power . . . In modern life a thousand accidents may intervene to defraud an artist's talents of fruition, but if only fate and his temperament are not adverse, we hardly dare confess how high are the hopes of Mr John's future which his paintings this year have led us to form . . .'[10]

With supporters like Fry and Sickert, 'an amusing and curious character',[11] who came down to Matching Green to look at his drawings; with his small additional income from the Chelsea Art School and from exhibitions at the Carfax Gallery, he could surely afford to dispense with Rothenstein's favours. He had further strengthened his position when, late in 1904, he was elected as one of the original members of the Society of Twelve, a group of British draughtsmen, etchers, wood-engravers and lithographers. The secretary of this group was Muirhead Bone, who organized its exhibitions at Obachs in New Bond Street. For Augustus this was another valuable outlet for his work; for Rothenstein, who was also an original member, it was a new arena in which to display, like an inverted Iago, his apparently motiveless generosity. His methods of alienating everyone were particularly adroit. To the Society of Twelve he proposed electing a thirteenth member, Lucien Pissarro, who, not being British, was ineligible for membership. It was a master-stroke. Inevitably, when Pissarro failed to gain the necessary vote, Will resigned. Augustus, who hated being dragged into these affairs, was persuaded to use his influence to bring him back, and this, somewhat improbably, he achieved. But no sooner was Will re-elected than he was at it again, returning undaunted and unavailing for three years in succession to the same charge, resigning again, and throwing the whole group into confusion. 'I was tenacious,' he later owned, 'and many letters passed between Bone and myself, until Pissarro was admitted.' By which time the society was so shaken with squabbles it did not long survive Will's quixotic triumph.

Five years after Rothenstein died, Augustus wrote an appreciation of him in the Catalogue to the Tate Gallery Memorial Exhibition.[12] In this he paid tribute to him as a man 'always intransigent and sometimes truculent', subject to a rare disease, 'madness of self-sacrifice', and bound therefore to make enemies. He also described him as 'a generous, candid and perspicacious soul'. While walking round the exhibition the day before it opened, his eyes filled with tears and he admitted that he had sometimes been unjust to his old friend. Yet if Will had come tripping through the door just then, Augustus would soon have struggled out, infuriated by his admirer. For one of the persistent features of Augustus's character, arising from his difficulties with Edwin John, was a dislike of anyone who assumed the role of father-figure. Rothenstein, who came from an authoritarian family, was enraptured with the father-figure, feeling a need both to promote others in that part, and to assume it himself. Augustus would neither play the parent, nor swallow the well-meaning reprimands. They were incompatible; and yet each felt he needed the other.

A new strain had been placed on Augustus's financial resources by the birth of Robin that autumn. By the New Year, despite his success in the galleries, he was even more dependent on Rothenstein for help. For Dorelia was now pregnant.

2

AT THE CROSSROADS

'It is more difficult at first to be wise, but it is infinitely harder afterwards *not* to be.'

Ida John to Margaret Sampson (May 1905)

The baby must have been conceived in early August 1904, when Dorelia and Gus left Bruges – and for almost five months Dorelia seems to have kept her pregnancy a secret. 'I did not know you are making un petit, how could I?' Gwen wrote to her early in 1905. 'Are you glad? . . . When we continue our walk to Rome we will carry it by turns on our backs in a shawl . . .'[13]

Though she may have been glad for herself, Dorelia was apprehensive over the complications it might stir up, and the effect it could have on Ida. Already, by the end of 1904, violent scenes had broken out between them. Shortly after Robin's birth, Ida had made one of her 'little journeys' up to London for a few days, avoiding her friends, feeling strangely hysterical. 'I simply drifted – from one omnibus to another – without aim or intention,' she admitted to Alice (December 1904). Yet the sudden flow of freedom, the release from duty, appeared to have 'done me worlds of good'. She returned to Matching Green shortly before Christmas, to find that a double portrait Augustus was painting of her and Dorelia had gone wrong. In her absence, Augustus had altered the design and there was no room on the canvas for Ida at all. Instantly, and beyond anything this incident seemed to warrant, she was plunged into misery and anger. She had a demonic temper; she could not contain it and 'there was a black storm'. After the storm was over and, rather to their surprise, they were still all afloat, Ida felt easier and 'there was a fair amount of sunlight'. But over the rest of this winter quarrels erupted. One morning Augustus and Ida would take sides against Dorelia, and Augustus would volunteer that she could leave whenever she liked; but the following morning it was Ida who was invited to leave – 'pack up your luggage and take your brats with you!' Next day Augustus would suddenly announce that *he* was leaving for 'the Blue Danube'; after which it was once more the turn of Ida (who threatened to leave for Amsterdam); then again Dorelia. Finally: 'We are all thinking of going to the tropics.'

But no one left. Augustus went roaring from room to room driving the children before him, like cattle. 'Never had so wretched a time, even over the festive season,' he notified Sampson, ' – now its over & all right again.'[14]

But for Ida it was not all right. She was in a dilemma. She had invited Dorelia to Matching Green, because the two of them had a better hold on Augustus than Ida by herself would have had. But then she was consumed by jealousy. For Augustus made no attempt to conceal his infatuation for Dorelia; while to Ida he seemed for long periods blind. 'Have I lost my beauty altogether?' she asked Dorelia. Sometimes she appeared ill with depression, going down with a succession of minor ailments that conspired to make her feel more ugly still. 'I have *an eye*,' she wrote to the Rani. 'Dr says due to general weakness! It has a white sort of spot in it and runs green matter in the evening – which during the night effectually gums down the eyelids so that they have to be melted open! Isn't it too loathesome?' The *eye* was followed by a *throat* – 'dear me what next? Varicose veins probably.'

Jealousy infected everything. Since Dorelia had come Maggie, who had helped with the cooking and children, took herself off, disapproving of their immoral ways. It was natural that, to some extent, Dorelia should take her place. But Ida could not let her do too much in the house, partly, it seems, because Augustus thought she was treating Dorelia like a servant. Nor could she bring herself to speak about Dorelia's unborn baby; and she began to hate herself for this meanness of spirit. Obscure moods of attraction and revulsion mingled with her envy of Dorelia. Doubt and self-hatred, frustration and exhaustion so assailed her during these dark months that she emerged from the winter a changed person, her love for Augustus impaired, her attitude to herself and to Dorelia transformed.

It was to the Rani she confessed most. 'I feel simply desperate,' one of her letters begins; and another: 'My depression is so great as to be almost exhilaration.' As the days went by this depression deepened. 'I feel utterly – like this ☐ – square as a box and mad as a lemon squeezer. What is the remedy?' she asked her friend. '. . . Do you know what it is to sit down and be bounced up again by what you sat on, and for that to happen *continuously* so that you can't sit *anywhere*? Of course you do – I am now taking phenacetin to keep the furniture still.' Up till then she had used humour to preserve her detachment and energy. But the effect of her phenacetin tablets appears to have reduced this detachment. For the first time she contemplated suicide. The Rani sometimes knew more of what was happening than Augustus and Dorelia, from whom Ida camouflaged her emotions. She did not complain, but told the Rani: 'I live the life of a lady slavey. But I wouldn't change – because of Augustus – c'est un homme pour qui mourir – and literally sometimes I am inclined to kill myself – I don't seem exactly necessary.' She still admired him – but was no longer so intimate with him. Also he was 'impossible', and so life itself had become impossible. 'I long for an understanding face,' she wrote to the Rani. 'I am surrounded by cows and vulgarity here. Isn't it awful when even the desire to live forsakes one? I *cannot* just now, see any reason why I should. Yet I feel if I tide over this bad time, I shall be glad later on. What do you think?'

Believing that Ida must not be left alone, the Rani wired Augustus, who was then in London with Dorelia, to return home at once. She also wrote to Ida urging her to shake off ill thoughts of death. 'As to suicide,' Ida replied,

'why not? What a fuss about one life which is really not valuable! . . . Am I not a fool to make such a fuss about a thing I accepted, nay invited, but I have lost all my sense of reason or right. All that seems far over the sea and I can only hear sounds which don't seem to matter. It's so funny not to *want* to be good. I never remember to have felt it before. It is such a nice free feeling – animals must be like that.'

Augustus rushed back, the crisis lifted, and Ida confessed to the Rani:

'You know *I was very near* the laudanum bottle – somehow it seemed the next thing. Like when you're tired you see an armchair and sit down in it. Now you "know all" I feel a sort of support – it is funny. Others know, but no one has given me support in the right place as you have. One held up an arm, another a leg, one told me I wasn't tired and there was nothing the matter . . . With you I have something to *sit on!*'

Dorelia too was not happy. She felt responsible for the bickering, the guilt, the dissatisfaction that pervaded the house. There were times, she knew, when Ida must have wished her at the bottom of the sea. She began to think it had been a mistake leaving Bruges, coming to Matching Green. Then, early in 1905, while Gus was painting her portrait, she told him categorically that once this picture was finished she must leave. There was nothing to stop her; she had no wish to stay.

Augustus could hardly believe it. Their life together, of which he had had such splendid dreams, was failing. It should have been so natural. He felt wretched.

Shortly before Dorelia's baby was due, Ida went to stay with the Salamans at Oxford. But her imagination still stalked the rooms of Elm House, remembering so many sights and sounds she had never wanted to witness, imprisoning the details in her mind. No matter what her intelligence told her, she seemed affected biologically. In a remarkable letter she now sent privately to Dorelia, very long, but written hurriedly in pencil, she set down her conclusions.

'. . . I tried not to be horrid – I know I am – I never hardly feel generous now like I did at first – I suppose you feel this through everything – I tried to be jolly – it is easy to be superficially jolly – I hate to think I made you miserable but I know I have – Gus blames me entirely for *everything* now – I daresay he's right – but when I think of some things I feel I suffered too much – it was like physical suffering it was so intense – like being burnt or something – I can't feel I am entirely responsible for this horrid ending – it was nature that was the enemy to our scheme. I have often wondered you have not gone away before – it has always been open to you to go, and if you have been as unhappy as Gus says you should have told me. I do not think it likely Gus and I can live together after this – I want to separate – I feel sick at heart. At present I hate you generally but I don't know if I really do. It is all impossible now and we are simply living in a convention you know – a way of talking to each other which has no depth or heart. I should like to know if it gives you a feeling of relief and flying away to freedom to think of going . . . I don't care what Gus thinks of me now, of course he'd be wild at this letter. He seems centuries away. He puts himself away. I think he's a mean and childish creature besides being the fine old chap he is.

I came here in order to have the rest cure, and I am, but it makes things seem worse than if one is occupied – but of course it will all come all right in the end. I know you and Gus think I ought to think of you as the sufferer, but I can't. You are free – the man you love at present, loves you – you don't care for convention or what people think – of course your future is perilous, but you love it. You are a wanderer – you would hate safety and cages – why are you to be pitied? It is only the ones who are bound who are to be pitied – the slaves. It seems to me utterly misjudging the case to pity you. You are living your life – you chose it – you did it because you wanted to – didn't you? Do you regret it? I thought you were a wild free bird who loved life in its glorious hardships. If I am to think of you as a sad female who needs protection I must indeed change my ideas . . . It was for your freedom and all you represented I envied you so. Because you meant to Gus all that lay outside the dull home, the unspeakable fireside, the gruesome dinner table – that I became so hopeless – I was the chain – you were the key to unlock it. This is what I have been made to feel ever since you came. Gus will deny it but he denies many facts which are daily occurrences – apparently denies them because they are true and he wants to pretend they aren't. One feels what is, doesn't one? Nothing can change this fact – that you are the one outside who calls a man to *apparent* freedom and wild rocks and wind and air – and I am the one inside who says come to dinner, and who to live with is apparent slavery. Neither Gus nor I are strong enough to find freedom in domesticity – though I know it is there.

You are the wild bird – fly away – as Gus says our life does not suit you. He will follow, never fear. There was never a poet could stay at home. Do not think myself to be pitied either. I shudder when I think of those times, simply because it was pain . . . It has robbed me of the tenderness I felt for you – but you can do without that – and I would do anything for you if you would ever ask me to – you still seem to belong to us. I.'[15]

What Ida overlooked was that, during the first few months of 1905, Augustus had grown rather less attentive towards Dorelia, as if the wild bird being caged was no longer capable of extraordinary flight. It was true that he could not find freedom, or poetry, or love in domesticity. Not for long. Love was like fire to Augustus. Confined within the grate of marriage, it smouldered drearily, collapsing into ashes. Its smoke choked him and its dying coals were cheerless. He wanted to spread it around, let it take light where it would, to make a splendid conflagration – rather than sit fixed by its embers. And now Dorelia, whom he had once likened to a flame, was sinking into this domestic apathy. His poems dried up, his gaze fell vacant. What he needed from Dorelia, and also from Ida, was positively less of them. He needed distance and elusiveness to get his romantic view in focus. He was not really a demonstrative man and became impatient over homely displays of affection. Confused by this sudden heating and cooling of emotion, Dorelia grew defensive. Ida had hardened towards her; Augustus, at moments, appeared indifferent; neither of them mentioned her unborn baby, and, from Augustus, this hurt her. She confessed as much to Ida who, contradicting her avowed loss of tenderness, wrote back to reassure her:

'My dear, men always seem indifferent about babies – that is, men of our sort. You must not think Gus is more so over yours than he was over mine. He never said anything about David except 'don't spill it'. They take us and leave us you know – it is nature. I thought he was rather solicitous about yours considering. Don't you believe he came over to Belgium because he was sorry for you. He is a mean skunk to let you imagine such a thing. If ever a man was in love, he was – and is now, only of course it's sunk down to the bottom again – a man doesn't keep stirred up for long – and because we can't see it we're afraid it's not there – but never you fear.'[16]

This consolation, which was also needed by Ida herself, was to flower after the birth of Dorelia's baby, leading to a special affection between the two women. But, for the time being, it was another confusing factor. Like a lake, swollen by the rivers of their mixed feelings, their bewilderment rose. At times, it was the only thing the three of them shared. Augustus's pronouncements certainly sounded unmixed, but then they were so quick, and so quickly succeeded by other pronouncements equally strong and utterly different. Ida, for all her disenchantment, still harboured a deep affection for him – 'he's a mean and childish creature besides being the fine old chap he is' – as Dorelia was to do. Admiration and anger, jealousy and tenderness for Dorelia spun within her. Amid all this eddying of emotion, it was up to Dorelia to steer a firm course. But for her pregnancy, it seems likely that she would have slipped away without a word. Words were not her *métier* – words, explanations, all this indulgence, were not in her line. She was, so she always insisted, 'a very ordinary person', blessed with an extraordinary vicarious gift. She had little talent for making independent decisions: she excelled at making the best of other people's, and when, as now, no one made any decisions, she drifted without a compass. Hoping that Ida might decide for her – for the two of them had never been so intimate as by post – she wrote expressing her confusion. But when Ida replied, she saw her confusion faithfully reflected:

'About your going or not *you* must decide – I should not have suggested it, but I believe you'd be happier to go . . . Yes, to stay together seems impossible, only we know it isn't – I don't know what to say. Only I feel so sure you'd be happier away . . . I know I should be jolly glad now if we all lived apart – or anyway if I did with the children. Don't you think we might as well? – if it can be arranged.

I don't feel the same confidence in Gus I did, nor in myself.

Yes I know I always asked you to stay on, but still I don't see why you should have – you knew it was pride made me ask you, and because I wouldn't be instrumental in your going, having invited you – also because I didn't see how I could live with Gus alone again. All, all selfish reasons.

. . . I have often felt a pig not to talk to you more about the* baby, but I couldn't manage it. Also I always feel you *are not* like ordinary people and don't care for the things other people do. Gus says what I think of you is vulgar and insensible – I don't know – I know I'm always fighting for you to people outside, but probably what I tell them is quite untrue – and vulgar. I know I admire you immensely as I do a great river or a sunny day – or anything else great and natural and inevitable. But perhaps this is not you. I don't feel friendly or tender to you because you seem aloof and like some calm independent animal – you don't seem to need anything from me, or from any woman – and it seems unnatural and a condescension for you to do things for me. Added to all this is my jealousy. This is a true statement of why I am like I am to you . . .

As to Gus he's a poet, and knows no more about actual life than a poet does. This is sometimes everything, when he's struck a spark to illumine the darkness, and sometimes nothing when he's looking at the moon. As to me, we all know I'm nothing but a rubbish heap with a few buried treasures which will all be tarnished by the time they come to light.

This mistake I make is considering Gus as a man instead of an artist-creature. I am so sorry for you, poor little thing, bottling yourself up about the baby. Shall we laugh at all this when we're 50? Maybe – but at 50 the passions are burnt low. It makes no difference to now does it? . . . I do want to be there for your baby. I do want to be good, but I *know* I shant manage it.'[17]

But so much of Ida's analysis, it seemed to Dorelia, made 'no difference to now'. Dorelia needed to simplify things in order to act, not to investigate

---

* Ida crossed out the word 'your' and substituted 'the'.

them more minutely. So far as action was concerned, there was only one new simplifying factor in Ida's letter: she was no longer asking Dorelia to stay. Dorelia wrote back briefly and cryptically, stating that she would 'treat it as an everyday occurrence' and, she implied, wander off. But Ida, fearing that Dorelia would vanish before she got back, answered urgently:

'Do not go until we all go, it would be so horrid . . . I want to go out from Matching Green all together and part at a cross roads – don't you go before I get back unless you *want* to . . . We shall have dinner all together – no slipping away. My admiration of you does not prevent my hating you as one woman hates another. Gus doesn't seem able to understand this – & it is so simple.'

As an inducement for Dorelia to remain until she arrived back, Ida promised 'a bottle of olives . . . 2 natural coloured ostrich feathers and some lace!'[18]

So Dorelia was persuaded to wait. Augustus had by this time gone up to yet another new studio* in London, and the two women joined him there in the last week of March. This was to be the crossroads, the parting of the ways. He did not know that they had been corresponding, and seems to have believed that the crisis of Dorelia's departure had passed: after all, no one had said anything. What then happened surprised everyone. 'We had a *terrific* flare up,' Ida afterwards (27 March 1905) told Alice Rothenstein.

'. . . and the ménage was on the point of being broken up, as D[orelia] said she would not come back, because the only sane and sensible thing for us to do was to live apart. But I persuaded her to, for many reasons – and we settled solemnly to keep up the game till summer. Lord, it was a murky time – most sulphurous – it gave me a queer sort of impersonal enjoyment. After it we all three dined in a restaurant (which is now a rare joy) and drank wine, and then rode miles on the top of a bus, very gay and light hearted. Gus has been a sweet mild creature since.'

The 'many reasons' for Ida's change of attitude are nowhere specified. Certainly this change puzzled Dorelia and also, it appears, was not really understood by Ida herself. The 'queer sort of impersonal enjoyment' she felt may have been the exercise of power. Where Ida led, Gus and Dorelia followed, and the knowledge of this may have given her satisfaction.

---

* He moved from No. 4 to No. 9 Garden Studios in Manresa Road, Chelsea, during the spring of 1905.

But one of the 'many reasons' was Ida's dread of living alone with Augustus. If she remained with him, as she might have to do, then he would take other mistresses, and none of them was likely to match Dorelia. It had been Ida's love for Gus that had drawn all three of them under the same roof; but it was her feeling for Dorelia that now held them together.

Augustus saw things somewhat differently. This last year, he reflected, they had been living rather too conventionally. 'I get to think of London as Hell sometimes,'[19] he told Michel Salaman. Matching Green was better, but even there they were confined with ten perpetually growling cats, squeaking canaries, games of cricket and flocks of chickens outside, tadpoles within, and of course the children like acrobats forever falling into the coal scuttle. Perhaps it was the parrot that he had taught to swear in Romany that gave him the solution. 'I want to buy a van or two next year . . . I expect I'll take my family somewhere, Dorelia included,'[20] he had written to Sampson at the end of 1904. It would be just the thing for serious gypsy spotting, for hunting up bits and pieces of their vocabulary.

It was his old Slade friend Michel Salaman who came to the rescue. He had started out on his honeymoon in a smart new caravan, but for some reason decided a few miles into his marriage to sell it. Augustus bought it in the spring of 1905 for the handsome sum of thirty pounds, paid scrupulously over the next thirty years. But what was a caravan without a horse? Here too Salaman was able to help. 'I might well use your horse,' Augustus conceded. '. . . Before I take possession of it please give me some notion of his tastes & habits – I should not like to upset him by wrong treatment, and I know nothing of horses' ways.'[21]

By April all stood ready and the future shone bright. 'I look forward to being out with a van or two,' he wrote to Salaman, 'our . . . multitude of boys are an amusing lot.' The horse and van had halted near the centre of Dartmoor, a fine challenging place, if they could find it. 'Probably I shall have a Gipsy to help in these matters,' Augustus had speculated.

But for the time being horse and van were to have a more discreet role as Dorelia's shelter for the birth of her first child. Ida, who had gone to stay with the Dowdalls in Liverpool, wrote to ask whether Dorelia 'would like me to help you over the baby's birth or if you'd rather I kept out of the way', adding: 'I'd like to and I'd hate to. I would rather come, probably only because I don't like to be away from things.'

In the event Ida was not with Dorelia when the baby was born, and nor was anyone else. 'I was surprised to hear you had your baby so soon,' Gwen wrote from Paris. 'I'm so glad everything has gone well, & it is such a charming one, it seems to be a real gipsy. I should like to come over, but I don't suppose I shall . . . Goodbye & love to you.'[22]

It was a boy, born in circumstances deliberately made obscure so as to conceal his illegitimacy. For the occasion Dorelia assumed the name of 'Mrs Archibald McNeill', wife of a naval officer long at sea, while Augustus on his arrival posed as her solicitous brother. Later on their identities changed. 'I'm quite certain there is no penalty attached to having a bastard in the family,' Augustus reassured her from a Liverpool pub called The Duke. 'So better register him as my son – provided of course it isn't published next morning in the Daily Mail or Express – as your family and my father no doubt take in one of those journals and such advertisement would be very disturbing. Have you stuck to that list of names? A sensation takes possession of me that Pyramus may be omitted or Alastir . . . The parish of Lydford wasn't it?'[23]

Pyramus was born at Postbridge on Dartmoor in late April or early May. Though Dorelia was alone (except for a large herd of cows), she was not far from an inn owned by a friendly landlord and his wife, Mr and Mrs Hext, who saw to it that a doctor and nurse visited her. Both Augustus and Ida had planned to be there, but Augustus 'wearing my new suit so of course I cannot think very composedly' was fastened in Liverpool where Charles Reilly 'keeps at me about his scheme of a school of 10 picked pupils and walls and ceilings to decorate – and £500 a year'. Ida, meanwhile, was held at Matching Green in polite talk with her mother, who had determined to stay with her over Whitsun. In their absence Augustus and Ida both sent money, advice on diet ('don't live on potatoes'), and plenty of unanswered inquiries.

As soon as the telegram – in almost impenetrable Romany – arrived at Elm House saying Dorelia's baby was born, Ida abandoned her mother and with mixed feelings churning within her hurried down, travelling through the night by train and arriving by eleven next morning. She found Dorelia lying along the caravan shelf which served for a bed, with her infant – 'a boy of course' – beside her. Augustus, 'suave and innocent as ever', turned up the following day 'to kiss the little woman who is giving up much for love of him', Ida wrote to the Rani. 'The babe is fine, a tawny colour – very contented on the whole – we have to use a breast pump thing as her nipples are flat on the breast.'

A few days later the other children flocked down, shepherded by Maggie who had returned for the emergency, and they all settled down to graze upon the moor for two months, Augustus coming and going at intervals. 'It is adorable and terrible here,' Ida wrote. 'We work and work from 6 or 7 till 9 and then are so tired we cannot keep awake – at least I can't. Dorelia is more lively – owing perhaps to an empty belly.' All day they were out of doors, wearing the same clothes, going about barefoot, growing wonderfully sunburnt – 'at least the women and children are – the Solitary Stag does not show it much' – and eating double quantities of everything.

Ida seemed transformed in this new climate. They were in a wide valley, with dramatic distant hills and never-ending skies. It was not simply the open-air life that transformed her, but a change in Augustus's attitude in the open air. 'Gus is a horrid beast,' she eulogized in another letter to the Rani, 'and a lazy wretch and a sky blue angel and an eagle of the ranges. He is (or acts) in love with *me* for a change, it is so delightful – only he *is* lazy seemingly, and when not painting lies reading or playing with a toy boat. Then I think well how could he paint if he has to be on duty in between – duty is so wearing and tearing and wasting and consuming – only somehow it seems to build something up as well which is so clever.' Ida hardly knew how to interpret this change. At the very moment one might have expected him to give his fullest attention to Dorelia, he had turned to Ida herself. She had lost confidence in herself to such an extent that she could not believe he loved her. But then what was Gus's love? What was anyone's love? 'We had one flare up – nearly 2,' she confided to the Rani,

'. . . owing to Gus's *strange* lack of susceptibility – or possibly by some human working, his being too susceptible. It is a difficult position for him. He is so afraid of making me jealous I believe – and he was not wildly in love with her – nor with me, only quite mildly. With the result that he appeared indifferent to her, while really feeling quite nice and tender, had I not been there. But Lord – it *is* impossible but interesting and truth-excavating.'

Despite the difficulties, and odd flare-ups, this was a marvellous summer for Ida. She adored living in the van. All their worries seemed to lose themselves among the rocks and heather of this open country, to float away with the procession of clouds across the great sky. Yet Ida knew they would have to work out something more permanent than this.

For Augustus too it was a happy summer. He was free to work, and work went well. 'I have made a step forwards but what infinite worlds before me!'[24] he had written to Sampson. And to Michel Salaman also he wrote that summer: 'I know now infallibly what is good painting, good imagination & good art.'[25] He was doing many etchings – romantic pieces entitled 'Out on the Moor' and 'Pyramus and Thisbe' and a good study of Dartmoor ponies. Close by their camp was a spring for washing and drinking, which the women and children used; while in the evenings Augustus would stride off out of sight to the Hexts, sit in their plain flagged kitchen and warm himself before the peat fire. Back at the camp he erected a tent of poles and blankets after the gypsy fashion and, like the Hexts, lit peat fires – but they were 'usually all smoke'. At night they would retreat into the tent to sleep 'and you can hear the stream always and always'.

The rest of this summer Ida and Dorelia passed together at Matching Green, while Augustus roamed the country between his school in London and his prospective school in Liverpool. In his absence the two women grew extraordinarily close. The whole basis of their friendship was shifting. They managed the house, looked after the children, made each other clothes and in the evening played long games of chess which Ida always won – 'except once', Dorelia remembered. Towards Augustus, it appeared, they now occupied very similar positions. 'A woman is either a wife or a mistress,' Ida had written to Dorelia.

'If a wife, she has (that is, her position implies) perfect confidence in her husband and peace of mind – not being concerned about any other woman in relation to her husband. But she has ties and responsibilities and is, more or less, a fixture – and not free. If a mistress she has no right to expect faithfulness, and must allow a man to come and go as he will without question – and must in consequence, if she loves him jealously, suffer doubt and not have peace of mind – *but* she has her own freedom too. Well here are you and I – we have neither the peace of mind of the wife nor the freedom (at least I haven't) of the mistress. We have the evils of both states for the one good, which belongs to both – a man's company. Is it worth it? Isn't it paying twice over for our boon?

Our only remedy is to both become mistresses, and so at any rate have the privileges of the mistress.

Of course I have the children and perhaps, being able to avail myself of the name of wife, I ought to do so, and live with G[us]. But I shall never consider myself as a wife – it is a mockery.'[26]

The need to free herself from being Augustus's wife ran very strong in Ida. She relinquished for a time the name Ida, calling herself Anne (or Ann), the third of her Christian names; and then, to escape further from her past self, signed some letters Susan.[27] Her mounting attraction to Dorelia in a curious way drew her closer to Augustus again. Like Gwen (whom she had also wanted to call Anne), she grew fascinated by Dorelia. 'I know it makes you mad to hear me rave on about her,' she teased Alice Rothenstein. 'Dear old darling pure English Alice – I can't help loving these fantastics however abnormally their bosoms stick out . . . as Gus says, she has the gift of beauty.'

Alone with Dorelia, Ida was as happy as she had been for a long time.

Envy and jealousy melted into love: she disliked their being apart even for a few days. 'Darling D,' she wrote while on a short visit to her mother, 'Love from Anna to the prettiest little bitch in the world . . . I was bitter cold last night without your burning hot, not to say scalding, body next me – . . . Yours jealously enviously and adoringly Ida Margaret Ann JOHN.'

To establish their new regime Ida now came out with the proposal that she and Dorelia, the two mistresses, should leave England and, with their children, live together in Paris. The lease of Elm House was up that autumn so that in any case they must move from Matching Green. She had loved Paris while living there with the two Gwens, and the Parisian atmosphere, she felt convinced, was capable of sustaining their *ménage* better than anywhere in England. What a brave new start it would be! They would find an inexpensive studio for Augustus who could make little journeys between London and Paris. They would all continue seeing one another – preferably not too much of one another. Money would certainly be a difficulty, but Ida would practise the severest economies and earn money from modelling again. She was determined to take Dorelia with her and had already written a letter to Gus, telling him she wanted to live apart – not because she didn't love him but because living together on a day-after-day basis was impossible. And he, still 'a sweet mild creature', who would bring her anything she asked for – 'a dictionary, an atlas and a toothpick' – had not sought to excuse himself, but blamed his 'nervous aberrations' for their troubles. For although he did not say so, he wanted much the same as she did. 'Dearest of Gs,' she had replied to him:

'With people one loves one does not suffer from "nervous aberrations". And peace with Dorelia would never bring stagnation, as you know well. For a time that spiritual fountain, at which I have drunk and which has kept me hopeful and faithful so many years, seems dried up – I think lately I have taxed it. I think it would be a good thing, when it can be arranged, for us all to live quite apart, anyway for a time. You will not mind that – you know we never did intend to live together. I shall have to sit – there's no other means of making money – mais tout cela s'arrangera.

Yes, there is in those letters [to Dorelia] something you never did and never will write for me – I think it is because I love you that I see it. And I think if I had known it before I should not have wanted us all to live together. It has been a straining of the materials for you and I ever to live together – it is nature for you and her.

I am quite sure you will visit me and I will receive you, oh my love . . .

By rights Dorelia is the wife and I the mistress. *Is it not so?* Arranged
thus there would be no distress ... Tu me comprends comme toujours
parce que tu es bon et doux. Aurevoir – we will see later on what can be
arranged –
Ever yours Sue.'[28]

What Ida now arranged was a variation of this 'two mistresses' scheme.
They would not calculate things precisely, but simply find out how the
details best sorted themselves out. 'Dodo says we can't trouble about
"turns",' she told Augustus. Also: 'you know you will be happy alone.'
The nucleus of this French plan was Ida and Dorelia's closeness. 'I do
not know rightly whether Ardor [Dorelia] and I love one another,' Ida
explained to Augustus. 'We seem to be bound together by sterner bonds
than those of love. I do not understand our relationship, but I feel it is
necessary for us to live [together].'[29] Whether or not they loved each
other, they both, in their fashion, loved Gus who, at one time or another,
sincerely loved one of them or the other. With so much love surging
between the three of them surely it must be possible, if only accidentally,
to hit upon some way of life that satisfied everyone? 'We *must* go,' Ida
announced. And as always her decision, plunging through the ocean of
indecision, was conclusive.

As always, too, they began by trying to make the best of anything
new. Dorelia's silence was enthusiastic; while from the north of England
Augustus exuded amiability. Unless some ungovernable mood was on him,
he felt nervous of opposing Ida. He had been shocked by her contemplated
suicide, and all the more alarmed at having to be told this by the Rani.
The news sobered him. 'My imagination is getting more reasonable and
joyous now,' he wrote, 'I wish to God it would be one thing or the other
and stay! I have longings to sculpt – it's been coming on for years.
Paris!!! ... I hope to paint two orange girls if I can get them. Before
actual life at any rate moods and vapours vanish. Suppose I came back to
the Green soon ... I look to you, Ardor, to restrain Ann's economical
fury.'

But Ida would not allow him back just then. His moods were so strong,
so unintentionally destructive, so – as he admitted – unreasonable that
the best-laid schemes might be finished off by them. She wanted to fix
everything unalterably before accepting such risks. She wrote off to hos-
tels, made travel arrangements, gave the servants notice, contracted to sell
all the furniture they could not take with them, and booked two taxis.
She also told the Rothensteins. 'I expect you'll think we're mad,' she
invited Alice (July 1905).

'We are going to live all together for a time again – it is pleasanter really and much more economical. We shall only need one servant. We shall do the kids ourselves – meaning Dorelia and me. Her baby is weakly, but a dear little thing – not much trouble. Gus of course will live mostly in London . . . I feel this living [in] Paris is inevitable, and though there are 10000 reasons in its favour I will not trouble you with them. The reason really is that we're going.'

Alice's reaction, predictably, was one of extreme horror. She wondered whether Ida had taken leave of her senses. Paris! So it had come to that. She knew what Ida should do. Her duty was to return at once to London and take a 'cheap flat' there. Anything else would be unfair to Augustus. 'Alice Rothenstein is simply indescribable,' Ida wrote to the Rani. '. . . She and I always feel quite opposite things. Lord! . . . I can't think of the tight, smiling life which London means to me now. Were I alone it would be different.'

Will appears to have agreed with Alice. Indeed it may have been his opposition to the Paris scheme that helped to reconcile Augustus to it. 'It is mostly on your account that they [Will and Alice] are so against Paris,' Ida told Augustus. 'Alice says "you do not quite realise what it means to a man!" Does she mean in the nights? Anyway I cannot, dare not, allow her ideas of comfort etc to influence me at all . . . if anything would keep me it would be Mother.'

She was still encumbered by her family. 'It *is* selfish,' she admitted to the Rani, 'because of my Mother – but I can't help it.' Mrs Nettleship's strong sensible middle-class standards were like chains upon Ida's freedom, and she had resolved to cut them. For, since they had settled to 'keep up the game', nothing could be concealed from Mrs Nettleship any longer – even that Dorelia had a baby of her own. Their departure called for drastic explanations, and as soon as everything was irreversibly arranged Ida broke the news. 'I have taken rooms at a little hotel where they make it cheaper as we travel with children,' she wrote. 'Aren't they mad?'[30]

The attitudes of Alice Rothenstein and Mrs Nettleship, representing those of society and the family, were very similar. It was Ida, they thought, who was mad. But to all Mrs Nettleship's objections Ida returned one answer: that it was unreasonable to blame her for not placing her mother's welfare above that of her husband, or, for that matter, above her own. Since her daughter's marriage Mrs Nettleship had, despite herself, begun rather to like Augustus. He was not so *absolutely awful* as she had once feared. He amused her, even charmed her. 'They get on quite well in a queer way,' Ida had noted with surprise. '. . . What an instinct many – I suppose most – people have for keeping "on good terms". It necessitates such careful walking – and fighting would be so much more amusing – or perhaps not.' Now Ida had a real fight on her hands. Mrs Nettleship blamed Augustus. She had always known what he was like, behind the charm and amusement. But she also blamed Ida for giving into him. Then there was the blameworthy figure of Dorelia. In the end she blamed all of them for exposing this wretched state of affairs to the public gaze. Why couldn't Dorelia live a little way off, if such things must be? Why make themselves a subject for squalid gossip – had Ida given no thought as to how it would affect her sisters? To which Ida replied that this was one of the reasons they were leaving the country. Exasperated, Mrs Nettleship declared that it was against the law to have two wives, and warned her daughter that she intended to institute legal proceedings. But no one took this seriously, and for Augustus ('my only husband' as Ida ironically called him) it completed the romantic comedy.

The Nettleship campaign continued to the end of the year. Mrs Nettleship called on her other two daughters, Ethel and Ursula, who now joined in with their own appeals to Ida. To them Ida was obliged to justify herself all over again. Her letters, injected with small shots of scepticism, are extraordinary for their forbearance. 'Dearest angel,' she wrote to Ursula:

'It is quite unnecessary for you to feel miserable about us unless of course your sense of morality is such that this ménage really shocks you. But as you say you know nothing of actual right and wrong in such a case I suppose you feel bad because you think I am unhappy or that Gus does not love me. I think I've got over the jealousy from which I suffered at first, and I now take the situation more as it should be taken . . . I don't know how they told you, but I suppose from your letter they made it pretty awful. As a matter of fact it is not awful – simply living a little more genuinely than would otherwise be possible – that is to say accepting and trying to digest a fact instead of hiding it away and always having the horrid consciousness of its being there hidden . . . I know in the end what we are doing will prove to be the best thing to have done. It is not always wisest to see most. Do you understand. Oh do you understand? I think really if you were left to yourself you would understand better than almost anyone – instinctively. If you were to begin to think of the reasons against our arrangement I should be afraid . . . It is a beautiful life we live now, and I never have been so happy – but that does not prove it is right. It seems right for us – but is it for the outside world? doesn't charity begin at home? and at most we only make people uncomfortable . . . do believe I no longer grudge Gus his love for Dorelia – I never did, but he was so much "in love" that no interested woman could have remained calm beholding them. But now that is over, and though he loves her and always must it is different – and we live in common charity, accepting the facts of the case – and she, mind you, is a very wonderful person – a child of nature – calm and beautiful and patient – no littleness – an animal if you will, but as wholesome as one – a lovely forest animal. It is a queer world.'[31]

These patient understanding letters called forth no answering sympathy from her sisters, both of whom were under their mother's control. If their *ménage* persisted, Ursula wrote, then she would never be able to see Ida again or give herself in marriage. Ida's immorality was like a blight, she declared, withering her own chances of fruitfulness – and those of Ethel.

Ida was stunned by this accusation. She could not believe it, did not know even whether Ursula herself believed it. In the past Dorelia had always left the house when any of Ida's family came to stay, but if they would not continue to come then Ida would simply have to go and visit them. 'As you can't accept her [Dorelia], I suppose it would be better,' she wrote. 'It *is* a queer world . . . As to your prospects of marriage – that is the one unsurmountable and unmeltable object – till you are both happily married! Do write again after thinking about it a bit – I mean the whole affair.'

Ursula needed no prompting. She wrote again the same week stating that, since Ida was unrepentant, she, Ursula, renounced marriage and resolved to live a spinster all her life.* Ida's reply, the final letter in this exchange, blended irony with tenderness but contained none of the guilt that the Nettleships had sought to implant within her.

'Darling Urla,

I was very glad to have your letter – I do think it was a little heroic. You have no business to feel so heroic as to be willing to give up marriage – or to say "what would it matter". Of course it might not matter – but dearest I understand you when you say that – it is like my painting – there are some things that seem so important which really don't matter in the least. It has cost me much pain to give it up – but it doesn't matter! It is part of the artist's life to do away with things that don't matter – but, as you say, it is unlikely you would love a man who couldn't at any rate be made to bear with our ménage. He needn't know us. You do astonish me with your idea of uncleanliness – I can't appreciate that – I am differently constructed. It seems to me so natural – and therefore not

* She did, and so did Ethel.

unclean . . . To me your thinking it so appears absurd and almost incredible – as if you'll grow out of it. A bit too "heroic". As to "doing away with the whole thing" you might as well say you'd like to do away with the sea because of wrecks and drowning.'

The long struggle seemed almost at an end. But throughout Ida's difficulties in carrying off Dorelia, persuading Augustus and resisting the Nettleships, there had been one factor which helped to blunt all opposition, and gave impetus to the setting up of a new *ménage*: she was again pregnant.

3

FROM A VIEW TO A BIRTH

'I marshalled my tribe over here [Paris] without mishap beyond a little inconsequent puking in mid-Channel.'
Augustus John to John Sampson (September 1905)

'Don't you too sometimes have glimpses so large and beautiful that life becomes immediately a jewel to prize instead of a burden to be borne or got rid of?' Ida had once asked the Rani. Regularly the darkness was shot through by these lyrical searchlights. Painting had been one source of happiness; marriage, initially, another. 'What great work is accomplished without a hundred sordid details?' she asked shortly after David's birth. 'To have a large family is now one of my ambitions.' But by the time Caspar was born, her ambition, still heroically proclaimed, sounded more hesitant. 'I should say more than I meant if I launched into explanations of why I want a large family,' she wrote again to the Rani. 'I know I do, but it may only be because there's nothing else to do, now that painting is not practicable – and I must create something.'

Babies, as a substitute for art, had failed even before Robin's birth. 'As soon as I am up,' she wrote to Margaret Sampson, 'I am going to climb an apple tree – and *never* have another baby.' For a time, cooking, gardening, even hens had become surrogates. Yet still the babies kept on coming and her disenchantment deepened: 'We are all such impostors!' she exclaimed. Then, in a letter from Paris in April 1906 Ida revealed to the Rani that she had made 'violent efforts' to dislodge her fourth child during early pregnancy. Her ambition to have a large family had died and was being replaced by something else.

They did not have, she and Gus, any skill or habit of contraception.

Nor did most people. Almost half a century after his marriage, Augustus was to make a quick sketch of the birth-control pioneer Marie Stopes, whom he portrayed as a beneficent 'witch'. But before the social revolution in family planning which Marie Stopes began in the 1920s, contraception was not easy for men and almost impossible for women. Neither men nor women were given any sex education and ignorance was equated with innocence. So they relied on the rumours of folklore, odd pieces of sponge and rubber, on periodic infertility and the split-second practice of *coitus interruptus*. Augustus was no good at this French-farce timing. There was only one time for him: the present. So he was seldom prepared. Condoms were in any case not openly for sale in pharmacies, and for someone prudish over such matters it was devilish awkward ordering these almost unmentionable provisions in a public place. Besides all these difficulties, he and Ida and Dorelia never knew when sexual intercourse would overtake them. They were all young, potent, fertile and, in their inevitable rebellion against the late-nineteenth-century culture of suppression, driven to act spontaneously.

Even before Dorelia had arrived at Matching Green, Ida had written to the Rani: 'It suddenly strikes me how perfectly divine it would be if you and I were living in Paris together. I can imagine going to the Louvre and then back to a small room over a restaurant or something . . . think of all the salads, and the sun, and blue dresses, and waiters. And the smell of butter and cheese in the small streets.' Conceived as fantasy, her romance was coming to life in fact. It represented for Ida a new attitude to the world and her place in it. 'I should like to live on a mountainside and never speak to anybody – or in a copse with one companion,' she wrote. 'I think to live with a girl friend and have lovers would be almost perfect. Whatever are we all training for that we have to shape ourselves and compromise with things all our lives? It's eternally fitting a square peg into a round hole and squeezing up one's eyes to make it look a better fit.'[32]

The girlfriend was different, but the philosophy was the same. In her experience, men were of two conditions: the artists and poets, who were beyond good or evil, and with whom one fell in love; and the others who mostly bored her. Both were impractical as husbands. With girls, however, she could develop an enduring intimacy. 'I wish I'd been a man,' she confessed to the Rani. 'I should then have felt at home in this infinitely simple world.' To some extent, it was the man's part she intended to play in Paris.

*

Augustus, Ida and Dorelia, with David and Caspar, Robin and Pyramus and Bobster their dog, set sail for France at the end of September 1905. The sea was rough, the boat rolled and Caspar (who was violently sick) declared in some alarm: 'We'd better go back.' Ida had taken two rooms for them all at the Hôtel St-Pierre in the rue de l'Ecole-de-Médecine. 'The hotel people are very kind and the food lovely,' she assured her mother. 'Children *perfectly* well and Tony [David] especially cheerful . . . [he] asked last evening if all the people in Paris talked nonsense.' Robin, however, seemed to pick up the new language astonishingly fast, and very soon was calling everyone *fou*, *sot* and *nigaud* in the most threatening manner.

From the hotel Ida sent Gus out to find a good cheap apartment for them all. 'I really feel more disposed to sit down comfortably & await the miracle rather than go through the faithless formality of climbing several thousand stairs a day, and arousing a thousand suspicions, a thousand vain hopes,' he wrote to Sampson. '. . . Ida has forbad me the Louvre till I bring home glad tidings. I admit I called on [Louis] Anquetin to-day . . . I went and had an ostentatious drink at the nearest café . . . and then bought a brown plush hat with a feather in it which must be very irritating seen from a bird's eye point of view.'[33]

These tactics were surprisingly successful and he soon came across what they wanted, near the Luxembourg Gardens. By the middle of October they had moved into 63, rue Monsieur-le-Prince, and engaged a young girl called Clara to look after them while they looked after the children. 'She [Clara] cleans a room thoroughly in the twinkling of an eye,' Ida informed Alice, 'cooks exquisitely, is clean to a fault, and can remember the exact mixture and amount and time of food for 3 babies under 1 year.' She was, moreover, not physically beautiful and seemed ideally suited to them.

Ida's fourth child, confidently referred to as Suzannah since its conception, was born on 27 November. It was 'another beastly boy – a great coarse looking bull necked unpoetical unmusical commercial snoring blockhead', she told Margaret Sampson. Yet he was the weakest of all her children and for over a year lived on bread, milk and grapes. 'He is called Quart Pot – as being a beery fourth,' Ida wrote to the Rani. '. . . After my experience I have quite given up the belief in a good god who gives us what we want. To think I must make trousers to the end of my days instead of the dainty skirt I long to sew . . . he is a difficult child like David was . . . Poor little unwelcome man.' Later called Jim, he finally settled, after gigantic difficulties in registering his birth, into the name of Edwin.

The world was fuller than ever of babies. But in these new surroundings, and fortified by her new outlook on life, Ida did not feel submerged. 'I almost think it worth while to live in this little world of children,' she confessed to the Rani. 'We are sometimes convulsed with laughter.' Laughter was the new ingredient in her life. 'Things mostly get worse in this world,' she had written to Margaret Sampson from Matching Green. Now, from Paris, she wrote to her: 'I've come to the conclusion that laughter is the chief reason for living . . . One is not bound to be too serious.' This was her new discovery, and with it rose 'those bubbles inside' that made her feel 'like a champagne bottle that wants to be opened'.

Dorelia was the centre of this happiness. While Augustus came and went, appearing over the horizon of London and Paris, she looked after Ida during her confinement and after Edwin's birth; she coped with the crises ranging from burst hot-water bottles to outbreaks of measles. Difficulties dwindled in her presence like weeds starved of nourishment: it seemed ridiculous to get worked up over such trivial affairs. 'My dear, you have no idea of the merits of Dorelia,' Ida confided to the Rani. 'Imagine me in bed, and she looking after the 4 others – good as gold – cheerful – patient – beautiful to look upon – ready to laugh at everything and nothing. She wheels out 2 in the pram, David and Caspar walking, daily, morning and evening – baths and dresses them – feeds them – smacks them.'

A few years back, Ida remembered, she had thought the Dowdalls very rich because they drank wine with their dinner. The food in Paris was so delicious and the wine so cheap that they ate and drank whatever they wanted, thanks to Gus's industry. 'I think we must be rich,' she wrote to Margaret Sampson, 'because though there is such a lot of us, we live very comfortably and are out of debt.'[34]

Their new life contained many aspects of the old, but the two mothers were better able to deal with it. Ida, in particular, regained her self-confidence. 'This place is divine,' she wrote to Margaret Sampson, 'and one can do everything – one feels so strong.' Outside the flat, their routine was of an almost bourgeois respectability. 'Time was spent taking the children out in a pram to the Luxembourg Gardens and in the evenings sitting in cafés or sometimes going to concerts, art shows, museums,' Dorelia remembered. 'How attractive Paris was in those days, separate tables outside the cafés and discreet lighting.'[35] On the surface, their days were 'fairly ordinary'. But those who called upon these bourgeois-bohemians at rue Monsieur-le-Prince saw something extraordinary. They had almost no furniture and only one bed between the lot of them – the children sleeping in boxes on rollers, the babies in baskets. 'Here is a picture of our life in one of its rarely peaceful moments,' Ida wrote to Alice early in 1906.

'Imagine a long room with bare boards – one long window looking on to a large courtyard and through an opening in the houses round to the sky and a distant white house, very lovely and glowing in the sun, and trees. In the room an alcove with a big wooden bed in it. At a writing table David doing "lessons" – on the floor two baskets – Pyramus intent on a small piece of biscuit in one – Edwin intent on his own hands in another. Robin in a baby chair with some odd toy – Caspar on the ground with another. The quiet lasts about ten minutes at the outside. Unless they are asleep or out there is nearly always a howling or a grumbling from one or more – unless a romp is going on when the row is terrific.'

Will Rothenstein, who looked in at their flat on his way to Venice shortly after they moved in, was deeply shocked by what he witnessed. The Johns seemed like a slum family with Augustus, on one of his visits, one of his bad days, a fearful figure, stamping around the bare boards. 'He is very impatient with his children and they are terribly afraid of him – the whole picture is rather a dark one,' Will reported to Alice (19 October 1905). '. . . I felt terribly sad when I saw how the kiddies were brought up, though anyone may be considered richly endowed who has such a mother as Ida. Ours seem so clean and bright compared with them just now.'

But in Augustus's eyes it was the children who terrorized him. They needed money, prevented work, wanted to be entertained, got on his nerves. One day, amid the uproar, losing his temper with David and Robin, he slapped both their faces: and then smarted with remorse. 'They will never really forget my having clouted them in the face like that,' he told Dorelia. 'I have never forgotten my father (whom I would give you for 2d) kicking me upstairs once – when I was almost Tony's [David's] age. Tell Tony I want him to enjoy himself – but to be somewhat useful and intelligent at the same time.' It was impossible to work in such an atmosphere and he returned after a fortnight to England.

Ida was now free to construct the life of which she had dreamed. Liberated from the man-dominated world, she struggled to escape the domination of children. In addition to the quick and intelligent Clara, she employed another servant, 'an old sheep' – 'which is why we can saunter out, and spend money to an outrageous extent . . . and we come in again, after an absence of 4 hours and find absolute tranquillity – babies everywhere asleep in cots (literally 3) and 2 virtuous little boys looking out of [the] windows at the rain from a house built of chairs – too sweet for words. Life is pleasant and exciting.'[36]

At last Ida seemed to have won that great luxury, time: time in which to read Balzac, Dostoevsky, Emerson and the *Daily Mail*; time to buy straw hats and cashmere shawls, to make clothes in which to sit for pictures which Gus might some day paint; time for music – Beethoven and Chopin; time to fill with talk and laughter and fantasy and sensuous laziness. They were not gregarious, the two of them: it was a secret life they led. 'It is, for 2 or 3 reasons, impossible to know people well here – so I keep out of it altogether,' Ida explained to the Rani. '. . . And it is just as nice in many ways not knowing people.' Not knowing people was part of Ida's detachment, her strength and freedom. 'How delightful not to care what the neighbours think!' she had sighed to Margaret Sampson at Matching Green. 'My utmost is to tell myself and others that I do not care – I do all the time.' In Paris she no longer cared so much. She had escaped from her family and the neighbours. She could be as free as Dorelia now: she felt sure she could.

Almost the only person they saw regularly was Gwen John – 'always the same strange reserved creature', as Ida described her.[37] Dorelia offered to sit again for Gwen and made a black velvet jacket for her. But this phase of Gwen's life was over – she was far from reserved with Rodin. Yet she was also strangely secretive. 'Gwen persists in Paris,' Augustus reported to Michel Salaman. 'I suppose she prefers penurious liberty to social dependence. She has several pictures which she never shows to anyone.' Gwen told Rodin nothing of the arrival of Ida, Dorelia and Gus in Paris (the new velvet jacket, she said, was made by a dressmaker), but wrote to him of her dreams and nightmares. Nevertheless, she would invite them over to her pretty new apartment at 7 rue St-Placide, a wide sunlit street of little shops on the northern boundary of Montparnasse. In the evenings they would dine with her on eggs and spinach and charcuterie in the room where she lived with her 'horrid' cat and where they would meet Miss Hart, an ex-pupil of Augustus's at Liverpool 'who has attached herself uncomfortably to Gwen'.[38] Gwen gave them three beautiful pictures for their bare flat: also, Ida wrote to Augustus, 'there was a head of Gwen by Rodin in the Salon'.

To be as irresponsible as she could allow herself, 'as gay as possible under the circumstances' – this was Ida's ambition. Dorelia took to wearing bright jerseys and short velvet skirts; Ida cut her hair short but did not look *very* 'new womanish, because it curls rather'. But who were the new women if not Ida and Dorelia and Gwen? Then David, presumably pursuing this fashion, cut off all his own and all Caspar's hair so that they were almost unrecognizable when Ida and Dorelia returned home. Released from the awful presence of their father – the eyes that stared, the voice that roared – the children had never been more boisterous. David, very light and springy, imitated bears and baboons; Caspar, very fat and solid in a sealskin cap, turned somersaults, and boasted that he was a king; Robin, who climbed and jumped a lot, was constantly teased by David and Caspar, constantly teasing the beautiful Pyramus; while Edwin, a long thin cross creature, howled independently in toothless rage. But though the 'acrobats', as Ida called them, had never been more lawless, yet 'I lose my temper less than of yore – Dorelia never did lose hers. We take it in turns to take them out.'

Other people's tempers were less shock-proof. After three months, the neighbours, unable to endure the reverberating wet tumult any longer, demanded their eviction. 'We shall probably take a small house,' Ida wrote (12 January 1906) to Alice who, in the confusion of breeding, had sent a bonnet for Pyramus, mistaking him for Ida's baby. Not living on a mountainside or in a copse, it seemed impossible to avoid compromise. In January they began house-hunting in the quarter beyond rue de la Gaieté. After exploring 'millions of studios' and a number of houses, they provisionally decided on 77 rue Dareau, where Augustus had already booked a studio for the spring. 'The concierge of your studio showed us his rez de chaussée [ground floor],' Ida wrote to Gus (January 1906). 'Do you think it would do?' There were many advantages: a garden, and the studio to sit in during the evenings, besides three living-rooms, a kitchen and scullery; the rent was low, they could take it on a quarterly basis, and they would still be near the Luxembourg Gardens. Best of all 'your concierge says there can be no objection to the kids – he says he understands "qu'ils crient – qu'ils ne chantent pas!" He was incredulous when I said the neighbours would object – and if they do they can go and we'll take their places.' Both Ida and Dorelia were convinced they would not 'find anything so good in every way as the R de C'. Their only doubt was Gus's attitude. 'If you dread having the kids and all at your place – if you think it will interfere with your work – we will find something else.' Ida's letter reached Augustus (who had just sold several pictures) in a jovial mood and he urged them to take the *rez-de-chaussée* at once. The clamour of the children seemed no great impediment now he could no longer hear it. 'I trust the family is well to the last unit,' he replied, enclosing a bundle of pound notes (February 1906). 'I hope to get everything done in a week and then back again my hearties! . . . Feed up well . . . and circulate the money.'

The new apartment would not be ready till April. Meanwhile Ida proposed taking the three eldest children to the South of France. Mrs Nettleship had not been well and was planning to go to Menton for three weeks' recuperation. To accompany her she invited her daughter Ursula together with Ida and the children. 'I cannot refuse can I?' Ida asked Augustus.

They set off early in March and spent the rest of the month at 'a highly respectable hotel' crowded with British gentlewomen of 'comfortable means' attended by their very correct daughters – prim little moppets in muslin. But the beauty of the country was heart-lifting. 'Shall I tell you of the mountains?' Ida inquired in a letter to the Rani (29 March 1906),

' – their grand grey forms right upon the clouds, the lower parts covered with trees – fir trees – and the lowest with Olive trees – and up at the top streaks of snow in the cracks (as seen from here) in reality masses of snow in the ravines and crevasses. And the town of Mentone all built up in piles against the hill and the sea – good old sea, ordinary old sea – spreading out at the bottom, with the steam yachts of the rich and the fishing boats of the poor and the eternal waves – so stupid and so graceful. And the mongrel population – selling in silly sounding French. They're all Italian or half Italian.'

In the sunlight of the hotel garden among the tulips and the wallflowers, the pansies, stocks and daffodils, Ida sat reflecting on how strange everything was and how happy she ought to have been, yet wasn't. Instead she fretted impatiently, filled with that familiar sense of exclusion that had devoured her at Matching Green. Gus had returned to Paris not long after she left for Menton. What was happening there? She longed yet dreaded to be back. These cushioned hotel days were a terrible waste of time. She felt like some general witnessing a battle swinging away from him, powerless to do anything about it. Good manners and an English sense of duty – all she had endeavoured to escape by coming to France – held her in check. If only she had been a different kind of person! 'I crave to go to school,' she told the Rani.

'Not quite literally, but to set about learning from the beginning – Lord, how I long to. The 3 kids are here, and very brave and jolly. Edwin is left in the care of the loveliest girl in the world God damn her. And I believe Gus has gone back to Paris to-day; so they'll all have a good time together, especially as his Poet Friend [Wyndham] Lewis is there, and great friends with Dorelia . . . I am here biting my nails with rage and jealousy and *impotence*. Because if I were there it would spoil the fun don't you see? Oh why was I not born otherwise?'

This was Ida's first setback since coming to France. Early in April she returned to Paris, and then she, Dorelia and their string of children moved into the rue Dareau.³⁹ The two women re-papered the walls of their new home, covering them with sketches, pictures, photographs. It was another fresh start, and hope rose again in Ida. Augustus came and went; the children ('it makes them all look very interesting') all caught colds; and Dorelia ('it's her turn') 'is decidedly enceinte', Ida informed Augustus.

4

CHANNEL CROSSING

'I think I shall be a supernaturalist in Paris, and in London a naturalist.'

Augustus John to Alick Schepeler (1906)

'About to embark shortly for England,' Augustus had written to Wyndham Lewis. 'I would be encouraged to the adventure by a word from you as to your welfare and whereabouts.' No sooner had he settled on a studio for his work in Paris than the work began to flow in – but from London. He hurried back. 'We had £255 [equivalent to £13,600 in 1996] in about ten days ago, to my amazement,' Ida wrote to him from Paris. 'You do make a lot.'

Augustus had hoped by this time to sell the Chelsea Art School to a Mrs Flower, 'a remarkable woman' and a cousin of Ida's, so that he could spend more time in Paris. 'The school has been very successful so far – I mean the first year was remarkably so – we have almost paid off our debts,' he wrote invitingly to Michel Salaman. 'No doubt there is a veritable goldmine in it, but the process of digging is long & tedious. Having prospected so successfully both Orpen & I would be happy to retire with all the glory & leave the yellow dirt for others to grab. We have the school with its lavish appurtenances, its golden prospects and a nucleus of brilliant pupils complete for sale & for a mere song.'[40]

Augustus hoped that Michel Salaman might hurry along the negotiations, but it was not until the summer of 1907 that they completed the sale. The delay did not please Orpen and irritated Augustus, who continued to be bound to the school, though 'only morally bound', he explained. In fact he was wonderfully neglectful after the first year. 'I hope the school will go on merrily,' he wrote cheerfully to Orpen in 1906. 'I thought it had stopped long ago.'[41] But Orpen too had been away, in Dublin. He did not like to be connected with something that might turn out to be a failure. Their gold-mine was tiresome for both of them. 'I am sick of the school and tired of Orpen,' Augustus wrote to Dorelia (1906). '. . . I think of chucking it – even if I have to pay off debts.'

That he did continue teaching at Rossetti Studios was partly due to an exciting new development early that winter. This was the acquisition of a gallery next to Chelsea Town Hall in the King's Road. Orpen, who largely financed it at the start, persuaded Knewstub to open the Chenil Gallery, as it was called – a small town house ideally suited, Knewstub saw, for accommodating his cultural dreams. Downstairs were two small rooms: one he converted into a 'shop' selling canvases, paints and all manner of artist's equipment; the other he established as an etching-press room for artists wishing to print from or prove their own plates. Upstairs there were two exhibition rooms, one of which held a permanent collection of work by the regular platoon of Chenil painters: Ambrose and Mary McEvoy, David Muirhead, William Nicholson, James Pryde, Orpen and Augustus himself. At the back was a large studio which Augustus was often to use in the years to come.

The first one-man show at the new gallery, in May 1906, was of etchings by Augustus, and this stimulated continuous work over the early months of this year. 'I have to spend days seeing to my etchings,' he explained to the pregnant Dorelia as the weeks passed and still he did not return to Paris, ' – a man has ordered a complete set. I find to my astonishment I have done about 100.' This man was the art historian Campbell Dodgson who, on 20 February 1906, had written to Will Rothenstein asking him to approach Augustus and find out whether he would let the British Museum (for which Dodgson worked) have a selection of his etchings and drawings. Rothenstein put Dodgson directly in touch with Augustus and a week later they met. 'I went to see John yesterday and looked through his etchings which interest me very much,' Dodgson reported to Rothenstein (28 February 1906). 'He is quite willing to give me specimens of his drawings hesitating only on the grounds that he hopes to do better, and would not like us to have things that he hopes to tear up some years hence; but there is not much fear of such a fate befalling certain things that I saw yesterday and would like to secure. But [Sidney] Colvin will go himself in a few days and settle the matter.'[42]

Once his initial interest in the plates had passed, Augustus was often careless about their preservation, allowing them to be scratched, battered and corroded by verdigris. So when Knewstub stepped forward to rescue these plates from further harm, and superintend their printing and publication in the catalogue of the coming exhibition, he found himself confronted by a vast salvage operation. He cleaned, he scraped, he searched, and as many plates as he could find (whether in sufficiently good condition to yield editions, or so badly treated that they had to be destroyed) he took over and numbered, together with all such early proofs as he could discover in Augustus's studio.

The Chenil exhibition 'far exceeded what I expected', Augustus told Charles Rutherston.[43] He would continue his experiments with needle and copper for another three years, though on a gradually diminishing scale. After 1910 he produced only half a dozen or so more etchings – a small group of portrait studies of a girl's head; a head of John Hope-Johnstone recovering from measles; and two self-portraits. His later work shows an advance from the sometimes rather laboured earlier efforts, with their ample use of dry-point, to the pure etched line of his most successful plates. But the medium was too slow, too small. The paraphernalia of needles and plates, of nitric and sulphuric acid, which had captured his interest at first, eventually fatigued him. He wanted to try something new.

*

Augustus's treatment of his copperplates was similar to the way he treated his friendships. He liked to keep an army of acquaintances in reserve, upon any number of which he could call when the mood was on him. He wanted fair-weather friends; he wanted them to be, like some fire brigade, in permanent readiness for his calls; and he enjoyed summoning them fitfully. Among the etchings at the Chenil Gallery were several portraits of friends who had already sped out of his life: Benjamin Evans, who had shot down the drain;[44] Ursula Tyrwhitt and Esther Cerutti, who had been outshone by later models. There were others, too, of whom he saw only little these days. Michel Salaman, who had graduated from art student into fox-hunting squire; 'little Albert' Rutherston, already partially eclipsed by little Will Rothenstein; the monkey-like Orpen, who had grown curiously attached to a gorilla in the Dublin zoo – 'perhaps the only serious love affair in his life';[45] and Conder, who in June 1906 had become so ill he was forced to relinquish painting.

There were two motives behind all Augustus's friendships: inspiration and entertainment. Either they stimulated him when at work, or they induced self-forgetfulness in the intervals between working. But none of them could live up to his veering needs. He knew this and mocked himself for it. 'I am in love with a new man,' he told Dorelia on 16 March 1906, 'Egmont Hake – a bright gem!' Such mysterious gems – and there were many of them – would glitter for a day and then be lost for ever. His most consistent relationships were those which were held together by humour or, more simply, renewed by imaginative periods of absence. He welcomed the retreating back, the cheerful goodbye, the disappearing companion whose tactful vanishing trick saved in the nick of time their comradeship from the terrible contempt that grew with familiarity. He relished people such as John Sampson, whom he could abandon 'in the Euston Road while he was immobilized under the hands of a shoe-black', and then meet again, their feelings charged with nostalgia; and of course Gwen, for whom, though she could not work under her brother's shadow, he continued to feel admiration shot through with exasperated concern.

What Gwen had known about Gus, others, such as Wyndham Lewis, were beginning to discover for themselves. 'I want also to do some painting very badly, and can't do so near John,' Lewis complained to his mother (1906). '. . . Near John I can never paint, since his artistic personality is just too strong, and he [is] much more developed, naturally, and this frustrates any effort.'[46] Partly because of this frustration, Lewis turned to his writing, being known by Augustus as 'the Poet' because he had produced, in next to no time, 'thirty sonnettes', some of them as good as Baudelaire's. Now that Augustus was jostling between Paris and London, he was able to see far more of Lewis, then on the move between England, France and Germany while brewing up his Dostoevskyan cocktail of a novel, *Tarr*. They would go off to nightclubs together, or sit drinking and talking at the Brasserie Dumesnil in the rue Dareau, recommended by Sickert for its excellent sauerkraut. 'Not that I find him absolutely indispensable,' Augustus conceded, 'but at times I love to talk with him about Shelley or somebody.'[47] Lewis himself preferred to talk about Apaches and 'to frighten young people' with tales of these Parisian gangsters. But what chiefly amused Augustus were Lewis's 'matrimonial projects' which formed part of his material for *Tarr*. If the artist, Lewis seems to argue, finds much in his work that other men seek in women, then it follows that he must be particularly discriminating in his love affairs, and scrupulously avoid sentimentality and all other false trails that lead him away from reality. It was a theme nicely attuned to Augustus's own predicament. 'I am like a noble, untaught and untainted savage who, embracing with fearful enthusiasm the newly arrived Bottle, Bible and Whore of civilization, contracts at once with horrible violence their apoplectic corollary, the Paralysis, the Hypocrisy and the Pox,' he wrote. '. . . So far I have been marvellously immune.'

Lewis's immunity appeared even stronger. Prudence, suspicion and an aggressive shyness ringed him about like some fortress from which he seldom escaped. 'Lewis announced last night that he was *loved!*' Augustus reported to one of their model-friends, Alick Schepeler.

'At last! It seems he had observed a demoiselle in a restaurant who whenever he regarded her sucked her cheeks in slightly and looked embarrassed. The glorious fact was patent then – l'amour! He means to follow this up like a bloodhound. In the meanwhile however he has gone to Rouen for a week to see his mother, which in my opinion is not good generalship. He has a delightful notion – I am to get a set of young ladies during the summer as pupils and of course he will figure in the company and possibly be able to make love to one of them.'

But when not in the vein to be amused by Lewis's eccentricities, Augustus would quickly get needled. It was almost as if his own easy romanticism was being caricatured. 'The poet irritates me,' he admitted, 'he is always asking for petits suisses which are unheard of in this country and his prudence is boundless.' The conclusion was obvious. 'What a mistake it is to have a friend – or, having one, ever to see him.'

The trouble was that Augustus could not be alone for long. Without an audience he disappeared. The dark interiors of the pubs and cafés were like wombs from which he could be reborn. He would saunter in as if on the spur of the moment, choose his companion for an hour or two, a Juliet for a night: then it was over and he could be someone else. Such encounters, with no hangover of duty, were marvellously invigorating. If friends were God's apology for families, it surely followed they should be as unlike one's own family as possible. But perfection could not be found in any single man, for perfection must suit all weathers. 'I cannot find my man,' he told Alick Schepeler, ' – hence I have to piece him together out of half a dozen – as best I can.'

Upon the construction of this composite friend Augustus spent much haphazard energy. A little less McEvoy, for example, was quickly balanced by more Epstein and the introduction of a new artist into his life, Henry Lamb. In his correspondence, Augustus sometimes has fun with Epstein. 'Epstein called yesterday and I went back with him to see his figure which is nearly done,' he wrote to Dorelia in 1907. 'It is a monstrous thing – but of course it has its merits – he has now a baby to do. The scotch girl [Margaret Dunlop] was here – she is the one who poses for the mother – he might at least have got a real mother for his "Maternity". He is going about borrowing babies. He suggested sending the group to the N.E.A.C.!! Imagine Tonks' horror and Steer's stupefaction!'

Augustus did some good etchings of Epstein. Most striking of all is a red-pencil drawing which Epstein himself much liked. By using the point of a very hard pencil Augustus gives this portrait a taut quality, a tightness of face and mouth indicating both intellect and temperamental force. The rhetorical pose of the head bends a little to the romantic conception of genius, but the drawing[18] also emphasizes the 'closed to criticism' nature of Epstein's personality.

He had much criticism to close his mind to. The 'monstrous thing' Epstein was working on in his studio in Cheyne Walk early in 1907 was almost certainly one of the eighteen figures, representing man and woman in their various stages between birth and death, that were to embellish the new British Medical Association building in the Strand. These figures, mostly nudes, caused much outrage when, in the spring of 1908, they were first thrust upon the public gaze. 'They are a form of statuary which no careful father would wish his daughter, or no discriminating young man, his fiancée, to see,' one newspaper informed its readers.[49] Other experts, including clergymen, policemen, dustmen and the Secretary of the Vigilance Society, were soon adding their voices to this vituperative hymn. The statues were 'rude'; they exerted a 'demoralizing tendency' and constituted 'a gross offence'. In short, they would 'convert London into a Fiji Island'. Who could doubt that these objects must become a focus for unwholesome talk, a meeting place for all the unchaste in the land?

Many artists defended Epstein. But Augustus, who privately did much to help him,[50] saw clearly that artistic support was irrelevant to moral indignation and would never impress the public. 'Epstein's work must be defended by recognised moral experts,' he wrote to the art critic Robert Ross. 'The Art question is not raised. Of course they would stand the *moral* test as triumphantly as the artistic, or even more if possible. Do you know of an intelligent *Bishop* for example? To-morrow there is a meeting to decide whether the figures are to be destroyed or not. Much the best figures are behind the hoarding which they *refuse* to take down. Meanwhile Epstein is in debt and unable to pay the workmen.'

Augustus's advice was quickly taken up, and the Bishop of Stepney, Cosmo Gordon Lang, later Archbishop of Canterbury, was persuaded to mount the ladders to the scaffolding, from where he inspected the figures intimately and, on descending, declared himself unshocked. His imperturbability did much to reassure the British public and soothe the Council of the British Medical Association, which instructed work to proceed.

Though Augustus admired Epstein's sculpture, he was impatient with some aspects of his personality and shocked to discover that this milk-drinker from America excelled in blowing his own trumpet.[51] 'I hope Epstein will find his wife a powerful reinforcement in his studio,' Augustus wrote to Will Rothenstein (19 September 1906) on learning of the sculptor's engagement to Margaret Dunlop. 'Perhaps she will coax him out of some of his unduly democratic habits.' As proud and touchy as Augustus was truculent, Epstein appeared determined to attract hostility. Augustus was able to oblige him here, and their friendship was often blown on the rocks.

But in these early days they got on well enough. Augustus's extravagance in the middle of so much polite good taste was refreshing to Epstein, and he admired Augustus's skill. Besides, Epstein needed encouragement and Augustus could afford to give it. Often they would be joined by

McEvoy in whose gentle company neither felt disposed to quarrel. Epstein also dropped round at the Chelsea Art School where he posed as a model for a shilling an hour, and afterwards there would be black periods of silence as he and Augustus leant against one of its walls: then a remark from Epstein – 'At least you will admit that Wagner was a heaven-storming genius.' Finally from Augustus an ambivalent grunt.

A witness to these exchanges, and much impressed by them, was Henry Lamb. Lamb had recently thrown up his medical studies in Manchester and, in a desperate bid to become an artist, turned up in London with an alluring wild girl called Nina Forrest whom, after Mantegna's Saint, he rechristened 'Euphemia'. While Lamb trained himself as an artist, Euphemia became an artist's model and was soon posing for Epstein. She had a natural sense of theatre, and drama perpetually hovered in the air around her. She was also 'a great romancer' and would grow famous for her amorous anecdotes. How interesting 'impure women are to the pure', Virginia Woolf later meditated over her. 'I see her as someone in mid-ocean, struggling, diving, while I pace my bank.'[52] Early in 1906 Euphemia discovered she was pregnant and, on 10 May, Henry and she were married at the Chelsea Register Office with Augustus as one of their two witnesses – shortly after which she appears to have had a miscarriage.

For the time being Augustus was no more than a witness to Euphemia's romances, but he involved himself quite seriously in Henry's career. While Euphemia somehow seemed 'always well supplied with money', Henry was impecunious. Arriving in London with a modest stipend and working intermittently as an illustrator for the *Manchester Guardian*, he enrolled at the Chelsea Art School at the beginning of 1906 and would sometimes sleep there on the model's throne. On coming in at night he would find a fresh cartoon done by Augustus during the evening – large works of many almost life-size figures that dazzled him. Occasionally Augustus, in his rumbling voice, would brood on these compositions: 'I think of taking out that figure and introducing a waterfall.' Lamb, wide-eyed, felt himself to be in the incalculable presence of genius.

Bernard Leach, the potter, remembered Lamb's first day at the Chelsea Art School. 'Augustus came in late straight from some party looking well groomed and remarkably handsome, picked up a drawing board, and instead of using it sat behind this new student and watched him for half an hour. They talked and Augustus invited Henry to his home.'[53]

Augustus had a powerful impact on Lamb, giving his draughtsmanship a technical fluency and professionalism, warming his rather clinical line, enriching it with new vitality. What Lamb lacked was confidence. 'The sight of my recent products fills me with dejection,' he wrote; 'my pictures . . . deject me beyond sufferance.' In Augustus's company this dejection lifted. He appeared 'a heaven-sent star destined to light the way for a beginner', wrote Lamb's biographer Keith Clements.

It was a matter of style and also of lifestyle. Another art student, Nina Hamnett, saw Augustus as 'a tall man with a reddish beard, in a velvet coat and brown trousers, striding along . . . a splendid-looking fellow and I followed him down the King's Road.'[54] Lamb too followed Augustus, modelling himself on his manner, his looks, his life. It was as if, for a time, Augustus imprinted his personality on him. 'I should have been Augustus John,' Bernard Leach recalled Lamb saying. Inevitably, Augustus was flattered by this talented follower. What could be more proper than a young man wishing to act apprentice to him? It was a concept he had always understood and needed to benefit from himself. He responded generously. 'I hope you are doing designs lightheartedly,' he wrote (24 October 1906). ' – What is so becoming as cheerfulness and a light heart? I think the old masters are apt to presume upon our reverence sometimes – one is always at a disadvantage in the society of the illustrious dead – perhaps it would be high time to bid them a reverent but cheerful adieu! since we have invented umbrellas let us use them – as ornaments at least.'

Lamb was not slow to respond to this message. He elected Augustus as a new master among the illustrious living. Confidence swelled within Augustus – confidence, but not conceit. If people believed in him, he believed in himself. He needed other people's faith to fortify his own will. 'Your letter thrills me somewhat,' he replied to Lamb (5 November 1906). 'I am not quite a Master – yet. I keep forgetting myself often. But I am learning loyalty. We must have no rivals – and no fickleness. I feel ashamed to go to sleep sometimes. I am learning to value my own loves and fancies and thought above all others. But Life has an infernal narcotic side to it – and one is caught napping and philandering – – – alas! alas! if one had some demon to whip one! I hardly believe you had faith in my possibilities – in my will. I am so glad.'

No friendship yet had begun in such promising style – none would lead to such complications or remain so long an embarrassment to both artists.

In London Augustus had found work and a few people to inspire him; in Paris entertainment and the promise of inspiration to come. Something of the awe and wonder that possessed him when he first went to the Slade now re-entered his life. Paris was 'a queen of cities' and 'so beautiful – London can't possibly be so nice'.[55] No atmosphere, surely, was ever more favourable to the artist. On the terraces of the Nouvelle Athènes or the Rat Mort it was not difficult to conjure up the spectres of Manet, Camille Pissarro, Renoir, Cézanne, Degas – figures from the last enchanted epoch, laughing and arguing across the marble tables. But the real heart of Paris lay further back; it belonged to the Middle Ages. Malodorous, loud with bells, its architecture full of passion, of the cruelty and splendour of ancient superstition, Paris seemed more dangerous than London. It was closer to Nature, to the earth itself, to man and woman's strange evolution from that earth. The murmur of the boulevards, deep and vibrant; the view of the city seen at dusk from Sacré-Coeur as the light receded to a pinpoint between the smoking of a thousand chimneys; the landscape of the Île de France with its opulent green as if depicted through medieval windows: such beauty seized him with a kind of anguish, confronted him with unanswerable questions: 'What will become of us? What could all this mean?'

For hours he would sit in the rue de la Gaieté, watching, talking, drinking, listening to the infernal din of a mechanical orchestra, and never wishing to go home – never going home. There was more dreaming of painting than pictures painted.

'They are playing in this café just now – so I expect I shall get rhetorical presently,' he wrote to Alick Schepeler. 'Yes, I shall paint yet: it is more like fighting than anything else for me now – it will be triumphant though . . . Civilization getting in my way and making a dreary hash of things – and wasting time. I'd like to be kept by a prince. It's not safe to let me loose about the place in this way – and then send me bills to pay.'

The cosmopolitan world of Montparnasse was a literary world. The talk was of Flaubert and Baudelaire, of Turgenev and Nietzsche, the excellent heathen entertainment of Huysmans and the newest Dostoevsky in French. Almost the only painter, living or dead, who is mentioned in his correspondence is Puvis de Chavannes. Augustus's Parisian friends were mostly writers, in particular the circle that gathered round the monocled, top-hatted figure of Jean Moréas at the Closerie des Lilas and which included Guillaume Apollinaire, Colette, Paul Fort, the wandering poet who, with his brother Robert, ran the journal *Vers et Prose*, and André Salmon, the literary spokesman of 'Les Jeunes'.

Of all this group his most valued friend was Maurice Cremnitz. Late at night, after the group had dispersed from the Closerie des Lilas, Cremnitz would lead Augustus off to louche areas of Paris and leave him with a Swedish lady famous for her exercises. At other times they would explore the old quarters of the city, 'visiting the wine shops where the *vin blanc* was good – and cheap';[56] and they would go to the little Place du Tertre, to the Moulin de la Galette and the Bal Tabarin, where such delightful songs as 'Petite Miette' and 'Viens pou-poule' were all the rage and where Cremnitz would sing, in amazing cockney English, 'Last Night Down our Alley Came a Toff.' 'I observed the true gaieté française last night,' Augustus wrote after their first expedition, 'a little femme de mauvaise vie had a new song she kept singing and teaching everybody else – no one could have been more innocently happy – and the song – !!'[57]

Innocent, too, at least in name, was an obscure subterranean *bouge*, the Caveau des Innocents, near les Halles, into which they descended one night, 'and, I must admit, drank great quantities of white wine. A drunken poet joined us there and declaimed Verlaine and his own verses at great length. As he had the impudence to take exception to my style of Beauty I said "Voulez vous venez battre avec moi, Monsieur l'Antichrist?" He got up and, having put himself into a pugnacious attitude, sat down again. Afterwards he was very affectionate, informing me that he and I had fought side by side in the Crimea – frères d'armes!' This robust shadow-boxing was marvellously congenial to Augustus. Paris seemed to unite those two aspects of his personality that could, in his work and friendships, so easily diminish each other: romanticism and wry humour.

So, for a season, Paris diverted him. 'I've been damnably lazy this summer,' he admitted to Will Rothenstein (19 September 1906), 'but am happily unrepentant. I fancy idleness ends by bearing [more] rare fruit than industry. I started by being industrious and lost all self-respect – but by now have recovered some dignity and comfort by dint of listening to the most private intimations of the Soul and contemning all busy-body thoughts that come buzzing and fussing and messing in one's brain.'

*

All his life Augustus lived under the influence of an impossible ideal. What he sought in men – inspiration and entertainment – he also looked for in women, though in a different form. Many of his finest male portraits are of writers and artists: Thomas Hardy, Wyndham Lewis, William Nicholson, Bernard Shaw, Matthew Smith, Dylan Thomas, Joseph Hone, W. B. Yeats. Other men – Trelawney Dayrell Reed, John Hope-Johnstone, Chaloner Dowdall – brought him alive by virtue of their eccentricities. The inspiration of women sprang from his belief that they were closer to Nature and to the mystery of birth: and this he celebrated most lyrically in small glowing panels showing young mothers and children as part of a natural landscape. But women also entertained him simply and obviously by their sexuality; for sex, which had so worried him while he was an adolescent, had become 'the greatest joke in the world':[58] and Augustus loved a joke.

As symbols of the miracle of life, women must guard their secret well. Yet the miracle of life, of which they were the custodians, depended upon the joke of sex. Inspiration and entertainment were therefore oddly harnessed, sometimes pulling in divergent ways.

No one, perhaps, catches this oddity and divergence so well as a woman he had recently come across in London. Her name was Alick Schepeler and, next to Dorelia herself, she became for a few years his supreme model. She was almost a parody of Augustus's romantic ideal. No one, it seemed, knew who she was. 'Are you a Pole?' he demanded – but in reply she would only smile. In *Chiaroscuro* he refers to her – 'Alick Schepeler, to whose strange charm I had bowed' – only once, and declares her to have been 'of Slavonic origin', adding that she 'illustrated in herself the paradox of Polish pride united to Russian abandon'. By naturalization she was in fact British, her mother, Sarah Briggs, being Irish and her father, John Daniel Schepeler, German. The facts of her life were unusual, though not extraordinary. Her real name was Alexandra, she was an only child and had been born on 10 March 1882 at Skrygalof, near Minsk in Russia, where John Schepeler worked as an industrialist. Her father died when she was five and she was taken by her mother to live in Poland. Here Sarah Schepeler found employment with a Polish family as 'English' governess, while Alexandra was boarded near by with a Mrs Bloch and her daughter Frieda. Some ten years later Sarah Schepeler died, and not long afterwards Alexandra, who had by now become part of the Bloch family, travelled to London with Frieda. The two girls, who were about the same age and had become great friends, lived together at 29 Stanley Gardens in Chelsea. Frieda went to the Slade but Alexandra, who appeared to have no special talent, took a course in typing and went to work as a secretary for the *Illustrated London News*. In her letters to Augustus she hints at leaving this paper and taking on grander work. In fact she never left. Her unsettled upbringing seemed to have implanted within her a fear of change, even change for the better. She lived in Chelsea and typed at the *Illustrated London News* for more than fifty years.

In the extent of her ordinariness lay her single extraordinary quality. She had nothing to hide, but from the presence of this nothing arose a mystery none could solve. Her talk was of her cat, her clothes, her office. She was unbelievably uninteresting – and no man could quite believe it. Augustus, in his pure wish to avoid intellectual passion, could not have chosen anyone better.

Yet she lived for passion. Love – physical and romantic love – was her escape from dullness. She had avoided the hockey-and-inhibition of a British education, and unlike many young girls in Edwardian London she was eager for love affairs. So her life became a fairy-tale. By night she was a coquette, abandoning herself anxiously to party-going pleasures. Day came, and she was translated once more into a pale contented secretary.

It is easy to understand why Augustus found her so interesting. Five feet five inches tall, she had sumptuous brown hair and pensive blue eyes. She was highly strung, easily pleased, equally easily offended. But her most bewitching quality was her gurgling voice, rich and soupy and full of flattering inflections.

It was through Frieda Bloch and her Slade friends that Alick, as everyone called her, got to know Augustus and subsequently many other writers and artists, from Wyndham Lewis to W. B. Yeats. Some of them treated her unkindly, though she never complained, never explained. When questioned about Yeats, she simply gurgled, her voice like hot air bubbling through lemonade: 'Ah Yeats – he was a won-derful man!' And Lewis? 'Yes – won-derful!' As for Augustus, he was 'won-derful!'

For such artists and poets her admiration was unfettered. While Ida and Dorelia were tucked up together in Paris, Augustus and Alick began to see a good deal of each other in London. Augustus was most surely himself when his hesitations were swept aside by a new passion. There was no hesitation over Alick Schepeler.

'You are one of the people who inhabit my world,' he wrote to her, ' – a denizen of my country, a daughter of my tribe – one of those on whom I must depend – for life and beyond life. I am subjected to you – be loyal to your subject.' Since Augustus had to spend much of his time in Paris, his infatuation for this 'jeune fille mystérieuse et gaie' intensified. Their relationship developed through a correspondence that was voluminous, purple, and of astonishing tedium. Augustus owned that he had to have a supply of brandy in order 'to continue this correspondence which bores me so much'. Boredom was an essential part of their intimacy. They were experts in the subject, connoisseurs; indeed they were competitors. In almost every letter he asks her urgently: 'Let me know if you are badly bored?' And in almost every answer she is able to boast of some new territory conquered by ennui. This ennui was an object of fascination to Augustus, who measures it wonderingly against his own until, reaching pathos, it becomes the essence of their love affair. 'Do you know I long to see you again,' he writes from France. 'You are such a love – your smile is so wonderful and nobody cries so beautifully as you. How bored are you Alick? I get quite desperate at times – really yesterday I caught myself in the act of beating my brow! All alone and quite theatrically – I tell you I was angry!' To paper up these areas of boredom, he begs her to 'cover six sheets with an embroidery of pretty thoughts and interesting information', and send them to him at once. 'Wrap yourself in the sheets, so to say, and leave the imprint of your adorable self behind for me.' But such an accomplishment is beyond Alick; she has nothing to say. He calls her 'Undine', after the female water-sprites or elemental spirits of the water in Paracelsus's system. To help him escape from himself, and assume another role in the theatre of their romance, he begs her: 'Do re-christen me!' But this feat too is beyond her; she can think of no names, her head is empty – and so, to his disappointment, Augustus remains inescapably Augustus. Nevertheless, by a fraction, she was more bored than he, if only because he wrote more letters than she did. 'Ah, Alick – writing so often as I do how can one avoid being a bore?' he demanded.

'I know what risks I run but still persist – it means talking to you vaguely, unsatisfactorily and blindly, but still some attenuated converse with you. I can't see the expression on your face nor hear the sound of your voice – it is worse than the telephone – and more open to misunderstandings. It is a kind of muffled dumbshow with hands tied.

How is it you mean so much to me – you are like a woman found on an island by one happily shipwrecked, who shows him the cave where she sleeps and the berries she eats and the pool in which she bathes herself – and in kissing her his soul flies to the moon henceforth his God as it is hers.'

Boredom was only to be outwitted by the most extreme romantics. As hypochondriacs of the soul, they searched for a magic paradox, the profundity of the superficial, adding from time to time some *nouveau frisson* to their medicine chest. 'I can tell you how to procure a new sensation,' Augustus prescribed in one of his letters. 'First of all get hot – undo your waistband – indeed it is better to remove your outer dress, then, seated on your bed, pour white wine very slowly down your neck, breathing regularly the while. But you must be at the proper temperature to commence with. If this doesn't please you I will tell you another method.'

Alick's letters almost always disappointed Augustus; but the posts that brought no letters from her stirred him marvellously. 'Alick – why don't I hear from you – won't you write even if you don't love me? Do not wait till you love me – it might take days to come on. What else can I say – nothing till I hear from you, my moon, my tender dove, rose of my soul. – John.'

Their correspondence was secret, and this secrecy gave excitement to the masquerade. Augustus never kept letters, he merely failed to lose them. Alick, who sensed this, is always rousing him to the point of destruction. 'Yes I burn your letters,' he prevaricated. 'Even the last, than which nothing less compromising could have been written, I took away to a lonely spot and consumed. I hope you dispose of mine with equal thoroughness. In case you are still without a cigarette I send you one – to be smoked with this letter.' But still Alick was not satisfied. She seemed to detect a bantering tone in this assurance, and on at least one occasion asked him to return her letters through the post.

'Here are your letters – you see I have destroyed many. My habit (an evil one of course) is to put them in my pocket where they remain safely till it gets too crowded – when I weed out a few . . . There is nobody here who would read *your* letters or understand them . . . Yes – you may trust to my honour to *burn* all letters I get from you in future *instantly* and if you like I will eat all the ashes as a further precaution. You don't realise what depths of discretion I am capable of, and I am improving in this respect – under your tuition.'

Alick distrusted flippancy. If Augustus had a fault, it was this disconcerting humour of his. She wished he were more straightforward, like herself. She told him plainly that she put every item of his correspondence to the flames. They may now be read in the Department of Manuscripts at the Huntington, California.

In his strangely muted world, isolated, swept by melancholia, Augustus welcomed Alick Schepeler as a fellow creature. His instinct was not wrong. She lessened his loneliness by being so inexplicably lonely herself. They were, he told her, both 'Keltic'. They seemed cut off from their childhoods, still curiously shy on occasions, reading widely as a refuge from solitude, taking their mental colouring from their friends. They shared an obsession with clothes. When Alick commanded Augustus to write and tell her all he was doing in France, he replied: 'I would rather talk about you and your beautiful underclothing.' At other times he would question her: 'Tell me, Undine, how are your shoes wearing? It seems so *fitting*, that you – a soulless, naked, immortal creature, come straight out of the water, should take to *shoes* with such passion!' She would fill the page with descriptions of her dresses, and he would ponder over which had demoralized him the most, the blue, the pink or the black-and-white.

There was something other than sexual excitement in these exchanges. 'I have bought a new hat and an alpaca coat,' Augustus announced, 'to give me confidence.' His clothes were like those in an actor's wardrobe. It was said that he modelled his appearance on Courbet, but in fact he had no single model in mind, for many transitory moods and influences claimed him. Parental disapproval was always a strong recommendation. One morning about this time old Edwin John read in a newspaper a description of his son's appearance as being 'not at all that of a Welshman, but rather a Hungarian or a Gypsy', and at once sent a letter of reproof which Augustus had no difficulty in treating as Alick Schepeler was always imploring him to treat hers. But the reproof did not go unheeded and, to caricature his father's wishes, he secured a complete Welsh outfit with which to flabbergast Montparnasse. Edwin John's wish was for gentlemanly inconspicuousness, and this perhaps was the starting point for his son's dramatic regalia. In these early days, Augustus's clothes, like his handwriting and the style of his pictures, were always changing as if in search of self-knowledge, or the avoidance of it. 'I am so mercurial,' he confessed. 'Really I must cultivate a pose. It is so necessary so often.' It was necessary for self-protection, and perhaps for finding direction in his rudderless progress.

'Méfiez-vous des hommes pittoresques,' warned Nietzsche. Augustus quotes this in *Chiaroscuro*, but adds that, though weary of his extreme visibility, he was unable to achieve unobtrusiveness. Sometimes he despised himself for this failure. 'I have half a mind to get shaved and assume a bowler,' he told Alick. 'My life seems more amazing everyday.' So he trimmed his beard and for a short time did wear a bowler – with the result that he grew more noticeable than ever: a victim of his own appearance, as Princess Bibesco later described him.

The man who sent Alick Schepeler so many letters during 1906 is a costume actor – but something kept pulling the masks a little from his face. 'The thought haunts me that in a gross state of satisfaction I have allowed myself to utter the most abominable sincerity,' he tells her. 'I ask you in your turn to make allowances.' But these letters are not insincere; they are elaborately undeceiving. They expose, perhaps more clearly than anything else he wrote, the fluidity of his character, with its hectic cross-currents of whim and temper. They show the urge to cover up his uncertainty with the hats and coats and hand-made shoes of the confident outer man. But what he intended as a means of self-confidence often made for agonized self-consciousness.[59] He was sometimes embarrassed by his sentimentality. In such a mood he later destroyed many of his letters to Ida, telling the Rani that 'they made me almost wither up in disgust'.

Augustus's infatuation with Alick Schepeler had at its source the knowledge that, for whatever reason, her face and figure could summon from him good work. For this paragon of boredom was forever Lady Enigma to him. In the years 1906 and 1907 he drew and painted her numerous times, the drawings displaying more than any other group the use of oblique-stroke shading, moving downward from right to left, reminiscent of Leonardo's silverpoints. His finest portrait of her in oils, entitled 'Seraphita', he accidentally set alight in the 1930s during one of his cigarette fires. But there are more than half a dozen remarkable drawings in galleries and private collections.[60] Alick Schepeler herself is said to have remarked that she had never noticed she was beautiful until Augustus drew her. Yet the drawings are in no way prettified. They show a haunting face which, though it may have some characteristic John features – a slight slanting of the eyes or high prominence of the cheekbones – is individual. The eyes drill through the spectator with peculiar insistence; the hair, like great flying fingers, is wild; the expression varies between animation, mischief and secrecy. Always enormous strength is conveyed – a reflection of the force of Augustus's feelings – without the cosiness occasionally present in his portraits of Ida and even Dorelia. Sometimes, as in a drawing entitled 'Study of an Undine', there is a hint of insanity. The face emerges out of soft contours and shadow, with its wispy strands of hair, like the head of Medusa. She is a cross between a witch and a nymph.

The letters he wrote to Alick Schepeler form a good commentary on these portraits. In the spring of 1906 he writes from Paris: 'Am I painting? – why yes – and I have burst certain bonds too that bound my brain with iron and now my bewildered eye mixes dream with reality . . .'

To mix dream with reality was his ambition. He saw in Alick a perfect focus for this ambition since she lived most intensely in his imagination. He observed her and painted her in England; but it was in France that his portraits were conceived.

'I see you standing on the summit of a sea-hill and, turning towards the sea with a gesture divinely nonchalant, project me a surreptitious yawn which, carried by the waves is at length deposited moistly yet merrily on my shore,' he wrote to her from across the Channel. 'I picture you extended, partly in and partly out of the water like an Undine hesitating between immortality and love, or like some sweet reptile of old discovering the first dry land or like some formerly aquatic species at the moment of differentiation. And how brown you are – O pray – retain the bloom till I come. Do not wash till I see you.'

On land he saw her, thought of her, as a witch:

'It is regrettable that I have not persevered with my occult studies,' he wrote in the summer of 1906. 'I used to wonder whether you were a young witch . . . given to broom-stick riding and Sabbats of a Saturday. Perhaps if I surprised you astrally at this moment I should detect you in the act of performing some diabolical incantation or brewing a hellish potion or suchlike. Sweet one! More probably I should find you sleeping soundly and I would be able to see how many kisses one required to wake you up.'

Dream and reality, the very mainspring of his art, seemed by June 1906 to have moved to the Sleeping Beauty of Stanhope Gardens. Paris, which was to have given him the impetus for so much new work, was already beginning to lose its glow.

5

A SEASIDE CHANGE

'We have a source in us that can only produce its own fruits.
Instinct is our genius.'

Gwen John

'A sojourn at Ste Honorine-sur-Mer, near Bayeux, was memorable for
little save the birth of my son Romilly,' Augustus recorded over thirty-
five years later.[61] In his correspondence at the time, and in that of Ida,
there is much that is memorable, though no mention of Romilly's birth
which, like that of Dorelia's first son Pyramus, was never registered.

Within two months of moving to the rue Dareau, though living there
only intermittently, Augustus was grumbling to Alick Schepeler (June
1906): 'So far rather gloomy here – I am decidedly sleepy and feel the
dullest of all devils.' He resolved to reconnoitre a long holiday by the sea
for himself and for what Wyndham Lewis had called 'a numerous retinue,
or a formidable staff – or a not inconsiderable suite, – or any polite phrase
that occurs to you[62] that might include his patriarchical ménage.' 'I am
off to-night,' Augustus signalled Alick one June evening, 'to find a place
by the sea, somewhere in Normandy I think. First of all I mean to go to
Caen. The poet [Wyndham Lewis] is coming with me . . . I shall be
moving about . . . Cher ange – why don't you come over too, as you
thought of doing? I will find a place. I will arrange everything . . .'

He roved the Normandy coast until he came to Ste-Honorine-des-
Perthes and fell in with a band of Piedmontese gypsies – about a hundred
vans packed with grand men and women with some sparkling children.
He took out his charcoal, began drawing,[63] and his spirits immediately
veered upwards. 'They spoke very good Romany,' he reported to Alick,
'and played very badly, alas. At Port-en-Bessin, near Ste-Honorine, there
are wonderful sea-women who collect shellfish – they are very tall and
quite pre-historic – just the sort you'd hate. I suppose I want to do a
painting of them all the same.' His mind was now made up. He would
lead his families to Ste-Honorine, and station Alick Schepeler off the
coast on Jersey. She could wear a beret and her splendid new pink dress
– and for good measure she could bring her friend Frieda Bloch too. It
would be a terrific summer. A 'glorious bathe in the sea' at Ste-Honorine
confirmed that this was the correct decision, and he hurried back to Paris
to fetch everyone.

'Gus has just come back from finding a little house by the sea for all of us to go to,' Ida informed Margaret Sampson. 'The kids ought to enjoy it.' Her implication seemed to be that the adults might not enjoy it. From July to the end of September they lived 'chez Madame Beck' at Ste-Honorine. 'It is a tiny village,' Ida told Alice Rothenstein. '. . . We are between Cherbourg and Caen. Bayeux is the nearest town, and we only get there by cart and steam tram.'

Here Ida had time to brood over the 'patriarchical ménage'. As Dorelia had looked after her during Edwin's birth, so now she looked after Dorelia. But the children, with whom Dorelia had dealt so calmly, rasped on Ida's nerves and the demon of discontent rose in her. Only four years ago, after David's birth, she had written to her sister Ursula: 'I *cannot* realize I have a little boy yet – I cannot believe I am his mother.' Now she had four boys and could hardly remember what it had been like without them. 'I don't care for them much,'[64] she admitted. David, who was 'very silly and not very interesting', seemed in the last year not to have advanced beyond making cheeky jokes or noises like an engine. Caspar spent his time dashing idiotically in and out of the water – up to his ankles; Robin still did little but climb and jump; Edwin, who now looked like a huge swollen doll – 'very ugly with tiny blue eyes' – had developed so red a face that 'we bathe him in sea weed';[65] Pyramus appeared more Wordsworthian than ever and, as ever, did nothing.

As at Matching Green, Ida's 'formidable staff' comprised two girls – Clara, who had joined them when they originally came to Paris, and Félice, a very ladylike woman who made disagreeable noises in her nose and suffered from palpitations. She screamed at mice, had fearful starts when failing to spot people approaching her, and yawned all day – huge, lionlike yawns. Yet she worked very well, though no one liked her, least of all Clara. The two of them were seldom on speaking terms – either it was ear-splitting peals of abuse rivalling the children's, or a disdainful silence. Their bad humour contributed to the tenseness of this holiday.

The confidence, the strength, even the humour of their life in Paris were ebbing. 'We are in a village miles from the railway and by the sea,' Ida wrote to the Rani that August. 'It is very relaxing and we all, except the children, feel awful.' What had gone wrong? At first it had promised so well. The sun shone gloriously and Augustus would lead off his sprightly troop on bathing parties, on long walks to pick blackberries for jam and 'English puddings', and to picnics along the sandy beaches or on the clifftops – 'there is a lovely place on the cliffs where we slide down. Gus goes head first.' These cliffs were 'full of arches & covered with pale green seaweed,' Dorelia wrote invitingly to Gwen as she waited for her baby to be born. 'We've got a tame rabbit – we were going to have it for dinner but it looked so pretty we kept it instead – it races madly about the field.'[66] They encountered several battalions of gypsies – 'glorious chaps' – and Augustus bought Ida a guitar which she promised she would 'learn to play well'. The poet Wyndham Lewis arrived – 'a nice beautiful young man', Ida called him – and stayed five weeks, grew a beard, let off cheap fireworks and made everyone cry with laughter[67] over his plans. He was 'a refreshment in the desert' for Ida. '. . . I love him as a brother.'

Gwen John also joined them with her cat, Edgar Quinet, otherwise known as Tiger, and bathed each day at Port-en-Bessin. She came, she said, for the sake of Tiger who had jumped out of a train and been lost for eleven days while Gwen, desperate and dishevelled and 'living like Robinson Crusoe' under a tree among nettles and rubbish, mice and owls, camped out on a piece of waste ground near St-Cloud. Still thin and nervous, Tiger needed a holiday: so Gwen allowed herself five days by the sea with the John tribe. She told Gus with justifiable pride that Rodin had declared her to be '*belle artiste*'. But actually Rodin had been angry with her over this matter of the cat. 'All is finished for me,' she told him before Tiger returned to her. 'I would like to live longer but I will not be pretty and happy for you without my cat.'[68]

Rodin did not understand that this cat was a love-object whose loss symbolized a loveless world in which she did not wish to live. 'Nobody suffered from frustrated love as she did,' Augustus wrote. She would send Rodin three letters a day, almost two thousand letters over two years, as she waited for his weekly visits to her room. Rodin had 'got in the habit of sleeping with her when the posing sessions were over', his biographer Frederick V. Grunfeld writes, and sometimes Hilda Flodin, a sculptress who had introduced them, 'would join in their lovemaking'. When the posing came to an end Gwen became his '*cinq-à-sept*, the lover one sees from five to seven, after work and before going home. In her case the caresses lasted barely an hour: he would make love to her, give her an orgasm, and then go instantly off.'[69]

She felt stupid in comparison to him, knowing so much less than he did – rather as she had felt with Gus in the days of their adolescence. He explained to her that 'a man could love many things in many women,'[70] her biographer Susan Chitty writes. But sometimes, like Ida, she was filled with 'a mad rage mounting from the heart to the brain' and would wonder if 'this monster [was] in all women's hearts to devour them and tear them to pieces?' At such times she felt like accusing Rodin of 'criminal cruelty and thoughtlessness',[71] as Gus still stood accused in her dreams. Then she would revert again to being Rodin's 'obedient model', the perpetually waiting woman who believed, as she told Ursula Tyrwhitt, 'one can be more free & independent in the mind & heart sometimes when one is tied practically.'[72]

Augustus, who was a prey to 'unreasonable desires' similar to Gwen's, could not master that paradox. Whenever he felt tied, panic would run through him, and he made another bolt for this elusive independence. He was sure he had cornered it against the sea at Ste-Honorine-des-Perthes. But then, abruptly, the sun went in; the gypsies vanished; Gwen left; Wyndham Lewis, after sitting for his portrait, failed to amuse any longer; and Augustus was 'plunged into gloom by a thousand tragedies'.[73] Instead of turning up in Jersey, Alick Schepeler had drifted north to, of all places, Cumberland, taking with her Frieda Bloch. Augustus shut himself away, refused to paint out of doors, refused even to bathe except after dark. 'I have had most horrible spells of ennui,' he admitted. 'I sat in a garden the other day and wondered what there was in the world at all tolerable. I examined a tree attentively to discover any beauty in it – without success. The sky seemed an awful bore and I wondered why it should be blue. If it had been dark indigo and the trees gold perhaps I should have been rather pleased.' He could not paint, could not 'get' the colour of trees and sky, could not stop trying to paint. He could not rest, he had no energy. His melancholia was not just the absence of high spirits: it was a disease that consumed his very talent. The one cure was a stimulus for his work, and the one stimulus just then was Alick Schepeler. Now that she was further off than ever, she began to obsess him.

'I have awful fits of boredom – *awful* . . . I dreamt such a dream of you last night', he confided to her,

' – and you had at last actually consented to take off your clothes – at any rate you were quite naked and quite beautiful . . . I would love to lie about with you – no, I mean walk long walks with you – and perhaps have a bathe now and then. The people I see on the beach don't please me . . . I am horribly restless – I wonder why the devil I came here now. I curse myself – and calculate the maximum of years I have to live . . . Kiss me Alick – if you love me still a bit – darling you strange one. It is time I went on with that portrait. I believe I shall do nothing before – almost. I am expecting a letter from you – Alick – I kiss your knees and eyes and mouth.'

He lived for her disappointing letters, wrote to her almost nightly, and composed sonnets to her in which he discovered (with apologies) her Christian name rhymed with 'phallic'.

Maddened by frustration – and insect bites – he could not wait to be out of 'this sea-side hole' and begin to paint 'Whitmanic' pictures. 'Just write, beloved,' he urged Alick, 'and keep my spirits up. I foresee dismal things if you don't. The sea is beautiful all the same – I would like to lie in the sun with you and let the water dry on us.'

The other side of these generous letters was a lack of generosity to those around him. He could not help himself. For day after day Ida, Dorelia and the children were subjected to his devouring apathy. Deprivation – if only as conjecture – restored the prevailing condition of his childhood: deprivation of a mother; deprivation of love. He reacted like a difficult adolescent, grew surly, then aggressive. After many dangerous days of simmering, he could hold himself back no longer. 'I have been dissecting myself assiduously here,' he informed Alick, 'and as a consequence have thrown overboard all self-respect and feel infinitely more comfortable and free and on excellent terms with the Devil.'

This allusiveness concealed a crisis that split apart the arrangements that Ida, with Dorelia's collaboration, had so carefully prepared. Augustus had no wish to hurt either of them, but misfortune moved in his blood like a poison, and he had to expel it or die. 'How I hate causing worry!' he exclaimed. And how much he caused! For he hated being 'unnatural', and he hated secrets, which were claustrophobia to him. But his awful melancholy made him 'careless of other people's feelings'. What he now did was to blurt out the truth to Ida and Dorelia – the unstable truth of the moment. He told them that domestic life, even the ramshackle variety with which they had experimented, smothered him; he told them of his liberating passion for Alick, how his painting could not advance without her. People said you could not have your cake and eat it: but what was the point of having a cake and not eating it? There was no personal criticism in all this – it was simply that he could not be restricted; he would explode. Boredom, guilt, frustration, sterility: to such morbid sensations had their *ménage* led him. 'I think I have about done with family life or perhaps I should say it has done for me,' he wrote to Alick, ' – so there is nothing to prevent us getting married now.'

Marriage to Alick was only another fantasy he sported because 'I wish to remain as respectable as possible in your eyes.' What in fact he proposed was something less original: to duplicate the arrangement he had with Ida and Dorelia in Paris, with a similar arrangement with Alick and Frieda Bloch. He was full of plans for them to join him. 'If I had a wish for the fairies to fulfil it would be that you would come to Paris with Miss Bloch before long and collaborate with me,' he tells Alick; and then: 'I begin to see very plainly that Miss Blocky will never get on unless she comes to Paris and brings you with her. I will find her a studio – and I will show her things I'm pretty sure she never suspected.'

Only now, for the first time, did Ida and Dorelia acknowledge that they could not contain Augustus. He was not proposing to leave them, simply to add to their number. He made no secret of it. 'John is taking a studio in Montmartre, where he thinks of installing two women he has found in England,' Wyndham Lewis confided to his mother; 'and I think John will end by building a city, and being worshipped as sole man therein, – the deity of Masculinity.'[74]

It was Dorelia who resolved that she wanted no place in this city. Once Romilly was three or four months old, she would 'buzz off'.[75] Ida too would have liked to leave. Her predicament is set out poignantly in a letter she wrote from Ste-Honorine to the Rani:

'Dearest, daily and many times a day I think I *must* leave Augustus. Isn't it awful? I feel so stifled and oppressed. If I had the money I think I really should do it – but I can't leave him and take his money – and I can't keep the kids on what I have – and if I left the kids I should not find peace – you must not mind these confidences, angel. It is nothing much – I haven't the money so I must stay, as many another woman does. It isn't that Aug is different or unkind. He is the same as ever and rather more considerate in many ways. It's the mental state – I don't understand it and probably I should be equally slavish – No – I know I am freer alone. However one has lucid moments anywhere. Don't think me miserable. All this is a sign of health. But it's a pity one's got to live with a man. I shall have to get back home sooner or later – not meaning 28 Wigmore Street – and it doesn't matter as long as I don't arrive a lunatic. It's awful to be lodged in a place where one can't understand the language and where the jokes aren't funny. Why did I ever go there? Because I did – because there lives a King I had to meet and love. And now I am bound hand and foot – darling how will it end? By death or escape? And wouldn't escape be as bad a bondage? Would one find one's way . . .'

At the end of September they all left Ste-Honorine and returned to the rue Dareau where the flowerbeds in their little garden had now been dug into mud-holes by the children. 'I get fits of depression about every two hours – alternately intervals of malign joy,' Augustus confessed to Alick. 'Paris is a queen of cities but I think Smyrna would suit me better.' Next moment he hankered after Italy – the Italians were surely the finest people in the world, and besides, he would be able to see in Italy 'my darling Piero della Francesca'. Genoa might suit him, of course, or 'Shall we go to Padua?' he asked Alick. But even before his invitation had arrived, several new brainwaves were upon him: 'I am inclined to take refuge in Bucharest at the nearest, to seek serenity in some Balkan insurrection, or danger in a Gypsy tent, or inevitable activity in Turkistan . . . I am horribly aware of the power of Fate to-night.' This self-destructive urge quickly passed and, in a more hibernating mood, he suddenly inquired: 'Perhaps I may depend on you for warmth this winter . . . I feel that once back in London I shall never leave it.' By now Alick was thoroughly confused. What really *was* happening? Augustus was astonished at her question. Surely everything was perfectly clear. 'As to my coming to London, is it not already definitely arranged?' he demanded. 'Haven't I said jusqu'à l'automne a dozen times? And is not my word unimpeachable – am I not integrity itself?'

He did return to London that October, while Dorelia prepared to move off the following month. Only Ida was to stay on at the rue Dareau – with her pack of boys, and two quarrelling servants. Her bondage there was now tighter than ever for, to add to the complications, Clara had become pregnant.

And, since it was her turn, Ida herself was again pregnant.

6

'HERE'S TO LOVE!'

'It was more circumstances than anyone's fault.'
Ida John to Alice Rothenstein (August 1905)

For the next six months, between October 1906 and the spring of the following year, Augustus, Ida and Dorelia tried for the last time to find a scheme of separate co-existing ways of life.

For Augustus the first taste of this new regime was indeed sweet. His depression lifted like clouds at evening, and exhilaration blazed through. The world was a grand mixed metaphor and he stood, in superb uncertainty, an extended simile at its centre. 'I feel recurrent as the ocean waves,' he noticed on arriving in London, 'blue as the sky, ceaseless as the winds, multitudinous as a bee-hive, ardent as flames, cold as an exquisite hollow cave, generous and as pliant as a tree, aloof and pensive as an angel, tumultuous as the obscenest of demons . . .'[76]

But how long would this combination of feelings persist? Augustus himself was as confident as a boy. 'I no longer suffer from the blues,' he told Alick, 'and my soul seems to have returned to its habitation. I think you are more adorable than ever.' Though painting some of the 'prehistoric sea-women' that summer, he had been damnably lazy but, as he explained, 'it is when I am not at work enough that I get bored'. The will to work throbbed through him. Seldom had he felt so vigorous.

But first there were some small practical matters to attend to. For while his soul had found its habitation, there was still no place to house his body. He required a new studio in London – a fine new studio to match his mood – and, while he was about it, should he not take another new studio in Paris? Then he would be free at last to paint. He wanted some place in Paris, 'remote and alone – in some teeming street – where I can pounce on people as they pass, hob-nob with Apaches [gangsters] and maquereaux [pimps] and paint as I can. Then of course the studio in London – the new one – in your [Alick Schepeler's] neighbourhood.'[77] He had found nothing in Paris before leaving. He now took up the search in London trusting to 'the Gods' to guide him to 'a studio I can live in and where you can come and sit without being spied on'. But the Gods, and estate agents, led him a complicated dance – to Paddington, Bermondsey and the East End: all without success. For the time being he still used his studio in the Chenil Gallery, which Knewstub offered to lease to him for a further year. But independence meant freedom from the Knewstubs, Orpens and Rothensteins, and so he refused it – while continuing to use it *faute de mieux*. For a short period he rented another studio in Manresa Road from the Australian painter George Coates. It seemed a splendid place – Holman Hunt had painted there – but Augustus did not stay long. Dora Coates noted that he had 'a compelling stare when he looked at a woman that I much resented'. She also resented his treatment of the studio – soiled socks and odd clothes lay thick upon the floor amid the dust of weeks, and by the time he left it was as 'dirty as a rag and bone shop' and had to be scrubbed with carbolic soap. He found no other place so good as this, and by February 1907 was reduced to a 'beastly lodging' at 55 Paultons Square, owned by Madame Herminie Considerant, corset-maker.

The only virtue of such a place was that, being in Chelsea, it was near Alick. They saw a lot of each other that winter. Often their meetings ended rowdily. She is always striking him in the face with her 'formidable fist', he apologizing too late for being 'so damnably careless'. Sitting to him, she discovered, like almost everything else, bored her excessively. Yet he had to paint her. His seriousness surprised her. 'You have not come to-day – but, dear, come to-morrow – You know I am not stable – my moods follow, but they repeat themselves – alas – sometimes – I must paint you dear – to-day – probably you don't quite like me – but do come to-morrow. Who knows? – You may find me less intolerable to-morrow . . . à demain, n'est-ce-pas chère, petite Ondine souriante. Soyons intimes – franches – connaissants – alors amants.' By the end of the year, feeling 'I want to wash myself in the Ocean', Augustus returned to Paris.

It was desperate work this seeking for studios. Gwen was also looking for a new place – her flowers at the rue St-Placide were dying for lack of light. Besides, her room there was too square, and Tiger had taken against it. Like Gus she found the seeing of 'horrible rooms' very depressing. 'Either the concierges were rude or their husbands lewd or there were single men among the *locataires*,' wrote her biographer Susan Chitty. Towards the end of the winter she found what she wanted, 'the prettiest ever room' on the fourth floor at 87 rue du Cherche-Midi, a wider street round the corner of rue St-Placide. Tiger was happy, sharpening her claws on the wicker chair, and so was Gwen. After almost three years, Rodin had asked her to model nude for him again.

At about the same time as Gwen was moving round on a horse and cart, Gus also struck lucky, finding a vast room off the boulevard St-Germain, in an old *hôtel* (town house) belonging to the famous Rohan family. 'I have taken a studio – with a noble address. Cour de Rohan [3], Rue du Jardinet,' he told Alick. By February 1907 the workmen were busy converting it – 'my studio commences to be magnificent' – and by March he had moved in – 'I will be about doing things in it soon.' But by March it was too late.

*

As soon as Augustus had returned to London, Dorelia made her move. Ida sublet the studio at rue Dareau, and the two women set off to find a *logement* for Dorelia. By the beginning of November they had found what she wanted at 48 rue du Château. 'It has 2 rooms and a kitchen and an alcove – one of the rooms is a good size,' Ida told Gus.

'It is in a lovely disreputable looking building – very light and airy, the view is a few lilac trees, some washing hanging up and a railway – very pleasant – and to our taste . . . The logement is 300frs a year. It is rather dear in comparison with ours, but we couldn't find anything better or cheaper, and there will be room to store all your things in it . . . Dodo and I had an amusing interview with the landlord and his wife of the logement last night at 9. We had to go down to his apartment near the Madeleine – a real French drawing-room with real French people – Very suspicious and anxious about their rent and Dodo's future behaviour – D. was mute and smiling. I did my best to reassure them that she was très sage and her man (they asked me at once if she was married or not and didn't mind a bit her not being) was "solvent". We said she was a model (she's going to sit again) and the wife wanted to know if the artists came to her or she went to the artists! The husband kept squashing the wife all the time though he called her in for her opinion of us. He was small and concise and sensible, and she was big and sweet and stupid.'[78]

Dorelia moved in with Pyramus and Romilly immediately. But Augustus was not wholly pleased. It had all happened so fast and while he was away. He signed the agreement, since women were not allowed to make agreements for such large sums, but he did not want Dorelia disappearing. She had started modelling again – though there was no mention of Leonard since her return to Paris. She also had a woman to mind the children during the afternoons. 'I think she is enjoying herself a bit in leaving the babies,' Ida told Gus. He did not know what to think. After all, it was not impossible that he had exaggerated Alick Schepeler's importance. There was certainly nothing exclusive about it. Besides, it was easy to exaggerate the significance of what he called his 'physical limitations'. At Matching Green when Ida had been suicidal over Dorelia, Augustus had explained his behaviour in a letter to the Rani – and in essence nothing had changed now that Dorelia was angry over Alick.

'One [i.e. Ida] must grow accustomed to the recurrence of these perhaps congenital weaknesses – which you must remember have not appeared with Dorelia's arrival only but date in my experience from the first moment of meeting Ida – which are indeed included in her system as a mark of mortality in one otherwise divinely rational. Don't please ever think of me as a playful eccentric who thinks it necessary to épater les bourgeois; things take place quite naturally and inevitably – one cannot however arrest the invisible hand – with all the best intentions – to attempt that is pure folly.'

But Dorelia was less tractable than Ida – and she had entered less deeply into the web. She saw no folly in his attempting to 'arrest the invisible hand' – everyone had to do that. She doubted his best intentions; she doubted his motives in writing to her now. Augustus was quick to protest. 'My beloved Relia, I don't write to you without loving you or wanting to write. Believe this and don't suspect me of constant humbuggery. Who the Devil do you think I'm in love with? If you think I'm a mere liar, out goes the sun. I've been thinking strongly sometimes of clearing back over the Channel to get at you, you won't believe how strongly or how often.'

And it was true: she didn't. But at Christmas he arrived and Ida gave a great party in the rue Dareau, 'immodestly' hanging up a big bunch of mistletoe in the middle of the room. Gwen John turned up and Wyndham Lewis and Dorelia with her children, and Ida's boys wrote a Christmas letter to Grandpa John in Tenby. They ate 'dinde aux marrons', plum pudding and 'wonderful little cakes'; and they drank quantities of 'punch au kirsch'. For the six children, instead of a plodding white-bearded

Father Christmas, they had 'le petit noël' who, though he descended the chimney, had 'a delicacy of his own entirely French'.[79] It was a happy time. 'The shops are *full* of dolls dolls dolls – it is so French and ridiculous and *painted*, and yet it doesn't lie heavy on the chest like English "good cheer",' Ida wrote to the Rani (December 1906). 'One can look at it through the window quite pleasantly instead of having to mix in or be a misanthrope as at home. Perhaps because one is foreign. It is delightful to be foreign – unless one is in the country of one's birth – when it becomes gênant [inconvenient].'

The holiday was delightful, but it solved no problems: it was simply a holiday. After all was over, Augustus returned to finish his portrait of Alick Schepeler; and Dorelia went back to her *logement*. Gradually she was growing more independent. Her sister Jessie came for a few weeks to help with the children; she began dressmaking; got one of Tiger's kittens from Gwen John; went on modelling. 'Dodo has just been to déjeuner, washed herself (1st time in 3 days) and gone off to sit at "Trinity Lodge",' Ida wrote to Gus. 'I'm afraid she's forgotten to take her prayer book. She says for her last pose she didn't have to wash – it was such a comfort. But for Trinity Lodge the outside of the platter must be clean.' Soon Dorelia had established her own routine of life. 'Dodo has only been once to déjeuner since she left,' Ida sadly observed. 'She is quite 20 minutes away.'

By March 1907 it seemed as if Dorelia had achieved her independence.

*

'I am alone again – and alone – and alone.' From Augustus, with his agreement, Ida was content to live apart – 'it is so easy to love at a distance,' she reminded him. And from a distance she still worshipped him. 'I say Mackay is 2nd rate,' she had written to the Rani in Liverpool.

'. . . I have always known it, but the other day it flashed on me. So is Sampson. There is no harm in being 2nd rate any more than being a postman. It is just a creation . . . Augustus has not that quality – he is essentially 1st rate . . . As to a woman, I know only one first and that is Gwen John. You and I, dear, are puddings – with plums in perhaps – and good suet – but puddings. Well perhaps you are a butterfly or an ice cream – yes, that *is* more suitable – but we are scarcely human . . . This sounds tragic, but I have been living with exhausting emotions lately and am – queer – Yours in a garden Ida.'

In all aspects of her life, it seemed to her, she had failed. She had failed as an artist – even as a musician; she had failed as a friend – she seldom saw her friends now; that she had failed with Gus was obvious; and, what was perhaps as painful, her relationship with Dorelia had failed – they were still friendly, but that sweet intimacy had gone. She had failed too – was in the very process of failing – as a mother. Her sister Ethel came to stay and they 'did nothing but alternately scratch out each others eyes and "die of laughing" '. She was reading Balzac's *Splendeurs et misères des courtisanes* and told Gus she would love to have a book about the Empress of China 'or, above all, a biography'. He was still her 'Darling G' or 'Dear Oggie', and she felt a sudden pang over him: 'Oh dear, do take care of yourself, cheer up . . .'

If Augustus that winter stood at the top of a great mixed metaphor, Ida seemed to be sinking into a huge bowl of cough mixture, dill water, cod-liver oil, milk of magnesia. The eldest children were getting to an age when they wanted more attention but she had no more to give them. Their future seemed bleak with such a mother. David, she told Margaret Sampson, was 'such a queer twisted many-sided kid. Horrid an[d] lovely – plucky and cowardly – cruel and kind – thoughtful and stupid, many times a day. He needs a firm wise hand to guide him, instead of a bad tempered lump like me.' She had begun to arrange their education, sending David and Caspar to the École Maternelle of the Communal School – 'there are about 300 all under 6', she told Gus, 'and they do nothing but shriek little ditties with their earless voices, and march about in double file'. But both boys were so unhappy there she had to remove them: another failure.

She was imprisoned during the children's pleasure, for so long as the mind could tell, the eye could see. 'Life here is so curious – not interesting as you might imagine,' she wrote to the Rani.

'I crave for a time when the children are grown up and I can ride about on the tops of omnibuses as of yore in a luxury of vague observation. Never now do I have time for any luxury, and at times I feel a stubborn head on me – wooden – resentful – slowly being petrified. And another extraordinary thing that has happened to me is that my spirit – my lady, my light and help – has gone – not tragically – just in the order of things – and now I am not sure if I am making an entrance into the world – or an exit from it! . . . As a matter of plain fact I believe my raison d'être has ended, and I am no more the inspired one I was. It seems so strange to write all this quite calmly. Tell me what you can make of it when you have time. My life has been so mysterious. I long for someone to talk to. I can't write now – another strange symptom!'

It was a sickness of living from which she suffered – quite different from the suicidal troughs of Matching Green. Then there had been rising waves of jealousy; now, though she often dreamed of Augustus and Alick Schepeler, they were absurd dreams, never tortured. 'Last night you were teaching her [Alick] french in the little dining-room here while I kept passing through to David who had toothache and putting stuff on his tooth.' It was as if she was too tired to feel anything more. On hearing that Augustus was coming over at Christmas, she had remarked to the Rani: 'Funny – I haven't been alone with him for $2^1/_2$ years – wonder what it will be like – boring probably.' Yet she had not been bored at all. She had been happy.

In Ida's letters, especially to the Rani, there is a fatalistic flirting with death: 'Oh Rani – Are you in a state when the future seems hopeless? I suppose things are never hopeless really are they? There is always death isn't there?' Except for death, there seemed no new thing under the sun. She lived in a pale stupor. 'The only way to be happy is to be ignorant and lie under the trees in the evening,' she had told the Rani. But she could not regain such green ignorance.

She had not counted on Augustus. Now that he had finished his portrait of Alick, now that Dorelia had inexplicably melted away, he suddenly proposed returning to live with Ida. Why not? They had come through so much. What else was there for them? Ida was dismayed. She hardly knew what to answer. Even if he was temporarily feeling dissatisfied with the present arrangement, surely he would not regret it later on. Had he considered the implications of living with her? What about the children – 'Can you really want to see them again?' she asked. 'You know they worry you to death.' But Augustus had no home. He could find nowhere to live in London, and he could not work. Was his request really so unsatisfactory? After all, they still loved each other in their fashion; why should they not settle down in London and be happy? Besides, he had given her scheme a long trial. What he said, and the troubled way he said it, did not sound unreasonable. She told him he would be happier alone, but some men were helpless when left to themselves. 'It may be I should come back to London,' Ida reluctantly agreed. 'You must tell me. I will come – only we get on so much better apart. But I understand you need a home. Dis moi et j'y cours. As to the love old chap we all have our hearts full of love for someone at sometime or other and if it isn't this one it's the other one over there.'

Her real feeling at the prospect of returning comes out in a letter she sent the Rani: 'Gus seems to hanker after a home in London, and I feel duties beating little hammers about me, and probably shall find myself padding about London in another $1/_2$ year – Damn it all.'

One factor that tied her to Augustus, as she had explained at Ste-

Honorine-des-Perthes, was financial dependence. Throughout the autumn and winter she had saved exorbitantly. To Augustus she represented such thrift as an art, parodying his own: 'Am still trying to take care of the pence with great pleasure in the feeling of beauty it gives – like simplifying an already beautiful, but careless and clumsy, work of art.' The impetus behind this economic activity was her desire to build some independence in the future. But the little hammers of duty were destroying this last dream. She had complained in the past of her own selfishness, but she was not selfish enough.

In a letter to Alice Rothenstein, Ida wrote: 'It chills my marrow to think of living back in England.' The Rothensteins were growing increasingly worried about her life with and without Augustus, and wrote to inquire, complain, praise and comfort her.

'My only treasure is myself,' she insisted to Will, 'and that I give you, as I give it to all men who need it . . . as to Gussie, he is our great child artist: let him snap his jaws. What does he matter? It is *you* who matters, and you dare not be frightened except at your own self. I am glad to have your letter: it is such a comfort to hear a voice. Life is a bit solemn and silent in the forest where I live, and the world outside a bit grotesque and difficult. Certainly there are always the gay ribbons you talk of but they are only sewn on and are there to break the intolerable monotony, for which purpose, darling Will, they are *quite inadequate . . .*'

Such gloomy letters worried the Rothensteins, who blamed Augustus. But this was too simple, and Ida would not allow it. Gus never treated women as if they were children or inferior to men. He treated them as adults, fully capable of looking after themselves in a difficult world. Nor did he lie to them or seriously mislead them. He was transparent. The advantages and disadvantages he offered were immediately obvious. 'I must write to say it is not so,' she firmly answered Will. The devil, she explained, was in herself – 'and as soon as you wound it, it heals up and you have to keep on always trying to find its heart.' This devil had so many names: it was jealousy (which had driven Dorelia away); a vanity which masqueraded as duty; finally sloth. Would she ever kill it? 'When one fights a devil does one not fight it for the whole world? It is the most enchanting creature, it is everywhere. God, it seems to spread itself out every minute. Sometimes I do find its miserable fat heart and I give it a good stab. But it is chained to me. I cannot run away.'

*

All of them were in Paris during February: Augustus moving into his new studio, and Gwen in hers; Dorelia in her *logement*; Ida still at the rue Dareau. 'Let's go up the Volga in the sun,' Augustus entreated Alick. But it was no more than a gesture: he could not run away now from Ida. At moments he might have liked to. Paris that winter seemed crowded with the bourgeoisie, and he blamed them for his ill thoughts. 'I am much depressed to-day by the aspect of civilization – never was human society so foully ugly, so abysmally ignoble – and I have also had a cold which doesn't improve matters.' He revisited all the places which had so delighted him less than a year ago – the Louvre, the Luxembourg Gardens, the Panthéon ('to encourage myself with a view of Puvis's decorations') – but everywhere seethed with masses of people which 'brought my nausea to a climax'. The whole French nation oppressed him. 'I went into the morgue and saw 4 dead men,' he told Alick; 'they looked *awfully well* really – the only thing impressive I found today . . . These four unknown dead men, all different, seemed enlarged by death to monumental size, and lacking life seemed divested only of its trivialities.'

To be reborn was what he longed for – not through death, but in the birth of Ida's fifth child. 'Oh for a girl!' she had written to him, yet he knew that 'I *always* have boys'. She referred to the unborn baby as Susannah, but noticed that she was 'pushing about in a fearfully strong masculine way'. The contemplation of another boy, which still had the power to excite Augustus, only caused her heartache. 'In 3 weeks – si on peut juger – a new face will be amongst us – a new pilgrim. God help it,' she wrote to the Rani. 'What right have we, knowing the difficulties of the way, to start any other along it? The baby seems so strong and large I am dreading its birth. How pleasant it *seems* that it would be to die.'

Wyndham Lewis – whom Augustus was now accusing of 'the worst taste', but whom Ida still liked – had spent much of his time recently at the rue Dareau. 'Mrs John and the bonne [Clara] will have their babies about the same time I expect,' he wrote to his mother, ' – I suppose beneath John's roof is the highest average of procreation in France.'

As it turned out neither of these babies – nor yet a third one that Wyndham Lewis had so far failed to spot – were born under Augustus's many roofs. After some hesitation Ida decided to have her child in hospital. 'It is much simpler and I don't pay anything,' she explained to her mother. 'I just go when it comes on without anything but what I'm wearing!'

Clara and Félice had by now both left,[80] and Ida engaged a new nanny called Delphine for the children. 'Gawd knows if she's the right sort,' she reported to Augustus, ' – one can but try. She's fairly handsome 22 years old.' Under these circumstances Ida was obliged to send word to Dorelia asking whether she would return to the rue Dareau while she was in hospital; and Dorelia, in agreeing, walked back into the web.

'Augustus is well in his studio now and a beauty it is – and he has plenty of models just at present . . . Dorelia – and all the kids – to say nothing of me in spreading poses,' Ida wrote to the Rani late that February. Although the writing of letters made her feel 'pale green', she continued her correspondence right up to the time of her confinement. To lighten the black humour of some of these letters, she had told the Rothensteins: 'we shall come up again next spring you know'. After which, she promised, all their worries 'would melt away like the mist when the sun comes out'. But to the Rani, with whom she felt less need to dissemble, she confessed that it was not to the spring she was looking forward, but 'to the winter for some inexplicable reason'. She was suffering from an 'egg-shape[d] pessimism' and 'I am dreadfully off babies just now . . . in a fortnight or so the silent weight I now carry will be yelling its head off out in the cold.'

There was one further item of recurring news in the new year that seemed to promise, for all their heroic efforts over the last months, an indefinite spinning out of the complex network of their lives. Dorelia was again pregnant.

*

In the first week of March 1907, Ida walked round to the room she had engaged at the Hôpital de la Maternité, ten minutes away in the boulevard du Port-Royal. Nothing, as she had predicted, could have been simpler. The baby was born in the early morning of 9 March: it was a boy.

The complications began immediately afterwards. Mrs Nettleship, who had gone over to Paris partly for business and partly to see Ida, bringing with her on Ida's instructions parcels of magnesia and dill water, special soaps and strong building bricks ('by strong I mean unbreakable'), explained to her daughters Ethel and Ursula what was happening:

'My dears, Ida is to have a slight operation. It is serious but not very dangerous. In 48 hrs she will be quite out of danger. It will be to-night – I can't come home for a few days . . . They think a little abscess has formed somewhere and causes the pain and the fever. She has to go to a Maison de Santé [private nursing home] and one of the best men in Paris will do it. I am glad I was here as I could help . . . I have been running about all day after doctors and people.'[81]

Augustus seemed paralysed by these events. The waiting, the suspense, above all the stupefying sense of powerlessness unmanned him. It was a nightmare, and he like someone half-asleep within its circumference. 'Apart from my natural anxieties,' he wrote, 'I was oppressed by the futility of my visits, by my impotence, and insignificance.'[82] Every decision was taken by Mrs Nettleship from her headquarters at the Hôtel Regina. It was she who chose a specialist and arranged to pay him sixty pounds – 'I would have paid him £600 if he had asked it'; it was she who organized Ida's move to the new hospital and paid sixteen shillings a day for her room there (each sum scrupulously noted); it was she who wrote each day to family and friends keeping them informed of developments. She was particularly reassured that the specialist, besides being the best in Paris, was well connected (his wife was a niece, she ascertained, of a baronet) and had attended several diplomats at the British Embassy. When not busy at the hospital she would inspect the children at the rue Dareau, interview Delphine and even Dorelia, replant the entire garden there filling up the children's mud-holes, and conduct David to his new school. 'He talks about "the boys in my school" just like an Eton boy might,' she noted with approval. Between times she managed to keep her business affairs going, sending off satisfactory messages to various titled clients. Her energy was prodigious, and in complete contrast to Augustus's stupor. 'Gus looks quite done up,' she confided to Ursula. 'He has the grippe and he is terribly upset about Ida. He does everything I suggest about Doctors and things, but has not much initiative – he has no experience.'

The *maison de santé* to which Ida had been removed was a light spacious building in the boulevard Arago. Somehow the atmosphere here engendered optimism. 'The place is the very best in Paris,' Mrs Nettleship reported. '. . . The nuns who nurse her are the most experienced and so quiet and pleasant. If it is possible for her to recover she will do it here.'

The crisis, which so galvanized Mrs Nettleship and demoralized Augustus, was seen by them at each stage differently. Where she is hopeful, he is pessimistic. 'Ida has got over her operation better than we expected,' she writes to her daughters, while Augustus the same day tells John Sampson that Ida 'is most seriously ill after an operation'. While Mrs Nettleship busied herself with complicated plans for Ida's recovery, Augustus would scribble out wan messages to the Rani: 'She is a little worse to-day.'

But on one subject they were agreed: the baby. Augustus indeed was the more enthusiastic: 'The new baby is most flourishing so far. I really admire him,' he told Margaret Sampson. '. . . He has a distinct profile. We called him Henry as it was the wish of Mother Nettleship to memorialize thus her great friendship with [Sir Henry] Irving.' But on Dorelia and on Mrs Nettleship Henry imposed an additional strain. 'He sleeps all day and cries all night,' Mrs Nettleship wrote to Ursula. 'Someone has to be awake with him every night.' He was, she added, 'a great beauty';

but 'I hope he will turn out worth all this trouble and anxiety.' This pious hope was to echo, like a curse, down his life.

Ida was suffering not from 'a little abscess' but puerperal fever and peritonitis. 'It all depends on her not giving way,' Mrs Nettleship explained. 'She is no worse to-night than she was this morning and every hour counts to the good – but she might suddenly get worse any minute.' The main hope of her pulling through lay with what Mrs Nettleship called her 'natural vitality', but this had been worn away through the years to a degree that her mother did not know, and it was Augustus who saw what was happening more clearly. To Mrs Nettleship her daughter's recovery was, once the doctors had done their best, a matter of simple determination. It did not occur to her that Ida might not want to live, that she could consent to die.

She was in pain and fever much of the time. Except while under the anaesthetic, she did not sleep night or day following Henry's birth. Mrs Nettleship maintained a whirl of cheerfulness revolving round her bedside, almost a party, so that Ida should not realize the gravity of her illness. But Augustus had little heart for this charade. 'I do everything that is possible,' Mrs Nettleship assured Ursula. 'She is very unreasonable as usual and wants all sorts of things that are not good for her. I have to keep away a good deal as she always begs me to give her something she must not have and I can't be always refusing.' Augustus could refuse her nothing. She made him ransack Paris for a particular beef lozenge; she demanded violets; asked for a bottle of peppermint, a flask of *eau de mélisse*: he got them all. She seemed to understand that any definite activity came as a relief to him, and when she could invent nothing else for him to be doing she made him go and have a bath. To Mrs Nettleship it sometimes appeared as if he were acting quite irresponsibly, but she made no move to stop him. Perhaps Ida sensed some friction between them. 'Either you're all mad or I am,' she told them.

But on the morning of 13 March she demanded something that even Augustus could not do for her. Sitting up in bed, she declared her determination to leave the hospital and go to Dorelia in the rue du Château. There she would cure herself, she said, 'with a bottle of tonic wine, Condy's, and an enema'. Augustus, in a panic, 'got the doctor up in his motor car' and at last he managed to dissuade her. But this was a bad day for Ida, and having relinquished the hope of joining Dorelia, her spirit seemed to give up the struggle.

'I adore stormy weather,' she had once written to the Rani. On the night of 13 March there was a violent storm, with thunder and lightning, lasting into the early morning. Lying in her hospital bed, Ida longed to be in the middle of it, somehow imagining that she was. 'She wanted to be a bit of the wind,' Augustus wrote to the Rani. 'She saw a star out of the window, and she said "advertissement of humility". As I seemed puzzled she said after a bit "Joke".'

The hospital staff tried to remove him, but Augustus stayed with her that night. Sometimes she was highly feverish, 'her spirit making preparatory flights into delectable regions',[83] but there were periods of contact between them. He rubbed her neck with Elliman's Embrocation and, when she asked him, tickled her feet. She pulled his beard about. To the sisters she remarked: 'C'est drôle, mais je vais perdre mon sommeil encore une nuit, voyez-vous.' In a delirium she spoke of a land of miraculous caves, then, with some impatience, demanded that Augustus hand over his new suit to Henry Lamb, who had recently turned up in Paris. Despite the fever, the pain had vanished and she felt euphoric. 'How can I speak of her glittering smiles and moving hands?' Augustus afterwards told the Rani. And to Margaret Sampson he wrote of that night: 'Ida felt lovely – she was so gay and spiritual. She had such charming visions and made such amazing jokes.'

In the morning, after the storm was over, she roused herself and gave Augustus a toast: 'Here's to Love!' And they both drank to it in Vichy water. It was a fitting salute to a life that had steered such a brave course between irony and romance. Mrs Nettleship came in shortly afterwards with Ethel her daughter, who had arrived from England. 'We are just waiting for the end,' Ethel wrote to her sister Ursula. 'Ida is not really conscious, but she talks in snatches – quite disconnected sentences. Mother just sits by her side and sometimes holds her hand – she has some violets on her bed. I am just going to take the children for a walk – they are not going to see her as they would not understand, and she cannot recognize them.'

She died, without regaining consciousness, at half-past three that afternoon. 'Ah well, she has gone very far away now, I think,' Augustus wrote to Margaret Sampson. 'She has rejoined that spiritual lover who was my most serious rival in the old days. Or perhaps she is having a good rest before resuming her activities.'

*

The relief was extraordinary. As he ran out of the hospital on to the boulevard Arago, Augustus was seized with uncontrollable elation. 'I could have embraced any passer-by,' he confessed.[84] He had had enough of despair. It was a beautiful spring day, the sun was shining, the Seine looking 'unbelievable – fantastic – like a Chinese painting'.[85] He wanted to strip off the immediate past, wash away the domination of death; he wanted to paint again, but first he wanted to get drunk. 'Strange after leaving her poor body dead and beaten I had nothing but a kind of bank holiday feeling and had to hold myself in,' he told the Rani.

Many of his friends were mystified and shocked. 'John has been drunk for the last three days, so I can't tell you if he's glad or sorry,' Wyndham Lewis reported to his mother. 'I think he's sorry, though.'[86] Not everyone was so charitable. They blamed Ida's death on Augustus, hinted at suicide, and attributed his 'Roman programme' to justifiable guilt. Guilt there must often be with death – guilt, grief and aggression. Augustus's drinking was a desperate bid to recover optimism. When his friend, John Fothergill, wrote to express sympathy, adding that one had only to scratch life and underneath there was sorrow, Augustus replied: 'Just one correction – it is *Beauty* that is underneath – *not* misery, which is only circumstantial.' This he *had* to believe; it was his lifebelt. What confused him about Ida's death, adding to his natural grief, was that it had come through childbirth, and that his children had been deprived of a mother as he had been. It seemed, then, that he was no better than his own father. He struggled against the tide of melancholia. But as the days passed he drank more.

Ida was cremated[87] on the Saturday following her death, 16 March 1907, at the crematorium of Père Lachaise. Almost no one was there – certainly not Augustus. A number of people had written from England offering to come, but Augustus, who disliked formal exhibitions of sentiment, refused them all. 'People keep sending me silly sentimental lamentations,' he complained to the Rani. 'I really begin to long to outrage everybody.' The worst offender was poor Will Rothenstein who 'never forgave'[88] himself for not having gone out to Paris, and wrote long 'Uriah Heep-like' letters which Augustus found 'unintelligible'.[89]

One man defied Augustus's instructions and arrived in Paris on the morning of the cremation. This was Ambrose McEvoy, who 'had the delicacy to keep drunk all the time and was perfectly charming'.[90] He had come for the day, intending to go back to London the same night, but became incapable of going anywhere for a week. 'He will lose his return ticket if he doesn't pull himself up within a day or so,' Wyndham Lewis predicted.[91]

Henry Lamb, who had taken Ida to a music hall the night before she entered hospital, did go to the cremation. When the coffin and the body were consumed, and the skeleton drawn out on a slab through the open doors of the furnace, Lamb and McEvoy were still able to recognize the strong bone structure of the girl they had known. An attendant tapped the slab with a crowbar, and the skeleton crumbled into ashes. The ashes were then placed in a box and taken round to Augustus. Later an informal memorial was held in Lamb's rooms.[92]

One of the few people who understood Gus's feelings after Ida's death was Gwen. Like him, she had no time for the mere politeness of things, and wrote to Rodin telling him not to bother with condolences to her brother but remember to save himself for their next lovemaking. Then she went round to look after Gus for a few days at his new studio in the cour de Rohan. 'She was one of those who *knew* Ida,' Augustus explained to Margaret Sampson; one who knew that 'Ida was the most utterly truthful soul in the world.'

Gwen also knew that Ida never had serious regrets, even if, as she had once admitted: 'Our marriage was, on the whole, not a success.'[93]

FIVE

Buffeted by Fate

I

THE BATTLE OF THE BABIES

'I have worked strenuously when I should have worked calmly – I have fought when I should have lain down – I have relied on my individuality instead of my reason – I have shouted and raged when I should have been listening attentively . . . Failing to paint beautifully we find something else and insist that it is just as good – and what unhappiness follows that lie!'

Augustus John to William Orpen

Ida was dead: but in many ways her influence lived on. 'Ida keeps teaching me things,' Augustus told Alice Rothenstein. It seemed to him that she was teaching him at last who he was, solving the everlasting problem of his identity. 'I don't know that I feel really *wiser* through my sorrows, perhaps, yes: but at any rate I feel more "knowing" – I also feel curiously more myself,' he wrote to Alick Schepeler. '. . . I also feel still greater admiration for my view of things as an artist . . .'

If his artistic aims had not altered, he saw them more clearly and was to pursue them with more determination. 'I still feel extremely confident that given the right woman in the right corner I shall acquit myself honourably,' he assured Will Rothenstein. '. . . I went to see Puvis's drawings in Paris. He seems to be the finest modern – while I admire immensely Rodin's later drawings – full of Greek lightness. Longings devour me to decorate a vast space with nudes and – and trees and waters. I am getting clearer about colour tho' still very ignorant, with a little more knowledge I shall at least begin . . .'

It was as if he could make sense of Ida's death only in his work. Many of his finest paintings, visionary moments of suspended time, matters of volume and reflected light – the liquidity of light spilling from one surface to another – were done in the following eight years. 'It is so difficult to realize that Ida has gone so far away,' he told Mrs Netttleship. '. . . If she could only just come and sit for me sometimes. I've never painted her – I thought I had so much time, and began by getting at sidelights of her only, counting on doing the real thing in the end – she was such a big subject.'

It was this sense of time lost that reanimated his need to paint, to seize every opportunity of doing so, to simplify life in order to do so. But with seven children to support, almost as many studios, and perhaps Dorelia (at least while she was still pregnant), how was he to start? His predicament was complicated by a new belief in his children. While Ida was alive, he had tended to look at them as interruptions to his work. But because of what they had lost, and what he had lost too, and the identification he felt for them through loss, he began to see them as the very subject-matter of his work. In order to paint them he must have them around him; but to have them around him he needed money; and to get money he would have to paint some commissioned portraits, which was a very hit-or-miss business. However this conundrum was to be worked out, he recognized the direction his painting must take. 'I must tell you how happy thoughts fill me just now,' he confided to Alice Rothenstein. 'I begin to see how it is all going to come about – all the children and mothers and me. In my former impatience and unwisdom I *used* to think of them sometimes as accidental or perhaps a little in the way of my art, what a mistake – now it dawns on me they are, must be the real material and soul of it.'

The sort of gossip from which Ida had partly shielded him now began to encircle him. He heard it everywhere – ill-informed, excited, curious, full of half-truths and sentimental platitudes.

'*Lady M.F. Prothero to Alice Rothenstein*:
I have been so much grieved to hear of Ida John's death. It sounds terribly sad, – and all those babies left behind! I hear that Mrs Nettleship was with Ida, so I feel she must have had care in her illness. But I wonder if she had been worn out lately in one way or another. The thought of her quite haunts me, – and her heroic conduct all through – I should so much have liked to hear something about her from you, and what is likely to become of those infants. – I suppose John is quite irresponsible and it will fall to Mrs Nettleship to mother them. She, poor soul, has already had a hard struggle, and this responsibility is a heavy one for her to bear . . .'

It was nevertheless a responsibility Mrs Nettleship resolved to shoulder. The fight between her and Augustus opened up as soon as Ida died. On the following day (15 March 1907) she reported the outcome to her daughter Ursula: 'Gus is quite willing for me to take them [the children] for the present but we have not made any plans for the future. I think he wants to get away to the country. I want to get a Swiss nurse for the children . . . They are very pleased to be coming with us.'[1]

Three days later, having arranged for a notice of Ida's death to be put in *The Times* and ordered mourning clothes for the family, she returned to Wigmore Street, carrying off the three eldest children. She was warm with plans for them – what they should precisely wear, what they must eat. The two babies, Edwin and Henry, she left in Paris, on the misunderstanding that they were to be looked after not by Dorelia but Delphine, who 'is a very good nurse: I don't mind leaving two babies with her.'

Augustus had not been 'quite willing' for his mother-in-law to take the children even on this temporary basis. But he had no alternative. 'I am nearly bankrupt at the moment,' he confessed to Will Rothenstein. It was out of the question to saddle Dorelia with more squatters just as her own, Pyramus and Romilly, were 'beginning to get wise'; and so he grudgingly conceded the first round in this contest. 'Mrs Nettleship and Ethel N. took David and Caspar and Robin back to London,' he announced to Margaret Sampson, ' – leaving us the incapables.'

He was determined to 'get them away again'.[2] To the Rani he confided: 'I have tried to make it clear that I shall kidnap them some day.' His plans were legion. His friends, none of whom lived so bourgeois an existence as his mother-in-law, could each take a child or two and Augustus would then rent a small studio or flat in their houses and travel round the country visiting them. It was not ideal, perhaps; but as a temporary solution it was, he flattered himself, pretty good. 'It is a pity to scatter them so,' he agreed with his outraged mother-in-law, ' – one will know what to do a little later.'

He could spot one difficulty. 'Everybody is asking for a baby and really there aren't enough,' he regretted, ' – but I should like Mrs Chowne to have a little one *if I can find one* . . . I wonder if Mrs Chowne can make Allenbury's and whether she understands the gravity of dill-water.'

The Chownes chiefly recommended themselves as prospective foster parents – probably for Ida's Henry – because Mrs Chowne was good-looking and her husband, besides being 'a nice chap', had 'painted some charming flower pieces'.[3] They had no children, lived in Liverpool where Augustus would enjoy seeing the Dowdalls and Sampsons; and they had known Ida, if only slightly. It was a pilot scheme for the whole exercise of adoption. But it failed, and for the most inconsequential of reasons. Both the Chownes welcomed the idea – *but never both at the same time*. As an example of diplomacy it was expert. 'I should hate to disappoint Mrs Chowne,' Augustus admitted to the Rani, who was acting as a broker in the arrangements. An unending stream of goodwill flowed between them without interruption or consequence, at the end of which there was no more talk of adoption.

The other practical matter that entangled Augustus was the future of the Chelsea Art School. The negotiations had been prolonged and for the most part unintelligible. This had been due to Knewstub's business methods, which involved muddling the school's money with that of the Chenil Gallery in such a way that his cheques from both school and gallery were returned to him. 'It is a great pity that Knewstub is such a tactless idiot,' Augustus had acknowledged to Trevor Haddon (4 February 1907). The reason why he was 'nearly bankrupt' was that Knewstub, who managed the shop at the Chenil Gallery, had lost some hundreds of pounds he had collected from the sale of John's pictures. 'I have always been anxious to avoid injuring the business or making things difficult,' Augustus assured Haddon, who had taken control of the gallery and from whom Augustus agreed to accept repayment at the rate of twenty-five pounds a month (equivalent to £1,215 in 1996). '. . . Believe me I shall not cease to regret the mistakes we made over the school and I wish above all things to avoid causing you embarrassment.'[4]

It was essential, nevertheless, to end this story of the school happily. He proposed giving it the use, for advertisement purposes, of his name and, if it provided him with a studio, he guaranteed to be on the spot – from time to time. As his understudy, elevated with the name of Principal, he recommended Will Rothenstein. The goodwill of the school had apparently been purchased for two hundred pounds by Mrs Flower, who intended removing it to Hampstead Heath and paying Augustus one guinea for each of his appearances there – provided his understudy turned up when he did not. The trouble was that Will would ask such damned pedagogic questions: What was the exact constitution of the school? Could he have more details of his status there? Was it 'honourable', of the first rank, and established on a proper economic footing? Augustus would meet such inquiries at a more personal level: Mrs Flower was 'a very nice woman – rather remarkable. I think one of those naked souls, full of faith and fortitude'; she therefore merited Will's collaboration. 'Knowing her pretty well,' Augustus added, 'I have not thought it necessary to treat her too formally – she would be perfectly ready to fall in with any views you or I held . . . she would give no trouble and understand she takes financial responsibility.' This responsibility embraced a fine new studio on the Heath 'she will erect for me, which will be an immense boon'; plus another, in a neighbouring pine grove, where the young pupils could pursue their studies under him. He would invite his friends, Lamb, Epstein, McEvoy, even Lewis, 'to roost among my trees'. Mrs Flower, he concluded, 'should consider herself lucky'.

Yet it was not to be. 'The school we might make of it is too good to let slip too hastily,' he urged Will Rothenstein (23 July 1907) as their plans for it began to fade. But truthfully he was no longer interested in teaching; only painting.

Without money from this school he had to rely more than ever on 'the asphyxiating atmosphere of the New English Art Club ... Its corrupting amenities – its traitorous esprit de corps – its mediocre excellencies even – !' he complained. 'I always want to slough my skin after the bi-annual celebrations and go into the wilderness to bewail my virginity for another reason than that which prompted Jephthah's daughter.'

Over the next years there would seldom be a time when his work was not being exhibited in London: at the Carfax and the Chenil, the Goupil and Society of Twelve shows, at groups, academies, clubs. Any new movement or gathering – the Camden Town, the Allied Artists – any mixed show of modern work, automatically invited him, however foreign its aesthetic programme might be. He was untouched by these movements and counter-movements – their interest for him was financial. But he was not hostile to them and they welcomed his co-operation. Fry and Tonks, Will Rothenstein and Frank Rutter – these and other painter-critic-politicians wooed him. He bowed to their solicitations to exhibit, to sit on hanging committees, to become president of societies: but he was above art politics, or at least to one side of them. They were simply a means to an end when other means failed. 'I am longing to borrow money so as to work till my show[5] comes, undisturbed by Clubs and Societies,' he hinted to Will (22 June 1907). It was the uncertainty of his life that forced him to rely so much on these institutions:

'Pendulous Fate sounds many a varied note on my poor tympanum – my darkness and lights succeed one another with almost as much regularity as if the sun and the Planetary system controlled them; and the hours of *moonless* nights are long dismal unhallowed hours. My life is completely unsettled; I mean to say the circumstances of my existence are problematic; but my art, I believe I can say, does not cease to develop ... I shall set about a composition soon – with a motive of action in it, controlling all – as in a Greek play.'[6]

Nothing could have been easier for Augustus, with his dexterity, than to follow with trivial variations the Post-Impressionists in Paris. But he already had enough influences to assimilate, and was not sure how to assimilate more. 'I want to start something fresh and new,' he told Will Rothenstein (April 1907). 'I feel inclined to paint a nude in cadmium and indigo and orange. The "Indépendants" is effroyable – and yet one feels sometimes these chaps have blundered on something alive without being able to master it.'

From the way in which he writes of pictures, Gauguin alone among near-contemporary French painters appears to inspire him.

'I should like to work for a few years entirely "out of my head", perhaps for ever. To paint women till their faces become enlarged to an idiotic inanimity – till they stand impassively, unquestionably, terrifyingly fecund – fetiches of brass with Polynesian eyes and dry imperative teeth and fitful craving of bowels that surge and smoke for sacrifice – of flesh and flowers. How delightful that sounds! Can you [Will Rothenstein] imagine the viridian vistas, can you hear the chanting in the flushing palm tree groves and the thumping of the great flat feet of ecstatic multitudes shining with the sacred oil. The "Ah Ah Ah" of the wild infant world?'

Primitive inspiration was not to be found in Paris. Parisian women were what Delacroix once described as 'on stage'.[7] There were those who would say that, by leaving Paris, Augustus turned his back on everything exciting that was happening in modern painting; that had he stayed he would have painted like Derain, who had something of the same panache. But he wanted to find somewhere uninvaded by the twentieth century, a place where the inhabitants still lived the life of their ancestors. He did not, however, plan to live in such a place, merely to spend a holiday there.

He set off in April, patrolling the north coast – 'right across the top of France', he reported to Will Rothenstein. Finally he came across what he was looking for: Equihen, a village of primitive fisherfolk not far from Boulogne. 'The fish women are simply magnificent,' he wrote to Dorelia. 'I must get a studio or shed here soon and paint 'em – there's money in it!' It was good to get away from the 'steam music, literary society, bugs and other embêtements' of Paris. At Equihen one could see the *marins* getting the fish out of the sea and the *matelots* selling them – 'and the women go about in wonderful groups. Just the stuff for me. They resemble a community that live on the river by Haverfordwest distinct from their neighbours – in a village called Langum. The women go all over Pembrokeshire selling oysters in a peculiar costume and the men are supposed to mind the babies.'

To this 'desolate little place'[8] in France he summoned Dorelia and the four babies, Pyramus and Romilly, Edwin and Henry, since there were 'nice soft sand dunes' for them to crawl on. After they had settled in, he proposed sending for Ida's other sons. 'I am working pretty hard,' he assured Will Rothenstein, 'now and then. Having a little studio here is a boon. I like the wenches here and the clothes they wear and I wish I had more money to spend on them . . . Pyramus grows more lyrically beautiful every day. He is like a little divine phrase from Shelley or Wordsworth. He is more flower-like and "meaningless" than any child I know. He is the incarnation of the daisy. I think I must try to do a "Mother and Child" of him and Dorelia.'

The Mother was now trying to bring about a miscarriage and for much of the time feeling too ill to sit to Augustus. Once more he experienced 'those submarine days when one begins to wonder what manner of beings live above the air'.[9] The frustration that had consumed him at Ste-Honorine began again to smoulder. 'Meet me at Boulogne next Saturday will you?' he suddenly invited Alick Schepeler. But she hurried north again. 'As to my work, I haven't got at it really,' he admitted to Henry Lamb (13 June 1907). 'But my "head" still yields enchanting suggestions. In fact call it what you will it is my best friend, tho' I have other loyal parts. Sometimes I feel myself as if slowly and surely settling down on some scrap heap.'

At this critical moment an invitation arrived from Lady Gregory. She asked him to come over to Ireland, stay with her at Coole, and do a portrait of her other guest that summer, W. B. Yeats. Augustus hesitated. 'It may be that I shall draw Yeats' portrait,' he wrote to Alick Schepeler, ' – I am so hard up.'

2

IMAGES OF YEATS

'Sin openly and scandalize the world.'
W. B. Yeats to John Quinn, describing Augustus John's moral code

The invitation to Coole Park originated from Lady Gregory's son, the artist Robert Gregory, at whose marriage Augustus had been best man. He had been helpful to Gregory over his work while in London, and this invitation was in the nature of a repayment. Appropriately, it was a business proposition. Yeats was then revising his collected works in preparation for A. H. Bullen's edition the following year. This edition was to contain a portrait by some contemporary artist. Yeats had wanted Charles Shannon to do an etching for the frontispiece, but 'Shannon was busy when I was in London,' he explained to the American art patron John Quinn (4 October 1907), 'and the collected edition was being pushed on so quickly that I found I couldn't wait for him.' It was then that Robert Gregory put forward Augustus's name, to which Yeats nervously agreed: 'I don't know what John will make of me.'

Augustus, too, was nervous – financially, 'I should like very much to visit you – and perhaps Yeats's drawing would make it possible,' he wrote from Equihen to Robert Gregory, 'but just now it is difficult for me. How much will the publishers pay, do you think? I would be glad to do the drawing. But as you see I am a long way off . . .' In reply, Lady Gregory sent him a fee of eighteen pounds in advance (equivalent to £875 in 1996), plus a suggestion that should he wish to draw some of the family, they might buy some of his drawings. The deal thus tentatively struck, Augustus sailed for Galway.

He arrived at Lady Gregory's big plain house in September, a flamboyant youth in a blue jersey and earrings, 'with all his luggage hanging from one finger'. Though he had met Yeats at the Nettleships' and at the Rothensteins', he had never studied him as a subject. 'Yeats, slightly bowed and with an air of abstraction, walked in the garden every morning with Augusta Gregory, discussing literary matters,' he remembered. It was as an embodiment of Celtic poetry that Yeats presented himself to Augustus. The flat dense colour areas of the oil portrait,[10] done as a preliminary study for the etching, suggest some comparison with Gauguin; and the design and colour are strong. Yeats, dressed in a white shirt and black smock, wears a loose cravat tied in a bow at the neck. Against the dark mass of his clothes and hair, the flesh-tones are wonderfully pale – a whitish-yellow; and this consumptive complexion with its dreamy expression is enhanced by a brilliant backcloth of emblematic viridian that isolates and freezes the poet by its density and airlessness. It is a romantic portrait: this is what Augustus did best. For a moment Yeats fulfilled his ideal of a poet, and this ideal has been beautifully caught.

Apart from the oil portrait, Augustus did numerous other studies[11] from which to work up his etching for the frontispiece. 'I felt rather a martyr going to him [Augustus],' Yeats had reported to John Quinn (4 October 1907). 'The students consider him the greatest living draughtsman, the only modern who draws like an old master. But he makes everybody perfectly hideous, beautiful according to his own standard. He exaggerates every little hill and hollow of the face till one looks a gipsy, grown old in wickedness and hardship. If one looked like any of his pictures the country women would take clean clothes off the hedges when one passed as they do at the sight of a tinker.'

Having glimpsed his studies with pen and brush, Yeats was certain at this stage that Augustus's 'best work is etching, he is certainly a great etcher with a savage imagination.' Shortly afterwards, to his horror, the etching arrived. It made him, he complained to Quinn, 'a sheer tinker, drunken, unpleasant and disreputable, but full of wisdom, a melancholy English Bohemian, capable of anything, except living joyously on the surface.'

Part of the trouble lay with the reactions of Lady Gregory and of Annie Horniman, who was financing the Bullen edition. 'I send one of the John etchings,' Yeats wrote to Lady Gregory. 'I admire it very much as an etching & shall hang it on my wall with joy but it is of course a translation of me into tinker language. I showed it to Miss Horniman . . . & she flew into a rage over it. If she could afford it she would buy up the plate and destroy it.'

Lady Gregory agreed with Annie Horniman. The etching was a horror. If it showed a tinker, then it was a tinker in the dock for chicken stealing. 'John has done a terrible etching of Yeats,' she had written to Quinn (22 December 1907). 'It won't do for the book but he may do another, he promised to do two or three. Meanwhile I am trying to get Shannon to draw him. It is rather heartbreaking about John's for he did so many studies of him here, and took so much of his time . . . But if they are not like Yeats, and are like a tinker in the dock, or a charwoman at a prayer meeting they and the plate shall go into the fire.'

Yeats, swinging this way and that, drifted into a complex panic. He could not use John's 'melancholy desperado' as the sole portrait. 'I confess I shrink before the John thing,' he told Florence Farr. But what should he say to John? 'I don't know what to write to John,' he confided to Lady Gregory, ' – whatever I say he will think I want to be flattered.' Eventually he wrote praising the etching but telling him that he expected a violent letter about it from his publisher – who indeed did refuse it in violent language.

Augustus seems to have remained philosophical – at any rate his confidence was unshaken. 'Lady Gregory, much as I love and admire her, has her eye still clouded a little by the visual enthusiasms of her youth and cannot be expected to *see* the merits of my point of view,' he explained to Alick Schepeler, 'tho' her intelligence assures her of their existence. Painting Yeats is becoming quite a habit. He has a natural and sentimental prejudice in favour of the W. B. Yeats he and other people have been accustomed to see and imagine for so many years. He is now 44 and a robust, virile and humorous personality (while still the poet of course). I cannot see in him any definite resemblance to the youthful Shelley in a lace collar. To my mind he is far more interesting as he is, as maturity is more interesting than immaturity.'

It was almost impossible for any artist to see Yeats as Lady Gregory saw him. If Augustus had portrayed him in her eyes as an ugly ruffian, Shannon, by an unlucky chance, was to make him look damnably like

John Keats; Jack Yeats, of course, could only see him through a mist of domestic emotion; Mancini turned him into an Italian bandit; Sargent into a dream creature. And so on. Yeats flirted with the idea ('it will be fine sport') of introducing the lot of them into his collected works, one after the other, 'and I shall write an essay on them and describe them as all the different personages that I have dreamt of being but never had the time for. I shall head it with this quotation from the conversation of Wordsworth: – "No, that is not Mr Wordsworth, the poet, that is Mr Wordsworth, the Chancellor of the Exchequer".'

In Bullen's edition a mild Sargent drawing took the place of Augustus's etching. But in subsequent editions it is most often one or other of Augustus's portraits that have been chosen as the frontispiece.* 'I enclose a photograph of a portrait painted by Augustus John in 1907,' Yeats wrote to Harold Macmillan on 2 October 1933; 'I suggest it as a frontispiece of my forthcoming volume of *Collected Poems* . . . John is, I think, more admired by the readers of books today than Sargent.'

Yeats was never really so opposed to Augustus's interpretation as Lady Gregory. This first etching had been a shock, but the more he looked at all the etchings and drawings and the portrait in oils, the more convinced he had become of their merit. On leaving Ireland he wrote to Quinn (7 January 1908): 'I would like to show you Augustus John's portrait of me. A beautiful etching, and I understand what he means in it, and admire the meaning, but it is useless for my social purpose.' Years later he wrote: 'Always particular about my clothes, never dissipated, never unshaven except during illness, I saw myself there an unshaven, drunken bar-tender. And then I began to feel John had found something that he liked in me, something closer than character, and by that very transformation made it visible. He found Anglo-Irish solitude, a solitude I have made for myself, an outlawed solitude.'

Though fearful of his 'savage imagination', Yeats was taken with Augustus. His attitude, like Augustus's towards him, mingled romance with an ironic perception of character.

'He is himself a delight,' Yeats told Quinn (4 October 1907), 'the most innocent, wicked man I have ever met. He wears earrings, his hair down to his shoulders, a green velvet collar and had two wives who lived together in perfect harmony and nursed each other's children on their

---

* 'The portrait was painted in 1907 at Coole by Augustus John,' Yeats wrote to Olivia Shakespeare on 13 November 1933, the year after Lady Gregory died. 'I am using it as a frontispiece for my collected volume of lyrics which you will get in a day or two.' When the etching was rejected, Yeats had written privately to his publisher A. H. Bullen (March 1908): 'The Augustus John is a wonderful etching but fanciful as a portrait. But remember that all fine artistic work is received with an outcry, with hatred even. Suspect all work that is not.'

knees till about six months ago when one of them bolted and the other died. Since then he has followed the lady who bolted and he and she are gathering the scattered families. Of course, nobody round Coole knew anything of these facts. I lived in daily terror of some benevolent gossip carrying on conversation with him like this,

"Married, Mr John? Children?"

"Yes." "How many?" "Seven." "You married young?"

"Five years ago." "Twins doubtless?" – after that frank horrifying discourse on the part of Augustus John, who considers himself a particularly good well-behaved man. The only difference is in code . . . He is the strangest creature I have ever met, a kind of fawn . . . a magnificent-looking person, and looks the wild creature he is.'

Augustus was on his best behaviour at Coole. Painter and poet would sit up late in intimate talk, each out-charming the other. 'He is most delightful,' Augustus told Alick Schepeler, 'nobody seems to know him but me – unless it is the Gregorys, but that is my conceit no doubt.' Except for these late-night conversations, Augustus spoke little, worked hard and would wander off for long solitary walks in the wooded park round Coole where he had located 'a region which is obviously holy ground'. Needing to escape out of doors, he passed many evenings rowing idly on the lake, with only the swans, which Yeats had celebrated, for company. Then, to the apprehensive admiration of Robert Gregory and the astonishment of everyone else, he would surge indoors, do wonderful athletic things on the drawing-room floor, rush out again and climb to the top of the tallest tree in the Coole garden, where he carved a cryptic symbol. Poets, playwrights and patrons struggled among its lower branches, but 'nobody else has been able to get up there to know what it is, even Robert stuck halfway.'[12]

By the time he left, Augustus had seen enough of Ireland to know that it was rich territory for him as a painter. Already he had vast schemes to paint all Galway. He would return, several times; and the last time he would again paint Yeats.

3

ALL BOYS BRAVE AND BEAUTIFUL

'God knows I am buffeted mightily by fate.'
Augustus John to Alice Rothenstein

At Equihen Augustus had left a situation full of passionate uncertainties.

Attended by one of her sisters – 'voluptuous Jessie'[13] – Dorelia had gone through an illness culminating, to the satisfaction of everyone, in a miscarriage. Nothing could be wrong with this unless it was the timing, which coincided with the arrival of Mrs Nettleship, bringing with her Ida's three eldest boys, David, Caspar and Robin.

Augustus had wanted to surround himself with all his children this summer, and to spend his time working over them and the admirable sea-girls. He had not reckoned on Mrs Nettleship's presence, nor on the unpainterly school clothes with which she had decked out her grand-children – quite wrong for late-fifteenth-century Italian work. It was a shock – yet he was determined to prove the optimist. 'This is a jolly place,' he wrote to Ursula Tyrwhitt. 'My numberless kids are all here now. I have a dilapidated studio to work in. The fish people here are very amusing. The girls look fine in their old costumes. Multitudes of children teem in the gutters together with the debris of centuries.'

He was resolved not to put up with the children's noise, but to *enjoy* it. After all, it was natural, and enjoyment was necessary for work – it accelerated his perceptions. Yet it was elusive. Everything seemed to rub away at this quality of enjoyment at Equihen, and in the most abrasive manner. Before Mrs Nettleship's commanding presence, the beauty of Nature seemed to hesitate and retreat; even alcohol could no longer call forth those 'delightful sensations old Debaucheries used to procure me . . . angelic glimpses secreted like pearls in piggeries.'[14]

In a letter to Henry Lamb (5 August 1907) he wrote: 'I wish this house were on wheels.' Wherever he was he wanted to move on. He had been enchanted by the magic lake or *turlough* at Coole, islanded, and mysteri-ously rising and subsiding. What he desired now was a miraculous encamp-ment that contained all possibilities, that moved yet rested, that congregated the right people – artists and comedians, women and children – but that had hidden places into which he could retire. In such a place the tension between the necessities of involvement and solitude would disappear.

'I understand that solitude is not always and ever good for a man,' he advised Henry Lamb. 'Are we not much too solitary? . . . I think company is better medicine than loneliness. Let us see new faces, lest the old ones grow old under our tiring eyes, and damn it we are artists not misanthrop-ists. Anthropology is our business. Solitude be damned. One seeks solitude – with one's woman only.'

These were brave-sounding words, but they trumpeted a virtue of what, for Augustus, was becoming a necessity. He needed more solitude, not less; more opportunity to train his memory in recapturing the fleeting moment; more emphasis on sustained imagination. But this gypsy way to artistic fulfilment was new and needed to be worked out.

Henry Lamb was 'no ordinary personage', Augustus was to assure the art patron Lady Ottoline Morrell (20 September 1908), 'and has the divine mark on his brow'. Lamb was still taking his apprenticeship to Augustus very seriously. While Euphemia was becoming the very model of a John model, Henry was allowing the John style to grow over him. His drawings resembled Augustus's, and so did his clothes. He had let his hair grow long; he failed to shave; he fastened on gold earrings. He was spectacularly handsome. With his hypnotic deep-blue eyes he fascinated men and women alike, and his entrance into any gathering was almost as striking as that of the *maître*. When the Chelsea Art School went into a decline – or rather when Augustus's attendances there declined – Lamb quitted it and with Euphemia followed him to Paris. By the beginning of 1907 he was living in the rue Cels and studying under Jacques-Émile Blanche at L'École de la Palette, an *académie* of some twenty students which included Duncan Grant.

Ida had liked Lamb. It would be 'rather nice to have a Lamb on the doormat', she had written to Augustus, on hearing at the end of 1906 that Lamb was coming over. When he did come, they discussed the French translations of Dostoevsky. Dorelia liked him too: they often played the piano together. After Ida's death, Dorelia and Henry drew closer. 'Dorelia will I hope buck up under your sunny influence,' Augustus encouraged him (13 June 1907), ' – yours is evidently the touch. My person is like a blight on the household.' Meanwhile Augustus was doing countless studies of the alluring Euphemia. She was an excellent model, especially when nude. The presence of this girl, with her pale oval face, husky voice and honey-coloured hair, had already provoked a rather sharp inquiry from Alick Schepeler. 'I have never had time or inclination to consider her very seriously,' Augustus airily defended himself. 'I have simply taken her for granted. It is true I have thought her rather eccentric . . .' Then, in Paris, immediately following Ida's death, time and the inclination had coincided. So the two households, the Lambs and the Johns, mingled, amoeba-like, revolved and came together again in a forma-tion of rich complexity. 'Could we not form a discreet form of colony', Lamb soon began wondering, '. . . in couples. For the sake of symmetry I could double myself no doubt at suitable intervals.'[15] To those looking on their fantasies appeared madness. 'Do you think he [Henry] is all right in his intellect?'[16] his brother Walter Lamb had asked Clive Bell, who was spending part of his honeymoon in Paris. But it was Euphemia's scattiness that struck Vanessa Bell as being so extreme, and her sister Virginia agreed ('my head spins with her stories'[17]). As Maynard Keynes later remarked to them, Euphemia enjoyed more sexual life 'than the rest of us put together'.[18]

'What will Mrs Lamb do?'[19] Ida had asked before Euphemia arrived in Paris. What she did was to fight with Henry ('using dinner plates and knives in their battles'), drift uncomfortably apart from Augustus, and fall in to the thankless arms of Duncan Grant. 'That Lamb family sickens me,' Grant complained to Lytton Strachey (7 April 1907),

'and that man John. I'm convinced now he's a bad lot. His mistress, Dorelia, fell in love with Henry and invited him to copulate and as far as I can make out John encouraged the liaison and arranged or at any rate winked at the arrangements for keeping Nina [Euphemia] out of the way, although Henry didn't in the least want to have any dealings with Dorelia. However it was apparently all fixed up that they should "go on the roads" together when Nina was (according to her own story) found with a loaded revolver ready to shoot herself (and Henry as far as I could gather). So Henry was left by himself . . . Dorelia and John seem to be the devils and the others merely absurd . . .'

This account, which suffers from being overcoloured by Euphemia's testimony, nevertheless indicated how Augustus remained separated from Fry's group of Bloomsbury painters. He felt ill-at-ease in their educated presence; and they were disconcerted by his deliberate thoughtlessness and irrationality. There seemed no common ground between his pursuit of 'meaningless' beauty, and their imposition of 'significant form'. To Bloomsbury, Augustus John was a meteor, dazzling and self-destructive, a brilliant phenomenon that was burning itself out. 'Oh John! Oh . . . what a "warning"! as the Clergy say,' Lytton Strachey exclaimed in reply to Duncan Grant (12 April 1907). 'When I think of him, I often feel that the only thing to do is to chuck up everything and make a dash for some such safe secluded office-stool [the Treasury] as is pressed by dear Maynard's [Keynes's] happy bottom. The dangers of freedom are appalling! In the meantime it seems to me that one had better immediately buy up every drawing by him that's on the market. For surely he's bound to fizzle out; and then the prices!'

To Bloomsbury eyes, Augustus appeared to live a life based upon the casual whim. They could not know the annihilating force of his solitude, or sense the panic. He seldom defended or explained his way of life. It was based upon a natural law of self-interest. If some desire swept through you, then you gave expression to it with all your being – physically, vocally, at once and until it was exhausted and you were left empty or filled by another desire. Lock antlers, copulate and procreate; work, accept risks and avoid deceits. Those who acted upon their emotions lived longer because they lived by a deeper biological reality than social convention. However admirable your motives for bottling up feelings might be, the contents of the bottle often turned to poison. There was a danger in modern society of the animal in man being neglected, and human history dwindling into devious tributaries. Such pollution of nature and exploitation of human nature revolted John. He preferred the simple life.

Yet it was surprisingly difficult to achieve the simple life. What could be more simple, for example, than to invite Henry Lamb to Equihen? And what, in the society of Mrs Nettleship, could be more amusing? 'I hope you will come and bathe here,' had run his innocent invitation. But instead of Henry, Euphemia arrived, dressed rather improbably as a young man and followed by an enthusiastic, but bankrupt, Swede. Having relieved Augustus of some of his Irish money, the Swede hurried on to Paris, while Euphemia, falling ill with a mysterious disease, was condemned for a week to bed. 'She makes an irresistible boy,' Augustus admitted to her husband, ' – I feel, myself, better after assisting at her recovery.'

According to Euphemia, she had been given a knife by Madame Maeterlinck with which to kill Dorelia. But while she lay asleep under a van, Augustus had joined her and they had both been arrested as practising homosexuals. In gaol she was obliged to take off her clothes to prove their innocence. But how much could you believe such stories from someone who also claimed to have been responsible for Ida's death ('I got a *sage femme* for her, but she was dirty and infected Ida. Her hair turned quite white in one night and her head shrank . . .'[20])?

Although she was not to allow him a divorce until the late 1920s, Euphemia had already parted from Lamb and was starting out on an exotic career. 'Henry has left Nina perhaps for ever,' Duncan Grant wrote to Lytton Strachey, 'and the white haired whore still goes on eating "*crèmes nouveautés*".' Her adventures were to lead her, in one guise or another, into many memoirs – as 'Dorothy', for example, in the *Confessions* of Aleister Crowley, the Great Beast 666, who wrote that she 'would have been a *grande* passion had it not been that my instinct warned me that she was incapable of true love. She was incomparably beautiful . . . capable of stimulating the greatest extravagancies of passion.' For Augustus, who gave her the name 'Lobelia', these extravagancies were wonderfully comic. 'She has made the acquaintance of a number of nations,' he assured Lamb (5 August 1907); and he told Dorelia (April 1908) that 'Lobelia had 6 men in her room last night, representing the six European powers, and all silent as the grave.'

For Lamb himself, Euphemia remained a unique experience. 'I always

250

feel grateful for the privilege of having been so closely associated with so much beauty & genius & glorious energy of character,' he wrote fifty years later. But the great figure of Lamb's life was to be Dorelia. It was almost inevitable, fulfilling his role as Augustus's *alter ego*, that he should fall in love with her. Since he was an artist, this also made destiny-sense to Dorelia. Already they had begun a love affair – the second of Dorelia's two 'discreditable episodes' – that was to continue, with intervals, over twenty years. During those years, Lamb never lost hope that she would free herself from 'the August clutches' and come to live with him. 'There is a fair chance of it all coming off some day,' he was still writing in the summer of 1926.

For the time being their involvement remained part of the *entente cordiale*, an agreeable *échange* that had no unpleasant repercussions: except with Mrs Nettleship. Ada Nettleship had never liked Dorelia, and everything she learnt this summer confirmed her in this dislike. Obviously Dorelia was quite the wrong person with whom to entrust Ida's boys. It was not simply a matter of immorality: it was incompetence – an incompetence so superlative it made Mrs Nettleship dizzy. It was out of the question for her grandchildren never to be washed, never brushed or combed, decked out in fanciful rags and left unsuperintended. Their bedrooms were full of unchecked frogs, absurd grasshoppers and other scattered atrocities: it was bedlam. Even Augustus was forced to own that 'this crèche-like establishment is a little too heroic – in the long run'.[21] Within a week of arriving at Equihen, the boys had been drowned *en masse* – or rather almost drowned, being uniquely rescued by a local fisherman who 'was getting food for his rabbits on the cliff when he heard their screaming', Mrs Nettleship explained to her daughter Ursula (19 July 1907). 'He has never saved anyone before and he hopes to get a medal.'

So different were these goings-on from the calm atmosphere at Wigmore Street, she felt as if she had landed on a distant world where no one knew what was right or wrong, and no normal standards applied. Every day was a carnival, and the amoral beauty of it all drove her frantic. 'There never seems time for anything here,' she complained to Ursula, ' – the weather is so lovely, we are out all day and in the evening we are too sleepy to do anything. It is almost irritating that this place is so lovely – I hate it all for being so placid and "only man is vile" . . . Something must come to relieve this tension.'

Something did come and it brought the tension to breaking point. Dorelia had succeeded in not telling anyone that her children this summer were suffering from ophthalmia, a painful eye disease. She had even forgotten it herself and, by arranging for all the children to share a single sponge and towel, had spread the infection to two of Ida's children, Edwin and Robin. Mrs Nettleship was appalled. Here was actual proof that Dorelia could not be trusted. She dismissed Dorelia's argument that many of these sicknesses cured themselves, and briskly herding Ida's untainted sons together she drove them out of the infected area. 'I should like to bring them back right away,' she told Ursula in London, 'but Gus does not think it matters! . . . He says the village children get over it all right and so will ours! . . . He is nearly driving me mad . . . I have never known anyone so impossible to deal with.' At the same time, fearing to lose the boys altogether, she had to check her temper. Nor could she leave while the ophthalmia persisted, since no one did anything to cure the disease unless she herself insisted on it being done – Dorelia still preferring what she called 'natural methods'. At first, Mrs Nettleship's monumental diplomacy seemed to be effective, especially when Augustus, responding to the strain of their holiday, remarked that the two families could never be brought up together. 'If either of our boys [David or Caspar] get ophthalmia I shall use it as a weapon,' Mrs Nettleship promised.

Twelve days later, diplomacy had disappeared and 'it is war to the knife'. Each side had marshalled a team of doctors with strongly opposing advice. 'Gus is hopeless – just one mass of selfishness – not thinking of anyone, but his own desires – and so surly and cross,' Mrs Nettleship reported to Ursula. 'How Ida can have endured it I can't imagine – he has no heart at all.'

Another twelve days and Mrs Nettleship had returned to Wigmore Street, triumphantly carrying off with her David, Caspar, Robin, and the urn containing Ida's ashes. 'We had a healthy respect for Grannie Nettleship,' Caspar remembered. This tubby woman with grizzled hair and plump face was strict but not ungenerous. The boys were chiefly looked after by Ursula, the elder of their two aunts. 'We had to wash and scrub thoroughly in preparation for an inspection by Ursula before being accepted as adequately clean,' Caspar wrote. 'We wore shoes and socks regularly and had our straggling locks cut short.'[22]

All this was distressing for Augustus. 'I am saddened to realise that I have allowed an immoral and bourgeois society of women to capture my 3 eldest boys,' he admitted to Henry Lamb (17 July 1907). 'It will be the devil to get them back again but it must be done when opportunity offers. Perhaps I may ask you to assist me one day in recovering them. Can you shoot? I cannot stand finding those chaps in the hands of people among whom I shall always be a stranger, and no longer in the brave and beautiful attire their mother gave them to wear. I cannot leave them with people who although they are Ida's mother and sisters did not even know her.'

Mrs Nettleship was used to getting her own way and, once back in

Wigmore Street, she set about consolidating her advantage. She knew that Augustus did not want to prolong the present arrangement, yet sensed he was somehow in two minds. His uncertainty was catching and she could not make up her own mind as to what her best tactics should be. If she wanted to mollify him she might approach him via her daughter Ursula; if she wanted to frighten him she would appeal to Edward Nettleship – 'Uncle Ned of Nutcombe Hill', said to be a dragon of a man. Finally, after canvassing opinion among various aunts and cousins, she did both. Ursula acted at once, writing to assure Augustus that, if the children were left with the Nettleship family, she would see to it that their education was not old-fashioned and would look after them herself. In his reply, Augustus sets down his feelings with unusual explicitness:

'Be sure that if any consideration could induce me to part with the children it would be the fact that *you* alone would have them. The *immediate* future has an unsettled aspect for me. Homeless, penniless and lawless I present a pretty spectacle of a paterfamilias! But thanks to you things begin to look much more tractable.

I want badly to retain the children as Ida's and mine – to keep them in the atmosphere they were born in – a delightful atmosphere and not at all dreadful you know – and to think of them being educated into ordinary little early Victorian bourgeois prigs is a horrid thought! You have eased me of that apprehension at least . . . and you would have some of Ida's sublime gigantic composure in dealing with them – I really was beginning to fear I shouldn't recognise them in a year or so, or they me. I was preparing myself for the moment when they would approach me and earnestly implore me to get my hair cut!

In addition to these perhaps morbid fancies the spirit of opposition was kindled somewhat on finding my section of the family treated to a kind of super-discreet aloofness – and the three kids in question hardly to be viewed and that only under formidable escort . . . I must have a try at getting people to know that Dorelia is a Person and a very rare and respectable being, to wit full of sense and sensibility, having no shams in her being, indeed a kind of feminine genius I fancy. I would like to mention that had she been only my "mistress" we would not be together now. Had she not been a worthy soul, do you think I could have stood it so long? I say this as no superior person, believe me – I might say like Hamlet "I am myself indifferent honest, but yet I could accuse myself of things it were better my mother had not borne me. I am proud, revengeful, ambitious, with more offences at my back than I had thought to put them in, imagination to give them shape, or time to act them in. What should such a fellow as I do, crawling between heaven and earth!"

But Dorelia was loved of Ida and her very good friend in spite of appearances and all great mistakes not withstanding. Barring their mother she had more to do with the children than anyone else; and because Ida happened to die it doesn't strike me as indispensable to hurry D. out by the back stairs. In a word she has been and so far remains part of my family and I should like her always to continue to give the children the benefit of her honesty and simplicity and affection, and help to dress them bravely too – as she knows how to. For without brave attire I can't put up with them.

It would be a frightfully difficult thing to take them away from you even now: but I don't want to. They can always pay you visits . . . But I suppose it's not impossible that you may have babies of your own some time and you might think that better than having other people's babies . . . since my proposal to reassume the parental responsibilities sooner or later – friendliness and Patience have to become established . . .'[23]

While Augustus was writing this letter to Ursula, Uncle Ned was sharpening his pen up at Nutcombe Hill. With long-drawn-out relish he was preparing himself 'a good slapping letter' for Augustus. It was congenial labour. He lingered lovingly over the vituperative phrases, savouring them, hardly liking to let them go. He was still remorselessly chewing over all this when he received from Ursula Augustus's letter and, as he read through it, it occurred to him that his carefully charged time bomb fell 'rather flat'. It was a sad waste, but at least a little of his invective could be discharged vicariously.

The letter he now (28 September 1907) addressed to Ursula shows between what bewildering changes of background some of Ida's sons were to pass their formative years. At first, Uncle Ned allowed, he had thought the fellow must have been mad drunk when he wrote, 'but on re-reading, there is too much essential coherence for that. He [Augustus] whines that he is penniless and homeless and lawless (the last evidently, like the other two, from his misfortune doubtless, not from any preventable fault!). He wants to keep the children for himself and Dorelia, but he wants you with your gigantic composure to carry on their Bohemian Education when in the intervals of their home life they pay you visits in some place where the atmosphere is "anti-Wigmorian".' Such a response, Uncle Ned urged, called in question the whole policy of conciliation. Instead, he would like to hear that Augustus was being instructed 'in quite simple words that it is his business to put his back into his work to maintain his children'; that no Nettleship worth the name would be a party to brave attire – if ' "brave" means (as I am told it does) squalid or dirty or gutter-snipe attire'; and that to talk of the inhabitants of Wigmore Street as bourgeois prigs was 'impudent nonsense' for which an instantaneous apology was required. This, like music, was what Uncle Ned would like to hear – but it would have to come now from Ursula, since she had opened the negotiations. She must change the tune – but he, if called upon, would conduct her playing. It must, however, be a solo programme – they couldn't have every aunt and cousin chiming in. Then the dragon roared his last paragraph of flame:

'I think that subtle, absolutely selfish and introspective as he is, and morose and bad tempered to boot, he is a coward at any rate when dealing with women; and that hard hitting, at any rate now, is at least as likely to succeed with him and Dorelia (who of course is doing her best as wire-puller) as any other plan . . . Dorelia wants to keep him; she does not really want Ida's children.'[24]

So with both sides convinced of the other's immorality as parents, the autumn passed; and, for their winter quarters, they took up entrenched positions in this war to the knife.

4

OR SOMETHING

'Do we not rise on stepping stones of our dead selves – or am I wrong?'

Augustus John to Caspar John

In one respect at least Uncle Ned had misunderstood the situation. He had attributed calculation to Augustus and Dorelia, and in doing so had stumbled on an untruth that made his generalship of incalculable value to the enemy. 'Wire-pulling' or any other species of long-term cunning had no part in Dorelia's make-up. Her gift was for taking things as they came – and when they didn't come, but hung around some distance off, she had little talent for advancing on them. The present suspended state of affairs did not bring into play her best qualities. To a degree, her desires were the very opposite of what Uncle Ned had represented: as her affair with Henry Lamb showed, she did not inevitably want to keep Augustus. But she did want one or two of Ida's children. Her point of view was beyond the comprehension of the Nettleships.

Over the summer, over the autumn, Dorelia and Augustus had debated the situation as fully as two inarticulate people could. They hit on all manner of schemes for taking care of the future, but without Ida they were strangely undecided and, despite much activity, made little progress. There were two main plans: first that they should continue living together; and secondly that they should not. The first plan came in many forms. One night, for example, Dorelia dreamt of 'a lovely country . . . terrific mountains and forests and rivers – the people were Russians but I think it must have been Spain';[25] and next day they were hot for setting off to find this place. Then, their mood changing, they thought of settling for a house in England. 'We must have an aquarium in the country,' Dorelia affirmed. 'We might get one in exchange for a baby or something.'[26] It was that continual 'or something' that foxed them.

Dorelia's difficulty was the adoring Henry Lamb, whose presence acted like that of a magnet upon a compass. She simply did not know what to do. 'I haven't the faintest wish to get married,' she informed Augustus (September 1907). 'I think it would be best if I went on the road and left you in peace which I should be only too glad to do if you would let me have one of the children – Caspar or Robin – he would be better with me than in that virginal atmosphere [Wigmore Street].'[27]

Lamb, who was to walk through Brittany from inn to inn the following summer with Caspar in a sack over his shoulders, had already been sounded out by Augustus in connection with the children. The argument was simple. Since Lamb was apprenticed to Augustus, what could be better than apprenticing one of Augustus's sons to Lamb? It was a merry scheme. 'I found Robin overwhelming!' he recommended. 'When one sings or even whistles to him, he lies back and closes his eyes luxuriously. It is he who should be your pupil . . .'

During the next three years, the relationship between Augustus and Dorelia was to be more fluid and circumstantial than at any other period. Sometimes they lived on wheels together, sometimes the Channel flowed between them. Sometimes they were close; sometimes they seemed to move apart, carried this way and that by currents they could not control. 'Don't worry,' Dorelia reassured him, 'as I think either plan extremely desirable.' There were indeed times when *any* plan seemed desirable – but still they could not decide. Yet whenever Dorelia drifted too far away, Augustus would suddenly be resolute: 'Beloved, of course it's you I want.'[28]

*

One thing at least had been agreed: they could no longer afford, scattered through two countries, quite such a multitude of unsuitable flats and studios. On returning to London, Augustus wrote to Lamb ('mon cher Agneau') asking him to sell the lease of his studio in the cour de Rohan.

Though he would make other parts of France his second home in the future, he was never again to live in Paris. Ironically, perhaps, this parting was to coincide with his meeting with Picasso. 'I saw a young artist called Picasso whose work is wonderful in Paris,' he had written that summer (5 August 1907) to Lamb. And two months later, once his studio was let and all connections with Paris severed (4 November 1907), he had become convinced that 'Picasso is a wonder'. The two painters, fellow-sympathizers with society's outcasts, had visited each other at their studios, and Augustus who saw 'Les Demoiselles d'Avignon', was greatly impressed by Picasso's work, chiefly because, like his own, it was steeped in the past, drew part of its inspiration from Puvis de Chavannes, and revealed 'elements derived from remote antiquity or the art forms of primitive peoples'.[29] Some of Augustus's paintings done at this time, such as the 'French Fisher-boy'[30] and 'Peasant Woman with Baby and Small Boy',[31] show resemblance to Picasso's Blue Period, and indicate a direction his work might have taken had the circumstances of his life been different.

But only in London could he sell his work. Lack of money was the Nettleships' best weapon and he was determined to disarm them. However, for the first few days, having nowhere else to go, he was obliged to put up in, of all places, Wigmore Street. 'I took a small studio here (28 Wigmore Street) which I now see is quite impossible,' he informed Lamb (25 September 1907). After a short period of 'perfect hell', he stopped off with Ambrose McEvoy's playwright brother Charles at 132 Cheyne Walk, then landed up at Whistler's old studio in 8 Fitzroy Street, 'a fine place', where he stayed, intermittently, for almost a year. It was his sole foothold in London, from where, at the prompting of his spirit, he liked to wander off to pubs and music halls, to the Café Royal or, in some painted wagon, to remoter spots.

'I am thinking of raising a little money with a preliminary show of drawings alone,' he notified Lamb on 11 November 1907. The results of this exhibition at the Carfax Gallery that December were encouraging. 'The show opened most successfully,' he told Dorelia. 'I sold about £225 [equivalent to £11,000 in 1996] worth the first morning. 'Twas a scene of great brilliance. Epstein and his wife looked grand.' After it was over he wrote to Lamb: 'I hope now to paint pictures for the rest of my life.' But he had other plans too. 'I *must* have a press,' he told Dorelia. 'I long to bring out a book of etchings. It might be called "etchings of Innocence" or "Phantasmagoria" or "The Simple Way" . . .'

Over the next months there were plenty of opportunities to sell his work: etchings and drawings at the Society of Twelve into which he was planning to elect Lamb; drawings and paintings at the NEAC, which had opened that winter with the 'paltriest of shows'. He was arranging a one-man summer show at the Chenil Gallery, and hoped to send in something big to the celebrated 'Exhibition of Fair Women' to be held by the International Society of Sculptors, Painters and 'Gravers in February and March 1909 at the New Gallery. It was the field work for this last affair that gave him most trouble. He had been presented with a huge canvas by William Nicholson: the problem was how to fill it. 'I have a scheme for a picture of fair women [the virgins of Damascus suing Tamburlaine for money] in which Lobelia ought to figure,' he apprised Lamb (24 December 1907). But Lobelia, alias Euphemia, had temporarily vanished and he had to look elsewhere. 'I just passed Bertha in the street (the girl in black tights),' he wrote hopefully to Dorelia. But Dorelia, unlike Ida, was determined to be firm with him. 'That barmaid has disappeared from my ken,' he reassured her. Next he unearthed 'La Seraphita', his still unfin-ished (as he now thought of it) portrait of Alick Schepeler, named after Balzac's ambiguous novel. 'Having changed the background it now looks rather remarkable,' he wrote to Lamb (10 January 1908), ' – her face embodies all that is corrupt, but the thing has a monumental character and the pose is perfect I think.' The picture showed Alick in a tight black dress, standing on a mountain top with strange ice-floes growing at her feet. It needed only a few more sittings. 'Seraphita still stands upon her crest and smiles her smile of specious profundity to a nervous and half-credulous world,' Augustus assured Alick. 'I hope you will come and see me here . . . when I will show you some things.' But again Dorelia, who particularly disliked Alick, put her foot down, and again Augustus yielded: 'I have written to the Schepeler and said goodbye so now you cheer up and get well, there's an angel.' Finally it was a superb picture of Dorelia herself, 'The Smiling Woman', which he submitted to the Exhibition of Fair Women.[32]

Though he himself was doing good work, the English art world depressed him. Of many fellow artists, with names like Bone and Dodd, he held no high opinion. In his letters over this period he seems to have been most excited by some drawings of Alfred Stevens, and some 'reproductions of wonderful pictures by Gauguin'. Of his contemporaries, Gwen was still the best. He had persuaded her to exhibit two pictures, both oil on canvas, at the NEAC show in the spring of 1908: her first portrait of Chloë Boughton-Leigh, and 'La Chambre sur la Cour' with herself seated, sewing at a window opposite her cat at the rue St-Placide. 'Gwen's pictures are simply staggering,' he told Dorelia. 'I have put up the prices to £50 [equivalent to £2,400 in 1996]. They will surely sell.'

As for his own work, 'I seem to make millions as usual,' he apologized to Lamb (10 January 1908) to whom, out of the blue, he sent a present of five pounds. But although no one exhibited more than he, no one in certain moods disliked it more. 'Would that I could leave exhibiting alone for years and years,' he confided to Lady Ottoline Morrell (20 September 1908). 'Perhaps some day I may be able to buy back the rubbish I have sold and have a grand auto-da-fé.'

The English art scene was dim, but there were some bright stars. 'It is surprising to find men in England apparently alive to the tendency of modern art to symbolism,' he wrote (17 January 1908) to Lamb, who had recently been telling him about the work of Van Gogh.

'I met [Roger] Fry the other night and he is quite a lively person – on the other hand "Impressionism" is still lectured on as the new gospel by certain persons of importance. I feel utterly incompetent to cope with problems outside art – without my wife, whom I want. Terrible glooms and ennuis visit me in the evenings when I can think of no one I want to see and am yet tormented in solitude. Sometimes I have tried seeing how much I can drink in one night but it's a dismal experiment. At any rate I have nearly done a large painting which I think is lovely – a nude virgin by a lake. I am thinking of giving up models altogether.'

He suffered very energetically from the great malaise of the times, Edwardian neurasthenia, treating it with complex diagnoses, simple pre-scriptions. 'I am myself a prey to chronic pulmonary bronchial and stomach catarrh but occasional spells of country air keep me going.' His symptoms were tremendous, and he became the very battleground for contests between his valiant phagocytes and every marauding macrophage. 'My macrophags are having a fight for it,' he reported back from the front line of this war. But the real culprit was that malign monster, London. 'The London people are sickening,' he informed Ottoline Mor-rell (20 September 1908). He had taken up riding, and this stirred his blood about a bit. 'You must come and ride over the downs with me,' he invited Lamb (14 December 1907). But Lamb always fell off his horse and Augustus got so hot riding, and afterwards so cold – it could not be good for his 'corpuscles'.

After the banishment of Alick Schepeler he felt more hemmed in than ever. He could not help thinking of the clairvoyant Ida sometimes. 'It is terrible,' he told Michel Salaman. 'I can't realise she is gone so very far away.' The only way to make sense of her death was to paint as she would have wished him to paint. But so much seemed impractical without her. He was seeing Dorelia only intermittently: it was an impossible situation. So he turned to Ida's Liverpool friend the Rani: 'La plus chère de toutes les dames!!' he greeted her in his wildest handwriting. 'Let me have a word, please – I live here [8 Fitzroy Street] now. They tell me you are coming to London for the Slade dance – if that's true – mightn't I see you – yourself. I have heard with incredible joy how much better you are for Canary carryings-on. Let me then assure myself – formally – visually – tangibly of your well-being . . . After the ball come and rest under my lofty roof – there's a little angel.'

Like a Colossus chained, he seemed incapable of independent action except under the impulse of terrific necessities; while by others, for a time, he could be led as simply as a child. Only at present he had no one to lead him, no one opposite whom to play a new Augustus. Self-escape, by one means or another, was essential. 'For the moment dreadful glooms blot out the glittering vistas of life – even debauch would afford me no illusion,' he confessed to Lamb (14 December 1907), '. . . nor bring back a sense of triumphant reality. In a word I am in a sorry state. Perhaps the fog will lift before to-morrow . . .'

He was about to meet a woman altogether different from any he had known before who, opening up the panoramic comedy of his life to new ironies, would dispel this fog. And for special reasons, Dorelia could not object.

5

ETHICS AND RAINBOWS

'You are able to do so much for me in spirit. And I, what can I do for you?'

Augustus John to Ottoline Morrell

Lady Ottoline Morrell had already heard about Augustus John before she met him. The artist Jimmy Pryde had described him in his black billycock hat as looking like 'Christ come to Chicago', and living a 'here to-day and gone-to-borrow sort of life'.[33] She had seen some of his paintings at Charles Conder's Chelsea studio in 1906 and been startled by the expanses of bare flesh. But Conder said John was a great artist, a great man, a man who would dare anything. She listened and longed to meet him. For she too dreamed of doing daring acts in some great cause. 'Conventionality is deadness,' she counselled herself in her diary. 'Your life must break bounds set by the world.'[34]

She met him not long afterwards with Conder. Tall and intensely silent, he had an air that was somehow *méfiant*. Gold earrings he wore, and a suspiciously dark sweater. His hair was shaped like that of some figure in a Renaissance picture, and he watched everyone with a curious intentness.

It was the eyes that first mesmerized her – his eyes, then his voice, then his hands.

'They were remarkably beautifully-shaped eyes,' she recalled,

'and were of that mysterious pale grey-green colour, expanding like a sea-anemone, and more liquid, more aesthetically and poetically perceptive, than any of the darker and more definite shades. His voice, when he did speak, was not very unlike Conder's, only rather deeper and more melodious, but like Conder's hesitating – and he also had the same trick of pushing his hair back with one of his hands – hands that were more beautiful almost than any man's hands I have ever seen.'[35]

Lady Ottoline was every inch as strange a figure as Augustus. When they met again early in 1908 at a smart dinner party in Lowndes Place, he felt self-conscious in his uncomfortable dinner jacket, shy and rather aggressive, until he caught sight of Ottoline: then he forgot himself. Tall, with deep mahogany red hair, a prognathous jaw, swan's neck and bold baronial nose, she had the features to command his self-forgetfulness. She was, he later calculated, 'a yard or two too long', but he liked people who were 'over the top'.[36] In a high-voltage oil portrait, painted nearly a dozen years later, he depicts her as some splendid galleon in full sail, triumphantly breasting the high seas. Her head, under its flamboyant topsail of a hat, is held at a proud angle and she wears, like rigging, several strings of pearls (painted with the aid of tooth powder) above a bottle-green velvet dress. Her eyes are rolled sideways in their sockets like those of a runaway horse and her mouth bared soundlessly. This portrait, though not unfriendly, produced a furore, and people asked themselves how Lady Ottoline could have allowed the artist to paint such a fantastic likeness of her. 'I hope it will give you pleasure, that you won't think it ill-natured as some foolish people did,' he wrote. *Truth* had called it 'witch-like', *Everyman* 'snake-like and snarling', *The Star* a 'grotesque travesty of aristocratic, almost imbecile hauteur', and the *Daily News* concluded: 'she is not flattered'.[37] Eventually Augustus was to grow rather nervous over her reaction to this press comment. 'I would like you to have that portrait but I don't think it's one you would like to hand down to posterity as a *complete* representation of you,' he told her (10 February 1922). He need not have worried.[38] She brushed aside the paper storm, went on to buy another portrait and hung it for all to see over the mantelpiece in her drawing-room. 'Whatever she may have lacked it wasn't courage,' Augustus acknowledged in *Chiaroscuro*; 'in spite of a dull and conventional upbringing, this fine woman was always prepared to do battle for Culture, Freedom and the People.'

Lady Ottoline was to stimulate Augustus as she did many novelists and painters: Aldous Huxley and D. H. Lawrence; Simon Bussy and Duncan Grant. To stimulate the imaginations of such men was her talent – almost her genius. She had crossed over from her aristocratic homeland (she was the daughter of a duke) to this country of art and letters, and she offered those artists and authors whom she admired excursions to her native country. 'We were all swept in to that extraordinary whirlpool where such odd sticks and straws were brought momentarily together,' wrote Virginia Woolf. 'There was Augustus John very sinister [?] in a black stock and a velvet coat; Winston Churchill very rubicund all gold lace and medals on his way to Buckingham Palace . . . There was Lord Henry Bentinck at one end of a sofa & perhaps Nina [Euphemia] Lamb at the other . . . There was Gilbert Cannan who was said to be in love with Ottoline. There was Bertie Russell, whom she was said to be in love with. Above all there was Ottoline herself.'[39]

At her house in Bedford Square – a symphony of pale grey walls and yellow taffeta curtains – Augustus first made contact with the smart world, for which, in years to come, he would develop such an intermittent taste. It was like a rich food that melted in the imagination but, in larger quantities, sickened the stomach. Yet in 1908 this drawing-room world was appealing, offering him an attractive theatre where he could assume a different role. He needed to move from one self to another, to play many parts like a travelling mummer. He also needed to come under the influence of someone he could admire.

Ottoline provided just such a potent theatrical influence. Sitting next to each other at dinner in Lowndes Square they talked of troubadours and Romanies, of Balzac and Dostoevsky, French Primitive painters and Russian anarchists; and then, abruptly, Augustus demanded: 'Will you sit to me? Come and see me tomorrow in my studio.' This signalled the beginning of a friendship, important to each of them, that was to last until Ottoline's death in 1937. The very next morning she went round to Fitzroy Street chaperoned by the Member of Parliament for South Oxfordshire, her husband Philip Morrell. 'We knock, and John himself appeared – in his usual clothes; a greyish suit, the coat long and full in the skirts, and with a bright green velvet collar, a large silk handkerchief round his neck. He waved us in.'[40] After inspecting his pictures and making arrangements for sittings, they were introduced to Clive and Vanessa Bell. 'Vanessa had the beauty of an early Watts portrait, ' Ottoline recorded, 'melancholy and dreamy. They stood in front of the picture of the lake ['The Childhood of Pyramus'], Clive Bell gesticulating in an excited way, showering speechless admiration, Vanessa, head bent, approving.'[41]

Augustus fulfilled Ottoline's pictorial notion of genius, and she was soon deeply enamoured. The impression she gives of his appearance speaks eloquently of her excitement. 'His dark auburn hair was long and cut across the front like a fringe, and with a square beard, his curious pale face and sea-anemone eyes, he might have been a Macedonian king or a Renaissance poet. He had a power of drawing out all one's sympathy.'[42]

Over these first months he did many pen-and-wash watercolour drawings of her; and she grew more infatuated by him. She did not really see herself as the sibyl Augustus saw, but his sketches were so ravishing she could not resist them. Nor could she resist going again and again to his studio though, preferring to be either upright or recumbent, she was 'not much good at sitting', Augustus noted. Each visit to Fitzroy Street sent her into a turmoil of emotions. With every step along the short walk from Bedford Square what tension there was! Before advancing, she would bombard him with a heavy artillery of gifts – fine editions of Wordsworth and Goethe, Browning and Plato, even Euripides, the works of Synge and eventually of Strachey. Augustus fell back. She was, he told her, 'the most generous woman in the world'. Perhaps too generous. 'You keep giving me things,' he remonstrated (8 June 1908). But she could not stop, and the first trickle of presents became a downpour. There was about their relationship a curious reversal of roles: it is Ottoline who plays the masculine part, bold and despairing, almost aggressive at times. Augustus is shy, rather coyly flattered by all these attentions, sometimes embarrassed, usually cautious. She invites him to concerts of love music, and to tragic melodramas. She sends him a little watch which keeps breaking – a kind of stop-watch; she sends him rings for his fingers and assorted jewellery including a magnificent opal. By every post the presents pour in – lilies (which Romilly ate) for his studio, and lotions for his hair; variously coloured scarves and cloaks for his hypochondria; a green shawl, a rug, and a capacious wool quilt for his bed which, he claims, will keep his whole family warm. If Augustus created the John-girl with her characteristic tight bodice, long-waisted full skirt and broad-brimmed peasant hat, Ottoline must have contributed generously to Augustus's own appearance. Her most triumphant adornment was a large replica of Thomas Carlyle's hat which 'is stupendous', he proclaimed (24 May 1909). 'It reduces even the rudest street gamin to speechlessness. But it is not a hat for every day of the week.'

Nor was their romance an everyday affair. His rapid mobility and hibernating illnesses made him an elusive lover. Yet this elusiveness only scalded her imagination the more. She was haunted by thoughts of him: his poverty, his vagabond freedom, the complex simplicity of his life, the poetry in his paintings; those mesmerizing eyes and long fine sensitive hands; his deep resonant voice echoing in her mind. At parties she would introduce his name into the conversation for the pleasure of hearing people talking about him. But so often what they said distressed her. Most conventional Englishwomen looked on her as affected or even amoral simply for knowing such a raffish creature. Even other artists and writers failed to hit the right note – Henry James, for example, who produced an off-key *mot*: 'John paints human beings as if they were animals, and dogs as if they were human beings'; or Lytton Strachey, who likened him to Byron. Ottoline could accept that some people thought Augustus mad – perhaps he was divinely mad. But was he also 'bad, and dangerous to know'? It was natural that Henry James should think so, for Henry James was already out of date, and Ottoline welcomed the new moral climate. 'The age of Augustus John was dawning,'[43] Virginia Woolf wrote of this time. But Virginia also thought that 'the wonderful Ottoline Morrell', with her open-eyed, open-armed worship of the arts, was 'very simple and innocent'. And so, in his complex and wicked fashion, was Augustus.

Despite her intoxication, there is shrewdness in Ottoline's observations. Her heart might beat for the legendary Augustus, but her intelligence comprehended the man. 'Engagements were intolerable to him. When I mixed in an ordinary London life, the figure of this man, so unques-tionably remarkable, living a life so completely different from anything I saw around me, haunted and disturbed me'.[44]

Mysteriousness, which he so highly prized in women, she had dis-covered in him. It was like a grain of love-powder that itched and irritated, that stimulated and would not leave her in peace. Above all, it was his melancholia that affected her, the silence that alternated with his flashing high spirits, the sudden boldness that interrupted his courtly manner with women.

Perhaps the most astonishing aspect of their relationship was that they hardly ever quarrelled. His moodiness and her possessiveness seemed made for difficulties, but she could not get past his melancholy and her possessiveness had little to feed on. Often he would call her 'an angel' – yet with the knowledge he could not travel with an angel very far. They remained on friendly but still quite formal terms until 30 May 1908. That day Ottoline sailed across to his studio and told him frankly of her love. He was unlike anyone she had met. She felt excited by his 'direct, ruthless, animal gypsy side, loving primitive men and women, and things ugly and cruel'; and she was even more responsive to his 'simple nervous sensitive side – the imaginative, idealist poet'. Without knowing it, he had become the most important person in her life. She felt sure she could 'develop' him, form a 'creative flame' between them, share their 'experi-ences of the soul'. She wanted to be his inspiration – and she wanted something else. Talking to him she began to lose the burden of her loneliness. She saw that he was lonely too – otherwise he could not listen to her so sympathetically. She felt she could ease his loneliness. She wanted to be his lover. Later that night, after she had left, Augustus wrote to her:

'When you were in my studio to-day I wished I could cry – I should have felt more intelligent – perhaps – with the delicatest and noblest woman loving me so infinitely beyond my deserts. Do you know what a horror I have of hurting a hair of your head and bringing a shadow into your thoughts . . . and you are trying to assure me you are just like others are! Is it not something to realise that change and development is possible still – that one is not yet altogether finished and one is still young! still adolescent! still living . . .'

Four pages he wrote that night, and he ended with a sentiment that might have drawn a rueful smile from Ida: 'Since my wife's death there have been few opportunities of excitement or intoxication that I have let pass . . .' Nevertheless, he concludes: 'We *can't* go on thus, darling that you are . . . Good-night, angel.'

Yet the affair did go on. Like the little watch she gave him, it was always stopping: then starting again. So far as was possible, Augustus acted honourably. He discouraged her quite gently, and from reasonable motives. 'You must know that I do care for you,' he told her (17 June 1908), '. . . and how I hate to pain you . . . but I see the inevitable . . . Forgive me Ottoline.' It is possible, of course, that, though she was an eyeful, he was not sexually very attracted to her, but some of his letters suggest an attraction. It is also possible that, seeing her as a patron for his work and as someone who would introduce him to prospective purchasers, he was at pains to avoid a situation that, by promising too much, might alienate her. But again his correspondence does not corroborate this. It is true he did benefit a little through Ottoline's friendship,[45] but those letters in which he writes of pictures invariably petition help for his friends, particularly Epstein and Lamb.[46]

For Augustus love affairs were explorations within himself of new possibilities, symbolized by his request to each woman to rechristen him. Ottoline called him Elffin. When he no longer signed himself Elffin, their affair (though not their friendship) was at an end. Each love affair was an opportunity to get away from the dull old stamping grounds and make new discoveries. But when the new continent had been thoroughly explored, the new discoveries mapped and assimilated into the central empire of the self, there was no more renewal: and interest died. Once the passion had gone, the dead-end of a relationship would depress him dreadfully. It is this he sees as the inevitable outcome of his affair with Ottoline – unless, that is, like some of his best pictures, they could end it while it was yet unfinished.

He warns her clearly that prolonged contact between them can only lead to disenchantment. He needs her – as a model. 'I am aware of my brutalities – and all my agonies and joys, and will continue as God made me,' he writes (28 July 1908), '. . . and will do yet the work that no one else can do *quand même.*' He blames his character for their difficulties. 'I should be called Legion and you know only one or two of me yet.' Some of these selves were not attractive – and he had no control over their comings and goings. 'I felt I was *fated* to cause you in the long run more pain than happiness – and that I could not acquiesce in,' he writes in another letter (21 December 1908). 'I dislike sailing under colours none of my hoisting . . .

'With every wish to be honest I suppose I cannot escape those notorious disabilities which I must share with all true Welshmen . . .'

Truth gradually gives way before the romantic assumptions held by each of them on behalf of the other. 'You are the most generous soul in the world and I the mouldiest,' he asserts (June 1908). But Ottoline maintains that it is *she* who is worthless – worthless without him. He is a genius: what do her petty pains and cares matter beside his needs? She will come to him tomorrow. Her letter awaits him when he gets back very late to Fitzroy Street, and at four in the morning (4 June 1908), in some panic, he replies: 'Ottoline, Don't come to-morrow. I am not able – yes you are too great for me, vulgarly tragical or unhappy.' But Ottoline only wants to serve him. She feels humbled before his goodness, his concern and tenderness for her. If only she had *more* to offer him. The postman hurries back and forth with their bits of paper, delivering questions, answers, counter-questions, often whole conversations on a single day. Even so, in their haste, they cannot always wait for him but must dash out to convey some vital postscript by hand. 'It is you who crush me with your goodness – no, exalt me!' Augustus contradicts her (3.45 p.m. 4 June 1908). 'Never will I cease to love and honour you, dear Ottoline. It is you have genius . . . Elffin.'

Truth gives way: but it never disappears beneath the haze of protective romance, for other people are involved. One of these is Ottoline's husband, Philip Morrell. Augustus's attitude to him had commenced jocular: 'Keep Philip happy,' he counsels her (9 June 1908), 'and make him blow up the houses of Parliament.' But Ottoline cannot conceal her feelings and soon the situation grows awkward. 'I think it is evident that your husband don't like me,' Augustus protests (8 January 1909). The possibility of a scandal that, since it involved a Member of Parliament, would hit the headlines alarms him to the point of pomposity. 'I was not really surprised that Morrell should have been out of humour,' he informs Ottoline (18 December 1908). 'I felt I was cutting rather an offensive figure in your house. I should be very sorry to disturb so admirable a personage as your husband. I have nothing but respect for him and would never question his right to object to me . . .'

The other person involved was Dorelia, whom Augustus was anxious to avoid offending. Whenever he sees Dorelia, he reassures Ottoline: 'Do *not* harbour the thought that I am going to forget you'; or 'I hope you will never suspect me of indifference'. But there is never any doubt, particularly after her return from Paris to London, that the incorruptible Dorelia comes first – about this he is specific: 'I love no one living more than Dorelia, and in loving her I am loyal to my wife [Ida] and not else,' he explains to Ottoline – then adds: 'You are certainly wonderful – Ottoline . . . There *will always* be that infinitely precious cord between us – so fine, so fragile that to strain it would break it . . . Bless you, Ottoline. Elffin.'

Although Dorelia was very strict at this time, and very suspicious, there were several reasons why she did not object to Ottoline. Their relationship was partly a business one; and besides, Lady Ottoline Morrell was utterly unlike the barmaids, actresses and models Dorelia had so far come up against. Then, until March 1909, she had not met Ottoline.

They met for the first time in Augustus's studio one day while Ottoline was sitting for her portrait. Dorelia seemed to take little notice of Ottoline; but Ottoline studied Dorelia keenly. 'She had the dignity and repose of a peasant from a foreign land,' Ottoline noted in her diary, '. . . nonchalance and domination towards the children, a slightly mocking attitude to John, and shyness, *méfiance*, towards me, which melted by degrees. Between my sittings we sat round the large table for tea, the children eating slices of bread and jam, John looking a magnificent patriarch of a Nomad tribe, watching but talking very little. I saw that in every movement Dorelia made there was such grace and rhythm that she was indeed a stimulating model for any painter.'[47]

From this day Ottoline set out to make a friend of Dorelia. It was uphill work. The two women were so different – Ottoline sophisticated and histrionic; Dorelia simple and laconic. To complement Augustus's Carlyle, Ottoline bought Dorelia a large straw hat. She put it on without a word, but with her special smile, and looked beautiful. Yet despite all Ottoline's overtures of friendship, Dorelia remained unforthcoming, and when Ottoline invited her with Augustus to a dinner party with the stars of Bloomsbury, Virginia Stephen, Roger Fry, Clive and Vanessa Bell, she received a disconcerting refusal:

'Dear Lady Ottoline. Thank you very much for your invitation but I cannot come as I think it rather ridiculous to be introduced to people as Mrs John. I do not know the Bells.

John asks me to say that he will be pleased to come. I'm afraid you'll think I'm rather ungracious.'

While Dorelia was still in Paris, Augustus and Ottoline had seen each other several times a week. But even then Ottoline had come to realize that 'what I can give him is not what he wants. He calls for something strong, reckless and rampant, which will carry him off his feet, and he knows too well that it is not mine to give.'[48] What he gave her was a tantalizing glimpse of another world. 'He would appear in my imagination as if he passed through the room, suddenly making the conventional scene appear absurd.'[49] He gave her this glimpse, but he did not take her into his unconventional world – or at least not for long. And Ottoline, who seemed ready to risk everything, wanted more.

According to one of Ottoline's biographers, Sandra Jobson Darroch, their affair 'reached its peak around July 1908';[50] according to another, Miranda Seymour, 'the relationship appears to have reached a climax in December 1908.'[51] Both biographers agree that it was on the wane after Dorelia had returned to London and met Ottoline.

'I have always been so excessively anxious to feel myself quite alive that I have plunged with needless precipitation into the most obviously fast flowing channels where there are rocks & bubbles & foam & whirlpools,' Augustus had written to Ottoline in the summer of 1908; '. . . this plan has saved me from deadly morbidity at any rate if it has not improved my complexion.'[52]

There is no telling where this plan might have led Augustus and Ottoline had not Dorelia brought them to land with what may have been a shrewd stratagem or an instinctive move, merging the troublesome subplots of their lives.

In September 1909, the two women were shopping in London – Dorelia loved pretty shoes, Ottoline noticed – and stopping their taxi at 8 Fitzroy Street, Dorelia went in for a couple of minutes, leaving Ottoline in the taxi. Ottoline knew the Fitzroy Street studio intimately. It was here that Augustus had begun painting her; here that she had declared her love to him. But Augustus had recently handed over the place to Henry Lamb on his return from Paris, and it was Henry who suddenly appeared at the window of her taxi and invited her in.

Arrayed in tobacco-coloured frock coat and breeches, Lamb had flowered into an astonishing spectacle since parting from Euphemia. Ottoline could not take her eyes off his slim visionary figure, his almost translucent face and hair like pale flames. She took him and Dorelia and a girl who was in the studio, Lamb's mistress Helen Maitland, who was a friend of Dorelia's, back to her home in Bedford Square for tea.

Soon Ottoline and Henry were in friendly correspondence. Fortunately Henry found it easier to decipher her letters than Augustus had done, and could be more precise in his answers. 'You say my friends can be yours, if I will,' he replied to her, 'yes, but are you ready to make enemies of my enemies?'[53] By this time Augustus was becoming one of those enemies as Henry struggled to escape the straitjacket of imitation. 'John and his set have done much to ruin and deface him and make him disbelieve in good,'[54] Ottoline decided. Henry had all Augustus's moodiness, and she was filled with a similar desire to 'develop' him into a happier person. 'If God will work in me I may be able to help him.'

Early in 1910, Henry was to give up the Fitzroy Street studio. 'Apparently vagabondage is my destiny,'[55] he proclaimed to Ottoline. But his destiny still seemed to lie in Augustus's footsteps. By the spring he was established among the rich coloured rugs and exotic flowers, the silks and stoves, of a coach house rigged up by Ottoline as a studio next to her country house at Peppard. While Philip Morrell went electioneering, Henry sketched Ottoline naked in the beechwoods, and was enveloped in her erotic maternal embrace. It was the start of a complex love affair full of the rocks and whirlpools Augustus had warned her against. That spring and summer Henry replaced Augustus as the most important person in Ottoline's emotional life. 'I burn to embrace you & cover all of your body with mine,' Henry wrote to her. '. . . I kiss your face & your body all over but your face – where your beautiful spirit is most expressed – I return to & kiss all over again.'[56]

But even at the height of their passion, Ottoline still knew that 'all his heart is given to Dorelia'.[57]

Despite this, and the disappearance of 'Elffin' from her life, Ottoline remained a useful friend to Augustus and Dorelia. Not the least of her uses – and the one that first melted Dorelia – was to the children. And with these they needed all the help available.

6

INLAWS AND OUTLAWS

'Though I admire children, I wouldn't care to take charge of a
nursery.'

Augustus John to John Davenport

Like a pair of skilled jugglers, Augustus and Dorelia had kept revolving
in the air every one of the schemes they had introduced into their act at
Equihen. To be or not to be married; to live together, or apart, or both –
and where or anywhere: the range of alternatives spun before their faces
ever more fantastically.

For much of the winter of 1907–8 Dorelia had stayed on in France.
There were many matters to occupy her: sorting out 'clothes, curtains,
cushions etc.' from the studios – 'and then there is the accordion and
various musical instruments', including the gypsy guitar Ida had never
really learnt to play. Dorelia gave up her apartment and, with Pyramus
and Romilly, moved through a series of hotels. She was seeing a good deal
of Lamb and something of Gwen, spending much time 'making clothes
for the kids' of the most anti-Wigmorian cut. She ordered Augustus to
send her supplies of wool, money and tobacco; and she waited.

Augustus had begun to 'look for a house about London', he told her.
He relied for success on a coincidence between what he happened to find
and what his dreams of the perfect life happened to be. While exploring
Hampstead Heath he dreamed fervently of Toulouse. Wyndham Lewis
was thinking of going there, and anything Lewis could do . . . But then a
brilliant notion seized him. Spain! A young friend, the celebrated practical
joker Horace de Vere Cole who, in the guise of the Sultan of Zanzibar,
had ceremonially inspected Cambridge, now (with a perfectly straight
face) recommended a castle in Spain. 'I met the Sultan of Zanzibar in
Bond Street,' Augustus reported to Dorelia. 'He said he was going to
Spain with Tyler.' Royall Tyler,[58] he added, was 'my latest friend', a
Bostonian and a profound student of Spanish matters. 'He is going to go
mad one day,' Augustus predicted, ' – I saw it in his hand and he knows
it.' The more he thought of Spain, the less attractive Hampstead or even
Wantage (which he also scrutinized) appeared.

By April 1908 he had set off in pursuit of some Spanish gypsies,
picking up Dorelia in Paris on the way. From the Hôtel du Mont Blanc
in the boulevard Edgar-Quinet, where Gwen and Dorelia had stayed when
they first came to Paris, he wrote to Ottoline (28 April 1908): 'Spain is

cruel – but I have blood-thirsty moments myself . . . Have you ever found it necessary to strangle anybody – in imagination? There is indescribable satisfaction in it. At other times I feel more like bringing people to life. My Variability is rather disconcerting and hardly makes life easier. I must learn discipline and consistency.'

Spain, which had seemed for a few moments a likely winner among his many schemes, now began to fall back. In fact he got no nearer the Spanish border on this occasion than Paris itself, and it took him almost another fifteen years to complete the journey. His indecision was assisted by Dorelia who was preparing to 'wander about' France with a few of the children. 'It would I think be out of the question to allow her to take Edwin for the reason that her own two boys are quite enough to keep her busy,' Augustus appealed to Mrs Nettleship, 'although she could cheerfully take charge of the whole lot . . . I know no princess with maternal instincts unsatisfied, unfortunately, who would open her gates to my poor boys. Perhaps I may meet one . . .'

Some final decision was becoming urgent. 'Travel as we may,' Augustus wrote to Dorelia, 'we want a pied-à-terre *somewhere*.' In the interval there was nothing for him to do but go back to Fitzroy Street. 'I haven't taken the house yet – it seems to me sometimes quite unpractical without Ida,' he wrote to Mrs Nettleship.

So far as the children were concerned, Augustus was considering farms. He bundled them along to stay with various friends, including Michel Salaman, now a country gentleman, and Ottoline at Peppard, Edna Clarke Hall at Upminster and Charles McEvoy,[59] who lived 'in a pigstye' at Westcot in Berkshire. But he went there mainly for the sake of the 'grand' Berkshire backgrounds which lent themselves to 'noble decoration', he informed Lamb. 'It is unfortunate that the peasants have taken to motor caps and bicycle shirts.' Then, on his way back with the children, he fell in with a man who told 'me about the country near Naples [where] he used to live', Augustus wrote to Dorelia. 'I asked him how much one could live [on] there with a family – he said £250. I have ordered a passport. It will be ready the day after to-morrow . . .'

An actual decision could only be wrung out of Augustus by some crisis, and it was Dorelia who now presented him with one, as he began to suspect she might never return from her wanderings.

'I wish you were here – if you want to be absolutely independent I don't want to be dependent,' he wrote to her. '. . . Will you come over? or will I come back? Doing nothing is killing me. I wish you would come south with me. I can't stand the thought of separating – only if you *want* to I can do nothing.'[60]

The danger of losing Dorelia, like another death, concentrated Augus-

tus's mind. 'C'est bien que toi que je désire – mon ange,' he declared,
' – c'est bien que toi.' Whenever Augustus was decisive, Dorelia fell in
step with him. Between their various schemes it was now a photo finish,
which revealed – a dead heat! For they agreed to marry, and yet not to
marry; to marry, so far as the Nettleships were concerned, almost at once;
but not to translate this policy very urgently into legal fact. Augustus
promised 'to raise the wind' in Wigmore Street 'which is quite willing to
blow just now', and added: 'I'm beginning to feel myself – ten times as
efficient as anybody else.'

This policy of 'marriage' was to convince the Nettleships that they
proposed taking away the children and making a home for them. Believing
that her son-in-law's life was falling apart, Mrs Nettleship had recently
swung into the attack, apprising Augustus that 'a woman who kills an
unborn child is not fit to have the care of children.' In a heated exchange
between the two of them Augustus felt able to answer that, in accusing
Dorelia of bringing about a miscarriage, she was condemning Ida, 'who
had tried the same thing'. He himself took the other view – that by
'annihilating a mass of inchoate blubber without identity at the risk of
her life to spare me further burdens', Dorelia had proved 'her unusual
fitness for the bringing up of children'. Was it not Mrs Nettleship herself
who had first 'instructed Ida in the mysteries of child prevention? –
mysteries which she was evidently not equal to mastering, thank God! . . .
I would have killed many an unborn child to keep her [Ida] alive – and
even have felt myself perfectly fit to take charge of children.' Both of
them having lost their tempers, Augustus notified Mrs Nettleship that he
'was taking all the children away and was at last happy at the thought of
resuming our ménage where it left off – with Ida there in spirit and in
the blood of her kids.'[61]

By treating Augustus in the way Uncle Ned had prescribed Mrs
Nettleship had committed a bad error of tactics. Realizing this, she then
sent him a conciliatory letter in which she allowed that to marry Dorelia
was 'obviously the correct thing to do'. But this irritated Augustus further:

'It is by no means from a desire to be "correct" that I am going to marry
Dorelia. It is precisely because she is the only possible mother to Ida's
children now Ida has gone, since I love her, knowing her to be such. And
for no less reason would she consent to marry me, or I her. She is entirely
and absolutely unselfish as Ida was and as their life together proved, with
such proofs as stagger the intelligence. She is besides the only woman
who does not stifle one in domesticity and who is on my own plane of
intelligence (or above it) in a word the one woman with whom I can live,
work and still be a father to all the children. Without her I would have

to say good-bye to the children, for I cannot recognize them or myself in a house and an atmosphere which will ever be strange and antipathetic to me as it was to their mother . . .

If I were not supremely confident that Dorelia and I are able to bring up the children immeasurably better than you or anybody else, I would not hesitate to leave them where they are. But as I distinctly object to the way they are being brought up with you, as I see quite clearly it is *not* a good way, nor their mother's, Dorelia's or my way, I am going to take them away at once . . .'

By now events had gained a momentum of their own, pulling in Dorelia, who 'suddenly turned up here [8 Fitzroy Street] to help with the children'. Together they would roam France with four kids, two of Ida's and Dorelia's two, he explained to Ottoline. 'They are not going to be brought up by Philistines any longer. I tell you I had to fight to come to the point.'

From Mrs Nettleship, however, he received literally more than he bargained for. At the end of June he had written to her outlining his plans: 'I am off to France in a few days and want to take David and Caspar with me – I would *like* to take them all of course – but am not quite ready for that. I think we may go to Brittany for the summer . . . I hate the thought of leaving Robin behind – and Edwin – and Henry!' Events now followed with what he called 'admirable briskness'.[62] Mrs Nettleship replied that she was holding on to the children, and that if Augustus attempted to abduct them she would have him committed to prison. As for Dorelia, she would prefer to see her dead than in charge of Ida's sons. To this, Augustus sent back an ultimatum: *'Take your proceedings at once, but deliver up all my children in your charge by tomorrow morning.'*

Next morning no children arrived at his studio, and Augustus marched round to Wigmore Street. He gave a version of what then happened in a letter to Wyndham Lewis (28 June 1908). Mrs Nettleship tried 'to take refuge in the zoo with my 3 eldest boys and only after a heated chase through the monkey house did I succeed in coming upon the guilty party immediately behind the pelicans' enclosure. Seizing two children as hostages I bore them off in a cab and left them in a remote village for a few days in charge of an elderly but devoted woman. The coup d'Etat was completely successful of course. Dorelia appears on the scene with almost miraculous promptitude and we take off the bunch of 4 to-morrow morning . . .'

Ida's son Henry, who was only fifteen months old, missed this escapade and was exempted from the bargaining. For all of them, the results of that morning's manoeuvres round the zoo were permanent. Though they visited Wigmore Street in their holidays, Ida's four eldest boys, David, Caspar, Robin and Edwin, were to be brought up by Augustus and Dorelia, along with her children, Pyramus and Romilly; while Henry, the odd one out, was brought up by the Nettleships. 'It certainly might have been rather better for all of you boys if Ida could have lived,' her sister Ethel Nettleship wrote many years later to Caspar. '. . . If only Mother [Mrs Nettleship] had been a wise woman instead of being completely haywire through those 7 years. If Father had been alive too – & lots of other ifs . . .

'You know Gus really *tried* with Mother – I mean he was willing to be helped and a wise woman could have done him no end of good – he was so young & I think he longed for it, but his tremendous vitality and passions used to get the better of him.'[63]

7

IN THE ROVING LINE

'I shall always be more or less suspect.'
Augustus John to Dorelia McNeill

'Paris is amazingly beautiful and brilliant . . . Was it not mad of me to abduct my children in this way?' Augustus asked Ottoline (1 July 1908). 'But I was provoked to the point of action.'

After a week in Paris, Augustus led his troupe off to Rouen, and from there they went by boat to Cherbourg, the appearance of which 'pleased me well'.[64] He had money to last them all three months, and confidence enough to take them anywhere. Leaving Dorelia and the six boys in Cherbourg, he set off on a walking reconnaissance. 'If my stars prove favourable I shall, I hope, start some beasts and vehicles and what not,' he explained to Wyndham Lewis.

But his stars glimmered luridly. At Les Pieux he was seized by the police and interrogated on suspicion of loitering with intent, though he had been plainly walking without much intent. Later he was robbed of his money in a restaurant and, without funds, was refused a bed – 'so I stole into the country by bye-ways and slept under a hedge,' he told Lamb (July 1908), ' – got down to a place called La Royel in the early morning, bathed my poor sore feet and . . . was refused milk and coffee'. It was not before he reached Flamanville that his luck began to turn. Here he caught up with 'a modest circus and a number of revellers keeping it up, was recognised by a charming circus man I met at Bayeux 2 years ago . . .

274

There was also a little Gypsy girl black as night who did the fil de fer. An intoxicated man conducted me down to Dielette where I finished him off with a bottle of wine. In the evening the crazy band drove round in a kind of box emitting gusty strains from various base instruments, the aged philosopher still capering and kissing his hand to the girls – a very wonderful company this – a very wonderful meeting.'

Next day he was again stopped by the police, and it became clear that any crime committed in the neighbourhood would be credited to him. For the rest of his journey he 'took tortuous ways to avoid the police', he told Dorelia, sleeping in ditches and fields, under bridges and hedges, often walking through the night. In a revealing letter to Dorelia, written from Diélette (to which, in his efforts to throw off the police, he had secretly doubled back), he confessed:

'My love of my kind had already vanished and I was becoming a rooted pessimist – as for J. F. Millet, he seemed to me a damned blagueur – a bloody romanticist and liar – as he was in fact. But Dielette renews me – it is astonishing – it is even better than my native town where I ought to have stopped . . . The place is lovely – so varied – sandy beaches, rocks, harbours and prehistoric landscape behind . . .

I shall probably be about here all to-morrow, so send me some calculations, I pray you, to guide me a little . . . You have only to lose your temper to gain everything you want with people.'

To Will Rothenstein he had explained: 'I don't want to fix myself long in hired rooms.' Yet his designs to gather beasts and vehicles together and follow a nomad life through Europe had been hit hard by the police hostility, and he reluctantly decided to assemble Dorelia and the boys in seaside apartments.

They moved into the Maison Delort late that July and stayed there until the end of September. 'The boys are exceedingly well,' Augustus reassured Mrs Nettleship, 'so don't be anxious.' They looked, so he boasted to Ottoline (September 1908), 'like healthy vagabonds'. He himself was anxious about Henry. 'I trust he is not over-clothed,' he warned Mrs Nettleship. 'It is wonderful how children can stand cold if they wear few things.'

The sun shone and he worked hard and happily. 'I am working up to colour at last,' he wrote to Ottoline (20 September 1908). 'Do you know Cézanne's work? His colours are more powerful than Titian's and searched for with more intensity.' His own colours he was now restricting to three primary ones represented by ultramarine, crimson lake and cadmium, with green oxide of chromium. It was with these that he painted 'Girl on the Cliff', another exploration of the link between landscape and the human figure.

The model for 'Girl on the Cliff' was Edna Clarke Hall. Three years earlier, in 1905, with 'a happiness that is beyond words', Edna had given birth to a son. But, like Ida, she soon found motherhood a demanding business that left her no time or energy for painting. 'It's a dull life I lead now,' she told one of her sisters. It might have been all right if her husband Willie had loved her. As it was, life 'goes on OK as long as I keep quiet and live without thinking or worrying or drawing or reading or anything else'.[65]

Ida's death had devastated Edna. 'I loved her more deeply than I realized – I realize it now,'[66] she wrote. Ida was the special 'friend of my youth' whose death seemed to symbolize the death of Edna's own youth.

Noticing her sadness, Willie arranged a holiday for them in France that summer of 1908. He had a 'peculiar gift for finding places no one had heard of', and at the end of a tortuous sixteen-mile cart ride through the night from Cherbourg, he found Diélette. Waking the next morning, Edna was charmed to see 'wide stretching sands and beautiful sand dunes, lonely and full of sunshine and blue butterflies and streams that are guarded by masses of flowers, purple ones, and flag leaves.'[67]

She also found that the sands around the sunlit village were teeming with Johns, and suspected that Willie would be angry. But he accepted the facts peacefully enough, and even allowed her to join the reprobates on their bathing and sketching parties.

As Ida's friend, Edna felt ill at ease with Dorelia. 'She never spoke very much to me,' she remembered, '. . . and she never called me Edna.' Nevertheless Edna was pleased to be posing for Gus. She seemed a perfect model for him. Something about her beauty in this summer landscape, to which she had so briefly come from the emotional aridity of her home, stirred him. Later, when he showed her the oil painting of his 'Girl on the Cliff', her face turned to the sky with the eyes closed, it seemed to her 'to have in it the spirit of myself – he has put the figure on a cliff with bright green grass full of wild flowers and the sea is blue but dark and the sky almost gloomy.'[68]

A number of Augustus's preliminary sketches had been done indoors, the only free area being his bedroom. But the children would keep dashing in and out, excited and uncontrollable, and so he was obliged to lock the door. 'He showed me two or three rather nice drawings he had done of me,' she recalled, 'and then he kissed me in the most enchanting way. There was something very lovely about it. But I drew back – because just then I was in rather a disturbed emotional condition – I had so little of what I needed [and] wanted so much that I wouldn't let anyone touch me.'[69] But when Edna drew back after their kiss he suddenly began to cry, explaining that he had kissed her because the poses she was taking for him were so beautiful.

During the next days, he seemed to be struggling to keep his feelings on that 'spiritual plane' he had appealed to when guarding himself against Ottoline's advances. But Ottoline was 'rather awful to examine closely',[70] while Edna's 'disturbed emotional condition' seemed to add to her attractiveness.

A few days later, Edna joined Gus and Dorelia for a walk along the cliff top to the next village where Henry Lamb had arrived. Then the four of them went off to an inn where Gus began drinking and, perhaps provoked by Lamb's company, concentrating all his attention on Edna, his eyes fixed upon her face. Finally, in his deep voice, he began serenading her.

Suddenly Dorelia stretched out her arms in a curious protecting gesture towards Edna, took her hand and hurried her outside. They ran, stumbling along the dark cliff top, back to Diélette, Augustus careering after them, Lamb left by himself. Next day, and during the remainder of the holiday, no one mentioned this episode, and Augustus, smiling and sympathetic, was back at work painting the children and Dorelia.

'Girl on the Cliff' was shown at the New English Art Club exhibition at the end of 1909. 'I am *longing* for it,' Edna wrote. But it was bought for £40 and 'I hadn't got £40.'[71] The buyer was Ottoline, who re-titled the picture 'Nirvana', the state of beatitude where all passions are dissolved.[72]

*

Though he had not liked the idea of taking seaside rooms again ('It would be cheaper and infinitely better to have a few houses about the place to go to'), Augustus profited by his season at Diélette. 'I have got, it seems to me, much further,' he told Ottoline. But the prospect of a London studio and dingy London streets was not alluring. 'I wanted to get to the Pyrenees or further instead of lingering in the chilly north, but I lack the necessary millions. So back again to the horrors of a Cockney winter. Are there no millionaires of spirit?' he asked Will Rothenstein.

He returned to London early in October, and within a month he had found a house 'in Chelsea with a big studio'.[73] This was 153 Church Street, off the King's Road – 'a good house', Dorelia decided.[74] They took a two-and-a-half-year lease and moved in shortly before Christmas. 'There is plenty of room and a piano,' Augustus invited Lamb (23 December 1908). '. . . I hope you will come at once. You'll have a room to yourself.'

It was also a jolly good place for the boys because of the patch of waste ground, littered with bricks and bushes, that ran beside the King's Road and was ideal for games. Round the corner, in Beaufort Street, was Epstein's studio where they would help themselves to clay from the metal tins, roll the pieces into pellets and expertly flick them at one another. They were still sometimes farmed out to friends: to Ottoline (or 'Ottofat' as they called her), and to Edna Clarke Hall, who thought they looked somewhat forlorn. But it was a useful arrangement for Augustus who could paint their guardians whenever he came to fetch or deposit them.

London that winter of 1908 was 'very hostile and the English sillier than usual'.[75] Jobless men roamed the towns in their thousands, and Members of Parliament warned one another that blood would soon be flowing in the streets. 'I hope blood will flow as nothing good can happen without,' Augustus declared.[76] Meanwhile, despite his mood of anarchy, he settled into the shell of his new home as if for protection against storms to come. 'Perhaps the Epsteins may come to dinner to-day,' he wrote to Ottoline (26 December 1908), ' – now that we are bourgeois folk with carpets and front doors and dining-rooms.'

> Wanderers, you have sunrise and the stars;
> And we, beneath our comfortable roofs,
> Lamplight and daily fires upon the hearth,
> And four walls of a prison, and sure food.
> But God has given you freedom, wanderers![77]

A broken collarbone partly accounts for Augustus having ceased wandering and turned bourgeois that winter. But, with the coming of spring, mended and eager, he resolved to abandon his carpets and comfortable roof. For three months, he had chafed within his prison walls, finding some relief in reading Dostoevsky's *Les Possédés*, 'a wonderful book', and submitting himself to be 'overhauled' by a new doctor, 'a celestial emissary in disguise', recommended by Ottoline. 'I am tired of nerves and glooms,' he confided to her (13 January 1909), 'and one could certainly surmount them, unhandicapped physically.' By February he was already feeling 'dangerously healthy', the proper condition in which to take the open road.

During this interval, while dreaming of the freedom which would soon overtake him, he threw off a wonderfully dandified and belligerent portrait of the painter William Nicholson. 'I have started Nicholson,' he wrote to Ottoline on 8 January 1909, ' – as a set off to his rare beauty I am putting in a huge nude girl at his side. This will add to his interest, I feel . . .' Eventually, as one of several cross-references between the two artists, he put in one of his own paintings – a girl, fully clothed, against a mountainous landscape at the lower right-hand corner of the composition, where his signature would have been.

The bold composition, with its low-key palette and associations with the royal pictures of Velázquez, was a style much favoured by Nicholson himself, who seems to stare from the canvas in alarm. There are also ironic references to William Orpen, who specialized in this genre of grand-manner portraiture, and had painted Augustus in a similar pose in 1900 as well as the Nicholson family in 1908. 'William, overcoated, yellow-gloved, the picture of a Georgian buck, glares from the corner of an overdark eye at the beholder,' wrote Marguerite Steen: 'a superb piece of coloratura painting . . . one of the finest of John's portraits, though not quite convincing as a likeness of the sitter. Still, perhaps in those days William did look like a gentleman pugilist, or perhaps this aspect of his personality was called out by their mutual fondness for the ring.' For several years Augustus himself believed this to be his best portrait which, in the words of Andrew Wilton, 'set the standards of his career as portrait painter: ambitious, slightly scandalous yet old masterly, respectful of mind and character rather than social rank, and not too serious'.[78] He had recognized in Nicholson an excellent subject, but unless commissioned he could not afford to paint him. So Nicholson himself provided the canvas and commissioned the painting for a hundred pounds (equivalent to £4,700 in 1996), which he nevertheless forgot to pay and for which Augustus forgot to ask. It was a gentleman's agreement, and when, some years later, the Fitzwilliam Museum at Cambridge bought the portrait for a thousand pounds, the two painters happily pocketed five hundred each.

Even before this portrait was finished, there came over him the absolute necessity to travel. Ever since the birth of Pyramus, the caravan which Augustus was buying from Salaman had lain gently disintegrating on Dartmoor. But recently he had moved it up and anchored it strategically at Wantage, where it was given a lick of fresh paint. A brilliant blue, it stood ready for adventurings. On his first expedition, he took along John Fothergill, architect and innkeeper, as companion. They trundled off on 1 April. 'I called on [Roger] Fry at Guildford and found him in a state of great anxiety about his wife who had just had another attack,'[79] Augustus reported to Ottoline (8 April 1909).

'He sent off his children that day. I was sorry as I wanted to take them on the road a little. Fry came down and we sat in the caravan awhile. Next day I hired a big horse and proceeded on through Dorking and up to a divine Region called Ranmore Common . . . I called at the big house to ask for permission to stop on the common and was treated with scant courtesy by the menials who told me their man was out. So on again through miles of wild country to Effingham where, after several attempts to overcome the suspicion attaching to a traveller with long hair and a van, I got a farmer to let me draw into one of his fields. At this time the horse was done up and my money at its last.'

So he left his van in the field, along with the sleeping horse and the sleeping Fothergill, and caught the milk train up to London. He had covered eighty miles on the road and it had been highly satisfactory. But this was a mere beginning, a mere flexing of muscles. The summer must be passed with all his family away from front doors and dining-rooms; with the wind in the night outside and the stars in the wind; with the sun and the rain on his cheek.

Ever since the market days at Haverfordwest, since his first visits to the circus and his sight, on the wasteland outside Tenby, of the gypsy encampment with its wagons and wild children, its population of hard high-cheekboned men and women with faces dark as earth, he had felt attracted to travellers and show people. Destiny had drawn him closer to them after meeting that 'old maniac' John Sampson when he had begun to pick up their language. Since leaving the art sheds at Liverpool, he had revisited Cabbage Hall on 'affairs of Egypt'. Elsewhere, encounters with such people as W. B. Yeats, with his addiction to tinkers as well as countesses, and Lady Gregory, with her studies of local myth and dialect, had helped to widen his knowledge. But it was not until the summer of 1908 that he had begun to dream of living as one of them. Two happenings that summer had nourished this idea. While in Paris he had met the gypsy guitarist Fabian de Castro in the luxurious apartment of Royall Tyler. The two of them entered into a deal where Augustus taught the guitarist to paint, while de Castro passed on to Augustus some of the songs from his voluminous repertoire. During these reciprocal classes, de Castro told Augustus something of his background. Now forty, he had been born at Linares in the Province of Andalusia. While still very young he was seized with the *Wanderlust*, forsaking his respectable family to take up with *gâjos* and others in the roving line. His conviction that he was of noble descent from the Pharaohs grew fierce and unalterable. He had travelled alone and in strange company, by foot and on the carpet of his imagination, through many lands plying many trades and practising many arts, to which he now intended to add the art of painting. Augustus was enchanted by his stories told with that serious self-mocking gypsy humour which found fun in the most unexpected places. After a day spent in talk, song, paint and laughter, towards evening they would be joined by other dreamers and jokers and exorbitant cronies, 'Dummer' Howard, Tudor Castle, Horace de Vere Cole, and together they would set off to see

La Macarona and El Faico, the flamenco artists. This was Augustus's introduction to the flamenco tradition of music and dancing. The intricate rhythms stirred undercurrents of anguish and regret that astonished him. The harsh outcry of the singers, rising convulsively and merging with the insistent humming of strings into an extraordinary ululation, sounded like the lamentations of beings thrust out of Heaven and debarred from all tenderness and hope. Yet the dancers themselves illustrated, with superb precision, the pride and glory of the human body.

After a week was up, Fabian de Castro left for Toledo where, having painted after Augustus's prescription a huge and unorthodox Crucifixion, he was rewarded with imprisonment for committing an act of blasphemy. Augustus took something of a vicarious pride in his pupil's accomplishment, though imprisonment in Spain, he admitted, like lunching in England, was a thing that might happen to anyone.

By this time Augustus, reaching Cherbourg, had fallen in with a raucous band of coppersmiths from Baku. 'I was thrilled this morning – and my hand still trembles – by the spectacle of a company of Russian Gypsies coming down the street,' he had illegibly informed Will Rothenstein. 'We spoke together in their language – wonderful people with everyone's hand against them – like artists in a world of petits bourgeois.' At once he set about compiling word-lists of their vocabulary, and noting down their songs. This parcel of scholarship he dispatched to Liverpool. 'It was a difficult job getting the songs down,' he reported to Scott Macfie (11 August 1908), ' – everybody shouting them out, with numerous variations – but they showed the greatest satisfaction on my reading them out . . . I don't like extracting words by force from Gypsies – it is too much like dentistry. I prefer to pick them up tout doucement.'

Back at Liverpool, a deep plot had been discovered to expel the gypsies from Europe. This hideous news, reaching Augustus, lodged in his imagination. He followed these children of nature because it seemed to him they had true freedom. 'In no part of the world are they found engaged in the cultivation of the earth, or in the service of a regular master; but in all lands they are jockeys, or thieves or cheats,' wrote George Borrow, who inspired a generation of late Victorians and Edwardians to leave their studies for the sunrise and the stars. These gypsies were the supreme anti-capitalists whose belongings were always burnt at death. Augustus's urge to be closer to them stemmed from his preoccupation with the primitive world from which we all derive. In taking to the road he was not following an isolated whim. He was reacting, as others were beginning to, against the advance of industrialized society, with its inevitable shrinking of personal liberty, its frontiers barbed-wired by a rigmarole of passports and identity cards, by indecipherable rules, reparations, indemnities,

by the paraphernalia of permits and censuses. Living in a gypsy community, mastering their ancient tongues, penetrating behind the false
glamour to join them round their camp fires in the night, Augustus was
searching for a way of holding in equilibrium contradictory impulses in
his temperament. His love of travelling people recalls the passion of
Jacques Callot, but it was also finding a parallel in contemporary literature,
from Arthur Ransome's *Bohemia in London* (1907) to the pastoralism of
the Georgian poets, the chunky anthologies in paperboards produced
by the Poetry Society,[80] and in the recovery of folk songs by Percy
Grainger, who played a number of them to Augustus on his phonograph
('he says that England is richer than the continent in folk music'). No
wonder the chief ornament of the Georgians, Eddie Marsh, lost sleep
wondering whether he could afford a second Augustus John for his
collection; and Rupert Brooke, seeing an Augustus John picture at the
New English Art Club (1909), felt 'quite sick and faint with passion'.[81]
To such poets and impresarios, no less than to art students, Augustus,
'with his long red beard, ear-rings, jersey, check-suit and standing six feet
high, so that a cabman was once too nervous to drive him', as Edward
Thomas reported[82] to Gordon Bottomley, seemed a natural leader. Their
movement, which was to be shattered by the Great War, sought as if by
some spell to freeze the tread of industry across the country. But the best
they could hope to win was a little extra time:

> Time, you old gipsy man,
>   Will you not stay,
>   Put up your caravan
>   Just for one day?[83]

'They're not Gypsies until they start moving.' But already, with his
comings and goings, Augustus had grown 'so damned Gypsy like', in the
words of Scott Macfie, 'that unless one writes at once one runs the risk
of missing you'. On his return to London in the autumn of 1908, harried
by gendarmes, an event occurred which persuaded him that he had
penetrated to the body of the gypsy world.

'This morning I find a parcel which opened – lo! the ear of a man with
a ring in it and hair sprouting around lying in a box of throat pastilles,'
he wrote to Wyndham Lewis, ' – nothing to indicate its provenance but
a scrawl in a mixture of thieves' cant and bad Romany saying how it is
the ear of a man murdered on the highroad and inviting me to take care
of my Kâri=penis, but to beware of the dangers that lurk beneath a
petticoat. So you see even in England, I cannot feel secure and in France

the Police are waiting for me, not to speak of armed civilians of my acquaintance.'

His broken collarbone that winter and removal to Church Street had enabled him to pursue his gypsy studies at a more bookish level. *The Journal of the Gypsy Lore Society*, first born in 1888 and soon issuing songs transcribed by John Sampson 'on the highroad between Knotty Ash and Prescot', had died only three years later. But now, like some sleeping beauty, it was being reawakened by the kiss of scholarship and, what it had lacked before, the oxygen of money. They were, as the Devil is said to have remarked when he glanced down the Ten Commandments, 'a rum lot', these Edwardian gentlemen: a cosmopolitan band of madcaps and idealists led by the portly and pontificating Sampson and assisted by various willing girls indispensable, in Sampson's view, to serious gypsy studies. Folklorists and philologists, Celtic lexicographers, Scottish phoneticians and bibliographers from the United States drew together to investigate the gypsy question. The tentacles of the society stretched out to reach anthropologists in Switzerland and linguists in India, embracing on the way such odd bards as Arthur Symons, expounder of French symbolism to the English, and (still at No. 2 The Pines) Theodore Watts-Dunton, author of the sultry bestseller *Aylwin*, now, in his middle seventies, about to be released from tending the sexually blighted Swinburne and – a final brilliant touch – married to a girl of thirty. Most prominent among them was an intimidating vegetarian 'Old Mother' Winstedt, the finest scientific authority on gypsies' poisons John Myers, and, from Lincolnshire, the Very Reverend George Hall, expert poacher and approver of plural marriages, whose sport was collecting pedigrees. Sampson had hoped that the presence of a parson might give a collar of respectability, so far absent, to the gang's Borrovian escapades – instead of which, his tattered clerical coat, huge bandage over one eye and habit of smoking a short pipe while drinking beer, produced quite the reverse effect.

All this was made possible by the new honorary secretary of the Gypsy Lore Society, Robert Andrew Scott Macfie, in truth the most endearing of men: and rich. Now in the prime of life, tall, dark and modest, of rueful and compassionate charm, he displayed a chivalry counted upon by the others – and not in vain – to bring in more lady members. He possessed the talent for getting on with everyone, the qualities (much exercised by Augustus) of tact and patience. His interests were wide and his abilities various. A skilful musician, expert in typography and proven bibliographical scholar, he was also a fluent linguist and had soon learnt the Romany tongue. He also claimed authorship of an authoritative and absolutely unobtainable work on Golden Syrup and, after the Great

War (during which he served as a regimental quartermaster-sergeant), an inventory of military recipes.

Macfie had been the head of a firm of sugar refiners in Liverpool before being led by Sampson into his gypsy career. Boarding up his large house near the cathedral, he moved to 6 Hope Place, which became the head-quarters of the society. Augustus, on his many trips to Liverpool, would often call on him there and was usually relieved of some frontispiece or article for the journal.[84] Fired by Macfie's enthusiasm, he was transformed into a vigorous recruiting officer. Patrons, dealers, Café Royalists and society hostesses who wished to preserve diplomatic relations with him were obliged, as an earnest of their goodwill, to keep up their gypsy subscriptions. All manner of Quinns and Rothensteins found themselves enrolled, and some, for extraordinary feats, were decorated in the field.*

By April 1909, having put his affairs in order, Augustus was more than ready, in Sampson's words, to exchange 'the flockbed of civilisation for the primitive couch of the earth'. He had made what passed for elaborate preparations, obtaining letters of introduction 'from puissant personages to reassure timid and supercilious landowners, over-awe tyrannous and corrupt policemen and non-plus hostile and ignorant county people in general'.[85] He had done more. To the sky-blue van still stationed at Effingham he added another of canary yellow and a light cart, a team of sturdy omnibus horses, a tent or two, and eventually Arthur, a disastrous groom. They mustered at Effingham – a full complement of six horses, two vans, one cart, six children, Arthur, a stray boy 'for washing up', Dorelia, and her virginal younger sister Edie. 'We are really getting a step nearer my dream of the Nomadic life,' Augustus told Ottoline. 'The tent we have made is a perfect thing and the horses I bought are a very good bargain . . . I would like all the same a few little girls running about. Will you lend me Julian[86] for one?' Their camp was like a mumper's, only, he boasted, more untidy. Undeterred by the scorn of the local gypsy, the convoy moved off to Epsom, where Augustus hit the headlines by protest-ing against the exclusion of gypsies from the racecourse on Derby Day. Then, the race lost, he set his black hunter's head towards Harpenden which after many adventures they reached on 9 July. Augustus was exhilar-ated by their progress. 'It's great fun,' he reassured his mother-in-law. 'The boys have never looked better.' And to Ottoline he wrote: 'It's

---

* 'I have recently taken it upon myself (with what share of justification I know not) to confer the title Rai upon a friend of mine – one Percy Wyndham Lewis – whose qualifications – rather historical or anthropological than linguistic viz. – the having coupled and lived in a state of copulation with a wandering Spanish romi in Brittany – seemed to me upon reflection to merit the honourable and distinctive title of our confraternity,' Augustus informed Scott Macfie (6 November 1908). '. . . I may add that my friend appears fully to appreciate the value of his new dignity. He remarks: "Henceforth, my brother, my seed is implicated with that of Egypt".'

splendid . . . I ride sometimes by the side of the procession, but for the last two days I've been drawing the big van with two horses. It's always a question of where to pull in for the night. Respectable people become indignant at the sight of us – and disrespectable ones behave charmingly . . . I'm acquiring still stronger views regarding landlords.'[87]

His next stop was Cambridge, where he secured a commission to paint a portrait of the classical anthropologist Jane Harrison, 'a very charming person tho' a puzzle to paint'.[88] Yet it was a puzzle he solved beautifully. He had been offered this job on the recommendation of D. S. MacColl, who described him as 'the likeliest man to do a really good portrait at present', and who gave him preference over Wilson Steer 'whose tastes lie in the direction of young girls'. With this opinion Jane Harrison appears to have agreed, writing to Ruth Darwin, the promoter of the portrait: 'I personally should take his advice . . . he [Augustus John] seems to me to have a real vision of "the beauty of ugliness" . . . What I mean is that he gets a curious beauty of line: character, I suppose it would ordinarily be called, that comes into all faces however "plain" that belong to people that have lived hard; and that in the nature of things is found in scarcely any young face. Now this interests some people – I don't think it ever did interest Steer. If I were a beautiful young girl I should say Steer . . .'

Augustus's painting, 'the only existing humane portrait of a Lady Don' as David Piper described it,[89] pleased its sitter, in particular because Augustus used Steer's 'Yachts', which Jane Harrison owned, as part of the background. To D. S. MacColl she wrote (15 August 1909) in praise both of the picture and the artist.

'Thank you for finding Mr John. He was delightful. I felt spiritually at home with him from the first moment he came into the room: he was so quiet and real and sympathetic too . . . He was perfect to sit to; he never fussed or posed me, but did me just as I lay on the chair where I have mostly lain for months. I look like a fine distinguished prize-fighter who has had a vision and collapsed under it . . . it seems to me beautiful, but probably as usual I am wrong!'[90]

Augustus and his retinue had encamped in a field by the river at Grantchester, and every day he would drive to Newnham, 'working away in utter oblivion',[91] while Jane Harrison smoked cigarettes and chatted with Gilbert Murray. 'Although a complete dunce,' he recalled, 'I enjoyed their learned conversation while I was painting, for in no way did it conceal the beautiful humanity of both.'[92] Even so, he was not tempted to advance further into Cambridge and, apart from a visit to James

Strachey at King's to spread the word of Dostoevsky, he made little contact with the university. 'The atmosphere of those venerable halls standing in such peaceful and dignified seclusion seemed to me likely to induce a state of languor and reverie,' he wrote in *Chiaroscuro*, 'excluding both the rude shocks and the joyous revelations of the rough world without.'[93]

He was already providing a rude shock to Cambridge life. 'John is encamped with two wives and ten naked children,' Maynard Keynes inaccurately reported from King's College (23 July 1909). 'I saw him in the street to-day – an extrordinary spectacle for these parts . . . He seems to have painted Jane Harrison at a great rate – 7 sittings of $1\frac{1}{2}$ hours each. She is lying on a sofa in a black dress with a green scarf and a grey face on cushions of various colours with a red book on her lap.' Two days later Keynes was writing to Duncan Grant: 'All the talk here is about John . . . Rupert [Brooke] seems to look after him and conveys him and Dorelia and Pyramus and David and the rest of them about the river . . . According to Rupert he spends most of his time in Cambridge public houses, and has had a drunken brawl in the streets smashing in the face of his opponent.'

Brooke excitedly invited them all over for meals at Granchester and took them up the river in punts. Augustus John was, he reminded Noël Olivier, 'the greatest painter', and 'the chief wife' Dorelia 'a very beautiful woman', and the boys 'brown wild bare people dressed, if at all, in lovely yellow, red or brown tattered garments . . . They talked to us of an imaginary world of theirs, where the river was milk, the mud honey, the reeds and trees green sugar, the earth cake, the leaves of the trees (that was odd) ladies' hats . . . To live with five wild children in a caravan would really be a very good life.'[94] Brooke was soon leading special parties from the colleges to the Johns' field to catch a glimpse of Dorelia making a pair of Turkish trousers, or the children gnawing bones for their supper then falling asleep on straw round the camp fire – and other marvels. 'We cause a good deal of astonishment in this well-bred town,' Augustus observed.[95]

The resurrection of the 'two wives' legend seems to have arisen not only because of Edie McNeill, but because of the more improbable presence of Ottoline Morrell who, dressed in her finer muslins, had hesitantly accepted an invitation to join them. 'Come any day,' Augustus had wired. '. . . In case of any mistake our field is at Grantchester . . .' And he sent her a photograph of some wild-looking people.

After three months in London entertaining her mother-in-law, who had recently been converted to Catholicism, it would be refreshing, Ottoline thought, to be with these 'scallywags', as Virginia Woolf called them. She took the train to Cambridge and was met by Augustus with a horse and high gig. 'Directly I climbed up into the cart the horse, which was a huge ungainly half-trained animal, began to back, slipped and fell down,' Ottoline recalled.

'John rapidly descended from our high perch; he stood calmly smoking a cigarette, looking at the great brute kicking and struggling, but made no attempt to help. However, station loafers came to the rescue, and we adjusted the horse and harness. Up we got again, and slowly trotted through Cambridge to a meadow . . .

How damp and cold and cheerless and dull it seemed. John was morose, with a black eye, the result of a fight . . . Dorelia and her sister, absorbed in cooking and washing . . . made no friendly effort to make me feel at home. But after all it would have perhaps been a difficult task to be at home in a melancholy, sodden meadow outside a caravan.'[96]

The boys, it was true, crowded round 'Ottofat' enthusiastically – she was excellent ballast for their kite-flying. But Dorelia, 'very Leonardo's Mona Lisa', Ottoline recalled, 'very passive, almost oriental – *very* inarticulate', left her alone. There was nothing to do but walk up and down in the damp trying to get warm until dinner, which was a crust of bread and some fruit. 'We did treat her badly,' Dorelia remembered. 'We couldn't imagine what to give such a grand lady to eat, so all she got was an apple. Heard after that the poor dear's favourite dish was kippers.' So Ottoline called it a day and hurried back to London 'chilled and damp and appreciative of my own home and Philip'.

Augustus's famous fight had been with Arthur, the groom, who had been flung into a pugnacious attitude by the notion of leaving Cambridge. It fell to Augustus to correct him, and between pub and trap they rained blows on each other, Augustus eventually carrying the day. Once recovered he led his troupe off and gained a piece of waste ground near Norwich, where he suddenly abandoned them for an urgent appointment in Liverpool. 'I hope to camp near the sea near Liverpool,' he had written to Mrs Nettleship, 'and ride up to the Town Hall to paint the Lord Mayor.'[97] But calculating from recent experiences, 'it'll take me 3 weeks to get to you by road,' he told the Rani (July 1909), 'so I fear I must give up the plan and come by train.' So, leaving his women and children with instructions 'to come on steadily' or not at all, he walked into Norwich and caught a train on his way to paint one of the most notorious portraits of his career.

*

It was the custom in Liverpool for members of the city council to raise a private subscription of one hundred guineas and to present the retiring Lord Mayor with a ceremonial portrait. The Mayor in 1908–9 had been Augustus's friend Chaloner Dowdall. Usually the Chairman of the Walker Gallery was invited to choose the artist, but Dowdall had so often collected the money for previous incumbents that when the deputation came to see him he at once asked it to let him handle the matter, 'and you will have the biggest gate the Autumn Exhibition has ever had – and I shall have a picture worth five hundred guineas within five years time.' He then offered the commission to Augustus, who willingly consented: 'I'ld like very much to stay with you,' he wrote to Dowdall's wife, the Rani. '. . . Don't let Silky [Chaloner Dowdall] worry any more. Tell him I'm coming . . .'

Augustus was full of notions for this portrait. He proposed to Dowdall, as they went together to buy the canvas, painting not only the Lord Mayor but his whole retinue of attendants which went with him on state occasions. Dowdall, slightly alarmed, demurred on the grounds that his house, though large, could hardly contain so monumental a masterpiece. Augustus, while nodding his head in agreement, nevertheless bought the biggest canvas available. 'I was an ass not to agree,' Dowdall afterwards claimed.[98]

That afternoon Augustus made a rapid watercolour sketch, about twenty-four inches by eighteen, and next morning when the canvas had arrived he set to work, beginning with the two lines – the wand and the sword – on which the design was based. By lunch it was all drawn in. 'He worked like a hawk on the wing,' Dowdall observed, 'and was white, sweating and exhausted.'[99] The two of them repaired for 'a good lunch' which was served by Smith, the Lord Mayor's footman. Noticing that Smith and Dowdall got along very well, Augustus suggested that the footman should be included in the picture, and to this Dowdall and Smith jovially agreed. 'The whole thing was drawn in on the canvas at a single sitting,' Dowdall recalled, 'and painted with extraordinary rapidity.'

What struck Dowdall as being so remarkably rapid lasted an eternity for Augustus: which was to say a fortnight. Initially it went 'without a hitch'. 'It'll be done in a few days,' he promised Dorelia. 'It's great sport painting jewels and sword hilts etc. My Lord sits every day and all day and I've been working like a steam engine.' The town hall itself made 'a devilish fine studio', and he reckoned that the portrait would be 'a shade better than Miss Harrison's'.[100] His only trouble was the background, 'which I didn't have the foresight to arrange first'. After a week this trouble had advanced to the foreground, mainly because Dowdall would assume 'such an idiotic expression when posing'. This spirit of idiocy seemed to fill the town hall during his second week. 'It was frightful there,' he complained to Ottoline (9 September 1909), 'made all the more impossible by his lordship's inability to stand at ease. No more Lord

Mayors for me. I used to be so glad to get out of the town hall that I roamed about the whole evening not returning till very late. I had but one desire: to submerge myself in crude unceremonious life.' The formality of it all was soon 'taking the sawdust' out of him. Instead of cruising the Chinese opium dens with a notorious character called Captain Kettle, Augustus was expected to spend every evening and night with the Dowdalls, and to voyage back and forth with his subject in an official carriage and pair with two footmen. The Liverpool police had appealed to Dowdall never to let Augustus out of his sight lest his excursions after dark be made a 'subject of comment in the town, and . . . be held to prejudice in some way the dignity of his Office'.[101] After tasting the freedom of the road, Augustus found this confinement intolerable. He bubbled with impatience, and the result was a curious inspiration: the portrayal of Dowdall as a civic Don Quixote attended by his doubtfully obsequious Sancho Panza, Smith.

Towards the end of the portrait, the municipal strain becoming too much for him, Augustus absconded to Wales. His friend Sampson had recently rediscovered the celebrated gypsy storyteller and great-great-grandson of Abraham Wood, King of the Gypsies: one Matthew Wood who, since 1896, had vanished from the face of the earth. To Sampson he was invaluable, being the last of his race to preserve the ancient Welsh Romany dialect in its purity. Like some hedgehog, he had been quietly grubbing along in a village 'at the end of nowhere'[102] and seven miles from Corwen, called Bettws-Gwerfil-Goch. It was vital to get a haul of his lovely words, ablatives and adverbs ending in ' *-od*', sense riddles, folk tales spoken as pure Indian idiom, a veritable mother tongue. Having triumphantly tracked him down, like an 'old grey badger to his lair', Sampson resolved not to lose such a valuable creature again till he had got to know him 'as well as his own boots'. He therefore rented a couple of hideous semi-detached Welsh suburban villas set on the hillside overlooking the village from the spur of Bron Banog, and having knocked them into one, moved in two imposing pantechnicons full of chattels, together with Margaret his wife, a dwarf maid named Nellie, their sheepdog Ashypelt, and three children, Michael, Amyas and Honor in the charge of two young 'secretaries', the fair Kish and the dark Dora. And Augustus.

He arrived one evening 'in the best of spirits', determined to profit by his freedom from Liverpool town hall, and signed the visitors' book with a flamboyant sketch of himself. The waterfalls and streams, the luxurious green woods below, the three shining peaks of Aran to the south, and the distant sight of Snowdon, delighted him. 'Matthew Wood with his fiddle and I with my voice entertained the company till late – and there was great hilarity,' he wrote to John Quinn (September 1909).

'There were two young ladies present, secretaries of the Rai. After going to bed I became possessed of the mad idea of seeking one of them – it seemed to me only just that they* should do something in the way of entertaining *me*. I sallied forth in my socks and entered several rooms before I found one containing a bed in which it seemed to me I discerned the forms of the two girls. I lay down at their sides and caressed them. It was very dark. Suddenly a voice started shrieking like a banshee – it might have been heard all over Wales. I thought then I had stumbled upon Sampson's boys instead of them I sought. I told the voice not to be silly and went away. On the landing appeared the two girls with a candle and terror in their eyes. I scowled at them and returned to bed.'

Next morning at breakfast, the maid Nellie demanded an explanation for his presence in her bed that night. Augustus, who had not seen her before, was horrified to observe that she was four feet tall. He explained his mistake was due to the peculiar pitch of Welsh darkness and the odd character of the house which together had left him entirely dependent on his sense of touch. Nellie, very dignified, remarked that this hardly explained the nature of the caresses he had lavished upon her – and the little girl with whom she slept, Miss Honor. Each revelation seemed to make the business worse, and Augustus could only fall back on the claim that he must have been dreaming. He had begun his adventurings like Tom Jones and ended them like Mr Pickwick. By lunch, the atmosphere in the house was so constrained that he decided to slip away. His exertions to make a joke of the matter by suggesting it might have been worse – supposing it had been Sampson's arms he had blundered into! – were met with silence.

He left without a word, walking down to the village to see about a horse and trap. Here Sampson overtook him to make it clear that he need not return to the house, and upon Augustus assuring him that 'nothing could have been further from my thoughts'[103] and that he was even then on his way, Sampson relented and proposed a drink. 'We passed several hours with drinks and gypsies,' Augustus told the Rani. The inn resounded to the melodious din of richly inflected Romany but soon a discord was introduced by Matthew Wood's half-brother, Howell, a hefty brute who began trying to pick a quarrel with Sampson. Feeling he might owe his friend a good deed, Augustus offered to begin matters by turning

---

* The words 'one of them' have been crossed out, and 'they' more accurately substituted.

Howell out of the pub. 'This I did and shot him into the road. Then ensued a bloody combat.' Within the sunlit square each stripped to the waist and, in the style of the old-fashioned prizefight, began battle. After two long rounds Augustus had him on the ground 'but he was biting my legs. Up came the others, Sampson vociferating blood and death! And the poor Gypsy was led off streaming with gore, howling maledictions in three languages.'

It was well past midnight when Augustus arrived back in Liverpool to find the Dowdalls' house, out of which he had been so eager to escape, impossible to enter. 'I climbed over the fence and tried all the windows at the back. I tried to pull down one of those damn lamps,' he told the Rani. 'Your house is like a fortress. So I went into Sefton Park and lay under a laurel bush till dawn . . . about 6 [I] went and washed my gore and grime in the Central Station.'

Though much revived by experiences that would have half killed another man, Augustus was in no frame of mind to do justice to his model, the Lord Mayor, and despite the head not being quite all there to his satisfaction,[104] he got off that same day back to Norfolk.

The reception given to the portrait when it was first shown that autumn was extreme. The press called it 'detestable', 'crude', 'unhealthy', 'an insult', 'a travesty in paint', and the 'greatest exhibition of bad and inartistic taste we have ever seen'. The art critic of the *Liverpool Daily Post* (18 September 1909) felt able to describe it as 'a work worse painted and worse drawn than any modern picture we can remember', and suggested that it was 'an artistic practical joke' which gave Smith grounds for legal action. Another critic (19 September 1909) detected moral danger in the canvas. It was, he declared,

'an attenuated specimen of what Mr John chooses to call a man, over 20 heads in length, all legs, the pimple of a head being placed on very narrow shoulders and by his side, in a ridiculous attitude, a figure that I fancy I have seen before in a Punch and Judy show. All painted in rank, bad colour and shockingly badly drawn . . . The public have none too great knowledge of art as it is; to publicly exhibit the work is calculated to do immense amount of harm to the public generally and the young art students who go to galleries and museums for guidance and help.'

'You are being pounded and expounded (which is worse) in the *Liverpool Post* just now,' Scott Macfie informed Augustus (21 September 1909). A strong body of supporters soon counter-attacked. The *Liverpool Courier* (25 September 1909) interpreted it as a 'topical allegory' which had a 'symbolic value as representing the characteristic relationships of the

Labour-Socialist Party and the Liberal Government'. While in the *Western Daily Press* T. Martin Wood, who described Augustus as 'the most revolutionary' of 'all the revolutionaries who are now alive', reflected upon the 'expression of countenance, in which a soul is to be seen'.

Liverpool was sent into an extraordinary commotion by this controversy, the echoes lasting many years. Day after day the Walker Art Gallery was packed with people coming in to ridicule or admire this 'Portrait of Smith', as it was now called. Letters of anonymous indignation were everywhere posted in haste, and feelings of fury, adulation and merriment were kept at a high level by all manners of Tweedledum cartoons, satirical verses and stories to the effect that Dowdall had commissioned a gang of burglars to make off with it, only to find they had taken the valuable frame and left the canvas. Though the picture represented a serious attempt, dignified yet witty, to come to terms with *grand salon* portraiture, Augustus did not immediately help his supporters by stating that he had introduced Smith into the picture 'for fun'[105] – and at no extra cost! But he was obviously taken aback by the venom of some attacks, which he described as 'stupid, disgusting and unnecessary'.

After its showing at Liverpool, the picture toured the country, always followed by a wake of argument. 'There is nothing to justify the indignation expressed by the Liverpool worthies,' one paper proclaimed after it was shown at the NEAC Winter Exhibition in 1911. But the *Athenaeum* (2 December 1911), as at some new Bonnard, could still 'marvel somewhat at Mr John's innocence of the science of perspective', while other critics invoked the names of Gainsborough, Sargent, Velázquez and Whistler.

One man who stood up for the portrait from the beginning was Dowdall himself. On all public occasions he announced that it was splendid, and went so far as to supplement Augustus's honorarium out of his own pocket. 'I consider it a great picture, and for what my opinion is worth, I am prepared to go nap on it,' he was reported as saying.[106] Nevertheless it was to prove something of a white elephant to the Dowdall family, following them from house to house in its atrocious golden frame and dominating their lives. 'You will have to build a special room to hold it,' advised a friend.[107] Such friends had to enter through the back door at Liverpool since the portrait blocked the entrance hall. It also cost a fortune to insure, required the hiring of a special railway truck to move and, when stationary, attracted crowds of Augustus's devotees who would call round demanding to view it, making the Dowdalls' lives a torment. Eventually, in 1918, Chaloner Dowdall decided to sell it. Liverpool, despite its hostility, still felt a proprietary right in the picture and was critical of this decision. But Augustus took a different line: 'I'm glad to hear you found the old picture useful at last,' he wrote to him (14 October 1918), 'and that it fetched a decent price. It was really too big for a private possession of course, failing the possession of a palace to hold it. I don't forget how well you acted by me at the time.'

The National Gallery had offered Dowdall six hundred and fifty pounds (equivalent to £14,200 in 1996) but E. P. Warren, a private collector who lived with John Fothergill at Lewes House in Sussex, topped this with an offer of one thousand four hundred and fifty pounds (equivalent to £31,700 in 1996). Dowdall asked the Rani whether their son (then aged ten) would prefer to see his father enshrined in the National Gallery at a fairly nominal price or enjoy the proceeds of the full market price – to which she replied, 'Don't be a fool!' So the portrait went to Warren's beautiful eighteenth-century house where it joined a Lucas Cranach, a Filippino Lippi and, in the garden, Rodin's 'Le Baiser'. With his money Dowdall then bought a house, Melfort Cottage, in Oxfordshire with three acres of land where he lived for the next thirty-five years. But the picture had not come to rest. When Warren died, his heir Asa Thomas lent it to the Walker Gallery where it was exhibited in 1932. But Liverpool was still dead set against it, and the gallery's director refused to buy it. Not for another six years was it bought. 'I have now to make a confession,' Sydney Cockerell then wrote to Dowdall (2 June 1938). 'As London Adviser to the Felton Trustees of the National Gallery of Victoria I am guilty of having caused the banishment to Melbourne of your magnificent portrait by Augustus John. It is really too bad as it is perhaps his masterpiece and it certainly should have remained in England. How mad your fellow citizens of Liverpool were to allow it to go out of their hands!'

The price this time had risen to two thousand four hundred pounds (equivalent to £68,500 in 1996) – twenty-four times the original fee. It was shown at the Tate Gallery in London for a month, then left for Australia. Sixteen years later it returned to Liverpool, and to the Walker Art Gallery where, for six weeks in 1954, it was the centrepiece of an Augustus John show having Liverpool connections. 'It may well be that something of this conflict, aligned in the same way, will divide Liverpool again now,' wrote Hugh Scrutton with a nostalgia for the aggressive past. '. . . At all events visitors to the Walker Art Gallery can now see this stormy petrel of a picture returned to its original place of showing. And it may be their last chance. For the picture will return to the National Gallery of Victoria, Melbourne, in September and it is anybody's guess whether it will return again within their lifetime from Australia.'[108]

*

Returning to camp, Augustus found that everything was not well. Arthur had misbehaved with the harness, and Augustus fired him on the spot.

They were now, with their various caravans, carts, animals and boys, immovable. In desperation, Augustus wired an SOS to his friend Charles Slade,[109] who lived not far off at Thurning. '*Have fired Arthur can you come help love conveniently at once John.*' Slade galloped over and shepherded the convoy back to his farm. But the travelling life was taking a heavy toll of them. Slade took a number of photographs that September exhibiting the brave equipment with which they had encumbered themselves. The vans, still bright, were in the 'cottage' style, with ornate chip-carved porch brackets projecting at the front and rear, and steps which, when the horses had been unharnessed and put out to graze, fitted between the dipped shafts. The tents, to judge from Augustus's drawings, were of the traditional gypsy construction – a single stout ridge-pole carrying five pairs of hazel-rods shaped into a cartwheel, over which framework blankets could be fastened by skewers or pinhorns.[110] There are no horses in the photographs, possibly because they had begun to die off. One stumbled and fell *en voyage*, projecting Augustus over its head; another collapsed while standing in the shafts 'and I sold it to the knacker for a sovereign'. Photographs of Dorelia and Edie suggest that they too were worn out by the rigours of road life. The boys, while at Thurning, all caught whooping cough, which they communicated to the Slade children; and the general discomforts of their camp even reached Augustus himself. 'I shall be damn glad to get on with my own work,' he grumbled to John Quinn (September 1909). He returned thankfully to Church Street, having agreed to decorate the Chelsea house of Lady Gregory's nephew, Hugh Lane. He would never go on such a rough-and-tumble journey again, but it was not long before he began speculating about agreeable variants. 'I don't suppose we shall return this summer,' he admitted to Slade, with whom he had left a number of his vans and sons. 'I wish I had the vans in France. Do you know how much it would cost to heave them over the Channel?'

8

FATAL INITIATIONS

'John is – has always been – one of my greatest friends, the only man who now has imaginative genius.'
Arthur Symons to Gwen John (27 October 1919)

'I have been seeing a lot of Arthur Symons lately,' Augustus wrote to Ottoline (1 October 1909). 'I'm afraid he's about to break down again and that will be the end. He reads me poems that get more and more lurid.'

They were an ill-assorted pair. The son of a puritanical Wesleyan minister, Arthur Symons had been brought up along nervously conventional lines and indoctrinated with a vast dose of the Knowledge of Evil. Against the effects of this upbringing he had received a vaccination at the hands of Dr Havelock Ellis who, during a week's visit to Paris, introduced him to the debauchery of cigarettes and wine. Upon such weeds and fruit was Symons's celebrated *Knowledge of French Decadence* brought to birth. He was a man, in George Moore's words, 'of somewhat yellowish temperament', who, according to Will Rothenstein, 'began every day with bad intentions . . . [and] broke them every night'. His spirit was eager enough, but his body, undermined by the chronic illnesses which afflict those who will outlive their contemporaries, was weak. Though much obsessed with notions of sex, he was not a passionate man but something different: a passionate believer in passion. The rhyme was preferable to the deed, and he would dizzy himself, in verse, with visions of belly dancers, serpent charmers and other exotic temptresses. More prosaically, he had married Rhoda Bowser, a strong-willed scatterbrain and occasional actress. He needed about him people who were strong, people who had an appearance of strength greater than his father's had been. It was this quality that attracted him to Augustus.

They had met in Gordon Craig's studio in Chelsea early in 1903 – 'one of the most fortunate events of my life', as Symons remembered. The following spring, when Augustus held his show at the Carfax Gallery, Symons wrote a glowing appreciation of it in the Anglo-French paper, *Weekly Critical Review* (2 April 1903). Many years later, in an article entitled 'The Greatness of Augustus John', in which he selected Augustus as 'the greatest living artist', Symons recalled his first reaction to the Carfax exhibition. Two sentences from Baudelaire had occurred to him: 'Je connais pas de sentiment plus embarrassant que l'admiration'; and 'L'énergie c'est la grâce suprême'. These two sentences sum up very well the commerce of their relationship. Symons traded his admiration in exchange for Augustus's stimulating treatment. He set out to please, sitting for Augustus, dedicating books to him, deferring to his literary taste, assailing him with congratulatory poems; and he set out to take from him something he badly needed: energy. Wilde had once described him as 'an egoist without an ego'. Augustus appeared to supply this ego from the dynamo of his overcharged personality. It was not difficult for Symons to identify himself with Augustus. 'I knew that he, like myself, was a Vagabond, and that he knew the gypsies and their language better than anyone else,' Symons wrote. And then, as he told John Quinn (30 January 1914),

'I was born at Milford Haven in Wales – oddly nine miles along the coast from where Augustus was born.' Were they not blessed then, or afflicted, with the same Celtic blood? Had they not endured similar upbringings? In his diary Symons noted:

'John's fascination is almost infamous; the man, so full of lust and life and animality, so exorbitant in his desires and in his vision that rises in his eyes.

His mother, who died young, was artistic, did some lovely paintings his father still keeps in Tenby. There he got some of his gift – as I did from mine. I for verse, he for painting. Our fathers never really understood us . . . John's father hated art and artists; the mother, imaginative. So was mine: both imaginative: one derives enormously from one's mother.'

Augustus lived vividly in Symons's imagination. 'Arthur Symons has sent me a poem he had dedicated to me – all about bones and muscles and blatant nakedness,' Augustus wrote to Alick Schepeler. 'I ask myself what I have done to merit this?' The poem, 'Prologue for a Modern Painter: to A. E. John' is a hymn to vitality, a declaration of his faith in the kind of life he could never make his own, except through someone else:

> Hear the hymn of the body of man:
> This is how the world began;
> In these tangles of mighty flesh
> The stuff of the earth is moulded afresh . . .
>
> Here nature is, alive and untamed,
> Unafraid and unashamed;
> Here man knows woman with the greed
> Of Adam's wonder, the primal need.
>
> The spirit cries out and hymns
> In all the muscles of these limbs;
> And the holy spirit of appetite
> Wakes the browsing body with morning light.[111]

But what *had* Augustus done to merit such a rhapsody? For one of the paradoxes of their friendship was that where Augustus dreamed, Symons, in his tireless search for 'impressions', often acted. He had breathed in the fantastical air of Dieppe deeper than Augustus, stopping impatiently for a night while in pursuit of some prehistoric fishwomen, could ever have done. And he had actually gone to many of the places, especially in

Italy, that Augustus had merely read about. Yet because Symons dreaded action 'more than anything in the world',[112] he was determined to see Augustus as a great man of action. What mesmerized him was the apparent lack of that guilt which so weighed down his own actions wherever he went.

The flow of poems was for some years their main line of communication. It formed, for Symons, a kind of umbilical cord attaching him to a creative source of life. 'Dear Symons,' Augustus replied from Church Street, 'To-day I've just come back to find another beautiful poem for me! I would have written columns of gratitude for the others you sent, only the words, not the will, failed me.'*

Then, in 1908, disaster had overtaken Symons: he had gone mad in Italy. From Venice, urged on by exasperation, he fled to a hotel in Bologna where his wife Rhoda, dressed like a dragonfly, hurried to his side. She found him racked by terrible phantoms, but her concern seemed only to sharpen his torment. For repeatedly she would demand: 'Do you *really* love me, Arthur?' One night he disappeared: he had given his answer. 'So it has come at last!' she soliloquized. 'He no longer loves me!' Next morning, however, Symons returned and created some dismay by failing to recognize his wife, and then, with foul curses filling his mouth, rushing off chased by horrible shapes and shadows. The hotel manager then explained to Rhoda: 'Madam, your husband is mad. He has bought three daggers.' In hysterics she raced back to England, to be arraigned by a herd of Bowsers for having deserted her husband. Symons, meanwhile, had lost himself, drifting day after day in ever-increasing fatigue from one ominous spot to another. 'I walked and walked and walked – always in the wrong direction.' At last he was arrested in Ferrara, manacled hand and foot, and thrown into a medieval gaol. It was only with great difficulty that his friends and family got him released and dispatched back to England where, in November 1908, he was confined to Brooke House, a private mental home.

The doctors were confident they could not cure him. They had diagnosed 'general paralysis of the insane', which could proceed, they confirmed, through hopeless idiocy to death. They spoke matter-of-factly, were kind, but firm: all hopes, they promised, were ignorant and vain. Symons (who lived thirty-seven more years in perfect sanity) had, they declared, a life expectancy of between two months and two years – it could not be more. His manner of life at Brooke House, though described by the specialists as 'quiet', was in some ways unusually active. He took

---

* Yet the words, so failing in gratitude, were more forthcoming in parody. John wrote a number of verses in the Symons style. See Appendix Four.

off his clothes and assumed the title of Duke of Cornwall. He frequently dined with the King and kept forty pianofortes upstairs on which he composed a prodigious quantity of music. He rose each morning at 4 a.m., and worked hard on a map of the world divided into small sections; he also wrote plays, devoted endless time to the uplifting of the gypsy, and, when not occupied as Pope of Rome, involved himself in speculations worth many thousands of pounds. But his main duty as a lunatic was to arrange for Swinburne's reception in Paradise, and when Swinburne died in 1909 the pressure of these delusions began to ease. 'Had it not been for [Augustus] John,' he wrote later, 'whose formidable genius is combined with a warmth of heart, an ardent passion and will, at times deep, almost profound affection, which is one of those rare gifts of a genius such as his, I doubt if I could have survived these tortures that had been inflicted upon me.'

Already by the summer of 1909, Symons was being allowed out from Brooke House in convoy, followed by Miss Agnes Tobin, a West Coast American lady bitten with a passion for meeting real artists, and, at some further distance, a hated 'keeper' from the asylum. This procession would make its serpentine way to the home of Augustus who, after losing the keeper 'without compunction or difficulty', would set them high-stepping to the Café Royal, where he prescribed for Symons medicines more potent than any administered at Brooke House. 'At the Café Royal, between five and eight, we each drank seven absinthes, with cigarettes and conversation,' Symons wrote excitedly.[113] There were many of these splendid occasions: visits to the Alhambra Theatre and to the Russian ballets; glorious luncheons at the Carlton and sumptuous suppers with young models in Soho; all for the sake of what Symons called 'la débauche et l'intoxication'.

Augustus was good to Symons. 'Although I like him,' he later explained to his sister Gwen, 'I find it difficult to support his company for more than 5 minutes.'[114] Nevertheless, under the impression that the poor man was shortly to die, he set out to make his last few weeks enjoyable. 'I have seen Symons a good deal,' he informed Quinn (25 October 1909) ' – he keeps apparently well but one can see all the same that he is far from being so. The doctors give him 2 or 3 more months . . . he reads out his latest poems – which are all hell, damnation and lust.'

Augustus had not calculated that, a dozen years later, he would still be entertaining Symons 'a good deal', and that Symons would still be counting on him to be (14 April 1921) 'as wonderful as ever'.

What he did for Symons was to blow into his life and keep blowing, ventilating it with humour, filling it with people, elbowing out Symons's morbid introspection. The delusions melted into nothing before the heat of actual events. But part of Symons's recovery was due, Augustus maintained, 'to the kindness and devotion of Miss Tobin'.[115] She was forty-five with the light behind her, hailed from San Francisco, had translated Petrarch, and now lived at the Curzon Hotel in Mayfair. She was observed to be 'a little bit flighty'.[116] Conrad (who dedicated *Under Western Eyes* to her) called her Inez; Francis Meynell, however, called her Lily 'because of the golden and austere delicacy of her head and neck'; and she called Augustus 'my poor butterfly'. He stood up to it well. 'I've been seeing Symons and Miss Tobin,' he told John Quinn (18 December 1909). Symons, he added, 'keeps pouring out verses'.

The three of them had been brought together (while Augustus was briefly in London following his escape from Liverpool's Lord Mayor) by John Quinn, the New York lawyer reckoned to be 'the twentieth century's most important patron of living literature and art'.[117] Quinn arrived in England that summer to buy some pictures by Charles Shannon, Nathaniel Hone and 'Augustus John, the artist who is much discussed in London now'.[118] He had heard tell of both Symons and Augustus from W. B. Yeats and, not content to meet them separately, had arranged for them to see one another too. There appeared to be advantages in this for everyone. Miss Tobin, who was coming into contact with more artists and authors than she could have dreamed possible, made the suggestion that Quinn acquire manuscripts by Symons and her friend Conrad. 'Your bringing A.S. and Mr John together was a miraculous success and will, I think, be an immense solace to A.S.,' she assured Quinn (16 September 1909). 'Mr John told me he would keep up the friendship – and wants A.S. to sit for him.' Augustus's portrait of Symons, one of his subtlest interpretations of writers, was delayed until the autumn of 1917 when, though described by Frank Harris[119] as showing 'a terrible face – ravaged like a battlefield', it was warmly praised by the Symons family. 'John has done a fine portrait of A[rthur],' Rhoda confided to Quinn (29 October 1917). '. . . What an odd fish he is; but he has great personal qualities. He has been true to A[rthur] all thro' these years, and it's few who have . . . he's a great artist, isn't he? . . . A[rthur]'s portrait is very El Grecoish!'

Of Quinn Augustus did a number of drawings (one of them described by a friend as 'the portrait of a hanging judge') and a large formal portrait in oils – all during a single week in August 1909. On the fifth and final sitting, as Augustus was about to take up his brushes, Miss Tobin stepped forward and exclaimed that the canvas was perfect – 'at the razor's edge'. Augustus at once laid down his brushes and began drinking – so the picture was perforce finished.[120]

Although Quinn affected to think well of his portrait – 'I liked the portrait John made of me,' he wrote calmly to Lady Gregory (21

December 1909). 'And I liked John himself immensely' – it was not an encouraging likeness. When it was exhibited that autumn at the NEAC under the title 'The Man from New York', the critic of the *English Review* (January 1910) wrote: 'The peculiar note of hardness which Mr. A. E. John has could not have found a better subject than "The Man from New York". It shows exactly that hardness which we look for and find in this type of American.'

Quinn insisted that, on reading this, 'I howled out loud with glee'.[121] There are few more doleful sounds than the laughter of a man without humour. Quinn's lack of humour was a very positive quality and he enjoyed drawing attention to it by cracking jokes.[122] His response to Augustus's portrait was indeed partly the result of its being a very funny picture. It presents him at three-quarters length, seated with his left hand on his hip and his right hand extended, resting on a cane. The shape of his figure is that of a tent and upon a face of tiny proportions at the apex of this design there sits an expression of the sternest vacancy, the mouth of the 'garrulous Irish American' for once firmly sealed. Quinn, his biographer B. L. Reid tells us, 'felt baffled and unhappy about it',[123] though Symons, Pissarro and others considered it 'extremely good'.[124] Bravely, he hung it over his mantelpiece for as long as he lived, but would indignantly protest that Augustus 'painted me as though I were a referee or umpire at a baseball game or the president of a street railway company with a head as round and unexpressive and under-developed as a billiard ball. Thirty or forty years of life in school, college, university and the world has I hope put a little intelligence into my face. Intelligence is not predominant in the John painting of me, but force, self-assertion and a seeming lack of sensitiveness which is not mine!'[125]

Quinn's interpretation of the portrait was right. 'Do not expect any subtle intelligence from him [Quinn] or any other Yankee,' Augustus warned Will Rothenstein (20 September 1911). '. . . Money has literally taken the place of brains and character, and the American mind is a metallic jungle of platitude and bluff.'

In an earlier letter to Rothenstein Augustus had lamented the dearth of 'millionaires of spirit'. In Quinn he had found a millionaire of the purse. He would have liked to like him. 'We became very friendly,' he wrote after their first meeting.[126] But they valued each other for qualities other than friendship. 'He's a treasure,' Augustus told Dorelia (August 1909). 'He's offered me £250 [equivalent to £11,800 in 1996] a year for life and I can send him what I like. He's a daisy and will do much more than that.' It seemed to Augustus that so liberal a patron, and one tactful enough not to inconvenience him by living in the same country, presented an ideal solution to his problems. This extra money would release him from a lot of commissioned work and allow him to paint imaginative pictures. 'I can tell you honestly you did me a lot of good that week in London,' he wrote in his first letter to Quinn (September 1909), 'and that quite apart from pecuniary considerations. You will help me to keep up to the scratch.'[127]

The figure of Quinn, hopelessly beckoning, stood at the end of a long road lavishly paved with good intentions. When, for example, he asks for a complete set of etchings, Augustus willingly consents, adding (4 January 1910): 'I mean to methodize my work more and put aside say one or two months every year to etching – it can't be done every day or any day.' In another letter (25 October 1909) he tells Quinn: 'I am extremely anxious to study Italian frescos as I am fired with the desire to revive that art . . . I am quite ready to say goodbye to oil painting after seeing the infinitely finer qualities of fresco and tempera.' But when Quinn replies with dismay, Augustus hurriedly gives way (18 December 1909):

'What you say about my remarks on fresco and oil-painting are words of wisdom – I wrote under the enthusiasm of the moment. But I have had time to realise that oil-painting has its own virtues and have given up despising my own past – a thing one is too apt to do, when struck with a fresh idea. I suffer from being unduly impressionable – and often forget the essential continuity of my own life: the result being I am as often put back on my beam's ends rather foolishly. What you say is true that one is apt to despise one's own facility – whereas one should recognise it as the road to mastery itself. I shall keep your letter and read it over whenever I feel off the track – *my own track*. It will be medicine for me who am occasionally afflicted with intellectual vapours.'

One of the contradictions of Quinn's character was that, while being financially generous, he was a triumphantly mean man. His letters to Augustus and other artists and writers are always business letters, and almost always interchangeable – what has been the main body of one is quoted in another. Essentially this correspondence is a form of memoranda for his files; it is pitted with headings and sub-headings, listings and recapitulations of earlier correspondence. He is not afraid of recounting events out of which he comes extremely favourably and everyone else greatly to their disadvantage. He confesses being partial to 'juicy girls', but at the same time he is a sexual puritan much given to amatory philosophizing, for which Augustus seemed an obvious target.

Quinn perfected the art of boredom. Dullness by itself was not enough. He ensnared his victims in the web of his money and inflicted on them his terrible jokes, appalling lectures, his deathly political harangues. Many of his 'friendships' disintegrated under this treatment, invariably, on Quinn's part, with a sense of moral relish. He fed greedily on gossip, extracting confidences and, 'in confidence', passing them on. It continually amazed him how extraordinarily stupid people were, and sometimes he wrote to tell them so – though he preferred telling their friends.

But in Miss Tobin, Quinn had met his match. Before long she was seeking to employ him for legal advice about her nightmares. 'I had a frightful dream which told me efforts were being made to make me out mentally unbalanced at some time or other,' she informed him (24 July 1911). 'This is a dreadful stigma. But . . . the only side of it that is of importance is the legal side. Can you find out for me if I have been found "incapable" at any time for any cause – that is the legal term ("incapable") isn't it? Irresponsible, I mean.' This was a subject upon which Quinn found some difficulty in taking instructions. Miss Tobin was sympathetic. She would cross the Atlantic and call at his office. She would travel with an English nanny who would be seasick. So would he please 'have a man sent out on a pilot- boat'. There is real pathos when Quinn suddenly cries out: 'I am a dreadfully driven man!' But in his legal opinion to Miss Tobin can be detected the seeds of his own lunacy: 'My conviction [is] that the origin of most dreams is in the stomach or intestines.'

Quinn had rapidly diagnosed Symons's complaint as venereal disease. Symons might 'fool them all yet', he guessed, but Quinn himself would not be fooled. His duty was clear: CABLED FIFTY POUNDS PLEASE WARN FRIEND AGAINST DANGER VENEREAL INFECTION ITALY.

Such cables, which were intended for Augustus and no 'friend', reached him wherever he travelled. However far he went, however fast or uncertainly, by van or train or erratically on foot, the venomous torrent of Quinn's goodwill, choked with the massive boulders of punning and unintentional double entendres, overtook him. At Arles, for instance, Augustus read (February 1910):

'For God's sake look out and protect yourself against venereal disease in Italy. Remember the Italians aren't white people. They are a rotten race. They are especially rotten with syphilis. They don't take care of themselves. They are unclean. They are filthy. Whatever their art may have been in the past, to-day they are a degenerate, filthy, diseased race. They are professional counterfeiters, professional forgers, habitual perjurers, blackmailers, black-handers, high-binders, hired assassins, and depraved and degenerate in every way. I know two men who got syphilis in Naples . . . I know another man who got syphilis in Rome. Therefore for God's sake take no chances. Better import a white concubine than take chances with an Italian. The white woman would be cheaper in the end ... Your future is in your own hands, my dear friend. I am convinced you have the intellect to keep the rudder true.'[128]

In time, Quinn's medical lunacy took a deeper hold on him, spreading from venereal disease to diseases of the feet and teeth. He became a specialist in sciatica ('sciatica is a term of ignorance and a disease arising from ignorance'); in lumbago ('lumbago is a term of ignorance and a disease arising from ignorance'); and in the relationship between fornication and eye strain. The cure for such distempers was soup, eight glasses of water a day and plenty of X-rays. In dentistry, a new American science 'like chiropody', lay the secret of 'healthful' life. To all writers and artists he was generous with his expertise. Whether they had bad eyesight or bad feet, he would urge them to visit their dentist. 'I think I wrote to you two years ago I told [James] Joyce that the trouble with his eyes was due to his teeth,' he reminded Symons (15 November 1923). 'I could see it.'

What was common to both Symons's and Quinn's relationship with Augustus was a form of vicarious living. In Symons this vicariousness is plain: 'What I am certain of is that John – of all living men – has lived his life *almost* entirely as he wanted to live it,' he wrote to Quinn (21 October 1915). 'So – he is the most enviable creature on earth.'

The vicarious quality in Quinn is more complicated. He led two lives. In the present he worked hard as a lawyer and amassed a considerable fortune; and with this fortune he bought his paintings for the future. He had a good eye for pictures, but he neither enjoyed them much aesthetically nor treated them primarily as financial investments. He collected them so as to shore up his immortality. 'All my life, or rather for twenty years, it seems to me I have been doing things for others,' he wrote to Will Rothenstein (25 March 1912). The thought gave him no pleasure.

Augustus was one of those for whom, Quinn later came to believe, he had done too much. He initially cast Augustus as an angel on whose back he would ride heavenwards – only to discover that this was not necessarily Augustus's destination. By 1910 Quinn had arranged to pay him three hundred pounds a year (equivalent to £14,100 in 1996) for the pick of his own work, and a further two hundred pounds to select, on his behalf, work by other British artists. In short, Augustus was to act as his patron's agent. Quinn's delusion, almost as fundamental as Symons's, was that a man who, by his own admission, was inconsistent, temperamental and had different tastes from his own, would be a good choice as his British representative. Nevertheless the plan worked reasonably well for a few years, and it was the eccentricities of Augustus that killed it.

Augustus's eccentricity was compounded of several ingredients. Between his promise and the fulfilment of that promise fell an almost endless pause. His incompetence over small matters tuned Quinn up to a marvellous pitch of exasperation. What should have been simple was made complicated with radiant ingenuity: paintings were sold twice, or painted over, set fire to, sunk, never begun, or lost for ever. But there was another ingredient – a motive, for all this purposeless perversity. Augustus hated these patron-and-artist dealings: they reminded him of father-and-son arrangements, and he felt an increasing itch to behave badly. He attracted hero-worship – then punished it.

'We were rather afraid he'd go mad again,' Augustus wrote to Dorelia about 'poor Arthur'. He was certainly 'very gaga' sometimes. But, from among the four of them – Augustus, Quinn, Symons and Miss Tobin – it seems that Symons, protected by an official certificate, was suffering less grievously from 'intellectual vapours' than his friends.

9

ITALIAN STYLE, FRENCH FOUND

'What's the good of being an island, if you are not a *volcanic island*?'

Wyndham Lewis to Augustus John (1910)

'I am overwhelmed with work just now,' Augustus wrote to Alick Schepeler, 'and have to scorn delights (or pretend to) and live laborious days.' He had it in mind during the autumn of 1910 to prepare a catalogue of his etchings, and to make a book about the gypsies of Europe; he would exhibit some paintings at the NEAC and drawings at the Chenil; and then he would paint all his children, separately and together. He had already started a large new portrait of Dorelia – 'it ought to be one of the best portraits of a woman in the world,' he told Quinn (4 January 1910), ' – the woman at any rate is one of the best.' Newest and best of all were two other big enterprises. 'There's a millionairess from Johannesburg [Mrs Lionel Phillips] who proposes sending me abroad to study and do some decorations for a gallery at Johannesburg which she is founding,' he wrote to Quinn (25 October 1909). 'If she is sufficiently impressed by what I will show her all will be well.' This opportunity had almost certainly come through Sir Hugh Lane, who was then forming the collection at the Johannesburg Municipal Gallery. Augustus had started work this autumn decorating Lindsay House, Lane's home in Cheyne Walk – 'exciting work', he told Ottoline Morrell (1 October 1909). Wyndham Lewis wrote to encourage him: 'Let it be an authentic earthquake.'[129]

Suddenly, at the beginning of December, he was attacked by the most dreadful melancholia. 'I have been working at little Lane's walls,' he explained to Ottoline (4 December 1909). 'It is an absolutely futile thing to undertake that kind of work in a hurry. I should like to have years to do it in – and then it might *last* years. Lane himself is a silly creature and moreover an unmitigated snob. It seems my fate to be hasty but I have serious thoughts of quitting this island and going somewhere where life is more stable and beautiful and primitive and where one is not bound to be in a hurry. I want absolutely to grasp things plastically and not merely glance at their charms, and for that one needs time. – As for these commissions such as Lane's or Phillips', they are misleading entirely – one is not even asked to do one's best – merely one's quickest and convenientest.'

He went on being misled by this 'house job' for another two weeks of deepening gloom: then came the earthquake. 'I have made a drastic move as regards Lane's decorations,' he confided to Quinn (18 December 1909). 'I found doing them in his hall impossible, subjected to constant interruption and inconsequent criticism as I was. Lane himself proved too exasperating in his constant state of nervous agitation . . . So I exploded one day and told him I'ld take the canvases away to finish – which I have done.'

In a letter Dorelia sent to Ursula Slade at about this time, she reveals that Augustus had spotted 'a lovely gypsy girl and asked her to sit for him'. This sitting took place next day at Lane's house, where the two of them were soon joined by 'a whole band of ruffians' who made merry in every room and 'nearly frightened Lane out of his wits'. When the danger had passed and they were gone, Lane 'was very angry and said it wasn't at all the thing to do'. It was after Lane's protest that Augustus erupted against 'this island' and carried off his canvases; while Lane himself, in high dudgeon, descended into Monte Carlo.

Dissatisfaction was everywhere. There seemed no light in England, no space in Church Street. 'Il me faut de l'air, de l'air, de l'air,' Augustus cried out to Wyndham Lewis. By Christmas, his son Robin had fallen ill with scarlet fever. He sat quarantined in one corner of the room with Dorelia's sister Edie, while the rest of them huddled in the opposite corner. When the Rothensteins, with implacable timing, called round bearing the compliments of the season they were shooed from the door. 'Our house', Augustus apologized (4 January 1910), 'was more hospital than hospitable, I fear.'

Even Dorelia's cheerful detachment faltered. She felt unwell and, to Augustus's fury, refused to see a doctor. It was as if she cherished her symptoms, like a list of unspoken complaints. In retaliation he developed catarrh: but as an argument it was hardly satisfactory. Dorelia's lethargy drained all energy from him, as if she were an electric current and he a mere bulb, growing dimmer. 'The days are leaden as a rule,' he confided to Quinn (18 December 1909). '. . . I don't seem to be cut out for family life . . . The crisis which takes place at least weekly leaves me less and less hopeful as regards this ménage. It is a great pity as I am fond of the missus and she of me.'

Despite all they had come through together, Augustus felt that they must now live separately. He would take a studio; she could remain at Church Street. Of course they must see each other, but not live together. 'I think it would be fairer on us both to avoid the day to day test,' he wrote, 'and I should work with less preoccupation. You would scarcely believe the violence of the emotional storms I go through so often – and worst of all those gloomy periods that precede them.'[130]

Yet a curious adhesiveness somehow kept them together. The discord was often loud, but always tenderly resolved with a forgiveness merging into forgetfulness. For it was not as though they were against each other: they fought a common enemy seeking to divide them.

'It was a horrible pity we got into that state,' he wrote to her after one row. '. . . I don't know what precisely brought it on. It was a kind of feeling you were tugging in the wrong direction or exhibiting a quite false aspect of your nature – not the real one which never fails to bowl me over, but like the moon suffers an occasional eclipse.

'By living together too casually our manners deteriorate by degrees, "inspiration" ceases to the natural accompaniment of irritation and dissatisfaction till at last the awful storms are necessary to restore us to dignity and harmony and equilibrium. You know very well that "expression" in you or state of mind I shall always love as the most beautiful thing in the world and hate to see supplanted by something less divine and you know how mercurial I am, veering from Heaven to Hell and torn to pieces by emotion or nerves or thoughts – is it any wonder we can't always be happy? I acknowledge my grievous shortcomings as I acknowledge your superior vision to which I owe so much (that's what I meant by "being useful"!). I never liked any "tart" as a "tart" but for some suggestion of beauty – and even some faint delusive charm is a concrete fact to a poor artist (!). I can't help thinking we *can* go on better than we have been by using our wits.'[131]

The explanation for Dorelia's 'false aspect' tugging 'in the wrong direction' was another pregnancy. 'So, you are in for another brat,' Augustus remarked. He needed all her devotion, faith, energy; he needed her as mother as well as mistress. But during pregnancy it was not possible for her to provide all this. By the end of the year they had come, somewhat hesitantly, to the conclusion that during the second or third month, she must have had a miscarriage. Augustus seemed rather mystified by this pregnancy ('I can't imagine what could be the cause of it'), and Henry Lamb, who had ended his affair with Ottoline, appeared as much concerned as he was.

The New Year promised new hope. Quinn, who attributed their matrimonial difficulties to bad dentistry, had nevertheless sent a Christmas cake to Dorelia and, to Augustus, his first cheque – a magic remedy. 'I feel by no means dreary now,' he replied (4 January 1910). '... Frank Harris has written me from near Naples[132] asking me to come out for a spell – I think I may manage a few weeks off profitably.'

By the second week of January they had drawn up a plan. They would part – but only for a month or so. Augustus would plunge south to escape the winter darkness and, putting Quinn's money to good uses, explore the French and Italian galleries. Dorelia's sister Edie, whom Lamb was using as a model, would mind the children, and Dorelia herself, who was still not well, would have an eye kept on her by her friend, and Lamb's ex-girlfriend, Helen Maitland. Then, once she felt better, Dorelia would leave with Helen and some children to join Augustus – while Edie, as a substitute for her sister, went to stay with Lamb. It seemed an obvious solution to all their problems.

*

Augustus set out by train in the middle of January to explore Provence. In bright sunlight he descended at Avignon and 'as if in answer to the insistent call of far-off Roman trumpets ... I found myself, still dreaming, under the ramparts of the city by the swift flowing Rhône.'[133] To Dorelia he sent his first impressions of the place with an illustration of himself approaching a castle across a mountainous landscape (10 January 1910): 'This is a wonderful country and a wonderful town Avignon. I'm beginning to feel better ... The people are certainly a handsome lot on the whole. I see beautiful ones now and then ... We could camp under the city walls here.'[134]

Everything delighted him. Across the Rhône the white town of Villeneuve-lès-Avignon shone like an illumination from some missal; and in the distance, as if snow-covered, Le Ventoux unexpectedly raised its creamy head. Near by, like a noble phalanstery, stood the Popes' Palace where Augustus went to admire the fragmentary frescoes of Simone Martini. But it was not the works of art that excited him most: it was the country and its people. 'I get tired of museums,' he wrote to Dorelia (17 January 1910). 'The sun of Provence is curing me of all my humours.' Of wonderful naïvety and charm were the gitano children. 'I never saw such kids – one of them especially broke my heart he was so incredibly charming, so ceaselessly active and boiling over with high spirits. He was about Robin's age, but a consummate artist. I went down first thing this morning to see them again but I fancy they have disappeared in the night for one of their hooded carts had gone. It's so like them to vanish just as you think you've got at them.'

His travels took in more encampments than galleries. 'Nothing so fills me with the love of life as the medieval – *antique* – life of camps,' he had (2 October 1909) told Scott Macfie, 'it seems to shame the specious permanence of cities, and tents will outlast pyramids.' Already he was feeling miraculously restored. 'I was in the last extremities of depression before getting here,' he wrote to Arthur Symons (January 1910), 'and now I begin to feel dangerously robust.' From Avignon he advanced to Nîmes and then hurried on to Arles, celebrated for the special beauty of its girls, where he was detained longer. 'The restaurant cafe where I am stopping here would not be a bad place for us to put up,' he reported to Dorelia. He was missing her. 'I can't sleep alone,' he complained, 'and when I do I dream of Irish tinkers and Lord Mayors.' Surely she would come to rescue him soon? 'What do you think about coming down here with P[yramus] and R[omilly]? I would love it. We would be quite warm in bed here.'

He made Arles his headquarters for the rest of this month. 'Arles is beautiful – Provence a lovely land,' he wrote to Ottoline (18 January 1910). '. . . What a foetid plague spot London seems from this point of vantage. It takes only this divine sunlight to disperse the clouds and humours that settle round in England. I never want to stop there again for all the winter.' But wherever he went in Provence he was tempted to stop – and would write to Dorelia telling her so. At Paradou he noticed 'an excellent bit of land to stop on, but we must have light wooded carts and tents – no heavy wagons please.' There were many such places in France. 'There's plenty of sand one could camp on all over the Camargue which is as flat as a pancake and mostly barren,' he reported to Dorelia.[135] 'I've been talking to a young man, a cocker, about getting a cart to move about in.' Meanwhile he walked huge distances – 'I have bought the largest pair of boots in the world' – and sometimes, in bourgeois fashion, travelled by train.

One village that enchanted him was Les Baux – 'an extraordinary place', he wrote, 'built among billows of rocks rather like Palestine as far as I remember. The people of Les Baux are pleasant simple folk – a little inclined to apologise for their ridiculous situation. We could have a fine apartment there cheap. There are plenty of precipices for the boys to fall over.'[136] It was at Les Baux that he met Alphonse Broule, 'a superb fellow' who claimed to be a friend of the great Provençal poet Mistral whose statue, overcoat on arm, reared itself at Arles – 'a man singularly like Buffalo Bill'. Broule – 'a poet', Augustus first hazarded: 'an absolute madman', he later concluded – offered to introduce him to the master, and a few days later they met near Maillane.

'The country I saw on the way made me wild,' he wrote to Dorelia, ' – so beautiful – a chain of rocky hills quite barren except for olives here and there . . . finally we came to Mistral's house; by this time my host was getting very nervous. But we found the master on the road, returning home with his wife . . . and he was so feeble as to receive us into his house. Mrs Mistral was careful to see that we wiped our feet well first. My companion talked a lot and wept before the master, a large snot hanging from his nose. Mistral listened to him with some patience. On leaving I asked him if he would care to sit two seconds for me to draw him when I passed that way again. He refused absolutely and recommended me to go and view his portrait at Marseilles. I . . . was enchanted with his answer which showed an intellect I was far from being prepared to meet.'[137]

Mistral later regretted having forbidden Augustus to do his portrait, he told Marie Mauron,[138] but their meeting had horrified him. First there was this terrible man Broule; and then there was his forbidding companion. Let a man like this begin to draw you, he reflected, and you would find him living with you for the rest of your life.

'I don't see how Italy could be much better than this,' Augustus wrote from Arles. Nevertheless he decided to push on to Marseilles, 'and so to Italy and get through some of the galleries studiously'. The first stage of this journey was to yield a marvellous discovery. Leaving Arles for Marseilles, the railway skirts the northern shores of the vast blue Étang de Berre, bordered by far-off amethyst cliffs. As he travelled along this inland sea, through the pine and olive trees, the speckled aromatic hills, he saw from the window, in the distance, the spires of a town appear, built as it seemed upon the incredible waters. The sensation which this sight, now gliding slowly away, produced on him was like that of a vision. He made up his mind to find out what this mysterious city might be.

At Marseilles another surprise: the town was teeming with gypsies. From the *terrasse* of the Bar Augas he watched groups of Almerian gitanos lounging at the foot of the Porte d'Aix, staves in their hands, their jet-black hair brushed rigidly forward over the ears and there abruptly cut, like nuns from some obscure and brilliant order. One figure specially caught his attention – a tall bulky man of middle age wearing voluminous high boots, baggy trousers decorated at the sides with insertions of green and red, a short braided coat garnished with huge silver pendants and chains, and a hat of less magnificence but greater antiquity upon his shaggy head, puffing at a great German pipe. Recognizing him as a Russian gypsy, Augustus accosted him in Romany. He had just received from Quinn another fifty pounds (equivalent to £2,350 in 1996) and with some of this he proposed celebrating their meeting, in return for which he was invited back to camp. They arrived, with a certain éclat, in a cab, ate supper round an enormous bonfire and ended the evening amid songs and dances in the Russian style. Augustus, who had come for dinner, stayed a week at this camp. 'I cannot tell you how they affect me,' he wrote to Ottoline (February 1910). '. . . I have an idea of dyeing myself chocolate pour mieux poser à Gitano.'

'Last night Milosch and Terka, my hosts, showed me all their wealth – unnumbered gold coins each worth at least 100 francs, jewels, corals, pearls. This morning came 3 young men, while we were still lying a-bed on the floor, bearing news of the death of a Romany. Terka wept and lamented wildly, beating her face and knotting her diklo [scarf] round her neck and calling upon God. At the station we found 20 or 30 Romanichels seated on the floor drinking tea from samovars. Beautiful people – amongst them a fantastic figure – the husband of the deceased – an old bearded man, refusing to be comforted.'[139]

Augustus did not draw much, feeling he gained more from watching. 'I tried to draw some of them,' he told Dorelia, 'but they never look the same when they're posing. All the same it's worthwhile trying.' What he hoped to do was to make very rapid sketches from which to work later. 'When people notice they are being drawn,' he explained to Ottoline, 'they immediately change expression and look less intelligent.'

He was learning more Romany every hour, and sending copious word-lists and notes on songs in the direction of Liverpool. What he jotted down in a few hours was enough to keep the best gypsy brains there at work for months. Scott Macfie was gratified by the demoralizing effect of Augustus's researches. 'This new dialect seems pretty stiff stuff to work out,' he wrote gleefully, 'and it is a pleasure to see signs of exasperation in Winstedt's remarks. He complains that in consequence of the strain his morals, his habits and his manners have become disgusting.'

Augustus too was happy – although Italy seemed as far off as ever. 'I'm not particularly impatient to do Italy,' he reminded Dorelia. 'Already I've seen a good many sights, but no pictures it is true, except the Avignon ones.' It is possible he would never have crossed the border but for the fact that the gypsies had elected to go there themselves.

'I may get off to-night to Genoa,' he eventually informed Dorelia, 'as the Gypsies are going to Milan I shall see them again. They also mean to come to London.* They could give a good show in a theatre. Terka, the woman in whose room I am staying, has a baby 10 months old who I think may die to-night. We went to a doctor to-day who seemed anxious to get rid of us. The little creature bucked up a bit to-night but was very cold. I'm going back now with a little brandy, all I can think of ... I might take a room in Milan for a few weeks and try and paint some of these folk.'[140]

He travelled by night to Genoa, his head still full of gypsies, his bearded and bedraggled appearance itself very gypsy-like. 'Why was I not warned against coming here,' he immediately complained to Dorelia. '... Wonderful things happened at Marseilles the last two days. I haven't had my clothes off for a week ... I'm sick of Italy.' But it was really Genoa he disliked. Though it had *sounded* warm, it was a cold place – 'a place to avoid'.[141] The streets crawled with people, like lice, and 'the pubs are horrid little places mostly art-nouveau'. Of course the country was better, and the Italian working classes had wonderful faces – virile, martial, keen as birds. But the bourgeois were not fit to be mentioned: and they swarmed everywhere. 'I took a second class ticket – hoping to get along quicker,' he told Ottoline (11 February 1910), 'but I couldn't put up with the second-class people (not to speak of the first). I had to take refuge in the third class – and was happy then. The 3rd class carriages have a hard simplicity about them which was infinitely comfortable.' He aimed to 'get through' Italy as fast as he could – a week, he calculated, should do the job.

'As to my handkerchiefs I have two with me, simply foul; socks I have given up; you could grow mushrooms in my vest,' he wrote to Dorelia. All this contributed to his Italian difficulties. His whirlwind flight, pursued everywhere by Quinn's venereal imprecations, lasted a full fortnight, but had an effect out of all proportion to this time. Though he disliked the big towns which, after the roughness of Marseilles, struck him as 'overcultivated', he loved the country. There were hillocks of brown earth on the way to Siena – 'things one might invent', he described them to Ottoline, 'without ever expecting to see'. The Tuscan landscape seemed not to have changed since the fourteenth century. 'You know those earthen mounds, gutted with the rains,' he wrote to Arthur Symons, ' – and those

---

* They turned up in the summer of 1911 at Liverpool and were infiltrated by several members of the Gypsy Lore Society in costume.

mountains, like women in bed, under quilts? What a lusty land it is!'
From Siena, where he was greatly attracted by the frescoes of Pietro
Lorenzetti, he came to Orvieto – 'do you know it?' he asked Symons.
'Splendid! The frescoes there break your heart – so beautiful, so magnificent.' He sped on – to Perugia ('no shape of a place . . . nothing but some
Perugino frescoes, and Perugino . . . was rather a soft growth'), and then
to Florence which, he told Ottoline (11 February 1910) was 'magnificent
and uncomfortable for a vagrant like myself – and too much to see – too
many masterpieces to digest at one meal'. All the same, simply because
of the rush, he was seeing things with an intensity that would keep these
sights vividly before him.

Deciding to postpone Rome, he turned north and travelled between
thick gloomy mountains with half-melted snow on them, through a grey
mist hiding the sky, to Ravenna. 'The mosaics here are superb,' he wrote
to Dorelia. 'Westminster Cathedral ought to be done in the same
manner.'[142] He had intended only to change trains at Ravenna, but it was
difficult to relinquish the Court of Justinian and Theodora, and so he
stayed on several days. The Tomb of Theodoric, with its echoes of Gothic
heroes, gave a sense of semi-barbaric splendour compared with which the
modern world seemed pale. Padua, his next halting place, and the paintings
of Giotto also slowed down his progress. He had seen so much he was
growing confused. 'Was it here I saw Piero della Francesca's majestic
Christ rising from the tomb?' he wondered.[143] 'I think not.'

But what did it matter, the provenance? Italy, he was discovering,
represented for him the authentic tradition to which, undismayed by its
splendour, he meant to dedicate himself. But it was in Provence that he
was to find another home – 'I love that patch of ground,' he told Symons
– and it was to the Provençal landscape, and to the landscape of North
Wales, that he would look for his finest pictures. In such an atmosphere,
less charged with the accumulated glory of the past and where there were
no masterpieces to overawe him, Augustus would set to work: but enriched
by what he had seen during these two brilliant weeks in Italy. For to
Giotto of Padua, to Duccio, Masaccio and Raphael, to Piero della Francesca wherever exactly his resurrected Christ might be, and to Botticelli
whose 'Primavera', lovely beyond compare, was the brightest jewel of
Florence, he would ultimately trace his own cultural beginnings.

And so to Milan. A vast assembly of gypsies – twenty tents of pleasure
– occupied a field outside the city. Work was in progress when Augustus
approached, and the air rang with the din of hammering and the cries of
these wild tribes. To his astonishment he found not only his Marseilles
friends but also the coppersmiths he had met two years previously in
Cherbourg – and there was a grand reunion. That evening a party filled

the principal tent. Black-bearded, sharp-eyed, fierce and friendly, the men
had dressed themselves in the costumes of stage brigands. They carried
long staves, and their white-braided tunics were decorated with silver
buttons as large as hens' eggs. The women were mostly in scarlet, and
each had threaded twenty or more huge gold coins in her hair and on her
blouse – a total, in sterling, of at least a hundred pounds. As the great
celebration proceeded, these young girls were called upon to dance to the
accordions, while the men lifted up their voices in melancholy song. The
dancers, without shifting their position on the carpet, agitated their hips
and breasts in a kind of shivering ecstasy. Cross-legged at a low table,
Todor, the elderly chief next to whom Augustus sat, beat time until the
bottles leapt, sometimes in sudden frenzy shattering his great German
pipe – immediately to be handed another. Solid silver samovars littered
the floor, and on the tables stood elaborately chased silver flagons a foot
high and filled with wine and rum. Troops of old men were seated round
them in a state of Bacchic inspiration, while outside the tent a crowd of
gâjos looked on as if in a hypnotic trance. 'The absolute isolation of the
Gypsies seemed to me the rarest and most unattainable thing in the world,'
Augustus wrote to Scott Macfie (14 February 1910). 'The surge of music,
which rose and fell as *naturally* as the wind makes music in the trees or
the waves upon the shore affected one strangely. It was *religious* – orgiastic.
I murmured to my neighbour "Kerela te kamav te rovav" ["It makes one
want to cry"].'

Late that night, while the festivities were in full swing, he tore himself
away and, returning the next morning to annotate some songs, found the
party still going strong – together with the rattle of twenty hammers
beating out copper vessels, and the yelling of youths with shining eyes
swaying together in a vast embrace. 'If ever my own life becomes insupportable I know where to turn for another,' he wrote to Quinn (3 March
1910), 'and I shall be welcomed in the tents.'

*

Back to Marseilles. 'In some respect it beats Liverpool even,' he wrote to
Chaloner Dowdall. He relished the roughness of the place. 'You ought
to let me take you round Marseilles one day,' he offered the Rani. 'There
are things there to raise the hairs on Rothenstein's back.' Now he knew
the night spots 'I feel ready to live here,' he told Dorelia. 'One sees
beautiful Gitano girls about with orange, green and purple clothes . . .
Hundreds of people to paint . . . One of the women, without being very
dark, is as splendid as antiquity and her character is that of the Mother
of God.'

But his letters to Dorelia were filled with anxiety. For however urgently he wrote, she did not answer him. When, for example, he asked for a bundle of postal orders and blank cheques to be sent, a registered envelope arrived at the poste restante which, since he still travelled without a passport, could not be released to him. After summoning two stalwart gypsies to swear in strange tongues as to his identity, he was eventually allowed to open the envelope, which was found to contain a dentist's bill. He began besieging Dorelia with telegrams. 'As you don't answer my three telegrams I conclude you have had enough of me.' What trickle of news did come through worried him. 'You had better see a doctor about your poor tummy,' he had written near the start of his journey, ' – and so leave nothing undone that might be good for you. Tell him you thought you had a fausse couche the other day. *Now do!*' The only information he had received since then was a note telling him she was suffering from mysterious pains in her side. 'Your belly is very enigmatic,' he replied. 'You'd better come this way at the next period and make sure. You'd don't want to have any more babies just yet. I don't suppose you'ld better Pyramus and Romilly. Don't forget to write . . . Au revoir, my love, I wish you were here.'

Finally she wrote. 'I was overjoyed to hear from you,' he answered. 'I was steeling myself for another disappointment.' The news itself was bad – and good. She *was* pregnant again: it had been a 'false miscarriage'. She would join him in Provence, together with her friend Helen Maitland and a detachment of family. 'This is splendid news!' Augustus wrote back cheerfully. 'I hope it'll be another boy! Glad your belly has settled down to proper working order. I wonder what part of the babe will be missing. Its kâri perhaps, in which case it may turn out to be a girl after all.'

'Certainly she deserves a rest & holiday,' Lamb remarked, but 'travelling with Augustus is a rather doubtful way of getting it.' As for Dorelia herself, she seemed neither happy nor unhappy. Pregnancy was no mighty matter. 'The terrible thing is I am going to have another infant in August (I don't really mind),' she wrote to Ottoline (February 1910). '. . . It is sure to be another boy.'

In view of what was to happen, and of the criticism voiced by Henry Lamb that Augustus was endangering Dorelia's life, as he had done Ida's, it is important to establish facts. An unusually intimate letter ('to no one else could I write so intimately') which Augustus sent Quinn (3 March 1910) reveals an aspect of what happened that seems to have been unknown to Henry Lamb and others. It also reveals a concern over this new pregnancy that Augustus was careful to keep veiled from Dorelia.

'The infernal fact is that she is in for another baby sometime this summer. God knows I've got plenty of kids as it is, and worst of all Dorelia is not in robust health. Her inside bothers her. I tried my best to avoid this – but she hates interfering with nature. All I hope is that she will at least get strong here. She insisted on bringing 3 of the youngest kids here; 3 remain in London and go to school.'

In his fashion he had been faithful to her, and besides she could always bring him to heel. Almost always. 'I went through Italy without sampling a single Italian female,' he gravely reassured Quinn. 'I saw, however, many with whom I slept (with my eyes open) in fancy.' He was to rejoin Dorelia at Arles. Travelling up there slowly from Marseilles, he wrote to Ottoline:

'These really barren hills round here *enchant* me . . . I visited this evening two bordels here . . . the ladies were not very beautiful, strictly speaking – but I found them very aimable . . . There was a mechanical piano which my acquaintance played with the utmost dexterity. I was thoroughly interested and lost more money than if I had been a "client sérieux".

At Avignon also I introduced myself into a bordel – "une maison très sérieuse". The ladies of these establishments are absolute slaves. The patron took all this money and the travailleuses are not allowed to quit the house without permission. However they don't complain – si le patron est gentil et pour vu qu'il y aurait beaucoup de clients. They are excessively simple.'

Two days later, 'looking incredible with some white veil over her head',[144] Dorelia arrived.

*

She came with Pyramus, Romilly and Edwin; and with Helen Maitland. Helen was now her closest friend. She was a striking girl, with clear grey-blue eyes, a rosy complexion and finely formed features. Rather small, she held herself upright and moved with a slow, purposeful stride. The set of her face expressed a somewhat daunting determination; her tone of voice, flavoured with irony, was sometimes harsh: and she had a hard energy within. But it was her smile that was remarkable, softening her expression, sending out a challenge, an air of complicity. And it was this smile, which she offered like a bouquet of flowers, that made people pour out their troubles to her. For herself, she seldom spoke of her own difficulties. Like Dorelia, she was a listener.

Like Dorelia, too, she saw her life as a vocation to be fulfilled among artists. She was a woman who preferred, in a maternal fashion, to give love than to have the responsibility of receiving it. She was to marry, eight years later, the brilliant and burly Russian artist in mosaic, Boris Anrep – reputed to be the only man in London capable of standing up to Augustus in a fist fight; and in 1926 she was to leave him to live with

Roger Fry,[145] many of whose ideas on modern art she was said to have 'invited' out of his head. But now she was in love with Henry Lamb.

It was galling to Augustus that, even though Helen's love might not primarily be a thing of the senses, she should prefer the understudy to the star.[146] Besides, in her loyalty to Dorelia, she was quick to be critical of him. His sense of the ridiculous often reduced her to tears of laughter, but though she laughed, she was not happy. Her love affair with Lamb was going badly and she blamed this on his erratic moods which, she believed, he had picked up from Augustus. She disapproved of the insensitive treatment of women on the excuse that they were raw material for art. Such masculine self-importance stirred her fighting qualities. Men she treated as children, and children as nonentities. She preferred men who sustained her belief that women were the more practical sex and should manage things. It was a belief shortly to be tested.

They assembled, the six of them, at Arles and caught the same train south which Augustus had taken the previous month along the Étang de Berre. Like a jewel in a chain changing colour and extending between the barren hills, the great lake seemed to mesmerize them all. 'I have seen this Etang de Berre looking wonderful,' Helen wrote to Lamb, 'it has these pale brown hills all around and it's small enough to get perfectly smooth the moment the wind is down and then the colours are lovely – very brilliant green one evening with a blue sky. All the way from Arles I was ecstatic with delight . . . simply speechless with astonishment at the curious light blue of one Etang we passed. It was so bright that it made the sky look dull and dark. They had planted cypresses all along the line so we only saw it for a moment or two now and again through a break in them. But I doubt if any mortal could have stood such loveliness much prolonged. On the other side was a vast stony plain, quite limitless and bare except for sage bushes and sheep. '

They were en route for the town whose spires Augustus had briefly seen rising from the waters on his first journey to Marseilles. At Pas des Lanciers they descended, ate their food squatting in a circle on the platform, then changed to a little railway line whose train skirted the Étang, passing close under hills of extraordinary shape, some very thin with jagged edges stacked one behind another and all bare except for grey aromatic herbs in patches – thyme, lavender and sage. At every orchard, at almost every cowshed, the train would stop. But at last they came to Martigues.

*

'An enchanting spot this, situated in the water at the mouth of an island sea where it joins the Mediterranean,' Augustus wrote to Ottoline. '. . . I have seen so many powerful women whose essential nudity no clothing can disguise. In the little port at hand are found sea-farers from all the shores of the Mediterranean.'

For several days they stayed at a hotel, then moved into 'an admirable logement unfurnished and unwallpapered, with a large room in which to paint'. This was the Villa Ste-Anne, a house they were to keep, using it intermittently, for the next eighteen years. On the outskirts of Martigues, along the route to Marseilles, it stood upon a steep yellow bank overlooking the blue waters of the lagoon. From the terrace stretched a plantation of pine trees, and all around were trackless stones, and rocky grey hills interfused with heather and sweet-smelling herbs. To Dorelia's delight, they had a large wild garden with olives, vines, almonds, figs and 'weeds all over the ground which is covered in pale coloured stones'.[147]

For the time being they shared the villa with its proprietor, a hawk-faced Huguenot with a passion for flying named Albert Bazin. Over twenty experimental years he had constructed a squadron of aeroplanes, all of which *flapped their wings*. From time to time, while Mme Bazin delivered a narrative of proceedings from the shore, he would launch one of them, like some enormous gnat, across the waters where at a desperate rate it would rise fractionally from the waves, sweep through a wide arc, then plunge into the bosom of the lake. Although these machines were always reduced to salads, Bazin himself was miraculously unhurt. With the arrival of Augustus his aviation fantasies soared to their highest altitude. For he recognized in this painter the perfect 'jockey' for his machines, and a source of revenue with which to continue his inventive industry. Augustus was delighted with this philosopher of the air and promised to sound out various art patrons on his behalf. Bazin needed, initially, a mere two hundred pounds (equivalent to £9,400 in 1996) to take off and 'it must be found', Augustus informed Ottoline (May 1910), since he was the 'finest man and aviator in France'. But it was Quinn who, through many months, bore the brunt of Augustus's enthusiasm. In letter after letter he was buried under information about this 'real savant as regards flying matters', flooded with journals that contained articles by Bazin proving that he 'has got ahead theoretically at least of the other men' such as Blériot. Augustus's appeals took many forms. Would Quinn like 'to collaborate with him and his machine No. 8 which ought to be ready in the autumn, if he finds the cash?' Could some 'American energy' be harnessed for 'my bird-like neighbour'? Perhaps someone from 'the Land of Enterprise' might investigate his 'case'. 'I wrote to you lately as longwindedly as I could about Albert Bazin,' Augustus reminded him (23 May 1910). '. . . Do not be bored with Bazin yourself but bore your friends as much as you can.' Quinn alternated between alarm on Augustus's behalf

– 'don't you attempt to go out on Bazin's machine' – and alarm on his own: 'Personally I can't afford to "take a flyer" now myself.' Although any appeal to bore his friends was irresistible, he disliked such methods when applied to himself. 'Say at once if you are not interested in the matter,' Augustus would beg him like someone stone deaf, 'and I will cease to bore you.' 'I am afraid it is hopeless!' cried Quinn. But Augustus, approaching the problem from a different angle, urged: 'He [Bazin]'s got a fine young daughter of 18 summers. The fact might as well be mentioned – in view of the collaboration.' 'I'd rather collaborate with his daughter than I would with the old man,' Quinn conceded, adding however that 'Marseilles seems to be far off'. But though the geography might be poor, the biology was strong enough, he insisted: 'I may tell you that not eating much meat and not drinking lessens the strain on the testicles . . . I have doubled my efficiency since I quit eating so much and since I stopped drinking. If only I could cut out smoking entirely, I would treble my efficiency.'

The pattern of life at the Villa Ste-Anne, though confused a little by good intentions, was straightforward. 'I am installed in this little house with a batch of family and hard at work,' Augustus promised Quinn (2 April 1910). 'The weather has been glorious and we have been out of doors all day for weeks.' They bought a boat and spent many days dreamily rowing across the glass-like surface of the lake. 'From time to time, as with dread I looked down into the bottomless void beneath us,' Romilly John recalled, 'an enormous jellyfish of a yellowish grey colour sailed by, trailing in gentle curves long streamers decorated with overlapping purple fringe: it seemed to emphasize the spatial quality of the blue depths.'[148]

This was a good place for the children. There was a donkey, plenty of berries, the stretch of salt water and 'a rock we play on', Caspar explained in a letter to his aunt, Ursula Nettleship. For Caspar especially this was a magical holiday as, naked and starry-eyed, he watched the fanatical birdman skimming over the lagoon in his primitive machine, and dreamed of growing wings himself and flying. It was 'the tender age of aerial experimentation' and these pioneers, the Wright brothers 'hopping like wounded birds among the sand dunes of North Carolina',[149] and Blériot the previous year making the first aeroplane crossing of the English Channel, and Bazin ('a crank but he was not mad'), dedicating their lives to this dream of flight, were all heroes to Caspar who, during the 1930s, would be the top aviator of the Fleet Air Arm.

While Dorelia took the children off for water-picnics, Augustus would harness the donkey and go on long sketching expeditions. 'One sees much more by these means,' he told Quinn (2 April 1910), 'and one doesn't go to sleep.' At night, while Dorelia cooked and the children eventually fell

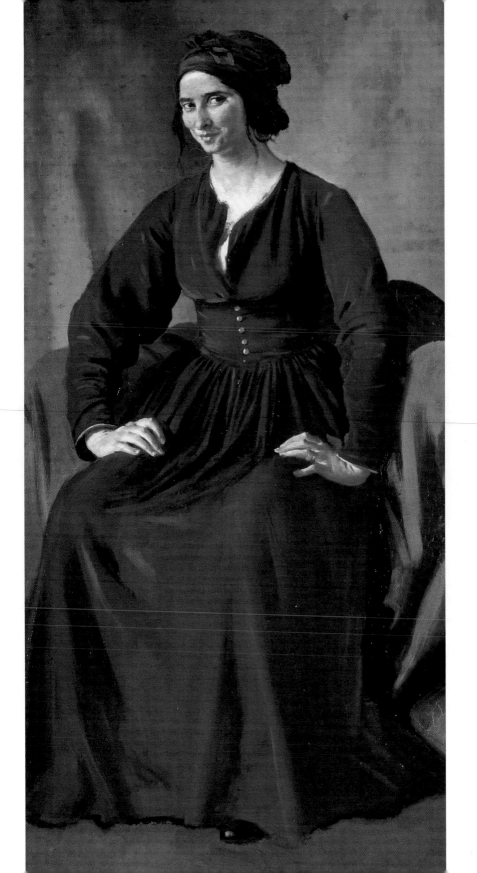

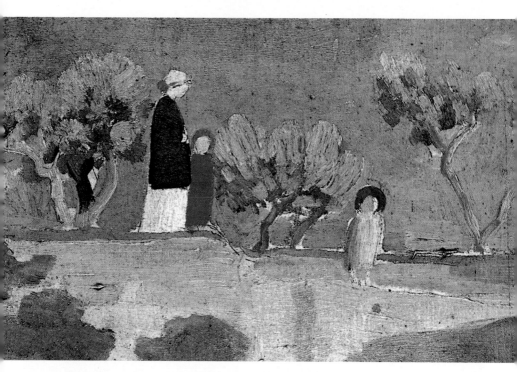

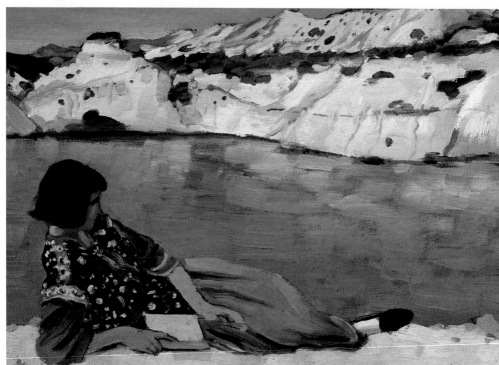

PREVIOUS PAGE The Smiling Woman, *portrait of Dorelia* (1909).
TOP Near the Villa Ste-Anne *(Martigues, 1910).*
ABOVE The Blue Pool *(Furzebrook, Dorset, 1911).*

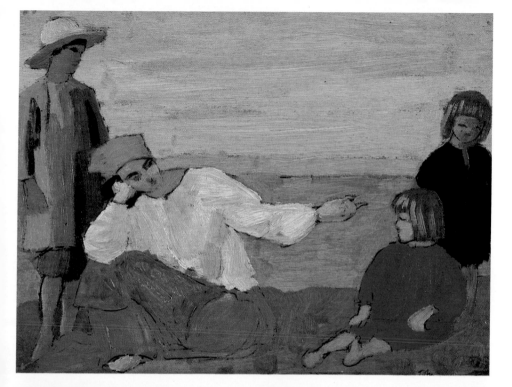

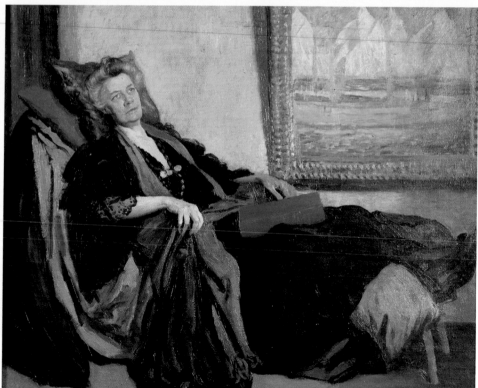

TOP Dorelia with Three Children (*Martigues, 1910*).
ABOVE Jane Harrison, *Lecturer in Classical Archaeology at Newnham College* (1909). *The painting on the wall is Wilson Steer's* Yachts.
OVERLEAF The Marchesa Casati (*Paris, 1919*).

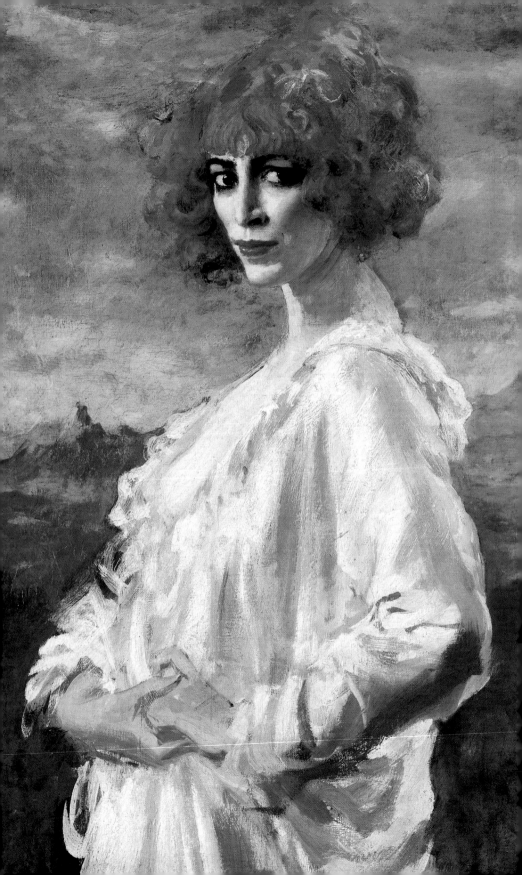

into bed, Augustus would read: gypsy literature from Liverpool, Provençal masters such as Daudet and Mistral, poems from Symons and prose from Wyndham Lewis, the works of Léon Bloy, and old copies of the *New Age*.

Gypsies would sometimes pass the door, be invited in for a drink and a talk, and stay several days. Somehow there was always enough food for them. 'We had the house full of gypsies for about a week,' Dorelia wrote to Ottoline (May 1910). '. . . It was great fun. They would dance and sing at any hour of the day.'

At intervals, when the supply of gypsies grew scarce, Augustus would take himself off to Marseilles and team up with 'some Gitano pals' who were teaching him to play the guitar. From here he could keep watch on a piece of waste ground outside the town over which passed a strange procession: bear-leaders from the Balkans; wagon-loads of women; Russians 'fresh from Russia'; a pantalooned tribe of Turkish wanderers from Stamboul 'in little brown tents of ragged sacking far from impervious to the rain', waiting for a boat to Tangier; a band of mumpers from Alsace ('a low unprofitable company'); Irish tinkers, Dutch nomads, French Romanichels, travellers from southern Spain, Bosnians, Belgians, Bohemians, Bessarabians – 'the travelling population of France is enormous.'[150] If only he could import some into Surrey, and let them breed!

His word-lists grew longer and his calligraphy more fevered. Of everyone he inquired about Sainte Sara and the gypsy pilgrimage to Saintes-Maries-de-la-Mer. 'This pilgrimage may be the last of the old pilgrim mysteries of the gypsies,' he assured Scott Macfie (14 May 1910). He ransacked the library at Aix; he reverently inspected the bones of the Egyptian saint at Saintes-Maries. But beyond various stories of miraculous cures he could discover little. It did not matter. For though Sainte Sara was a problem to be solved by the Gypsy Lore Society, to Augustus she remained a symbol, and the annual fête at Saintes-Maries a renewed act of faith. As such, it presented itself to him as a picture by Puvis de Chavannes, and would dominate the last years of his life.

His letters to Scott Macfie intersperse gypsy scholarship with exploits among the 'inveterate whores of Marseilles'[151] whom he contemplated introducing into his decorations for Hugh Lane. They were everywhere, like an army of occupation. To run the gauntlet of what he called 'this fine assortment of Mediterranean whores',[152] he resorted, Wyndham Lewis-style, to the protection of a voluminous cloak – 'a cloak albeit of stout fabric' – like a bandit. 'Why does the employment of a prostitute cause one's last neglected but unbroken *religious* chord to vibrate with such terrifying sonority?' he suddenly demanded (16 March 1910). From Liverpool came little response to these Dostoevsky-like rumblings, and Augustus was left to ponder them alone.

'As to whores and whoredom, considered from the purely practical point of view (never really pure) as a utility it is an abomination which stinks like anybody else's shit,' he volunteered (30 March 1910); 'considered morally it is a foul blasphemy which must make Christ continually sweat blood: but without either point of view, there is an aspect of beauty to be discovered – which indeed jumps at one's eye sometimes – whores, especially at 20 sous la pusse, have often something enigmatic, sacerdotal about them. It is as if one entered some temple of some strange God, and the "intimacy" really doesn't exist except to reveal the untraversable gulfs which can isolate two souls.'

To 'know' someone in the biblical sense, and to know her otherwise not at all; to preserve the stranger-element in a physical union; this symbolized, without speech, the loneliness of human beings. No one said anything, and nothing was expected. The relationship was a single act with no descent into tedium, no clash of wills. It was the implications of the act rather than the act itself that lived in the imagination. A number of times this spring and summer Augustus took off for Marseilles, drank whisky, 'misbehaved', and returned to Martigues the better for it. But this was, he admitted to Scott Macfie (3 April 1910), 'a dangerous subject'.

*

Henry Lamb had recently written to Ottoline Morrell suggesting a *ménage-à-six*. There would be the two of them, and of course her Philip and naturally his Helen Maitland. And then inevitably, for the sake of continuity, there would be Augustus and Dorelia. He illustrated the proposal with a diagram of himself as a bee, flitting round the circle. It was not the sort of joke that much amused Ottoline. Perhaps Henry, in his efforts to free himself of Augustus, was becoming too greatly influenced by Lytton Strachey.

Ever since they had settled into Martigues, Augustus and Dorelia had been inviting Ottoline to visit them in their new villa. But she remembered that damp meadow outside Cambridge. However, she did agree to meet them at Cézanne's house in Aix-en-Provence.

Augustus and Dorelia travelled all day in their donkey cart. Ottoline found them sitting outside a café, Dorelia very beautiful in a striped cotton skirt, a yellow scarf covering her head; Augustus, his square-cut beard now pointed in the French manner, 'which made him look like a dissipated Frenchman, as his eyes were bloodshot and yellow from brandy and rum'.[153] Together they went to Cézanne's house on the outskirts of Aix, which still contained a number of his pictures including the murals of the four seasons mysteriously inscribed 'Ingres'; and the next day they explored the town. Augustus, Ottoline observed, was a bored and weary sightseer.

'In the afternoon when we returned we found him sitting outside a café drinking happily with the little untidy waiter from the hotel and a drunken box-maker from the street nearby. In his companions he requires only a reflecting glass for himself, and thus he generally chooses them from such inferiors. He seems curiously unaware of the world, too heavily laden and oppressed with boredom to break through and to realize life.'[154]

Ottoline left Aix with the secret conviction that she, rather than Dorelia, could have guided Augustus 'into greatness such as Michelangelo, Cézanne or Van Gogh'.

His second expedition that summer could only have confirmed Ottoline in this conviction. It was to Nice – 'a paradise invaded by bugs (human ones)'[155] – and involved what he called 'some mighty queer days' with Frank Harris. He had first met Harris in Wellington Square, Chelsea, with Max Beerbohm, Conder, Will Rothenstein and others. With his booming voice and baleful eye, Harris imposed himself upon the company by sheer force of bad character – or so it appeared to Augustus, whose attention was taken up with the stately figure of Constance Collier, the flamboyant actress somewhat improbably engaged to Max Beerbohm. While Harris was holding the floor, Augustus suggested to this 'large and handsome lady' that she sit for him, adding, perhaps tactlessly, that he would have to find a bigger studio. 'Why not take the Crystal Palace then?' boomed Harris, suddenly exploding into their conversation: and everyone laughed. He was, Augustus rather sourly observed, very much the *pièce de résistance* of the party, a position Augustus preferred to occupy himself. Like Augustus, Harris presented a bold front to the world. 'Stocky in build, his broad chest was protected by a formidable waistcoat heavily studded with brass knobs,' Augustus wrote. 'With his basilisk eyes and his rich booming voice he dominated the room. Hair of a suspicious blackness rose steeply from his moderate brow, and a luxuriant though well-trained moustache of the same coloration added a suggestion of Mephistopheles to the *ensemble*.'[156]

Harris took an apparently flattering interest in Augustus, claiming in return that 'he praised my stories beyond measure' – the sort of high-flown approval he regretted being just unable to accord Augustus's paint-ings. This was a preliminary exercise in psychological outmanoeuvring. In fact Augustus had not greatly admired Harris's fiction, but praised *The Man Shakespeare* as 'a wonderful book', in what Harris called a 'most astonishing letter' which he would put with his 'collection of letters from Browning, Matthew Arnold, Carlyle, Coventry Patmore, Huxley, Swinburne and Wilde'. To this literary judgement Harris also responded with a burst of artistic criticism: 'The quality of his [John's] painting is poor – gloomy and harsh – reflecting, I think, a certain disdainful bitterness of character which does not go with the highest genius.' Then, describing Augustus as 'a draughtsman of the first rank, to be compared with Ingres, Dürer and Degas, one of the great masters', he bought a drawing, persuaded Augustus fulsomely to inscribe it to him, then sold it for a nice profit to a dealer where, to his irritation, Augustus later stumbled across it.

In an unfair world, where it was always necessary to turn the tables on those who were over-gifted, Harris saw Augustus as a potentially superior version of himself – a deep lover of women, a lusty drinker, a creature of fantasy and talent, a rebel Celtic artist who disdained the social successes that Harris had coveted. Lunching at the Café Royal at the time *The Man Shakespeare* was published (autumn 1909), Harris was struck by Augustus's height, beauty and 'great manner' which, he wrote, 'swept aside argument and infected all his hearers. Everyone felt in the imperious manner, flaming eyes and eloquent cadenced voice the outward and visible signs of that demonic spiritual endowment we call genius.'[157]

Harris was then considering himself in the role of prosperous gallery owner. His blandishments, mixed in with pious references to Jesus Christ, continued to arrive by post that winter, first from Ravello, then from Nice. He believed Augustus might do worse than illustrate his story 'The Miracle of the Stigmata', and urged him: 'Don't be afraid of telling me of any faults you may see' in his books, however difficult this might be. Eventually in the spring of 1910 Augustus agreed to visit him. He arrived at Nice station dressed in corduroys and with his painting materials in a small handbag. On the platform he was met by Harris decked out in full evening dress, apparently disconcerted by his guest's lack of chic, yet determined to carry him off to the Opera House where he had a box lent to him by the Princess of Monaco. Here his wife Nellie awaited them 'attired for the occasion in somewhat faded and second-hand splendour'. The composer of 'the infernal din' to which they were subjected soon joined them and, taking a dislike to Augustus on sight, restricted his compliments to Harris. Augustus gathered that 'I was assisting at a meeting between "the modern Wagner" and "the greatest intellect in Europe".'[158]

What happened later that night and on subsequent nights back at Harris's home was peculiar. 'I was shown my room which, as Frank was careful to point out, adjoined Nelly's, his own being at a certain distance, round the corner . . . Before many hours passed in the Villa, I decided I was either mad or living in a mad-house. What I found most sinister was the behaviour of Nelly and the female secretary. These two, possessed as it seemed by a mixture of fright and merriment, clung together at my approach, while giggling hysterically as if some desperate mischief was afoot.' Ten years later Nellie Harris hinted to the biographer Hesketh Pearson that she had repulsed Augustus's advances during this visit.[159] Whatever the facts, Augustus came to an opposite conclusion, sensing a deeply laid Harris plot.

What is so strange in testing for the truth of this episode is that Harris was extremely possessive of Nellie; while Augustus, though he often gets details wrong (such as Harris's house at Nice) and embroiders facts, had little gift for invention. He had come to suspect that, by taking advantage of Nellie's night-time propinquity, he would lay himself open to Harris's 'requests' for money. That Harris was keen on raising funds is undeniable, yet Augustus's interpretation of what was in his mind was probably wrong. Harris was, in the view of the artist J. D. Fergusson, a Robin Hood robbing the rich in order one day to reimburse the poor. His vendetta was carried on against the socially successful for the ostensible benefit of the writer and artist. That he himself was poor and a writer enabled him to begin and end many of these charitable exercises at home. Although Augustus could congratulate himself on having 'failed' Harris, it seems more likely that he played up perfectly. From Carlyle onwards, Harris sought to humiliate, usually in some sexual context, those he admired. Such men pointed the way to all that Harris prized – power and the love of women – but at their own risk, for Harris's route was paved with their exposed lives. He resented that his own notoriety as a biographer should depend upon the fame of other men. Shakespeare was beyond his reach, if only in time; but his books on Shaw and Wilde, and his series of 'Contemporary Portraits', ring loud with this rival-complaint. His novels and short stories reveal Harris's hopes of self-greatness. In *Undream'd of Shores*, for example, there is an account of a great Mogul ruler, curiously similar to Harris, who tells the girl he loves that there are many men handsomer and stronger than he. But she denies this, asserting that he is the most splendid man in the Court, for 'although he was only a little taller than the average' there was, she reminds him, his 'black eyes and hair and his loud deep voice'. Harris set up situations which allowed him to score off those who were publicly acknowledged to be handsome, talented, tall and romantic. Harris's Contemporary Portrait of Augustus reveals his attraction and resentment unashamedly.

'It was Montaigne who said that height was the only beauty of man, and indeed height is the only thing that gives presence to a man. A miniature of Venus may be more attractive than her taller sisters, but a man must have height to be imposing in appearance, or indeed impressive.'

Harris then goes on to portray Augustus as a perfect example of the male species.

'Over six feet in height,* spare and square shouldered, a good walker who always keeps himself fit and carries himself with an air, John would draw the eye in any ground. He is splendidly handsome with excellent features, great violet eyes and long lashes . . . he is physically, perhaps, the handsomest specimen of the genus homo that I have ever met.'

Yet this was the man who, three nights in succession, had been rejected by Nellie; who had failed precisely where Harris was successful. His pitfall, Harris insists, 'is not drink'. Jesus drank. No: if he fails 'it will be because he has been too heavily handicapped by his extraordinary physical advantages. His fine presence and handsome face brought him notoriety very speedily, and that's not good for a man. Women and girls have made up to him and he has spent himself in living instead of doing his work.'

By the third night at Harris's villa Augustus had had enough and, shouldering his belongings, stole out at dawn and made his way down the hill to Nice harbour, where he laid up in a sailors' café. 'Ah! the exquisite relief! To be alone again and out of that infected atmosphere, that mad-house!'[160] It was an instance of that 'certain abruptness of manner' without which, Harris gleefully noted, 'he would be almost too good-looking'.

In his amusing descriptions of Harris thirty years later, Augustus attempts to get something of his own back by taking it out of him *visually*. Harris, he observes, 'was looking his ugliest' by the third day; while Nellie (then in her thirties and not unattractive) is converted into a middle-aged matron. But when, in 1929, Augustus first read Harris's Contemporary Portrait of him, he was not amused. In a letter to Harris's biographer Elmer Gertz (25 May 1929), he explains that he had left Harris's villa 'because I found the moral atmosphere of the place unbearable . . . I could not consent to stay as the guest of a cad and bully posing as a man of genius.' Besides, his host's habit of dragging the name of Jesus Christ into any conversation was obnoxious 'coming from a man of Harris's moral standards'.[161] Here, unmistakably, is the pomposity of Edwin John, his father. His fear of blackmail marks the first hereditary pull towards that inflated caution with which, in later years, he sought to protect himself. 'It seems hopeless for me ever to attempt to conceal even the secrets of the water-closet from the outside world,' he complained to Wyndham Lewis (July 1910). 'There will still be an industrious person with a rake stationed at the other end of the sewer. It is true that I don't

---

* Augustus was actually just under six feet, but walked tall.

put myself out for secrecy . . .' But the superficial film of secrecy had already begun to grow.

*

The effects of his visit to Nice lingered with Augustus like a bad hangover. 'I expect he would be less gloomy with just his Family,' Helen Maitland confided to Lamb. Soon afterwards she left Martigues to join Lamb, having assured herself that Dorelia 'seems better. She doesn't get a pain in her side anymore.'

A few weeks later, in the early morning of Monday 1 May, Dorelia gave birth prematurely to a dead child at the Villa Ste-Anne. Throughout that day her life hung agonizingly in the balance. 'She *nearly* died afterwards of loss of blood and was really saved by having sea-water injected into her body,' Augustus wrote to Quinn (5 May 1910). '. . . The child, which was a girl, would have been welcome 3 months hence. It had got displaced somehow.' Pale and weak, Dorelia kept to her bed for a month. 'Happily she has more common sense than would be needed to fit out a dozen normal people and doesn't worry herself at all, now that she is comfortable.'

Augustus was less calm. The hideous threat of puerperal fever which had killed Ida terrified him – 'I know that demon already too well.' He was seized with a panic of guilt and helplessness. Now that his family was so scattered – three children in France, three in London, and one, Henry, in Hampshire – he needed more than ever a strong centre to his life. If Dorelia died, everything fell apart. Being 'totally without help except for the neighbours', he wired Helen Maitland, who returned bringing with her Henry Lamb. 'We made an amnesty for these peculiar conditions,' Lamb explained to Ottoline. With Dorelia and Helen in the house, Lamb assumed a very John-like role, and it was difficult for Augustus to object, though he feared, in Lamb's wake, tremors of gossip.[162] Only when it was clear that Dorelia was 'on the high road to recovery' did Lamb leave, after which Helen kept him informed by letter. 'Her lips are dreadfully pale but I think she's getting better really' (19 May 1910). In another letter she observed: 'Dorelia, you know, doesn't care for herself and if she thinks she does for other people I am sure it's a mistake and it's something else that she minds.'

Though she had brought a packet of tea with which to combat the crisis, Helen was handicapped by being unused to children and cooking.[163] Her meals may well have helped to subdue the boys, and they began to tell even on Augustus's constitution. 'He is very saintly the way he eats the strange food put before him and even finds ways of pretending to like it,' she wrote to Lamb.

By 25 May, Augustus reported that Dorelia 'is getting strong. She is gay to ravishing point.'[164] They had emerged at last from their 'awful adventure' but, anxious to avoid any possibility of a relapse, Augustus planned to import 'a sturdy wench' into the house to do the work as soon as Helen left. 'We have an abominably pretty housemaid,' he was able to complain a little later that summer.[165]

Dorelia's illness overshadowed the rest of that summer at Martigues. For a time Augustus took a studio in Marseilles – 'an astonishing town', he assured Quinn (28 May 1910), 'probably the dirtiest in Europe'. But he grew ill with a series of stomach disorders cheerfully diagnosed by Dorelia as appendicitis, cancer and ulcers. Personally he blamed the climate, which was too hot, too dry and too windy. By July the other four children arrived – something Augustus strongly welcomed in theory – and their complaints were added in chorus to his own. 'I have my whole family over here now, and it's a good deal,' he conceded.[166] Regular cheques from Quinn and Hugh Lane arrived; but he was more resistant to this medicine now. He found himself a martyr, suddenly, to homesickness. 'There are no green fields here,' he noticed (5 August 1910), 'scratch the ground and you come to the rock . . . a green meadow smells sweet to me . . . This place doesn't succeed in making me feel well – but I have intervals of well being.'[167] A curious longing for the west of Ireland swept over him, and for the people of Ireland with their wry ramshackle ways, so much more appealing than the complacent natives of Provence. 'These people are too bavard [talkative],' he told Ottoline (5 August 1910), 'too concrete – too academic even. They all look as if they've solved the riddle of the universe and lost their souls in the process.'

In this mood he decided to return to London before the end of September and, though he at once regretted this decision, it gave a zest to his last month there. He was working once more against time, and this suited him. Although little finished work had been possible – or so he believed – he had lightened his palette and made many brilliant little studies that would, he calculated, be useful for his Hugh Lane decorations. He felt that he had begun something new 'with all the lust and keenness of a convalescent'.[168]

'What I have been about here is rapid sketching in paint,' he told Quinn (25 August 1910), 'and I can say (with some excitement) that it's only during the last week or two that I have made an absolute technical step . . . I want to live long!'

That November the fruits of Augustus's nine months abroad were shown at the Chenil Gallery in a one-man show entitled 'Provençal Studies and Other Works'. At the same time, a mile away, another exhibition had just opened: Roger Fry's 'Manet and the Post-Impressionists'.

SIX

Revolution 1910

WHAT THEY SAID AT THE TIME

'It is impossible to think that any other single exhibition can ever
have had so much effect as did that on the rising generation.'

Vanessa Bell

There can have been few more unfortunate times for a British painter to
have been born than in the 1870s. At home, he would have passed his
youth in an atmosphere of genteel tranquillity and then, at the onset of
middle age, been overtaken by changes unprecedented for their speed and
significance. It was difficult for such a painter not to be at some period
out of step with his age. For even in 1910 it was still possible to believe
one was living in Victorian times. Nothing very much had changed.
Victorianism had hardened into a tiny Ice Age, impervious to the intellectual fires that were lighting up the Continent.

Fear was the artificial stimulant that had kept nineteenth-century values
alive beyond their natural life span: fear of national decline and the rise
of the degenerate lower classes; fear of sex and the desire for birth control;
fear that the very implements of fear, poverty and religious superstition,
were losing their power; fear of foreigners.

Then, 'in or about December 1910 human character changed.' The
date was not arbitrary. Announcing[1] this change fourteen years later,
Virginia Woolf chose it so as to make Roger Fry's exhibition 'Manet and
the Post-Impressionists' (which actually opened on 8 November 1910) a
symbol of the way in which European ideas invaded English conservatism.
For the first time people in Britain saw the pictures of Van Gogh, Gauguin
and Cézanne, and in or about December 1910 the character of British art
changed. The Second Post-Impressionist Exhibition which, two years
later, admitted British artists, signalled the last opportunity for them to
choose the path they would follow and the view posterity would take of
them.

The 'awful excitement' which erupted after 'Manet and the Post-
Impressionists' was a journalistic freak diagnosed by Roger Fry as an

327

outbreak of British philistinism, more extreme than anything since Whistler's day. *The Times* critic declared a state of anarchy;[2] Robert Ross warned readers of the *Morning Post*[3] that the exhibiting artists were lunatics, and Charles Ricketts wrote to congratulate him on his percipience. Doctors were called in to pronounce on the pictures; Philip Burne-Jones saw in the show 'a huge practical joke organised in Paris at the expense of our countrymen', though Wilfrid Blunt could detect 'no trace of humour in it', only 'a handful of mud': and he summed up the exhibits as 'works of idleness and impotent stupidity, a pornographic show'. It was left to a Royal Academician, the 'desecrator' of St Paul's, Sir William Richmond, to strike a note of pathos: 'I hope that in the last years of a long life', he wrote, 'it will be the last time I shall feel ashamed of being a painter.'[4]

'Why do people get so excited about art?' asked Lytton Strachey. '. . . I must say I should be pleased with myself, if I were Matisse or Picasso – to be able, a humble Frenchman, to perform by means of a canvas and a little paint, the extraordinary feat of making some dozen country gentlemen in England, every day for two months, grow purple in the face!'[5]

The answer was that, in Frances Spalding's words, 'art is a carrier of ideology.'[6] Roger Fry succeeded as no one else had done in smoking out British philistinism from its lair. It was especially irritating to find this modern movement heralded by an acknowledged authority on the Old Masters. Fry used his exhibition of foreign artists, with their rearrangements of visual facts, their unconventional structures, their slapdash lack of finish, their provoking incorrectnesses and appalling liberties, to disturb ordinary comfortable ways of seeing things. Their strange relations of form suggested all sorts of exciting new possibilities. 'Perhaps no one but a painter can understand it and perhaps no one but a painter of a certain age,' wrote Vanessa Bell. 'But it was as if one might say things one had always felt instead of trying to say things that other people told one to feel.'[7]

Reading the newspapers, led by ponderous jokes in *The Times*, Hugh Blaker predicted the reversal of attitudes to come. 'Cultured London is composed of clowns who will, by the way, be thoroughly ashamed in twenty years time and pay large sums to possess these things. How insular we are still.'[8]

This extravaganza of journalism presenting the first draft of art history was to give critics a quick device with which to begin the story of twentieth-century art in Britain. But the two Post-Impressionist shows actually confused the art scene in London dramatically. That Sir William Richmond should find these exhibitions 'unmanly' was to be expected. What was unexpected was the reaction of Henry Tonks, who came to recognize in Roger Fry the counterpart of Hitler and Mussolini. Fry, to the irritation of Will Rothenstein and the amusement of Walter Sickert, became the leader of a band of young rebellious painters – before splintering from Wyndham Lewis and his regiment of Vorticists. The repercussions from these shows did not divide the sheep from the goats. As Eric Gill observed to Will Rothenstein: 'The sheep and the goats are inextricably mixed up.'

In this mix-up Augustus John's position was perhaps the most difficult of all to define. He had long been someone who said things he felt rather than what was expected of him. Indeed he was part of the change that was happening in human character. He was a pupil of Tonks, Fry's enemy, yet provoked the same feelings of shame and outrage as Fry did in many Royal Academicians, including Sir William Richmond who called him 'loathesome'. He admired Cézanne, was already influenced by Gauguin, but agreed with Sickert that Matisse was full of 'the worst art school tricks'. There seemed to be two opposing views of John's work during the first dozen years of the twentieth century. Surveying French trends from a British point of view in 1913, the art critic James Bone saw the new movement in English art as being 'largely influenced by the Pre-Renaissance Italian masters, by archaic Greek, Byzantine, Egyptian, and Assyrian art, and by the art of the Far East.

'Mr Augustus John, its leader, already occupies a position for which there is no parallel in our history in that his art, which is supported by many of the most fastidious and erudite connoisseurs of the time, has for its content democratic and revolutionary ideals of the most uncompromising kind ... [His art] has much in common with the French Post-Impressionists, although Mr John's development seems to have no connexion with their experiments; but the plastic freedom of Puvis de Chavannes undoubtedly gave importance to both schools. It is noticeable that they have sought in the first place to simplify their technical method as well as their representations. They use tempera, and in their experiments with oil have often reduced their colours to a few tints prepared beforehand ... they have stripped art of much that was comfortable and informing, of many graces and charms ... and it is natural enough that in the eyes of the older generation the result should have a naked, disquieting look. Mr John's masterpiece, *The Girl on the Cliff,* is like nothing else in English painting in the pure keenness of its imaginative invention. The master draughtsman of his time, he has been strong enough to yield up every appearance of skill and of grace, and to limn his idea with the fresh, short-cut directness of a child.

... His poetry is his own ... The old men look cunning and tough, the children untamed and fierce, the women deep-breasted, large-bodied, steady-eyed, like mothers of a tribe . . . John rarely shows a figure at work . . . He makes you see that his strong men and women in poor clothes, standing with beauty under cold skies, have chosen their part . . . The distrust of comfort, of cities, of society in its present organisation, even of civilisation, and the desire for a simple life and the recovery of the virtues that lie in a more physical communion with the earth, are all questions of the time [that] . . . many are putting to the test of experiment.'[9]

Such was the ideology of John's art. In 1909, when his pictures appeared along with those of Robert Bevan, J. D. Fergusson, Harold Gilman, Spencer Gore, Kandinsky and Sickert at the second Allied Artists' Association exhibition, he seemed a focus for all that was most modern in Britain. But Clive and Vanessa Bell who had earlier bought John's big decoration 'The Childhood of Pyramus' were to sell it in 1913. 'I wish we could get a Cézanne,' Vanessa wrote to Clive. 'It would be a great thing to have one in England.'[10] Once she had praised John's influence on Lamb ('His drawings are much freer than they were and have lost their rather unpleasant hardness');[11] now Lamb's work appeared to her deadly academic, and John himself somewhat sentimental. Clive Bell was to relegate John, along with Stanley Spencer, into nursery provincialism. Mature European art had 'jumped the Slade and Pre- Raphaelite puddles'.

'Manet and the Post-Impressionists' divided critics into those who, like Laurence Binyon, felt that 'none of these paintings could hold a candle to the *Smiling Woman* of Augustus John,'[12] and the art critic of *The Times* who wrote that, compared to the revolutionary painting in Paris 'the most extreme works of Mr John are as timid as the opinions of a Fabian Socialist compared with those of a bomb-throwing anarchist.'[13]

Like the Post-Impressionists, John was simplifying his forms and intensifying his colour. But Post-Impressionism had moved away from a reliance on subject-matter because, Fry explained to Vanessa Bell when he took her round the Grafton Gallery, 'likeness to nature was irrelevant in art unless it contributed to the idea or emotion expressed.'[14] Though John never used storytelling or moral emphasis, he relied on nature – on the non-dramatic theatre of nature – and the ideas and emotions arising from this staged subject-matter. The question was: had he failed to put his talent to the test of painterly experiment, or had he been able to achieve a good deal of what the Post-Impressionists achieved without breaking tradition? In short, was he a 'Post-Impressionist without knowing it'?

The trouble was, as the art critic Frank Rutter explained, 'nobody but

Mr Roger Fry and Mr Clive Bell can tell us who is a post-impressionist and who not.'[15] But Roger Fry and Clive Bell did not inevitably agree. 'I have always been an enthusiastic admirer of Mr John's work,' wrote Fry in the *Nation* on 24 December 1910. 'In criticising the very first exhibition which he held in London I said that he had undeniable genius, and I have never wavered in that belief, but I do recognise that Mr John, working to some extent in isolation, without all the fortunate elements of comradeship and rivalry that exist in Paris, has not yet pushed his mode of expression to the same logical completeness, has not yet attained the same perfect subordination of all the means of expression to the idea that some of these artists have. He may be more gifted, and he may, one believes and hopes, go much further than they have done; but I fail to see that his work in any way refutes the attainments of artists whom he himself openly admires.'[16]

Such isolation, which would eventually be perceived as a strength in Gwen John, was to be an increasingly unhappy and incomplete condition in Augustus, gradually removing him, a prominent but lonely figure, to the margins of the modern movement. What Virginia Woolf had called 'the age of Augustus John' was reaching its zenith, and over the next few years would rapidly fade away, leaving an unanswered question hanging in the air: was that legendary reputation of his early years a mirage or was the posthumous decline of that reputation 'a quirk of our own time'?[17]

*

In these years before the Great War, as the republican revolution in art spread from these two Post-Impressionist exhibitions around Britain, Wilson Steer seemed like an old king about to enter retirement, while Sickert occupied the role of Regent, and Augustus John, in his early and middle thirties, was the heir apparent. Whatever he did was news, and whatever he did added not so much to his achievement as to his promise of future achievements. 'Promise' was a word that was invariably applied to his work; he was credited and debited with it; it hung like a label round his neck, and eventually like a stone. Ever since the Slade days, he had been dogged by an enviable and excessive facility. His admirers were encouraged to detect in his drawings and paintings signs of infinite potential. However good a particular work might be – his 'William Nicholson', 'W. B. Yeats', 'Jane Harrison', 'The Smiling Woman', his drawings of Ida and Alick, his dream picture of Dorelia standing before a fence – it added only to the weight of his future. 'He seems always on the brink of tremendous happenings,' wrote the art critic of the *Pall Mall Gazette*.[18]

For the last dozen years these happenings had been constantly in the public mind, associated with everything romantic, brilliant and scandalous. 'He is the wonder of Chelsea,' exclaimed George Moore in 1906, 'the lightning draughtsman, the only man living for whom drawing presents no difficulty whatever.' Two years later (10 June 1908) the painter Neville Lytton, describing him as 'an anarchistic artist', told Will Rothenstein: 'I think John's daring and talent is an excellent example for us and shows us in which direction it is expedient for us to throw our bonnets over the windmills.' Some indication of the kind of fame he had achieved before 1910 is given by an exhibition of Max Beerbohm's caricatures in May 1909 at the Leicester Galleries. One of these, as described by Max himself, showed Augustus 'standing in one of his own "primitive" landscapes, with an awfully dull looking art-critic beside him gazing (the art-critic gazing) at two or three very ugly "primitive" John women in angular attitudes. The drawing is called "Insecurity"; and the art-critic is saying to himself "How odd it seems that thirty years hence I may be desperately in love with these ladies!" '[19]

Max's ambiguous attitude to Augustus's work reflected that of many contemporaries. At the Leicester Galleries his caricatures had been interspersed with pictures by Sickert and other artists – and 'John has a big (oils) portrait of Nicholson,' Max told Florence Beerbohm, ' – a *very* fine portrait, and quite the *clou* of the exhibition.'[20] Four months previously Augustus and Max had dined with the Nicholsons and Max afterwards described Augustus as 'looking more than picturesque ... [he] sang an old French song, without accompaniment, very remarkable, and seemed like all the twelve disciples of Christ and especially like Judas!' Admiration for his personality and for his painting were shot through with suspicion. 'I've got a very fishy reputation,' Augustus conceded. His appearance suggested some betrayal and his paintings caused bewilderment. 'He [John] has a family group at the Grafton,' Max wrote to Florence (April 1909), ' – a huge painting of a very weird family. I wish I could describe it, but I can't. I think there is no doubt of his genius.' Max considered 'The Smiling Woman' 'really great',[21] but many of the paintings, especially of women, struck him as crude and ugly. At the same time he believed, like his art critic, that he would be 'converted' to them and that future generations would acknowledge their lasting value. The 'promise' which he attributed to Augustus was a symptom of an age that had not adjusted its focus and did not really know what to think.

To what extent this faith in Augustus's work depended upon his glamorous personality is difficult to calculate. The artist Paul Nash, who did not know him and had 'a deep respect for John's draughtsmanship especially when it was applied with a paint brush', observed that 'technical power rather than vision predominated'.[22] But critics were disconcerted by his love of bravura and theatricality, his impromptu effects so prolific and unpredictable, and the emphasis he placed as a portraitist on candour and informality. He was worshipped by the young, and, until the 1920s, would remain a cult figure among students. The futurist painter C. R. W. Nevinson, to whom Augustus was 'a genius', noted that 'though I am always called a Modern, I have always tried to base myself on John's example'.[23] 'I like success, occasionally,' Augustus remarked. But he appeared to have achieved too easy a success – at the age of twenty-two, he was sharing a long notice with Giorgione. By the time he was thirty, critics had begun sprinkling their commendations with caveats. In 1907, in an article entitled 'Rubens, Delacroix and Mr John', Laurence Binyon wrote:

'Mr John has shown such signal gifts, and has such magnetic power over his contemporaries, that he might to-day be the acclaimed leader of a strong new movement in English painting; only he seems to have little idea as to whither he is himself moving . . . he will never know the fullness of his own capacities till he puts them to a greater test than he has done yet, till he concentrates with single purpose instead of dissipating his mind in easy response to casual inspirations of the moment . . .'[24]

Few questioned that here was a great draughtsman – but his work was felt to be too 'unconventional'. It was not 'normal' to search for distortion as he persistently did. What was this 'affectation' that made him deliberately misplace 'the left eye in the "Girl's Head"?' asked the *Magazine of Fine Arts*; '. . . it is difficult to follow the aim of the artist'.[25] The critic of *The Times* (3 December 1907) expressed, in a genial way, what many senior art critics thought about John's work: 'The artist, as is well known, is a favourite among the admirers of very advanced and modern methods; and, if he were a dramatist, his plays would be produced by the Stage Society. That is to say he is very strong, very capable, and very much interested in the realities of life, the ugly as well as the beautiful.'

Another critic, heralding what was to come, announced: 'One must go to Paris to see anything approaching the nightmares that Mr John is on occasion capable of.'[26]

By 1910 the Americans were discovering Augustus. His flamboyant portrait of William Nicholson was seen to be one of the strongest paintings at the International Exhibition held by the Carnegie Institute at Pittsburgh in 1910. When Quinn sent him a batch of notices from Philadelphia for Dorelia's 'scrapbook', Augustus replied (4 January 1910) that 'she don't keep one – when she *does* read my notices, it's with a smile.' She had begun, he added, to complain that they were no longer rude enough, and therefore not fun. 'I've never kept any of my press notices yet,' he told Quinn (23 May 1910), ' – doubt if I could find storing room for them, but I have a habit of sending some of them to my father, who likes it; reserving the scornful and abusive ones for my own delectation till I light my pipe or otherwise utilize them . . . The only ones who count are the inspired critic-clairvoyant and fearless – and the conscientious and equally fearless Philistine – and praise and blame from either are equally welcome and stimulating.'

By 1910 Augustus John dominated the New English Art Club to an extent where his failure to send in work to their exhibitions itself became headline news. Though still assailed by critics for his wilful distortion – an opinion that seems extraordinary today – he was generally considered the most avant-garde artist in the country.

'There are two artistic camps in England just now,' W. B. Yeats advised Quinn in 1909, 'the Ricketts and Shannon camp which carries on the tradition of Watts and the romantic painters, and the camp of Augustus John which is always shouting its defiance at the other. I sometimes feel I am divided between them as Coleridge was between Christianity and the philosophers when he said "My intellect is with Spinoza but my whole heart with Paul and the Apostles".'

Quinn's intellect too, supported by his purse, was with Augustus. At the famous Armory Show in 1913, the equivalent in the United States of the two Post-Impressionist shows in Britain, there were fourteen drawings, three works in tempera, and twenty oil paintings (including fifteen Provençal studies) by John. The American critic James Huneker declared that the three biggest talents among living European artists were Matisse, Epstein and Augustus John.

'It was not until 1911–12 that the gap widened considerably between the conservative New English and the committed progressives,' wrote the art historian Richard Shone.[27] Many critics who up to the autumn of 1910 had supported progressive art now found themselves agreeing with Wilfrid Blunt that the Post-Impressionist daubs at the Grafton Gallery were like 'indecencies scrawled upon the walls of a privy'. In retrospect it may appear that, in the last weeks of that year, the enlightened élite of Britain were reduced to half a dozen Bloomsbury intellectuals drawn up about the frail defiant figure of Roger Fry, while Augustus John fell away as a Little Englander. But it was not exactly so. Augustus's fifty Provençal studies at the Chenil Gallery seemed to many people more eccentric than those of 'the Frenchmen at the Grafton'. Reviewing his show, which he summed up as being 'a mystery', *The Times* critic asked (5 December 1910): 'What does it all mean? Is there really a widespread demand for these queer, clever, forcible, but ugly and uncanny notes of form and dashes of colour? . . . For our part we see neither nature nor art in many of these strangely-formed heads, these long and too rapidly tapering necks, and these blobs of heavy paint that sometimes do duty for eyes.'

These controversial pictures included primitive portrait-busts of his children which recall Tuscan work of the late fifteenth century; small rapid sketches in oil which suddenly made the British palette brilliant with blues and greens and crushed strawberry pinks before Spencer Gore and Harold Gilman began similar experiments with the Camden Town Group; glowing figures in landscapes that tell no story but simply show them bathing in or walking by the Étang de Berre, sitting in the sun or on the shaded steps of the Villa Ste-Anne. They were drawn on the wood in pencil and sometimes redefined over a thin skin of pigment, which produced a jewelled and painterly effect in the relation of the figures to their background of trees and sky, sand and water.

In notice after notice, critics linked these exquisite panels to the concurrent show of Post-Impressionists at the Grafton, and their tone is almost as hostile. 'At his worst he can outdo Gauguin,' wrote a critic in the *Queen* (10 December 1910), '. . . uncouth and grotesque . . . It is unfortunate that Mr John should go on filling public exhibitions with these inchoate studies, instead of manfully bracing to produce some complete piece of work.' Two years later, when the Second Post-Impressionist Exhibition coincided with the showing of Augustus's vast schematic decoration, 'Mumpers' at the NEAC, it was the latter which was seen by many critics to be the significant masterpiece in British painting. The *Sunday Times* and the *Daily Chronicle* both compared it to 'The Dance' by Matisse; the *Spectator* described it as a 'Déjeuner sur l'Herbe' 'more startling than Manet'; the *Manchester Guardian* stated it had won 'a new freedom for the artist'; the *Daily Mail* called it 'one of the greatest decorative works of our age'; the *Observer* declared it to be 'the first mature masterpiece of Post-Impressionism'; and *The Times*, in a leader, announced that it marked 'a turning-point in English painting'.[28]

Public opinion in these two years was turning towards Post-Impressionism, but not in its placing of Augustus's work as more 'advanced' and, in some cases, more incomprehensible than that of the Post-Impressionists. For many he was the last word in modernity. 'After Picasso,' wrote one critic, 'Mr John.'[29]

It was to be the war, galvanizing *avant-garde* art among British artists, that finally detached John's work from the modernist movement. The younger artists had formed up behind him, but he had had nowhere to lead them and they clocked in instead at Fry's Omega Workshops. Contemporary art critics, such as D. S. MacColl, had celebrated his bravura feats of draughtsmanship for the liberating effects they brought from Whistlerian 'daintiness' and their power to recapture the tradition of Rubens. Then art critics towards the end of the twentieth century, such as Simon Watney in his *English Post-Impressionism* (1980), reacted against this assessment and identified John as the victim of 'a highly exclusive connoisseur-orientated approach to art education',[30] which between 1910 and 1912 showed younger artists into what doldrums such acclaimed graphic dexterity led. But these critical assessments were confined to John's drawing and by default undervalued his early panels in oil as simply 'brilliant historicism'. Critics were in part influenced by two facts and a misinterpretation of those facts. The first of these was Augustus's description of 'Manet and the Post-Impressionists' as 'a bloody show'; the second was his refusal in 1912 to send in any pictures to the Second Post-Impressionist Exhibition, which included work by Epstein, Gilman, Gore and Nevinson.

The very time when he had begun to fulfil his much-trumpeted promise was the year that contemporary critics renewed their hostility to him and art historians have removed him from the forefront of British art. But in 1910, working independently in France and taking his inspiration from Italy, he had launched a private revolution of his own.

2

WHAT HE SAID

'Since the advent of Post-Impressionism Mr John has been almost forgotten . . . Many of his erstwhile champions have been so eager to uphold the fantastic banner of Matisse and Picasso's Falstaffian regiment that they have neglected the old leader who led them into unknown paths of danger . . . "Where is he? What is he doing?" At last he himself has answered in decisive fashion.'

Morning Post (23 November 1912)

'Is it that the atmosphere of England is oppressive?' Augustus asked Quinn (25 May 1910). 'Stendhal said a man lost 50% of his genius on setting foot on that island.' Almost fifty per cent of Augustus's post-Slade work had been done in France. He had met Picasso, seen the work of Cézanne in Provence and of Matisse in Paris. He had even read the novels of Dostoevsky before they had been put into English. Yet in two respects the Slade had held him back. He had been trained in a climate so regulated that it admitted only two schools of rival art; the academic art taught by Tonks and Brown based on classical and Renaissance models; and the academizing process carried on by the Royal Academy 'by which', Harold Rosenberg has written, 'all styles are in time tamed and made to perform in the circus of public taste.'[31] Augustus had learnt his lessons well and it had taken him time to 'see' a non-academic form of art that matched his talent.

Despite the time he had spent there, Augustus remained something of a foreigner in Paris. But in Provence he had come home. There was something of Wales here, he felt, something to which he responded instinctively. The country was rooted in a past to which he belonged and with which he could connect the work of Puvis de Chavannes and the great Italian masters he had been studying. He suddenly saw himself as being part of a tradition in painting, as being able to add to that tradition; and this feeling of belonging steadied him. Everything fell into place; what he had seen, where he worked, who he was.

'I am certain I have profited greatly by my visit to Italy,' he told Quinn on reaching Martigues (3 March 1910).

'My imagination and sense of reality seems to me just twice as strong as it was before – and no exaggeration . . . I tell you frankly and sincerely, I feel *nobody* dead or alive is so near the guts of things as I am at present . . . *What is surprising*, together with this infallible *realism* my sense of beauty seems to: *has*, grown simultaneously. All this remains to be proved of course. I give myself till the end of the year to prove it up to the hilt. And this comes, it seems to me, from being suddenly *alone* for some months, and seeing – and rubbing against (without committing myself too far) new people and also seeing certain pictures which crystallize the overwhelming and triumphant energy of dead men – like Signorelli for instance.'

There had been plenty of happenings to interrupt this stern pro-gramme, and the mood of confidence and resolution that supported it: drunken days with gypsies; irrelevant sorties with his bird-like neighbour and the air-machines; that distressing ambush of hospitality prepared for him by Frank Harris; Dorelia's illness and family complications. Yet this season there was more optimism, more resolve to say the word 'no'. He admits to 'floundering' at times, but returns stubbornly to his work and makes genuine progress. 'I wish to God I was born with more method in my madness – but it's coming,' he tells Arthur Symons. And, he confides to Quinn, 'I'm beginning to take a really miser's interest in my own value.' One of his problems is that, in periods of enthusiasm, he is inclined to turn away from his past to pursue anything new. 'I think little of my etchings so far,' he informed Quinn (28 May 1910), who had bought almost all of them, ' – but I'm keen to do a set of dry-points soon.' Temptation came to him in the form of an invitation to South Africa, where he was asked to found a school, decorate Parliament and paint ten portraits of South African celebrities for one thousand pounds (equivalent to £47,000 in 1996). These offers he turned down.

He was helped in his resolution by a book that Quinn had sent him early in May: James Huneker's *Promenades of an Impressionist*. He had been prepared to dislike it. At first sight there appeared too many Parisian anecdotes, too many picturesque phrases, and eulogies of bad artists such as Fortuny and Sorolla. But it was characteristic of his new seriousness this year to get beyond first sight. He persevered with the book and found it useful. 'He [Huneker] reminded me of many a thing I used to know but had, to my shame, forgotten,' he explained to Quinn (25 May 1910).

'His fresh and unfailing enthusiasm for a crowd of merits lesser minds think mutually destructive, is splendid . . . it is the gesture of a generous and hearty man – who seems to overflow with intellectual energy and does not husband it like poorer men . . . This book gives me the courage and humility of my boyhood. It is strong crude air after the finicking intellectuality of London which drives a sensitive spirit into subterranean caverns where thoughts grow pale like mushrooms. I have been assailed with manifold doubts and have taken refuge in dreams when I should have sharpened my pencil and returned to the charge. An artist has no business to think except brush in hand.'

'I am keen on a good show in the autumn,' Augustus had told Quinn (19 May 1910). The show which opened at the Chenil in December contained thirty-five drawings and etchings in the upper rooms, and downstairs fifty small 'Provençal Studies' in oils. It was the drawings upstairs that tempered the hostility of critics with a tone of regretful wonder; but it was the oils that represented his new achievement. Sometimes he saw these panels as preliminary studies for a set of complete fresco works on a magnificent scale, for he had been fired by Roger Fry's call in the *Burlington Magazine* the previous year for him to be given a great wall in some public building and a great theme to illustrate it. 'In Watts we sacrificed to our incurable individualism, our national incapacity of co-operating for ideal ends, a great monumental designer,' Fry had written. 'A generous fate has given us another chance in Mr John, and I suppose we shall waste him likewise. What would not the Germans do for a man of his genius if they ever had the chance to produce him?'[32] Such stirring words rang sweetly in John's ears; but they took no account of his lack of consistency, the fact that he painted best when in the grip of some intense but fleeting mood – the intensity arising from its very transitoriness. Fry, in many ways the greatest and most influential critic of his age, had little sense of individual talent in relation to particular theories. John was an unlikely person to co-operate, publicly and for any length of time, for civic ends. But Fry's commendation had a heroic tone that went on echoing in Augustus's imagination. Besides, it came on top of the big ambitions of Will Rothenstein and the immeasurable hopes of Hugh Lane on his behalf, as well as Charles Conder's view that large decorations were John's forte. In 1939, when opening an exhibition of photographs of contemporary British wall paintings at the Tate Gallery, he remarked: 'When one thinks of painting on great expanses of wall, painting of other kinds seems hardly worth doing.' Shortly afterwards, in a restaurant, he asked: 'I suppose they'd charge a lot to let Matt Smith and me paint decorations on these walls.'[33] Later still Joyce Cary was to use this frustrated longing to be a painter on a monumental scale in the creation of Gulley Jimson, the ebullient artist of his novel *The Horse's Mouth* (1944).

The oil sketches at the Chenil Gallery revealed, for the first time, a gift for colour. The pale hills of Provence with their olives and pines and their elusive skies, the summer light across the Étang mysteriously moving with sun and shade, seemed to have brought Augustus into a more vivid contact with nature. These figures or groups of figures reflect life as in a ballet – the girl on the sea's edge poised like some dancer, her hand on the barre of the horizon. The colour is clear and untroubled, brushed on with hasty decision – there is no niggling detail: they are austere, these panels, and often shamelessly unfinished. 'The technique appears to be, at its simplest, to make a pencil drawing on a small board covered with colourless transparent priming,' commented David Piper; 'then the outlines are washed in with a generous brush loaded with pure and brilliant oil colour – and there's a happy illogicality about it, for the lines of the drawing . . . are those of any John drawing, subtly lapping and rounding the volume they conjure up, but they are obliterated by the oils, and the result for effect relies on the inscape of vivid colour, on contrasting colour, and the broad flattened simplified pattern.'[34]

Never in his work had the tension between dream and reality, the ideal and the actual, been presented so lyrically by means so simple; never had the content been raised so free of a mere imitation of nature. John has no message for us. A painter, he told John Freeman, 'leaves his emotion behind so that people can share it'. The emotion in these pictures comes from the choreography and reflected light, from a sense of volume and outline. His method seemed far removed from the ordinary language of British art, and critics argued that he was using a curious shorthand. The most appreciative was the poet and dramatist Laurence Binyon, who had recently been appointed Assistant Keeper in the Department of Prints and Drawings at the British Museum. 'Somehow everything lives,' he wrote after seeing this Chenil Gallery exhibition.

'Even the paint, rudely dashed on the canvas, seems to be rebelling into beauties of its own. Mr John tries to disguise his science and his skill, but it leaks out, it is there . . . I do not know how it is, but these small studies, some of them at least, make an extraordinary impression and haunt one's memory. A tall woman leaning on a staff; a little boy in scarlet on a cliff-edge against blue sea; a woman carrying bundles of lavender: the description of these says nothing, but they themselves seem creatures of the infancy of the world, aboriginals of the earth, with an animal dignity and strangeness, swift of gesture, beautifully poised. That is the secret of Mr John's power. He is limited, obsessed by a few types . . . his ideas are few . . . But in it there is a jet of elemental energy, something powerful and unaccountable, like life itself.'[35]

In the course of this review Binyon compared these Provençal Studies to the brilliant colour and simplified form of Gauguin. Other critics compared this new work to that of Matisse,[36] Van Gogh[37] and Jules Flandrin,[38] all of whom were then exhibiting at the Grafton Gallery. The coincidence points to a parallel development in the minds of John and Roger Fry. In the month that John first saw the wall paintings of Luca Signorelli, Fry was writing of Signorelli as 'one of the family of the great audacious masters'.[39] The names of both Fry and John had, in the past, been primarily associated with those of the Old Masters. What they believed they had discovered was the *modernity* of certain Old Masters, such as Masaccio and Signorelli. Their enthusiasm for modern French painters sprang from their new understanding of the Italian Primitives.

John thought of Fry as a powerful writer, a disappointing artist and a man of credulous disposition who had nevertheless discovered 'wonderful things'. It was, as Quentin Bell wrote, 'remarkable' for a man of Fry's temperament and training to have realized that 'Cézanne and his followers were not simply innovators but represented also a return to the great tradition of the past, for such a conviction, which does not seem wonderful to-day, required an extraordinary effort of the mind in the year 1910'. It was perhaps even more remarkable that Augustus John should independently have guessed at a similar connection at the same time.[40]

3

WHAT HE SAID ABOUT THEM

'I seem to find I can paint better in France – and I meet a few people after my own heart.'

Augustus John to John Sampson (September 1919)

'It is good for him [Augustus] to be over here and meet such different people . . . I don't want to see any English pictures again except those by 2 or 3 artists.'

Gwen John to Ursula Tyrwhitt (February 1918)

'A bloody show!' John's words, reverberating down the decades, have been hailed as the first cry of the future Royal Academician.

He did say them – to Eric Gill who reported them by letter to Will Rothenstein. They represented his first reaction, not so much to the pictures themselves but to the chatter and outcry that rose from the first Post-Impressionist exhibition. From this time on he was to become increasingly touchy about publicity. It seems certain, from the date Gill must have written to Rothenstein, that Augustus had denounced the exhibition before going to see it. Certainly his first sight of it was distorted by all he had heard and read which, like a film, seemed to come between him and what he saw. He did not visit the Grafton until the show had been running a month. 'There is a show of "Post-Impressionists" now on here,' he noted in a letter to Quinn (December 1910), 'and my post-impression of it is by no means favourable.' That was all. Perhaps he was fearful of Quinn transferring his agency fees to Fry. However, in the last week of the exhibition, when the noise had died down, he went again. His opinion of the pictures is set out in a long letter to Quinn (11 January 1911).

'I went to the "Post-Impressionists" again yesterday and was more powerfully impressed by them than I was at my first visit. There have been a good many additions made to the show in the meanwhile – and important ones. Several new paintings and drawings by Van Gogh served to convince me that this man was a great artist. My first view of his works disappointed and disagreed with me. I do not think however that one need expect to be at once charmed and captured by a personality so remarkable as his. Indeed "charm" is the last thing to talk about in regard to Van Gogh. The drawings I saw of his were splendid and there is a stunning portrait of himself. Gauguin too has been reinforced and I admired enormously two Maori women in a landscape. As for Matisse, I regard him with the utmost suspicion. He is what the French call a fumiste – a charlatan, but an ingenious one. He has a portrait here of a "woman with green eyes" which to me is devoid of every genuine quality – vulgar and spurious work. While in Paris the other day I saw a show of paintings by Picasso which struck me as wonderfully fine – full of secret beauty of sentiment – I have admired his work for long . . . I forgot to mention *Cézanne* – he was a splendid fellow, one of the greatest – he too has work at the Grafton.'

It would take another ten years for him to come round to Matisse. Meanwhile he helped Quinn to buy a Gauguin ceiling (July 1913), and recommended (3 December 1912) work by Manet and Degas. He also wrote about the work of Maurice Denis and others (17 May 1912):

'I think Denis has a certain talent . . . I think him an intelligent, ingenious, and sincere man who makes the most of his gifts within the contemporary field. He is not, in my opinion, great by any means. Picasso now has genius, albeit perhaps of a morbid sort . . .

I wish we had gone to see Anquetin while in Paris. A man of immense gifts. Bye-the-bye if you come across a painting by Daumier, freeze on to it! One of the great Frenchmen. El Greco too is now coming into his own. A terrible, mysterious Spaniard – or rather Greek.'

He was interested by his British contemporaries too, writing copiously about their work to Quinn so that, in this way, he could help them without reprisals of gratitude. Such methods appealed alike to his generosity and secretiveness, and accurately reflected his attitudes from 1910 into the 1920s. For himself he bought work by, among others, Epstein, Wyndham Lewis, William Roberts and Christopher Wood. But about Ricketts and Shannon, artists who seemed to have more in common with himself (such as a reverence for Puvis de Chavannes), he was lukewarm: 'I have never succeeded in feeling or showing any great interest in *his* [Shannon's] work tho' I have remarked that personally he shows himself a man, one would say, of character,' he wrote to Quinn on 25 August 1910. 'He has a reserve which contrasts with the funny effervescence of Ricketts – who is the cleverer chap; but as for him, he has lost his innocence, he is corrupt . . . A man of his intellectual parts should keep himself straighter – at the risk of being stupid even.'[41]

Quinn relied on Augustus for information about contemporary British art. The first artist he recommended was Gwen who, like himself, was absorbing aspects of Post-Impressionism into her work, flattening the contours, emphasizing surface pattern. He was concerned, not about her artistic reputation, which was secure in his eyes, but her economic survival and her morale. 'I am touched by your gentle solicitude,' she told him in 1910. 'I think it would be wise to shake off this funeste fatigue.'[42]

In her dealings with Quinn, Gwen is in many respects the reverse of her brother. From Quinn's point of view, it was like looking towards their pictures through opposite ends of a telescope: his so awfully near, hers infinitely distant. Yet he was not a man to give up. He began in 1909 by offering her thirty pounds (equivalent to £1,400 in 1996) for any picture she cared to send him, and when that failed he paid her in advance and arranged for her to have an annual stipend. He badgered and bullied her until she felt breathless. After eight years of financial support he possessed only four of her paintings; after more than twelve years he owned six paintings and a few drawings. She was an extraordinary challenge to him, but he persevered, and eventually succeeded in buying almost every picture she sold. She thought him acquisitive and domineering, and 'he bores me'. Yet his patience, financial generosity, genuine interest and enduring encouragement stimulated her and during a period of six months in the last year of his life she sent him half a dozen paintings and five drawings. Meanwhile, watching their negotiations anxiously from the sidelines, Augustus continued counselling Gwen to retain Quinn's goodwill, while triumphantly forfeiting it himself.

He recommended work by John Currie,[43] Epstein and Jacob Kramer, the early paintings of Mark Gertler and the later carvings of Eric Gill, as well as pictures by Harold Gilman, Charles Ginner, Spencer Gore,[44] Derwent Lees, C. R. W. Nevinson, Wilson Steer and Walter Greaves.[45] Often he would write enthusiastically about painters working in styles very different from his own. Alvaro ('Chile') Guevara he described as 'the most gifted and promising of them all' (16 February 1916), but he was also impressed by Henri Gaudier-Brzeska who, he wrote (3 April 1915), 'is a man of talent. His things look as if they have been sat on before they got quite hard. Some of them look like bits of stalactite roughly resembling human forms. But they are wittily conceived.' Most of all he wrote about David Bomberg. 'You ought to get more Bombergs,' he advised Quinn[46] (26 January 1914), 'he is full of talent.' Following the lead of Marinetti, the initiator of Futurism – 'a common type of the meridional; naif, earnest, and ignorant. But we are very friendly' – Bomberg's painting took a course that was ultimately unsympathetic to Augustus. But, with reservations, he continued to praise him (in company with 'another Futurist called Giacomo Balla who is good') – singling out his famous 'Mud-Bath'.

There is no mention of Bomberg in *Chiaroscuro* or in *Finishing Touches*, the two autobiographical volumes Augustus wrote late in his life; and almost none of the other artists upon whose behalf he had secretly exercised himself. He took to writing only in his early sixties at the end of the 1930s, and, by the time his fragments of autobiography were put together as books in the 1950s and early 1960s, he was distrustful of his own spasms of generosity, and no longer interested in the unfamiliar. Of Picasso, for example, he wrote: 'Such ceaseless industry, leading to a torrent of *articles de nouveauté*, may seem to some, capricious and rootless, but it undoubtedly deserves its reward in the greatest snob-following of our time' – a sentence that was rewarded by Picasso's classification of Augustus as: 'The best bad painter in Britain'.

It can therefore be misleading to reconstruct the young man from what was written by the disaffected older man. As a guide to his artistic taste, there exist eight long articles[47] he wrote for *Vogue* in 1928 on modern French and English painters. These articles demonstrate how catholic and near-contemporary his taste remained until his fifties – though he had grown resentful of the power of fashion in art, for which he blamed the dealers. The value of the French tradition, which depended upon 'the unceasing enthusiasm of French painters towards a personal expression', was beyond fashion. Those French painters he pointed to as having created a climate favouring innovation were Manet, Monet ('in the entrancing waterlilies of his later years'), Alfred Sisley and Camille Pissarro – 'these are the pioneers who led painting from the halting deliberation of David to the courageous or even risky contact with the open air. Monet, Renoir, Degas not tentatively, but with conscious authority, released that long-confined expression of instant response to the aspect of the visible world.' The battle of the Impressionists had long ago been fought and won, but he deplored the labelling of Post-Impressionism applied to the later Van Gogh, Gauguin and Émile Bernard because 'their work and their own individuality was much more significant than, and much more distinct from, the work of the Impressionists themselves.' After Gauguin and Van Gogh, the next painters in the grand line of French art were rather less to his liking. The atmosphere had become too cultured. He praises, with reservations, the work of that 'lazy giant' Derain, but deprecates his pedantry; while the developments since 1912 in the styles of Picasso and Matisse seem to have reversed his attitude to them. Picasso, whose Blue and Rose periods he had loved, appeared to be growing metaphorically false. 'Matisse remains the best, the most sensitive, of French painters, for Matisse having abandoned his early essays in imbecility, has by dint of assiduity and method achieved the foremost place in his generation as an exquisite paysagist and painter of *genre*.'

He also picks out 'three old gentlemen', Bonnard, Jean-Louis Forain and Georges Rouault, as being above competition – 'individual and isolated examples of the glory of French painting'. And among the younger ones he chooses Marc Chagall for 'his admirable handling of paint', Othon Friesz and, above all, André Segonzac, who 'conceived the landscape in its fundamental unity and basic rhythm . . . setting free its deep burden of emotion in low and thrilling chords of colour'.

His criticism of British painters is more complicated since it sews together paragraphs of interrupted friendship with passages of tentative appreciation – the two sometimes embroidered with double entendre:

'With Mr Henry Lamb we have another type of mind, more self-conscious but less free [than Matthew Smith's]. He seeks, with an almost mathematical ingenuity, to invent new harmonies of colour in combination with a most searching analysis of character. This passionately serious painter, for whom any intellectual concession is an impossibility, remains still insufficiently recognised. For so many amateurs, an easy and comforting facility is more attractive than Mr Lamb's *intransigence* and the almost moral integrity of his art.'

The theme which emerges from this art criticism is a belief in individual accomplishment independent of art trends. Augustus comforted himself with the notion that posterity amends the injustices of contemporary neglect and that no effort of creative merit could fail to be recognized in the course of time: but he did not really believe it. There was no sign, for instance, that the work of Paul Maitland or W. E. Osborn would be revived. Yet there was a certain luxury in protesting against the inevitable.

His protest lay against Paris: not as a symbol and repository of the great French tradition of painting by which he himself had profited, but as a forcing house of the international picture bourse. Paris had become the world's greatest stock-exchange for art, the Mecca of the amateur, the student, and above all the dealer. A great machinery for the encouragement of the young was centred there and people arrived from all over the world in search of revelation. That a great tradition had made Paris famous was taken to imply that it was Paris which had made the tradition. Yet many painters had had a bitter struggle to establish themselves in the city of which, after their deaths, they were the pride. Constantin Guys had been, in Baudelaire's words, 'le peintre inconnu'; Honoré Daumier a political suspect and journalist-illustrator to the end of his life. The Post-Impressionists found it no easier. Biographies of Cézanne, Gauguin and Van Gogh all told a similar story of derision, lack of understanding. Henri Rousseau 'le Douanier' and Modigliani, whom in great poverty Augustus visited a few years before his death, were two recent victims of incomprehension on the part of 'the great art city of the world'. By the late 1920s their pictures all fetched enormous prices, and Paris, on their posthumous behalf, did herself great honour. The huge combination of studio and dealer's shop that had been constructed there was an empty shell: the goddess of art had paused – and now moved on.

There is a danger of the individual and national voice being lost in an international lingua franca.' This became the basis of Augustus's complaint against Roger Fry and his Omega Workshops which, full of bright 'rhombuses, rhomboids, lozenges, diamonds, triangles and parallelograms',[48] had been set up shortly before the Great War to give young artists the chance to earn money from many sorts of commissions – for murals, painted furniture, rugs and carpets, mosaics, pottery or stained glass. Augustus came to believe that the gifts of the Bloomsbury painters were misappropriated by Fry (though he did not see that this might also be partly true with regard to himself). Duncan Grant, for instance, had 'an innate sense of decoration [and] . . . exhibits a natural lyricism in his work which appears to owe less to definite calculation than to irrepressible instinct for rhythmical self-expression'. But his talent was misdirected by Fry's critical ideology, so that his versatile temperament absorbed 'with an ease nearly related to genius the most disconcerting manifestations of the modern spirit'.

A better course, Augustus believed, was exemplified by an artist whose work had something in common with Duncan Grant's, Matthew Smith. He too was influenced by the modern spirit, but had taken from it only what was useful:

'French influences are inevitably to be noted in his work, but the fulness of form which characterises so many of his figures has a distinct relationship with Indian and Persian drawings. With a cataract of emotional sensibility he casts upon the canvas a pageant of grandiose and voluptuous form and sumptuous colour, which are none the less controlled by an ordered design and a thoroughly learned command of technique. This makes him one of the most brilliant figures in modern English painting. Aloof and deliberately detached from the appeals of ordinary life, he sits apart and converts what to other men are the ever-partial triumphs of passion into permanent monuments of profound sensory emotion. In flowers, fruit and women he finds the necessary material for his self-expression, and from them he has evolved a kind of formula which represents his artist's inner-consciousness. And he has never risked the danger which threatens those who make bargains with society by attempting the almost impossible task of combining fine painting with satisfactory portraiture.'

Of all living British painters Matthew Smith was the one whose abilities Augustus most admired. The nature of his admiration, as revealed here, was partly a stick with which to beat himself. The source of Augustus's own inspiration was South Wales, but he felt he was denied access there by the presence of his father. He had found in Provence, and very soon would find in North Wales too, landscapes that through a mysterious process of self-identification and self-abandonment liberated his imagination. He had found also an artist, another Welshman, with whom he now entered a brief period of mutual apprenticeship, radiant, and unique in his career.

4

WHAT HAPPENED

'When shall I come to Wales again?'
> Augustus John to John Sampson (undated, *c.* May 1910)
'Since I left it I find myself to be very much of a Welshman and would like to be back.'
> J. D. Innes to Augustus John (4 August 1913)

During 1910, the first of Augustus's Slade contemporaries, William Orpen, quietly joined the Royal Academy. This appeared the dull side of Virginia Woolf's brilliant Post-Impressionist symbol. With extraordinary precision art history was repeating itself and the *enfants terribles* of a decade ago were starting on their journey to become respectable Old Men. Their rebel headquarters, the New English Art Club, was now twenty-four years old. French-built to withstand the assaults of British Academicism, it now stood, a British fortress against the advance of French Post-Impressionism. What was needed, apparently, was a newer Salon des Refusés to oppose the old Salon des Refusés, whose tyrannical rule was felt by younger artists far more acutely than the remote indifference of Burlington House.

The first expression of this need had been Frank Rutter's Allied Artists' Association, a self-supporting concern modelled on the Parisian Société des Artistes Indépendants. All artists, by paying an annual subscription, could exhibit what works they pleased without submitting them to a censorious jury. Founded in 1908, in July of which year it held its first mammoth show at the Albert Hall, it soon gave birth to the 'Camden Town Group' and the 'London Group', which in 1914 was to swallow them both. Augustus was a founder member of the Allied Artists' Association, though he seldom exhibited. 'John never does exhibit anywhere unless you go and fetch his pictures yourself,' Rutter explained. '. . . He joined because, like the good fellow he is, he thoroughly approved of the principles of the A.A.A., and knew it would help others though he had no need of it himself.'[49]

The ideals of the Allied Artists' Association were soon immersed in combative art politics. On Saturday nights its members – usually Augustus, Robert Bevan, Harold Gilman, Charles Ginner, Spencer Gore, Lucien Pissarro, Rutter himself and Sickert – would meet at a little hotel in Golden Square, then go on afterwards to the Café Royal. And almost always the talk would turn, and return, to the question of whether they should capture the New English Art Club or secede and set up a rival society. Augustus was what Rutter called 'consistently loyal' to the NEAC. In several respects his position was closest to the Protean figure of Sickert. Both were opposed to 'capturing' the New English, and Augustus believed furthermore that any other group they might found must be truly indepen-dent rather than a rival. Only in that way could it faithfully represent their ideal of exhibiting freely, and plot a course of tolerance and diversity between the various rocks of art fashion. The result of these talks was the formation in 1911 of the Camden Town Group, dominated by Gilman, Ginner, Bevan and Gore, and watched over by the benevolent eye of Sickert. Though unconnected with Camden Town, Augustus was admitted to this group, which marked an important defection from the New English Art Club whose original aims it nevertheless almost exactly reproduced. He exhibited only once with them, though he liked to look in on their weekly meetings at 21 Fitzroy Street, and surreptitiously buy pictures both for himself and for Quinn.

Then, in 1912, two things happened: he turned down Clive Bell's invitation to show work at the Second Post-Impressionist Exhibition; and, leaving the Camden Town Group, he 'flew back to the New English'. When, in 1914, the London Group emerged as the spearhead of mod-ernity, Augustus's name was, for the first time, not among Britain's avant-garde.[50]

It is easy to draw from these two acts a false conclusion. Augustus was prolific; he had a wealthy American patron, and the use of a London gallery where he could show his pictures. With his large family, he needed more money than many other artists, but his work was now fetching good prices – the small oil panels at the Chenil had sold for forty pounds (equivalent to £1,800 in 1996) each and some of them were soon changing hands for seventy and eighty pounds. He was deeply uninterested in art politics. What he wanted was as many alternatives as were practicable – all sorts of exhibitions where, irrespective of style, artists could display and sell their paintings. But the Camden Town Group – named, in deference to Sickert, after the working-class area which provided subject matter for many of its members' pictures – though it contained better painters, seemed narrower than the New English. Besides, John's vibrant landscapes were quite out of place in a Camden show. The decision to show nothing at its two exhibitions in 1910 had not been one of art policy: no one could 'go and fetch his pictures' while he was abroad that year. The year had ended with his one-man show at the Chenil for which he reserved all his recent work; but in 1911 he was again exhibiting with the NEAC. Nevertheless he had not quarrelled with the Camden Town painters, whose work he continued recommending to Quinn.

Yet behind his decision to withhold work from the Second Post-Impressionist Exhibition there lay Augustus's involuntary involvement in a sudden clash between Roger Fry and Will Rothenstein. The enmity which flared up between these two didactic painter-politicians seems partly to have arisen from Rothenstein's attitude to the new power Fry was exercising on behalf of the younger contemporary artists. Fry had been given temporary control of the Grafton Gallery which, he innocently told Rothenstein, 'seemed to me a real acquisition of power'. He planned to stage there a large exhibition by living British artists and, very late in the day, invited Rothenstein to submit – adding by way of inducement: 'John has promised to send.'[51] This invitation, however, was not only delayed but also restricted to Rothenstein's recent Indian work, which Will knew in his heart was far from being his best. Worse still, he himself had been pondering upon a similar plan; but while he pondered Fry had gone ahead with his own arrangements without benefit of Rothenstein's collaboration. Many years later (27 July 1920) Fry admitted to Virginia Woolf that 'I used to be jealous of Prof. Rothenstein, who came along about four years after me and at once got a great reputation, but', he added triumphantly, 'I wouldn't change places with him now.'[52] From all sorts of people Rothenstein was picking up rumours of Fry's schemes. He felt offended. 'I have heard no details of your Grafton schemes at all and was waiting to hear what it is you propose,' he pointed out to Fry (30 March 1911). '. . . You have been too busy to tell me of a thing which is of some importance.' Fry, however, seems to have been anxious to establish his Grafton Group to a point where Rothenstein, once admitted, could not alter it. 'Do let us, however, get rid of misunderstandings,' Rothenstein pleaded, under the threat of being left out altogether (4 April 1911): 'we are both of us working for the same thing and it seems absurd that there should be anything of the kind . . . But I don't think you realise how ignorant I am of your intentions and of your powers.'

It was this fact of their 'working for the same thing' that divided them.

Rothenstein felt that if Bloomsbury was sponsoring the Grafton Group, he would be at a disadvantage. He therefore sought to discover a point of principle with which to misunderstand Fry's intentions. Since Steer and Tonks had already refused to let their pictures be shown in company with those of younger artists, there seemed a good chance that Fry's scheme could be halted. The particular point of principle that Rothenstein turned up concerned the selection of the show, which apparently was to be made by Fry alone. In place of such dictatorship, Rothenstein suggested an 'advisory committee of artists', and recommended the sort of people – Augustus, Epstein, Eric Gill, Ambrose McEvoy – who might sit on it. These were all artists, friendly to Rothenstein, whose work Fry wanted to include. By refusing this suggestion Fry ran the risk of alienating them. In his reply to Rothenstein (13 April 1911) he insisted that it was 'inevitable that I should appeal to various artists to trust me with large powers since I have the actual control and responsibility on behalf of the Grafton Galleries. Now you know me well enough to know that I am not unlikely to listen to advice from you and that I should give every consideration to any suggestions which you or John or McEvoy might make and I should be delighted if you would co-operate; at the same time I could hardly go to the other groups of younger artists, who are quite willing to trust me personally, and say to them that their work must come before such a committee as you suggest for judgement; nor can I possibly get rid of my responsibilities to the Grafton Galleries.'

But Rothenstein resented being made, as it were, a mere minister without portfolio in Fry's new government: he wanted a cabinet post – preferably that occupied by Clive Bell. Was it not he, Will Rothenstein, who had first established lines of communication between France and England while Fry was director of the Metropolitan Museum of Art in New York? Although, in the past, Fry had written generously in praise of his work, Rothenstein refused to trust his judgement.[53] Didn't everyone know how naïve he was, how credulous? But Fry was at a loss to account for Rothenstein's non-cooperation. 'I gather you are very much annoyed with me,' he wrote to him (13 September 1911), 'but I simply can't disentangle the reason. No doubt it is all quite clear in your mind, but I haven't a clue.'

Although Rothenstein was out of things after he left for the United States in October 1911, his tactics affected Fry's Second Post-Impressionist Exhibition, which eventually included only a small British group among French and Russian sections. If McEvoy seems to have been a pawn in the complicated chess game that had developed between these two painter-impresarios, Augustus had been a knight who found himself being moved strongly about the board forwards and sideways on behalf of Rothenstein's team. Great efforts were made to capture him. As late as the summer of 1912, Fry was writing to Clive Bell: 'I'm delighted that John wants to show.' But in the event he did not do so. His letter of refusal was sent not to Fry but to Clive Bell:

'Dear Bell,

I received your very enigmatic letter. I am sorry I cannot promise anything for the "Second Post-Impressionists". For one reason I am away from town, and for another I should hesitate to submit any work to so ambiguous a tribunal. No doubt my decision will be a relief – to everybody.

Yrs truly, Augustus John.'[54]

It was a relief, primarily, to Augustus himself. 'I am conscious that the various confabulators find the question of my inclusion embarrassing,' he had confided to Wyndham Lewis, 'and I would wish to liberate their consciences in the matter if I could find adequately delicate means of doing so.' Once he was clear of the whole bloody show he felt marvellously disencumbered. He had owed some loyalty to Will Rothenstein, though he might feel closer to Fry and some of the Camden and London Group painters. He was not, however, close to Clive Bell, who was to launch upon his later work a strong attack,[55] valuing it as 'almost worthless'. It was one of those pieces of Bell's journalism that, Fry complained,[56] 'have done me more harm than all the others'.

The consequences of an artist's absence from the Second Post-Impressionist show were 'swift and severe'. He was simply 'not a Post-Impressionist according to the definition which Bell put forward in his selection of English artists', S. K. Tillyard wrote in *The Impact of Modernism*.

'When, for instance, Augustus John was left out of the show, his work was no longer described as being connected with Post-Impressionism. But such painting was obviously not Academic . . . The absence from the 1912 show of John and some members of the Camden Town group increasingly left critics and public without any acceptably "modern" language of description to apply to their work and in particular to their subject matter. Hence John, and, as time went on, Sickert too, became increasingly difficult to evaluate and categorise. As the Post-Impressionist version of the past became gradually accepted, the two artists also became hard to place within any "development" of English painting, and impossible to "rehabilitate" without a re-evaluation of the past.'[57]

John had no modern group, society or workshop from which to conduct such an exercise in re-evaluation. His two pictures, 'Lynn Cynlog' and 'Nant-ddu', listed as numbers 1 and 2 in the first Camden Town Exhibition of 1911, were Welsh landscapes which illustrated his distance from this metropolitan group. For John, the right place was far away from the metropolitan art world, in North Wales or southern France, not alone, but with J. D. Innes.

*

James Dickson Innes was nine years older than Augustus. 'Born and bred in Wales,' Augustus wrote, 'to which country he felt himself bound by every tie of sentiment and predilection',[58] he had nevertheless practised eating black ants at school in order to establish his French ancestry.[59] By the autumn of 1907, when he first met Augustus, Innes was living in Fitzroy Street. 'A Quaker hat, coloured silk scarf and long black overcoat set off features of a slightly cadaverous cast with glittering black eyes, wide sardonic mouth, prominent nose, and a large bony forehead invaded by streaks of thin black hair. He carried a Malacca cane with a gold top and spoke with a heavy English accent which now and then betrayed an agreeable Welsh sub-stratum.'[60]

It was during his first visit to France with John Fothergill in April and May 1908 that Innes's painting life really began. They travelled to Caudebec, Bozouls and ('because it looked so good on the map', Fothergill explained) to Collioure, where Derain and Matisse had worked two or three years before. The impact of southern light upon Innes increased his awareness of colour and intensified his involvement with Nature in a manner similar to Augustus in Provence. Having fallen ill, apparently with spots arising from his failure, over a long period, to wash, he returned alone via Dieppe and was found to be suffering from tuberculosis. Such a diagnosis meant probable death. Almost the only treatment was rest. Innes was not the person to accept such passive medical advice. The TB had attacked his teeth so that he could not chew properly: but he could drink, and sometimes did so heavily. There was one other pleasure the disease did not quench (as a romantic adventure with a young Algerian carpet weaver was to demonstrate): tuberculosis was said to stimulate sexuality.

Early in 1909 Innes had visited Paris with Matthew Smith, but does not seem to have been particularly interested in the French painters who (some of them posthumously) were about to invade England. Once again illness curtailed his visit and he was sent to convalesce at St Ives. But in the spring of 1910 he was back in Paris and it was here, at a café in the boulevard du Montparnasse, that he met and fell in love with Euphemia

Lamb. Together they made their way back to Collioure, Euphemia dancing in cafés to help pay their way.

As with so many British artists, this year was crucial for Innes. He had looked for guidance to John Fothergill. But Fothergill himself was in need of guidance. A romantic-looking young man, lithe and elegant 'like a young fawn', with almond-shaped eyes and a light curling beard, he had been admired by Oscar Wilde and by the surrealist lesbian painter Romaine Brooks. Caught in the cross-currents of his sexual ambiguities, he then came under the protection of E. P. Warren and his brotherhood of aesthetes. Early in 1910 Fothergill and Innes ended their friendship. It seems that Fothergill's relationship with Innes was to some degree homosexual. There was a self-destructive aspect to Fothergill – an artist, gallery proprietor and classical archaeologist – who took up innkeeping. Such a masochistic vein Innes, with his violent Swiftian imagery, had been well fitted to exploit.

'[Derwent] Lees tells me strange things about Innes,' Fothergill complained to Albert Rutherston, ' – in short – [Euphemia] Lamb off – (sounds like 11 o'clock p.m. at a nasty eating house) and also his allowance from mother – gone to Paris, his savings gone also. Knocked a bobby on the head and arrested. He was also wounded in the head in a back street in Chelsea along with John in a fight. What stupidities some people allow themselves to indulge in because they call themselves artists.'

And the company he kept! Drunkards, practical jokers, loose women, known eccentrics. No wonder his mother had cancelled his allowance – Fothergill knew just how she must be feeling. One day when Innes, Horace de Vere Cole and Augustus were in a taxi they 'bethought themselves of the rite of "blood brotherhood" . . . Innes drove a knife right through his left hand. One of the others [Augustus] stabbed himself in the leg and was laid up for some time afterwards. Cole made a prudent incision, sufficient to satisfy the needs of the case. The driver was indignant when he saw the state of his cab and its occupants, but the rite had been performed and no lasting damage was done.'[61]

Both Innes and Augustus, as John Rothenstein observed,[62] were obsessed 'by a highly personal conception of the ideal landscape which also haunted the imaginings of Puvis de Chavannes'; both, in the brilliant Mediterranean light, were working rapidly in high-key colours, and rediscovering what they felt they had first known in their sunlit days as children in Wales. Both were looking for what Augustus, writing about Innes, called 'the reflection of some miraculous promised land'.[63]

It was in the autumn of 1910 that Innes and Augustus began seeing a lot of each other. Augustus's exhibition at the Chenil in December 1910 was followed by a one-man show of Innes's watercolours, and Augustus immediately wrote to Quinn advising him to buy some of them.

'He's a really gifted chap and shows a rare imagination in his landscapes. It is true he has not done much yet, being quite young, but if he can keep it up there can be no doubt about his future. London doesn't do for him and he's off to Wales and later to the south.'[64]

It was a relief to leave London and paint their way over the moorland and mountains from Bala to Blaenau Ffestiniog, where there were no theories of what should be painted or why. Innes visited London for exhibitions and would sometimes stay on, obeying what he called the 'stern call of dissipation'. These were innocent romps. 'Innes has just been given the option of 40/- or a month [in jail] for pulling Bells in the King's Rd,' Augustus wrote to Sampson after one episode. Innes was by now a bearded figure, still with his wide black Quaker hat, but permanently covered with paint, permanently ill and permanently out of doors, preferring to live rough and sleep under the stars. One night, wandering upon the moors of North Wales, he had come upon the lonely inn of Rhyd-y-fen and been cared for by its landlord, Washington Davies. Waking up next morning Innes had seen the mountain of Arenig against the sky and fallen in love. 'Mynedd Arenig remained ever his sacred mountain and the slopes of the Migneint his spiritual home.'[65] Upon the summit of this mountain, under the cairn, he was to bury a silver casket containing his letters from Euphemia.[66] For him she *was* Arenig. This was the magnetic point to which, like the needle of a compass, he always returned.

Compelled, like a lover, to broadcast his feelings, Innes confided to Augustus about Arenig, and the two of them made a plan to meet at Rhyd-y-fen that March. 'Our meeting was cordial,' Augustus remembered, 'but yet I felt on his part a little reserve, as if he felt the scruples of a lover on introducing a friend to the object of his passion.'[67] Behind the inn, to the south, rose the flanks of Arenig Fawr, and beyond the little lake of Tryweryn they could see in the distance the peaks of Moelwyn. 'This is the most wonderful place I've seen,' Augustus wrote to Dorelia (March 1911). '. . . The air is superb and the mountains wonderful . . . We are now off for a week to see a waterfall that falls 400 feet without a break.' They decided to look for a cottage and found one some three miles from Rhyd-y-fen on the slopes of the Migneint by a brook called Nant-ddu. They furnished it sparsely and moved in when Augustus returned during May. 'I think Innes was never happier than when painting in this district,' Augustus wrote.[68]

'But this happiness was not without a morbid side for his passionate devotion to the landscape was also a way of escape from his consciousness of the malady which then was casting its shadow across his days . . . This it was that hastened his steps across the moor and lent his brush a greater swiftness and decision as he set down in a single sitting view after jewelled view of the delectable mountains he loved before darkness came to hide everything . . .'

'Before working with John,' wrote the art critic Eric Rowan, 'Innes had been painting in water-colour . . . After John's arrival in North Wales, Innes began to copy his technique of making quick sketches in oil paint on prepared wooden panels.'[69] Though rapidly done, these panels had often entailed long expeditions over the moors looking for that moment of illumination which would suddenly burst through the procession of clouds. He worked like a man condemned. The effect of this upon Augustus was extraordinary. Never before had he met someone whose swiftness exceeded his own. What he had once done at the Slade for others, Innes, acting as a pacemaker, could now do for him.

But there was another way in which Innes helped. 'He was an original, a "naif",' Augustus wrote[70] – and in a letter to Quinn (15 June 1911) he describes him as an 'entirely original chap and that's saying a lot. He is not the sort who learns anything. He will die innocent and a virgin intellectually which I think a very charming and rare thing.' Augustus did not imitate Innes or seek to learn from him any very painterly secrets. It was Innes's example that inspired him. He had felt recently that his own innocence, the quality which W. B. Yeats had found so remarkable, was in jeopardy. Innes helped him to repossess it – so much is evident from his letter to Quinn in which, passing from Innes to himself, he adds: 'I am on my way I think to get back (or forward) to a purely delightful way of decorating which shall in no way compete with the camera or the coal-hole. But one has a lot to unlearn before the instinct or the soul or what you call it can shine out uninstructed.'

It was ironic that their chief disciple should have been a copycat of genius, the Australian painter Derwent Lees. 'I tire of seeing my own subjects so many times,' Innes wrote of Lees's pictures. Besides Inneses, Lees could paint McEvoys and Johns[71] fluently. He had come from Melbourne, after a duty stop in Paris, to London, and now taught drawing at the Slade. A fair-complexioned man, rather thin yet somehow giving an impression of plumpness, he was remarkable, in the days when artificial limbs were still unusual, for a fine and exciting false right foot, complete with wooden toes in which, amid much giggling, a Slade girl once got her finger caught.

The pictures which these three painted before the war mark a short phase in British art which, though it has been labelled 'Post-Impressionist', belongs more properly to the tradition of the symbolist painters.

But the war was to signal the end of their landscape painting.

5

WHAT NEXT?

'There is no doubt that he pines for comrades & is sick of his chance pub acquaintances ... but [I] much doubt whether he has not become inaccessible.'

Henry Lamb

'It was cruel to leave Provence,' Augustus had complained to Ottoline on his arrival back in England in September 1910. Only a month before he had started to feel homesick – but for what home? London really suited neither Dorelia, nor himself, nor the children who, especially Ida's David, fell far too readily under the sway of Mrs Nettleship. 'Dorelia (my missus) is very keen on a house in the country,' Augustus reminded Quinn (December 1910), 'and we shall have to look out for one soon. She tends to get poor in London.'

He had recommended work on Hugh Lane's decorations – no longer in Lane's house but at the Chenil Gallery. 'I think you will find Chenil's quite a good place now,' he reported with some optimism to Will Rothenstein, 'and Knewstub is improving.' Determined to get Lane's pictures done by the spring 'or perish', he several times gave up 'touching a drop of liquor' and felt 'exceedingly good'.

Having the Chenil as his office brought some alleviation to their Church Street problems, but it fell far short of solving them. The old difficulties crowded in. 'Do you want a ring?' Augustus suddenly invited Dorelia: but answer there came none. He had moved up his squadron of caravans to Battersea 'so that we may turn into the van any hour'. As soon as spring came they might begin trekking over England: the possibilities were endless.

Some days over these next twelve months, Augustus would leave for the Chenil in the morning – a distance of five hundred yards – and not return that night at all. Next day Dorelia would receive a note from Essex, Berkshire or Brittany: 'the country is so beautiful – you wouldn't believe it – I suddenly quitted London.' In October he went to France; in November he took off to see Eric Gill at Ditchling, discussing there the question of a New Religion and a co-operative scheme for taking a house from which their work could be sold independently of the dealers. In December he hurried back to Charlie McEvoy's 'pig-stye' at Wantage: 'Mrs McEvoy frequently wishes you were here,' he wrote to Dorelia – adding hastily: 'So do I.'

A family Christmas at Church Street being obviously unsupportable, he once more set off for the Chenil and arrived this time in Paris. 'I have been so embêté lately and have taken refuge in Paris and have neglected all my pleasures,' he explained to Ottoline (27 December 1910). '. . . I found London quite deadly and think of going south again till England becomes more habitable. I hear Lamb has been doing your portrait[72] – le salaud!' He dined with Royall Tyler off stuffed pigs' trotters; saw Epstein and Nevinson, and squared up to Boris Anrep;[73] searched in vain for Gwen; attempted to teach Euphemia to ride a bicycle; was chased by a Swedish tiger-woman from whom he escaped through a smoke screen of Horace Cole's practical jokes (including, apparently, a mock operation for appendicitis); and with devastating innocence concluded: 'Paris is certainly preferable to Chelsea. I think I'd like to live here.'[74]

For most of this time he stayed at 40 rue Pascal with Fabian de Castro, the Spanish guitarist who, having outwitted his gaolers in Madrid, was now writing his autobiography. 'He has wandered all over Europe,' Augustus warned Quinn, 'and even across the Caucasus on foot and speaking only Spanish – and has done everything except kill a man.'

He was thinking of passing on to Marseilles with a Miss George, possibly Teresa George who had called on him to say that Edwin, his father, was seeking her hand in marriage. 'He and I had something in common after all, then,' Augustus concluded. At any rate, he asked in a letter to Dorelia, she 'might be useful, posing?' But instead of Marseilles, he arrived in London leading, like small deer behind him, a troupe of his cronies up to the front door of Church Street. What with the cook's two children to reinforce Augustus's six, and the intermittent appearances of Helen Maitland and Edie McNeill to reinforce those of Fabian de Castro and Miss George, the place was crowded as for war. One packed night during the first week of January 1911, fire broke out in the house, and Augustus, wakened by screams, 'leapt out of the room half-crazy and found our servant on top of the stairs burning like a torch. I happened to have been sleeping in a dressing-gown by some happy chance and managed to extinguish the poor girl with this. But it was a terrible moment . . . fortunately her face, which is a good face, was untouched. She was burnt about the arms, legs and stomach . . . She had come up the stairs from the dining-room, blazing – the smell nearly made me faint afterwards. It was the hottest embrace I've ever had of a woman.'[75] They summoned a 'smart little doctor' to do the repairs to the girl and to Augustus himself, whose left hand and leg and areas nearby had got toasted without, he was anxious to demonstrate, putting him 'out of action in the slightest degree'.[76] He was, however, ordered to stay in bed. 'This will mean keeping quiet for a few days,' he told Quinn (5 January 1911), 'after which I want to take one of my vans on the road for a week or so and then get back to work with full steam up.'

For Dorelia it was not these conflagrations so much as the convalescences that were arduous; not the explosive rows but the periods of 'keeping quiet'. She, who could enjoy-and-endure so much of the heroic, found herself strangely vulnerable to the trivial. A small thing it was that finally cracked her: the matter of spitting. Fabian de Castro was a splendid guitarist, but he *would spit in the bath*, and this infuriated Dorelia. She lay awake thinking about it, and finally she put up a notice: PLEASE DO NOT SPIT IN THE BATHROOM. Then, when he took no notice of it, she left.

She left for Paris, and she left with Henry Lamb. It was a casual business. 'Dorelia is in Paris for a few days and I in London,' Augustus remarked in the course of a letter to his old Slade friend Michel Salaman dealing with the more pressing matter of ponies. But it was not casual for Lamb. 'I stayed more than a week,' he wrote to Lytton Strachey (1 February 1911): 'seeing for the first time the city in all its glamour of history, art and romance. But I should explain Dorelia was there and that I came back with her in a motor car belonging to an American millionairess [Mrs Chadbourne]. Now I am completely rejuvenated and working with tenfold industry.' Intermittently Dorelia would have this effect on him, but his love for her in the shadow of Augustus caused him much pain and perhaps accounted for the wounds he inflicted on those, like Lytton Strachey, who fell in love with him. On the evening of their return, after they had parted, Lamb wrote to Ottoline:

'I arrived about 6 this evening having travelled since very early on Sunday with Dorelia, Pyramus and Mrs Chad, in her motor. The excitements of Paris came in an unusually trebled dose, and the final shaking of the journey have reduced me too low . . . I have lived too giddily these last days to give them the thought they must have. It is an odd and desolate sensation to spend the evening alone. I must turn into bed immediately in the hope of a braver morning moral.'

By the time Dorelia arrived back in Church Street, 'full steam' was up. Augustus and his friends had journeyed into Essex for a gypsy evening during which Euphemia executed a fantastic belly dance, writing her name and address on the shirt fronts of those she favoured as she whirled past them. Then, on their return, Horace Cole charged his motor car into a cartload of miscellaneous people injuring many, one severely. Innes, too, had 'been doing la Bombe lately by all appearances', Augustus advised Dorelia; and McEvoy, in her absence, had sprouted 'a moustache like an old blacking brush'. Now there was the Gauguin Ball in London; and after that Lady Gregory had invited him back to Coole. But first, he decided (10 February 1911), 'I want to go south again and work in the open.' This was his way of announcing he was going west to meet Innes. But after returning from some intense days round the lakes and mountains of old Merionethshire, he found Dorelia had gone off with Lamb again. 'Dorelia did come the last day at Peppard,' Lamb wrote to Strachey (11 May 1911); 'we walked through divine woods and lunched in an exquisite pub with the politest of yokels and I . . . got of course quite drunk. Then I had another evening with her all alone at Bedford Square. It was more than the expected comble [climax].'

Lamb's original fantasy of 'a discreet form of colony' which he had illustrated in his letter to Ottoline with an amoeba-like drawing of Johns, Maitlands, Morrells and himself, was almost being translated into fact. Like a rock-pool by the sea, the colony was sometimes teeming, sometimes vacant. Innes and Euphemia and Epstein (whose 'weak point', Augustus disapprovingly noted, was 'sex'); Alick Schepeler and Wyndham Lewis – all these and countless others would float in and be carried out from time to time, causing a little ripple. But for Lamb there was no one so important as Dorelia. He writes about her in a tone – rueful, tender, oblique – he reserves for no one else. He saw and heard too little of her; but he felt hopelessly in her debt.

When Augustus returned to North Wales in May he took Dorelia with him. But she did not like the bare unruly place and came back alone. 'We are getting restless about moving,' Augustus had confided to Quinn (10 February 1911). Dorelia was certainly restless. Cut off from the country she seemed to lose strength. There was no sun in London, no air, no time, no involvement with real things. She had to get away.

They had written to a number of friends asking them to look out for a house in the country. Investigations had not begun well. Pursuing a house in the west with Charlie Slade, Augustus tripped, fell, damaged his leg and returned home an invalid. 'Please get me a house, John,' he had desperately wired to his friends the Everetts. In reply he received a list of questions with intervening spaces, which he loyally filled in and sent back. Shortly afterwards, Katherine Everett came upon Alderney Manor, a strange fortified bungalow, larger than most houses, which had been built by an eccentric Frenchman. It was set in sixty acres of woodland near the Ringwood road outside Parkstone in Dorset, included a walled garden, cottage and stables – all for a rent of fifty pounds a year (equivalent to £2,290 in 1996). The owner, Lady Wimborne, a keen Liberal and evangelical leader, insisted in conversation with Katherine Everett that 'we should be pleased to have a clever artist for a tenant.'[77] Dorelia was ready to take the house sight unseen, but Augustus, in the guise of a practical man, cautioned her: 'The house is no doubt lovely in itself, but it must be seen – so much depends on the placing of it.' They therefore went down to spend a few days with the Everetts, who lived some three miles from Alderney.

'I can still visualize the group coming up our pine-shaded, sun-dappled drive,' Katherine Everett wrote. 'Mrs John, who was leading a grey donkey with a small boy astride it dressed in brilliant blue and another equally vivid small boy at her side, wore a tight-fitting, hand-sewn, canary-coloured bodice above a dark, gathered, flowing skirt, and her hair very black and gleaming, emphasized the long silver earrings which were her only adornment.'[78]

'It's a good find,' Augustus informed Quinn, 'any amount of land with pine woods goes to it, and inexpensive.'[79] Some repairs and alterations were needed and, while these were being arranged, the Johns camped in the Everetts' grounds, amusing themselves by decorating the small empty gardener's cottage where they ate, painting the walls black and the furniture scarlet.

'One afternoon,' Katherine Everett remembered, 'the children decided to get the red and black paint off their persons, so they all undressed and, with turpentine soap and scrubbing brushes, set to work to clean themselves up. It was while they were so occupied that Lady Wimborne paid her first call.'[80]

For a moment Alderney seemed to tremble in the balance, but Lady Wimborne, her liberal principles fully extended, sailed past this test and all was settled. Over these summer months, Dorelia spent her time preparing for their move. 'D. has gone to live for ever near Poole,' Lamb wrote in despair to Lytton Strachey. But already, in the second week of July, he had joined her there for what he called 'a supreme time'. In a letter to Strachey (24 July 1911) he described what was to become for him a second home.

'She [Dorelia] lives in an amazing place – a vast secluded park of prairies, pine woods, birch woods, dells and moors with a house, cottages and a circular walled-garden. And, pensez, all these you could have possessed for £50 a year – *we* could have possessed them!! It was very hot when I was there and lovely naked boys running about the woods. John was away.

In the course of some almost endless conversations with D. I thought her as superior as ever, but in danger of becoming overgrown in such isolation.'

On leaving Alderney, Lamb crossed over to France, a sudden enterprise inciting him to carry off with him Dorelia's sister, poor picturesque Ede' – a substitution he instantly regretted.

'Funny things continue to happen,' Augustus told Ottoline (14 July 1911). While Lamb was lingering at Alderney, Augustus had been in Liverpool finishing his portrait of Kuno Meyer – a good portrait though painted in an 'awful cellar' at the Sandon Studios Society. He liked to keep up his Liverpool associations. 'I am really attached to Liverpool,' he told his friend, the architect Charles Reilly with whom he was lodging, 'and I would rather paint a Liverpool portrait than another.' Reilly was roused from sleep one night by Augustus climbing through his bedroom window; next day the playwright Harley Granville Barker was surprised at finding himself cross-examined over dinner on the subject of 'a horse and trap'; then Innes was infuriated on being joined at Nant-ddu by the painter Albert Lipczinski and his beautiful wife Doonie, sent expressly from Liverpool – 'they are incredibly poor', Augustus explained; the Sampsons and Dowdalls were of course visited, and Susan their maid. And all Liverpool was praised and blamed: 'The Mersey is a grand thing. The ordinary Li-pool population is awful – hopeless barbarians.'[81]

Though nothing appeared to have altered, the acquisition of Alderney marked the beginning of a new pattern in the lives of Augustus and Dorelia. They moved in during August, though he kept on his studio at the Chenil Gallery. 'We have left Church Street for this place which does well for the kids,' he announced to Quinn (16 August 1911). '...My studio here is still unfinished and this has lost me a lot of work. My missus is well and gay but I very much fear she is in for something rather unnecessary.'

Augustus could not help responding optimistically to everything that was new. But to Henry Lamb the future seemed black: 'One of the chief temptations,' he confessed, '[is] to succumb to the general pressure of the news that Dorelia is enceinte again, which means she may die at any minute.'[82]

PART II

'Moral sentiment corrupts the young. Children are the first to lose their innocence, artists the second: idiots never.'

Augustus John, *Chiaroscuro*

THE YEARS OF EXPERIENCE

SEVEN

Before the Deluge

I

A SUMMER OF POETRY

'I saw in Augustus and Dorelia two of that rare sort of people, suggestive of ancient or primitive themes, whose point lay rather in what they were than in what they said or did. I felt that they would have been more at home drinking wine under an olive tree or sitting in a smoky mountain cave than planted in this tepid English scene. But at least they were bohemians and kept up with style and lavish hospitality the old tradition of artistic life that had come down from William Morris or Rossetti. This I thought was important . . .'

Gerald Brenan, *A Life of One's Own*

That summer of 1911 was oppressively hot. The heathlands of the Wimborne Estate were turning brown, and from time to time fires would break out sending columns of smoke far up into the blue skies.

The carts and wagons, with their wildly singing children, rattled past in the sun. Then, swerving off the narrow road, they entered a drive lined, like a green tunnel, with rhododendrons tall as trees. They turned left; and there, before them, lay a curious low pink building, a bungalow with Gothic windows and a fantastic castellated parapet: Alderney Manor.

It looked like a cardboard castle in some Hans Andersen story – a fragile fortress, square, strangely misplaced, from which an army of toy soldiers might suddenly emerge, or a puff of wind might knock flat. The smooth stucco surface, once a proud red, had faded leaving patches here and there of the cardboard colour. With its single row of windows pointing loftily nowhere, the house seemed embarrassed by its own absurdity. 'But its poetry even outdid its absurdity . . . There was something fantastic and stunning about it.'[1]

Alderney was to be the Johns' home for the next sixteen years. Like Fryern Court, into which they moved afterwards, it became Dorelia's creation and an eloquent expression of her personality. The rich colours – yellows, browns and mauves – the arrangements of flowers everywhere lighting up the rooms, the delicious meals – huge soups, stews and casseroles with rough red wine, fish with saffron and Provençal salads with plenty of garlic, tomatoes and olive oil – the wood fires filling the air with their fragrance, contributed to its happy disorder. For they were not tidy places, these houses. Lord David Cecil remembers leaving his hat on the floor one evening, and returning six weeks later to find it undisturbed. Nor were the manners formal: guests were seldom introduced to one another and might be confronted on arrival by an animal silence from the whole John pack. Sometimes visitors would find no one in the house at all, though all doors and windows lay open as if everyone had suddenly vanished through them. When the Spencer brothers, Gilbert and Stanley, came to stay

'we found the children frightening. At bed time everyone seemed to fade away but no one attempted to "show us to our bedrooms" until we decided that you slept as you fell but took the precaution of falling on odd pieces of furniture which made things easier . . . Requiring a lavatory I decided to seek one unaided. Having no luck I opened the front door very quietly and crept out into the darkness. Dorelia went into another room and noticing a bowl of dead flowers, opened a window and flung them out smack into my lap.'[2]

Yet there was a quality to the house. 'It was like a royal household in the heroic age,' wrote Romilly John, 'at once grand and simple.'[3] For many it became a place to run away to, a place where someone, calling for tea, might hang on a week, a month, even a year. These visitors perpetually filled Alderney, overflowing into the blue-and-yellow caravans and the 'cottage' – a red-brick building, actually larger than the 'Manor', standing invisible a hundred yards off behind a range of rhododendrons. 'This intervening vegetation made comings and goings difficult on wintry nights,' Romilly recalled: 'those unfamiliar with the route would bid a cheerful good night to the house-dwellers, launch out into the dark, and presently find themselves struggling amid a wilderness of snaky boughs.'

Alderney had eight rooms. At one end was the dining-room with its long oak table and benches, and a row of windows through which, at mealtimes, the horses would poke their heads, and doze. At the other end, looking on to beech trees, towards the orchard and the walk to the sandpit, was the kitchen. In between lay the bedrooms, and below them capacious cellars.

The kitchen, noisy with helpers, was ruled over by Dorelia's sister Edie. She was small, with black-brown hair and large brooding eyes, their upper lids curiously straight giving them a strange rectangular shape. Her mouth was rather prominent, curving downwards, and her expression sardonic yet vulnerable – an index of her life to come. Into her care were given the youngest children and some of the cooking until a local woman, Mrs Cake, was engaged.

By helping to run things inside the house, Edie enabled Dorelia to give more time to the gardens. Her first venture was, appropriately, with an Alderney cow which provided colossal quantities of cream so rich it had the taste of caramel. This cow was soon followed by 'a large black beast called Gipsy, an adept in the art of opening gates and leading off the increasing herd to unimagined spots in the remote distance',[4] where a team of children would be sent off to shepherd them home. The children were also trained to help Dorelia milk the herd, to skim the milk and make butter. 'We'd skim the cream out of shallow metal vats,' Caspar remembered. '. . . Then we poured the cream into an eccentric hand-rotated churn . . . We then took the lump [of solidified cream] into the kitchen and squeezed out all the buttermilk with rolling pins and patted the butter into rounds or cubes.'[5]

To the cows, at one time or another, were added, less successfully, a dovecote of pigeons (which all flew away); and, briefly, a 'biteful' monkey; then an entire breeding herd of pedigree saddleback pigs; various donkeys, New Forest ponies and carthorses, all with names; miscellaneous dogs, including a fat dachshund called Sonny which looked like a sack of potatoes on wheels; and, among the teacups, endless cats – Siamese, white, tabby and black – which bore unheard-of relationships to one another. Finally came twelve hives of dangerous bees that stung everyone abominably.

'People who were staying at Alderney would come and watch the operations from a distance, whereupon a detachment of bees made a bee-line for them, alighting on their noses and cheeks and in their hair, which would cause them to rush round and round the field beating their heads like madmen. The next day everybody would present an extraordinary and uncharacteristic appearance. People who had usually long solemn faces would appear with perfectly round ones, and a perpetual clownish smile. Eyes would vanish altogether, and once or twice the victims retired to bed with swollen tongues, convinced . . . they would be choked to death . . . At last we resorted to a couple of old tennis racquets . . . Anybody at a little distance might have imagined that we were playing some very intricate kind of tennis, with special rules and invisible balls.'[6]

In all things Dorelia seemed to rely on instinct rather than planning. She invented as she went along, ignoring the occasional disasters. 'With an air of complete ease and leisure, without hurrying or raising her voice, her long Pre-Raphaelite robes trailing behind her as she moved, she ran this lively house, cooked for this large family and their visitors, yet always appeared to have time on her hands,' wrote Gerald Brenan. '. . . I remember her best as she sat at the head of the long dining-table, resting her large, expressive eyes with their clear whites on the children and visitors and bringing an order and beauty into the scene.'[7] Through these surroundings she moved with an effortlessness compared with which others appeared bustling and vociferous. The windows at Alderney stood open, and into the house flowed the produce of Dorelia's 'home farm' – piles of fresh vegetables from the kitchen gardens; blue and brown jugs of milk and cream; jars of home-made mead tasting like a light white wine; the honey and the butter; lavender in the coarse linen – and everywhere a profusion of flowers.

Almost every kind of tree and shrub flourished at Alderney: ilex and pine, apple and cherry and chestnut, pink and white clematis. The circular walled-in garden, with its crescent-shaped flowerbeds over which sim-mered the bees and butterflies, became an enchanted place. 'The peculiar charm of that garden was its half-wild appearance,' wrote Romilly John.

'. . . great masses of lavender and other smelling plants sprawled outwards from the concentric beds, until in some places the pathways were almost concealed. Tangled masses of rose and clematis heaved up into the air, or hung droopingly from the wall . . . [which] was overtopped most of the way by a thick hedge formed by the laurels that grew outside, and a eucalyptus, which had escaped the frosts of several winters, lifted high into the air its graceful and silvery spire.'[8]

Dorelia's influence extended far beyond the walls of this garden. For three decades her taste in clothes was followed by students. She ignored the manners and fashions of London and Paris, and the brash styles that succeeded them. Her style was peculiar to herself. 'She was the most beautiful woman I have ever seen,' wrote the children's author Kathleen Hale.

'. . . I remember one Christmas at Alderney, when all the decorations were fixed and everything set for the fun and sing-song, the last to arrive was Dorelia. She appeared on the top step of the room in a white woollen gown, her dark hair looped and braided as always, but so different to the arty hair-do's of the artistic set. Her warm brown skin glowed in the whiteness of her softly gathered white bodice. Translucent green earrings dangled from her ears – they may have been only of glass but no emerald could have been more beautiful. They were the only colour she wore. She stood quietly surveying us, unaware of the impact she made.'

From cotton velveteen or shantung in bright dyes and shimmering surfaces; from unusual prints, often Indian or Mediterranean in origin, she evolved clothes that followed the movement of the body, like classic draperies. Her flowing dresses that reached the ground, with their high waistline and long sleeves topped by a broad-brimmed straw hat, its sweeping line like those of the French peasants, became a uniform adopted by many girls at art colleges, and a symbol, in their metropolitan surroundings, of an unsevered connection with the country. In the mythology of the young, Dorelia and Augustus were seen as representing the principle of living through your ideas, not merely conveying them to canvas or on paper.

For the boys Dorelia invented a costume which, with its long-belted smock over corduroy trousers, together with their bobbed hair, gave them the appearance of fierce dolls. 'Our hair was long and golden,' Romilly remembered, 'with a fringe in front that came down to our eyebrows; we had little pink pinafores reaching to just below the waist, and leaving our necks bare; brown corduroy knickers, red socks and black boots completed the effect.'[9] Later on, Dorelia dressed her daughters in buff-coloured woollen dresses, rather draughty, with thin crisscross lines, saffron-yellow ankle socks and square-toed black slippers. Their hair, also bobbed, was shoulder length, and their frocks, which they learnt to manipulate with dexterity when climbing off floors or clambering into chairs, reached almost down to their feet. It was as if Augustus's pictures had come alive. Here, in a coach house converted to a studio, he painted 'Washing Day',[10] 'The Blue Pool',[11] and made innumerable drawings and panels of the children alone or in groups, portraits of the many visitors from Francis Macnamara[12] to Roy Campbell,[13] and studies for the figures in his large decorative groups 'Forza e Amore',[14] 'The Mumpers'[15] and 'Lyric Fantasy'.[16]

Augustus kept himself in the background. His presence, like that of a volcano, was often silent and sometimes menacing. A swiftly moving, dark bearded figure, with a wide-brimmed hat, tweeds and a pipe, he patrolled Alderney, watching everyone, disconcerting them with his stare, his sudden eruptions. No longer was he the wild youth 'Gus John'; he had flowered into the full magnificence of 'Augustus John', soon to be truncated to the moody monosyllabic 'John'. In the mornings he was morose, merely issuing a rumbling summons 'Come and sit!' He would collect some guest, or a bunch of children, take them off and in a couple of hours produce a panel of one of the boys with a bow and arrow, or Dorelia leaning against a fir tree, or a series of drawings.

As the day wore on his mood lightened. Often he would suggest taking out the pony trap and driving through the country lanes to the White Hart or King's Arms, small favourite pubs with sawdust on the floors and the reek of shag and cool ale, where he would drink beer and play shove-ha'penny ('I play myself. Play alone'). The two eldest boys, David and Caspar, who were in charge of the stabling and grooming, would 'harness the ponies into their traps, ready to drive up to the front door where Augustus and Dodo would be waiting, he for a round of the nearer pubs, she for a round of the shops', Caspar wrote. 'We two would sit on the rail boards, ready to feed and water the ponies at each stop, most of which they knew without being reined.'[17]

But it was in the evening, seated at the head of the refectory table, that Augustus came into his own. A central passage in the house, with bed-rooms on both sides, led down some steps to a large living-room where everyone dined. It had a wide open fireplace, its burning logs lying on soft grey ash. Within this arena of hospitality, melancholy would thaw, allowing his good humour to come out. Sometimes he would permit the children to stay up on these gorgeous occasions and wait at table. 'The table seemed to groan under the weight of innumerable dishes,' Romilly remembered, 'and be lighted by a hundred glittering candles in their shining candlesticks of brass. Dorelia and John appeared, for the first time in the day, in their true characters and proportions; they were like Jove and Juno presiding over the Olympian feast.'[18] Sometimes, too, there were terrific parties with bonfires and dancing, and John, rolling his lustrous eyes like marbles, an enigmatic smile on his face, would in his growling voice sing songs between long puffs of pipe smoke.

> In Jury town I was bred and bornn
> In Newgate gaol I'll die in scornn.

He delivered these highwayman's songs with intense concentration; but it was a strange thing, one of his listeners noticed: 'as he sang his body seemed to grow small. It was as if it all went into his voice. He dwindled.'[19]

> At seventeen I took a wife
> I loved her as I loved my life.

It was often a point of honour that these parties continue till early morning, and so many people came that huge wigwams had to be con-structed from branches and brown blankets, like the tents in *Prince Igor*, to accommodate everyone in the garden. On hot nights they would make up a communal bed in the orchard, nine wide and full of bracken that crackled when anyone moved. Then, first thing in the morning, John would be towering over them, and, while others were still lying where they had fallen, lead off some child to his studio.

The children played a natural part in this community. There were signs of them everywhere, such as the uncertainly chalked notice in the lavatory: PLEASE PULL THE CHAIN JENTLY. But most often they were out of doors, immersed in their secret games. From the dark undergrowth they would suddenly shin up the trees in bare feet, run with a pack of red setters, plunge into the frog-laden pond and, to the distress of the parson, dash naked round the garden getting dry. Sometimes they played hide-and-seek on the horses, or harnessed a tin bath to one of the pigs which towed them across the grass. One favourite place was the brickyard over the road with its great claypit and little trolleys pulled along miniature railway lines; and another, a large sandpit enclosed by pine trees. The many-shaded sand-cliffs could be tunnelled into and carved out in paths and bear-holes. At the top where the sand joined silver-grey and black earth, and the smell of heath and dank sand had a peculiar quality, they would set up shop with different-coloured sands and play an absorbing game. Then the lunch bell, erected at the top of a high post at the back of the house, echoed across the fields, and they would pelt back through the orchard. On windless days this bell could be heard all over the estate, alerting whole troops of poachers and stealers of wood, who were chased off between courses.

After lunch, they were off again, fighting a fire on the heath or, more mysteriously, entering their private world of rites and humours, games of their own invention such as 'Bottom First' and cults that embraced strange moaning choruses, 'Give us our seaweed!', accompanied by side-splitting yells of laughter.

They were not pampered, these children, but increasingly as time went on put to work sawing logs, digging, grooming the horses, collecting hens' eggs, tarring fences, minding the farm and doing all the chores of the house. It was an unorthodox upbringing, permissive yet sometimes oppressive. But this first summer, while the house was still empty and they slept in tents and every day the sun shone, Alderney was idyllic.

2

THE SECOND MRS STRINDBERG

'Am I a Don Juan? How sad!'
Augustus to Dorelia (1911)

Keeping his studio at the Chenil Gallery, John stayed for much of the week in London; then, at weekends, or in moments of revulsion from town life, he would show up at Alderney to go on with his work inside the converted coach house. It suited him in many ways, this dual existence, giving a constructive pattern to his restlessness. Alderney was a harbour, and Dorelia his anchor.

'He behaves very well,' Dorelia admitted to Charles Tennyson, ' – *if I keep my eye on him.*' The eye she kept on him was tolerantly fierce. Over the early years at Alderney a pattern of existence developed between them that became roughly acceptable to both. He carried on two lives; and so, eventually, did she. In London he enjoyed affairs and flirtations with models, actresses, dancers – anyone new. These amatory exercises seemed almost obligatory. 'The dirty little girl I meet in the lane', he declared, 'has a secret for me – communicable in no language, estimable at no price, momentous beyond knowledge, though it concern but her and me.'[20] It was of some concern to Dorelia, nevertheless, when these girls appeared at Alderney. For she would surrender easily to nothing, knowing that were she to do so John, like a child, would seek to push things further. 'I want to live with you when I come down,' John wrote from London, 'but I don't like imposing myself on you.' From Dorelia's point of view this seemed a promising start. Her most useful card was Henry Lamb. Whenever Lamb wanted to see her, she would ask John, almost formally, whether he minded. Surprised, he would disclaim any objection to 'the poor agneau' coming to Alderney – provided, of course, Dorelia didn't mind. But when he inflicted his girls on her, or too inconsiderately hared off in pursuit of them, he would find at moments particularly inconvenient to himself Lamb happily installed there again, playing Bach duets with her. He hadn't imagined Lamb's company was so 'indispensable', he sarcastically remarked.

Many of John's romances were short;* others, drifting into the mellower

---

* The painter Jean Varda remembered a characteristic affair with the extravagant dancer Lady Constance Stewart-Richardson – reputedly 'the worst dancer in the world but one of the most remarkable athletes', as described by Aldous Huxley, 'whose strength is as the strength of ten'. Their liaison began in 1914 and 'for being unrequited lasted longer than his [John's] periodic infatuations. At Lady Constance's studio (in her performance of the sword dance) he took a violent dislike to me

waters of affection, lasted years. 'You may be sure I want you a great deal more than any other damsels,' he assured Dorelia: but he wanted them as well. In all his painting, whether landscapes or portraits, he depended upon some instinctive relationship that would take hold of him and guide his paintbrush. In the case of women, this miracle was difficult to achieve if his concentration was constantly fretted by unsatisfied desire. Under such conditions, his shyness stood like a barrier between him and his sitter. It was to this argument that Dorelia listened with most attention. No worthwhile man, she told Amaryllis Fleming, was easy. By such a definition John was extremely worthwhile. There were those who wondered how, stoical and accepting of life as she was, Dorelia could put up with as much as she did. She did not do so without a struggle. In their long tug-of-war, the rope between them almost snapped. She endured what she did less for love than from belief. She believed him to be a good, perhaps a great artist; and she scorned conventional indignation, expressed on her behalf, about his 'goings-on'. But if he were not to prove a good or great artist, she told Helen Anrep, then her life had been wasted.

She saw her job as lifting some of the responsibilities, irrelevant to painting, from John's shoulders. She would untie the cords and give him back part of his freedom. When he had illegitimate children she did not leave him, but sometimes helped to look after them, as she looked after Ida's legitimate children. He could go where he wanted, do what he wanted, but must come to heel when she called.

It seemed, at times, as if Dorelia had entered the plant world more completely than the world of human beings, as if flowers meant more to her than people: perhaps, eventually, they did. There were terrifying fights with John: but over such issues as whether or not, on some half-forgotten occasion, Ida's Caspar had suffered from toothache. Dorelia examined small things under a microscope, but appeared to look at the large events of life through the wrong end of a pair of binoculars so that they never came too close. This protective strategy is well caught by a conversation she later had with the novelist Richard Hughes. One afternoon, when the two of them were walking in the garden with a boy of about four believed to be John's youngest illegitimate son, Dorelia suddenly came out with: 'There's one thing about John I've never got used to, not after all these

and in fits of prodigious eloquence cursed me with a wealth of abuse and vituperation, the like of which I never encountered in my life . . . It was a great treat to hear these gorgeous syllables delivered with the grandiose emphasis of a Mounet Sully of the Comédie Française.' Varda at that time was Lady Constance's perspiring partner in the dance. A few years later a calm seems to have descended and at Evan Morgan's birthday party in July 1917 Aldous Huxley records: 'in one corner of the room Lady Constance supported John on her bosom.' She was, he adds, 'profoundly exhausting company'.

years.' Richard Hughes glanced apprehensively at the child, and braced himself. Then she continued: 'I don't know what to do about it. Time after time, *he's late for lunch.'*

The girls John brought down to Alderney were accepted coolly by Dorelia and were not helped much by John himself. It was as if they knew a different John, while, in the words of the poet Iris Tree, 'she guarded his higher ghost'. Some she frightened away, being known by them as 'the yellow peril'; others, through their exceptional qualities, she came to see as allies. But there were limits. Her censure usually fell hardest on the girls themselves rather than on John, for it was not justice that interested her but what was practical. A friend who lived near by remembers one incident that shows her methods of dealing with anything unacceptable:

'One afternoon I had gone up to Alderney Manor to learn from Dorelia how to "turn a heel", so I would be able to knit socks for my two boys. We were having tea when a vehicle came to the front door. Dorelia went to see who it was, some luggage was dumped in the passage, a girl was brought in, introduced, and politely asked to have some tea. The conversation dragged, neither Dorelia nor I were any good at "chatting". Soon I got up to go, but Dorelia asked me to stay on . . . Dorelia then turned to the girl. "What train are you catching?" she said. The girl looked surprised. "There is a good train to Waterloo you can get if you go now, the next one is much later. I will see that you are driven to the station." Before Dorelia had reached the door, the girl blurted out in an offended voice: "Augustus asked me to stay." "But Augustus is not here," answered Dorelia calmly, and went out . . . She politely and firmly got the girl and luggage out of the house without raising her voice, without losing her temper, without even looking upset, so it all seemed a most ordinary affair. "I am not going to have Augustus's girls here when he is not present" – and that was all she ever said about that interlude.'[21]

*

It was this version of a welcome (emphasized when one of the children shot an adhesive dart at her) which was extended to the second Mrs Strindberg, who, rising vigorously from her deathbed in the Savoy Hotel (upon which, she boasted, John had deposited her), called on Dorelia one Christmas Eve. She arrived, wearing a nightdress in the snow. Her visit was brief, and represented the latest in 'a long series of grotesque and unedifying adventures'[22] to which this tiger-woman from Vienna was, John claimed, subjecting him. For two years, in Paris, Liverpool and London, she had dogged his heels, buying up pictures that were not for sale and presenting large cheques that baffled Knewstub at the Chenil, infuriated Quinn in New York, and eventually found their way, via her maid, back into her own pocket.

By all accounts Frida Strindberg was a remarkable woman. After ten years in a convent 'among the brides of Christ', she had been let out to serve, for a further two years, as 'the beautiful jail keeper' of Sweden's chief dramatist. Their marriage had been an exhausting comedy of love, the tone of which was set at the wedding when the parson, addressing his question to Strindberg rather than to Frida, demanded: 'Will you swear that you do not carry another man's child under your heart?' While Strindberg nervously denied being pregnant, Frida interrupted with a volley of hysterical laughter.

A determined admirer of the hero in man, Frida had sharpened up a ravenous appetite, given somewhat to indigestion, for men of genius. On catching sight of a specimen she would burrow ruthlessly under his spell, and there was little he might do to extricate himself from the rigours of her devotion. As she grew older she gathered force until she arrived in London an Amazon. She had become aware within herself of brilliant gifts as a journalist and now conducted her life as if it were the daily material for front-page headlines. In 1910, while on the track of the fleeing Wyndham Lewis, she had called at Church Street and, expecting to corner him there, found herself in bed with John. 'I then dismissed the incident from my mind,' he recorded,[23] 'but it turned out to be the prelude to a long and by no means idyllic tale of misdirected energy, mad incomprehension, absurdity and even squalor.'[24]

What happened over the next two years has been summarized by Strindberg's biographer John Stewart Collis:

'If, without telling a soul where he was going, he sought refuge in some obscure café in Paris or London, Frida would know and appear on the scene. If he boarded a train for the country, there she would be on the platform to bid him good-bye or to follow him. And it was advisable for him to watch his step in his treatment of her even when dining with her in company, for if he were discovered paying too much attention to another female member of the party she would pay a man to take up a concealed position and aim a champagne bottle at his head; and on one occasion, in Paris, when he imagined that he had been successful in eluding her by a series of swift changes of scene, he was informed through an anonymous and illiterate note that he would *again* be beaten up if his behaviour towards a certain lady did not improve – for evidently someone had been mistaken for John and had innocently suffered the attack.'[25]

Mrs Strindberg saw herself as John's benefactress. In her late thirties, she was still a very cordial woman, her face wreathed in dangerous smiles and, we are told, with 'eyes of that shade of dark and lively brown which so often prove irresistible to men'.[26] John felt intimidated. 'I admit', he conceded, 'that the sight of Mme Strindberg bearing down on me in an open taxi-cab, a glad smile of greeting on her face, shaded with a hat turned up behind and bearing a luxuriant outcrop of sweetpeas – this sight, I confess, unnerved me.'[27] He held his ground – then ran; but whichever way he goes, there she is with arms outstretched to welcome him. 'I am worn out!' she cries. 'I am suffering more than I have strength to bear!!' But he too is suffering: 'Can you seriously think I *enjoy* this business,' he demands, 'that I glory in it???' Their reproaches and punctuation marks multiply. She speaks of love and death, and swears that he does not understand her. He hears the voice of power, and objects: 'It is this *constant* misunderstanding of my character which is the fatal element in the whole affair.' Their accusations turn towards the thickets of legality. 'They are serving you a subpoena or will try to do so to-day,' she promises him. 'I want to attack you by the Law!!!' he bursts out.

What has survived of their correspondence reveals the secret of Frida's ubiquity. When unable to accompany John on his wild flittings to and fro, she would arrange for him to be shadowed by a private detective, and it is round the competence of this man's reports that many of their arguments revolve.

Each claimed that the other was making a public exhibition of them both. 'If all Chelsea is aware of your existence it is simply because you have a genius for advertising it,' John blandly concluded. Frida's chief complaints centred on the company he kept other than her own. 'You write love letters to all the girls in London, which they all read aloud,' she objected. One girl, in a leopard skin, had recited nine pages to music; and another, unaccompanied, had danced a dance of jealousy. Was it any wonder, then, that Frida 'felt like murder yesterday – I was mad, mad, mad'. It was untrue, she added, that Edith Ashley ('a silly Kensington girl from a penny novel') had 'been bribed by me not to see you, that I had twice tried to murder her, once by poison, once by pushing her from a cliff'.

John refused to disbelieve her. 'You are determined to be melodramatic to the last!' He felt imperilled by her threats of love, recognizing 'an audacious attempt at intimidation'. For she had sensed his fear of publicity and was constantly playing on it. 'I was born as the only woman of one man,' she was to write in her autobiography.[28] That man was temporarily John. She therefore promised to 'unmask' his other women. 'I have shunned it until now for your sake,' she added, '. . . for your wife and children's sake.'

John feared that she would, by means of the courts and press, try to disrupt his life at Alderney. To forestall this he had already made Frida a figure of fun. She has 'gone off her head again,' he told Dorelia. '. . . The waiters in the Café Royal look at me with discreet sympathy.'[29] She had one very potent weapon: death. It happened that she was strong on suicide, swallowing down regular doses of Veronal mixed with Bovril, then dispatching her abominably pretty maid to John with the news that she had tossed down this fatal cocktail and was about to die. But when, in terror of some farewell message for the coroner and press, he hurried to her bedside, there would always ensue an intolerable interview; and on one occasion, having seized his hat and bolted down the hotel corridor, he was overtaken by the dying woman in the lift.

In *Chiaroscuro* John makes well-rehearsed comedy out of such episodes, though it appears from contemporary documents that he was sometimes seriously disturbed by them. To John Quinn, revisiting London at the beginning of September 1911, he unburdened himself. Quinn's diary entry for 3 September records that John, at the Café Royal, 'sober but normal looking', told him that, in response to four or five pleading letters from Frida, he had just gone to see her at the Capitol Hotel. He advised her that she had made 'a damnable nuisance of herself', and that their relationship must end. She 'clutched and raved', but though he felt sorry for her, he steeled himself not to surrender. Later that night, in his studio at the Chenil, he learnt that she had again killed herself and was not feeling well. She is 'pegging out in earnest this time', he warns Dorelia. Next morning Quinn called round: 'Awful tale about Madame Strindberg all right,' he confirmed in his diary. '. . . Mme S. had taken poison and the doctor said she would not last the night. John shaken but game & determined not to give in. I felt sorry for him and did my best to brace him up. I don't think he had slept very much. This damned Austrian woman has wasted John's time – upset his nerves – played hell with his work.' The two men walked to the Queen's restaurant near Sloane Square and 'I advised John if Mme S. *did* die to "beat it" – clear out of the country,' Quinn continued. '. . . John is really a combination of boy and man – but a man of the highest principle.'

As a result of their discussion, John made up his mind, whatever happened, to accompany Quinn to France. 'Would you come over too?' he asked Dorelia. '. . . We could persuade Quinn to eat in modest restaurants.' But Dorelia was involved in her vegetable garden and could not join them. Disappointed, John met Quinn at the Café Royal next evening to call the journey off, but changed his mind on hearing reports of Frida

Strindberg's worsening condition. In place of Dorelia, he arranged for the two of them to be accompanied by Euphemia Lamb and another model, Lillian Shelley, 'a beautiful thing . . . red lips and hair as black as a Turk's, stunning figure, great sense of humour'.[30] Exhilaration and exhaustion struggled for possession of Quinn. At midnight, he allowed himself to be guided by Lillian and Euphemia to John's studio. 'All drunk,' he rejoiced, 'and John sang and acted wonderfully. Two divans full – L[illian] the best natured.' After breakfast Quinn ordered four tickets, and John bought 'a swell automobile coat & cap'.[31]

John was looking forward to 'a few days' peace'; Quinn, more apprehensively, hoped that 'the trip will be pleasant'. The two of them arrived punctually at Charing Cross station, but the girls did not. Instead, upon the platform stood Frida Strindberg, her only luggage a revolver. Quinn's notes at this stage become shaky, though the word 'carnage' is deceptively clear. 'Only by appealing to the guard,' John wrote, 'and the use of a little physical force were we able to preserve our privacy.'*[32] Undeterred she followed them on to the boat at Dover. John locked himself into his cabin, but Quinn, relishing this contact with Bohemian life, bravely offered the huntress a cup of tea. John was appalled when he heard of this errand: 'She spoke to Quinn on the boat and tried to get him into partnership with her to run me!!' he protested in a letter to Dorelia. To this purpose she had made an appointment to see Quinn the following day in Paris. But in the interval, Quinn lost his nerve and instead of keeping his appointment he took John to the Hotel Bristol to meet an American copper king, Thomas Fortune Ryan; a tall elderly Southerner who talked wearily in immense sums of money and pessimistically chewed upon an unlit cigar. That evening they went to the Bal Tabarin and were joined by a young Kabyle woman. 'This dusky girl's whole person exhaled a delicious odour of musk or sandalwood. A childlike candour illuminated her smouldering eyes.'[33] At two o'clock that morning they returned to their hotel: 'finally to Pl. Panthéon,' Quinn noted wearily, '& John went with the girl.'

By now Madame Strindberg had reached their hotel and 'committed suicide'. There was not a moment to lose. 'We shall throw her off the scent by means of the car,' John assured Dorelia.[34] Hurriedly borrowing Ryan's seventy-five-horsepower Mercedes manned by 'the best chauffeur in Europe',[35] a German, Quinn and John set off and 'careered over France ruthlessly'.[36]

The prospect of a week with Quinn in such delightful country depressed

* In *Chiaroscuro*, John was careful to write of 'passive yet firm resistance' at the railway station. But in a letter to Dorelia he is more direct: 'I shoved her out.'

John, and he proposed reviving their earlier scheme by fetching over Lillian and Euphemia. Quinn was game, but Dorelia, to whom John suggested this by letter, was not: and the plan was reluctantly abandoned. For much of the time John was sullen and aggressive. 'O these Americans!!!' he burst out. 'I don't think I can stand that accent much longer . . . their naiveté, their innocence, their banality, their crass stupidity is unimaginable.'[37] Yet Quinn stayed doggedly optimistic. 'John and I had a great time in France,' he loyally declared.[38]

What they achieved in this breathless ellipse to and back from the Mediterranean was a forerunner of the modern package tour.[39] 'It was like a nightmare.' At the start they fuelled themselves with prodigious quantities of champagne. 'The first day out we started on champagne at lunch,' Quinn told James G. Huneker (15 November 1911):

'That night at dinner, feeling sure that I would be knocked out the next day, I might as well go the limit and so we had champagne at dinner. I slept like a top, woke up feeling like a prince, and did a hundred and fifty miles next day, and from then on and every day till we returned to Paris we had two and sometimes three quarts of champagne a day – champagne for lunch, champagne for dinner, liqueurs of all kinds, cassis and marc, vermouth, absinthe and the devil knows what else.'

For John, who had counted on Quinn retiring to bed most days with a hangover, such resilience was disappointing. But there were many hair-raising misadventures to enliven the excursion. Their progress was punctuated by several burst tyres and encounters with chickens and dogs. At one place they knocked down a young boy on a bicycle and themselves leapt wildly down a steep place into a ploughed field. 'We landed after about three terrific jumps,' Quinn reported, '. . . just missed bumping into a tree which would have smashed the machine . . . the kid's thick skull that got him into trouble saved him when he fell.'[40] Having deposited the child with a doctor, they raced on expecting at every town to be arrested. 'Quinn's French efforts are amazing,' John wrote in a letter to Dorelia. 'Imagine the language we have to talk to the chauffeur. Desperando!' Descending a tortuous mountain road, Quinn had inquired the German for 'slow'. 'Schnell,' John replied. 'Schnell!' Quinn shouted at their burly driver, who obediently accelerated. 'Schnell! Schnell!' Quinn repeatedly cried. They hurtled down the mountain at breakneck speed and arrived at their hotel 'in good time for dinner' – though on this occasion Quinn immediately retired to bed.

In a letter to Conrad[41] Quinn recalled 'feeling like a fighting man' during this journey. But the points were massing up against him. At night he was haunted by 'horrible shapes – stone houses, fences, trees, hay stacks, stone walls, stone piles, dirt walls, chasms and precipices advancing towards us out of the fog all to fade away into grey mist again'. On one occasion, John recounts in *Chiaroscuro*, 'when the car was creeping at a snail's pace on an unknown road through a dense fog in the Cévennes, the attorney [Quinn] suddenly gave vent to a despairing cry, and in one masterly leap precipitated himself clean through the open window, to land harmlessly on the grass by the road-side! He felt sure we were going over a precipice.'[42]

Quinn secretly, and John openly, were much relieved when their tour came to an end. 'We were not quite a success as travelling companions,' John conceded.[43] The motor car, he concluded, 'is a damnable invention'. Travelling on foot or by caravan was the proper progress for a painter. 'Motoring is a fearfully wrong way of seeing the country but an awfully nice way of doing without railway trains,' he instructed Dorelia. 'It makes one very sleepy.' Nevertheless, it had been impossible to overlook everything, the countryside, the cathedrals at Bourges and Chartres 'veritably miraculous and power-communicating. The Ancients', he told Will Rothenstein, 'did nothing like this.'

Another success had been their final shaking-off of Mrs Strindberg. Two days after their return, Quinn embarked for New York; and John, having heard that Frida was again becoming 'very active in London', slipped quietly off to Wales. 'It has been impossible to do any work travelling this way,' he had complained to Dorelia from a brothel in Marseilles, 'but one can think all the same.' Now, in the peace of Wales, he could transfer these thoughts to paint.

3

CAVALIERS AND EGGHEADS

'*Non Scholae sed vitae.*'
Dane Court School motto[44]

One of the earliest visitors to Alderney was John's father. He was a model of patience. For hours he would sit motionless and then move quietly about the garden, hoping to be photographed. Every day he put on the same costume he wore for promenading the beach at Tenby: a sober suit, leather gloves, dark hat, wing collar and spats. He too had recently moved, a distance of several hundred yards, to 5 Lexden Terrace, overlooking the sea. In this desirable residence he was to linger a little uncertainly some thirty years, with the weather, a few illnesses and his 'specimens of self-photography' as companions. Occasionally he was looked in on by his grandchildren, and more occasionally by Augustus himself. It was a life spent patiently waiting, filling the long intervals with letters to Winifred to say he was writing to Gwen, and to Augustus saying he was writing to Thornton: and variations on this pattern.

From Dorelia's family there came, among others, her mother – a very straight-backed old woman with shiny white hair and a comforting round face. She spent her days quilt-making, and in the evenings would take a hot brick from the fireplace, wrapping it in cloth to warm her bed.

From 1912 onwards the guests, many of them subjects for portraits and testifying to the rich variety of the human species, began to assemble at Alderney. Not everyone was immediately welcome. Wyndham Lewis 'had an inner door slammed in my face' by Dorelia who was nevertheless the object of his 'most sympathetic admiration'. But this was because of his 'empty abuse of Lamb' which she had perhaps mistaken for 'strenuous plotting'.[45] And then, 'Did you turn away Lord Howard de Walden & his wife one day at the door?'[46] John mildly inquired. Perhaps she had, but if so it was because this valuable patron and important sitter (who was pregnant) looked like obvious troublemakers.

But many people found a home from home at Alderney. There was Iris Tree, with her freckles and blue shadows, gliding between the trees in a poetic trance; Lytton Strachey, who amazed the children by claiming he felt so weak before breakfast that he found it impossible to lift a match; Fanny Fletcher, a poor art student later revered for her wallpapers, who arrived for a few weeks, knitted herself into the household with her cardigans and gained the reputation for being a rather inefficient witch whose salad dressings were said to contain spells; there was also a Polish doctor of music, Jan Sliwinski, who became expert at tarring fences, mending walls and cataloguing books; the Chilean painter Alvaro Guevara with tales of terrific boxing matches in Valparaiso, where he had been a champion; and an 'unknown quantity', Haraldar Thorskinsson, called 'the Icelander', a speechless, hard-drinking Icelandic poet with bright carmine cheeks and stark black hair, who had written a play in which angels somehow figured and who was now heavily involved in defeating the law of gravity. Very often Henry Lamb (or 'Arry Lamb' as John called him) would ride over on a pony cart to play duets with Dorelia at the upright piano. Sounds of Mozart and of Bach fugues would float out of the open windows into the garden, sometimes followed by heated words as to who had played the wrong note and, more implausibly, whether or not there was a deity – for Dorelia was an agnostic and Lamb an atheist, and the two of them often argued over what neither of them believed. Horace de

Vere Cole, the country's most eminent practical joker and inventor of turned-up trousers, who claimed descent from Old King Cole, would invite himself over, 'such a hopeless child', but always bringing a 'Grand New Hoax'.

More cavalier still was the farmer, archaeologist* and anti-aircraft pioneer, Trelawney Dayrell Reed, who dropped in for a cup of tea one afternoon, hung on a few years, then bought a farm near by into which he settled with his grim mother, unmarried sister and some eighteenth-century furniture. Black-bearded and fanatic, he looked like a prince in the manner of El Greco, and was much admired for the violence of his Oxford stammer, his loud check tweeds, and socks of revolutionary red. An occasional poet, he also took to painting, executing in his farmhouse a series of vigorous and explicit frescoes. He was attended by two spaniels and his 'man', a wide-eyed factotum named Ernest. His air of refinement infuriated John. 'Huntin' does give one the opportunity of dressin' like a gentleman,' he would drawl. 'But I've always thought the real test was how to undress like a gentleman.' When asked whether he had pigs on his farm, he had replied: 'No. The boys have the pigs. I have the boys.' He liked to sing ballads of extreme bawdiness, accompanying his tuneless voice with free-flowing gestures. A great hero to the children, he was master of many accomplishments from darts to the deepest dialect of Dorset. He was also a landscape and market gardener with a special knowledge of hollyhocks and roses – his chief love. It was in defence of these blooms, his dogs, pigs and an apple tree that he later served his finest hour. Every afternoon he would go to bed, and every afternoon he was woken by aeroplanes which had selected his cottage as a turning point in their local races. He wrote letters, he remonstrated, he complained by every lawful means: but the flying monsters still howled about the chimney pots, creating havoc among his cattle and female relatives. Then, one afternoon, awakened by a deafening racket, he sprang from his bed and let fly with a double-barrelled shotgun, winging one of the brutes. Although no vital damage was done, Trelawney was arrested and tried at Dorchester Assizes on a charge of attempted murder. In opposition to the judge, a man much loved for his severity, the jury (being composed mostly of farmers like himself) acquitted him. It was a triumph for the individual, amateur and eccentric against the ascent of technology; and there was a grand celebration.

To be brought up amid such people constituted an education in itself. John, however, pressed matters to extremes: he hired a tutor. As long ago as May 1910 he had been persuaded that 'the immediate *necessity* seems

---

* He was the author of *The Battle of Britain in the Fifth Century; an Essay in Dark Age History.*

to be an able tutor and major-domo for my family.'[47] If the search had been long and hesitant, this was because he needed someone exceptional. On 16 August 1911 he reported to Quinn that 'I have just secured a young tutor who really seems a jewel'; and a month later[48] he was telling Ottoline Morrell that 'our tutor is an excellent and charming youth.'

His name was John Hope-Johnstone. He was then in his late twenties, a man of many attainments and no profession, an adventurous past and a waxed moustache. He had been educated between Bradfield, Hanover and Trinity College, Cambridge, which he had been obliged to leave prematurely when his mother abandoned her second fortune to the roulette wheel. From this time onwards he lived by his wits. But, as Romilly John observed, 'he was very fortunate in combining, at that time, extreme poverty with the most epicurean tastes I have ever known.'[49] He had a hunger for knowledge that ranged from the intricacies of Arabic to the address of the only place in Britain where a certain toothpaste might be bought. It was part of a programme of self-perfection to which he had dedicated himself pending the death of eleven persons which, he calculated, would bring him into a fortune with a title. Undeterred by a lack of 'ear', he mastered the penny whistle and then, by sheer perseverance, the flute.* He was a confirmed wanderer. Before taking up his post as a tutor, he had spent some years pushing a pram charged with grammars and metaphysical works through Asia, reputedly in pursuit of a village where chickens were said to cost a penny each.

He never found it, but arrived instead at Alderney into which, for a time, he fitted very well. Slim and well built, with finely cut features, dark hair and pale skin, he wore heavy hornrimmed spectacles, an innovation at the time. It was not long before he conceived an immense admiration for John and Dorelia and the romantic life they led around their battlemented bungalow, with their entourage of gypsy caravans and ponies and naked children. As a mark of admiration he took to wearing a medley of Bohemian clothes – buff corduroy suits cut by a grand tailor in Savile Row after the style of a dress suit, with swallow tails behind, a coloured handkerchief or 'diklo' round his neck and, to complete the bizarre effect, a black felt hat of the kind later made fashionable by Anthony Eden when

---

* He was drawn by Wyndham Lewis playing the flute. Later, with Compton Mackenzie, he became joint editor of the *Gramophone*, in which he reviewed the latest records under the pseudonym 'James Caskett'. In Octave 5 of *My Life and Times*, Compton Mackenzie recounts that he first met Hope-Johnstone in Greece in 1916. 'John Hope-Johnstone had arrived by now from Corfu with a kitbag containing a few clothes, one top-boot, several works on higher mathematics and two volumes of Doughty's *Arabia Deserta*, a pair of bright yellow Moorish slippers, a camera and a flute . . . He enlisted at the beginning of the war, somehow cheating the military authorities over his eyesight; then his myopia was discovered by his having saluted a drum he had mistaken for the regimental sergeant-major.'

Prime Minister, though with a broad rim. To John's eyes he was every inch a tutor.

It is doubtful if his pupils benefited as much as John and Dorelia did from his encyclopedic tutelage. 'For Hope the argument – long, persistent, remorseless, carried back to first logical principles – was an almost indispensable element in the day's hygiene,' his friend the 'bright young intellectual' Gerald Brenan recorded.[50] The day began at first light. He would sit over the breakfast table dilating upon Symbolic Logic or Four Dimensional Geometry while the children fled on to the heath. Then Dorelia, who in any case did not believe in education, would murmur: 'Never mind. Leave them for to-day,' and the tutor would be free to retreat into the cottage kitchen, which he had converted, with retorts and bottles of coloured fluid, into a laboratory for malodorous experiments. At other moments, possibly when it was raining, he would lead the older boys off and propound to them Latin gender rhymes and the names of the Hebrew kings. They learnt to write Gothic script with calligraphic pens and black ink. He also made a speciality of the Book of Job, parts of which he encouraged them to learn by heart to train their ears for sonorous language, give them a sense of the remote past, and instil patience.* He was not entirely popular, however, with the children, chiefly because of his greed. At table, when the cream jug was passed round, he would 'accidentally' spill most of it over his own plate, leaving nothing for them.

To Dorelia, with whom he was a little in love, he made himself more helpful. He was a scholar of ancient herbs and jellies, and she made use of his book-knowledge in the kitchen and when laying out her garden. To John also he tried to make himself useful by persuading him to buy an expensive camera with which to photograph his paintings. But Hope's technique of photography – 'losing bits of his machine & tripping over the trypod continually'[51] – led to a gradual fading away of all the prints into invisibility. It was an accurate record at Alderney of his waning popularity. John had warmed to him at first as an authentic dilettante – someone magnificently irrelevant to the commerce of modern life. He had been impressed by his mathematics and had liked the way he dived into their rigorously easygoing way of life, accompanying, unshaven, the barefoot boys through the Cotswolds to North Wales with pony and cart. Then John began to tire of him, as he did of everyone whom he saw regularly. He had encouraged Hope as an entertainer, and within a year

---

* 'Hope-Johnstone used to try and explain relativity to me when I was about 10,' Romilly John recalled. 'I still remember the horror of his subsequent discovery that I had not wholly mastered vulgar fractions.'

his repertoire of tricks and stories had run out. 'He's a garrulous creature and extremely irritating sometimes,' John admitted to Dorelia. 'The way he makes smoke rings with a cluck.'[52] John was never one for encores. The tutor's capacity for absorbing knowledge, which appeared so limitless, was replenished by his growing library and by John's depleted one. As a future editor of the *Burlington Magazine*, it was necessary that he should study art, but not perhaps by the method of absconding with John's own pictures, of which he amassed a good private collection. His passion for argument pierced through the growing barrier of John's deafness, especially when it developed into vast literary quarrels with Trelawney or with Edie, whose reading was confined to the *Daily Mirror* and romantic novels from the lending library at Parkstone station. So it was with some relief on all sides that in the last week of August 1912, with his entire capital of sixteen pounds, camel-hair sleeping bag and a good many grammars, he wheeled his perambulator off once more in the direction of China. Although he had been tutor for little more than a year, he was regularly to re-enter the lives of the Johns, in Spain, in Italy, at the corner of Oxford Street. Gerald Brenan, with whom he set out for the borders of Outer Mongolia, gives as Hope's reason for this sudden journey the rainy weather – though it was also rumoured that John had hit on a plan to marry him off to one of his models who was soon to give birth to a child.

After Hope's disappearance the children's education stumbled into slightly more conventional lines. 'The boys go to a beastly school now and seem to like it,' John complained to their ex-tutor (20 November 1912). Dane Court had been founded at Hunstanton in Norfolk in 1867 by a vicar, with the novelist-to-be Henry Rider Haggard as his solitary pupil. It had moved to Parkstone at the turn of the century and recently been taken over by a newly married couple, Hugh and Michaela Pooley. Hugh Pooley, a hearty player of the piccolo with a rich baritone voice, took music classes. 'He lectured us in the dormitory on the dangers of masturbation I now realize,' recalled Romilly, 'though I was puzzled at the time.'[53] If Hugh was the symbol of a headmaster, his wife, a devotee of bicycling with a weakness for astonishing hats, was the 'progressive' force in the school and taught French. It was disconcerting for her to find that the Johns already spoke the language. She was a Dane,* the

---

* 'We considered her rather a witch-like figure, though I daresay she was quite handsome in a Danish way,' Romilly John wrote. '. . . On parents' day Mrs P. invariably gave the same speech, in which she told, with considerable emotion, how she was enlightened as to the meaning of the word "gentleman", presumably there being no equivalent in Denmark either of the word or the thing. One day she had seen from an upstairs window one of the 12 older boys (*not* a John) stealing gooseberries. This boy had subsequently owned up to the theft, an instance of gentlemanliness the like of which Denmark could afford no equal. It was this boy who at a later date was employed as tutor to Edwin and me.' Romilly to the author, 15 November 1972.

daughter of Pietro Köbke Krohn, an artist and director of the Künstmuseum in Copenhagen. On the strength of her parentage she would bicycle up uninvited to Alderney with her husband and a tin of sardines to supplement the rations, and seemed deaf to the loud groans which greeted her arrival. While Hugh sang in his baritone for supper, Michaela would swivel her attentions upon John himself. The retired colonels and civil servants with which Hampshire and Dorset seemed filled were little to her taste, whereas John was an 'attractive man, who made one feel 100% woman – a quality I missed in most Englishmen at that period'.

Dane Court had eleven pupils and, since its future depended upon swelling this number, the Pooleys had been delighted to receive one morning a letter of inquiry from Alderney Manor – a property, they saw from the map, on Lord Wimborne's estate. An interview was arranged, and the Pooleys prepared themselves to meet some grand people. 'From our stand by the window we saw a green Governess cart drawn by a pony approaching up the drive,' Michaela remembered.

'A queer square cart – later named "The Marmalade Box" by the boys in the school – and out stepped a lady in a cloak with a large hat and hair cut short . . . After her a couple of boys tumbled out, their hair cut likewise and they wore coloured tunics. For a moment we thought they were girls . . . It was soon fixed that the three boys aged 8, 9, 10 should come as day boys. When Mrs John was going, she turned at the door and said: "I think there are two more at home, who might as well come." '[54]

That was the beginning and it was not easy for them, knowing only the Latin gender rules, French, and part of the Book of Job. But they were quick to learn, being, the Pooleys judged, 'a fine lot . . . intelligent and sturdy, good at work and good at games'. With their long page-style hair and belted pinafores (brightly coloured at first, then khaki to match the brown Norfolk suits the other boys wore) they felt shamefully conspicuous. Yet since they numbered almost half Dane Court and stood shoulder to shoulder against any attack, their entrance into school life was not so painful as it might have been. They formed a community of their own, a family circle with doors that could be opened only from inside. But gradually they edged these doors ajar, Eton collars giving way, under Michaela's reforming spirit, to allow corduroy suits and earthenware bowls to become the order of the day.

'David and Caspar now are expert cyclists,' John reported to Mrs Nettleship after their first term (8 January 1913). '. . . Mr Pooley wants them to be weekly boarders, he thinks they'd get on much faster – and I think it's no bad idea.' First the three eldest, then the others, boarded.

Because of their strange ways, they became known as 'the Persians'. 'But we shone on the playing fields and won many games of cricket and football for the school', Caspar remembered. '. . . Augustus once scored a goal – palpably offside – playing for the parents and Old Boys. Unhappily I was the goalkeeper . . .'[55]

On visiting days, they grew self-conscious, more vulnerable to parent-embarrassment and so far as was possible they tried to keep the parts of their lives – the Nettleship part too – within separate compartments. Details of their home life were guarded from their friends, while about Dane Court they were seldom pestered for information by John and Dorelia.

'I was especially afraid that one of my brothers would let out some frightful detail of our life at Alderney, and thus ruin us for ever,' wrote Romilly; 'a needless alarm, as they were all older and warier than I. I contracted a habit of inserting secretly after the Lord's Prayer a little clause to the effect that Dorelia might be brought by divine intervention to wear proper clothes; I used also to pray that she and John might not be tempted, by the invitation sent to all parents, to appear at the school sports.'[56]

During the holidays, Ida's children often went to stay with Grannie Nettleship. She would see that they had their hair cut and were indistinguishably fitted into regular boys' uniforms. With their aunts, Ethel and Ursula, they travelled to seaside resorts, spending their days breathing fresh air on long walks, their evenings playing Racing Demon and Up Jenkins – then early to bed.

The boys did pretty well at school; especially David, who was head boy for two years. As the eldest he felt himself to be at least as much a Nettleship as a John and was more successful when away from Alderney. But it was Caspar, Ida's second son, who cut loose. At the beginning of the Great War he was given a copy of *Jane's All the World's Fighting Ships* and, looking through the lists of warships, two-thirds of them British, decided that this 'new and orderly society . . . was the world for me'.[57] All the boys were talking of the army, the navy and the Royal Flying Corps. With Hugh Pooley's encouragement, Caspar eventually approached his father with the notion of making the navy his career. It was a difficult interview. John felt bewildered. He could remember himself having decided at this age to trap beaver on the Arkansas River. David, who had been reading *Coral Island* and who wanted to go to sea on the chance of getting wrecked on such a charming spot, he could understand. But Caspar seemed unaccountably serious. John plainly thought it stupid to subject oneself to such harsh discipline, and he did not scruple to say so. 'Think again,' he advised, and brushed the idea aside. 'I had no encouragement at home,' Caspar remembered; 'I felt a lonely outcast.' But he persisted, and came against other obstacles – the cadet's uniform alone cost a hundred and fifty pounds. But once John saw that his son was set on the navy, he paid all bills without objection. It was Dorelia who engineered this change of mind. She had no more interest in the sea than in schooling, but she wanted to get at least one boy off her hands and see him settled. So she organized it all. In September 1916 they harnessed the pony and trap and, she in her long skirts, Caspar in his bright new uniform, they travelled the thirty-five miles to Portsmouth and 'I was dumped through the dockyard main gate.'[58]

Caspar was the only one of John's children brought up at Alderney who, like Thornton, Gwen and Winifred, left home and made a life elsewhere. The others left too late or too incompletely, as perhaps John himself had done. Although one or two later illegitimate children, raised with their mothers, felt themselves deprived by not living at Alderney or Fryern, Ida's and Dorelia's children needed to escape these places – and for many of the same reasons that old Edwin John's family had fled Tenby. The atmosphere was powerful and, as the boys grew older, it seemed to become less sympathetic. 'He was extremely strict at table,' one of John's children wrote, 'and we were hardly allowed to say a word – which resulted in one of us getting the giggles, which was fatal, because that infuriated him . . . Perhaps it was because of his own very strict upbringing with his father.'[59]

John loved babies. When they were very small he used to bath them and play with them, and in such a role they preferred him to anyone else. But he found it hard to bear the physical presence of his maturing sons. Overawed, they fell, one by one, into lines of self-preservation. It was the beginning of a long defensive war no one could win. 'He always liked to have children around, plenty of them, not necessarily his own,' Caspar remembered. '. . . He enjoyed children to that extent, but he was never a warm-hearted man, really, to us; he was a tremendously difficult sort of fellow to understand for a kid. I don't think he ever understood himself, come to that.'[60]

Dorelia, too, was not good at demonstrating her love. She was not unfair, but only her own children seemed able to sense her fondness for them. John himself was inhibited from expressions of tenderness. 'He intensely disliked seeing parents *fondling* their children and this may partly have accounted for my mother's inhibitions in respect of us children,' remembered his daughter Vivien. 'In fact we never embraced our mother until the ages of 12 and 15, when [my sister] Poppet and I made a pact to break this "spell" in order to be like other families.'[61] But this was later, and for the time being the regime, for all its Bohemian tone, was almost Victorian in its rules of reticence.

Dorelia's pregnancy, in the autumn of 1911, being against her doctor's advice, was a time of anxiety. In the event everyone except Dorelia felt ill.[62] By the end of February 1912, John was already confessing to 'feeling so sick . . . Dorelia is expecting a baby momentarily . . . Pyramus mysteriously ill.' In the following week this illness came to be diagnosed. 'Little Pyramus is fearfully ill – meningitis, and I can't believe he can recover, though I do hope still,' John wrote to Ottoline Morrell (5 March 1912). 'Last night I thought he was about to die but he kept on. Dorelia behaves most wonderfully – though she is expecting her baby at any moment. It will be terrible to lose Pyra . . .' In desperation John had tried to get 'the best specialist in London, perhaps in Europe', but the man was in Europe, not London – and besides what was there he could do? 'There is no treatment for the disease.'[63] In a wobbly handwriting John wrote to his old crony John Sampson to tell him what was happening. 'We are in a sad way here. Pyramus is frightfully ill . . . Dorelia about to have a baby. The doctor tells me he thinks she has postponed the event for 2 or 3 weeks so as to look after Pyramus – he says this has been known to happen.'[64]

On 8 March Dorelia's labour pains began and she 'had to take leave of Pyramus and go and have her baby' which 'turned out a big nice girl'. They told Dorelia that Pyramus was dead, but for four more days the child lay on his bed quite close to her, still just alive. 'Pyra is still breathing feebly but happily has been unconscious for the last 2 or 3 days,' John told Ottoline on 10 March. 'I do not think he will outlive to-day. He was indeed a celestial child and that is why the Gods take him . . . The mind refuses to contemplate . . . such an awful fact.' While Dorelia grew stronger, John continued to sit by their son, waiting for the end. 'It was a terrible event,' he wrote afterwards (9 May 1912) to Quinn. '. . . I must say the Missus behaved throughout as I think few women would – with amazing good sense and a splendid determination not to give way to the *luxury* of the expression of grief.' It was this code of silence they shared. 'I can't talk about Pyra,' Dorelia told Ottoline a year later (10 March 1913): and John wrote to Albert Rutherston: 'It is indeed a terrible thing to have lost darling little Pyramus – the most adorable of children. Of course I can't find words to say what I feel.' Dorelia's silence was natural and eloquent, and her grief was private. John recognized this. But when he spoke of feeling, as from time to time he was tempted to do, he always regretted it for the words seemed to let him down, making the reality something acted. When unhappiness threatened, he feared giving way to it because he knew the depths of depression to which his nature was susceptible. No one could reach it, though 'your wire was so welcome', he told Sampson. 'These things are stupefying.'⁶⁵ So he concentrated on the birth of his daughter: 'le roi est mort, vive la reine.'⁶⁶ They called her Elizabeth Ann or Lizzie – at least that was their intention. But somehow these names never stuck. Then, one day, after contemplating her sometime, her half-brother Caspar chanced to remark: 'What a little poppet it is!': after which she was always known as Poppet.

Pyramus was cremated at Woking. Returning by train with the ashes – 'one more urn for my collection'⁶⁷ – John placed the receptacle carefully on the rack above his seat, and then forgot it. It was found further along the line and sent to Alderney.

4

CHRONIC POTENTIAL

'People were getting too silly'.
Augustus John to Gwen John (24 October 1914)

'All are well at home,' John reported philosophically, ' – the baby-girl a god-send. My missus keeps fit. We have disturbances of the atmosphere occasionally but have so far managed to recover every time.'⁶⁸ He seldom remained long at Alderney, preferring to visit rather than to stay there. 'It is pleasant enough down here,' he remarked to Ottoline Morrell (25 July 1913), 'but a little uninspiring.'

Inspiration lay further off, waiting to be taken unawares. In the summer of 1912 he had set off with his family to Wales – then, abandoning them in the desolate valley round Nant-ddu, hurried on to Ireland. 'Like a lion' he entered Dublin, remembered Oliver St John Gogarty;⁶⁹ 'or some sea king' . . .

> 'Or a Viking who has steered,
> All blue eyes and yellow beard.'⁷⁰

This was John's first meeting with stately, plump buck Gogarty, the quick-witted and long-talking professional Irishman of many parts – poet and busybody, surgeon, litigant and aviator, wearer of a primrose waistcoat and owner of the first butter-coloured Rolls-Royce. John had sought him out in the Bailey Restaurant, Dublin's equivalent of the Café Royal, on the advice of Orpen and, despite Gogarty's 'ceaseless outpour of wit and wisdom', confessed to being 'immensely entertained'.⁷¹ 'All agog with good humour', Gogarty fell headlong under John's spell, describing him as 'a man of deep shadows and dazzling light . . . I noticed that he had a magnificent body . . . He was tall, broad-shouldered and narrow-hipped. His limbs were not heavy, his hands and feet were long.'[72] 'The aura of the man! The mental amplitude!' Even so, Gogarty could not fail to notice that he was 'a moody man'. There was always the problem of what to do with him.

An ear-nose-and-throat specialist, Gogarty examined John's ears and pronounced them to be the very Seat of his Melancholy: in which case, John felt, he had much to answer for. Gogarty was a hectic monopolizer of all conversation. If he did not have enough words of his own, he borrowed other people's, and so was never at a loss. Only once did John arrest him – by 'flinging in his face a bowl of nuts'.[73] He 'is a brick but such a mad hatter', John confided to Dorelia. He was also 'rather awful sometimes', and 'dreams of the days when gentlemen addressed their wives as "Madam" and all was dignity and calm'. Not surprisingly it was difficult to make such a man 'see one's problems'.[74] But often his problems sailed out of sight as he accepted Gogarty's invitation to 'float his intellect' while in Dublin, and drink huge tumblers of whisky until the chatter retreated to a distant murmur. Bottles of John Jameson were what Gogarty was 'inspired to give' with almost sinister generosity. 'It was very pleasant, this bathing in the glory of Augustus,' Gogarty remembered[75] – adding, to John's chagrin: 'I felt myself growing so witty that I was able to laugh at my own jokes.'

But still there was the problem of what to do with John. Gogarty put him up in lodgings next to the Royal Hotel, Dalkey, overlooking Shanagolden Bay. His presence there, at the window, was a constant invitation to take the day off. 'We would pick up Joe Hone, who lived at Killiney, and go to Glendalough, the Glen of the Lakes, in Wicklow,' Gogarty wrote. '. . . On through the lovely country we went. Augustus, who was sitting in the back, could not be distracted by scenery, for beside him sat Vera Hone.

'. . . We bowled along the Rocky Valley. Suddenly I heard the word "Stop". As it evidently was not meant for me, I didn't stop. Joe Hone did not turn his head, so why should I?'[76]

This was the beginning of a lifelong infuriating friendship commemorated by John with two portraits[77] of Gogarty, and by Gogarty with two of his 'Odes and Addresses'. In a fragile verse at the end of his poem 'To Augustus John', Gogarty recorded how much, despite all its difficulties, this friendship meant to him:

When my hawk's soul shall be
With little talk in her,

391

> Trembling, about to flee,
> And Father Falconer
> Touches her off for me,
> And I am gone –
> All shall forgotten be
> Save for you, John!

Meanwhile there was the problem of what to do. John had been offered the freedom of Ireland by another bizarre new friend, Francis Macnamara, 'poet, philosopher and financial expert',[78] and though payment for such freedom could be heavy, he willingly accepted it. Macnamara was an extra 'bright gem' for John to add to his adornment of friends: at times simply 'a queer fish, not like a man at all';[79] and then, when John recovered his admiration, a 'warrior poet'. From a career in the law, from Magdalen College, Oxford, from his father the High Sheriff of County Clare, Francis Macnamara had turned to a career of literary and philosophical speculation. Over six feet tall, golden-haired and with blue-bright eyes, he carried himself (as John's portrait of him eloquently reveals) 'like a conqueror'.[80] Famous for his wild deeds, he subsisted on theories embracing many subjects from Bishop Butler to tar water, admitted to having poetry as a vocation and claimed, by way of trade, to teach the stuff. 'He has shown me a manuscript which seems to me most remarkable,' John confided to Quinn (6 August 1912), whom he hoped might buy his friend's jottings. 'He has put soliloquies into the mouths of personages from the Irish legends and he has made them talk quite modern language albeit in free verse – the result is amazingly vivid and vital. The people live again!'

It was Francis's pride, his daughter Nicolette later wrote, 'to introduce Augustus to Ireland, to County Clare, Galway and Connemara; the land the Macnamaras had roamed since history began'.[81] Though living in London, he owned a house in Doolin, a small fishing village in County Clare 'seven Irish miles away from Ennistymon', and it was here that John arrived at the end of July.

It was a lonely place, and wild. The troughs and furrows of the land, 'like an immobilized rough sea',[82] were crested with outcrops of grey rock and ridden by a net of stone walls. Except for an obstinate few trees, stunted and windswept like masted wrecks, and sudden calm surges of lush green grass, it was a barren landscape, frozen from times of primitive survival: the very place for painting. Macnamara would harness his horse and ride off with John for days on end. Several times, either by steamship or, more recklessly, by native currach, they crossed over to the Aran Islands. The great Atlantic waves that thundered in from Newfoundland and Greenland and charged against the granite boulders of the coast had protected the islanders from invasion. They lived among the same rocks and wind and weather that had long enveloped their families and seemed, as John sometimes felt himself to be, throwbacks to an earlier century. Grave dignified people, speaking English when unavoidable with a rich Elizabethan vocabulary, they wove their own garments and supported themselves without interference from the mainland. 'The smoke of burning kelp rose from the shores,' John wrote. 'Women and girls in black shawls and red or saffron skirts stood or moved in groups with a kind of nun-like uniformity and decorum. Upon the precipitous Atlantic verge some forgotten people had disputed a last foothold upon the ramparts of more than one astounding fortress . . . who on earth were they?'[83]

It was a mystery which the bleakness of their lives made beautiful to him. They represented an ideal, a dream without a dream's surreal exactness, never disappearing but growing dimmer as his actual life became more episodic and confusing.

It had been a reconnaissance. To these islands, to Doolin House, County Clare, as the guest of Macnamara, to Renvyle House, County Galway, where Gogarty lived, and the speckled hills of Connemara John was soon feeling impatient to return. He would get a studio and paint a big dramatization of the landscape, he told Quinn, and 'some of the women' who belonged to it.[84]

*

But in order to return he had first to leave. Innes, who was staying with Lady Gregory, had suddenly appeared – 'God knows how'[85] – and together the two painters crossed back into Wales. John had been invited by Lord Howard de Walden, despite his having been turned away from Alderney, to stay at Chirk Castle and paint his wife. Having separated from Innes and returned his family, safe and disgruntled, to Alderney, he rushed back to Wales again to find Lady Howard de Walden powerfully pregnant and unable to stand. No foreigner to this condition, he took up his brushes and started work on her, full length. But she was horrified, protesting that the picture was cruel, while he endeavoured to explain that 'lots of husbands want it like that, you know'.[86] In the saga of this picture, and John's many visits to Chirk in order to complete it, lies much of the pattern his life would follow. After this first visit he wrote to Quinn (11 October 1912): 'I enjoyed my stay at the medieval Castle of Chirk. I found deer stalking with bows and arrows exciting. Lord Howard goes in for falconry also and now and then dons a suit of steel armour . . .' In such an atmosphere there was room for ideas to expand. 'Howard de W ought to be taken in hand,' he was soon telling Dorelia. His host had allowed second-rate people to 'impose themselves on him'. By way of a new regime he suggested substituting himself in their place as artist-in-residence. He would decorate the Music Room at Chirk: it was a grand scheme. But first there was the problem of her ladyship's portrait. It was, he told Quinn, extremely promising. He waited patiently till after the birth of her twins, started again, exhibited it half-finished, recommenced, changed her black hair to pink and threatened to 'alter everything'. Years went by: war came. Her ladyship's nose, John complained, was an enigma, and he temporarily turned to her athletic antiquarian husband, his portrait giving 'his lordship the severest shock he has experienced since the War began'.[87] The Music Room was never begun. But he was not idle at Chirk; he painted all the time – small brilliant panels of the Welsh landscape which he conceived to be preliminary studies for his Music Room decorations but which were his real achievement.

'I would much rather just do the things I want to do and leave people to buy if they want . . . I am not likely to make a success of fashionable people even if I tried to,' John later wrote to Quinn (29 September 1913). But Chirk Castle witnessed John's beginning as an erratic portrait painter of fashionable sitters, and his last phase as a brilliant symbolist painter. 'Do you mind if I bring a friend?' he asked Lady Howard de Walden. This was Derwent Lees. Recently John's opinion of Lees had risen. He had been active at the Chenil Gallery where Orpen had apparently aimed a gun at Knewstub and shot a hole through one of his own pictures. Then Lees, despite his wooden leg, had climbed up the outside of the gallery and entered into combat with Knewstub: it was impossible to think badly of such a man even when, to everyone's surprise, he suddenly got himself married to a model. 'I too was astonished by the Lees marriage,' Innes admitted to John (4 August 1913). '. . . I think I felt rather jealous of him. Well they looked very happy and so good luck to them.' A year later Lees looked lost and white when John brought him to Chirk during a smart weekend party. He was under the impression he had arrived at a chic lunatic asylum. At night he would stand rigid in the corridors, a helplessly pyjama'd figure, whispering: 'Frightened. Can't sleep.' He had developed a shorthand method of speaking, like a child. 'Want to go for walk,' he would say. But when Lady Howard de Walden offered to accompany him, Lees objected: 'Can't. No gloves.' He did not feel safe without gloves. His illness put an end to his career as a painter, and eventually to his life.

For his security John needed plans; but he also needed to avoid the implications of these plans unless they were to become prisons for the future. He had not grasped the trick of saying no. He was impelled to say yes even when no one had asked him anything. He said yes now to the prospect of Lord Howard de Walden becoming a new patron. The difficulties that might follow with Quinn or even with Hugh Lane, whom he had similarly elected, were of little account. He would need a new house – somewhere close to Chirk. On his first visit he had been introduced to the composer Joseph Holbrooke, 'an extraordinary chap . . . funniest creature I've ever met'.[88] With Holbrooke's friend, the illustrator and editor of *The Idler* Sidney Sime, they had set off on a number of wild motor rides around Wales, knocking up Sampson at Bala, descending on Lees at Ffestiniog, resting a little with Innes at Nant-ddu 'where I always keep a few bottles of chianti'; then scaling the park gates at Chirk at three o'clock in the morning. 'The country round Ffestiniog was staggering,' he reported to Dorelia (September 1912), '. . . I have my eye on a cottage or two . . . I feel full of work.'

Having exhausted the possibilities at Nant-ddu, John decided to throw in his lot with Holbrooke and Sime, and the three of them took Llwyny-thyl, a 'delightful' corrugated-iron shanty with a large kitchen and 'great fireplace', living-room and four small cabins containing bunks, the upper ones reached by wooden ladders. Dorelia had disliked Nant-ddu and would not visit Chirk Castle; but Llwynythyl, John told her, was 'not half a bad place'. On the inside it was lined with tongued-and-grooved pinewood planking, lightly varnished but otherwise left its natural colour. Into this bungalow above the Vale of Ffestiniog Holbrooke, who was collaborating with Lord Howard de Walden on an operatic trilogy, imported a piano with all the bass notes out of tune, and John imported Lily Ireland, a model of classic proportions who had never before strayed beyond London. The bungalow, which was reached by a steep climb from Tan-y-grisiau up an old trolley shaft with a broken cable-winch at the top, stood on a plateau looking across the valley to the range of mountains above which the endless drama of the sky unfolded itself.

The place was almost ready, and John prepared himself for a long stint of painting. In December he set off: for France. The weather was so gloomy he had suddenly veered off south 'with the intention of working out of doors'.[89] At the New Year, Epstein reported him passing through Paris 'in good spirits'.[90] He planned to link up with Innes and Lees in Marseilles. From the Hôtel du Nord there he wrote to Dorelia:

'Innes came yesterday morning. He looks rather dejected. Lees doesn't appear to be well yet. He is going back to London. We have been wandering about Marseilles all day. When you come we might get another cart and donkey. I have advised Innes to go to Paris and get a girl as he is pretty well lost alone and must have a model . . . I don't know who you might bring over. Nellie Furr, that girl you said one day might be a bore although she has a good figure and seems amiable enough. It could of course make a lot of difference to have several people to pose.'[91]

Marching off each day into the country to 'look about', John would return late at night to Marseilles – and to Innes who, though invariably talking of his departure, would not leave. 'He is insupportable – appears to be going off his head and stutters dreadfully,' John complained.

It was now Dorelia's turn to come south, bringing with her money, underclothing, handkerchiefs, a paintbox, some hairwash – but no model: and the three of them moved, in some dejection, to the Hôtel Basio at St-Chamas. 'It is a beautiful place,' John reassured Mrs Nettleship, 'on the same lake as Martigues but on the north side.' No sooner had they settled in than Innes fell seriously ill. 'He had had a very dissipated time at Perpignan and was quite run down,' John explained to Quinn (2 February 1913). 'Finally at St Chamas . . . he was laid up for about a week after which we took him back to Paris and sent him off to London to see a doctor . . . The company of a sick man gets on one's nerves in the end.'

Though he spent part of August in Paris in the company of Epstein, J. C. Squire and Modigliani (from whom he bought two prodigiously long and narrow stone heads which 'affected me deeply'),[92] John did use his new Welsh cottage during the summer of 1913, passing all July there and all September. The paintings he completed in these two months were exhibited during November in a show at the Goupil Gallery. He was working in tempera, a technique of painting that put him in closer contact with the fifteenth-century Italians from whom he sought inspiration, and his own recipe for which he passed on to younger British artists such as Mark Gertler.[93] 'I have been painting in tempera to my infinite delight,' he told Michel Salaman early in 1912. This quick-drying, hard-setting medium made possible the building up of a picture in superimposed masses. He was also attempting to work on a larger scale than before. At the end of 1911 his adventurous 'Forza e Amore' had been hung at the New English Art Club to the bewilderment of almost everyone. At the end of 1912 he showed his first major essay in tempera, the controversial 'Mumpers'. 'The N.E.A.C. has just been hung,' he wrote to John Hope-Johnstone (20 November 1912). 'I suddenly took and painted my cartoon of Mumpers – in Tempera, finished it in 4½ days, and sent it in.[94] In spite of the hasty workmanship, it doesn't look so bad on the whole. I have also an immense [charcoal] drawing of the Caucasian Gypsies ['Calderari'].' Again, in the late New English show of 1913, he exhibited another huge cartoon, 'The Flute of Pan', with three female figures, four male and a boy, all life size. 'Some say it is the best thing I've done,' he told Quinn (26 January 1914), 'and some the worst.' All these years, too, he had been struggling with Hugh Lane's big picture, subsequently called 'Lyric Fantasy'. On 28 October 1913 he was writing to Ottoline Morrell:

'I am overwhelmed with the problems of finishing Lane's picture.' He had hoped to show it at the next New English. On 29 December he confided to Quinn that it 'will soon be done'; and again on 16 March 1914 he is 'actually getting Lane's big picture done at last'. So it went on until, in May 1915, Lane was drowned on board the *Lusitania* when it was torpedoed by a German U-boat, at which opportunity John ceased work on 'Lyric Fantasy'. Had it been Quinn who died, there seems every likelihood that his big picture 'Forza e Amore' would not have been painted into oblivion.[95]

In these years before the war, John was producing his best work. This was often achieved as preliminary studies for larger decorations, panels knocked off while on holiday, or pictures done as designs for Dorelia's embroidery. He held shows almost every year at the Chenil, sometimes covered whole walls at the New English, struggled on with his private commissions, and regularly sent work in to the Society of Twelve and the National Portrait Society of which, in February 1914, he was elected President. What caused the muddle in his life was also a stimulus for his best work – a sense of urgency, often assisted by financial pressure. John made a habit of externalizing his problems. But what he grappled with was some phantom rather than the problem itself. Whenever he felt dull or ill he fixed the blame on people and places, and would demand a change. These changes often brought with them an immediate lifting of his spirits, but would rapidly lead on to still worse complications.

For a short time early in 1913 he populated a bewildering number of houses acquired through this process of change. There was Alderney, which he shared with Dorelia and his family; Nant-ddu, which he shared with Innes; Llwynythyl, which he shared with Holbrooke and Sime; the Villa Ste-Anne at Martigues which he shared with the birdman Bazin; and 181A King's Road, Chelsea, which he shared with Knewstub. Yet somehow he felt unaccommodated. Entering a public house in Chelsea, he demanded to know whether there was an architect present, and then commissioned a Dutchman who happened to be drinking at the bar to design a new house and studio for him in London. The simple part of the business was now over.

The house was to be built in Mallord Street, a new road which had recently been created parallel to and north of the King's Road, over the waste ground where the John children used to play cowboys and Indians when they lived at Church Street. Van-t-Hoff, as this architect was called, 'takes the studio very seriously', John promised Dorelia. '. . . He is going back to Holland to *think hard*.'[96] After an interval of slumbering thought, John was obliged to summon him back by cable. By 13 May 1913 he confidently reported to Quinn: 'My Dutch architect has done his designs for my new studio with living rooms – and it will be a charming place. They will start building at once and it'll be done in 6 months. How glad I shall be to be able to live more quietly – a thing almost impossible in this studio. My lawyer strongly urges me to try and find the money for the building straight away instead of saddling myself with a mortgage. The building will cost £2,200 [equivalent to £98,000 in 1996].' John would have liked to offer the responsibilities for this property to others – looking in occasionally to pass, over the rising pile, his critical eye. But lawyers, estate agents, builders and decorators were constantly importuning him. 'I can't be rushing all over London and paint too, not having the brain of a Pierpont Morgan,' he complained to Dorelia. Nor was it just his time for which these people were so greedy. 'I shall want all my money and a good deal of other people's,' he explained to John Hope-Johnstone (8 September 1913). His letters to Quinn are congested with money proposals, the nicest of which is a scheme to save costs by building two houses, the second (at some considerable distance from the first) for his patron. 'The materials will be of the best,' he assures him, 'and I think it will be a great success.' His own house continued to rise, his funds to sink and his spirits to oscillate between optimism and despair. By late summer he had decided that Van-t-Hoff's house was 'very good and amusing'. But was the amusement at his expense? He had decided to move in during the autumn, but when autumn came the house still had no roof. 'It'll be ready in January,' he declared: adding with some desperation, 'I feel rather inclined to try another planet.'[97] By early January it was 'getting on well'; by late January it was 'rising perceptively [sic]'. By February 1914 he had not retreated an inch, or advanced. It 'will be done in three weeks Van-t-Hoff thinks', he informed the silent Dorelia.[98] By the middle of March it was still 'nearly done' and even being 'much admired'. By April John is again ready to move – but to Dieppe where he aims to hold out until the house is equipped to receive him. After what turns out to be a fortnight round Cardiganshire and, in June, one week at Boulogne he returns to Chelsea and, though the house is certainly incomplete, decides to occupy it and hold a party 'to baptize my new studio'.[99] This party, a magnificent affair in fancy dress, lasts from the first into the second week of July.

'The company was very charming and sympathetic, I thought,' wrote one of the guests, Lytton Strachey, ' – so easy-going and taking everything for granted . . . John was a superb figure. There was dancing – two-steps and such things – so much nicer than waltzes – and at last I danced with him [John] – it seemed an opportunity not to be missed. (I forget to say I was dressed as a pirate). Nini [Euphemia] Lamb was there, and made effréné love to me. We came out in broad daylight.'[100]

It was like a dolls' house. Steep steps led up to the front door, behind which the rooms were poky and, in spite of the sun streaming in from the south over the market gardens, rather dark. The windows were long and thin and well proportioned; yet when children appeared behind them, they looked like iron-barred cages. The best feature was the staircase, which was copied from Rembrandt's house. In the drawing-room Boris Anrep designed a superb mosaic, a pyramid of wives and children with John at its apex, glowing a dull green as if from the depths of the sea. At the back lay the great studio. With its sloping ceiling, deep alcove, and two fires burning at opposite corners, 'The studio looks fine,' John told Quinn on 24 June 1914. But even in these early days he recognized the prison-like atmosphere of the place. 'It is quite a success I think. It has nearly ruined me,' he wrote to John Hope-Johnstone. '. . . It certainly is rather Dutch but has a solidity and tautness unmatched in London – a little stronghold. I hope I shall find the studio practical.' The studio was perhaps the most practical area – an excellent place for parties.

One of John's motives for commissioning this house had been to please Dorelia. Their correspondence in these years before the war shows her reluctance to go on accompanying him on his jaunts to windswept areas of Wales or Ireland, or join him roaming after gitanos and mumpers anywhere between Battersea and Merseyside. He *had* to be on the move; but she needed to settle herself and the children at Alderney: and this was putting their relationship under new strain. 'I think you are anything but morbid. I get that way far too often I fear,' he assures her in the summer of 1912. He was painting her less frequently. But '. . . I'm sure I could paint a good picture of you if you wouldn't mind letting me try.'[101] He sends her loving letters – 'I wish to God you were here,' he writes from Galway. '. . . wish I was going to sleep with you'[102] – and his tone is sensitive, even at times humble. But she is less available now, having so much work of her own to do at Alderney. Since she will not travel with him he must take other models – Nora or Lillian, Nelly or 'Katie with Songs' from the bar at the New Docks in Galway City, though whenever Dorelia objects, John quickly comes to heel again.

But sometimes Dorelia did not object soon enough. Surely then she would be better placed to do so if they shared a house in London as well as in the country? There would be advantages too for him, comforts such as Dorelia's cooking. The housekeeper she had engaged at Mallord Street intimidated him. 'Her puddings with froth on the top make me rather self-conscious,'[103] he complained. He was sure that one or two bouts of illness he suffered had never been due to alcohol, as malicious people alleged, but to the fact that this housekeeper 'doesn't think things are ready to eat till they begin to decompose'.[104] But Dorelia remained unmoved by his pleas.

As a means of bringing them closer together and the symbol of a conventional union, the house in Mallord Street* was a failure. Within two years the 'little stronghold' had become 'this damned Dutch shanty'.[105] John attributed his dissatisfaction to the Dutch architect's 'passion for rectangles'.[106] Dorelia blamed the roof garden, which faced north.

Mercifully John had begun shedding his Welsh cottages before occupying Mallord Street. Nant-ddu went first. Between February 1913 and August 1914 he did not see Innes who, attempting to regain his health, had gone to Tenerife with Trelawney Dayrell Reed. Llwynythyl was given up with its debris of painting materials in 1914.[107] The place had gone sour on him. He tracked down the source of the trouble to the noise that Joseph Holbrooke made at meals. 'I don't think I can stand him and will probably leave at the end of the week . . . I could get on with Sime but Holbrooke is too horrible.' Holbrooke dedicated his piano ballad 'Tan-y-grisiau' to John. 'Most of your Welsh titles of your things are misspelt,' John told him. Besides, he had the disadvantage of 'a tune constantly playing in his left ear'. But the 'man Sime' was one of Nature's gentlemen – strongly built, with a cliff-like forehead, eyes of superlative greyish-blue and a look (which grew fixed at Llwynythyl) of heroic patience.[108]

In place of Wales, John had hit upon 'the only warm place north of the Pyramids'[109] during winter: Lamorna Cove, near Penzance in Cornwall, where he met 'a number of excellent people down in the little village . . . all painters of sorts'[110] – John Birch, Harold and Laura Knight, and Alfred Munnings[111] – 'and we had numerous beanos'. John was later said to have indecisively remembered a party that began in Haverfordwest one Thursday and ended the following Tuesday somewhere in Hungary. A number of his Cornish 'beanos' were also pretty terrifying affairs. 'We feared', Dame Laura Knight recalled, 'to shorten our lives.'[112] John would perform amazing tricks – tenderly opening bottles of wine without a corkscrew; flicking, from great distances, pats of butter into other people's mouths; dancing, on point in his handmade shoes, upon the rickety table, and other astonishing feats. Then, while the others collapsed into exhausted sleep, out he would go in search of Dorelia, and do little studies of her in various poses on the rocks: 'He never did anything better.'[113] John was delighted with the place. 'I found Cornwall a most sympathetic country,' he wrote to Quinn on his arrival back at Alderney (19 February 1914). '. . . There are some extraordinarily nice people there among the artists and some very attractive young girls among the people.'

---

* It was originally No. 5, but the numbering was changed in 1914 and it became No. 28.

'It seems your appearance at the Café Royal caused a great sensation,' John had told Dorelia after one of her rare appearances in London. He himself was in the Café Royal on 4 August 1914, the night war was declared. 'I remember our excitement over it.'[114] One of their friends carried the news among the waiters, and John, suddenly perturbed, turned to Bomberg: 'This is going to be bad for art.'

Much of that month he spent with Innes who was to die of his tuberculosis on 22 August. 'He cannot be said to have fulfilled himself completely,' John was to write in his first draft for an Innes Memorial Exhibition at the Chenil Gallery in 1923; 'he died too young for his powers to have reached their full maturity – and for that matter does not everyone?

'But by the intensity of his vision and his passionately romantic outlook, his work will live when that of many happier and healthier men will have grown, with the passing years, cold and dull and lifeless . . . the cruel fate so soon to overtake him spurred him into frenzied activity which used up all those hours so often with others devoted to dreams or talk or recreation.'

*

One of the first things Augustus did after the declaration of war was to send a letter to his sister Gwen. 'I wonder if you are going to remain in Paris during the war,' he wrote on 4 August. 'I hope not. You will have to suffer great hardships I fear if you do and it is not too late to come back here . . . food will be awfully dear and most likely communication will be stopped and in any case sending money over will be difficult if not impossible . . . Let me know what you decide and if I can help in any way. With love, Gus.'[115]

But he already knew what she would decide. At the Guildhall that autumn, Winston Churchill, newly appointed First Lord of the Admiralty, declared the maxim of the British people to be 'business as usual'. In their own curiously detached yet conventional ways, it was to be business as usual for both Gwen and Gus. She insisted that she would be safer in France; and besides, she could not leave Rodin. Yet if it became impossible for her to receive her mother's quarterly allowance from Britain, or to send her pictures to Quinn in the United States, how would she subsist? There was little Gus could do. He sent her train times and offered to fetch her over to stay at Alderney, 'but of course she won't', he told Dorelia.[116]

EIGHT

How He Got On

I

MARKING TIME

'Kennington and John: both hag-ridden by a sense that perhaps their strength was greater than they knew. What an uncertain, disappointed, barbarous generation we war-timers have been. They said the best ones were killed. There's far too much talent still alive.'

T. E. Lawrence to William Rothenstein
(14 April 1928)

'[Edward] Wadsworth, along with Augustus John and nearly everybody, is drilling in the courtyard of the Royal Academy, in a regiment for home defence,' wrote Ezra Pound that autumn to Harriet Monroe. It was the last occasion John would find himself so precisely in step with other artists. His letters soon grew more portentous, nearer in tone to those of his father: full of the stuff to give the troops. Already in the first month, the sight of fifteen hundred Territorials plodding up Regent Street swells him with pride: 'they looked damn fine.'[1] And by the end of the war he was anxious lest the Germans be let off too lightly. 'The German hatred for England is the finest compliment we have been paid for ages,' he assures Quinn. To some extent he seems to have fallen victim to war propaganda, though never to war literature. 'The atrocities of the Germans are only equalled in horror by the war poems of the English papers,' he writes to Ottoline Morrell in 1916. 'What tales of blood and mud!' In addition to what he reads in the papers, he absorbs confidential whispers from his various khaki sitters, repeating stories of lunatic generals on whom he fixes the blame for early defeats. 'As for the men, they are beyond praise.'[2] By the spring of 1916 he is looking forward to being able to 'swamp the German lines with metal'.

John's attitude to the war remained consistent: but his emotions, as he lived through it, veered hectically. At first he is excited; by the end it has aged him, and he is no longer quite the same person. Starting out smartly in step, he was left behind struggling to find a world where he could be at ease. From the beginning he wanted to 'join in' – 'it's rather sickening to be out of it all.'[3] His predicament is set out in a letter (10 October 1914) to Quinn:

'I have had more than one impulse to enlist but have each time been dissuaded by various arguments. In the first place I can't decide to leave my painting at this stage nor can I leave my family without resources to go on with. I feel sure I shall be doing better to keep working at my own job. Still all depends on how the war goes on. I long to see something of the fighting and possibly may manage to get in [in] some capacity. I feel a view of the havoc in Belgium with the fleeing refugees would be inspiring and memorable. Lots of my friends have joined the army. The general feeling of the country is I believe quite decent and cheerfully serious – not at all reflected by the nauseating cant and hypocrisy and vulgarity of the average Press. There is no lack of volunteers. The difficulty is to cope with the immense number of recruits, feed and clothe and drill them. There are 20,000 near here, still mostly without their uniforms but they have sing-songs every night in the pubs till they are turned out at 9 o'clock.'

The war intensified John's sense of exclusion. There was his deafness 'which is very bad now', he wrote in 1917. 'I can't hear anything less than an air-raid.'[4] By curtailing freedom of movement, the war also aggravated his tendency to claustrophobia.

He was being badgered by their old friend Ursula Tyrwhitt to make sure Gwen was all right. Gwen had written to Ursula describing the bombing raids on Paris and the cattle trucks at the Gare Montparnasse 'crammed with frightened people'. But though she became a little frightened herself by what she was to read in the newspapers, especially by the massacre at Ypres, she felt 'more and more disinclined to go'.[5] The Germans of course were 'brutes and vandals' and it would be 'dreadful' if they won; yet England had become 'quite a foreign country to me'. In a sense she had no country outside the dark first-floor room she now inhabited at 6 rue de l'Ouest and the flat she had rented on the top storey of an old house near the bois de Meudon, in the south-west suburbs of Paris.

In December 1914 Gus came striding up the rue Terre-Neuve in Meudon, 'tall and broad-shouldered', Gwen's biographer Susan Chitty writes, 'wearing a loose tweed suit with a brightly coloured bandanna round his neck'.[6] After having registered as an alien, Gwen told him, she was doing work as an interpreter for English officers; and Gus approved. 'The soldiers must be glad of your help as an interpreter. I suppose even the officers don't know a word of French.' He suggested she might try Red Cross work – certainly any sustained painting seemed 'impossible' for both of them during the war. He also explained why he could not join a fighting regiment (his 'establishment would go bust if I did'); and Gwen understood. 'Will the world be very different afterwards?' Gus was brimful of confidence. 'It might do people a world of good,'[7] he asserted. In any event he was certain Britain would benefit. For Gwen, who had feared Britain would be invaded, there was comfort in the feeling that the English would 'come up to the mark'.

Gus's invitation to England remained open; and Gwen remained in France. 'Ici tout va bien, surtout la petite fille,' he wrote to her from Alderney.[8] '. . . The children obstinately keep up the Xmas traditions. They are all flourishing & Dorelia too . . . Don't let yourself get frozen dearest. Take exercises. Love from Gus.'[9] Dorelia sent over some money and clothes; Gus sent Sanatogen tonic wine and copies of A. R. Orage's *New Age*. He could tell Ursula Tyrwhitt, and also his father, that he had done what was possible; and old Edwin John could pass the news on to Winifred and Thornton.

Winifred had made her final visit to Europe shortly before Ida's death. In January 1915 she married – and Thornton, perhaps the loneliest of all these Johns, returned to England. In a letter to Gwen, Winifred had described Thornton as a 'thought reader'.[10] But though he could trespass into her secret thoughts he never seemed to know what other people were thinking and he was, she told Gus, 'very unlucky in his partners'.[11] His twelve years in North America had been disappointing. He worked hard at mining gold in Montana, but found only hostility among the farmers, who disliked the holes he dug in their land and threatened him with writs. Then he got a job ploughing with three horses in British Columbia, but had fallen ill. After that he built a boat which he sailed on Lake Kinbasket, planning to make good wages washing the gravel for gold. He loved his boat and the work suited him, but there was only gravel. By now he had run out of partners and eventually spent his solitary days on his boat, fishing. He was fishing near Lasquet Island when war broke out. He had been so long alone, and the world had changed so much, he was astonished by the news when he went to buy provisions in Vancouver. He applied to join the Canadian Army – nearly all the Canadian troops, he believed, were English-born – but was rejected on account of his broken foot.

Winifred was now a United States citizen, settled in California and pregnant with her first child, a daughter who was to be born in November 1915. She had begun a new life, but there seemed no more life for Thornton in North America – he hated peddling his fish for money. So he came back, paying a duty call on his father in Tenby, walking in the woods with Gwen at Meudon, seeing Gus at Alderney and in London. 'The little girl Poppet and I are good friends and I hauled her about the studio on a mat,'[12] he wrote to Gwen. This was the one of the few gleams of happiness in his letters. He was to spend part of the war in a munitions factory at Woolwich Arsenal. Working along with conscientious objectors and rejects from the armed services was 'an abomination, but there is nothing to do but hold on grimly,' he told Gwen. 'I try to do as much as I can with as little thought of reward as possible . . . I know I am not liked.'[13] Eventually he found work as a shipwright at Gravesend, and there at last he was in the open air. His boat lay afloat in a basin near by and he managed to work on it nearly every day.

'The war probably makes France impossible for holidays,'[14] Augustus had written to Dorelia, whom he advised to plan as if for a siege. After his visit to Gwen he did not return to France for more than three years. 'I feel the nostalgie du Midi now that there's no chance of going there,' he told Ottoline. '. . . I commence the New Year rather ill-temperedly.'[15] There was no easy escape from these dark days of civilian incarceration, and he began to develop symptoms around the head and legs that 'put me quite out of action'.[16]

Ireland now took the place of France. He made several visits to Dublin, to Galway and Connemara. 'John was a good friend of Ireland,' Christine Longford remembered. 'We bobbed our hair because Augustus John girls had short hair; and anyone who had red hair, like the picture of Iris Tree in Dublin, was lucky . . . He knew Galway well, "the shawled women murmuring together on the quays, with the white complex of the Claddagh glimmering across the harbour".'[17] The men were going off 'to fight England's battles', and there was a great wailing on the platforms as their women saw them off. They were consoled by government grants, and 'the consequence is an unusually heavy traffic in stout,' Augustus told Dorelia when inviting her over, adding that she 'would hate it here'. In her absence he was stalked by 'my double' who went everywhere spreading legendary rumours. It became all the more important to get himself settled. 'I have found a house here,' he wrote to Dorelia from Galway City,[18] 'with fine big rooms and windows which I'm taking – only £30 a year . . . I had a bad attack of blues here, doing nothing, but the prospect of soon getting to work bucks me up.' This house was in Tuam Street and owned by Bishop O'Dea, who leased it to John for three years on the understanding that no painting from the nude was to be enjoyed on the premises. John's plan was to execute a big dramatization of Galway bringing in everything characteristic of the place. He explained this scheme to Dorelia:

'I'm thinking out a vast picture synthesizing all that's fine and characteristic in Galway City – a grand marshalling of the elements. It will have to be enormous to contain troops of women and children, groups of fishermen, docks, wharves, the church, mills, constables, donkeys, widows, men from Aran, hookers* etc., perhaps with a night sky and all illuminated in the light of a dream. This will be worth while – worth the delay and the misery that went before.'[19]

He went out into the streets, staring, sketching: and was at once identified as a spy. Bathing – 'the best tonic in the world' – was reckoned to be a misdemeanour in wartime; and sketching in the harbour a treason – 'so that is a drawback and a big one'. In a letter to Ottoline Morrell he complained: 'There are wonderful people and it is beautiful about the harbour but if one starts sketching one is at once shot by a policeman . . . It would be worth while passing 6 months here given the right conditions.'

But the right conditions were elusive. Without disobeying the letter of Bishop O'Dea's injunction, 'I had two girls in here yesterday,' he admitted to Dorelia, 'but they didn't give the same impression as when seen in the street. I could do with some underclothing.' He was anxious not to return to Alderney 'till I've got something good to take away'. Every day he would go out and look, then hurry back to Tuam Street and do drawings or pen-and-wash sketches. 'I've observed the people here enough,' he eventually wrote to Dorelia. 'Their drapery is often very pleasing – one generally sees one good thing a day at least – but the population is greatly spoilt now – 20 years ago it must have been astonishing . . . Painting from nature *and* from imagination spells defeat I see clearly.'

Imagination meant memory. His imagination was kindled instantly: then the good moment went. He had to catch it before it began to fade, rather than recollect it in tranquillity. Yet now there seemed no alternative to a retrospective technique – what he called 'mental observation'.[20] He had found himself painting portraits of the Ladies Ottoline Morrell and Howard de Walden while they were 'safely out of sight'. But this was not why he had come to Galway. After vacillating for weeks between the railway station and the telegraph office, he left. 'It was in the end', he explained to Bernard Shaw, 'less will-power than panic that got me away.'[21]

He had been at Galway two months. After his return to Alderney he began to work feverishly at a large cartoon, covering four hundred square feet in a single week. Once again he was racing against time. He wanted to bring all those one-good-things-a-day together in a composite arrangement of the ideal Galway: a visionary city locked deep in his imagination.

---

* A two-masted fishing-boat of Dutch origin used off the west coast of Ireland. John had a scheme for buying one for fifty pounds.

War gives some painters an opportunity to record and interpret the extremities of human behaviour. Lamb, Wyndham Lewis, Paul Nash, C. R. W. Nevinson, William Roberts and Stanley Spencer were among the artists who grasped this opportunity. Others, such as McEvoy, succumbed to fashionable portraiture. John, like William Nicholson, also painted commissioned portraits to earn money; but they were erratically fashionable. By 1914, in a hit-or-miss fashion, he was still painting in his best vein. 'Of course painters as good as John will always sell,' Sickert assured Nan Hudson, 'war or no war.' But the war put pressures on him. 'I'm afraid we are in for thin times over here,' he explained to Quinn. 'No one will want luxuries like pictures for awhile.'[22] Nevertheless he continued painting those large decorative groups, such as 'Galway', for which, he felt, his talent was best suited: also, for a year or two, those bold and glowing landscapes with figures, often on small wooden panels, sometimes with children, which were inspired by private affections, and which show his talent at its most direct and engaged. In the past he had sold such work better than any of his contemporaries, but after 1914 this was no longer possible. Partly for financial reasons, but also because he did not want his work to be wholly irrelevant to the contemporary business of this war, he began to paint a different sort of picture. 'I am called upon to provide various things in aid of war funds or charities connected with the war,' he told Quinn.[23] Among his sitters were several staff officers and, in 1916, the bellicose Admiral Lord Fisher who brought in tow the Nelsonically named Duchess of Hamilton[24] ('You won't find as fine a figure of a woman, and a Duchess at that, at every street corner'), to whom John transferred part of his attentions, while Fisher explained how to 'end the war in a week'.[25] When this portrait was shown at the NEAC, Albert Rutherston noted that it was 'careless and sketchy',[26] and *The Times* critic observed that John had really painted a zoo picture of Fisher as a 'Sea-Lion . . . hungering for his prey'.[27] Yet it has lasted better than the formal portrait by Herbert von Herkomer and the Epstein bust. John's depiction of Fisher's face 'shows it looking wryly over the viewer's left shoulder,' wrote Jan Morris,[28] 'its eyebrows raised in irony, its round eyes alert, its mouth mocking, cynical and affectionate, all at the same time. It is a quirky and highly intelligent face.'

But on the whole these public portraits of war celebrities are not satisfactory, perhaps because John could not match his public sentiments to private feelings. In his correspondence he is often approving of these statesmen and soldiers; but when he actually came face to face with them he felt unaccountably bored. He did not think it proper to caricature them as he had done the Lord Mayor of Liverpool. Some satire, in a muted form, does come through: but seldom convincingly.

Perhaps the most biographically interesting of these war pictures was that of Lloyd George, who had 'introduced himself to me' at the Park Hotel in Cardiff in the early summer of 1914. Towards the end of 1915, having recently been appointed Minister of Munitions, he agreed that John should paint him. A suitable canvas had been bought by Lieutenant-General Sir James Murray, Chief of the Imperial General Staff, in aid of Red Cross funds, the arrangement being that John would paint whomever Murray designated. Like a marriage broker, Murray settled the agreement between them, then discreetly retired, confident that the two Welshmen would hit it off like fireworks. In fact they seem to have had just the wrong things in common and did not take to each other. The poetry of their natures was rooted in Wales: England had magnetized their ambitions. But their ambitions were different. Happy as a child, pampered by his family, Lloyd George was greedy for the world's attentions. John in his childhood had felt deprived of love, and now grasped at it while seeking to evoke a romantic world set in those places of natural beauty politicians call the wilderness. 'I feel I have no contact,' Lloyd George told his mistress Frances Stevenson. John too had no contact by the end: but he had been reaching for other things.

In public, John admired Lloyd George. He was 'doing good work over Munitions' and would surely have made a better business than Asquith, then the Prime Minister, of leading the country to victory. 'One feels that what really is wanted is a sort of Cromwell to take charge,' he told Quinn, 'having turned out our Parliamentarians into the street first.'[29] The Welsh wizard who was to play the part of Cromwell had agreed 'to sit for half an hour in the mornings' but, John complained, was 'difficult to get hold of'.[30] The portrait lurched forward in short bursts during December, January and February. On 16 February 1916 John wrote to Quinn: 'I have finished my portrait of Lloyd George. He was a rotten sitter – as you say a "hot-arse who can't sit still and be patient".' It was a restlessness that consumed them both. Lloyd George may not have appreciated being placed, in order of priority, behind the actress Réjane whom John was then also painting, and indiscriminately shoulder to shoulder with 'some soldiers'. According to Frances Stevenson, 'the sittings were not very gay ones.'[31] Lloyd George was 'in a grim mood', suffering, in addition to toothache, from the latest Serbian crisis. Nevertheless, this cannot wholly account for the 'hard, determined, almost cruel face,' Frances Stevenson noted angrily in her diary, 'with nothing of the tenderness & charm of the D[avid] of everyday life'.[32] 'Do you notice what John says about pictures which he does not like?' Lloyd George had asked her. 'Very pleasant!' He was 'upset', she realized, 'for he likes to look nice in his portraits!' Another worry was Frances herself. Though professing to find

John 'terrifying', she acknowledged him to be 'an uncommon person . . . extraordinarily conceited . . . nevertheless . . . very fascinating'. Lloyd George persuaded her not to have her own portrait painted by John and, to her disappointment, prohibited her from going to his parties. Confronted by John's 'unpleasant' portrait he reverted to nursery tactics, gathering his family round him (much to John's irritation) in a chorus of abuse over the object, and drawing from 'Pussy' Stevenson her most maternal protectiveness. To account for the cunning and querulous expression, he suggested calling the picture 'Salonika'. Then he affected to forget about it.[33] But John remembered. Announcing his first portrait to have been 'unfinished', he caught up with Lloyd George nearly four years later in Deauville,[34] drew out his brushes and began a second canvas. Under his fierce gaze Lloyd George grew restless again, hurried back to London and, wisely, did not honour his promise to continue the sittings at Downing Street. For John this was a foretaste of how his career as a professional portrait painter would proceed.

In Winston Churchill, whom he drew after the Second World War, John was to observe the same inability to keep still. Under his scrutiny, Churchill seemed reduced to the condition of a child. His concern was for his 'image'. How else to explain, John wondered, 'these fits and starts, these visits to the mirror, this preoccupation with the window curtains, and the nervous fidgeting with his jowl?'

A less quick-footed target was Ramsay MacDonald, whom John vainly attempted to paint on a number of occasions. The difficulty here seems to have been that the sitter proved too dim a subject to illuminate the romantic interpretation of a 'dreamy knight-errant, dedicated to the overthrow of dragons and the rescue of distressed damsels' which John insisted upon trying to fix on him. 'I have fallen into troubled waters and I do not know when on earth I shall be able to see you,' MacDonald wrote from Downing Street on 8 April 1933, two days before the Labour Party moved a vote of censure on the all-party government of which he was Prime Minister over unemployment. A fortnight later, MacDonald admitted in a letter to Will Rothenstein that 'John's portrait was a melancholy failure. It really was a terrible production, and everybody who saw it turned it down instantly. He wants to begin again, but I am really tired. The waste of my time has been rather bad. He made two attempts and an earlier one some time ago. In all I must have given between 20 and 30 sittings of $1\frac{1}{2}$ hours' average, and I cannot afford going on unless there is some certainty of a satisfactory result . . .'

The most satisfactory of John's Prime Ministers was achieved at the expense of A. J. Balfour, who appeared to fall asleep. His philosophy of doubt, which always appealed to John, seemed to reach a culmination in his slumbering posture. 'I set to,' John records, 'and completed the drawing within an hour.'

He relished the prospect of meeting the famous. But invariably the prospect was better than the experience – except in the case of artists and writers. These portraits, especially of writers, comprise a separate section of his work – not private in the same way that 'Washing Day' or 'Woman Knitting' or 'The Red Feather' or 'The Mauve Jersey' are private, but not to be classed among what Quinn fretfully described as his 'colonels and fat women, and . . . other disagreeable pot-boilers'.[35] Among the writers who sat to him in these war years were W. H. Davies,[36] Ronald Firbank, the gregarious Gogarty and the ailing Arthur Symons. Perhaps the most celebrated was Bernard Shaw, of whom, during May 1915, he did three rapid portraits in oil.

Shaw was staying at Coole over Easter with Lady Gregory when his industry was suddenly halted by an atrocious headache. 'Mrs Shaw was lamenting about not having him painted by a good artist,' Lady Gregory wrote to W. B. Yeats, 'and I suggested having John over, and she jumped at it, and Robert [Gregory] is to bring him over on Monday.'[37] In the event John seems to have travelled more erratically, catching 'a kind of cold'[38] in Dublin, falling into convivial company and arriving 'in a contrite and somewhat shattered condition'[39] a week late. His symptoms deepened on discovering that Lady Gregory (who 'is just like Queen V[ictoria] only uglier') had used Shaw as bait for a portrait of her grandson 'little Richard'[40] whom, until now, he had successfully avoided. Although John made no secret of his preference for little Richard's sister, Anne Gregory, 'a very pretty little child with pale gold hair', Lady Gregory insisted that it must be the son of the house who was honoured. So he began this 'awful job', producing what both children found 'a very odd picture . . . [with] enormous sticky-out ears and eyes that sloped up at the corners, rather like a picture of a chinaman . . .'[41, 42]

Meanwhile, in his bedroom, Shaw was preparing himself. He had recovered from his headache to the extent of having his hair cut, but in the excitement, Lady Gregory lamented, 'too much was taken off'.[43] Despite Shaw's head and John's cold, both were at their most winning by the time the sittings began.

Each morning John would strip off his coat, prop his canvases on the best chairs and paint several versions at one sitting. But at night he would, 'like Penelope', undo the work of the previous day, washing the canvas clean and then starting another portrait in its place. 'He painted with large brushes and used large quantities of paint,' Shaw remembered.[44] Over the course of eight days he painted 'six magnificent portraits of me', he told Mrs Patrick Campbell.[45] '. . . Unfortunately as he kept painting them on top of one another until our protests became overwhelming, only three portraits have survived.'

Between sittings John went off for 'some grand galloping'[46] with Robert Gregory, or, more sedately, would row Mrs Shaw across the lake. 'Mrs Shaw is [a] fat party with green eyes who says "Ye-hes" in an intellectual way ending with a hiss,' he divulged to Dorelia. Over thirty years later, in *Chiaroscuro*, John described Shaw as 'a true Prince of the Spirit', a fearless enemy of cant and humbug, and in his queer way, 'a highly respectable though strictly uncanonical saint'.[47] In his letters to Dorelia at the time he refers to him as 'a ridiculous vain object in knickerbockers' and describes the three of them – Lady Gregory and the Shaws – as 'dreadful people'. Such discrepancies were odd notes played by John's violently fluctuating moods, which were agitated at Coole Park by the fact that, though there was plenty to eat, nobody smoked or drank. 'I smoke still,' he reassured Dorelia, 'but only touch claret at meals. In Ireland claret is regarded as a T[emperance] drink.'[48] His admiration of Shaw, whom he intermittently thought 'very pleasant company', was qualified by the extreme awe radiated towards GBS from the women in the house. This veneration combined with John's hearty silence to stimulate in Shaw the kind of brilliant intellectual monologues which put John in the shade, and which may have prompted him to paint over the portraits (a sort of silencing) so many times.

'I find him [Shaw] a decent man to deal with,' John notified Quinn,[49] after Shaw had decided to buy one of these emphatic portraits for three hundred pounds (equivalent to £10,800 in 1996) – the one with the blue background.[50] He had been reminded by Wyndham Lewis that Shaw's beard 'protrudes for several feet in front of his face', unlike Darwin's which 'grew into his mouth'.[51] The head, as Shaw himself pointed out, had two aspects, the concave and the convex. John produced two studies from the concave angle, and a third (with eyes shut as if in aching thought) from the convex – 'the blind portrait' Shaw called it; adding in a letter to Mrs Patrick Campbell that it had 'got turned into a subject entitled Shaw Listening to Someone Else Talking, because I went to sleep . . .'[52] With this sleeping version John was never wholly satisfied. 'It could only have happened of course in the dreamy atmosphere of Coole,' he suggested to Shaw.[53]

Though he had sometimes bridled at having his portrait washed out by John, and rebelled against 'being immortalised as an elderly caricature of myself', Shaw was generally pleased with these poster-portraits, especially the one he bought and kept all his life – 'though to keep it in a private house seems to me rather like keeping an oak tree in an umbrella stand'.[54] In the regular Irish manner, like Yeats, he boasted that 'John makes me out the inebriated gamekeeper'; but in later life he would tell other artists wishing to paint him that since he had been 'done' by the two greatest artists in the last forty years, Rodin and John, there was no room for more portraits.[55]

John exhibited the portrait with the blue background at the summer show of the NEAC in May and June 1915; and in February 1916 he held an exhibition of twenty-one paintings and forty-one drawings at the Chenil Gallery.[56] It was, perhaps, his last effort to pursue something of what he had been doing before the war, an anthology of past and present, landscape and portrait. Ursula Tyrwhitt made a point of writing to Gwen to say how much she had liked Gus's drawings. But they had little connection with the war. 'Mr Augustus John continues to mark time with great professional skill,' wrote the art critic of *The Times*. The eyes of critics and painters were now fixed on him to see in what new direction he would go.

2

THE VIRGIN'S PRAYER

'Mr John, one feels somehow, does not spend all his vitality on painting.'

Manchester Guardian (23 November 1912)

'A house without children isn't worth living in!' John had once pronounced. His sons, no longer to be classed simply as children, now passed much of their time at schools and colleges: but the supply of fresh children to Alderney continued unchecked. In March 1915, in a room next to the kitchen, John presiding, Dorelia gave birth to a second daughter, described as 'small and nice',[57] whom they named Vivien. By the age of two she had grown into 'a most imposing personage – half the size of Poppet, and twice as dangerous'.[58] Through the woods she liked to wander with 'a beautiful Irish setter called Cuchulain . . . he patiently bringing me home for meals at the toll of the great bell'.[59] Unlike the boys, neither Poppet nor Vivien was sent to school. 'We roamed the countryside,' Vivien recalled, 'and a tutor cycled over from Bournemouth to teach us. Finally we punctured his bicycle . . .'

In 1917 four more children joined the Alderney gang – John, Nicolette, Brigit and Caitlin. These were the son and daughters, 'robust specimens' aged between seven and three, of Francis Macnamara who, after seven years of unfaithful marriage, had left home permanently to live with

Euphemia Lamb (who had briefly left someone else's home to live with him). His children had circled slowly in the wake of their mother, who was eventually towed down to Alderney out of range of the German Zeppelins. One of the children, Nicolette, elected John as her second father, conceiving for the John *ménage* an exaggerated loyalty not whole-heartedly welcomed by them. Yet her feelings, despite some lapses from fact, give an intensity to her memories of Alderney.

'In my memory the bedrooms were small boxes with large double beds. Poppet and Vivien shared one of these. On occasions, we three Macnamara girls squashed in beside them for the night. In the morning we always woke up with hangovers from an excess of giggling . . .

. . . Poppet and Vivien, the younger boys, my sisters, splashed naked in the pond, while my mother and Dodo stood by with their arms full of flowers. Edie held out a towel for a wet child. And like some mythical god observing the mortals, Augustus the Watcher, sat on a bench leaning forward, his long hair covered by a felt hat, his beard a sign of authority.

It was in this garden that I first experienced ecstasy . . . There has never been another garden like it; it excited me in such a way that it became the symbol of heaven.'[60]

For those who, like the Macnamara or Anrep children, continually came and went, Alderney seemed an Eden; but for the John children themselves it was an Eden from which they needed to be expelled in order to be born into the world outside. While for a third group, a race of demi-Johns, it was also an Eden, but seen from a place of exile.

The first of this race 'not of the whole blood' was the daughter of a music student of generous figure and complexion called Nora Brown-sword, twenty years younger than John and known, bluntly, by her sur-name. On a number of occasions she had posed for him mostly for wood panels, and on 12 October 1914 he wrote in a state of some financial panic to Quinn: 'By-the-bye I've been and got a young lady in the family way! What in blazes is to be done?' Quinn suggested exporting the lady to France. This advice, which arrived safely at Alderney almost five months later, was invalid by the time John read it. Yet the problem remained. What in blazes *was* to be done?

John explained the position as clearly as he could in another letter to Quinn: 'Some while back, I conceived a wild passion for a girl and put her in the family way. She has now a daughter and I've promised her what she asks: £2 a week and £50 to set up in a cottage. I never see her now and don't want to, but I'm damned if I see where that £50 is to be found at the moment. Her father is a wealthy man. He has just tumbled to the situation and I suppose he'll be howling for my blood.' Dorelia's attitude was one of sternness and calm. If matters were made too easy, then the same thing might happen many times. So she hardened herself. In John's letters to her at this time there is a new note of diffidence mingling with reminders that 'I cannot exist without you for long, as you know.' He is apologetic too for not meanwhile having painted better. 'Sorry to be so damn disappointing in my work. It must make you pretty hopeless at times, but don't give me up yet. I'm going to improve.' It was, to a degree, for the sake of his work that Ida had died and Dorelia risked her life: for his work and himself and themselves all together.

As a civilian in wartime John felt at the dead centre of a hurricane. It was this awful sense of deadness, this curious uselessness, that tempted him to rush into new lovemaking, as the only means of self-renewal available. Extricating himself from the consequences of his affair with Brownsword seems to have taken longer than the affair itself. She had often visited Alderney during her holidays from music college; but after the birth of her daughter she did not go back there. 'She must on no account come to Alderney,' John instructed Dorelia. '. . . For God's sake don't worry about it – don't think about it.'

This advice John made several lusty attempts to pursue himself. It was not easy. Brownsword had been anxious to shield the news from her parents – which, since they could far better afford to look after the child than he, dissatisfied John. In due course she went to live in Highgate, where John sometimes turned up – Brownsword hiding herself away at his approach. She had become extraordinarily elusive even when John pursued her with genuine offers of help. He felt deeply impatient. 'I dined with her and wasn't too nice,' he admitted to Dorelia, 'but tried to keep my temper and it's no use allowing oneself to be too severe . . . She showed every sign of innocent surprise when I asked her why she had bunked away without warning.'[61] In a less severe mood still, he confided on one occasion to Theodosia Townshend: 'I'd marry her if necessary – Dodo wouldn't mind.' To what extent he believed this it is impossible to be sure: probably a little, once it was out of the question. In any event the ceremony of marriage meant less to him than it did to many people. Besides, there were other more fantastic plans to fall back on. 'The Tutor's plan I think the best,' John had affirmed in another letter to Dorelia. After leaving Alderney, the boys' ex-tutor, John Hope-Johnstone, had gone 'tramping to Asia', as John explained to Sampson, 'got as far as Trieste, & then was arrested as a spy, spent 8 days in chokey along with a dozen other criminals mostly sexual, & then was liberated. He doesn't think he'll go no further.' Stopped in his tracks by the world war, he reappeared in London and secretly offered himself in the role of the baby's legal father. 'I must say,' John acknowledged, 'the tutor is behaving with uncommon decency.' From Brownsword's point of view this 'best plan' contained disadvantages. Although Hope-Johnstone entertained some romantic attachments for young men of under twenty, he was physically attracted to girls of ten or twelve, towards whom he would proffer timid advances, placing his hand on their thighs until, their mothers getting to hear of it, he was expelled from the house. The prospect of having a young daughter in his own house was certainly inviting; and it seems probable that he scented money in this *mariage blanc* – to the extent at least of making a household investment, 'a most expensive frying pan'. But Brownsword was not a party to this. The surname she gave her daughter, the painter Gwyneth Johnstone, suggests that no hope had entered this relationship.

In his letters to Dorelia, John makes no reference to Nora Brownsword that can be construed as sympathetic. But then Dorelia was not in the business of easy sympathy. He himself appears to have believed that he offered Brownsword money, but that she accepted nothing. She remembered asking for £4 a week for the baby, not herself: and receiving nothing. That nothing positively changed hands on a number of businesslike occasions appears indisputable. Having a musical degree she was just able to support herself and her daughter, and their independence was complete. It was only casually, years later, that John learnt she had married. As for Dorelia, she provided Brownsword with a ring; and within limits she was kind. But she was not welcoming. She offered to take the baby and bring it up as one of the family, provided Brownsword never saw the girl again. But since that was unacceptable to Brownsword, she took no further interest in the matter.

The Brownsword affair shot a warning across John's bows.[62] Through the deep gloom of war he needed, like pilot lights, a girl to call and a girl to play. After one party at Mallord Street, Dorelia and Helen Anrep could hear him shuffling about in the entrance hall and, with hushed comic intensity, confiding to a procession of female guests: 'When shall I see you again? . . . You know how much it means to me . . . I never cease thinking of you . . . Relax a little and inspire your poor artist with a kiss . . . Or shall I drown myself?' Each time, for a moment, the tone carried conviction. His need seemed, if almost indiscriminate, almost real. Without these girls he was in the dark. He could not stop himself. At the beginning and in the end, he drank: first to make contact, then to forget.

The roll-call reverberated on. Lady Tredegar, with her strange gift for climbing into trees and arranging nests in which polite birds would settle; Iris Tree, with her pink hair and poetry, 'someone quite marvellous'; Sylvia Gough, with her thin loose legs, whose husband later paid John the compliment of placing his name on the list of co-respondents in her divorce case; Sybil Hart-Davis, nice and apologetic and also 'determined to give up the drink';[63] a famous Russian ballerina, from whose Italianate husband John was said to have 'taken a loan of her': these and others were among his girlfriends or mistresses over these few years. Not all the voluminous gossip that rose up round him was true: but the smoke did not wholly obscure the flames. Even before the war his reputation, along with that of Ezra Pound, had been popularly celebrated in the 'Virgin's Prayer':

Ezra Pound
And Augustus John
Bless the bed
That I lie on.[64]

Of such notoriety John was growing increasingly shy. 'The only difference between the World's treatment of me and other of her illustrious sons is that it doesn't wait till I am dead before weaving its legends about my name,' he complained (February 1918) to Alick Schepeler. By becoming more stealthy he did not diminish this legend, but gave it an infusion of mystery. The addict's spell is written in the many moods of revulsion and counter-resolution, the promises, promises, that chart his downhill flight. Sometimes it seemed as if Dorelia alone could arrest this descent. 'If you come here I'll promise to be good,' he wrote to her from Mallord Street at the end of the war, '. . . I am discharging all my mistresses at the rate of about 3 a week – Goodbye Girls, I'm through.'

3

CORRUPT COTERIES

'Do you manage to get any work done in spite of the war?'
Augustus John to Gwen John (18 November 1918)

Alderney was also changing with the war. Visitors no longer floated in and out in such abundant numbers. Henry Lamb had left. 'We are square enough I suppose,' he had written to John before the war. But in truth, Lamb never felt square with John. After drawing up his first Will and Testament, and handing it to Dorelia during a farewell party at Alderney,[65] he was gone, looking 'very sweet in his uniform', to serve as an army doctor in France. Deprived of 'poor darling Lamb',[66] Dorelia dug herself more deeply still into the plant world. Assured by John that 'in a week or two there'll be no money about and no food,'[67] she surrounded herself with useful vegetables. They clustered about the house giving her comfort. 'It's rather a sickening life,' she confessed to Lytton Strachey, 'but the garden looks nice.'[68]

God came to Alderney less often these days: God was Dorelia's new name for John. The war had thrown shadows over both their lives, as well as between them. 'Do you feel 200?' he asked her, ' – I feel 300.' While Dorelia was immersing herself in the life of the soil, John sought distraction at clubs and parties in London. He went everywhere and belonged nowhere. Though he still drank elbow-to-elbow with poets and prostitutes under the flyblown rococo of the Café Royal, the place was beginning to revolve almost too crazily. There were raucous-voiced sportsmen; alchemists and sorcerers sitting innocuously over their spells; a grave contingent from the British Museum; well-dressed gangs of blackmailers, bullies, pimps and *agents provocateurs* muttering over plans; intoxicated social reformers and Anglo-Irish jokers with their whoops and slogans; the exquisite herd of Old Boys from the Nineties 'recognizable by their bright chestnut wigs and raddled faces' whispering in the sub-dialect of the period; a *schlemozzle* of Cubists sitting algebraically at the domino tables; and, not far off, under the glittering façade of the bar, his eye fixed on the fluctuating crisis of power, the leader of the Vorticists kept company with his lieutenants. Decidedly the place was getting a bit 'thick'[69] for John.

Throughout London a bewildering variety of clubs and pubs had sprung up offering wartime consolations. There was the Cave of the Golden Calf, a cabaret club lodged deep in a Soho basement where the miraculous Madame Strindberg had been resurrected. As queen of this vapid cellardom, wrapped in a fur coat, her face chalk white, her hair wonderfully dark, her eyes blazing with fatigue, she drifted among her guests diverting their attention from entertainments that featured everything most up to date. Under walls 'relevantly frescoed' by Spencer Gore and Charles Ginner, beside a huge raw-meat drop curtain designed by Wyndham Lewis, and watched over by the heads of hawks, cats and camels which, executed by Epstein in scarlet and shocking white, served as decorative reliefs for the columns supporting the ceiling, couples went through the latest dances, the bunny hug and turkey trot. There were also experiments in amateur theatre, foreign folk songs led by an Hungarian fiddler, and the spectacle of performing coppersmiths. Everything was expensive, but democratic. Girls, young and poor, were introduced to rich men on the periphery of the art world; various writers and artists, including John, found themselves elected honorary members 'out of deference to their personalities' and given the privilege of charging drinks to non-artistic patrons in their absence. Into its holes and corners slunk the Vorticists, 'Cubists, Voo-dooists, Futurists and other Boomists'[70] for whom it was transfigured into a campaign headquarters. But not for long. As war advanced from the East, so Madame Strindberg went west. 'I'm leaving the Cabaret,' she wrote to John. 'Dreams are sweeter than reality.' Stripping the cellar of everything she could carry, she sailed for New York. 'We shall never meet again now,' she wrote from the ship. '. . . I could neither help loving you, nor hating you – and . . . friendship and esteem and everything got drowned between those two feelings.'[71]

Even before Madame Strindberg left, John had absconded to help set up a rival haunt in Greek Street. 'We are starting a new club in town called the "Crab-tree" for artists, poets and musicians,' he wrote to Quinn. 'It ought to be amusing and useful at times.' The Crabtree opened in April 1914, and for a time it tasted sweet to him: the only thing wrong with it, he hinted darkly, were the crabs. Like the Cave of the Golden Calf it was a very democratic affair, and provided customers with what John called 'the real thing'. Euphemia Lamb, Betty May, Lillian Shelley and other famous models went there night after night wearing black hats and throwing bottles: and for the men there were boxing contests. Actresses flocked in from the West End theatres to meet these swaggering painter-pugilists and the atmosphere was wild. 'A most disgusting place!' was Paul Nash's recommendation in a letter to Albert Rutherston, 'where only the very lowest city jews and the most pinched harlots attend. A place of utter coarseness and dull unrelieved monotony. John alone, a great pathetic muzzy god, a sort of Silenus – but also no nymphs, satyrs and leopards to complete the picture.'

Much the same spirit saturated the atmosphere of the Cavendish Hotel in Jermyn Street which was owned by Rosa Lewis, a suave and sinister nanny, who ran it along the lines of a plush asylum in her own Welfare State. For connoisseurs there was nothing like the Cavendish, with its acres of faded red morocco, and hideous landscape of battered furniture, massive and monogrammed. Beneath every cushion lay a bottle, and beside it a girl. The place flowed with brandy and champagne, paid for by innocent millionaires. Much of this money came from the United States, among whose well-brought-up young men, bitten with the notion of being Bohemians Abroad, Rosa Lewis became a legend. Financially it was the artists, models and other poorer people who benefited: but for those who did not have John's constitution it was a risky lair.[72]

In quieter vein, he would appear at the Café Verrey, a public house in the Continental style in Soho; then, for the sake of the Chianti – though he always 'walked out nice and lovely' – at Bertorelli's; and, a little later, also in Charlotte Street near the Scala Theatre, at the Saint-Bernard Restaurant, a small friendly place with an enormous friendly dog that filled the alley between the tables to the exclusion of the single waiter and Signor del Fiume, its gesticulating owner. But of all these restaurants the most celebrated was the Eiffel Tower in Percy Street, 'our carnal-spiritual home' as Nancy Cunard called it.[73] The story is that one stormy night, John and Nancy Cunard found refuge there, and taking a liking to its genial Austrian proprietor, Rudolph Stulik, transformed the place during these war years into a club patronized chiefly by those who were connected with the arts. Its series of windows, each with a daffodil-yellow half-blind looking wearily up Charlotte Street, became a cultural landmark of the metropolis. The décor was simple, with white tablecloths, narrow crusty rolls wrapped up in napkins beside the plates and long slender wine glasses. The food was elaborate ('Canard Pressé', 'Sole Dieppoise', 'Chicken à la King' and 'Gâteau St-Honoré' were among its specialities); and it was costly. For the art students and impoverished writers drinking opposite in the Marquis of Granby it represented luxury. To be invited there, to catch sight of the elegant figure of Sickert amid his entourage; and the Sibyl of Soho, Nina Hamnett, being helped home, a waiter at each elbow; of the Prime Minister's son Herbert Asquith in poetic travail; of minor royalty slumming for the evening; of actresses and Irishmen, models, musicians, magicians; a pageant of Sitwells, some outriders from Bloomsbury: to be part of this for a single evening was to feel a man or woman of the world.

Those who were well looked upon by Stulik could stay on long after the front door had been closed, drinking into the early hours of the morning mostly German wines known collectively as 'Stulik's Wee'. Stulik himself spoke indecipherably in galloping broken-back English, hinting that he was the fruit of an irregular attachment 'in which the charms of a famous ballerina had overcome the scruples of an exalted but anonymous personage' – a story that was attributed to the fact that he had once been chef to the Emperor Franz Josef to whom he bore an uncertain resemblance. He was assisted in the running of the place by a team of tactful waiters, a parrot and a dog.

Upstairs lay the private dining-room, stuffy with aspidistras, glowing dully under a good deal of dark crimson. Here secret liaisons took place, grand ladies and raffish men entering by the side door and ascending the hen-roost stairs. Those modestly sitting below could feel tremors of activity and hear scufflings up and down the narrow staircase. Then, on the topmost floors, 'dark and cluttered with huge articles of central European furniture',[74] lay the bedrooms.

The high prices were partly subsidized by young diplomats on leave, and the tariff was tempered to the visitor's purse. John was a popular host, sometimes even in his absence. 'Stulik's friends could run up enormous bills,' Constantine FitzGibbon recalled.

'Augustus once asked for his bill after a dinner party, Stulik produced his accumulated account, and Augustus took out £300 from his pocket with which to pay it . . . Stulik himself was sometimes penniless. On one occasion when John Davenport ordered an omelette there, Stulik asked if he might have the money to buy the eggs with which to make it. On another occasion, when Augustus grumbled at the size of his dinner bill, Stulik explained calmly in his guttural and almost incomprehensible English that it included the cost of Dylan [Thomas]'s dinner, bed and breakfast the night before.'[75]

Such bursts of generosity were followed by bouts of financial remorse deepened by the weight of Dorelia's disapproval. But for John money was freedom, and he could not tolerate being imprisoned by the lack of it. Money worries buzzed about him like flies, persistent though unstinting. A request by post from a deserving relative, if it arrived in the wrong hour, would detonate a terrifying explosion of anger. But he did not covet money. One day at Mallord Street, when he was grumbling about money, his friend Hugo Pitman offered to search through the house and found, in notes and uncashed cheques, many hundreds of pounds.

His generosity was unpremeditated. Money was important to him for his morale, not his bank account. He needed it about his person. All manner of creditors, from builders to schoolmasters, would queue for their bills to be paid, while he entertained his debtors at the Eiffel Tower. In times of war, he would explain severely, it was necessary for everyone to make sacrifices. But he himself did not sacrifice popularity. Among the art students he was now a fabled figure, a king of Chelsea, Soho and Fitzrovia. 'I can see him now walking . . . beneath the plane trees,' recalled the sculptor Charles Wheeler.

'. . . He is tall, erect and broad-shouldered . . . He is red-bearded and has eyes like those of a bull, doubtless is conscious of being the cynosure of the gaze of all Chelsea and looking neither to the left nor the right strides on with big steps and at a great pace towards Sloane Square, focusing on the distance and following, one imagines, some beautiful creature he is intent on catching . . .'[76]

Dorothy Brett, the painter, remembers her first sight of him from a bus in the King's Road 'with a large black homburg hat at a slight angle on his head, some kind of black frock coat. I think I must have been staring with my mouth open at him, he shot me a piercing look, and the bus rolled away.'[77] Later on, he would call at the Slade for Brett and two other students, Ruth Humphries and Dora Carrington, and take them to the Belgian cafés along Fitzroy Street, and once to call on a group of gypsies, 'beautiful, dark-haired men and women and children, in brilliant-coloured clothes', Brett recalled, in a room full of bright eiderdowns.

Best of all were the parties in Mallord Street. Invitations would arrive on the day itself – a telephone call or a note pushed under the door or a shout across the street urging one to 'join in' that evening. Carrington, in a letter to Lytton Strachey (23 July 1917), gives a voluptuous description of one of these events:

'It had been given in honour of a favourite barmaid of the Pub in Chelsea, near Mallord St, as she was leaving. She looked a charming character, very solid, with bosoms, and a fat pouting face. It was great fun.

Joseph, a splendid man from one of those cafés in Fitzroy St, played a concertina, and another man a mandolin. John drunk as a King Fisher. Many dreadfully worn characters, moth eaten and decrepit who I gathered were artists of Chelsea . . .

John made many serious attempts to wrest my virginity from me. But he was too mangy to tempt me even for a second. "Twenty years ago would have been a very different matter my dear sir" . . . There was one magnificent scene when a presentation watch was given the barmaid, John drest in a top hat, walking the whole length of that polished floor to the Barmaid sitting on the sofa by the fireplace, incredibly shy and embarrassed over the whole business, and giggling with delight. John swaggering with his bum lurching behind from side to side. Then kneeling down in the most gallant attitude with the watch on a cushion. Then they danced in the middle of the room, and every one rushed round in a circle shouting. Afterwards, it was wonderful to see John kissing this fat Pussycat, and diving his hand down her bodice. Lying with his legs apart on a divan in the most affected melodramatic attitudes!!'[78]

The Mallord Street studio was really a wonderful place for parties. All sorts of creatures turned up there. 'I suppose they were Bohemians,' Caspar, on leave from the navy, hazarded. With their old songs, new dances, sudden collapses, unexplained disappearances, these crowded gatherings looked to Caspar like complex experiments conducted in the laboratory of this studio. John would stare at it all with his wild eyes as if trying to discover 'which way life led', Caspar observed. 'I think he was experimenting the whole time, trying to find out what the hell it was all about.' But despite the activity, it was always the same. 'How it brought back another world!' Carrington exclaimed after a later party (2 November 1920).

'. . . Dorelia like some Sibyl sitting in a corner with a Basque cap on her head and her cloak swept round her in great folds, smiling mysteriously, talking to everyone, unperturbed watching the dancers. I wondered what went on in her head. I fell very much in love with her. She was so amazingly beautiful. It's something to have seen such a vision as she looked last night . . . I had some very entertaining dialogues with John, who was like some old salt in his transparent drunkenness.

"I say old chap will you come away with me?"

D.C. "But you know what they call that."

"Oh I forgot you were a boy."

D.C. "Well don't forget it or you'll get 2 years hard."

"I say you are insinuating," drawing himself up and flashing his eyes in mock indignation, "that I am a Bugger."

D.C. "My brother is the chief inspector of Scotland Yard."

"Oh I'm not afraid of him." But in a whisper. "Will you come to Spain with me? I'd love to go to Spain with *you*."

D.C. "This year, next year, sometime."

John. "Never." Then we both laughed in a roar together.'

The spirit of artistic London during the war, its spiral of gaiety and recrimination, is well caught by the affair of the Monster Matinée performed on 20 March 1917 at the Chelsea Palace Theatre.[79] This jumbo pantomime had been organized in aid of Lena Ashwell's Concerts at the Front. 'It was to be a sort of history of Chelsea,' Lady Glenavy wrote, 'with little plays about Rossetti, Whistler and others, with songs and dances ending up with a grand finale in praise of Augustus John.' Everyone in the polite world was soon elbowing his way and hers into this charity rag; a committee of duchesses gave birth to itself; and sub-committees proliferated through many smart houses. During rehearsals fashionable ladies gathered in groups for gossip about the notorious John, vying with one another to tell the most succulent story of his dreadful deeds. But when he appeared, 'Birdie' Schwabe noticed, such was his presence that they would all stand up to greet him with their best smiles. The last scene of the show featured 'Mrs Grundy and the John Beauty Chorus',* in which a band of Slade girls – Dorothy Brett, Carrington, Barbara Hiles and others – shouted out:

* See Appendix Five.

John! John!
How he's got on!
  He owes it, he knows it, to me!
Brass earrings I wear,
And I don't do my hair,
And my feet are as bare as can be;
When I walk down the street,
All the people I meet
  They stare at the things I have on!
When Battersea-Parking
You'll hear folks remarking:
'There goes an Augustus John!'[80]

But not everyone was approving. Peering out from the jungle of the art world, Epstein spied a plot within the matinée, with John its Machiavelli. At the start of the war Epstein had written to Quinn: 'Everybody here is war-mad. But my life has always been war, and it is more difficult I believe for me here to stick to the job, than go out and fight or at least get blind, patriotically drunk.'[81] He seemed determined to be disliked: 'As an artist I am among the best-hated ones here,' he boasted, 'and the most ignored.'[82] Perhaps through negligence, John and he seem nevertheless to have remained on good terms. In January 1917 Epstein finished a sculptured head of John. 'I wanted to capture a certain wildness,' he explained, 'an untamed quality that is the essence of the man.'[83] Seen from one angle, this head has the aspect of a devil; and this, a little later that year, was what John became. Compulsory conscription had now been introduced and Epstein found himself called up. He saw immediately that it was the result of this monster pantomime.

'My enemies have at last succeeded in forcing me into the army . . . John has been behind the whole nasty business ever since the war started, but I first found it out when in a theatrical show got up for charity, he had me caricatured on the stage; he was one of the chief organizers of this dastardly business and ever since then I understand the low, base character of the man. This so-called charity performance was the work of our "artists" mostly hailing from Chelsea, and I was chief butt, partly on account as I take it, of the great public success of my exhibitions.'[84]

The conspiracy, to the extent that it existed, was a conspiracy of one – the professional joker Horace de Vere Cole. Making a tour of rival sculptors, he had guided their hands in the drafting of some extraordinary letters to the *Sunday Herald*[85] opposing Epstein's military exemption.

Walter Winars, a sculptor of horses, wrote from Claridge's; Derwent Wood went on record as disliking Epstein personally, and John Bach came up with the notion that there were too many artists in the country anyway. In a sane world, such a correspondence could have done no harm to Epstein. But the world was not sane, it was at war; and this anti-Epstein conspiracy was now rampant. The deeply laid pantomime revealed its leader to be the most popular artist of the day, Augustus John. Nothing less would satisfy Epstein.

Though John was certainly capable, when the mood was on him, of doing ugly things, he had no part in Cole's joke, and his letters show that he wanted Epstein to escape conscription. Quinn, who gave generous support to Epstein's fantasy, calling John 'malicious, for what you describe is pure malice and meanness and dirt', failed to tell Epstein that John had written to him on 18 August 1916: 'I saw Epstein lately: he is in suspense about being taken for the army. I sincerely hope they'll let him off.'

Friends did bring the two artists together and a reconciliation was arranged at a hotel in Brighton. Unfortunately a parrot belonging to the hotel exploded with some abusive remarks just as Epstein entered the restaurant, and he rushed out swearing that John was up to his tricks again.[86]

Epstein objected to John's untroubled exemption from conscription. While in Ireland with Gogarty, John had injured his knee jumping a fence. Despite months encased in plaster of paris, the knee had not mended. In exchange for a portrait or two, he consulted Herbert Barker, the specialist in manipulative surgery. 'The celebrated "bone-setter" having put me under gas . . . carrying my crutches, I walked away like the man in the Bible.'[87] Not long afterwards, with another insufficient leap, he damaged the other knee – 'bang went the semi-lunar and I nearly fainted.' Again he sought out Barker, this time at a remote village in North Devon.

'I invited him to my private sitting-room and examined his knee,' Barker records. 'It was swollen, bent to a considerable angle and both flexion and extension were painful even to attempt. It was a typical case of derangement of the internal semi-lunar cartilage.'[88] This time there was no anaesthetic and the knee snapped back into place while John smoked a cigarette. 'I feel rather like a racehorse come down in the world and pulling a fourwheeler must feel,' he wrote afterwards (18 August 1916) to Quinn. 'But both knees will get strong again in time.'[89]

They were not strong enough for the medical authorities who examined him later that year at the barracks in Dorchester and who, while insisting that he be re-examined periodically, rejected him for military service. There followed a year in limbo, with the constant threat of being compelled to do office work – a prospect more alarming than trench warfare. On the bright surface of things he was enjoying a brilliant career in London, admired by the young and pursued by the wealthy. But below this surface, despair was forming. He was petted and flattered; he still roared, but he had been coaxed into a cage and the door was closing behind him. All the sweetmeats poked through the bars he gobbled up at once: he liked them, but they did not satisfy him, so he ate more until they began to sicken him. He was painting less well, and though he could blink away this fact he could not blind himself to it. 'I wish it were not necessary to depend so much on rich people,' he confessed to Handrafs O'Grady. 'They don't really buy things for love – or rarely.' He had developed a technique of 'boldly accelerated "drawing with a brush" '.[90] Once he had mastered this, he could almost never unlearn it because anything else was slower.

In November 1917, at the Alpine Club, he held the largest exhibition of his pictures ever assembled. He was now, in the words of *The Times*, 'the most famous of living English painters'.[91] But he had reached a watershed in his career. He did not paint to please the public nor whole-heartedly to please himself, but as if he were simply passing the time. 'He seems to have, with the artistic gifts of a man, the mind of a child,' wrote one critic of this show.

'. . . Life to him is very simple; it consists of objects that arouse in him a *naïve* childish curiosity and delight; but he has been artistically educated in a modern, very unchildish, world, and has learnt very easily all the technical lessons that the world has to teach. The consequence is that he is too skilful for his own vision, like those later Flemish Primitives who were spoilt by acquiring the too intellectual technique of Italy. Constantly one feels the virtuoso obtruding himself into a picture that ought to be as *naïve* in execution as it is on conception; and often, where there is no conception at all, one sees the virtuoso trying to force one.'

The change in his painting may be measured by a differing quality of interest it excited. Shortly before the war Osbert Sitwell had visited the Chenil Gallery,

'. . . and saw a collection of small paintings by Augustus John: young women in wide orange or green skirts, without hats or crowned with large straw hats, lounging wistfully on small hills in undulating and monumental landscapes, with the feel of sea and mountain in the air round them . . . By these I was so greatly impressed that I tried to persuade my father to purchase the whole contents of the room . . . Alas, I did not possess the authority necessary to convince him . . ."[92]

This new exhibition in the autumn of 1917 was also impressive, like a cocktail party with windows on to past countries; the west of Ireland, South of France, North Wales, Cornwall and the Aran Islands. Next to Dorelia in a yellow dress or orange jacket and the children (one of which, of Ida's Robin, was bought for the Tate Gallery) were allegorical groups of gypsies, tinkers, 'philosophers in contemplation'; the familiar faces of old friends such as Ambrose McEvoy and Arthur Symons; smart old buffers who appeared indifferently on donated canvases in aid of the Red Cross; the more formal shapes of titled ladies and gentlemen such as Lady Tredegar, Sir Edwin Lutyens and the two somewhat unfinished Howard de Waldens; and various servicemen ranging from the fat artilleryman to a colonel and an admiral. It was an admirably democratic group, a sociological record of types and individuals that would have been invaluable before the age of photography. 'If you will go to the Alpine Club on Mill Street off Conduit Street you will see an unprecedented exhibition of paintings of Augustus John,' wrote Lord Beaverbrook (then Sir Max Aitken) to F. E. Smith (28 November 1917). 'Every picture in the room is painted by John. If you judge for yourself you will conclude that John is the greatest artist of our time and possibly of any time. If you refuse to follow your own judgement you must listen to the comments of your fashionable friends who are flocking to John's Exhibition. I saw some of the female persuasion there to-day gazing on John rather than on his pictures.'

It was Sickert, the previous year, who had warned his fellow painters against the mistake of inverted snobbery: 'you are reflecting whether it is not high time to throw Augustus John, who has clearly become compromising, overboard. Take my tip. Don't!'[93] But the war had dimmed John's imaginative world. The future seemed to be with those who looked for a new art dominated by the functions of machinery rather than the organic forms of nature. Over the last half of his career, there was, as Herbert Read wrote, 'little in his work to show that he has lived through one of the most momentous epochs in history'[94] – a limitation that could also be fixed on Gwen John.

The war was initially seen as the enemy of all artists. They had come together in a profusion of groups and movements: collided: flown apart. Marinetti's Futurists, Wyndham Lewis's Vorticists, Roger Fry's Omega Workshops: all were adjusting to a competitive age, to discord, to the conditions of war. In the histories of modern art, John has no place with these movements. But he did maintain contacts on the periphery. When in the autumn of 1914 Wyndham Lewis's Rebel Art Centre in 38 Great Ormond Street destroyed itself, another less well-publicized centre at 8 Ormonde Terrace replaced it. This was led by Bomberg, Epstein and William Roberts: and John was asked to be its first president. In their derelict house, leased by 'a dear old humorist with a passion for vegetables',[95]* these artists took aggressive refuge from the war, teaching, and employing the rooms as studios. In a letter to the young Evan Morgan (Lord Tredegar), John (who refused the presidency) explained his views in a manner that defines his relation to almost all the new movements:

'I confess I was always shy of the Ormonde Terrace schemes when approached before . . . *I do still think the idea is a very good one.* I only have my doubts of our carrying it to success when hindered by certain personalities – given a nucleus of serious and sensible persons or enough of such to *predominate* I would not refuse my name for any useful purpose. It was for this reason I was so keen to get Ginner and Gilman on the Committee. They are both able men especially the former and would not be likely to wreck or jeopardize our plans by childish frivolity or lack of savoir-faire. Given such conditions, I say, B[omberg] and the rest could take their chance . . . I am quite game to go on with the affair and do all I can. But I can't go and identify myself publicly with a narrow group with which I have no natural connexion. You must see that I have arrived at greater responsibilities than the people we are dealing with. My own "interests" lie in *isolation* as complete as possible. I have never studied my interests but experience teaches me at least to avoid misunderstandings. I would be quite ready to waive my "interests" damn them! pour le bon motif, but I don't want a fiasco . . . It's impossible for a painter to be also a politician and an administrator. We ought to have [A. R.] Orage as dictator . . . I was loath to act as captain to a scratch crew and seeing nothing but rocks ahead.'[96]

This letter points to several developing strains in John: the superstitious fear of failure, of contagious 'bad luck', and an impatience with himself for succumbing to this; an apprehension of press and publicity; the film of 'greater responsibilities' that was clouding his natural vision; and some common sense. Only isolation could uphold this talent, he believed, but to isolation he was by temperament unsuited. The groups and movements he avoided had, as they exploded, flung their adherents into the forefront of the war where they found inspiration. John too had wanted to hurry to the front.

* Stuart Gray, an ex-lawyer, hunger marcher and future 'King of Utopia'.

'I have had the idea of going to France to sketch for a long while and I have hopes now of being able to do so,' he had written on 26 April 1916 to Will Rothenstein.

'But I am still in suspense. I have applied for a temporary commission which I think indispensable to move with any freedom in the British lines where the discipline is exceedingly severe . . . there's enough material to occupy a dozen artists. Of course the proper time for war is the winter and I very much regret not having managed to go out last winter. I cannot say I have any personal influence with the powers that be . . . I have been advised at the same time to keep my business quite dark. You might suppose I could do something with Lloyd George but I fear that gentleman will never forgive me for painting a somewhat unconventional portrait of him . . .'

Another winter came and went, and John continued to keep his business dark, remaining sombrely at home. During 1917 he began to drift, not altogether gracefully, into the McEvoy world of 'Duchesses'. One sitter who occupied him that year was Lady Cynthia Asquith, who had sat to McEvoy, Sargent and Tonks. Her diary entries give revealing glimpses of him in this new milieu.

'*Friday 27 April 1917*
. . . His appearance reduced Margot [Asquith]'s two-year-old girl to terrified tears. I like him but felt very shy with him . . . Mary [Herbert] and I both exhibited our faces, hoping he might want to paint us. He is doing a portrait of Margot and at one time asked her to sit for the "altogether", saying she had such a perfect artist's figure . . .
. . . Margot once asked John how many wives he really had (he is rather a mythical figure), saying she heard he was a most immoral man. He indignantly replied, "It's monstrous – I'm a very moderate man. I've only got *one* wife!"

Tuesday 9 October 1917
. . . He has a most delightful studio – huge, with an immense window, and full of interesting works. The cold was something excruciating . . . I felt myself becoming more and more discoloured. His appearance is magnificent, straight out of the Old Testament – flowing, well-kept beard, hair cut *en bloc* at about the top of the ear, fine, majestic features. He had on a sort of overall daubed with paint, buttoning up round his throat, which completed a brilliant picturesque appearance. He was "blind sober" and quite civil. I believe sometimes he is alarmingly surly. Unlike McEvoy,

he didn't seem to want to converse at all while painting and I gratefully accepted the silence. He talked quite agreeably during the intervals he allowed me. He made – I think – a very promising beginning of me sitting in a chair in a severe pose: full face, but with eyes averted – a very sidelong glance. He said my expression "intrigued" him, and certainly I think he has given me a very evil one[97] – a sort of *listening* look as though I was hearkening to bad advice.

Thursday 1 November 1917
Bicycled to John's studio. John began a new version of me, in which I could see no sort of resemblance to myself. The [D. H.] Lawrences turned up. I thought it just possible John *might* add another to the half dozen or so people whose company Lawrence can tolerate for two hours. It was quite a success. John asked Lawrence to sit for him,[98] and Lawrence admired the large designs in the studios, but maintained an ominous silence as regards my pictures. He charged John to depict 'generations of Wemyss disagreeableness in my face, especially the mouth', said disappointment was the key-note of my expression, and that what made him "wild" was that I was "a woman with a weapon she would never use" . . . He thought the painting of Bernard Shaw with closed eyes very true symbolism.'

'*Come quickly*, like Lord Jesus,' John had urged her, 'because I've got to go away before long.' After eighteen months at the starting line he was still waiting his call to the front – or, better still, to several fronts with intervals in England during which he would work up the results of his sketching into pictures. 'I very much want to do a great deal in the way of military drawings and paintings,' he told the publisher Grant Richards,[99] who had proposed a book of these drawings. The authorities, however, held out against granting permanent exemption from military service. Its rule was that artists must be called up, after which the War Office could then apply to the army for their artistic services. Because of his recurring exemption, John was unable to force his way into the army in order to get seconded out of it. He had become a bureaucratic paradox.

On 7 September 1917 he underwent another medical examination. 'I was not taken on the 7th,' he wrote to Campbell Dodgson. 'On leaving, my leg (the worst one) "went out" so I had physical support for spiritual satisfaction.'[100] He had already informed the War Office that he had no objection to his work being used for government publications, and had produced for a Ministry of Information book, *British Aims and Ideals*, a hideous symbolical lithograph, 'The Dawn'. In a letter to the writer, journalist and politician C. F. G. Masterman, Campbell Dodgson wrote:

'I am of opinion that it might be the making of John to be brought into contact with reality and the hard facts of warfare, instead of doing things out of his own head as he does at present, except when he has a portrait to paint.' Impressed by these arguments, and by John's obvious eagerness, the War Office capitulated, finally inviting him to act as one of its official artists: and John refused.

The invitation had come only just too late. Through the good offices of P. G. Konody, the art critic of the *Observer*, John had volunteered to work for the Canadian War Memorials Fund, a scheme started by Lord Beaverbrook to assemble a picture collection that would give a record of Canada's part in the war. The Canadian War Records Office now granted him, with full pay, allowances and an extra three hundred pounds (equivalent to £7,500 in 1996) in expenses, an honorary commission in the Overseas Military Forces of Canada, in return for which John agreed to paint a decorative picture of between thirty and forty feet in length. 'I had almost forgotten about this project . . . I had given up hope of it,' he explained to Campbell Dodgson. '. . . The Canadians would be, I imagine, far more generous than the British Government.'

London that autumn saw the sight of John absorbed in *Jane Eyre* ('what a wonderful work!') and attired as a Canadian major. 'Yes, I am told I look very beautiful in uniform,' he wrote to a girl called Kitty. 'I wish you could see me.'[101] But others who did see him were dismayed. 'I have lunched at the Café Royal with Major John in Khaki!' exclaimed Arthur Symons in a letter to Quinn. 'The uniform does not suit him . . . I never saw John more sombre and grave than to-day. He is brooding on I know not what.'[102] The conscientious objector Lytton Strachey, who had observed him looking 'decidedly colonial' at the Alpine Club, took a more hostile view of this development. 'Poor John,' he lamented. '. . . Naturally he has become the darling of the upper classes, and made £5,000 out of his show. His appearance in Khaki is unfortunate – a dwindled creature, with clipped beard, pseudo-smart, and in fact altogether deplorable.'[103]

Strachey was one of those who 'joined in' a farewell party at Mallord Street. Early next morning, John's military figure, greatcoated, with leather gloves, a cane, riding boots laced up to the knee, and spurs, picked its way between the prostrate bodies, and strode off to the war.

4

AUGUSTUS DOES HIS BIT

'The dawn of peace breaks gloomily indeed.'
Augustus John to John Sampson (1919)

'John is having a great time!' William Orpen, now an official war artist, wrote excitedly from Amiens. '. . . in the army [he] is a fearful and wonderful person. I believe his return to "Corps" the other evening will never be forgotten – followed by a band of photographers. He's going to stop for the duration.'[104]

He was billeted on the Somme front at Aubigny, a small village that had been designated a 'bridgehead'. Though there were intermittent shelling and occasional air raids, one of which removed the roof of the hut where he lived, Aubigny was 'a deadly hole'. Nevertheless he felt 'overjoyed to be out here'.[105] Over the last two years John's letters had been weighed down with a despair that leaves 'me speechless, doubting the reality of my own existence'.[106] He complained of a 'sort of paranoia or mental hail-storm from which I suffer continually',[107] and of curious states of mind when he was 'not myself'. 'I like John,' D. H. Lawrence wrote in November 1917, ' – but he is a drowned corpse.'[108] Often he felt 'horribly alone',[109] knowing that 'there is no one I can be with for long.'[110] In a letter to Cynthia Asquith he accused himself of owning 'a truly mean and miserable nature. Obviously I am ill since I cannot stand *anybody*.' This meanness infected whatever he looked at until he could see 'no good in anything'.[111] While submerged in such moods he had a way of hopelessly shaking his head like an animal in a zoo. Observing him closely one evening at the Margaret Morris Theatre 'with two very worn and chipped ladies', Katherine Mansfield had written to Ottoline Morrell (August 1917):

'I seemed to see his [John's] mind, his haggard mind, like a strange forbidding country, full of lean sharp peaks and pools lit with a gloomy glow, and trees bent with the wind and vagrant muffled creatures tramping their vagrant way. Everything exhausted and finished – great black rings where the fires had been, and not a single fire even left to smoulder. And then he reminded me of that man [Svidrigailov] in *Crime and Punishment* who finds a little girl in his bed in that awful hotel the night before he shoots himself, in that appalling hotel. But I expect this is all rubbish, and he's really a happy man and fond of his bottle and a goo–goo eye. But I don't think so.'[112]

He was now in his fortieth year, and age had begun to inflict upon him its humiliations. 'I am waiting for a magic elastic belt to prevent me from becoming an *absolute* wreck at 35!' he had written to Ottoline. 'It doesn't sound very romantic does it?' His deafness too partly accounted for his bravery during bombardments. 'I'm stone deaf myself,' he shouted into Dorothy Brett's hearing aid, 'besides having a weak knee and defective teeth and moral paralysis.'[113] This last condition was aggravated by the war. 'As for me I can only see imminent ruin ahead – personal I mean, perhaps even general,' he had confided to Evan Morgan. Inevitably the war, with its regimentation and officiousness, subordinated the individual to the state. In such an atmosphere John was 'neither fish, flesh, fowl nor good red herring'.[114] His work too afforded him little certainty – painting for money, against time: an abuse of his skill. Something had to change. His translation into a Canadian major appeared to offer him a new life, a fresh stimulus for his painting. It had arrived barely in time.

To be caught up by events, to be on the go again was exhilarating. The blood began to move more swiftly through his body. Cheerfulness broke through. With his rank came a car and a melancholy batman. Before long they were patrolling the Vimy front held by the Canadian Corps like Don Quixote and Sancho Panza. The Canadians were 'excellent fellows' though the work of the Canadian painters was 'extremely bad'. 'I go about a good deal and find much to admire,' he wrote.[115] After an immense fall of snow everything looked wonderful. He had discovered 'quite a remarkable place which might make a good picture'. This was a medieval château, converted into a battery position, with towers and a river running through its grounds, at Lieven, a devastated town opposite Lens. Near by were several battered churches standing up amid the general ruin and, further off, a few shattered trees and slag heaps, like pyramids against the sky. It was here, among this strange confusion of ancient and modern, that he planned his big 'synthetic' picture, bringing in tanks, a balloon, 'some of the right sort of civilians', and a crucifix. 'There is so much to do out here,' he wrote to Arthur Symons. 'All is glittering in the front; amidst great silence the guns reverberate. I shall take ages to get all I want done in preparation for a huge canvas. France is divine – and the French people.'[116] The desolation seemed to hearten him. It was 'too beautiful', he told Dorelia, adding: 'I suppose France and the whole of Europe is doomed.'

Also stationed at the château was Wyndham Lewis. For both these war artists it was an untypically peaceful time: guns were everywhere, but for painting not firing. John, Lewis noted with approval, did not neglect the social side of military life and was everywhere accorded the highest signs of respect, largely on account of his misunderstood beard. 'He was the only officer in the British Army, except the King, who wore a beard,'

Lewis explained. 'In consequence he was a constant source of anxiety and terror wherever he went. Catching sight of him coming down a road any ordinary private would display every sign of the liveliest consternation. He would start saluting a mile off. Augustus John – every inch a King George – would solemnly touch his hat and pass on.'[117]

On one occasion, after a successful party, the two war artists commandeered a car and careered off together almost into enemy lines. It was probably the closest John got to the fighting, and Lewis, the ex-bombardier, was soon poking fun at his friend's mock-war experiences. But John, noticing that Lewis had retreated home following their exploit, pursued him vicariously. 'Have you seen anything of that tragic hero and consumer of tarts and mutton-chops, Wyndham Lewis?' he asked their mutual friend Alick Schepeler. 'He is I think in London, painting his gun pit and striving to reduce his "Vorticism" to the level of Canadian intelligibility – a hopeless task I fear.'

Occasionally John would 'run over' to Amiens, Paris or, more surreptitiously, back to London. At Amiens he 'found Orpen',[118] whose welcome seemed a little agitated. 'They are trying to saddle me with him [John],' Orpen protested to Will Rothenstein, ' – but I'm not having any! Too much responsibility.' He also came across the painter Alfred Munnings who was there to 'do some horse pictures'.

In Paris he put up at the Palais d'Orsay as the guest of Lord Beaverbrook, who had arranged a special entertainment for his 'Canadians' in a suite at the Hotel Bristol.[119] At supper, John recalled, 'the guests were so spaced as to allow further seating accommodation between them. The reason for this arrangement was soon seen on the arrival of a bevy of young women in evening clothes, who without introduction established themselves in the empty chairs.' These girls, the pick of the local emporium, came strongly recommended: 'one or two of them were even said to be able to bring the dead to life.' Beaverbrook, at this critical moment, tactfully withdrew, and was followed by the impetuously cautious Orpen ('I'm afraid he's a low lick-spittle after all,' Augustus wrote to Dorelia). Bottles of champagne then appeared and the atmosphere became charged with conviviality. 'Yet as I looked round the table, a curious melancholy took possession of me,' John recorded. '. . . I had no parlour tricks, nor did my companions-in-arms seem much better equipped than I was in this line; except for one gallant major, who, somehow recapturing his youthful high spirits, proceeded to emit a series of comical Canadian noises, which instantly provoked loud shrieks of appreciative laughter.' To keep his melancholy at bay, John also attempted an outburst of gaiety, raising 'in desperation' one of the girls to the level of the table and there effecting 'a successful *retroussage*, in spite of her struggles'.

Despite all this 'rich fun', he felt curiously islanded. Before starting out, he had promised Cynthia Asquith to keep a diary while at the Front, but 'the truth is I funk it! . . . I am in a curious state,' he had explained from Aubigny,

' – wondering who I am. I watch myself closely without yet being able to classify myself. I evade definition – and that must mean I have no *character* . . . To be a Major is not enough – clearly – now if one were a Brigadier-General say – would *that* help to self-knowledge if not self-respect . . .? I am alone in what they call the "Château" in this dismal little town. I am very lucky, not having to face a *Mess* twice a day with a cheerful optimistic air. When out at the front I admire things unreasonably – and conduct myself with that instinctive tact which is the mark of the moral traitor. A good sun makes beauty out of wreckage. I wander among bricks and wonder if those shells will come a little bit nearer . . .'

The wearing of a uniform seemed to have imposed another self on him, and he had no centre from which to combat this imposition. The devastation of the fields and trees reflected a devastation within him. At Beaverbrook's party or in the mess, he could not lose himself; alone, in the château where there was 'no romance', he felt characterless. Yet to paint he had to establish a sense of character, and if he could not do this then he felt it might be better to be killed, suddenly, pointlessly, by some shell. A sudden bellicose joy surged through him at the great news that thirty German divisions had been repulsed with 'colossal slaughter'. There was 'a wonderful show last night', he wrote to Dorelia, 'when we discharged five thousand gas drums at the Boches followed by an intense bombardment. Things are getting interesting out here.' But this joy quickly passed and he fell into 'a horrible state of depression'.[120]

The crisis erupted in a sudden act of self-assertion when he knocked out one of his fellow officers, Captain Wright. 'The gesture had only an indirect relation to my codpiece,' he assured Gogarty.[121] Captain Wright had said something that, interpreted by John as an insult, acted as the trigger for this explosion. The situation was serious and John was rushed out of France by Lord Beaverbrook. 'Do you know I saved him [John] at a Court-martial for hitting a man named Peter Wright?' Beaverbrook complained in a letter to Sir Walter Monckton, the lawyer and politician who had been serving in France (30 April 1941). 'I cannot tell you what benefits I did not bestow on him. And do you know what work I got out of John? – Not a damned thing.'

John arrived back in London at the end of March 'in a state of utter mental confusion'.[122] There was no chance of getting back to France, and for four months the threat of military punishment hung over him. 'I think this trouble must be over,' he eventually wrote to Gogarty on 24 July 1918. 'The Canadian people seem to think so, and it's now so long since.'

It remained to be seen whether he could salvage something from his few months at the front. 'I am tackling a vast canvas,' he had told Innes Meo (22 February 1918), ' – that is, I shall do.' Cynthia Asquith, who saw this canvas on 29 July, recorded her impression in a diary: 'It is all sketched in, but without any painting yet . . . it rather took my breath away – splendid composition, and what an undertaking to fill a forty-foot canvas!' On 18 November he is writing to Gwen: 'I am hard at work on the Canadian war picture. The cartoon will be finished by Xmas after which there will be an exhibition.'[123] This cartoon went on view in January 1919 when the *Observer* art critic P. G. Konody organized a Canadian War Memorials exhibition at Burlington House showing war pictures by Bernard Meninsky, C. R. W. Nevinson, William Roberts, the Nash brothers and others. 'Even Mr Paul Nash may grow old-fashioned with the years,' commented *The Times*, 'but it is hard to imagine a time when Major John's cartoon (not yet finished) "The Pageant of War" will not interest by its masterly suggestion of what war means.'[124] In an article for *Colour Magazine*, Konody described John's summary of all he had witnessed during his five months in France, and his portrayal of it as a vast gypsy convoy.

'His picture may be described as an epitome of modern war. In it are introduced crowds of refugees, men, women and children with their carts and cherished belongings, detachments of soldiers in their trench outfits, officers on horseback, trucks carrying soldiers to the front line, wounded sufferers and stretcher-bearers, a camouflaged gun position, bursting shells, an observation balloon, a ruined chateau, Vimy Ridge, all the movement and bustle, all the destruction and desolation of war. But this astounding accumulation of motives is organized with classic lucidness, with a sense of style unrivalled by any other living painter. Full of animation, movement and seething life, the design is controlled by a rare sense of order.'

Konody, who wrote books on Velázquez, Filippo Lippi and Raphael, as well as a study of C. R. W. Nevinson's war paintings, believed that John's prodigious decoration would stand comparison with the work of 'Michelangelo, Signorelli, Raphael or Leonardo, to whose best tradition John is faithful in spite of his essential modernity . . . [if he] has the staying power to carry out consistently with the brush what he has so triumphantly accomplished in charcoal'.[125] Intermittently during that year

John grappled 'with my Canadian incubus . . . I must try to get quit of the whole business. No more official jobs for me.'[126] He did not have the staying power. The erection of the art gallery in Ottawa, planned to house the entire Canadian War Memorials collection, was postponed, and forty years on Beaverbrook and John were still in correspondence, Beaverbrook asking after the picture, John parrying with inquiries about the gallery.[127]

But there is one large oil painting, 'Fraternity',[128] at the Imperial War Museum in London, that seems to justify the time he spent in France. Executed in muted greens and browns, it depicts three soldiers against a background of ruined brickwork and shattered trees, one giving another a light for his cigarette. It is a touching picture, emotionally and literally in the swirl of arms and the two cigarettes held tip to tip. But though the background is an authentic record of what John actually saw in France, the figures are a straight copy of a mass-circulation postcard from the *Daily Mail*'s Official War Picture Series 2, No. 11 – 'A "Fag" after a Fight'. It is a studio artist's picture.

The fact was that John had little aptitude as a war artist. A caricature by Max Beerbohm that appeared in *Reveille* in 1918 shows him in his neat uniform and tin hat behind the front lines staring into a field of French peasants in Johnesque attitudes with spades, buckets and hoes, exclaiming: 'Ah, now there really is a subject.'

*

'Peace has arrived,' Gus wrote to Gwen on 18 November. 'London went mad for a week & Paris too I suppose.'[129] He had called on Gwen in December 1917 on his way to the Canadian headquarters at Aubigny and 'at the fourth call caught her & we dined together' at the Café de Versailles in Montparnasse. The change in her since he had last seen her four years ago was rather terrible. Before the war Henry Lamb had thought her 'really quite a gay person who could be full of fun';[130] and Duncan Grant, seeing her 'living with her cats on the old fortification',[131] did not find a recluse but someone eager to go out picnicking and talk of Rodin. But Rodin had died on 17 November 1917 and Gwen, so Gus reported to Dorelia the following month, 'has been getting more and more hypochondriac'.[132] During these war years she had not seen much of Rodin, though they corresponded and she still thought of herself as his 'true wife'. But then she did not see much of anyone over these years. The fortifications rose. 'I don't like meeting people,' she explained to Quinn. In 1913 she was admitted into the Catholic Church. As Rodin was a Catholic, she explained, this made no difference to their relationship. 'I was born to love,' she had written. The advantage of loving God was that He did not fall ill, get old, die. 'He loves me,' she wrote in her child's hand. But

He could not protect her from grief over Rodin's death. 'I don't know what I am going to do,'[133] she admitted to Ursula Tyrwhitt five days after he died. 'I have not seen Gus yet.'

Gus trusted to Gwen's 'esprit' not to get morbid over Rodin. Yet he was bothered by her. 'I trust you to believe that my infrequent letters don't mean that I don't think of you very often,' he assured her.[134] The morning after their dinner, he drove round to her 'garret at Meudon' and borrowed five pounds off her. 'She says my visit did her a lot of good,'[135] he assured Dorelia. That sounded like typical bravado, almost comic in its insensitivity. Yet it was true. Gwen confided to Ursula that she had surprisingly enjoyed his visit. Somehow he broke the spell of death and connected her again, however randomly, with living energy. By February 1918 she was feeling 'nearly normal' and beginning to paint again. She had particularly liked learning about Gus's family (and was 'surprised to hear of Vivien's existence').

'She utterly neglects herself,' Gus had complained to Dorelia, whom he asked to send Gwen photographs of the children 'and perhaps a Jaeger blanket as she admits the cold keeps her awake at night. The Lord only knows how she passes her days.'[136] He had promised to come back and see her again soon, but after his stand-up fight with Captain Wright and the threat of a court martial, he was not allowed into France for the duration of the war. He seems to have been too embarrassed to tell Gwen the facts. 'My authorities wouldn't send me back to France as I expected & wanted,' he wrote. 'They preferred to keep me at work here [Mallord Street] which was very silly . . . I will try to get to Paris early next year [1919] . . . One will be able to fly over in 2 or 3 hours! I cannot come before.'[137]

In the last months of the war, as Paris came under bombardment from German and American troops, Gwen had abandoned her room in the rue de l'Ouest and, under 'balls of fire' from the planes and the awful 'Gottas [i.e. Gotha heavy bombers] with torpillos', she travelled back and forwards on the train moving her possessions to Meudon. Gus had renewed his invitation to Alderney. Dorelia, he said, 'would love to see you again'. But if he could not lure her into England, he did at least persuade her to go off a few times to Brittany.

During 1918 she found rooms in the Château de Vauxclair, an empty, silent, sixteenth-century house behind tall iron gates, with a neglected garden, near a 'wild lonely bay' at Pléneuf. 'I think I shall be alone there,' she wrote to Ursula Tyrwhitt. 'I could work.'[138] But in the spring of 1919 the house was bought by speculators. Gwen stayed on as a squatter, hoping that Gus might buy it. He tried, but at fifty thousand francs it became too expensive for him. 'Just at present debts & responsibilities are rather overwhelming,' he apologized to her that summer.' '. . . As you say it takes a lot of money to keep my family going.'[139] She also appealed to Quinn, but he complicated everything with his businesslike questionnaires and plans to move in Arthur Symons as caretaker. Men always became entangled in money like this.

Before the end of 1919 Gwen returned to Meudon. At last it was business as usual. Winifred had given birth to a second child in the United States. Thornton, after a short stay in Tenby, was mining oil shale at Deer Park in Newfoundland. 'I suppose later he will live in his boat and catch fish,'[140] Gus accurately predicted in a letter to Gwen. He himself was also planning to spend a week or two round Tenby. 'I wish you were coming too.'[141]

This concern for her, tinged obscurely with guilt, agitated Gwen. Gus had written to Quinn saying that she 'wasn't looking at all fit'. But he wanted things for her that she didn't want herself, or at least not often, not much. So she made an effort to reassure him, explaining the nature of her independence. 'When illness or death do not intervene, I am [happy],' she wrote. 'Not many people can say as much.

'I do not lead a subterranean life . . . Even in respect to numbers I know and see more people than I have ever. (Some of my friendships are nothing to be proud of by-the-bye.) It was in London I saw nobody. If in a café I gave you the impression that I am too much alone, it was an accident. I was thinking of you and your friends and that I should like to go to spectacles and cafés with you often. If to "return to life" is to live as I did in London, merci Monsieur! There are people like plants who cannot flourish in the cold, and I want to flourish.'[142]

Admiration, exasperation, attraction, temptation confused their feelings. If they could have shuffled the cards, dealt new ones from the pack they both held, then they might truly have helped each other. As it was they could do very little, though that little was sometimes useful. In their separate ways, now that the war was over, Gus wrote to Gwen, 'one will work better I hope.'[143]

*

On Armistice Day, 11 November 1918, John made his appearance at a party in the Adelphi 'amid cheers, in his British [sic] officer's uniform, accompanied by some land-girls in leggings and breeches who brought a fresh feeling of the country into the overheated room'.[144] He seemed to be enjoying himself, and communicating enjoyment, more than anyone. The following month he wrote to Quinn: 'London went fairly mad for a week but thank the Lord that's over and we have to face the perils of Peace now.'

He had, he reminded Dorelia, 'an odd nervous system'. His 'bad period', that had begun in France, persisted. 'Rather dreadful that feeling of wanting to go somewhere and not knowing where,' he noted. 'I spend hours of anguish trying to make a move – in some direction.'[145] In this sinking uncertainty he grew more dependent on other people. One was Lady Cynthia Asquith. 'Of you alone I can think with longing and admiration,' he declared. 'You have all the effect of a Divine Being whose smile and touch can heal, redeem and renew.' For Cynthia Asquith, herself close to a nervous breakdown, admiration was a medicine to be swallowed as 'dewdrops' – though when it took the form of 'an advance – clutching me very roughly and disagreeably by the shoulders – I shook myself free and there was no recurrence'.[146] What John responded to was the unhappiness below her giddy exterior. He understood her need for such an exterior and found he could talk with her. 'I bucked up somewhat,' he told her. 'Such is the benefit we get from confessing to one another.'

The war was over, but the trappings of war remained. In the spring of 1919 he was invited to attend the Peace Conference in Paris. Lloyd George proclaimed that the conference should not be allowed to pass 'without some suitable and permanent memento being made of these gatherings'. The British Government had therefore decided to 'approach two of the most famous British artists and ask them to undertake the representation of the Conference'. The two selected were John and Orpen, and both accepted. They were to get a subsistence allowance of three pounds (equivalent to £62 in 1996) a day, expenses, an option whereby the Government could purchase each of their pictures for three thousand pounds, and a five-hundred-pound option price for the portraits of visiting celebrities. Many of these celebrities, the Government was assured by Sir George Riddell, Chairman of the *News of the World*, who was acting as liaison officer between the British delegation and the press, 'are most anxious to be painted'. In John's case there was an immediate obstacle. Unaccountably he was still in the Canadian Army, and special arrangements were rushed through enabling him officially to be 'loaned to the War Office'.

He dreamed of being flown to France but, after three days of waiting in foggy weather, went by train. 'I am over here to paint something to commemorate the Conference. No small job!' he wrote to Sampson. '. . . This is my first day in Paris and a full one its been . . . There seem to be ructions brewing in the Conference.'[147] He found himself in 'a delightful apartment', 'almost too dream-like' on the third floor of 60 avenue Montaigne. Here, as the guest of Don José-Antonio de Gandarillas, a charming opium-eater with dyed hair who was attached to the Chilean Legation, he stayed during February and March. The conference hall was just across the river and he went over in search of profitable celebrities. Though he 'managed to collar a Belgian representative', he was worried over how he was to get hold of the statesmen for sittings. 'A certain delay at the start is to be expected no doubt,' he hazarded in a letter to Frances Stevenson,[148] with whom he was angling for a weekly allowance. It was Gandarillas who speeded things up. He knew everyone, and invited everyone to his flat. The parties they gave in the avenue Montaigne were soon the talk of Paris. 'My host Gandarillas leads a lurid and fashionable life,' John admitted.[149] An orchestra played ceaselessly all night and the spacious apartment was thronged with the *beau monde*. Rather nervously John began to infiltrate these parties, entering for the first time 'as dream-like a world as any I had been deprived of'.[150]

He had not thought of promoting himself – certainly he had no wish to dance: he had come prepared to 'stand apart in a corner and watch the scene'. What happened astonished him. He talked, he laughed, he danced: he was an extraordinary success. Paris this spring was the vortex of the social and political world; and at its centre this son of a Pembrokeshire solicitor stood out as 'easily the most picturesque personality', Frances Stevenson recorded. 'He held court in Paris.'

All red carpets led to him. The Prime Ministers of Australia, France, Canada and New Zealand submitted to his brush; kings and maharajas, dukes and generals, lords of finance and of law froze before him; the Emir Faisal posed; Lawrence of Arabia took his place humbly in the queue – and Dorelia wrote to inquire whether he had yet been knighted. More wonderful still were the princesses, infantas, duchesses, marchesas who lionized him. His awkwardness departed, and a sudden confidence surged through him. They were, he discovered, these grandiloquent ladies, all too human: they 'loved a bit of fun'. Under a smart corsage beat, as like as not, 'a warm, tender even fragile heart'. It was a revelation.

He was born quite suddenly into a new world, but it did not take full possession of him. Even now, at the height of this triumph, his 'criminal instincts' reasserted themselves, and he hurried away to 'my old and squalid but ever glorious quarter . . . and sat for a while in the company of young and sinister looking men with obvious cubistic tendencies'.[151] A few old friends still roamed Montparnasse, but something had been extinguished, something was vanishing for ever. Jean Moréas was dead; Modigliani, addicted to drink and drugs, would die within a year; Paul Fort had become respectable and the *cercle* of the closerie des Lilas was disbanded. Maurice Cremnitz was there, only slightly damaged by the war; but he, who had once likened Augustus to Robinson Crusoe, now gazed at Major John with suspicion. 'I was conscious of causing my friends embarrassment,' John admitted. A doubt sailed briefly across his mind. Was he too becoming respectable?

He was doubtful also about his painting. He had begun the Peace portraits grudgingly, but his accelerated technique worked well. 'I think I have acquired more common skill,' he wrote to Cynthia Asquith on 24 July 1919, ' – or is it that I have learnt to limit my horizons merely?' In the immense conference hall he had found a room with a high window niche, and from here he made sketches of the delegates. It was a curious assignment. 'All goes well,' he reassured Dorelia, ' – except for the poor old Conference.' Sometimes he felt like throwing a bomb into the chamber. Amid the ghastly talk of reparations and indemnities, the British contingent showed signs of despair, 'all except L[loyd] G[eorge] who looks bursting with satisfaction'. He and President Woodrow Wilson 'apparently boss the whole show'. General Smuts from South Africa appeared overcome with misgivings; William Massey, Prime Minister of New Zealand, described the proceedings as farcical; Balfour slumbered; the Prime Minister of Australia, William Hughes, looking like a jugged hare, was learning French. Speech followed speech in a multiplicity of languages: the assembly wilted in boredom. For John, who had arrived with 'my eyes open and brain busy', these interminable rows of seated figures offered no pictorial possibilities. But he badly needed the three thousand pounds and decided to attempt a more fanciful interpretation of what he saw. 'I do not propose to paint a literal representation of the Conference Chamber,' he promised the Ministry of Information, 'but a group which will have a more symbolic character, bring in motifs which will suggest the conditions which gave rise to the Conference and the various interests involved in it.' It did not augur well.

In April he moved from Gandarillas's apartment to a private house at 3 quai Malaquais belonging to the Duchess of Gramont, whose portrait he was painting. By May he had resolved to quit Paris. 'I was pretty busy in Paris,' he told Gwen, '& had a queer time.' He had been spoilt, pampered, dazzled. But now he had had enough: strangers would make better company, or perhaps solitude itself might be best. 'Life in Paris was too surprising,' he afterwards confided to Cynthia Asquith. 'I long for some far island, sun and salt water.' He had had too much work of the wrong sort. 'I am very helpless and desolate,' he confessed.[152]

He was still in khaki. Until the autumn of 1919, and to everyone's consternation, he continued to receive pay and allowances from the Canadians, and also for almost seven months from the British War Office. 'I must drop this commission and get into walking clothes again,' he told Dorelia. Everyone agreed. 'Would it not be more satisfactory for you to be demobilized?' the authorities tactfully persisted. But each time he prepared to return to civilian life a curious reluctance, not wholly financial, overcame him.[153] Had he not been 'going for a soldier' even before deciding on the Slade? The uniform, which had caused such embarrassment in Montparnasse, had given him confidence in the Champs-Élysées, and he enjoyed the pantomime. Besides, he had two medals.

But his inability to finish either the big Canadian war or Paris Peace Conference pictures made him 'very unstable'. He tried several methods of restoring this stability. To reimburse the British Government for the expenses it had paid him, he gave the Imperial War Museum eight drawings relating to the war, and allowed the museum to buy at an almost nominal price, one hundred and forty pounds (equivalent to £2,900 in 1996), his painting 'Fraternity'. He felt better too once he began travelling again. In September 1919, he turned up at the Villa La Chaumière at Deauville as the guest of Lloyd George.

'What a monde he lives in!' he exclaimed in a letter to Cynthia Asquith. '. . . My fortnight here has been fantastic . . . It's a place I should normally avoid. I have been horribly parasitical. I began a portrait of a lady here which promised well – till I gathered from her that if I made her *beautiful*, it might turn out to be the first step in a really brilliant career.'[154]

But he had left many unfinished things in Paris from the conference days and had no idea how to deal with them. 'Here I have met the Duchesse de Guiche who invites me to store my things in her house,' he wrote from Deauville to Gwen. 'You see in what exalted company I move!'

In March 1920, again at the Alpine Club Gallery, John exhibited his war and peace portraits. They were not flattering likenesses, nor were they satirical: with few exceptions they were neutral. The tedium released by the company of this exalted band is very adequately recorded, and to that extent he remained uncorrupted. But he had succumbed to the temptation to waste time. His two exhibitions at the Alpine Club were exercises in the higher journalism of art – commissions that gave little evidence of his special talent. John knew this himself. No amount of social success could conceal the truth for long. His melancholia deepened. In April 1920 he entered the Sister Carlin Hospital for an operation on his nose to make breathing easier. He had been 'in a state of profound depression', he told Ottoline Morrell. '. . . I feel always as though practically poisoned and must not shirk the operation. I look forward to it indeed as a means of recovering my normal self.'[155] It was essential to keep morale high. 'It took an uncommon amount of ether to get me under,' he bragged to Eric Sutton.[156] Under the ether, with a deep sigh, he uttered one remark: 'Well, I suppose I must be polite to these people.' He recovered with his usual facility and 'am doing rather brilliantly'.[157]

For his convalescence he went with Dorelia and some of the family to stay with his father in Tenby. A new era was beginning in Britain, and many were curious to know what part John would occupy in it. He was no longer the leader, as the *Observer* art critic had reported in 1912, of 'all that is most modern and advanced in present day British Art'. Nor, in his forty-third year, was he yet a Grand Old Man. To the younger artists he had once been the apostle of a new way of seeing: now he was the embodiment of a way of living. He wanted to start again and be more like Gwen. 'I want to dig myself up and replant myself in some corner where no one will look for me,' he declared to Cynthia Asquith. 'There perhaps – there in fact I know I shall be able to paint better.'

NINE

Artist of the Portraits

EVERYBODY'S DOING IT

'Après la guerre
There'll be a good time everywhere.'

And there was. Everyone wanted to be young again, and to forget not only the war but the ideals that had been contaminated by it. Enjoyment was to be the new currency – enjoyment spent as an unprecedented freedom to act, to experiment, to travel. The Continent became transformed from a battlefield into a playground. It was as if youth had suddenly been invented and pleasure become compulsory. There was no one who had been unaffected by those four years of terrible fighting: the whole country was scorched. Now it set about applying a balm.

To no category of people did this freedom seem to apply more directly than the New Woman. During the war her capabilities had been astonishingly displayed in the police, the munitions factories, and on the land. In the twenties she changed into a boy. No longer did she take up her hair and let down her hems to signify at sixteen that she was an adult: her hems went farther up and her hair was cut, redefining the frontiers of gender and adulthood.

People began exploring new entertainments – nightclubs, cocktails, cinemas, open-air breakfast parties and the *thé dansant*. 'I have a thé dansant to-morrow,' John announced from Mallord Street, ' – about 3,000 people are coming.' Parties grew more informal and gyrated to more syncopated rhythms, jazz on the gramophone and exotic dances – the shimmy, the charleston, the black bottom, the foxtrot. The handsome woman in the hansom cab was overtaken by a fast woman in a fast car. Glamour had come to London. There was a whirl of glass beads and pearls, sparkling paste, rouge, plucked eyebrows, brilliantined hair, sticky scarlet lips, surprised faces. Coloured underclothes broke out in shades of ice-cream: peach, pistachio, coffee. Young men sported plus-fours, big bow ties, motoring caps, gauntlets, co-respondent shoes. John himself sprouted a dazzling waistcoat and suits of decisive check tweed.

There was an epidemic of health. 'Vapours' were no longer admired, neurasthenia went out of date. Young wives drilled themselves in natural-childbirth exercises, practised art and craftwork for charity. At weekends everyone seemed to stay with everyone else in draughty country houses, playing bridge and tennis. Nature was again important: a million women cycled out beyond the suburbs.

The twenties was not a cynical but a sentimental decade. Under the high kicks lay a deep disillusionment, beneath the quickstep slow disintegration. Social divisions were being creakingly readjusted. The social centre of gravity in Britain was on the move.

To the Old Guard, those dinosaurs from Victorian and Edwardian England, Augustus John was still 'disgusting John', a rascal in sinister hirsute league with those other dangerous spirits – D. H. Lawrence, Bernard Shaw, Lytton Strachey – all of them plotting to do away with what was decent in the country. But to the Bright Young Things, John was a ready-made hero, one of the pioneers of the new freedom. This post-war mood seemed sympathetic to him. He appeared to recover himself and gain a second wind. He travelled greater distances, drank greater quantities, made more money, did more portraits. He painted popular people: film actors, airmen, matinée idols, beauties and beauticians, Greek bankers, infantas, Wimbledon champions, novelists, musicians. The Emperor of Japan called one morning and was polished off in an hour. The new cosmetics made a false barrier between the painter and his subject, but John knew about barriers. His most glittering portraits – of the smouldering Marchesa Casati posed before Vesuvius, and of Kit Dunn seen as the arch flapper, and Poppet as a provocative sex-kitten – are extraordinarily vivid.

The spirit of the age was a fair-weather friend to John. The sun shone, the breeze blew, he sped along: it did not matter where. He was invited everywhere, though the weather of his moods made the journey tempestuous. Wherever he went, his gift for boredom dramatically asserted itself. 'What a damnable mistake it is to go and stay with anybody,' he cried out in one letter to Dorelia. Many of the London hostesses were too sophisticated for his appetite. He was sometimes abominably rude to them, but his apologies were full of charm, and all was forgiven this half-tamed society artist.

He had become one of the most popular men in the country. In Soho restaurants 'Entrecôte à la John' was eaten; in theatres any actor impersonating an artist was indistinguishable from him; in several novels he was instantly recognizable as 'the painter'.[1] He began to use a secretary. 'Is there room for Kathleen Hale?'[2] he asked Dorelia somewhat desperately. There was, and he started to employ this twenty-two-year-old girl (later to become celebrated herself as the creator of the marmalade cat Orlando) primarily, he explained, gesturing his hand across his stomach as though guarding against onslaught, to provide a barrier between him and the hostesses, journalists and probationary models who solicited him.

'He offered me £2 a week, a spare bedroom in his Chelsea house, and meals,' Kathleen Hale remembered. When she took up her duties, she found piles of unanswered letters (often commissions for portraits), unpaid bills and beautiful drawings lying all over the table, chairs, piano, floor, mostly stained by teacups, marked by wine and whisky glasses, dusted with cigarette ash. 'We had lots of silly fun, but getting him to start work was always a tussle of wills,' she wrote. 'The minute he had finished his morning painting session, his only idea was to join his friends at a local pub . . . There were moments of leisure when he taught me how to play chess . . . and how to play shove-ha'penny . . . jabbing at those highly polished ha'pennies, skidding them across the slippery wood.'

After a few days Dorelia came up to inspect John's new secretary. Seeing them teasing each other, 'she looked piercingly at me as if she doubted our relationship. A moment later the suspicion had changed.' But it was some time before Dorelia trusted her; though Kathleen Hale was captivated by Dorelia who 'was to have more influence on me than anyone I had ever met'.

Though John was then at the height of his fame, he seemed unspoilt. To his new secretary he appeared tired, his moustache tobacco-stained, beard grizzled. 'But the man had panache, and his character was magnetic,' she wrote. 'He was a bit of a dandy, only wearing . . . the best silk shirts, and wonderful wide-brimmed hats . . . He was broad-shouldered, and muscular, and moved surprisingly lightly on his small feet . . . He had a feminine ability to draw people out.' Nevertheless he always seemed on 'a knife-edge of sensibility', she saw, 'poised to take things the wrong way and snap off a few heads. I never heard him shout; rather he would rumble, puff, or growl.'

But the overriding impression John made on her was of a paralysed giant. 'I always felt that there was more to Augustus than he could ever express, and, though he appeared uninhibited, he seemed to me to be always trying to break through tremendous frustration – as if there was a volcano inside him that might erupt at any moment,' she wrote. '. . . To his little daughter Vivien, Augustus was "the King of Men"; but I thought him a king in captivity, hounded by two black dogs: one his shyness, the other his despair.'[3]

He seemed best able to escape these two black dogs in the blurred tobacco smoke of his Mallord Street parties. They would begin at five and last till five, and they appeared to have what the painter Christopher

Letter from Ida and Augustus to Gwen John (Matching Green, December 1903).

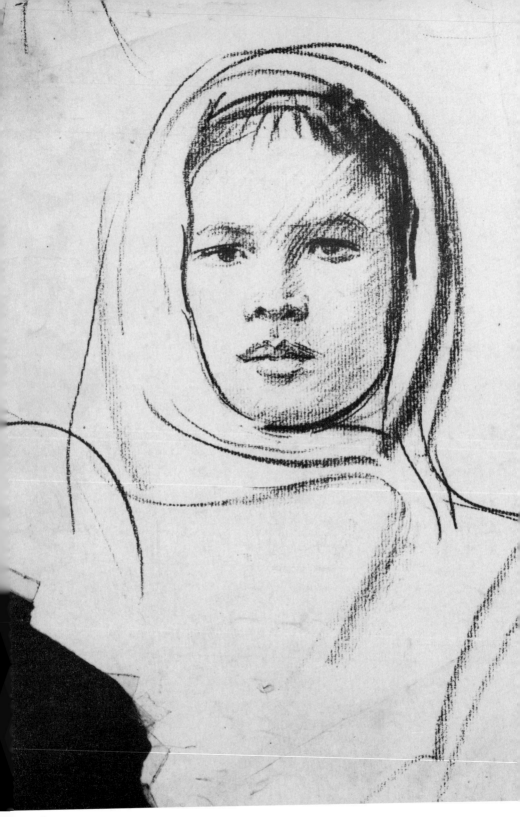

Ida.

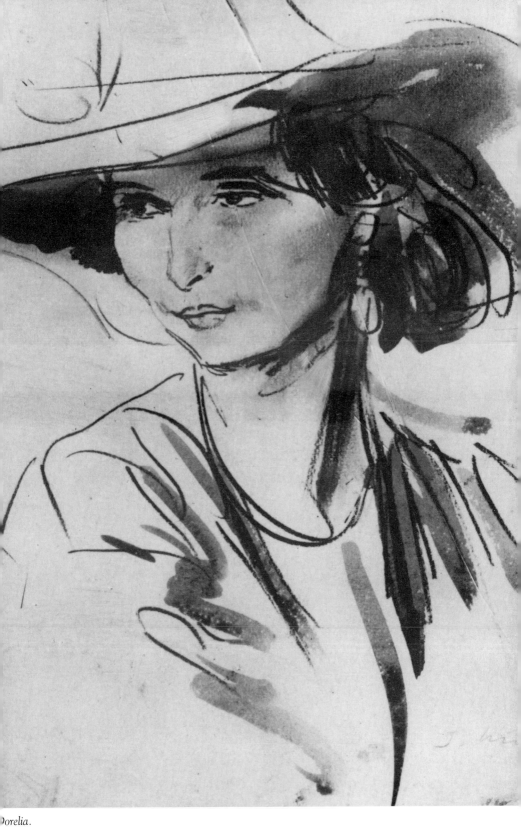

Dorelia.

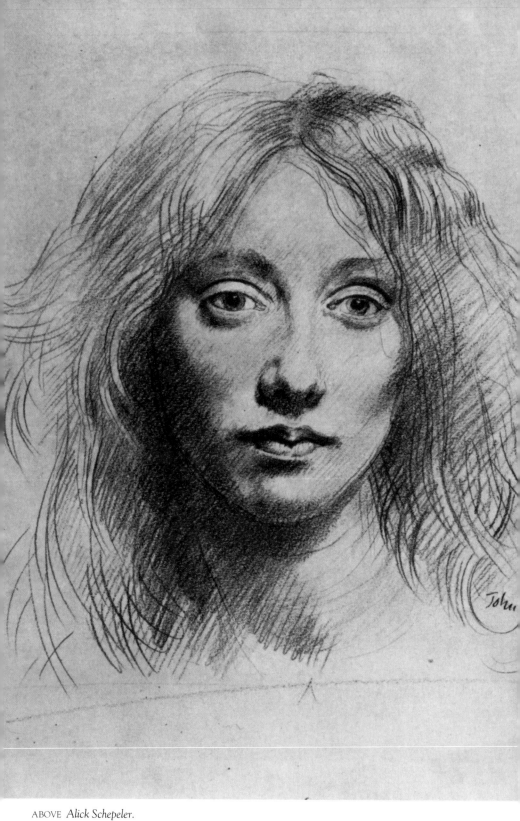

ABOVE *Alick Schepeler.*

OPPOSITE *Augustus's drawings of some of his children.*

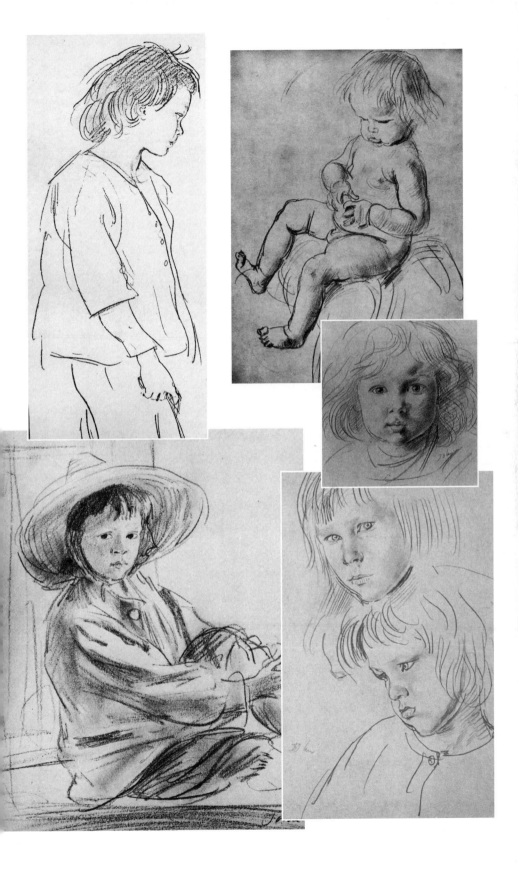

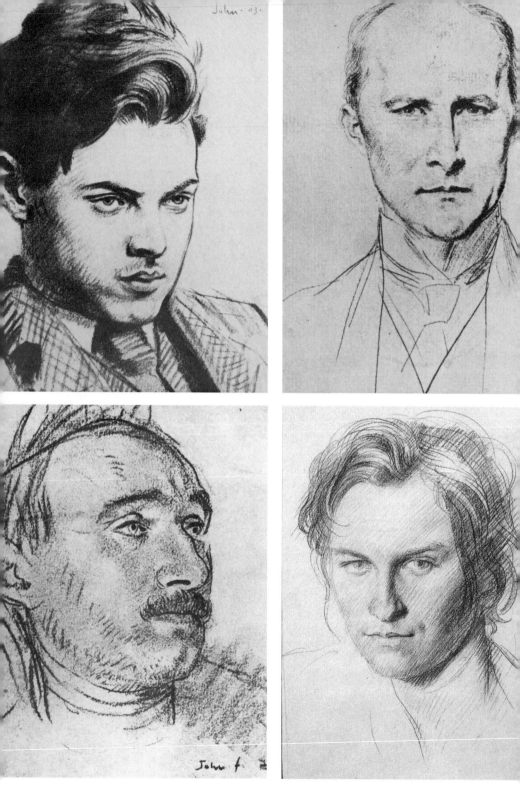

CLOCKWISE FROM TOP LEFT *Wyndham Lewis, John Quinn, Henry Lamb, John Sampson.*

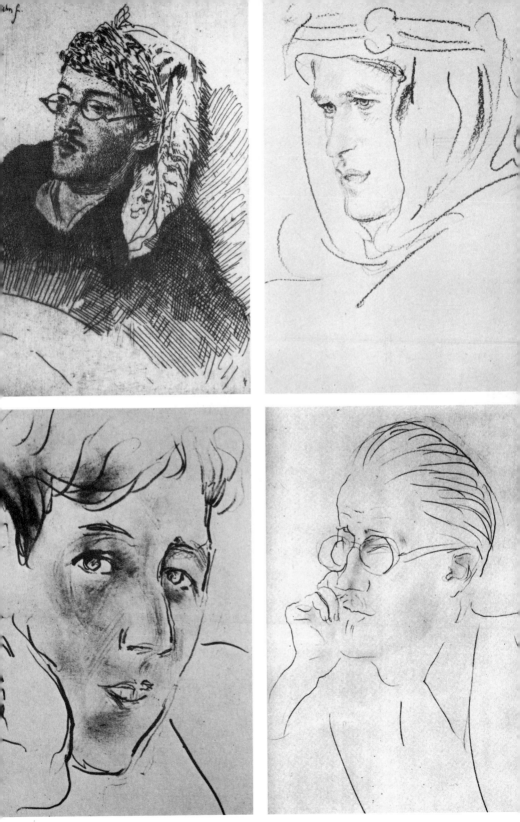

CLOCKWISE FROM TOP LEFT *John Hope-Johnstone, T. E. Lawrence, James Joyce, Ronald Firbank.*

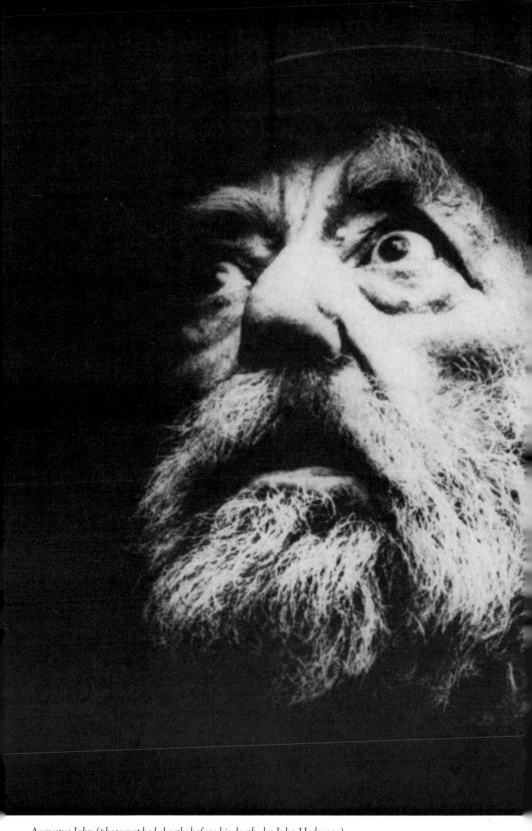

Augustus John (photographed shortly before his death by John Hedgecoe).

Wood called 'a remarkable feature ... there was not one ugly girl, all wonderfully beautiful and young'. Though they regularly ended 'in the most dreadful orgy I have ever seen', Christopher Wood concluded: 'One always enjoys oneself so much at his house, he is such a thorough gentleman.'[4]

More coveted still was an invitation to Alderney. 'He has lots of ponies, dogs and all kinds of animals which roam quite wild all round the house,' Christopher Wood explained to his mother (11 October 1926).

'... We arrived to find old John sitting at his long dining table with all his children and family followers. We took our places quite naturally at the table where there was a perfect banquet with all kinds of different drinks, which everyone – even the children going down to ten years of age and even seven, and all the cats and dogs partook of. Afterwards we took off our coats and waistcoats and had a proper country dance. John has a little daughter of fifteen, like a Venus, whom he thinks a lot of ... [He] is the most delightful person.'

Dancing and motoring were the obsessions of the twenties. 'We often had afternoon jazz sessions,' Vivien wrote, 'dancing the Charleston, Black Bottom, or anything new.'[5] Dorelia never danced, though she was often near by, watching and smiling. John could not be prevented from taking the floor. 'The tango can't be resisted,' he admitted. More irresistible still were motor cars. He had first been infected with this virus in 1911 when, throwing Mrs Strindberg off the scent, he was chauffeured through France with Quinn. 'It can't be denied there's something gorgeous in motoring by night 100 kilometres an hour,' he told Ottoline Morrell.[6] Two or three years later he had had a whack at steering Gogarty's canary-coloured Rolls-Royce through the west of Ireland, and concluded that he 'must get a Ford'. But it was not until 1920 that he acquired, in exchange for a picture, a powerful two-seater Buick with yellow wheels and a dicky. After enduring half an hour's lesson in London, he filled it with friends and set off for Alderney. Apart from barging into a barrel organ and, so far as the passengers could judge, derailing a train, the car enjoyed an immaculate journey down – and this despite the fact that John's lesson had not touched upon the philosophy of gear-changing, so that it had been in first gear from start to finish. 'The arrival at Alderney was rightly considered a great triumph,' Romilly John recalled.

All his sons insisted on being taught immediately – in fact they taught one another. It was then Dorelia's turn. By evening the house was full of brand-new drivers. 'After that we always seemed to be whizzing ... up to London,' Romilly remembered. 'In those days the roads were still fairly empty, and motoring was still a sport. We nearly always came up with another fast car, also on its way to town, and then we would race it for a hundred miles. No matter who was driving, we made it a point of honour never to be outdone, and we very seldom were. When our car and its rival had passed and repassed each other several times, emotion would work up to a white-heat, and every minor victory was the signal of a wild hilariousness.'[7]

Though the family inherited his talent, the John style of motoring was seen in its purest form whenever Augustus took the wheel. In fine country, on a good day, he was apt to forget he was driving at all, allowing the car to pelt on ahead while he stared back over his shoulder to admire some receding view. Indeed the car often performed better like this than when he bent upon it his fullest attention. Then, roaring like a wounded elephant, it would mount hedges, charge with intrepid bursts towards corners, or simply explode. Once, when hurtling towards a fork in the road, John demanded which direction to take, and, his passenger hesitating a moment, they bisected the angle, accelerating straight into a ploughed field until brought to a halt by the waves of earth. Another time, he 'awoke to find himself driving through the iron gate of a churchyard'.[8] Because of feats like these, the car soon began to present a dilapidated appearance, like an old animal in a circus: the brakes almost ceased to operate, and the mechanism could only be worked by two people simultaneously, the second taking off the handbrake at the precise moment when the first, manipulating the knobs, pedals and levers as if performing on an organ, caused the engine to engage with the wheels. But though he occasionally admitted it to be suffering from a form of indigestion known as 'pre-ignition' or to be unaccountably off colour ('pinking somewhat'), John would loyally insist that his Buick was 'still running very sweet'. It was true that sometimes, 'like a woman', the car refused to respond and had to be warmed up, cajoled, petted, pushed. At last, yielding to these blandishments, she would jerk into life and, with her flushed occupants, drag herself away from the scene of her humiliation to the dispiriting cheers of the assembled voyeurs. In her most petulant moods, she would react only to the full-frontal approach. But once, when John was winding the crank (the car having been left in gear on the downward slope of a hill), she ran him down. His companion, the music critic Cecil Gray, 'frantically pushing and pulling every lever I could lay my hands and feet on',[9] was carried off out of sight.

> Not that I would cast a slur
> No; but accidents occur,

And your driving not your drawing
Was what there might be a flaw in.[10]

Even if accidents were plentiful, as Gogarty acknowledged, there were almost no deaths and the Johns themselves seemed marvellously indestructible. They were, however, extremely critical, even contemptuous, of one another's skill. Dorelia, for example, would not applaud John's inspired cornering: while he irritably censored her triumphant use of the horn. She was, so Kathleen Hale remembered, like a lion at the wheel, brave and imperturbable. 'She didn't seem to understand the danger.' But none of them 'felt safe' while being driven by the others, and did not scruple to hide this. 'I will not attempt to conceal,' wrote Romilly John, 'that some of us were secretly glad when some others incurred some minor accident.'[11]

Towards people outside the family, though dismissive of their ability, they were nervously polite. An episode from Lucy Norton's motoring career shows John's kindness on wheels at its most characteristic. The incident happened in 1926 or 1927 when she was in her early twenties.

'I had recently purchased a motor-car, and John thought a long country drive would be the thing to give me experience. Night-driving experience, he said, was very important. I picked him up at Mallord Street early on a May morning. He appeared in a beautiful Harris-tweed coat, his usual large gypsy hat, several scarves with fringed ends, a bottle of whisky in case of need, and a bottle of gin for a friend.

All seems to have gone well until we reached Winchester, when I was turning to the right as John was saying "turn left", and we mounted, very slowly, a lamp-post. John said nothing but I could see he was shaken. We . . . had a superlative lunch and about six o'clock started for home.

I suppose we must have gone about ten miles or so, when I was overcome with the strong suspicion that the back door of the four-doored Morris Cowley (I had bought the cheapest car, so that it would not matter if I hit things) was not shut. I turned to shut it – not realising that, as I pivoted with one hand back, the other on the steering wheel would follow me round. The next thing was a mildly terrific crash, as the car hit the soft bank at right angles on the other side of the road. John rose upright in his seat, lifted me also to a standing position behind the wheel, and clasping me to his shoulder said in tones of sympathetic disgust: "You simply cannot trust the steering of these modern cars! It's too bad!" '[12]

Such imaginative courtesy was often useful in court. The biographer Montgomery Hyde, who happened to be passing one day, observed how

John, coming out of his drive 'fairly rapidly',[13] cannoned into a steamroller which was doing innocent repairs to the road outside his gate. Very correctly John reported this incident but the police, having their own ideas, replied with a summons. In due course he appeared before the local Bench but was acquitted because, the magistrate explained, he 'behaved in such a gentlemanlike manner'.

As it whizzed through the twenties this car took on many of John's characteristics. It became, in effect, a magnified version of himself, and its exploits drew attention to a developing feature of his life. He seemed to have no sensitivity to danger. 'How we never got killed in this car was a miracle,' Poppet recalled.[14] The detached feeling that had first invaded John at the front during the war – the calm knowledge that he might be struck dead at any second – grew more established. 'He might easily have been killed,' the music critic Cecil Gray calculated, '. . . but Augustus has always lived a charmed life where cars are concerned.'[15]

To more than one person in his later years John spoke of suicide: how he must resist the temptation to give into it. His carelessness seemed deliberate. But Dorelia helped to keep him ticking on. Sometimes he longed – or so it appeared – to make what haste he could and be gone: but she never let him.

In spite of all vicissitudes, the Buick continued to function with increasing noise and pathos 'and was only abandoned at last', Romilly remembered, upside-down and panting terribly 'somewhere near London'.[16]

2

SURVIVING FRIENDS, WOMEN AND CHILDREN: AN A TO Z

'If it's beauty, it's love in my case.'
Augustus John to John Freeman
'The women! ah! the women!'
Arthur Symons to Augustus John

He had said goodbye to his mistresses and, by the end of the war, taken leave of friends. 'What casualty lists!' he exclaimed in a letter to Quinn.[17] 'How can it go on much longer? Among my own friends, and I never had many – [Dummer] Howard, [Ivor] Campbell, Heald, Baines, Jay, [Tudor] Castle, Rourke, Warren, Tennant . . . We must be bleeding white – and it seems the best go down always.' The eccentrics survived: Trelawney Dayrell Reed, aloof and stammering, to be the perfect subject for John's El Greco phase; Horace de Vere Cole, to become a victim of his own sinister practical jokes; the odd and fascinating Francis Macnamara, with his soft Irish voice, blue eyes, string-coloured fringed hair and small trim beard, who, surrounded by bottled ships and thundering treatises and rejuvenated by monkey glands, became Dorelia's brother-in-law and eventually the father-in-law of Dylan Thomas. The boys' old tutor, John Hope-Johnstone, also danced back 'like an abandoned camel'[18] and re-engaged himself as Robin's philosopher and guide. Henry Lamb, too, his health fearfully damaged after being gassed in the war, floated back into the orbit of their lives, a dry and caustic figure now, furtive and uneasy, like a ghost of the dazzling youth who had served Augustus and who still trailed after Dorelia as she helped to nurse him into health.

Another damaged survivor was the great Rai, John Sampson, torn for years between patriotic pride and parental anguish as his elder son, after being wounded four times, emerged from the war gloriously decorated; while his younger son, reported missing early in 1918, was killed somewhere in France. He had separated from his wife Margaret who continued living in Wales with their daughter, while Sampson himself lodged with one unfortunate landlady after another in Liverpool. But Liverpool after the war was tense and discontented. 'The streets are intolerable now,' he wrote, 'with all sorts of motor traffic . . . [and] heaps of accidents.'[19] Illness, age and poverty prevented him from adjusting to these post-war times as John appeared to have done. He envied his friend's success: 'John must now be at the top of his profession,' he wrote to Margaret, 'but what I envy him most is meeting all these interesting people on the free and easy terms that obtain between artist and sitter. [Admiral] Fisher's conversation must have been worth listening to.' But with all John's gifts – 'friends, freedom, genius, wealth, fame' – Sampson sometimes wondered 'whether he is happy'.[20]

The two friends kept up their intermittent correspondence, often falling into Romany, 'this dear language of ours'. 'Your letters charm me as they always did,' John assured Sampson, because 'our friendship has meant a very great deal to me and our gypsing together [is] one of the major episodes in my blooming life.'[21] Whatever changes were spreading across the world, Sampson went on 'putting luxuries before necessities' – that is, his work before comfort. He soldiered on with his great *The Dialect of the Gypsies of Wales*, carrying his assault on reflex verbs during the early stages of the war, conquering word-formation and taking on inflexion. By September 1916, as British troops captured Dar-es-Salaam and introduced tanks on to the Western Front, Sampson 'completed the imperative', his grandson Anthony Sampson writes with justifiable pride, 'and was advancing upon the present tense'.[22]

In July 1917 he finally handed in his dictionary to Oxford University

Press. It 'should prove to the judicious reader a complete guide to sorcery, fortune-telling, love and courtship, kichimai [inns], fiddling, harping, poaching and the life of the road generally,' he told John, ' – in fact I hope it may prove the Romani Rai's Bible.'[23]

John was all impatience. 'I hope your publisher will hurry up . . . The news that we may soon see the proofs of the book is great,'[24] he wrote in 1919. By then the dictionary had already been at the publisher two years and seemed miraculously suspended there 'like Mahomet's coffin', as Sampson described, 'balanced between earth and heaven'.[25] A year later some specimen sheets appeared. 'It's always a joy to me to read a word of the old tongue,' John replied after seeing these sheets on 14 July 1920, 'and now we shall soon have the big book at last.' Three-and-a-half years later, on 25 January 1924, he was enquiring: 'When will the book be out? *I WANT IT.*'[26] So did Sampson. After putting his whole life into this work, it was a torment to have it halted in this way. It had only been by 'not looking at the task ahead' that he had been able to complete it. 'There may be three people in England who will buy a copy,' he had written to his son Michael, 'but I doubt it.' One of those who did buy a copy when it eventually came out in 1926 was John, though the book took a further year to reach him. 'It will be my livre de chevet [bedside book],' he promised Sampson.[27]

How was it that this exploration of a fast-dying secret language, spoken by a few score of persons in the heart of Wales, which had been pursued with so comprehensive a neglect for remuneration, could bring such pleasure? It was a work of unfathomable love. The book's strange spell shines through Sampson's autobiographical preface.

'My collections have been gathered in every part of Wales where members of the clan were to be found, following the Gypsy avocations of harpers, fiddlers, fishermen, horse-dealers, knife-grinders, basket-makers, wood-cutters, fortune-tellers, and hawkers. From ancient men and women, their faces a complex of wrinkles, to tiny children out of whose mouths Romani falls with a peculiar charm, all have been laid under contribution . . .'

One of those who understood what Sampson had achieved with this 'piquant blend of sound science and inconsequent levity' was that other great Rai, Scott Macfie. In his review for the *Journal of the Gypsy Lore Society*, Macfie introduced readers to some of the people they would meet in this vocabulary:

'Black Ellen the teller of tales, Alabaina the sorceress with her hollow voice, William who had the misfortune to be transported, Hannah who when her child died suckled two bloodhounds . . . We are invited to their lodging, "the barn of laughter", become their friends, discover the nicknames, and admire the diabolical tones of the Gypsy voice in moments of ironic pleasantry. They tell us . . . : "We are all wanderers: the dear Lord created us so." '

John still felt a kinship with these wanderers who could thaw his loneliness as could few of the interesting sitters he painted, whose company Sampson sometimes envied him. But he was no longer painting gypsies, or Dorelia, or his children, Kathleen Hale observed, 'nor living in Romany style. All this had been overtaken by the need to support his increasing family, and the growing demands on him both socially and financially.'[28] His success was a veneer that did not please him, but which he made little effort to strip off. Sometimes he pretended to find satisfaction in it. 'Having been regarded as a kind of "old master" for a long time,' he wrote in 1928, 'I am now hailed as a "modern" which you must admit is very satisfactory.'[29] This was the same year as he admitted to Ada Nettleship: 'I don't find it at all amusing to paint stupid millionaires when I might be painting entirely for my own satisfaction.'[30] From a superficial point of view his career bloomed in the 1920s while that of Sampson withered. But in his heart he agreed with the implication of the dictionary, where Sampson had questioned whether 'Madam Civilisation may not have put her money on the wrong horse?'

*

John appeared superior to the needs of ordinary friendship. 'Is it because I seem an indifferent friend myself?' he asked Will Rothenstein. 'I know I have moods which afford my friends reason for resentment; but I love my friends I think as much as anybody – when they let me.'[31] What he needed in the way of friends was variety, from which, like notes on a piano, he could select any tune of his choice. Though many had gone down, more were stepping forward, like the fresh row of a chorus, to fill their places. There was Joe Hone, rare phenomenon, an Irishman of silence; Roy Campbell, the big-action maverick poet from South Africa, with his black cowboy hat, white face and flashing blue eyes, dressed in clothes that 'appeared to have been rescued from the dustbin';[32] T. W. Earp, ex-President of the Oxford Union, a soft-spoken, gently humorous man, his hair close-cropped, his head shaped like a vegetable, who had taken his lack of ambition to the extreme of becoming an art critic; Ronald Firbank,[33] his nervous laugh like the sound of a clock suddenly running down, his hands fluttering with embarrassment, trying to live down 'the dreadful fact that his father had been an M.P.'; and A. R. Orage, John's 'man of sense',[34] the wayward editor of the *New Age* and advocate of the Douglas Credit Scheme.

Such friends provided new worlds for John. He was easily transplanted. Having been a Welshman, gypsy, nomad, teacher, he was soon to turn Academician, illustrator for Ronald Firbank, and stage designer for Sean O'Casey and J. M. Barrie. He had been on amicable terms with Bloomsbury, still maintained good relations with the Sitwells, and was an intermittent comrade-in-arms of Wyndham Lewis. By the 1920s he had moved into the land of the affluent upper classes – of Lord Alington, Lord Tredegar (Evan Morgan) and Lord Berners. It was not true that he never looked back – such was not his nature. But the distance over which he had to look to connect other parts of his life lengthened.

He had crossed into this aristocratic world at the Paris Peace Conference. It was here that his friendship began with T. E. Lawrence who, singling him out as the perfect image-maker, returned again and again (concealing his 'hideous' motorbike behind the bushes) for 'fancy-dress'[35] portraits of himself as Café Royal Arab or pale aircraftman. But it was the Marchesa Casati, of the archaic smile and macabre beauty, who beckoned him into international high society. As Luisa Ammon, daughter of a Milanese industrialist, she had been, it was said, a mousy little girl. But, inspired by the example of Sarah Bernhardt, she decided to turn herself into a theatrical work of art and her world into a stage. As the young wife of Camillo Casati Stampa di Soncino, noblest of Roman huntsmen, she pounced like a panther on to life: and somewhat overshot it. The mousy hair burst into henna'd flames; the grey-green eyes, now ringed with black kohl and treated with toxic belladonna, expanded enormously, fringed with amazing false eyelashes like peacock's feathers. Her lips were vermilion, her feet empurpled, her sphinx-like face, transformed by some black-and-white alchemy, became a painted mask. By taking thought she added a cubit to her stature, raising her legs on altitudinous heels, and crowning her head with top hats of tiger skin and black satin, huge gold waste-paper baskets turned upside down, or the odd inverted flowerpot from which gesticulated a salmon-pink feather. It was for her that Léon Bakst, soaring to his most extravagant fantasies, designed *incroyable* Persian trousers of the most savage cut; for her Mariano Fortuny invented long scarves of oriental gauze, soaked in the mysterious pigments of his vats and 'tinted with strange dreams'.[36]

She lived, this decadent queen of Venice, in the roofless 'Palazzo Non Finito',[37] on the Grand Canal where Bakst choreographed her *bals masqués*. She would appear with a macaw on her shoulder, an ape at one arm, or a few cobras. As a backdrop she redesigned her ballroom with caged monkeys which gibbered among the branches of lilac as she floated past, pursued by a restive ocelot held on its leash by a black keeper, his hand dripping with paint. But there were failures. The 'slaves', painted with gold, collapsed; her costume – an affair of armour pierced with a hundred electric arrows – short-circuited. By the spring of 1919 she had left Venice and her husband, achieved poetic status as mistress of the symbolist 'Prince of Decadence' Gabriele d'Annunzio and, having exhausted one huge fortune, was preparing to demolish a second.

Casati's witch-like aspect often provoked terror. But John, unlike most of her admirers, was a romantic only by instalments. Visually she stimulated him, but in other ways she made him 'laugh immoderately'.[38] Where T. E. Lawrence beheld a 'vampire', John saw only 'a spoilt child of a woman' ringed about with the credulity and suspiciousness of a savage. Yet, as the vigour of his two portraits shows, he found her dramatically exciting.

She had been painted by innumerable artists as Joan of Arc, Pulcinella, Salome, the naked Eve. To Marinetti and the Futurists, she was their Gioconda; to Boldini, who portrayed her smothered in peacock feathers and arched over cushions like a pretend-panther, she was Scheherazade; to Alberto Martini, she became an art-nouveau Medusa. But to John, who painted her twice in April 1919[39] in the Duchess of Gramont's apartment on the quai Malaquais, she was something else again: a pyjama'd figure, with dramatic mascara, poised with a provocative elbow before a veiled view of Vesuvius where, as the unbidden guest of Axel Munthe, she overstayed her welcome by some fifteen years. Romanticism and irony were perfectly blended to produce what Lord Duveen was to call 'an outstanding masterpiece of our time'.[40]

'He painted like a lion,' sighed Casati. 'Le taxi vous attend,' he writes to her from Paris. 'Venez!' They flung themselves towards each other. Sex was not the real attraction between them. Casati took other people's admiration for granted, like a perpetual chorus singing invisibly while she stood on stage alone. For she was intensely narcissistic. John responded to her exhibitionism. It was her sheer extraordinariness he loved – she was more tempestuous and terrifying than Ottoline had ever been. Though Marinetti dedicated his Futurist *Dance Manifesto* to her in 1917, she lived always for the present, converting everything she touched into make-believe, using all her camp artillery to keep reality in retreat. John relished her gypsy-like fervor and, under the brazen theatricality, what he judged to be her 'perfect naturalness of manner'.

She wanted for nothing until the 1930s when the last penny of the last fortune had been squandered and the curtain came down on her performance. She fled from her Palais Rose at Neuilly to England. In England there was charity, a pale but persistent kindness, first from Lord Alington, then, for the last dozen years of her life, from a Wodehousian platoon of old fellows – the Duke of Westminster, Baron Paget-Fredericks, Lord Tredegar and, most constantly, John himself with whom she stayed for a time in Chelsea. 'Je serai ravi de vous revoir, carissima,' he gallantly welcomed her, enclosing 'un petit cadeau'. He warned her that 'Londres n'est pas gai en ce moment', but she knew there was nowhere else she could shelter. She lived in a small dirty flat within, however, a house that had once been Byron's. The layers of powder grew thicker; the stories of Italy longer; her clothes more faded and frayed; her leopard-skin gloves spotted with holes; her thin figure, subsisting on opium and cocaine, turned into an assemblage of bones. But she had never valued comfort and did not miss it now. Despite the squalor, she played, to the last notes, this ghostly echo of the d'Annunzian heroine. 'Bring in the drinks!' she would call, and a bent Italian servant would shuffle forward with a half-empty bottle of beer. What money came in she tended to spend at once, shopping in Knightsbridge and Mayfair for Spider, her Pekinese. Her one asset was absolute helplessness, which threw responsibility for her survival on to everyone else. Her friends paid an allowance each week into her bank from where she would collect it by taxi. The bank statements show that, for over a decade, John was her most persistent source of income. She did not need very often to beg from him: he gave spontaneously, regularly, small sums with a there-but-for-the-grace-of-God generosity. 'Ayez courage, carissima, et croyez à mon amitié sincère.' It did not occur to her to do otherwise. 'Je suis bien triste que vous êtes toujours dans les difficultés,' he wrote again, with more apprehension. But when, during the early 1940s, she asked for more money to remove these difficulties, he fell back into explanations: 'Le gouvernement prend tout mon argent pour ce guerre et j'ai des grandes dépenses comme vous savez.' The aphrodisiac notes now gave way before a crisp commercial correspondence – 'Voici le chèque'. But she did not embarrass him with gratitude and they remained friends until her death in 1957. His last portrait, painted in 1942, shows her wearing a half-veil, the elaborate golden fichu gathered at her chest matching the eyes of the staring black cat on her lap. She is seated in an upright chair against a theatrically stormy sky – a sad, sinister, witch-like figure still held together with some vestiges of dignity.[41]

Casati occupied a unique place in the latter part of John's life. She should, he once suggested to Cecil Beaton, have been shot and, like Spider, stuffed – she would have looked so well in a glass case. The other women in his life were for more active employment and, from the 1920s onwards, began to arrange themselves into a pattern. There were the occasional models; there was the chief mistress who looked after him in town and abroad when Dorelia was absent; and there was the Grand Lady, to be defined neither as model nor mistress, who conducted his life in society.

John's principal mistress during these years was Eileen Hawthorne, 'an uncommon and interesting type', he suggested to Maurice Elvey, ' – at any rate she would like to do some work in films.' Pictures of her constantly appeared in the press – a new portrait by Lewis Baumer or Russell Flint; an eager advertisement for bath cubes, lingerie, eau-de-cologne; or simply as 'Miss 1933'. The most extraordinary feature of these pictures was that, though she appeared forever young and glamorous, none of them looked the same. As queen of the magic world of cosmetics she could change her looks from day to day. This was her 'mystery'. She was known by the newspapers as the girl of a thousand faces. Each morning she re-created herself, and again each evening. Superficially, it was impossible to tire of her.

But she was not a good model for John. Hardly had he begun to apply his brushes than her features would start to re-form themselves. She was always painting herself more fluently, it was said, than he was.

There were other problems too. He suspected that she did not possess a flair for discretion. The man who, twenty years before, advised Sampson to 'sin openly and scandalize the world' had grown timid of scandal himself. Experience, like a great wall, shut off his return to innocence. His letters to Eileen Hawthorne exhibit more anxiety than enjoyment. He asks her, because of Dorelia, not to telephone him in the country; he begs her to avoid journalists – especially on those occasions when she happens to be missing a tooth or is unable to conceal a black eye. He wishes he could trust more wholeheartedly her ability to hide things: for example, pregnancies. Though he shared her favours with the composer E. J. Moeran, it was John who, after some grumbling, paid for the abortions. He had no choice. Otherwise her mother would get to hear of them, and then the world would know.

This climate of secrecy did not suit John, but it was necessary. He divided his life into compartments as irretrievably lonely people do. It is unlikely, for instance, that Eileen Hawthorne ever met the redoubtable Mrs Fleming. She was the widow of Valentine Fleming, a millionaire Yeomanry officer and Member of Parliament for Henley: 'one of those rare, slightly baffling Edwardian figures of whom nothing but good is ever spoken',[42] who had been killed after winning the DSO in the Great War. She was rich; she was handsome – dark, with a small head, large eyes and autocratic features. The three portraits he painted of her in her forties show 'a Goyaesque beauty, hard, strong-featured, the self-absorbed face of an acknowledged prima donna used to getting her own way'.[43] Upon her four 'shiny boys' (as John called them) – Peter the author and explorer,

Ian the creator of James Bond, Richard a prosperous banker, and Michael who died of wounds as a prisoner of war after Dunkirk – she had laid an obligation to succeed. She believed in success, and herself led a successful life in society. In 1923 she moved to Turner's house at 118 Cheyne Walk, a few minutes' walk from Mallord Street. It was a luxurious place, superb for entertaining, with a large studio at the back, all drastically improved since J. M. W. Turner had lodged there in old age. Sitting at the bar of the Aquatic Stores next door 'fortifying the inner man' against his entry into Mrs Fleming's luncheon parties, John sometimes thought of Turner – how he would have preferred the grosser amenities of Wapping. Often John needed drink to confront these social occasions, but the money, the aura of success, the opportunities – these could not be denied. Eve Fleming passionately admired him, he could not help feeling some admiration for her, and many people who came to Cheyne Walk admired them both. In such company it was possible to forget a bad day's work.

In his biography of Ian Fleming, John Pearson describes Mrs Fleming as 'a bird of paradise', extravagant, demanding, a law to herself. She was, he wrote, 'a rich, beautiful widow – and, thanks to the provision of her husband's Will, likely to remain one.' In order to ensure that his millions remained within the family, Val Fleming had left her almost all his wealth on condition that she remained a widow. If she remarried, most of the money would pass to her sons. Nevertheless, such was her attachment to John that, despite everything, she dreamed of taking him away from Dorelia and having a child by him. She would turn up at Alderney, drive him off in her Rolls-Royce, and tell him that she would give up her fortune if he would give up Dorelia. Poppet remembered that her mother 'hated' Eve Fleming 'and suffered quite a lot'.[44] For Eve was a most insistent woman. She could not endure coming second to anyone. After one of her Rolls-Royce tutorials, John suggested that he might briefly marry Eve, have a child by her, then obtain a quick divorce and return to Alderney, all for the sake of a quiet life – in which case, Dorelia replied, she would no longer be there. She might have left with Henry Lamb.

What appeared to be a solution to their problem had already been brought to the door of Mallord Street one afternoon in the late spring of 1921 by John Hope-Johnstone. He arrived with a girl of sixteen – a little old for his own taste since he was one of those people for whom time passes too rapidly. He had seen her at the Armenian café in Archer Street, introduced himself, then taken her in a cab to meet Compton Mackenzie. They'd had a grand time. Now, since she was an avid admirer of John, they'd come to see him too. Her name was Chiquita. John grunted and let them in.

She was an engaging creature, very tiny, with a dark fringe and a low rippling laugh, and she specialized in 'cheekiness'. While the men growled away in conversation, she flitted round the enormous studio, aware of John's eyes, like searchlights, travelling all over her as she moved. Soon she began to chatter, telling stories about herself – how her mother had run away to New Orleans with a Cuban leaving her to be brought up by a funny old man with whiskers; how she had been a tomboy, climbing trees, stealing apples, getting spanked and, at the age of fifteen, ran away from school to join a travelling theatre company.

'When can I paint you?' John interrupted. 'Come to-morrow at four.'

'I'll come at five,' Chiquita retorted.

It was agreed that she should wear the same clothes – a blue blouse, black stockings, red skirt – and that he would pay her a pound for each sitting: handsome wages. She came at five, carrying as a weapon and badge of her sophistication a long cigarette holder.

As a sitter she was frightful. She chattered all the time, while John's expression darkened dreadfully. She could not understand why he seemed so 'terribly ratty'. One afternoon he interrupted her by demanding to know whether she would take off her clothes. She agreed, provided there was somewhere private to undress. Then she came back into the studio wearing a dressing-gown. He began to work – and after a few minutes, while she lay there nakedly chattering, he pounced. She remembered him being so old, the coarse beard, smell of whisky and tobacco, no words, just grunting and snorting . . .

Later, on discovering she was pregnant, Chiquita approached Dorelia. It seemed the natural thing to do. They arranged that she should have an abortion, but Chiquita did not take to the specialist and eventually refused to go through with the operation. 'It was a very drastic time in my life but I was too young to be unhappy,' she remembered.[45] The atmosphere at Alderney where she went was wonderfully comforting. 'It was a lovely summer,' she wrote, 'and we slept outside in the orchard in the communal bed there . . . We used to light a little bonfire down our end . . . it was fun – there weren't any strict rules, one could get in through the window without being nagged at.' Pigs and red setters stalked the garden; there were picnics, rides in the pony cart and, under a sign that read 'Bathing Prohibited', there was bathing. Dorelia was always near 'and she always looked pretty super especially when she wore her sun bonnet and picked currants'.[46] Dorelia never referred to her pregnancy, suggesting, after a few months, that Chiquita wear a cloak 'because she would look so fine in one, and they were becoming very fashonable'.

At the beginning of March they took her to a nursing home where, on 6 March 1923 she gave birth to a daughter whom she called Zoë. John arrived bringing masses of flowers, but when Chiquita came out he tactfully withdrew to Spain.

She had a little money, and quickly got some jobs as a photographer's model. Zoë meanwhile was fostered in Islington by a policeman and his wife whose own daughter, 'Simon', was later to marry Augustus's eldest son David. One day Chiquita received an invitation to call on Mrs Fleming. The meeting was not easy. Eve Fleming's imperious manner brought out everything that was rebellious in Chiquita, and when she offered to adopt the baby, provide it with a good home and education, Chiquita refused – though accepting some clothes and the assistance of a nanny. It seems that Mrs Fleming hoped to increase the pressure of her persuasion, but before she had any opportunity a row broke out over the clothes, all of which were marked 'Fleming'. From this time on the two women were enemies. 'If she [Chiquita] had a million pounds a year, I still should not alter my opinion that she ought not to have the bringing up of that baby or of any other,' wrote Mrs Fleming.[47]

Each weekend Chiquita would call at Islington and pick up Zoë. One Saturday the baby was collected early – by Mrs Fleming, who rushed her off to North Wales in the hope that Chiquita would not trouble to pursue them. Over the crisis lawyers soon began to circle. John, innocently returning from Spain, was horrified. He had supported, in his absence, Mrs Fleming's plan and arranged anonymously through her and a solicitor to offer Chiquita twenty pounds down and a pound a week thereafter in exchange for the baby. What could be fairer? But instead of this quiet 'baby agreement' he was confronted with a *cause célèbre*. There was no alternative but to return the baby.

Chiquita had various allies, in particular Seymour Leslie ('a grinning society microbe' John called him) to whom she blurted out her story one evening at the Eiffel Tower. She was determined to 'fight like a tiger' to keep Zoë, she insisted. 'I trust no one with Zoë's happiness as I do myself. I am waiting for Mrs Fleming to return. I would like to kill her . . .' Vowing indignantly to help, Seymour Leslie called for pen and ink and drew up a contract, signed by the proprietor Stulik and the head waiter Otto, undertaking to pay for Zoë provided Chiquita agreed to live with him as his mistress. This settled, they hurried off to Paris for four days of celebration.

The agreement lasted some six months. 'I used to lead him a pretty good dance,' she recalled, '. . . tho' he made me happy in a strange sort of way.' He let her have fun, but what she really wanted was marriage. When Seymour Leslie returned from a visit to Russia in the autumn of 1923, he found her married to Michael Birkbeck, a friend of John's, and living with him and Zoë in the country.

Mrs Fleming was not used to being worsted. 'My dreams of a happy home', she wrote, '. . . have fallen to the ground.' In place of dreams she was surrounded by clouds of 'reprehensible gossip'. 'It seems to be a mistake to be the good Samaritan or to feel things,' she complained to Seymour Leslie. 'People don't seem to understand either, and only to imagine the worst motives for one's actions.' The deplorable affair had made her ill. 'I have done my best,' she declared, 'and have had to retire to bed, really exhausted with this worry.' At night she would dream 'of drowned babies with dead faces and alive eyes looking at me'. She had sons, but she wanted a daughter: John's daughter. It should all have been so easy. John himself felt exasperated. 'There's no peace for a *man* at all,' he complained to the Rani. Had Ida lived, he sometimes thought, it might have all been different. 'Failing her, one simply tries all the others in rotation – I've nearly reached the limit.'

But the game had to be played 'to the last spasm'. Eve Fleming wanted a child: she must have one.

In March 1925, when John went to Berlin to paint Gustav Stresemann, the German Foreign Minister (and a former Chancellor), Eve, who was a friend of the British Ambassador in Berlin, Lord D'Abernon, went too and stayed with John at the British Embassy. Early that summer she called together the staff at Cheyne Walk, announced that she was closing the house and going on a long cruise. A postcard of snow-capped mountains that December informed John of the birth of a daughter. At the end of the year she returned with her 'adopted' daughter wrapped in a shawl – the adoption, she let it be known, having been arranged by the Royal Physician, Lord Dawson of Penn. On 18 June 1926, the child was baptized Amaryllis Marie-Louise Fleming at a private ceremony in Cheyne Walk, the word 'unknown' being entered against the parents' names on the certificate. After a public baptism a fortnight later another certificate was issued identifying Amaryllis as the 'adopted daughter of Mrs Valentine Fleming'.

Amaryllis's childhood was very different from Zoë's, but both girls grew up not knowing who was their actual father. Rumours of their parentage, fanned by John's intermittent forgetfulness as to its secrecy, blew around them and eventually reached Zoë in her late teens, Amaryllis in her early twenties. After an initial smokescreen of indignation, John was happy to accept them both as part of the tribe. 'You were found in a ditch,' he told Amaryllis at the beginning of a dinner in the Queen's Restaurant in Sloane Square. But at the end of the dinner, he gave her a great slap on the back: 'So you're my little girl, are you? Well, don't tell your mother.'[48]

Zoë and Amaryllis felt wonderfully at home with Augustus and Dorelia in the country. Once they turned up on the same day, and John, his eyes glinting, airily introduced them: 'I believe you two are related.' Amaryllis's career as a cellist gave him much pleasure. He would listen to her on the radio and write her letters of congratulation on her 'howling success'. He also turned up at her first promenade concert, where he judged her triumph in terms of the number of people in tears during the slow movement. He felt proud that she with her red hair and the black-haired Zoë were such fine-looking wenches. Each of them sat for him. 'I could paint you on your back . . .' he offered Amaryllis. Zoë, too, who had gone on the stage and was everybody's understudy, was 'a first-rate sitter, and useful', he judged, 'in other ways too'.[49] But neither of them would ever understand the need for so much secrecy, and both despised their mothers for the years of lying.

3

FACES AND TALES

'You will be a giant again.'
T. E. Lawrence to Augustus John (19 April 1930)

'I kept procrastinating.'
John to Ottoline Morrell (27 March 1929)

'Augustus John, whose brain was once teeming with ideas for great compositions, had ceased to do imaginative work and was painting portraits,' wrote Will Rothenstein of these years between the wars.[50] Though he was to return over the next two decades to 'invented' landscapes on a large scale, and though he continued to paint at all times from nature, adding, on Dorelia's instructions, flower pictures to his repertoire in the 1920s, portraits dominated John's work until the Second World War. He was always 'dying to get through with them and tackle other things', but 'Alas! that seems to be my perpetual state!'[51]

The most celebrated portrait of this period was of Guilhermina Suggia, the exotic Portuguese cellist under whom Amaryllis Fleming briefly studied in the late 1940s. John began this work early in 1920 and, after almost eighty sittings, finished it early in 1923.[52] It took so long and involved her calling at Mallord Street so incessantly that a rumour spread that they were living there together – and Amaryllis was their daughter. The portrait had been begun at the suggestion of the newspaper owner Edward Hulton who was briefly engaged to Suggia and who intended the picture to be a betrothal offering. By the time the engagement lapsed, John was committed to the painting.

'To be painted by Augustus John is no ordinary experience,' Suggia allowed. '. . . The man is unique and so are his methods.'[53] Throughout the sittings she played Bach, and this forestalled conversation – John continuing to hum the music during lunch. 'Sometimes', Suggia noticed, 'he would begin to walk up and down in time to the music . . . When specially pleased with his work, when some finesse of painting eyelash or tint had gone well, he would always walk on tiptoe.'[54] As a rule she posed for two hours a day, but by the third year she would sit for another two hours in the afternoon.

Those who visited the studio during these years were aware that a terrific struggle was taking place. John was attempting to paint again: that is, not simply draw with the brush. From week to week the picture would change: sometimes it looked good, sometimes it had deteriorated, and at other times, in spite of much repainting, from gold then to white then to red, it appeared almost unchanged. As with a tug of war, tense, motionless, no one could tell which way it would go.

Suggia herself was 'more delighted with the result than I should have thought possible'. It is a rare, full-length profile portrait which shows her holding the cello between her legs, like a male player, instead of in the side-saddle position women were then expected to use. Not being a commission, it had been painted for exhibition and sale, and as Andrew Wilton writes, 'to create a striking image, and to cause a stir that would promote both sitter and artist'. In these aims it was immediately successful. It was bought for three thousand guineas (equivalent to £80,600 in 1996) from the Alpine Gallery by an American collector in 1923, shown in 1924 at the Pittsburgh International Exhibition, where it won first prize, and the following year acquired by Lord Duveen who presented it to the Tate Gallery in London.

It was to be a popular painting. Though it does not possess the overwhelming power of 'The Smiling Woman', painted in John's prime, with which it has sometimes been compared, it is nevertheless a spectacular essay in painterly rhetoric, and catches very memorably the exotic image of a performer who, during her residence in England between 1912 and 1923, often lifted audiences – including even such a reputedly cold fish as Lytton Strachey – into 'a state of ecstasy'.[55] With her head so erect, her eyes closed in concentration, her right arm theatrically extended to form a dramatic V-shape (the echo of which in the sitter's neck, the background drapery and long ruby-red skirt gives the composition its aesthetic unity), Suggia embodies the romantic idealization of musicianship. In the emphasis which John throws on the visual drama of her performance, in its very excess, there is an agreeable suggestion of irony. For though Suggia looked every inch a prima donna and gave an impression of romantic boldness her playing was actually 'calculated, correct and classical', her accompanist Gerald Moore remembered,[56] and her bow-hold, clearly to be seen in John's portrait, could not deliver the power her attitude proclaimed.

Even in this accomplished big work, six feet tall and almost as wide, the painting of the long train of the skirt is uneven. This was a result of his impatience of which he tried to make a virtue – the virtue of concentrating on essentials. 'There are coarse passages to be found even in those pictures generally reckoned to be among his successes,' wrote the art critic Richard Shone. 'The shoes of William Nicholson, for example, are more like Sargent at his worst, and John seems to make very little of the draperies in the background.'[57]

Something seemed to have snapped in John as a result of the extended effort he put into this picture. Never again did he seriously attempt anything so ambitious. The portrait of Thomas Hardy, for example, done some six months after the completion of 'Suggia', is a dry impasto laid straight on to the canvas, which is barely covered in parts (the hairs of the moustache are attached to a piece of unprimed canvas). In treatment and colour scheme it is reminiscent of his three emphatic studies of Bernard Shaw.

John had met Hardy at Kingston Maurward on 21 September 1923 and, after several visits to Max Gate, the house in Dorset that Hardy had designed himself, polished off the portrait by the middle of the following month. Hardy was then eighty-three. 'An atmosphere of great sympathy and almost complete understanding at once established itself between us,' John recorded.[58] They did not talk much, but John felt they were of a kind:[59] 'I wonder which of the two of us was the more naïve!' He painted Hardy seated in his study, a room piled to the ceiling with books 'of a philosophical character'. Hardy wears a serious, querying expression; he looks stiff, but is bearing up. It is the portrait of a shy man, full of disciplined emotion. 'I don't know whether that is how I look or not,' he said,[60] 'but that is how I *feel*.' The picture was painted at the suggestion of T. E. Lawrence and bought by Sydney Cockerell for three thousand pounds on behalf of the Fitzwilliam Museum in Cambridge. 'If I look like that the sooner I am under the ground the better,' Hardy remarked to Cockerell. But in fact 'the old man is delighted, & Mrs Hardy also,' T. E. Lawrence told his mother. 'It is seldom that an artist is so fortunate in his sitter's eyes.'[61] After his death in 1928, Hardy's widow Florence reported him as having said to her that he would rather have John's portrait in the Fitzwilliam than 'receive the Nobel Prize – and he meant it'.

In a letter to Hardy, John suggested that this portrait was 'merely preparatory to another & more satisfactory picture which I hope to do with your help, later on'.[62] It was only by labelling his paintings as preliminary studies for more elaborate compositions that he could decide to stop working on them. Where there was infinite time there was infinite delay, infinite painting out and indecision. Some critics interpreted this dissatisfaction as a quest for perfection. But he painted without premeditation, asking his sitters sometimes what background colour they would like, at other times whether they thought he should introduce a flower or a bowl of fruit, or simply demanding: 'Tell me what's wrong with this arm.' When Lord David Cecil inquired what aesthetic motive there had been for making the colour of his tie darker than it actually was, John replied that some black paint had accidentally got mixed into the red, and he thought it looked rather good. He liked, starting perhaps with an eye, to exaggerate the figure as he worked downwards, as El Greco or Velázquez might, for grand manner. His unfinished work is often better in these later years because it manages to convey powers, latent in him, on which he could no longer call. It must be 'hard', T. E. Lawrence sympathized (9 April 1930), 'to paint against time'. But time was a false friend to John – a substitute for concentration. It remained to Dorelia and close brave friends to rescue, by one subterfuge or another, what pictures they could before they were painted into oblivion.

The longer he worked the more difficult it became to persuade him to stop. With commissioned portraits there was often some limitation that imposed a discipline, though it afforded little pleasure. Of all these 'boardroom' portraits, his favourite was of Montagu Norman, Governor of the Bank of England. Begun on 1 April 1930, it was completed a year later, Norman's hair subsiding in the interval from grey to white. To John's mind he was 'an almost ideal sitter', taking apparently no interest whatever in the artist or his picture. 'It was in a spirit of severe reserve that we used to part on the doorstep of my house,' John recorded, 'whence, after looking this way and that, and finding the coast clear, Mr Norman would venture forth to regain his car, parked as usual discreetly round the corner.'[63] What John did not know was that, on arriving back at his office, Norman was transformed, regaling everyone with descriptions of the Great Artist at work. 'It's marvellous to watch him scrutinizing me,' he would rhapsodize, '. . . then using a few swift strokes like this on the outline and dabbing on paint like lightning. What a heavenly gift!'[64]

John represents the two of them as sharing a sense of isolation. Though the banker seemed 'troubled with graver problems than beset other men', it was not difficult, John recalled, 'to offset Mr Montagu Norman's indifference to my activities by a corresponding disregard of his'.[65] At rare moments 'our acquaintance seemed to show signs of ripening', and then, so he told Michael Ayrton, a curious attraction would rise up in him for this dry, preoccupied, semi-detached figure. To John Freeman he later remarked: 'It seemed to give him pleasure.' But he was referring to the sittings, not the portrait itself which, with its hard eyes, nervously taut mouth and haunted expression, shocked Norman so much that he refused to let it hang either in his home or at the Bank of England – where, nevertheless, it now hangs.

'Sometimes', John recalled, 'Lord D'Abernon would come to chat with my sitter. The subject appeared to be High Finance. I was not tempted to join in these discussions.'[66] D'Abernon, a trustee of the National Gallery in London, was another of John's subjects; his portrait, completed after Montagu Norman's, had been started early in 1927. As the second ceremonial portrait of John's career, it invites comparison with 'The Lord Mayor of Liverpool' but falls incomparably short. It is neither caricature nor straight portrait study: it is a false creation. John himself affected to believe it a finer painting than 'Suggia', but this judgement rested on the greater time it had taken him, and on his wish to obtain for it the same price – three thousand pounds (equivalent to £79,500 in 1996). Sometimes, during this five years' marathon, he was tempted to give up: then another cheque, for five hundred or a thousand pounds, would arrive and he was obliged to paint wearily on. 'I hope', he wrote rather unconvincingly to Dorelia, 'old D'Abernon won't peg out before the portrait is done.'[67] To gain wind it was necessary for him to puff enthusiasm into the ordeal. On 18 December 1927 he writes to D'Abernon that the portrait is 'too fine a scheme' to take any 'risks' with. Since Lady D'Abernon had a villa in Rome, might it not be 'a practical plan', John wondered, 'for me to come to Rome in February where I could use a studio at the British School'?[68] Two years later, on 8 December 1929, Lord D'Abernon notes in a letter to his wife: 'The Augustus John portrait at last improving – the face less bibulous. Seen from five yards off – it is a fine costume picture.'[69] John had brought in a stalwart Guardsman to stand wearing the British Ambassador's elaborate uniform, but eventually this soldier collapsed and John fell back on a wooden dressmaker's dummy, the character of which is 'well conveyed in the completed work'. By the autumn of 1928 he is begging Dorelia to 'undress that awful dummy and put d'Ab's clothes in his trunk'.[70] But still the work went lamely on. Like Macbeth, he had reached a point from which it was as tedious to retreat as to go on. He put the best face he could on it: 'Things bad begun make strong themselves by ill.'

The portrait, now in the Tate Gallery, is dated 1932, in which year it was finally handed over to Lord D'Abernon. 'There are only two styles of portrait painting,' says Miss La Creevy in *Nicholas Nickleby*: 'the serious and the smirk'. 'Lord D'Abernon' is not smirking and he is not serious. He is nothing. A photograph of Lord D'Abernon posing for the picture 'shows how unlike him the "parade" portrait was and is', his wife noted on the back.

On other occasions, when his soul revolted against such formal work, John could be less accommodating. After finishing the portrait of the Earl of Athlone, he agreed to show it the following day to the sitter's wife. She arrived with her husband and went into his studio. Two minutes later they burst out, looking furious. John stood in the doorway quietly lighting his pipe as they drove off. Egerton Cooper, who had watched the incident from his studio near by, hurried over to ask what was wrong. 'I tore the painting to pieces,' explained John. 'I suddenly couldn't bear it.'

Another time it was the sitter who dismantled a portrait. During part of the summer of 1920, John had been at work on 'His Margarine Majesty', the fish and soap millionaire Lord Leverhulme. Although 'strongly inclined' to have his portrait done by John, Leverhulme had begun the first sitting by warning him he could spare little time and that he was an almost impossible subject, no artist (excepting to some degree Sir Luke Fildes) having done him justice. When the time was up, great praise was lavished on the picture: by John. It seemed, he said, to breathe with life and self-satisfaction and only lacked speech. Leverhulme himself did not lack speech, and finding the portrait very 'humbling to pride' and a 'chastening'[71] reflection, argued that neither the eyes, nor yet the mouth, nor even the nose were his, though it was probably the bloated face and grasping fingers that hurt him, if not the informality and small size for 'under a thousand pounds' commission. Whatever the deficiencies, John, proffering his palette, invited His Lordship to make the amendments himself. This offer was declined and the picture, with all its alleged faults intact, paid for and dispatched.

John had then gone down to Tenby. Returning to Mallord Street late in September he discovered the portrait had been returned to him – at least, that part representing Lord Leverhulme's stomach, shoulders, arms, hands and thighs, though not his head, which had been scissored out. That evening (31 September 1920) John sat down and wrote: 'I am intensely anxious to have your Lordship's explanation of this, the grossest insult I have ever received in the course of my career.'

Leverhulme's reply four days later shone with friendliness. He felt 'extremely distressed at the blunder that has occurred', but added: 'I assure you it is entirely a blunder on the part of my housekeeper.' He had intended hanging the painting in his safe at Rivington Bungalow, but overlooked 'the fact that there were internal partitionings and other obstacles that prevented me doing this'. After a bold prognosis, he settled on a surgical operation, removing the head, 'which is the important part of the portrait', and storing it safely away. This letter, culminating with an urgent request to keep the matter dark, was succeeded by an invitation to 'dine with my sister'. To his surprise, John appeared dissatisfied with this answer, and the correspondence between them persisted in lively fashion over the next ten days until suddenly appearing in full on the front page of the *Daily Express*.[72] It was a case of the Baronet and the Butterfly in reverse. 'I actually frightened him into violence,' John told T. E. Lawrence.[73] Leverhulme insisted that he had a right to deal with his own property – a little trimming here or there – as he chose. Even the copyright, he hazarded, belonged to him. As for the publicity, it was not of his choosing: 'all that I am impressed by is that Mr John can get his advertising perfectly free . . . whereas the poor Soap Maker has to pay a very high rate for a very bad position in the paper.'

For John it had begun as a matter of principle. He took the Whistlerian view that money purchased merely the custodianship of a picture. Whatever the legal rights, he was convinced of his moral right. 'Formal portraiture implied a subservience of artist to patron increasingly unacceptable to artists imbued with a romantic concern for expression, particularly self-expression,' wrote the art historian Edward Morris.[74] The history of John's 'Leverhulme' was to take its place between Sargent's 'Henry Irving' and Graham Sutherland's 'Winston Churchill'.

The excitement provoked by this beheading was tremendous. Newspapers throughout Britain, the United States, Europe and as far off as Japan trumpeted their reports of the affair. Students of the London art schools marched on Hyde Park 'bearing aloft a gigantic replica of the celebrated soap-boiler's torso, the head being absent'.[75] In Paris there was furore; in Italy a twenty-four hour strike was called involving everyone connected with painting – even models, colourmen and frame-makers. 'A colossal effigy entitled "IL-LE-VER-HUL-ME" was constructed of soap and tallow, paraded through the streets of Florence, and ceremoniously burnt in the Piazza della Signoria, after which, the demonstrators proceeded to the Battisterio where a wreath was solemnly laid on the altar of St John.'[76]

Appalled by the rumpus, John backed away to Lady Tredegar's home, near Broadstairs; but the reporters, discovering his hiding place, besieged him there. 'I did not want this publicity,' he prevaricated. 'I get too much as it is.' Nevertheless, some papers were announcing that he intended to press the matter to the courts so as to establish a precedent for the protection of artists. 'The bottom fact of the case is that there is something in a work of art which, in the highest equity as distinct from the law, you cannot buy,' declared the *Manchester Guardian*. '. . . Whatever the law may allow, or courts award, the common fairness of mankind cannot assent to the doctrine that one man may rightfully use his own rights of property in such a way as to silence or interrupt another in making so critical appeal to posterity for recognition of his genius. The right to put up this appeal comes too near those other fundamental personal rights the infringement of which is the essence of slavery.'

The country waited for this Wilberforce of the art world to act. But after this great roll of drums, there was nothing. For John, unlike Whistler, had no relish for court work. He did not have the stamina of his own indignation, and his sense of humour outran his sense of honour. He ended the affair with a joke, exhibiting his portion of the portrait above the title 'Lord Leverhulme's Watch-chain'. For years he patiently preserved this decapitated torso while the missing head continued to stare unseen in its depository. Then, in 1954, by what Sir Gerald Kelly, the President of the Royal Academy, described as 'hellish ingenuity',* the two segments were sewn together and the picture elevated to a place of honour in the Leverhulme Art Gallery at Port Sunlight.

Some sitters were pleased with John's portraits of them – Lord Conway of Allington was 'as proud as a peacock with two tails to be thus glorified by you'.[77] But generally John was suspicious of praise and would tell admirers that they 'didn't know a painting from a cowpat'. It was surprising how much controversy his portraiture attracted. 'I painted what I saw,' he remarked of Lord Spencer's portrait. 'But many people have told me I ought to have been hung instead of the picture.' Men he was tempted to caricature, women to sentimentalize. For this reason, as the examples of Gerald du Maurier and Tallulah Bankhead suggest, his good portraits of men were less acceptable to their sitters than his weaker pictures of women.

John had painted du Maurier in four sittings during 1928, but the picture had lain in his studio in Mallord Street until Tallulah Bankhead

---

* The operation was performed by Dr Johann Hell after Kelly 'laid the fire' to which John and Leverhulme's grandson 'put the match'. 'Sir Gerald Kelly has talked to me about the portrait of your grandfather,' John wrote to Viscount Leverhulme in May 1953. 'I had the lower part of it knocking about for years but I haven't seen it lately . . . Kelly said he liked the head very much, and it would be very satisfactory if it could be restored to its proper position.' At the beginning of April 1954 John sent Kelly a 'rapturous letter' saying that he had found the late Lord Leverhulme's belly. The headless torso and the head were joined together 'in hospital' later that month. 'It was a great pity that when the head alone was framed the edges were turned back around the panel thus destroying two strips, but the reconstruction of these two narrow pieces has been beautifully done by the ingenious Dr Hell. The picture is now very much more worth looking at than it was . . . [it is] the best possible solution to what was a very difficult problem.' The complete picture was first shown at the 'Exhibition of Works by Augustus John, OM, RA' in the Diploma Gallery of the Royal Academy of Arts in 1954. The painting is privately owned.

found it there early in 1930. At her insistence it was shown, with her own portrait, at the Royal Academy Summer Show that year when together they caused a sensation. Tallulah reserved her portrait for the special price of one thousand pounds, but the du Maurier was for sale. Since his knighthood in 1922, du Maurier had become the acknowledged sovereign of the British theatre. But in John's portrait, one of his more sombre studies, the actor-manager's expression appeared almost criminal. Du Maurier had prayed never to see the picture again, and after it was exhibited at Burlington House he issued a distressed statement proclaiming that it 'showed all the misery of my wretched soul . . . It would drive me either to suicide or strong drink.'[78] John, apparently at a loss to account for this response from so fashionable an actor, suggested that perhaps it was insufficiently permeated with sex appeal: 'In my innocence I had omitted to repair his broken nose.'[79]

John had imagined the picture hanging at the Garrick Club, but Tallulah herself bought it ('even though I had to go in hock'[80]) and carried it off to the United States. It was, however, her own portrait that, as her legend grew, became the more celebrated. 'My most valuable possession is my Augustus John portrait,' she wrote in her autobiography:[81] and since Lord Duveen had offered her one hundred thousand dollars for it, this may have been literally true. Opinion since then has moderated. The judgement of one critic in 1930 – that it was 'the greatest portraiture since Gainsborough's "Perdita" ' – now looks excessive.[82] According to some who saw it, John's first image of Tallulah – a thin face blown lightly on to the canvas – had been exquisite. But the finished work was a little disappointing. 'Perhaps she has just that initial quality and no follow through,' T. E. Lawrence tactfully suggested.[83] Tallulah's friends objected that the baleful fragility of the painting had little connection with her ravishing beauty – the blue eyes, voluptuous mouth and honey-coloured hair falling in waves on to her shoulders. Yet over the years she suffered a curious change into the very replica of this picture – either an act of will on her part or, on John's, of foresight.

'I'm not a fashionable portrait painter,' he told John Freeman.[84] Perhaps the most endearingly deficient picture of his career was the painting of the Queen (now the Queen Mother) he failed to finish between the years 1939 and 1961.

John had been tentatively suggested as a royal portrait painter by Lord D'Abernon as early as 1925. In his shocked rejection, King George V's Private Secretary, Lord Stamfordham, replied (11 December 1925): 'No! H.M. wouldn't look at A.J.!! and so A.J. wouldn't be able to look at H.M.!!' The notion merited only a joke. Then, in 1937, shortly after George VI had come to the throne, Hugo Pitman (who had been in love with her and become her stockbroker) nervously invited John to meet the new Queen – provided he arrived dead sober. The implication angered John. For a moment he looked murderous, then, his face clearing, he inquired: 'Must I be dead sober when I leave?' One way or another the meeting had gone well. The possibility of a portrait was touched on, though nothing decided. 'It is very nice to know that the Queen still wants me to paint her,' John wrote to Maud Cazalet two years later. 'Needless to say I am at her service and would love to do her portrait whenever it is possible.' In September the outbreak of war seemed to put an end to this plan. 'No chance of doing Her Majesty now . . .'[85]

But to John's surprise, the Queen did not see the war as an obstacle. 'The Queen is going to sit for me,' he wrote on 23 November 1939, '. . . I shall probably start on it in a few days.'[86] At this time of crisis, an inspiring new picture of the Queen in Garter robes was what the nation needed. John, who had overlooked the national significance such a portrait might have, was thinking more informally. The Queen could sit, he thought, during weekends at Windsor Castle – it would be 'a well-earned rest' for her. 'I would stay in some pub,' he explained to Mrs Cazalet, 'and no doubt there's a suitable room at the castle for painting.'[87] If not, doubtless there'd be something at the pub – 'one could keep it very dark'. The Queen, he hoped, would wear 'a pretty costume with a hat': something 'décolletée'. She would be a tremendous success in Hollywood – the destination he vaguely had in mind for the portrait.

Arrangements were completed in October. The portrait was to be painted in Buckingham Palace, where a room with a north-east aspect had been set aside. All painting equipment must be dispatched in advance. John himself should seek admittance by the Privy Purse entrance. It was possible that Her Majesty might be graciously pleased to accept the picture as a token of the artist's 'deep admiration and respect'. The first sitting was scheduled for Tuesday, 31 October 1939 at eleven o'clock, but the Queen would consent to receive him at two forty-five on the Monday afternoon for a preliminary interview.

John was horrified. By the time Monday came he felt 'very odd' and wired to call the meeting off. It had been, he diagnosed, an attack of the influenza, though with a slip of the pen he described himself as suffering from 'the influence'.

The Palace, meanwhile, awaited news from him 'to say when you will feel yourself available again'.[88] Sittings began next month. 'I'm dreading it,' John told Egerton Cooper as he set off in a taxi. What should the Queen wear? At last an evening gown was agreed on, but an extraordinary eagerness to discover fresh difficulties possessed John. 'Is there a platform available at the Palace?' he suddenly demanded. 'It should be a foot from the ground or slightly more.' Could they, he also wanted to know, import an easel with a *forward lean*? By the beginning of 1940, the sittings were transferred to another room, where John had installed a new electric daylight system. 'I feel sure it will prove a success and will illuminate Your Majesty in a far more satisfactory way besides rendering one independent of the weather.' It was the weather,[89] nevertheless, that offered the next interruption. 'The temperature in the Yellow Room is indistinguishable to that reported in Finland,' the Queen's Private Secretary advised, 'and Her Majesty would like therefore to wait until some temperature more agreeable . . . makes resumption of the portrait possible.' There was no difficulty here: John knew how to wait. But when sittings started again in March fresh difficulties had bloomed. Though there was much chinoiserie 'from the Brighton Pavilion. Quite amusing in itself ',[90] there was 'lack of back-ground,' John ejaculated. '. . . What is wanted is a tapestry of the right sort – with a bit of sky and landscape. Perhaps I shall have to invent one.' The Palace, anxious for John to avoid invention, hurried in tapestries and decorations. These, at John's request, were subsequently removed, and afterwards at John's insistence returned. With and without them, he struggled on. 'I wouldn't be surprised if people have been peeping at the beginning of it and seeing it merely sketched out in *green*,' he suspected. '. . . I loathe people peeping . . .' Green, he had decided, was a mistake. But when he arrived at the Palace to change it to blue, Her Majesty was not there. 'As the Queen understood from you that you were going to have your tonsils out, Her Majesty made other arrangements,' her secretary explained.

The trouble was John's paralysing shyness. He could not overcome it. 'She has been absolutely angelic in posing so often and with such cheerfulnes,' he told Mrs Cazalet on 13 June 1940. But he could make no contact with her – she was not real. He wanted to make her real . . . Good God! It was an impossible situation.

Something of these inhibitions was sensed at Buckingham Palace. In next to no time sherry was introduced into the sittings; and then, in a cupboard reserved for John's painting equipment, a private bottle of brandy. As a further aid to relaxation, the Griller Quartet (unnervingly misheard by John as the 'Gorilla Quartet') was wheeled into an anteroom to play works by English composers. Eventually it was Hitler who came to the rescue, his blitz on London providing the ostensible motive everyone had been seeking to end the ordeal. 'At this moment, what is described as "the last sitting" is proceeding,' the Queen's Private Secretary wrote on 26 June 1940. John put his bravest face on the matter: 'it looks very near done to a turn,' he told Mrs Cazalet.

During the summer he described the portrait as 'lingering', adding that

'H.M. is the best of women and I am very devoted to her.' That autumn it was moved to his studio in the country where he continued to brood over it. 'I can see a good Johnish picture – *not* a Cecil Beaton creation or anything of that sort,' he had claimed. Later, on 10 February 1941, he evolved a new plan 'to bring Mr Cecil Beaton to the Palace to take some photographs of Her Majesty, which should help me to complete her picture'. The Queen agreed to this. She did more: the following year she wrote to remind John of her portrait, suggesting that it might help matters if she wore a hat. 'If you are in London, I could come to your studio if you have any windows, for we have none in Buckingham Palace, and it is too dark and dusty to paint in anyway.'[91]

John felt acutely his sense of failure. He shut away the portrait and no one was allowed to see it. In December 1948, the Queen wrote again suggesting a drawing of her daughter Margaret: 'I could easily bring her to your studio, and I promise that I won't bring an orchestra with me!'[92] Nothing came of this or of her wish to commission a cartoon from him for a tapestry, and it was not until the early 1960s that the Queen Mother, as she had become, finally took possession of the portrait. Under thick dust and massed cobwebs, in a world of rats and spiders, it had lain with canvases from all periods in one of the cellars below John's studio. Here in 1960 a foraging West End dealer stumbled across it. 'Perhaps the Queen Mother would not mind deferring the completion of her portrait till next spring when the light would be more favourable,'[93] John urgently requested on 30 July 1960. In March 1961, at a show of John's 'Paintings and Drawings not previously exhibited', and despite a desperate last-minute attempt by John to withdraw it, the portrait was revealed to the public. Shortly afterwards a shipping company, to commemorate the launching of a large tanker, presented it to the Queen Mother. 'I want to tell you what a tremendous pleasure it gives me to see it once again,' she wrote to John on 19 July 1961. 'It looks so lovely in my drawing-room, and has cheered it up no end! The sequins glitter, and the roses and the red chair give a fine glow, and I am so happy to have it . . .'[94]

After almost twenty-two years the portrait had come home where, greatly loved, it remained. It is not the picture of a queen, nor of a woman: but of a fairy princess. It is disarmingly unfinished, and no masterpiece. Stern critics have condemned it. Yet the sitter has seen something to which others are perhaps blind.

4

METHODS AND PLACES

'I believe Papa's chief ambition in life is to see me an R.A. I fear
he will die a disappointed man.'

Augustus John to Gwen John (May 1920)

From commissioned portraits, with all their rules of vanity and forced
politeness, John turned with relief back to the ranks of his family. For
them there was little relief. The ordeal of sitting had begun at the age of
two-and-a-half. To the girls, Poppet and Vivien, he was a fearful figure.
Each morning they would wait to discover which of them was doomed
for the day. Their tears were stemmed with lumps of sugar: and the
painting went remorselessly on. The slightest movement of the head or
body was immediately corrected with the point of the brush used like a
conductor's baton.

The studio was John's battlefield. His preparatory drill never changed.
Though he might debate with a woman about the wearing, or not, of a
dress, he seldom posed his subjects. 'Sit down!' was his instruction to
men on leading them up to the platform. After that the sitter was merely
an 'object', an arrangement of shapes, surfaces and colours. John would
come up very close, too close, and glare. It was difficult not to start back
at the ferocity of those glaring eyes an inch away. Then with a grunt he
retreated: and battle began.

He painted with intense physical concentration, working without words,
breathing heavily, occasionally stamping his foot, drawing on his pipe
which uttered small bubbling sounds. Sometimes it appeared as if he had
stopped breathing altogether, and then everything seemed to stop – the
clocks, the bees, the birds on the trees. Perspiration broke out on his
temples, the pipe trembled between his lips, and the only sound for miles
seemed to be the brush jabbing on the canvas. Suddenly he would jump
backwards, knocking over a chair; there was a crash and a curse, and he
would begin pacing back and forwards. The sitter, his body aching as if
on a rack, appeared forgotten. Finally a rest was called, like half-time at
a football match, and John would sit down for a long look at the canvas.
Two or three minutes later he was up and at it again.

There were variations in this drill. Occasionally he played music on the
radio, or if things were going well the silence might be splintered by a
Welsh poem or a snatch of song. Sometimes he smoked cigarettes instead
of a pipe, and as he advanced and retreated before the canvas, he would

throw the stubs into a corner, unerringly missing the ashtray and waste-paper basket, and a few times starting a small fire. For those who were practised sitters it was possible to tell which part of them he was working on, and to keep that part alive: and invariably when he came to the mouth he would summon his own lips into a rosebud.

Whatever the variations, it was the bursting effort to concentrate that impressed his subjects. The studio seemed to throb with energy as he worked. But somehow the moment of finishing never quite arrived and then, at the bell for tea, he would stop instantly, like a cricketer drawing stumps.

These seemed the methods almost of an action painter rather than the Royal Academician he had recently become. Over a number of years his election as an Associate had been painfully imminent – so much so that it had become his habit to leave the country at the time elections took place. 'Noticed with the greatest relief that I was not elected,' he wrote from Dieppe to Cynthia Asquith in May 1920. Yet by this time his persistent non-election had in itself become considerable news, pulling the headlines from under the feet of those who had been chosen. 'We learn', announced *The Times* in 1920, 'that Mr Augustus John has received no direct intimation of any decision of the Royal Academy to open its doors to him.'[95] People looked to his election as a symbol of Burlington House being prepared to accept what were called 'broader views and wider sympathies'. In a letter to his sister Gwen, he makes it clear that he had allowed his name to be put up, 'but made sure they wouldn't elect me by making certain uncomplimentary statements in the press. It has been an amusing history altogether.'[96] Yet when the offer did come in April the following year, he decided to accept. Then he grew defensive. 'To many', he wrote, 'it seemed to be not a triumph but a surrender. Had I not been a Slade student? Was I not a member of the New English Art Club? Did I not march in the front ranks of the insurgents? The answer to these questions *is* "yes". But had I cultivated the Royal Academy in any way? Had I ever submitted a single work to the Selection Committee? . . . History answers "no". Without even blowing my own trumpet the walls of Jericho had fallen! . . . I acknowledged and returned the compliment.'[97]

But the fact was that John had taken pride in being outside the Royal Academy. 'Never exhibited at R.A.', he scrawled across the form when sending five pictures to the 'Exhibition of Works by Certain Modern Artists of Welsh Birth or Extraction'. Old Edwin John would sometimes write to Gwen telling her how 'very sorry' he was that Gus had not become a Royal Academician. 'He practically asked not to be elected.'[98] Did his election as an Associate mean that Gus was moving in his father's direction? In any event he had made his father a happy man.

In December 1928 he was elected to full membership and the process of 'self-sacrifice', as he called it, was complete. But his passage with the RA was far rougher than his autobiographical writings allow. To start with his father wrote to congratulate him on achieving the crown of his career. Then Sean O'Casey wrote to commiserate with him on being 'soiled' by contact with the World, the Flesh and the Devil – 'three excellent things,' John retorted. '. . . I assure you that it won't make the slightest difference to me . . . at any rate, it will be a useful disguise. Cézanne longed for official recognition and the Legion of Honour – and didn't get either. Van Gogh dreamt of electric light, hot and cold water, w.c's and general confort anglais. I have them all and remain unsatisfied.'[99]

The chief use of Burlington House lay in providing a new market for his wares at a time when the New English Art Club had faded.* It was, as he explained to his old Slade friend Ursula Tyrwhitt, 'the cheapest & probably the best place to show at'.[100] But he hated sitters who were anxious to have their portraits shown at the Academy. 'Kindly get it into your head that the R. Academy is not the important thing,' he instructed one of them. 'What is important is to do the picture.'[101] T. E. Lawrence had the right attitude. 'Damn the Academy, please, for me!'[102] John's view depended partly upon the President. In 1928 he was reasonably happy exhibiting pictures there; in 1938 he rebelled. It was in this year that Wyndham Lewis painted his portrait of T. S. Eliot. In the spring it was submitted to the Hanging Committee of the Royal Academy which, to Eliot's relief and Lewis's indignation, rejected it. On learning this, John at once issued a statement full of powerful negatives for the press:

'I very much regret to make a sensation, but it cannot be helped. Nothing that Mr Wyndham Lewis paints is negligible or to be condemned lightly. I strongly disagree with this rejection. I think it is an inept act on the part of the Academy. The rejection of Mr Wyndham Lewis's portrait by the Academy has determined my decision to resign from that body . . . I shall henceforth experience no longer the uncomfortable feeling of being in a false position as a member of an institution with whose general policy I am constantly in disagreement. I shall be happier and more honest in rejoining the ranks of those outside, where I naturally belong.'

This statement provoked an extraordinary response in the press in Britain, the United States and, breaking through the walls of art insularity, France. 'Premier May be Questioned', ran a headline in the *Morning Post*. 'He has been meaning to [resign] for years,' Dorelia wrote to his son

* See Appendix Six.

Edwin. 'There was a devil of a fuss.'[103] With some bewilderment, it was reported that the Academy itself had received no notification of John's resignation. In fact he had written a formal letter to the President, Sir William Llewellyn, three days beforehand, but neglected to post it. 'After the crowning ineptitude of the rejection of Wyndham Lewis's picture I feel it is impossible for me to remain [any] longer a member of the R.A.,' he told Llewellyn. He had been searching round for an escape partly because he disliked Llewellyn. The Eliot portrait provided him with a perfect motive, and he wrote to Lewis to thank him: 'I resign with gratitude to you for affording me so good a reason.'

Lewis was delighted, suggesting that all sorts of politico-artistic activities should issue out of this rumpus, including the formation by the two of them of a new Salon des Refusés. But John demurred, delivering instead a neatly placed blow, just below the belt, when he let it be known that he had not seen the portrait of Eliot at the time of its rejection. 'I wasn't thinking of doing anybody a kindness and I don't give a damn for that picture,' he assured Laura Knight, 'but I acted as a better R.A. than you and others who let the show go to pot from year to year. I know I haven't done anything directly to affect the policy of the Institution. It seemed pretty hopeless to oppose the predominant junta of deadly conservatism which rules. If by my beastly action I shall have brought some fresh air into Burlington House I shall feel justified.'[104]

Two years later, Llewellyn having left, he accepted re-election to become what Lewis described as 'the most distinguished Royal Academician . . . of a sleeping-partner order'. In 1944 he almost woke up to find himself President. Once again the romance of honour attracted him, but common sense counselled refusal: once again he prevaricated. 'I would of course like to do my best for the R.A.,' he confided to Philip Connard, 'and would be fully conscious of the honour of such a position but am only doubtful of my ability to cope with the duties, official and social, it would entail. Here's the snag. Apart from this, as P.R.A. is only an extension of R.A. I would have no logical reason to refuse.'[105] This snag was successful enough to stave off his election, and by seventeen votes to twenty-four he secured second place. 'I was in grave danger of being elected PRA recently,' he told Edwin, 'but to my great relief [Alfred] Munnings quite rightly was preferred.'[106]

During the 1920s, John had allowed himself to be overtaken by several major changes in the gallery world. Once the war was over, Knewstub, slightly bombed, emerged to dream again. From his upstairs room at the Chenil he gazed across Chelsea and saw in his mind a great art centre with himself at its summit.[107] The idea was irresistible. Although he had no head for business, he was possessed of a genius for advertisement. He whispered into the ears of the wealthy; he wrote well-directed letters of indignation and enthusiasm; he interviewed himself in newspapers. News of his dreams travelled to Boston and Calcutta.[108] Then, towards the end of 1923, vast notices began to spread themselves across the press.[109] His arguments were simple. The galleries of London were closing. The old Grosvenor Gallery had long ago collapsed and its successor, the New Gallery, been converted into a cinema. The Grafton Gallery, until recently the home of the International Society of Sculptors, Painters and Gravers, was now a dance hall. The Doré Gallery and Messrs Dowdeswell's in Bond Street, the Dudley Gallery in the Egyptian Hall: all had disappeared. The Society of British Artists and the Royal Society of Painters in Water Colours, in Suffolk Street and Pall Mall East respectively, were threatened with demolition. In such conditions living artists had almost nowhere to exhibit their pictures. 'The root of the difficulty is obvious,' Knewstub proclaimed, 'as is the remedy.' The difficulties were rates and rents; the remedy decentralization. 'A new and commodious Art Institution, *untrammelled by the impossible burden of West End expenses*, has become an urgent need of the day.' Chelsea, with its literary and artistic traditions, was 'unquestionably the alternative'.

The New Chenil Galleries was an enlargement of the old Chenil on a Napoleonic scale. The adjoining premises were taken over and, with the aid of George Kennedy, the Bloomsbury architect, robust plans were planted for a 'temple of the muses'. 'Under three spacious new roofs', explained Knewstub, 'are to be large and small galleries for paintings, drawings, prints, and sculpture; a musical society; a literary club or institution, a school of art, a large block of private studios, a first-class restaurant, a café or lounge, a library, and a hall that may be let for lectures, concerts, dancing, and other social gatherings.'[110]

In a letter (30 January 1924) written for publication, John applauded Knewstub: 'I consider you deserve great credit for showing the imagination to conceive and the business ability to bring to fruition so ambitious an undertaking.' With the significant exception of *The Economist*,[111] congratulations flowed in from every quarter. Knewstub was beside himself. He published a prospectus; he held meetings; he offered large quantities of shares for subscription; he invented several 'honorary advisory councils' on which John's name was prominent; and he appointed directors including (besides himself) an editor of the *Queen*, the proprietor of a defunct rival gallery, an eminent conductor and a catering expert. On Saturday, 25 October the foundation stone was laid. After a few words from John Ireland representing music, John himself entered the ring amid cheers, smoking a cigarette and with marks of deep concentration on his brow. Baring his head, he spoke. Though inexperienced in laying stones, he had read that it was customary on these occasions to slay a man and lay his corpse in the foundation of the building, so that his spirit would guard the place from malevolent influences: he now appealed for volunteers whom (raising a mason's mallet) he could offer an expeditious exit and any amount of posthumous glory. His large uneasy eyes contemplated a crowd that numbered the leonine belletrist Augustine Birrell, the Sitwell brothers in plain clothes, and James Pryde wearing a blue Count d'Orsay coat and soft travelling hat. No one coming forward, John (hoping this would 'do the trick') placed a George V half-crown on the lower stone and energetically applied the mortar, bespattering the noblemen and art-ist's models in the front row. Suddenly a choir, conjured up by Knewstub, broke into a rendering of 'Let us now praise famous men', while John and the other famous men stiffened to attention. 'In Paris', commented the *Manchester Guardian Weekly*, 'such a figure would be continuously before us on the revue stage and the comic press.'[112]

A year later the building was ready. Much impressed by its 'solidity and elegance', John assured Will Rothenstein that 'Knewstub with all his faults deserves considerable credit.' Knewstub not only deserved it, he needed it. By the end of 1926 he was bankrupt, and had resigned his managing directorship – 'taking a very necessary and long overdue rest and medical treatment', was how he phrased it in a rather desperate letter to John. The fact was that financial humiliation had finally sent him mad. Searching for someone on whom to stick his own incompetence, he settled collectively for the Bloomsbury Group which, he revealed to John, was scheming to get control of 'this enterprise of mine'. If it succeeded, 'there would be a pitiable outlook both for you and for the Company's liability to you.' Such financial threats were familiar to John from the days when he had lost money in the original Chenil Gallery and the Chelsea Art School through Knewstub, who 'was the curse of the place', as he now told his American dealer Mitchell Kennerley.'[113] Nevertheless, Knewstub had a final plan for making the New Chenil 'one of the most vital Art interests in the world'. Since he had 'spared no effort whatever and . . . involved myself substantially in debt', why should not John and a few other well-known artists 'get together', sell their pictures and hand him the money: in short, hold 'an Exhibition for my benefit'?[114] When John declined, Knewstub suddenly realized it had been his disloyalty that, on top of the General Strike, was responsible for the débâcle. 'I've known John for twenty-five years,' he said. 'If you'd known him for half that time you'd realise what a feat it was.' To long service, honour is due. But Knewstub's complaint that John abandoned him in this year of need was a more complicated matter.

On 22 October 1925 John had received a letter from Dudley Tooth explaining that his gallery in Bruton Street was no longer to be exclusively associated 'with the academic works of deceased masters of the British School', but intended to 'deal in the best modern art of to-day'. The letter, asking John to let the gallery handle his future work, apparently went unanswered. Then, in 1926, John held a joint exhibition with his sister Gwen at Knewstub's New Chenil Gallery. When Dudley Tooth wrote again, on 9 February 1928, Mrs Fleming, acting as go-between, gave him little chance of success. But by that time Knewstub had collapsed and John, who had tried unsuccessfully to find someone to take over the Chelsea art emporium, finally decided to invade the West End. At a meeting on 12 March 1928, Tooth proposed setting up an agency to deal with all John's pictures (excluding portraits painted to private commission), and holding a one-man show to identify the gallery as John's sole agents. To these proposals John agreed, his first exhibition at Tooth's being held in April 1929. It was into this exhibition that Virginia Woolf dashed and 'was so shocked that I came out again', she told her sister Vanessa Bell (28 April 1929). 'You can't conceive – if I'm to be trusted – the vulgarity, banality, coarseness and commonplaceness of those works, all costing over £400 [equivalent to £10,800 in 1996] and sold in the first hour.'[115] Though he could still rake in the money, the 'age of Augustus John' was well and truly over.

All this postdated Knewstub's period of utmost need. After 1927 his friendship with John ceased. When J. B. Manson appealed for a fund to assist him, he received from John a categorical reply: 'I shall certainly not help Knewstub or any other crooked swine.'[116] To many this smelt of ingratitude. But he believed that, in addition to making a hole in his own pocket, Knewstub had taken advantage of Gwen John's financial innocence to cheat her of fifty pounds. Yet he did help Knewstub's wife and at least one of her children 'on the understanding that K[newstub] is to know nothing,' he instructed Manson. 'I gather that K's family see nothing of him and don't particularly want to.'[117]

For years Knewstub had modelled himself on John, training his wife to resemble Dorelia; and now John had deserted him. He retired to Hastings, to the singing of the birds and of his kettle. 'A well-fitted cellar of the best would certainly rejuvenate me,' he suggested. But in vain. He fell back pitiably on tea. 'Possibly', he estimated, 'the outstanding comfort I have is being able to make good hot tea *very easily* in the morning . . . It is an almost indispensable stimulant and restorative.' He luxuriated in the 'humiliation' of National Assistance – which showed how far 'on the downward path' he had travelled. He threatened to 'sell my few pos-sessions', even his 'worn out lot of rubbish and rags'; he threatened to live to a hundred so that he might receive a royal telegram for his 'dear ones the generations ahead'; he threatened, most embarrassingly, to start again: 'I think I must somehow refit myself with Evening Dress,' he calculated. Refitted thus, he proposed to write doggerel for charity, in particular the Women's Voluntary Service. Or else: 'A lavatory attendant would not be too great an effort,' he told one of his sisters, 'and would allow me ample time for quiet meditation.' But when the family, responding to this blitzkrieg, implored him to visit them, he shook his head. 'I have had nearly half-a-gallon of my blood drawn from my arm by way of donation to the Blood Transfusion Service,' he explained, refusing the invitation. '. . . I am by far and away the oldest in the whole of this South-East Area Service. The true "Blue Blood" is graded "O" – as mine is – and is the most suitable for a child, or even the most delicate of patients. So you will understand, my dear, that I cannot abandon my interests in this town – only a fortnight ago I was called upon for another pint . . . Courage as always, until the final peace comes to us.'

So he lived on, an old man 'making my own bed; blacking my own grate; washing my own shirt; darning my own socks; and doctoring myself'. Upon his family, he took revenge for the bitterness of his life, smiling with self-pity, bragging of his modesty, rubbing his poverty into their faces like an enormous scab. Had he mentioned the time, he often wondered, Augustus John 'said to me nearly forty years ago that in his opinion your tactfulness was the greatest of your many charms'? He would have liked to remind John of that now, face to face, here in Hastings.

But John had escaped and was moving into new territories.

5

UNDISCOVERED COUNTRIES

'I am employed mainly in accepting invitations & getting out of keeping them.'

Augustus to Dorelia (27 April 1924)

'Whenever I see a bottle of Chateauneuf du Pape I am reminded of him,' wrote the painter A. R. Thomson. Most years, 'to refresh myself', John would ease his way down to Provence, taking the wine 'with great gusto'.[118] One day he would suddenly announce that they were off, and everything was dropped. Cats, daughters, perhaps a son or governess – all filed into the train and by night meandered through the charging carriages, while John sat peacefully asleep in the corridor.

But Martigues was no longer the place it had been before the war.

More cafés were opening up on the cours de la République, more motor cars herded under the plane trees. A new bascule bridge was put up, useful but unbeautiful. Creeping industrialism was beginning to mar that air of innocence which had first attracted John to this little community of fishermen. Progress did not stampede through Martigues: it infiltrated. For ten years he and his family continued to come and then, submitting to the advance of commercialism, left for ever.

Bazin, that essayist of the air, was now dead and his daughter, it had to be admitted, 'rather mad'.[119] Once intended as mistress for Quinn, she was recast as Poppet and Vivien's governess. The two girls loved the Villa Ste-Anne. 'It seems to me', wrote Poppet,[120] 'that life went by very smoothly on these visits to Martigues. There were great expeditions round the country and picnics as many as we could wish for ... Saturday nights were very gay', dining 'chez Pascal', then descending to the Cercle Cupidon and dancing to their heart's content while John, a glass of marc-cassis at his elbow, sat proudly watching them. Like the village girls, Poppet and Vivien danced together until, tiring of this, Poppet took to lipstick. 'After that we hardly missed a dance with the young men.' These young men would present themselves at John's table to ask for his permission then, after the dance was over, escort the girls back to him. 'Augustus seemed to enjoy watching us and sometimes would whirl us round the floor himself,' Poppet remembered.

'Then suddenly one Saturday night at dinner he looked at me with a glaring eye and growled: "Wipe that muck off your face!" Whereupon Vivien piped up with: "But she won't get asked to dance without it – they'll think she's too young." Augustus was furious. "Wipe it off!" he shouted, "and stop ogling the boys!" Then I lost my temper (always a good thing to do I later found) and I flew at him, telling him it was he who ogled all the time and that I must have picked up the habit from him – also that I noticed the girls he ogled used lipstick and I was jolly well going to do so too! This made him laugh, the whole thing passed off and I continued to dance with le joli garçon every Saturday night ... So life went on.'[121]

For John, life depended upon weather, flowers, girls. If the sun shone there was a chance of happiness. Though 'there was a brothel near John's villa I always found him playing draughts,' protested A. R. Thomson. '... He liked to wander in back streets of old France, smell of wine-and-garlic or wine-and-cheese in his nostrils.' Then, if he spotted an unusual-looking woman he would rise and with swollen eyes, pursue her. But more often he found the models he needed from among his family, posing them in a setting of olive or pine trees, the speckled aromatic hills beyond and, further off, bordering the blue Étang, distant amethyst cliffs.

But there were other days when the sun refused to shine and he would energetically tinker with plans to be off elsewhere, anywhere. 'The weather is cold and grey,' he wrote to Dorelia. '. . . There's nothing much in the way of flowers here and I have no models. I might as well be dead.' He would decide to leave, return to London, paint portraits; then the clouds dispersed and he was suddenly negotiating to buy another house there. 'Martigues is like some rustic mistress one is always on the point of leaving,' he confided to Mitchell Kennerley, 'but who looks so lovely at the last moment that one falls back into her arms.'[122]

*

John's scheme, 'quite wise for once',[123] was to pass his winters in Provence painting intermittently out of doors, and then, in the spring or summer, explore new regions. In May 1922 he found himself in Spain. His son Robin was then in Granada studying Castilian affairs with the tutor. 'I don't know if I can get painting materials in Spain,' John had hesitated; and then: 'Spanish people, I imagine, are hideous.'[124] But he went.

But he went first to Paris for a hectic week with Tommy Earp, then descended south. 'Down here in the wilds life is much calmer,' he assured Viva Booth, 'indeed there are perhaps too many vacant moments and unoccupied gaps.' Like all his random travels, there was no plot or continuity. Spain was a series of impressions: in Madrid the sight of Granero, the famous matador, limping from the ring where, the following Sunday, he would be killed; at the Café Inglés other heroes of the bullring in Andalusian hats and pigtails 'looking rather like bulls themselves',[125] vibrating with energy; the blind, hideously deformed beggars crouching in the gutters and appealing for alms; and, at evening, the ladies of the bourgeoisie collecting in the pastry-shops to 'pass an hour or two before dinner in the consumption of deleterious tarts and liqueurs'.[126] Then, in the Alhambra, a glimpse of two friends: Pepita d'Albaicin, an elegant gitana dancer, and Augustine Birrell again, until quite recently Chief Secretary for Ireland – 'a surprising combination'; and at Ugijar the spectacle of Robin full of silent Spanish and the tutor taking very bad photographs.

By mid-June his white paint had 'just about come to an end'[127] and he started back, crossing the Sierra Nevada and descending on the north to Guadix, where he was to catch a train to Barcelona.

'The ascent was long. Snow lay upon the heights. At last we reached the Pass and, surmounting it, struck the downward trail. A thick fog veiled the land. This suddenly dispersed, disclosing an illimitable plain in which here and there white cities glittered. The distant mountains seemed to hang among the clouds. At our feet blue gentians starred our path, reminding me of Burren in County Clare . . . the country became more and more enchanting. As we rode on, verdurous woods, grassy lawns and gentle streams gladdened our eyes so long accustomed to the stark and sun-baked declivities of the Alpujarras.'[128]

Spain, John told Dorelia, was 'very fine in parts, but there are *immense* stretches of nothing'. The spirit of the counry had come near, but it had not taken hold of him. 'Art, like life, perpetuates itself by contact,' he wrote. The moment of contact came as he was leaving Barcelona. 'I was walking to the station, when I saw three Gitanas engaged in buying flowers at a booth. Struck numb with astonishment by the flashing beauty and elegance of these young women, I almost missed my train.' He went on to Marseilles, but the vision of these gitanas persisted: 'I was unable to dismiss it.' In desperation he hired a car and returned all the way to Barcelona. But 'of course I did not find the gypsies again. One never does.'

Spain incubated in his mind, but never hatched. When he flew back there in December 1932 on his way to Majorca, rain was to make the world unpaintable; after which Franco, like a hated bird of prey, kept him off until too late.

'I am sure it will stimulate me,' he had written to Ottoline Morrell, 'and I shall come back fresher and more myself.'[129] In fact he came back as someone else. He had seen many pictures in Spain. 'At the Prado I found Velasquez much greater and more marvellous than I had been in the habit of thinking,' he told Dorelia. 'There is nobody to touch him.' He went to the Academy of San Fernando and the shabby little church of San Antonio de la Florida to see the Goya frescoes of the cupola: 'My passion for Goya was boundless.' The streets of Madrid seemed to throb and pulse with Goyaesque characters afterwards, bringing the place alive for him. There were other paintings too that 'bowled me over': Rubens's 'The Three Graces' and, 'a dream of noble luxury', Titian's 'Venus'. Only El Greco, at the Prado, disappointed him. Yet, mysteriously, it was El Greco who was to affect his painting. John's 'Symphonie Espagnole' of 1923 is a self-confessed essay in the El Greco style that marshals all the mawkishness and conveys little of the ecstatic rhythm. These weeks in Spain form a parallel to his journey through northern Italy in 1910. From Italy he had discovered a tradition to which he belonged; in Spain he lost himself. 'He is painting very much like El Greco now since his visit to Spain,' Christopher Wood noted in December 1922. This influence of El

Greco became a mannerism. The lengthening of the head worked well for few of his sitters, and the elongation of the body seemed to draw life out of it. It was an attempt by John to speak a new language, but he could say little in it that was original.

*

It was as a Distinguished Guest of the Irish Nation that in the summer of 1924 John went with Eve Fleming to Dublin. The occasion was a festival of 'fatuous self-glorification' called the Taillteann Games. Oliver St John Gogarty, as commander of the social operations, had billeted him with Lord Dunsany in County Meath. 'Here I am entrapped,' John wrote desperately from Dunsany Castle. '. . . Mrs Gogarty has developed into a sort of Duchess. I must get out of this. It was very fool-hardy to have come over.'[130] Gogarty had warned Dunsany not to give John any alcohol – which made Dunsany determined to offer his guest as much as he could want. This would have suited John well, had Gogarty not confided to him that Dunsany was a fierce teetotaller. The result was that, in an agony of politeness, John persisted in refusing everything until, according to Compton Mackenzie, 'Dunsany started to explain how to play the great Irish harp . . . After they went to bed Augustus climbed over the wall of Dunsany Park and walked the fourteen miles to Dublin.'[131]

During the festival banquet the Commander-in-Chief of the Irish Free State Army delivered a long speech in Gaelic during which the municipal gas and electricity workers decided upon a strike. Unperturbed by the blackness, the Commander spoke on. After a minute, John leant over to Compton Mackenzie, and whispered: 'What's going on?' Mackenzie explained. 'Thank God,' breathed John. 'I'm only drunk then. I thought I'd gone mad.'

*

For one month in the spring of 1925 John stayed at the British Embassy in Berlin and, with a key to the side entrance, was free to explore this 'strange and monstrous city' at all hours. His impressions were scattered: Max Liebermann at eighty painting better than ever; 'some marvellous wall decorations brought back from Turkistan by a German digger';[132] beer 'like nectar'; and girls, 'hearty creatures and sometimes very good looking' who, on a more vital inspection, were revealed as being men 'devoted to buggery' and 'furnished by the police with licences to adopt female attire'.[133] As for embassy life, it was all very swell but 'too strenuous for me . . . there are hours of *intense* boredom.'

Of the three portraits John painted while in Berlin with Eve Fleming, the most important was of Gustav Stresemann, the German Foreign

Minister. It was Lord D'Abernon who arranged the sittings during which the Locarno Treaties advanced to the point of signature. In Lord D'Abernon's diplomatic language, Stresemann's 'lively intelligence and extreme facility of diction' inclined him 'to affect monologue rather than interchange of ideas'.[134] The British Ambassador could not get a word in. By early March, when sittings began, their negotiations had reached the verge of collapse. It was then that he had his idea. Since John knew little German, D'Abernon reasoned, there could be no grounds for not carrying on their discussions while he worked. The advantage was that Stresemann would be 'compelled to maintain immobility and comparative silence'. John, by treating the German Foreign Minister as one of his own family, exercised his role strongly. At the first sitting, after a sentence or two from Lord D'Abernon, Stresemann broke in and was about to go on at his customary length when John 'armed with palette and paint-brushes' asserted his artistic authority. 'I was therefore able to labour on with my own views without interruption,' D'Abernon records. '. . . The assistance given by the inhibitive gag of the artist was of extreme value . . . Reduced to abnormal silence . . . Stresemann's quickness of apprehension was such that he rapidly seized and assimilated the further developments to which the Pact proposals might lead.'[135]

The Locarno Pact, for which Stresemann was awarded the Nobel Prize, was eventually less controversial than the portrait. Stresemann faced it bravely and 'even his wife', John reported, 'admits it's like him at his worst'.[136] To Dorelia he wrote: 'I like Stresemann. He is considered the strongest man in German politics.' But Lord D'Abernon, who now felt some tenderness for Stresemann, thought the painting 'a clever piece of work' though 'not at all flattering: it makes Stresemann devilishly sly.'[137] This proved an accurate foretaste of popular reaction. Nobody much liked Stresemann, and no party trusted him. When the portrait was shown in New York in 1928, John was much acclaimed for his 'cruelty'. Modestly he rejected this praise. 'I have nothing to do with German politics, but I thought Stresemann an *excellent* fellow, most sympathetic, intelligent and even charming,' he wrote on 13 March 1928 to Mitchell Kennerley,[138] adding with less modesty: 'One must remember that even God chastises those whom he loves.'

*

Apart from Stresemann's silences, John had not greatly relished Berlin. The motor cars, the hard-boiled eggs, combined with a lack of handkerchiefs, unnerved him. He felt 'very impatient' to go somewhere new, and paint. 'For God's sake learn up a little Italian,' he urged Dorelia. It was May when he boarded the train for Italy, with Dorelia, Poppet and Vivien.

Romilly too was coming. 'In a fit of megalomania',[139] he had decided to cross the Alps on foot, aided by the tutor with fourteen schoolgirls 'on their way to spend a week-end in Paris'.[140] Drifting through Italy at the head of the main party John lost his wallet with all their money in it. This calamity, though credited to the quick fingers of Italian train thieves, may in fact have been attributable to Eileen Hawthorne's abortion for which urgent funds had just then been prescribed. For some days John's party were luxuriously stranded in the most expensive hotel in Naples (the only one that would accept their credit), and when they finally approached the 'barbarous island' of Ischia, their destination, they were irritated to see Romilly, his feet in ruins, waving to them from the harbour.

Skirting the shores, John sought anxiously for some pictorial motif. They were to stay at the Villa Teheran, a little wooden house with a veranda, that stood by itself on a miniature bay. It belonged to Mrs Nettleship and, being loaded with fleas, proved uninhabitable: 'it was clear this place offered nothing to a painter.'[141] John marched his family off to Forio, the next town along the coast, and quartered them more happily above some vineyards overlooking the sea. The oleander, nespoli, quince, orange, lemon and pepper trees, 'with the addition of a bottle of *Strega*', contributed greatly, John recalled, 'towards our surrender to the spirit of the place. Indeed, at night, when the moon shone, as it generally did . . . resistance had been folly.'[142] But it was as holiday-maker, not primarily as painter, that John surrendered. He would float on his back in the phosphorescent sea for hours, while Dorelia bathed more grandly in a black silk chemise that billowed about her as she entered the waves. There were picnics on the beach, sunbathing on the long flat roof of their new villa, and expeditions through the island behind a strongly smelling horse. 'Apart from drowning, life on the island presented few risks,' John grumbled.[143] Even the werewolves, reported to range the mountain, remained invisible. So, it was back to portrait painting, 'finding myself very well occupied here with the two superbly fat daughters of the local Contessa'.[144] The cook's little girls also came to sit, side by side in a window, wearing alarmingly white-starched dresses. But a portrait of Mussolini, arranged by an ardent Fascist they had met, fell through. In his place Dorelia assembled various exotic blooms: and so John added to his flower pictures, the best of which, wrote the art critic Richard Shone, have 'something of the freshness of Manet's late flower paintings'.[145]

*

John was destined to cross the Atlantic six times; and, in one form or another, the United States visited him several times more. The purpose of all this traffic was the innocent one of 'making a useful bit of money'.[146]

He had first attracted attention in the United States when, in 1910, his portrait of William Nicholson was shown at the Carnegie Institute's International Exhibition in Pittsburgh. Travelling there for the first time thirteen years later it was as the guest of the Carnegie Institute, which had invited him to act as the British representative on its jury. He embarked on 28 March 1923, elated to be on his way at last to the land of his boyhood day-dreams. 'The Americans all wear caps and smoking-suits in the evenings, and smoke very long cigars,' he wrote to Dorelia from the SS *Olympic*. 'They are very friendly people.' When his hat flew off into the sea, they rushed up in numbers to offer him their own which, one by one as he accepted them, also flew off. 'There must be a continuous track of caps along our route.' On board he met several passengers who petitioned him to paint portraits: Mrs Harry Payne Whitney, 'quite a pleasant woman but infernally lazy'; a 'big fat sententious oil king . . . who argues with me'; and Sir Arthur Conan Doyle, who told him 'startling things about the spook world. It really seems quite a good place somewhat superior to this one in fact . . . Lady Conan Doyle is like people I've met in my youth – all spiritual love and merriment and dowdy clothes.'

Of all contemporary British artists, John was then the best known in northern America. At the famous Armory Show of 1913 in New York no other modern painter, with the exception of Odilon Redon, had been so well represented.[147] The huge Armory had been packed with the élite of New York 'cheering the different American artists, cheering Augustus John, cheering the French . . .'[148] Critics and journalists had soon been dispatched to interview John, and many reports of his 'recent activities' appeared in American papers. 'Augustus John is now at the height of his fame,' the New York magazine *Vanity Fair* had declared in June 1916. 'Not even the war . . . has taken public attention off Britain's most conspicuous native painter.'

On arriving, hatless, in New York harbour he was penned down by a press of journalists who, like pirates, boarded the ship even before it berthed. 'They sought to get a "story" out of me. I stood them a drink instead.'[149] They were delighted by his appearance – 'thoroughly consistent in living up to what he ought to look like'; he thought them 'nice boys'.

That evening, after dinner at the Coffee House, Frank Crowninshield whirled him round the city and eventually landed him back at the Biltmore Hotel 'exhausted and bewildered by an orgy of colour, noise, smartness and multitudinous legs'.[150]

Of Pittsburgh, where he arrived next day, John remembered little but the boundless hospitality of its natives and the 'infernal splendour' of their steelworks. He did not stay long. He had been invited to Buffalo to paint an impeccable old lady, Mrs Goodyear. On the station platform at Buffalo the sitter's son, Conger Goodyear, was surprised to see hovering at John's elbow the Assistant Director of the Carnegie Museum, John O'Connor. O'Connor whispered that he had come to explain away the 'extraordinary capacity' of John's drinking habits. 'I replied, somewhat haughtily that I thought Buffalo men could take care of themselves in the drinking line,' Goodyear reported. 'Pittsburgh might have suffered but I had every confidence in my fellow citizens. I was wrong.'[151]

John was lodged at the Saturn Club, reputedly – in those days of Prohibition – 'the most bibulous of our social institutions'. He appreciated the compliment. 'This club is a very good place', he acknowledged, 'full of determined anti-Prohibitionists . . . There is a little back room with lockers all round the walls in which the members keep their "hootch". About 6 o'clock this room gets densely packed with a crowd of vociferating men wildly mixing cocktails. I have the freedom of Conger Goodyear's locker.'[152] For part of the first evening, about which he could recall nothing, his host 'participated lap by lap'. 'The following afternoon and evening I decided to stay aloof and keep count,' Goodyear wrote. 'Some of my friends formed relay teams to pace the visitor. The official score showed seventeen cocktails for our guest without visible effect other than a slight letting down of British taciturnity. There were a few highballs during dinner and after and we sat in a respectful silence as the champion walked a straight path bedwards.'[153]

Work on the portrait sped along intermittently, and sometimes John would escort the old lady politely to the shops. One morning, as she was emerging from her dressmaker, Mrs Goodyear cracked a joke, fell down a flight of stairs and broke her ankle. 'Just my luck!' commented John.[154] That afternoon he left for New York.

Over the next weeks a gradual disenchantment with American life may be traced in his letters. Like his brother Thornton, he had hoped to ride over the American West, he told a reporter from the *New York Times*, to set up camp along the prairies, push up the Mississippi, mix with the black workers on the cotton plantations. His plans were greeted with bewilderment. 'The prairies had been ploughed; the backwoods levelled; the Indians mostly tamed or exterminated; the frontiersmen replaced by "regular fellows".'[155]

In a letter to the ten-year-old Poppet (28 April 1923) he gives a child's-eye view of New York.

'This is a strange country. There are railways over your head in the streets and the houses are about a mile high . . . The policemen chew gum and hold clubs to knock people down. The people don't say "yes". They say instead Yep, yeah, yaw, yawp, yah and sometimes yump. Otherwise they simply say "you bet" or "bet your life". They eat clams, fried chicken, chives, slaw soup and waffles with maple syrup. They drink soda-ices all the time. The rich people drink champagne and whisky for dinner and go about with bottles of gin in their pockets. When a policeman catches them they have to pay him about 1,000 dollars after which he drinks their gin and locks them up.'

John did not seek publicity in New York: the more publicity, the less freedom. So far as possible he kept his whereabouts secret from journalists.[156] He put up initially at the Plaza Hotel on Fifth Avenue, then at the Hotel des Artistes at sixty-seventh and Central Park, and finally moved to a studio owned by Harrington Mann. To this studio numbers of Americans trekked, convinced that they were discovering a new Sargent, the famous American portraitist. 'It's been a fearful grind,' John wrote to Dorelia. Everyone wanted to give parties for him. 'The telephone rings continuously.' There was always something to do: a boxing match, a cocktail party, the theatre, a trip to Philadelphia, another party. His best hours were in the company of a decorative artist called 'Sheriff' Bob Chanler, 'a Gargantuan creature, as simple as a babe', with great flapping arms and hands, 'indescribably improper but . . . as good as gold' at whose house he met 'easy-going ladies, eccentrics and hangers-on'. It was almost like home. But John was cautious. 'I walked down Fifth Avenue,' he told Dorelia,

'there were a number of rather tarty-looking damsels walking about giving glad or at any rate significant eyes – of course one mustn't respond, for if you as much as say "how do you do" to a woman, you are immediately clapped into gaol for assault or otherwise blackmailed for the rest of your life. The country is chiefly controlled by a villain named [Randolph] Hearst who owns most of the papers . . . This city at night is dominated by a stupendous scintillating sign advertising Wrigley's chewing gum. The poor bewildered multitude seethe aimlessly below.'[157]

He saw the Americans as 'inconceivably naif' though 'not unattractive'. But it is possible to see John himself as floundering naïvely within the bowl of this artificial society. Despite all the hectic enjoyment he was never quite at ease, except in Harlem. It was with great difficulty at first that he could persuade anyone to take him there. After that he went alone and sometimes stayed all night. 'The dancing that took place in these Harlem clubs was brilliant beyond description . . . I was immensely pleased.'[158]

Harlem at that time was not known in polite society and when John spoke of his plans to paint New York's black population there was some high-pitched embarrassment. 'Do you like the mulattoes, or the brown or black Negroes?' one incredulous journalist asked. 'I like them all,' he growled. He was questioned on Harlem as if it were some far-off planet. 'They seem to be natural artists,' he told the New York press. 'It seems too bad that when any of them in this country show talent in the graphic and plastic arts, or in any line of artistic endeavour, they are denied an equal chance with other artists.'[159]

John's other area of criticism was Prohibition. 'There's a new rich class springing up,' he told Dorelia, ' – the *bootleggers*. They are the strongest advocates of Prohibition and extremely powerful.' In public he aimed his protest at what appeared to him the most appropriate point. The Secretary of the Independent Society of Artists in New York had been convicted for hanging a picture by François Kaufman that showed Christ being prevented by some Prohibitionist politicians from changing water into wine, a joke that appealed to John. 'The conviction was an outrage on liberty and art,' he thundered. 'Your prohibitionists seem the richest subjects for satire . . . Prohibition is more than a farce – it is a tragedy. I agree with those who say it breeds disrespect for all laws. It is unjust to the poor, because one doesn't have to be in this country long before discovering that anyone with money can get all the liquor he wants, while it's beyond the reach of those with little money.'[160]

These were scarcely the tones of a new Sargent. Nevertheless, New Yorkers liked him. He was wild but, like the Indians, he could be tamed. 'I could get *any number* of portraits to do if I liked,' he informed Dorelia. The idea of having done them, swiftly, painlessly, profitably, was attractive; but the work itself was 'sweat and travail'. Letters from Dorelia arrived, describing the flowers in her garden, the girls' new pony, the dogs, cats and vegetables. Amid the canyons of New York, all this seemed infinitely green and desirable, and he longed to be back.

Before leaving, he saw for the last time his old patron John Quinn. Quinn had been dreading this encounter. Having largely lost interest in John's painting, he was then arranging to sell off most of his pictures on the open market. To his relief John 'was very pleasant and did not allude to the episode of my selling the paintings at all', he confided to Percy Moore Turner. 'I took him out riding with a lady . . .' By admiring his new pictures and his special friend, the beautiful Jeanne Foster (to whom he made amiable advances), John charmed Quinn. But the following year, Quinn was dead. The doctors had given him up months before, but once again he knew better than any of them, and simply would not die. They told him he was suffering from a hardening of the liver; he shook his head. Barely alive, hardly able to move, his body skeletal though swollen with fluid and yellow all over, he admitted to a small glandular disorder. He was 'run down', he believed, and must be careful not to catch a cold. He was to die on 28 July 1924. 'He had cancer of the liver but never knew it and so had hope to the end and made plans for the future,' Jeanne Foster wrote to Gwen John. For three months she had scarcely left him. 'He suffered greatly . . . He was so thin I could lift him.'[161] No longer did he want to look at Picasso's work, or Braque's, Rousseau's or anything by Augustus. But he kept a few of Gwen's pictures near him, as well as some by Matisse, Arthur Davies and Nathaniel Hone, and some sculpture by Brancusi and Gaudier-Brzeska. Towards the end he grew strangely fond of flowers, having never much cared for them during his life. But he had been frightened of his emotions, and perhaps it was this which had made Jeanne Foster afraid of declaring her love for him. 'He was a strange man,' Mitchell Kennerley wrote to John; 'led a strange life; died a strange death. Properly handled his Collections will ensure his fame.'[162]

In the last week of June, John sailed back on the *Berengaria*. 'The first few days he seemed quite low,' noted Conger Goodyear, who was with him on the boat. 'He said he thought he had rather overdone it in New York and he was glad to be getting back from American Prohibition to England and temperance.'

By April the next year he was back in New York in a big bare studio in the Beaux Arts Building at 80 West Fortieth Street. 'It is a very beautiful high building on Bryant Park – near our Public Library and not far from Fifth Avenue – quite fashionable in fact,' Jeanne Foster wrote to Gwen. This second coming, which has been described as 'an electric event . . . that enriched the great saga of John's career',[163] was largely indistinguishable from the first. 'All the newspapers reproduced photographs of him,' Jeanne Foster wrote.[164] The Mellons and the Wideners queued up for the society portraits; Harlem, all aglow at night, again bewitched him. But he was less cautious. He began painting black girls 'semi-nude'; and he began quarrelling with American dealers from whose 'unctuous greetings' he protected himself with a 'cold zone'. There was something about New York, he discovered, that for all its speed and activity deprived him of initiative. All around throbbed an air of industry: yet it was impossible to work.

'Life', he warned Homer Saint Gaudens, 'is full of pitfalls (and gin).' At the end of one dinner he broke his silence and, to everyone's amazement, apologized in booming tones for having 'monopolized the conversation'. At a lunch he was seated next to a lady who pressed him about young artists: whose pictures could she buy that would multiply in value ten times within five years? 'But is there no one?' she finally asked, 'is there no one whom *you* are watching?' His reply ended their conversation: 'I am watching myself, madam, with considerable anxiety.'

John's reputation in the United States was built largely on hearsay. The Carroll Gallery and the Photo-Secession Gallery in New York; the Boston Art Club, the Art Institute of Chicago, the Cleveland Museum of Art and numerous other galleries had been endeavouring over several years to hold John exhibitions. The Carnegie Institute itself had offered to set up a one-man show that would tour the country. All these establishments had the burden of John's active co-operation. He was, as one gallery director put it, always 'cordial . . . but persistently indefinite'.[165] When his first one-man show in New York was held early in 1928 at the Anderson Gallery, John inadvertently was in Martigues and never saw it. Stevenson Scott, who had brought him over in 1924 to 'secure commissions for the paintings that commemorate his American period', and had undertaken to show the fruit of this period at Scott and Fowles, did not live to see the exhibition take place. It opened, a quarter of a century later, in the spring of 1949.

Perhaps John's best portraits of Americans were done in Europe: of Tom Mix, the movie actor, who visited Mallord Street with a camera team to film the event; and of the McLanahans from Philadelphia, at their aptly named house in the Côte d'Or, Château de Missery. His portrait of Frances McLanahan,[166] a large-eyed oval-faced beauty, is a Swedish study, blue and yellow, of peach-fed innocence. It was eventually completed in London where, about the same time, he was failing to finish a portrait of Governor Fuller of Massachusetts.

It was in pursuit of Fuller that he made his last voyage to the United States in 1928 – a journey he never failed to regret. 'Come over and rescue me!' he appealed to Carrington. He had been carried off to the Fullers' country house, some fifty miles from Boston, and presented with the task of painting the Governor and his problematic children. 'This sort of work is very ageing,' he grieved. 'I have practically no hair left.' One difficulty was that the Fullers 'do not yet grasp the difference between a hired photographer and an artist. As I am their guest I cannot point out the difference as forcibly as I should like.'[167] The children were impossible – in John's picture the son ('who blacked his sister's eye') has no feet because 'that boy drives me crazy, swinging his legs about all the time'; and one of the daughters ('a nice young bitch . . . if one could catch her on the hop') he dismissed altogether because 'neither she nor I could concentrate'. Mrs Fuller, a good soul brimming over with cheerfulness, had 'designs on my virtue', making his position in the house tricky. 'I can't stick this,' he wrote darkly to Dorelia. 'I *can't* tell you *all*.' The

Governor himself, John decided, 'is the best of the lot . . . I could make Fuller the most ridiculous figure in two hemi-spheres if I wanted to.'

As the weeks flowed by, his lamentations reached a comic intensity. 'It's hell and damnation here!' he cried. 'Everybody I meet seems half-witted.' The prolonged meals with sweet food and iced-water; the gramophone gabbling all day its muddled melodies; the political guests with their recreational tales of golf and fish; the 'advice' on painting; the labour-saving devices including a 'ridiculous old ass of a butler' with a pseudo-cockney accent who, John believed, 'was suffering from a disease of the spine till I realized his attitude was merely one of deference'; all these conspired to make the months of August and September 'the most hideous ordeal of my life'.

In the second week of October they moved, en masse, to Boston. The Fullers expected John to stay at their official residence in Beacon Street, but he had been lent a studio in the Fenway by Charles Woodbury, the marine artist, 'a perfect old dear . . . I could have embraced him'. Though the walls were covered with alarming pictures of sharks leaping from the Caribbean Sea, 'I think I shall recover here,' he assured Dorelia. 'That stay with the Fullers pulled me down terribly. The darkest passage of my life undoubtedly.' He had, he added, devised a 'good method of doing portraits with much use of toilet-paper'.

Offers for portraits still poured in – 'there are millions to be made . . . but I would rather paint vegetables.'[168] He took up his brushes and produced four cyclamen, two begonias and a chrysanthemum. It was a long way to have come for such work. Among his few exciting portraits was one of a black elevator girl who offered to return with him to England. Wherever he went he could see nothing but 'masses of full-grown men dismally guzzling soda-ices'. 'This city is a desert,' he concluded. But no longer did he have to rely on charity for a glass of wine. A coffin-like object in his studio had been filled with drink. He began to suffer from terrible hangovers. Worse still, he had picked up 'a little actress' with whom he was seen in public. This was Harriet Calloway, the star of *Blackbirds* and famous for her 'Diga Diga Do'. By December the Fullers were as eager as John himself for his departure. 'They seem to think I'm a comic here,' he grumbled. The last laugh was theirs. When the portrait was finished, an official telegram of congratulation was sent from the Governor's residence to Augustus's father in Tenby.

'How happy I shall be to get on the Ocean,' John had written to Dorelia on 28 November, ' – even if the ship sinks it will be better than staying here, where one sinks only less quickly.' He sailed from New York on 14 December. 'I am a complete wreck,' he warned his family. '. . . Be ready to meet me at Southampton with a drink.'

John's chief endowment to the United States was his unfinished work. Over the next thirty years, numbers of ageing Americans continued to throng the Atlantic in pursuit of their portraits. One was Mrs Vera Fearing, a niece of Whistler's. John had begun to paint her in October 1928, but not having completed the portrait to his satisfaction by the time he left, he refused to sign it. She promised to come over. The first time she came, he was ill. Later she followed him to Connemara and then back to England. From August to December 1931 she stayed at Fryern, being painted in the tool shed. In the course of these sittings she changed her dress, he changed his studio. She learnt to drink, helped Dorelia with the housework, met Lytton Strachey, Carrington and Lawrence of Arabia, went for death-defying drives to London. Then, in 1935, she tried again – as Mrs Montgomery with a husband and two children. Everyone was extremely kind, John himself offering to give her a child of their own. But one day – 'one of the worst days I've ever been through' – John decided his studio was haunted and disappeared at midnight to London. So it went on. Telegrams and letters flowed between them, and ruses of all dimensions were engineered to lever the picture from John's grasp. He worked on, sometimes using photographs and the clothes of other sitters, grappling with the abominable job of fitting someone else's body on to her head. 'I want to work some more on your extremities,' he pleaded. She waited: was divorced, remarried, became a grandmother. Her father-in-law, who had originally commissioned the portrait, died without ever having seen it. War came. War went. 'Augustus means you to have it,' his friend Reine Pitman assured her on 13 July 1959, 'but is already slightly baulking, and saying he wants to show it before sending it off.' That autumn it had reached 'an electric fire having its signature dried! So it won't be long now . . .' Then, in 1960, Vera Stubbs (as she had now become) was repossessed of her picture. But her new husband didn't care for it and it was hung in a disused hut.

There was another aftermath to John's American period. Ann and Joan from New York, Doris from Massachusetts, Karin in *Runnin' Wild*, wrote giving times and addresses. Myrtle, a music student 'particularly interested in art', wondered 'if you would like to see me'; Margaret and her friends wished to know whether he would 'consent to stimulate our interest in art'; could he, another correspondent inquired, 'spare a few moments to look at four paintings by my sister, who is in a lunatic asylum?' Some letters, mentioning cocktails, are anonymous; others, providing names and ages of children, affectionate. Others again, containing financial calculations, were torn up. A 'celebrated squawker' offered her services as vocalist 'at any social function'. Another Vera, who had stopped him in the street one day to demand his 'opinion as to the future of art' wrote to inform him that 'I interrupted my artist's career in order to find out the meaning of things', adding: 'It seems to me that a great figure in the art world like yourself ought to give your contribution to this problem.'

And it was true that, in some manner, John was still seen as 'a great figure in the art world', with all the clarity of a mirage. Whenever his name burst into their newspapers – on the cover of *Time* magazine and of *Life*, or as the first artist to wireless a drawing across the Atlantic – curiosity was quickly rekindled. But there was too little of his best work on public view to sustain interest, so there remained only a vague impression of his bloodshot personality, some memory of those powerful party manners, a rumour of exploits; then a vanishing trick.

*

On one of his voyages back from the United States, the ship touching at Cherbourg, John had disembarked. 'I was unable to resist the urge to land first of all on the soil of France,' he wrote.[169] It was soothing after the glitter and turmoil of New York to find himself in the quiet of a Norman town such as Bayeux and taste again a dish of moules marinière with a litre of *rouge*. The gentle aspect of the country, the leisureliness of life, the detachment and intimacy mixed; these were virtues of the Old World that now appealed to him. In the past, he had speculated on the existence of a better land to the west. After 1928 he knew it did not exist. When asked whether he would return to the United States, perhaps to paint Franklin D. Roosevelt, he replied no: Goethe's dictum 'America is here' was turning out to be literally true, and saved him the journey. It was the answer of someone who felt himself to be getting old.

The New World, once it invaded Europe, revealed itself as his enemy. Like a Canute, John held his hand up to halt the tide of history; and such was the force of his personality and the sphere of his influence in style and fashion that, for a time, he appeared to succeed. The waves held back, there was a frenzied pause – then the sea of modern life flooded past him and he was in retreat.

'We have to give up Alderney Manor or buy it,' he had written to Gwen. 'We have been looking about in Dorset & elsewhere for another house without success.'[170] In March 1927 they finally packed up and moved on. For a while the strange castellated bungalow, in which they had lived for more than fifteen years, stood empty, a shell behind its broken-down garden wall and the rising screen of rhododendrons. Then it vanished altogether, and in its place rose a brand-new housing estate. The old site, purged of its pagan associations, became consecrated ground, the site of Alderney Methodist Chapel.

By April the following year, 'in submission to the march of progress as conceived by business men or crooks', the Johns also left the Villa Ste-Anne. It was later converted into the Hostellerie Ste-Anne, credited with three knives and forks in the *Guide Michelin*, though still with its '*vue exceptionelle*' over the blue Étang de Berre.

It was the same story in Mallord Street. The Chelsea fruit and flower market opposite their house was obliterated; blocks of flats and a telephone exchange blotted out the sun. In the early 1930s they sold the house to the singer Gracie Fields; the Anrep mosaics were covered up, the structure altered, the house and its surroundings becoming almost unrecognizable.

Everywhere the old world was vanishing, and John was part of it. Though he might blare his defiance, though he would heave out an announcement from time to time about 'turning a corner', there seemed only one direction for him to go. The retreat was sounded on all fronts, and everything would depend upon the subtlety with which he conducted it.

TEN

The Way They Lived Then

I

FRYERN COURT

'I got stuck here.'
Augustus John to Bill Duncalf
(23 May 1959)

Fryern Court had originally been a fourteenth-century friary which, in the early nineteenth century, was converted into a farmhouse. Later a Georgian-style front had been stuck on to the old farm building, and it was transformed into a manor house.

It was on the edge of the New Forest, a mile from Fordingbridge. A porch 'like a nose'[1] divided the windows that reached almost to the ground. At the rear of the house stood a whitewashed courtyard with a figtree and stables, a garage and outhouses stretching away into garden and meadow. The sitting-room and dining-room, the dark pantry with its slate floor and a fourteenth-century kitchen with carved stone heads (then heavily painted over) protruding from the walls – all had their floors level with the ground. The cellars were crammed with wine, apples and cobwebs. Upstairs there was more the feel of the old farmhouse than the manor, the passages rambling crookedly past eight bedrooms.

They moved there early in 1927. Augustus descended from London and 'like the traditional clown'[2] busily did nothing. Everything that could be prised from Alderney was taken. Poppet and Vivien, in great excitement, rode over on their horses; the old vans and carts, soon to be embedded as garden furniture, set out on their last rusty journey; cats, dogs, pigs joined in the stampede past the large copper beeches, magnolias, yellow azaleas up the curving gravel drive to their new home.

The routine and rituals at Fryern were to be arranged as a supportive background for John: but, as with Alderney, it was Dorelia's arrangement and far removed from the wild emptiness that stimulated his painter's imagination. He saw, with despair, all round a beauty he could not use. 'Here', exclaimed Cecil Beaton,[3] a frequent visitor, 'is the dwelling place of an artist.' The irony seemed invisible, though the changes that were made to Fryern, in particular a mammoth new studio, on stilts like a child's playhouse and 'entirely based on mathematical calculation',[4] were expressions of John's discontent. In an agony of guilt, disappointment, incomprehension, suddenly released in thunderous bursts of temper, he worked on amid these tranquil surroundings.

Meanwhile Dorelia 'busies herself in the garden', John noted. She spent hours studying horticultural catalogues, ordering plants and bulbs. It was a grander garden than at Alderney, and more formal. The avenue of dark yew trees was neatly clipped; the lawn, with a pond converted from a tennis court at its centre, was enclosed by hedges; in the orchard, the pear and apple trees were hung with little bags against the wasps. Up the walls of the house roses and clematis twined, the matted stems making nests for cats; and on the north side, a hazard for drivers, bunched the holly and laurels. There were garden seats, tables of stone and teak, a hammock strung between the Judas and an apple tree, medlars, and little chequered fritillaries in the grass. It was a place for animals and children to play, a place to relax in and read.

It was also a place to be used for keeping the house replenished with fruit and herbs, bright yellow goat's butter, quince and raspberry jam, grape juice from the vine in the greenhouse, sweetcorn, lavender, flowers. During the 1930s Dorelia was helped by two gardeners. One, a fine man, landed up in hospital. The other was Mr Cake. He and his wife, Mrs Cake the cook, had been brought from Alderney and, though often promising to leave, remained with the family for over thirty years. Old Cake was a small man with a limp and a bright buttonhole who would go swinging off each evening to the pub over a mile away. He seldom spoke, and his wife, who 'did wonders' with fish, could not read. Larger and more voluble than her husband, and always grinning, Mrs Cake appeared (on account of her wall eye) a fearsome creature. 'Trouble with 'im', she was heard to say of John, 'is 'e's got too many brains and they've gone to 'is 'ead.' Mrs Cake was immensely proud of her hair, which was long and thick and washed, she would explain, in juice of rosemary. She spoke with a strong Dorset accent. 'Old Cake was very lucky to get me,' she would say. 'All the boys were after me. It was my hair.' Old Cake, pursued by several goats, said nothing.

There were the same smells of beeswax, pomanders and lavender, wood- and tobacco-smoke, coffee, cats as at Alderney; the same disorder of vegetables, tubes of paint, nuts from the New Forest, saddles, old canvases, croquet mallets, piles of apples. The furniture was not grand nor the pictures specially valuable: it was the opposite of a museum. Alongside those paintings of John's which had eluded fire and finish were some lovely Gwen Johns, including one of her paintings of Dorelia at Toulouse, a watercolour by Augustus's son Edwin, a Henry Moore sketch, small Wilson Steers and Conders, an Alvaro Guevara, a beach scene by Boudin and some Matthew Smiths. An Epstein head of a small child stood on a table, and in the hall, crowned with a cactus, one of the two Modigliani stone heads John had bought in Paris. In her bedroom, Dorelia hung some tinfoil pictures by Carrington and two drawings by Augustus of Pyramus. Then there were paintings by friends: Eve Kirk, Adrian Daintrey and a passing number of gypsy artists.

It was not a smart house, and it had much of the farm about it. The colours were rich, the atmosphere lavish yet shabby. 'There is no beguiling, ready-made impact of beauty,' wrote Cecil Beaton; 'rather, an atmosphere of beauty is sensed. No intention to decorate the house ever existed. The objects that are there were originally admired and collected for their intrinsic shape. They remain beautiful . . . the colours have gratuitously grown side by side. Nothing is hidden; there is an honesty of life which is apparent in every detail – the vast dresser with its blue and white cups, the jars of pickled onions, the skeins of wool, the window sills lined with potted geraniums and cacti . . .'[5]

Fryern was the most open of houses, a mandatory first stop between London and the west. Many were invited, many more came. But the informality was testing and the welcome to strangers deceptive. Hugo Pitman remembered every window of the house lit up (though it was still light) when he first approached: 'It was like arriving at a stage set'. Through the long windows of the dining-room, he saw two figures sitting by a blazing fire. On the other side of the front door, some children moved about in the drawing-room. 'Upstairs, Augustus could be seen in bed . . .' The bell did not work, so they rattled the front door. 'Instantly every light in the house went out, except Augustus's – and his blind came down immediately.'[6]

John was emphatic about people enjoying themselves. He liked anyone who was good-looking, anyone who made him laugh. Though quickly bored he was a keen listener, shooting out scornful comments and darting from subject to subject in search of relieving entertainment. His speech was somewhat formal, old-fashioned, full of rounded phrases, though he was a good mimic and could give a wonderfully fruity impersonation of Oscar Wilde during his last years in Paris. Up in London, his deep laugh volleying round the Eiffel Tower; or seen striding about the sunlit gymkhanas where Poppet and Vivien loved to ride; or picnicking with the family on the phallic giant of Cerne Abbas; or in the evenings, seated at one end of the long scrubbed oak table opposite Dorelia, with twenty people between them, and candles, bottles of wine, he seemed lit up by joie de vivre. Broad-shouldered, athletic still in his fifties, capable of princely gestures, there was yet 'a touch of tragedy in his appearance', Adrian Daintrey observed.[7]

Parties were conspiracies of self-forgetfulness. At Fryern someone would put on the gramophone or begin playing the guitar, then singing and dancing would break out round John's Jove-like figure. Fierce fits of depression had made him dependent upon the momentary gaiety of a clamorous public whom he did not honestly admire but whom he allowed to play him out of his gloom. Hating publicity, he had become an object of this gala-world's 'image-making'. But the praise was counterfeit: fan-club hot air. As numerous letters of apology testify, he could behave rudely when drunk, but there was some integrity in this rudeness. The good things they said about him he did not believe. He could suspend disbelief, but never for long. '*La bonne peinture* is all the praise I want!' he wrote to Will Rothenstein (26 May 1936). 'I am painting better than ever before,' he growled one day to Lady Waverley. But when she congratulated him – 'How happy you must be' – he snapped back: 'You have never said anything more silly!'

That it became, with time, more difficult to flatter him stood awkwardly to his credit. But it did not make him easier. False praise, like alcohol, was ultimately a depressant, allowing him briefly to 'take off' while it drilled a deeper cavity into which he fell back. Among his family who, reflecting only distorted versions of himself, provided no escape, he was often most hostile. 'Daddy has returned to the scene so it will be gloom, gloom, gloom,' Vivien wrote in one of her letters from Fryern. Meals could be 'absolute killers' with the silence and fear that had filled his father's dining-room at Tenby. When the going was bad, John would sit, a crazed look on his face, his eyes staring. Something odd was going on inside him as he sat watching the gangway of brooding children. Almost anything they did could provoke him – the way a knife was held, the expression of a face, a chance sentence. To others he spoke in a mild cultivated voice, volunteering academic speculations about the birth of language or the origin of nomads. Then he would relapse into silence, and again something nameless appeared to be torturing him. But sometimes, when he thought no one was observing him, his whole body quivered with silent laughter.

The house was controlled by these moods. Intrigues and hostilities moved through the rooms, threatening, thundering, blowing over: and all the time something within John was shrinking. His generosity, the largeness of his attitude, these he still communicated. 'I never met any man who gave me such an immediate effect of being a great man,'[8] remembered Lord David Cecil. He was a big man: but inside the magnificent shell his real self was diminishing. One sign of this was his handwriting, which had been wild in youth, handsome and expansive in middle-age, and from the 1930s began to contract until it grew tiny – a trembling crawl across conventional small-scale writing-paper. Fryern remained a beautiful cobweb spun by Dorelia round John. Like a fly, suspended, exposed, he buzzed and was silent, buzzed and grew smaller.

Dorelia was caught too. After the war, Henry Lamb had been invalided back to England 'in a desperate state'.[9] From the General Hospital at Rouen he was sent to a hospital in London where Dorelia went to see him. 'He's not allowed more than one visit a day so it's very maddening,' she had written to Lytton Strachey (11 December 1918). '. . . His heart and nerves are in a very bad state. He's in a very comfortable place [27 Grosvenor Square] which is a blessing, and being looked after properly for the first time.' In so far as she could – though 'it's very difficult for me to get away' – Dorelia had helped him back to health. He was often at Alderney, and to be near her he set up house at No. 10 Hill Street in Poole. To the children he had been an uncle; to Dorelia he was still her other artist, the theoretical alternative reconciling her to actual life. But for John, who knew his clever criticisms, Lamb was a sparrow imitating an eagle.

There were not many opportunities for Lamb and Dorelia to escape together. After a few precious hours, 'that old tarantula Augustus' would reappear 'in his customary nimbus of boredom, silence and helpless gloom'. Dorelia would then step back into the shadows and Lamb retire bitterly alone. A drawing he did of her in 1925 shows the poignant feelings she aroused in him, and his letters to Carrington (who was herself very close to Dorelia) declare them.[10] Her sexuality trapped him. A photograph he took of her with an inviting expression, sitting naked on the wooden edge of a bath, still had the power to startle the novelist Anthony Powell over sixty years later. 'I saw at last her charm,' he wrote,[11] 'sexual attraction, hitherto hidden from me, as a force people used to talk about.' She continued to absorb Lamb's waiting life. When she fell ill he felt 'terrified', blaming John for thoughtlessly loading her with work. He tried to extricate her from the 'cataract' of hangers-on in the country, to rescue her when 'bemallorded with the old monster' in London. 'I find her quite inaccessible,' he sighed to Carrington (12 September 1925), 'and of course she makes no effort.' But there were glimpses of her, secret times when she would slip away to him, bringing plants for his garden or accompanying him to concerts.

He thought her 'as supreme as ever'. A letter from her would make him 'more éperdument [madly] amoureux than ever'; and after a telegram telling him to meet her at the station 'imagine the volcano in my soul'. It was amazing how, after a few days in his company, she would recover from 'that old wreck of a millstone round her neck'. When conducting her home to 'a very copious bed' and spending four nights with her while John was away, he felt 'some tremendous affirmation of that Spring that glimpsed on me with curious rays . . .'

Then there would be the prolonged anguish of separation. What aggravated everything was his sense that, by making Dorelia one of the most famous icons in twentieth-century British art, John had forever tied her to him. 'I have had some glimpses of her,' Lamb wrote. 'But in spite of some occasional gleams I cannot escape from the terrible feeling of a great cloud descending – dark & immoveable.'[12]

Still he persisted in the hope that she would come to him, 'and then perhaps part of the day dream could be realised . . . when that strange woman is less perplexed and all our nerves less raging.'[13] Seeing her with John's friends, it was inexplicable to Lamb why Dorelia 'willingly inflicts herself with such trials'. But by the summer of 1926 it seemed as if she were finally ready to leave. He came for her and they set off together. But 'it was no use,' Lamb wrote afterwards, 'the rain & the hopelessness of the houses seemed to penetrate her and she wanted to turn back at Salisbury. Although I carried out the plot to programme, waiting till the last minute at Upavon before springing it on her she flatly refused.' It was not until the next day that she gave Lamb the reason why she would not run off with him: 'we should never have been able to get away,'[14] she said. It would have been like her escapade with Leonard all those years ago in Bruges.

Lamb's hopes were finally extinguished by the move to Fryern. 'I think she [Dorelia] is already pretty well bored there,' he wrote sourly to Carrington not long afterwards. He had managed at last to get a divorce from Euphemia, and the next year, 1928, he married Pansy Pakenham, the eldest daughter of the sixth Earl of Longford, springing the news on Dorelia a few days beforehand.

Dorelia's life with John had been growing more difficult. She made at least two attempts to leave. Once she got so far as the railway station. A pony and trap was sent off in scalding pursuit, arriving just before the train, and she was persuaded to return. The letters John wrote whenever he was abroad reveal his dependence on her, and it was this need that held her back. Finally it was too late, too unthinkable that 'Dodo', as everyone now called her, should not always be there. She grew more fatalistic, relying on the swing of her pendulum – a ring harnessed to a piece of string – to decide everything from the wisdom of a marriage to the authenticity of a picture. From anything that might cause pain she averted her attention, though she might seem to stare at it without emotion. The range of her interests narrowed. She had stopped drawing, now she read less, and eventually would give up the piano. Nothing got on top of her, nothing came too near. She grew more interested in the vegetable world. The sounds at Fryern matched her equanimity: no longer the jaunty duets with Lamb, but a softer noise, the purring, amid the pots and plants, of the sewing-machine as she sat at it, for life as it were.

2

A LONG LOVE AFFAIR WITH DRINK

'They don't give it a name, but it seems to me rather like Winston [Churchill]'s complaint.'

Augustus John to Caspar John

In the first four years at Fryern a physical change came over John. 'He had aged very much in those years,' Diana Mosley remembered. '. . . John was fifty-three in 1931, but he seemed old, his hair was grey, his eyes bloodshot, and he already looked almost as he did in the cruelly truthful self-portrait he painted after the war.'[15]

The immediate cause of this change was alcohol. 'I drink in order to become more myself,' he stated once to Cecil Gray.[16] At Fryern he was king of the castle; but outside this castle he felt ill-at-ease. He remained loyal to one or two places – Stulik's, or the Queen's Restaurant in Sloane Square – he had made homes-from-home.

Drink changed him into a different person. It was the passport that enabled him to go anywhere, giving him the gift of tongues. After a glass or two the terrible paralysis lifted, and the warmth that had been locked up within him flowed out. But then there was a third stage, when the geniality and amorousness gave way to senseless aggression – such as punching out a cigarette on someone's face – about which he would afterwards feel baffled and ashamed.

Though he nowhere laments his mother's death when he was six, his obsessive theme as a painter – a mother with her children in an ideal landscape – illustrates the lasting effect this loss produced. If his father represented the actual world, the deprivation of his mother became the source of that fantasy world he created in its place. It was an attempt to transmute deprivation into an asset. He was still haunted by those 'delectable regions' into which Ida had disappeared. To recreate this miraculous promised land in his large-scale imaginative work – a simple, self-sufficient, tribe-like way of living, vital and primitive – within the pressure of the contemporary world, with its bureaucracy and bombs, soap kings and tax inspectors, was a lonely struggle. But alcohol, which blurred the distinction between dream and reality, lessened this sense of loss. Ida 'will always live on in your drawings',[17] Will Rothenstein had assured him. About her death, as about his mother's, he was reticent, but she had been a casualty in the warring of these worlds, committing him, if he were to find any justification for it, more deeply to the fantasy of his art.

But alcohol fulfilled another function: it screened the truth. It did so in many ways, numbing his disappointment, leading him into moods of self-deception. In the fictitious jollity of the bar, he acted happy and almost felt so. Acting, which had begun as a means to self-discovery, became a method of self-forgetfulness. It was this remoteness that people sensed about him. 'I'm sure he has no human heart,' noted Hugh Walpole in his diary (3 July 1926), 'but is "fey", a real genius from another planet than ours.'[18] But if he was not of this planet, he did not now belong to any other. 'Sometimes one feels positively the old *horror vacui* overwhelming one,' he admitted to Christabel Aberconway.[19] Although alcohol promoted a temporary sense of well-being, John had long recognized it as an enemy. 'I have never really been captured by alcohol,' he had told John Quinn in 1910, 'and I'm not going to run after it. I think any sport can be overdone; and I'm taking a real pleasure in dispensing with that form of entertainment. In a short while I shall be able to get as drunk as I like on green tea.' He made many of these 'experiments in temperance', but his drinking had got worse in the war, and worse still during his trips to the United States which seemed to prohibit temperance. Driving home in the pink light of dawn, he had been shocked to see a small herd of elephants, not realizing that they belonged to a travelling circus. He tried to pull himself together, but towards the end of the 1920s he began to have attacks of delirium tremens and appeared to be suffering from some sort of breakdown. Lamb believed these were 'some of his melodramatic methods' for stopping Dorelia from leaving him. 'I think Augustus's threatened breakdown is all fiddle dedee,' he wrote to Carrington, '. . . though I suppose he is quite plainly, though slowly, breaking up if not down.' Treatment was made difficult because John never admitted his addiction to alcohol. He prevaricated, referring to 'Neurasthenia' or even (to account for his unsteady walk) 'water on the knee'. 'There's nothing the matter with me except occasional "nerves",' he diagnosed in a letter to Ottoline Morrell (8 June 1929). On this matter of nerves he consulted Dr Maurice Wright who was 'very eminent in his own line – psychology, and he is already an old friend of mine'.[20] According to Leonard Woolf, Wright was 'an exceptionally nice and intelligent man'. He had failed to cure Leonard of his trembling hands and Virginia of her suicidal troughs of depression, though he was a man of high principle who 'knew as much

about the human mind and its illnesses'[21] as any of his contemporaries –
which, Leonard Woolf adds, 'amounted to nothing'. Discussing his difficulties with Wright, John used a rich supply of euphemisms, inviting
the psychologist to treat symptoms which, masking the real complaint, he
saw as diseases in themselves. Some of them were so bad, he joked, they
could drive a man to drink. 'You are quite right,' he wrote to Dr Gogarty,
'catarrh makes one take far more drink than one would want without it.'
Pretending to treat a variety of sicknesses, from lumbago to sinusitis, while
achieving a cure for alcoholism, was too stern a test for even so eminent
a psychologist, and these consultations came to nothing. But by the end
of March 1930, on the advice of Ottoline Morrell, John was attending
her doctor. 'Dr Cameron has done me worlds of good,' she assured him.
'He is the only really honest doctor I have found, and I have tried so
many! . . . So do, dear John, give Cameron a trial.'[22]

Dr Cameron, 'nerve specialist', was fairly knowledgeable about alcohol.
When drunk one day he ran over a child, and was sent to gaol. But he
was a persuasive man, with a nice bedside manner, and many of his
patients returned to him. Later, after a number of them had died from
his drugs, he committed suicide.

John took to Cameron at once. 'I shall bless you to the end of your
days for sending me to Dr Cameron,' he thanked Ottoline. 'Would that I
had seen him years ago. He put his finger on the spot *at once*. Already
I feel happy again and ten years younger.' The treatment involved no
surrender of pride, and John's relief came from having escaped a long
process of humiliation. Both he and Cameron knew that alcohol was the
real cause of his 'nerves', but they entered a conspiracy to gloss over this
truth. 'The defect in my works has been poisoning me for ages,' John
reported. 'It explains so much . . .'[23] Cameron's diagnosis was delivered
with a vagueness very dear to alcoholics. John had been 'overdrawing his
bank account' and should go to a convalescent home where (though
expensive in terms of money) he would make a sober investment. Under
the guise of tackling a rigorous rest cure, John allowed himself to be sent
to Preston Deanery Hall in Northampton, a briefly fashionable private
nursing home full of fumed oak, leatherette, beaten copper and suburban
mauve walls, that had opened in 1929 and was to close in 1931. Here, as
if by accident, he was removed from all alcohol though permitted to
equivocate as much as he liked. He was 'travelling in the midlands' or
suffering from a 'liver attack' or undergoing 'a thorough spring-cleaning'
because 'my guts weren't behaving harmoniously'. His friends were generally optimistic. 'Any place apart from the world is a good idea for a bit,
and it will do no harm to try it,' Eve Fleming wrote to him. 'You must
get well, & I do hope this will do the trick.'[24] Expressing her gratitude

for Ottoline's 'great brain wave', Dorelia wrote on 5 May 1930: 'Of course J. would be perfectly well without wine or spirits. Many a time I've managed to keep him without any for *weeks* and then some idiot has undone all my good work in one evening. He may be impressed this time. All the other doctors have said the same, Dr Wright included. One can only hope to do one's best . . .'

What Dorelia did not perhaps appreciate was that the first phase of a successful cure must be the patient's admission that he needs special treatment for alcoholism. This admission John was never required to make. He stayed at the nursing home a month, and his treatment appears to have been largely custodial, with a few vitamin supplements, nuts, caraway seeds and some tranquillizing drugs served on silver platters by footmen. 'They are making a good job of me, I feel,' he announced.[25] '. . . I am a different being and they tell me in a week or two I'll be as strong again as a horse.' He was allowed out with another inmate for a 'debauch of tea and toast' and by himself to Cambridge for a drink 'of coffee with Quiller-Couch and a bevy of exquisite undergrads', as well as for walks to the church and, more recklessly, drives in his car. In the absence of gypsies, he made friends with 'some nice animals', cows and sheep mostly; while indoors there were erotic glimpses of a remarkable chambermaid. He read voraciously, but was sometimes 'rather forlorn'. 'If I were not beginning to feel as I haven't felt for years I *might* be bored,' he threatened in a note to Ottoline, who had entered the nursing home herself for a few days, ' – as it is – I am smiling to myself, as at some huge joke.'

The presence of Ottoline helped to reconcile John to Preston Deanery Hall. He insisted that she came and sat by his bed and, after his morning exercises on the 'electric belly-waggler', photographed his new ethereal-ized figure. Ottoline was likewise convinced that she looked 'much younger since I went to Dr Cameron. Everyone exclaims so.' It was, she added, 'so depressing to look like a wreck'. John gallantly affirmed that she was 'more paintable than ever', at which she suddenly took fright. So they discussed other people such as Henry Lamb, who was said to be curing himself of his Augustus John 'infection' in the company of Stanley and Gilbert Spencer, but whose case (so Dorelia had told Ottoline) 'was more serious than John's'.[26] As for John himself, Ottoline couldn't help reflecting 'how like he has become to Asquith, who had his two failings, drink and women.' Every day he entreated her to keep him company, and when Philip Morrell arrived to fetch her away, he came down to the front door to wave them off. He looked, she thought, 'like the boy who had been left behind at the school gate'.[27]

After Ottoline had gone, John could not stay there long. Instead he 'had it out with the doctor' and left a week earlier than planned. 'No doubt I'll have to follow a regime for a while,' he warned Dorelia. 'They say I'll be marvellously well in about 10 days after leaving.'[28] His aftercare came in the form of a diet. 'Unfortunately I have lost that almost ethereal quality which I had so welcomed,' he told Ottoline (23 May 1930). '. . . I blame the cook for giving me unauthorized potatoes and beef steak.'

'You'd be all right if you lived sensibly,' Eve Fleming instructed him. 'You're as strong as twelve lions by nature.'[29] But sense of this sort was unavailable to him: 'I who always live from hand to mouth and have so little practical sense.'[30] He was awash with optimism. His strong constitution, with its extraordinary powers of recovery, quickly misled him. Austerity, he claimed, had made him 'much more like myself' – though he had also bought a new hat which was making him 'a different person and a better'. One way or another he felt like 'a giant refreshed'.[31]

It was not long before he relapsed into drinking, and the deterioration went on. 'John is in ruins,' T. E. Lawrence noted in 1932, 'but a giant of a man. Exciting, honest, uncanny.'[32] He never quite became a chronic drinker – 'I was never a true alcoholic,' he admitted to Mavis Wheeler. From time to time he went back to doctors who tried to remove him from alcohol altogether. But Dorelia's tactics worked better. She rationed him with lock and key at home, and in restaurants would furtively empty his glass. Without drink he tended to avoid people: 'I find my fellow-creatures very troublesome to contend with without stupéfiant,' he told Christabel Aberconway. He still retreated into the comforting womb of pubs 'to get alone for a bit'.[33] A solitary figure in a muffler, booted and corduroyed, he sat quietly in a corner, drinking his beer. Latterly he consumed far less, because his tolerance to alcohol had diminished. Conger Goodyear, who had been so struck by his capacity at the Saturn Club in the 1920s, was regretting by the 1940s that 'his ancient alcoholic prowess had departed', and after a few drinks 'Augustus did not improve'.[34]

The loss of confidence, the upsurges of temper, the tremulousness of his hands, his inability to make decisions – all grew more pronounced. He knew the truth, but would not hear it from anyone. But it amused him sometimes to make people connive at his inventions – then, with disconcerting relish, come out with the facts. 'I have heard of a new treatment for my complaint – it consists of total abstention from liquor.'[35] At other times he would innocently complain of Dodo that she smoked too much; or of J. B. Manson (who was dismissed as Director of the Tate Gallery) that 'the fellow drinks', deliberately slurring his words as he spoke.

Intermittently between bursts of renewed effort, he drank to destroy himself. If he could not paint well, and could not disguise his inability to do so, then he was better dead. But Dorelia, who had tolerated so much, would not tolerate this. Her watchfulness, care, relentless programme of regular meals and early nights, propped him up and pulled him through – the ghost of an artist he had once been.

3

IN SPITE OF EVERYTHING OR BECAUSE OF IT

'I still draw a little.'
Augustus John to T. E. Lawrence

The first test came that summer of 1930. He had been invited by Gogarty to assist at the opening of his hotel, Renvyle House, in Connemara. Yeats was also coming, and Gogarty arranged for John to do a 'serious portrait' of him. 'I would think it a great honour,' Yeats had murmured. But standing before the mirror, he began to examine himself with some apprehension, 'noticing certain lines about my mouth and chin marked strongly by shadows', and to wonder 'if John would not select those very lines and lay great emphasis upon them, and, if some friends complain that he has obliterated what good looks I have, insist that those lines show character, and perhaps that there are no good looks but character.'[36]

Early that summer Yeats learnt that the city of Cork had rejected John's earlier portrait of him 'because of my attack on the censorship & my speech about divorce', choosing instead 'as an expression of Cork piety and patriotism'[37] a picture of the Prince of Wales by the Irish painter James Barry. At about the same time he received a letter from Gogarty saying that John wished to paint a portrait of him in his maturity. 'John is to paint me at Renvyle,' he wrote from Italy to Lady Gregory (27 June 1930), 'and I will try to go there at once . . .' The sittings began in the third week of July, and Yeats himself was soon writing that it 'promises to be a masterpiece – amusing – a self I do not know but am delighted to know, a self that I could never have found out for myself, a gay, whimsical person which I could never find in the solemnity of the looking-glass. Is it myself? – it is certainly what I would like to be.'[38]

But a couple of days later, John 'somewhat spoiled that portrait & has laid it aside', so Yeats reported; adding, ' – I like him will endow it later with vice or virtue according to mood . . . He started another much larger portrait to-day which is more "monumental" – his word – [and] has less comedy. It is a fine thing.'[39] It was at this point that John laid down his brushes and, joined by Caspar, who had flown over in his little Avro

Avian, went off for three days to 'Galway races & attendant activities' where the enjoyment rose to such a level they 'had the ambulances out'.[40]

John seems to have been in two minds about Yeats. He noticed, with surprise, that Yeats had made the mistake of growing older, and was 'now a mellow, genial and silver haired old man'.[41] He had put on weight, seemed vaguely distrustful and, despite the vastly poetical manner, looked somehow less Yeats-like. Yeats himself had noted 'marks of recent illness, marks of time, growing irresolution, perhaps some faults that I have long dreaded; but then my character is so little myself that all my life it has thwarted me.' This was a development very close to John's own, explaining why observers such as Robert Graves could dismiss them both as poseurs. 'Lord and Lady Longford had fetched him [Yeats] over to be painted,' John remembered.

'The conversation at dinner consisted of a succession of humorous anecdotes by Yeats, chiefly on the subject and at the expense of George Moore, punctuated by the stentorian laughter of his Lordship and the more discreet whinny of his accomplished wife. I was familiar with most of these stories before, or variants of them: for the Irish literary movement nourished itself largely on gossip . . . My difficulties while painting Yeats were not lightened by the obligation of producing an appreciative guffaw at the right moment, and I fear my timing was not always correct.'[42]

It was Yeats's melancholy that John recognized, and shied away from. 'The portrait represents the poet in his old age,' Gogarty records. 'He is seated with a rug round his knees and his broad hat on his lap. His white hair is round his head like a nimbus, and behind him the embroidered cloths of heaven are purple and silver. It is the last portrait of Yeats.'[43]

Once this portrait was finished, John was free to do whatever he wanted. What he wanted was to go to Galway City. Denouncing Renvyle as too 'new and raw', off he went. From O'Flaherty's bar and from parties flowing with barmaids on and around Francis Macnamara's boat *Mary Anne*, he was eventually fished up and carried back to Renvyle where an admiring entourage had assembled – the painters Adrian Daintrey and George Lambourn, and any number of painterly girls including 'the ladies Dorothea and Lettice Ashley-Cooper', and their sister Lady Alington who 'has been posing for him and does not confine it to that'.[44] To this number a beautiful American, Hope Scott, added herself, arriving in Dublin straight from Pennsylvania and being rushed across Ireland in a hearse. Her first sight of John, his beard caught by the sun, his eyes gleaming with anticipation, was at a ground-floor window. The hearse door was flung open, and 'I fell out on my head.'[45]

John painted most days, Adrian Daintrey and George Lambourn acting as pacemakers. But every evening there were parties, and the effect of these began to infiltrate the day. His seclusion in Preston Deanery Hall seems to have precipitated two reactions: a greater urgency in his pursuit of girls, and a crippling anxiety over his work. 'Though I was sitting, I did not lack exercise. Most of Augustus's models found themselves doing a good bit of sprinting round the studio,' recalled Mrs Scott, the original for the heroine in Philip Barry's play *The Philadelphia Story* (later refilmed as *High Society*), into whose bed John was prevented from blundering by the presence of a bolster he angrily mistook for Adrian Daintrey. But Hope Scott also noticed: 'He was enormously concentrated, at times he seemed actually to suffer over his work.'

Dodo and Poppet, who had gone with him to Ireland, left early. To them, arranged as a compliment, he confided his depression: 'J'étais dans un gloom affreux quand tu et Dodo êtes parties. Tu pourrais bien m'avoir embrassé . . .'

To shed this black mood in some new climate became the theme of this decade. He travelled to the Hebrides, to Jersey, Cornwall and, for short visits, back to Wales. Now that he no longer had the Villa Ste-Anne, he stayed during part of two winters at Cap Ferrat with Sir James Dunn 'the friendly financier'.[46] But John failed to please Dunn. 'Dunn's quarrels with John over the various portraits were furious,' Lord Beaverbrook wrote, 'and much tough language was tossed to and fro, without reaching any conclusion . . . John, however, gave as much as he got.'[47] These fashionable pleasure grounds, full of millionaire property owners flying like migratory birds of prey back to Big Business after the season was over, increased John's depression. 'I could find nothing in Cap Ferrat to excite me, and with a violent effort of will we pulled ourselves together and decamped.'

Other journeys were rather more productive. In October 1930 he set off with Dodo to see a 'tremendous' Van Gogh exhibition in Amsterdam, and from there went on alone to Paris, where he polished off some drawings of James Joyce. 'He sits patiently,' John noted in a letter to Dodo. A photograph of the two of them, in which John appears the more anxious to take part, shows Joyce as upright and foursquare, his head rigidly tilted back and with dark glasses ('his mug is largely occluded by several pairs of powerful lenses,' John told T. E. Lawrence) – and John gripping him, brandishing his pipe, apparelled in a pugilist's dressing gown. Joyce wanted a drawing for what John called his 'quite unsingable "Pomes"', which had been set to music by various composers and edited for the Sylvan Press by Herbert Hughes under the title *The Joyce Book*. But had John done justice to the lower part of his face? Some of the

drawings were so spare, so 'School of Paris', that Joyce could hardly make
out the lines at all. 'Praise from a purblind penny poet would be ridiculous,' he later wrote when thanking John for the portrait in the book.
'. . . Do you remember that you promised my wife one of the others you
made – the one that made her cry?'[48]

All these places – France, which he loved; Wales, where he belonged;
Ireland, which had once suggested great pictures to him – recalled a past
John could not re-enter. What he now sought was somewhere without
associations. It was this need that persuaded him, in December 1932, to
try what he described as a 'health trip'[49] to Majorca. But there had been
rain and heavy air. The island might have been what he was looking for,
but 'big operations' were going on 'with screeching rock-drills and a
general banging of machinery'. The developers had arrived; he was too
late. Feeling 'like death', he returned with the news that Majorca was 'not
paintable'.[50]

Back in the mellowness of Fryern Court, he racked his brains, consulted
maps, looked up trains and boats, and, retrieving a plan from the spring
of 1912, settled on Venice. His last illuminating weeks in Italy had been
nearly twenty-two years ago. Now, entering at another great centre of
Italian painting, he seems to have tried a similar experiment. With him
travelled his daughter Vivien, aged eighteen, 'to keep an eye on the
money'.[51] John, 'determined to see all the famous paintings', spent hours
in the Venetian churches, looking at the Tiepolo frescoes at San Francesco
della Vigna, the Titians and the Bellini triptych at the Frari, the huge
works by Tintoretto at Santa Maria dell'Orto, the Veronese ceiling in San
Sebastiano. He was curious about the Ferrarese painters of the fifteenth
century with their unusual dry style, and made expeditions to Ferrara to
study Pisanello and Piero della Francesca, and the grand fantasies of
Francesco del Cossa with their vivid naturalistic detail. There was much
to enchant him, but past masterpieces no longer seemed capable of reviving
his own work. 'I rather felt I was a few centuries late for Venice,' he
wrote, 'but all the same it was wonderful.' Possibly these pictures showed
up his limitations too painfully; or perhaps he had cast a shadow over the
past, or simply let trivialities and enjoyments get in the way. 'I saw many
pictures but left many unseen,' he wrote, 'and I met a lot of people I
knew there some of whom I would prefer to have avoided.'[52]

On landing at the steps of his hotel the first day, he had been hailed
from a passing gondola by Sacheverell Sitwell's wife, Georgia. From that
moment, word getting round, he was sucked into 'the maelstrom of
Venetian society', he wrote to Dodo (29 August 1933). '. . . the place is
full of bores, buggers and bums of all kinds. Vivien is greatly in request
and there are various optimistic members of the local aristocracy on her

tracks. Conditions are not favourable for painting and money goes like water, so I think an early return is indicated.' Much of this time Vivien was in tears, and John, though generally protective, burst into sudden fits of anger, complaining that her clothes were *too smart*. 'The air of Venice was getting me down,' he acknowledged. 'I became more and more indolent . . . it was the people I tired of most. My God, what a set! . . . I was seeing less of Vivien . . . but at last even my daughter agreed it was time to depart.'[53]

He had done little painting. What eluded him lay in his receding imagination. A yearning for distant scenes and the impulse towards flight overwhelmed him. They overwhelmed him, but he could not act on them. Like a giant ship stranded in shallow water, its propellers gyrating in the air, he stayed.

But one last voyage awaited him – had awaited him, by the time he embarked, for twenty-six years. 'I think Jamaica would be a nice place to go and work,' he had written to Dorelia. That was in September 1911. 'I think of going to Jamaica,' he repeated in a letter to Vera Stubbs on 4 June 1929. By 1936, the effects of his renewed drinking had led him to consult an occultist who proposed casting John's horoscope. This exercise led to the prediction that he would turn up soon in one of the British colonies. 'I would have been sorry to leave the astrologer's forecast unful-filled and his prophetic gift in dispute,' John wrote. '. . . I decided [on] a visit to Jamaica.'

Dodo was set on joining the adventure. With them went Vivien, Francis Macnamara's daughter Brigit, now 'une grosse blonde . . . très aimable',[54] and a mysterious child called Tristan, also blond but aged two and a half, who 'imagines himself to be the Captain of this ship'.[55] The tropics suited John. Though the island was 'altogether too fertile', parts of it reminded him of North Wales. The internal conflict he carried wherever he went externalized itself in Jamaica very satisfactorily. The enemy were the bridge-players, golf club members, and the management of the American United Fruit Company. His allies were the natives. There were similar distractions to those in Venice, but he controlled them better. 'We are in some danger of being launched into the beau monde of Jamaica. Nobody believes I am serious when I tell them I am only interested in painting the coloured people,' he wrote to Tristan's mother, Mavis de Vere Cole (10 March 1937). '. . . I shall have a mass of work done before I am finished.' Jamaica activated him more than Italy had done, perhaps because the past could speak to him more immediately through these living models than through the pictures of Renaissance Venice. It appeared to him that these Jamaicans still inhabited a freer, more natural world than the embattled, illiberal, over-policed states which modern industrialized countries had created and were attempting to impose on them.

To gain extra time for himself, Jamaica being so expensive, he dispatched 'the females and Tristan' back to England after a month, and continued working alone until the rains came six weeks later. 'I hated leaving you,' Dorelia wrote on board the SS *Aciguani*, 'but doubtless you are getting on very well and doing the work you wanted to.' In *Chiaroscuro*, where he devotes over ten pages to this time,[56] John records that he felt 'anything but satisfied' with his painting. Like gypsies, the native Jamaicans were elusive. In a perfect world he would have built a 'house of mud, mahogany and palms' and lived there as one of them. Instead – the ultimate degradation – he was taken for a visiting politician. Yet, the place 'suits me and stimulates me', he decided. 'I am painting with a renewal of energy quite remarkable and will not cease till I have accomplished much.'[57]

With the rains 'a great gloom descended upon me, almost depriving me of volition'. He returned on a banana boat to England and Fryern and struggled to work up these pictures before his memories slid behind an invisible screen of habit. His portraits of 'Aminta', 'Daphne', 'Phyllis' and many others delighted London when they were exhibited at Tooth's Gallery in May and June 1938. The show, Dudley Tooth noted in his diary, 'has been a tremendous success, nearly everything having been sold at prices between £200 and £550' [equivalent to between £5,700 and £15,600 in 1996]. Among the purchasers were J. B. Priestley, Mrs Syrie Maugham, Vincent Massey, Oswald Birley, Sir Lawrence Phillips and Sir Stafford Cripps, the announcement of whose purchase was, to his horror, splashed across the *Evening Standard*.

These Jamaican pictures, constructed rather as a modeller builds up his clay to make shapes, represent the most vigorous body of John's work over the last thirty years of his career. The exhibition gave art critics an opportunity to reflect upon the curious narrative of his career and find reasons for its decline.

The most hostile critic was Clive Bell. 'If only Augustus John had been serious,' he wrote in the *New Statesman*,[58] 'what a fine painter he might have been.' Bell's review was an attempt to reconcile his early admiration for John's paintings with this later disappointment. In a few of the Jamaican portraits, where the 'impression though banal is vivid, the execution telling, and the placing happy, one finds the ghost of that great talent with which Augustus John was blest,' Bell argued. 'As a rule, however, there is less talent than trick; and there is no thought at all.' Bell's conclusion was that John lacked the intellectual powers of composition that were the mature test of an artist's ability. Undoubtedly he scored some successes, but they had 'the air of a fluke'.

In the *Spectator*,[59] Anthony Blunt confronted the same question with more difficulty. 'Everyone is agreed on the fact that Augustus John was born with a quite exceptional talent for painting – some even use the word genius, – and almost everyone is agreed that he has in some way wasted it,' Blunt began. '. . . [But] it is extremely hard to see just where John's paintings fail. For myself I find it impossible to put my finger on the point.' Instead of a point, Blunt drew a line of gradually lessening vitality and concentration along John's career. For him the great work, akin to that of masters from the past, was 'represented by the portrait heads in two coloured chalks which date from the turn of the century.

'In these drawings John gave proof of a quality which does not seem to reappear in his work, namely, humility in the face of nature. He is not prepared to take nature as the basis for a technical experiment, but is willing to follow her in all her tiresome intricacies. These early drawings have a sort of industrious observation which distinguishes them from all the later productions. For even in the oil sketches of the next period John is already letting himself go in a sort of mannerism, though the mannerism is so brilliant that one is at first willing to accept it as a serious basis for painting.'

John portraits, Blunt argued, were based on a sound technical brilliance that 'will stand the most minute study, and even study over a long period, without becoming thin. It is only in his methods of dealing with the psychological problems presented by his sitters that his shorthand appears. Even in such a masterly work as the Suggia one grows tired of the over-emphatic gesture before one has finished admiring the brilliance of the drawing and the brush-work.'

John's recent work, his portraits and figure-studies, were solidly constructed, Blunt acknowledged, but had lost the brilliance of his earlier paintings without regaining the meticulous care of his initial drawings. Blunt likened his last landscapes to work by Matisse and Derain: 'to Matisse in the insubstantial flatness of the objects, to Derain in much of the colour.'

Blunt ended his review more handsomely than Bell. 'It is only because his gifts are so great that one is forced to judge him by the very highest, that he seems to fail.' Both Bell and Blunt were attempting to come to terms with the corrosion of a predominantly lyrical talent which had interpreted landscape, and figures in landscape, or the solitary figure drawn in preparation for placing in the landscape, through poetic or visionary eyes. But as Richard Shone later pointed out, 'this lyrical mode belongs essentially to youth (as so often in poetry) and it is rare . . . for the artist to effect a successful transformation as he grows older'[60] – though this was the transformation Yeats had achieved.

To his old sparring partner Wyndham Lewis, John appeared to have briefly regained something of his youth, and he gave these Jamaican pictures a splendid celebration in the *Listener*:

'As one passes in review these blistered skins of young African belles, with their mournful doglike orbs, and twisted lips like a heavyweight pugilist, one comes nearer to the tragedy of this branch of the human race than one would in pictures more literary in intention . . .

Mr John opens his large blue eyes, and a dusky head bursts into them. His . . . brushes stamp out on the canvas a replica of what he sees. But what he sees (since he is a very imaginative man) is all the squalor and beauty of the race – of this race of predestined underdogs . . .

Nature is for him like a tremendous carnival, in the midst of which he finds himself. But there is nothing of the spectator about Mr John. He is very much a part of the saturnalia. And it is only because he enjoys it so tremendously that he is moved to report upon it – in a fever of optical emotion, before the object selected passes on and is lost in the crowd.'[61]

Over thirty years earlier, in the second issue of *Blast*,[62] Lewis had faulted his friend for his *fin-de-siècle* leanings, lack of discipline and premature artistic impotence. In a letter written shortly afterwards he went on to accuse him of dropping into the rather stagnant trough that followed the heights of Victorianism. 'You begin by shipwrecking yourself on all sorts of romantic reefs,' he had written. '. . . Whether a craft is still sea-worthy after such buccaneering I dont know. But lately you have not, to put it mildly, advanced in your work. That you will enter the history books, you know, of course! Blast is a history book, too. You will not be a legendary and immaculate hero, but a figure of controversy, nevertheless.'[63]

It was John's place in art history that Lewis now began to re-examine. When looking back along 'a narrative of my career up to date' in *Rude Assignment*, he told a story from the Great War. 'When Mars with his mailed finger showed me a shell-crater and a skeleton, with a couple of shivered tree-stumps behind it, I was still in my "abstract" element. And before I knew quite what I was doing I was drawing with loving care a signaller corporal to plant upon the lip of the shell-crater.'[64] In other words, he was doing a John drawing and placing John's work in the margins of Vorticism.

Four years later, in *The Demon of Progress in the Arts*, Lewis drew a lesson from this experience in a passage that explains how John's example at its worst – the attitudinizing properties of 'your stage-gypsies . . . [and]

your boring Borrovian cult of the Gitane' – off which Lewis had ricocheted into Vorticism in 1913, later helped him in its better aspects to escape from the inhumanity of prolonged abstraction. 'What I was headed for, obviously,' he wrote, 'was to fly away from the world of men, of pigs, of chickens and alligators, and go to live in the unwatered moon, only a moon sawed up into square blocks, in the most alarming way. What an escape I had!'[65]

John had long ceased to be a champion of the young. To them he appeared a figure without modern interest, someone who had 'made a pact with social success at the expense of painting', though he barked beautifully before parties of lion hunters. But when Lewis's young disciples such as Geoffrey Grigson questioned his good opinion of such a 'vulgar art-school draughtsman with a provincial mind',[66] Lewis found it difficult to make them understand what John represented to artists of his generation. He had buried 'the mock naturalists and pseudo–impressionists' and, as the legitimate successor of Beardsley, had contributed a new vitality to the last few years of the nineteenth century and the first dozen years of the twentieth.

No one cared very much in the last twenty-five years of John's life how he drew and painted: it was what he stood for, as the most celebrated British artist in the first part of the twentieth century, that counted. This was why, for example, he was formally associated (along with John Nash, Vanessa Bell and Duncan Grant) with a new school of drawing and painting, started in 1937 by Claude Rogers, Victor Pasmore and William Coldstream to free the study of drawing and painting from the teaching of the applied arts and commercial and industrial design. He had become somewhat ludicrously what Yeats called 'a public event': the sort of famous person for whom admirers liked to knit 'tortoiseshell earflaps' or a 'pair of blinders' to wear 'when Ladies invite you to teas'; someone asked to paint the portrait of a dog ('I could bring him to see you at any time'), or to judge the Fordingbridge Cricket Club's Beauty Competition ('select at your leisure among all the ladies in the room, during dances and intervals').[67]

This comic celebrity irritated young people, but amused Lewis. In the course of their teasing and testing relationship, Lewis often mocked John for having become 'an institution like Madame Tussaud's', inquiring at one point if he was yet 'a Futuriste' or whether he planned to advance on the Louvre and 'put your foot through the Mona Lise'. And John would intermittently acknowledge that such thrusts were 'salutary and well-deserved'.

In *Rude Assignment* Lewis pays tribute to John's intelligence and wide reading. Yet John's art was curiously unallied to his intelligence. He was,

Lewis told Grigson, 'an Eye' and if the Eye 'happened to fall on the right object' the results were good. Both of them did too many potboilers, too much undistinguished work for money – John more than Lewis. But for all their quarrelling, this patriarch and his cadet were kindred spirits with a common 'Enemy' in the previous generation, and they reinforced in each other Oscar Wilde's belief that 'it is only shallow people who do not judge from appearances. The mystery of the world is the visible, not the invisible.'

*

As if to avoid comparison with past work, and bring about a rebirth of his talent, John occasionally tried out new genres. In 1929 the theatre producer C. B. Cochran had agreed to employ him as designer for the controversial second act of Sean O'Casey's play *The Silver Tassie*. John had got to know O'Casey through a Belfast friend of Gogarty's called William McElroy ('a kind of minor Horatio Bottomley', John called him), who occupied himself as coal merchant, impresario and part-racehorse owner ('the left hind leg, I think it was'). The three of them would dine together at the Queen's Restaurant off Sloane Square, and despite the fact that both John and O'Casey liked to dominate the conversation, they got on well. 'He's a splendid fellow, & utterly unspoilt,' O'Casey wrote in 1926. 'Says I'm a great Dramatist & slaps me on the back for breaking every damned rule of the Stage.'[68] That year John painted two portraits of O'Casey, one of them completed in an all-day sitting between eleven o'clock in the morning and half-past four in the afternoon. 'Uncanny, powerful, embarrassingly vivid,' O'Casey described it: 'an alert concentration wearing a look of (to me) shuddering agony'.[69] O'Casey already owned a John 'Head of a Gitana' and, on his marriage to the beautiful Eileen Reynolds, John gave the couple one of his portraits – 'a princely gift' which they hung in their sitting-room over the mantelpiece.[70]

It was Eileen O'Casey who had put forward John's name for *The Silver Tassie*. She called on him at Mallord Street like 'an angel rushing in where a devil feared to tread'.[71] There was, she noticed, 'a debutante trying to get in, ringing the bell, appearing at various windows'. John ignored this as they talked over the project. The play was fine, but he had qualms. 'I have never done one before; I don't really think I could.' He was, Eileen remembered, 'extremely shy, though as ever courteous and complimentary, for he liked good-looking women. This helped me to plead my cause.' At the end of the afternoon, she asked: 'Have I persuaded you?' 'I'm afraid you have,' he replied.[72]

Everything seemed to go with surprising ease. 'I have the Silver Tassie with me,' he had written from Cap Ferrat on 3 February 1929, 'and I don't see much difficulty about the second act'. O'Casey had described this act in detail: a War Zone, its 'jagged and lacerated ruin of what was once a monastery', the life-size crucifix, stained-glass window, and great howitzer with 'long sinister barrel now pointing towards the front at an angle of forty-five degrees'. In a note he had added: 'Every feature of the scene seems a little distorted from its original appearance.' All this approximated closely to what John had wanted to depict as a war artist and, given this new impetus, he turned to his sketchbooks of France. But when Raymond Massey, who was directing the play, called on John in September, he found him distracted and nervous, with 'not only an open mind but a blank one'. He was shown some of the large charcoal drawings John had done as a war artist, and they settled on one of a ruined chapel as the basis of the design. Massey gave a number of John's war sketches – 'frightening, grizzly and jagged, O'Casey's scene was there' – to the scene painters and builders, but he wanted John himself to paint the Madonna for the stained-glass window. His hopes ran out on set-up day when he made alternative arrangements for a scene painter to do the work – at which point John, 'his great black hat cocked over his forehead', lurched into the theatre, sauntered down the aisle, climbed unsteadily on to the stage flooded in harsh work-lights, and silently surveyed the bone-yard scene. Then he took up a stick of charcoal, moved towards the window frame lying on the floor, and made a firm stroke on the oiled silk.

'He worked as though possessed and for more than two hours he never looked up,' Raymond Massey remembered. '. . . the crew watched in fascination. At last it was done. He moved to the side of the stage and stood waiting. Without a word, two stagehands lifted the window piece and braced it in position. The master electrician connected the cable and set the lights for act 2. And there shone the Madonna of *The Silver Tassie* . . . We cheered Augustus John. He did not hear us; he just stood there looking at his scene. He was pleased with it. He left, swaying slightly.'[73]

O'Casey too was pleased. He had been nervous of Eileen's impetuosity, then anxious over John's commitment to his play. But the overpowering[74] effect of the design delighted him, – and also Bernard Shaw, who pronounced 'the second act a complete success for both of you'.[75]

John also felt excited by what seemed a new arena in which to exercise his talent. He was starting to design the sets of Constant Lambert's ballet *Pomona* for the Camargo Society, when he went into Preston Deanery Hall. In the following years there were many rumours of his re-entry into the theatre, but all came to nothing until, in 1935, at Cochran's suggestion, he agreed to do the scenery and costumes for J. M. Barrie's *The Boy David*.

The changes that had overtaken John in the seven years between the two plays are very clear. On 25 October 1935, Cochran sent John a letter confirming the details of their arrangement. Less than two months later, he was sending out an SOS for Ernst Stern, who had been the chief designer to Max Reinhardt and was the most professional artist in the theatre of his day. With the exception of Barrie, everyone in the production had taken to John at once. 'John, in his extraordinary innocence of the theatre, was never too proud to defer to their expertise,' recorded Malcolm Easton. 'On them, and on all Cochran's brilliant band of technicians, he smiled benevolently. From the benevolence, however, proceeded few practical results ... John's efforts to envisage Barrie's characters rarely got further than the upper half of the body. When it was a question of the precise cut of the skirt of a tunic, exact length of a cloak, or clothing of the legs, it seemed that, like Byron, he *never looked so low*.'[76] These tactics had driven the needlewomen to despair, given Barrie a high temperature and aggravated Cochran's arthritis for which, at rehearsals, he wore a splint. It was to everyone's relief, John's included, that Stern took over these costumes.

To Barrie's irritation, John had depicted Bethlehem as a Provençal village, decorated with terraces, boulders and cypress trees. The principal set, and John's main contribution to the play, was the Israelite outpost of Act II, scene ii. For this he provided 'a dark and lowering sky, with immense rocks in the foreground, from which descended a slender waterfall, giving rise to the brook from the bed of which David chose the pebbles he was to sling at Goliath'.[77] Although attending a few rehearsals – 'an impressive figure splendidly sprawled across two stalls'[78] – he did not travel up to see the opening night at Edinburgh. The greatest problem that night had been how to force the actors on and off stage. 'Having delivered their exit line,' John Brunskill, the scenery builder, remembered, 'they were forced to clamber over a number of rocks before getting off stage.' By the end of the scene the stage was crowded with these bruised and scrambling actors attempting to reach or retire from their lines. In a desperate move to halt these gymnastics, Cochran again called on Stern, this time to redesign the set. Numbers of rock units were scrapped, the sky was replaced with a white canvas cloth, the inset scenes altered and, worst of all, John's waterfall – 'how charmingly it glittered and fell!' – dried up. Stern, who respected John, describing him as 'the typical painter, and we understand one another', hated this work which, he felt, went against the 'artists' freemasonry'. Such was the guilt that no one dared to tell John of the alterations. He arrived at His Majesty's Theatre for the London première on 12 December 1936 happily ignorant of the fearful mutilations.

The change to Act I had been minimal, and John sat through it undisturbed. But when the curtain rose on Act II, he rose from his seat, left the auditorium, and stayed for the rest of the performance in the bar, pondering this betrayal. 'This play was a complete flop from the start, and I wasn't sorry.' But later, having been handsomely paid by Cochran, he admitted: 'It dawned on me too late that I had neither the technique nor the physical attributes for this sort of work, apart from the question of my artistic ability.' Stern's final comment, which achieves unconscious irony, corroborates this: 'How I envy John, as he stands in front of his easel, palette and brushes in hand.'

Alone with his easel, palette and brushes, John could only point to failures in geography, to weather and viruses. Also studios. 'A sympathetic studio is *very* hard to find,' he admitted to Lord Duveen's daughter, Dolly. In June 1935 he borrowed Vanessa Bell's studio; by November that year he had moved into Euphemia's house at 49 Glebe Place, Chelsea (later owned by Gerald Reitlinger and by Edward Le Bas); and in March 1938 he rented the 'cottage' in Primrose Codrington's estate, famous for its garden, at Park House in South Kensington. From these places he came and went, tampering with their lighting then leaving them for good. In 1940, when bombs began falling on London, the top windows of Park Studio, fantastically illuminated in the night sky, were smashed, and John moved on to 33 Tite Street, in Chelsea, where Whistler and Sargent had lived, and where he rested in battered comfort throughout the Blitz.

'My life seems to get more and more complicated,' he wrote wonderingly.[79] The multiplicity of studios, reflecting this confusion, extended beyond England. In 1936 Dorelia had rented, 'for the large sum' of twelve pounds a year, the Mas de Galeron, a little farmhouse 'au ras des Alpilles' behind 'les Antiques' at St-Rémy-de-Provence.[80] Though it was merely a modest grey old building, 'I really couldn't resist it,' she wrote to him from Cannes. 'There are 3 large rooms and one smaller one,' she added. 'One would make a good studio for you. It is quite isolated with a rather rough track ... There are grey rocks on one side, vines and olives and an immense view from the north ... Why not come down?'

John went down for the first time in September 1937 and, despite his worst fears (imagining Dorelia might have gone mad), he loved it. The house was built into the hillside, its floors uneven, with small surprising rooms turning up round corners and down steps. Outside, a hot aromatic terrace, flanked by pine trees, overlooked a field of stones, olives and euphorbias. Above ran the chain of rocky Alpilles, dotted with green scrub and the plumes of cypress trees – 'an endless sequence of exquisite landscapes'.[81] Anyone who knows and likes this landscape will enjoy John's paintings of it, recognize how accurately he has observed it. Yet these paintings lack the inspirational quality of his early landscapes, and he confessed to his neighbour there, Marie Mauron, that 'ces Alpilles attendent encore *leur* peintre – mais ce n'est pas moi. Regardez! Ces jeux de gris, de bleu, de rose, ces touffes de plantes aromatiques, en boules, taches, traits sur le roc de toutes couleurs insaisissables, me désespèrent.'[*][82]

The next year he went again, and once more in July 1939 with Dorelia, Vivien, Zoë and Tristan, intending to stay there three months. 'Il n'y aura pas de guerre,' Derain scoffed as the two artists sat peacefully drinking on the terrace of the Café des Variétés and watching the soldiers and horses crowd through the streets. 'C'est une blague.' But it was becoming, John suspected, 'necessary to make a decision'. Eventually, responding to urgent telephone calls from Poppet ('I told them there was a man called Hitler . . .'), Dorelia decided they must leave. They set off, John gaining maximum delay with the aid of dictionaries, by sending a long telegram to England in very correct French. 'C'est la guerre! C'est la guerre!' the farmers greeted them, as they fumed and thundered through the villages in a furious convoy of two cars. At Orléans they put up for one night, and while Dorelia and Tristan slept, John escorted Vivien and Zoë to a club run by a couple of spinsters from Kensington, and full of the jolliest girls. 'And what do you do, sir?' one of them asked John. 'I am a ballet dancer,' he replied.

Le Havre, which they reached on 2 September, was in terrible confusion. There were no porters, the last boat was preparing to leave and passengers were told they must abandon their cars and take only what luggage they could carry. John's car had now run dry of petrol and rested on a rival passenger's baggage. Money changed hands, and somehow the cars were hauled on board. John, in a huge chequered overcoat, was the last to embark, tugging a large travelling rug out of which splashed a bottle of Châteauneuf du Pape. 'Really it was a magnificent exit,' wrote Vivien, 'if one hadn't already been overdosed with similar rich occurrences . . .'[83]

They motored back to Fryern. Next morning John was painting 'plump little' Zoë in the orchard studio. During a rest, he switched on the radio and they listened to Chamberlain's speech announcing that Britain and France had declared war on Germany. Then he turned it off and without a word went on painting until the bell rang for lunch.

---

[*] But, Marie Mauron went on, 'ce désespoir-là éclatait d'un grand rire car, lui, savait qu'il recommencerait une toile le lendemain. Avec la même obstination, le même "désespoir", le même enthousiasme, le même amour, vif et sans amertume, rancune ou vanité devant, tout de même, de magnifiques réussites!'

4

HIS FIFTIES, THEIR THIRTIES

'[Augustus's] varnish was cracking visibly.'
Dylan Thomas to Henry Treece
(1 September 1938)

'The disastrous decade', Cyril Connolly called the 1930s.[84] For John, if
in no other way a thirties figure, it was truly disastrous – 'the worst spell
of my bloody life', he called it.

The world around him, as it plunged towards war, had grown horrific,
and in its place he had created little. Once the early lyricism had faded,
his flashing eye, searching for new wonders, found little on which to
focus. The happy accident, travelling through the dark, came to him less
often. And beyond this dark, lending it intensity, rose the shadows of
fascism and Nazism. In such circumstances John's pretty girls, wide-eyed
and open-legged, his vast unintegrated and unfinished compositions, his
vacant landscapes, gaped irrelevantly.

Yet he worked hard. Reviewing his exhibition at Tooth's in 1938, *The
Times* critic had expressed 'admiration for what is achieved and regret,
with a touch of resentment, that so great a natural talent for painting,
possibly the greatest in Europe, should have been treated so lightly by its
possessor . . . This is not to accuse Mr John of idleness . . . As everybody
knows there is a kind of industry which is really a shirking of mental
effort . . .'[85]

In the opinion of the poet and artist David Jones, who admired John,
it was the company he kept that finally ruined him: in particular 'that
crashing bore' Horace de Vere Cole. John had known Cole since before
the Great War. He was a commanding figure, with needle blue eyes, a
mane of white hair, bristling upswept moustaches and the carriage of
a regimental sergeant-major. This exterior had been laid on to mask the
effects of having only one lung, a shoulder damaged in the war and, like
John himself, encircling deafness. Fighting pomposity was what he claimed
to be doing, repunctuating life with absurdity so that it no longer read
the same. His whoops and antics were often better to hear about than be
caught up in. When John learnt how Cole, dressed as 'the Anglican Bishop
of Madras', had confirmed a body of Etonians, he laughed out loud. But
when Cole took some of John's drawings, sat in the street with them all
day in front of the National Gallery, and, having collected a few coppers,
came back with the explanation that this was their value on the open

market, John was less amused. Cole liked to ruffle John's feelings, 'for I think he gets too much flattery'. Rivalry and rages interrupted their friendship, but the bond between them held. John used Cole as his court jester; while Cole 'seemed to have no friends – except John', the painter A. R. Thomson noted. 'People who knew him avoided him.'

In the autumn of 1926 they had set out together on a walk through Provence. 'Horace was a famous walker in the heel and toe tradition,' John recorded, 'and, with his unusual arithmetical faculty, was a great breaker of records, especially when alone.'[86] Their expedition quickened into a fierce walking match and, in the evenings, contests for the attentions of village girls. It was an exhausting programme and Thomson, who joined them for part of this competitive tour, remembered, 'in the bright moon, Horace flanked by John and I marched along the bridge over the Rhone – swinging arms, hats tilted, cigars. John's swaggers were natural, not put on. I watched Horace impersonating John. His plenty white hair, busy moustaches, fierce eyes. He was "Super-John".'[87] A caricature that Thomson drew, 'John and Super-John', catches much of their pantomime relationship – John leading, Cole an extravagant shadow behind, mocking, but needing John to parody.

It was a fantasy friendship they enjoyed, part of a make-believe life; and when it collided with the actual world there was trouble. In 1928, at the Café Royal, Cole had met Mabel Wright. 'Mavis', as she was always to be called, was a strikingly tall girl of nineteen with big brown eyes, curly blonde hair, wonderful legs and a forthcoming manner. About her background she was secretive, confiding only that her mother had been a child stolen by gypsies. In later years she varied this story to the extent of denying, in a manner challenging disbelief, that she was John's daughter by a gypsy. In fact she was the daughter of a grocer's assistant and had been at the age of sixteen a scullery maid. During the General Strike in 1926, she hitchhiked to London, clutching a golf club, and took a post as nursery governess to the children of a clergyman in Wimbledon. A year later she was a waitress at Veeraswamy's, the pioneer Indian restaurant in Swallow Street.

John was one of those that night at the Café Royal who had witnessed Cole break through a circle of men and make an assignation with Mavis. 'To a great extent we get on splendidly ... but our pitched battles are devastating affairs,' Cole later wrote to John. Nevertheless, 'Mavis and marriage is the only logical outcome.'[88] For two years they lived together and in January 1931, after Cole obtained a divorce from his first wife, he did marry Mavis. From that time on everything went wrong for him. But not for Mavis. On coming to London she had learnt the astonishing power of sex. She had an extraordinary talent for it. Already a winner of beauty contests, she was naturally affectionate and liked touching people. But sex appeal, she felt, was not enough; she must acquire education, and she selected Cole to play Professor Higgins to her Eliza Doolittle. To have married him was a triumph, for was he not a famous Old Etonian, a cousin of Neville Chamberlain (who in 1937 was to become Prime Minister), and a cultivated aristocrat whose ancestor Edward de Vere, seventeenth Earl of Oxford, had written all Shakespeare's plays?

Cole, now fifty and a sufferer from what John called 'pretty-girl-itis', was very possessive of his twenty-two-year-old wife. But Mavis had no wish to be restricted, and their marriage was full of plot and tension. Under this strain, Cole's antics grew more extreme. After a hard day's joking, he would set out late at night to haunt houses. Then, a last bad joke, he had lost almost all his first wife's money in an unlikely Canadian venture and was obliged to leave Mavis immediately after their marriage to live in France.

It was soon afterwards that John stepped forward to help. 'You must be frightfully lonely I fear,' he sympathized with Mavis, who was spinning back and forth across the Channel. In 1934, she became his mistress and on 15 March 1935 she gave birth to a son, Tristan Hilarius[89] John de Vere Cole. 'What a whopper!' John exclaimed in delight. One thing was certain: Horace, disconsolately exiled in France, could not have been Tristan's father. John himself immediately brushed aside other candidates and assumed that role. In a letter to Wyndham Lewis, he explained: 'Tristan is not Cole's son, though born in wedlock ... at my last meeting with Cole, before he departed for France, he stung me for £20 which, of course, he never repaid. So when Mavis deserted him after four years of matrimonial bliss, I felt no compunction in taking it out in kind.'[90]

But the initiative was less with John than he cynically suggests. Mavis was not only affectionate, she was shrewd. She knew how potent her attractions were for John. She was his 'sweet honey-bird', eye-catching and easy going. She brought a zest to his life, made him feel young again. He sent her 'tasty poems' about orgasms, did drawings of her with legs kicked high and wide. 'She is really a good wench,' he urged Dorelia, 'and has a good deal of *gumption*.' But Dorelia saw a different Mavis: someone who was using her sex appeal to lure John away from Fryern. One of the guests there, Andrea Cowdin, remembered Mavis playing on the floor with Tristan, rolling about and laughing and 'being delightful', but always with an eye on John who sat there gloomily without a word or sign. If only for the sake of his 'nerves', John wished Mavis and Dodo to be friends. But they were never more than outwardly polite.

Mavis was not 'mysterious' but she could be elusive. She would disappear down to her cottage in the west and suddenly stop answering letters. In her absence John became an old man. There were weeks of suspense, and 'I cannot bear it'. He knew she had affairs with other men and would imagine her in bed with all manner of travellers. The trouble was that everyone liked her. 'She seemed so amiable and gay and I was rather taken by her,' admitted Carrington. But so too was Carrington's lover Beacus Penrose. There was no telling in what plot or story Mavis would land up. 'Try to hold yourself in till our next,' John would beg. Then she would return to London, generous, beautiful, irresistible; so the sun would shine again and he was young.

Nevertheless, though Mavis pulled hard, and John wobbled a little, she could not pluck him from Dorelia. By 1936 she had switched tactics. Putting Tristan into a children's home, she went down to Cornwall from where she announced her impending marriage to a man she called 'the Tapeworm', six feet seven inches tall, who 'looks as if he has come from another planet'.[91] Dorelia's response was an offer to bring up Tristan at Fryern.

Because of Mavis's indecisiveness, John proposed legally adopting her son. 'Are you clear about adopting Tristan?' he asked Dorelia (September 1936). She was. But Mavis was not clear, and when Tristan went to Fryern in 1937 it was under an informal arrangement. Mavis herself was now free to cast her eyes on a target even loftier than her tapeworm. One day in the summer of 1937 John had taken her to Maiden Castle, where the archaeologist Mortimer Wheeler was working. 'I was wandering about at the eastern end of Maiden Castle when I saw a curious entourage on its way towards me,' Mortimer Wheeler recalled. 'It consisted of Augustus John and his party, in the odd clothes they always wore. Mavis was skipping in front on long legs; very distinctive that skipping walk of hers – I was greatly taken with her straight away. All work stopped as the cavalcade arrived.'[92]

The following year Mavis elected to marry Mortimer Wheeler and let him 'run in harness' with John. 'It will be like an amputation to let you go,' John protested. '. . . I felt you were part of *me*.' He did not accept this operation without a fight. Now in his sixtieth year and seeing himself *in loco parentis*, he declined to give Wheeler his consent: 'You must wait. I haven't finished with her yet.' On one occasion, reduced to 'a mass of nerves and brandy' by Wheeler's 'grinning mask', he most alarmingly lost his temper. Next day he sent an apology. 'I was in a wrought-up state and have been for some time . . . Do write and say you will be friends again.' In a desperate moment, after Wheeler had climbed into Mavis's room at Fryern, John had challenged his rival to a duel. 'As the challenged party,' Wheeler related, 'I had choice of weapons. Being a field gunner I chose field guns.'[93] John, declaring this to be 'very ungentlemanly conduct',

bowed to the inevitable, and, putting the best face on it, advised Mavis
to accept this 'distinguished personality' as her husband. He might be a
cad, but at least he had been Director of the National Museum of Wales.
They were married in March 1939,* occasioning a brief interlude in
John's relationship with Mavis.

But there was an awkward corollary. In many of his letters to her, John
assures Mavis that Tristan is 'full of beans', 'in the pink', 'incredibly
beautiful' and 'eating well'. 'Don't disturb yourself,' he urges her. 'Dodo
seems absolutely stuck on him.' But Mavis was never reconciled to leaving
Tristan at Fryern, and one day in January 1941 she abducted him. John
at once sent off an indignant letter protesting at this 'Rape of Tristan' to
Mortimer Wheeler who in his tactful reply (31 January 1941) explained:
'Mavis has always regarded Fryern Court as her real home and you and
Dodo as an integral part of her life. This little episode is entirely subordinate to that overwhelming factor . . . The fact is, Mavis does not want to
feel that T's destinies are completely beyond her control and that she is
merely a name in the visitors' book.'

'The Battle of Fordingbridge', as Wheeler called it, was quickly over.
John and Dorelia had no legal rights and in any case Tristan continued
to spend numerous holidays at Fryern. 'The violent offence which you
will give', Wheeler had advised Mavis, '. . . will disappear in time.' And
so it turned out. 'The incident is closed,' John assured Mavis. Almost at
once they were back on friendly terms. But he remembered – this and
much else that he tried to banish into oblivion.

*

Mavis was John's chief mistress-model in these years. 'Soon I will be
ready to paint you off in *one go*,' he had written to her. 'That is what I
live for.' But though he drew and painted her often, this 'supreme
picture . . . which I know would come off at the right time' never did
come off. On almost any occasion, in taxis or at dinner parties, she rejoiced
in flinging off her clothes. She would strike provocative attitudes before
John who, when severe, restricted his drawing to her face. In Cornwall or
Provence he led her out into the country, posed her achingly against some
expert expanse of rocks and trees, then painted landscapes without a
figure. Yet he needed her company: she still gave him the 'authentic thrill'.
'I cannot forget that last marvellous embrace,' he was still writing to her
in the 1940s. 'A real wonder! How was it possible? . . . I don't know what
I should do without you.' His feelings were intensely sentimental. Though
Mavis could disguise the fact, the pictures proclaim it: he was losing his

---

* John and the writer A. P. Herbert were witnesses and the guests included Agatha Christie and her
husband, the archaeologist Max Mallowan.

sexual drive. At the beginning of the war he was in his sixty-second year. His age, the psychological uncertainty of his work, and alcohol which 'provokes the desire and takes away the performance' had left their mark. His letters to Mavis, with their vigorous signing off, 'Yours stiff and strong', urge a degree of potency that she alone could summon up. 'I drink but I am not a "Boozer". I have affairs of the heart but I do not womanize,' he wrote to the art critic D. S. MacColl. 'Drinking helps (for a time) to overcome the horrors of a world into which I rarely seem to fit; love renews (alas for a time) the divine illusion of beauty. By which you may perceive that my soul is sick.'[94]

A pessimistic sentimentality was replacing the lyrical romanticism of his early years and the 'hectic sexuality' of the 1920s. His portraits of women between the 1930s and late 1940s are sweet and feeble echoes of eroticism. Far better were his paintings of exotic flowers which did not agitate him.

His emotionalism over Mavis became one reason 'why I haven't had much success painting of late'. Other models were sometimes less unsettling. Two of them were daughters of his old friend Francis Macnamara.

John's involvement with the Macnamara family was working steadily through the generations. 'I love him above all men,' Francis Macnamara had declared. This hero-worship was a guiding force in Macnamara's life as he took on several mistresses including, it was rumoured, Euphemia Lamb, and also Alick Schepeler's friend Frieda Bloch. The most extraordinary of these women was Erica Cotterill, who had previously chosen Rupert Brooke and then Bernard Shaw as 'the gorgeous thing I have to live for and love with every atom of my soul'. But Francis Macnamara was not so gorgeous, and in her anonymous book *Form of Diary* (1939) Erica laid a trail of clues pointing to his cruelty before he left her to marry Dorelia's sister Edie.

John himself had incidentally enjoyed a brief affair with Macnamara's first wife Yvonne, and indeed with her sister Grace. Both of them were, he assured Dorelia, 'beyond praise'.[95] But this intermingling was so indiscriminate and comprehensive that the Macnamara children sometimes wondered whether they were actually John children. The eldest daughter Nicolette, on her visits to the family, had certainly 'adopted' Augustus as her father – going on to the Slade School and later marrying two artists, first Anthony Devas, then Rupert Shephard who had been in love with her sister Caitlin.

John seems to have grown fonder of Caitlin Macnamara and her sister Brigit as they grew into their late teens. Everyone trusted Brigit. She was good with animals, good with children (Mavis was always happy to leave Tristan in her care), and especially good to John. In his portrait of her she appears, clasping a tankard of ale, as a companion fit for Falstaff.[96] She seemed in some respects rather a masculine countrywoman, yet was shy, sensitive, oddly reliable for a Macnamara, and the repository of many secrets. She felt an instinctive sympathy for John, independent of words. 'An intonation, a pause, a movement from Brigit's . . . hand was answered by Augustus with a smile that started slowly all over his face and faded in his beard,' Nicolette observed. '. . . In this shorthand of long-term sympathy, the eaves-dropper might catch a hint or two, yet the depth of the meaning was a secret kept between them.'[97]

Brigit saw the terrifying glare, the tremendous male arrogance: but she saw through them to someone more complex and interesting. Intermittently over many years they kept up a love affair. Even at sixty, she remembered, his body was good – well-shaped hands and feet, narrow hips, small bones. Unfortunately Brigit was also engaged to Augustus's son Caspar – at least, everyone expected them to marry. In the late 1930s Dorelia, who was fond of Brigit, wrote to ask Augustus why the marriage 'seems indefinitely postponed'.[98] There is no record of his answer, though the probable reason was Caspar's inability to accept Brigit's sexual intimacy with his father. According to Brigit herself, she and Caspar were in bed 'at the home of one of his sisters when, two days before the wedding, he told her he couldn't or wouldn't marry her'.[99]

Caitlin, the youngest sister, was also caught between father and son. Augustus did several nude drawings of her, some unfinished oils, and a couple of completed portraits, the best of which shows a sparkling eyeful of a girl, pink and precocious.[100] But she failed to entrap Caspar John even when, 'all dolled up and ready' at the age of fifteen, she came to his bed wearing her special négligé.

Remote, handsome, a powerful man who would subdue her to his will, Caspar stood in her imagination as a prince in the fairy tale of her life. Only her life was not a fairy tale. Having been neglected by her father, and then being cut off from her mother (who was absorbed in a lesbian relationship), Caitlin needed attention – the dramatic attention of a romantic rescuer. She wanted to give herself to Caspar, but he had only thoughts of the navy in those days. Besides, she was too young.

She was not too young, however, for Augustus. Unlike Nicolette, Caitlin did not treat Augustus as a father: she physically hated her father. But having been rejected by Caspar she turned to Augustus, flirting with him, enjoying the glamour of his fame. She was a luminous girl, spectacular, and he could not stop staring at her. She led him on; and, as she bitterly remembered in the leftover years of her life, then or later he raped her.

'Caitlin's relationship with John is important and difficult to unravel,'[101] wrote her biographer Paul Ferris. Unlike Brigit, she was not trustworthy, and her later memories of John were opposite to those of her sister: he was simply an 'old goat', a 'hairy monster', 'a disgusting old man who fucked [everyone]'. And of course it was true that he did 'pounce' on attractive girls. 'I felt a frisson whenever he came into the room,' Kathleen Hale remembered of the 1920s. '. . . Sometimes there would be mock battles between us, when he would try to "rape" me, scuffles that always began and ended in laughter – hardly the atmosphere for passion. I have always found laughter as good as a chastity belt. Once, though, out of curiosity, I allowed him to seduce me. The sex barrier down, this aberration only added a certain warmth to our friendship.'[102]

But such sophisticated laughter did not come naturally to very young girls like Chiquita and Caitlin. And perhaps, in any case, there was less laughter in the 1930s. As late as 1929 Augustus still appeared an attractive man. Describing a party given in June that year by the writer Arthur Machin and his wife, Sylvia Townsend Warner wrote:

'Then Augustus John came, and I could have no other eyes. He is very long and lean, his hair is grey, his eyes are bright, he was rather drunk, he is the Ancient Mariner . . . He is perfectly young still, and with a sad drunken youthfulness and guileless-ness he embraced my waist in the taxi, and begged me to go to Wales with him . . . I loved him terribly, he is so simple, intent in the true world, astray in the real. It is awful to think that this youth must go down quick into the pit of senility.'[103]

This descent accelerated after he left Preston Deanery Hall, and his pouncing on women seemed to grow cruder. 'Not the best introduction to the carnal delights of the marriage bed,' wrote Caitlin – for she was perhaps sixteen and he was over thirty-five years older. In his poem 'Into her lying down head', written almost three years after he married Caitlin, Dylan Thomas conjures up the priapic figure of John:

> A furnace-nostrilled column-membered
> Super-or-near man
> Resembling to her dulled sense
> The thief of adolescence.

The affair continued spasmodically over several years, each using the other, neither very happy about it. John seems to have felt some affection for 'my little seraph', especially when, in his confusion, he 'thought she was his daughter as well'.[104] Caitlin later denied any feeling for John, claiming only one 'luridly vivid memory . . . pure revulsion . . . and inevitable pouncing . . . an indelible impression . . . of the basic vileness of men'.

She was, John noted, 'apparently in a perpetual state of disgust with the world in general'.[105] But he had no sense of contributing to that disgust. She came to see herself as 'the Avenger of wrongs'. The 'merciless vengeance' she had sworn on Francis Macnamara embraced John and almost all men.

It was John who introduced Caitlin to Dylan Thomas. In Constantine FitzGibbon's version John had met Dylan at the Fitzroy Tavern and it was at another pub, the Wheatsheaf, that he brought the two of them together: 'Come and meet someone rather amusing.' Caitlin, 'quite mute',[106] nervously approached Dylan and 'within ten minutes' they were in bed together, spending several days and nights at the Eiffel Tower and charging everything to John's account. But however 'deaf and obtuse' John might be, Caitlin explained, there was a danger he might find out. So they parted, Dylan for Cornwall, she back to Fryern Court.

They met again in the summer of that year, 1936, in the novelist Richard Hughes's castle at Laugharne, Dylan in the interval having contracted gonorrhoea.

Caitlin, Hughes remembered, was very pretty and gauche and, though now twenty-two years old (she concealed her age from Dylan), impressed him as being about 'the equivalent of eleven years of age'.[107] She arrived with John in July and during their stay there was much giggling and kissing in the passages, and no visible evidence, at least to his eyes, of Caitlin disliking this. One morning John (possibly at Caitlin's prompting) suggested that the Hugheses invite Dylan (who had written to say he was 'passing awfully near Laugharne') over for lunch. He came, and stayed the night. Dylan and Caitlin gave no sign of knowing each other.*

John was judging a painting competition at the National Eisteddfod in Fishguard, and motored there next day in his six-cylinder Wolseley, 'the Bumble-Bee'. Dylan and Caitlin went too; but when John arrived back at Laugharne that night he was alone with Caitlin who looked, Hughes noticed, 'like a cat that's been fed on cream'. 'Where's Dylan?' Hughes asked. 'In the gutter,' drawled John, slurring his words horribly as he lurched in. 'What happened?' 'I put him there. He was drunk. I couldn't bring a drunk man to a house like this.'

It transpired that at Carmarthen there had been a fight. All day John

---

* John, however, was not taken in by this pantomime. In a letter to Dorelia (20 July 1936) he wrote: 'I drove down to Wales taking Caitlin who wanted to see Dylan Thomas. We stayed at Laugharne Castle and the next day by a strange coincidence Dylan turned up out of the blue! . . . I drove them to Fishguard, Caitlin and Dylan osculating assiduously in the back of the car.' NLW MS 22778D fols. (cf. Notes) 136–7.

had felt irritated by Dylan and Caitlin's lovemaking. It may also have been that, knowing of Dylan's gonorrhoea, he felt justified in protecting Caitlin. At Carmarthen, Dylan had insisted that John drive him back to Laugharne. But John refused and, tempers rising, they raised their fists in the car park.

Caitlin remembered John being 'on top of me' that night. The following morning as John was stepping outside into the sunlight, Dylan turned up and the stage was set for a spectacular castle farce. Laugharne, though somewhat roofless, had a good cellar, a watchtower, plenty of surrounding shrubbery which was said to be haunted, and three entrance doors. No sooner had Dylan gone out by one of these doors than John would appear through another. Though the plot was confused, a tremendous atmosphere of melodrama built up. Caitlin was on stage for most of the performance, but when the exigencies of the theatre demanded it, she would make a quick exit, while the two men made their entrances. The timing throughout was remarkable, and there were many rhetorical monologues in the high-flown style. To the spectators, wiping their eyes, the outcome appeared uncertain. But, a year later, Caitlin married Dylan at Penzance Register Office; and when their first child was born, Richard Hughes and John were godfathers.*

They had then moved, the Thomases, to Laugharne and, as neighbours of Richard Hughes, were understandably 'nervous' of John's visits there. John too seemed nervous. He put up at their house, Sea View, for a night or two 'in circumstances of indescribable squalor'.[108] It had been to relieve this austerity that he gave them some furniture, including 'a wonderful bed'. At night, when he went up to his room, Mervyn Levy remembered, John 'used to stuff ten-shilling notes and pound notes in his pockets, rich sort of reddy-brown notes, and hang this vast coat of his over a chair. Then we would creep upstairs and nick a few, because it was the only way of gaining any money from Augustus.'[109] Though 'bloated and dumb from his deafness'[110] John was well aware of these raids. In *Finishing Touches* he remarks that Dylan had once been a Communist, and 'could always be relied upon as a borrower . . .'[111]

There is a grudging tone to everything John wrote of Dylan who, he owns, was 'a genius' – though his shove-ha'penny was superior to *Under Milk Wood*, in which 'there is no trace of wit'. Such sallies were themselves attempts at wit which misfired. 'There is no *rancour*,' he explained to D. S. MacColl, 'only a little playful malice.' The affection between them,

---

* 'Last week we christened the baby,' Dylan Thomas wrote to Veronica Sibthorp early in 1939. '. . . Augustus could not follow the service, although he had the text, and broke in with the refrain "I desire it" at intervals.'

much enlivened by this malice, lurked behind a prickly barricade of gibes. 'Dylan has a split personality of course,' he wrote to Matthew Smith's mistress Mary Keene. 'He can be unbearable and then something else comes out which one loves.'

Of the two oil portraits John did of Thomas in the late 1930s one, now in the National Museum of Wales, is possibly his best painting of this period – a 'diminutive masterpiece', as Wyndham Lewis described it, that matches his pen-portrait in *Finishing Touches*: 'Dylan's face was round and his nose snub. His rather prominent eyes were a little veiled and his curly hair was red, or auburn rather. A pleasant and slightly sardonic smile registered amusement and, I think, satisfaction. If you could have substituted an ice for the glass of beer he held you might have mistaken him for a happy schoolboy out on a spree.'

Both John and Dylan were 'bad Welshmen' whose ruin was hastened by their visits to the United States, where they broke records in drinking. There are passages in John's essay on Dylan in *Finishing Touches* that could equally well refer to himself since, perhaps unconsciously, he identified himself with the younger man. Having passed on some of his own traits in this way, he is able to deplore them more wholeheartedly. It was a technique he often used to pep up his writing, and accounts for his sharpest sallies being directed towards those with whom he had most in common.

5

CHILDREN OF THE GREAT

'Tottering under the burden of parental responsibilities.'
Description of Augustus John by Trelawney Dayrell Reed (1952)

When walking the streets of Chelsea, so the story goes, John had a habit of patting local children on the head 'in case it is one of mine'.* Calculations over the number of these children floated high into fantasy, reaching, in James Laver's autobiography, three figures at which, in the opinion of Max Beerbohm, John stopped counting.[112]

He was never quick to deny fathering a child. Improbable rumours, incapable of proof, seethed around him, agitated by the readers of news-

---

* But Romilly John remembers that 'as a small boy I frequently encountered Augustus striding arrogantly down the King's Road on his way to the Six Bells. He never deigned to notice one on these occasions. Nor did it occur to me to claim any relationship. We passed as perfect strangers.' Romilly John to the author, 25 January 1973.

papers in which he featured as an archetypal father figure. Adolescents with a liking for art or a connection with Wales, as they grew up and away from their parents, sometimes speculated over their hidden kinship with Augustus John. One middle-aged woman in North Wales has written in a Welsh magazine the elaborate story of John's friendship with her mother, ingeniously tracing her own family connections with the Johns to show that, in addition to being her father, John was a cousin. Every detail that can be checked pushes this narrative further into invention.

Another example is sadder and more revealing. In about 1930, Sheila Nansi Ivor-Jones, a schoolgirl, was sent by her parents to see a Dr Clifford Scott. Although she was not unintelligent, Sheila had done badly at school. She could not stick to any routine. Her father, Robert Ivor Jones, headmaster of West Monmouth School at Pontypool, and his wife Edwina Claudia Jones (née Lewis) were worried. But Sheila did display some artistic ability and, after going up to an art school in Tunbridge Wells, her troubles seemed over. In October 1937 she transferred to the Slade and by the 1940s had become an art instructor at the Chelsea School of Art. Then, on 15 February 1948, she again consulted Dr Scott, complaining of terrible nightmares about horses, fighting and hysterical love scenes; and adding that she had discovered herself to be the illegitimate daughter of Augustus John – to which she attributed this trouble. The nightmares and delusions persisted throughout this year, growing worse. She seems to have neglected herself, lost her job, and in February 1949 was admitted to West Park Mental Hospital, Epsom, where on 28 February she died. The cause of her death was recorded as bronchial pneumonia and acute mania.

Sheila Ivor-Jones (she hyphenated her name in London) had been born at Llanllwchaiarn in Montgomeryshire on 28 September 1912 and, from the evidence that exists, it seems most unlikely that John could have been her father. If, then, this was fantasy, it seems to have taken possession of her after the death of her real father. She may have seen John fairly frequently in Chelsea, since she lived round the corner from Mrs Fleming's house (and no distance from John's various studios) at 77 Cheyne Walk above the Cheyne Buttery – tea and supper rooms and a guest house run by a man called Stancourt, whose christian names were John Augustus.

Whatever the source of her delusion, it represents, in an extreme form, a tendency that was surprisingly widespread. The irony was that, as an actual father, John was extraordinarily difficult. 'I have no gifts as a paterfamilias,' he admitted.[113] For all his children self-help was the only salvation – the key for entry into, as to liberation from, the powerful John orbit. Fryern Court 'wasn't my home', wrote his daughter Amaryllis Fleming, 'but it was the only place I ever felt utterly at home in'.[114]

Another daughter who was not at Fryern felt her exclusion to be a paralysing deprivation of love, leaving her 'doubting my own validity as a human being, a boring thing to feel'. But the magnetic field rejecting her threatened to devour others, Ida's sons and the son and daughters of Dorelia, who needed supreme willpower to escape.

John was like a Victorian father. Children were to be seen and not heard, painted and glared into silence. An incorrectly pronounced syllable would provoke pedantic wrath. 'I apologise for my poor handwriting, syntax, spelling (probably) and faults of style and punctuation,' David ended a letter written when in his early fifties. One morning when Poppet arrived at breakfast wearing her dress the wrong way round, she was picked up, deposited behind some curtains, and left. Another time when Vivien was at fault, John refused to speak to her and all communication had to pass via a third party. 'As a child I can only say I feared him greatly,' Vivien wrote, 'and if spoken to by him would instantly burst into tears.' But he was proud, if a little disturbed, when his two daughters, aged seventeen and fourteen, saved a young man from drowning. 'They dived into the river at Fordingbridge and fished him out and applied artificial respiration and kissed him so frantically', Ralph Partridge told his friend Gerald Brenan, 'that he returned from unconsciousness to find he had an erection.'[115]

John was even more severe with the boys. The tension between them was sometimes agonizing. Edwin had a habit of smelling his food before starting to eat, and this infuriated Augustus so much that he pushed the boy's face hard into the plate. His son retaliated by flinging the plate out of the window, but Augustus made him go out, collect every morsel from the gravel and eat it. It was a battle of wills and Augustus, with all the advantages, won. As for Dorelia, she 'had a mysterious way of disappearing when anything troublesome cropped up'.[116]

Augustus's silences could last thirty hours or more and were echoed back at him by his pack of brooding sons. 'Why don't you say something?' he growled at David, whose silence darkened. But it was the quality of Robin's silence, grimmer than any of the others', seeming to accuse him of something literally unspeakable, that maddened Augustus most. 'He hardly utters a word and radiates *hostility*,' he wrote to Mavis. 'I fear I shall reach a crisis and go for him tooth and nail. That happened once here and I soon floored him on the gravel outside.' He affected to believe that all his sons were slightly mad. Should he hire straitjackets? 'Do you think it would be a good idea', he asked Inez Holden, 'to have the lot of them psycho-analysed?'

'As children,' Romilly acknowledged, 'we made no allowances for, since we had no conception of, the despairs of an artist about his work.'

Augustus's glooms, charged with an intense hostility to those near by, cut him off from easy companionship. Yet he resented not being confided in, and wanted in a discreet way to be loved by all of them. 'On rare occasions when Augustus and I talked, it was almost invariably about Sanskrit,' remembered Romilly, 'a subject neither of us knew much about.' When another of his sons wrote to him in personal distress, Augustus confined his reply to matters of prose style which 'I find overweighted with latinisms', and to the envelope itself upon which 'you have, either by design or carelessness, omitted to place the customary dot after the diminutive *Hants*. In an old Dane Courtier this seems to me unpardonable but I put it down to your recent bereavement.' Nothing intimate could be spoken. At the end of a letter to a Dartmouth schoolmaster (a retiring bachelor of thirty-eight) Augustus had added a timorous postscript suggesting something might be mentioned to his son Caspar about sex: 'Boys of Caspar's age stand particularly in need of help and enlightenment on certain subjects, don't you agree?' The best he could do was to use conversation as a neutral territory where he and his sons might guardedly meet without giving anything away. It was a tragedy, Caspar thought, that, by the time they could talk on easier terms, his father was so deaf that everything had to be shouted.

To his severity Augustus added a bewildering generosity and freedom. He gave all his sons good allowances into their twenties and thirties when he could not well afford it. He also allowed them at the ages of ten or twelve to choose their own schools. If 'all that is learned at public schools is football, cricket and buggery', he wrote to Dorelia after reading Alec Waugh's *The Loom of Youth*, 'I cannot see that these accomplishments need be so expensive myself even if they *are* indispensable.'[117] Nevertheless he always stumped up the fees. David had gone to Westminster, Caspar to Osborne, Robin ('the slackest youngster I've ever come across') briefly to Malvern and then to Le Rosey in Switzerland, Edwin and Romilly to a strange school, the Collège de Normandie, near Rouen. As for the girls, when asked at the ages of nine and seven whether they would like to go to school, Vivien again burst into tears and Poppet said 'No'. A procession of tutors and governesses (one of whom Romilly married) were erratically employed, but the two sisters passed more of their time with ponies than people. Augustus showed interest only in their art work, though when Vivien went up to the Slade she was under specific orders that there was to be no instruction. 'Little', she remembered, 'came of this.'

The sisters had served almost as stern an art apprenticeship as the boys. 'I had to look at him,' wrote Poppet, 'and if I caught his eye he would ask me very politely to come and pose for him, and this would mean the whole morning gone . . . all our plans for swimming at Bicton or riding in the forest with Vivien . . .' These 'gruellings', as Vivien called them, continued until the girls married, 'then ceased abruptly'. A considerable number of nude drawings of them both were hurried off to Australia, Canada, Japan.

As they grew up their relationship with their father became more complicated. Vivien, like Caitlin Macnamara, wanted to be a dancer. In 1930 the two of them caught the Salisbury bus to London, hoping to start their careers with C. B. Cochran's 'Young Ladies' on the revue stage. Arriving at the door of Ethel Nettleship's house, they sent a reassuring telegram to Augustus and Dorelia back at Fryern: 'DON'T WORRY, WITH RELIABLE FEMALE'. But Augustus objected to Vivien going on the stage, and it was a relief to him when she took up painting. She received some help from Matthew Smith and the Euston Road artists William Coldstream and Victor Pasmore before going on to the Académie de la Grande Chaumière in Paris. 'You can do it,' Augustus wrote encouragingly.

Towards both Poppet and Vivien he was jealously possessive. No boyfriend was good enough. 'Why should you bother with boy-friends when you have such a magnificent father?' he once asked Mollie O'Rourke, and this appeared to be his general attitude. After Poppet's wedding to Derek Jackson, he hopped into the car at Fordingbridge beside his daughter and, happily acknowledging the cheers, was driven off with her while Jackson took his place disconsolately next to the chauffeur.[118] 'He was like an old stag,' Poppet's second husband Villiers Bergne observed, 'with his herd of women and children round him. Interlopers were beaten off.'[119]

It had been hard for boyfriends, and it was harder still for husbands. Vivien's husband, a distinguished haematologist, was known as her 'medical attendant'. At least, Augustus reminded the family, he could congratulate himself on not having gone to their wedding. Why such a gorgeous girl as Vivien, or an enchanting creature like Poppet, who had given exquisite relief after the death of Pyramus, should want to end up as a *hausfrau* was inexplicable to him. At meals, he would sometimes draw caricatures of his in-laws, passing them round for comic appreciation; and his letters to all the family contain many invitations to disloyalty between his sons and daughters, their wives and husbands who, at one time or another, were 'revolting', 'villainous', or 'repulsive little swine' and who would generally learn this through some third party. His daughters-in-law ('no oil-paintings'), who he affected to believe had been chosen for their plainness so that his sons 'need fear no competition from me', had a scarcely easier time of it. A recurring question was how to do away with all this proliferating family. He had a double-barrelled gun ready in the house, but was open to other suggestions. 'I know little of toxicology but have heard the merits of *ratsbane* well recommended. The only question is: should the whelps be included in the purge? Personally I am all for it.'[120]

Possessive over his daughters, he was fiercely competitive with his sons; and it was with them that the most bitter battles were fought. One developed an eczema that would visibly spread over his skin during a quarrel. 'He is quite insupportable. I shall kill him soon,' Augustus promised Dorelia. In certain moods this did not seem an exaggeration. He genuinely wanted all of them to succeed yet could not prevent himself putting obstacles in their path.

Outside the family, the sons were treated like a branch of the nobility. When they were due to arrive at a party, the news was buzzed about, *Augustus John's sons are coming!* They grew anxious to disguise themselves, to avoid this vicarious limelight, play down the possession of the awful name John. The eldest son David, for example, never referred to 'my father' but always to 'John' as if to underline his detachment.

All of them were good looking and all of them had talent but, in the shadow of the Great Man, they dwindled. At Dane Court, David had been considered 'a dreamer'. But his dreams of becoming an aviator like his brother Caspar (a 'regular boy') flopped. Influenced by the Nettleships, he took up music and played the oboe in several orchestras before giving it up and becoming a postman. 'David has not been in the public eye recently,' Augustus commented to his brother Edwin.

Romilly, who had joined Francis Macnamara on the River Stour for philosophical explorations of *Robinson Crusoe* and the Book of Genesis, later became apprentice to a farmer, then a teetotal innkeeper at John Fothergill's public house the Spread Eagle at Thame, before 'commencing author' with a volume of poems, some detective works and a minor masterpiece of autobiography, *The Seventh Child*, which Augustus advised him not to publish.[121] When Romilly pressed for a reason, his father looked harassed and, after casting round for several minutes in silent agony, thundered out that Romilly had misspelt the name of a Welsh mountain. Besides, the title was of dubious accuracy. To which Romilly replied he would be 'the last to assert that my book is perfect'.[122] His book did not make much money and he sometimes felt 'rather a lout having to be subsidised'. But he was the humorist in the family, and in the company of literary friends – Gerald Brenan, Gamel Woolsey and the Powys brothers – he began to feel better. 'It's a wicked world, and yet, well, is it?' he asked Augustus. 'Personally I'm beginning to enjoy it.'[123]

'But for the sobering presence of Robin,' Augustus wrote to one of his brothers, 'we might all go, momentarily, off the rails.'[124] Robin, it was held, achieved the most bizarre reaction against their father. After leaving school he became assistant to Sir Charles Mendel, Press Attaché at the British Embassy in Paris. Despite his dislike of the press, Augustus accepted this as a fairly honourable beginning. When Robin gave it up to study painting, Augustus was still obstinately delighted, believing that his son had a talent for drawing. Robin, however, concentrated on the study of colour, especially blue, 'from the scientific or purely aesthetic angle',[125] eventually making 'an important discovery on the mixing of blue and yellow' about which he thought of writing a book. It was this apparent neglect of natural ability, infuriating to Augustus, that Robin appeared to perfect. He travelled widely, mastered seven languages, and was silent in all of them. Maddened by this misuse, as he saw it, of 'linguistic genius' Augustus struggled to find him employment – with Elizabeth Arden. Indeed he took up the matter of Robin's future with everyone, 'even with the Prime Minister'.[126] Appropriately Robin took a job 'in the censorship', about which he 'held his tongue'. He was transferred to Bermuda and Jamaica where (care of the Royal Bank of Canada) he farmed fruit and flowers in the hills, dabbling on lower levels in real estate. Over the years he wandered invisibly from place to place and job to job (architecture, publishing and, as a 'more immediate means of earning money', films). Back in England during the war, he spent much of his time, according to his brothers David and Edwin, 'gazing intently at a pot of marmalade'. Then he was off again and in 1956 he married. By this time he was working as a travel agent in Spain where the papers reported him as having formerly been a matador. 'He has kept this very dark hitherto,' Augustus commented. 'I'm sure he [Augustus] regretted our inability – as I did – to achieve a friendly and easy relationship,' Robin wrote. 'But the main obstacle was that he – fundamentally – was a rebel against established society and most conventions, while I hated Bohemianism and yearned for a normal life – which made me in my turn also a rebel – but in reverse.'[127]

Then there was Edwin. His gift, in his father's eyes, was for clowning, and the stage (which had been forbidden Vivien) was recommended. 'I feel strongly you yourself could make a great success on the stage,' Augustus advised. 'You have a good voice and ear and an unusual comedic sense.' After studying art in Paris, Edwin accidentally fell into professional boxing, winning, as 'Teddy John of Chelsea', seven of his first nine fights. 'Edwin fought a black man last Monday and beat him,' his father wrote proudly to a friend. On one occasion Augustus entered the ring himself, squared up opposite his son and had his photograph taken, bulging with satisfaction. 'I like him [Edwin] immensely,' he wrote to his son Henry. '. . . He has become a tall hefty fellow full of confidence, humour and character.' His delight at Edwin's success was redoubled by his own father's horror. Old Edwin John, he told David, 'is outraged in all his best feelings that Edwyn has adopted the brutal and degrading profession of prize-fighter but everybody else seems pleased except some Tenbyites who, according to Papa, have decided that *my* little career is at an end in consequence of Edwyn's career in the Ring.' But one other person disapproved: Gwen John. She told her nephew he was wasting his time boxing and should become a serious artist – and to Augustus's dismay Edwin threw in the towel. Gwen's influence was to fall awkwardly between father and son, multiplying their many misunderstandings.

Caspar, the one who, from earliest days, had kept away, was the exception. By 1941 he was a naval captain; by 1951 a rear-admiral; by 1960 First Sea Lord and Chief of Naval Staff; and by 1962 he had become Admiral of the Fleet Sir Caspar John, GCB. Of his son's enthusiasm for aeroplanes, ships and the sea Augustus understood nothing: but he understood success. 'My son Caspar hasn't done too badly,' he remarked to Stuart Piggott. Of course he would make fun sometimes of 'the gallant admiral . . . looking like a Peony in full bloom', but such sallies had no poison in them. He often proposed painting Caspar 'with all your buttons', but never caught him decked in his 'stripes and all'. Their relationship remained a staccato affair, neither giving ground, but the more senior Caspar became the more his father thawed. 'Still in the navy?' he would ask when Caspar returned on leave. But though he took this success lightly, seldom embarrassing Caspar with compliments, it gave him satisfaction. 'You can't go any further without damaging the ceiling,' he pointed out. He even gave grudging approval when in 1944, after a larky wartime courtship on two bicycles, Caspar married Mary Vanderpump, known as 'Pumpy' (she was an ambulance driver and also worked on the Grand Union Canal). 'I disliked P[umpy] less than I expected,' he wrote to Poppet's second husband, whom he was beginning to dislike rather more. 'Caspar at any rate looks better on it which is something.'[128]

There was another son, Ida's fifth child, Henry: the odd one out who had become separated from the others after the chase round London Zoo in the summer of 1908. He had been brought up by a cousin, Edith Nettleship, in the village of Sheet, near Petersfield. It was an energetic upbringing: long walks in the open, long prayers indoors. ('She prays an awful lot,' Henry complained.) While serving as a nurse during the Great War, Edith had been converted to Catholicism, and had then sent Henry to Stonyhurst College, a superior Catholic school. Sometimes in the holidays he would climb on to the backs of lorries and be driven to Alderney and to Fryern, entering for a week or two the amazing world of his brothers and half-sisters. 'He had an adventurous, not to say reckless, spirit just below the surface,' observed his schoolfriend Tom Burns,[129] which these visits brought forth. Vivien was 'great', Poppet a 'great flirt', and the two of them together were 'perfect sisters'. 'What more perfect sisters could one deserve?' He longed to see more of them. Among his brothers he particularly envied David with his oboe and his country dancing. Henry didn't play a musical instrument and 'I can't dance even the one-step yet. I always used to be occupied at Stonyhurst when they danced.'[130] His holidays with the Johns were like a dream – the riding and tree-climbing; the invention with his half-brother Romilly of a machine that *thought*; the urgent swopping of stories, information, books; the pictures, the endless talk of love and philosophy that continued in Henry's illustrated letters and included his poem about Eden in the style of Edward Lear and a complicated theological essay on 'Girls' Bottoms', much criticized for its inaccuracy. He was a strangely attractive figure to the Johns, with striking good looks, a vehement personality, his laugh fierce, his manner harsh and precise. As William Rothenstein noticed, he was 'startlingly like Ida'. 'Henry is a wonderful boy,' Augustus told Gwen.[131] He was particularly pleased when Henry showed an interest in Romany matters. At Stonyhurst he had gained a reputation as a brilliant scholar, actor and orator, and at weekends would mount a platform at Marble Arch to argue dramatically on behalf of the Catholic Evidence Guild. But he was too unconventional to be a popular boy. The problem was: with all his energy and gifts, what should he do? He wanted to 'have a shot at being a Jesuit', he told Augustus. 'But I would like to go to China first.' Father Martin D'Arcy, who had been a pupil and teacher at Stonyhurst, was sent to interview him and, if he judged him sufficiently remarkable, groom him for the Jesuit priesthood. 'I was captivated by Henry John,' he wrote. '. . . He was an absolute genius . . . handsome, looking like an angel (except he was dark) . . . absolutely irresistible . . . I had very close to a father's feeling for him, an affection such as I don't think I've ever had for any other boy.' In Father D'Arcy's opinion and that of Father Cyril Martindale, the prominent Jesuit hagiographer, Henry was a miraculous boy 'devastating for the enemies of the faith'.[132] In 1926, Father D'Arcy carried him off to Rome, where he lodged at the Beda College and attended lectures at the Jesuit university, the Gregoriana. Henry's letters from Rome to his father show how his Catholic training and John-like paganism were fusing into fantasy.

'Another thing which is absorbing is how I am going to bring up my children and how I am going to spend my honeymoon (supposing I don't become a p[riest]). I think the most awful thing that could happen to anybody would be to have horrible children . . . I should bring them up in some sunny place by the sea, pack their heads with fairy-stories and every conceivable pleasant Catholic custom, be extremely disciplinary when need arose, and make them learn Japanese wrestling, riding, prize-fighting (i.e. not boxing), swimming, dancing, French, Latin, and acting from the cradle. We would have the most glorious caravan expeditions (like you used to do, didn't you?) in Devonshire and France and Wales. The catechism lesson, once a week, given by myself, would be a fête. At Christmas – Xmas tree, stockings, crib, miracle-play, everything. I would take them somewhere where they could play with poor children . . . on at least one day of the week they would be allowed to run about naked and vast quantities of mud, soot and strawberries etc. would be piled up for their disposal. All the apostolic precepts would have to be encouraged . . . Tell me . . . what amendments you suggest. Quick, else I shall be having them on my hands. The first Communion of the ten small Johns will be a magnificent affair; if possible it will be on the sands in the sun, and afterwards the whole family will sit round having great bowls of bread and milk. Then we shall go out in sailing ships and have dances when we come back and a picnic with a terrific stew ending up with Benediction and bed.'[133]

Henry had not liked Rome, but everywhere he went there at his side was Father D'Arcy, 'who is the *paragon*', he told Augustus, ' – he sees every conceivable point of view without being the least bit vague or cocksure, and allows himself to be fought and contradicted perhaps more than is good for me.' In an ejaculation of enthusiasm he invited Augustus swiftly to 'come to Rome' so that he could 'cheer up D'Arcy and paint the Pope (green) and the town (red)'.[134]

Father D'Arcy, with his 'blue chin and fine, slippery mind',[135] was already famous for his brilliant converts, the best known of whom was to be Evelyn Waugh (who portrayed him as Father Rothschild in *Vile Bodies*). On his return from Rome, Henry decided to 'do a D'Arcy' and commit himself to the priesthood. In 1927 he entered as a novice the Jesuit House, Manresa, at Roehampton as the first stage of thirteen years' training. He suffered and survived this noviceship, but it altered him. By the time he went up to Heythrop College he had become a passionate theologian. No longer did the worlds of the two fathers, D'Arcy and Augustus, mingle in happy fantasy; they frothed within him in a continuous chemical antipathy. 'You are like Fryern,' he wrote to Vivien. 'Fryern is a sort of enchanted isle – very beautiful and nice and kind and fantastic; but nobody ever *learns* anything there.' It was strict neo-Thomist learning that, like a missionary gospel, he strove to implant there. Summoning up all the resources of Farm Street, the English Jesuit headquarters in May-fair, he rained on them books, pamphlets, words. With time these proselytizing exercises grew more frantic. 'Acquaint yourself with Romilly,' he ordered Father D'Arcy. 'Write to him. Save him from Behaviourism . . . send him something on psycho-analysis . . . Start on immortality.' And then: 'There is no reason why David should travel separately. Therefore *get hold of him on the platform* and talk to him all the way. [Christopher] Devlin can go to the W.C. Hint forcibly to him that he should seek companions among the other youths . . .' But for conversion, the Johns seemed very unripe fruit, and the only result of his efforts was that 'our vocabularies have increased'.

Top of this Tree of Ignorance was Augustus himself, a mighty plum. This 'great character' with his 'thunderous voice' appeared to Father D'Arcy 'a wholly fantastic figure'. He was 'never a Catholic', Father D'Arcy admitted, 'though I always felt there was a chance he might become one'. If anyone could perform this miracle it was Henry. He did not hesitate.[136] At times, it even seemed to him he was gaining. 'Daddie says there might be "some small corner" for him in the Church,' he hopefully advised Father D'Arcy. But hope sank eternal. 'I'm afraid though we're at a deadlock. He spurns revelation entirely – says he's just as religious as we are.'

Nevertheless, Henry wanted to provoke a continual discussion with Augustus over what he believed or condemned. 'You seem so aimlessly erudite, so irresponsibly appreciative,' he challenged him, '. . . you never think – you just observe things aesthetically – you like the sound and colour of theories. In you Beauty has not travailed into truth, nor diversity into unity.'[137]

These philosophical speculations jostled with offers to buy his father 'a penis-ring after the fashion of the Brazilian Tupis', and advice to 'tattoo your privies and migrate to the South Seas'.[138]

Henry's career bewildered the Johns. 'They all seem to miss Henry a lot & cannot, I think, understand much of what took him to Man[resa], & what makes him happy there,' Tom Burns wrote to Gwen John. 'I told Augustus to write to him: because I [don't] want him – or any of them to become all embittered by what must seem to them an inhuman thing – this isolation.'[139]

But Augustus regarded the Catholic Church in history as a reactionary power. He retaliated to Henry's sermonizing by trying to undermine his faith. 'What do you believe in?' he demanded.

'What you're told I suppose. It would be a grand training for you to get out of your church and take your chance with common mortals. When I'm well and sane I detest the anti-naturalism of religiosity and become a good "Pagan". Chastity and poverty are horrible ideals – especially the first. Why wear a black uniform and take beastly vows? Why take your orders from a "provincial", some deplorable decrepit in Poland. Why adopt this queer discredited premedical cosmogony? Why emasculate yourself – you will gradually become a nice old virgin aunt and probably suffer from fits which will doubtless be taken for divine possession. Much better fertilize a few Glasgow girls and send them back to Ireland – full of the Holy Ghost.'

In the expectation of miracles, and with the encouragement of Father Martindale, Henry persuaded John to paint him in the robes of a Jesuit saint, Aloysius Gonzaga, to celebrate the two hundredth anniversary of his canonization. 'Do not discover in this Jesuitical suggestion a conspiracy to baptize you (by immersion),' he adds.[140] But neither Jesuitically nor aesthetically was the experiment a success.[141] The struggle between them, for all its ludicrous aspects, was serious. 'I am a person of absolutely feverish activity . . . I am madly impatient and madly irritable and appallingly critical . . . yet I have an immense desire to be exactly the opposite of what I tend to be,' Henry had written. The Jesuit training, he believed, would teach him the secret of self-renunciation, the absolute submission of his rebellious spirit to the Will of God as manifested in Superiors. Was this not similar to what his aunt, Gwen John, had done? Yet while the rest of his family remained blatant 'bloody fools' basking in 'flashy old paganism', they were an intolerable irritant. He had elected to read philosophy at Campion Hall where Father D'Arcy was the new Master, but he could find nothing to calm his turmoil. His letters, written in a shuddering hand, and relentlessly illegible, are saturated with violence, page after page of it, like a protracted scream. Watching him, Father D'Arcy (who had advised against philosophy) was increasingly worried by what he called 'your periods of heats . . . the temperature you rise to, the complications . . .'

At the end of his time at Campion Hall, Henry gained Second Class Honours in philosophy. But this was not good enough. 'I often long very greatly to see you and the others,' he wrote to Augustus from Campion Hall. '. . . There is such an enormous amount I can learn from you.'[142] Should he 'stick to the J[esuit]s or no'? He needed advice. He was reacting against the scrupulous discipline of his training, but feared he would be misunderstood. 'He had not lost his faith,' one of his friends remarked, 'but maybe he had a bit lost his head.'[143] In the summer of 1934, he submitted a dispensation of his vows. 'The Jesuit life is not any longer my cup of tea', he wrote. 'I am not leaving for intellectual reasons but for physical ones i.e. I do not think I am meant to lead a *life of books only* . . . nor can S.J. [Society of Jesus] Superiors, generous as they are, be expected to cater for a permanent eccentric . . . Having had a determined shot, I failed. I don't think the chastity question comes into it very much at all – at any rate disinclination for a life of chastity is not a prominent reason in my mind, though of course it is present . . . I should not mind if people said I was funking disobedience – for that's quite plausible.'

This letter, far more controlled than anything he usually wrote, was sent to Augustus via Henry's Provincial 'to make sure things are quite clear'. But other writings, that sit less politely upon the page, affirm a different truth. Henry appears to have been 'girl-shy' but highly sexed. At school there had been a devastating infatuation for another boy; and during his noviciate he seems to have become painfully involved, though in a more sophisticated way, in another unrequited passion. But he was not homosexual: it was simply that he was always in the society of other men. His correspondence to his Provincial and Superiors was preoccupied with birth control and questions of sexual ethics; while to others, such as his friend Robert McAlmon, it was 'one long wail about carnal desire . . . and the searing sin of weakening'.[144] Henry also did a series of drawings, harshly pornographic, depicting a Jesuit entering heaven by violently explicit sexual means.

He had won the high opinion of G. K. Chesterton and of Wyndham Lewis, but to follow them would be once more to 'lead a *life of books only*'. To Augustus, he insisted: 'I have got to make what amounts to a fairly big fresh start, do a lot more "abdicating".' This took the form of plunging into the East End of London among the poor. 'He seems as mad as a hatter,' was Augustus's verdict. '. . . He is studying dancing – for which he shows no aptitude – and the price of vegetables.'[145] In the newspapers it was announced that, like his brother Edwin, Henry had become a boxer and would wear the papal colours on his pants. Augustus was not pleased. In the past he had often urged his son to 'quit this stately Mumbo Jumbo'. Yet he had not relished the manner of his quitting: it reeked of failure. Now he poured scorn on Henry for not discovering 'your own Divinity', and for still carrying out to the letter the injunction of Loyola by failing to look 'directly at any female'.[146] The novelist Julia Strachey, who saw him in November 1934, also observed this curious obliqueness:

'Henry John to tea . . . Sitting down in the small chair – which he placed sideways on to me – beside the bookcase, he conducted the whole conversation – metaphysical almost entirely – with his face turned away, and looked round at me only three times, I counted, during the whole session, which lasted from 4.30 till 7. What lies behind this habit? Is it, as with Ivor Novello and Owen Nares, to display his profile, which is beautiful, the shape of his head as in a Renaissance painting. It would be pleasant to indulge my daydreams about him, inhibit my critical faculties and concentrate on – say – his profile, forgetting that his full face is disappointing and makes a certain impression of insensitiveness... He refused both butter, and jam, for his scone.'[147]

His experiments at moving from the metaphysical to the physical world over the next six months were unhappy. His chief girlfriend at this time was Olivia Plunket-Greene, a disconcerting creature with bobbed hair, 'pursed lips and great goo-goo eyes'.[148] She belonged to a generation that had found in the 1920s a new emancipation; but her crazy party goings-on overlaid a character that was strange, snobbish and secretive. She was more fun-loving than loving, more intimate with crowds than single people, a sexual adventuress and religious fanatic with a love of drink, whose mute white face and slim figure dressed in black captivated many men. Among them, most unhappily, had been Evelyn Waugh. But she played him off against a formidable rival, the black singer Paul Robeson, and then sent him for religious instruction to Father D'Arcy. For she had recently 'gone over' to Roman Catholicism herself, unable to resist its 'great, tremendous and dazzling lure'. It was said that, one evening, as she was dressing for a party, the Virgin Mary dropped in with instructions to pursue an anguished life of chastity. This experience, in Waugh's judgement, was to make her 'one third drunk, one third insane, one third genius'.[149] She still appeared a fun-loving, party-going raffish girl. But she was now a saint too, who read St John of the Cross as well as *Vogue*. Whenever she began taking off her clothes she would hear the Virgin Mary's voice, and dress again. It was with her that Henry now sought to make his 'big fresh start'.

They held hands; she wrote poems; they talked; she let him kiss her: and then there were her love letters.

'You are rather a darling with your long legs, and your jerky sensitive notions and your mind busy with acceptance, I would like to give you breasts and knees and curved embraces... Wish you hadn't made me think of loving. I need to be loved, charms and skin and embraces soft and strong... But if I let you hold me in your arms, it is for a variety of reasons... Your embraces are lessons, but most enjoyable, like lessons in eating ice-cream or treacle.'

They had planned to spend part of June at a bungalow belonging to Henry's aunt, Ethel Nettleship, near Crantock in Cornwall. In the first week of June he received a six-page letter from Olivia explaining some of the reasons why she could not have sexual intercourse with him. 'I never knew how anti-birth control I was before but evidently I am.' He argued abstractedly; she promised to write again. He drove down to Cornwall; she did not come. On the evening of 22 June 1935 he bicycled to a desolate stretch of the cliffs. He was seen walking along, swinging a towel, his aunt's Irish terrier at his heels. Then he vanished.

Within forty-eight hours police were methodically searching the cliffs; scouts were lowered down on ropes to explore the caves, aeroplanes circled round, and motor boats manned by coastguards with binoculars patrolled the seas. Augustus, who had rushed down, joined in the hunt. 'I'm searching for my blessed son who's gone and fallen in the sea,' he explained to Mavis. 'I have no hope of finding him alive. His corpse will come to the surface after nine days. A damn shame you are not hereabouts . . . I suppose I'll be here a few days although corpses don't interest me.' The description of these few days he gave in *Chiaroscuro* has been criticized for its callous tone. Partly this was the result of press reporters tracking him for a 'story'; and their melodramatic accounts of the artist 'speechless with grief' and Henry's 'disconsolate terrier' that went on appearing in the newspapers. Augustus never revealed grief or guilt; he buried it away to reappear as other things. 'Henry was a wonderful fellow,' he wrote to Michel Salaman. '. . . As Ida's last child I thought of him as compensating somehow for her loss – and now . . .'[150] That the son Ida had died giving birth to should so recklessly have lost his own life troubled him, but he resolved to force the matter from his mind. For the sake of appearance, he stayed in Cornwall a week exploring the coast, but directing much of his attention to the cormorants, puffins and seals. There was some cheerful weather for the search, and almost without thinking he took a pad of paper and began sketching . . .

On 5 July, thirteen days after his disappearance, Henry's body was washed up on the beach at Perranporth, dressed only in a pair of shorts. 'Though it was without a face, from the attention of birds and crabs, I was able to identify it all the same.'[151]

In the press Father D'Arcy was quoted as saying that there could be no possibility of Henry's death having been anything other than an accident. 'In many ways he was a cheerfully irresponsible young man, and I only wonder that he has not had a serious accident before. He always took risks and loved adventure.'[152] His old schoolfriend, Tom Burns, agreed. 'Suicide was suggested. But to me that was totally out of the question: he was a lover of life if ever there was one, but from his schooldays he had been madly reckless.'[153]

John suspected otherwise. In 1943, travelling from London to Salisbury, the train being held up by an air raid, he suddenly became very talkative with the young man sharing his compartment about 'the suicide'[154] of his son. Otherwise he showed his thoughts little enough, even when a fantastic figure from the past, Mrs Everett, wrote from the Portobello Road urging him to 'send for Mr Littlejohn of Exeter, the greatest Psychic we have'. To many people who wrote offering their sympathy he replied it was a tragedy that, having climbed out of the Society of Jesus, Henry should have fallen into the sea. Dorelia too stayed calm. 'It's perfectly all right,' she assured Lady Hulse. 'Henry wasn't mine.'

They invited Father D'Arcy to say a requiem mass. 'I feel very much the cutting short of so much promise,' he wrote to Augustus. 'He & I were such friends when he was young, and I thought the world lay at his feet. He changed much & I did not for a while see eye to eye with him. But only at Whitsuntide did he come to see me. It looked as if he were beginning to recover that spontaneous & happy character with all its brilliance which he had seemed at one time to choke . . . You have had some wonderful children & he was not the least.'[155]

6

BARREN OUR LIVES

'As to "going slowly" don't we all have to sooner or later?'
Augustus John to Charles Reilly

'In spite of all,' a friend noted in her diary, 'he wasn't dead yet.' It was the others, family and friends, who kept 'popping off'. 'People seem to be dying off like flies,' he complained.[156] In December 1932 it was Mrs Nettleship. Over the years John and she had reached some sort of understanding – particularly strong when they could unite in disapproval of something, such as Henry's Catholicism. As she lay dying at her home, John burst in with two of Ida's sons and a supply of beer. He settled down by the fire in her bedroom, Ursula Nettleship remembered, 'and talked about his life in France, about French literature, what he had read, about the quayside at Marseilles and the people he'd known there, all night replenishing our glasses from the beer bottles, watching mother . . . had she been conscious she would have vastly appreciated both his presence and the completely unconventional Russian play atmosphere. And somehow, again in all simplicity, proving a very real support . . . a good memory to treasure up.'[157]

The previous year it had been his old crony, the gypsy scholar John Sampson. 'It's a ghastly blow to me,' John wrote to his widow Margaret

Sampson, 'for the Rai was so much part of my life.' In his will, Sampson left John 'as a small memento of long friendship my Smith and Wesson Revolver No. 239892'. He was cremated on 11 November 1931 and ten days later his ashes were carried to Wales. In those ten days mysterious messages passed between the gypsies, and the private ceremony was crowded with Woods and Lees, Smiths and Robertses, the men wearing red bandannas, the women in tattered dresses, their hair jingling with spangles and coins. Farmhands and village girls mingled with illustrious members of the Gypsy Lore Society: judges, architects, professors, ladies in fur coats and gentlemen in plus-fours, and then that other great Rai, Scott Macfie, ill but indefatigable, mounted on a Welsh pony. 'There is no one I have quarrelled with more often,' he wrote to Sampson's son, 'and nobody whose loss I feel more.'[158] The straggling procession, trailed at a cautious distance by a platoon of pressmen and British Movietone News, was overtaken along the way by John in his ulster and scarlet-spotted scarf, who had been chosen to act as Master of Ceremonies. He led them panting up the slopes of Foel Goch, a mountain where Sampson had often rallied his crew. Here, eyes fixed in the distance, in his hand a smouldering cigarette, he delivered his eulogium.[159] It was a blue day, his words rang out over the bright green fields, the brown woods below. After this oration, a powerful silence. The Rai's son, Michael Sampson, expressionless, scattered handful on handful of the ashes which swept in showers of fine white dust down the mountainside. The sun shone, the wind lifted their hair a little, blew the ashes round to land, like dandruff, on their shoulders. Then John, 'with his right hand out-stretched in a simple gesture as if actually to grasp that of his old friend',[160] spoke a poem in Romany. Everyone murmured the benediction *Te soves misto* ('Sleep thou well') and, as the words died away, the music began – first the strings of the harp, then the fiddles, mouth organ, clarinet and dulcimer. Someone lit a match, started a pipe; and 'we each found our own way down the hilly slopes,' Dora Yates remembered, '. . . I myself saw the tears rolling down Augustus John's cheeks as he tramped in silence back to Llangwm.'[161] Then they gathered for the funeral feast at the White Lion at the hilltop town of Cerig-y-Drudion, and there was dancing, merriment and singing. 'Wouldn't the Master have been pleased with the scene in that oak-beamed kitchen afterwards?'[162] Dora Yates asked John. But they both knew that with Sampson dead, 'half or more of the fun has gone out of Gypsying'.[163]

In 1935, Horace Cole died in exile at Ascaigne. 'I went to his funeral,' John wrote, 'which took place near London, but I went in hopes of a miracle – or a joke. As the coffin was slowly lowered into the grave, in dreadful tension I awaited the moment for the lid to be lifted, thrust aside, and a well-known figure to leap out with an ear-splitting yell. But my old friend disappointed me this time. Sobered, I left the churchyard with his widow [Mavis] on my arm.'[164]

Shortly afterwards Mavis, in silver fox furs, turned up at 11 Downing Street, the official residence of the Chancellor of the Exchequer, then Neville Chamberlain, to collect Horace's belongings from his sister Annie Chamberlain – fighting her way through the crowds that had assembled next door to find out what the Cabinet were doing over the King's threat to marry a divorced American commoner.

But there was one who refused to die, obstinately, year after year: John's father. Often he had given notice of doing so; and, summoning his courage, John would journey across to Wales. He liked on these death trips to make use of Richard Hughes's castle as an advance base, inviting himself to tea, arriving shortly after closing time and stabling himself there for ten days or so. 'My father', he would say, 'is on his death-bed, but refuses to get into it.' Every morning he set off for Tenby in his 'saloon' car with a bottle of rum, stopping on the way to sketch and then, after a telephone call, arriving back at Laugharne. Hughes, watching these forays, concluded that he must fear his father. Then, one day he would finally reach Tenby, find old Edwin John miraculously recovered, and at once motor back to Fryern, his duty accomplished.

'My father writes of the uncertainty of life and his Will – so I suppose he is thinking of moving onwards,' John notified Dorelia. That had been in 1925. Shortly afterwards the old man added by way of postscript that 'he would prefer to wait till Gwen and I have returned.' No obstacle, John considered, should be put in his way.

Augustus and Dorelia regularly invited Gwen over to stay with them, urging her to come and see, if not her father, then 'our Siamese cats' or even the children before they all grew up and went their ways. But when, after seventeen years, Gwen finally returned to England in the summer of 1921 it was to stay with Arthur and Rhoda Symons at their cottage in Kent. 'I wish you had agreed to stay with us in Dorset – where there is much more room and we would have made you quite at home,'[165] Gus wrote on learning that she was coming over.

But there was an exceptional reason for Gwen's visit to the Symonses. Rhoda Symons was the sister of Gwen's friend Isabel Bowser, who had died of cancer in 1919. Gwen had often slept in Isabel's rooms when difficulties arose between Rodin's furious American lover, the so-called Duchesse de Choisseul, and herself. 'I adore your devotion for Isabel . . . for you and me to have known Rodin is a certain link between us,'[166] Arthur Symons wrote. He bought three of her drawings in 1919, and the following year Gwen met him and Rhoda in Paris. Isabel had often told them of Gwen, and Rhoda insisted that 'I love you . . . because of your understanding of – & love of – Isabel . . . are you coming sometime to stay with us?'[167]

So Gwen made an exception. But it did not seem as if she would travel again to England. In the autumn of 1924 she reminded Gus of a huge portmanteau, miraculously full of her possessions (a dressing case, writing desk, paintbox and pictures), together with some ancient chairs and a chest of drawers, all of which she had left with Charles McEvoy in 1903 to keep for her 'till my return from Rome'. She wanted Gus to transport everything to her in France. It would, she mysteriously explained, 'be very useful now'.[168]

She still lived in the rue Terre-Neuve in Meudon, but in the autumn of 1926 she also bought a derelict shack (which she used as a studio) and a patch of overgrown ground (where she sometimes slept) near by at 8 rue Babie.

One of the reasons she did not tell Gus of this acquisition was probably that he was beginning on her behalf the purchase of Yew Tree Cottage at Burgate Cross, not far from Fryern Court, advancing her most of the purchase money of five hundred pounds. 'The cottage is yours,' Dorelia wrote to her in May 1927. 'So will you send as much money as you can spare to me. What more is wanted Gussie can lend you. I went over the cottage again yesterday . . . the whole place can be made delightful without much money.'[169] By the beginning of May the sale was completed, Dorelia had the keys and was taking measurements for curtains.

'I don't mind seeing Gus now or that family,'[170] Gwen wrote to Ursula. But there were few people she did want to see. For many years Gus had been sending her admiring letters and advice about the sale of her work. 'Instead of £50 you ought to get at least 3 times as much for a picture, and would easily if you sent some to England where I know several people who are most anxious to possess things of yours. There is no reason why you should have to submit to any discomfort or privation any longer. It can't be any good for your health or your work. I'm sure Quinn wanted to help you & get your work as long as you'ld let him.'[171] After Quinn's death, Jeanne Foster had volunteered to take his place and send her a retainer from the United States. But 'I would rather follow your advice,' Gwen told Gus, 'and send my paintings to England.'[172]

Such an arrangement might have surprised anyone who had only read Gwen's references to her brother in her correspondence to others ('he is offended by everything I do or don't do'). Gus had really become something of a scapegoat for her. Whatever the emotional disturbances between them, there also existed an emotional affinity. As a Christmas present in 1925 he sent her some earrings. 'My ears are pierced but I thought the time for earrings was over for me,' she replied. 'But these are so lovely I must wear them. If you don't like them on me when you see me I will exchange them for something else.'[173]

But when would she see him? He wanted her to hold an exhibition of her work at the New Chenil Gallery. 'Chenil writes that Gus would like a one man show with me if it's agreeable in the galleries in April,'[174] Gwen explained to Ursula Tyrwhitt on 10 November 1925. Ursula and Gwen were still 'part of each other's atmosphere'. 'If you will exhibit with me I will write & say it's not agreeable,'[175] Gwen promised. But Ursula refused to give her friend such an alibi. 'This exhibition is a nightmare,' Gwen complained.

'Paintings and drawings by Gwen John' was held at the New Chenil Gallery between May and July 1926. 'My thoughts went back to our youth with its aims and hopes,' Michel Salaman wrote to her after seeing these pictures, ' – and you seemed to be the only one of that eager band who had been utterly faithful to those aspirations, who not only had not failed them but achieved more than we dreamt of.' The girls had appeared supreme at the Slade, at least in Augustus's memory. But their advantages 'for the most part came to nought', he later wrote, 'under the burdens of domesticity which . . . could be for some almost too heavy to bear . . . "Marriage and Death and Division make barren our lives." '[176]

Though he must have been thinking of Ida, this was also largely true of her Slade contemporaries. Edna Clarke Hall's talent went into decline under her husband's discouragement. Gwen Salmond had reignited Matthew Smith's self-confidence, but the failure of their marriage and the bringing up of their two sons had made painting additionally difficult for her – and this had been compounded by the connection between Smith's success as a painter and other women. Ursula Tyrwhitt also married, but she had altered neither her name (her husband was a cousin called Walter Tyrwhitt) nor her life. 'Fortunately and by a great piece of luck I'm not at all unhappy,'[177] she told Edna Clarke Hall.

Ursula Tyrwhitt was the only friend from the Slade Gwen John consented to see when she eventually came to England for two months during the summer of 1927. '*I count on you not to tell anyone,*' she wrote, '*I will not be troubled by people.*'[178] Her nerve had almost failed, but when she did arrive she was enchanted by Yew Tree Cottage. 'I looked in through the window & saw a lovely dresser & the ground on one side is bordered by lovely little fir trees!!' she wrote to Ursula. '. . . My cottage is furnished so far only by a little picture of Gus's & the dresser . . . I am going over for a few days to whitewash the rooms.'[179]

She stayed at Fryern that summer, and so did many other people. 'As she was extremely shy, this made it necessary for her to have her meals in her bedroom,' her thirteen-year-old niece Vivien remembered. '. . . I was terribly struck by her appearance – so very like my father, but very very tiny, like a miniature Augustus, with eyes that filled with tears almost continuously as she talked; very pale, bluey eyes and she wore dark dark clothes.' She insisted on speaking French to the children, though with a Pembrokeshire accent Gus could not remember her having when they were children. There was much to do at the cottage, but Gwen was always ready to go and look at the sea at Bournemouth. Henry Lamb, who came over to Fryern, found 'a little old lady in a shawl' who, sitting beside him in the car, clutched his arm feverishly. 'He interpreted this gesture as an amorous advance,' writes her biographer Susan Chitty. 'It seems more probable that Augustus was driving.'[180]

'It is nice here,' Gwen decided. She liked the Dorset country more than Gus did, and 'the cottage has very much beauty . . . It is quite a big house too, but it looks small outside.' Dorelia and she bought furniture together, and Ursula gave her a carpet and a counterpane. But it took longer to get settled there than she expected. 'I have been sleeping here a few days,' she told Ursula.[181] But the workmen bothered her. She planned to stay until 19 September, but 'I don't want Gus to know I shant be there this winter.' She intended to return after she had finished some paintings at Meudon. 'I cant say how long they will take.'

They took a year. She returned to her cottage in 1928 and seems to have narrowly avoided her father who, she feared, might want to stay with her. 'Of course we will put up your father [at Fryern] if he will only consent,' Dorelia assured her. '. . . Do come & I want to invite your Da.'[182] She came to England once more, briefly in May 1931, to see the dying Edith Nettleship – Ida's cousin.

'I sometimes want to be there very much,' Gwen had written to Ursula Tyrwhitt. Augustus and Dorelia kept on urging her to come. 'Are you ever coming again?' Dorelia asked at the beginning of 1933. '. . . Would you like to have a show in London? Augustus's agents are anxious to have one & I think you ought to, you have many admirers over here.'[183] But Gwen had by then given up painting which she likened to housework – more tiring than it used to be and not much pleasure. Never again would she waste time promising pictures for exhibitions. For she had rather more money now. In 1930, after the death of the last surviving child of her maternal grandfather Thomas Smith, master plumber of Brighton, it had been decided to wind up the estate and dispose of the properties at auction. Over the next year Gwen received nine hundred and fifty pounds (equivalent to £26,600 in 1996) of which she transferred two hundred pounds to Dorelia for Yew Tree Cottage.

Some more family income became available later in the 1930s.

Old Edwin John still kept in remorseless communication with his children. His letters showed an unyielding devotion to the weather. 'What is the weather like in Paris?' he would ask urgently. News of its behaviour in parts of the United States and Canada were passed anxiously on to France. 'The climate is very hot,' he instructed Gwen of conditions in Jamaica while Augustus was there, ' – but usually tempered by a breeze from the sea.' At home he often found himself dramatically overtaken by some 'nice breeze', afflicted with 'unbearable heat waves', or 'in the grip of a fierce blizzard'. 'Typical November weather' did not go unobserved, nor the curious fact that 'the cycle of time has brought us to the season of Christmas again.' As he advanced into his young nineties, so the climate hardened, 'the present weather being the worst I think I have ever experienced in my life'. 'How', he demanded, 'is it going to end?' After each winter, with its unexampled frosts and snows, he revived. 'I am making good progress to recovery of health,' he assured Gwen on 28 March 1938 after an attack of bronchitis. 'I eat and sleep well and take short walks daily . . . How near Easter has become has it not? I must really purchase some Easter cards . . .' On the afternoon of 7 April, while he was resting in bed, his housekeeper heard him call out: 'Good-bye, Miss Davis. Good-bye.' When she went up to see him, he was dead.

They buried him in the cemetery at Gumfreston, a tiny damp grey church two miles from Tenby where he had played the hymns on Sundays. After some delay, an inscription, suggested by Thornton and considered to be definitive, was cut upon his gravestone:

Edwin William John
1847–1938
With Long Life will I satisfy
Him and show Him my Salvation

Augustus, Caspar and the housekeeper attended the funeral; Thornton and Winifred were too far off; and Gwen did not come. She seldom went anywhere now. Besides, Gus only sent her the news a few days after the funeral. 'I am writing to tell you of Father's death,' he announced on 16 April.

'I, Thornton & a solicitor of Haverfordwest are appointed executors & Trustees of the Estate which is of the value of some £50,000 [equivalent to £1,400,000 in 1996]. I am sending herewith a copy of the Will. As far as I can make out we, his sons & daughters, are entitled to an equal share of the Income from the Estate, which at the death of the last survivor will be divided equally between the two families of grandchildren which now or shall exist, irrespective of their numbers.'[184]

It had seemed a pity to leave her cottage empty for so long, so Gus had asked Gwen's permission to lease part of it to Fanny Fletcher. For years she had been helping Gus and Dodo, looking after the children and animals, doing the wallpapers. Now she wanted to use the cottage as a teashop. 'The suggestion is that you should [have] two rooms to yourself and your own staircase and that Fanny should pay you say £12 a year while looking after the garden & raising vegetables & flowers. She understands that you want to be left alone and thinks you need not be at all interfered with by the customers she would expect about tea-time. There seems a good chance of her making a success of this scheme if you agreed and the place would be well looked after in your absence.'[185]

Gwen agreed that this was a sensible arrangement, but when she did not come back, Augustus and Dorelia began to wonder if they had done the right thing. 'I hope you won't regret giving up half the cottage, but it will be much better to have someone there,'[186] Dorelia explained. And Gus assured Gwen that 'Fanny Fletcher will vacate your cottage whenever you want to come to it.'[187]

For more than ten years Dorelia continued giving Gwen news of her cottage. Few people came to the teashop and 'your rooms are just as they were except there is a round table and armchair . . . The garden is lovely in the front thanks to Fanny . . . Your blue room is just the same except that Fanny has taken off the cement on the floor. The bricks look much nicer . . . It's such a pity you cannot come sooner . . . A bit of your roof was blown off in a great hurricane but has been mended . . .'[188]

By 1933 Dorelia was asking: 'Are you ever coming again? Don't you think you had better sell the cottage?'[189] But evidently Gwen did not want to sell it. She often thought of Dorelia and Gus and the family, and thinking of them was less fatiguing than travelling across the Channel to see them. Besides, she occasionally saw one or other of them in France on their way to St-Rémy. It would probably have been easier for her if Gus had bought a house he coveted in Equihen that had belonged to the painter Cazin, but old Mrs Cazin still occupied it in the 1920s and would not sell.

And nor would Gwen sell since, though she was ill, she had not ruled out the possibility of going back to England until Dorelia wrote to her with a definite proposal on 30 May 1939. 'I don't suppose you will use it again, and wondered if you would sell it for the price it cost, £500 . . . Fanny is in very bad health & I should like to think she had somewhere to live if anything happened to me.'[190] So Gwen agreed, pretending to make a gift of the cottage to reduce expenses.

On 10 September, a week after Britain and France declared war on Germany, Gwen made her will in Meudon. She was sixty-three. Then, overcome by a longing for the sea, she caught a train to Dieppe, but on arrival collapsed in the street. Though she had 'not forgotten to make provision for her cats',[191] she had brought no baggage with her and was taken to the Hospice de Dieppe in the avenue Pasteur where, knowing herself to be dying, she gave a lawyer there her will and burial instructions. She died at 8.30 a.m. on 18 September. No cause of death was given on the certificate, and no one knows where she is buried.

ELEVEN

Things Past

I

BLACK OUT

'I am trying to live down my adolescent past, but find I cannot bury it altogether. I have great hopes of my maturity though.'

Augustus John to John Davenport

The hectic drive from St-Rémy to Fordingbridge in the late summer of 1939 had been for John a journey into old age. The Second World War cut off his retreat and confined him to a narrow routine. On the surface there seemed little change: it was business as usual again. 'I don't see what I can do but go on painting.'[1] But there was a difference. In the past he had often worked 'like blazes' in fits and starts ('mostly fits'). Now he began to feel 'ashamed of wasting my time . . . thinking that life went on almost for ever'. He had been studying the papers that were coming to light from Gwen's studio. 'Astonishing how she cultivated the scientific method,' he exclaimed in a letter to his daughter Vivien. 'I feel ready to shut up shop.' His own *premier coup* days were long past, and he sought to acquire some of Gwen's patience, investing time in one or two large imaginative pictures, writing a simple message on the landscape. 'I want a good 20 years more to do something respectable,' he had told Herbert Barker.[2]

During the 1940s he laboured hesitantly over a cartoon in grisaille twelve feet long called 'The Little Concert'. 'I'm doing a huge picture of imaginary people – about 25 or 30, life size,' he told his son Edwin in the summer of 1944. 'I've just provided the females with Welsh top-hats which stiffens things up greatly.'[3] The picture represents three itinerant musicians entertaining a group of peasants on the fringe of a landlocked bay. 'Though the conception is romantic, it is carried out with a classic authority of form,' wrote T. W. Earp when it was first shown at the Leicester Galleries in 1948, 'and is easily the most important achievement in English painting since the war.'[4] Wyndham Lewis, reviewing the same exhibition, described it as being 'as fine an example of Augustus John's large-scale decorative work as I have ever seen'.[5] But John himself felt unsatisfied, snatched the picture back and after some revision re-exhibited it at the Royal Academy in 1950, after which it went to a private collection. Even then he could not think of it as 'finished', and as late as 1957 was proposing to 'warm up' the monochrome. Fortunately he was prevented, and coming across this 'almost forgotten and very big composition' unexpectedly in 1961, 'I was very bucked I can tell you,'[6] he reported to his son Caspar.

Over the last twenty years of his life there was always one of these decorative compositions 'cooking' in his studio. 'Imaginative things occupy me mostly now,' he wrote to Conger Goodyear.[7] He worked on them laboriously, with much anguish and persistence, continually revising and from time to time challenging the public to see in them his finest achievement. 'They interest me very much and take up a lot of my time,' he wrote. 'What will become of them God knows.'[8] Commissioned portraits, he told Dudley Tooth, had rarely paid off and he was tired of making promises he was unable to keep. 'The artist doesn't consider the "Public" – which is the concern of the theatrical producer, the journalist, the politician and the whore.'[9] The Great War had obliterated the visionary world he had created in his painting; the Second threatened to devastate the world itself. He resolved therefore to use the opportunity war provided to retire into greater privacy; there, by the magical operation of his art, to re-illumine a peaceful paradise of sea and mountain, women, children, age and youth, music, dancing. From the age of sixty till he died at eighty-three this task overwhelmed all others.

It overwhelmed but it never eliminated his portrait painting, for he was still caught by the visible world. In these war years his portraits were of pretty girls and public men. Drawing girls he could not resist. They were to be seen – 'living fragments of my heart'[10] – in shows at the Wildenstein, Redfern and Leicester Galleries: magnified faces, almost identical, large-eyed and honey-lipped, a parody of his past. 'My drawing rather large heads appears to synchronize with wearing spectacles which do distinctly magnify,' he told the critic D. S. MacColl (17 January 1945). '. . . It often takes me ½ dozen tries before I get anything satisfactory: at any rate one can choose the best' (16 February 1940).

After weeks of refuge 'from contact with a depressing epoch', weeks in his studio spent painting 'decorations as remote as possible from the world we precariously live in',[11] a longing to paint people again, to be swept back into the world as an artist-biographer, would gain on him. It was an honourable pursuit in wartime, he believed, for an artist to paint those men who were leading the fight for one's country. He accepted a number of such commissions, but a lack of interest in his sitters helped to make this wartime portraiture unsatisfactory. 'He [John] was usually asleep when I arrived at Tite Street,' Lord Portal, Marshal of the Royal Air Force, remembered, 'and loud knocks were required to rouse him. When roused he came noisily to the door, greeted me gruffly and started clearing the space for my chair by kicking away any pieces of furniture that were in the way . . . I did not get the impression that he enjoyed painting me, but he certainly got a wonderful picture after 5 or 6 sittings. He then asked that my wife should come and look at it, which she did and admired it. She told me that while she was actually watching him at work he turned the portrait, in the course of a few minutes, into the "caricature" which she and others think it now is . . . I don't think he ever asked me what I thought . . . A powerful character, but I don't think we attracted each other.'

He did not set out to caricature; he wanted to produce noble painting. But the difficult short sittings and the lack of intimacy with his beribboned subjects would tempt him into ambiguously exaggerated concoctions of paint that pleased no one. The most celebrated of these portraits, mopped up shortly before the Normandy landing, was of General Montgomery. At first glance he looked 'a decent chap', John told his son Edwin. 'Without being a great scholar, he is polite, speaks up clearly and to the point and sits still . . . He is also apparently good at his job.' Montgomery would motor in his Rolls-Royce each day to Tite Street and sit 'as tense as a hunting dog on a shoot'[12] upon the dais John had positioned for him. 'Monty has been sitting like a brick,' John reported to Mavis, 'and the picture progresses.' But it did not progress well. Montgomery felt down-right suspicious of the whole business. John lurched around dropping cigarette ash into his paints, and Montgomery complained that 'my right ear was not in the right place.'[13] Matters deteriorated after John turned up for one sitting with a broken rib. It smelt very fishy to Monty. 'Who is this chap?' he demanded. 'He drinks, he's dirty, and I know there are women in the background!'[14] John painted away in a spirit of deepening gloom. 'It's rather unfortunate the Colonel has to be in the room while I'm working,' he lamented, 'as I feel his presence through the back of my head which interferes with concentration. I seem to be a very sensitive plant.'[15] To improve the atmosphere between the two men, another figure was imported: Bernard Shaw. 'Fancy a soldier being intelligent enough to want to be painted by you and to talk to me.' For an hour Shaw 'talked all over the shop to amuse your sitter and keep his mind off the worries of the present actual fighting'.[16] 'Little was done by me on that occasion,' John remembered. Monty hadn't been able to get a word in, but old Shaw liked 'this soldier who knows his job so well (and doesn't smoke or drink)'.[17] Then, his hour up, Shaw was driven home by Montgomery's chauffeur (whom he goaded into reaching ninety miles an hour) and sat down to write John two brilliantly nonsensical letters about the portrait. 'The worst of being 87–88 is that I never can be quite sure whether I am talking sense or old man's drivel,' he admitted.[18]

According to John, Shaw 'has a wild admiration for Monty';[19] whereas, in Shaw's view, John really was not 'interested' in him. Nevertheless, 'I don't think the result is too bad,' John hazarded after the sittings were over, 'though I haven't got his decorations exact.' Not knowing what time Montgomery could give to the painting, 'I couldn't launch out on a full length in the desert. Besides he only bargained for a head and shoulders,' John explained to Shaw. '. . . I have been concerned with his remarkable bony structure: a queer combination of massiveness & delicacy.'[20] Montgomery was appalled when he finally saw the portrait. An alcoholic blue cloud was suspended over his head, he declared, and it wasn't 'the sort of likeness he would want to leave to his son'. 'I daresay', commented John, 'I stressed the gaunt and boney aspect of his face – the more interesting one I thought.'[21] But he was familiar with dismay from his sitters, accepting it with particular geniality when, as in this instance, it enabled him to sell the picture for more elsewhere.[22]

Such work still loomed large in the public mind where even his worst failures were regarded as 'controversial'. The peculiar conditions of war held him in the limelight. He was asked to open exhibitions, to donate pictures for war victims. But it was on behalf of artists he exercised himself most energetically. He had been one of those, along with Eric Gill, Henry Moore and Ben Nicholson, who in 1933, the year of Hitler's ascendancy, had helped to form the Artists' International Association. The aim of this body had been to establish an army of artists opposing the advance of 'philistine barbarism' with periodic exhibitions 'Against Fascism and War' to which John prominently contributed. He also presented several pictures to sales for war funds and used his influence to free a number of German and Austrian refugee artists who had been interned by the British government.[23]

He joined (rather late in the day) the Voluntary Contraception League, the committee of the National Campaign for the Abolition of Capital Punishment and, though not interested in party politics, he persistently petitioned Members of Parliament on behalf of the gypsies.* He also kept in faithful correspondence with Sampson's Liverpool friend Dora Yates

---

* 'After my election to the House of Commons in 1950,' Montgomery Hyde wrote to the author, '. . . I took up the cause of gypsies. At that time they were being pushed around by the police, particularly in Kent, and Augustus took a lot of trouble in briefing me on the subject of their troubles. He was convinced that their periodic clashes with the police which were reported in a not too favourable press at the time were largely due to a misunderstanding.' Hyde's campaign ranged from an article in *Encounter* (1956) to an appeal for help to Barbara Cartland and physical intervention in the case of Sven Berlin, whose house the authorities were attempting to convert into a public lavatory.

who, since the death of Scott Macfie, was 'the best Romani scholar going'.[24] The gypsies still looked on John in good times as a brother and in bad times as their champion; and he had felt genuinely honoured in 1936 to be elected President of the Gypsy Lore Society. 'It is a distinction I had never dreamt of attaining,' he told Dora Yates.[25]

Dora Yates came to depend on his commitment, reinforced by a 'noble cheque' now and then, to this society which 'keeps alive the great work of the Baro Rai [Sampson]'.[26] Without gypsies, and this centre for gypsy scholarship, 'life indeed would be bleak for me,'[27] she admitted. And he responded: 'Be sure that I (and others) know you to be a very precious person.'[28] Though they almost never met these days, they had become curiously indispensable to each other. As academic and economic official-dom in Liverpool trampled over 'the great Sampsonian tradition', she sometimes needed John to pull her 'out of the gulf of dark despair'.[29] On reading through her letters, her 'Recollections of a Romani Rawnie [Lady]' called *My Gypsy Days*, and the *Journal of the Gypsy Lore Society* which she regularly sent to Fryern, the clamorous affairs of Egypt would rise up in his mind, reminding him of his ups and downs with Sampson, filling him 'with mixed regret and elation',[30] until he felt 'a good deal younger than I am'.[31] Then the clock would jerk forward again and 'I hardly ever see a Gypsy now-a-days.'[32]

The war affected everyone. 'People carry on marvellously through it all I must say,' he wrote to Conger Goodyear on 19 April 1941. '. . . Life in London goes on much as usual except that people don't go out so much at nights – though I do.' It was an uneventful time, 'punctuated with pin-pricks'. There was less to eat and drink, but they had plenty of vegetables at Fryern and from friends and family in the United States came parcels of food, whisky, pipes. No longer could he rove and ramble round France, but there was Mousehole in Cornwall where one of his daughters-in-law now lived – 'very pleasant. I go to Penzance for my rum.' Petrol rationing had made travel even in England difficult ('we hardly move a yard'), but the trains still ran between London and Fordingbridge, and since his journeys were 'really necessary' he could admit to being 'moderately gregarious'.

The country, in wartime, was 'like a paddock which one grazes in, like a cow, but less productive'. To enliven the scene at Fryern 'we must get a lot of children', he announced.[33] He was particularly keen to attract black children – 'darkies' as he called them – and by the spring of 1940 he and Dodo had five evacuees, all white. Dodo herself appeared to take no notice of the war, spending it in the garden; but John's letters are full of gibes against 'old Schicklgruber' (Hitler). In London no one could ignore the bombardment. 'London is being badly bombed,' he wrote to his sister Winifred on 18 October 1940. 'I was up there with Vivien the other day and saw a good deal of devastation . . . The row at night is hellish.'

He was determined not to allow these disturbances to interrupt his work even if it sometimes endangered his sitters. One of them, Constance Graham, remembers posing for him when an air raid started. John 'was utterly unperturbed, and we were seated by the enormous studio window while the bombs buzzed overhead. They might have been blue bottles for all he cared so of course I felt obliged to remain equally unmoved.'

London had become a village. People stopped each other in the streets, swapped stories about last night's raid, drank together, made one another laugh. John, 'the oaktrunked maestro' as Dylan Thomas called him, swaying between one pub and the next, was a cheerfully reassuring sight. 'He is like some great force of nature,' noted Chips Channon, 'so powerful, immense and energetic.'[34] It was out of the question that anything Hitler could do might disturb him. While the 'doodle-bug' or 'buzz-bombs' were falling, twice 'buggering up' his Tite Street studio, he would sit with Norman Douglas and Nancy Cunard in the Pier Hotel at Battersea Bridge, where the 'drink supply had generously expanded – to steady the clients' nerves'.[35] There was a marvellously enhancing quality about his presence. After an evening here, or at the Gargoyle Club in Dean Street, or the Antelope in Chelsea, he liked to invite his companions back to Tite Street for a last drink or two. At such times there seemed something undeniably lovable about him; by turns generous then angry, an old gentleman wobbling through the black-out. Back at Tite Street, on one fuddled occasion, he laid himself down vaguely on top of the artist Michael Ayrton, as if, Ayrton recalled, quite shocked, 'I were his daughter'. The third member of the party, Cecil Gray, snatched up his Quaker hat, shouted: 'I'm not going to remain here to watch this', and opening a door, walked into the broom cupboard. 'He's gone into the broom cupboard,' John declared, sitting up. 'By God he has!' Ayrton agreed, also sitting up. They stared at the closed door from which faint scufflings could be heard. Then Cecil Gray knocked, came out and took off his hat: 'I think I'll stay after all.' After which they all went to sleep.

Such stories, revealing an innocence not altogether lost, endeared him to his friends. 'Look at Augustus John!' proclaimed Norman Douglas. 'Take away his beard, close-crop his hair and Augustus would be as impressive as before. Him I admire not only as a fine man but for his way of thinking about life. Alas! I fear *he's* the last of the Titans.' In wartime John's stature appeared to grow. He was unafraid, almost grateful, for there was an external enemy to account for his look of suffering. People needed parties, drink and the boosting of their morale in much the same way as he needed these things in peacetime. Homes and buildings were everywhere being destroyed; friends, families, lovers killed. The marks of torture on John's face reflected what everyone was feeling. But his real enemy was invisible. Late one night, when Michael Ayrton was being driven home, his taxi, swerving suddenly to a halt, nearly ran over a pedestrian. It was John. Tears were streaming down his face. At Ayrton's insistence he got into the taxi to be taken back to Tite Street. 'It's not good enough,' he kept murmuring to himself. Disliking histrionics, and believing the old actor to be up to his tricks again, Ayrton tried to tease him out of this mood. 'What girl is that, Augustus? What girl's not good enough?' John gave a dismissive wave. 'My work's not good enough,' he said. Nor would he be comforted: 'My work's not good enough.'

It was seldom he could speak of anything about which he felt deeply. 'The only English thing about me is my horror of showing emotion,' he confessed to Mary Keene.[36] 'This makes my life a hideous sham.'[37] This 'sham' was a necessary covering over 'the ghastliness of existence'. He hated this war. His five adult sons were in different services; Vivien had become a nurse, Poppet worked in a canteen. Everyone, even the girls, seemed to be in uniform. In such circumstances it was 'not amusing' to remain a civilian. 'I think of joining the Salvation Army,' he joked, 'though I believe the training is severe.'[38] What depressed him was 'this foul and bogus philosophy of violence'.[39] It was a world war to end all worlds he could recognize as his own. 'I can hardly bear to think of France being overrun by those monsters,' he told Will and Alice Rothenstein.[40]

He kept working. 'What else is there to do?' he wrote to Conger Goodyear in the first week of October 1943. But he feared that his painting might become impossible. 'There seems nothing (in my line) in London just now,' he told Emlyn Williams. Yet the war, which was to transform the art world, eroding the influence of figurative painters and setting up an international style of abstract art, at first produced the reverse effect. Owing partly to Britain's isolation and the difficult conditions for young painters, the public's attention was forced back to previous generations of artists, to Whistler, Sickert and John himself.

A black-out stretched over London. 'It extended to every form of pleasure, recreation or enlightenment,' wrote Kenneth Clark, Director of the National Gallery.[41] 'Theatres and concert halls were in darkness, museums and galleries were closed, most art dealers shut up shop.' The permanent collection at the National Gallery was evacuated to an 'unknown destination' (Wales), and the building was used as a canteen for war workers. But every lunchtime concerts were put on and, 'to uphold the traditions of art in the winter of the Blitzkrieg',[42] special exhibitions were also held. The most popular of these exhibitions was 'British Painting since Whistler', to which one hundred and twelve Augustus John drawings were added between 21 November 1940 and 22 March 1941. Twice the opening was delayed by bombs which destroyed part of the roof and courtyard and some of the galleries themselves, and the drawings were moved for safety into the ground-floor room of the east wing previously reserved for Dutch pictures. Over eleven thousand people made their way round the craters and down into the long room divided into bays where John's drawings, 'representative of various aspects of my draughtsmanship from student days to the present', were hung. 'It is an astonishing record,' wrote Herbert Read, 'and it is doubtful if any other contemporary artist in Europe could display such virtuosity and skill.'[43] A year later Lillian Browse produced her volume of *Augustus John Drawings*, and in 1944 Phaidon Press published John Rothenstein's *Augustus John* which, despite wartime paper restrictions, went into three editions in two years.

Rumours of a knighthood had been blowing around, and when it was offered to John early in the war he felt unaccountably pleased. Unfortunately there was a fly in the ointment. Buckingham Palace soon discovered that he was not officially married to Dorelia, and he was discreetly requested to put matters on a regular footing. He had no objections. Dorelia and he might well have married if there hadn't been so many paintings to finish and so much work to do in the garden. But the thing had to be done properly. So, after almost forty years and the birth of four children, he went down on one knee and formally asked for her hand in marriage – and she turned him down! It was ridiculous to marry so late and for such a reason. Besides, she had no wish to be known as 'Lady John'. So the knighthood receded and, brooding in the pub, John felt strangely out of sorts. Then in 1942, three months after the death of Wilson Steer, he was offered the Order of Merit – a much more distinguished award, it was explained, which did not have repercussions on one's marital status. He brightened at once. 'It is of course a matter both of pride and humility to succeed Steer in this order,' he instructed D. S. MacColl on 25 June 1942.[44] 'Daddy got what Tristan calls his "medal" on Thursday,' Dorelia wrote to Edwin on 4 July 1942, '& the ceremony went off quite well.' He was engulfed with congratulations. 'I knew it was a great distinction,' he told John Freeman, 'and I thanked them for it, whoever they were. But I wasn't oppressed by the grandeur.' There were some, however, who deplored the old republican having accepted recognition from the monarch. His response to all criticism was that people should be allowed to do whatever they liked, and benefit by whatever gave them pleasure. He disapproved of hereditary titles but found in other awards a romantic appeal. He supported Anthony Wedgwood Benn's fight against disqualification as a Member of Parliament because of his inherited peerage,[45] but also defended Herbert Read's 'courageous decision' to take on a knighthood in 1953 when his fellow anarchists were sharply critical. 'Although we may diverge in some matters, I think you were quite right to accept a knighthood (though I feel it should have been a baronetcy),' John wrote to him. 'If there is one thing certain, it is that there is no such thing as "equality" in human society, and your Order, symbolizing this truth, justifies itself in admitting you.'[46]

As for his own award, though not to be overvalued, it gave him a momentary glaze of harmless pleasure. 'Would you believe it?' he asked in a letter to his sister Winifred. 'It is the rarest of all orders.' He treated it in the manner of a private transaction between himself and George VI – and particularly good of the monarch considering how much of his wife's time he had squandered. But he discouraged outsiders from concerning themselves with it. 'I only remember the O.M.,' he reprimanded D. S. MacColl, 'when others forget it.'

2

FRAGMENTS

'I feel writing a great labour and takes up too much time when I
should be painting. However it is often too dark to paint.'
Augustus John to Sean O'Casey (1952)

'I am two people instead of one: the one you see before you is the old painter. But another has just cropped up – the young writer.' With these words at a Foyle's Literary Lunch in March 1952, John announced the publication of *Chiaroscuro*, his 'fragments of autobiography'. It had been a lengthy cropping-up – a month or two short of thirty years. 'I think we must all write autobiographies. There would be such side-splitting passages,' he had urged Henry Lamb on 13 June 1907. But it was not for another fifteen years that he was seriously importuned by publishers. 'I've been approached by another firm on the subject of my memoirs,' he wrote to the publisher Hubert Alexander on 21 February 1923. The approaches multiplied, grew bolder; the delay lengthened, became confused. A synopsis – three-and-a-half sides of Eiffel Tower paper in fluent handwriting reaching forward to 1911 – was probably done before the end of 1923, but sent to no one; and another fifteen years slipped by before a contract was signed. The interval was full of speculations: the whispering of vast advances[47] and extraordinary disclosures.

'Other people's writing has always interested me,' runs the first sentence of *Chiaroscuro*. He was surprisingly well-read – surprisingly because he was never *seen* with a book. At Alderney and Fryern visitors were made to feel it was somehow reprehensible to be caught in the act of book-reading. John himself read in bed. He devoured books voraciously, reading himself into oblivion, to escape the horrors of being alone. His library reflected the wide extent of his tastes – occultism, numerology, French novels, Russian classics, anthropology, anarchy, cabbala – and the ill-discipline with which he pursued them all.

He had long dreamed of writing. Privately he composed verse – ballads, sonnets, limericks – and was immoderately gratified when Dylan Thomas exhorted him to pack in painting for poetry. But he had also written for publication: first, with the encouragement of Scott Macfie, for the *Journal of the Gypsy Lore Society*; then, with the approval of T. E. Lawrence, a preface for a J. D. Innes catalogue; some pieces for A. R. Orage's *New Age*; a few pages, under the guidance of Cecil Gray, about the composer 'Peter Warlock' (Philip Heseltine); and, with the help of T. W. Earp, eight articles on painting for *Vogue*. More recently, with Anthony Powell's support, he had completed an essay on Ronald Firbank. He needed encouragement. 'I have not a practised hand at writing & am quite aware of the howlers a novice is capable of,'[48] he told Cecil Gray. In the spring of 1930 Jonathan Cape wrote to say that he 'would be very proud to be the publisher' of his reminiscences. Eight-and-a-half years later, in the autumn of 1938, John was able to assure him: 'I have thought of a good opening – which was holding me up.'

Their contract was an engaging work of fantasy. John would deliver his completed manuscript by All Fools' Day 1939 'or before'. The length was to be 'at least 100,000 words' and it should be 'copiously illustrated'. The prospect excited everyone. 'I believe this to be a big book on both sides of the water,' enthused his publisher in the United States.[49] Much correspondence crossed this water over the next twelve months from one publisher to the other and back: but from John, nothing. He had equipped himself with a literary agent[50] to whom, on 2 May 1939, he expressed his appreciation of their dismay. Nevertheless 'the idea of the book has developed and interests me more and more,' he maintained. '. . . When I am quite myself again it will unroll itself without much difficulty and turn out a success.' The war, seen by his publishers as a cause for acceleration, he saw as a fresh reason for delay. He continued distressingly to play the optimist. Already by January 1940 he had made 'an important step forward in destroying what I have already written', he promised Cape. In vain his agent would expound John's method of allowing 'his work to accumulate until everybody loses patience and subsequently complete it in an incredibly short time'. It was a case of 'this year, next year, sometime – ' growled Cape.[51] 'Each time I have seen him [John], he has told me how busy he is, painting portraits.'[52] The publishers formally conceded defeat in the autumn of 1940, the fabulous contract expired and this first stage of negotiations was at an end.

But Jonathan Cape himself had not surrendered. 'I have the strong conviction that John is a natural writer,' he had told the United States publisher Little, Brown and Company. The book had been conceived; what it now needed was a team of midwives to nurse it into the world. First of these *aides-mémoire* was Cyril Connolly, who had recently launched his monthly review of literature and art, *Horizon*. In conversation with Connolly one day, John volunteered to write something for the review, and this led to an arrangement whereby Cape allowed Connolly to have, without fee, what amounted to serial rights in John's autobiography. Between February 1941 and April 1949, John contributed eighteen instalments to *Horizon*.[53] He liked writing in short sections and, knowing how 'a little food and drink [can] make things move along', every time he had a few pages ready he would arrange an evening in London with Connolly, without whose support it is unlikely that the book would have been written. John's letters are full of author-complaints. He seized upon air raids, black-outs, apple-tree accidents, electricity cuts, bouts of 'Mongolian' or 'Korean' flu, broken ribs, dislocated fingers, operations, thunderstorms – any narrow squeak or Act of God that made painting impracticable – to turn to 'my literary responsibilities'. Over a decade of such setbacks he gradually edged forwards.

At the beginning of 1949 Jonathan Cape tiptoed back into the arena, and John was persuaded to reorganize his *Horizon* pieces into a book. He made heavy weather of this 'colossal task'.[54] 'I lack paper,' he cried out. Secretaries were provided; he changed his agent and joined the Society of Authors. He was full of ideas, eager for advice (with which he sometimes lit his pipe). In place of Cyril Connolly, Jonathan Cape dispatched John Davenport, a friend of Dylan Thomas, to be his literary philosopher and the two of them 'spent many pleasant days together at odd intervals'.[55] As a way out of his difficulties Davenport proposed that John simply abandon the autobiography, and instead commission him to write a biography. But John reluctantly demurred. 'I feel if anybody is to do it, it will have to be myself.'

Back in London, Cape was foaming with impatience. He began to petition some of John's friends and, a bad blunder, girlfriends. Learning this, John fell into a passion. His publisher was excavating for 'scurrility and scandal which I'm not able or willing to provide'. He would stand no nonsense. 'I've done nothing drastic about Cape yet,' he threatened. '. . . I would have to seek advice.' To John Davenport he pointed out the terrible lesson this had taught him against overfamiliarity with tradespeople. 'I regret having been inveigled into getting on friendly terms with this business man . . . He had incidentally an eye on Mavis.'

In 1950 Cape sent his last ambassador to Fryern, the tenacious Daniel George. 'My function was merely that of the tactful prodder, the reminder of promises, the suggester of subjects, the gentle persuader,' Daniel George wrote.[56] John's writing technique, similar to his method of painting, depended upon short bursts and timeless revision. 'I would receive from him two or three quarto sheets of small beautifully formed and regular script,' Daniel George remembered. '. . . On one such sheet now before me are twenty-five lines, only seven of which are without some emendation. One line reads: "I am a devil for revision. I cannot write the simplest sentence without very soon thinking of a better one." Here the words "very soon" have been changed to "at once".'

John called it 'putting my stuff in order'. Once a few pages had been typed, they were sent back to him, and after further copious corrections ('I keep thinking of fresh things') he would submit them for retyping. They were then returned to him and he would set about 'improving certain recent additions and making a few new ones'.[57] This process would jog on until the typescript was mislaid. 'I am most unmethodical,' John admitted, 'and have been troubled too by a poltergeist which seizes sheets of writing from under my nose and hides them, often never to reappear.'[58] It was Daniel George who released him from this predicament by inventing a conspiracy of forgetfulness. He 'forgot' to send the revised revisions back to John who forgot never having received them. It worked perfectly. After this John's area for revision was restricted to the title, which he altered a dozen times before uniting everyone in opposition to his final decorative choice, *Chiaroscuro*, 'a forbidding mouthful for the timid bookbuyer'.

The book was reviewed widely when it appeared in 1952. Lawrence Hayward in the *Guardian* called John 'a writer of genius'. Desmond MacCarthy, Sacheverell Sitwell and Henry Williamson also praised what Will Rothenstein had called the 'splendidly baroque' quality of his prose style.[59] 'Augustus John is an exceptionally good writer; and upon this most reviewers have dilated, with a tendency to compare him with other painters who have written books,' criticized Wyndham Lewis in the *Listener*. 'This is the obvious reaction, it would seem, when a painter takes to the pen: to see a man of that calling engaged in literary composition, affects people as if they had surprised a kangaroo, fountain-pen in hand, dashing off a note. The truth is that Augustus John is doubly endowed: he is a born writer, as he is a born painter . . .'[60]

These reviews were a measure of the affection in which John was now held in the country – an affection that ignored the unhappy complications of his character. 'What a pleasure it is to read this robust autobiography of a man who has achieved all he has desired from life,' exclaimed Harold Nicolson in the *Observer*. To such devastating irony many readers were blind. *Chiaroscuro* presents John as an enigma. It gives a sense of his powerful personality and a feeling of great waste. It is 'a tragic record', in Quentin Bell's words. John 'had gained the whole world and lost his talent'. The atmosphere is of expanding fame and deepening loneliness, a general disgust, and a sardonic humour through which he gave that disgust expression. 'A great character emerges, a giant covered with the dust of a falling world,' wrote a reviewer in the *Twentieth Century*. '. . . A Celtic melancholy underlies all: Chiaroscuro is an apt title.'

Tom Hopkinson in Britain and Geoffrey Grigson in the United States attacked the book in print; otherwise criticisms were voiced in private. One of the more severe critics was the man who, perhaps more than any others, had helped to get it written: Cyril Connolly. In Connolly's view, despite the long years of preparation, John had not gone through enough agony. 'For someone who was such a brilliant conversationalist he was terribly inhibited when he wrote . . . He would fill his writing with the most elaborate clichés. He couldn't say "She was a pretty girl and I pinched her behind". He would say: "The young lady's looks were extremely personable and I had a strong temptation to register my satisfaction at her appearance by a slight pressure on the *derrière*." '[61]

Only in the opening pages, recalling his boyhood in Pembrokeshire, did John achieve sustained and imaginative narrative. The rest of the autobiography arranges itself into a scrapbook, brief brilliant moments and haphazardly plotted incidents with little reference to their sequence. Increasingly he relied on indistinct anecdotes relating the misfortunes of his friends and the loss of their women implicitly to him – traits that were to be amusingly parodied by Julian Maclaren-Ross.[62] Sometimes he felt like writing 'with less bloody diffidence and reserve', but usually found he had hidden more than he revealed. In a passage which the editor, J. R. Ackerley, removed from Wyndham Lewis's review in the *Listener* (20 March 1952), Lewis asked: 'Why should there not be something in the way of a "Confession"? He informs us at the end of "Chiaroscuro" that he does not lay bare his heart, which, he adds, concerns no one but himself. I think he is wrong there, everyone would be delighted to look into his heart; and so great a heart as his is surely the concern of everybody.' But John did not wish, he claimed, to 'spoil other people's fun' later on. 'Much of the portraiture in the book is sketchy and incomplete,' he admitted to Dora Yates (10 March 1952). 'Perhaps a kind of shyness has often led me to conceal my true feelings or camouflage them under a show of bravura & high-spirits I was far from feeling.'

John's preference for a combination of reverberating syllables to a single short word encumbers his prose, but does not conceal his genuine enjoyment of language. There are many passages of sudden beauty, of wit and penetrating irony: but being unattached to anything they do not contribute to a cumulative effect. Also: 'There is too much facetiousness', he told John Davenport, '. . . this is a form of evasion'. He had laboured long at these fragments, but never to connect them, and the result, he concluded, was 'a bit crude and unatmospheric'. Contrasting Caitlin Thomas's *Leftover Life to Kill* with *Chiaroscuro*, he wrote to Daniel George: 'As a self-portrait it's an absolute knock-out. Unlike me she cannot avoid the truth even at its ghastliest.'

As soon as *Chiaroscuro* was published he started 'writing on the sly'[63] a second series of fragments. 'I'll get on with the next with renewed energy,' he promised Caspar. John Lehmann, editor of the *London Magazine*, and Leonard Russell at the *Sunday Times* assisted one section or another into print, and 'Book-lined Dan', as he now called Daniel George, continued with him to the end. As with *Chiaroscuro*, there are good pages.[64] But generally this second volume is scrappier than its predecessor. John had become so 'literary' that he had lost the innocent style. Compared to his paintings, simple and primitive at their best, the deviousness of this writing is extraordinary. In the book he focused his mind retrospectively on the actual world which, in these last years, held for him a lessening interest. 'My second book languishes,' he reported to John Davenport. It was uphill work. In almost ten years he completed a hundred and ten pages. Early in 1960 Jonathan Cape died, but his partner wrote to assure John that the company's policy and plans remained unaltered. So did John's until his own death eighteen months later. Not until 1964 was this doubly posthumous work published.

There could be no amendments this time to the title, which pointed to what for so many years had troubled him most: *Finishing Touches.*

*

Gwen's will surprised everyone. 'It could hardly have been more succinct,' Augustus remarked. She left a small legacy to Thornton, and made her nephew Edwin her heir and executor. 'Our meetings were few and far between & more often than not my communications by letter remained unanswered,' Edwin had told his brother Henry early in the 1930s. The reason she 'shunned my society', he explained, was that 'I indulged in the horrible and degrading pursuit of boxing.'[65]

But by the mid-1930s Edwin was no longer 'Teddy John of Chelsea', the hefty humorous fellow whom Augustus had so much liked. He had taken up painting instead of boxing, and gone to live in Paris for three years with his wife and small son. Gwen was still rather suspicious of him. When she had told him that she believed Georges Rouault to be 'the greatest painter of our day',[66] it seemed to her that he had given a contemptuous snigger – though later, having perhaps heard Rouault praised by others, he volunteered that at the exhibitions Rouault put everyone else in the shade. Coming up with her opinions as if they were his own discoveries was merely the awkward process of his education. By the time he left Paris in 1938, he had picked up a good deal of artistic knowledge. The following year, when she died, he was still only thirty-three.

Edwin went over to France in September 1939 to wind up Gwen's estate. 'I retrieved a mass of beautiful drawings in various mediums, pencil, gouache, water colour, charcoal, etc.,'[67] he wrote to Maynard Walker, a gallery owner in New York. Augustus was 'deeply impressed'[68] by these pictures when Edwin brought them to England. A number of galleries wanted to show Gwen's work, and the Matthiesen Gallery in London was chosen to represent her estate. In 1940 Matthiesen held an exhibition of her paintings and drawings at the Wildenstein Gallery in Bond Street. 'I am flummoxed by their beauty,'[69] wrote Augustus, who offered to pay for the mounting and framing of the pictures. Because of the war it was impossible to show more of her work for another half-dozen years. The easy beginnings were now over and difficulties began to accumulate.

During the war Augustus and Edwin got terribly on each other's nerves. 'What's eating you?' Augustus demanded. Edwin was vexed by the feeling that his father treated him 'like muck' because he was a 'miserable private' in the Military Police. 'Come off it!' Augustus exclaimed. But it was true that he had always felt the police to be his natural enemies, and hated thinking of his son among them. 'It is an impossible situation,' he protested. '. . . The Police is hardly the correct service for an old Collégien de Normandie and Pooleyite.'[70] But it was no joking matter for Edwin. He attributed his difficulties to the carelessness Augustus had lavished over his education. 'Forget it!' Augustus commanded. When Edwin somewhat unrealistically asked his father to 'pull some strings' on his behalf with General Montgomery during one of their portrait sittings, Augustus bluntly answered: 'I did mention your case [to Monty] but failed to interest him.'[71]

They could not avoid paining each other. Though they tried to make peace, spending 'some precious beer-time' together in pubs that had escaped the Blitz and swapping useful wartime tips ('Bird's Custard

Powder is the best lubricant'), provocation and insult were as natural as breathing to them. Both suffered from 'neurotic inversion', Augustus diagnosed after reading a book by the Russian émigré philosopher Nicholai Berdyaev. 'It's a pretty prevalent complaint among people with over delicate sensibilities,' he explained.[72] Edwin could no more escape this complaint than he could escape being Augustus's son – indeed they were virtually the same thing. Throughout their long correspondence, he tried calling his father 'Augustus', but almost always it came back to 'Dear Daddy'.

After the war their battle centred itself on Gwen's affairs. The struggle as to who could serve her reputation the better reached deep into them, and was aggravated by legal complexities. Edwin, as the executor and chief legatee, was in authority; which is to say he occupied the father's role – he even had the same name as Augustus's father. Augustus himself felt an instinctive protectiveness towards Gwen arising from their childhood days together. In 1946 Edwin gave Matthiesen permission to hold a large memorial exhibition of Gwen's paintings and drawings in London, and Augustus (who had written an article on his sister for the *Burlington Magazine* in 1942) agreed to contribute a foreword to the catalogue. 'I don't fancy strangers writing about her somehow,' he told Edwin. 'As I blame myself continually for having even appeared to be unkind to her at times, the task seems doubly fitting.'[73]

His unkindness now turned towards Edwin, and he took offence at the Matthiesen catalogue for which he had eventually 'coughed up' an introduction. 'While this fiasco has been arranged,' he chided Edwin, 'I presume you have been conspicuously absent in your mousehole.'[74] He needed to make an imaginative act of reconciliation with Gwen, and proposed publishing a memoir of her. 'I am prepared to do this myself,' he announced to Edwin at the end of November 1946, 'being the sole person living competent to do so. If there were anyone else equally or better equipped I would gladly retire as writing is a great labour.'[75]

Edwin appeared anxious to relieve Augustus of this great labour. But the suggestion that Romilly's wife publish a memoir of Gwen infuriated him; while a more interesting proposition for a volume by Wyndham Lewis about both Gwen and Augustus came to nothing. It seemed to Augustus that his son was continually frustrating the act of atonement he wished to make with Gwen. 'I am perplexed to know what it is that is expected of me,' Edwin protested. In fact they were both profoundly perplexed. Whatever they did ended up with 'brickbats', and though the 'door to conciliation is never closed',[76] neither of them could walk through it. It was acutely distressing. Sarcasm had become their form of intimacy, and like a poison it paralysed them.

So, through a fog of pomposity, father and son went on exchanging brickbats, both of them perpetually outraged by the misery of it all. 'Obviously you have completely misunderstood my letter . . . If I have failed to get the correct meaning of your letter you have equally misunderstood mine . . . I had no idea that my last communication, re the book, was going to arouse so foul an exhibition of bad taste (and worse). It is an unpleasant surprise . . . Your reasoning faculties are still in eclipse . . . Is your presence really necessary? . . . my advice is, Keep away . . . Let us call it a day then . . . One has, so far as possible, to protect one's peace of mind.'[77]

Augustus finally gave up his idea of writing a memoir of Gwen after Winifred appealed to him to give it up. 'There is no one in the world who would be more averse to having their private life made public,' she wrote in 1956. 'Gwen would wish to be forgotten. I think I knew her better than anyone else ever did, and now I know this to be true. Thornton feels the same way.'[78]

Later scholarship has shown up factual errors in the pages about Gwen that appear in *Chiaroscuro* and *Finishing Touches*.[79] But these glimpses from their shared attic in Tenby and rooms in London, his oblique references to her passions at the Slade and in France, the clues about her nature scattered through notes and letters which he quotes, and his celebration of the talent she so methodically disciplined, are illuminated by genuine understanding and happiness. 'Few on meeting this retiring person in black, with her tiny hands and feet, a soft, almost inaudible voice, and delicate Pembrokeshire accent, would have guessed that here was the greatest woman artist of her age, or, as I think, of any other.'[80]

3

THE MORNING AFTER

'Our late Victory has left us with a headache, and the Peace we
are enjoying is too much like the morning after a debauch.'
Augustus John, 'Frontiers', *Delphic Review* (Winter 1946)

For John, the war had been a winter, long, dark, 'immobilizing me for a devil of a time'. Six years: then all at once 'a whiff of spring in the air, a gleam of blue sky . . . renewal of hope and a promise of resurrection'.[81] It was impossible not to feel some tremor of optimism: 'the age-old fight for liberty can recommence.' Though the world had been spoilt 'there must be some nice spots left.'[82] He was still able-bodied – it was time to be on the move again. 'We sometimes refer to St-Rémy,' John wrote to his son Edwin, 'and, in monosyllables, wonder if we might venture there with car.' It was not until the late summer of 1946 that he came again to the little *mas* 'au ras des Alpilles'.

He had raced away in 1939, after much anguish and delay. 'I think of it as a shipwreck, this journey,' Van Gogh had written to his brother Theo on leaving St-Rémy fifty years earlier. 'Well, we cannot do what we like, nor what we ought to do, either.' That was very much how John felt at the beginning of the war. 'Il regarda au mur les toiles qu'il laissait inachevées,' his neighbour Marie Mauron remembered, 'les meubles qui avaient charmé sa vie provençale de leur simplicité de bon aloi, les beaux fruits de sa table et de ses "natures mortes", ses joies et ses regrets . . . Sur quoi, Dorelia et lui, émus et tristes mais le cachant sous un pâle sourire, nous laissèrent les clés de leur mas pour d'éventuels réfugiés, amis ou non, qui ne manquèrent pas, et de l'argent pour payer le loger, chaque année, jusqu'à leur retour.'[83]

Seven years later they collected their keys. St-Rémy had been a place of no military importance and the damage was not spectacular. Yet 'everything and everybody looked shabbier than usual,' John noted.[84] The *mas* had been broken into and a number of his canvases carried off: one of a local girl – 'a woman at St-Rémy I simply can't forget' – he missed keenly. French feeding wasn't what it had been and the wine seemed to have gone off. But in the evening, at the Café des Variétés, he could still obtain that peculiar equilibrium of spirit and body he described as 'detachment-in-intimacy'. The conversation whirled around him, the accordion played, and sometimes he was rewarded 'by the apparition of a face or part of a face, a gesture or conjunction of forms which I recognize as belonging to a more real and harmonious world than that to which we are accustomed'.[85]

To fit together these gestures and faces so that they came to reveal a harmony below the discord of our lives – that was still John's aim. 'I began a landscape to-day which seemed impossible,' he wrote to Wyndham Lewis in October. 'At any rate I will avoid the *violence* of the usual meridional painter. In reality the pays est très doux.' For two months he went on painting out of doors, and the next year he painted in Cornwall. Then in the summer of 1950, in his seventy-third year, he returned to St-Rémy, tried again, 'and I despair of landscape painting'.[86] That summer, they gave up the lease of the Mas de Galeron. After this there was little point in travelling far. Each summer they would prepare for a journey west or south; the suitcases stood ready but the way was barred by unfinished pictures; autumn came, the air grew chill, and they began unpacking.

There seemed so little time. John could seldom bear to leave the illusory lands he was striving to discover in his studio; for the actual world had little to give him now. 'After the Hitler war he seemed a ghost of himself,' Hugh Gordon Proteus remembered. He moved about it uncertainly. The writer William Empson recalled a last meeting with him in the 1950s.

'I came alone into a pub just south of Charlotte St, very near the Fitzroy Tavern but never so famous, and found it empty except for John looking magnificent but like a ghost, white faced and white haired . . . it was very long after he had made the district famous, and I had not expected to see anyone I knew. "Why do you come here?" I said, after ordering myself a drink. "Why do you?" he said with equal surliness, and there the matter dropped. I had realized at once that he was haunting the place, but not that I was behaving like a ghost too. It felt like promotion . . .'[87]

For John, as for Norman Mailer, the fifties was 'one of the worst decades in the history of man'. Industrial corrosion seemed to have attacked everything in which he once took pleasure. 'Our civilization grows more and more to resemble a mixture of a concentration and a Butlin camp,' he wrote to Cyril Connolly.[88] Even the public houses were being made hideous by 'manifestations of modern domestic technology'. Young girls walked about dressed like the Queen Mother. The food, the rationing and economic restrictions all contributed to 'the sense of futility and boredom which, together with general restlessness and unease, marks the end of an epoch'.[89]

'My outlook on life or rather death . . . [assumes] a Jeremy Bentham-like gloom,' John told Tommy Earp.[90] 'We shall have little to do with the New World that approaches and, by the look of it, it is just as well.' He saw a special danger in the effect of architecture upon the conduct of our lives. Already 'Paris at night has the aspect of a vast garage'; and as for London 'either it or I or both have . . . deteriorated greatly since our earlier associations which I so much loved.' He was 'reconciled', he told Thelma Cazalet, 'to a change of planet in the near future. If we are due to be blown to Kingdom Come, it may be our only chance of getting there after all.'

The anxiety people were feeling about their future under the shadow of the hydrogen bomb was something to which John was acutely sensitive. 'The bombs improve,' he wrote to his son Robin, 'the politics grow worse.' He had never been interested in party politics. 'I've got a clean slate,' he swore to Felix Hope-Nicholson. 'I've never voted in my life.' The endlessly depressing news from the radio increased his despair. He felt a mounting dislike of professional politicians. If he had sympathy for any party, it was for the Liberals, perhaps because they never got into power these days.

But he was more deeply attracted to the concepts of anarchy ('Anarchism is the thing, anarchism and Bertrand Russell') and communism, deploring the failure of Britain's two Prime Ministers in the late forties and early fifties to differentiate between communism ('which surely lies at the basis of all human society') and Soviet Kremlinism under Stalin and his successors.

In his years of haphazard reading John had come across the philosophical writings of the nineteenth-century French social reformer Charles Fourier, and saw in his Utopian theory of gregarious self-governing social groups something similar to what he was trying to depict in his large decorations. Despite some socialist pedantry, there was, he believed, 'a strain of wisdom' in Fourier.

'This is shown by his elimination of the state, of national frontiers, armies & trade barriers and in his principle of co-ownership of his Phalansteries without either levelling down or subjection to High Finance. He was indeed "an original" with a touch of genius. As for his oddities, I find them charming and égayant . . . eg his proposal to harness the Aurora Borealis so as to convert the Arctic regions into a suitable terrain for market-gardening . . . His "Harmony", at any rate, has its funny side which is more than can be said for our civilization.'[91]

Fourier became the hero of John's later years, uniting the principles of anarchy and communism, comedy with idealism; while in the world of contemporary politics his special villain was General Franco. In 1942 he had joined the Social Credit Party, 'our only certainty',[92] and in 1945, after the National Council for Civil Liberties had temporarily become a Communist Front organization unhelpful to anarchists, he joined Benjamin Britten, E. M. Forster, George Orwell, Herbert Read and Osbert Sitwell in sponsoring the Freedom Defence Committee 'to defend those who are persecuted for exercising their rights to freedom of speech, writing and action'.[93]

But John was not a man for committees. The best elucidation of his beliefs appeared in the *Delphic Review*,[94] a magazine edited in Fordingbridge. 'We are not very happy' – this was his starting point. Looking round for a cause of this unhappiness, he sees the threat of 'extinction not only of ourselves, but of our children; the annihilation of society itself'. Left to themselves, he believed, 'people of different provenance' would not 'instinctively leap at each other's throats'. The atmosphere of political propaganda which we constantly breathed in from our newspapers, radios and television sets had set off a reversal of our instincts. 'Propaganda in the service of ideology is the now perfected science of *lying* as a means to power.' For someone passionately neutral like himself and 'no great Democrat either', the best course had been silence. But silence was no longer a sufficient safeguard to neutrality. So in the age of microphone and media 'I have decided that a practice of ceaseless ... loquacity should be cultivated.'

By the end of the 1940s he was publishing and broadcasting his message. National sovereign states, he argued, were by definition bound to fall foul of one another. All nationalities are composed of a haphazard conglomeration of tribes. But the state, originating in violence, must rely on force to impose its artificial uniform on this conglomeration, transmitting its laws and class privileges like a hereditary disease. 'The State', he warned, 'must not be judged by human standards nor ever be personified as representing the quintessence of the soul of the people it manipulates. The State is immoral and accountable to nobody.' The real quintessence of all people lay in their 'needs and in their dreams' – their need 'to gain their living; freedom to use their native tongue; to preserve their customs; to practise any form of religion they choose; to honour their ancestors (if any); to conserve and transmit their cultural traditions, and, in general, to mind their own business without interference.' Their need also to feel planted in the land: though many would not know what to do if they found themselves there.

John's alternative to 'the collective suicide pact' of the 1950s was for a breaking down of communities into smaller groups – the opposite of what has taken place in the last forty years. He began with hedges. The modern hedge, with which the country had been parcelled out by financial land-grabbers, must be dug up:

'Hedges are miniature frontiers when serving as bulkheads, not wind-screens. Hedges as bulkheads dividing up the Common Land should come down, for they represent and enclose stolen property. Frontiers are extended hedges, and divide the whole world into compartments as a result of aggression and legalized robbery. They too should disappear. . . They give rise to the morbid form of Patriotism known as Chauvinism or Jingoism. Frontiers besides are a great hindrance to trade and travel with their customs barriers, tariffs and *douanes* . . .'

Without frontiers, John reasoned, the state would wither and the whole pattern of society change from a heavy pyramid to the fluid form of the amoeba, 'which alone among living organisms possesses the secret of immortality'. Our monstrous industrial towns, our congested capital cities with their moats of oxygen-excluding suburbs would melt away, and a multiplicity of local communities appear, dotted over the green country, autonomous, self-supporting, federated, reciprocally free. 'Gigantism is a disease,' he warned. '. . . Classical Athens was hardly bigger than Fordingbridge.'

Such beliefs, later commonplace among those advocating an alternative society to capitalism, sounded eccentric in the late 1940s. During the last dozen years of his life John found himself part of a gathering minority. What joined him to others was the atomic bomb. Progress by massacre, historically so respectable, seemed no longer morally acceptable.

'In the practice of some primitive "savages", warfare is a kind of ritual: should a casualty occur through the blunder of an inexperienced warrior, a fine of a pig or two will settle the business and everybody goes home (except one). Modern warfare is different. We'll all be in it, the helpless as well as the armed . . . There will be no quarter given, for the new Crusaders have no use for "Chivalry". War will be waged impersonally from the power-house and the laboratory . . . and mankind will survive, if at all, as brute beasts ravening on a desert island.'

Nuclear bombs had been hatched in a climate of self-destruction. 'With only a limited capacity for emotion, a surfeit of excitement and horror induces numbness, or a desire for sleep: even Death is seen to offer advantages.' The malignant gloom against which John had partly anaesthetized himself, the anxious uncertainties, ill thoughts of death – these that he had lived with so long he now saw reflected in the faces of young people.

By the late 1950s John's beliefs had brought him in contact with Bertrand Russell, whose anti-nuclear movement of mass civil disobedience, called the Committee of 100, he joined. This brought him some middle-class hostility. He was called a traitor and told that the sooner he 'stand in the dock at the Old Bailey on a charge of treason the better it will be for this country'. But 'you may count on me to follow your lead,' John assured Russell on 26 September 1960, '. . . it is up to all those of us above the idiot line to protest as vigorously as possible.' He had planned to participate in the demonstrations against governmental nuclear policy held on 18 February 1961 and on 6 August 1961, 'Hiroshima Day', but early in February suffered a thrombosis that 'forbids this form of exercise'.[95] 'As you see,' he scribbled almost illegibly, 'I cannot write; still less can I speak in public, but if my name is of any use, you have it to dispose of.' Later he made a partial recovery, and against doctor's orders came quietly up to London for the great sit-down in Trafalgar Square on Sunday 17 September. 'I have quite lost my hearing and am becoming a nuisance to myself and everybody,' he told Russell. He had not seen

Trafalgar Square so full of people since Mafeking Night over sixty years earlier when, feeling rather scared, he had extricated himself from the pandemonium and crept home. He still loathed crowds, feared policemen, and 'didn't want to parade my physical disabilities'. But he would 'go to prison if necessary'. The public assembly began at five o'clock, and until that time John hid. Unprecedented numbers took part in this demonstration. 'Some of them were making what was individually an heroic gesture,' Russell wrote. 'For instance, Augustus John, an old man, who had been, and was, very ill . . . emerged from the National Gallery, walked into the Square and sat down. No one knew of his plan to do so and few recognized him. I learned of his action only much later, but I record it with admiration.'[96]

A month later John was dead.

4

A WAY OUT

'P.S. Is the world going mad?'
Augustus John to Caspar John
(29 December 1960)

He had shrunk into old age. Over his lifetime the changes had been remarkable. Emerging from the little renaissance of the nineties, a romantic Welshman in a Guy Fawkes hat, he had imposed a new physical type, almost a new way of life, on British Bohemia. 'Under his influence', wrote the novelist Anthony Powell, 'painters became, almost overnight, a bearded, silent, unapproachable caste . . . Huge families, deep potations were the order of the day. A new race of models came immediately into being, strapping, angular nymphs with square-cut hair and billowing smocks. The gipsies, too, were taken over wholesale, so that even today it is hard to see a caravan by the roadside without recalling an early John.'[97]

Then, in his middle years, he had moved from the roadside into town, a commanding personality in shaggy well-cut suits, embracing whole parties at the Eiffel Tower or in Mallord Street. He had swelled into a national figure, one of the legendary demigods round which the post-war carnival was danced.

But after the Second World War there had been no carnival. The caravans halted; the fierce nights in Chelsea and Fitzrovia drifted into dreams; the national figure itself was whitewashed and transformed into a monument to be photographed on birthdays. One art student, visiting

579

Fryern in 1948, found him 'old and very deaf . . . It was rather like visiting Rubens . . . I noticed various goats and people dotted about in the sun. I noticed too, as we stepped into his surprisingly small and cluttered studio at the end of the garden, that he came alive, his rambling memory returned and he moved about the canvases with the agility of youth.'[98]

Most of his days were passed in this little studio. 'I am immobilised with work,' he wrote to Dora Yates. He painted there each morning, and in winter Dodo would send in a little milk-and-whisky. After lunch he slept for an hour, then returned to the studio until late afternoon when he would come stumping across to the house for two cups of tepid tea. His mood depended upon his work. He would sit, growling complaints, with his hands round the cup. In summer he often went back to the studio again and continued painting until half-past six or so. Then out would come the wine bottles from the telephone cupboard, perhaps a visitor or two would call, and he relaxed.

Dodo, who he claimed was becoming more 'tyrannical', sent him to bed at about eight and he would have his dinner brought to him on a tray. He listened to the radio at night, growing frantic with the knobs on the contraption and the wilful obscurities of the *Radio Times*. In bed he would wear his beret at a revolutionary angle or, when it was mislaid, a straw hat, and often fell asleep in it, his pyjamas smouldering gently from his pipe, the radio blaring around him with competing programmes.

In these last years John and Dodo were represented as Darby and Joan. The 'resentments had faded away with the years,' Nicolette Devas wrote.[99] They were 'enviable in the peace between them'. There were days like this, and there are photographs that catch these moments of tranquillity. But difficulties persisted almost to the end. Outrage was never far below the surface of John's melancholia. 'He said he hated London . . . he hated where he lived in Hampshire . . . he hated settling down, and that he was thinking of leaving his family,'[100] Stephen Spender recorded after an evening in 1955. He looked 'quite magnificent' with his mane of white hair, but his fanatical stare put some people in mind of Evelyn Waugh. 'Shocked by a bad bottle of wine, an impertinent stranger, or a fault in syntax, his mind like a cinema camera trucked furiously forward to confront the offending object close-up with glaring lens'; Waugh's description of himself closely fits John.

He found it difficult to accept the limitations of old age. The world closed in on him. 'Age in my case brings no alleviation of life's discomforts,' he told Sylvia Hay, 'and the way to the grave is beset with potholes.'[101] He was often breaking fingers, ribs, legs. 'I am too old for these shocks,' he admitted.[102] But it was less the accidents that tormented him than the galling disabilities. He hated having to rely on spectacles to see, a hearing aid to understand. He would borrow other people's spectacles – 'I say, these are rather good. Where did you get them from?' But his hearing aid infuriated him and he would hurl it across the room into a corner where it would lie feverishly ticking. The trouble, he explained to friends, was that Dodo grudged spending the money on batteries: it had come to that. He had reached the age 'when one is far too much at the mercy of other people. I shall never get used to it – nor will they.'[103]

Old age had become his schoolmaster but he was always playing truant, darting up to London. Some of these trips were memorable for others, if not himself. After one terrific beano at a Chelsea pub, the crowds 'gathered together to do me honour ... some of them claiming *intimate* acquaintance', he woke up 'safely in bed at my dosshouse' next morning completely mystified. He sometimes claimed 'my tempo has slowed down,' but 'when he comes to town, [he] seems to set a terrific pace,' Mavis wrote admiringly in the 1950s. 'I wonder how the old boy doesn't drop dead in his tracks.' Almost always he would demand her presence for 'an hour or two's sitting and a sweet embrace'. 'Must get hold of the old cow,' he would gruffly tell other people. She could still – 'how was it possible?' – make him forget his years, and their battles at the bar of the Royal Court Hotel, or at the Queen's Restaurant, were precious to both of them.

He had given up Tite Street in the autumn of 1950 'and am on the pavement till I find another studio'.[104] The new studio he found was in Charlotte Street, the very one he had shared with Orpen and Albert Rutherston after leaving the Slade in 1898. It belonged now to his daughter Gwyneth Johnstone, who lent him a room there. For an easel he turned a chair upside-down, but the light was not good and he did little work in town.

He came to London to escape the 'decrepit' household at Fryern and, by implication, his own decrepitude, and would put up at 14 Percy Street, where Poppet kept a flat. He never gave warning of these trips, but expected everyone to fit in with him the moment he arrived. Otherwise he would grow depressed and begin dialling old cronies – anyone who might be free to lead him astray for a few hours. Robert and Cynthia Kee, who had a room next to his at Percy Street, could sometimes hear the stentorian blast of his snores, mixed with powerful swearing, through the dark. At night, it seemed, he fought again the old campaigns, vanquished long-dead rivals. But during the day his manner was guardedly courteous, sinking periodically to disconcerting troughs of modesty.

He was still, even to the age of eighty, apparently in the thick of life. 'He could outdrink most of his companions and engage in amorous – if that is the word – relations that would have debilitated constitutions generally held robust,' remembered Will Rothenstein's son John.[105] The two of them would go off into Chelsea and be joined by others. 'After a longish visit to a bar he would apprehend that his guests might be inclined to eat. "I want to stay here for a bit longer. There's a girl who's going to join us. Sturdy little thing . . ." We would wait. Sometimes she would turn up and sometimes not. Augustus did not seem to mind, assured that before the evening was finished there would be others.'

He still distributed love poems – only now it was the same poem he shamelessly handed out to everyone; he was still given to sudden lunges at women, but took no offence at their rebuffs. 'A little of Augustus went a long way,'[106] wrote Diana Mosley. With his sparse hair and bloodshot eyes he was no longer attractive, especially to women who did not relish pubs and shove ha'penny. 'May I fig-and-date [fecundate] you?' he politely inquired of Sonia Brownell. These days he felt relief at being spared such duties, but he was seldom so discourteous as to forget them. Nor were they always refused. Late one night at Percy Street a girl with long fair hair came beating on the door, shouting that she loved him and must be let in. The Kees cowered beneath their bedclothes, and the old man's snoring halted and he eventually heaved himself downstairs. There followed a series of substantial sounds, then silence. Next day several of the banister supports were missing, there seemed to be blood on the floor and, more mysteriously, sugar. John looked sheepish. "Fraid there was rather a rumpus last night,' he muttered. Later that day he visited the girl in hospital and came back elated. 'Said she still loved me,' he declared wonderingly.

There is no greater misfortune, Disraeli said, than to have a heart that will not grow old. This was John's misfortune. 'No Romanichale can fail to diagnose my trouble on sight,' he wrote to Dora Yates in November 1959, 'a trouble which he would do nothing to allay, but on the contrary, will at once set about adding coals to what should rightly be a dying flame.' To everyone's consternation he had fallen for an art student in 1950. To separate them, Poppet dragged him and Dodo through France to her house at Opio. John arrived very crestfallen. For days he was abominably rude to Dodo, who sat silently absorbing his insults. Eventually Poppet flared up into a red-hot temper. 'Didn't know you had it in you,' John exclaimed, beaming. He quickly regained his spirits. 'Not going to lose your temper again, are you?' he asked hopefully from time to time during the rest of their holiday.

From the prison of old age, he treated his family as gaolers. Dodo, he complained, kept everything dark, barred all visitors, never spoke, was 'illiterate, dumb and ill-natured', and had made Fryern into a tomb. 'No gatherings of the clan – no community singing after breakfast – no wrestling on the green after dinner.' On good days he took most delight in his grandchildren and liked to league with them against their 'respectable' fathers. On bad days it was often Dodo he attacked, because she was there. 'She comes from a stinking cockney breed,' he wrote to Robin on 3 September 1961. Gwen, he seemed to remember, had felt the same. When the two girls had 'walked to Rome', Dorelia had preferred to take a passport than a pistol. It proved what 'a fishy lot' the McNeills were. 'I'm glad you at least are a true-bred Nettleship,' he congratulated his eldest son David (27 October 1956). This querulousness showed his agony: his vanished talent and the irreversible change of life. Who was there to blame except Dodo, who had kept him alive and so helped to make him old? By identifying her as an enemy and deliberately making his complaints absurd, he tried to numb the truth and lessen the pain. But the side-effects were unpleasant. Then the effects would wear off and he was confronted by the full horror of his condition. 'Hell seems nearer every day. I have never felt so near it as at Fryern Court. There must be a bricked-up passage leading straight to it from here. I see no way of escape. Meanwhile I have to pretend to work away gaily and enjoy my worldwide renown . . .'

The pretence, though still accepted by the world, had become very brittle. It took little to crack it. Cyril Connolly remembered him having lost his temper with a taxi-driver, bursting out of the taxi and measuring up to fight him in the road.[107] 'I'm sorry, but it's the right fare,' insisted the driver. 'Why, so it is,' hesitated John, lowering his fists. 'I apologize.' In a moment he had changed from an angry giant to a Lear-like old man, confessing his error and touchingly polite to the driver, who was himself overwhelmed with remorse.

In 1951, though warned by mutual friends against it, Alan Moorehead suggested to John that he write his biography. 'I was captivated by John at that time,' Moorehead records, '. . . and I believed that my genuine admiration for him would smooth over any difficulties that arose between us.' At John's suggestion they met in the saloon bar of the Royal Court Hotel, a quiet spot, he described it, where they could chat undisturbed. 'Directly he walked in . . . all conversation among the other customers ceased while they gazed at the great man and listened with interest to the remarks I shouted into his hearing-aid.'

John was inclined to think a biography not possible. He had no head for dates and many of his friends were dead, 'usually through having committed suicide'. Yet the past for him was not a different country. 'He appeared to look back on his life as he might have looked at a broad large painting spread out before him, all of it visible to the eye at once, and having no connection with time or progression,' Moorehead noticed. 'It was the sum of his experiences that counted, the pattern they presented . . . Once one grew accustomed to this approach it had a certain coherence and I believed that with persistence I could enter, in terms of writing, into that close relationship that presumably exists between a painter and his sitter.' It was agreed he should start work at once, calling on those friends who had so far failed to commit suicide and seeing John from time to time to check his notes. After several months Moorehead ventured fifteen thousand words on paper 'as a sort of sample or blue-print' of the projected book, and sent them to John. 'This typescript', he records, 'came back heavily scored with a pen, whole pages crossed out and annotated with such comments as "Wrong" and "Liar".' It was accompanied by a letter: 'All your statements of fact are wrong. I prefer the truth. Your own observations I find quite incredibly out of place. I must refuse to authorize this effort at biography.'[108]

'I can remember', wrote Moorehead, 'feeling appalled and humiliated – indeed after all these years the rebuff is still fresh and it remains in some ways the worst set-back I have ever experienced in my attempts to write.'

The two of them were due to meet that March at a Foyle's lunch. Moorehead was 'determined to go to this lunch and to have it out with him'. As soon as the speeches were over John made for the door, with Tommy Earp growling out at Moorehead as he passed: 'Come on.' The three of them went by taxi to a Soho wine shop, and there Moorehead tackled him. 'I thought for a moment he was going to strike me. Where, he demanded, had I obtained the information about his father's Will? I had gone to Somerset House, I replied, and had got a copy. What business had I going to Somerset House? That was spying . . .'

The argument went on long, reaching nowhere, until Moorehead revealed that he had abandoned the biography and was sailing to Australia next week. John then grew calmer, the eyes glared less, and when they said goodbye he was gruffly amiable. A week later Moorehead's ship reached Colombo. There was a cable waiting for him from John: 'For heavens sake lets be friends.' 'I remember now the feelings of intense relief, contrition and happiness with which I read those few words,' Moorehead wrote. 'In an instant all was well again . . . After all these years I am left admiring him as much as I ever did. If there was pettiness in his life and much ruthlessness, he was also a mighty life-enhancer and a giant in his day . . . Reflecting, long after our contretemps, about his really passionate anger at my mentioning such matters as his father's Will, I saw that in a way he hated his own wealth and notoriety. These things diminished his true purpose which was to paint to the final extent of his powers.'

Difficulties lay like watchdogs about his work and it was almost impossible not to stir them up. Over a book of fifty-two of his drawings that George Rainbird published in 1957, no one escaped censure, because as usual no one was 'able to tell the difference between a drawing and a cow-pat'.[109] Lord David Cecil, who contributed an introduction, came from a good family but clearly knew nothing about art; Rainbird was a philistine businessman; and from the expert advice of Brinsley Ford, John sought relief through referring to him by his initials. 'I prefer', he told Joe Hone, 'to make my own mistakes.'[110] To other people's eyes these mistakes arose from his preference for his current work. 'References to my early efforts sometimes make me sick,' he grumbled to D. S. MacColl, ' – as if I had done nothing since.'[111]

The contrast between the old and new was often painfully marked, particularly when, in 1954, four hundred and sixty exhibits from all periods of his career were shown together in the four rooms of the Diploma Gallery in Burlington House. It was almost unprecedented for the Royal Academy to hold an exhibition of work by a living artist. John, however, initially failed to answer the formal invitation. 'I don't repudiate the great compliment but only doubted my capacity for deserving it,' he later explained. '. . . I'ld love to make the show you suggest more than anything in the world, now that I am (apparently) on the way to a kind of rebirth.' Nevertheless, he queried, might it not be 'more safely deferred till after my death when [my] responsibilities will be lessened?' But for the President of the Royal Academy, Sir Gerald Kelly, the arranging of this show was a lifetime's ambition and he would not be deterred. 'I have good reason to beware of hurry,' he was warned by John, who succeeded in delaying 'this threatening show' of the 'collection of my misdeeds' by two years. What he feared were the 'appalling distractions, fatal to the activities which still lie ahead and which may lead me a little nearer to the light'. The Royal Academy was also eager that he should not be distracted. 'We should never have got anywhere if it had been left to John,' Kelly explained to Tommy Earp. For months, to everyone's dismay, John worked feverishly to have as many of his recent pictures as possible ready for the exhibition. 'If I survive the strain,' he told Kelly, 'I shall need a powerful restorative followed by a trip to the South Seas where, I am told, work is at a discount.' Everyone was exhausted by the time of the opening. 'I hope John won't come up when we are hanging the show,' Kelly nervously wrote to Earp. But he did come, twice, and took advantage of these visits for 'weeding' out a dozen early canvases ('by no means enough'), modestly claiming some of them to be forgeries – a charge that, as soon as it was too late to reintroduce them, he withdrew. 'I sometimes wonder if all artists are not the worst judges of their own work,' John's friend Hugo Pitman commiserated with Kelly. '. . . I can well imagine how in need of a holiday you must feel.'[112]

John had not received much serious critical attention since the 1930s. This Royal Academy exhibition gave critics an opportunity to estimate his work after a long interval. 'The freedom, sureness, versatility and sheer voluptuous accomplishment' of the early drawing, wrote John Russell in the *Sunday Times*, 'befit them to hang in great company.

'They have, moreover, a note of wonder and bemusement which is carried over into the group of panel-paintings . . . these radiant Tennysonian panels are Mr John's great accomplishment, not only to English painting, but to the English poetic imagination. It is in them, and in the drawings . . . that his private mythology comes wonderfully to fruition and he persuades us that the whole of life may be illumined by what happened to him, and his family, and his closest friends, in the Welsh mountains and around Martigues.'[113]

Gerald Kelly had assured John that 'the show is going to be really fine'. In fact it turned out to be 'a far greater success than any of us had dared hope', as he wrote to Liza Maugham. 'No one-man show has had a tithe of the success or attraction which yours has,' he told John. Almost ninety thousand people came, and the catalogue had to be reprinted twice. 'It is surprising how the young came along,' Kelly wrote. The Queen also came and, John falling ill that day, she told Kelly that 'she wished you had painted the King'.[114]

And John too came away in high spirits. 'It was such a relief to see Augustus was really pleased,'[115] Dorelia confided to Kelly. 'I have had a wonderful press,' John acknowledged. '. . . I see some chance now of living down my somewhat lurid reputation.'[116] Perhaps the fairest summary of his career appeared in *The Times*.[117] The display at Burlington House, this critic wrote, made his 'neglect seem outrageous, but at the same time explains it.

'The effect of the drawings, when seen in such abundance, is overwhelming. They do more than explain why Mr John's contemporaries were convinced that here at last was a great modern artist in England; they suggest even now that a genius of that order had really appeared . . . His power of draughtsmanship would have fitted him to work in Raphael's studio, but in 1900 there was no way in which it could be used directly and with conviction.'

With the panels came John's poetry. Their colour was

'radiant and clear, and the paint, which has aged very beautifully on almost all the small panels of this time, is laid with a sweet and sensitive touch. At the same time Mr John now found expression for the vein of true poetry that runs through the best of his work. In part the sentiment of these pictures is Celtic, other-worldly, and ideal, but never for a moment did he paint in a Celtic twilight. To these blue distances and golden suns Mr John transferred, not some wraith of the literary imagination, but quite simply and in literal fact his family and friends.'

Finally there was his gift for catching a likeness – at its best not simply a superficial resemblance but that physical identity imprinted upon the features from childhood to old age. As a portrait painter he had chosen an art that was guided by fewer standards than formerly. In consequence he was thrown back on his own judgement 'and quite clearly Mr John is not a good critic; the unevenness of his later work is really startling, and this even in the simplest technical matters'. Even so, *The Times* critic concluded, 'he remains a force and a power and every now and then there is a picture, a landscape or a portrait of one of his sons, in which all has gone brilliantly well. But though it is impossible not to see that here is a great man, this is too great a man, one sometimes feels, to practise the painter's slow and nine-tenths mechanical art.'

Yet since the war John had been applying himself to these mechanical matters as never before. He lacked only the one-tenth of inspiration. However long he waited in his studio, it did not visit him. The only remedy he understood was time; to stay by his easel endless hours, hoping for a miracle. But the hit-or-miss stage was over – it was all miss now. His unfinished canvases lay around him. 'I fear I shan't accomplish as much as I intended,' he confessed to Tommy Earp. 'Life is definitely too short.' He had begun to learn something of physical exhaustion through the multiplying illnesses that consumed days and weeks. In November 1954 he entered Guy's Hospital for a double operation. 'My bloody old prostate might need attending to and also a stone in my bladder,' he told Hugo Pitman. 'Together they are responsible for my condition which has become very troublesome.'[118] He lay in a modest room where 'there is no room for modesty',[119] surrounded by flowers and sending out in vain for bottles of wine. 'I have instructed . . . [the surgeon] not to make a new man of me but to do what he could to restore the old one to working order,' he informed John Davenport. He hated being confined 'in this horrible place', watched over by 'a dozen vague females in uniform. I have considered getting away but it's difficult . . .' After the operation, his relief flowed out unchecked. He inflated himself with optimism: the vague females blossomed, the invisible future glowed. 'I had a most successful op. and am still considered the prize boy of the hospital,' he boasted.[120] 'The only snag is it seems to have increased my concupiscence about 100%! What makes my situation almost untenable is the arrival of a pure-blooded African nurse from Sierra Leone . . . you may imagine the difficulties with which I am constantly confronted . . .'

Though he had made a 'wonderful' recovery, he was still very weak. His doctor, he later told Caspar, 'has banned all my favourite sports, such as football, golf etc'. Both he and Dodo, too, needed a convalescence. While grappling with some garden creature, a goat or lawn mower, she had broken her arm. They decided to go away and, on the advice of Gerald Brenan, submitted to Spain. It was a victory of climate over politics, and therefore partly a defeat. 'I would love to visit Spain again,' John had written many years earlier to Herbert Barker, 'but not during the horrible regime of General Franco.' Like many artists he had backed the Republican cause, but his hatred of Franco was personal and recurs obsessionally through his correspondence over twenty years. He believed that Britain's failure to come out against the insurgents had led to the Second World War. 'With our backing the Spanish people would rise and throw Franco and the Fascists into the sea and chase the Germans out of the country,' he had written to Maud Cazalet on 4 December 1940. '. . . Spain is the key country and our potential friend. Meanwhile Franco continues to murder good men . . . Remember the Spanish War was the preliminary to this one and our benighted Government backed the wrong horse. We are now expiating that crime.' With rare passion, too, he spoke of Vichy's handing over to Germany of Republican refugees in France. 'What is he [President Roosevelt] or what are we doing for Franco's million prisoners, imprisoned and enslaved by that foul renegade and his Axis allies?'[121] After the liberation of France ('a real re-birth') and the defeat of Germany, he looked for the freeing of Spain. 'When we have dealt with Franco in his turn Europe will be a hopeful continent again and fit to travel in.'[122] He attended anti-Franco meetings and contributed pictures for the relief of prisoners (though 'I cannot approach anything like the munificence of Picasso or any other millionaire'[123]) up to the end of his life. But in the winter of 1954–5 he spent four convalescent months in Spain, during which the outpouring of criticism continued – 'Franco is beneath contempt, he "knows nothing of nothing" I think is the general view.'[124]

Their son Romilly had bought the tickets and driven them to Heathrow. 'Almost the last time I saw this remarkable couple together,' he remembered, 'they were standing arm in arm, at the entrance to the airport, quite clearly petrified by the monstrosities that, unknown to them, had sprung up since the days of their youth. Augustus was glaring angrily at me for having got them into this fearful situation, while Dodo, thinking I was about to desert them, cried out in anguish, "Don't leave us, don't leave us!" '

They flew to Madrid, travelled by train to Torremolinos where they took rooms at a hotel, the Castello Santa Clara, belonging to Fred Saunders, a castrated cockney who had served with T. E. Lawrence. 'They have a bed-sitting-room and a private balcony looking over the sea,' wrote Gerald Brenan who had taken them from the station to their hotel. '. . . They seemed cheerful and to like the place.'[125] But both of them were fragile. They were looked after by a staff of sturdy Spanish women, 'fine girls all', and visited by a local doctor who was 'quite a celebrity in the medical world' on account of having been thrown into gaol as a 'political firebrand'. 'This is a Paradise of convalescents, full of elderly English rentiers,' John recommended on his arrival. '. . . The Bar is hideous', but 'the Rioja wine very palatable.'[126] Gerald Brenan, whose house they visited at Yegen (the 'garden made us green with envy'), noted that 'Augustus had become very genial in his old age'.[127] But much of this mildness was attributable to post-operative fatigue – 'weaker than any cat and hardly able to eat a thing'.[128] After a single debauch amid rear-admirals in Gibraltar, he collapsed. The sun shone every day, the roses flowered, there was not a breath of air, and he cast lustful eyes at the 'superb landscape back of here',[129] but contented himself with Edie, Fred Saunders's wife – though 'my bedroom proved unsatisfactory as a studio'.[130] Vowing to return to his unfinished canvases in Spain, he left with some relief for Fryern.

'I get anchored down here', he had told Matthew Smith, 'with some endless work.'[131] It was to Matthew Smith in France that he cast off for his last journey abroad in 1956. Tickets were bought for him, money of various denominations placed in his pockets, his clothes in a suitcase, and reminders hummed about his ears. A network of old girlfriends along the route was alerted. Most of this planning was conducted in whispers, for John would vastly have objected to the fuss. In Paris, where he was obliged to change trains, it had been arranged that the artist William de Belleroche would meet him as if by accident and chaperone him from one station to the other. John blandly accepted the coincidence. 'Extraordinary! When I stepped out of the train, there was Belleroche who happened to be passing.' Even so, he lost his tickets. After a few nights with Matthew Smith and his friends John and Vera Russell at Villeneuve-lès-Avignon, he pressed on to Aix to see Poppet, but failed to turn up at the agreed meeting point. They found him, not far off, grazing over lunch, and took him for a few days to their house near Ramatuelle. But he felt physically ill away from his paints and insisted on being driven to St-Raphael so as to catch a train direct to Calais. 'I would have liked to have stayed in

Provence,' he told William de Belleroche, 'but felt still more drawn to my work here. I find I cannot stop working . . .'[132] Yet it had been a good expedition because of a Cézanne exhibition at Aix. 'The Cézanne show was overwhelming,' he wrote to Matthew Smith on his return to Fryern, 'and painting seems more mysterious than ever if not utterly impossible. Only the appearance of a young woman outside, with very little on, restored me more or less to normality and hope. But she belonged to an earlier and more fabulous age than ours.'[133]

Most fellow creatures from that age were dead. Among the artists and writers, Will Rothenstein had 'pegged out' in 1945, 'a severe loss'; Dylan Thomas died in 1953, which 'greatly saddened me';[134] Frank Brangwyn in 1956, though 'he was a courageous man who made the best use of his talents and could have nothing to regret.'[135] Gogarty had long before gone to the United States, a fate worse than death (he died in 1957). Among the women, the Rani had 'popped off'; Alick Schepeler had disappeared with all her illusory charm, something she had always been threatening to do, suddenly dying after leaving the *Illustrated London News* and bequeathing her tiny savings to a cats' home; and Dorelia's sister Edie faded sadly away as Francis Macnamara's neglected wife.

One of those whose company John missed most was Tommy Earp who pursued his solitary recreation, silence, to its ultimate lair in 1958. He was buried at Selborne. 'John came with Dorelia – a quiet elderly lady by then,' the critic William Gaunt remembered.[136] He wore a black-varnished straw hat, headgear venerable enough for a dean, yet at a rakish angle. 'Painted it myself,' he boasted. 'Best thing you've done for years,' a friend retorted. William Gaunt murmured something about it being a sad occasion. 'Oh, awful!' John thundered enthusiastically. 'I noticed at the same time,' Gaunt records,

'how the artist's eye professionally functioning in a separate dimension was observing the architectural and natural details of the scene: and when all the mourners were assembled in Selborne Church and all was hushed, suddenly a roar reverberated along the nave. It was Augustus with a superb disregard of devout silence. "A fine church", he roared. There was . . . a shocked rustling through the interior. With perfect sang-froid he went on with his meditations aloud. "Norman!" the word pealed to the rafters. There were some who seemed to scurry out into the open with relief at no longer being subjected to this flouting of convention.'

Of the survivors, those who had strayed prehistorically into the bland 1950s, he still saw something of Wyndham Lewis. The jousting between these two artists-in-arms continued to the end. Passages of complimentary abuse were interrupted by sudden acts of kindness. When Lewis went blind in 1951, John bragged that he had sent him a telegram expressing the hope that it would not interfere with his real work: *art criticism*. When pressed to account for this message, he declared that he wasn't, through sentimentality, going to lay himself open to some crushing rejoinder. In fact his letter had not been unsympathetic. 'I hope you find a cure as did Aldous Huxley,' he wrote. 'Anyhow indiscriminate vision is a curse. Although without the aid of a couple of daughters like Milton, I don't really see why you should discontinue your art criticism – you can't go far wrong even if you do it in bed. You can always turn on your private lamp of aggressive voltage along with your dictaphone to discover fresh talent and demolish stale.' At other times he treats this blindness as a gift of which Lewis has taken full advantage. Lewis received these 'impertinent' congratulations with an appreciative silence. Never once did he allude to his blindness, preferring to make any accusation obliquely: 'Dear John, I'm told you've mellowed.' John hotly denied the charge, but Tristan de Vere Cole remembers him taking Lewis out to dinner shortly before his death, seeing that his food was properly cut up, deferring to him in their talk.

Wyndham Lewis died in 1957; Matthew Smith two years later. The war had devastated him. Evacuated from France, he had abandoned many canvases and later lost his two sons on active service. In 1944 he came to Fryern for some months, and in October that year the two artists painted each other. Smith's three portraits of John are wild-eyed and florid – John called them 'landscapes';[137] John's picture of Smith is full of quietness and sympathy – perhaps his last interesting portrait.

They were often seen about Chelsea in those years after the war: a curious couple – Smith, 'whose canvases suggest that a stout model has first been flogged alive, then left to bleed to death, slowly and luxuriously, on a pile of satin cushions',[138] looking timid and myopic, a pale, spindly specimen like some bankrupt financial expert; John, with his late-flowering addiction to anaemic prettiness, like an ageing lion full of sound. 'It is always an amusing experience to see them together,' Peter Quennell observed, Matthew Smith 'shrinking into his chair and glancing nervously about the room, John looking too large for the table and ordering the wine in a voice of rusty thunder'.

They went regularly to the Queen's Restaurant, where the atmosphere – a little French, a little Edwardian – suited them well. John hated dining in a restaurant where he did not know the waiters. Here everything was the same, the waiters, the menu, the tired flowers on the tables, the potted palm at the foot of the staircase. Having a large but dispersed clientele, it was haunted by the past – old friends you could have sworn were long dead appearing there from time to time like spectres: 'They were easily distinguishable,' Lucy Norton remembered:

'John with his lion-coloured hair, the wisps drawn thinly over the top of his head, and the numerous mufflers that he never seemed to take off . . . the cavalier-puritan hat on the antlers of the old hat stand, and the black coat below, could have prepared anyone for the sight of him. Matthew Smith was always in the best place, against the wall, facing the room, looking very old now, but serene and gentle, seeming to say very little but a very bright smile unexpectedly lighting up his face . . . What struck me was John's attitude, his care for the other old man, the way he turned his attention upon him, leaning forwards towards him over the table, encouraging him to talk and listening to everything he said . . . I used to join them a moment before I left . . . and I remember talk about Sickert and his odd clothes (no odder than Augustus's), of Paul Nash's illness and death . . . It was a totally different side to all that I had ever known of John. He had always been the focus of attention whenever I had seen him. In the very distant past, with a circle of people round him, women particularly, trying to flatter him; in later years, when he was growing old, sitting against a wall muzzy and fuddled with drink, waiting to be rescued, to be taken safely home. To see him thus sober, in command, so wrapped up in someone who took all his interest, was extraordinarily moving.'[139]

The Royal Academy, that 'asylum for the aged',[140] put on a memorial show after Matthew Smith's death. 'Bloody marvel,' John grunted. Some days it seemed he really wanted to die himself but did not know how to go about it. During a television interview with Malcolm Muggeridge in 1957 he demanded 'another hundred years' to become a good painter.[141] Otherwise it was a dog's life, an agony from start to finish. If he had it all over again he would probably do the same.

Early in the 1950s, in an effort to break new ground, he had taken to sculpture 'like a duck to water'. He had first felt 'longings to sculpt' in the summer of 1905, but it was not until 1952, when he met the Italian sculptress Fiore de Henriques, that this 'new phase in my history opened up'.[142] She was a wild young woman 'of robust physique', he noted, savagely featured, with coal-black hair, stalwart legs and a grip of iron. She came to Fryern late in 1952 shortly after her monument to the humanist philosopher Don Giovanni Cuome in Salerno had been blown up, and 'has done a very successful bust of me'.[143] He could not keep his hands, while she worked, off the clay, and eventually she gave him some with which to experiment. The result was 'a prognathous vision of the young Yeats',[144] followed by busts of some of his family, friends and a model. 'Getting the hang of this medium', as he called it, was exciting for John. 'I visited the Foundry where my busts are being cast,' he told Lord Alington's daughter, Mary Anna Marten, '...I feel all the excitement of a Renaissance artist who happened on a head of Venus of the Periclean age while digging in his back garden.'[145]

It may have been that John hoped to overcome in sculpture some of those muscular vagaries that were so affecting his draughtsmanship and painting. In the opinion of Epstein it was 'the sculpture of a painter; it's sensitive, but you could stick your finger through it. It's interesting, but it's not real sculpture.'[146] John had many mighty plans, from a 'colossal statue' of St Catherine at the summit of St Catherine's Rock at Tenby, to a towering statue of the mature Yeats to confront all Dublin – 'Would you advise trousers,' he questioned Yeats's biographer, Joe Hone, 'or a more classic nudity?'[147] But within eighteen months this 'new phase' was over, and he was free to pursue with fewer interruptions the big composition upon which the reputation of these post-war years would depend.

The only other interruption was portraiture – often drawings of famous men such as Thomas Beecham, Frank Brangwyn, Walter de la Mare, Charles Morgan, Gilbert Murray, Albert Schweitzer ('sat like a brick he did'). These drawings provided John with 'outings', moments of adventure and respite. His studies of these 'old buffers' are probably his best work in these last years. Of the original talent little remains: yet a certain ingenuity has developed, the skill of using a restricted vocabulary. The trembling contours, the blurred and fading lines convey poignantly the frailty of old age. Some, who guarded their public image scrupulously and would have given much for a John portrait before the war, now refused his requests: among them J. B. Priestley and A. L. Rowse. Others refused because of their own great age. 'I am too old for sittings,' Shaw wrote (10 May 1949). '... I have no longer any outline and am just like any other old man with a white beard. At 90 one must be counted as dead ...'[148]

But one who welcomed him enthusiastically was John Cowper Powys. 'Here is Augustus John Himself with his daughter [Vivien] as his driver,' he wrote to Phyllis Playter (26 November 1955). 'Hurrah! Hurrah! Hurrah! – He himself is a splendid picture.' In an hour and a quarter John polished off two drawings, retired for the night to the Pengwern Hotel, then 'like Merlin' returned next morning for another session. When he rose to depart, Powys told Louis Wilkinson, 'I leapt at him exactly as a devoted Dog of considerable size leaps up at a person he likes, and kissed his Jovian forehead which is certainly the most noble forehead I have ever seen. I kissed it again & again as if it had been marble, holding the godlike old gent so violently in my arms that he couldn't move till the monumental and marmoreal granite of that forehead cooled my feverish devotion. His final drawing was simply of my very soul – I can only say it just *awed* me.'[149]

Almost his last outing, in October 1959, was to Tenby, which had conferred on him the Freedom of the Borough. It means 'simply civil amour propre, something good to drink, a few little speeches and jokes, a write-up in the papers,' Thornton wrote from Canada. But, he warned, Augustus would 'have to get a new suit'.[150] Dodo, 'under the impression that it rains perpetually in Wales', did not go, and he was accompanied by his daughter-in-law, Simon John, who 'was very much admired'.[151] He had been quite afraid to go back, but the morbid associations with Tenby had now vanished. The Prescelly Mountains where he had been taken by his nurse, and the Cleddau valley where he had walked with his father were 'more beautiful than ever . . . all, all was perfect.'[152] He also liked the people, 'particularly one', he told Caspar, 'a blonde of truly classic proportions. With the backing of the mayor, a past owner of the hotel where this paragon works as a waitress I hope to succeed in over-coming this young lady's scruples, and putting her to the acid test of my brush.'[153]

He lingered over dinner with the Mayor while a large audience, waiting impatiently for them in the town hall, was assailed by Mussorgsky's *Pictures at an Exhibition*. At last, to the sound of cheers, the diners clambered on to the flower-camouflaged platform with, the *Tenby Observer and County News* reported, 'an air of deep sincerity and of historic significance'. John, though 'the piercing eyes still flashed', seemed envel-oped by benevolence. Sandwiched between the Mayor and Town Clerk, flanked by aldermen, councillors and burgesses, buffeted by sonorous compliments, he looked 'deeply moved and at times somewhat overcome by . . . an emotion that he did not try to conceal'.[154] As he rose to sign the Freeman's Roll, the audience rose too, singing 'For he's a jolly good fellow!' In a speech of stumbling thanks, he spoke of his walks as a boy over the beaches and burrows: 'I could take those walks again now and I don't think I would get lost,' he declared defiantly. 'I can find my way about still.'

But to many, in these last years, he looked pitifully lost, the beard stained with nicotine, the listening eyes glaring, the slurred actions menacing the traffic. He was shepherded back by Simon 'my eldest son's wife', he explained to his sister Winifred, 'or rather ex-wife for I think they are now divorced'. Simon had come to live at Fryern in 1956 'and to my astonishment is quite a success'.[155] He relied on her as a model (his voluptuous portrait of her, very dashing *en déshabillé*, was shown at the Royal Academy in 1959); and she was devoted to him, though there was a number of what he lightly called 'fracas' – matters of words and tablets, after which they would all return to 'friendly terms' again.

John's face – 'one of the most remarkable old faces I have ever seen', the writer Maurice Collis called it[156] – appeared on television, was splendidly photographed for the newspapers, and occasionally seen at galleries being 'assaulted' by some old lady 'whose summer costume quite concealed her identity till a warm embrace on parting brought me to my senses'.[157] He had little to say. Every birthday the journalists telephoned and every time they reported his words: 'Work as usual'. No one seemed interested in this work – it was the past for which he was famous. From time to time phantoms from that past would overtake him, dragging his name into the headlines. He was reported as racing to Devizes Hospital after Mavis Wheeler suddenly shot her current lover, Lord Vivian, in the stomach. She was charged at the Assize Court in Salisbury with attempted murder and found guilty of unlawful and malicious wounding. 'Heard from Mavis, very cheerful and cock-of-the walk at her new prison,' John told their son Tristan.[158] Then Eve Fleming, aged over seventy, began a series of 'foolish' court battles, drenched by gusts of public laughter, against one of John's models, a voluble overweight daughter of a Parsee high priest, and author of *Heroines of Ancient Iran*, for the affection of a penniless nonagenarian aristocrat, the sixteenth Marquis of Winchester, known harmlessly as 'Monty'. John advised Eve to 'drop that discredited old ass', but she persisted, eventually winning her case on appeal, carrying her elderly prize to the Hotel Metropole in Monte Carlo, and steering him into the *Guinness Book of Records* as the oldest peer in history. 'How pleased you must be to hear that Mama is about to join the aristocracy,' John wrote to their daughter Amaryllis.[159]

But it was to a remoter past that he felt himself tied. The subject of his gigantic triptych, 'Les Saintes-Maries de la Mer with Sainte Sara, l'Egyptienne', had first fired his imagination when, with the encouragement of Scott Macfie in 1910, he became involved with the pilgrim mystery of the gypsies. In the years between the wars, the dreams symbolized for John by this legend paled. Then, with the Second World War, he turned back to them. 'I have begun a picture of Les Saintes Maries de la Mer with Sainte Sara l'Egyptienne,' he wrote to Dora Yates on 13 March 1946. His first attempt to re-illumine this miraculous land had been 'The Little Concert' which, he told William de Belleroche on 1 April 1948, 'will never be really finished as I want to alter it every time I see it'. He could resign himself to its inconclusive state only by becoming more interested in variation. It was then, in the late 1940s, that his long-slumbering interest in Sainte Sara awoke. It was as if, on opening his eyes, she mesmerized him. 'I am astonished at my own industry,' he declared. She became his reason for not travelling, not taking on profitable portrait work. For over a dozen years, with few pauses, she held him, like some siren, calling him back to his studio day after day, and making his nights sleepless. She enchanted and tortured him; she was to be his resurrection or his death.

The saga of this vast mural and John's 'dreadful expenditure of time and effort' over it can be assembled from his letters. 'There will soon not be an inch of wall-space left for me to disfigure,' he had joked to Doris Phillips on 24 July 1951. By 1952 the three compositions appeared to be combining harmoniously. 'So much depends on them,' he confessed to Daniel George. 'They wax and wane like the moon.'[160]

The spirit in which he met this challenge is conveyed in a letter to the artist Alfred Hayward: 'It seems to me one wasted most of one's time when young. At last I feel myself interested only in work and feel always on the brink of discovery. That surely is excitement enough. We are left very much in the dark and have to find a way out for ourselves. One thing becomes clear – nothing worth doing is easy – though it may and should look so, after ages of effort and god knows what failures!'[161]

The months moved on and 'I work from morning to night on the big panels which are developing well but seem to need *years* of work.'[162] In May 1954 he reported that they were showing 'signs of "coming out" like a game of Patience'.[163] Four years later, however, he was still labouring at them and admitting: 'Unfinished things are often the best.' But there was no chance this time of supplanting his obsession with another. For this was love and must give birth to beauty. 'My wall decorations keep changing and evolving like life itself,' he had told Cecil Beaton. But 'the sureness of hand and mind', Sir Charles Wheeler records, '. . . was waning and more than ever he scraped, altered and hesitated . . . I was charmed by the design which had all the Celtic poetry so characteristic of his figure work. Each time I saw it, it became less and less resolved . . .'[164]

At Fryern he could sometimes be heard alone in his studio, roaring in distress. 'What the hell do I know about art?' His right hand was partly crippled with arthritis and, as he smoked, it trembled. Canvases lay everywhere, hanging on the walls, stacked in cupboards and on ledges, propped up or lying on the floor. People scurried in and out taking what they wanted. John stood, a skullcap on his head, dressed in a woollen sweater and jeans, scraping and hesitating before the triptych, caring for nothing else. Sometimes he drew in chalk on top of the paint; sometimes he splashed on gold and silver paint, or pasted it over and over again with dozens of pieces of paper to try out modifications; sometimes it seemed to him that even now, after all these years, he was about to pull it back from the precipice and have a 'triumph of a sort'.[165]

He was impatient with sympathy, but longed for the expert encouragement of another artist. After seeing the work, the gallery owner Dudley Tooth wrote to him calling it 'magnificent . . . among the finest things done in this generation'. But John was not fooled, knowing Tooth was simply a 'man of affairs' interested in the money. In 1960 a private collector offered him up to eight thousand pounds (equivalent to £99,500 in 1996), but John would not let it go. Over the last two or three years he relied increasingly on the President of the Royal Academy, Charles Wheeler. 'I think he needed someone to lean on,' Wheeler wrote, 'so that I received many letters begging me to visit him at Fryern Court.'[166] They would lunch together with Dodo, then pass most of the afternoon in John's studio discussing the composition. 'When it was time to leave Augustus would hug us and, standing side by side with Dorelia at the tall Georgian windows, wave us goodbye.' He had undertaken to show his triptych at the Royal Academy Summer Exhibition of 1960. The sending-in day was 22 March. On 10 February 'a strange thing happened', he told Philip Dunn. 'I rapidly made some bold changes and the results have delighted me beyond measure!'[167] But a month later he was writing to Wheeler: 'I think it *impossible* to finish the triptych in time . . . I shall have to keep the big panels for another time.'[168]

Early in 1961, on the evidence of some photographs[169] of the cartoon, the Edwin Austin Abbey Memorial Trust offered to purchase the central panel for five thousand pounds and present it for the decoration of Burlington House. It was hoped that this 'magnificent proposal'[170] would give John the stimulus he needed. But after five agonizing days, he could not keep back the truth any longer: *the triptych was not good enough and never would be.* Before, locked up with his fantasies, he could pretend and try to conjure something from this pretence. But studying the panel with the objectivity that the Abbey Trust's offer now compelled, he could see only the truth. The letter he wrote 'in great distress' to Wheeler on 9 March 1961 bows to this truth:

'I have some bad news for you. After working *harder than ever* I have come to the conclusion that I cannot continue without ruining whatever merit these large pictures may have had, nor can I expect to recover such qualities as have already been lost. I want to ask you to release me from my promise to have these things ready for the coming show while there is still time to replace them. *I cannot work against time.* That is now quite obvious: it will be a disappointment for you, and perhaps a disaster for me . . . I will not again make unnecessary promises but will return to the work I love with renewed zest and confidence . . .'

Wheeler at once replied with a wire, following this up with a letter accepting John's reasons and absolving him from his promise: 'They saved me and I am almost myself again,' John answered.

But nothing could be the same. In a real sense it had been *against time* he sought to work: to reach out and reassemble the past – a legendary past that had never existed otherwise than in his imagination. 'This working from the imagination is killing me,' he had written on 5 May 1960. 'I find myself so variable that sometimes I lose all sense of identity and even forget my name.' So, at the end, he had been brought back to the central predicament of his life: 'Who *am* I in the first place?' In the early visual lyrics, he had revealed a paradise composed in the image of his desire which, though mysterious in its origin, was immediate and actual in its observation. But his desire, arising perhaps from the loss of his mother, had been overlaid by other desires. What had been damped down could not now be rekindled. In his triptych the dream paled into nebulous shadows miming the sensuous beauty and stately gestures of earlier days.

John never abandoned the triptych, but was freer in this final year to turn to 'lesser and handier things'. Almost his last portrait was of Cecil Beaton. It had been begun in June 1960, but much to John's fury Beaton left shortly afterwards for the United States. John felt mollified, however, on being introduced to Greta Garbo. 'I fell for her of course,' he assured Beaton. '. . . Quel oiseau! . . . I really must try to capture that divine smile but to follow it to the U.S.A. would kill me. I wouldn't mind so much dying *afterwards* . . .'[171] The sittings started up again after Beaton's return, and became increasingly painful for them both. John seemed at his last gasp. The portrait would change and change again. John daubed it with green paint like a cricket pavilion, then with pillar-box red. He stumped about, lunging at the canvas to add a pupil to one eye or, it might turn out, a button. His hands shook fearfully, his beret fell off, he glared; and Beaton, exquisitely posed, watched him suffer. 'I think', John puffed, '. . . this is going to be . . . the best portrait . . . I have ever . . . painted.'

Sex had been one medicine that, in the past, could lift him clear of melancholia. In the summer of 1961, Simon John having left to marry a neighbour, John's daughter Zoë came to stay at Fryern. John, then in his eighty-fourth year, was sleeping on the ground floor. One night, carrying a torch and still wearing his beret, he fumbled his way upstairs to Zoë's room, and came heaving in. 'Thought you might be cold,' he gasped, and ripped off her bedclothes. He was panting dreadfully, waving the torch about. He lay down on the bed; she put her arms round him; and he grew calmer. 'Can't seem to do it now,' he apologized. 'I don't know.'

After a little time she took him down, tucked him up, and returned to her room. It was probably his last midnight expedition.

There was no escape now from the tyranny of the present, no land of hope in his studio, no forgetfulness elsewhere. 'I have been struck deaf and dumb,' he told Poppet, 'so that the silence here is almost more than I can bear.' Old age had become a nighmare. 'I feel like a lost soul at Fryern!' he cried out to Vivien. Honours, now that he cared little for them, came to him from the United States, Belgium, France.* 'I'd like to quit and get away from it all,' he told a friend. 'But where is there to go?'

The end, when it came, was simple. He caught a chill; it affected his lungs; and after a short illness he died of heart failure, his heart having been greatly weakened by previous illnesses.

During the last weeks, his abrupt exterior largely fell away and he revealed his feelings more directly. He was agitated at being a 'blundering nuisance' to Dodo and Vivien, worried lest they were not getting enough rest. The night he died, they left him alone for a minute and he at once got up and sat in an armchair, complaining that he could not sleep. 'You try it,' he suggested, indicating the bed. They got him back and when his eldest son David arrived later that evening, he was 'breathing very quickly and with difficulty but just about conscious'. Vivien told him that David had come, and he spoke his name. In his sleep he rambled about a picture of an ideal town which he claimed to have finished. The doctor came and John lay very quiet, rousing himself suddenly to remind the women 'to give the doctor a drink'.

Dodo, Vivien and David took turns sitting up with him that night. At 5.30 a.m. on Tuesday 31 October, with Dodo beside him, he died. 'His face looked very fine,' David wrote, 'calm and smoothed out, in death.'[172]

*

The funeral service was at Fordingbridge Parish Church. Apart from the many members of John's family, there were few people – Charles Wheeler and Humphrey Brooke from the Royal Academy; one or two students who had 'footed it' from Southampton. 'I didn't have any great feeling of disturbance or deprivation,' remembered Tristan. '. . . But suddenly half way through the service I burst into tears . . . I couldn't stop myself and it went on and on.' Afterwards, at Fryern, they had a party. Dodo, tiny but regal, seemed to have taken it wonderfully well, as if she could not believe yet that John was really dead.

He had been buried in an annexe of Fordingbridge cemetery, an allot-

* He had been elected an honorary member of the American National Institute of Arts and Letters in 1943; in 1946 he became an associate of the Académie Royale de Belgique; and in 1960 he was invited to join the Institut de France.

ment for the dead up one of the lanes away from the town. To this rough field, in the months that followed, odd groups of hard-cheekboned people, with faces like potatoes, silent, furtive-looking, made their pilgrimage. Sven Berlin, man of the road, took Cliff Lee of Maghull. Under the great expanse of sky they stood before the gravestone. 'He rested with councillors and tradesmen of the area,' Sven Berlin wrote. '. . . His name was carved in simple Roman letters.' Cliff Lee stood holding a rose he had torn from the hedge on the way.

' "The first time I've seen you take a back seat, old *Rai*," he said . . . "Here is a wild rose from a wild man." He threw the rose on the grave and turned away; perhaps to hide from me the grief in his dark face though he was not ashamed.'[173]

The newspapers were covered with obituaries, photographs, reproductions of pictures that would soon be hurried back to their dark repositories. 'A man in the 50 megaton range,' wrote Richard Hughes.[174] 'We lose in him a great man,' declared Anthony Powell.[175] He had personified 'a form of life-enhancing exhibitionism', said Osbert Lancaster, 'which grew up and flourished before the Age of Anxiety'.[176] His death was treated as a landmark. 'In a very real sense it marks the close of an era,' recorded the leader writer of the *Daily Telegraph*.[177] More remarkable, perhaps, was the admiration felt by artists, such as Bernard Leach and David Jones, whose work and manner of life were different from his own.

On 12 January 1962 a memorial service was held at St Martin-in-the-Fields. To the large crowd, many with curiously similar features, Caspar John read the lesson and Amaryllis Fleming played Bach's Prelude and Fugue from Suite No. 5 in C Minor for unaccompanied cello. In his address, Lord David Cecil spoke of the heroic scale of John's personality, the strength and sensibility of his imagination, and the pictures in which these qualities found expression. 'A visionary gleam pervades these rocky shores, these wind-blown skies . . . the earthy and the spiritual in his art expresses the essence of the man who created it . . . it was rooted in the sense that the spiritual is incarnate in the physical, that the body is the image of the soul.'

In questioning how future generations would assess his work, many agreed that it was essential to discount most of what he had done during the last twenty-five years. Public estimation even of his earlier pictures had changed, and would change again. But one day these pictures would be brought out again – 'Caravan at Dusk', 'Dorelia Standing Before a Fence', 'Ida in a Tent', 'The Smiling Woman', 'The Red Feather', 'The Red Skirt', 'The Blue Shawl', 'The Blue Pool', 'The Mumper's Child' – passing moods and moments of beauty that he had made permanent.

John's reputation was sent into a deep decline by the many sales and exhibitions that were held shortly before and following his death.[178] The market was flooded with very inferior work that he had never intended to be seen.

Romilly and his wife Kathie came to Fryern, and Dodo lived on. She still wore the same style of clothes, sitting as if posing for, walking as though out of, another John painting. At work in the garden, or seated at the refectory table over tea – Gwen John's 'Dorelia by Lamplight at Toulouse' behind her – she appeared extraordinarily like the mythical Dorelia of John's imagination. 'Her white hair', noted the Gwen John scholar Mary Taubman, ' – strange and unexpected but accentuating the unchanged features . . . very kind and smiled quickly . . . her whole face quick and intelligent. Self-contained, rather frightening, though charming. Conversation conducted very much on her terms.' Brigid McEwen, who visited Fryern in December 1963, observed her 'long dress of saffron cotton patterned in black, a neckerchief, long cardigan, long earrings, pierced ears, rings on wedding finger, white stockings & no shoes. She kept playing with her spectacles rather like an old man. Her asymmetrically done hair – a long plait & a white comb. Very young voice . . . and young expressions "Jolly difficult" (to write life of John so soon) . . .'

For years she had seemed pliant, sensible, undemanding. But following John's death she flexed her muscles and rather enjoyed being 'difficult'. Though she travelled more to France, staying with her daughter Poppet, for most of this time she remained at Fryern.

Fryern too was ageing. Dry rot burrowed through the house; the large studio stood deserted, like an empty warehouse; brambles made the path to the old studio impenetrable. Vandals had broken in and covered the vast triptych of Sainte Sara with graffiti and explosions of paint. Under Dodo's orders, Romilly laboured long hours in the garden among the giant weeds. Yet even in disarray, a magic atmosphere clung to the place. Kittens still nested in the stems of the clematis; the hammock still swung between the apple and the Judas tree; the pale brick, the long windows leading to dark rooms, the crazy paving inaccurately sprayed with weedkiller, the roses, magnolias, yellow azaleas and, outgrowing everything, the mountainous rubbish dump: all were part of this magic.

On 19 December 1968 Dodo was eighty-seven. She had been getting visibly weaker and, to her consternation, able to do less in the garden. On the evening of 23 July 1969, Romilly found her lying on the dining-room floor. He got her to bed, and she slept. Next morning when he went in she lay in the same position. She had died in her sleep.

APPENDICES

Appendix One

DESECRATION OF SAINT PAUL'S
To the Art-Students of London

Since the so-called decorations of Saint Paul's have been encroaching actually on the substructure of the mighty Dome itself, a great feeling of indignation has arisen. The atrocities of the design, the meanness of the patterns, the crudity of the colour, and the vulgarity of the whole is too evident to those who have inspected the results of Sir William Richmond's scheme of decoration. Even *good* decoration would be out of place, superfluous, and utterly contrary to the expressed wish of Wren.

But what are we to say to the treatment in Romanesque Style of a Renaissance building, the Petroleum Stencilled Frieze (already condemned), the false accentuation of architectural features nullifying the Master's intended effect, but, above all, the audacious demolishing of the stonework of the structure itself to provide a bed for these detestable Mosaics?

We feel assured none who have at heart the preservation of the Masterpiece can submit to see the glorious memory of its illustrious Author thus insulted, or can do less than their utmost to avert what can only be regarded as a National Calamity.

The initiators of this movement call upon the Students of the various Art Schools in London to send their representatives to join with them in determining the most effective means of making their protest.

A Meeting will be held to that end at Mr A. Rothenstein's Rooms, No. 20 Fitzroy Street, Fitzroy Square, W., on Saturday, May 6. from 5.P.M. till ——

Secretary, MAX WEST,
Slade School, Gower Street.

Appendix Two

JOHN'S PICTURES AT THE NEW ENGLISH ART CLUB

As a non-member, John exhibited the following pictures at the NEAC:

Summer 1899	Miss Spencer Edwards (drawing)
	Study (drawing)
Winter 1899	Study in Pen and Wash
	Study of a Lady Seated (drawing)
Summer 1900	Portrait of William Morgan
	Head of an Oriental
Winter 1900	Little Miss Pank
Winter 1902	The Signorina Estelle Dolores Cerutti
	Merikli

After his election to membership, he exhibited:

Summer 1903	A Girl's Head
	Haute-Loire
	Hark, the Lark
	The Wood Folk
	A Wild Girl
	Study of a Young Girl (drawing)
Winter 1903	Professor John MacDonald Mackay
	Portrait of a Man
	Head of John Sampson, Esq. (drawing)
	Study of a Girl's Head (drawing)
	Head of William Rothenstein, Esq. (drawing)
	Study of a Girl (drawing)
Summer 1904	The Daughter of Ypocras
	Dawn
	Joconda
	Girl's Head (drawing)
	Head of William Orpen (drawing)
	Head of Girl (drawing)
Winter 1904	Ardor
	Carlotta
	Dorelia
	A Portrait of an Old Man
	Study of a Girl (drawing)
	Goton (drawing)
Summer 1905	Professor J. M. Mackay
	Carlotta
	The White Feather
	Fantasie
	Study of a Girl's Head (drawing)
	John Sampson, Esq., Head (drawing)
	Head of Girl, Sanguine (drawing)

Winter 1905　Mother and Child
　　　　　　　Flora
　　　　　　　Bohemians
　　　　　　　Study (drawing)
　　　　　　　Cupid and Nymphs (drawing)
Summer 1906　A Man's Head (drawing)
　　　　　　　A Girl's Head (drawing)
　　　　　　　Sir John Brunner
　　　　　　　E. K. Muspratt Esq., Vice-President of the University of
　　　　　　　　　Liverpool
　　　　　　　The Meeting in the Lane
　　　　　　　Van Dwellers
Winter 1906　The Sea-Shore (drawing)
　　　　　　　Study for a Portrait (drawing)
　　　　　　　The Crab (drawing)
　　　　　　　A Girl on the Moor
　　　　　　　The Camp
　　　　　　　In the Tent
Summer 1907　Study of a Girl (drawing)
　　　　　　　Study of a Girl (drawing)
　　　　　　　Portrait (drawing)
　　　　　　　Study for a Portrait (drawing)
　　　　　　　Study of a Head (drawing)
　　　　　　　Study of a Head (drawing)
Winter 1907　The River-Side (drawing)
　　　　　　　Mother and Child (drawing)
　　　　　　　Charles McEvoy (drawing)
　　　　　　　Nymph (drawing)
　　　　　　　The Nixie (drawing)
　　　　　　　The Old Girls of Kinbara
Summer 1908　Three Little Things (drawing)
　　　　　　　Study (drawing)
　　　　　　　Study (drawing)
　　　　　　　A Portrait (drawing)
　　　　　　　The Infant Pyramus
　　　　　　　Olilai
Summer 1909　The Way Down to the Sea
　　　　　　　Portrait of William Nicholson
　　　　　　　Eight Drawings (including four studies in colour; two pencil
　　　　　　　　　studies; one nude study)
Winter 1909　The Girl on the Cliff
　　　　　　　The Man from New York (John Quinn)
　　　　　　　The Camp (drawing)
　　　　　　　Head of a Girl (drawing)
　　　　　　　Wandering Sinnte (drawing)
Winter 1911　Dr Kuno Meyer
　　　　　　　The Rt Hon. Harold Chaloner Dowdall, Lord Mayor of
　　　　　　　　　Liverpool 1909
　　　　　　　Forza e Amore
Winter 1912　Calderari: Gypsies of the Caucasus
　　　　　　　The Mumpers
Summer 1913　The World
Winter 1913　Cartoon: The Flute of Pan
　　　　　　　Robin
　　　　　　　Six Drawings (three nude studies; Study for a Portrait; A Girl's
　　　　　　　　　Head; Head of an Architect)

Summer 1915   George Bernard Shaw, Esq.
Galway Group
Provençal Composition (drawing)
Galway Shawls (drawing)
Nude Sketch (drawing)
Group of Women (drawing)
Family Group (drawing)
Fisher Folk (drawing)
Nude (drawing)
Portrait (drawing)

Summer 1916   The Laughing Artilleryman
Fresh Herrings
Mr H. A. Barker, 'The Bone-setter'
The Girl by the Lake
G.B.S.
Five Drawings (three studies for a panel; two studies for a bronze)

Winter 1916   Admiral Lord Fisher of Kilverston
Summer 1918   A Dancer
Winter 1920   Iris Tree
Portrait of Marquise Salamanca
A Girl's Head (drawing)
L'Argentina

Summer 1920   Sketch for a Picture (drawing)
Nude (drawing)
Composition (drawing)
Nude Study (drawing)

Winter 1921   The Galway Women
Summer 1921   Cartoon for Decoration (fragment)
Winter 1923   Portrait of Two Boys
Portrait of the Artist's Son, David

Summer 1924   Roy Campbell
1925 Retrospective Exhibition
Merikli; Ardor; Woman and Boy on Shore; Professor J. M. Mackay; Ambrose McEvoy (all oil); Fisher Girls; Ida Nettleship; Wandering Sinnte; Gwen John; Girls at the Well; Head of a Girl; Two Girls (drawings)

Winter 1931   Magnolia
Winter 1933   Amaryllis
1935 (Summer) 50th Anniversary Exhibition
Head of a Girl
Portrait of Professor Oliver Elton
Auriculas and Geraniums
Rhododendrons

Appendix Three

THE CHELSEA ART SCHOOL
ROSSETTI STUDIOS
FLOOD STREET, CHELSEA EMBANKMENT

PRINCIPALS:
AUGUSTUS JOHN
WILLIAM ORPEN

YEAR 1904
FIRST TERM: MONDAY, JANUARY 11TH TO FRIDAY, MARCH 25TH.
SECOND TERM: MONDAY, APRIL 11TH TO FRIDAY, JUNE 24TH.
THIRD TERM: MONDAY, OCTOBER 3RD TO FRIDAY, DECEMBER 18TH.

THE STUDIOS SEPARATE TO EACH SEX WILL BE OPEN ON WEEK DAYS (SATURDAYS EXCEPTED) FROM 10 TO 5. AND MODELS WILL BE POSED DAILY. A LADY SUPERINTENDENT WILL BE PRESENT. SEATS AND EASELS WILL BE FOUND, BUT SUCH OTHER MATERIALS AND APPLIANCES AS MAY BE NECESSARY MUST BE PROVIDED BY THE STUDENTS.

FEES
FOR FIVE DAYS PER WEEK. SEVEN GUINEAS PER TERM, OR NINETEEN GUINEAS PER YEAR.
FOR THREE DAYS PER WEEK. FOUR GUINEAS PER TERM, OR ELEVEN GUINEAS PER YEAR.
ALL FEES MUST BE PAID IN ADVANCE. CHEQUES SHOULD BE DRAWN IN FAVOR OF THE SECRETARY AND CROSSED.

COMMUNICATIONS SHOULD BE SENT TO THE SECRETARY,

J. KNEWSTUB
18 FITZROY STREET, W.

IT IS TO BE UNDERSTOOD THAT MR JOHN AND MR ORPEN WILL FIND THEIR PART IN STIMULATING, BY ADVICE AND SUGGESTION, THE MOST PERSONAL ARTISTIC AIMS, AND THEY ARE BOLD TO HOPE THAT BY SYSTEMATIC DISCOURAGEMENT OF THE CHEAP AND MERETRICIOUS AND HEARTY PROMOTION OF THE MOST REAL AND SINGLE-MINDED VIEW OF LIFE, NATURE AND ART, THEIR EFFORTS WILL NOT TEND OTHERWISE THAN TO THE BEST PROGRESS OF THEIR STUDENTS IN ART, IN NATURE AND IN LIFE

MR AUG. E. JOHN and MR WILLIAM ORPEN desire to bring to your notice the ART COURSES to which they propose to give their assistance during the forthcoming year.

The CLASSES will consist of Drawing and Painting from Life (figure, portrait, and costume), Painting from Still Life, Figure Composition, Landscape and Decorative Painting, together with the usual Elementary Subjects where required.

The STUDIOS will be situated in Chelsea; classes will be held for ladies and gentlemen, and every arrangement will be made to meet the convenience of individual students. A Lady Superintendent will be present daily.

The SPRING TERM of Session 1904 commences on the 11th January, and intending students should give prompt notification as the numbers are strictly limited, and no application can be considered later than the 31st December.

The FEES are moderate, and particulars and all other information can be obtained by writing to

THE SECRETARY,
18 Fitzroy Street,
London, W.

Appendix Four

To Iris [Tree], A parody of Arthur Symons

To her foul breathing maw I hold
The guttering candle of my lust,
That smoketh like burnt offerings
Upon the altars of that old
Intoxicate goddess of the bust,
Multiple and indeterminate,
The fume whereof waxes and wanes
As spew upon the floor of Hell,
That bubbles with the heat of it;
Red lips that smack of carrion
And the faint penetrating smell
That comes of eating onions
That grow beside the lake of Sin;
And eager cloven tongue that laps
The froth from off the jaws of Shame;
(Ah God, ah God, the Joy thereof!)
Beneath the fulsome beaded paps,
Her devastated belly quakes
With the unmentionable aches
And agonies without a name,
As used to ravage and lay waste,
The carcase of Lucrezia,
When she lay panting with the Pope,
And thro' her burning violet veins,
The corpuscles of passion chased
The Molecules of virtue out;
Her heavy eyes quite glazed with Dope
And fume of the abominable wine,
That sinners serve to sinners, shine
With the extraordinary desire for trout
Caught by lost souls in Acheron;
The issue of her riven loins,
As evil monsters pullulate
About the shadow of her groin's
Unholy sanctuary; ululate
Like Hell's spawn unredeemable,
Brought forth to torment, damnably
And writhe and twist and turn again.
                                    SIMPLE SYMON

609

Appendix Five

'AUGUSTUS JOHN'

Sung by Mrs Grundy and the John Beauty Chorus

Music by H. Fraser-Simson

Words by Harry Graham

Some people will squander
    Their savings away
        On paintings by Rankin or Steer;
For Brangwyn or Conder
    Huge sums they will pay,
        And they buy all the Prydes that appear!
But if you'd be smart,
As patrons of Art,
    It's almost a *sine qua non*
To prove your discretion
By gaining possession
    Of works by the wonderful John!
              Augustus John!

Refrain
    John! John!
    How he's got on!
        He owes it, he knows it, to me!
    Brass earrings I wear,
    And I don't do my hair,
    And my feet are as bare as can be;
When I walk down the street,
All the people I meet
    They stare at the things I have on!
When Battersea-Parking
You'll hear folks remarking:
    'There goes an Augustus John!'

Chorus
    John! John!
    If you'd get on,
        The quaintest of clothes you must don!
    When out for an airing,
    You'll hear folks declaring:
        'There goes an Augustus John!'

Good people acquainted
    With Singer or Strang
        Will sit to them week after week!
It's nice being painted
    By Nicholson's gang,

And McEvoy's touch is unique!
But if 'in the know,'
You'll hasten to go
Where all the best people have gone;
His portraits don't flatter
But that doesn't matter,
So long as you're painted by John!
Augustus John!

Refrain

John! John!
If you'd get on,
Just sit for a bit, and you'll see!
Your curious shape
He will cunningly drape
With an Inverness cape to the knee!
What a wealth of design!
And what colour and line!
He turns ev'ry goose to a swan!
And though you're not handsome,
You're worth a king's ransom,
If you're an 'Augustus John!'

Chorus

John! John!
How he's got on!
He turns ev'ry goose to a swan!
You needn't be pretty,
Or wealthy or witty,
If you're an 'Augustus John!'

Our ancestors freely
Expressed their dislike
Of all unconventional styles;
They raved about Lely,
They worshipped Vandyke,
And Leighton they greeted with smiles!
To-day if one owns
A Watts or Burne-Jones,
Its subject seems bloodless and wan!
One misses the vigour,
The matronly figure,
That marks all the drawings of John!
Augustus John!

Refrain

John! John!
How he's got on!
He's quite at the top of the tree!
From Cotman to Corot,
From Tonks to George Morrow,
There's no-one as famous as he!
On the scrap-heap we'll cast
All those works of the past
By stars that once splendidly shone!
Send Hoppners and Knellers
To attics and cellars,
And stick to Augustus John!

Chorus　　　　　　　　John! John!
　　　　　　　　　　　How he's got on!
　　　　　　　　　　　　　No light half so brightly has shone!
　　　　　　　　　　　The verdict of Chelsea's
　　　　　　　　　　　That nobody else is
　　　　　　　　　　　　　A patch on Augustus John!

Chorus

Miss SILVIA FAUSSETT BAKER.
Miss FAITH CELLI.
Miss VERA BERINGER.
Miss BERYL FREEMAN.
Miss WINIFRED BATEMAN.
Miss MANORA THEW.
Miss ELLEN O'MALLEY.
Miss ELSIE MCNAUGHT.
Mrs. CAMPBELL.
Miss ETHEL MACKAY.
Mdme VANDERVELDE.
Mrs. GORDON CRAIG.
Miss SYLVIA MEYER.
Miss MARGARET GUINNESS.
Miss MARJORIE ELVERY.
Miss EVE BALFOUR.
Miss STELLA STOREY.
Miss DOROTHY GOODDAY.
Miss JANET ROSS.
Miss OLGA WARD.
Miss BARBARA HILES.
Miss PHYLLIS DICKSEE.
The HON. SYLVIA BRETT.
Miss IRENE RUSSELL.
Miss NORTH.
Mrs. HENDERSON.
Mrs. FRENCH.
Miss EMILY LOWES.
Miss DOROTHY CHRISTINE.
Miss D'ERLANGER.
Miss HONOR WIGGLESWORTH.
Mrs. HANNEY.
Mrs. NIGEL PLAYFAIR.
Masters GILES and LYON PLAYFAIR.
Mrs. DODGSON.
Miss FAUSSETT.
　and
CARRINGTON.

Appendix Six

1921 Elected Associate
1922   14 Mrs Valentine Fleming
        155 Capt. the Hon. Frederick Guest, MP
        637 The Rev. Padre Fray José-Maria Lozkoz Biguria de Elizondo
        639 Viva
        675 G. Bernard Shaw, Esq. (presented to the Fitzwilliam Museum, Cambridge)
1924   27 Princess Antoine Bibesco
        127 Robert Fleming
        630 Sir Charles Scott Sherrington, GBE, PRS, DSc.
1928 Elected Royal Academician
1929   67 Portrait of a Man
        177 J. L. S. Hatton, Esq., MA, Principal, East London College
1930   52 Miss Tallulah Bankhead (now at the National Gallery, Washington)
        222 Sir Gerald du Maurier
        232 Magnolias
        240 The Earl Spencer
        266 Portrait of a Young Man (Diploma Work)
      1205 Sketch for a Version of Omar Khayyam
1931   118 William Butler Yeats
        308 Brenda, Daughter of Senator and Mrs Oliver St John Gogarty
        318 The Viscount D'Abernon, GCB, GCMG
1934   3 Major Clifford Hugh Douglas
1935   194 Lord David Cecil (purchased by the President and Council of the Royal Academy under the terms of the Chantrey Bequest)
        224 T. Barclay, Esq.
        284 The Lord Conway of Allington
        288 Professor J. Cunningham M'Lennan, FRS
        376 Miss Thelma Cazalet, MP
      1214 James Joyce (chalk)
1936   57 Mrs Harry Sacher
        168 Thomas Barclay, Esq.
1938 Resigned
1940 Re-elected
        52 Blue Cineraria (Chantrey Purchase)
        60 H. S. Goodhart-Rendell, FRIBA
        94 The Rt Hon. Vincent Massey
        183 Mrs Oliver Harvey
        230 The Lord Alington
1941   3 W. B. Yeats (Chantrey Purchase)
        164 Major-General The Earl of Athlone, KG
1942   106 The Mask (Harry Melville)
        110 The Viscount Caldecote, CBE
1943   238 Air Chief Marshal Sir Charles F. A. Portal

1944 51 Dr H. H. E. Craster, Bodley's Librarian
   220 General Sir Bernard Montgomery
   989 Lawrence J. Clements, Esq. (chalk)
   990 Poppet (chalk)
   993 Lauretta [Nicholson] (chalk)
   994 Mary (chalk)
   997 General Sir Bernard Montgomery (chalk)
1945 1073 Mrs Michael Pugh (chalk)
  1090 General Sir Hastings Ismay (chalk)
  1094 The Duke of Alba (chalk)
  1098 Master Tom Pugh (chalk)
  1102 Master Tim Pugh (chalk)
  1106 The Duchess of Montoro (chalk)
  1125 Michael Pugh, Esq. (chalk)
1950 3 Matthew Smith (Chantrey Purchase)
   58 The White Feather Boa
   94 Henry Elphin John
  128 Gonnoske Komai
  148 The Little Concert
  1065 Portrait of a Woman (red chalk)
  1066 Walter de la Mare (chalk)
1951 129 Caspar John
  132 Mrs Robert Adeane
  135 Young Negress
  779 Reclining Nude
  879 Two Heads of Women (chalk)
  880 Sketch for Composition (pen and wash)
1952 1114 The Hurdy-Gurdy Man (red chalk)
    An Apostle (red chalk)
1953 980 Dr Hubert Noel (chalk)
  984 The Disciple (chalk)
1955 98 Gloxinia (Chantrey Purchase)
1957 89 Edward Grove (Chantrey Purchase)
1958 74 Theodore Powys (Chantrey Purchase)
1959 22 Dorelia
   91 Simone
1960 52 Portrait of a Man
  168 The Late Viscount D'Abernon
1961 Died 31 October
1962 123 Dorelia
  124 The Blue Lake
  125 Portrait of the Artist
  876 Lady with a Scarf
  877 Family Group
  878 Ursula Tyrwhitt

Appendix Seven

1878   4 January, born at Tenby, Pembrokeshire, Wales.

1884   August, mother dies. Family move from Haverfordwest to Tenby.

1894–8   Slade School of Fine Art, London.

1897   Bathing accident.

1898   'Moses and the Brazen Serpent' wins the Summer Composition Prize. Visits Holland with Ambrose McEvoy.

1899   First one-man show at Carfax Gallery. Makes £30 and goes to Vattetot-sur-Mer with William Rothenstein, William Orpen, Charles Conder. Meets Oscar Wilde in Paris. Begins exhibiting at New English Art Club.

1900   Goes to Swanage with Conder. 'Walpurgis Night'. Visits Le Puy-en-Velay with the Rothensteins and Michel Salaman. Painted by Orpen.

1901   12 January, marries Ida Nettleship. Moves into 18 Fitzroy Street, London.

1901–2   Art instructor at Liverpool. Meets John Sampson and the Dowdalls. Etchings.

1902   6 January, David born.

1903   Elected to NEAC.

       January, meets Dorothy McNeill in London. March, Carfax Gallery: 'Paintings [3], Pastels [8], Drawings [21] and Etchings [13] by Augustus E. John'; 'Paintings [3] by Gwen John'.

       22 March, Caspar born.

       August, Gwen and Dorelia's 'walk to Rome', via Toulouse. Augustus and Ida move to Elm House, Matching Green, Essex.

1903–7   Involved with Orpen and Knewstub in Chelsea Art School, Rossetti Studios.

1904   Gwen and Dorelia arrive in Paris. Dorelia elopes to Bruges.

       August, Dorelia returns and lives at Elm House.

       Augustus elected to membership of the Society of Twelve.

       23 October, Ida's Robin born.

1905   April–May, on Dartmoor. Dorelia's Pyramus born.

       September, emigration to rue Monsieur-le-Prince, Paris.

       November, Chenil Gallery: 'Drawings by Aug. E. John [42] and William Orpen [22]'.

       27 November, Ida's Edwin born.

1906   January, move to 77 rue Dareau, Paris.

       May, Chenil Gallery: Eighty-Two Etchings. First drawings of Alick Schepeler.

       August, at Ste-Honorine-des-Perthes with Wyndham Lewis. Dorelia's Romilly born.

       November, Dorelia detaches herself and moves to 48 rue du Château.

1907   February, Augustus and Ida move to 3 Cour de Rohan.

       9 March, Ida's Henry born.

       14 March, Ida dies.

       Summer at Equihen with Dorelia.

September, visits Lady Gregory at Coole, Ireland. Paints W. B. Yeats. Moves to 8 Fitzroy Street, London.

November, Carfax Gallery. Eighty-one drawings.

1908   Gets to know Lady Ottoline Morrell. Starts off for Spain, via Paris.

July–September, at Dielette with Dorelia and children. Visited by Mrs Nettleship.

Autumn, moves into 153 Church Street with Dorelia and families.

1909   January, paints William Nicholson. Takes studio at 181a King's Road.

July, caravans to Cambridge. Paints Jane Harrison. August, paints 'His Worship the Lord Mayor of Liverpool, and Smith'.

Meets John Quinn in London.

September, agrees to decorate Hugh Lane's house.

1910   January–September, travels, at Quinn's expense, to Italy and Provence. Visits Frank Harris at Nice.

April, Villa Ste-Anne, Martigues.

October, 'The Smiling Woman' becomes the first purchase of the Contemporary Art Society (£225) and is later (1917) given to the Tate Gallery.

November–December, Chenil Gallery: 'Provençal Studies [48] and Other Works [35 drawings]'. Begins working with J. D. Innes.

1911   Elected to the Camden Town Group.

May, rents cottage with Innes in North Wales.

July, paints Kuno Meyer in Liverpool.

August, moves to Alderney Manor.

September, in France with Quinn.

October, in Wales.

December, Chenil Gallery: Paintings, Drawings and Etchings.

1912   March, Pyramus dies. Poppet is born.

Summer, west coast of Ireland with Francis Macnamara and Oliver St John Gogarty.

September, stays at Chirk Castle with the Howard de Waldens.

1913   January, in South of France with Innes.

February, Armory Show, New York (23 paintings, 14 drawings).

Spring, Madam Strindberg's cabaret club opens.

July, North Wales with Holbrooke and Sime.

August, visits Modigliani in Paris.

September, North Wales.

November, Goupil Gallery: Fifteen Panels.

1914   February, elected President of the National Portrait Society. In Cornwall with Laura Knight and others.

April, Crab Tree Club opens.

May, Cardiganshire. Gives up studio at 181a King's Road, moves into 28 Mallord Street.

June, one week in Boulogne.

August, Eilean Shona, Archarcle, Argyllshire. Last visits to Innes at Brighton and Swanley in Kent before his death.

October–November, drilling with Wadsworth in the courtyard of the Royal Academy.

December, sees Gwen John in Paris. Fails to persuade her to return to England.

1915   March, Vivien born.

May, Hugh Lane drowned in *Lusitania*.

June, at Coole. Paints three portraits of Bernard Shaw.

October, Aran Islands and Galway.

1916   February, Chenil Gallery: Paintings (21) and Drawings (41). Portrait of Lloyd George.

May, Chenil Gallery: 'Etchings by Augustus E. John'.

July, goes to Herbert Barker for knee operation.

August, rejected for military service. 'Galway' shown at Arts and Crafts Exhibition, Burlington House.

Starts experiments in lithography. Bust by Jacob Epstein.

1917   20 March, Monster Matinée at Chelsea Palace Theatre.

27 April, meets Lady Cynthia Asquith.

August, portrait of Oliver St John Gogarty.

9 October, begins portrait of Lady Cynthia Asquith ('Lady in Black').

November–February (1918), Alpine Club: pictures and decorations (67 exhibits).

December, advances to Aubigny as a Canadian Army major.

1918   March, retires from France after knocking out Captain Wright.

May, starts Canadian cartoon (National Gallery of Canada) and 'Fraternity' (Imperial War Museum, London).

8–28 August, represented at 'Englische Moderne Malerei', an exhibition organized by the Contemporary Arts Society at the Kunsthaus, Zürich.

1919   February–May, in Paris as official war artist. Paints Marchesa Casati and Duchess of Gramont. First drawing of T. E. Lawrence.

March, Chenil Gallery: 125 etchings.

September, at Deauville with Lloyd George.

1920   *Augustus John* by Charles Marriott published by John Lane in the 'Masters of Modern Art' series. Elected Fellow of University College, London.

March, Alpine Club: War, Peace Conference and Other Portraits (39 exhibits).

April, Sister Carline Hospital. Operation on nose.

May, Rouen and Dieppe.

October, rumpus over Lord Leverhulme's decapitated portrait.

Campbell Dodgson's *Catalogue of Etchings by A. E. John* published.

1921   22 April, elected Associate of the Royal Academy. Begins painting of Mme Suggia.

June, portrait of Herbert Barker.

1922   March, the Sculptors' Gallery, New York: works by Epstein, Gaudier-Brzeska, Innes, Augustus John and Wyndham Lewis from Quinn Collection (7 paintings, 7 drawings).

April, Paris.

May, arrives in Spain.

1923   March, Alpine Club Gallery: Paintings and Drawings. First showing of 'Mme Suggia'.

28 March–23 June, United States.

June, Beaux Arts Gallery: paintings (29).

Augustus John by A.B. [Anthony Bertram] published by Benn.

21 September, meets Thomas Hardy at Kingston Maurward.

October, completes portrait of Hardy at Max Gate.

1924   'Mme Suggia' wins first prize at International Exhibition, Carnegie Institute, Pittsburgh.

April–June, United States.

July, in Dublin for Taillteann Games. Stays with Lord Dunsany.

September–October, Paris.

1925   February, Lord Duveen gives 'Mme Suggia' to the Tate Gallery.

March–April, in Berlin. Paints Gustav Stresemann and Lali Horstmann.

May–June, Ischia with T. W. Earp.

Italy. Starts flower painting.

1926   February–March, Albright Art Gallery, Buffalo Fine Arts Academy, United States: drawings.

February–April, France.

April, Elected member of Royal Society of Portrait Painters.
May, New Chenil Gallery: Paintings (47) and Drawings (35); Gwen John, paintings (44) and 4 albums of drawings.
17 June, begins portrait of Hugh Walpole.
9 July, 'Art and the Public', BBC talk. Meets and paints Sean O'Casey.
October, walks from Avignon to Marseilles with Horace de Vere Cole and A. R. Thomson.
December (till February 1927), at Villa Ste-Anne.

1927   Begins portrait of Lord D'Abernon.
March, moves from Alderney Manor to Fryern Court.
June–July, at Château de Missery.
July, helps Gwen John buy Yew Tree Cottage, Burgate Cross, Fordingbridge.
December (till January 1928), South of France.

1928   14 January–4 February, Anderson Gallery, New York: Paintings and Drawings.
April, Villa Ste-Anne sold.
August–December, in United States. Portrait of Governor Fuller.
5 December, elected Royal Academician.

1929   February, at Cap Ferrat with James Dunn.
4 April–17 May, Tooth's Gallery: Recent Paintings (27).
May–June, designs sets for Act II of Sean O'Casey's *The Silver Tassie*.
July, Château de Missery.
September, Rheims.
October, paints T. E. Lawrence at Fryern Court.
November, drawing of Frederick Delius.
December, designs Noah's Ark for Chelsea Arts Club Ball at Albert Hall.

1930   Contributes reminiscences to Ifan Kyrle Fletcher's *Ronald Firbank*.
April, Harlow, McDonald & Co, New York: Etchings and Drawings.
1 April, begins portrait of Montagu Norman.
April–May, in hospital, Preston Deanery Hall, Northampton.
July–September, Ireland. Portraits of W. B. Yeats and Brenda Gogarty.
October, Kiddalton Castle, Port Ellen, Isle of Islay. In Amsterdam with Dorelia.
November, Paris, James Joyce drawings.
December (till February 1931), Cap Ferrat.

1931   21 November, funeral of John Sampson who bequeaths John under Clause 8 of his will, 'my Smith and Wesson Revolver No. 239892'.

1932   February–March, in Jersey with Sir Herbert Barker. More attention to knee. Lord D'Abernon's portrait signed.
May, portraits of Joe Hone and T. W. Earp.
June, represented at XVIII Biennial International Art Exhibition, Venice.
July, France.
August, Cornwall. Romilly John's *The Seventh Child* published by Heinemann.
December, Majorca.
Death of Mrs Nettleship.

1933   January, Leicester Galleries: Sixty Etchings. LL D Cardiff University.
August, appointed trustee of the Tate Gallery (to 1941). Venice.

1934   *Augustus John* by T. W. Earp, published by Nelson.
21 May, elected President of Royal Cambrian Academy of Art.
September, Paris.
October (to February 1935), 'Etchings at the National Museum of Wales' (catalogue by Kighley Baxandall). Mallord Street sold to Gracie Fields. New studio built at Fryern Court.

1935 30 April, 'La Séraphita' and other paintings destroyed in fire at Fryern.

14 May, letter to *The Times* about Stanley Spencer's works.

June, borrows Vanessa Bell's studio for one month.

22 June, Henry John missing. Body found drowned on 6 July.

November, takes studio at 49 Glebe Place.

1936 5–29 February, Adams Gallery: Forty Etchings.

April, Paris.

25 April, Laugharne Castle, Carmarthen. Portrait of Dylan Thomas.

26 May, fined £5 for drinking after hours at the Old Mill Club, Salisbury.

June, represented at XX Biennial International Art Exhibition (4 paintings).

Autumn, British Empire Exhibition, Johannesburg. Works (later with Ernst Stern) on designs for costumes and scenery for C. B. Cochran's production of J. M. Barrie's *The Boy David*, which opened on 14 December.

1937 Associated with new school of drawing and painting under the direction of Claude Rogers, Victor Pasmore and William Coldstream. Elected President of the Gypsy Lore Society.

March, Wildenstein Gallery, London: Thirty Drawings.

February–May, Jamaica. Travels back on a banana boat via Rotterdam.

September, rents Mas de Galeron, St-Rémy-de-Provence. Visits Matthew Smith at Aix-en-Provence.

1938 February, one of three British artists (with Sickert and Steer) represented at Exhibition of British Art at the Louvre, Paris.

March, Leicester Galleries: Drawings. Takes Park Studio, Pelham Street, London.

7 April, father dies in Tenby.

28 April, resigns from Royal Academy following its rejection of Wyndham Lewis's portrait of T. S. Eliot.

19 May–11 June, Tooth's Gallery: Latest Paintings (32), including Jamaican pictures.

18 June, Dorelia's mother dies following a fall from the balcony of her bedroom at Fryern Court on 20 May.

4 July, opens Exhibition of Twentieth-Century German Art at Burlington House.

July, signs contract with Jonathan Cape for autobiography.

August, at Laugharne with Richard Hughes.

27 August, goes to Mas de Galeron.

1939 February–March, Redfern Gallery: Exhibition of Paintings by John, Innes and Derwent Lees.

July–August, Mas de Galeron.

18 September, Gwen John dies at Dieppe.

Autumn, begins painting the Queen. Represented at British Council Exhibition, New York.

1940 Honorary Member of the London Group.

16 February, re-elected to the Royal Academy.

July, moves to studio at 33 Tite Street, Chelsea.

November, National Gallery: 'British Painting Since Whistler: Drawings of Augustus John' (112).

December, exhibition at the Francis Taylor Gallery, Hollywood.

1941 February, starts writing for Cyril Connolly's *Horizon* (until April 1949).

June, Redfern Gallery: Drawings (40).

July, joins the Green Shirts and 'throws in his lot' with the Social Credit Party.

October, Augustus John *Drawings*, edited by Lillian Browse, published by Faber and Faber.

1942　March, etchings collected by Gerald Brockhurst shown at Boston Library, Massachusetts.

11 June, awarded Order of Merit (investiture 2 July).

31 June, writes to *The Times* deploring the lack of interest shown by press and public in Ethel Walker's exhibition at the Lefevre Gallery.

October, article on Gwen John published by *Burlington Magazine*.

1943　January, elected Honorary Member, American National Institute of Arts and Letters. Artists' International Association (1 painting).

May, Leicester Galleries: 'Drawings by Augustus John, Paintings by Gilbert Spencer'.

1944　Matthew Smith stays at Fryern; he and John paint each other.

14 March, Alfred Munnings 24 votes, John 17 in elections for the presidency of the Royal Academy.

7 June, in a light fawn tropical suit opens Exhibition of Indian Art for the Mayor of Calcutta's Relief Fund.

2 August, appointed First President of the Central Institute of Art and Design.

October, *Augustus John* by John Rothenstein published by Phaidon and Allen & Unwin as Phaidon Press Art Books: 'British Artists' series, No. 2.

1945　In Wales with the Howard de Waldens.

July–November, Tite Street studio under repair.

1946　Introduction to Gwen John exhibition (Arts Council). Elected chairman of the Contemporary Art Society for Wales. Elected member of Académie Royale de Belgique. Jeu de Paume, Paris: represented in 'Exposition de peinture anglaise du XX siècle' (portraits and a composition).

24 July–31 August, Temple Newsam House, Leeds: Exhibition of Paintings and Drawings (124 exhibits).

24 December, letter to *The Times* about the dangers of picture cleaning at the National Gallery.

1947　A long convalescence. September–October, Mousehole, Cornwall.

1948　May, Leicester Galleries: Exhibition of work from previous fifteen years (52 exhibits), including 12-foot canvas 'The Little Concert' (grisaille).

31 May, on the cover of *Time* magazine, USA.

10 July, elected President of the Royal Society of Portrait Painters.

30 July, Welsh National Eisteddfod, Bridgend. Arts Council Exhibition: Paintings (61) and Drawings (65).

October, American-British Art Center: Drawings.

1949　7 March, 'Engaged on a long and vast composition' (letter to Wyndham Lewis).

21 March–12 April, Scott & Fowles, New York: Exhibition of Works in American Collections (23 paintings).

9 September, radio talk for BBC, Far Eastern Service, 'I Speak for Myself'.

November, Lefevre Gallery: 'Works by Augustus John and Ethel Walker'. 'Frontiers' published by *Delphic Review*.

1950　30 April, profile in London *Observer*.

June–July, Mas de Galeron given up.

July–August, Hôtel de Bourgogne, Paris: 'a course of injections'.

29 August, letter to *The Times* on art students at the National Gallery. Castello San Peyre, Opio, France.

October, Paris.

1951　15 January, Café Royal closes. Leaves Tite Street studio.

17 August, letter to *The Times* about the Arts Council of Great Britain.

1952　28 January, on the cover of *Life* magazine.

3 March, *Chiaroscuro* published by Jonathan Cape (by Pellerini & Cudahy in United States).

5 March, appointed Vice-President of the Artists' Benevolent Institution.

28 March, Guest of Honour at Foyle's Literary Lunch: 'I am two people instead of one: the one you see before you is the old painter. But another one has just cropped up – the young writer.'

October, Introduction to the catalogue of Ulrica Forbes Exhibition, Walker Art Gallery, Liverpool.

1953   Resigns as President of Royal Society of Portrait Painters.

Begins sculpture with Fiore de Henriques.

1954   March–April, Royal Academy, Diploma Gallery: Exhibition of Works by Augustus John OM, RA (460 exhibits). Portrait of Lord Leverhulme repaired. Walker Art Gallery: Exhibition of Augustus John pictures with Liverpool associations.

November, Nuffield House, Guy's Hospital, prostate gland operation.

December (till March 1955), Spain.

1955   February, 'Some Portraits from Memory' published by the *London Magazine*.

March, bronze head of Yeats purchased for the Abbey Theatre, Dublin.

19 September, letter to *The Times* on the rights of gypsies.

November, Wales. Drawings of John Cowper Powys.

1956   August, France.

September, Graves Art Gallery, Sheffield: Paintings (43), Drawings (88) and Prints (15).

1957   4 November, interviewed by Malcolm Muggeridge on BBC TV *Panorama*: 'Have you always wanted to be a painter?' 'Give me another hundred years and I would become a very good one.'

December, *Fifty-two Drawings*, with an Introduction by Lord David Cecil, published by Rainbird.

1958   Joins British Peace Committee.

1959   29 October, given the Honorary Freedom of Tenby.

1960   Elected first president of the Contemporary Art Society for Wales.

4 January, eighty-second birthday. 'Work as usual' (*Daily Telegraph*).

12 May, interviewed by John Freeman on BBC *Face to Face* television programme.

14 October, letter praising the work of Matthew Smith in the *Daily Telegraph*.

1961   15 March–30 March, Tooth's Gallery: Paintings and Drawings not previously illustrated.

31 October, dies at Fryern Court.

5 November, obituary programme, BBC TV *Monitor*.

1962   20 July, Christie's first studio sale.

Augustus John by John Rothenstein published by Beaverbrook Newspapers Ltd.

1963   21 June, Christie's second studio sale.

1964   12 November, *Finishing Touches* published by Jonathan Cape.

1965   1–30 April, Upper Grosvenor Galleries: Loan Exhibition of Drawings and Murals by Augustus John OM, RA, in aid of the Augustus John Memorial Appeal.

1967   *The Drawings of Augustus John*, with an Introduction by Stephen Longstreet, published by the Borden Publishing Company, California.

1 October, memorial statue by Ivor Roberts-Jones unveiled by Lord Mountbatten at Fordingbridge.

1968   18 July, Harlech Television, *Augustus John* programme.

1969   24 July, Dorelia dies at Fryern Court.

1970   25 October–14 November, The University of Hull: 'Augustus John: Portraits of the Artist's Family'.

1971	2–28 December, Lefevre Gallery: Drawings by Augustus John (36 pictures).

1971   2–28 December, Lefevre Gallery: Drawings by Augustus John (36 pictures).

1972   Over 1,000 drawings, 110 paintings and 3 bronzes, the last remains of the artist's studio, purchased by the National Museum of Wales.

November, Dalhousie Art Gallery, Halifax, Nova Scotia: Augustus John (40 pictures, catalogue by Ernest W. Smith).

1974   September, Malcolm Easton and Michael Holroyd, *The Art of Augustus John* published. Colnaghi's: 'Augustus John: Early Drawings and Etchings' (162 exhibits, catalogue essays by Malcolm Easton and Michael Holroyd).

October, London Weekend Television *Aquarius* programme, *Augustus John*, with Richard Burton (producer, Humphrey Burton).

1975   25 March–31 August, National Portrait Gallery, London: 'Augustus John, Paintings and Drawings'.

30 May–26 October, National Portrait Gallery, London: 'Augustus John. Life and Times' (catalogues for both exhibitions by Malcolm Easton and Romilly John).

1978   15 April–21 May, National Museum of Wales Centenary exhibition, 'Augustus John: Studies for Compositions' (catalogue by A. D. Fraser Jenkins).

October–December, Fitzwilliam Museum, Cambridge: 'Augustus John: Paintings, Prints and Drawings in the Fitzwilliam Museum' (128 exhibits, catalogue Foreword by Michael Jaffe). BBC TV South, *Augustus John* (producer John Coleman).

1979   *Augustus John* by Richard Shone published.

17 December, Augustus John papers sold at Sotheby's for £52,000 to anonymous buyer in the United States.

1982   August, Mostyn Art Gallery, Llandudno: 'Some Miraculous Promised Land: J. D. Innes, Augustus John and Derwent Lees in North Wales 1910–13' (catalogue by Eric Rowan).

1985   21 November–9 February 1986, Manchester City Art Gallery: 'Augustus John and Friends'. Exhibition in conjunction with 'Gwen John: an Interior Life' (28 November–26 January 1986).

1988   June, Augustus John papers sold by private treaty at Sotheby's to National Library of Wales, Aberystwyth. National Museum of Wales: 'Portraits by Augustus John: Family, Friends and the Famous' (50 exhibits, catalogue by Mark Evans).

1991   3–27 July, Piccadilly Gallery, London: 'Augustus John Paintings, Drawings, Etchings' (4 oils, 38 drawings, 12 etchings, catalogue by Rebecca John). Ceridwen Lloyd-Morgan's *Augustus John Papers* published by the National Library of Wales.

21 September–17 November, Glynn Vivian Art Gallery, Swansea: 'Passionate Visions. Gwen John and Augustus John' (52 exhibits, catalogue by David Fraser Jenkins).

1994   29 July–4 August, Mercury Gallery, London: single work exhibition, cartoon of 'The Mumpers'.

December, HTV Wales, *Augustus John: King of Bohemia* programme.

1995   Mark Lewis, *Augustus John* (pamphlet published by Tenby Museum & Art Gallery, including list of works in the gallery's collection).

1996   July–September, National Museums and Galleries of Wales, Cardiff 'Themes and Variations: The drawings of Augustus John 1901–1931'. *Augustus John. Papers at the National Library of Wales* by Ceridwen Lloyd-Morgan published.

Appendix Eight

The story of how the main collection of Augustus John Papers reached the National Library of Wales is told in my preface. There are, however, many other John letters and manuscripts in Britain and abroad. I have not been able to trace all the correspondence that was privately owned twenty-five years ago, though correspondence that I did not see then I have now seen in galleries, libraries and museums. The following list of John papers held in public collections will I hope be useful, but I do not claim it is definitive.

WALES
The National Library of Wales, Aberystwyth
The catalogue of Augustus John papers purchased and donated between 1988 and 1991, compiled in 1991 by Ceridwen Lloyd-Morgan, provides a calendar of letters from Augustus John to Dorelia McNeill (NLW MSS 22776–8) and various other correspondents (NLW MS 22775); letters to Augustus John (NLW MSS 22779–87) and to Dorelia McNeill (NLW MS 22789); two groups of letters from Ida John (NLW MSS 22788, 22798); miscellaneous letters (NLW MS 22790); sketchbooks (NLW MSS 22791–4); prose and verse (NLW MSS 22795–6); Nettleship and John family papers (NLW MSS 22799–803); and miscellaneous papers (NLW MS 22797).

The catalogue also refers to other Augustus John material at the library, including seventy-one letters to Michel Salaman (NLW MS 14928D); one letter to J. C. Squire (NLW MS 16098E); seven letters to Mrs Goeritz and Ruth King, together with ten letters to Peter Heseltine, 'Peter Warlock' (NLW MS 18909D); ten letters with sketches to Ursula Tyrwhitt (NLW MS 19645C); thirty-seven letters, together with autograph drafts of verse, to John Sampson (NLW MS 21459E); three letters to Ernest Forbes, one letter to Eric Kennington, two letters to C. K. Ogden and one letter to Robert Gregory (NLW MS 21482D); twenty-eight letters to various correspondents including Laura Knight and Frances Stevenson, together with some autobiographical writings (NLW MS 21570E); fifty-nine letters to John Davenport (NLW MS 21585E); twenty-one letters to Bapsy Pavry and three letters to her brother (NLW MS 21622D); one letter to Caitlin Macnamara (NLW MS 21698E); one letter to 'Kitty' [McGee] (NLW MS 21818D); one letter to John Cowper Powys (NLW MS 21872D); ten letters to Sean O'Casey and seven letters to George Bilainkin (NLW MS 21980C); four letters to Villiers Bergne (NLW MS 22022C); one letter to the Rev. R. J. Jones (Papers of the Rev. R. J. Jones, Cardiff); eighteen letters and four telegrams to Alicia Gower Jones (Miss Olive Mary Jones Bequest).

There are also two letters from Augustus John to Ceri Richards at the library (NLW MS 23007E); one letter to Keidrych Rhys (NLW MS 22745D); one letter to Hugh Blaker and one letter to R. A. Maynard (Dr Thomas Jones Collection); one letter to Emlyn Williams (Emlyn Williams Scrapbook II); one letter to Port Talbot Forum (NLW MS 23186E); an appreciation of J. D. Innes (NLW MS 11067C); and papers relating to exhibitions from the Welsh Arts Council Archives.

Ten letters from Augustus John to the composer Joseph Holbrooke were bought

623

at Sotheby's on 24 July 1995 (lot 540) and one letter to Charles Conder (21 June 1901) bought at Phillips on 9 November 1995 (lot 425). Both purchases are in a volume, NLW MS 23410C, which also contains a recent donation of two letters from Augustus to Dorelia.

The catalogue also refers to some Augustus John correspondence within the Gwen John Papers, including twenty-seven letters from Augustus to Gwen (NLW MS 22305D); forty-eight letters from Augustus to his son Edwin (NLW MS 22312D); and one letter to Dorelia McNeill (NLW MS 22311D). In the Gwen John Papers these items are listed with a C and not a D.

The Schedule of Gwen John papers purchased in 1984 and 1987, compiled by Ceridwen Lloyd-Morgan in 1988, lists diaries (NLW MSS 22276–8A); notebooks (NLW MSS 22279–92); loose notes (NLW MSS 22293–6); sketches (NLW MS 22297–9); draft letters from Gwen John (NLW MSS 22300–3); letters to Gwen John (NLW MSS 22304–11); miscellaneous letters (NLW MS 22311C); letters to her nephew Edwin John (NLW MSS 22312–13C); Estate of Gwen John correspondence (NLW MSS 22314–15); photographs (NLW MS 22316C); and miscellaneous papers (NLW MSS 22317–18). Included as an appendix is a calendar of other Gwen John letters at the National Library of Wales: seven letters to Michel Salaman (NLW MSS 14930C, 14931C); approximately seventy letters to Ursula Tyrwhitt (NLW MS 21468D); three letters to Augustus John; and four letters to Dorelia McNeill (NLW MS 22155B). See also Ceridwen Lloyd-Morgan, *Gwen John Papers at the National Library of Wales* (1988), and *Augustus John Papers at the National Library of Wales* (1996).

Pembrokeshire Record Office, Haverfordwest
Correspondence to Douglas James.

Glynn Vivian Art Gallery, Swansea
Two letters to Grant Murray, and one (copy) to Winifred Combe Tennant.

Tenby Museum and Art Gallery
Two letters to Wilfred Harrison, one to the museum, one to his father E. W. John (22 September 1934), and one letter to Mrs Cazalet (23 September 1939). There is also a box of miscellaneous items, including books won by Augustus at school and some music composed by E. W. John.

SCOTLAND
Special Collection Library, University of Glasgow
Thirty-six letters to D. S. MacColl, 1900–45.

IRELAND
National Library of Ireland, Dublin
Letter to Hugh Lane (Hugh Lane Papers MSS 13071–2).

ENGLAND
British Library, London
Correspondence to: Lady Aberconway (formerly McLaren) 1924–59, Add. MS 52556 ff. 25–114; Cecil Gray 1933–41, Add. MS 57785 ff. 72–7; Bernard Shaw 1915–44, Add. MS 50539 ff. 28–38; T. E. Shaw (Lawrence) 1929, Add. MS 45904 f. 83; Society of Authors 1944–7, Add. MS 63278 ff. 112–20; Marie Stopes 1943–56, Add. MS 58543 ff. 105–40. There is also correspondence from Augustus, Dorelia, Edwin, Poppet, Romilly and Caspar John to Lytton Strachey 1913–31, Add. MS 60672 ff. 1–45.

Dorset County Museum, Dorchester
One letter to Thomas Hardy.

Modern Archive Centre, King's College Library, Cambridge
Correspondence to Clive Bell, Vanessa Bell, J. M. Keynes, Rosamond Lehmann, Lydia Lopokova. There are also references to John in Duncan Grant's 'Paris Memoir'.

Liverpool City Library
Correspondence to Harold Chaloner Dowdall and the Hon. Mary Dowdall 1901–54 (920 DOW). See also Sandon Studies Society papers (Acc. 4096).

Liverpool University Library
Reilly papers. Seventeen letters from Augustus John to Charles Reilly and one from Dorelia (D.207/40/51–67. D.207/40/68).
Gypsy Lore Society Archive. Correspondence to Dora Yates and John Sampson (GLS D.Y., D.9).
John Sampson Library. Letters on Sampson's retirement, death and sale of books (S.P.11,12,14).
Liverpool University Library MSS letter to William Garmon Jones (MS 5.26).
Scott Macfie Collection. Correspondence to Scott Macfie.

Imperial War Museum, London
Correspondence to Campbell Dodgson and Grant Richards.

National Portrait Gallery, London
Correspondence to Evan Charteris (NPG 2362) and single letters to Charles Kingsley Adams (NPG 2910) and Mrs Dorothy Garthwaite (later Burns).

The Royal College of Surgeons of England, London
Correspondence to Herbert Barker.

British Broadcasting Corporation Written Archives Centre, Caversham
Correspondence to the BBC 1941–61. There is also the script of a talk John gave in the Far Eastern Service series *I Speak for Myself* (10 September 1949), as well as scripts for his television interview with John Freeman in the *Face to Face* series (1960) and with Malcolm Muggeridge for *Panorama* (1957). There is also a programme production file for an abortive film profile in 1951–2.

Royal Academy of Arts, London
Correspondence with Gerald Kelly and one letter from Dorelia to Kelly.

Royal Society of Portrait Painters, London
One letter to Maurice Codner.

Special Collections, National Art Library, Victoria and Albert Museum, London
Correspondence to Boris Anrep (86.PP.12), Sydney Cockerell (86.UU.3–4), I. Spielmann (86.PP.17), and two unknown correspondents (MS.L. 49–1984; 86.WW.1).

Department of Western Manuscripts, Bodleian Library, University of Oxford
Single letters to Isidore Spielmann, 1905 (MS. Eng. misc.d.87, fol.323), J. L. Boston, 1949 (MS. Autogr. d.30, fol.63), Lionel Curtis (with two letters from Curtis regarding John's 1919 sketch of T. E. Lawrence. MS. Curtis 97, fols.31–40). There is also a letter of reference from John for Ernst Stern, 1940 (MS. S.P.S.L.

555, fol.344), and a reference to John in a letter of W. B. Yeats, 1927 (MS.Eng.lett. c.650, fols.1–2).

University of Reading Library, Whiteknights, Reading
In the Jonathan Cape archive there are approximately one hundred and thirty letters (with some copies of replies and supporting material such as book reviews) from Augustus John to Cape himself, his business partner George Wren Howard, John's editor Daniel George, and Cape's secretary Menina Mesquita. There are two letters from John to Chatto & Windus, and one to Professor D. J. Gordon. There are also copies of some of John's contracts and a report by William Plomer on an early draft of *Chiaroscuro*.

Leeds City Art Gallery
One letter to Philip Hendy.

Record Office, House of Lords, London
Correspondence with Lord Beaverbrook (1918 and 1928, and one reference by Beaverbrook to *Finishing Touches* in 1964). There is also an exchange of letters in April 1941 between Beaverbrook and Walter Monckton, who suggested John be commissioned to paint portraits of cabinet ministers (Beaverbrook Papers D.344).

Tate Gallery Archives, London
Correspondence to Henry Lamb 1907 and 1913–14 (TAM 15B 32–43/52) and to Charles Rutherston 1902–6 (TAM 49 49/2); autobiographical fragments, articles, press cuttings and manuscript drafts of John's writings (TAM 21E and 21F 3–38/67); letters to Dorelia 1930–3 (TAM 21H 67/67). There are also letters to John from Wyndham Lewis with transcriptions 1948–52 (TAM 21D 1–2/67) and one hundred and forty-three letters from other correspondents (TAM 21G 39–66/67).

UNITED STATES
Humanities Research Center, University of Texas at Austin
Correspondence to Jocelyn Brooke, [Dora] Carrington, Willard Connely, Cyril Connolly, Rupert Croft-Cooke, Nancy Cunard, St John Ervine, Richard Garnett, Nina Hamnett, Barbara Hiles (later Bagenal), J. M. Hone, David Hughes, Mary Hutchinson, Robin John, John Lehmann, E. V. Lucas, Lillah McCarthy (a.k.a. Granville-Barker, later Lady Keeble), Compton Mackenzie, J. B. Manson, Ottoline Morrell, Philip Morrell, Edward Nehls, Herman Ould of PEN, Mr Pickward, T. F. Powys, Grant Richards, R. A. Scott-James, Edith Sitwell, John Symonds, H. M. Tomlinson, Henry Tonks. There are also some fragments of John's autobiography at Texas.

New York Public Library, Department of Manuscripts and Berg Collection
Correspondence to Ronald Firbank, Lady Gregory, Robert Gregory, Tania Jepson, John Quinn, Edith Sitwell. There is also John's contribution to Max Beerbohm's Eightieth Birthday Album; and two letters to J. B. Manson in the Mitchell Kennerley Papers.

American Archives of Art, Detroit, Michigan
Correspondence to John Beatty and Homer St Gaudens.

McFarlin Library, University of Tulsa, Oklahoma
Correspondence to Cyril Connolly.

Vassar College Library, Poughkeepsie, New York
Correspondence to William Kent Rose.

University of Delaware Library, Newark, New Jersey
Correspondence to Ulick O'Connor.

Library of Congress, Washington, DC
Correspondence to Elmer Gertz.

Special Collections, University of Michigan Library, Ann Arbor
Sonnet to 'Alick [Schepeler]'.

Division of Special Collections, New York University Libraries
Correspondence to Ronald Firbank.

Houghton Library, Harvard University, Cambridge, Massachusetts
Correspondence to William and Alice Rothenstein (bMS Eng 1148 [772], 1148.1 [151–153]). There are also letters from Ida John and Gwen John to the Rothensteins. One letter from Augustus John to George Reavey (bMS 943.9 [19]).

Widener Library, Harvard University, Cambridge, Massachusetts
Correspondence to Theodore Spencer.

University of Illinois, Urbana-Champagne
Correspondence to Grant Richards.

University of Cincinatti, Ohio
Correspondence to Dorothy Brett.

Morris Library, Southern Illinois University, Carbondale
Correspondence to Aleister Crowley.

Department of Special Collections, University of California, Los Angeles
Correspondence to Emery Walker.

Department of Manuscripts, The Huntington, San Marino, California
One hundred and six letters and two poems to Alick Schepeler.

Buffalo and Erie County Historical Society, Buffalo, New York State
Correspondence to Conger Goodyear.

Cornell University Library, Ithaca, New York State
Correspondence to Wyndham Lewis (ninety-eight letters and two from Dorelia), also manuscript entitled 'The Cerements of Gold' and one letter headed 'To Whom It May Concern'). See *Wyndham Lewis: A Descriptive Catalogue of Manuscript Material in the Department of Rare Books, Cornell University Library*, compiled by Mary F. Daniels (1972).

Bertrand Library, Bucknell University Library, Lewisburg, Pennsylvania
Correspondence to Oliver St John Gogarty (1917–55) and two letters from Dorelia to Gogarty.

Schlesinger Library of the History of Women in America, Radcliffe College, Cambridge, Massachusetts
One letter to Dorothy Ardlow, and one letter to Florence Cary Koehler.

Boston University Libraries, Massachusetts
Correspondence to Catherine and Mikaly Karolyi, and one letter to Stuart Cloete.

Yale University Library, New Haven
Correspondence to John Drinkwater, Norman Douglas, Sylvia Hay and Mr Stewart-Jones (all in the Beinecke Rare Book and Manuscript Library). There is also a letter from John to James Rockwell Sheffield in the Sterling Memorial Library.

CANADA
National Gallery of Canada, Ontario
One letter to the gallery concerning copyright (copy, June 1922), and correspondence (1923–71), including letters from Lord Beaverbrook, Vincent Massey and the Hogg Museum at Harvard, regarding John's cartoon 'Canadians at Lens' (charcoal on paper, 12feet by 40feet). There are also letters from Caspar John about other pictures (the National Gallery of Canada owns nine oil paintings, fifteen etchings, and sixteen drawings, watercolours and other works by Augustus John).

Mills Memorial Library, McMaster University, Ontario
Correspondence to Bertrand Russell.

University of Victoria, British Columbia
Letter to Herbert Read.

AUSTRALIA
State Library of Victoria, Melbourne
Correspondence to and about Basil Burdett.

FRANCE
Musée Aéronautique, Paris
Correspondence with M. Bazin.

NEW ZEALAND
Dunedin Public Art Gallery
One letter to Frank Lewis.

My indebtedness to the many people, galleries, libraries and museums that helped me to write my original biography of Augustus John is recorded in the first edition. In the preparation of this revised edition I have been further assisted by Nicola Beauman; John Beynon and Marion Hutton, Curator and Hon. Art Curator of Tenby Art Gallery; Jane Bond; Michael Bott, Keeper of Archives and Manuscripts at the University of Reading Library; Annette Bradshaw, Deputy Exhibitions Secretary at the Royal Academy of Arts, London; Sally Brown and T. A. J. Burnett in the Department of Manuscripts and Manuscript Collections at the British Library; Mrs Robin Paisey and Alison Lloyd at the Glynn Vivian Art Gallery, Swansea; David Carver, Archivist at the National Gallery, London; Charles Cholmondeley; Honor Clerk and Jonathan Franklin at the National Portrait Gallery, London; Caroline Cuthbert and David Fraser Jenkins at the Tate Gallery; Roy Davids, formerly at the London office of Sotheby's; Mark Evans, Assistant Keeper (Fine Art) at the National Museums and Galleries of Wales, Cardiff; Patrick Farndale; Jerome Farrell, City of Westminster Archivist; Susan Flint; Sir Angus Fraser; Cathy Henderson, Librarian at the Humanities Research Center, University of Texas, Austin; Jane Hill; Sara S. Hodson and Mary L. Robertson, Curators of Manuscripts at the Huntington; Francesca John; Rebecca John, who gave me access to the papers of her father, the late Sir Caspar John; John Kelly, who gathered for me all references to Augustus John in the letters of W. B. Yeats; Erika Kruger, Registrar at the Johannesburg Art Gallery; Cecily Langdale at the Davis & Langdale Company, New York; Linda Lloyd Jones, Head of Exhibitions and Susanna Robson, Assistant Curator, Special Collections, at the Victoria and Albert Museum, London; Ceridwen Lloyd-Morgan, Assistant Archivist in the Department of Manuscripts and Records, the National Library of Wales, Aberystwyth; Edward Morris, Curator of Fine Art at the Walker Art Gallery, Liverpool; Hayden Proud, Curator of Paintings and Sculpture at the South African National Gallery, Cape Town; Dr D. M. Pugh, who was for a time Augustus John's doctor and also for a time my own; Gillian Raffles at the Mercury Gallery, London; Ian Rogerson, who let me see the text of his introduction to a forthcoming edition of John Sampson's *Welsh Gypsy Folk-Tales*; Anthony Sampson, who showed me the typescript of his book on his grandfather, John Sampson; Richard Shone, Assistant Editor of the *Burlington Magazine*; Greg Spurgeon, Head of Documents and Storage and Cindy Campbell, Archivist, at the National Gallery of Canada, Ottawa; Mary Taubman; Daphne Todd, President of the Royal Society of Portrait Painters, London; S. R. Tomlinson, Assistant Librarian at the Bodleian Library, Oxford; Joan Winterkorn at Bernard Quaritch Ltd, London.

I would also like to record my gratitude to the late Vivien White, Augustus John's daughter, who, as owner of the copyrights, renewed the permission first given to me by her mother, Dorelia John, to quote from Augustus John's writings and reproduce his pictures.

I am grateful to Alison Samuel, my editor at Chatto & Windus, for passing her critical eye over the old and new portions of my text and helping me to harmonize them. I am also indebted to Toby Buchan for his valuable policing of my typescript. I have retained what Willa Cather called 'the irregular and intimate quality of things made by the human hand', and I owe much to Sarah Johnson for transferring my prehistoric manuscript on to post-modernist disks.

Finally I must pay tribute to my wife, who propped me up and pulled me through when I fell ill, enabling me to complete this book.

MICHAEL HOLROYD
Porlock Weir, September 1995

NOTES

PREFACE

1 Stephen Spender *World Within World* (1951), p. 76.
2 Mary Taubman to the author, 6 March 1995. See also her introductions to the Gwen John exhibitions organized by Faerber and Maison Ltd (1964), the Arts Council of Great Britain (1968) and Anthony d'Offay (1976). Her *Gwen John* was published by the Scolar Press in 1985.
3 Now in the National Library of Wales. NLW MS 22802D.
4 *Portraits by Augustus John: Family, Friends and the Famous* (National Museum of Wales 1988), p. 11.
5 Romilly John to David Fraser Jenkins, 3 March 1979. National Museum of Wales.
6 'Photocopy and be damned: literature and the libraries', *Sunday Times* (2 September 1984).
7 Philip Larkin *Required Writing: Miscellaneous Pieces 1955–1982* (1983), p. 99.
8 Some John and Nettleship papers were purchased from Caspar John's daughter Rebecca John in October 1988, and two small groups of correspondence and drafts of Augustus John's autobiographical writings for the *Sunday Times* were bought at Sotheby's in April and December 1989. All these were incorporated into the main archive, but other odds and ends of correspondence acquired since then have been catalogued separately.
9 NLW MS 22305C fols. 5–6.
10 Richard Shone *Augustus John* (1979), p. 3.

CHAPTER I: LITTLE ENGLAND BEYOND WALES

1 This lodging house was Corporation property owned by Ancient Grant. Its lease was assigned to William John on 23 October 1877. Two years later, on 17 December 1879, the lease was devised to William Willams.
2 After Augustus John's death in 1961 a plaque commemorating the place where he spent his early years was fixed by the Haverfordwest Council at No. 5 Victoria Place. On neither his brother's nor his sisters' birth certificates had any number been given. Winifred, who was still alive in the United States, could not remember the number; Thornton, nearing ninety and living in Canada, appears to have copied down the number 5 from the address (5 Tower Hill) of the solicitor who wrote to him asking after his birthplace.

No. 7 Victoria Place is now part of Lloyds Bank. The John family leased it from a Mr Joseph Tombs, and the number is confirmed by several directories of the period. No. 7 Victoria Place is also given on the birth certificate of Augustus's youngest uncle Frederick Charles John, born on 20 September 1856. In 1995 the Civic Society Guild of Freemen put up a plaque marking the birthplace of Gwen and Augustus on Lloyds Bank, a few yards from the rogue plaque on the Victoria Bookshop next door.

3   The dates of their births were: Thornton, 10 May 1875; Gwendolen Mary, 22 June 1876; Winifred Maud, 3 November 1879.

4   Until 1850 the abominable crime of 'associating with gypsies' was punishable by hanging.

5   Winifred John to Gwen John, 10 July 1910 (National Library of Wales MS 22307 fols. 119–23).

6   *Horizon* Volume III No. 14 (February 1941), pp. 98–9.

7   This house, though altered and precariously named 'Rocks Drift', still stands. It has a large entrance hall and stairwell, drawing-room, dining-room and six bedrooms. It was built using the stone from Settlands, the next bay.

8   Besides being a labourer, William John was a violin player. 'I am hoping that the musician will turn out to have been a wandering minstrel,' Augustus wrote to H. W. Williams on discovering this fact (16 May 1952). '. . . His musical gifts reappeared in one or two of my descendants.' Perhaps the most celebrated musician among these descendants is the cello player Amaryllis Fleming. Augustus's sister Winifred played the violin, and her daughter Muriel Matthews is a respected cellist in America. Augustus's son David was for many years an oboist in the Sadler's Wells orchestra, and another son, Edwin, played the flute.

9   His obituary in the *Haverfordwest and Milford Haven Telegraph* (9 July 1884) notes that 'The funeral was largely attended by the principal professional men, as well as the leading tradesmen of the town and neighbourhood.'

10   Joanna (b. 1840), Emma (b. 1842), Alfred (b. 1844), Edwin, and Clara Sophia (b. 1849).

11   William John used to describe Alfred as a solicitor, though in fact he never passed the law exams, and probably acted as managing clerk, a position he could hold without legal qualifications.

12   Alfred John, with his haggard good looks and air of impoverished innocence, came to fulfil Augustus's ideal of a Bohemian English gentleman. Visiting his nephew one hot summer day, he accidentally revealed by a spontaneous gesture that, underneath his mackintosh, he wore no clothes at all. With equal transparency, he added to his family name a 'St' and, as Alfred St John, was rewarded with a very fine funeral service, free of charge, by the clergy of St David's Cathedral.

13   It was not until the removal of the Sex Disqualification Act in 1919 that women were permitted to qualify as solicitors. The first woman was admitted in 1922.

14   Benjamin died on 12 January 1856 of hydrocephalus and convulsions, aged two months; William had died six days earlier from the same cause, aged one year and eleven months; Sydney died after fourteen days of diarrhoea on 13 August 1861, aged five weeks; and Thornton died on 15 May 1861, aged eleven years, of congestion of the brain, fever and debility.

15   Now in the Tenby Museum. It is a copy of a David Cox. The picture of cattle is owned by Muriel Matthews, Augusta's American granddaughter.

16   Alison Thomas *Portraits of Women* (1994), p. 71.

17   The death certificate inaccurately gives her age as thirty-four.

18   William John died of cerebral softerina on 6 July 1884.

19   Aunt Leah went straight to the United States, where she picked up a slight American accent and a large band of disciples. Aunt Rosina's travels were

more circuitous, and her destinations always preceded by a series of brown-paper parcels. Sustained by a diet of over-ripe fruit and protected by a dense fur muff, she set off for Switzerland from where she wrote a number of letters in purple ink testifying to her brief enthusiasm for Dr Coué, who believed that if people repeated 'Every day in every way I am getting better and better' many thousands of times, the world might become a more cheerful place. From here she went to Japan, where she collected a miniature Japanese maid, and later, improbably passing through Mason, Nevada, married Owen H. Bott, a druggist with two sons. Under the pitiless blue of the Californian skies, she caught up with Winifred, terrifying her children with her cotton-wool hair, her humped back and restless scuttling from place to place.

20 Gwen, Augustus and Winifred were baptized at St Mary's Church, Tenby, on 21 January 1886.

21 William John's will is dated 14 June 1881, a little over three years before his death from a disease that would have made him legally incompetent.

22 NLW MS 22782D fols. 115–16.

23 *Chiaroscuro* p. 28. All page numbers are taken from the first Jonathan Cape editions of *Chiaroscuro* and *Finishing Touches* (1952 and 1964). The two books were republished, with an additional chapter, under the title *Autobiography* in 1975.

24 Letter to the author, 18 October 1968.

25 *Chiaroscuro* p. 25.

26 Later the Sea Beach Hotel, Tenby.

27 This building (the original house of which was built by Edward Morgan in the 1830s) was later converted into a public library. In the cemented grounds two trees were planted, an oak in memory of Augustus, and a birch in memory of Gwen. Greenhill School later moved to the outskirts of Tenby.

28 *Chiaroscuro* p. 36.

29 At the junction with South Cliff Street. Later the property became the Hallsville Hotel.

30 Letter to the author, 18 October 1968.

31 *Chiaroscuro* p. 37.

32 *Ibid.* p. 19.

33 *Ibid.* pp. 31–2.

34 Thornton John to Augustus John, 3 February 1959. NLW MS 22782D fols. 115–16.

35 Augustus John to Caspar John, 16 August 1952. NLW 22775C fol. 7.

36 Augustus John to John Davenport n.d. (late 1940s). NLW MS 21585E.

37 Winifred John to Augustus John, 8 January 1906. NLW MS 22782D fol. 124.

38 Winifred John to Augustus John, 3 March 1956. NLW MS 22782D fol. 125.

39 Cecily Langdale *Gwen John* (1987) p. 115.

40 Anthony d'Offay *Gwen John: 1876–1939* (1982).

41 Thornton John to Augustus John, 3 March 1948. NLW MS 22782D fol. 111.

42 Thornton John to Gwen John, 7 September 1935. NLW MS 22307C fol. 88.

43 Winifred John to Gwen John, 10 July 1910. NLW MS 22307C fols. 122–3.

44 Thornton John to Gwen John, 14 July 1920. NLW MS 22307C fols. 71–2.

45 Gwen John to Ursula Tyrwhitt, summer 1910. NLW MS 21368D fol. 46.

46 Gwen John to Ursula Tyrwhitt, 1908. NLW MS 21468D fol. 25.

47 Ceridwen Lloyd-Morgan *Gwen John. Papers at the National Library of Wales* (1988), p. 11.

48 Augustus John to Dorelia McNeill n.d. (July 1908). NLW MS 22776D fols. 89–90.

49 Letter to the author from Darsie Japp, 13 December 1968.

50 *Chiaroscuro* p. 12.
51 Augustus John to Bill Duncalf, 22 May 1959 (privately owned).
52 Augustus John to John Sampson, n.d. (*c.*1912). NLW MS 21459E fol. 46.
53 Augustus John to John Sampson, 13 March 1912. NLW MS 21459E, fol. 44.
54 Entry for 22 June 1919 in *The Diaries of Sylvia Townsend Warner* (ed. Claire Harman 1994), p. 37.
55 Augustus John to Ada Nettleship n.d. NLW MS 22775C fol. 81.
56 The word *petulengro* means horseshoe-maker or smith. It was T. W. Thompson who first identified Borrow's Jaspar Petulengro with a certain Ambrose Smith.
57 William Rothenstein to Max Beerbohm, 24 July 1941. Quoted in Robert Speaight's *William Rothenstein* (1962), p. 402.
58 *Evening Standard* (19 January 1929).
59 *Horizon* Volume XIX No. 112 (April 1949), p. 295.
60 Ceridwen Lloyd-Morgan *Gwen John. Papers at the National Library of Wales*, p. 9.
61 Letter to the author, 18 October 1968.
62 *Chiaroscuro* p. 35.
63 *Evening Standard* (19 January 1929).

CHAPTER II: 'SLADE SCHOOL INGENIOUS'

1 BBC talk first transmitted on 17 November 1967. Augustus's eyes were actually blue.
2 George Charlton 'The Slade School of Fine Art' *The Studio* (October 1946).
3 In his inaugural lecture, *Systems of Art Education*, Poynter had attacked the current methods of English art teaching in which 'a trivial minuteness of detail [was] considered of more importance than a sound and thorough grounding in the knowledge of form', and only at the end of the course was the student allowed to do what he should 'have been set to do the first day he entered the school, that is to make studies from the living model'. He himself intended to 'impress but one lesson upon the students, that constant study from the life-model is the only means they have of arriving at a comprehension of the beauty in nature . . .' See Edward Poynter *Lectures on Art* (1879) and also Andrew Forge *The Slade 1871–1960*.
4 *Men and Memories* Volume I (1931), pp. 22–5.
5 George Charlton 'The Slade School of Fine Art' *The Studio* (October 1946).
6 *Horizon* Volume III No. 18 (June 1941), p. 394.
7 *Chiaroscuro* p. 41.
8 Some of John's music hall sketches made at the Alhambra were exhibited at the Mercury Gallery, London (15 January–10 February 1968). John also made a portrait of Arthur Roberts dated, almost certainly inaccurately, 1895, now in the National Portrait Gallery. 'I consider him [Arthur Roberts] about the most important buffoon England has ever produced – a born comedian and a most accomplished artist,' he wrote to the National Portrait Gallery (14 May 1929). In Henry Savage's autobiography, *The Receding Shore*, there is a brief mention of John doing a portrait of Arthur Roberts in about 1922.
9 *Chiaroscuro* p. 42.
10 *Ibid.* p. 44.
11 *Finishing Touches* p. 29.
12 Letter to the author, 1969.
13 Letter to Ursula Tyrwhitt. Augustus's letters to Ursula Tyrwhitt are at the National Library of Wales, NLW MS 19645C; and so are Gwen John's letters to Ursula Tyrwhitt, NLW MS 21468D.

14 Famous People, No. 31 of a series of 50. Illustrated by Angus McBride and described by Virginia Shankland. A secondary John legend involved Augustus's son Caspar who dived on to a rock in 1930 and emerged from the waves a potential admiral.

15 *Daily Telegraph* (1 November 1961).

16 *Augustus John: Studies for Compositions. Centenary Exhibition National Museum of Wales 1978.*

17 Spencer Gore to Doman Turner, 25 January 1909. See John Rothenstein *Modern English Painters* Volume I *Sickert to Smith* (1976 edn), p. 177.

18 *Evening Standard* (19 January 1929).

19 This portrait is now in the National Portrait Gallery, London. Many years after it was painted John described it in *Finishing Touches* as 'most regrettable'. Orpen had painted it in imitation of Whistler's 'Carlyle', and at the time John wrote of it to Michel Salaman: 'Orpen's portrait of me extracts much critical admiration. It is described in one notice as a clever portrait of Mr John in the character of a French Romantic.

'One far-seeing gentleman hopes that I will emerge from my Rembrandtine chrysalis with a character of my own! I have just been to the Guildhall and return exalted with the profound beauty of Whistler's Carlyle.'

20 *Finishing Touches* p. 30.

21   'Augustus Caesar,' so the poet said,
   'Shall be regarded as a present god
   By Britain, made to kiss the Roman's rod.'
  Augustus Caesar long ago is dead,
  But still the good work's being carried on:
  We lick the brushes of Augustus John.
      Punch 27 February 1929

22 *Rude Assignment* (1950), pp. 118–19.

23 This letter was written to John Rothenstein (14 May 1952) after having read Rothenstein's essay on Gwen John in *Modern English Painters*. Gwen 'was never "unnoticed" by those who had access to her', he corrected Rothenstein.

24 *Chiaroscuro* p. 49.

25 Augustus John to Robert Gregory n.d. (1909). NLW MS 21482D.

26 Augustus John to Michel Salaman, August 1902. NLW MS 14928D fols. 59–60.

27 Gwen John to Ursula Tyrwhitt n.d. NLW MS 21468D.

28 Quoted in Susan Chitty *Gwen John* (1981), p. 142.

29 Possibly Grace Westray, a Slade student who lived with Gwen, Augustus and Winifred at 21 Fitzroy Street for a time and whom Gwen painted as 'Young Woman with a Violin' (Cecily Langdale *Gwen John* [1987] pl.5 cat. no. 4) and Augustus drew (Fitzwilliam Museum, Cambridge PD 942). Her addresses up to 1914 are remarkably similar to those of Ambrose McEvoy and his wife. After the war she appears to have married a Mr Reardon and by 1930 was widowed and living in Wiltshire. 'She and Mary McEvoy have both visited,' Louise Bishop wrote to Gwen (22 October 1930). NLW MS 22304C fol. 50.

30 *Chiaroscuro* p. 249.

31 See *Gwen John* Retrospective Exhibition Catalogue, Arts Council, 1968. Introduction by Mary Taubman.

32 Gwen John to Ursula Tyrwhitt, 22 July 1936. NLW MS 21468D fol. 179.

33 Letter from Gwen John to Ursula Tyrwhitt n.d. NLW MS 21468D.

34 Gwen John to Ursula Tyrwhitt, 23 July 1927. NLW MS 21468D fol. 160.

35 Gwen John to Ursula Tyrwhitt, 6 June 1936. NLW MS 21468D fols. 140–2.

36 NLW MS 14928D. The picture was bought by Frederick Brown at the Slade, and, a year after his death in 1941, was purchased by the Tate Gallery.

37 *Table-Talk of G.B.S.* (ed. Archibald Henderson 1925), pp. 90–1.

38 *Modern English Painters* (1976 edn) Volume I, 'Gwen John', pp. 160–1.
39 In his obituary notice (*The Times*, 1 February 1958) of Lady Smith, Augustus wrote: 'The death of Lady (Matthew) Smith has removed one of the last survivors of what might be called the Grand Epoch of the Slade School. Gwen Salmond, as she then was, cut a commanding figure among a remarkably brilliant group of women students, consisting of such arresting personalities as Edna Waugh, Ursula Tyrwhitt, my sister Gwen John, and Ida Nettleship.
   'Gwen Salmond's early compositions were distinguished by a force and temerity for which even her natural liveliness of temperament had not prepared us. I well remember a Deposition in our Sketch Club which would not have been out of place among the *ébauches* [sketch, rough draft] of, dare I say it, Tintoretto!
   '. . . "Marriage and Death and Division make barren our lives". Gwen Smith had reason to know this but she also had the pluck to face it bravely, which is what made all the difference.'
40 See Alison Thomas *Portraits of Women* (1994), pp. 24–9.
41 Quoted by Alison Thomas in *Edna Clarke Hall*. Milne & Moller, Max Rutherston, catalogue (1989).
42 Alison Thomas *Portraits of Women* p. 55.
43 Bruce Arnold *Orpen. Mirror to an Age* (1981), p. 237.
44 *Ibid.* p. 234.
45 *Modern English Painters* Volume I, 'William Orpen', p. 227.
46 *Men and Memories* Volume I p. 334.
47 See *The Listener* (23 November 1967).
48 Unpublished reminiscences. But see 'Edna Clarke Hall: Drawings and Watercolours 1895–1947' in the catalogue of the Slade Centenary Exhibition at the d'Offay Couper Gallery, October 1971.
49 'The Slade Animal Land', a notebook of caricatures of staff and students at the Slade in 1898, shows the BEARDGION, a cartoon of Augustus John by Logic Whiteway with the explanatory caption: 'This simple creature is so accomplished that, according to the Tonk, Michael Angelo isn't in it.' See National Library of Scotland Acc. 3969 1965.
50 Gwen also won a certificate for figure drawing, while Augustus after his second year was awarded a second certificate for advanced antique drawing, a £3 prize for the study of a standing male nude, a certificate for head painting, and a £6 prize for figure painting.
51 *Men and Memories* Volume I p. 333.
52 Mary Taubman *Gwen John* (1985), p. 15.
53 See John's Introduction to the Catalogue of Drawings by Ulrica Forbes, Walker's Galleries, 118 New Bond Street, London, 17 October 1952.
54 'A Note on Drawing', from *Augustus John: Drawings* (ed. Lillian Browse 1941), p. 10.
55 *Chiaroscuro* p. 46.
56 *Augustus John: Studies for Compositions* (National Museum of Wales 1978) pls. 1–3. The text for 'Moses and the Brazen Serpent' came from Numbers 21:9. 'And Moses made a serpent of brass, and put it upon a pole, and it came to pass, that if a serpent had bitten any man, when he beheld the serpent of brass, he lived.' The painting is owned by the Slade School.
57 *Chiaroscuro* p. 48.
58 *Rude Assignment* p. 119.
59 *Men and Memories* Volume I p. 333.
60 *Chiaroscuro* p. 36.
61 *Ibid.* p. 27.
62 Jack Nettleship wrote a biography of Browning. One of his brothers, Henry, was Corpus Professor of Latin at Oxford; another, Richard, was a Fellow

and Tutor at Balliol, and a friend of Benjamin Jowett; and the third, Edward, a prominent oculist. Jack regretted not having done the lions in Trafalgar Square, of which, he believed, he could have made a far better job than Sir Edwin Landseer.

63   Ethel Nettleship to Caspar John, 27 June 1951. NLW MS 22790D fols. 34–9.

64   W. B. Yeats *Autobiographies* (1955), p. 271.

65   See NLW MS 22798B fols. 11–15, 55–71.

66   Ada Nettleship's maiden name was Hinton, and she was the sister of James Hinton who wrote an enormous philosophical work and then, according to David John, went off his head. 'I had an idea of "discovering" him,' Romilly John records (1 August 1972), 'but have always been completely baffled after reading two sentences and had to start again, and so on indefinitely. James Hinton's son was the author of a book on the fourth dimension, involving the construction by the reader of hundreds of cubes with differently coloured surfaces and edges.'

67   Ethel Nettleship to Caspar John, 27 June 1951. NLW MS 22790D fols. 34–5.

68   W. B. Yeats *Autobiographies* p. 193.

69   *Ibid.*

70   *Chiaroscuro* p. 48.

71   This synopsis was done for Hubert Alexander, who had got to know Augustus through Dorelia McNeill. In the 1920s Alexander had turned publisher and approached John for his memoirs. 'I've been thinking of the book and will send you shortly a provisional synopsis,' John wrote to him on 21 February 1923. Alexander believes he may have got the synopsis about 1927, but since there is a holograph synopsis among Augustus's papers, it may never have been sent. Certainly by 1932 negotiations were still continuing and Sir Charles Reilly remembered that year 'a publisher came down [to Fryern Court] and offered him great sums for his autobiography, finally reaching £13,000 [equivalent to well over £400,000 in 1996] the sum I heard him say Lady Oxford got for hers, but he nobly turned it down.'

72   *Chiaroscuro* p. 48.

73   *Finishing Touches* p. 40.

74   *Chiaroscuro* p. 147. In 1941 Sir John Rothenstein came across this picture at the Leger Galleries, bought it for the Tate Gallery, and showed it to John for identification. At first he failed to recognize it, but later did acknowledge it to be his. In his *Modern English Painters*, Rothenstein described it as a rather fumbling and pedestrian essay and, though probably a fair example of his painting at this time, laboured, niggling in form, hardly modelled at all. But John himself, on reading this, objected: 'The "Old Lady's" head is very well modelled: the hands unfinished yet expressive. She couldn't move them easily.'

75   Ida Nettleship to Ada Nettleship, 18 September 1898. NLW MS 22798B fols. 18–19.

76   Letter from Ida Nettleship to her mother n.d. NLW MS 22798B fols. 16–17.

77   Ida Nettleship to Ada Nettleship, 20 September 1898. NLW MS 22798B fols. 20–1.

78   Ida Nettleship to Ada Nettleship, December 1898. NLW MS 22798B fols. 30–1.

79   *Chiaroscuro* p. 250.

80   Ida Nettleship to Ada Nettleship n.d. (late September 1898). NLW MS 227988 fols. 22–4.

81   Gwen John to Michel Salaman n.d. (spring 1899). NLW MS 14930C.

82   Fothergill's inn was the Spread Eagle at Thame in which, for a time,

Augustus's son Romilly worked, and for which Dora Carrington painted an inn sign (now gone). He was the author of *Confessions of an Innkeeper, John Fothergill's Cookery Book, The Art of James Dickson Innes, My Three Inns,* etc.

83 Rothenstein had first heard of Ibsen through Conder, and in his *Men and Memories* (Volume I p. 56) writes: 'We were all mesmerised by Ibsen in those days.' The picture, now in the Tate Gallery, expresses the tension of Act III of *The Doll's House* when Mrs Linden and Krogstad are listening for the end of the dance upstairs. Subsequently it became famous as a 'problem picture' mainly perhaps on account of its dark colour. 'I am portrayed standing at the foot of a staircase upon which Alice has unaccountably seated herself,' John wrote in his Introduction to the Catalogue of the Sir William Rothenstein Memorial Exhibition at the Tate Gallery (5 May–4 June 1950). 'I appear to be ready for the road, for I am carrying a mackintosh on my arm and am shod and hatted. But Alice seems to hesitate. Can she have changed her mind at the last moment? . . . Perhaps the weather had changed for the worse . . .' The picture, painted between June and October 1899, was exhibited in the British section of the Paris Exhibition in 1900, where it won a silver medal.

84 Introduction to the William Rothenstein Memorial Exhibition Catalogue, Tate Gallery (May–June 1950).

85 *Men and Memories* Volume I p. 352.

86 *Horizon* Volume III No. 18 (June 1941), p. 400.

87 Oscar Wilde to William Rothenstein, 4 October 1899. See *The Letters of Oscar Wilde* (ed. Rupert Hart-Davis 1962), p. 811.

88 John Rothenstein *Modern English Painters*, Volume I p. 179. Rothenstein instances 'The Rustic Idyll' of about 1903 as having been done under the immediate impact of Daumier. This work – possibly watercolour on damp-ened cartridge – is now in the Tate Gallery, and is called 'Rustic Scene'. It has an unusual texture – soft, blurred contours – and is more dramatic than most of John's work. ' "The Rustic Idyll" I remember well,' John wrote to the Tate Gallery (16 March 1956). 'It is one of several pastels I did soon after leaving the Slade. Though hardly an Idyll, it has dramatic character . . . I don't consider it has merit as a *pastel*.'

89 Everett, who had been baptized Herbert, registered at the Slade as Henry Everett, but he always called himself John Everett. He added to the confusion by marrying his cousin – Mrs Everett's niece – Kathleen, who altered her Christian name fractionally to Katherine. A dedicated marine painter, John Everett never sold a marine painting during his life, but bequeathed them all (1,700 oils and a larger number of drawings and engravings) to the National Maritime Museum, which held a memorial exhibition of his work in 1964.

90 *Men and Memories* Volume I p. 352.

91 *Ibid.*

92 Rothenstein's portrait of Augustus is at the Walker Art Gallery, Liverpool.

93 Augustus John to Michel Salaman, February 1900. NLW MS 14928D.

94 Gwen John seems to have been living at 122 Gower Street illegally and without furniture. The house was officially inhabited by a woman called Annie Machew, who since October 1898 had paid no rates. The rating authorities who attempted to collect the money owing to them throughout 1900 reported that there were 'no effects' there. For this reason the house does not appear in *Kelly's Post Office Directory* until three years later, when it had been taken over by the National Amalgamated Union of Shop Assistants, Warehousemen and Clerks.

95 Three of Conder's paintings of Swanage are in the Tate Gallery.

96 What became of the large decoration is not known, though a number of

small versions of the subject exist, showing the influence of Goya and Delacroix. One is an oil which belonged to Humphrey Brooke, Secretary of the Royal Academy (1952–68); another, a wash drawing in the Quinn Collection in New York, was sold by the Fine Art Society at the Slade Centenary Show (autumn 1971); a third, a pen and wash drawing, is in the Tate Gallery (reproduced in *Modern British Paintings, Drawings and Sculpture* Volume I 1964, pl. 51).

97 *Horizon* Volume III No. 18 (June 1941), p. 401.
98 Letter from Augustus John to Michel Salaman n.d. NLW MS 14928D.
99 *Horizon* Volume III No. 18 (June 1941), p. 401.
100 *Chiaroscuro* p. 38.
101 NLW MS 19645C.
102 John's drawing of the Château de Polignac, done with black crayon on white paper and very Flemish in its atmosphere, is now in the Manchester Art Galleries. It is reproduced in *Augustus John. Fifty-two drawings* (1957), pl. 5.
103 *Men and Memories* Volume I p. 358.
104 Some pages from his sketchbook at this time were exhibited at the Mercury Gallery, London, 15 June 1967–10 February 1968.
105 *Chiaroscuro* p. 49.
106 E. Fox-Pitt 'From Stomacher to Stomach' (unpublished autobiography).
107 *Men and Memories* Volume II p. 1.

CHAPTER III: LOVE FOR ART'S SAKE

1 From an essay Osbert Sitwell did not include in *A Free House*. It will be found in André Theuriet *Jules Bastien-Lepage & his Art* (1892), pp. 139–40. See also Malcolm Easton *Augustus John* (1970).
2 Alfred Thornton *Fifty Years of the New English Art Club* (1935).
3 Augustus John to Michel Salaman n.d. (spring 1900). NLW MS 14928D.
4 *Cambridge Review* (March 1922).
5 Quentin Bell *Victorian Artists* (1967), p. 91.
6 *The English Review* (January 1912).
7 *The Burlington Magazine* (February 1916).
8 *New Age* (28 May 1914).
9 Letter from Augustus John to Lady Ottoline Morrell, 5 August 1910. This correspondence is at the University of Texas, Austin.
10 This and other unpublished Orpen letters were owned by Miriam Benkovitz, the biographer of Ronald Firbank.
11 Herbert Jackson was Professor Walter Raleigh's brother-in-law, while D. S. MacColl was connected by marriage to Oliver Elton, who succeeded Raleigh as Professor of Modern Literature at Liverpool.
12 Dora E. Yates *My Gypsy Days* (1953), p. 74.
13 Anthony Sampson 'Scholar Gipsy. The Quest for a Family Secret' (unpublished), Chapter 2.
14 *Lytton Strachey by Himself* (ed. Michael Holroyd, 1994 edn), p. 104.
15 Augustus John to Michel Salaman n.d. (April 1900). NLW MS 14928D fol. 39.
16 This portrait, which hung in Liverpool University Dining Club, was later the cause of a historic decision. First exhibited at the NEAC in the Winter Show of 1903, it was to have been awarded the Gold Medal for Painting at the International Exhibition at St Louis, Missouri, in the following year. Learning that this prize was to go to so young and relatively obscure an artist, the President of the Royal Academy and the English members of

the international jury took the astonishing step of withdrawing, without explanation, the entire British section.

17 *Chiaroscuro* p. 60.

18 Augustus John to Will Rothenstein, 9 March 1902. He continues: 'I felt inclined to add my patch of homemade sienna in reference to the past.'

19 Anthony Sampson 'Scholar Gipsy. The Quest for a Family Secret' Chapter 2.

20 *The Letters of Sir Walter Raleigh 1879–1922* (ed. Lady Raleigh 1926), Volume II p. 333.

21 Geoffrey Keynes *The Gates of Memory* (1981), p. 112.

22 Augustus John to John Sampson n.d. (*c*.1914). NLW MS 21459E fol. 50.

23 Augustus John to John Sampson, 22 October 1902. NLW MS 21459E fols. 2–3.

24 Augustus John to John Sampson n.d. (1907). NLW MS 21459E fols. 21–2.

25 Augustus John to John Sampson, 23 February 1911. NLW MS 21459E fol. 32.

26 Augustus John to John Sampson n.d. (December 1904). NLW MS 21459E fol. 13.

27 John Sampson to Augustus John, 22 November 1930. NLW MS 22785D fols. 42–3.

28 Augustus John to John Sampson, September 1911. NLW MS 21459E fol. 33.

29 Geoffrey Keynes *The Gates of Memory* p. 379.

30 John Sampson to Augustus John, 2 February 1924. NLW MS 22785D fols. 29–30. Sampson had finished the letter R in 1911 and started S. 'Scanning this new sea anxiously from the mast-head,' he wrote to Augustus (30 August 1911), 'I see it simply bristles with rocks not indicated on the charts.' He sent the completed work to the Clarendon Press in July 1917, and though 'a little wearied by the severity of Indian phonology' was confident that the great work should prove 'a complete guide to sorcery, fortune-telling, love and courtship, kichimas [inns], fiddling, harping, poaching and the life of the road'. NLW MS 22785D fol. 22.

31 W. B. Yeats to John Quinn, 4 October 1907. Berg Collection, New York Public Library.

32 Anthony Sampson 'Scholar Gipsy. The Quest for a Family Secret' Chapter 3.

33 Ethel Nettleship was a cellist who, in the First World War, became an ambulance driver and nurse in Italy and Malta and who had such a bad time there that, on her return, she took to lacemaking for her nerves. 'Untidy and gay,' Sir Caspar John remembered, ' – always hard up – accessible and directly interested in all our lives.' Ursula, the third sister, was rather stern and aloof compared with Ethel. An adventurous mountaineer and skier, she became a singer and teacher of singing. She was for a long time closely connected with the Aldeburgh Festival, at which Benjamin Britten dedicated his *A Ceremony of Carols* to her. 'Her energy, her eagerness, her determination to be satisfied with nothing less than the best, forced those she taught to give of their best, and produced remarkable results,' wrote Ann Bridge (*The Times*, 7 May 1968). 'Moving about, gesticulating, her greying hair wild, Ursula Nettleship conducting her choir was in fact an inspiring sight – lost in the music, utterly unselfconscious, dragging the sounds she wanted out of, often, very unpromising material.'

34 This building, which has now been destroyed, was between No. 2 Rodney Street and the hospital at the corner of Mount Pleasant.

35 Augustus John to Will Rothenstein. See *Men and Memories* Volume II p. 9.

36 The Sandon Studios Society, of which John was elected an honorary member, was later set up in opposition to the University School of Art, to encourage freer and more vigorous draughtsmanship and a less restrictive attitude to painting. It was officially opened at 9 Sandon Terrace on 5 December 1905,

but 'any formality intended', records R. H. Bisson in *The Sandon Studios Society and the Arts* (1965, p. 18), 'was dissipated by Augustus John, who got very cheerful and fell headlong down the stairs'.

37 *Saturday Review* (7 December 1904), p. 695.

38 William Rothenstein *Men and Memories* Volume II (1932), p. 3.

39 Two Liverpool models who later went 'to breed in the colonies. May they raise many a stalwart son to our Empire!' John wrote to the Rani.

40 Campbell Dodgson *A Catalogue of Etchings by Augustus John 1901–1914* (1920), pl. 14. (Hereafter referred to as CD, with the number.)

41 One of his subjects, for instance, was 'A Rabbi Studying', from a drawing by Rembrandt. CD 73.

42 Some of the plates would have been better if they had been left in the pure etched state, without being carried to a finish by lavish use of drypoint, which sacrificed their original crispness, leaving them soft and veiled. A number of the best ones are incomplete studies or sheets of studies, where the needle has been used like a pencil and the emphasis is on line; where, with a minimum of cross-hatching, the face has been left free from the rubberized pockmarks of dots and dashes intended to suggest variations of surface and of tone. These studies are often less self-conscious than the finished products, picked out more precisely in order to stress a curve or a fold. Some of the series of heads form a natural design on the page, and some of the studies give the impression of a fine watercolour wash. But John is at his best with single figures, and to his Liverpool period belong several good portraits including 'The Mulatto'; 'The Old Haberdasher'; 'The Jewess' with her shrewd suspicious gaze; and 'Old Arthy', where the effect of strong light behind the head creates a silhouette which the dense cross-hatching emphasizes without negating the figure, since the lines become part of the creases of the face and the shadows cast by it.

43 Introduction to *Augustus John: Fifty-two drawings*, Lord David Cecil (1957), p. 12.

44 The Walker Gallery was soon to return this compliment. When, in 1902, a group of subscribers gave William Rothenstein's portrait of John to the gallery, it was catalogued anonymously as 'Portrait of a Young Man'. When offered John's official portrait of Chaloner Dowdall as Lord Mayor of Liverpool in 1918, the gallery refused it. The first example of his work it bought was 'Two Jamaican Girls', in 1938.

45 To Will Rothenstein, 9 March 1902.

46 To Will Rothenstein n.d.

47 Ida John to Ada Nettleship, 16 October 1901. NLW MS 22798B fols. 38–9.

48 Ida John to John Trivett Nettleship, 24 December 1901. NLW MS 22798B fols. 72–4.

49 These included a rather military portrait of Oliver Elton, the English Literature don; a curious King Lear impression of Edmund Muspratt, Pro-Chancellor of the University of Liverpool, emerging from the shadows of a dark background; a sombre Victorian impression of Sir John Brunner, the radical plutocrat, with mother-of-pearl flesh tones, a white beard and a moustache slightly ginger on one side; a likeness of Sir John Sherrington, the scientist and a special friend of Ida's, a timid, gauche figure, his eyes distrustfully peering through weak spectacles; and a comfortable spongy portrait of the architect Charles Reilly, rather sadly wrapped in a black-and-white scarf. 'I took great pride & pleasure in painting Elton & shall look forward to documenting you with equal zest,' Augustus wrote to Sir Charles Reilly on 15 May 1931, recording his wish to 'keep up my old Liverpool associations'. Twenty-six years earlier he had written to Reilly, 'I don't remember Mr Muskpratt [*sic*] but crossed eyes are always good to paint as Raphael knew.'

The portrait of Chaloner Dowdall (1909) is now at the National Gallery of Victoria, Melbourne; of Kuno Meyer (1911) at the National Gallery of Ireland, Dublin; those of Mackay, Elton, Muspratt, Brunner and Sherrington at the University College Dining Club, Liverpool; and that of Reilly at the School of Architecture in Abercrombie Square, Liverpool.

50 Ida John to Michel Salaman n.d. (July 1902). NLW MS 22788C fols. 69–70.

51 In his preliminary synopsis for an autobiography, 1923.

52 One impression, at least, is dated 1902. CD 47.

53 'I would subscribe to make Augustus John Director of a Public House Trust,' Walter Raleigh wrote to D. S. MacColl (27 May 1905). John's time at Liverpool was later commemorated by a new public house, The Augustus John, which was erected next to the postgraduate club.

54 Augustus John to Michel Salaman, July 1902. NLW MS 14928D fol. 57.

55 Unpublished diaries of Arthur Symons.

56 Ethel Nettleship to Sir Caspar John, 27 June 1951. NLW MS 22790D fols. 34–9.

57 Unpublished diary of L. A. G. Strong, in the possession of B. L. Reid, biographer of John Quinn.

58 Augustus John to Michel Salaman, 1902. NLW MS 14928 fols. 52–3, 67–8.

59 Osbert Sitwell *Laughter in the Next Room* (1975 edn), p. 29.

60 *Men and Memories* Volume II p. 4.

61 'I Speak for Myself', recording for BBC Far Eastern Service, 10 September 1949.

62 *Ibid.*

63 *Chiaroscuro* p. 100.

64 Walter Pater *Studies in the History of the Renaissance* (1873).

65 In January 1903 John did two etchings of Lewis, and in the same year an excellent drawing and one of his very best oil portraits 'full of Castilian dignity', as John Russell described it, ' – displayed in a moment of repose'. Lewis did a drawing of John that is reproduced in the former's volume of memoirs, *Blasting and Bombardiering* (1937).

66 Wyndham Lewis to Augustus John n.d. (April 1910). NLW MS 22783D fols. 28–31.

67 'I called you poltroon for not daring to let me know before in what contempt you held me – when I had admitted you – fondly – almost to my secret places, for not honouring me so far as to be frank in this,' John wrote (June 1907) in a letter that gives the flavour of their explosive friendship. 'I called you mesquin [shabby] for jesting at my discomfiture, for playing with words over the stricken corpse of our friendship, ever sickly and now treacherously murdered at a blow from you, poor thing! And I called you bête for so estimating me as to treat me thus – cavalierly – for though my value as a friend has not proved great, it is neither nil nor negligible. And I say this from the very abysm of humility. Nor am I one to be dismissed with a comic wave of the hand . . .

'The wall you think fit to surround yourself with at times might be a good rampart against enemies, but its canvas bricks cannot be considered insurmountable to friends, and indeed (imagining them detachable) it would be an impertinence to level them in all seriousness at one's devoted head. I am as little inquisitive by habit as secretive by nature . . . I have never committed the indecency of trespassing on the privacy of your consciousness, of which you are rightly jealous. But in a *friendly* relationship I expect, yes, I expect, a frankness of word and deed as touching that relationship – an honest traffic – within its limits – a plainness of dealing, which is the politeness of friends. *That* we have never practised – you have never – it seems to me – given the Index of friendship a chance. It would appear that you live in fear of intrusion and can but dally with your fellows momentarily as Robinson Crusoe with his savages before running back to his castle . . .'

68 'Now, as for your recent drawings of which you sent me photostats, I must at once admit my inability to discover their merits, qua drawings,' John wrote to Lewis (undated). 'They lack *charm*, my dear fellow (from my point of view that is).' In *Blast*, No 2 (1915), Lewis wrote an article called 'History of the Largest Independent Society in England', in which he called John 'a great artist', adding that he was lacking in control and prematurely exhausted – 'an institution like Madame Tussaud's'. He also credits John with bringing some exotic subject matter into English painting, before going on to describe his gypsy cult as hothouse and *fin de siècle*. Shortly after this article appeared the two painters met one night at a restaurant. John, all smiles at first and with a 'woman-companion', invited Lewis to join them, but later in the evening, when the talk turned to *Blast*, he lost his temper.

Next day John wrote to apologize. 'I must have been positively drunk to assume so ridiculously truculent an attitude upon such slender grounds. Your thrusts at me in "Blast" were salutary and well-deserved, as to the question of exact justice – any stick will do to rouse a lazy horse or whore and the heavier the better. I liked many of your observations in Blast if I don't feel the particular charm of those designs which last night I characterized as "pokey". Probably "charm" is quite the last thing you intend. I think pokiness is an excellent and necessary element of design and I understand and admire your insistence on it. But I deplore your exclusion of all the other concomitants provided by an all too lavish creation – and with which I imagine none is better able to deal than you.'

69 Rebecca John *Caspar John* (1987), p. 17.
70 *Finishing Touches* p. 26.
71 The painting was bought by Charles Rutherston and now belongs to the Manchester City Art Gallery.
72 *Modern English Painters* (1976 edn) Volume I p. 179. The picture is in the Manchester City Art Gallery.
73 Called simply 'Esther'. CD 1903.
74 Tate Gallery, London, Modern British Paintings, Drawings and Sculpture, Catalogue no. 3171.
75 *The Burlington Magazine* (May 1909).
76 They were married on 31 August 1870 at the Register Office in Camberwell when he was twenty-two and she eighteen.
77 Ida John to Michel Salaman n.d. (September–October 1902). NLW MS 22788C fols. 79–80.
78 *Journal of the Gypsy Lore Society* Volume XLIX 3rd Series parts 1–2.
79 'Miss McNeill', Manchester City Art Gallery.
80 Now in the Manchester City Art Gallery.
81 Malcolm Easton *Augustus John* (1970), p. 43.
82 Arthur Ransome *Bohemia in London* (1907; 2nd edn, 1912), p. 89. See also Malcolm Easton *Augustus John*.
83 Charles McEvoy (1879–1929), the brother of Ambrose McEvoy, a village playwright and gifted clown.
84 *The Burlington Magazine* No. 475 (October 1942), p. 237.
85 *Gwen John*, Exhibition Catalogue, Arts Council, 1968. Introduction by Mary Taubman.
86 Ida John to Gwen John n.d. (1903). NLW MS 22307C.
87 Ida John to Gwen John (August 1903). NLW MS 22307C fols. 8–16.
88 Gwen John to Ursula Tyrwhitt, 3 September 1903. NLW MS 21468D fols. 2–6.
89 Gwen John to Ursula Tyrwhitt n.d. (late 1903). NLW MS 21468D fols. 7–8.

90 Augustus John to Dorelia McNeill n.d. (October 1903). NLW MS 22776D fol. 19.
91 In an undated letter to Mrs Hugh Hammersley.
92 Edna Clarke Hall's unpublished diary for 1898. Quoted in Alison Thomas *Portraits of Women* p. 62.
93 Ida John to Mary Dowdall (the Rani), March 1903.
94 Edna Clarke Hall to Ida John. Quoted in Alison Thomas *Portraits of Women* p. 85.
95 Augustus John to Michel Salaman n.d. (late 1902). NLW MS 14928D fol. 67.
96 Alison Thomas *Portraits of Women* p. 86.
97 Augustus John to Gwen John n.d. (autumn 1903). NLW MS 22311D fol. 135.
98 Ida John to Gwen John n.d. (late December 1903). NLW MS 22397C fols. 19–20.
99 Ida John to Winifred John n.d. (spring 1904). NLW MS 22311D fols. 138–9.
100 Augustus John to John Sampson n.d. (late 1904). NLW MS 21459E fol. 12.
101 Ida John to Dorelia McNeill n.d. (autumn 1903). NLW MS 22311D fols. 136–7.
102 Ida John to Gwen John and Dorelia McNeill n.d. (spring 1904). NLW MS 22207C fols. 21–2.
103 Ida and Augustus John to Gwen John and Dorelia McNeill, December 1903. NLW MS 22307C fols. 17–18.
104 In May 1904 Lady Gregory sent Augustus a copy of her *Poets and Dreamers*, an 'astonishing book', he called it. In a letter to Lady Gregory (25 May 1904) he wrote: 'Mr John Sampson of Liverpool know[s] more than any man about the Tinkers. He has collected a considerable vocabulary of their words besides tales and rhymes, and was the first to solve the mystery of their language and its origins. I have only known some English Tinkers whose language is but a debased and impoverished derivative of the Irish Tinkers' . . . If you would care I would willingly send you the hundred words or so I know of English Shelta but I feel it is the richer Irish dialect you ought to come across and Mr Sampson is its custodian.' Berg Collection, New York Public Library.
105 Augustus John to Gwen John, 28 March 1904. NLW MS 22305D fols. 96–8.
106 Ida and Augustus to Gwen and Dorelia, December 1903. NLW MS 22307C fol. 18. Essex County Council has placed a commemorative plaque on Elm House.
107 Augustus John to John Sampson n.d. (1903). NLW MS 21459E fol. 7.
108 Dorelia to John Rothenstein (19 January 1951). See *Modern English Painters* (1976 edn), 'Sickert to Grant', p. 187.
109 'Dorelia by Lamplight at Toulouse' (privately owned); 'The Student' (City of Manchester Art Gallery); and 'Dorelia in a Black Dress' (Tate Gallery, 5910).
110 Ida John to Gwen John n.d. and 24 August 1903. NLW MS 22307C fols. 8–16.
111 Augustus John to Gwen John, 28 March 1904. NLW MS 22305D fols. 96–8.
112 Augustus John to Gwen John, 28 March 1904. NLW MS 22305D. fols. 96–8.
113 Dorelia's words, spoken to the author, while describing this time.
114 Ida John to Gwen John and Dorelia McNeill n.d. (spring 1904). NLW MS 22397C fols. 21–2.

115 Augustus John to Gwen John, 28 March 1904 and 16 May 1904. NLW MS 22395D fols. 96–101.
116 Dorelia to the author, 3 July 1969.
117 Ida John to Gwen John n.d. (May/June 1904). NLW MS 22307C fol. 23.
118 *Ibid.*
119 Gwen to Dorelia n.d. (May/June 1904). NLW MS 22789D fols. 58–9.
120 Dorelia McNeill to Gwen John n.d. (May/June 1904). NLW MS 22308C fols. 9–10.
121 *Ibid.*
122 Gwen John to Dorelia McNeill n.d. (May/June 1904). NLW MS 22789D fols. 60–1.
123 Leonard to Gwen John n.d. (June/July 1904). NLW MS 22305C.
124   'Love seeketh not itself to please,
       Nor for itself hath any care,
       But for another gives its ease,
       And builds a Heaven in Hell's despair.'

       So sang a little Clod of Clay,
       Trodden with the cattle's feet,
       But a Pebble of the brook
       Warbled out these metres meet:

       'Love seeketh only Self to please,
       To bind another to its delight,
       Joys in another's loss of ease,
       And builds a Hell in Heaven's despite.'
125 Gwen John to Dorelia McNeill n.d. (July 1904). NLW MS 22799D fol. 35.
126 'Miss Dorelia Ardor, Pirini, I must keep writing,' he wrote from La Place Verte in Antwerp. 'You have not written to me yet. Do you not believe you are precious to me, invaluable one! I am alone and what can I do but think, and thoughts of all sorts come to me. I know if I don't hear from you to-morrow I will come to find you again. I can always claim you; I will have you for myself . . . I have tears of love for you and yet I am not drunk. Sweet I have met you on the high-way and I have recognised you and kissed you and you have fled into the woods and I have followed you at last and found you again. My girl, my sweet friend whom I love so much can you withhold your lips your eyes and your heart and your mind from me your lover – he who will take no denial – no denial. No denial is valid with him henceforth. It is useless – my lady, Sibyl, Dryad, form without circumference, incomprehensible simplicity, earth and air –
    'Ardor McNeill, it is you I love – Gustavus.' NLW MS 22776D fols. 29–30.
127 *Ibid.*
128 Augustus John to Dorelia McNeill n.d. (July 1904). NLW MS 22776D fols. 32–3.
129 Augustus John to Dorelia McNeill n.d. (July 1904). NLW MS 22776D fol. 34.
130 Dorelia McNeill to Gwen John, 1 August 1904. NLW MS 22308C fol. 11.
131 Gwen John to Dorelia McNeill n.d. (September 1904). NLW MS 22789D fol. 62.
132 Augustus John to Gwen John, 28 March 1904. NLW MS 22305D fols. 96–8.
133 Gwen John to Ursula Tyrwhitt n.d. NLW MS 21468D fol. 15.
134 Augustus John to Gwen John, 28 March 1904; September 1904. NLW MS 22305 fols. 96–8, 106.

135 Augustus John to Gwen John, 29 August 1904. NLW MS 22305D fols. 104–5.
136 Augustus John to Gwen John, September 1904; 24 October 1904. NLW MS 22305D fols. 106,109.
137 Gwen John to Auguste Rodin n.d. Musée Rodin, Paris. See Cecily Langdale *Gwen John* (1987), p. 28.
138 NLW MS 22393C fols. 4–5. See Ceridwen Lloyd-Morgan *Gwen John. Papers at the National Library of Wales* p. 9. The passage has been translated from the French by Ceridwen Lloyd-Morgan.
139 Winifred John to Gwen John n.d. (1903/4). NLW MS 22307C fols. 116–17.
140 Winifred John to Gwen John n.d. (1905). NLW MS 22307C fol. 118.
141 Winifred John to Gwen John, 10 July 1910. NLW MS 22307C fols. 119–23.
142 Auguste Rodin to Gwen John, 14 September 1907. Quoted in Cecile Langdale *Gwen John* p. 33.
143 Quoted in Susan Chitty *Gwen John* p. 70.
144 *Ibid.* p. 121.
145 *Gwen John Memorial Exhibition*, Catalogue, Matthieson Ltd, 1946, p. 4.
146 Gwen John to Michel Salaman, 17 January 1926. NLW MS 14930C.
147 Mary Taubman *Gwen John* p. 25.
148 Augustus John to Gwen John, 29 August 1904. NLW MS 22305D fols. 104–5.
149 Gwen John to Dorelia McNeill, August 1904. NLW MS 22155B fols. 1–2.
150 Augustus John to Gwen John n.d. (autumn 1903). NLW MS 22311D fol. 135.
151 Augustus John to Gwen John, September 1904. NLW MS 22305D fol. 106.
152 Ida John to Gwen John n.d. (summer 1904). NLW MS 22207C fol. 24.
153 Augustus John to Gwen John, 29 August 1904. NLW MS 22305D fols. 104–5.
154 Gwen John to Dorelia McNeill, August 1904. NLW MS 22155B fols. 1–2.
155 Augustus John to Gwen John, 29 August 1904. NLW MS 22305D fols. 104–5.
156 Ida John to Gwen John n.d. (summer 1904). NLW MS 22207C fol. 24.
157 Ida John to Gwen John, 21 September 1904. NLW MS 22207C fol. 28.
158 *Ibid.*
159 *Ibid.*
160 Ida John to Gwen John, 29 September 1904. NLW MS 22207C fols. 29–31.
161 Augustus John to Will Rothenstein n.d. (September 1904).
162 *Ibid.*
163 Entry for 26 February 1968 in *The Diaries of Sylvia Townsend Warner* (ed. Claire Harman) p. 318.
164 Gwen John to Ursula Tyrwhitt, 21 December 1910. NLW MS 21468D fol. 15.

CHAPTER IV: MEN MUST PLAY AND WOMEN WEEP

1 Ida John to Winifred John n.d. (October–November 1904). NLW MS 22311D fols. 143–6.
2 Ida John to Gwen John, 2 November 1904. NLW MS 22207C fols. 32–4.
3 Ida John to Margaret Hinton n.d. (spring 1905). NLW MS 22788C fol. 1ᴿ.
4 Augustus John to Ottoline Morrell, 30 November 1908.
5 William Rothenstein to Gwen John, 30 May 1926. NLW MS 22311C fols. 1–2.
6 Gwen John to Dorelia McNeill n.d. (*c.* 1909). NLW MS 22115B fols. 7–8.
7 See Mary Lago *Imperfect Encounter* (1972), p. 207.

8   An article Rothenstein wrote about the Slade celebrated Augustus for many of those buccaneering qualities that fed the John legend. But Augustus objected to this. 'Your all too picturesque treatment of me, leaves me in any posture but that of the penitent. Tho' you have been good enough to clothe me in "Bravest green", I find myself much more comfortable in my own less operatic habiliments and much more likely to face with fortitude and detachment the kind of music you bring to bear on me; – I have heard such strains before – but never! oh never! did I expect to find you in the position of band master – you my dear Will, whose flair and vision have been among the conditions which make life tolerable in this island . . . Differing with you, I think that the artist may *not* without shame join with his fellow men. His isolation indeed grows more complete as his art becomes more pure, nor is it the "ultimate usefulness" of the art which ever inspires him. His goal lies within himself – nor in his audacity is he deterred or terrified or bewildered for more than one sickly moment by the clamour and bustle and siren voices that come to him from without.'

9   *Men and Memories* Volume II p. 166.

10 *Athenaeum* (19 November 1904), p. 700.

11 'Sickert is certainly an amusing and curious character – amiable withal. But it offended me to hear him cast off his old master so lightly and perfunctorily the other day – after all, Whistler wasn't a bad artist. Sickert probably never saw his real merits, but he is singularly inept at times, for instance having once and for all disposed of poor Whistler he goes on to discover Robert Fowler Esq! But anybody who has served on a Jury with him must know he is quite futile . . .'

12 Sir William Rothenstein Memorial Exhibition, Tate Gallery, 5 May–4 June 1950.

13 Gwen John to Dorelia McNeill n.d. (early 1905). NLW MS 22789D fol. 63.

14 Augustus John to John Sampson n.d. (end of 1904). NLW MS 21459E fol. 13.

15 Ida John to Dorelia McNeill n.d. NLW MS 22789D fols. 66–70.

16 Ida John to Dorelia McNeill n.d. (March/April 1905). NLW MS 22789D fols. 73–6.

17 *Ibid.*

18 Ida John to Dorelia McNeill n.d. (1905). NLW MS 22789D fols. 71–2.

19 Augustus John to Michel Salaman n.d. (1905). NLW MS 14928D fol. 73.

20 Augustus John to John Sampson n.d. (December 1904). NLW MS 21459E fol. 13.

21 Augustus John to Michel Salaman, 9 February 1905. NLW MS 14928D fol. 69.

22 Gwen John to Dorelia McNeill, May 1905. NLW MS 22155B fol. 3.

23 Dorelia disliked certificates, and the birth was never registered. In a letter that would make a biographer's heart sink, Augustus advised her: 'There is no need to register Pyramus at all – or anybody else – you *may* register him for *nothing* within 6 weeks but after that you pay so much to do so. But you are not bound to register him. Sampson told me this. He has not registered Honor. So you can write to the registrar and tell him you have decided not to.'

24 Augustus John to John Sampson n.d. (December 1904). NLW MS 21459E fol. 13.

25 Augustus John to Michel Salaman n.d. (summer 1905). NLW MS 14928D fols. 73–5.

26 Ida John to Dorelia McNeill n.d. (March/April 1905). NLW MS 22789D fols. 77–8.

27 A number of Augustus's etchings of Ida call her Anne; for example, 'Anne with a Feathered Hat' (CD 59) and 'Anne with a Lace Shawl' (CD 46). Ida

also began renaming her friends – the Rani, for example, who became Lady Polly. 'Lady Polly is such a much more suitable name for you than Rani,' she explained. 'You are quite like lots of Lady Pollies in cheap novels . . . of course you will think it atrocious.'

28 Ida John to Augustus John n.d. (late summer 1905). NLW MS 22782D fols. 65–6.

29 Ida John to Augustus John n.d. (late summer 1905). NLW MS 22782D fols. 67–8.

30 Ida John to Ada Nettleship n.d. (late September 1905). NLW MS 22789B fols. 40–1.

31 Ida John to Ursula Nettleship, 6 December 1905. NLW MS 22788C fols. 12–16.

32 In an undated letter to the Rani. Ida John's correspondence with both the Dowdalls is in the Liverpool City Libraries.

33 Augustus John to John Sampson n.d. (September/October 1905). NLW MS 21459E fol. 19.

34 Ida John to Margaret Sampson n.d. (July 1906). NLW MS 22798B fols. 77–8.

35 Letter to the author, 23 November 1968.

36 Undated letter from Ida John to the Rani.

37 In an undated letter to Margaret Sampson.

38 Extract from an undated letter from Ida John to Augustus John.

39 In a letter to his mother, Wyndham Lewis primly reported John's move 'with his families' to this new home. 'He [John] has an apartment, garden and studio all together, parterre. The elder of his children, that I hadn't seen for some time, are becoming excessively interesting personalities: but their conversation, although sparkling, is slightly disgusting to a person of pure mind . . . They call me a "smutty thing" and a "booby" because I insisted that a lion could climb up a beanstalk, nay, *had* done so, in my presence! – and one of the first wife's children has contracted the indelicate habit of spitting at one of the second wife's children while having his bath: – by the way, Miss MacNeill is producing another infant.' *The Letters of Wyndham Lewis* (ed. W. K. Rose 1963), p. 31.

40 Augustus John to Michel Salaman n.d. (summer 1905). NLW MS 14928D fols. 73–5.

41 Bruce Arnold *Orpen. Mirror to an Age* (1981), pp. 192–3.

42 Campbell Dodgson (1867–1948) had entered the Print Room of the British Museum in 1893, and in 1912 he succeeded Sir Sidney Colvin as Keeper of Prints and Drawings. He became particularly well known as an expert on early German art and a collector of nineteenth-century prints and drawings. His catalogue of Augustus's etchings appeared in 1920. He married in 1913 the artist Frances Catharine Spooner, daughter of Canon W. A. Spooner, of Spoonerism fame.

43 The Chenil exhibition catalogue lists eighty-two etchings, the number of prints varying but never exceeding twenty-four. A significant quantity of these plates, Dodgson noted, mostly nudes, were etched 'somewhat hurriedly and in several cases without genuine inspiration', in order to be ready for the show. About fifteen were produced in the early months of this year, sometimes more than one plate being etched on the same day. It seems possible, too, that several numbers were added to the exhibition after the catalogue was printed: about seven are dated precisely (thought possibly without accuracy) as having been done in the last week of May; while three excellent portraits of Stephen Grainger which Augustus appears to have completed that spring are not listed. Among those shown, some of the portraits, and a few of the groups in a landscape setting, are striking. Many of the numbers in the exhibition were

a frank act of homage to Rembrandt, one of them being a translation on to copper of a Rembrandt pen-and-ink drawing.

44 Augustus's claim that Evans became a sanitary engineer seems to have been a metaphorical way of expressing his disappointment ('I held him in the highest regard and perhaps on insufficient grounds considered him immensely gifted'). Evans was briefly employed in the food industry and in about 1911 emigrated to British Columbia and lived on a ranch. After the First World War (in which he was wounded), he went on painting but did not show his work, little of which apears to have survived his death in 1958.

45 Augustus John to Ulick O'Connor. See the *Spectator* (10 November 1961).

46 *The Letters of Wyndham Lewis* (ed. W. K. Rose 1963), p. 39, where this letter is wrongly guessed as *c.* 1908.

47 Augustus John to Alick Schepeler n.d. (1907).

48 Now in the National Portrait Gallery, London, No. 4119.

49 *Evening Standard and St James's Gazette* (19 June 1908).

50 For example, he wrote to the poet Arthur Symons: 'Perhaps you may not have seen or heard of the sculptured figures on a new building in the Strand by a man called Jacob Epstein, which are in imminent danger of being pulled down or mutilated at the instigation of the "National Vigilance Society" of sexual maniacs, supported by tradesmen in the vicinity – and the police. These decorations seem to me to be the *only* decent attempt at monumental sculpture of which the streets of London can boast. A few of the nude male figures however have been provided by the artist with the indispensable apparatus of generation, without any attempt having been made to disguise, conceal, or minimise the features in question. This flagrant indelicacy has naturally infuriated our susceptible citizens to such an extent that without the most sturdy exertions of the intelligent lovers of Art and truth, the figures will be demolished.

'. . . If you would view the works, or those which are visible, for the hoardings are not yet all down, I feel sure you will share some of my feelings and will do something in defence of Epstein and Art itself – Yrs Augustus E. John.'

To Dorelia, Augustus wrote: 'Epstein wrote to me in despair, his figures are being threatened by the police! It is a monstrous thing . . . I sent him a fiver on account of Rom[illy]'s portrait and have written to a few people. On comparing his figures . . . with the squalid horde that pullulate beneath, leering and vituperative, one is in no doubt *which* merit condemnation, sequestration and dismemberment . . .'

51 But he was always a good subject for anecdotes. 'I don't believe in the modern ideal of living in a cow-shed and puddling clay with somebody else's wife concealed in a soap-box, like our friend Epstein,' Augustus wrote to Alick Schepeler (summer 1906). A few days later he amended this to an explanatory passage: 'The soap-box or packing-can is well known in Bohemia as a substitute for a bed – and if turned over might very well be used to conceal somebody else's wife, provided she were not too fat – I was wrong however to provide Epstein with this piece of furniture. I forgot that he used to keep somebody else's wife in his *dustbin* – I hear recently that he has married her – so it's all right.' Epstein and Margaret Dunlop (known as 'Peggy') were not married until 13 November 1913 at the Chelsea Register Office.

52 *The Diary of Virginia Woolf* Volume II *1920–1924* (ed. Anne Olivier Bell 1978), p. 54.

53 Bernard Leach *Beyond East and West* (1978), pp. 31–2.

54 Nina Hamnett *Laughing Torso. Reminiscences* (1932), pp. 26–7.

55 Letter to Alick Schepeler n.d. (*c.* autumn 1906).

56 *Chiaroscuro* p. 68.

57 Letter to Alick Schepeler n.d.

58 *Chiaroscuro* p. 26.

59 For example: 'An English fool, whom I had observed eyeing me in Rouen Cathedral to-day, rushed up to me outside, and started addressing me with extreme nervousness in lamentable French. He asked me if I were a Russian. I said "Mais non monsieur". He then began excusing himself so painfully that I invited him to speak English. He was thunderstruck and asked if I were a socialist. "No, are you?" "Er, no, I'm a Christian – first of all etc." He explained he was so struck by my appearance, the ass! He was a pitiable sight. His deplorable condition when I left him made me almost *feel* Christlike. Indeed I was about to make him the repository of the newest Beatitude. "Blessed are the ridiculous, for they shall entertain the Lord," when he oscillated confusedly and disappeared in a pink mist.' John to Alick Schepeler n.d.

60 At the Fitzwilliam Museum, Cambridge, there is 'Study of an Undine' (PD 155), dated 1907, and 'Portrait of Alexandra', 1906 (PD 154–1961). At the Manchester City Art Gallery there is 'Study for Undine' (1182) and 'Miss Schepeler'. 'Alick Schepeler', a black-pencil portrait on grey paper owned by Mrs H. Alexander, is reproduced as pl. 18 in *Augustus John: Fifty-two drawings*. A full-length drawing (5³⁄₈ x 13 inches) described as 'A lady with left hand raised to her cheek' – a very deliberately enigmatic pose – is probably a study for the burnt oil painting 'La Seraphita'. It was owned by Mrs Charles Hunter and later bought by Vita Sackville-West, who left it to her son Benedict Nicolson. 'I have a certain tenderness for this drawing,' Augustus wrote on 9 June 1938. 'It is of Miss Alick Schepeler.'

61 *Horizon* Volume V No. 26 (February 1942), p. 125.

62 Anne Stuart Lewis, his mother. See *The Letters of Wyndham Lewis* p. 12.

63 A large charcoal drawing he did of these gypsies, 'Wandering Sinnte', is now in the Manchester City Art Gallery. Though the figures are unrelated psychologically, they have a compositional unity and a community of feeling that makes it one of the best of Augustus's groups.

64 Letter from Ida John to Margaret Sampson n.d.

65 Letter from Ida John to Alice Rothenstein n.d.

66 Dorelia McNeill to Gwen John n.d. (June/July 1906). NLW MS 22308C fol. 12.

67 'The poet astonished the beach by appearing in a Rugby blazer and a cholera belt,' Augustus reported to Alick Schepeler. '. . . He came back full of the beauties of sea-bathing – that is to say: he had been viewing the girls frolicking in the water from a prominent position on the beach. He assures me there were at least 10 exquisite young creatures with fat legs, and insists on my accompanying him tomorrow . . . He wants me to go to Munich in January for the Carnival – he assures me I will dance with the Crown Princess.'

   Lewis's more laconic description of this long vacation was: 'I wrote verse, when not asleep in the sun.' See *Rude Assignment* p. 120.

68 Susan Chitty *Gwen John* p. 88.

69 Frederick V. Grunfeld *Rodin. A Biography* (1987), pp. 479, 481.

70 Susan Chitty *Gwen John* p. 82.

71 *Ibid.* p. 83.

72 Quoted in Frederick V. Grunfeld *Rodin. A Biography* p. 482.

73 Letter to Alick Schepeler n.d.

74 *The Letters of Wyndham Lewis* p. 31.

75 Dorelia to the author, July 1969.

76 To Alick Schepeler.

77 Letter to Alick Schepeler n.d.

78 Ida John to Augustus John, 10 November 1906. NLW MS 22782D fols. 86–7.

79 Letter from Ida John to the Rani, December 1906.

80 'Clara is enceinte and will have to leave end of January,' Ida had written to Augustus. 'It is so disappointing. She is such a good nurse. Félice is going to snort over needles and thread and be a dressmaker – I bravely gave her notice and had to bear a scene of tearful reproach – but within the week she found a genteel place as mender to a school . . . Poor old Clara is cheerful over her affair but she would much rather not have it, and says had she been in Paris when she found out she would have gone and had it destroyed.' NLW MS 22782D fols. 90–1.

81 Ada Nettleship to Ursula and Ethel Nettleship n.d. (10 March 1907). NLW MS 22799D fols. 36–7.

82 *Finishing Touches* p. 45.

83 Letter from Augustus John to the Rani, March 1907.

84 *Finishing Touches* p. 46.

85 Letter from Augustus John to Margaret Sampson, March 1907.

86 *The Letters of Wyndham Lewis* p. 36.

87 Five years later Augustus abruptly gave Mrs Nettleship notice that he was coming to fetch Ida's urn 'but not the half-ton of lead with which it appears to be ballasted'. NLW MS 22775C fol. 89. Early in April 1912 Henry Lamb came across Augustus on the platform of Waterloo station. He said 'he was travelling 1st because he had an urn with him,' Lamb wrote to Lady Ottoline Morrell (6 April 1912). '. . . At Poole we found each other & went to a pub . . . then we came back to the station & got our luggage on board. J. flabbergasted me when they bumped a dull looking wooden box beside the coachman by suddenly announcing that it contained Ida's ashes.' See Keith Clements *Henry Lamb. The Artist and his Friends* (1985), p. 54.

88 See *Men and Memories* Volume II p. 90.

89 Letter from Augustus John to William Rothenstein, 20 March 1907.

90 Letter from Augustus John to the Rani, March 1907.

91 *The Letters of Wyndham Lewis* p. 36.

92 Information from 'Augustus John', an unpublished typescript by Alan Moorehead, whose source was Henry Lamb.

93 Unpublished diaries of Arthur Symons: 'Gwen and Doulia' (*sic*).

CHAPTER V: BUFFETED BY FATE

1 Ada Nettleship to Ursula Nettleship, 15 March 1907. Written from the Hotel Regina. NLW MS 22799D fols. 46–8.

2 John to Alice Rothenstein.

3 John to Chaloner Dowdall.

4 John to Trevor Haddon, 4 February 1907. NLW MS 21570. See also letter of 12 July 1907: 'I wonder if it has occurred to you to think of replacing Knewstub as manager of the shop; as a shareholder I should be in favour of that step, tho' no doubt it would be difficult to find a suitable man.'

5 'Drawings by Augustus E. John' at the Carfax Gallery, December 1907. 'Knewstub's peculiarities have ended by tiring me out,' he had written to Trevor Haddon (11 February 1907), 'and I have arranged for my next show to be elsewhere.'

6 John to Will Rothenstein.

7 Delacroix to Félix Guillemardet, 1 December 1893.

8 John to Will Rothenstein, April 1907.

9 John to Alick Schepeler from Equihen.

10 Now in the Manchester City Art Gallery. An unfinished study, one of several, is in the Tate Gallery (5298).

11 One of these, in pencil and wash on tinted paper, is at the National Portrait

Gallery, London. It has what appear to be spots of Beaujolais on it. Yeats is wearing a mackintosh.

12 W. B. Yeats to John Quinn, 4 October 1907.
13 John to Henry Lamb, 24 August 1907.
14 John to Henry Lamb.
15 Keith Clements *Henry Lamb. The Artist and his Friends* (1985), p. 49.
16 *Ibid.* p. 35.
17 *The Flight of the Mind. The Letters of Virginia Woolf* Volume I *1888–1912* (ed. Nigel Nicolson 1975), p. 215.
18 *The Diary of Virginia Woolf* Volume II *1920–1924* (ed. Anne Olivier Bell 1978), p. 54.
19 Ida John to Augustus John n.d. (November 1906). NLW MS 22782D fols. 84–5.
20 Frances Partridge *Everything to Lose. Diaries 1945–1960* (1985), p.192.
21 John to Henry Lamb, 25 June 1907.
22 Rebecca John *Caspar John* (1987), pp. 21–2.
23 John to Ursula Nettleship n.d. (September 1907). NLW MS 22775C fols. 84–7.
24 Edward Nettleship to Ursula Nettleship July 1907. NLW MS 22790D fols. 66–8.
25 Letter (undated, but probably September 1907) from Dorelia to Augustus. NLW MS 22783D fols. 112–13.
26 *Ibid.*
27 Dorelia to Augustus n.d. (September 1907). NLW MS 22783D fols. 110–11.
28 Augustus to Dorelia. NLW MS 22776D fols. 55–6.
29 *Chiaroscuro* p. 69.
30 'French Fisher-boy' was owned for many years by Judge Stephen Tumim, and is now in the National Museum of Wales, Cardiff.
31 See Malcolm Easton and Michael Holroyd *The Art of Augustus John* (1974), pls.7 and 42.
32 Originally called 'Woman Smiling', it reversed its title in 1910 when it was shown at the Manchester City Art Gallery in a loan exhibition of John's work. It was the first picture bought (for £225 [equivalent to £10,600 in 1996] at Manchester) by the Contemporary Art Society, founded that year to acquire works by living artists for loan or gift to public galleries. It was also the first picture presented by the Society to the Tate Gallery (3171).
33 Miranda Seymour *Ottoline Morrell. Life on the Grand Scale* (1992), p. 71.
34 *Ibid.* p. 74.
35 *Ottoline: The Early Memoirs of Lady Ottoline Morrell* (ed. Robert Gathorne-Hardy), p. 141.
36 Augustus to Dorelia n.d. (May 1908). NLW MS 22776D fol. 79.
37 *Truth* (6 March 1920), *Everyman* (13 March 1920), the *Star* (11 March 1920), *Daily News* (2 March 1920). See also *Manchester Guardian* (1 March 1920: 'it makes life more exciting and fantastic and unlikely'), and *Spectator* (6 March 1920): 'a brilliant performance . . . one of those pictures we recognise at once as a new thing, with a distinct life of its own, come into the world').
38 'I am delighted you snubbed those stupid and impertinent journalists,' Augustus wrote to her (14 March 1920). 'I have kept them at bay as far as possible but they are very persistent. Even if one is induced to express an opinion it is sure to appear in a distorted form and minus the points.' Two years later, on 1 February 1922, he wrote in answer to a letter from Ottoline about the picture: 'I still have your portrait. People don't often buy other people's portraits. It's rather a cruel predicament as you know and yet I like it. I think I had priced it at £500 at the show but you can have it for much less. Would £200 be too much?' Ten days later he is hedging: 'In the

meanwhile I have collected some pictures for a show at Pittsburgh U.S.A. and I thought of including your portrait among them as I think with all its deficiencies (and tooth-powder) it is one of my best in some ways. Would you mind letting it go for the show, and then we could decide later if you really wanted it, or try another.' On 9 January 1925 he informs her: 'The price I have put on your portrait is £400 [equivalent to £10,000 in 1996]. Is that too much?' Eight months later (2 September 1925) he writes: 'I am delighted that on seeing the portrait again you still think well of it. It isn't good enough but I think it has distinction. I am sorry the price I put on it is too much – but I would not part with it to anyone else for less than twice that sum – and I know I shall be able to get it or more one day.' The following month, some seventeen years after he had begun this portrait, their transactions were at an end – and at once he suggested beginning another picture. 'Oh yes – your portrait is full of faults and I know I should love to do another.' By now Ottoline was middle-aged, and feeling perhaps that there was not enough time left for another portrait, she did not accept this offer.

39 Quentin Bell *Virginia Woolf* Volume I (1972), p. 145.
40 *Ottoline: The Early Memoirs of Lady Ottoline Morrell* p. 157.
41 *Ibid.*
42 *Ibid.* p. 158.
43 Quentin Bell *Virginia Woolf* Volume I p. 124.
44 *Ottoline: The Early Memoirs of Lady Ottoline Morrell* p. 159.
45 'How good of you to get the Duke of Portland to buy my drawings,' Augustus to Ottoline Morrell (7 July 1908). The 6th Duke of Portland was Ottoline's half-brother.
46 'My friend Lamb has just 40 francs left to carry him through the summer . . . Epstein is slowly being killed in London. It seems to be a general superstition that artists can live on air – whereas the truth is their appetites, like their other capacities, are exceptionally good,' Augustus wrote to Ottoline (20 September 1908). Later that month he wrote: 'You were good sending that cheque to my friend Lamb . . . Epstein is I think still very hard put to it . . . It would be grand if Portland or anyone else gave him a commission.' With characteristic generosity Ottoline gave Epstein an order for a garden statue and took likely clients to visit him, including W. B. Yeats and Lady Gregory, who commissioned him to do a bust of herself.
47 *Ottoline: The Early Memoirs of Lady Ottoline Morrell* p. 163.
48 *Ottoline: The Early Memoirs of Lady Ottoline Morrell* p. 158. See also Sandra Jobson Darroch *Ottoline. The Life of Ottoline Morrell* (1975), p. 66.
49 *Ibid.* p. 155; *ibid.* p. 67.
50 Sandra Jobson Darroch *Ottoline. The Life of Ottoline Morrell* p. 65.
51 Miranda Seymour *Ottoline Morrell. Life on the Grand Scale* p. 84.
52 John to Ottoline Morrell, 30 May 1908.
53 Henry Lamb to Ottoline Morrell n.d. Quoted in Sandra Jobson Darroch *Ottoline. The Life of Lady Ottoline Morrell* p. 76.
54 Ottoline Morrell's diary May 1910. Quoted in Miranda Seymour *Ottoline Morrell. Life on the Grand Scale* p. 98.
55 Keith Clements *Henry Lamb. The Artist and his Friends* (1985), p. 147.
56 *Ibid.* pp. 146–7.
57 Quoted in Miranda Seymour *Ottoline Morrell. Life on the Grand Scale* p. 97.
58 Royall Tyler was the author of *Spain: A Study of Her Life and Arts*, 'a capital straightforward business-like book . . . My only objection is to the title, as I think Spain is a neuter noun,' A. E. Housman wrote to the publisher Grant Richards (6 July 1909). Richards himself had more to object to, since Tyler then ran off with his wife.
59 'Charlie McEvoy nearly killed me in the evening by his drolleries,' Augustus

wrote to Lamb (24 August 1907) after an early visit to Westcot. 'He has recently had a play put on by the Stage Society which was a great success, the most enlightened critics combining in a chorus of praise. He sketched me the plot of his next play which also endangered my life. It is regrettable I am at the mercy of these comedians.' In 1907, McEvoy had written 'David Ballard' and he was also the author of 'The Village Wedding', which was performed by the village players at Aldbourne. In 1908 Augustus had done an etching of him (CD 20) described by Campbell Dodgson as 'a wonderful example of direct and unprejudiced portraiture, a perfect likeness and a masterly, though by no means beautiful, etching, which ranks by general consent as one of the best of Mr John's plates'. It was first shown at the fourth exhibition of the Society of Twelve in 1908.

60 Augustus to Dorelia n.d. (April 1908). NLW MS 227760 fols. 75–6.
61 Augustus to Dorelia n.d. (May 1908). NLW MS 22775C fol. 73.
62 John to Wyndham Lewis, 28 June 1908.
63 Ethel Nettleship to Caspar John, 27 June 1951. NLW MS 22790D fols. 34–7.
64 John to Ottoline Morrell, 7 July 1908.
65 Alison Thomas *Portraits of Women* (1994), pp. 96, 97.
66 Edna Clarke Hall to Rosa Waugh, 15 March 1907. Quoted in Alison Thomas *Portraits of Women* p. 105.
67 Alison Thomas *Portraits of Women* p. 110.
68 *Ibid.* p. 111.
69 *Ibid.* p. 112.
70 Augustus to Dorelia n.d. (September–October 1915). NLW MS 22777D fol. 90.
71 Alison Thomas *Portraits of Women* p. 111.
72 A pencil-and-watercolour study for this picture is in the Tate Gallery (3198).
73 John to Ottoline Morrell, 11 November 1908.
74 Letter to the author, 25 November 1968.
75 John to Lamb, September 1908.
76 *Ibid.*
77 From 'The Wanderers' by Arthur Symons in *Amoris Victima* (1897).
78 *The Swagger Portrait. Grand Manner Portraiture in Britain from Van Dyck to Augustus John* (Tate Gallery 1992), pl. 76, p. 214.
79 Helen Fry suffered from an incurable thickening of the bone of her skull and in 1910 was consigned to a mental home until her death in 1937.
80 Malcolm Easton *Augustus John: Portraits of the Artist's Family* (1970).
81 Christopher Hassall *Edward Marsh* (1959), pp. 145, 148.
82 *Letters from Edward Thomas to Gordon Bottomley* (ed. R. George Thomas 1968), p. 144.
83 'Time, You Old Gipsy Man' by Ralph Hodgson.
84 John's contributions to the *Journal of the Gypsy Lore Society* are: *New Series*, Vol. 2, 'Wandering Sinnte' (frontispiece), pp. 197–9; *Russian Gypsy Songs*, Vol. 3, pp. 251–2; *French Romani Vocabulary*, Vol. 4, pp. 217–35; *Russian Gypsies at Marseilles and Milan*, Vol. 5, pp. 135–8; *The Songs of Fabian de Castro*, pp. 204–18; *O Bovedantuna*, 'Calderari Gypsies from the Caucasus' (frontispiece). *Third Series*, Vol. 7, 'Portrait of Dr. Sampson' (opp. p. 97); Vol. 17, 'Self-Portrait' (frontispiece), p. 136; *Le Château de Lourmarin*, Vol. 23, pp. 120–22; *Portrait of a Russian Gypsy*, Vol. 27, pp. 155–6; *Keyserling on Hungarian Gypsy Music*, Vol. 36, pp. 81–2; *Miss Jo Jones's Frontispiece*, Vol. 39, 'Les Saintes-Maries de la Mer, with Sainte Sara, l'Égyptienne, and a Child' (opp. p. 3), pp. 3–4, 'Dora E. Yates'.
85 John to Ottoline Morrell, 8 April 1909.
86 Ottoline's daughter.
87 John to Ottoline Morrell, 9 July 1909.

88　John to Ottoline Morrell, 22 July 1909.

89　*Augustus John – the pattern of the painter's career*, BBC Third Programme (15 April 1954).

90　Jessie G. Stewart *Jane Ellen Harrison: A Portrait from Letters* (1959), pp. 129–30. The portrait was hung in Newnham College, Cambridge. See also Sandra J. Harrison *Jane Harrison. The Mask and the Self* (1988), pp. 162–3. The painting is still at Newnham College. It greatly shocked the Provost of Eton, M. R. James, this being 'one of the rare occasions when I saw him in a temper,' Sir Gerald Kelly wrote to the Principal of Newnham, Dame Myra Curtis (21 January 1954). 'We regard it as one of our treasures,' she replied. '. . . The cause of the shock to Montague James remains mysterious.' (25 January, 5 June 1954). This correspondence is in the archives of the Royal Academy in London.

91　Jane Harrison to D. S. MacColl, 15 August 1909.

92　John to Jessie G. Stewart, October 1957.

93　*Chiaroscuro* pp. 64–5.

94　*Song of Love. The Letters of Rupert Brooke and Noël Olivier* (ed. Pippa Harris 1991), pp. 14–15.

95　John to Ottoline Morrell, 22 July 1909.

96　*Ottoline: The Early Memoirs of Lady Ottoline Morrell* pp. 181–2.

97　Augustus John to Ada Nettleship, n.d. (July 1909). NLW MS 22775C fols. 78–9.

98　Chaloner Dowdall to Vere Egerton Cotton, 6 November 1945.

99　*Ibid.*

100　Augustus to Dorelia n.d. (August 1909). NLW MS 22776D fols. 93–4.

101　*Chiaroscuro*, p. 154.

102　Dora E. Yates *My Gypsy Days* p. 71.

103　John to the Rani n.d.

104　He later reversed this opinion. In 1911, when he had an opportunity to add to the head, he decided against doing so. 'I sent your portrait to the N[ew] E[nglish],' he wrote to Dowdall. 'I couldn't decide to touch it, merely gave it a thin coat of varnish. I think it looks well.'

105　*Daily Dispatch* (4 October 1909).

106　*Scotsman* (September 1909).

107　Albert Fleming in a letter to Dowdall, 16 December 1911 (Liverpool Public Library).

108　In July 1911 Augustus painted another Liverpool portrait that, amid much controversy, was exiled overseas. This was of the Celtic scholar Kuno Meyer. It shows him lolling in a chair, his waistcoat thrown open and also part of his trousers ('this I really must get him to change', Meyer ineffectually wrote) to display a large expanse of shirt and a claret-coloured tie. It is a weighty and effective piece of portraiture, highly praised by the art critic Sir Claude Phillipps, and 'all agree that it is a masterpiece', wrote Meyer rather dubiously. Presented, through subscription, by some two hundred Liverpool friends, and shown at the NEAC (winter 1911) and the National Portrait Society (spring 1915), it was much admired by Sir Hugh Lane who, Lady Gregory told Quinn (16 March 1912), 'hopes to buy John's picture of Kuno Meyer for the [Irish National] Gallery. The Liverpool people don't like it, and he could sit to someone else for them. It is a fine thing.' But once again, though Liverpool did not like it, the city did not especially want others to enjoy it elsewhere. Then, at the beginning of the Great War, Kuno Meyer came out on the side of the Germans, and left Britain for the United States. The portrait continued to hang at the Liverpool University Club, greatly to the embarrassment of the authorities who, by way of compromise, turned its face to the wall. Though it still belonged to the absent professor, Liverpool in its anxiety now to be rid of the traitorous object tried to remove it to the care of the Public Trustee as the property of an alien enemy. As the war continued, Ireland, England, America and Germany fought for the right not to have it, and it remained in a state of suspended ownership. 'I have been thinking that I ought to sell John's portrait of me,' Kuno Meyer innocently wrote to Quinn on 3 November 1915, 'although this is not the best time to do so. Besides, John wouldn't like it, and I should be very sorry to hurt his feelings. For, unlike most of my English friends, he is one who will not put politics – and such dirty politics – above friendship . . . the portrait (which my English friends no longer care for) is unsuited to my small flat and – entre nous – not liked by my family as a portrait, while it is one of John's masterpieces, as everybody admits.'

The portrait which Augustus had begun at Dingle Bank, a 'Rotten' place, and finished in two sittings at Gethin's studio in the Apothecaries Hall at the corner of Bold Street and Colquitt Street, went after the war to where Lane had originally wanted to send it: the National Gallery of Ireland in Dublin. See Seàn Ó Lúing *Kuno Meyer* (1991), pp. 98–9, 113, 203.

109   Charlie Slade, whose brother Loben had married Dorelia's sister Jessie, was known as 'the half-a-potato man' on account of his curious mysticism which, Romilly John explains, 'originated in an experience of his own nothingness in the ruins of Pompeii, and the revelation that came to him that the cut surfaces of a potato sliced in half, however asymmetrical in shape the potato, were exactly similar. He was subsequently promoted to station master at Cambridge, where I became deeply involved in his ideas and was urged (in vain) to produce a book on the subject.' Romilly John to the author, 28 July 1972. Felix Slade, Charles Slade's son, objects that 'the half-a-potato man exists only in Romilly's imagination. My father did, however, often propound informal theories, which were put to us for study and topics of conversation . . . I remember the potato theory but was only slightly intrigued by it . . . My father was the District Engineer, Cambridge (1924–27), and not the Station Master.'

110   See Malcolm Easton *Augustus John: Portraits of the Artist's Family* p. 52.

111   Arthur Symons *The Fool of the World* (1906), p. 69.

112   Arthur Symons to Rhoda Bowser, 6 May 1900. See Roger Lhombreaud *Arthur Symons: A Critical Biography* (1963), p. 175.

113   Arthur Symons to John Quinn, 29 June 1914 (Berg Collection, New York Public Library).

114   Augustus to Gwen, 23 June 1920. NLW MS 22305D fol. 133.

115   See *Agnes Tobin: Letters, Translations, Poems. With some account of her life* (Grabhorn Press for John Howell, San Francisco 1958), p. xii.

116   Quinn to Joseph Conrad, 12 April 1916.

117   Alice B. Saarinen *The Proud Possessors* (1959), p. 206.

118   Quinn to Josephine Huneker, 10 April 1909 and 14 July 1909.

119   '[Augustus John] has painted Symons with the relentless truth we all desire in a portrait,' Harris wrote: 'the sparse grey hair, the high bony forehead, the sharp ridge of Roman nose. The fleshless cheeks; the triangular wedge of thin face shocks one like the stringy turkey neck and the dreadful claw-like fingers of the outstretched hand. A terrible face – ravaged like a battle-field; the eyes dark pools, mysterious, enigmatic; the lid hangs across the left eyeball like a broken curtain. I see the likeness, and yet, staring at this picture, I can hardly recall my friend of twenty-six years ago.'

120   John's portrait of Quinn now hangs in the New York Public Library. In a letter to his wife (25 August 1909) Symons gives rather a different account to Miss Tobin's. 'We went to John's studio at 3. The Quinn was finished: a very fine portrait: 5 days!'

121   Quinn to John, 31 January 1910.

122   A fair example may be taken from a letter Quinn wrote to James Huneker,

the American art critic (4 February 1913): 'In my cable to Fry I expressly said that I bought the picture on your recommendation only so that if you have any fish to fry or bones to pick with Roger of the same name, then why not fry Fry. Personally, I never take fries; I always go in for roasts or broils . . .'

123 B. L. Reid *The Man from New York. John Quinn and His Friends* (1968), p. 73.

124 *Ibid.* p. 76.

125 *Ibid.* p. 77.

126 *Horizon* Volume IV No. 20 (August 1941), p. 125. This descripton and comment were omitted from *Chiaroscuro* twelve years later.

127 This letter is not in the Quinn Collection at the New York Public Library, but belongs to the author.

128 In a letter sent the previous day (31 January 1910) Quinn had written: 'Syphilis is the national disease of Italy. Before a white man has intercourse with an Italian woman or a white woman with a "dago" (our word for an Italian) male or female should be examined by a physician, a non-Italian of course, to see there is no gonorrhoea or syphilis . . . and even *then* there is danger. For Heaven's sake, if you do go to the rotten place look out for this. Whisky and syphilis are two of the greatest enemies of the human race and the latter often follows indulgence in the former . . . Youth is a precious thing.'

129 Wyndham Lewis to John n.d. NLW MS 22783D fol. 32.

130 John to Quinn, 18 December 1909.

131 Augustus to Dorelia n.d. NLW MS 22777D fols. 12–14.

132 From, in fact, Lord Grimthorpe's villa at Ravello.

133 *Chiaroscuro* pp. 104–5.

134 Augustus to Dorelia n.d. (January 1910) from Hôtel Olympia, Place de l'Horloge. NLW MS 22776D fol. 104.

135 Augustus to Dorelia, 27 January 1910 from Restaurant Gelet, Aux Lices, Arles. NLW MS 22776D fol. 111.

136 Augustus to Dorelia n.d. (January 1910) from Café Gilles Roux, Paradou, Bouches-du-Rhône. NLW MS 22776D fols. 107–8.

137 Augustus to Dorelia n.d. (January 1910) from Grand Bar des Glaces, Avignon. NLW MS 22776D fols. 109–10.

138 Interview with Marie Mauron, September 1971.

139 Augustus to Dorelia n.d. (February 1910) from Grand Bars des Cinq Parties du Monde, Marseilles. NLW MS 22776D fol. 117.

140 Augustus to Dorelia n.d. (February 1910). NLW MS 22776D fols. 118–19.

141 John to Ottoline Morrell, 11 February 1910.

142 Augustus to Dorelia n.d. (February 1910). NLW MS 22776D fols. 125–6.

143 *Horizon* Volume VI No. 36 (December 1942), p. 422.

144 Helen Maitland to Henry Lamb, 23 February 1910.

145 Like Augustus, Boris Anrep had landed himself with two wives in the same house – number two being useful, it was said, for selecting books from the public library for Helen on the principle of their not being the sort she would choose for herself. But Boris disappointed Helen 'by his literary philistinism and preference for legshows to those concerned more with the head', Romilly John remembered (29 July 1972). '. . . It was rumoured that she came from California which might account for her devotion to Culture and her eventual rejection of Boris and Hampstead in favour of Roger Fry and Bloomsbury.'

146 In the first draft of his autobiography, Augustus referred to Helen as 'censorious', adding: 'I have always disappointed her, being somewhat earth-bound and unable to rise to the lofty stratosphere, where, without oxygen, she seems most at home . . . For, feeling myself accursed, her strictures left me

subdued but with an inkling at least of higher things beyond my grasp.'
Dorelia, however, considered these observations too sarcastic and they do
not appear in *Chiaroscuro*.

147 Dorelia to Ottoline Morrell, February 1910.
148 Romilly John *The Seventh Child* (1932), p. 8.
149 Rebecca John *Caspar John* pp. 26–8. After Augustus's death, Caspar made
arrangements for the correspondence between his father and Bazin to be
given to the Musée Aéronautique in Paris.
150 John to Scott Macfie, 2 May 1910.
151 John to Arthur Symons n.d.
152 John to Scott Macfie n.d.
153 *Ottoline: The Early Memoirs of Lady Ottoline Morrell* p. 199.
154 *Ibid.* p. 200.
155 John to Chaloner Dowdall n.d.
156 *Horizon* Volume VI No. 32 (August 1942), pp. 135–8.
157 Frank Harris *Contemporary Portraits: Third Series* (1920), pp. 181–9.
158 *Chiaroscuro* p. 128.
159 Hesketh Pearson *Extraordinary People* (1962), p. 212. Also private
information.
160 'I WENT TO NEECE TO STAY WITH SOME PEOPLE BUT I FOUND
THEY WERE SO HORRIBLE I RAN AWAY ONE MORNING EARLY,
BEFORE THEY WERE UP NEECE IS A LOVELY PLACE FULL OF
HORRIBLE PEOPLE.' Augustus to David John, March 1910.
161 The Gertz papers are in the Library of Congress, Washington, DC.
162 'I wired to a young woman to come and assist,' he gruffly explained to
Wyndham Lewis (July 1910), 'Lamb accompanied the young woman and
spent 2 or 3 days in this town; possibly with the object of making himself
useful or perhaps with some purely sentimental motif or both.' In fact
Lamb seems to have spent about ten days there. 'John's alarm was naturally
exaggerated by past experience,' he explained to Ottoline Morrell.
163 'One evening Helen experimentally served up an untried Greek vegetable
which I rashly pronounced delicious. A deathly silence ensued. It was as if
I had praised Alma Tadema. Such are the pitfalls of associating with the
aesthetes!' Romilly John wrote (29 July 1972).
164 John to Quinn, 25 May 1910.
165 John to Quinn, 25 August 1910.
166 John to Quinn n.d.
167 John to Ottoline Morrell n.d.
168 John to Quinn, 25 May 1910.

CHAPTER VI: REVOLUTION 1910

1 In her lecture 'Mr Bennett and Mrs Brown' delivered on 18 May 1924 at
Cambridge.
2 *The Times* (7 November 1910), p. 12.
3 *Morning Post* (1 November 1910), p. 3.
4 *Ibid.* (16 November 1910), p. 3.
5 Michael Holroyd *Lytton Strachey* (1994 edn), p. 271.
6 Frances Spalding *Vanessa Bell* (1983), p. 91.
7 *Ibid.* p. 92.
8 Diary entry 14 December 1910. See Richard Shone *Bloomsbury Portraits*
(1993 edn), p. 61.
9 James Bone 'The Tendencies of Modern Art' *Edinburgh Review* (April 1913),

pp. 420–34. Collected in *Post-Impressionists in England – The Critical Reception* (ed. J. B. Bullen 1988), pp. 433–47.

10 Frances Spalding *Vanessa Bell* p. 109.

11 Vanessa Bell to Margery Snowden, 21 October 1908. *Selected Letters of Vanessa Bell* (ed. Regina Marler 1993), p. 75.

12 Laurence Binyon 'Post-Impressionists' *Saturday Review* (12 November 1910), pp. 609–10.

13 'The Autumn Salon' *The Times* (2 October 1908), p. 8.

14 Frances Spalding *Vanessa Bell* p. 93.

15 Frank Rutter 'An Art Causerie' *Sunday Times* (10 November 1912), p. 19.

16 Roger Fry 'A Postscript on Post-Impressionism' *Nation* (24 December 1910).

17 Grey Gowrie 'The Twentieth Century' *The Genius of British Painting* (ed. David Piper 1975), p. 302.

18 *Pall Mall Gazette* (25 November 1912).

19 In a letter dated March 1909 to Florence Beerbohm. David Cecil Transcripts, Merton College, Oxford.
'Max has done a very funny caricature of me – dozens of awful art students in the background,' Augustus wrote to Dorelia. Besides 'Insecurity' (now owned by the National Gallery of Victoria, Melbourne), Sir Rupert Hart-Davis has 'run to earth' another five Beerbohm caricatures.

20 Max Beerbohm to Florence Beerbohm, 22 May 1909.

21 'In the Fair Women Show, by the way, John has a portrait in oils – a full length – of "A Smiling Woman" – which seems to me really great – quite apart from and above anything else there; and you behold in me a convert.' Max to Florence Beerbohm, March 1909.

22 Paul Nash *Outline* (1949), p. 7.

23 C. R. W. Nevinson *Paint and Prejudice* (1937), p. 189.

24 *Saturday Review* (7 December 1907), pp. 694–5.

25 *Magazine of Fine Arts* (May–August 1906).

26 Quoted by David Piper in *Augustus John – the pattern of the painter's career*, BBC Third Programme (15 April 1954).

27 Richard Shone *Bloomsbury Portraits* (1993 edn), p. 61.

28 See *Sunday Times* (1 December 1912), *Daily Chronicle* (26 November 1912), *Spectator* (30 November 1912), *Manchester Guardian* (25 November 1912), *Daily Mail* (23 November 1912), *Observer* (24 November 1912), *The Times* (23 November 1912).

29 See John Woodeson 'Mark Gertler. A Survey' (1971).

30 Simon Watney *English Post-Impressionism* (1980), p. 21.

31 'The Academy in Totalitaria' *Art News Annual* (1967).

32 *Burlington Magazine* Volume XV No. 73 (April 1909), p. 17.

33 John Rothenstein *Modern English Painters* Volume I, *Sickert to Grant* (rev. edn 1962), p. 207.

34 *Augustus John – the pattern of the painter's career*, BBC Third Programme (15 April 1954).

35 *Saturday Review* (10 December 1910), p. 747.

36 *Pall Mall Gazette* (11 December 1910).

37 *The Queen* (10 December 1910).

38 *Daily Graphic* (10 December 1910).

39 *Burlington Magazine* (February 1910), p. 267.

40 It is this shared discovery, as well as his own independence, that Augustus signified in a letter to Quinn (10 February 1911): 'I don't think we need Fry's lead: he's a gifted obscurantist and no doubt has his uses in the world. He is at any rate alive to unrecognised possibilities and guesses at all sorts of wonderful things.' Elsewhere in this letter he writes: 'If you sent him [Fry] a gilded turd in a glass case he would probably discover some strange poignant

rhythm in it and hail you as a cataclysmic genius and persuade the Contemporary Art Society to buy the production for the Nation.'

41 He had also recommended Mark Gertler's early work – which hung alongside his own at the Chenil Gallery – but by 16 February 1916 he is telling Quinn that 'Gertler's work has gone to buggery and I can't stand it. Not that he hasn't ability of a sort and all the cheek of a Yid, but the spirit of the work is false and affected.'

With Eric Gill it was the other way about. On 10 February 1911, he is advising Quinn against buying his work. 'Personally I don't admire the things and feel pretty certain that you wouldn't neither. I admit that Gill is an enterprising young man and not without ability. He has been a carver of inscriptions till quite recently when he started doing figures. His knowledge of human form is, you may be sure, of the slightest and I feel strongly that his experience of human beings is anything but profound. I know him personally. He carves well and succeeds in expressing one or two cut-and-dried philosophical ideas. He is much impressed by the importance of copulation possibly because he has had so little to do with that subject in practice, and apparently considers himself obliged to announce the gospel of the flesh, to a world that doesn't need it. Innes calls him "the naughty schoolmaster", Gore calls him the "precious cockney" and I call him the "artist of the Urinal" . . . I'll let you know when I see a thing of Gill's which I can really respect and desire. His present things are taking at first glance as they look so simple and unsophisticated – but, to me at least, only art at first glance.' As Fiona MacCarthy remarks in her biography of Gill (1989), 'For Augustus John to claim crassly that Gill was impressed by the importance of copulation because he had so little to do with it in practice was to misread Gill's whole outlook.' But three years later his opinion of Gill's work had risen. 'I also ordered you one of Gill's things, a dancing figure in stone,' he wrote to Quinn (26 January 1914). '. . . Gill has made good progress and his things are admirable now, both in workmanship and idea.'

42 Gwen John to Augustus n.d. (c. 1909–10). NLW MS 22782D fols. 29–30.

43 John Currie, who appears as 'Logan' in Gilbert Cannan's novel *Mendel* (1916), shot himself and his mistress in a fit of jealousy. 'You remember Currie, some of whose works you bought?' Augustus asked Quinn (10 October 1914). 'He shot his mistress dead yesterday and then himself. He has since died of four bullet wounds in the chest. The girl [Dolly Henry] was staying here [Alderney Manor] lately carrying on a futile love affair with another young man. We all got sick of her. She was an attractive girl or used to be when I knew her first, but seemed to have deteriorated into a deceitful little bitch.

'It is a terrible affair and it's a good thing I suppose that Currie died. He was an able fellow and would have had a successful career.' Augustus's portrait of Dolly Henry (sometimes called O'Henry) is in the South African National Gallery at Cape Town, entitled 'The Woman in Green'. The gallery also owns his portrait of Wilson Steer's most celebrated sitter, Rose Pettigrew.

44 Spencer Gore, whose work Augustus recommended to Quinn as 'good and promising'. In 1928 (*Vogue*, 25 July) he wrote: 'The work of Spencer F. Gore, although [attracting] the admiration of a small body of genuine picture-lovers, undoubtedly failed to reach its deserved favour with the general public on account of the war following so soon after his death, which befell when he might be said to have arrived at the prime of his accomplishment. But this unconscious injustice was repaired by the April [1928] exhibition [at the Leicester Galleries], when it was realised that Gore was one of the most notable landscape painters of his time.' And again in 1942 (*Horizon* Volume VI No. 36, December 1942, p. 426) he wrote: 'The industrious apprentice is a type to be admired rather than loved. In Spencer Gore's case, however, immense industry was coupled not only with a rare and ever-ripening talent;

he possessed in addition an amiable, modest and upright nature which elicited the deep affection and respect of all those who knew him.'

45 'He [Greaves] is a real artist-kid, with Chelsea in his brain. I shall never cease to appreciate his work – *so* unlike Whistler's at bottom.' John to Quinn, 17 May 1912.

46 On 19 December 1913, Augustus had written to Quinn urging him to buy a Bomberg drawing, 'extremely good and dramatic representing a man dead with mourning family, very simplified and severe. I'ld like you to have it.' Quinn bought it for fifteen pounds (equivalent to £670 in 1996).

47 *Vogue*, 11 January 1928, 'The Paintings of Evan Walters'; 7 March, 'The Unknown Artist'; 18 April, 'The Woman Artist'; 27 June, 'Paris and the Painter'; 25 July, 'Three English Artists'; 22 August, 'Some Contemporary French Painters'; 3 September, 'Five Modern Artists'; 31 October, 'Interior Decoration'. The series was originally intended to comprise twelve articles but, even with the help of T. W. Earp, Augustus did not get beyond eight.

48 Arnold Bennett *The Pretty Lady* (1918).

49 Frank Rutter *Since I Was Twenty-five* (1927), pp. 191–2.

50 He was, however, elected with Oscar Kokoschka and Jack Yeats as an honorary member of the London Group in the Second World War.

51 Roger Fry to Will Rothenstein, 28 March 1911. *The Letters of Roger Fry* (ed. Denys Sutton) Volume I (1972), p. 344.

52 27 July 1920. See *The Letters of Roger Fry* Volume II (1972), p. 486.

53 See Mary Lago *Imperfect Encounter* pp. 10–13.

54 The Library, King's College, Cambridge.

55 'Seriousness' by Clive Bell, *New Statesman and Nation*, 4 June 1938, pp. 952–3. 'If only Augustus John had been serious what a fine painter he might have been . . . in my opinion "the latest paintings of Augustus John" at Tooth's gallery in Bond Street are almost worthless.

'They are not serious: in the strict sense of the word they are superficial. The painter accepts a commonplace view and renders it with a thoughtless gesture. And even that gesture is not sustained . . . the picture crumbles into nothingness. Nothingness: at least I can find nothing beneath the general effect . . . there is less talent than trick; and there is no thought at all . . . the master has preferred carelessly to dash on the canvas a brushful of colour which at most indicates a fact of no aesthetic importance . . .'

Elsewhere in the article, which refers to John's talent, charm, personal beauty, detestation of humbug and, perhaps optimistically, his sense of decency and magnanimity, and calls him 'a national monument', his work is unfavourably compared to that of Paul Nash, Xavier Roussel and Claire Bertrand.

56 Roger Fry to Jean Marchand, 19 December 1921. *The Letters of Roger Fry* Volume II p. 519. 'I do not exactly find him [Clive Bell] spiteful. He hasn't much personal judgement and he's a terrible snob . . . it is not by personal antipathy that he castigates a painter but rather by his over-preoccupation to show himself in the forefront of the trend. And since he is an admirable journalist and expresses himself forcefully he inflicts much distress without exactly meaning to.' Later in this letter, Fry suggests that Bell was not fundamentally a 'serious' art critic – 'he does not make a serious effort to understand it but collects hearsay and remarks from other artists etc.'

57 S. K. Tillyard *The Impact of Modernism* (1988), pp. 182–3.

58 'J. Dickson Innes', an unpublished essay by Augustus John (formerly owned by William Gaunt).

59 Information from Charles Hampton, to whom I am indebted for many facts concerning Innes's career.

60 Augustus John 'Fragment of an Autobiography', *Horizon* Volume XI No. 64 (April 1945), p. 25.

61 Randolph Schwabe 'Reminiscences of Fellow Students' *Burlington Magazine* (January 1943), p. 6.
62 *Modern English Painters* Volume II *Innes to Moore* (1962), p. 25.
63 Introduction to Catalogue of 'J. D. Innes Exhibition', Graves Art Gallery, Sheffield, 1961.
64 Augustus John to John Quinn, 10 February 1911. Quinn bought four of Innes's watercolours.
65 Rough draft for his Introduction to the Catalogue of the Innes exhibition of 1923 at the Chenil Gallery.
66 The cairn was destroyed by a USAAF Flying Fortress bomber that crashed on the peak of Arenig Fawr in 1946.
67 *Horizon* Volume XV No. 64 (April 1945), p. 255.
68 William Gaunt holograph *loc. cit.*
69 'Some Miraculous Promised Land. J. D. Innes, Augustus John and Derwent Lees in North Wales 1910–13'. Mostyn Art Gallery, Llandudno, 1982.
70 'The Late J. D. Innes. A Short Appreciation' by Augustus John, ARA.
71 For a Derwent Lees 'John' see 'The Round Tree' at the Aberdeen Art Gallery, which may be compared with John's own 'Gypsy in the Sandpit' at the same gallery.
72 'My immense picture of Ottoline is to begin: so my respiration may be audible in Dorset.' Henry Lamb to Lytton Strachey, 10 April 1910.
73 Boris Anrep recorded this first encounter with Augustus (in a letter to Henry Lamb) thus: 'If you could creep in my heart and memory which you honoured by some particulars of your relation to John's – you would feel sike and poisoned by the byle which turns round in me when I first saw John. That was a night-mare, with all appreciation of his powerful and mighty dreadedness, and some ghotic beaty, I could not keep down my heat to some beastly and cruel and vulgar look of brightness which I perceived in his face and demeanour . . .' Augustus relished Anrep's personality and admired his work. In 1913 he persuaded Knewstub to arrange an exhibition of Anrep's drawings at the Chenil Gallery, and in later years put him in the way of several commissions, from Lady Tredegar and others, for his mosaics.
74 Augustus to Dorelia, from the Hôtel Camille. Probably December 1910. NLW MS 22776D fols. 128–9.
75 John to Quinn, 5 January 1911.
76 John to Quinn, 11 January 1911.
77 Katherine Everett *Bricks and Flowers* (1949), p. 232.
78 *Ibid.* pp. 232–3.
79 15 June 1911. 'It's an excellent place for the boys and I think we are pretty lucky to have got it. The towns near are perfectly awful, being horrible conglomerations of red brick hutches.'
80 Katherine Everett *Bricks and Flowers* (1949), p. 232.
81 Augustus to Dorelia from Dingle Bank, July 1911. NLW MS 22776D fols. 143–4.
82 Henry Lamb to Lytton Strachey, 18 October 1911.

CHAPTER VII: BEFORE THE DELUGE

1 Romilly John *The Seventh Child* (1932), p. 21.
2 Gilbert Spencer to the author, 3 November 1968.
3 Romilly John *The Seventh Child* p. 25.
4 *Ibid.* p. 109.
5 Rebecca John *Caspar John* (1987), p. 31.
6 Romilly John *The Seventh Child* pp. 116–18.

7   Gerald Brenan *A Life of One's Own* (1962), pp. 241–2.
8   Romilly John *The Seventh Child* p. 134.
9   *Ibid.* p. 58.
10 Tate Gallery (3730).
11 Aberdeen Art Gallery.
12 National Gallery of Ireland.
13 Pittsburgh Art Gallery.
14 This composition, bought in advance by Quinn, 'after undergoing continual alterations became gradually unrecognizable and finally disappeared altogether.' *Horizon* Volume VI No. 36 (December 1942), p. 430.
15 Detroit Art Gallery. 'So that's what became of "the Mumpers",' John wrote to Homer Saint Gaudens. 'They will feel more than ever out of place in that hot bed of Ford's.' The picture had been bought at the Quinn sale of 10 February 1927 by René Gimpel. See his *Journal d'un Collectionneur* (1966), p. 327.
16 Bequeathed by Hugo Pitman to the Tate Gallery. See Nicolette Devas *Two Flamboyant Fathers* (1966), pp. 103–7.
17 Rebecca John *Caspar John* p. 31.
18 Romilly John *The Seventh Child* p. 54.
19 Oliver St John Gogarty. See his *It Isn't This Time of Year at All* (1954), p. 181.
20 John to Alick Schepeler n.d.
21 Michaela Pooley to the author, 1969.
22 *Chiaroscuro* p. 103.
23 The source for this is Quinn's diary – John having told him. In John's published account he relates that 'my caller, though uninvited, entered the house and with great good-nature made herself at home.'
24 *Horizon* Volume V No. 26 (Februry 1942), p. 127.
25 John Stewart Collis *Marriage and Genius* (1963), pp. 117–18.
26 *Ibid.* p. 64.
27 *Chiaroscuro* p. 116.
28 Frida Strindberg *Marriage with Genius* (1937), p. 20.
29 Augustus to Dorelia n.d. (September 1911). NLW MS 22776D fols. 155–6, 158.
30 John Quinn to Jacob Epstein, 7 August 1915. Quinn Collection, New York Public Library.
31 Quinn's unpublished diary, p. 16.
32 *Horizon* Volume VI No. 32 (August 1942), p. 131.
33 *Ibid., loc. cit.*
34 Augustus to Dorelia n.d. (September 1911). NLW MS 22776D fol. 162.
35 B. L. Reid *The Man from New York* (1968), p. 105.
36 John to Ottoline Morrell, 27 September 1911. University of Texas.
37 Augustus to Dorelia (September 1911). NLW MS 22776D fols. 160–1.
38 Quinn to James Gibbons Huneker, 15 November 1911.
39 In a letter to Huneker (15 November 1911) Quinn gave the inventory of this tour. 'We did Chartres, Tours, Amboise, Blois, Montélimar, Le Puy (a wonderful old place), Orange, Avignon, Aix en Provence (where we saw some of the most wonderful tapestries in the world), Marseilles, Martigues (where John spent over a year), Aiguemortes, Arles and Nîmes; back by way of Le Puy, St Étienne, Moulins, Bourges and into Paris by way of Fontainebleau. John knew interesting people at Avignon, Aix, Marseilles, Martigues, Arles and Nîmes . . . We careered through the heart of the Cévennes twice . . .'
40 Quinn to Huneker, 15 November 1911.
41 Quinn to Conrad, 17 November 1911.
42 *Chiaroscuro* p. 122.
43 *Horizon* Volume VI No. 32 (August 1942), p. 133.

44 The motto comes from line 12 in the 106th letter of Seneca to Lucilius, 'Non Scholae sed vitae discimas' ('Not for school but for life we learn').

45 Wyndham Lewis to John n.d. (April 1910). NLW MS 22783D fols. 28–31.

46 Augustus to Dorelia n.d. (*c.* September 1913). NLW MS 22777D fols. 25–6.

47 John to Quinn, 23 May 1910.

48 On 27 September 1911.

49 Romilly John *The Seventh Child* p. 62.

50 Gerald Brenan *A Life of One's Own* p. 147. See also Augustus to Dorelia n.d. (January–February 1915). NLW MS 22777D fols. 63–4.

51 Augustus to Dorelia, 20 May 1922. NLW MS 22778D fols. 33–4.

52 Augustus to Dorelia n.d. (August 1912). NLW MS 22777D fol. 11.

53 Romilly John to the author, 9 December 1972.

54 In a letter to the author, January 1969.

55 Rebecca John *Caspar John* p. 36.

56 Romilly John *The Seventh Child* p. 62.

57 Tom Pocock 'A Name to live Up to' *Evening Standard* (5 June 1967).

58 Rebecca John *Caspar John* pp. 41, 42.

59 Poppet John 'The Fire and the Fountain' *Listener* (20 March 1975), p. 361.

60 *Ibid.* p. 360.

61 Vivien White to the author, 1971.

62 John to Ottoline Morrell, 28 February 1912.

63 John to Quinn, 9 May 1912. Meningitis was afterwards treated with streptomycin and penicillin. 'It's maddening to think that Pyramus could have been cured of meningitis a few years later,' John wrote to his son-in-law Bill Bergne in 1941. NLW MS 22022C.

64 John to Sampson, March 1912. NLW MS 14928D fol. 99.

65 John to Sampson, 13 March 1912. NLW MS 21459E fol. 44.

66 John to Ottoline Morrell, 10 March 1912.

67 John to Quinn, 9 May 1912.

68 John to Quinn, 8 May 1913.

69 Oliver St John Gogarty *It Isn't This Time of Year at All* p. 180.

70 'To Augustus John' by Oliver St John Gogarty in *The Collected Poems of Oliver St John Gogarty* (1951), pp. 27–30.

71 *Horizon* Volume IV No. 22 (October 1941), p. 289.

72 Oliver St John Gogarty *It Isn't This Time of Year at All* pp. 178, 181.

73 Ulick O'Connor *Oliver St John Gogarty* (1964 edn), p. 149. See also Ulick O'Connor 'Blue Eyes and Yellow Beard' *Spectator* (10 November 1961).

74 Augustus to Dorelia 1912, 1915. NLW MS 22777D fols. 10, 86, 97–8, 99–100.

75 Oliver St John Gogarty *As I was Going Down Sackville Street* (1954 edn), p. 247.

76 Oliver St John Gogarty *It Isn't This Time of Year at All* p. 183.

77 Painted in August 1917, one portrait depicts Gogarty as a rather flagging dandy lit up with what Ulick O'Connor called 'elfin vitality' – though to Gogarty himself this image looked

> like Caesar late returned
> Exhausted from a long campaign.

In his poem 'To My Portrait, By Augustus John', he reveals that the painting provoked some deep questions.

> Is it a warning? And, to me
> Your criticism upon Life?
> If this be caused by Poetry
> What should a Poet tell his wife?

78 *Horizon* Volume I No. 22 (October 1941), p. 286.

79 Augustus to Dorelia n.d. (October 1915). NLW MS 22777D fols. 99–100.

80 Nicolette Devas *Two Flamboyant Fathers* p. 21. There is a reproduction of this portrait, which is in the National Gallery of Ireland, facing p. 32.

81 Nicolette Devas *Two Flamboyant Fathers* p. 28.

82 *Ibid.* p. 25.

83 *Horizon* Volume IV No. 22 (October 1941), p. 287.

84 John to Quinn, 6 August 1912.

85 *Chiaroscuro* p. 93.

86 John had painted a full-length portrait of Ida when she was pregnant. It is now in the National Gallery of Wales, Cardiff. 'It is a picture of a pregnant woman, painted with the assured brushwork of Hals or Manet, and a tenderness reminiscent of Rembrandt's,' wrote R. L. Charles, the Keeper of Art: 'mastery, depth and intimacy combined in a way hardly paralleled in British painting of its time.' *Amgueddfa: Bulletin of the National Museum of Wales* No. 12 (Winter 1972), p. 29.

87 John's portraits of Lord Howard de Walden and Lady Howard de Walden are now in the National Museum of Wales, Cardiff. The latter is dated 1912–22. In her autobiography, *Pages from my Life* (1965), Lady Howard de Walden wrote that after innumerable sittings over ten years, John ended up with 'a horrible picture' which he painted over. 'I'm very sorry Margot takes so pessimistic a view of her portrait and that her nerve has gone,' John wrote to Howard de Walden on 22 September 1923. 'I'm quite sure I can hit her off now and am anxious to retrieve my character and incidentally earn my hire (paid).' To make amends he offered to give Lady Howard de Walden another picture, a canvas 12 feet by 15 feet showing two Welsh gypsies, a mother and daughter, in a mountainous landscape 'talking to a life-sized obviously German professor in a bowler hat!' But it was too big to get out of the house. See *Portraits by Augustus John: Family, Friends and the Famous* (National Museum of Wales 1988).

88 John to Quinn, 11 October 1911. It is an impression of Holbrooke quite different from Beatrice Dunsany's description of 'a pathetic, good-natured deaf child' who played the piano beautifully. See Mark Amory *Lord Dunsany: A Biography* (1972), pp. 104–6.

89 John to Mrs Nettleship, 8 January 1913.

90 Epstein to Quinn, 11 January 1913.

91 John to Dorelia n.d. (January 1913). Written from Hôtel du Nord, Cours Belsance, Marseilles. NLW MS 22777D fol. 16.

92 'For days afterward I found myself under the hallucination of meeting people on the street who might have posed for them.' John remembered the studio as being 'covered with statues', and Modigliani as 'a naive and modest boy *when not on the hashish*'. These were the first sculptures Modigliani had sold and he was much encouraged. According to one source, 'he was found unconscious in an abandoned shack in Montparnasse, and was rescued and cared for by Epstein and the painter Augustus John.' See Pierre Sichel *Modigliani* (1967), pp. 213–16. After the war John painted 'In Memoriam Amedeo Modigliani', an arrangement of book, cactus, guitar, tapestry and one of the two heads he had bought. 'The book represents his Bible – Les Chants de Maldoror,' John explained to the art critic D. S. MacColl; 'the cactus, Les Fleurs du Mal; the guitar, the deep chords he sometimes struck; the fallen tapestry, the ruins of time.'

93 In the summer of 1912, Gertler wrote that John 'proceeded to give me some very useful "tips" on tempera,' and by September he was writing: 'Just think, I have actually done a painting in that wonderful medium tempera, the medium of our old Great friends! . . . I love tempera.' See John Woodeson *Mark Gertler* (1972), pp. 81, 100.

94 This cartoon, measuring 92$^1/_2$ by 232 inches, depicting a family group resting and cooking at their camp fire, was drawn in charcoal on paper laid on linen, but not squared for transfer or pricked through for tracing. It was shown as a single-work exhibition from 29 July to 4 August 1994 to mark the thirtieth anniversary of the Mercury Gallery in Cork Street, London.

95 This picture had originally been promised to Quinn in 1910. Quinn's inquiries about it met with little response until 19 February 1914, when John announced that he was now able to 'simplify the problem by confessing that I have *painted it out* some time back. I had it down here [Alderney] to work on, and after reflection decided I could not finish it to my satisfaction (without the original models) and thought I would paint you another picture which would be a great deal better. The cartoon lately at the N. English [The Flute of Pan] was started with that object. In course of doing it I added the right portion of the design, consisting of landscape which makes it about a third larger than "Forza e Amore". As to Lane's claim to this last – it originally formed part of a much larger scheme which on my break with him I did not carry out . . . I am damn sorry you were so set on the "F. e A". I was merely conscientious in painting it out as I did. But you will like The Flute of Pan better and the price of course will be the same.'

Quinn was horrified at this news, and John assured him (16 March 1914) he was not alone. 'I was at Lane's lately and told him I had painted out "Forza e Amore". Words failed him to express his horror . . . He implored me to send it up to him and let him have the coat of white I gave it taken off. Shall I? I suppose I was a bloody fool to do it.' Three months later (24 June 1914) he confirmed that Quinn had 'the only real claim to the picture' – adding that he was now certain the white coat could not be removed successfully.

96 Augustus to Dorelia n.d. (spring 1913). NLW MS 22777D fol. 20.
97 John to Hope-Johnstone n.d.
98 Augustus to Dorelia January–February 1914. NLW MS 22777D fols. 34, 36, 39.
99 John to Ottoline Morrell, July 1914.
100 In a letter to his brother James Strachey. British Library.
101 Augustus to Dorelia (summer 1912). NLW MS 22777D fols. 9, 11.
102 Augustus to Dorelia (1915). NLW MS 22777D fols. 87–8, 89.
103 Augustus to Dorelia (June 1916). NLW 22777D fols. 120–1.
104 Augustus to Dorelia (summer 1916). NLW MS 22777D fol. 130.
105 John to Hope-Johnstone, 1916.
106 *Horizon* Volume VIII No. 44 (August 1943), p. 140.
107 Llwynythyl was later taken by the composer Granville Bantock. His daughter remembers that John 'had drawn an enormous mural in white chalk of angel figures covering the entire end wall of the sitting-room . . . We discovered a whole pile of discarded oil paints and brushes, together with many crumpled sketches. We salvaged and smoothed out two of these sketches and I still have one of them . . . an amusing cartoon of a woman sitting at a table and trying to work; around her pots and pans are flying through the air, a tradesman presents bills and a half-naked baby screams on the floor.'
108 See Mark Amory *Lord Dunsany: A Biography* (1972), pp. 73–4.
109 John to Hope-Johnstone, 20 February 1914.
110 John to Quinn, 19 February 1914.
111 John went out sketching with Munnings, listening carefully to Munnings's theory that a horse's coat reflects the light of day, and then, after silent reflection, gruffly demanding: 'If you see a brown horse, why not paint it brown?' Many years later John told E. J. Rousuck that Munnings's horses had 'better picture quality, better groupings' than Stubbs's. See Reginald Pound *The Englishman* (1962), pp. 59, 61, 201.

112 Interview with the author, 1969. See also Margaret Laing 'Dame Laura Knight' *Evening Standard* (5 November 1968), p. 12.

113 Dame Laura Knight to the author. She recalled that they were living in three cottages knocked into one, which made a room thirty feet in length. A panel of Dorelia at Falmouth that winter is called 'The Mauve Jersey'.

114 *Horizon* Volume XI No. 64 (April 1945), p. 258. In *Chiaroscuro*, p. 205, 'our excitement' has been changed to 'the general excitement'.

115 Augustus to Gwen John n.d. NLW MS 22305C fols. 114–16.

116 Augustus to Dorelia, 6 August 1914. NLW MS 22777D fols. 52–3.

CHAPTER VIII: HOW HE GOT ON

1 Augustus to Dorelia, from Mallord Street n.d. (5 August 1914). NLW MS 22777D fols. 59–1.

2 John to Quinn, 12 October 1914.

3 John to Quinn, 13 August 1915.

4 John to Dorelia n.d. (summer 1917). NLW MS 22777D fol. 138.

5 Gwen John to Ursula Tyrwhitt n.d. (September 1914). NLW MS 21468 fols. 76–8.

6 Susan Chitty *Gwen John* (1981), p. 136.

7 Augustus to Gwen John, 24 October 1914. NLW MS 22305D fols. 118–19.

8 *Ibid.*

9 Augustus to Gwen John, 25 December 1914. NLW MS 22305D fols. 120–21.

10 Winifred John to Gwen John n.d. (*c.* 1904). NLW MS 22307C fols. 116–17.

11 Winifred John to Augustus John, 8 January 1906. NLW MS 22782D fols. 121–4.

12 Thornton John to Gwen John, 7 February 1917. NLW MS 22307C fols. 51–3. Thornton came back twice to Europe. The first time was in the autumn of 1910 (when he was thinking of getting work in Ireland and brought back one of Gwen's pictures of Fenella Lovell). The second time was at the beginning of 1915. 'Factory work is an abomination,' he wrote to Gwen, 'but there is nothing to do but hold on grimly.'

13 *Ibid.*

14 Augustus to Dorelia n.d. (31 August 1914). NLW MS 22777D fol. 56.

15 John to Ottoline Morrell, 1 January 1915.

16 John to Quinn, 15 February 1915.

17 *Irish Times* (21 November 1964).

18 Augustus to Dorelia, from the Railway Hotel in Galway City n.d. (13 October 1915). NLW MS 22777D fols. 103–4.

19 Augustus to Dorelia n.d. (17 October 1915). NLW MS 22777D fols. 105–6.

20 John to Quinn, 15 November 1915.

21 John to Shaw, from Mallord Street, 18 December 1915. BL Add. MS 59539.

22 John to Quinn, 19 October 1914.

23 John to Quinn, 12 October 1914.

24 This commission to paint Lord Fisher had come through Epstein, who had recently done a bust of Fisher for the Duchess of Hamilton. His three-quarter length portrait of Fisher, which was shown at the Alpine Club in 1917–18 and priced at seven hundred guineas (equivalent to £18,500 in 1996), is owned by the National Gallery of Scotland at Edinburgh, and a half-length portrait is in the Leicester Museum and Art Gallery.

25 Augustus to Dorelia n.d. (*c.* June 1916). NLW MS 22777D fol. 119.

26 Albert Rutherston to William Rothenstein, 8 December 1916.

27 *The Times* (3 March 1920).

28 Jan Morris *Fisher's Face* (1995), pp. 132–3; see also p. 221.
29 John to Quinn, 19 January 1916.
30 John to Ottoline Morrell n.d.
31 Frances Lloyd George *The Years That Are Past* (1967), p. 84.
32 Frances Stevenson *Lloyd George. A Diary* (ed. A. J. P. Taylor 1971), pp. 83, 103–4; entry for 12 March 1916.
33 It is now in the Aberdeen Art Gallery.
34 At the Villa la Chaumière in September 1919.
35 Quinn to Kuno Meyer, 10 May 1916.
36 See W. H. Davies *Later Days* (1925), pp. 177–84.
37 Berg Collection, New York Public Library.
38 John to Dorelia, from Coole Park n.d. (May 1915). NLW MS 22777D fols. 80–85.
39 Bernard Shaw to Francis Chesterton, 5 May 1915. *Bernard Shaw. Collected Letters* Volume 3 *1911–1925* (ed. Dan H. Laurence 1985), pp. 294–5.
40 Lady Gregory remembered this rather differently. In *Coole* (1971) she wrote: 'John asked while he was here if he might paint Richard, and I, delighted, reading a story to the child, kept him still for the sitting. I longed to possess the picture but did not know how I could do so without stinting the comforts of the household, and said no word. But I think he must have seen my astonished delight when he gave it to me, said it was for me he had painted it. That was one of the happy moments of my life.' She also added: 'I had from the time of his birth dreamed he might one day be painted by that great Master, Augustus John, yet it had seemed but a dream.'
41 Anne Gregory *Me and Nu: Childhood at Coole* (1970), p. 47.
42 'Augustus John had been very annoyed at being thwarted, and had given Richard that funny look to pay Grandma out! The picture of Richard was hung in the drawing-room, on the left of the big fireplace.' Anne Gregory also remembered that John 'was large and rather frightening to look at, and we felt he might step on us, as he seemed to stride about not ever looking where he was going.' *Me and Nu*, Chapter VII.
43 Lady Gregory to W. B. Yeats n.d.
44 S. Winsten *Days with Bernard Shaw* (1948), p. 164.
45 *Bernard Shaw and Mrs Patrick Campbell: Their Correspondence* (ed. Alan Dent 1952), p. 175.
46 Augustus to Dorelia n.d. (May 1915). NLW MS 22777D fols. 82–3.
47 *Chiaroscuro* pp. 96–9.
48 Augustus to Dorelia n.d. (May 1915). NLW MS 22777D fols. 84–5.
49 John to Quinn, 15 November 1915.
50 To his secretary, Ann Elder, Shaw described John (30 April 1915) as 'a painter of intense reputation among advanced people'. Of the three portraits Shaw temporarily owned two. In 1922 he presented one of these to the Fitzwilliam Museum, Cambridge. 'I note that you are keeping the best – with the blue background – which I suppose still adorns one of the top corners of your rooms at Adelphi Terrace,' John wrote to him (24 March 1922). This portrait is now at Ayot St Lawrence and belongs to the National Trust.
51 Wyndham Lewis to John, from 19 rue Mouton Duvernet, avenue d'Orléans (Paris) n.d. NLW MS 22783D fols. 19–20.
52 Shaw to John, 6 August 1915.
53 He attributed the expression to Shaw's midday intake of vegetables, though admitted (16 May 1915) that 'the one in which you have apparently reached a state of philosophic oblivion is perhaps liable to misinterpretation'. It was originally credited with the title 'The Philosopher in Contemplation' or 'When Homer Nods'. It was bought by an Australian who later sold it in

London where it was purchased by the Queen. It now (1995) hangs in Clarence House as part of the Queen Mother's collection.

54 Shaw to John, from the Hydro, Torquay, 6 August 1915.

55 Between John's portrait and Rodin's bust, which had been done a few years earlier, Shaw differentiated. 'With an affectation of colossal vanity, Shaw gestured and genuflected before the Rodin bust of himself when I once visited him,' Archibald Henderson wrote (*George Bernard Shaw: Man of the Century*, 1956, p. 789); 'but during a later visit delightedly rushed me into the dining-room to see the Augustus John poster-portrait, in primary colours – flying locks and breezy moustaches, rectangular head, and a caricaturishly flouting underlip. To the John portrait he pointed with a delicious chuckle: "There's the portrait of my great reputation"; then pointing to the Rodin bust, he breathed: "Just as I am, without one plea".' But it is arguable that, by 1915, Shaw's protective covering, which he called 'G.B.S.', was complete.

56 It was at this exhibition that the famous 'ladies of Gregynog', Gwendoline and Margaret Davies, acting on the advice of Hugh Blaker, Curator of the Holburne Museum at Bath, bought their first Augustus John pictures – ten oils (including the self-portrait on the jacket of the Chatto & Windus hardback edition of this book) and a drawing – for £2,350 (equivalent to £84,500 in 1996). In 1918 Margaret Davies bought another oil ('Study of a Boy' [Edwin]), and in 1919 added John's portrait of W. H. Davies (whose *Selected Poems* and *The Lover's Song Book* were published by the Gregynog Press) as well as a portfolio of ten drawings to their joint collection. This collection was eventually given to the National Museum of Wales at Cardiff.

In October 1920 John dispatched a complete set of his etchings to the National Museum of Wales, the only other public collections having this suite of etchings being Cambridge and Berlin (and in 1949 the British Museum, to which Campbell Dodgson bequeathed his collection). Though the National Museum of Wales was given two John pictures by the Contemporary Art Society in 1936 and 1942, it was not until the end of the 1940s that it bought its first John work (a flower painting, 'Cineraria', in 1948 and a nude design in 1949). In 1962 the museum bought the full-length painting 'Dorelia in the Garden at Alderney Manor' at the Christie's sale of John's work. It also bought portrait drawings of John Cowper Powys and Frank Brangwyn in the 1960s, and then the small oil paintings of Caitlin Macnamara and Ida John and the 'French Fisher-boy' of 1907 (owned by Judge Stephen Tumim), some studies for his Slade School 'Moses and the Brazen Serpent' and miscellaneous studies and sketchbooks that had been owned by Michel Salaman, all in the 1970s. From the estate of Dorelia in 1972 the museum purchased over one thousand drawings, one hundred and ten paintings and three bronzes, making it, in the words of the Assistant Keeper, Mark L. Evans, 'the principal repository of John's work and the main centre for research on his art'.

57 Dorelia to Lytton Strachey, 16 March 1915. British Library.

58 Lytton Strachey to Carrington, 8 March 1917. 'At first she [Vivien] completely ignored me. She then would say nothing but "Oh no!" whenever I addressed her. But eventually she gave me a chocolate – "Man! Have a chockle," – which I consider a triumph.'

59 'Vivien John. Malaysia: its People and its Jungle'. Upper Grosvenor Galleries, 19 January–6 February 1971.

60 See Nicolette Devas *Two Flamboyant Fathers* (1966), pp. 36–49.

61 John to Dorelia, April 1915. NLW MS 22777D fols. 74–5.

62 Some years later, when John was visiting the composer Jack Moeran in Norfolk, he called on Brownsword; and continued seeing her later still after she was widowed, 'always on friendly terms'.

Gwyneth became a talented painter, and mixed with the Johns after she had grown up, but remained outside the family circle. She was always fond of Augustus, would frequently see him in London, and lent him her studio to work in occasionally. 'He was a unique and wonderful man,' she wrote after his death.

63 John to Quinn, 13 August 1915. In *The Arms of Time. A Memoir* (1979), pp. 63–72, her son Rupert Hart-Davis wrote, 'the two people who most often advised her to give up alcohol altogether were John and her brother Duff, two of the most persistent drinkers of their time.' John also introduced her to Wyndham Lewis with whom, 'her heart as always too soon made glad', she had an affair. John, too, was fascinated by her and 'after his fashion, loved her. She thought him a genius.' He drew several pencil heads of her and of her two children, Deirdre and Rupert, for whom he recommended John Hope-Johnstone as a holiday tutor. 'He challenged all comers to box with him,' Rupert Hart-Davis remembered, 'and the milkman, who was a much better performer, repeatedly knocked him down, saying "Sorry, sir" each time.'

64 According to Ezra Pound, this verse sprang from 'the Castalian fount of the Chenil'. In a letter to Wyndham Lewis (13 January 1918) Pound noted: '(Authorship unrecognised, I first heard it in 1909). It is emphatically NOT my own, I believe it to have come from an elder generation.'

65 In the last week of January 1915. Lamb had been in Guy's Hospital for an operation. 'I have written to Dodo to know if she can pick me up . . . It all depends on whether J[ohn] will be gone: his temper not being considered good enough to stand the strain of a visit from me,' Lamb had explained to Lytton Strachey (15 January 1915). After his visit, he wrote (31 January 1915): 'They have been discussing the moral effects of being in hospital, saying that one's sensitiveness is apt to become magnified. I wonder if that is the reason why I was miserable at Parkstone.'

66 Dorelia to Lytton Strachey, 13 September 1916.

67 Augustus to Dorelia n.d. (31 August 1914). NLW MS 22777D fols. 48–9.

68 Dorelia to Lytton Strachey, 10 May 1916.

69 John to Quinn, 26 January 1914. See also John's Foreword to Cecil Gray's *Peter Warlock, A Memoir of Philip Heseltine* (1934), pp. 11–12.

70 John to Evan Morgan (Lord Tredegar) n.d.

71 Frida Strindberg to John n.d. NLW MS 22785D fols. 150–3.

In *Chiaroscuro* John records: 'I received a letter from her, written on the ship. It was a noble epistle. In it I was absolved from all blame: all charges, all imputations were withdrawn: she alone had been at fault from the beginning: though this wasn't true, I was invested with a kind of halo, quite unnecessarily. I wish I had kept this letter; it might serve me in an emergency.' The letter, written from the RMS *Campania*, has since come to light. In it she writes: 'The chief fault others had, who interfered with lies and mischief. The rest, I take it, was my fault – and therefore I stretch out my heart in farewell . . . You are the finest man I met in this world, dear John – and you'll ever be to me what the Sun is, and the Sea around me, and the immortal beauty of nature. Therefore if ever you think of me, do it without bitterness and stripe [*sic*] me of all the ugliness that events have put on me and which is not in my heart . . . Goodbye John. I don't know whether you know how awfully good at the bottom of your heart you are – *I* know. And that is why I write this to you – Frida Strindberg.'

72 See *Finishing Touches*, pp. 84–5.

73 'To the Eiffel Tower Restaurant', in *Sublunary*, pp. 93–5.

74 Constantine FitzGibbon *The Life of Dylan Thomas* (1968), p. 163.

75 *Ibid., loc. cit.*

76 Charles Wheeler *High Relief* (1968), p. 31.

77 Letter from Dorothy Brett to the author, 7 August 1968.

78 See *Carrington, Letters and Extracts from her Diaries* (ed. David Garnett 1970), pp. 74–5, where this letter is incorrectly dated 25 July 1917.

79 And repeated on 29 July at the Lyric Theatre. It had been organized in conjunction with the Ladies Auxiliaries Committee of the Young Men's Christian Association. See the Enthoven Collection at the Victoria and Albert Theatre Museum, Covent Garden.

80 See Appendix Five.

81 Epstein to Quinn, 12 August 1914.

82 Epstein to Quinn, 4 September 1914.

83 *Epstein. An Autobiography* (1955), p. 89.

84 Epstein to Quinn, 20 July 1917.

85 See, for example, *Sunday Herald* (10 June 1917).

86 Information from Sir Sacheverell Sitwell. Later in life, while not seeing much of each other, Epstein and John remained friendly. Kathleen Epstein remembered that they met once in a street and, in answer to a question, Epstein said he was doing good work but could not sell it and was very poor. John at once took out a chequebook and wrote him a cheque 'which we will never refer to again'. This was in the 1930s.

87 *Chiaroscuro* p. 125.

88 Sir Herbert A. Barker *Leaves from My Life* (1927), pp. 263–5.

89 By way of payment John offered to 'do a head' of Barker. 'If you will rattle my bones, I should be more than repaid!' This portrait, the first of two painted during the war, is now in the National Portrait Gallery, London. Barker, who often slept during the sittings, nevertheless observed: 'It was a wonderful thing to watch John at work – to note his interest and utter absorption in what he was doing . . . The genius of the born craftsman was apparent in every look and movement. He had a habit when most wrapped up in some master-stroke or final touch of running backwards some feet from the canvas with his critical eyes bent upon the painting. Once when doing this he tripped and almost fell heavily over the stove near by.' The portrait used to hang in Barker's waiting-room to encourage the patients. Variously described as 'Satanic' or like 'a Venetian Doge', it was, Barker bravely maintained, one of John's 'best male portraits': adding 'I look upon John as one of the greatest portrait painters who has ever lived.' John himself described the painting, in a letter to Hope-Johnstone, as 'just like him, stuffy and good'. Early in March 1932 John saw Barker again, this time in Jersey. 'You have always done me good, and I feel it is high time I put myself in your hands again,' he had written (17 September 1931). During this visit he began a third portrait. See Reginald Pound *Harley Street* (1967), pp. 80, 123–4. Also unpublished correspondence at the Royal College of Surgeons.

90 The phrase is Malcolm Easton's. See his *The Art of Augustus John* (1974).

91 *The Times* (27 November 1917).

92 Osbert Sitwell *Great Morning!* (1948), p. 248.

93 In the *Burlington Magazine* (April 1916). See also his article for February 1916 on the New English Art Club.

94 *Burlington Magazine* (December 1940), p. 28.

95 John to Evan Morgan, December 1914.

96 December 1914.

97 'You are too much like the popular idea of an angel!' John wrote to her (5 October 1917), '(not *my* idea – which is of course the traditional one).' This portrait (oil 34 by 25 inches) was bought in 1933 from Arthur Tooth and Sons for £1,400 (equivalent to £44,500 in 1996) by the Art Gallery of Ontario. 'At the time of purchase we were requested to hang it as *Portrait of a Lady in Black*,' the Curator wrote, 'and not refer to the fact that it was a portrait of Lady Cynthia.' In 1968 it was reproduced as the frontispiece to Cynthia Asquith's *Diaries*.

98   In *Chiaroscuro* John reveals that Lawrence, despite his eagerness to have Cynthia Asquith portrayed disagreeably, protested that he himself was 'too ugly' to be painted. 'I met D. H. Lawrence in the flesh only once,' John wrote, and adds that Cynthia Asquith 'treated us to a box at the Opera that evening'. In fact he and Lawrence met twice, the visit to *Aida* taking place twelve days later, on 13 November – a meeting Cynthia Asquith describes in *Haply I May Remember* and Lawrence in *Aaron's Rod*.

Of John's portrait Lawrence remarked that it had achieved a certain beauty and had 'courage'. In 1929, when Lawrence's pictures were seized from the Warren Gallery and a summons issued against him, John added his name to the petition in Lawrence's support and stated that he was prepared, if it came to trial, to go into the witness box.

99   John's letters to Grant Richards are in the University of Illinois Library, Urbana.

100   John to Campbell Dodgson, 11 September 1917. Imperial War Museum, London.

101   NLW MS 218180 fol. 125.

102   Arthur Symons to Quinn, 22 November 1917.

103   Lytton Strachey to Clive Bell, 4 December 1917.

104   William Orpen to William Rothenstein, 23 February 1918.

105   John to Tonks, 21 February 1918. The Library, the University of Texas at Austin.

106   John to Lady Cynthia Asquith, 5 October 1917.

107   John to Alick Schepeler, 2 February 1918.

108   D. H. Lawrence to Cynthia Asquith, 2 November 1917. *The Letters of D. H. Lawrence* Volume III *1916–21* (ed. James T. Boulton and Andrew Robertson 1984), p. 176.

109   John to Evan Morgan, 27 October (1915).

110   Augustus to Dorelia n.d.

111   Augustus to Dorelia n.d.

112   *The Collected Letters of Katherine Mansfield* Volume I *1903–7* (ed. Vincent O'Sullivan and Margaret Scott 1984), pp. 316–17.

113   From the Dorothy Brett Papers, Department of English, University of Cincinnati, Ohio.

114   John to Quinn, 13 December 1918.

115   John to Evan Morgan, 1 March 1918.

116   John to Arthur Symons, 22 February 1918.

117   *Blasting and Bombardiering. An Autobiography 1914–26* (1927), p. 198.

118   Augustus to Dorelia, 3 February 1918.

119   'Lord Beaverbrook Entertains' was intended to occupy pages 79–81 of *Finishing Touches* but, for reasons of libel, was dropped at proof stage and the chapter 'Gwendolen John' was substituted. This was done by Daniel George, of Jonathan Cape, after John's death. It was subsequently published in the amalgamated *Autobiography* (1975), pp. 369–71.

120   Augustus to Dorelia n.d. (February–March 1918). NLW MS 22778D fols. 6–9.

121   John to Gogarty, 24 July 1918. This correspondence is at Bucknell University.

122   John to Cynthia Asquith, (April) 1918.

123   Augustus to Gwen John, 18 November 1918. NLW MS 22305D fols. 122–4.

124   *The Times*, 4 January 1919, 'War Story in Pictures – Canadian Exhibition at the Royal Academy'.

John Singer Sargent was less impressed. 'I have just come from the Canadian Exhibition, where there is a hideous post-impressionist picture, of which mine ['Gassed'] cannot be accused of being a crib,' he wrote to Evan Charteris. 'Augustus John has a canvas forty feet long done in his free and script style, but without beauty of composition. I was afraid I should be depressed by seeing something in it that would make me feel that my picture is conventional, academic and boring – whereas.' But William Rothenstein thought it 'superb'. See his *Men and Memories* Volume II p. 350.

125 P. G. Konody 'The Canadian War Memorials' *Colour* (September 1918). See also P. G. Konody *Art and War* (1919). John's decoration, eventually called 'The Canadians opposite Lens', is now in the National Gallery of Canada, Ottawa, together with four compositional studies for the picture, numerous solid drawings of soldiers, and some oils done in thick juicy textures.

126 John to Cynthia Asquith, 24 July (1919).

127 'My dear Comrade,' Beaverbrook wrote to John on 26 August 1959, '. . . I was quite willing to build a Gallery in Ottawa but the Canadians did not have a suitable site and also there seemed little enthusiasm for the project.

'Now there is a beautiful Art Gallery by the River in Fredericton built by me and in it you will find two John drawings and two John paintings with a third on the way.

'How I wish that big picture might be handed over to us for exhibition there.'

Among those pictures now at the Beaverbrook Gallery, New Brunswick, is a small version (oil on canvas 14'/₂ by 48 inches) of his large war picture, entitled 'Canadians at Lieven Castle'.

128 Now in the Imperial War Museum, London. Oil on canvas, 93'/₂ by 57 inches.

129 Augustus to Gwen John, 18 November 1918. NLW MS 22305D fols. 122–4.

130 Keith Clements *Henry Lamb* (1985), p. 50.

131 Richard Shone *Bloomsbury Portraits* (1993), p. 45.

132 Augustus to Dorelia n.d. (December 1917). NLW MS 22777D fols. 148–9.

133 Gwen John to Ursula Tyrwhitt, 22 November 1917. NLW MS 21468 fols. 109–10.

134 Augustus to Gwen John, 18 November 1918. NLW MS 22305D fols. 122–4.

135 Augustus to Dorelia n.d. (mid-December 1917). NLW MS 22777D fols. 148–9.

136 *Ibid.*

137 Augustus to Gwen John, 18 November 1918. NLW MS 22305D fols. 122–4.

138 Gwen John to Ursula Tyrwhitt (September–October 1918). NLW MS 21468D fols. 121–2.

139 Augustus to Gwen John, 20 August 1919, 17 September 1919. NLW MS 22305D fols. 126–7.

140 Augustus to Gwen John, 18 November 1918. NLW MS 22305D fols. 122–4.

141 Augustus to Gwen John, 23 June 1920. NLW MS 22305D fol. 133.

142 *Chiaroscuro* pp. 254–5.

143 Augustus to Gwen John, 18 November 1918. NLW MS 22305D fols. 122–4.

144 Beatrice, Lady Glenavy *To-day We Will Only Gossip* (1964), p. 111.

145 In a letter to Cynthia Asquith.

146 Lady Cynthia Asquith, *Diaries 1915–18* (1968), p. 471.

147 John to John Sampson n.d. (February 1919). NLW MS 21459E fol. 58.

148 John to Frances Stevenson, 13 February 1919. NLW MS 21570E.

149 John to Cynthia Asquith n.d.

150 *Horizon* Volume VIII No. 48 (December 1943), p. 406.

151 John to Cynthia Asquith, 1 February 1919.

152 John to Cynthia Asquith n.d.

153 His secondment for duty with the War Office was terminated on 22 September 1919; and then, without delay (on 23 September) he was struck off the strength of the Canadian War Records – though with two medals: the British War Medal and the Victory Medal.

154 John to Cynthia Asquith, 17 September 1919.

155 John to Ottoline Morrell, 14 March 1920.
156 John to Eric Sutton, 6 April 1920. Written from the hospital, 12 Beaumont Street, London W1.
157 John to Cynthia Asquith, April 1920.

CHAPTER IX: ARTIST OF THE PORTRAITS

1   In Aldous Huxley's *Point Counter Point*, for example, where he appears as the forty-seven-year-old John Bidlake 'at the height of his powers and reputation as a painter; handsome, huge, exuberant, careless; a great laugher, a great worker, a great eater, drinker, and taker of virginities'. Professor Grover Smith, editor of *The Letters of Aldous Huxley*, writes (22 February 1970) that 'it is said that John was indeed the prototype of the artist John Bidlake in *Point Counter Point*. Aldous nowhere wrote that this was the case; but he was extremely cautious and tactful where his literary models were concerned.'
    John is said to be the prototype of characters in several novels – the artist in Margery Allingham's *Death of a Ghost*; Struthers in D. H. Lawrence's *Aaron's Rod*; Tenby Jones, the 'lion of Chelsea', in Henry Williamson's *The Golden Virgin* and *The Innocent Moon*; the sculptor Owen in Aleister Crowley's *The Diary of a Drug Fiend* (Crowley noted this in his own copy of the novel); the musician Albert Sanger in Margaret Kennedy's *The Constant Nymph* (though in part this may be based on Henry Lamb). Gulley Jimson in Joyce Cary's *The Horse's Mouth*, though popularly supposed to be based on Stanley Spencer, also contains some aspects of John – in particular the urge to paint large murals. Cary and John knew each other a little in Paris, when Cary was studying art there. Cary mentions John in his letters and diary of 1909–10; and in the autumn of 1956, writing to Ruari Maclean, he suggested John might do illustrations for the Rainbird edition of *The Horse's Mouth*. Nothing came of this, though John admired the novel. Judy Johncock in Ronald Firbank's *Caprice* (for which John designed a book jacket) also owed something to him.
    Of Somerset Maugham's *The Moon and Sixpence* John Quinn wrote (9 September 1919): 'The description of the artist, red beard and all, and his words and manner and the first part of the book up to the time he leaves France, is obviously based upon a superficial study of Augustus John. The second part of the book, the Tahiti part, is obviously based upon the life of Gauguin.'
2   See 'Cat's Whiskers: Philip Oakes talks to Kathleen Hale' *Sunday Times* (19 March 1972).
3   Kathleen Hale *A Slender Reputation* (1994), pp. 85–90.
4   Christopher Wood to his mother, September 1925.
5   Vivien John 'Memories of Carrington and the John Family' *The Charleston Magazine* (Spring/Summer 1995), p. 33.
6   John to Ottoline Morrell, 29 September 1911.
7   Romilly John *The Seventh Child* (1932), pp. 165–6.
8   *Ibid.* p. 167.
9   Cecil Gray *Musical Chairs* (1948), p. 228. It was because of such behaviour that Gerald Summers addressed his 'Lines to Augustus John's Car'.

> Thou miscreant, who, forgetful of thy freight,
> Leapt from the level stretches of the road,
> Scaled the steep bank and met thy certain fate,
> O'erturned and spilled thy all too precious load ...
> Let yokels leave their furrows on hot heels,

With anxious arms to place thee on thy wheels.

10 *The Collected Poems of Oliver St John Gogarty* (1951), p. 27.
11 Romilly John *The Seventh Child* p. 167.
12 Lucy Norton to the author n.d.
13 Montgomery Hyde to the author, 17 November 1969.
14 Poppet Pol to the author, 27 February 1970.
15 Cecil Gray *Musical Chairs* pp. 228–9. Another description of this incident is given in Adrian Daintrey's autobiography *I Must Say* (1983), p. 126.
16 Romilly John *The Seventh Child* p. 168.
17 John to Quinn, 20 April 1917.
18 Augustus to Dorelia n.d.
19 Quoted in Anthony Sampson 'Scholar Gypsy. The Quest for a Family Secret' (unpublished), Chapter 2.
20 *Ibid.* Chapter 8.
21 John to Sampson, 30 December 1930 and n.d. (Liverpool University Library).
22 'Scholar Gypsy. The Quest for a Family Secret' Chapter 6.
23 Sampson to John, 21 November 1918. NLW MS 22785D fols. 21–2.
24 John to Sampson, 6 January 1919. NLW MS 21459E fol. 56, and 7 September 1919 (Liverpool University Library).
25 Sampson to John, 26 August 1919. NLW MS 22785D fols. 27–8.
26 John to Sampson, 14 July 1920, 25 January 1924. NLW MS 21459E fols. 61–3.
27 John to Sampson, 29 January 1927. NLW MS 21459E fol. 64.
28 Kathleen Hale *A Slender Reputation* p. 92.
29 John to Conger Goodyear, 4 January 1928. See Conger Goodyear *Augustus John* (privately printed).
30 John to Ada Nettleship n.d. (1928).
31 John to William Rothenstein, 29 September 1921.
32 Romilly John *The Seventh Child* p. 169. The portrait of Roy Campbell is in the collection of the Carnegie Institute, Pittsburgh.
33 John's essay on Firbank was written for Ifan Kyrle Fletcher's *Ronald Firbank* (1930); see pp. 113–15. 'In his life as in his books he left out the dull bits and concentrated on the irrelevant.'
34 See John's tribute to A. R. Orage in the *New English Weekly* (15 November 1934).
35 T. E. Lawrence to William Rothenstein, 25 April 1925.
36 Philippe Jullian *D'Annunzio* (1971), p. 182.
37 Originally called the Palazzo Venier dei Leoni, it was begun in 1749 and intended as the grandest palazzo of them all, though stopping at ceiling level when the Venier family ran out of money. Along the entrance terrace are the heads of eight stone lions which gave the palazzo its name. In 1949 it was bought by another exaggerated figure devoted to the Pekinese dog, the American art collector Peggy Guggenheim (1898–1979). The house still holds her art collection and is owned by the Solomon R. Guggenheim Foundation.
38 *Horizon* Volume VIII No. 48 (December 1943), p. 413.
39 John's half-length portrait (privately owned) was probably painted first and left unfinished. The more famous and flamboyant picture (Art Gallery of Ontario, Toronto, Canada), 'originally full-length in pyjamas', Sir Evan Charteris noted, 'was cut in half by John himself'. A laboratory examination showed a 'single, bold brushstroke traversing the full width of the canvas which marked the new lower extremity'. In 1942 John painted a final portrait of Casati (National Museum of Wales, Cardiff), a less assured handling of a

less dominating figure, seated in a chair, a black cat on her lap, done in his El Greco manner.

40   Of the two versions of this picture, one, which John presented to Casati, was bought by Lord Alington and passed into the collection of his daughter, the Hon. Mrs George Marten. The other, which is misdated April 1918, was first exhibited at the Alpine Club in London early in 1920. 'It's a most marvellous show,' T. E. Lawrence wrote to John, adding the information that 'the Birm[ingham] F[ine] A[rt] Gallery say it would be bad for the women of the town to hang ['La Marchesa Casati'] there.' The picture was acquired in 1934 by the Art Gallery of Ontario from Sir Evan Charteris, through Lord Duveen, for £1,500 (equivalent to £47,000 in 1996). In a letter (26 February 1934) to the gallery, Duveen wrote: 'I consider it to be an outstanding masterpiece of our time. It is no exaggeration to say this will live forever, which is true of very few pictures of modern times. You have bought a masterpiece for practically nothing ... Such painting of the head, for instance, I have never seen surpassed by any artist, and you can safely place it for comparison alongside the great Velasquez, Giorgione or even Titian! That is what I think about this picture.' In 1987 it was voted the most popular painting in the gallery.

41   This portrait is in the National Museum of Wales.

42   John Pearson *The Life of Ian Fleming* (1966), p. 13.

43   *Ibid.* p. 15.

44   Fergus Fleming *Amaryllis Fleming* (1993), p. 20.

45   Chiquita to the author n.d.

46   Chiquita to the author n.d.

47   Mrs Val Fleming to Seymour Leslie, 16 May 1923.

48   Fergus Fleming *Amaryllis Fleming* p. 119.

49   John to Viva King n.d.

50   William Rothenstein *Since Fifty: Men and Memories* Volume III *1922–38* (1939), p. 19.

51   John to William Rothenstein, 6 May 1929.

52   The picture (73$^1/_2$ by 65 inches) now belongs to the Tate Gallery (4043) which also owns a charcoal study (4448).

53   Mme Suggia 'Sitting for Augustus John' *Weekly Dispatch* (8 April 1928).

54   Suggia continued: 'Directly I heard his footsteps hush and his tread lighten I strained all my powers to keep at just the correct attitude. In a picture painted like this, a portrait not only of a musician but of her instrument – more of the very spirit of the music itself – the sitter must to a great extent share in its creation. John himself is kind enough to call it "our" picture.'

55   See Michael Holroyd *Lytton Strachey* (1994 edn), pp. 435–6.

56   Gerald Moore *Am I too Loud?* (1962), pp. 108–9.

57   *Burlington Magazine* CXX 909 (December 1978), p. 869.

58   *Horizon* Volume VIII No. 36 (December 1942), p. 424. See also Michael Millgate *Thomas Hardy. A Biography* (1982), p. 552. There was a curious aftermath in which John reappeared, his identity merged with that of George Meredith, author of *Modern Love*, in a dream where Hardy found himself carrying a heavy child up a ladder to safety, while the John–Meredith chimera looked on unconcernedly. Hardy, who must have known John's prowess as a father, had no children – though always wished to have had them. See *Times Literary Supplement* (16 June 1972), p. 688.

59   In a letter to John, Florence Hardy wrote (8 February 1929): 'He [Hardy] had the greatest respect and *liking* for you not only as an artist but as a man. I can think of few people he liked so much.' NLW MS 22781D fols. 90–1. John last met Hardy at Dorchester 'during a performance of "Tess". He introduced me to the leading actress, a Miss Bugler ... whom he greatly admired. He told me her husband, a respectable butcher at Bridport, "was

quite inadequate" and pointed out that her figure was perfect if only she could be persuaded to remove her clothes'. John to Christabel McLaren (later Lady Aberconway), 5 February 1928. British Library Add. MS 52556 fol. 72.

60 See Cyril Clemens *My Chat with Thomas Hardy* (1944), Introduction by Carl J. Weber. The picture was formally presented by H. T. Riches to the Fitzwilliam Museum, Cambridge, after J. M. Barrie had refused Sydney Cockerell's petition to present it ('I don't think they ought to ask me to do these things.' See Basil Dean *Seven Ages* [1970], pp. 212–13). See also *Friends of a Lifetime: Letters to Sydney Carlyle Cockerell* (ed. Viola Meynell), p. 310. The Fitzwilliam also has a drawing of Hardy by John.

61 T. E. Lawrence to his mother, 22 November 1923. *The Letters of T. E. Lawrence* (ed. Malcolm Brown 1988), p. 250.

62 John to Hardy, 20 November 1923. Thomas Hardy Memorial Collection, Dorset County Museum, Dorchester.

63 *Chiaroscuro* pp. 148–9.

64 Andrew Boyle *Montagu Norman* (1967), pp. 218–20; see also p. 252.

65 *Horizon* Volume X No. 56 (August 1944), pp. 132–3.

66 *Ibid.* p. 132.

67 Augustus to Dorelia n.d. (1 November 1928). NLW MS 22778D fols. 121–2.

68 Lord D'Abernon Papers, British Library 48932.

69 *Ibid.* 48936.

70 Augustus to Dorelia n.d. (3 September 1928). NLW MS 22778D fols. 95–6.

71 Lord Leverhulme to A. Wilson Barrett, editor of *Colour*. Blumenfeld Papers, House of Lords Library.

72 *Daily Express* (15 October 1920). See also the editions of 8 and 9 October. Also the *Literary Digest* (27 November 1920) and *American Art News* (13 November 1920).

73 John to T. E. Lawrence n.d. NLW MS 22775C fol. 58.

74 Edward Morris *Lord Leverhulme* 'Painting and Sculpture' (Royal Academy of Arts, 1980). See also Nigel Nicolson *Lord of the Isles* (1960), p. 11, and W. P. Jolly *Lord Leverhulme* (1976), pp. 190–6.

75 *Chiaroscuro* pp. 150–1. See also *Horizon* Volume X No. 56 (August 1944), pp. 134–5.

76 *Ibid.*

77 Lord Conway of Allington to John from the Imperial War Museum, 5 May 1935. NLW MS 22779E fol. 173.

78 *Sunday Dispatch* (28 September 1930). See also *News Chronicle* (29 September 1930); *Daily Mail* (29 September 1930), and *The Scotsman* (30 September 1930).

79 *Chiaroscuro* p. 147. See also *Horizon* Volume X No. 56 (August 1944), p. 131.

80 Tallulah Bankhead *Tallulah, My Autobiography* (1952), p. 156.

81 *Ibid.* p. 154.

82 See Lee Israel *Miss Tallulah Bankhead* (1972), p. 127. Also Brendan Gill's *Tallulah* (1973), in which a letter and photograph of John are reproduced on p. 130, and a drawing on p. 131. After Tallulah Bankhead's death, both her John pictures were sold at the Parke-Bernet Galleries, New York. Her own portrait, appraised at $15,000, was sold for $19,500 and is now in the National Gallery in Washington, DC. The portrait of Gerald du Maurier, appraised between $9,000 and $12,000, fetched only $5,000 and later passed into the collection of Gerald du Maurier's daughter, Jeanne du Maurier.

83 T. E. Lawrence to John, 19 April 1930. NLW MS 22783D fol. 12.

84 Interview on *Face to Face*, BBC Television, 15 May 1960.

85 John to Maud Cazalet, 3 March 1939.

86 John to Kassie, 23 November 1939. NLW MS 21570E.

87   John to Maud Cazalet, 23 September 1939.
88   Letter from A. Penn, the Queen's Private Secretary, to John, 1 November 1939. Clarence House.
89   John to HM Queen Elizabeth, 20 January 1940.
90   John to Gerald Kelly, 7 April 1954. Royal Academy.
91   HM Queen Elizabeth to John, 16 October 1942. NLW MS 22780E fols. 73–4.
92   HM Queen Elizabeth to John, 2 December 1948. NLW MS 22780E fols. 75–6.
93   Augustus to Caspar John, 30 July 1960. NLW MS 22775C fol. 45.
94   HM Queen Elizabeth the Queen Mother to John, 19 July 1961 from Clarence House. NLW MS 22780E fols. 77–8.
95   'Mr Augustus John and the Royal Academy' *The Times* (31 March 1920).
96   Augustus to Gwen John, May 1920. NLW MS 22305D fols. 130–2.
97   *Horizon* Volume X No. 56 (August 1944), p. 146.
      In a letter to his mother, Christopher Wood wrote (22 May 1922): 'Augustus John has been admitted to the Academy this year. They wouldn't have him before. I don't think he takes this as an honour in the least, as it doesn't matter much to him whether he is an A.R.A. or not. He is unquestionably the greatest painter in England to-day and if he hadn't drunk so much would have been greater than Leonardo da Vinci or Michelangelo.'
98   Edwin William John to Gwen John, 1 May 1920. NLW MS 22306D fols. 28–9.
99   John to Sean O'Casey n.d. (1928–9). There are ten letters from John to O'Casey (1926–52) at the National Library of Wales. NLW MS 21980C.
100 John to Ursula Tyrwhitt, 7 April 1958. NLW MS 19645C.
101 John to Bapsy Pavry, 8 October 1948. NLW MS 21622D.
102 T. E. Lawrence to John, 9 April 1930. NLW MS 22783D fol. 11.
103 Dorelia to Edwin John, 3 May 1938. NLW MS 22313D fols. 8–9.
104 John to Laura Knight, 9 April 1938. In another letter to Laura Knight (3 May 1938. NLW MS 21570E) John wrote: 'Although I did so little directly to affect the general policy of the Academy, always feeling somewhat ill-at-ease within those sacred precincts, my views as to a more liberal though *not* less critical an attitude to outside activities must have been well known and, I felt sometimes, even regarded with grave suspicion . . . The President, I know, had the courage to advocate a more enlightened attitude towards modern painting & I can assure you it was a particularly painful experience for me to take so violent a step . . . What you say is quite true of the necessarily slow & belated movement towards reform in a body like the R.A. The fact is it will always be too slow . . .'
105 John to Philip Connard, 18 January 1944.
106 Augustus to Edwin John, 5 July 1944. NLW MS 22312C fol. 52.
107 See *Daily Graphic* (14 June 1924).
108 *Christian Science Monitor*, Boston (17 December 1923); *Statesman*, Calcutta (12 October 1924).
109 See, for example, *Colour* (November–December 1923 and January 1924).
110 Eugene Goossens 'Culture in Music' *Daily Express* (19 July 1924).
111 *The Economist* (15 March 1924), p. 592.
112 *Manchester Guardian Weekly* (3 October 1924).
113 John to Mitchell Kennerley, 22 November 1926. New York Public Library.
114 Knewstub to John from King's Nursing Home, 22 December 1922. NLW MS 22782D fol. 167.
115 Quoted in Richard Shone *Augustus John* (1979), p. 10.
116 John to J. B. Manson, 2 July 1927.
117 John to J. B. Manson, 4 July 1927.
118 John to Wyndham Lewis, 9 December 1927.

119 Augustus to Dorelia n.d.
120 Poppet Pol to the author, March 1970.
121 *Ibid.*
122 John to Mitchell Kennerley, 22 November 1926.
123 John to Mitchell Kennerley, 22 November 1922.
124 John to Viva Booth, 14 May 1922.
125 Augustus to Dorelia, 13 May 1922. NLW 22778D fols. 31–2.
126 *Horizon* Volume VII No. 37 (January 1943), p. 60. Cf. *Chiaroscuro* p. 181.
127 Augustus to Dorelia, 13 June 1922. NLW MS 22778D fol. 35.
128 *Horizon* Volume VII No. 37 (January 1943), pp. 63–4.
129 John to Ottoline Morrell, 1 February 1922.
130 Augustus to Dorelia n.d. (June 1924). NLW MS 22778D fol. 55.
131 Sir Compton Mackenzie *My Life and Times* Octave 6 (1963–71), pp. 39–40, and Ulick O'Connor *Oliver St John Gogarty* (1964), p. 212. But for an amended version of this story see Mark Amory *Lord Dunsany: A Biography* (1972).
132 Augustus to Dorelia n.d. (April 1925). NLW MS 22778D fol. 68.
133 *Horizon* Volume X No. 56 (August 1944), p. 129.
134 Lord D'Abernon's diary, *An Ambassador of Peace* Volume III *The Years of Recovery January 1924–October 1926* (1930), p. 15.
135 *Ibid.* p. 16.
136 Augustus to Dorelia n.d. (April 1925). NLW MS 22778D fol. 68.
     'The sittings for this portrait took place mostly at 3 o'cl. p.m. and already at that time I have asked Sir Augustus to put below the portrait: The German Minister for Foreign Affairs at 3 o'cl in the afternoon, for I don't think that I am really so sleepy and broken down as I am represented on this picture.' Stresemann to Dr Ruppel, 12 June 1926. The portrait of Stresemann is now in the Albright-Knox Art Gallery, Buffalo, NY.
137 Lord D'Abernon *An Ambassador of Peace* Volume III p. 152.
138 Publisher, and director of the Anderson Gallery, 489 Park Avenue, New York.
139 *Horizon* Volume XI No. 64 (April 1945), p. 242.
140 Romilly John *The Seventh Child* p. 218.
141 *Chiaroscuro* p. 190.
142 *Horizon* Volume XI No. 64 (April 1945), p. 244.
143 *Ibid.* p. 244.
144 John to Oliver St Gogarty, 22 May 1925. The two girls, Cleves and Pita, were the daughters of Countess Stead.
145 Richard Shone *Augustus John* p. 10.
146 Augustus to Dorelia n.d. (April 1923). NLW MS 22778D fols. 39–40. But he came away 'feeling considerably older & less wise than before, and certainly not much richer,' he told Christabel McLaren. British Library Add. MS 52556 fol. 60.
147 For a list of John's works shown at this exhibition, see Milton W. Brown *The Story of the Armory Show* (1963), pp. 253–5.
148 B. L. Reid *The Man from New York* (1968), p. 152.
149 *Horizon* Volume X No. 56 (August 1944), p. 141.
150 *Chiaroscuro* p. 160.
151 Conger Goodyear *Augustus John* p. 29.
152 Augustus to Dorelia n.d. (April 1923). NLW MS 22778D fols. 41–2.
153 Conger Goodyear *op. cit.* p. 29.
154 Augustus to Dorelia, 17 April 1923. NLW MS 22778D fol. 43.
155 *Horizon* Volume X No. 56 (August 1944), pp. 141–2.
156 See, for example, his letter of 16 February 1923 to Homer Saint Gaudens (American Archives of Art). Most of the articles written about him show

little evidence of his co-operation – see 'A Much-Talked of Painter' *New York Times Magazine* (24 June 1923).

157 Augustus to Dorelia, 17 April 1923. NLW MS 22778D fol. 43.
158 *Horizon* Volume XII No. 72 (December 1945), p. 418.
159 *Art News*, New York (16 June 1923), pp. 1, 4.
160 *Ibid*. p. 4.
161 Jeanne Foster to Gwen John, 14 August 1924. NLW MS 22305D fol. 66.
162 Mitchell Kennerley to John, 13 August 1924. NLW MS 22782D fols. 151–2.
163 Introduction by E. J. Rousuck to Catalogue for 'Augustus John', Scott & Fowles, 21 March–12 April 1949: 'an electric event which produced not only a new group of paintings, but countless anecdotes, legends, friendships that enriched the great saga of John's career.'
164 Jeanne Foster to Gwen John n.d. (April 1924). NLW MS 22305D fol. 63.
165 Homer Saint Gaudens to Martin Birnbaum, 23 June 1924. American Archives of Art.
166 Now in the National Gallery, Washington, DC.
167 John to Mitchell Kennerley n.d.
168 John to Christabel Aberconway, 29 September 1928. This correspondence is in the British Library. See also the correspondence with Nina Hamnett at the University of Texas.
169 *Horizon* Volume XII No. 72 (December 1945), pp. 419–20.
170 Augustus to Gwen John, May 1920. NLW MS 22305D fols. 130–2.

CHAPTER X: THE WAY THEY LIVED THEN

1 Nicolette Devas *Two Flamboyant Fathers* (1966), p. 65.
2 John to Christabel Aberconway. British Library Add. MS 52556.
3 Cecil Beaton *The Glass of Fashion* (1954), p. 156.
4 For a full analysis of this studio, which was designed by Christopher Nicholson, see *Architectural Review* Volume LXXVII (February 1935), pp. 65–8.
5 Cecil Beaton *The Glass of Fashion* p. 158.
6 Nicolette Devas *Two Flamboyant Fathers* p. 66.
7 Adrian Daintrey *I Must Say* (1963), p. 75.
8 BBC Home Service, 8 November 1963.
9 Dorelia to Lytton Strachey, 4 December 1918.
10 Henry Lamb's letters to Carrington are in the University of Texas Library, Austin, Texas.
11 Anthony Powell *Journals 1982–1986* (1995), pp. 115–16, entry for 30 June 1984.
12 Keith Clements *Henry Lamb. The Artist and his Friends* (1985), p. 57.
13 Lamb to Carrington n.d.
14 Keith Clements *Henry Lamb* p. 60.
15 Diana Mosley to the author, 5 January 1970.
16 Cecil Gray *Musical Chairs* (1948), p. 278.
17 William Rothenstein to John, 25 March 1907. NLW MS 22784D fols. 135–6.
18 Rupert Hart-Davis *Hugh Walpole: A Biography* (1952), p. 272. John's portrait of Walpole (Fitzwilliam Museum, Cambridge) is reproduced opposite this page, and a chalk drawing as frontispiece.
19 John to Christabel Aberconway, 3 November 1928. See also Christabel Aberconway *A Wiser Woman? A Book of Memories* (1966).
20 John to Ottoline Morrell n.d.
21 Leonard Woolf *An Autobiography* Volume 2 *1911–1969* (1980 edn), pp. 114, 128. See also Volume I p. 64.

22 Lady Ottoline Morrell to Augustus John, 31 March 1930, 1 April 1930, from Gower Street. NLW MS 22783D fols. 162–5.
23 John to Ottoline Morrell n.d.
24 Eve Fleming to John, 8 April 1930. NLW MS 22780E fols. 95–6.
25 John to Ottoline Morrell n.d.
26 Sandra Jobson Darroch *Ottoline. The Life of Lady Ottoline Morrell* (1975), p. 273.
27 Miranda Seymour *Ottoline Morrell. Life on the Grand Scale* (1992), p. 386.
28 Augustus to Dorelia, 16 April 1930. NLW MS 22778D fol. 133.
29 Eve Fleming to John, 8 April 1930. NLW MS 22780E fols. 95–6.
30 John to Ottoline Morrell, 20 July 1932.
31 John to Tallulah Bankhead, 12 May 1930.
32 T. E. Lawrence to G. W. M. Dunn, 9 November 1932. *The Letters of T. E. Lawrence* (ed. David Garnett 1938), p. 752.
33 John to Al Wright, 13 August 1946. *Time* magazine 'morgue' (8 June 1948).
34 Conger Goodyear *Augustus John* (privately printed), p. 35.
35 John to Viva King n.d.
36 W. B. Yeats 'Pages from a Diary Written in Nineteen Hundred and Thirty'. The Cuala Press (September 1944).
37 W. B. Yeats to Lady Gregory, 25 May 1930, from via Americhe, Rapallo.
38 W. B. Yeats to George Yeats n.d. (*c.* 25 July 1930).
39 W. B. Yeats to George Yeats (27 July 1930).
40 W. B. Yeats to George Yeats, 3 August 1930. This big picture, which Yeats used as frontispiece for his philosophical works *A Vision*, is at Glasgow City Art Gallery. 'John has done a fine portrait – a large oil. I am sitting on a chair in the open air with my legs in a fur-bag,' Yeats wrote to Lady Gregory (30 July 1930). 'There is also an amusing smaller portrait but John no longer likes it so it may remain unfinished.'
41 *Horizon* Volume IV No. 22 (October 1941), p. 291. For a variant description see *Chiaroscuro* p. 101.
42 *Horizon* Volume IV No. 22 (October 1941), p. 291.
43 Oliver St John Gogarty *It Isn't This Time of Year at All* (1954), p. 242.
44 Hope Scott to her mother n.d.
45 Hope Scott to the author, 29 November 1968.
46 *Horizon* Volume XII No. 72 (December 1945), p. 428.
47 *Courage. The Story of Sir James Dunn* pp. 247–8. See also *The Diaries of Sir Robert Bruce Lockhart 1915–38* (ed. Kenneth Young 1973), 25 January 1931, p. 149.
48 James Joyce to John, March 1933, from 42 rue Galilei, Paris. NLW MS 22782D fols. 132–3.
49 *Daily Telegraph* (1 December 1932).
50 *Ibid.* (20 December 1932).
51 Vivien White to the author, June 1973.
52 John to Bapsy Pavry, 1 December 1933. NLW MS 21622D.
53 *Horizon* Volume XIII No. 73 (January 1946), pp. 51–2.
54 John to Casati n.d.
55 John to Mavis de Vere Cole n.d. (January 1937).
56 *Chiaroscuro* pp. 264–74.
57 John to Mavis de Vere Cole, 22 February 1937.
58 *New Statesman and Nation* (4 June 1938), pp. 952–3.
59 *Spectator* (27 May 1938), p. 96.
60 Richard Shone *Augustus John* (1979) p. 3.
61 *Listener* (25 May 1938), pp. 1105–7.
62 'History of the Largest Independent Society in England' *Blast* No. 2 (July 1915), pp. 80–1.
63 *The Letters of Wyndham Lewis* (ed. W. K. Rose 1963), pp. 70–2.

64 Wyndham Lewis *Rude Assignment* (1950), p. 128.
65 Wyndham Lewis *The Demon of Progress in the Arts* (1954), p. 3.
66 *Listener* (13 July 1972).
67 NLW MS 22780E fol. 139, 22787D fol. 43, 22780E fol. 100.
68 O'Casey to Gabriel Fallon, 13 May 1926. Quoted in Garry O'Connor *Sean O'Casey. A Life* (1988), pp. 213–14.
69 Garry O'Connor *Sean O'Casey* p. 213.
70 The other portrait is in the Metropolitan Museum of Art, New York. The one which he gave to O'Casey as a wedding present is now at the Abbey Theatre, Dublin. 'Blue-green coat, silver-grey sweater, with a gayer note given by an orange handkerchief flowing from the breast-pocket of the coat,' O'Casey described it; 'the face set determinedly in contemplation of things seen and heard, the body shrinking back right to the back of the chair, as if to get further away to see and hear more clearly; a sensitive and severe countenance with incisive lines of humour braiding the tightly-closed mouth.' 'He [John] is evidently intensely interested in what he sees behind what is understood as my face,' Sean O'Casey wrote on 16 May 1926.
71 Sean O'Casey to John, 15 January 1929. NLW MS 22784D fol. 12.
72 Eileen O'Casey *Sean*, edited with an Introduction by J. C. Trewin (Pan edition 1973), p. 77.
73 Raymond Massey *A Hundred Different Lives* (1979), pp. 90–91.
74 The set proved too heavy for the scene-shifters. It was designed, like an oil painting, on canvas stretchers. 'John's scene was an exterior with a derelict church, with a fine stained glass window,' Alick Johnstone, the scene painter, remembered. 'He designed this originally on cartridge paper . . . and I suggested he should do it on a linen panel in thin oils or aniline dye; which he did, and it was an enormous success, and, as it was in scale to the scene, was inserted in the church construction.' *Apollo* (October 1965), p. 324 n.3.
75 Shaw to John, 31 October 1929.
76 Malcolm Easton 'The Boy David: Augustus John and Ernst Stern' *Apollo* (October 1965) pp. 318–25.
77 *Finishing Touches* p. 89.
78 Lady Cynthia Asquith *Portrait of Barrie* (1950), p. 206.
79 John to John Davenport n.d.
80 Later renamed 'Mas de la Fé', it was taken over by Alphonse Daudet's granddaughter-in-law.
81 *Chiaroscuro* p. 257.
82 Marie Mauron to the author, 1969.
83 Vivien John to Edwin John, September 1939. NLW MS 22312C fol. 123.
84 Cyril Connolly *The Modern Movement* (1965), p. 67.
85 *The Times* (12 May 1938).
86 *Horizon* Volume VIII No. 44 (August 1943), p. 136.
87 A. R. Thomson to the author n.d.
88 Cole to John, 17 July 1930. See Roderic Owen with Tristan de Vere Cole *Beautiful and Beloved* (1974), p. 43.
89 He was born in the Parish of Woodstock St Hilary: John had suggested the names Iolo Gabriel Augustus Caesar Imperator while Mavis was pregnant.
90 John to Wyndham Lewis, 15 August 1954.
91 Augustus to Dorelia n.d. (1936).
92 See Roderic Owen with Tristan de Vere Cole *Beautiful and Beloved* pp. 89–90.
93 He later attributed this procedure to a speech made by Shaw's Captain Bluntschli: '. . . I'm in the artillery; and I have the choice of weapons. If I go, I shall take a machine gun . . .' (*Arms and the Man*, Act III).
94 John to D. S. MacColl, 14 January 1945.

95 Augustus to Dorelia n.d. (September–October 1915). NLW MS 22777D fol. 93.

96 John's portrait of Brigit is at the Southampton Art Gallery.

97 Nicolette Devas *Two Flamboyant Fathers* pp. 269–70.

98 Dorelia to Augustus n.d. (1938), from Mas de Galeron. NLW MS 22783D fols. 122–3.

99 Paul Ferris *Caitlin. The Life of Caitlin Thomas* (1993), p. 34.

100 This portrait, painted in 1937, is at the Glyn Vivian Art Gallery, Swansea. The National Museum of Wales, Cardiff, has four nude drawings of Caitlin, two unfinished oils, and a portrait of her wearing a striped cardigan dated *c*.1930.

101 Paul Ferris to National Museum of Wales, 27 June 1992.

102 Kathleen Hale *A Slender Reputation* (1994), p. 91.

103 *The Diaries of Sylvia Townsend Warner* (ed. Claire Harman 1994), p. 37.

104 Caitlin Thomas to the author, 16 September 1968. 'It was merely a question of a brief dutiful performance for him to keep up his reputation as a Casanova ogre,' Mrs Thomas hazarded. '. . . I may add that this lofty favour was not reserved for me alone, but one and all of his models, of whatever age and social category, suffered the identical treatment. I hope I have been able to add a drop of at least truthful spice, no doubt unprintable, to enliven your cleaned-up eminently respectable book, plodding in the heavy-going dark (God help you and your public).'

105 *Finishing Touches* p. 114.

106 *Aquarius*, ITV, 3 March 1972.

107 In an interview with the author.

108 Augustus to Vivien John, August 1938. In a letter to Dorelia (NLW MS 22778D fol. 138) he described Dylan and Caitlin as 'living in frightful squalor and hideousness . . . The Dylans are impossible to stand for long.'

109 *Listener* (5 October 1972), pp. 433–4.

110 Dylan Thomas to Henry Treece, 1 September 1938. *Dylan Thomas. The Collected Letters* (ed. Paul Ferris 1985), p. 324.

111 *Finishing Touches* p. 111.

112 *Museum Piece, or The Education of an Iconographer* (1963), p. 95.

113 John to Amaryllis Fleming, 27 November 1953.

114 Amaryllis Fleming to the author, 25 July 1969.

115 Ralph Partridge to Gerald Brenan, 22 July 1929. *Best of Friends. The Brenan–Partridge Letters* (ed. Xan Fielding 1986), p. 84.

116 Vivien John 'Memories of Carrington' *The Charleston Magazine* (Spring/Summer 1995), p. 35 col. 1.

117 Augustus to Dorelia n.d. (August 1916). NLW MS 22777D fol. 130.

118 These were John's usual tactics. In a letter to Frances Hughes (29 March 1939), Dylan Thomas wrote that Augustus is 'out and more or less about now, although Mavis's wedding put him back a few beds. We saw the newsfilm of the departure from the registry office, and Augustus, blowing clouds of smoke, hopped in the first car before bride and groom could get in . . .'

119 'I hope it will be their last visit,' he wrote after Poppet and Bergne had gone to Fryern for the first time. But he made an exception of Wilhelm Pol, the Dutch painter who became Poppet's third husband. 'This time I favour the match,' he told Caspar (1 March 1952). '. . . Poppet, a thorough bourgeoise, provided there is plenty to laugh at, reasonable access to food and drink, and of course the indispensable privileges of matrimony, will stay put.' NLW MS 22775C fol. 5. To others he exclaimed, with an oblique slap at Edwin, Robin, Vivien and perhaps himself: 'Thank God there is a painter in the family at last!' In David Herbert's autobiography, *Second Son* (1973),

p. 61, Poppet is described as 'extremely attractive, she had almost as many boy friends as her father had mistresses.'

120 Augustus to Caspar John, 13 November 1956. NLW MS 22775C fol. 26.

121 Augustus was pleased to accept compliments from others on behalf of Romilly John's book. 'It has been very well reviewed but badly advertised,' he wrote to Charles Reilly (7 November 1932), 'so do recommend it if you get a chance.'

122 Romilly John to Augustus n.d. (1936). NLW MS 22782D fols. 106–7.

123 Romilly John to Augustus n.d. (1936). NLW MS 22782D fol. 108.

124 Augustus to Edwin John n.d. (1940). NLW MS 22312C fols. 19–20.

125 Robin to the author, 13 January 1969. See also *Horizon* Volume VII No. 37 (January 1943), pp. 65–6: 'Robin displayed also, or rather attempted to conceal, a remarkable talent for drawing; but in the course of his studies lost himself in abstraction, which he pushed finally to the point of invisibility. Thus his later efforts, hung on the walls of his studio, presented no clear image to the physical eye. Refinement carried to such a pitch ceases to amuse. Art, like life, perpetuates itself by contact.'

126 George Popoff to John, 5 February 1935. NLW MS 22784D fol. 62.

127 Robin John to the author, 13 January 1969.

128 John to Villiers Bergne, 15 February 1945. NLW MS 22022C.

129 Tom Burns *The Use of Memory* (1993), p. 17.

130 Henry John to Augustus n.d. (May–June 1926). NLW MS 22782D fol. 39.

131 Augustus to Gwen John, 18 November 1918. NLW MS 22305 fols. 122–4.

132 Martin Cyril D'Arcy *Laughter and the Love of Friends* (ed. William S. Abell 1991), pp. 36–41.

133 Henry John to Augustus, 11 March 1926, from 67 via San Niccolò da Tolentino, Rome.

134 Henry John to Augustus n.d. (*c.* March 1926). NLW MS 22782D fol. 37.

135 See Selina Hastings *Evelyn Waugh. A Biography* (1994) p. 225.

136 Martin Cyril D'Arcy *Laughter and the Love of Friends* pp. 41–2.

137 Henry John to Augustus n.d. (April–June 1924). NLW MS 22782D fols. 35–6.

138 Henry John to Augustus n.d. (July 1926), from Chalet des Mélèzes. NLW MS 22782D fols. 43–4.

139 Tom Burns to Gwen John, 6 November 1927. NLW MS 22305D fol. 15.

140 Henry John to Augustus, 26 July 1926. NLW MS 22782D fol. 44.

141 More successful was John's portrait of Martin D'Arcy painted in 1939, which is at Campion Hall, Oxford. 'Genuinely alive and as enigmatic as he really is,' D'Arcy's friend Father B. C. Gurrin called it, though 'it doesn't seem to me to be very much like me', Father D'Arcy wrote.

142 Henry John to Augustus n.d. (*c.* 1932). NLW MS 22782D fols. 50–4.

143 James Strachey Barnes to John n.d. (*c.* 1935). NLW MS 22779E fols. 50–2.

144 Robert McAlmon and Kay Boyle *Being Geniuses Together* (revised edn 1970), p. 26.

145 John to Father D'Arcy n.d.

146 *Chiaroscuro* p. 212.

147 Julia Strachey's diary, 3 November 1934. This version was given to me by Julia Strachey. But for a slightly different version, see *Julia. A Portrait by Herself and Frances Partridge* (1983), p. 143.

148 Harold Acton *Memoirs of an Aesthete* (1948), p. 146.

149 'The Private Diaries of Evelyn Waugh' (ed. Michael Davie), *Observer* magazine (6 May 1973), p. 28.

150 John to Michel Salaman, 4 September 1935. NLW MS 14928D fol. 111.

151 *Chiaroscuro* p. 213.

152 *Daily Mail* (24 June 1935).

153 Tom Burns *The Use of Memory* p. 21.

154 The Rev. Canon K. J. Woolcombe to the author, 24 December 1968.
155 Father D'Arcy to John, 28 June 1935. NLW MS 22780E fol. 5.
156 Augustus to Dorelia n.d.
157 In an unrecorded BBC script.
158 'I'm a miserable old crock now, unlikely to live to be undertaker to any more pals, but quite content to toddle about a shamelessly unkempt garden and enjoy the sound of my living waterfall and the ever changing view of Wild Boar Fell.' Scott Macfie to John, 8 October 1932, from Shaws, Lunds, Sedburgh, Yorkshire.
159 The words of this eulogium are given in Dora E. Yates *My Gypsy Days* (1953), pp. 119–20; also, in a slightly different form, in the *Daily Mirror* (23 November 1931).
160 Dora Yates *My Gypsy Days* p. 120.
161 *Ibid.* p. 121.
162 Dora Yates to John, 22 November 1931, from Class Office Libraries, The University, Liverpool. NLW MS 22782D fols. 51–2.
163 John to Dora Yates, 6 December 1936.
164 *Chiaroscuro* pp. 89–90.
165 Augustus to Gwen John, 23 June 1920. NLW MS 22305D fol. 133.
166 See Cecily Langdale *Gwen John* (1987), p. 220. Letter written in 1919.
167 *Ibid.*
168 Gwen John to Augustus, 1 and 8 September 1924. NLW MS 22782D fols. 31–2.
169 Dorelia to Gwen John, May 1927. NLW MS 22308C fol. 21.
170 Gwen John to Ursula Tyrwhitt, 23 July 1927. NLW MS 21468D fols. 160–1.
171 Augustus to Gwen John, 29 December 1924. NLW MS 22305D fol. 136.
172 Gwen John to Augustus, 22 March (1925). NLW MS 22782D fol. 33.
173 Gwen John to Augustus n.d. (1925). NLW MS 22782D fol. 34.
174 Gwen John to Ursula Tyrwhitt, 10 November 1925. NLW MS 21468D fols. 146–7. See also fols. 148–9.
175 Susan Chitty *Gwen John* (1981), p. 173.
176 Obituary of Gwen Smith, *The Times* (1 February 1958).
177 Alison Thomas *Portraits of Women* (1994), p. 128.
178 Gwen John to Ursula Tyrwhitt, 23 July 1927. NLW MS 21468D fols. 160–1.
179 *Ibid.*
180 Susan Chitty *Gwen John* p. 179.
181 Gwen John to Ursula Tyrwhitt, 15 September 1927. NLW MS 21468D fol. 164.
182 Dorelia to Gwen John, 28 June 1928, 14 September 1928. NLW MS 22308C fols. 29–30.
183 Dorelia to Gwen John, 11 January 1933. NLW MS 22308C fols. 47–8.
184 Augustus to Gwen John, 16 April 1939. NLW MS 22305C fol. 147.
185 Augustus to Gwen John, 21 June 1928. NLW MS 22305C fols. 144–5.
186 Dorelia to Gwen John, 28 June 1928. NLW MS 22308C fol. 29.
187 Augustus to Gwen John n.d. (October–November 1930). NLW MS 22395C fol. 146.
188 Dorelia to Gwen John, 28 June 1928, 14 September 1928, 22 July 1929, 15 December 1930, n.d. (c. 1932). NLW MS 22308C fols. 29–46.
189 Dorelia to Gwen John, 11 January 1933. NLW MS 22308C fol. 47.
190 Dorelia to Gwen John, 30 May 1939. NLW MS 22308C fol. 55. See also letter of 15 June 1939, fol. 56.
191 *Chiaroscuro* p. 256.

CHAPTER XI: THINGS PAST

1   John to Mrs W. M. Cazalet, September 1939.
2   John to Herbert Barker, 4 February 1938.
3   Augustus to Edwin John, 22 August 1944. NLW MS 22312C fol. 53.
4   *Daily Telegraph* (5 May 1948).
5   *Listener* (13 May 1948), p. 794.
6   Augustus to Caspar John, 14 April 1961. NLW MS 22775C fol. 50.
7   John to Conger Goodyear, 10 January 1948.
8   John to Conger Goodyear, 8 August 1949.
9   John to T. W. Earp, 6 June 1944.
10 John to Mrs W. M. Cazalet, 10 May 1943.
11 John to Kit Adeane n.d.
12 'Augustus John', unpublished monograph by Alan Moorehead.
13 Tom Pocock *Alan Moorehead* (1990), pp. 181–2.
14 *Sunday Times* (22 July 1973), p. 34.
15 John to Mavis Wheeler n.d.
16 Shaw to John, 26 February 1944. See Alan Moorehead *Montgomery. A Biography* (1967), pp. 187–90. See also *Bernard Shaw Collected Letters* Volume 4 *1926–1950* (ed. Dan H. Laurence 1988), pp. 700–1.
17 Augustus to Edwin John, 23 February 1944 and 22 August 1944. NLW MS 22312C fols. 51 and 53.
18 *Bernard Shaw Collected Letters* Volume 4 *1926–50* (ed. Dan H. Laurence 1988) pp. 700–1.
19 Augustus to Simon John, 15 April 1944.
20 John to Bernard Shaw, 29 February 1944. British Library Add. MS 50539 fol. 38.
21 Augustus to Simon John, 14 September 1944.
22 The painting is reproduced in Alan Moorehead's *Montgomery. A Biography*, and a drawing, which was exhibited in May 1944 at the Royal Academy, is reproduced in Nigel Hamilton's *Monty. Master of the Battlefield* (1983). Montgomery, Hamilton wrote, 'never saw this fine crayon sketch – perhaps the only portrait ever to capture the ascetic missionary behind the soldier's mask' (see facing p. 544). There is a conversation piece drawn by James Gunn showing John painting Montgomery in the presence of Bernard Shaw. See Brian Montgomery *Monty. A Life in Photographs* (1985), p. 102. John's oil portrait belongs to Glasgow University.
23 Among John's papers was a letter from Oscar Kokoschka thanking him for his attempts to help him escape from Prague.
24 John to Leonard Russell, 31 September 1953. NLW MS 21570E.
25 John to Dora Yates, 28 July 1936.
26 Dora Yates to John, 25 November 1959. NLW MS 22787D fols. 102–3.
27 *Ibid.*
28 John to Dora Yates, 29 November 1956.
29 Dora Yates to John, 22 August 1952. NLW MS 22787D fol. 78.
30 John to Dora Yates, 13 October 1953.
31 John to Dora Yates, 30 June 1960.
32 John to Dora Yates, 13 March 1946.
33 John to Mrs W. M. Cazalet, 16 June 1941 and 26 September 1941.
34 *Chips. The Diaries of Sir Henry Channon* (ed. Robert Rhodes James 1967), p. 389.
35 Nancy Cunard *Grand Man* (1954), p. 195.
36 John to Mary Keene, 26 January 1948.
37 Augustus to Vivien John n.d.
38 John to Winifred Shute, 21 June 1942.
39 John to Winifred Shute, 18 October 1940.

40 John to Will and Alice Rothenstein, 15 June 1940.
41 Kenneth Clark *The Other Half. A Self-Portrait* (1977), p. 1.
42 *Country Life* (7 December 1940).
43 *Burlington Magazine* (December 1940), p. 28.
44 Augustus to Dorelia, 21 May 1942.
45 'I am thoroughly in sympathy with your determination to remain a commoner in spite of antique conventions. May you win the battle!' John to Anthony Wedgwood Benn, 16 March 1961.
46 John to Sir Herbert Read, 18 January 1953. This letter is in the Collections Division of the University of Victoria, British Columbia. Some of the matters in which they diverged are given in a review Read wrote in the *Burlington Magazine* (December 1940, p. 28) where he criticized John's tendency to idealize his types. 'We must say "idealize" in preference to "romanticize" because one has only to compare such drawings with the superficially similar drawings of Picasso's "blue" period to see that, while Picasso has a particular brand of romanticism (a Baudelairean romanticism), he never palliates the underlying drabness and horror. John's gypsies are too coy, and they share this quality with his religious and allegorical figures . . . "Le dessin, c'est la probité de l'art" – Mr John quotes this saying of Ingres' at the head of his catalogue, but it is a maxim with a double edge. In the sense that draughtsmanship is an index to the sensibility and skill of the artist, these drawings are a triumphant vindication; but the maxim might also mean that an artist's drawings betray his limitations – the limitation of his interests no less than the degree of his skill. John is a typical studio artist, and there is little in his work to show that he has lived through one of the most momentous epochs of history. An artist creates his own epoch, it will perhaps be said, his own world of reality; and this is true enough. But surely that world, if it is to compete in interest with the external world, must be inhabited by figures somewhat more substantial than John's appealing sylphs.'

About John's portraits, however, Read admitted 'there is no denying his superb mastery of this form . . . the pencil already prepares us for that balance out of psychological insight and formal harmony which his brush secures with such instinctive facility.'

47 'Did I tell you about August[us] John, whom I duly tackled or rather sounded, weeks ago? He said lots of publishers had been at him. One offered him £10,000 [equivalent to £308,000 in 1996] in advance for his memoirs. He said, "Oh, that's not enough: I want £20,000." They rose to £13,000.' T. E. Lawrence to Jonathan Cape (September 1932). See Michael Howard *Jonathan Cape, Publisher* (1971), p. 151.
48 John to Cecil Gray, 'Wednesday 1933'. British Library Add. MS 57785 fol. 72.
49 Alfred McIntyre of Little, Brown and Company to Jonathan Cape, 27 June 1938. The contract with Little, Brown, dated 26 July 1938, gave John an advance on royalties of $5,000 and provided for delivery of the manuscript by 1 January 1940. The Jonathan Cape contract, dated 2 May 1938, allowed John an advance of £2,000 (equivalent to £57,000 in 1996). Both advances were payable on the day of publication, and both contracts lapsed in 1940.
50 M. S. Wilde of the British and International Press.
51 Jonathan Cape to Alfred McIntyre, 24 January 1940.
52 Jonathan Cape to Alfred McIntyre, 15 August 1940.
53 February, Vol. III, No. 14, 1941, pp. 97–103; April, Vol III, No. 16, 1941, pp. 242–52; June, Vol. III, No. 18, 1941, pp. 394–402; August, Vol. IV, No. 20, 1941, pp. 121–30; October, Vol. IV, No. 22, 1941, pp. 285–92; February, Vol. V, No. 26, 1942, pp. 125–37; August, Vol. VI, No. 32, 1942, pp. 128–40; December, Vol. VI, No. 36, 1942, pp. 421–35; January, Vol. VII, No. 37, 1943, pp. 59–66; August, Vol. VIII, No. 44, 1943, pp. 136–43; December,

Vol. VIII, No. 48, 1943, pp. 405–19; August, Vol. X, No. 56, 1944, 128–46; April, Vol. XI, No. 64, 1945, pp. 242–61; December, Vol. XII, No. 72, 1945, pp. 417–30; January, Vol. XIII, No.73, 1948, pp. 49–61; October, Vol. XIV, No. 82, 1946, pp. 224–31; June, Vol. XVII, No. 102, 1948, pp. 430–41; April, Vol. XIX, No. 112, 1949, pp. 292–303.

54 John to T. W. Earp, 20 March 1947.

55 Introduction by Daniel George to *Finishing Touches*, p. 9.

56 *Ibid.* p. 11.

57 John to Daniel George, 19 October 1950.

58 John to Clare Crossley, 9 May 1952.

59 'Augustus John' by Sir Desmond MacCarthy, *Sunday Times*, 2 March 1952; 'Memories of a Great Artist' by Sacheverell Sitwell, *Spectator*, 7 March 1953, p. 302; 'Augustus John's Self-Portrait' by Henry Williamson, *John O' London*, March 1952, pp. 296–7. See also 'Self-Portrait' by Harold Nicolson, *Observer*, 2 March 1952; 'Augustus John: A Self-Portrait' by Denys Sutton, *Daily Telegraph*, 8 March 1952; *The Times*, 5 March 1952; 'Painting with a Pen', *Times Literary Supplement*, 21 March 1952. The book was also well received in the United States where it was published by Pellegrini and Cudahy. See, for example, 'Magic-Lantern Show' by Joseph Wood Krutch, *Nation*, pp. 277–8. See also Quentin Bell in the *New Statesman* (20 November 1964), p. 797.

60 *Listener* (20 March 1952), p. 476.

61 Harlech Television, 18 July 1968.

62 Julian Maclaren-Ross 'Sfumato' *The Funny Bone* (1956), pp. 25–9.

63 John to Daniel George, 11 August 1954.

64 'The piece called "The Girl with Flaming Hair" – a young woman picked up in Tottenham Court Road – might very reasonably be allowed a place in Villiers de L'Isle-Adam's "Contes Cruels",' wrote Anthony Powell in the *Daily Telegraph* (3 December 1964). For some of John's correspondence with Daniel George over *Finishing Touches* see Catalogue 158 (1981), Rendells Inc., Newton, Massachusetts.

    The first impression of *Chiaroscuro*, costing 30 shillings (£1.50), was 10,000 copies. It was published on 3 March 1952, the unsold stock being converted on 25 April 1955 to a cheap edition costing 15 shillings (75 pence) which went out of print on 4 November 1968. An edition published by the Readers Union early in 1954 of 31,792 copies was produced independently of Jonathan Cape. *Finishing Touches* was published on 12 November 1964 and cost 25 shillings (£1.25). The first impression ordered was for 3,000 copies, and a second impression of 750 copies was printed on 8 June 1965. The two volumes were amalgamated in 1975 and brought out by Cape under the title *Autobiography* in an edition of 2,000 copies costing £6.50.

65 See Cecily Langdale *Gwen John* (1987), p. 130 n. 11.

66 Gwen John to Ursula Tyrwhitt, 17 July 1930. NLW MS 21468D fol. 176.

67 Cecily Langdale *Gwen John* p. 130 n. 1.

68 Augustus to Edwin John n.d. (1 January 1940). NLW MS 22312C fol. 19.

69 Augustus to Edwin John n.d. (1 May 1940). NLW MS 22312C fols. 28–9.

70 Augustus to Edwin John, 22 January 1942. NLW MS 22312C fol. 49.

71 Augustus to Edwin John, 5 July 1944. NLW MS 22312C fol. 52.

72 Augustus to Edwin John, 22 August 1944. NLW MS 22312C fol. 53.

73 Augustus to Edwin John, 4 March 1946. NLW MS 22312C fol. 57.

74 Augustus to Edwin John, 11 September 1946. NLW MS 22312C fol. 62. Edwin John was then living in the village of Mousehole, Cornwall.

75 Augustus to Edwin John, 30 November 1946. NLW MS 22312C fol. 65.

76 Edwin John to Augustus, 24 December 1951. NLW MS 22782D fols. 20–1.

77 See NLW MS 22782D fols. 18–25, 22312C fols. 27–77.

78 Winifred Shute to Augustus John, 3 March 1956. NLW MS 22782D fol. 125.

79 Instead of a memoir Augustus reworked his Matthiesen catalogue essay as an article in *Horizon* Volume XIX No. 112 (April 1949), pp. 295–303, and this, with some revisions, appeared in *Chiaroscuro* pp. 247–56; later his *Burlington Magazine* contribution (Volume LXXXI No. 475 [October 1942]) was reprinted in *Finishing Touches* pp. 79–81.

80 *Finishing Touches* p. 81.

81 John to Pamela Grove, 25 February 1945.

82 John to Sylvia Hay, 5 June 1959.

83 Marie Mauron to the author, 1969.

84 *Chiaroscuro* p. 261. See also *Horizon* Volume XVII No. 102 (June 1948), p. 438.

85 *Chiaroscuro* p. 262.

86 *Horizon* Volume XVII No. 102 (June 1948), p. 440. In a letter to Matthew Smith (5 December 1946) he wrote: 'I thought the country as good as ever but didn't do anything with it.'

87 William Empson to the author, 6 December 1968. See also Hugh Gordon Proteus *Listener* (3 December 1964), pp. 902–3.

88 John to Cyril Connolly, 5 November 1949. McFarlin Library, University of Tulsa.

89 *Chiaroscuro* p. 264.

90 John to T. W. Earp, 20 March 1947.

91 Augustus to Edwin John, 29 November 1947. NLW MS 22312C fol. 72.

92 Augustus to David John, 22 June 1942.

93 *Socialist Leader* (18 September 1948). See also *The Collected Essays, Journalism and Letters of George Orwell* Volume 4 *In Front of Your Nose 1945–50* (1970 edn), pp. 595–6.

94 There were only two issues of the *Delphic Review*, Winter 1949 and Spring 1950. John's article 'Frontiers' occupies pages 6–11 of the first issue.

95 John to Bertrand Russell, 6 February 1961. 'Very disappointed,' he had cabled Russell. 'Had looked forward to jail.' See Caroline Moorehead *Bertrand Russell* (1992), p. 509.

96 *The Autobiography of Bertrand Russell* Volume III *1944–67* (1969), p. 118. See also p. 146.

97 'The Great Bohemian', *Time and Tide* (9 November 1961).

98 Breon O'Casey to the author, 7 September 1969.

99 Nicolette Devas *Two Flamboyant Fathers* (1966), p. 277.

100 *Stephen Spender Journals 1939–1983* (ed. John Goldsmith 1985), 1 July 1955, p. 157.

101 John to Sylvia Hay, 7 September 1956. In the collection of Professor Norman H. Pearson, Yale University, New Haven.

102 John to Cyril Clemens, December 1955.

103 John to Sylvia Hay, 7 January 1959.

104 John to Hope Scott, 3 October 1950.

105 John Rothenstein *Time's Thievish Progress* (1970), pp. 24–5.

106 Diana Mosley *A Life of Contrasts* (1977), p. 89.

107 Harlech Television, 18 July 1968.

108 John to Alan Moorehead, 31 March 1952.

109 John to John Davenport, 11 March 1956.

110 John to Joe Hone, 4 February 1956.

111 John to D. S. MacColl n.d.

112 John to Kelly, 23 July 1952, 20 May 1952, 2 July 1952, 15 March 1952; Kelly to Earp, 20 January 1954; John to Kelly, 30 September 1953; Kelly to Earp n.d. (1954); Hugo Pitman to Kelly, 12 August 1952. Royal Academy.

113 *Sunday Times* (14 March 1954).

114 Kelly to John, 10 February 1954; Kelly to Lady John Hope (Liza Maugham), 2 June 1954; Kelly to John, 28–9 June 1954; Kelly to John, 1 April 1954. Royal Academy.

115 Dorelia to Kelly n.d. (March 1954). Royal Academy.

116 John to Kelly, 16 March 1954. Royal Academy.

117 *The Times* (13 March 1954).

118 John to Hugo Pitman, 27 December 1952.

119 John to Hugo Pitman, 10 November 1954.

120 John to Dorothy Head, 16 November 1954.

121 John to Mrs W. M. Cazalet, 16 June 1941.

122 Augustus to Simon John, 14 September 1944.

123 John to Michael Ayrton, February 1961.

124 Augustus to Caspar John, 7 January 1955.

125 *Best of Friends. The Brenan–Partridge Letters* (ed. Xan Fielding 1986), p. 209.

126 Augustus to Edwin John n.d.

127 Gerald Brenan *A Personal Record* (1974), p. 356.

128 Augustus to Caspar John, 7 January 1955.

129 John to Clare Crossley, 12 January 1955.

130 John to Sylvia Hay n.d.

131 John to Matthew Smith, 22 December 1948.

132 John to Count William de Belleroche, 5 September 1956.

133 John to Matthew Smith, 5 September 1956.

134 John to Matthew Smith, 24 December 1953. In a letter to Caspar John of about the same date (NLW MS 22775C fol. 10) John wrote: 'I have been much distressed by the death of Dylan Thomas and have managed to write a note about it for a paper called *Adam* in an edition wholly devoted to the Poet.' John's essay, 'The Monogamous Bohemian', appeared in the January 1954 issue of *Adam Literary Magazine*, and was reprinted in E. W. Tedlock's *Dylan Thomas – the legend and the poet* (1960). Another essay by John, originally appearing in the *Sunday Times* (28 September 1958), was reprinted in J. M. Brinnin's *A Casebook on Dylan Thomas* (1960), and in *Finishing Touches* pp. 108–15.

135 John to Count William de Belleroche, 21 June 1956.

136 William Gaunt to the author, 16 October 1971.

137 One of Matthew Smith's portraits of John is at the Montreal Museum of Fine Art; another at the Scottish National Gallery of Modern Art; and the third, which was sold at Sotheby's on 13 May 1987, is privately owned. John's portrait of Matthew Smith is in the Tate Gallery.

138 Peter Quennell 'Augustus John' *Harper's Bazaar* (February 1952), p. 45. Photographs by Cartier-Bresson.

139 Lucy Norton to the author, 1973.

140 John to Matthew Smith, 1 July 1959.

141 BBC *Panorama*, 4 November 1957.

142 *Sunday Times* (18 January 1953).

143 John to Eric Phillips, 9 December 1952.

144 John to Joe Hone, 9 February 1956. It was purchased by a number of subscribers, headed by Hugo Pitman and Lennox Robinson, and unveiled at the Abbey Theatre, Dublin, in November 1955.

145 John to Mary Anna Marten, 31 January 1953.

146 John Rothenstein *Time's Thievish Progress* p. 15.

147 John to Joe Hone, 9 February 1956. See also *Tenby Observer and County News* (15 October 1954).

148 *Bernard Shaw. Collected Letters* Volume 4 (ed. Dan H. Laurence 1988), p. 794.

149 *Letters of John Cowper Powys to Louis Wilkinson 1935–1956* (1958), p. 336–7, 8 December 1955. The drawing is reproduced as frontispiece to this volume.

Powys reckoned John to be 'one of the 3 great men I've met in my life', the other two being Thomas Hardy and Charles Chaplin. He was particularly pleased that John had also done a portrait of his brother T. F. Powys (1933). 'So two of the Brothers Powys will be seen by the next and the next generations as the great artist saw them,' he wrote to G. Wilson Knight (14 July 1958).

150   Thornton John to Augustus, 25 June 1959. NLW MS 22782D fols. 119–20.

151   Augustus John to Winifred Shute, November 1959.

152   John to John Davenport n.d. NLW MS 21585E.

153   Augustus to Caspar John, 6 May 1960. NLW MS 22775C fols. 41–2.

154   *Tenby Observer and County News* (30 October 1959).

155   John to Tristan de Vere Cole, 5 February 1956.

156   *Maurice Collis: Diaries 1949–1969* (ed. Louise Collis 1977), p. 55, 9 September 1953. 'His face was very expressive, like an actor's. He had very great charm. Affection, intimacy, indignation, sadness flitted across his features. There was emotion of some kind showing all the time . . . not intellectual, not kind, not even very intuitive or sympathetic for others but human and greatly experienced in life. One sees very few Englishmen with such faces in the upper classes, but tramps, beggars and poets (old style) sometimes have that look.'

157   John to Sir Charles Wheeler, 11 April 1960.

158   Roderic Owen with Tristan de Vere Cole *Beautiful and Beloved* (1974), p. 225.

159   Fergus Fleming *Amaryllis Fleming* (1993), pp. 150–1. See also pp. 179–81, 199. Eve Fleming did not in fact marry Lord Winchester, who remained married to Bapsy Pavry. 'When I saw the announcement in the Times I received quite a shock,' John had written to her (23 July 1953). '. . . As the Marquess remarked to some journalist it was quick work on his part.' NLW 21622D.

160   John to Daniel George, 28 September 1952.

161   John to Alfred Hayward, 13 June 1952.

162   John to Doris Phillips, 9 December 1952.

163   Augustus to Edwin John, 30 May 1954.

164   Charles Wheeler *High Relief* (1968), p. 116.

165   Augustus to Edwin John, 1 December 1960.

166   Charles Wheeler *High Relief* p. 116.

167   John to Sir Philip Dunn, 11 February 1960.

168   John to Sir Charles Wheeler, 8 March 1960.

169   Now in the Royal Academy Library.

170   John to Sir Charles Wheeler, 4 March 1961.

171   John to Cecil Beaton n.d.

172   David John to Robin John, 20 November 1971.

173   Sven Berlin *Dromengro: Man of the Road* (1971), pp. 196–7.

174   Richard Hughes 'Last Words from Augustus' *Sunday Telegraph* (5 November 1961).

175   Anthony Powell 'The Great Bohemian' *Time and Tide* (9 November 1961).

176   Osbert Lancaster 'Last of the Great Unbeats' *Daily Express* (1 November 1961).

177   *Daily Telegraph* (1 November 1961), p. 12.

178   Tooth's Gallery, 15–30 March, 'Paintings and Drawings not previously exhibited'. Christie's, First Studio Sale, 20 July 1962 (115 drawings, 70 paintings) £99,645 (equivalent to £1,200,000 in 1996). Christie's, Second Studio Sale, 21 June 1963 (103 drawings, 62 paintings) £33,405 (equivalent to £391,200 in 1996). Both studio sales were held primarily to pay off death duties, John's estate having been valued at approximately £90,000 (equivalent to £1,119,000 in 1996).

INDEX

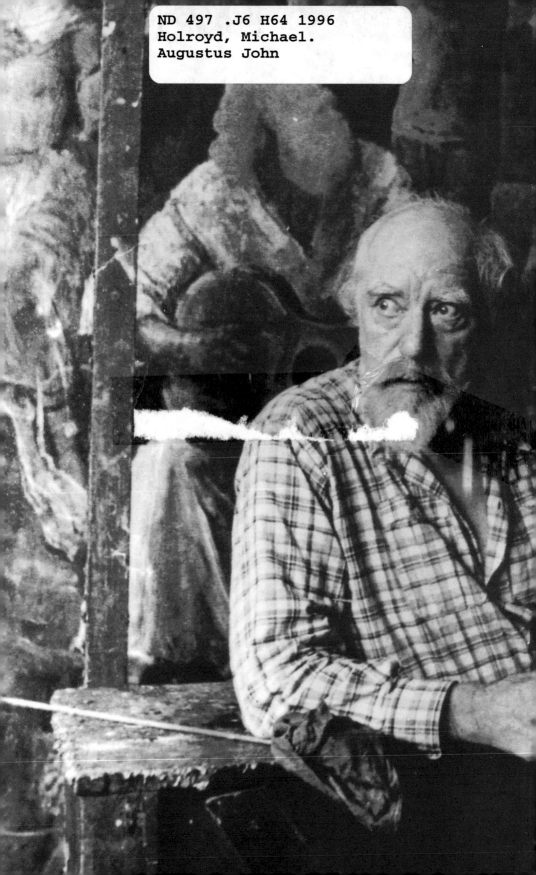